10,000 Rare Books
Published before 1860

A CATALOG
FOR COLLECTORS
AND HISTORIANS

Compiled by
Bernard Quaritch

Wexford Press
2008

TABLE OF CONTENTS.

	PAGES
EUROPEAN MANUSCRIPTS, ILLUMINATED MISSALS, etc.	1—9
Autographs 9	
Palaeography, Catalogues of MSS.	10—13
PERIODICALS, ENCYCLOPÆDIAS, Society Publications, Issues of Private Presses .	13—55
Directories, Calendars, Peerages . . . 54—55	
RELIGIOUS WORSHIPS, Philosophical Sects, Secret Associations	55—62
THEOLOGY, ECCLESIASTICAL HISTORY	62—70
HORAE, MISSALS, PASSIONALES, and Liturgical Literature	71—74
BIBLES and TESTAMENTS in all languages	74—88
CLASSICS, GREEK AND LATIN PHILOLOGY, Ancient History	88—112
Latin and Greek Miscellanies, Mediaeval Writers . 108—112	
BIBLIOGRAPHY, LITERARY HISTORY, TYPOGRAPHY	112—124
GAMES, SPORTS, EXERCISES	124—127
MUSIC AND SONGS	127—130
POLITICAL ECONOMY, JURISPRUDENCE, DIPLOMACY	130—135
MILITARY SCIENCES and History	135—137
NAVAL AFFAIRS	138
ORIENTAL LITERATURE	138—190
Oriental History, Polyglotts, Oriental Societies' Transactions . . . . . 138—146	
Assyria 146	
China . . . . . 146—147	
Egypt . . . . . 147—149	
India . . . . . 150—153	
Japan 154	
Palestine 154	
Turkey 154	
Oriental Manuscripts . . . . 155—166	
Illuminated MSS., Drawings . . 155—156	
Arabic . . . . . 156—161	
Assyrian, Burmese, Hebrew . 161	
Hindee, Hindustani, Mahratti . 161	
Pali . . . . . 161—162	
Persian . . . . . 162—166	
Punjabi or Sikh . . . 166	
Sanscrit, Tibetan . . . 166	
Turkish 166	

TABLE OF CONTENTS.

	PAGES
ORIENTAL LITERATURE—*continued*—	
Oriental Languages, printed books	166—190
Amharic	166
Arabic	166—172
Armenian, Assyrian	172
Berber	173
Chinese	173—175
Circassian	175
Cochin-Chinese	175
Coptic	175
Ethiopic	175
Georgian	175—176
Hebrew, Chaldee, Syriac	176—179
Indian Languages	179—182
Bengali	179
Burmese, Canarese, Gujarati	179
Hindustani, Hindee, Urdu	179—181
Mahratti	181
Malayalim, Manipuri, Orissa	181
Punjabee, Sindhi, Singhalese	181
Tamul	181—182
Telugu	182
Jakout	182
Japanese	182
Javanese	182
Malay	182
Maltese	182
Mantchu, Mongolian	183
Pali	183
Persian	183—185
Phœnician, Pushtu	185
Sanscrit	185—188
Siamese	188
Tatar	188
Tibetan	189
Turkish	189—190
Zend	190
AFRICAN LANGUAGES	190
AMERICAN LANGUAGES	190—192
POLYNESIAN AND AUSTRALIAN LANGUAGES	192—193
EUROPEAN PHILOLOGY	193—200
Polyglotts, Comparative Grammar	193—196
Albanian	196
Basque	196—197
Celtic Languages	197—202
Breton	198
Cornish	198—189
Gaelic	199—200
Irish	200—201
Manx	201
Welsh	201—202

TABLE OF CONTENTS.

	PAGES
FINE ARTS, &c.—*continued*—	
Pageants	371
Portraits	373—375
Spain, Spanish Art	379—380
Xylography, Woodcuts	384—387
Emperor Maximilian's Publications	386
Catalogues of Pictures and Works of Art	387—388
ARCHITECTURE, ENGINEERING, MACHINERY	388—393
Landscape Gardening	390
Turning	392
CURIOSA	393—402
Manuscripts	393—394
Early Prayer Books	394—395
Varia, Miscellanies, Magic, Early Science	395—397
Early Printed Books, Romance Literature	397—401
France	397—398
Germany	398—400
Holland and Belgium	400
Italy	400—401
Sweden	401
Shorthand, Steganography	401—402
PROVERBS of all Nations	402—404
FRENCH LITERATURE	404—422
French Language	404—405
GERMAN LITERATURE	422—428
German Language	422
ITALIAN LITERATURE	428—444
Italian Language	428—429
Italian Dialects	441—444
ENGLISH LITERATURE	444—514
English Language and Dialects	444—447
England	489
Ireland	489—493
Scotland	493—495
Wales	495—497
Art and Architecture	497—499
Bibliography	499
Geography and Travels	499—503
India and Indian Publications	501—503
Philological Works	503—507
Science and Natural History	507—513
Theology and Bibles	513—514
SPANISH LITERATURE	514—547
Spanish Language	514—515
Spanish Dialects	545—546
Spain, Works relating to	546—547
PORTUGUESE LITERATURE	547—550
Portuguese Language	547—548
Portugal, Works relating to	550

TABLE OF CONTENTS. vii

	PAGES
EUROPEAN PHILOLOGY—*continued*—	
Germanic Languages	202—209
Anglo-Saxon	202—204
Teutonic	204—207
Dutch, Flemish, Frisic	207—209
Scandinavian Languages	209—214
English	210—211
Icelandic, Old Norse	211—213
Swedish	213—214
Romance Languages	214—216
Romansch, Wallachian	216
Romaic or Modern Greek	217
Sarmatian Languages	218—219
Bohemian, Croatian, Illyrian	218
Polish, Lithuanian	218
Russian	218—219
Servian, Slovak	219
Slavonic Church Language	219
Wendish	219
Ugrian Languages	219—220
Hungarian	219
Finnish, Lapponic, Gipsy	220
NATURAL HISTORY, SCIENCES, MATHEMATICS	220—264
Watchmaking	257—258
GEOGRAPHY, VOYAGES, TRAVELS	264—318
Atlases and Maps	282—284
Eastern Europe	284—288
Bohemia, Dalmatia, Esthonia (and Finland)	285—286
Hungary	286
Poland	286—287
Russia	287—288
Scandinavia	288—289
Africa	289—290
America	290—306
Asia	306—318
Philippine Islands	312—313
Japan	313—314
Palestine	315—316
Australasia	318
HERALDRY, ANTIQUITIES, CHRONICLES, GENEALOGY, Mediaeval History	319—339
CHRONOLOGY, HISTORY OF THE CALENDAR	340
DIPLOMATICS, MEDIAEVAL GLOSSARIES	340—341
NUMISMATA, AND MEDALLIC HISTORY	341—349
FINE ARTS, BOOKS OF PRINTS, PAINTINGS	349—388
Bible Illustrations	351—352
Christian Art	355
Costume	356
Emblems	357—358
Gems	361—362
Ornaments	370

BERNARD QUARITCH'S
CATALOGUE OF BOOKS.

EUROPEAN MANUSCRIPTS.

**Early Codices of the BIBLE and of CLASSICS on Vellum;
Important HISTORICAL Documents; Inedited Works;
ILLUMINATED MISSALS; Original DRAWINGS.**

1 ALBUM. 165 Water-Color Drawings by English and Foreign Masters (Canaletti, Pinelli, Della Gatta, Cozens, Stothard, Worledge, Dallas, Page, Rowlandson, Gilpin, Thrale, Koenig, Serres, Fergola, etc.) mounted on thick paper of different hues, and bound in 3 vols. atlas 4to. *morocco extra, two of them in morocco cases,* £25. *ca.* 1770-1840

Containing some beautiful sketches of Scenery and Figures, chiefly Italian; some of the maritime scenes and studies of Vesuvius in 1835 are exquisite. There are also English and German landscapes, and some elegantly finished drawings by Stothard, apparently in illustration of Don Quixote or some similar work; and by Cozens and Mortimer, executed during the latter part of the 18th century.

2 ANTIPHONALE ECCLESIÆ ROMANÆ, *with the Music in Neumes;* Orationes in Diebus Sanctis; LIBER SACRAMENTORUM (*probably the rarest of the Roman Service Books*), folio, MANUSCRIPT ON VELLUM, *written in a singularly clear Roman character, with a slight mixture of the Carlovingian type of the X-XIth Century, the Music written in Neumes, and ornamented with several Initial Letters illuminated in gold, silver and colours, in a fine state of preservation, and rendered complete at end, on paper, in a German handwriting of the XVth Century, in the original oak boards, with brass bosses,* £16. 16s *Sæc.* X.—XI.

On the verso of leaf 86, at the foot of the page, occurs the name "Frideric' D," and on the verso of 94, " Frideric' Diacon.' "

3 ANTIPHONARIUM CUM NOTIS MUSICIS, MANUSCRIPT ON VELLUM, folio, 165 *leaves, with very quaint painted capitals, the musical notes written in Neuma or Neumes (with only one central line), old red morocco gilt, in good preservation,* £40. *Sæc.* XI.

This VENERABLE and highly interesting relic of antiquity—800 years old—is similar in character to a Graduale, bearing date of 1071, bought by Mr. Boone for 80*l*. (No. 154, at Payne's sale, Sotheby's, June 20, 1860), and probably came from the same church. For the History of Sacred Music this is one of the most important volumes, as in the Antiphonarium are preserved those beautiful Chants which the Venerable Bede was so anxious to introduce into our cathedrals, and which admirers of solemn grandeur consider were no way improved when Guido d'Arezzo introduced, in this same century, his newly invented system of sol-fa-ing.

4 BERNARDI (S.) Opusculum de Laudibus Virginis Matris; Sermones LXV. et Institutio quomodo canere et psallere debeamus, 4to. MANUSCRIPT ON VELLUM, *with the* INITIAL LETTER *containing portrait of the Saint, illuminated in gold and colours, in the original oak bds. in a fine state of preservation,* £4. *Sæc.* XV.

5 BIBLIA LATINA (Gen. xxxv. 11, usque ad IV. Reg. xviii. 27), *a venerable* MANUSCRIPT ON VELLUM, folio, 238 *leaves, with Capitals, in the original oak boards, covered with stamped leather,* £30. *Sæc. XII.*

This important and valuable Manuscript is that cited by C. Vercellone in his "*Variæ Lectiones Vulgatæ Latinæ Bibliorum Editionis,*" as Codex U. It belongs to what is usually termed the "*Recensio Alcuina,*" with which it generally agrees, but exhibits some few important readings not to be found therein. The commencement, and also the continuation as far as I. Chronicles, 6, are supplied in MS. of the fifteenth century.

6 BIBLIA LATINA, à Regibus I. usque ad librum Hester, cum prologis Sancti Hieronymi, large folio, *a beautiful German MS. of* 165 *leaves, on* VELLUM, *with thirteen elaborate Miniatures within large initials (mostly* 3½ *inches square), eight of them richly illuminated with gold and colours, the other five etched, the writing large and clear, in an elegant Gothic character, bound in the original oak boards,* £50. *ca.* 1440

Though valuable in itself, the chief feature of interest in this MS. is the fact that the fly-leaves of the binding which are pasted down upon the inner covers, contain two large specimens of XYLOGRAPHY or BLOCK PRINTING, each 14¾ inches by 10. They are colored, and signed by "MICHEL SCHORPP, *Maler, zu Ulm.*" The first represents St. Jerome kneeling at the foot of a Crucifix, behind which there is a lion *couchant*, with a landscape of trees and a distant city, and an owl perched on a bough above the Saint's head. The second represents Christ upon a mount, blessing the twelve Apostles, who are taking leave of each other before departing to preach the Gospel in distant lands; and above them is a legend in the Swabian dialect of Upper German, "Der Zwölff botten Usstailung, etc." They are, perhaps, not quite so early as the MS., but their large size renders them singularly interesting as specimens of early Block-printing.

B

7 **BONAVENTURA** (Saint) **Life of Christe**, and other Devout Pieces of the XVth Century, An EARLY ENGLISH MANUSCRIPT, on VELLUM.

A perfect and very extraordinary volume, containing the following pieces, written in Gothic Letter, in double columns, viz.:—

I. The Booke that is cleped "**the Mirrour of the blissed Lyfe of Jhesus Crist**," *from the Speculum Vite Christi* of Bonaventure, with a **Shorte Tretice of the Wieste and moste worthy Sacrament of Criste is blissede body, and the merbelous thereof.**

On the recto of the second leaf is a remarkable note, *in Latin*, of which the following is a translation:—
"Memorandum: that about the year of our Lord One thousand four hundred and ten, the original copy in English of this book (Speculum Vite Christi) was presented at London, by its compiler, to Lord Thomas Arundel, Archbishop of Canterbury, for his inspection and approbation before it was generally circulated; who, after a due inspection, and keeping the book several days, expressed an unqualified approbation of it and by his metropolitan authority, commanded that it should be circulated as an orthodox work for the edification of the faithful and the confutation of heretics or Lollards. Amen." The Translator's name is unknown, At the end of the Short Tretyes is "Jhu Lorde thi blissede life helpe and comforte our wretched life. Amen. Explicit Speculum Vite Christi, complete."

II. **Here begynneth the Boke of the Crafte of Dyinge** (Ars Moriendi), with a **Tretyse of Gostely Bataple right deboute.**

A very popular production of the middle of the XVth century. Caxton *is said to have translated* it for his own impression, but whether he only improved on the present Version, which there is little doubt preceded his, could only be arrived at by comparing the two: the lingual differences appear to be many, but as the English language was undergoing great change at the period this volume was written, a collation of the pieces alone would remove all doubt on the matter.

III. **A Lytil Shorte Tretyce, that telleth how ther were VI Masters assembleve togeder, and iche askede othir what thynge thei myght beste speke of that myght beste please God, and were most prosytabil to the people, and all thei were accordid to speke of tribulacion.** *At the close,* "Thus is endede a shorte Tretyes of the XII profytes of tribulacion right devoute."—*The transla*' name of this is unknown—in one large vol. folio, 168 *leaves of vell*·· columns, antique calf, £50.

A VENERABLE, AND TO THE PHILOLOGIST ALMOST PRICELESS ENGLISH MAN· ·· ·· been offered for sale for many years past. The whole of the pieces were printed at severa· ···e Father of English Printing, WILLIAM CAXTON,—but whether he used any part of the contents of thi· ····me, must be only conjectured, but certain it is that these are not manuscript copies of his printed productions.

8 CASSIANI (Joannis) Constantinopolis Diaconi, Collationes Patrum, de Mortificatione, de Perfectione, de puritate cordis, de discretione, de tribus abrenuntiationibus, de VIII vitiis principalibus, de nece Sanctorum, de animæ mobilitate et Spiritualibus nequitiis, de principatibus, de Oratione, de Illusionibus Nocturnis, Collatio DANIELIS, etc., sm. folio, 201 leaves, FINE MANUSCRIPT OF THE XIIITH CENTURY UPON VELLUM, *written in a bold hand, the Initials colored, a few leaves supplied by a modern Scribe, otherwise in excellent preservation, original wooden boards, covered,* 36s *Saec. XIII.*

Bp. Burnet in his Exposition of the Thirty-nine Articles speaks of the Author as a Semi-Pelagian, and of his Collations as being much used for their piety and good sense.

9 CICERONIS (M. T.) DE ORATORE, AD QUINTUM FRATREM LIBRI EXPLICIUNT, *Scripti per me Petrum Suuilden Leodien. Dyoc. Anno a nativitate domini* MCCCCLVIII. *tempore potestatorie Venerabilis ac egregii viri domini Antonii de Campanatiis Juris civilis doctoris famosissimi tunc t'pis co'is Medicine potestatis clarissimi*

Sallustii Crispi in M. T. Ciceronem Oratio et in Sallustium Oratio Ciceronis.
Epistola Lentuli ad Senatores Romæ.
Pontius Pilatus Regi Claudio.
Epistola Cæsaris *copiata ex Exemplari habito ex exemplari Petrarce, quam ipse Petrarca auream dicit*
Plutarchi Epistola ad Trayanum Imperatorem.
C. Fabricius et Q. Æmilius Consules Pirrho Regi.
Josephus de Christo—in 1 vol. 4to. *fine Manuscript of* 135 *leaves upon vellum, with elegant Arabesque initials illuminated in gold and colours, the first page adorned with a beautiful border of interlaced work, adorned with figures of birds, a butterfly and flowers,* having the arms *of* ANTONIUS DE CAMPANATIIS *painted in the lower compartment, an elegant Manuscript, in very fine preservation, calf gilt,* £15. *Saec. XV.*

10 DUGDALE (SIR WILLIAM). THE VISITATION OF THE COUNTY OF YORKE, begun in Anno Domini 1665, and finished 1666, by WILLIAM DUGDALE, Norroy King of Armes, stout folio, *drawings of the arms borne by the several families, several hundred in number, russia extra, gilt edges,* £100. *ca.* 1668

⁎⁎ This valuable volume, of nearly 300 leaves, prefaced by an elaborately compiled Index, was purchased

from the sale of Sir Mark Masterman Sykes in 1824 for 157*l*. 10*s*, since which time the pedigrees have been continued by Mr. W. Paver, of Clementhorpe, near York, for which a further payment of 10*l*. was incurred, as stated in Miss Currer's handwriting on the fly-leaf to the volume. It appears to have been purchased in 1797 of Mr. W. Prince of York by Sir M. M. Sykes.

This "noble" MS., as it has been justly designated by a high authority (Sir Chas. G. Young, Garter), contains the pedigrees of 472 families, a pen and ink drawing of the armorial bearings of each family being placed at the head of the pedigree.

Portion of the volume is in the handwriting of Dugdale himself, but the greater number of the pedigrees, and of the shields of arms which are executed with much artistic spirit and elegance, are undoubtedly the work of Gregory King, afterwards Lancaster Herald, who was in Dugdale's service and accompanied him in all his visitations of the northern counties.

The reprint published recently by the Surtees Society is not to be considered as diminishing the value of this book, when it is observed that the MS. contains not only the drawings of Arms, which are not reproduced in publication, but also possesses the valuable additions made by Mr. W Paver, Genealogist, of Clementhorpe. These additions, in many instances, trace the genealogies to a more remote date than originally done, as well as giving their continuation; and contain interesting historical details. The sum of 10*l*., said to have been paid for Mr. Paver's labor, must have been but a nominal payment; as its value far exceeds such a comparatively trifling remuneration. Mr. Paver has also added a copy of Dugdale's 'List of persons generally reputed Esquires or gentlemen, who having been unable or neglected to make proof of their gentility, on the Visitation, were forbidden to be addressed by those titles," with his notification to the Sheriff.

The Surtees reprint stops short with the genealogy of the "Davye of Fockerby" family; and omits the concluding portion of the MS., which proceeds from that, with accounts of the Boroughs of Pontefract, Leedes, Richmund, Kingston upon Hull, Beverley, Doncaster and York. Beautiful drawings of their Common Seals and Arms, are prefixed. The preface to the reprint contains an exact history and pedigree of this MS., but notwithstanding the Editor's anxiety to give a faithful reproduction, as stated, this omission (doubtless inadvertent, in consequence of some blank pages and portion of Mr. Paver's additions occurring between the Davye pedigree and the concluding portion of the MS.) makes the Surtees Society publication glaringly imperfect.

11 EARLY ENGLISH MANUSCRIPT, on vellum, of the XIVth Century, containing:
I. Meditacioūs and Cōnfessioñs of Seint Austyn
II. A Tretise that men callith Richarde of Seynt Victor (of the study of wysdome)
III. Carta redempcionis, *in English metre*
IV. Songe of Love to owre Lorde Jhesu Christe
V. Ave, Quene of heven, ladi of erthe, welle of all bounte
   Emperice of helle, & of mekenes the sov eynte
   Ryht briht sterre schynynge, of all fayrnes the flor
   Gracious moder of Jhū, throw you have we grace, counfort and socour, etc.
In English Metre, *divided into* 15 *sections, expounding on each of the principal words of the Ave Maria separately, commencing with Ave, then Maria, and so on*
VI. A Poem on the Passion of Christ, divided into various sections, and beginning:
   Whoso wole over rede this booke
   And with his gostly yze thereon loke
   To other scole thar he nat wende
   To save his sowle fro the feende
   Than for to do as this boke tellyth
   Ffor holy writte forsooth it spellith, etc.

sm. folio, a beautiful volume of 92 leaves, *in the finest state of preservation. With the exception of a few pages in long lines, it is written in double columns, the capital letters illuminated in gold and colours, probably from the Library of King Henry VIII, having the Crown and Tudor Rose stamped on the sides,* £28. Sæc. XIV.

The fifth piece in this volume, which apparently is not entirely complete, is a very remarkable production, and is apparently entirely unknown to poetical antiquaries.

The Meditations of St Austin end with the following address of the Scribe to the nuns by whom it seems he was employed to write the book.—

Thankyd be almyghti God, my gode sustren, I have now pformyd yor. desyre in englysshinge these meditacious etc. I have nat wrytin alway as it standith. Ffor in translatynge of oon langage to another, som wordis must be chaungyd & and some places moo wordes must be seyde Ffor Englysch is soo buystuy (?) of it self that ellis it wole be full unsavery to rede therfolwe as me semyth is most lisabel. And I have wryten in spekyng to God, for reverens, ye and youres & so I fynde in the frensche boke that I wrote after vo^s & vre, etc.

Much of the poetry is written with an ease and melody of versification which is remarkable in comparison with the rugged metrical efforts of the time; and on the whole this beautiful MS. is one of extreme interest for the light it throws on the history of the English language in its early development.

12 EARLY ITALIAN MS. ON NAVIGATION.—Cesareo (Agostino) l'Arte del Navigare con il regimento della Tramontana, e del Sole; e la vera Regola et osservanza del Flusso e Reflusso delle Acque sotto breve compendio ridotta, sm. 4to. 114 *pages neatly written, with* 9 *drawings,* 3 *of which have moveable parts attached, bds.* 32*s* *Dated at the end of the preface,* 1585

An interesting manuscript very neatly written and evidently prepared for publication. It is dedicated "allo illmo. Signor Ferrante Somma." Contents: on the North Pole; on the cross-staff, its manufacture, use, etc. *with diagram;* Ursa Major and Minor, *with moveable diagram;* on the Antarctic Pole; Rule for calculating distance; on oblique winds; on the navigation of the Levant; on the sun's altitude; on the sun's shadow; 16 pp. of tables of the sun's declinations; on Tides; Rule for Tides with lists of Tides on the Coasts of Spain, England, etc.; Rule to know the tides in all parts of the world, *with a curious diagram having two moveable pieces,*

13 EVANGELIA IV. graece, apparently written by GEORGE HERMONYMUS of SPARTA, the teacher of Budaeus and Reuchlin, sm. 4to. *a remarkably well written Greek MS. with 4 curious* DRAWINGS, *and Initial Letters in gold; quite perfect, and in excellent preservation,* olive morocco extra, by THOUVENIN, £8. 8s
Sæc. XV. XVI.

Though this MS. was probably written after the invention of printing, there is no doubt, that it was copied from a much earlier MS. Biblical writters are invited to examine this manuscript.

14 EVAGGELIA, Ta Hagia, small 4to. A FINE GREEK MS. of the 13th Century, *written upon* VELLUM, *rudely ornamented with* INITIAL LETTERS *and headings in red,* 324 *pp. not quite complete, in the original oak boards,* £36   Saec. XIII.

A curious and valuable MS. which has come from a Monastery in the East. It was selected by an English officer, as the most precious book in the library there, and obtained under very peculiar circumstances. The writing, which is not entirely that of one scribe, is in a fine bold hand; and the text is arranged not according to the usual form, but in chronological order. It begins with the first and second chapters of John, then proceeds with Luke; and alternates similarly all through the book. The chapters and verses are numbered; and dates are prefixed at each heading.

On the first page, above the ornamental border, is seen the inscription, (in contracted characters.) " Μνησθητη κυριε την Ψυχην τȣ δουλȣ τȣ θεȣ Μαρτηνȣ. Μνησθητη κυριε την Ψυχην της δουλης τȣ θεȣ Ελενης." [Remember, Lord, the soul of God's servant Martin. Remember, Lord, the soul of God's servant, Helena.]

15 EVANGELIUM S. Matthæi Græco-Latinum. Manuscript of the XVth Century, on Paper, with Miniatures, folio, *hf. vellum,* £17. 10s   Saec. XV.

A very interesting volume containing several very singular Miniatures executed in gold (in many places faded) and colours, in a style wherein may be traced the oriental influence. In 1465 this Manuscript was presented to the Convent of St. Epiphanius. It begins with two Epistles of Saint Jerome, after which follows a sort of commentary on the arrangement of the Gospels. An epistle of St. Ambrose in Latin, and the Nicene Creed in Greek; with a record of the donation of the book, are found at the end.

16 GALLEGO (Hernando, de la Coruña) Vyaie y Descubrimiento de las Yslas Salomon en el Mar de el Sur, (1566), smallest 4to. 87 *leaves, vellum,* £10. 10s ? 1570

The discovery of the Isles of Solomon, was one of the greatest achievements which marked the career of Spanish domination in America, during the sixteenth century. The accounts which the mariners brought back with them, concerning these islands were marvellously magnified; the rivers of their fertile soil were said to flow over sands of gold; and all the wonders of an El-Dorado were associated, in Europe, with the name of the Islands of Solomon. From them, it was believed, the Royal Sage of Judah had obtained the gold with which he glorified the Temple; and hence they received the appellation which they have retained, notwithstanding the designations bestowed by subsequent discoverers. They long maintained a fabulous character in the eyes of Europe, for the Spaniards who first discovered them, could not find them again; and little, beyond their name was known, till Surville re-discovered them in 1767, and they first became noted in France and England, as the Islands of the Arsacides, and as New-Georgia.

This valuable MS. which was never published, is probably the only existing authentic record (unless there be a copy in the archives of Spain) of the voyage in which they were first discovered. In Thevenot's collection, there was inserted a Spanish fragment (generally wanting), concerning these Islands, from which, apparently, the small information to be found upon the subject of that voyage, has always been derived. This fragment seems to have been written about 1620, when Luis de Velasco, Marquis de Salino, was Viceroy of Peru; and, although its first five columns are devoted to the first Voyage, yet it chiefly records the second enterprise, in which the Spaniards went out ineffectually, to seek again and colonize the Isles of Solomon.

In the year 1566, Don Lope Garcia De Castro, Governor of Peru, fitted out the expedition chronicled in the above MS.; Alvaro de Mendano, (called frequently Mendoza, Miranda, Mandana, etc. by other writers), being appointed Admiral, and Hernando Gallego the Piloto Mayor. On the 19th of November, 1566, they sailed in two ships from Callao; and after a voyage, styled by the *Biographie Universelle,* " one of the most remarkable since the discoveries of Columbus," they landed in Peru again on the 26th of July, 1569, bringing with them golden tales of the new found Islands in the Pacific. Mendano, or Mendana, was received by the Viceroy, with a complimentary speech, in which he compared him with Columbus and Cortes; and in the Spanish fragment in Thevenot, he is extolled by the side of Ulysses and Vasco de Gama. The discovery was considered of such importance by the Spanish government, that they determined to send him out again with a larger force, to colonise the islands. The political troubles of Spain prevented the immediate execution of this project, which lay in abeyance for twenty years; and in 1599, Mendana set out again on the unfortunate voyage, in which he sailed for some years round the world, unsuccessfully, in search of the Isles he had previously discovered.

Gallego's narrative is in a simple style, somewhat like a diary; and gives exact records from day to day of the progress they made. Several errors in date, which are generally received, from the statement of the Spanish fragment in Thevenot, may be corrected by the account of the Piloto Mayor, who probably prepared the above work for presentation to Philip II.

17 HAWTREY (Rev. Dr., *Provost of Eton*) Dissected Map of the Parish of Mapledherham, traced from the Rent-Charge Map 1859, with MS. reference or index, by the Rev. Dr. HAWTREY, 12mo. *morocco,* 20s   1859

18 HERALDRY. Coats of Arms of the Noble and Gentle Families of Great Britain and Ireland, upwards of Eight hundred neat and boldly executed pen and ink drawings of Armorial Bearings, executed about 1640, with an Index added about 1780, sm. 4to. *a few of the earlier drawings inlaid and slightly injured, an interesting MS. hf. bd.* £3. 10s   ca. 1640

There are also several MS. notes added in the commencement of this century by some learned hand.

19 HIERONYMI (S.) EPISTOLÆ, sm. folio, SPLENDID ITALIAN MANUSCRIPT, in Latin, *upon the* PUREST VELLUM, *of* 286 *leaves, in the most elegant character. The first page is encircled with the most beautiful* ITALIAN ARABESQUE BORDER, *with a small miniature by an artist of great merit, in the finest state of preservation, bound in vellum,* £12. 12s   J. Grassus Carpensis, Ferraræ, 1467

It may be remarked that this voluminous and interesting correspondence of St. Jerome is of very unusual occurrence in Manuscript.

EUROPEAN MANUSCRIPTS. 5

20 HOMILIÆ ET SERMONES, cum LECTIONARIO veterum Patrum; nempe Augustini, Bedæ, Leonis et Gregorii Paparum, Fulgentii, Maximi, Origenis, etc. large folio, MANUSCRIPT, ON VELLUM, OF THE VIIIth or IXth CENTURY, 289 leaves, meas. generally 18½ inches by 13, *in double columns, brown morocco, in compartments*, £180. SÆC. VIII.-IX.

A Magnificent Manuscript, in two columns, in Merovingian characters, with an admixture of Saxon and rude Gothic. It contains more than two hundred initials, some of which are upwards of half a foot in height, in various colours. The style of these initials is very singular, and they present to view a number of interlaced lines and crossbars similar to those seen in the famous Evangelistarium written by Bishop Eadfrith in honour of St. Cuthbert, between the years 698 and 720 of the Christian era, so admired in the British Museum. Although more square, the form of the letter G is the same as that indicated in the Saxon Alphabet represented in the second volume of the *Nouveau Traité de Diplomatique*, published by the Benedictines. The body of this Manuscript has a great resemblance to the one of St. Isidore ("Bibliothecæ Regiæ Parisiensis" No 2994 A), which is of the VII—VIIIth Century, and of which a facsimile can be seen in Plate LI of the third volume of the *Nouveau Traité de Diplomatique*, but the writing of this Manuscript is more regular and finer. The *Homiliæ* here described is a palæographic monument of the highest importance. At once a *Homiliarium* and a *Lectionarium*, it is doubly valuable as a monument of ancient Liturgy, and as containing a very large number of Pieces by the VENERABLE BEDE. It contains 289 leaves, with an ancient numbering, which proves that the first nine are deficient. This enormous volume has been admirably bound by Sumter, who has clothed it with one of those brown morocco bindings (called monastic, and so well executed in England), and surmounted the difficulties offered by so ancient a volume. Besides the Initials and the writing of the entire Manuscript, which is very fine, most remarkable are the numerous Rubrics, in red and blue, written in capitals interlaced in a peculiar style. The reverse of the 130th leaf is entirely occupied with a magnificent Initial in various colours, measuring 16½ inches in height, accompanied by an inscription in large letters, interlaced in the style of monograms to be found in certain very ancient Charters, and arranged by great lines alternatively in red and blue, commencing thus:

EXPLICIT LIBER HOMELIARUM PARTIS PRIMÆ, &c.

This magnificent page, which we have never seen surpassed, will be found facsimiled in *Libri's* INEDITED MONUMENTS.

The above is the description which Mr. Libri has given of this venerable MS., but he is manifestly wrong in attributing it to the Seventh Century; for BEDE died at the age of 63 in the year 735; and it is generally admitted now that he did not receive the epithet of "Venerable" (which is here given to him) till after his death. It is therefore probable that this MS. was not executed till late in the Eighth or early in the Ninth Century, and was probably the work of some Saxon monk upon the Continent, most likely in France. The shape of the letters partakes much of the Anglo-Irish and, in a less degree of the Roman style of Charlemagne's period, but is entirely without the rudeness of construction and irregular character of the writing which prevailed in France at that time. There is a singular exactness and equality of form throughout; and the writer must have been a man of refined taste, judging from the symmetry of his work, and the constant variations in the shape of the initials, which nearly all differ from each other, yet have a bold and felicitous elegance quite remarkable. The chief feature of the ornamentation is the multiplied interlacing, which was first used in Irish MSS., and introduced upon the continent during the seventh and eighth centuries; and which flourished there till the twelfth century, then dying out, to be reproduced as an accessory in the Italian MSS. of the fourteenth century. The green, purple, blue, and red colours used in painting the initials, are of that dark and peculiar tint only met with in the most ancient MSS.

There are some slight peculiarities in the orthography, not very frequent indeed, but which may be remarked. The letters B and V appear to be interchangeable; for instance the word *laror* is to be met instead of *labor*, and *Benerabi is* for *Venerabilis. Nihil* is spelt *Nicil*, and *charitas* begins with a *k* instead of *ch*. On leaf 34, at the commencement of one of Bede's Homilies is a heading which appears to read thus, in mingled Western and Greek characters: "Eabacthanse Prbcr." Its meaning is left to conjecture.

This Manuscript evidently formed at one time a valuable portion of some Spanish monastic library. On the first page (which was originally the nineteenth, being the obverse of the tenth leaf) there is a memorandum, in Spanish handwriting, possibly two hundred years old, which runs thus: "Sermones y Homilias de varios Santos Padres, de el tiempo, y festividades particul." On the front of leaf 30, at the beginning of a Sermon of "Fulgentius Episcopus," there is a Latin memorandum, also in a Spanish hand, which is as follows: "Sermo Fulgentii Ruspensis, vid. Tom. 3. Bibliothe. pp. f. 106. Vide Opera S. Fulgentii Ruspensis, p. 250, et in prefat. Oper. n. X. ubi cum hoc notantur reliq. 3 sermones reperti in hoc Lectionario, pp. 38-60 et 274."

As the mind looks back upon the probable history of this venerable Manuscript, and reverts to the vicissitudes through which its owners may have passed, a kind of reverential awe is awakened, and we seem to stand in the presence of Time, the Destroyer. Yet his hand has but lightly touched this relic of ancient days, it is in fine preservation; and is not much changed from what it was, when the great empire of Charlemagne was torn asunder, and deluged with bloodshed by his grandchildren. It passed unscathed through those stormy times, and through all the subsequent troubles of the Middle ages; and perhaps, was part of the treasures of the Holy Roman Empire till the days of Charles V. Upon his death, it is not unlikely that it came into the possession of Philip II. and remained in Spain till the present century.

I gave £161. for these "Homilies," at Mr. Libri's sale, and now offer it at the above slightly increased price, reserving to myself only a commission profit of 10 per cent. for expenses, and the honour of having possessed, even for a while, this venerable monument of the Carlovingian times.

21 HORÆ Beatæ Mariæ Virginis, cum Kalendario, Manuscript upon fine Vellum, in a large gothic hand, and richly decorated with 50 SUPERB MINIATURES, *illustrative of the Passion of Christ, the Lives of Saints, etc. thirteen of them large miniatures of nearly the size of the page, with borders, and thirty-seven small Miniatures with appropriate* SEMI-BORDERS, *the whole depicting a multitude of figures most admirably drawn and grouped, and highly interesting in their various accessories as Buildings, Costume, Beasts, Birds, Insects, etc. The preceding are all executed in the extremely rare* CAMAIEU GRIS, *with occasional relief of gold, ultramarine in the skies, etc. There are also a multitude of initial letters in rich gold and colours. The whole of* FRENCH *execution, in fine preservation, with ample margins, stout* 4to. *in old morocco, powdered with the fleur-de-lys, having impressed within the covers,* "Ce livre apartien a moy Vincent Guichard," £80. *circa* 1440

An extremely beautiful example of a very unusual style of art in Missal painting. There was no specimen of the *Camaïeu-gris* style at the recent magnificent exhibition of Illuminated Manuscripts in the rooms of the Society of Antiquaries.

22 HORÆ BEATÆ MARIÆ VIRGINIS, secundum Usum Romanum, cum Calendario, 16mo. MANUSCRIPT ON VELLUM, *with* 7 MINIATURES, *and with Borders and Capitals,* ILLUMINATED *in* GOLD *and* COLOURS, *having the arms of the original possessor,* (*a white dog surrounded by flames*) *under the first painting, calf, a very pretty volume,* £5. Sæc. XV.

23 HORÆ BEATÆ MARIÆ VIRGINIS secundum Usum Romanum cum Calendario, 8vo. MANUSCRIPT *partly in French,* UPON VELLUM, *by a French Scribe, adorned with* 6 MINIATURE PAINTINGS, *and numerous* CAPITAL LETTERS, *all richly illuminated in gold and colours, old French olive morocco, gilt edges,* £7. Sæc. XV.

24 HOROLOGIUM Magnum et Troparium, Horas Officii Divini continens, *Graece, exquisite Manuscript of the* FIFTEENTH CENTURY *upon Bombyx paper, dated in the year* 6982, A.M. *of the Constantinopolitan Era,* thick sm. 4to. vol. (meas. 8 inches by 5½), *in the original binding, having a portion of one leaf torn off,* £10. 1474

This most beautiful specimen of Greek Caligraphy is mentioned in Mr. Coxe's Report to H. M. Government on Manuscripts in the Levant.

25 **IRELAND.** STATE PAPERS and Records relating to IRELAND, a large collection of MS. official documents, chiefly from the Irish Rolls Office, with other documents, mostly on VELLUM, £3. 16s 1600-1800

Including—"Ledger of William Penn, Army Storekeeper in Ireland, of Charles II."—"Official Report as to importation of Gunpowder into Ireland."—"Accounts of the Earl of Fingall for Lord Killeen," curious bills of private expenses, 1713-16—Grants of forfeited Estates from James I., Charles I., Charles II. and William III., and other Grants from the Crown, relating to the title to the Annesley peerage, to the Gormanstown, Esmonde, and other Estates—Copies and translations of Charters to several Towns in Ireland—Inquisitions of Outlawry, as to Tythes, etc. A very valuable and interesting collection for those who are studious of Irish Antiquarian and Historical details. There is also a curious document in this collection, although not relating to Ireland, dated 1601, consisting of a statement of Queen Elizabeth's Order in Council, that all traffic between England and Scotland should pass through Warwick, so that Her Majesty should not be defrauded of her Customs.

26 **ITALIAN ART.** PRECES ET PRÆCEPTA HEBRÆORUM, *Hebraice,* small 4to. *a beautiful specimen of Caligraphy, written in very elegant Romano-Jewish Characters, with points, and having the commencing words in* LETTERS OF GOLD, *surrounded by ornamental borders, painted in various colours, upon vellum, richly bound in green velvet, the sides and edges thereof protected with centres,* (*having a lion rampant and three stars, as arms, engraved thereon*), *corners and clasps of solid silver,* £35. Sæc. XV.

Illuminated Hebrew MSS. by Italian Artists are of very rare occurrence. This elegant specimen of Italian Art was a marriage gift, it is in the purest state of preservation. Some of the Prayers are intermixed with Benedictions in Italian, but written in Hebrew characters.

Although the language is chiefly Hebrew, yet this beautiful MS. is entitled to a place in this class, inasmuch as the art and ornamentation, as well as the graceful execution of the Caligraphy, are entirely European in character and belong to the most flourishing period of Italian art.

27 JONES (J. M.) GRAMADEG CYMREIG YMARFEROL: a practical WELSH GRAMMAR, comprehending the substance of all Welsh Grammars, with original observations on the rudiments and characteristics of the Language, also the rules of WELSH POETRY, *a plainly written MS. on 192 pages, with a drawing of Beaumaris, Llanidloes,* 1847—Hughes' (Hugh) (Tegai) Welsh Grammar, namely, a Philosophical Grammar, in which the Laws of the Welsh Language are explained, *a legibly written MS. on 184 leaves, Caernarfon,* 1846—together 2 vols. 4to. hf. bd. 36s 1846-47

Two rival Welsh Grammars; at the end of one vol. is a sharp critique on the merits of the two productions. Both are evidently very valuable works.

28 JUSTINUS. CLARISSIMI HISTORICI JUSTINI super historiis Trogi Pompei Epythoma, *a beautiful MS. by an Italian Scribe, upon* VELLUM, 4to. meas. 10 *inches by* 7, 125 *leaves, the first leaf elaborately embellished by exquisite* ARABESQUE BORDERS, *in gold and colours,* ILLUMINATED CAPITALS *to each of the* 43 *books, the writing, as usual with early Italian MS. very legible, but with occasional contractions, bound in vellum,* £10. Sæc. XIII.

A desirable volume, in very fine preservation, marked "Volumen 7um. Bibliothecae Fr. Aloysii de Baronis Ord. Serv. 1748"

29 LATINÆ GRAMMATICÆ Compendia, 4to. *Manuscript on vellum, with the Initial Capital illuminated in gold and colours,* £4. Sæc. XV.

In the original Italian binding of the XVth century, with sides ornamented with gold tooling. This Manuscript is without the name of the author, and commences "Vox est Aer tenuissimus ictus." Spaces throughout have been left for filling in the Greek quotations. This abridgment, which seems to have been made from the original work in XVI. books, concludes with the following lines:—

"Cum legeris nostri compendia parva laboris
Dicere non pudeat gratia magna tibi :
Nam que vix poteras multis ediscere in annis
Mensibus hec paucis nunc meminisse potes."

30 LEYDEN unsers Herrn Jhesu Christi, 302 pp.—Bible Lessons in German, 32 pp. *with* 12 *extremely quaint and rudely executed* DRAWINGS, *resembling in style the* EARLY GERMAN ART, *as displayed in the Block-books,* sm. 4to. *original old oak binding,* £4. 10s Sæc. XV.

EUROPEAN MANUSCRIPTS. 9

SCRIPT, *beautifully written on* 145 *leaves of vellum, with finely illuminated Capitals (the last containing a characteristic portrait), and Headings in gold and colours, having* PAINTINGS OF THE CRUCIFIX, BEFORE WHICH DON MIGUEL WITH HIS WIFE AND CHILD *are praying, and of his Coat of Arms prefixed. Each leaf is officially stamped, and at the end are the Autograph Signatures of the Marquis del Arco and other Officials, oak bds.* £9. 9s
dated Valladolid, 20 *August*, 1695

Similar works of Spanish art are so rare, that this beautiful example ought to be looked upon as extremely interesting.

47 XENOPHON de VITA CYRI, translatus per POGGIUM FLORENTINUM, small folio, VERY BEAUTIFUL ITALIAN MANUSCRIPT, *upon the purest* VELLUM, 124 *leaves in Roman characters, with beautiful* ILLUMINATED BORDER *on the first page, and the* CAPITAL LETTERS *in the best Italian style, in the original stamped calf binding, perhaps the oldest specimen of ancient binding, in excellent preservation,* £10.
Sæc. XV.

An interesting monument of the famous Poggio Fiorentino, who filled the position of Apostolic Secretary to so many Popes,—amongst them, John XXIII; and whose name has descended to our time, not merely as the author of the "Facetiæ" afterwards used by La Fontaine, but as one of the most learned and energetic of the restorers of ancient literature. His visit to England about the year 1420 is also to be remembered; although he gained by it little beyond a flattering reception from the notorious Cardinal Beaufort.

This MS. translation of Xenophon was never printed, but it was used by one of Poggio's sons as the text from which to publish an Italian version of the Cyropædia, which appeared at Florence in 1521.

48 YUILLE'S (Robert) Missionary Journals, Letters and Reports from Selenginsk in Siberia, 1823-28 (a district of about 96,000 inhabitants, including 1500 Lamas) and addressed to the London Missionary Society, and to his friends in England, Scotland and Russia, giving various details of the Geography of SIBERIA, Mongolia, Tibet, and other Countries of Central Asia—A curious Meteorological Diary of the Weather at Selenginsk, 1822-28—together 7 vols. folio and 4to. 25s
temp. 1822-37

49 **SPANISH MS.** Sentencias y Carta executoria de Hidalguia a favor de CHRISTOVAL DE VILLALOVOS, vezino de la villa de Griñon, folio, *the entire first page beautifully illuminated with a fine large* COAT OF ARMS, *the final page surrounded by a light and graceful border, a well written MS. on* 46 *leaves of* VELLUM, *with many Autographs, old black calf tooled,* £2. 5s
Valladolid, 1571

An instance of Spanish art in its practical application, during the magnificent reign of Philip II.

50 **PORTUGUESE LAW.** In initio, "Sequitur Tt' Ff. Soluto Matrimonio explicatus,"—several MS. treatises in Latin on Portuguese Law, by Gabriel à Costa, Petrus Barboza, Alvaro Valasco, and Lopez da Veiga, written between 1570 and 1580, folio, *about* 600 *leaves, half of the top margins eaten away, and text slightly injured, with some curious initial letters,* 20s
Sæc. XVI.

51 **AUTOGRAPHS.** Bothwell. BOCCACCIO, il Decamerone, nuovamente stampato e ricorretto per Brucioli, 4to. 10 *and* 274 *leaves, portrait of Boccaccio on title, large margins, but of which the lower corners are stained nearly all through the book, with the autograph of* "*Borthwel*," *third husband of Mary Queen of Scots, limp vellum,* £3. 3s
Vinetia, G. G. da Trino, 1538

An excellent edition, regarding which Haym quotes Bonamici's observation upon its beauty and correctness; but of course, the chief interest attaching to this copy is the signature of James Hepburn, Earl of Bothwell, that cruel and turbulent successor of the unfortunate Darnley, and who also met the miserable fate which attended all the favourites of the unhappy Mary. It comes from the library of the "travelled Thane, Athenian Aberdeen," to whose family it has probably belonged for three centuries back.

52 **Maria Theresa** (Empress) Letters patent under Great Seal to Wenzl Graf von Sinzendorf, WITH HER AUTOGRAPH SIGNATURE, *countersigned* "Theodor Damian Monshaussen," 20s
dated 23rd *February*, 1764

53 **Melancthon.** BIBLIA HEBRAICA, cum commentariis David Kimhi, à Vatablo recognita, 24 parts in 3 vols. sm. folio, LARGE PAPER, *fine clean copy, in the original stamped hogskin,* £10.
Parisiis, Rob. Stephanus, 1539-44

Priced, 1854, £13. 13s. A book of the greatest beauty and rarity, but this copy is of the highest interest as having belonged to Melancthon. Inside the cover of the first volume is a precious memorial of the great Reformer, being an inscription in his autograph, first in Hebrew, then its translation (apparently) in Greek, viz.,

"Epiphanius
'Ου παντα τὰ θεῖα ῥήματα ἀλληγορίας δεῖται,
ἀλλ' ὡς ἔχει. Θεωρίας δὲ δεῖται καὶ αἰσθήσεως,
εἰς τὸ εἰδέναι ἑκαστης ὑποθέσεως τὴν δύναμιν.
Scriptū manu Philippi."

There is also another MS. note in Greek, quoted from Scripture, and signed "Paulus Eberus M. scribebat Vuiteb. vi die Maij Anno 1558." Paul Eber was the secretary and intimate friend of Melancthon, and was sent with him to the Diet at Worms, in 1541. He held the Hebrew professorship at Wittemberg, and made himself illustrious amongst the Reformers, by his learning and writings.

54 NETHERCLIFT'S Hand-Book to Autographs, a ready guide to the handwriting of distinguished men and women of every Nation, with biographical Index, sq. 12mo. *about* 600 *Autographs, cloth,* 18s
1862

PALAEOGRAPHY, CATALOGUES OF MANUSCRIPTS.

55 ADRIAN, Catalogus codicum Manuscriptorum Bibliothecae Academicae Gissensis, 4to. *facsimiles, sd.* 5s ; *or in red bds. gilt edges,* 7s 6d
Francof. ad Mænum, 1840

56 ALCOBATIÆ (in Lusitaniâ) BIBLIOTHECÆ INDEX Codicum, (MSS.) sm. folio, *Large Fine Paper, with two facsimiles, a beautiful copy in old red morocco gilt, Royal Arms on sides, gilt edges,* 32s
Olisipone, 1775
A careful and excellent Catalogue, with Index.

57 ANDERSONI Selectus DIPLOMATUM et NUMISMATUM SCOTIÆ Thesaurus cum Indice Nominum et expositione praecipuarum Familiarum cura Ruddimanni, royal folio, *containing* 183 *plates of* COINS, ANCIENT SEALS, CHARTERS, &c. *fine impressions, hf. bd.* £8. 8s ; *or whole russia,* £9. 9s
Edinb. 1739
The only record of the Genealogies of the Great Families of Scotland. Nearly the entire edition of this extremely scarce and valuable work was destroyed by fire. Hibbert's copy fetched 12*l.*

58 RUDDIMANN'S Introduction to Anderson's Diplomata Scotiæ, 12mo. *hf. bound,* 7s 6d
Edinb. 1782

59 ARTE de Escribir por reglas y sin muestras, 4to. *with plates of rudimentary Penmanship, bd.* 7s 6d
*Madrid, ?*1800

60 ASTLE on the Origin and Progress of Writing, illustrated by Engravings taken from Marbles, Manuscripts, and Charters, SECOND EDITION, *with additions, portrait, and* 31 *plates of facsimiles of MSS. Alphabets, &c.* 36s
1803
To all gentlemen engaged upon original researches of State Papers, Charters, and other Early Documents, Astle's work is indispensable.

61 BARROIS (J.) Eléments Carlovingiens, linguistiques et littéraires, 4to. *plates, hf. calf gilt,* 10s
Paris, Crapelet, 1846

62 BAURENFEIND'S Schreib-Kunst, von C. Weigel, oblong folio, 59 *engraved plates of every variety of style of Penmanship, including many very elaborate Initial Letters, vellum,* 18s
Nürnberg, 1716

63 BEAU CHESNE and BAILDON, A Booke containing divers Sortes of Hands, as well the English as French secretarie, with the Italian, Roman, Chancelry and Court hands ; also the true and just proportion of the capitall Romane, smallest 4to. *quite perfect, beautiful copy in russia extra, gilt edges by Lewis,* VERY RARE, £4. 4s
London, Richard Field, [1602]
Collation: woodcut-title, the oval centre printed ; rules for children to write by, 1 leaf ; 42 engraved leaves, the first of them has a woodcut "how you ought to hold your penne," and an engraved page on the other side. Each plate has a most elaborate capital letter, embellished with spirited and grotesque figures.

64 BIBLIOTHEQUE de l'ECOLE des CHARTES, Revue d'Erudition consacrée principalement à l'Etude du Moyen-Age, 15 vols. in 85 parts, royal 8vo. *uncut, very rare,* £5.
Paris, 1840-1854
This is one of the most important and interesting publications relating to Mediæval MSS. ; the present copy is complete to the above date, with the exception of the first vol. for 1840. The cost of publication was 12s a volume.

65 BOISSENII Grammato-graphices ; in quo varia scripturæ emblemata Belgicis, Germanicis, Italicis, Hispanicis, Gallicis, et Latinis characteribus exarata, oblong folio, 48 *plates of various styles of Penmanship with flourishes, including the title, fine copy of an elegant work on this subject, vellum,* 30s
Amst. 1605

66 BLACK (W. H.) Catalogue of the Manuscripts, bequeathed unto the University of Oxford, by Elias ASHMOLE, Windsor Herald ; also of additional MSS. 4to. 1522 pp. *cloth,* 24s
Oxford, 1845
A remarkably well-made Catalogue, descriptive, analytical and critical.

BODLEIAN LIBRARY Catalogues of MSS.—*see* Class "TRANSACTIONS OF SOCIETIES."
BRITISH MUSEUM Catalogues of MSS.—*see* Class "TRANSACTIONS OF SOCIETIES."

67 CHAMPOLLION, Paléographie des Classiques Latins, d'après les MSS. de la Bibliothèque Royale de Paris, avec introduction par Champollion-Figeac, Liv. I. *Introduction,* folio, 2 *plates of* 7 *facsimiles,* 7s 6d
1839

68 CHASSANT, Paléographie des Chartes et des Manuscrits du XIe au XVIIe siècle, roy. 8vo. *facsimiles of ancient writing, hf. morocco,* 10s
1839

69 CLARKE's Catalogue of the MSS. in the library of the late Adam Clarke, large 8vo. 7 *facsimiles, bds.* 5s
1835

70 D'ANISY, Extrait des Chartes et autres Actes Normands, et Anglo-Normands, qui se trouvent dans les Archives du Calvados. 2 vols. 8vo. *with 4to. atlas of engravings of* 503 SEALS, *hf. red morocco, uncut,* 34s
Caen, 1834-35

71 DELANDINE, Manuscrits de la Bibliothèque de Lyon, leur ancienneté, leurs auteurs, le caractère de leur écriture, etc. une histoire des anciennes Bibliothèques de Lyon, essai sur les MSS. et une Bibliographie spéciale, 3 vols. 8vo. *calf gilt,* 15s
Paris, 1812

EUROPEAN MANUSCRIPTS. 7

31 MAUNDEVYLL (Johñ, *Knygt*) Travels in the Holy Land, Hierusalem, with the Merveyles of Inde, etc.
   2. The Invencion of the Armite Seynt Antony, the whiche Seynt Jerome compownyd and translate out of Grec into Latten, and out of Latten into Englyshe, made by the holy Bysschop Teophile in the time of Constantyne
   3. That portion of the Monk's Tale from Chaucer, containing the Story of Ugo Earl of Pisa, "How an Erle was brought yn thral," but with alterations and additions, ending "Explicit quod B."
   4. The Passion of Christ versified
   5. A Lamentable Ballad on the Death of King Edward ye IVth, from Fabyan, (by John Skelton), *containing an entire Stanza not in the printed copies* ANTIENT MANUSCRIPTS ON PAPER, *written from about* 1480 *to* 1490 ; *formerly in the Collection of Lord Somers, afterwards in those of E. Umfreville, Esq.* [*circa* 1738], *then in M. Tulet's, very curious and interesting, russia neat, gilt edges*, £16. *Sæc.* XV.

32 MEIGCRATH. Dánta Eoghain Mhic Donchadh Mhaoil Mheigcraith ; Eoghain O'Dubhthair ; Taidhg O'Cobhthaig ; agus an chead bheatha naomh Brighid, le Brogán ; in 1 vol. sm. 4to. *hf. calf*, 12s   *Atha-Cliath (Dublin)* 1847
   Poems by Eoghan, son of Donogh Magrath the Bald, written about the year 1240 ; Eoghan O'Duffy's Poem on the Apostacy of Miler Magrath, Archbishop of Cashel ; Teague O'Coffey's Cross of Christ; St. Brogan or Breccan's Life of St. Bridget ; all transcribed by John O'Daly. The poems of Magrath are extremely rare.

33 ODDONIS CANTUARIENSIS COMMENTARII IN PSALMOS, MANUSCRIPT ON VELLUM, *by an* ENGLISH SCRIBE, sm. folio, 158 *leaves, with singularly grotesque capitals to each Psalm in the Anglo-Saxon style, some of them gilt and silvered, bound in green vellum, gilt edges, in the best state of preservation,* £40. *Sæc.* XII.-XIII.
   Oddo Wood, better known as Oddo Cantuariensis, was Prior of Canterbury at the time of the murder of Archbishop Thomas à Becket, and fought stoutly against the Court for the right of free election of a new Archbishop. He was subsequently in 1175 made Abbot of Battle Abbey. This valuable and highly interesting Manuscript presents a fine specimen of English Caligraphy at the end of the XIIth or commencement of the XIIIth century, having on the last leaf the name of the scribe: *Ego Dominicus Presbyter Alberici filius scripsi complevi et absolvi. Rogo vos omnes fratres quum hunc libel'um l gitis, Orate pro me peccatore, Secundum habentis Protectorem, &c.*" The author's name appears in the preface, where he says, "*tua tuique Oddonis pudica diligentia corrigat, abradat et opponat, &c*. The preface is addressed to some one whom he entitles, "præsul venerabilis," and by whose desire he states that he had performed the work, this " Davitica præda," as he calls it.

34 OFFICIUM BEATÆ MARIÆ, secundum Usum et Consuetudinem Romanæ Ecclesiæ, cum Calendario, thick 12mo. *a valuable* MANUSCRIPT ON VELLUM, *with many illuminated* CAPITALS *and* BORDERS, *adorned with* 7 LARGE MINIATURES *and* 17 SMALL PAINTINGS *in the margins, by a French artist, blue morocco extra*, £10.
   Sæc. XV.
   From some MS. memoranda in the Calendar, this Officium appears to have belonged to the Vatican family.

35 OFFICIUM BEATÆ VIRGINIS MARIÆ, secundum Consuetudinem Romanæ Curiæ, cum Calendario, 24mo. MANUSCRIPT ON VELLUM, *written by an Italian scribe, with* 20 *small* MINIATURES *within the initial letters, painted and bordered, and also two elegantly illuminated borders, of graceful design, in which children at play are introduced, morocco, gilt edges,* £3. 3s   *Sæc.* XV.

36 OFFICIUM sancte Marie virginis secundum ordinem romane curie, cum Calendario, VALUABLE ITALIAN MANUSCRIPT, square 8vo. (6½ by 5 inches) *written on* 260 *leaves of* VELLUM, *some of them slightly injured, embellished with* 26 *fine* MINIATURES, *surrounded by rich borders, besides* 24 BORDERS *round large Illuminated Capitals, bound in old Italian red morocco, with the Cypher M. A. under a Crown and surrounded by a wreath on the sides*, £10. 10s   *Sæc.* XV.
   Some of the Miniatures, such as "The CRUCIFIXION,' the Four APOSTLES, and ST. CATHERINE, are executed with especial artistic skill. Many of the Prayers are in Italian. The volume was written for a "LUCRETIA," as she calls herself "misera peccatrix Lucretia" (? Lucretia Borgia).

37 O'REILLY (E. author of the Irish Dictionary) Collection of the Ancient Names of Places mentioned in Irish History, with their more modern names, and those by which they are called at the present day, the names of the Princes or Chiefs, and notices of historical and remarkable events, folio, *an interesting volume of* 250 *pages, half bound,* 36s   *ca.* 1820
   This MS. would have been of much value to the late Dr. O'Donovan in preparing his edition of the "Topographical Poems," published lately by the Archæological Society; for it is stated to include the names of all the places in John O'Dubhagain's poem.

38 PAULI (S.) EPISTOLÆ, cum Commento et Glossis, folio, SPLENDID MANUSCRIPT ON VELLUM, *with grotesque painted capitals*, 141 *leaves, in the best preservation, bound in the original oak boards, covered with leather, elegantly blind tooled,* £10. 10s   *Sæc.* XIII.-XIV.
   This beautiful MS. is headed "*Liber Sci Ruphi. Si quis ei abstulerit Anathema sit.*" The binding, however, shows that in the XVth century it must have been transferred to those great collectors of Manuscripts, the illustrious family de Medici.

39 **PETRARCA** (Francesco) SONETTI, CANZONE E TRIONFI. "Francisci. Petrarce. poetae. clarissimi. Sonectorum. liber. foeliciter. incipit", MANUSCRIPT ON VELLUM, *written in the first half of the XVth Century*, royal 8vo. *old calf extra, dentelle borders, gilt edges*, £50. *Saec.* XV.

MAGNIFICENT MANUSCRIPT, admirably written on very white and very fine vellum, in perfect condition. The text is extremely pure, and the volume contains the Sonnets against the Court of Rome, which are so often deficient. At the end there is " Vita Francisci Pe. per Arretinum," in Italian, which occupies nearly 14 pages.
This Manuscript is ornamented with MINIATURES OF EXTRAORDINARY DELICACY and elaboration. The first page is surrounded by a border filled with figures (including a portrait of the Poet), birds, flowers, &c. &c. The title is written on letters of gold, on a blue and rose-coloured ground, producing a charming effect; the "Trionphi" are adorned with numerous borders and small emblematical miniatures of an amazing delicacy. The initial letters of each "Sonnet," and of all the "Canzoni," are chastely painted in gold and colours. It is one of the most beautiful manuscripts of Petrarch in existence. The binding appears to have been executed towards the end of the last century.

40 **PORTOLANO** ove si contiene tutto il costaggio di Terra Ferma cominciando dal Porto Santa Maria, dentro il Stretto di Gibilterra, e si gira sino alla montagna detta Erminia, with an INDEX, folio, *MS. upon paper, ornamental gilt binding*, £3. 10s *Saec.* XVII.

41 **PRISCIANI** GRAMMATICI ARTIS LIBRI XV. 4to. MANUSCRIPT ON VELLUM, WITH THE GREEK QUOTATIONS, 211 *leaves*, WITH ELEGANTLY FLOURISHED GROTESQUE CAPITALS, *in the original oak boards, covered with leather ornamented with blind tooling, and clasps, from the Library of the* "MAGNIFICO LORENZO DE MEDICI," £10. *Saec.* XIII.

A most valuable Manuscript with the inscription "*ad Julianum Consulem*," omitted by Krehl, and presenting many important various readings. The last two leaves are in a ruder style of penmanship than the rest of the work, and without commentaries.

42 **PRISCIANI** Cæsariensis Grammatici de Grammatica Libri XV. 4to. 243 *leaves of* VELLUM, *original binding*, £10. 10s *Saec.* XV.

"In a beautiful Italian hand, with illuminated capitals, and a fine PAINTED BORDER, *with figures*, on the first leaf, the initial containing a portrait of Priscian writing, somewhat Egyptian in character, having in front the inscription "ad Julianum Consulem ac Patricium," which Krehl omits, as he was unable to find it in any manuscript he collated.

This fine manuscript exhibits a very pure text, the Greek quotations being supplied in a different hand, and the correct digamma used whenever it occurs. As the XVth book in Krehl's edition is divided into two, in reality this manuscript ought to be described as exhibiting " Libri XVI." As a specimen of the various readings, we select a few occurring in the XVIth Book of Krehl, treating " De Conjunctionibus:"

MANUSCRIPT.	EDITION.
Vim vel ordinem demonstrans	Vim vel ordinationem
Non tamen motum omnimodo sequitur ambulatio	Non tamen etiam motum, &c.
Ambulare tamen sine motu non potest	Ambulare autem sine motu non potest
Accidunt conjunctioni figura et species	Accidunt igitur, &c.
Copulativæ sunt quæ copulant	Copulativa est quæ copulat
Hæc einem copulat	Hæc einem copulant
Utque invenitur non solum copulativa sed etiam completiva.	Utque invenitur etiam completiva.

A curious fact is that this manuscript does not contain any mention of Theodorus, and also that there is scarcely any division of the work into different books.

43 **PSALTERIUM**, Latinè, cum Calendario, square 12mo. a fine old English MS. ON VELLUM, *full length figure of an Apostle at the side of each month in the Calendar, with the signs of the Zodiac at foot, two Miniatures, and several large Capitals and Borders, enclosing smaller paintings, all illuminated, resembling the Anglo-Saxon style, in brown morocco antique*, £25. marked *Saec.* XII. (sed ca. 1320)

44 **SANCHEZ** (Mathias) SEMI-HISTORIA DE LAS FUNDACIONES, Residencias, o Colegios, que tiene la Compañia de Jesus en las ISLAS CANARIAS ; Origen, Progresos y estado presente de aquellas Islas, resumen de su Conquista y algunos Problemas concernientes a ellas, singularmente a la famosa Encantada, o de San Borondon, sm. 4to. 1036 *pages*, A HIGHLY INTERESTING MANUSCRIPT, STATED TO BE IN THE AUTOGRAPH OF THE AUTHOR, AND UNPUBLISHED, *from the Library of the Marquis of Loreto, vellum*, £2. 16s ca. 1720

45 **THERAMI** LIBER BELIAL. ANONYMI Flores Sacræ Scripturæ, pp. 1—39. JACOBI DE THERAMO, *Archidiaconi Aversani et Canonici*, Compendium breve de redemptione generis humani, Consolatio peccatorum nuncupatum et apud nonnullos BELIAL vocitatum sive processus Luciferi contra Jesum judice Salomone, pp. 41—118; *at the end,* "*Datum aversae prope Neapolis, anno Domini* 1382 *aetatis meae* 33o. *Ego scriptor, qui hunc scripsi, imposui extremam manum die* 16 *Juli* 1463. *Absque labore gravi vix munera magna dabuntur*," folio, *a well written MS. in a neat gothic hand, in excellent preservation, dark morocco extra, gilt edges, a handsome volume*, £6. *Saec.* XIV.—XV.

This second work, the "Belial" of J. Palladino Teramo, who was Archdeacon of Aversa, and became in 1400 Archbishop of Tarentum, is a grotesque romance, in which Christ, represented by Moses, is accused by Satan before the judgment seat of Solomon; and the style of argument used, with the curious illustrations from scripture, makes it one of the most singular works of the Middle Ages.

46 **VERDE BARAONA**. Carta executoria de Hidalguia de Sangre, &c. &c. de D. Miguel Verde Baraona Vecino de Sepulveda, folio, THE OFFICIAL MANU-

PALÆOGRAPHY, CATALOGUES OF MANUSCRIPTS. 11

72 DENIS (M.) CODICES Manuscripti Theologici Bibliothecae Palatinae Vindobonensis Latinæ aliarumque Occidentis linguarum, 6 vols. folio, *facsimile, calf,* £3. 10s *Vindob.* 1793-1802
Ouvrage très estimé des Bibliographes.—*Brunet.*
73 GIRARDOT, Catalogue des MSS. de la Bibliothèque des Bourges, royal 4to. 164 pp. *executed in lithography, with facsimiles, sd. only 90 copies printed,* 12s 1859
74 HAENEL, Catalogi Libr. Manuscriptorum, qui in Biblioth. Galliæ, Helvetiæ, Belgii, Britanniæ Magnæ, Hispaniæ, Lusitaniæ asservantur, 4to. *calf gilt, from Miss Currer's library,* 27s *Lips.* 1830
Contains Lists of Manuscripts existing in Public and Private Libraries in Europe.
75 HARRIS, Fragments of an Oration against Demosthenes, folio, 32 *facsimile fragments of Greek Papyri in* 11 *plates,* 2s 6d 1848
76 HAYTER's Report upon the Herculaneum MSS., with observations upon a Review, and a letter of Sir W. Drummond, 4to. *plates, hf. calf, Miss Currer's copy,* 7s 6d 1810-12
77 HUMPHREYS' (H. N.) ILLUMINATED BOOKS of the Middle Ages, with an Account of the development and progress of the Art of Illumination from the IVth to the XVIIth centuries, impl. folio, LARGE PAPER, *illustrated by a series of* 31 *examples of the size of the originals, selected from the most beautiful of the MSS. of the various periods, executed on stone, and most beautifully printed in gold, silver and colours by* OWEN JONES, *red mor.* (pub. at £16. 16s) £8. 8s 1849
An extremely low price for such a beautiful work. In 1855, Bernal's copy, mor. fetched £12.
The illustrations, all of the exact size of the originals, are from the most celebrated and splendid MSS. in the Imperial and Royal Libraries of Vienna, Moscow, Paris, Naples, Copenhagen, and Madrid; from the Vatican, Escurial, Ambrosian, and other great Libraries of the Continent; and from the rich Public, Collegiate, and Private Libraries of Great Britain.
78 IRIARTE (J.) Regiæ Bibliothecæ Matritensis Codices GRÆCI MSS. Vol. I. *all published,* folio, *whole bound,* 25s *Matriti,* 1769
Of this catalogue, the first volume only was published, it is a valuable and elaborate work.
79 INDEX to the Records, with explanations of Rolls, Writs, &c. 12mo. *calf,* 5s 1739
80 KELHAM'S Dictionary of the Norman or Old French Language, 8vo. *calf,* 20s; *calf extra,* 30s 1779
81 KOOPS (M.) Historical Account of the Substances which have been used to DESCRIBE EVENTS, and to CONVEY Ideas; from the EARLIEST DATE to the INVENTION OF PAPER, royal 8vo. 92 *pp. printed entirely upon* STRAW PAPER, *with a sample of a superior kind, hf. russia, with Hanrott's autograph, rare,* 18s *London,* 1800
A very interesting and valuable work, especially to Palæographers.
82 KOPP, PALÆOGRAPHIA CRITICA, 4 vols. 4to. (pub. at £16. 16s) *bds.* £3. 10s 1817-19
A most important and valuable work, containing several thousand new characters, expressly struck for it, to represent the endless varieties of styles, the abbreviations, etc. in the early Greek and Roman Writing. They are arranged in form of a Lexicon, explained in the regular Greek and Roman characters, and followed by reverse Indexes. The work further contains several large folding sheets of facsimiles. The cost of the publication amounted to several thousand pounds, and was entirely defrayed by the learned author, in whose lifetime only a few copies were circulated amongst Public Libraries and his friends.
83 LANGLOIS, Essai sur la Calligraphie des Manuscrits du Moyen-Age, et les ornements des livres d'Heures imprimés, large 8vo. *frontispiece, (slightly injured) and* 15 *plates of Initial Letters, Miniatures, etc. hf. calf neat,* 16s *Rouen,* 1841
In this volume are bound up, also, "JUBINAL, Tapisseries historiées, 4 *plates,* 1840;" and LICHTENBERGER, Invention de l'Imprimerie, *portrait of Gutenberg,* and 9 *plates, Strasb.* 1825."
84 LE LONG, Bibliotheque Historique de la France, contenant le Catalogue de tous les Ouvrages imprimés et Manuscrits qui traitent de ce Royaume; augmenté par Fontette, 5 vols. folio, *a beautiful copy from Miss Currer's library, in old French calf extra, with Arms on sides,* £10. 10s *Paris,* 1768-78
Priced, 1831, H. Bohn, £10. 10s.
"Le Long's historical library of France, if we except some errors, is a very curious and useful work."—*Voltaire.*
This is perhaps the most laborious and most able Bibliographical work which has ever appeared. It is scarcely possible to find a volume or a manuscript in the least connected with French History, not what is fully described here, and it frequently gives curious details respecting our English historians. Brunet says of it—
" Cet ouvrage est un des travaux les plus essentiels qu'ait produit la science bibliographique, et il doit se trouver dans toutes les Bibliothéques."
85 MASSEY (W.) Origin and Progress of Letters, manner of writing of different nations, etc. with an account of English penmen, 8vo. *plates of alphabets and contractions, old calf,* 7s 6d 1763
86 MACHHOLDTH (A.) Formular oder Schreiber Buch, black letter, *a curious work on writing, with* SINGULARLY FINE INITIAL LETTERS *of peculiar design, Eisleben,* 1559—Karls V., des H. Römischen Reichs peinlich Gerichts Ordnung, *woodcuts, Franckfurt,* 1558—Meischner (J. H.) Teutscher Nation Formular und Handbuch Teutscher Schreiberey, 4 vols. *ib.* 1562—in 1 vol. stout folio, *stamped pigskin,* 18s

87 MÖLLER, Schreib-Kunst Spiegel, sm. oblong 4to. *bds.* 27*s*   *Lübeck*, (1644-50)
   Collation: Ornamental bastard title, engraved title, dedication, 2 plates; printed text, pp. 1-16; a beautiful portrait of the Artist; 38 plates of Alphabets with very ingenious ORNAMENTS and FLOURISHES; text 1-119.

88 MONTFAUCON, Bibliotheca Bibliothecarum Manuscriptorum Nova: ubi, quae innumeris pene Msp. Bibl. continentur, ad quodvis literaturae genus spectantia describuntur et indicantur, 2 vols. folio, *neat in calf*, 25*s*   *Paris*, 1739
   Mead's copy fetched 37*s*; Heath's, 39*s*. "A learned and useful work, almost necessary for every man of letters."
Gibbon's Misc. Works, Vol. I. p. 341. See Dibdin's Dec. Vol. III. p. 207.

89 MONTFAUCONI Palæographia Græca, sive de Ortu et Progressu Literarum Græcarum, et de variis Scriptionis Græc. Generibus, itemque de Abbrevationibus, folio, *plates of facsimiles of Inscriptions, Monuments, &c. calf*, 25*s*   *Paris*, 1708
   "An invaluable work, which has done the same in reference to the discovery of the age of Greek MSS. that the *Re Diplomatica* of Mabillon has done for the Latin."—DR. CLARKE.
   "A work illustrating by a considerable number of plates, and learned dissertations, the whole history of Greek writings, with the variations of the Greek characters from the earliest times down to the present. This was almost the first work written upon the subject, and it has served as the text-book for all students of this branch of Greek Literature."—*H. L. Jones, Gent.'s Mag. Dec.* 1855.

90 NATURÆ et Scripturæ concordia: de literis ac numeris primævis, sm. 4to. *plates of ancient alphabets*, 5*s*   *Lips.* 1752

91 NESSEL (D. de) Catalogus, sive recensio specialis omnium Codicum Manuscriptorum Græcorum nec non Linguarum Orientalium Bibliothecae Caesareæ Vindobonensis, 2 vols. folio, *numerous facsimiles of early Greek and Byzantine Art, calf*, 21*s*   *Vindob.* 1690

92 NOTICES et EXTRAITS des Manuscrits de la Bibliothèque du Roi, et d'autres bibliothèques, publiés par l'Institut royal de France, faisant suite aux Notices et Extraits lus au Comité établi dans l'Académie des Inscriptions et Belles Lettres, Vols. I. to XIII.—13 vols. 4to. *plates and facsimiles, half bound calf, not uniform, the Earl of Munster's copy*, £6. 10*s*   *Paris*, 1787-1838

93 —— Tome XII. 4to. *containing* "De Sacy, Correspondance des Samaritains de Naplouse," *with the Samaritan, Hebrew, and Arabic Texts, etc. bds.* 15*s* *ib.* 1831
   As there is some irregularity in publication of the recent volumes, I give a statement of what has been done since volume XIII.; Vol. XIV. parts 1, 2; Vol. XV. not out; Vol XVI. part 2; Vol XVII. parts 1, 2. The "Notices et Extraits" form a desirable Supplement to the "Histoire de l'Académie des Inscriptions." The existence and continuation of this collection, exhibiting such noble proofs of French literary industry, are hardly sufficiently known or appreciated. How is it that so excellent an example is not followed by other European Governments?"—*Rev. Enc.* vol. 4, p. 508.

94 NOUVEAU TRAITÉ de DIPLOMATIQUE, où l'on examine les fondemens de cet Art, on établit des regles sur le discernement des Titres, et l'on expose historiquement les Caractères des Bulles Pontificales et des Diplomes, par deux Religieux Benedictins de S. Maur, 6 vols. 4to. *many plates of Ancient Writings, Charters, Diplomas, Documents, &c.* £8. 8*s*   *Paris*, 1750-65
   The best book on Diplomatics, indispensable to every Public Library.

95 PALATINO, Libro nel qual s'insegna a Scriver ogni sorte Lettera, Antica et Moderna, di qualunque natione, con le sue regole et misure et essempi, sm. 4to. FIRST EDITION, *woodcut portrait on title, numerous wood engravings of* ORNAMENTAL LETTERS, *Combinations, Rebuses, &c. vellum*, £2. 2*s*   *Roma*, 1561

96 —— Compendio del Gran volume de l'Arte del bene et leggiadramente Scrivere tutte le sorti di Lettere et Carattieri, sm. 4to. *woodcuts (rebus), ornamental letters, &c. vellum*, 36*s*   A later edition of the preceding.   *Roma*, 1566

98 RODRIGUEZ, Bibliotheca Universal de la Polygraphia ESPANOLA, royal folio, *with 126 plates, exhibiting specimens of the writing of different ages, hf. yellow morocco, uncut; or calf*, £3. 10*s*   *Madrid*, 1738
   This work is invaluable, and in fact indispensable to all collectors of, or any persons who are engaged in, manuscripts. The plates exhibit the various kinds of writings, from the earliest time down to the seventeenth century. "Cet ouvrage dont les exemplaires sont peu communs est precieux, a cause des modeles d'anciennes ecritures qu'il contient; les Benedictins auteurs du *Nouveau Traité de Diplomatique*, le citent avec eloge."—*Brunet*.

99 ROELAND'S PENMANSHIP: T'Magazin der Penn-const, 4to. *folding plates of every style of Writing of that period, every page embellished with wonderfully combined* FLOURISHES, *vellum*, 20*s*   *Antwerpen*, 1616

100 SANDERI, Bibliotheca Belgica Manuscripta: Elenchus Codicum MSS. in Belgii Bibliothecis adhuc latentium, 2 vols. in 1, sm. 4to. *vellum*, 30*s* *Insulis*, 1641-44

101 SERVIDORI (Domingo M. de) Reflexiones sobre l'Arte de Escribir, 2 vols. folio, *one consisting of* 105 *plates, calf*, £3. 10*s*   *Madrid*, 1789

102 SILVESTRE (J. B.) PALÉOGRAPHIE UNIVERSELLE. Collection de FACSIMILE D'ECRITURES de tous les peuples et de tous les temps, publiés d'après les modèles ecrits; accompagnés d'explications histor. et descriptives par MM. Champollion, 4 vols. atlas folio, *with about* 300 *magnificent plates of* FACSIMILES OF EVERY KIND OF MSS. *many* BEAUTIFULLY ILLUMINATED, *in gold and colours, a most sumptuous work, bound in blue* MOROCCO, *gilt edges, original copies like this are now* VERY SCARCE, £63   *Paris*, 1839-41

PALÆOGRAPHY, CATALOGUES OF MANUSCRIPTS. 13

102 SILVESTRE (J. B.) UNIVERSAL PALÆOGRAPHY, or Facsimiles of Writings of all Nations and Periods, copied from the most Celebrated and Authentic Manuscripts in the Libraries and Archives of France, Italy, Germany, and England, with Historical and Descriptive Text, and Introduction by Champollion-Figeac and Aimé Champollion, Fils, translated from the French and edited with corrections and notes by Sir Frederic Madden, 2 vols. impl. folio, with 2 vols. of text in 8vo. *half red morocco, gilt edges*, £26. 5s   London, 1850
Ouvrage capital éxécute avec le plus grand luxe et dont beaucoup de planches sont coloriées et rehaussées d'or. This splendid publication, alike interesting to the Antiquary, Scholar, and Man of Taste, has been got up regardless of expense by the Chevalier Silvestre, Professor of Calligraphy to the Royal Family of France, and cost to Subscribers 1530 francs. The copies of the Paintings are executed with great judgment, and for the Student of Art are nearly equal to the elaborate and costly originals. The excellent descriptions were contributed by Champollion-Figeac and Aimé Champollion Fils.

103 SILVESTRE, ALPHABET ALBUM, ou Collection de 60 feuilles d'alphabets historiés et fleuronnés, tirés des plus beaux manuscrits de l'Europe, des documens les plus rares, ou composés par J. B. Silvestre, professeur de calligraphie des Princes d'Orleans, folio (pub. at £3. 3s) *hf. morocco*, 30s   Paris, 1843-44

104 SMITH'S (C. J.) Historical and Literary Curiosities, consisting of Fac-similes of original Documents, and Autographs, Interesting Localities, and the Birth Places, Residences and Monuments of Eminent Literary Characters, 4to. 100 *plates of facsimiles of Manuscripts, Original Letters, Views, Antiquities, etc., some brilliantly illuminated*, (pub. at £3.) *cloth, uncut*, 36s   1840
"A rich and varied exhibition of literary relics."—*Gent.'s Mag.*
"There is not a page that does not affect the reflecting mind with melancholy emotion, and with imaginative ideas."—*Lit. Gazette.*

105 SPELMANNI Glossarium Archaiologicum continens Latina-barbara, peregrina, obsoleta et novatae significationis Vocabula; quæ post labefactas a Gothis, Vandalisque res Europaeas in scriptoribus, chartis et formulis occurrunt, folio, *best edition, portrait, calf*, 35s   Lond. 1687
Priced, 1832 and 1837, Payne and Foss, 3l. 13s 6d; 1848, Payne and Foss, 2l. 12s 6d; Brockett's copy fetched 3l. 16s; Bindley's, 2l. 17s; Tooke's with MS. notes, 3l. 17s. Large Paper, Heath's, 5l.; the Duke of Grafton's, 3l. 5s; Hibbert's, 4l. 14s 6d.
This valuable work is particularly directed to the illustration of Early English and Anglo-Saxon Words, Subjects, and Localities; it is indispensable to English Etymologists and Antiquaries.

106 TAGLIENTE (G. A.) la vera Arte de lo excellente Scrivere diverse et varie Sorti di Litere, small 4to. *a most curious book, printed in an immense variety of letters, apparently imperfect, vellum*, 18s   Venegia, 1547-8

107 THORPE'S Catalogue of Manuscripts, *mounted on small folio writing paper, upwards of* 700 *articles, with ample descriptions, total value*, £2987, *hf. bd.* 10s

108 TORIO, Arte de Escribir por reglas y con muestras, small 4to. 58 *plates of all manners of writing, vellum*, 12s   Madrid, 1802

109 TROMBELLI, Arte di conoscere l'Età de' Codici Latini e Italiani, 4to. *with* 2 *plates of facsimiles, bds.* 7s 6d—the same, *red morocco*, 9s   Bologna, 1756

110 VAINES (De) DICTIONNAIRE de DIPLOMATIQUE, contenant les Règles pour de- chiffrer les ancien Titres, Diplomes, et Monuments, ainsi qu'à justifier de leur Date et Authenticité, 2 vols. 8vo. *numerous plates of Charters and Facsimiles of MSS. calf*, 18s   1774

111 VAN PRAET, Recherches sur Louis de Bruges, Seigneur de la Gruthuyse, avec une notice des MSS. qui lui ont appartenu, impl. 8vo. *five plates,* LARGE THICK PAPER, *hf. morocco, uncut,* 25s   1831
Rempli de recherches curieuses.—*Brunet.* A catalogue of a large collection of the most valuable MSS.

112 VERIEN, Livre de trois Alphabets de CHIFFRES simples, doubles, et triples, avec un grand Nombre de Devises, Emblêmes et Médailles, sm. 8vo. *numerous plates of* CYPHERS, *Emblems and Devices, half bound,* 16s   Paris, 1686

113 VESPASIANO (Frate) Il perfetto modo d'imparare a Scrivere tutte le sorte di Lettere Cancellaresche, Corsive et moderne, colle Soprascrittioni di Lettere missive, oblong sm. 4to. 10 *pp. of letterpress, and* 85 *of engraved ornamental letters, etc. half calf, uncut,* £2. 10s   Venetia, 1620

114 WAILLY (Natalis de) Elements de PALÉOGRAPHIE, 2 vols. folio, or atlas 4to. *with two Series of plates:* FACSIMILES 1-17, SEALS A-U, *cloth bds.* £4. 5s Par. 1838

115 WALTHERI LEXICON DIPLOMATICUM, Abbreviaturas Syllabarum et Vocum in Diplomatibus et Codicibus a Seculo VIII ad XVI usque occurrentes exponens, junctis Alphabetis et Scripturae Speciminibus integris, cum prefatione J. H. Jungii, 3 parts in 1 vol. folio, *last edition,* 225 *plates of Mediaeval Alphabets and Contractions, and* 28 *plates of Facsimiles, all with explanations, calf, sound copy,* £2. 16s   Ulmae, 1756
A magnificent volume. In consequence of variations existing between copies, the collation of the above is given. Title and 11 prel. printed leaves; the Alphabet of Contractions in 459 columns, facsimile specimens of Early Manuscripts, Tab. 1-28; printed index, 19 leo

116 WESTWOOD'S PALÆOGRAPHIA SACRA Pictoria, being a Series of Illustrations of the Ancient Versions of the Bible, copied from Illuminated Manuscripts executed between the fourth and sixteenth centuries, impl. 4to. 50 *plates, beautifully coloured and illuminated in eact facsimile of the originals, now in the various public and private libraries in England and on the Continent* (pub. at £4. 4s) *half bound, morocco*, £2. 10s 1845
117 WRIGHT'S Court Hand Restored, or the Student assisted in reading OLD CHARTERS, Deeds, etc. with an Appendix containing the Ancient Names of Places in Great Britain and Ireland; Ancient Surnames, etc. *eighth edition, considerably improved*, sm. 4to. 23 *plates* (pub. at 21s) *cloth*, 10s 1846
A very important and useful work for reading old Charters, Manuscripts, Rolls, etc. containing examples of Old Court Hand, Set and Common Chancery, Secretary and other old Law Hands, and the Contractions used in Manuscripts, etc. with an Appendix containing the Ancient names of places in Great Britain and Ireland, and a Glossography of Latin words found in the works of the most eminent lawyers, and other ancient writings, but not in any modern dictionaries. A work not only useful to remind the learned, but absolutely necessary for young students and others who have occasion to consult Old Charters, Deeds or Records.

PERIODICALS, ENCYCLOPAEDIAS, PUBLICATIONS OF LEARNED SOCIETIES, ISSUES OF PRIVATE PRESSES.

ABBOTSFORD CLUB:
118 ROMANCES of Sir GUY of WARWICK, and Rembrun his son; now first edited from the Auchinleck MS. stout 4to. black letter, *plates, cloth*, 32s *Edinb.* 1840
119 THE CHARTULARIES OF BALMERINO and Lindores, now first printed from the original MSS. in the library of the Faculty of Advocates, 4to. *plate, cloth, uncut*, 14s *ib.* 1841
120 LIBER CONVENTUS S. Katherine Senensis prope Edinburgum, 4to. *plate on title, cloth, uncut*, 17s *ib.* 1841
121 GARDYNE'S (A.) Garden of grave and godlie flowers; GARDEN'S Theatre of Scotish Kings; with miscellaneous poems by J. LUNDIE, 4to. *finely printed within borders, hf. morocco, uncut*, 24s *ib.* 1845
122 OPPRESSIONS of the Sixteenth Century in the Islands of ORKNEY and ZETLAND, from original documents, with introduction, appendix, and a Glossary, 4to. *cloth*, 12s *ib.* 1859

ACADEMIE ROYALE DES SCIENCES [DE PARIS].
Mémoires de l'Institut:
123 MATHEMATIQUES et PHYSIQUES, pour les années VI. d. l. R.—1806 (Vols. I.—VI.); et 1806-15, 8 vols. in 13 parts—together 14 vols. in 19
Sold separately, vols. 1, 2, and 6. *Paris*, 1798-1818
MÉMOIRES présentés par DIVERS SAVANS: Sciences mathématiques et physiques, Tomes I. II. (all published) *ib.* 1806-11
Sold separately for 15s.
LITTÉRATURE et BEAUX-ARTS, Tomes I.—V. années IV.—XI. *an* VI.—XII.
Sold separately, calf, 15s per vol.
SCIENCES MORALES et politiques, Tome I.—V. *an* VI.—XII.
Sold separately, calf, 15s per vol.
Rapports et Discussions de toutes les Classes 1810
This finishes the FIRST SERIES of the work, it afterwards takes the title of:
Mémoires de l'Académie Royale des Sciences, du commencement en 1816, Tomes I.-XIX. XXI.—XXIV. XXVII. première partie 1818-54, 56
Sold separately, Vols. 1 to 17, 19, 21, 23, at £1. per volume, or £12. the series.
MÉMOIRES présentés par DIVERS SAVANTS à l'Académie des Sciences: Sciences mathématiques et physiques, Tome I.—XIV. 1827-1856
Sold separately, Vols. 1 to 10, 12, 14, at £1. per volume, or £5. the series.
COMPTES RENDUS hebdomadaires des Séances de l'Académie des Sciences, Août-Décembre, 1835, Nos. 1-22 et Tables alphabétiques, *wanting* No. 18, *or pp. 413-436, a very rare volume* 1835
—— Tomes VI.—XVII. avec les Tables des Matières 1838-43
—— Tome XXVI. 1848 1er. semestre 1848
COMPTES RENDUS des Séances de l'Académie des Sciences, le SUPPLÉMENT, Tome I. 1856
RECUEIL DES DISCOURS, Rapports et Pièces diverses lus dans les séances de l'Académie française, depuis 1820 jusqu'en 1839, 2 vols. 1847-50
Memoires de l'Academie Royale des Sciences Morales et politiques, Tomes I.-X. 1837-55
—— Savants-Etrangers, Tomes I. III. 1841-47

Mémoires de l'Institut National de France:
Academie des Inscriptions et Belles-Lettres, XVIII. XIX. XX. 2ème partie,
   XXI. XXIII. 2ème partie   1845, 1849-58-59
—— MÉMOIRES présentés par DIVERS SAVANTS à l'Académie Royale des Inscriptions et Belles-Lettres de l'Institut de France; PREMIÈRE SÉRIE: Sujets divers d'Erudition, Tomes II.—V.   1852-58
—— deuxième série: Antiquités de la France, Tomes I. III.   1843-54
Together 103 vols. 4to. *many plates*, (pub. at about £120.) *sewed, uncut*, £52.
Paris, 1798-1856

124 HISTOIRE de L'ACADEMIE ROYALE des SCIENCES, avec les Memoires de Mathematique et de Physique, from the commencement in 1699 to 1772 (*wanting the vol. for* 1747)   *Paris*, 1718-1775
Table générale, 1699-1734   *Amsterdam*, 1741
Table générale, 1681-90   1709
Discours, Tables générales, 1731-70, 4 vols. in 2   *Paris*, 1747-74
Suite des Mémoires de l'Academie Royale des Sciences, 1718, 1727 (Elements de la Geometrie de l'Infini), 1740 (Cassini et le Monnier, la Meridienne de l'Observatoire verifiée)   *ib.* 1720-44
Memoires donnés à l'Academie Royale des Sciences, non imprimés dans leurs temps, par Fontaine   *ib.* 1764
Gallon, Machines et Inventions approuvées par l'Academie, 1666-1734, 6 vols. *ib.* 1735
Ouvrages adoptez par l'Academie Roiale des Sciences, avant son renouvellement en 1699, 5 vols. *plates*   *La Haie*, 1729-31
Memoires pour servir à l'Histoire naturelle des Animaux et des Plantes, par Messieurs de l'Académie   *La Haye*, 1731
Memoires de Mathematique et de Physique tirez des Registres de l'Academie
Paris, 1692
In all 94 vols. 4to. *many plates, uniform in old French calf*, £10.   1692-1775

125 HISTOIRE et MÉMOIRES de l'Academie des Sciences, Années 1699-1744, 46 vols. 12mo. *many plates, calf*, 20s   *Amsterdam*, 1706-51

ACTA ERUDITORUM.—*See* LEIPZIG.

ÆLFRIC SOCIETY:
126 PUBLICATIONS of the ÆLFRIC SOCIETY, *the Complete Series*, the Homilies of Ælfric, parts 1-10—Poetry of the Codex Vercellensis, 2 parts—The Dialogues of Salomon and Saturn, 3 parts, edited by J. M. Kemble—together 15 parts, 8vo. £2. 10s   1843-48

AGRICULTURAL AND HORTICULTURAL SOCIETY OF INDIA:
127 TRANSACTIONS of the above, Vols. I.-VII. 8vo. *cloth*, 25s   *Calcutta*, 1838-49
_{^{The first volume of these Transactions was reprinted three times, hence the variation in the dates. Vol. 8 completing the Series appeared 1851.}}

128 MONTHLY JOURNAL, Vols. I.—V. part 2, in 27 parts, 8vo. *sewed*, 15s   1842-46
129 ALLIBONE'S (S. A.) Critical Dictionary of English Literature, and BRITISH AND AMERICAN AUTHORS, to the middle of the 19th century, containing 30,000 biographies and literary notices, Vol. I., A-Syl, *all published*, stout impl. 8vo. *cloth*, 20s   *Philadelphia*, 1859

AMERICAN ACADEMY:
130 TRANSACTIONS OF THE AMERICAN PHILOSOPHICAL SOCIETY held at Philadelphia, Vols. 1 to 4, Jan. 1, 1769 to 1799, *folding plates, Philadelphia*, 1771-99—Memoirs of the American Academy of Arts and Sciences, Vol. 1, 1780-3, *folding plates, Boston*, 1785—together 5 vols. 4to. 4 *in half calf, and* 1 *in calf,* £2. 10s   1771-99
_{The American Philosophical Society was the first, and the American Academy the second Literary or Scientific Society established in America. They received original contributions from Franklin, Priestley, Rittenhouse, Ewing, Bowdoin, Willard, and the most eminent men of the time. The transactions of both are very rare.}

131 TRANSACTIONS of the American Philosophical Society held at Philadelphia, Vol. 1, 1768-71, 4to. 7 *plates, calf,* 5s   *Philadelphia*, 1789
132 MEMOIRS OF THE AMERICAN ACADEMY of Arts and Sciences, *New Series*, Vol. I. II. III. IV. part 1, V. VI. part 1, 4to. *plates*, £7.
Cambridge, U. S. 1833-57
_{Mostly valuable Scientific Transactions by Worcester, Paine, Bowditch, Bond, Nuttall, Hale, Lovering, Captain Owen, Storer, Asa Grey, Everett, Haldeman, Leidy, Emory, Sargent, Burnett, Eustis, Jussieu, Bache, James Hall, and others. Vol. I. contains "A Dictionary of the Abnaki Language in North America by Father Sebastian Rasles, edited by Pickering."}

133 PROCEEDINGS, Vol. 1. 8vo. 4s   *Boston*, 1848

AMERICAN ANTIQUARIAN SOCIETY:
134 ARCHÆOLOGIA AMERICANA, Transactions and Collections, Vol. I., roy. 8vo. *plates, bds. uncut*, 10s   *Worcester, Massachusetts*, 1820
Containing vocabularies of the Shawnee and Wyandot languages.

AMERICAN ORIENTAL SOCIETY:
135 JOURNAL of the above, 5 vols. 8vo. *plates of facsimiles, etc. in* 11 *parts, sd.* £3. 10s; or 5 vols. *neatly half bound calf,* £4. 4s *Boston, New York, &c.* 1847-56
This periodical contains learned articles by Burnouf, Lassen, Whitney, and other eminent Orientalists.
136 AMERICAN JOURNAL of Science and Arts, conducted by Professor SILLIMAN, Vol. XXIV. 8vo. *presentation copy, plates, cloth,* 7s 6d *Newhaven*, 1833
137 AMERICAN JOURNAL of Science and Arts, conducted by Professor SILLIMAN, B. Silliman, Jr., and James D. Dana, SECOND SERIES, May 1846 to November 1860, being Vols. I to XXX. 8vo. *numerous plates, half bound green morocco,* £10. 10s   *New Haven*, 1846-60
138 AMERICAN Association for the Advancement of Science, *fourth Meeting, Newhaven*, 1850, 1 vol. 8vo. *plates, cloth,* 6s   *Washington*, 1851
139 AMERICAN SCIENTIFIC PERIODICALS, in 8vo.
American Academy of Arts and Sciences, 1848-52, Vol. III.   *Boston*, 1852
American Journal of Science, No. 9   *Newhaven*, 1821
American Philosophical Society's Proceedings, Vol. I.—VI. or Nos. 1-56 (*a few wanting)*   1848-55
Bahama Soc. Journal, Nos. 6, 11   1835-36
Boston Journal of Natural History, Vol. III. parts 1-4, IV. part I.   1840-42
New Orleans Academy of Sciences, No. 1   1854
New York Annals of the Lyceum of Natural History, Vol. III. Nos. 8-14, Vol. IV. Nos. 1-11, V. Nos. 2-3   1836-51
Philadelphia Academy of Natural Sciences, from Jan. 1856—April 1858, including Ruschenberger's Notice of the Academy and Meig's Catalogue of Human Crania, *with cuts, various parts*   1847-58
Quebec Transactions, Vol. III. p. 1, 2   1832
The whole lot, *containing many plates*, from the libraries of Dr. Horsfield and the Horticultural Society, £2.
140 AMERICAN ANNUAL REGISTER for 1825-31. Vols. I—VI, stout royal 8vo. *bds.* £2.   *New York*, 1827-32
Contains interesting information respecting the United States.
141 **AMERICAN ETHNOLOGICAL SOCIETY**, Transactions of the, 2 vols. 8vo. *plates and cuts, sd. rare*, 30s   *New York*, 1845-48
Comprises valuable Papers, including VOCABULARIES of the MEXICAN NATIONS.

AMSTERDAM SOCIETY OF NATURAL HISTORY:
142 BIJDRAGEN tot de Natuurkundige Wetenschappen, verzammeld door Van Hall, Vrolik en Mulder, *from the beginning*, Vol. I.-V. stout 8vo. *plates of Natural History, bds.* 18s   *Amst.* 1826-30

AMSTERDAM ROYAL INSTITUTE:
143 TIJDSCHRIFT TOT de Taal- Land- en Volkenkunde van NEDERLANDSCH INDIE: Bijdragen, Vols. I.-IV. in 3—Nieuwe Volgreeks, Vols. I, II.: together 6 vols. in 5, 8vo. *plates*, £2. 16s   *Amst.* 1852-58
144 WERKEN: Afdeeling II.: Müller, Reizen, 2 vols.; Vries, Reize, door Leupe en Siebold; Javaansche Woordenboek, 4 vols. 8vo. *sd.* 20s   1857-58

AMSTERDAM ACADEMY:
145 TIJDSCHRIFT voor de Wis- en Natuurkundige Wetenschappen, uitgegeven door de eerste Klasse van het Koninkl.- Nederlandsche Instituut van Wetenschappen, Letterkunde en schoone Kunsten, Vols. I.-V. in 9 parts, 8vo. *scientific plates, sewed*, 20s   *Amsterdam*, 1848-52
146 VERHANDELINGEN der Koninkl. Akademie van Wetenschappen, Vols. 1–6, in 5 vols.—Verhandelingen der eerste Klasse van het Koninkl.-Nederlandsche Instituut, 3de Reeks, Deelen 4, 5, 1851-2; together 8 vols. in 6, 4to. *plates of Anatomy, Zoology, Conchology, Ichthyology, and Botany, three vols. in cloth and three sd.* £3.   *Amsterdam*, 1851-58
147 —— the same, Vols. 1.—VI. 4to. *plates, sewed*, £2. 10s   1854-58
148 LACOSTE, Synopsis Hepaticarum Javanicarum, 4to. 22 *plates, bds.* 5s   1856
149 VERSLAGEN en Mededeelingen: Afdeeling NATUURKUNDE, Vols. I.—VII. 1853-58—Afdeeling LETTERKUNDE, Vol. I.—III. 1855-58—together 10 vols. 8vo. *plates*, £2.   1853-58

PUBLICATIONS OF LEARNED SOCIETIES, ETC. 17

150 AFDEELING NATUURKUNDE, 7 vols. in 4, stout 8vo. *plates, cloth*, £3.
   1853-58
151 ANNALEN DER PHYSIK, nach Gilberts Tode fortgesetzt von Poggendorf, Vols. 85-90, 94-103: Annalen der Physik und Chemie, (Vols. 9-14, 18-27) 16 vols. 8vo. *plates, cloth*, 30s *Leipzig*, 1827-33
152 ANNALEN DER PHYSIK und CHEMIE, herausgegeben zu Berlin von J. C. Poggendorff, Bande 82 to 111. (der ganzen Folge, 158-187) *numerous plates, twenty-four vols. are half bound, edges cut, and six vols. bds. uncut*, together 30 vols. 8vo. *numerous plates*, £6. 10s *Leipzig*, 1851-60

ANNALES DES MINES:
153 JOURNAL DES MINES, from the beginning in 1793 to Jan. 1812, Nos. 1-181, being Vols. I. to XXXI. 1. 8vo. *numerous plates, twelve vols. half bound, six in boards, the remainder in parts*, £5. *Paris*, 1793-1812
154 ANNALES DES MINES ou Recueil de Mémoires sur l'Exploitation des Mines et sur les Sciences et les Arts qui s'y rapportent, redigées par les Ingénieurs des Mines; *quatrième série*. Vols. 9 to 20, 12 vols. 1846-1851—*Cinquième série*, Vols. 1 to 8, 1852-55—Lois, Décrets, Arrets et autres Actes concernant les Mines et Usines, cinquième série, 4 vols. 1852-55—together 24 vols. 8vo. *numerous folding maps and plates*, 10 vols. *half calf*, 14 *in cloth, all uniformly lettered and gilt*, £8. 10s *Paris*, 1846-55
155 ANNALS OF NATURAL HISTORY; or, the Magazine of Zoology, Botany, and Geology, conducted by Sir W. Jardine, P. J. Selby, Sir W. J. Hooker, and others: SERIES I. *complete*, 20 vols. *cloth*, 1838-47, *numerous plates some* COLOURED—SERIES II. 20 *vols. complete, several hundred plates*, 16 vols. *cloth*, 4 vols. in 25 Nos. 1848-1858—SERIES III. Nos. 1 to 21, being Vols. 1. to part of Vol. IV. Jan. 1858—Sept. 1859, *numerous plates*—in all 36 vols. 8vo. *cloth*, and 46 Nos. COMPLETE, *from the commencement* in 1838 to Sept. 1859, *several hundred plates, some* COLOURED, £14. 14s 1838-59
156 ANNALS OF PHILOSOPHY, or Magazine of Chemistry, Mineralogy, Mechanics, Natural History, Agriculture, and the Arts, edited by Dr. Thomson, 16 vols.—New Series, The ANNALS of PHILOSOPHY, 12 vols.; together 28 vols. 8vo. 151 *plates, (pub. at* £21.) *bds. uncut*, £2.; or *half russia*, £2. 10s 1813-26
157 ARCHÆOLOGIA CAMBRENSIS, a record of the Antiquities of Wales and its Marches, and the Journal of the Cambrian Archæological Association, FIRST SERIES, 4 vols.—SECOND SERIES, 5 vols.—together 9 vols. 8vo. *many hundred plates of Coins, Views, Antiquities, etc. half calf gilt, a fine set*, £5. 10s 1846-54
   A very valuable and interesting publication, throwing great light upon the early history of Wales, by the discovery of early MSS. Antiquities, &c.
158 ARCHAEOLOGIA SCOTICA, Transactions of the Society of Antiquaries of Scotland, Vol. III. pt. 2, IV. pt. 2, 4to. *bds*. 15s *Edinb*. 1831-33
   Including, amongst other interesting matter, "Extracts from the Hawthornden MSS." and "Drummond's Notes of Conversations with Ben Johnson."
159 ARCHAEOLOGISCHE ZEITUNG, herausgegeben von E. GERHARD, Jahrgang 1-16, in 3 SERIES: Series I. 4 vols.—Series II. 2 vols.—Series III. with the additional Title: "Denkmaeler, Forschungen und Berichte," Vols. 1-10—together 16 vols. 4to. *with* 192 *plates of Ancient Art, (subscription price* 48 *Thalers), new and clean in parts, from the library of the late W. Hamilton, Esq.* £5. *Berlin*, 1843-58

ARCHITECTURAL PUBLICATION SOCIETY:
160 THE DICTIONARY OF ARCHITECTURE, including the Biographical and Poliographical, as well as the Technical and other portions of the Art and Science of Architecture, with a Series of Illustrative Plates, small fol. 9 years, (including the subscription for 1860) comprising TEXT (A—Felibien) 660 pp. 286 WOODCUTS, and 96 PLATES, £9. 9s 1852-59
   As a complete set of the first Four Years' works can only occasionally be obtained, a volume has been prepared entitled:
160* "DETACHED ESSAYS AND ILLUSTRATIONS issued during the Years 1848-52." The volume contains 28 plates, 175 pages of text, and 177 woodcuts: to Subscribers to the Dictionary, 31s 6d 1848-52
161 ART DE VERIFIER LES DATES des Faits historiques, des Chartes, des Chroniques, et autres anciens Monumens, *depuis* la Naissance de Notre-Seigneur (commencé par D. Maur, D. Fr. d'Antine, D. Clémencet et D. Durand, continué et publié par D. Fr. Clément), 3 vols.—L'Art de verifier les Dates, etc. *avant* l'Ere Chrétienne, par St. Allais, 1 vol. 1820—L'Art de verifier les Dates *depuis*

c

l'année 1770, jusqu'à nos jours, par le Chevalier de Courcelles, 3 vols. 1821-30 —together 7 vols. folio, BEST EDITION, *calf neat, carefully rebacked and gilt*, £24. *Paris*, 1783-1830

162 ART (L') DE VERIFIER LES DATES DES FAITS Historiques, des Inscriptions, des Chroniques et autres Anciens Monumens, avant l'Ere Chrétienne, mis en ordre par Mons. de Saint Allais, 1 vol. 1820—DEPUIS la Naissance de Notre Seigneur, par un Religieux Benedictin de la Congregation de S. Maur, 5 vols. 1818—Depuis l'Année 1770, jusqu'à nos jours, par M. le Chev. de Courcelles, 4 vols. 1821, Continuation, 1 vol.—togother 11 vols. impl. 4to. *calf gilt, fine set, rare*, £18. 18s *Paris*, 1818-28

"Comprenant les *Annales comparatives de tous les Peuples et de tous les Rois du Monde*; ouvrage qu'on peut, à juste titre appeler la clef de l'Histoire générale; car point de bons livres sans l'Art de Verifier les Dates; point de Bibliotheque s'il n'en occupe la premiere place: point d'homme sauvant s'il ne connait à fond ce precieux travail."

"For Chronology, use the great French Work, '*l'Art de Vérifier les Dates*.'"
Prof. Smyth's Lecture on Modern History.

"A splendid monument of learning, which has left little to be done by subsequent chronologists, besides the humble duties of translation and abridgement."—*Sir Harris Nicolas.*

"The great treasure of historical information."—*Sir Jas. Mackintosh.*

"This is the great collection of chronological tables, the great summary of all history, ancient as well as modern, the great *multum in parvo*, for which, if the Benedictines produced nothing else, the thanks of all subsequent scholars would be voted unanimously. It may truly be said that no book ever held so important a place in modern historical literature as this. It contains a most exact summary of the history of all nations; so exact, that to detect any error in it may, commonly speaking, be called an impossibility. The decisions of this book are always looked upon as final; he who possesses a copy of it, has indeed a treasure."

ARUNDEL SOCIETY:

163 PUBLICATIONS of the Arundel Society, from the beginning in 1849 to 1861 inclusive, (Subscription price, £13. 2s 6d) £15. 15s 1849-62

Complete sets are very rare, several volumes and many of the plates being out of print. Sets completed.

List of the Annual Publications of the Arundel Society, from the beginning to the present time:

FIRST YEAR (1849-50).

A plate by GRUNER, "The Distribution of Alms by St. Lawrence," one of the series of frescoes by FRA ANGELICO in the Chapel of Nicholas V. in the Vatican. The Life of Fra Giovanni Angelico da Fiesole translated from Vasari by Bezzi, with 21 plates. *Out of print.*

SECOND YEAR (1850-51).

Four plates from the same series of frescoes: "St. Stephen before the Council;" "St. Buonaventura;" "St. Matthew," and St. Thomas."

THIRD YEAR (1851-52).

Two engravings by SCHÄFFER:—A continuation of the same series, "Saint Lawrence before the Emperor Decius." The "Pieta," from the fresco by GIOTTO in the Chapel of S. M. dell' Arena at Padua.

FOURTH YEAR (1852-53.)

Eight engravings on wood, from the frescoes by Giotto in the Arena Chapel.

FIFTH YEAR (1853).

Six similar engravings from the same series of frescoes.
GIOTTO AND HIS WORKS IN PADUA, by JOHN RUSKIN. Part I.

SIXTH YEAR (1854).

Eight similar engravings from the same series of frescoes.
GIOTTO AND HIS WORKS IN PADUA, by JOHN RUSKIN. Part II.

SEVENTH YEAR (1855).

Four similar engravings from the same series of frescoes.
NOTICES of SCULPTURE in IVORY, being a Lecture on the History, Methods, and Productions of the Art, by M. DIGBY WYATT; and a Catalogue of Specimens of Ivory-Carvings, by Edmund Oldfield, with nine photographic illustrations. *Out of print.*

EIGHTH YEAR (1856).

View of the interior of the Arena Chapel, printed in colours. Two wood-engravings in continuation of the series from the frescoes in the same Chapel. Chromolithograph of the fresco by Pietro Perugino, "The Martyrdom of St. Sebastian." Five outlines of portions of figures in the same fresco. *Out of print.* MEMOIR on the "St. Sebastian" of Perugino, by LAYARD. *Out of print.*

NINTH YEAR (1857).

Two wood-engravings in continuance of the series from the Arena Chapel. Chromolithograph of the fresco, "Christ among the Doctors," by Pinturicchio, Spello Cathedral; Chromolithograph of the fresco by Ottaviano Nelli in the Church of S. Maria Nuova at Gubbio, the "Virgin and Child, with Saints and Angels."

MEMOIR on the fresco of Nelli, by LAYARD.
Four lithographic outlines of heads traced from these two frescoes.
TENTH YEAR (1858).
Four wood-engravings in continuation of the series from the Arena Chapel.
Chromolithograph of " The Nativity," by Pinturicchio, Spello Cathedral.
MEMOIR on the three frescoes by Pinturicchio, Spello Cathedral, by Layard.
Chromolithograph of the fresco by Luini, "St. Catherine buried by Angels," Brera Gallery, at Milan. Engraved outlines from tracings of two heads in the " Nativity," and two in the " St. Catherine," 3 *plates*.
ELEVENTH YEAR (1859).
Two wood-engravings in continuation of the series from the Arena Chapel. Chromolithograph of the fresco of the "Madonna and Child," by Leon. da Vinci, Church of S. Onofrio, Rome. Outline of the "Head of the Virgin," from this fresco. Chromolithograph of the fresco by Giov. Sanzio, at Cagli, " Madonna and Saints, with the Resurrection of Our Lord." Engraved outline of the head of of an Angel, traced from the last-mentioned fresco.
MEMOIR on the fresco of Sanzio, by LAYARD.
TWELFTH YEAR (1860).
Two wood-engravings in conclusion of the series from the Arena Chapel. Illustrated title-page, and list of the series of woodcuts from the Arena Chapel.
GIOTTO AND HIS WORKS IN PADUA, by JOHN RUSKIN. Part III.
Chromolithograph of the fresco by Ghirlandaio, in the Church of S. S. Trinita, Florence, " Death of S. Francis of Assisi. Chromolithograph of two Heads from the same fresco, on the scale of the original.
MEMOIR, entitled "Domenico Ghirlandaio and his Fresco of the Death of S. Francis," by LAYARD,
THIRTEENTH YEAR (1861).
Seven chromolithographs from frescoes in the Brancacci Chapel, Florence:—
" The Fall," by Filippino Lippi; " The Expulsion," by Masaccio; " The Tribute Money," by Masaccio; " S. Peter Preaching," by Masolino; S. Peter Baptizing," by Masolino; "Two Heads," on the scale of the originals, from the preceding subjects.

164 WYATT'S Notices of Sculpture in Ivory, 4to. 9 *photographic plates of print, half bound, rare*, 20s   1856
165 ASIATIC RESEARCHES, or Transactions of the Society instituted in England for inquiring into the History, the Antiquities, the Arts and Sciences, and Literature of Asia, A PERFECT UNMIXED SET, 20 vols. and Index, 1 vol.—together 21 vols. 4to. *many plates, calf gilt*, £30.   Calcutta, 1788-1836
166 ——— another set, 20 vols. and Index, 4to. *somewhat wormed, cloth, cut edges*, £18.   *ib.* 1788-1836

Complete sets are of very rare occurrence. Many separate volumes are kept in stock, and supplied for 30s each.
Contains the learned Essays by Colebrooke, Sir William Jones, Carey, Strachey, Dr. Wallich, Roxburgh, etc.
" They are full of the most curious and valuable intelligence, in every possible form and on every possible subject." *Dibdin.*
Continued in the Bengal Journal.

ASIATIC SOCIETY OF BENGAL:

167 BENGAL JOURNAL. JOURNAL OF THE ASIATIC SOCIETY OF BENGAL, *complete from the beginning to the present*, Nos. 1—284, forming 31 vols. 8vo. *with all the numerous plates and Tables of Contents, excessively rare both in India and Europe*, £36.   Calcutta, 1832-62

All the early volumes are out of print in Calcutta, and sell there at exorbitant prices. The Bengal Journal is a continuation of the "Asiatic Researches;" it is a most valuable periodical, devoted to Oriental Literature, Science, Antiquities, Geography, Art, &c. No public library can do without this important work; it forms, with the Asiatic Researches, one of the noblest monuments of British dominion in the East.

168 GLEANINGS IN SCIENCE, a monthly periodical, in 3 vols. 8vo. *numerous plates and woodcuts*, £5.   *ib.* 1829-31

These Gleanings, edited by PRINSEP, formed the forerunner of the Bengal Journal, and copies are now of the utmost degree of rarity.

169 PRINSEP'S Useful Tables, printed as an Appendix to the Journal of the Asiatic Society, 3 parts, 8vo. *containing the Indian Coins, Weights, and Measures, Chronological Tables, and the Generic Characters of Roxburgh's Flora Indica, with plates of Coins, &c.*   *ib.* 1834-36

This extremely rare work should be added to a set of the Bengal Journal.

ASIATIC SOCIETY OF GREAT BRITAIN AND IRELAND:

170 TRANSACTIONS of the above, *complete*, 3 stout vols. 4to. *plates of facsimiles, etc.* (pub. at £9. 7s) *sd.* or *hf. calf*, 24s   *ib.* 1827-35

Sets completed at a moderate rate.
This valuable publication upon the learning, languages, and antiquities of the East, contains amongst the

names of its contributors those of Professor Wilson, G. C. Haughton, Davis, Morrison, Colebrooke, Humboldt, Dorn, Grotefend, and most of the eminent Oriental scholars of the day. This may be called the *first* series of the Publications by the Royal Asiatic Society of England. The continuation or *second* series appeared in 8vo. as follows.

171 JOURNAL of the ROYAL ASIATIC Society of Great Britain and Ireland, from the beginning to 1861, 8vo. COMPLETE *as far as published*, Vols. I—X. Vol. XI. part 1, Vols. XII. XIII. Vol. XIV. part 1, XV. to XX. part 1, *complete as far as published, many plates*, (pub. at £11. 10s) sewed, £10. 1834-62

ASTRONOMICAL SOCIETY:

172 MEMOIRS of the Astronomical Society, complete from the commencement of the series in 1821 to 1857, Vols. I—XXVI. in 31 divisions, large 4to. *numerous plates*, (pub. at about £50.) *unbound*, £18. 1822-58

With this set is included an imperfect series of the "Monthly Notices," 8vo.

173 —— another set, Vols. I—IX. in 7 vols. 4to. *plates, neatly hf. bd. in calf*, £6.

Fetched, 1854, Puttick's, 16 vols. £11. 1822-36

174 ATHENÆUM (The) London Literary and Critical Journal, from the commencement, No. 1, Jan. 5, 1828, to No. 1731, Dec. 29, 1860, COMPLETE, 33 vols. in 36, stout 4to. (pub. at about £30.) *cloth*, £8. 10s 1828-60

The early volumes are very rare.

175 ATTI della terza Riunione degli Scienziati Italiani, large 4to. *plates, bds. uncut*, 7s 6d *Firenze*, 1841

AUSTRIAN IMPERIAL ACADEMY OF SCIENCES; *published as follows*:

176 Denkschriften der kaiserlichen Akademie der Wissenschaften:

MATHEMATISCH-NATURWISSENSCHAFTLICHE CLASSE: Band I. to VII. and IX. large 4to. *many beautiful plates, mostly coloured* 1850-55

PHILOSOPHISCH-HISTORISCHE CLASSE: Band I to VI. and VIII. large 4to. *many plates* 1850-57

Sitzungsberichte:

MATHEMATISCH-NATURWISSENSCHAFTLICHE CLASSE, Jahrgang 1849 to 1857, being Vol. I. to XXIV Heft 4 (1850, no Aug. Sept.) 8vo. 1849-57

PHILOSOPHISCH-HISTORISCHE CLASSE: 1848-49, 1849 to 1857, Vols. I. to XVII. XXI. part 3, XXII. and XXIII. (1849, no Aug. Sept.; 1850, no Aug. Sept.) 8vo. 1848-59

☞ The above series of the Denkschriften und Sitzungsberichte, folio, 4to. and 8vo. are sold together, price £25.

177 ARCHIV für Kunde österreichischer Geschichts-Quellen, 1848-1849, parts 1 to 5, Jahrgänge 1849-1857, being vols. I—XV part I, XVII parts 1 and 2, and XVIII part 1, 8vo. *numerous plates*, £3. 10s 1848-57

178 FONTES RERUM AUSTRIACARUM: Erste Abtheilung: Scriptores, Band I.; Zweite Abtheilung: Diplomataria et Acta, Band II.—X. XIII and XV., 12 vols. 8vo. £2. 10s 1850-57

Historische Commission:

179 MONUMENTA HAPSBURGICA: Actenstücken und Briefen zur Geschichte des Hauses Habsburg 1473-1576, parts I. II. in 4 vols. stout roy. 8vo. *sd*. 12s 1853-57

BANNATYNE CLUB:

180 LANERCOST: CHRONICON DE LANERCOST, A.D. 1201-1346 e codice Cottoniano, nunc primum typis mandatum, 2 parts in 1 vol. stout 4to. LARGE FINE THICK PAPER, Mr. EYTON'S COPY, *dark morocco super extra, joints inside, the sides and back elegantly tooled, edges gaufré and gilt, a very handsome volume*, £2. 10s

Edinburgi, 1839

Presented to the Bannatyne Club by W. MacDowall, Esq. The Chronicle of Lanercost, now printed for the first time, contains a general history of the affairs of England and Scotland, together with allusions to Continental proceedings, extending from the year 1201 to the year 1346.

181 LAUDER'S Historical observes of memorable occurrents in Church and State, 1680-86, 4to. 5s *ib.* 1840

182 TRACTS by David FERGUSON, Minister of Dunfermline (one of the fathers of the Reformation in Scotland) 1563-72, 8vo. *cloth*, 9s 1860

183 TRACTS by Dr. Gilbert SKEYNE, Medicinar to his Majesty (James VI.), 4to. *cloth*, 7s 6d 1860

184 BAPTIST MISSIONARY SOCIETY, Accounts relative to, 6 vols. 8vo. *portraits and maps, hf. calf, from Lord Calthorpe's library*, 36s *Clipstone*, 1800-17

A very valuable and rare publication, with contributions by Carey, Ward, Marshman, and other learned missionaries on the Religious Systems, the Antiquities, Natural History, &c. of India.

BATAVIAN ACADEMY TRANSACTIONS:

185 VERHANDELINGEN van het Bataviaasch Genootschap der Kunsten en Wetenschappen, Vol. I, III—IX, XII—XIV., with a separate vol. containing the "Javaansche Spraakkunst, door De Groot en Gericke," together 12 vols. 8vo. *plates, not uniform, Dr. Horsfield's copy, very rare*, £7. *Batavia*, 1771-1833

186 BENARES Magazine, Vol. I. (1848-49) and Nos. 29-35 inclusive (1851-53) 8vo. 30s
Calcutta, 1848-53
Contains amongst other interesting articles, Banergea on Vedantism, on Urdu Lexicography, Dr. Roth on Brahma and the Brahmans, etc,
187 BERKSHIRE ASHMOLEAN SOCIETY. Original Letters and documents relating to Archbishop Laud's benefactions, edited by Bruce, sm. 4to. *cloth*, 5s   1841

BERLIN ACADEMY TRANSACTIONS:

188 MISCELLANEA BEROLINENSIA ad Incrementum Scientiarum ex Scriptis Societati regiae Scientiarum exhibitis edita, *folding plates*, (*Tomus* 1)   *Berolini*, 1749
—— Continuatio I.—V., sive Tomi II.—VI. 5 vols. *plates*,   *ib.* 1723-40
—— Elsner, Schediasma Criticum (ad Continuationem Tomi VII.)   *ib.* 1744
Nouveaux Mémoires de l'Academie Royale des Sciences et Belles Lettres, avec l'histoire, 1771-1774 et 1779-80, 6 vols. *plates*   *ib.* 1773-6-82
Sammlung der deutschen Abhandlungen, welche in der K. Akademie vorgelesen worden, 1778-1803, 6 vols. *folding plates*   *ib.* 1793-1806
Mémoires de l'Académie des Sciences et Belles-Lettres depuis l'avènement de Frederic Guillaume II., 1796-7, 2 vols. *plates*   *ib.* 1792-1800
Abhandlungen der K. Akademie der Wissenschaften zu Berlin, 1820-1, 1824, 1825, 1826, 1827, 1828, and 1832, Theil 1, 7 vols. *plates*   *ib.* 1838
Philosophisch-historiche Abhandlungen der K. Akad. der Wissenschaften, 1836, *plates of Ancient Art*   *ib.* 1838
Together 28 vols. 4to. *plates, bds. uncut, sold separately*   *ib.* 1723-1838
189 COLLECTION (A) of 31 VALUABLE and IMPORTANT DISSERTATIONS and Works on Philology, Ancient Art and Literature, *with many plates*, in 2 portfolios, 4to. *red morocco*, 25s   *Berlin*, 1846, etc.
This collection includes, A. PHILOLOGY: Hagen, die Schwanen-Sage; Bopp, Georgische Sprache; Schott, das Altaische Sprachen-geschlecht; Hagen's Artus: J. Grimm's Deutsche Sprache; etc. in all, 13 parts.—B. ANCIENT ART: Gerhard's Agathodämon; Gerhard's Eros; Welcker's Lesche zu Delphi; Panofka, der Vasenbildner Panphaios; Panofka's Perseus; Gerhard's Kunst der Phoenizier; together 8 parts, with plates.—C. SCIENTIFIC; Karsten, die Vegétations Organe der Palmen, with plates, and others by Bessel, Encke, &c. together 10 parts.
190 BERLINER ASTRONOMISCHES JAHRBUCH, mit Genehmhaltung der Königl. Akademie der Wissenschaften herausg. von Encke, 1831-43, 1850-56, together 20 vols. 8vo. (pub. at about 66 thalers) *twelve hf. bd. eight unbound*, 25s   1829-53
A collection, important for the memoirs of practical Astronomy inserted by the editor. A set of 26 vols. priced, 1858, Friedländer, 32 thalers.
191 BIOGRAPHIE UNIVERSELLE, ANCIENNE ET MODERNE, 52 vols.—Mythologie, 3 vols.—Supplement, 30 vols.—in all 85 vols. 8vo. A COMPLETE SET, *sd.* £16. 16s   *Paris*, 1811-62
☞ Complete sets like the above are of the rarest occurrence, even in France. The last volume published brings the Supplement down to "Vil."
192 BIOGRAPHIE UNIVERSELLE, ancienne et moderne, ouvrage entièrement neuf, 52 vols. 8vo. *sd.* £4. 10s; or 52 vols. 8vo. FINE PAPER, *the genuine book, cloth lettered*, £6.   *Paris, Michaud*, 1811-28
None of the modern imitations of this valuable work have been completed yet, and none comes up to it in correctness: the Biographies, including those of Englishmen, were written with great care by most eminent writers.
193 BIBLIOPHILE (le) BELGE, 6 vols.—BULLETIN du Bibliophile Belge, fondé par M. le Baron de Reiffenberg, 4 vols.—together 10 vols. 8vo. *portraits and facsimiles, half calf gilt*, £2. 18s   *Bruxelles*, 1845-54
An interesting bibliographical periodical, containing notices of Early Printers, valuable articles on old Books, Manuscripts, Public Libraries, etc, Reviews of new Books, and other useful information.
194 BIBLIOTHEQUE DE L'ECOLE des CHARTES, Revue d'Erudition consacrée principalement à l'Etude du Moyen-Age, 15 vols. in 85 parts, royal 8vo. *uncut, very rare*, £5.   *Paris*, 1840-1854
This is one of the most important and interesting publications relating to Mediæval MSS.; the present copy is complete to the above date, with the exception of the first vol. for 1840. The cost of publication was 12s a volume.

BODLEIAN LIBRARY:

195 CATALOGUS impressorum librorum Bibliothecæ Bodleiana in Academia Oxoniensi, 2 vols. royal folio, *calf*, 12s   *Oxon.* 1738
196 CATALOGUS Codicum Manuscriptorum ARABICORUM, confecit Nicholl, roy. fol. *bds.* 7s 6d   1821
197 CATALOGUS LIBRORUM impressorum Bibliothecæ Bodleianæ, 4 vols. folio, *unbound*, £3. 5s; *bds.* £3. 15s   *Oxon.* 1843-50
198 CATALOGI Codicum MSS. Bibliothecae Bodleianae pars I., Recensio Codicum Græcorum, cum Indice, à H. O. COXE, 4to. 961 pp. *cloth*, 12s   *Oxonii*, 1853
199 —— Vol. II. pars 1, Codices G. Laud, 4to. 20s   *ib.* 1858
200 —— ejusdem pars 3, Codices Graeci et Latini Canoniciani, cum Indice, 4to. 918 pp. *cloth*, 10s   *ib.* 1854
201 —— Pars IV. Codices Thomæ Tanneri, confecit Hackman, 4to. 12s   *ib.* 1860

22   B. QUARITCH, 15 PICCADILLY, LONDON.

202 CATALOGUES of the Books purchased by the Bodleian Library, and the cost price of each article, from Nov. 8, 1841 to Oct. 11, 1856, 2 vols. 8vo. *hf. morocco, uncut,* £3.   NOT PUBLISHED, 1841-56
These Volumes abound in curious information to the Book Collector. From the late Dr. Bliss's library.

BOMBAY GEOGRAPHICAL SOCIETY:
203 TRANSACTIONS AND PROCEEDINGS of the Bombay Geographical Society, from the beginning, in 1836, to 1856, Vols. I—XII. (XI. wanting) 11 vols. 8vo. nine vols. *hf. bd. edges cut, and two unbound,* £7. 10s   *Bombay,* 1836-56
A scarce and valuable periodical, containing much historical and ethnological matter, Vocabularies and grammatical sketches of several Languages and dialects, etc. Sets completed.

BOMBAY LITERARY SOCIETY:
205 TRANSACTIONS of the above, Vol. II. 4to. *many Mythological and Antiquarian plates, hf. bd. rare,* 25s   1820

BONAPARTE (PRINCE LUCIEN). Publications of his Imperial Highness, Prince Louis Lucien Bonaparte:
206 PARABOLA de Seminatore, ex Matthæo, *in* 72 *Europæis linguas* ac dialectos versa, characteribus Romanis, 8vo. *sd. hf. bd. rare,* 25s   1857
207 SPECIMEN LEXICI COMPARATIVI omnium linguarum Europæarum, à L. L. Bonaparte, sm. folio, 15s   *Florence,* 1847
208 CATALOGUES des ouvrages de Linguistique Européene, édités par le Prince L. L. Bonaparte, 2 vols. 16mo. 7s 6d   1858
209 CANTICUM Canticorum Salomonis, 3 *Vasconicis dialectis Hispaniæ* versum, ab Uriarte et L. L. Bonaparte, 4to. 15s   1858
210 CANTICUM trium puerorum in 7 *dialectos Vasconicas* versum, 4to. 4s 6d   1858
211 —— idem, in 11 *dialectis Vasconicis,* à L. L. Bonaparte, 4to. 7s 6d   1858
212 PRODROMUS evangelii Matthæi octupli: oratio dominica, Hispanicè, Gallicè et omnibus *dialectis Vasconicis* versa, 4to. 1s 6d   1857
213 DIALOGUES BASQUES: Guipuscoans, Biscaiens, Labourdins, Souletins, par Iturriaga, Uriarte, Duvoisin, et Inchauspe, avec deux traductions Espagnole et Française, 8vo. 27s   1857
214 BIBLIA edo Testamentu: the Bible in the *Guipuscoan dialect* of Basque, by Uriarte, L. L. Bonaparte and Azpiazo, 2 vols. 8vo. *not yet completed,* £10. 1859
215 EVANGELIO segun San Mateo, traducido al Vascuence, *dialecto Guipuzcoano,* por Uriarte, 8vo. *only* 25 *copies printed,* £2. 14s   1858
216 APOCALIPSIS de San Juan, traducido al *Vascuence, dialecto Guipuzcoano,* por Uriarte, 16mo. *only* 50 *copies printed,* 27s   1858
217 APOCALIPSIS de San Juan, *Vascuence Vizcaino,* por Uriarte, 16mo. 51 *copies printed,* 27s   1857
218 DOCTRINA Cristiana, en el *Vascuence de Llodio,* provincia de Alava, 32mo. 50 *copies printed,* 15s   1858
219 BIBLIA, eta berria Duvoisin Kapitainak, etc.: Bible, traduit en *Basque,* dialecte du *Labourd,* 2 *vols.* large 8vo. *when completed,* £10.   1859
220 RUTH, le Livre de, traduit en *Basque Labourdin,* par Duvoisin, 32mo. 4s 6d 1860
221 CANTIQUE des Cantiques de Salomon, en *Basque Labourdin,* par Duvoisin, 16mo. 4s 6d   1859
222 APOCALYPSE de Saint Jean, en *Basque Souletin,* par Inchauspe, 16mo. 50 *copies printed,* 27s   *Londres,* 1858
223 VERBE BASQUE (Le) par l'Abbé Inchauspe, publié par le Prince L. L. Bonaparte, 4to. £3. 7s   *Bayonne,* 1858
224 CELTIC HEXAPLA: the Song of Solomon in all the living dialects of the Gaelic and Cambrian languages, (in English, Irish, Gaelic, Manx, French, Welsh, Breton, Vannetais), 4to. 20s   1858
225 APOCRIPHA, chum na *Gaelic Albannaich,* leis Alasdair Macgriogair, 8vo. £2.   1860
226 EVANGILE de Saint Mathieu, en *Breton de Vannes,* par Terrien, 16mo. 6s   1857
227 PARABOLA del Figliuol Prodigo, in *Greco di Cargese (Corsica)* da Stefanopoli, 4to. 1s 6d   1860
228 VANGELO di San Matteo, in *dialetto Milanese,* da Picozzi, 16mo. 15s   1859
229 —— in *dialetto Bergamasco,* da Locatelli, 16mo. 15s   1860
230 —— in *dialetto Piemontese,* 16mo. 6s   1861
231 —— in *dialetto Genovese,* da Olivieri, con osservazioni Linguisto-comparative sulla *pronunzia Genovese,* da L. L. Bonaparte, 16mo. 15s   1860
232 —— in *dialetto Veneziano,* da Fontana, 16mo. 15s   1859
233 —— in *dialetto Friulano,* dal Conte P. dal Pozzo, 16mo. 15s   1860

PUBLICATIONS OF LEARNED SOCIETIES, ETC. 23

234 VANGELO di San Matteo, in *dialetto Napolitano*, da un letterato di Napoli, 16mo.
15*s* 1861
235 LIBRO di Rut, in *dialetto Siciliano*, da Scalia, 32mo. 4*s* 6*d* 1860
236 CANTICO de' Cantici di Salmone, in *dialetto Siciliano*, da Scalia, 16mo. 4*s* 6*d* 1860
237 VANGELO di Matteo, in *dialetto Siciliano*, da Scalia, con osservazioni linguistico-comparative, da L. L. Bonaparte, 16mo. 15*s* 1861
238 STORIA di Giuseppe: Capi 37 e 39-45 della Genesi, in *dialetto Sardo Cagliaritano*, da Abis, 8vo. 15*s* 1861
239 LIBRO di Rut, in *dialetto Sardo meridionale*, da Abis, 32mo. 4*s* 6*d* 1860
240 CANTICO de' Cantici, in *dialetto Sardo meridionale*, da Abis, 16mo. 4*s* 6*d* 1860
241 PROFEZIA di Giona, in *dialetto Sardo Cagliaritano*, da Abis, 16mo. 4*s* 6*d* 1861
242 VANGELO di S. Matteo, in *dialetto Sardo Cagliaritano*, da Abis, 16mo. 15*s* 1860
243 STORIA di Giuseppe, Capi 37 e 39-45 della Genesi, in *dialetto Sardo Logudorese* da Spano, seconda edizione, 8vo. 15*s* 1861
244 LIBRO di Rut, *in dialetto Sardo centrale*, 32mo. 4*s* 6*d* 1861
245 CANTICO de' Cantici, *in dialetto Sardo centrale*, 16mo. 4*s* 6*d* . 1861
246 PROFEZIA di Giona, in *Sardo Logudorese*, da Spano, 16mo. 4*s* 6*d* 1861
247 VANGELO di S. Matteo, *Logudorese*, da Spano, 16mo. 15*s* 1858
248 LIBRO di Rut, *Sardo Settentrionale Tempiese*, da Spano, 32mo. 4*s* 6*d* 1861
249 CANTICO de' Cantici, *Sardo Settentrionale Tempiese*, 16mo. 4*s* 6*d* 1861
250 VANGELO di S. Matteo, in *dialetto Sardo Gallurese di Tempio*, da Mundula, con osservazioni da L. L. Bonaparte, 16mo. 15*s* 1861
251 VANGELO di S. Matteo, in *dialetto Corso*, 16mo. 15*s* 1861
252 —— in *dialetto Romano*, da Caterbi, con la cooperazione di L. L. Bonaparte, 16mo. 15*s* 1861
253 SONETTO *Romanesco*, 4to. 1*s* 6*d*
254 EVANGELIO de S. Mateo, en el *dialecto Asturiano*, por un natural de Asturias, con cooperacion de L. L. Bonaparte, 16mo. 15*s* 1861
255 COLLECÇAO de vocabulos e frases usados em *S. Pedro, Rio Grande, Brazil*, 4to. 25 *copies printed*, 7*s* 6*d* 1856
256 EVANGELIO de S. Mateo, traducido al *dialecto Gallego* por Santa Maria, con observaciones sobre la pronunciacion Gallega, Asturiana, Castellana y Portuguesa por L. L. Bonaparte, 16mo. 15*s* 1861
257 SALOMO's Hohe Lied in *Siebenbürgischsächsischer* Sprache, von Seivert, 16mo. 4*s* 6*d* 1859
258 PSALMS, the Book of, in *Lowland Scotch*, by Riddell, 8vo. 15*s* 1857
259 SOLOMON, the Song of, in *Lowland Scotch*, by Riddell, 4to. 4*s* 6*d* 1858
260 BOOK of Ruth, in the *Northumberland dialect*, by Robson, 32mo. 3*s* 1860
261 SOLOMON, THE SONG OF, *in twenty-five English dialects*: Lowland Scotch, three versions; of Northumberland; Newcastle, two versions; Cumberland, two varieties, North and Central; Durham, Westmoreland, North Yorkshire, Craven, North Lancashire, West Yorkshire, Sheffield, Lancashire (Bolton), Devonshire, East Devonshire, Somersetshire, Wiltshire, Dorset, Cornwall (living dialect,) Sussex and Norfolk, and Saxon-English; together 25 copies, 16mo. £3. 5*s* 1858-62
262 —— versified *in the dialect of the Colliers of Northumberland*, by Robson, 4to. 7*s* 6*d* 1860
263 SOMERSETSHIRE Dialect (the), its pronunciation, by Baynes, reprinted, 8vo. 4*s* 6*d* 1861
264 EVANGELII Matthæi Cap. I. *Neo-Frisicè*, à Halbertsma, 16mo. 100 *copies printed*, 3*s* 1857
265 —— Cap. II. 16mo. 25 *copies printed*, 7*s* 6*d* 1857
266 EWANGEELJE fen Matthéwes: Evangelie van Mattheus vertaald in *Land-Friesch*, door Halbertsma, 4to. 27*s* 1858
267 PESNI Pesnei tsara Solomona (*the Song of Solomon in Russian*), 16mo. 4*s* 6*d* 1858
268 PROPHÉTIE de Jonas, en Basque de la vallée de *Cize, Basse Navarre*, par Casenave, 16mo. 4*s* 6*d* 1862
269 STORIA di Giuseppe Ebreo, della Genesi, in dialetto *Sardo Tempiese*, da Porqueddu, 8vo. 15*s* 1862
270 PROFEZIA di Giona, in dialetto *Sardo Tempiese*, 16mo. 4*s* 6*d* 1862
271 GOSPEL of St. Matthew in *Lowland Scotch* by Henderson, 16mo. 15*s* 1862
272 VANGELO di San Matteo, in dialetto *Calabrese Cosentino*, da Lucente, con osservazioni dal Principe L. L. Bonaparte, 16mo. 15*s* 1862

273 CORNISH Literature, reprinted from the Cambrian Journal, 1861, 8vo. *two leaves*, 1s 6d 1861
274 LANGUE BASQUE et LANGUES FINNOISES, par le Prince L. L. Bonaparte, 4to. 24s 1862
275 VANGELO di S. Matteo, in *dialetto Bolognese*, da Pepoli, 16mo. 15s 1862
BONGARSIUS—*See* GESTA DEI.

BONN AND BRESLAU ACADEMY:
276 VERHANDLUNGEN der Kaiserlichen Leop. Carol. Akademie: Nova Acta Physico-Medica Academiæ Cæsareæ Leopoldino-Carolinæ naturae curiosorum, Vols. X. part 2; XVI. 2; XVII. 1, 2, and Supplement; XVIII. 2, and 2 Supplements; XIX. 1, 2, and 2 Supplements; XX. I, 2; XXI. 1, 2; XXII. Supplement; XXIII. 1, 2, and Supplement; XXIV. 1; XXV. 1, 2; XXVI. 1; in 24 vols. or *parts*, large 4to. *numerous plates, many coloured*, sd. £10.
Vratisl. et Bonn. 1821-57
277 SCHULTZ, die Cyklose des Lebenssaftes in den Pflanzen, 4to. 33 *plates, bds.* 7s 6d
Bonn (Vol. XVIII. Suppl.), 1841
278 LEHMANN, Revisio Potentillarum, large 4to. *with* 64 *plates*, 10s
Bonn (Vol. XXIII. Suppl.) 1856
279 BOREL D'HAUTERIVE, Annuaire de la Noblesse de France, et des Maisons souveraines de l'Europe, Vols. XI—XV. 5 vols. 12mo. *several hundred coats of Arms, plates, containing much historical, biographical, and bibliographical information*, sd. 20s Paris, 1854-58
280 BOUQUET. GALLICARUM ET FRANCICARUM RERUM SCRIPTORES; ou Recueil des HISTORIENS DES GAULES ET DE LA FRANCE, par Dom Martin Bouquet, et autres Religieux de St. Maur, et continué par MM. Daunou et Naudet, Guigniaut, De Wailly, etc. 21 vols. folio, *a fine tall copy, in French calf gilt*, VERY RARE, £110. Paris, 1738-1855
Copies are getting *scarcer* and *dearer* every year.

Tom. 1. Les Gaulois
Les François jusqu' à Clovis
2, 3. Rois de la *Première Race*
4. Lettres Historiques, Lois, &c.
5. *Seconde Race.*—Pepin et Charlemagne, A.D. 781-814
6. Louis le Debonnaire, 781-840
7. Fils et pet. fils de Louis le Debonnaire, 840-877
Capitulaires de Charles le Chauve
8. Diplomes des mêmes
Louis le Begue.—Louis V., 877-987

Tom. 9. Restes des Monumens de la *Seconde Race*, 877-991
10. *Troisième Race.*—Hugues Capet, Robert, 980-1045
11. Henri I., 1031-1060
12-16. Philippe I. Lous VI. et VII. 1060-1080
17-19. Philippe Auguste—Louis VIII., 1180-1226.
20. Louis IX.—Chas. IV., 1227-1328
21. Les mêmes, livraison II., 1328.

"Some years ago the design of publishing *Les Historiens des Gaules et de la France* was resumed on a larger scale and in a more splendid form; and although the name of Dom Bouquet stands foremost, the merit must be shared amongst the veteran Benedictines of the Abbey of *St. Germain des Prés* at Paris. This noble collection may be proposed as a model for such national works; the original texts are corrected from the best manuscripts; the curious reader is enlightened without being oppressed by the perspicuous brevity of the preface and notes. But a multitude of obstacles and delays seem to have impeded the progress of the undertaking; and the historians of France had only attained the twelfth century and thirteenth volume, when a general deluge overwhelmed the country and its ancient inhabitants."—*Gibbon's Miscellaneous Works*, vol. 2, p. 713.
"The tables of contents and the index are framed with so much minuteness as to bring, in a few minutes, before the reader's eye, all that can be found respecting any fact within the period of the collection, and the dissertations are so copious and ably executed, that there seldom is a point of importance where the writers have not collected the learning and sentiments of all preceding writers. Dom Bouquet lived to finish the first eight volumes; on his decease, the work was put into the hands of Dom Haudiquier, who had, in Dom Bouquet's life-time, learned the Arabic language, to enable him to print, with a translation, the authors who have written in that language upon the Crusades. Both writers were Benedictine monks of St. Maur; and invaluable as the work is, it is by no means the only work of the same calibre for which we are indebted to that learned community."—*Works of C. Butler*, vol. 2, p. 5. (Appendix).
"Bouquet is a name better known to the continental historian than any other compiler and editor, and indeed almost every one who has studied the earlier portions of English history, must be familiar with the sound. This Benedictine was commissioned by his order to draw up one of those immense works which, from time to time, have been the peculiar boast of the French literary world and to which we have nothing to compare in our country. It was considered desirable that all the ancient and mediæval writers upon the history of France should be collected into one immense corpus historicum for the good of the nation."—*H. L. Jones, in Gent.'s Mag.*, Dec. '55.

BRITISH ASSOCIATION:
281 REPORTS of the British Association for the Promotion of Science, from the commencement in 1831-1856, *wanting* 1838-40 *and* 1842-3) 21 vols. 8vo. 20 *vols. in calf neat and* 1 *in bds.* £9. 1833-56

BRITISH MUSEUM PUBLICATIONS:
282 CATALOGUE of the HARLEIAN MSS. now in the British Museum, with Indexes, 3 vols. folio, *calf gilt*, 25s 1808
283 COMBE (Taylor) Veterum Populorum et Regum Numi qui in Musco Britannico adservantur, royal 4to. *calf*, 25s 1814

PUBLICATIONS OF LEARNED SOCIETIES, ETC. 25

284 VETUS TESTAMENTUM, Graece e Codice MS. ALEXANDRINO, qui Londini in Bibliotheca Musei Britannici asservatur, Typis ad similitudinem ipsius Codicis Scripturae fideliter descriptum, cura et labore H. H. Baber, 3 vols. impl. folio, (pub. at £18. 18s) bds. £7. 7s; or *beautifully bound in russia extra, gilt edges, with blind-tooled sides, bordered with gold, a sumptuous copy*, £12. 12s   1816-21

Priced, 1834, Straker, £14. 14s; 1837 and 1840, Payne and Foss, russia, £26. 5s; Dr. Hawtrey's copy fetched, 1853, £13. 15s. The edition was confined to 250 copies. Woide's edition of the "NEW TESTAMENT" of the same Codex, bound uniformly, should be bought with this the "Old Testament."

285 NOVUM TESTAMENTUM Græcum, e Cod. MS· ALEXANDRINO descriptum a C. G. WOIDE, cum Appendice, royal folio, LARGE PAPER, *fine copy in russia extra, gilt edges*, £5.   1786

Of this very valuable work, presenting a facsimile of a very precious early Greek Manuscript, only 50 copies were printed on this fine large paper; 450 copies were printed of the regular edition, and TEN copies on vellum, but of these only 6 had the notes and illustrations.

286 BIBLIOTHECÆ REGIÆ Catalogus, 5 vols. *portraits*—Catalogue of the Maps, Prints, Drawings, etc. presented by George IV.: together 6 vols. royal folio, *bds.* uncut, £4. 10s   1820-29

287 CATALOGUE of MSS. in the British Museum, New Series, Vol. I. parts 1, 2, 3, the ARUNDEL and BURNEY MANUSCRIPTS and INDEXES, 3 vols. folio, *facsimiles*, (pub. at £3. 1s) *bds*. £2.   1834-40

288 ——— the same, Part I. The ARUNDEL MSS. *bds.* 10s   1834

289 CATALOGUS Codicum ORIENTALIUM Musei Britannici, tres partes, in 4 vols. royal folio, *facsimiles*, (pub. at £2. 10s) *bds*. £2.   1838-47

Contents; I Codd. Syriaci et Carshunici; II. Arabici, 2 parts; III. Aethiopici. Sets completed.

290 BONOMI (J.) and F. ARUNDALE, Gallery of Egyptian Antiquities in the British Museum, with Description by S. BIRCH, 2 parts in 1 vol. 4to. *with 57 plates, mostly coloured* (pub. at £2. 2s) *cloth*, poor copy, 20s; a good copy, 30s   (? 1840)

291 CATALOGUE of the Printed Books, Vol. I. A to Azz. sm. folio. *cloth*, 16s   1841

This volume contains 91 admirable rules for cataloguing. The article Academies supplies a valuable Bibliography of all the Transactions of Learned and Publishing Societies.

292 HIERATIC PAPYRI. Select Papyri in the Hieratic character from the collections of the British Museum, with Hawkins' prefatory Remarks, parts I. to III. royal folio, 168 *plates*, (pub. at £4. 7s) *bds.* £2. 12s   1841-44

293 BIBLIOTHECA GRENVILLIANA, Bibliographical Notices of the Library of the Right Hon. Thomas Grenville, by Payne and Foss, 1842, 3 vols. royal 8vo. *cloth, uncut*, very rare, Vols. *I. and II. are out of print, only a few copies were published*, £8.   1842-48

These books are now in the BRITISH MUSEUM, to which they were munificently bequeathed by the late owner.

294 CATALOGUE of the Manuscript Maps, Charts, and Plans, and of the Topographical Drawings in the British Museum, 2 vols. royal 8vo. (pub. at 20s) *cloth*, 15s 1844

295 INDEX to the Additional MANUSCRIPTS, with those of the Egerton collection, preserved in the British Museum, and acquired in the years 1783-1835, folio, *cloth, out of print*, £2. 2s   1849

296 CATALOGUE of Additions to the Manuscripts in the British Museum in the years 1841-45, stout royal 8vo. (pub. at 20s) *bds.* 15s   1850

297 LAYARD (A. H.) ASSYRIAN INSCRIPTIONS in the Cuneiform Character, recently discovered and now in the British Museum, impl. folio, 98 *plates, bds.* 18s 1851

298 CATALOGUE of the GREEK and ETRUSCAN VASES in the British Museum, Vol. I. (*all published*) impl. 8vo. LARGE AND FINE PAPER, *plates, cloth*, 12s   1851

299 LIST of the BOOKS OF REFERENCE in the Reading Room of the British Museum, 8vo. *plans, cloth*, 7s 6d   1859

British Museum Natural History Catalogues:
LIST OF CONTENTS.

300 CATALOGUE of MAMMALIA, 3 parts, *plates and woodcuts*, 17s 6d		1850-52
301 LIST of MAMMALIA, *plates*, 2s 6d		1843
302 CATALOGUE of MAMMALIA, and Birds of Nepal, presented by B. H. Hodgson		1846
303 CATALOGUE of MAMMALIA, and Birds of New Guinea, 8vo. 1s 6d		1859
304 CATALOGUE of the Birds of the Tropical Islands of the Pacific, 8vo. 1s 6d		1859
305 CATALOGUE of the Genera and Sub-Genera of Birds, 4s		1855
306 LIST of Birds, 4 parts in 5, 9s 3d		1848-59
307 CATALOGUE of Shield Reptiles, part 1, Tortoises, 4to. *plates*, £2. 10s		1855
308 CATALOGUE of Reptiles, 3 parts, 7s		1844-49
309 CATALOGUE of Colubrine Snakes, 4s		1858

310 CATALOGUE of Amphibia, part II. *all published, plates*, 2s 6d   1850
311 CATALOGUE of Batrachia Salientia, 8vo. *plates*, 6s   1858
312 LIST of Fish, part I. Chondropterygii, *all published, plates*, 3s   1851
313 CATALOGUE of Fish, by L. T. Gronow, 3s 6d   1854
314 CATALOGUE of Lophobranchiate Fish, *plates*, 2s   1856
315 CATALOGUE of Apodal Fish, 8vo. *plates*, 10s   1856
316 CATALOGUE of Acanthopterygian Fishes, 3 vols. 8vo. 29s   1859-61
317 LIST of Osteological Specimens, 2s   1847
318 CATALOGUE of Bones of Mammalia, 8vo. 5s   1862
319 LIST of Lepidopterous Insects, Papilionidae, Erycinidae, and Appendix, 3 parts, 3s 6d   1847-56
320 CATALOGUE of Lepidopterous Insects, part I, Papilionidae, 4to. COLOURED PLATES, £1. 5s   1852
321 SPECIMEN of a Catalogue of Lycaenidae, 4to. COLOURED PLATES, £1. 1s   1862
322 LIST of Lepidopterous Insects, 24 parts, £4. 9s   1854-62
323 LIST of Hymenopterous Insects, 2 parts, 3s 6d   1846-48
324 CATALOGUE of Hymenopterous Insects, 7 parts, 12mo. *numerous plates*, 34s 6d   1853-59
325 LIST of Dipterous Insects, 7 parts, *woodcuts*, 27s   1848-55
326 LIST of Homopterous Insects, 4 parts and Supplement, *plates*, 20s 6d   1850-58
327 LIST of Hemipterous Insects, 2 parts, *plates*, 11s   1851-52
328 CATALOGUE of Orthopterous Insects, part I. 4to. *plates*, £3.   1859
329 NOMENCLATURE of Coleopterous Insects, 6 parts, *plates*   1847-52
330 CATALOGUE of Coleopterous Insects, parts 7, 8, 9, *all published, plates*, 9s   1853-56
331 CATALOGUE of the Coleopterous Insects of Madeira, 8vo. 3s   1857
332 LIST of Coleopterous Insects, part I. *all published*, 6d   1851
333 CATALOGUE of Halticidae—Physapodes and Œdipodes, part I. 8vo. *plates*, 7s   1860
334 CATALOGUE of Hispidae, 8vo. *plates*, 6s   1858
335 LIST of Crustacea, 2s   1847
336 CATALOGUE of Crustacea, part I. *all published*, 6d   1855
337 CATALOGUE of Myriapoda, part I. *all published*, 1s 9d   1856
338 LIST of Myriapoda   1844
339 CATALOGUE of Neuropterous Insects, 4 parts, 8s 6d   1852-53
340 CATALOGUE of Neuropterous Insects, part I, *Termitina, all published*, 6d   1858
341 GUIDE to the Systematic Distribution of the Mollusca, part I, *all pubd.* 8vo. 5s   1857
342 CATALOGUE of the collection of Maratlan Shells, 8s   1857
343 CATALOGUE of Mollusca, parts 1, 2, and 4, *all published, woodcuts*, 8s   1849-53
344 LIST of Mollusca, part I, *all published*, 6d   1855
345 CATALOGUE of Bivalve Mollusca, part I, *all published*, 4d   1850
346 CATALOGUE of Conchifera, 2 parts, 3s 6d   1853-54
347 NOMENCLATURE of Molluscous Animals and Shells, part I. *all pubd.* 1s 6d   1850
348 LIST of Mollusca and Shells, collected, etc., by Eydoux and Souleyet, 8d   1855
349 LIST of Shells of the Canaries, 1s   1854
350 LIST of the Shells of Cuba, 1s   1854
351 LIST of the Shells of South America, 2s   1854
352 CATALOGUE of Phaneropneumona, 2s   1852
553 CATALOGUE of Pulmonata, part I. *all published, woodcuts*, 2s 6d   1855
354 CATALOGUE of Auriculidae, Proserpinidae, and Truncatellidae, 1s 9d   1857
355 CATALOGUE of Entozoa, *plates*, 2s   1853
356 LIST of British Animals, 17 parts, £1. 14s 2d   1848-55
357 CATALOGUE of British Hymenoptera, part I. *all published, plates*, 6s   1855
358 CATALOGUE of Fossorial Hymenoptera, Formicidae and Vespidae, *plates*, 6s   1858
359 CATALOGUE of Ichneumonidae, 1s 9d   1856
360 LIST of British Curculionidæ, 1s   1856
361 CATALOGUE of Recent Echinida, pt. I. *all pubd. plate*, 3s 6d   1855
362 CATALOGUE of Marine Polyzoa, 2 parts, *plates*, 32s   1852-54
363 LIST of British Diatomaceae, 1s   1859
364 CATALOGUS Concharum Bivalvium, pars I: Veneridæ, 12mo.   1853

BRUSSELS ACADEMY:

365 BULLETINS de l'Académie Royale de Bruxelles (de Belgique), 1835-50, Tomes 2-4, 6-11 pt. 1, (*tome* 9 *wanting No.* 3), 12 pt. 2, 14 pt. 2, 17 pt. 1 ; 20 vols. 8vo. *plates of Antiquities, Natural History*, £3.   *Brux.* 1835-50

PUBLICATIONS OF LEARNED SOCIETIES, ETC. 27

366 BULLETINS of the Campaigns, 1793 to 1832, 31 vols. 12mo. *hf. bd.* £2. 16*s*
                                            1793-1832
  There was no Bulletin published for 1802; and those for the years 1818-22, and 1824-26, are wanting to this set.
367 CALCUTTA JOURNAL, or Political, Commercial and Literary Gazette, from its commencement in 1818 to 1821, 14 vols.—Asiatic Department of the Calcutta Journal, 1821 to 1823, 7 vols.—together 21 vols. royal 4to. *maps and plates, not uniform, very rare*, £6.   *Calcutta*, 1818-23
  An important Indian periodical, almost unknown in Europe.
368 CALCUTTA JOURNAL OF NATURAL HISTORY, Nos. 11-16, 19-21, 8vo. *plates, sd.* 25*s*
                                       Calcutta, 1842-45
369 CALCUTTA MAGAZINE and Miscellany for 1814-15, 2 vols. 8vo. *hf. bd.* 20*s Cal.*1814-15
370 CALCUTTA REVIEW, from the beginning in 1844 to Dec. 1859, being Nos. 1—66 (without No. 39-40, intended for the Index), complete; together 33 vols. 8vo.—7 volumes neatly bound, *half calf, the remainder in quarterly parts, uncut*, £10.   *Calcutta*, 1844-59
        Numbers sold separately at 2*s*.

CALCUTTA MEDICAL AND PHYSICAL SOCIETY:
371 TRANSACTIONS of the above, 7 vols. 8vo. *bds.* £4.   *Calcutta*, 1825-35

CALEDONIAN HORTICULTURAL SOCIETY:
372 MEMOIRS of the above, Vols. I.—IV., 8vo. *plates, hf. bd. green morocco*, 10*s*
                                     Edinb. 1814-29
373 CAMBRIAN QUARTERLY MAGAZINE and Celtic Repertory, Vols. I—V. 8vo. *bds.* £2. 10*s*   1829-32
374 —— the same, Vols. I—IV. 8vo. *half calf*, 30*s*   1829-32
375 CAMBRIAN QUARTERLY MAGAZINE and Celtic Repertory, Nos. III.-VIII., X-XVI., XVIII.-XX.—together 16 Nos. 8vo. *sd.* 27*s*   1829-33
  The above contains much valuable information relative to the Language, Literature, and Antiquities of Wales.
376 CAMBRIAN Register for 1795, 8vo. *coloured map, calf, scarce,* 10*s*   1795
    Contains much valuable Antiquarian and Philological matter.
377 CAMBRIDGE MATHEMATICAL JOURNAL, edited by R. L. Ellis, SERIES I, 4 vols. 1839-45—CAMBRIDGE AND DUBLIN MATHEMATICAL JOURNAL, edited by W. Thomson, Vols. 1 to 7, 1846-52—together 11 vols. 4 vols. *half calf, the remainder unbound*, £7. 15*s*   *Cambridge*, 1839-52

CAMBRIDGE PHILOSOPHICAL SOCIETY:
378 TRANSACTIONS of the above, Vols. 1 and 2, 4to. *half calf,* 36*s Cambridge*, 1822-27
379 —— the same, Vol. 5, Parts 2 and 3, 4to. *sd.* 20*s*   1834-35
380 —— the same, Vol. 8, Part 5, 4to. *sd.* 12*s*   1849
381 CAMBRO-BRITON, from the Commencement in September, 1819, to June, 1822, 3 vols. 8vo. *half calf,* 34*s*   1820-22
  The above contains valuable articles on the Welsh Language, Welsh Poetry, Topographical and Biographical Notices, etc.
382 CAMDENI (Guil.) Anglica, Normannica, Hibernica, Cambrica, a Veteribus scripta: Asser Menevensis, Anonymus de Vita Gulielmi Conquestoris, Thomas Walsingham, Thomas de la More, Gul. Gemiticensis, Giraldus Cambrensis, plerique nunc primùm in lucem editi, fol. *best edition, old calf*, 30*s Francf.* 1603
  Priced, 1832, Payne and Foss, £3. 13*s* 6*d*; 1834, Arch, mor. £4. 10*s*; 1844, Rodd, £3. 3*s*.

CAMDEN SOCIETY:
383 PUBLICATIONS of the CAMDEN SOCIETY, being reprints of exceedingly rare and curious Books, and Publications of inedited MS., etc. with copious Introductions and Notes, 80 vols. small 4to. *new in cloth,* £10. 10*s*   1838-61

CONTENTS.

1838	Poems of W. Mapes	1845.
Edward IV.'s Restoration	Irish Narratives, 1641-90	Varney's Long Parliament
Bishop Bale's Kynge Johan	1842.	Bramstone's Autobiography
Maydiston's Richard II.	III Metrical Romances	James Earl of Perth's Correspondence
1839.	Diary of Dr. Dee	
Plumpton Correspondence	Apology for the Lollards	1846.
Anecdotes and Traditions	Rutland Papers	Liber de Antiquis Legibus
Political Songs	1843.	Chronicle of Calais
1840.	Diary of Bp. Cartwright	Polydore Vergil, an early English
Hayward's Annals of Elizabeth	Letters of Eminent Men	Translation, Books 1—8
Ecclesiastical Documents	Proceedings against A. Kyteler	1847.
Norden's Essex	Promptorium Parvulorum, Vol. 1.	Italian Relation of England
Warkworth's Chronicle (1839)	Suppression of Monasteries	Church of Middleham
Kemp's Nine Days Wonder		Camden Miscellany, Vol. I.
Egerton Papers	1844.	Life of Lord Grey
Chronica Jocelini de Brakelonda	Leycester's Correspondence	
Rishanger's Chronicle	French Chronicle of London	1848.
1841.	Polydore Vergil.	Diary of Walter Yonge
Travels of N. Nucius.	Thornton's Romances	Diary of H. Machyn

1849.	Camden Miscellany, Vol. II.	Dean Davies' Journal
Visitation of Huntingdonshire	Verney Papers	The Domesday of St. Pauls
Obituary of R. Smythe	Ancren Riwle	1858.
Twysden on English Government	1854.	Liber Famelicus of Sir J. White-
Letters of Elizabeth and James	Letters of Lady B. Harley	locke
Chronicon Petroburgense	Household Roll of Bishop Swinfield	Savile Correspondence
1850.	Grants of Edward V.	Blonde of Oxford
Q. Jane and Q. Mary	Camden Miscellany, Vol. III.	Camden Miscellany, Vol. IV.
Wills from the Registers of Bury St. Edmunds	Swinfield's Household Roll, Abstract and Glossary	1859. Richard Symonds' Diary
W. Mapes de Nugis Curialium		Papers relating to Milton
1851.	1856.	Letters of George Lord Carew
Pilgrimage of Sir R. Guylford	Letters of Charles I. 1646	1860.
Secret Services of Charles II. and James II.	English Chronicle, 1377-1461	Narratives of the Reformation Correspondence of James I. and
1852.	1857.	Cecil
Chronicle of the Grey Friars	Knights Hospitallers in England	1861.
1853.	Diary of John Rous, 1625-42, (1856)	Chamberlain's Letters, (1597-1602)
Promptorium Parvulorum, Vol. II.	Trevelyan Papers	Proceedings in Kent, 1640

This is a most important series of works, being reprints of exceedingly rare and valuable books, and publications of MSS. never before published; printed verbatim, with copious Introductions, Notes, and Illustrations by the learned members of the Society.

The following Nos. can be had separately.

384 DIARY of John Rous, 2s 6d   1856
385 PAPERS relating to Milton, 5s   1859
386 LETTERS of George Lord Carew, 5s   1859
387 NARRATIVES of the Reformation, 8s 6d   1860
388 CIVIL ENGINEER and ARCHITECT's JOURNAL, from the beginning in October 1837 to October 1861, Vols. I. to XXIV. 4to. *numerous plates and cuts, nineteen vols. bound in cloth, the remainder in 58 parts*, £12.   1837-61
A similar set, unbound, recently priced in a bookseller's catalogue £15. 15s

CELTIC ACADEMY—*See* MÉMOIRES.
CELTIC SOCIETY :
389 PUBLICATIONS of the CELTIC SOCIETY, founded MDCCXLV; the Complete Series of 6 vols. royal 8vo. *portraits* (sold to subscribers for £7.) *clean copy in cloth*, £2. 2s   1847-53
Incorporated with the IRISH ARCHÆOLOGICAL SOCIETY, which see.
390 CHALMERS' (Alex.) General BIOGRAPHICAL DICTIONARY, containing an Historical and Critical Account of the Lives and Writings of the most eminent Persons in every Nation, particularly the BRITISH and IRISH, from the earliest accounts to the present time, 32 vols. 8vo. *calf, very neat*, £5. 15s   1812-17
Still the best "English" Biographical Dictionary. Published at £19. 4s in boards, cost of binding, £9. 12s; 1855, Bernal's copy fetched £9. 17s 6d.
"In this much improved edition, Mr. Chalmers has taken more than common pains in giving accurate lists of the works of such as were authors, with the dates of the best editions, &c. &c. It is by far the most complete and copious biographical dictionary in our language."
"This work contains much information which will be useful and amusing to the generality of readers, and which could not be procured except in works which are now become both scarce and expensive."—*Quarterly Review*.
391 CHAMBERS' (R.) Biographical Dictionary of eminent SCOTSMEN, 4 vols. 8vo. 1835—Supplement by T. Thomson, 1 vol. roy. 8vo. 1855—together 4 vols. *numerous fine steel portraits, calf extra, gilt edges*, £2. 5s
392 CHINESE REPOSITORY (of facts and statements respecting the History, Statistics, Language, Trade, etc. of China and the adjacent countries), from the beginning in 1832, Vols. I—XX., a complete set, with the General Index, 21 vols. 8vo. *maps and plates, half calf neat*, £28.   Canton, 1832-51
392* —— the same, Vols. I—XV. XIX. XX. 8vo. *eleven vols. bound, and six in parts*, £18.   1832-51
An imperfect copy in stock, of which Numbers are sold separately.—The entire remaining stock of this valuable Repository was destroyed by the Chinese during their destruction of the British Factories near Canton.
"This work, edited by the late Dr. Morrison, contains a great variety of valuable and curious papers."
MacCulloch.
This valuable Repository is of great importance to Oriental scholars; its scarcity is so great that few of the public Libraries of England can boast of complete sets; on the Continent the work is vainly sought after. Abel Remusat could never get sight of it; and complains of it in his preface to his Chinese Grammar. China is a world of its own on this Globe; so much independent thought and so many wonderful achievements in Arts, Literature, and Industry, are entirely peculiar to the Chinese, that European readers will derive the greatest interest and profit from the careful study of this "Chinese Repository," which embodies the most accurate recent information on the Celestial Empire.

CHRONOLOGICAL INSTITUTE OF LONDON :
393 TRANSACTIONS of the above from the beginning in 1852 to 1861, 6 parts 8vo. *sd. an extremely valuable and important periodical*, 20s   1852-61
394 CLASSICAL JOURNAL, from the beginning in March 1810, Vols. I. to XVIII. in 36 Nos. with Index (to the first twenty vols.) bound in 9 vols. stout 8vo. *hf. calf*, 18s   1810-1818
A most valuable periodical containing Prize Essays, etc. by Whately, Blomfield, Sir W. Drummond, and other

PUBLICATIONS OF LEARNED SOCIETIES, ETC. 29

distinguished names; also contributions by continental savants. There are several pieces on the Ancient British language of Cornwall.

COLLEGE OF ARMS:
395 CATALOGUE of the ARUNDEL MANUSCRIPTS in the library of the College of Arms, [by Sir Charles G. Young] royal 8vo. *not published*, bds. 14s   1829
396 COLONIAL CHURCH CHRONICLE and Missionary Journal, from the beginning in July 1847 to December 1860, Vols. I—XIV. 14 vols. 8vo. *hf. calf neat*, £2. 10s   1848-61
    A receptacle of vast and varied information upon the people, habits, languages, and history of the world, especially America and the East.
397 COLONIAL INTELLIGENCER; or ABORIGINES' FRIEND, for 1847-52, comprising interesting intelligence concerning the ABORIGINES of various climes, and articles upon Colonial affairs, 4 vols. 8vo. *three in cloth, one in Nos.* 10s   1847-52

COPENHAGEN ACADEMY:
398 DET KONGELIGE DANSKE VIDENSKABERNES SELSKABS Philosophiske og Historiske Afhandlinger, Deel 1-5, 8 *plates*, 1823-36:—Naturvidenskabelige og Mathematiske Afhandlinger, 12 vols. *the complete series containing* 210 *plates and* 3 *maps*, 1824-46:—*Femte Række*, Naturvidenskabelig og Mathematisk Afdeling, Bind 1-3, 18 *tables*, 3 *maps, and* 37 *plates*, 1849-53: together 20 vols. 4to. *comprising upwards of* 250 *plates of Natural History, Mathematics and Antiquities, boards,* £6.   1823-53
399 NATURVIDENSKABELIGE og MATHEMATISKE Afhandlinger, Vols. I—VIII, 4to. *numerous plates of Natural History, etc. boards*, £2.   Kjöbenhavn, 1824-41

CORNWALL ROYAL GEOLOGICAL SOCIETY:
400 TRANSACTIONS of the above, Vols. III. IV., 2 vols. 8vo. *Geological Map of Cornwall, bds. uncut*, 30s   Penzance, 1828-32
401 CURTIS'S BOTANICAL MAGAZINE, from the commencement in 1786 to June 1860, COMPLETE SET. CONTENTS: 1786-1860
SERIES I. Vols. 1—53; *plates*, 1—2704, with text; General Index, 1 vol.   [1786] 1793-1826
    The last volume (53) ends also Dr. John SIMS' Series, called by him the NEW SERIES.
SERIES II. conducted by S. Curtis and Sir W. J. Hooker, Vols. 54-70; or New Series, Vols. I—XVII.; *plates*, 2705—4131, with text and Index, 17 vols.   1827-44
SERIES III. by Sir W. J. Hooker, Vols. 71—86, or Third Series, I—XVI.; *plates*, 4132—5212, with text   1845—June 1860
    This, the scarcest portion, was published at 2 guineas per volume, making 32 guineas.
Together, the 3 Series as described, £65.   1786-1860
    A fine complete set of Curtis's Magazine is seldom offered for sale.
402 DEZOBRY et BACHELET, DICTIONNAIRE GÉNÉRAL de BIOGRAPHIE et d'Histoire, de Mythologie, de Géographie ancienne et moderne comparée, des antiquités et des institutions Grecques, Romaines, Françaises et étrangères, 2 vols. roy. 8vo. *hf. morocco*, 35s   Paris, 1857
403 DICTIONNAIRE (NOUVEAU) D'HISTOIRE NATURELLE, appliquée aux Arts, à l'Agriculture, à la Médecine, etc. par une Société de Naturalistes et d'Agriculteurs, nouvelle édition, refondue et augmentée, 36 vols. 8vo. and ONE VOLUME *with several hundred plates, calf neat*, £4. 10s   Paris, 1816-19
Priced, 1824, £21. 12s; 1836, £8. 8s; 1847, £7. 17s 6d and £8. 18s 6d. With coloured plates, I sold a copy, 1856, hf. bd. £7. 10s.
    A valuable set of books for a Public Library. This Dictionary was compiled by the most eminent scientific men in France. each article was written by the most competent person in each branch of the subject he undertook, and their names are a sufficient guarantee for their excellence, viz.: Biot, Bosc, Chaptal, Desmarest, Du Tour, Lamarck, Latreille, Lucas, Olivier, Richard, Sonnini, Vieillot, Virey, and others.

EDINBURGH ROYAL SOCIETY:
404 TRANSACTIONS of the ROYAL SOCIETY of EDINBURGH, from the commencement in 1783 to 1857, 21 vols. 4to. *numerous plates*, 20 *vols. handsomely bound in calf gilt, the last in* 4 *parts, a fine set and now very scarce*, £21.   Edinb. 1788-1858
    The following parts can be had new, with a reduction from the affixed publishing price.
Vol. XV. pt. 1, 10s 6d; pt. 2, 4s; pt. 3, 6s; pt. 4, 10s 6d   Vol. XVIII. 42s
Vol. XVI. pt. 1, 5s; pt. 2, 18s; pt. 3, 10s; pt. 4, 5s; pt. 5, 7s   Vol. XIX. pt. 1, 42s; pt. 2, 18s
Vol. XVII. pt. 1, 15s; pt. 2, 30s   Vol. XX. pt. 1, 18s; pts. 2, 3, 4, each 10s
    Vol. XXI. pt. 1, 15s; pt. 2, 10s; pt. 3, 7s; pt. 4, 18s
405 ENCYCLOPÆDIA BRITANNICA, or Dictionary of Arts, Sciences, and General Literature, seventh edition, 21 vols, 4to. *numerous engravings, strongly half bound calf, a bargain*, £9. 9s   Edinb. 1842
406 ——— the same, EIGHTH AND LAST EDITION, 21 vols. 4to. *numerous plates, half russia*, £25.   1860
    This grand book is without a rival in the world; it is the best modern Encyclopaedia published in any language.

407 DUCHESNE (A.) HISTORIÆ NORMANNORUM SCRIPTORES Antiqui, Res ab illis per Galliam, Angliam, Apuliam, Capuæ Principatum, Siciliam et Orientem gestas explicantes, ab anno 838 ad 1220, ex MSS. Cod. fere omnes nunc primum editi, folio, *a fine copy in russia extra, from Miss Currer's library,* £5. 5*s*
Lutet. Paris, 1619

A cheap copy of this valuable set of all the Norman chroniclers. Priced, 1826-8, Payne and Foss, £6. 6*s* ; 1840-44, James Bohn, £6. 6*s*; in 1847, £7. 17*s* 6*d*; the Roxburghe copy fetched £6. 6*s*; Dawson Turner's 1858, £7. 7*s*; Purton Cooper's, 1853, £8. 5*s*.
Large Paper copies sold: The Marquis of Townshend's, £9. 15*s*; Hibbert's, £9. 5*s*; 1854, Gardner's, mor. £30. "Liber rarissimus, et in paucis bibliothecis obvius."—*Vogt.* Baron Maseres observes of this work, that "the tracts of which it is composed, give us the fullest and most authentic account of the Normans in France, Italy, and England, that is anywhere to be found." See also Dr. Dibdin's Library Companion, p. 159-60.

408 DU CHESNE (F.) Historiæ Francorum Scriptores, a Philippo Augusto Rege usque ad Philippi IV tempora cum Epistolis Regum, Pontificum, Ducum, Abbatum et aliis veteribus Rerum Francicarum Monumentis, 5 vols. folio, *hf. vellum,* £6. 6*s* ; *or, vellum, gilt edges,* £8. ; *or a fine copy in old calf gilt, from Miss Currer's library,* £8. 8*s*
Lutetiæ Paris, 1636-49

A most important work for English as well as French history ; and considered by Vogt and Reimman to be of the most extreme rarity. "Cette collection continent plusieurs écrits qui ne sont pas dans le recueil de Bouquet."—*Brunet.*
"Duchesne, un des plus savants historiens que la France ait produits, et qui par ces immenses travaux a mérité le titre glorieux de père de l'histoire de France, naquit en 1584.—Le Cardinal de Richelieu l'appelait toujours son bon voisin.—Le "Historiæ Normannorum Scriptores," est un ouvrage rare et curieux. Le premier volume de " Historiæ Francorum Scriptores," contient l'origine de la nation jusqu'à Pepin, le second va jusqu'à Hugues Capet, et le troisième jusqu'au roi Robert. Pendant l'impression de ce volume, (1640) Duchesne mourut; son fils en achevait l'édition, et publia les volumes IV. et V. qui contiennent les évènemens jusqu'à Philippe le Bel."—*Biog. Universelle.*

ENGLISH HISTORICAL SOCIETY:

409 The Fine Series of Chronicles, &c. as printed under the auspices of this Club, ON FINE LARGE PAPER, which was restricted to the number of Noblemen and Gentlemen composing the Society. The Complete Series contain the following:—

Bedæ Historia Gentis Anglorum et Opera Minora recensuit Stevenson, 2 vols. 1838-41
Chronicon Ricardi Divisiensis de Rebus gestis Richardi I. R. Angliae, ed. Stevenson 1838
Roger de Wendover. Chronica sive Flores Historiarum cum Append. edidit H. O Coxe, 5 vols. 1841-44
Willelmi Malmesburiensis, Gesta Regum Anglorum atque Historia Novella, recensuit Hardy, 2 vols. 1840
Codex Diplomaticus Ævi Saxonici Opera J. M. Kemble, 6 vols. 1839-48
Gildas de Excidio Britanniæ, recensuit Stevenson 1838
Nennii Historia Britonum, recensuit Stevenson 1838
Gesta Stephani Regis Anglorum et Ducis Normannorum ab And. Duchesne, recensuit R. C. Sewell 1846
Florentii Wigorniensis Monachi Chronicon ex Chronicis, edidit Thorpe, 2 vols. 1848-49

Chronicon Walteri de Hemingburgh de Gestis Regum Angliæ, recensuit H. C. Hamilton, 2 vols. 1848
Chronique de la Traison et Mort de Richart Deux, Roy d'Engleterre, avec un Glossaire, par Benj. Williams 1846
Henrici V. *Angliæ Regis* Gesta, cum Chronicâ Neustriæ, Galliæ, recensuit B. Williams 1850
Adami Murimuthensis Chronica sui temporis cum continuatione, ed. et recens. T. Hog 1846
Nicholai Triveti Annales sex Regum Angliæ, recensuit Hog 1856
Historia Rerum Anglicarum Willelmi Parvi, S. T. D. Ordinis Sancti Augustini Canonici Regularis in Cœnobio Beatæ Mariæ de Novoburgo in Agro Eboracensi, recensuit H. C. Hamilton, 2 vols. 1856

Together 29 vols. royal 8vo. *very elegantly printed, extra boards, complete sets have now become scarce,* £15. 1838-56

410 —— another set, 22 vols. 8vo. *small paper,* being the complete series, *without* Gesta Stephani, 1846 ; F. Wigorniensis, 2 vols. 1848-49 ; Walter de Hemingburgh, 2 vols. 1848 ; Chronique de Richart II., 1846 ; Adam Muremuthensis, 1846, *bds.* £9. 9*s* 1838-56

411 KEMBLE'S Codex, 6 vols. sold separately, *small paper,* £4. 4*s* ; LARGE PAPER, £6. 6*s* 1839-48

ENTOMOLOGICAL SOCIETY:

412 TRANSACTIONS of the above, Vols. I-IV, 1836-47, *calf gilt*—Proceedings, 1833-46, 2 vols. *half calf*— New Series, Vol. I. pts. 1—3 ; Vol. II. pts. 1, 5, and 6 ; Vol. III. pts. 1-7 ; Vol. IV. pts. 1-7 ; Vol. V. pts. 1 and 2—together 6 vols. and 22 parts, 8vo. *numerous beautifully coloured plates of Insects,* £7. 10*s* 1833-52

413 —— Transactions of, Vol. 1, parts 1 and 2, 8vo. *coloured plates,* 5*s* 1807-9

ETHNOLOGICAL SOCIETY OF LONDON:

414 JOURNAL of the above, FIRST SERIES *complete,* 4 vols. *cloth.* SECOND SERIES, Vol. 1, pts. 1 and 2—together 4 vols. and 2 parts 8vo. *rare,* £3. 16*s* 1848-61
A very valuable collection of papers upon the Ethnology of all parts of the world, *out of print, and scarce.*

ETHNOLOGICAL SOCIETY OF PARIS:

415 MEMOIRES de la Société Ethnologique de Paris, Vol. II. stout 8vo. *chiefly on the races and languages of Oceanica and America, sd.* 7*s* 6*d* *Paris,* 1845

416 BULLETIN de la Société Ethnologique de Paris, Vol. I. (*all published*) in 3 parts, 8vo. *sd.* 10*s* 1846-47

PUBLICATIONS OF LEARNED SOCIETIES, ETC. 31

417 FOREIGN QUARTERLY REVIEW, from its commencement in 1827 to 1843
inclusive, 31 vols. 8vo. (pub. at £18. 6s) *half calf neat*, £2. 16s 1827-43
This Journal embraces full and comprehensive views of the state of Continental Literature; and contains reviews on some of the most celebrated works of the age.

418 FRIEND OF INDIA, Quarterly Series, 3 vols. 8vo. *Professor Wilson's copy, half russia neat, rare and valuable*, 36s *Serampore*, 1821
Contains Rammohun Roy's original dissertations on Christianity; interesting Essays on Hindoo Polytheism, the Indian Archipelago, the Vedic Literature, etc.

419 FREEMASON'S QUARTERLY Magazine and Review, complete from the commencement in April 1, 1834, to April 1853, in sixteen volumes, *half calf neat*, and 13 *parts, rare*, £6. 1834-53

420 FREEMASON'S Monthly Magazine for 1855, 12 Nos. FREEMASON'S MAGAZINE and Masonic Mirror for 1856, 57, 58, 36 Nos.—together 48 nos. 8vo. (pub. at £3. 6s) *sd*. £2. 1855-58

421 GALE ET FELL, SCRIPTORES RERUM ANGLICARUM VETERES, 3 vols. folio, *fine copy in calf*, £8. 15s *Oxon*. 1684-91
Vol. I.—I. Ingulphi Croylandensis Historia. II. Petri Blesensis Continuatio ad Historiam Ingulphi. III. Chronica de Mailros. IV. Annales Monasterii Burtonensis. V. Historiae Croylandensis Continuatio.
Vol. 2.—I. Annales Marganenses. II. Chronicon Thomae Wikes, aliter Chronicon Salisburiensis Monast. III. Annales Waverleienses. IV. Itinerarium Regis Anglorum Richardi et aliorum in Terram Hierosolymorum, auctore Gaufrido Vinisauf. V. Chronica Walteri Hemingford de Gestis Regum Angliæ.
Vol. 3.—I. Gildas. II. Eddius. III. Nennius. IV. Asserius. V. Higden. VI. W. Malmsburiensis. VII. Anonymus Malmsb. VIII. Historia Remesiensis. IX. Historia Eliensis. X. Thomas Eliensis. XI. Joan. Wallingford. XII. Rad. de Diceto. XIII. De Partitione in Schiras, etc. XIV. Fordun Scoti Chronicon. XV. Alcuinus.
Priced, 1840, J. Bohn, *russia*, £12. 12s; 1841, Bohn, *morocco*, £13. 13s; fetched, 1853, Cooper, £9. 10s. "As in every monastery there was some curious mind, fond of noting the great incidents of his day, every country in Europe has such Chronicles. But I think with Dr. Henry, that upon the whole, our annalists are superior to any other nation at this period. Such a series of regular chronology and true incident; such faithful, clear, and ample materials for authentic history have scarcely appeared before the public. Nothing could be more contemptible as compositions; *nothing could be more satisfactory as authorities.*"—*Turner.*

GAZETTES AND NEWSPAPERS:

422 NOUVELLES Ordinaires et Extraordinaires de divers Endroits, de Novembre, 1630, à Decembre, 1658, 12 vols. *wanting the years* 1647-55, *Paris*—Gazette de Paris, de Juin 1691, à Decembre, 1715, 14 vols. *wanting the years* 1709-10, *Paris*— Nouvelles d'Amsterdam, 1739-42, 4 vols. *Amsterdam* — Nouvelles Extraordinaires, de Janvier, 1770, à Decembre, 1794, 24 vols. *half bound, uncut, Leyde*—together 54 vols. sm. 4to. and 8vo. *various bindings*, £10. 1630-1794
An extremely important and interesting collection, containing almost a complete History of the World, from the time of the Thirty Years War to the fall of Robespierre. It is the more valuable as containing those minute details of social life, and contemporary opinions which are so seldom found in the pages of professed history, but which are so vitally necessary for the information of the true historian. It may be confidently asserted that, without access to this or some similar collection of periodical documents, the history of Europe during the period embraced by it could not be written.
There are some few numbers wanting in the earlier volumes.

GEOGRAPHICAL SOCIETY:

423 JOURNAL of the Geographical Society of London, from its commencement in 1830 to 1859, Vols. I. to XXVII., with Indices to the first twenty volumes, 30 vols. 8vo. *numerous maps, fine set in hf. russ. ext. marb. edg.* £13. 10s 1832-59

424 ——— another set, Vols. I. to XVII. 8vo. *many maps, half calf neat, uncut, a desirable set*, £6. 15s 1832-47
The continuation from 1848 to the present time can be supplied at a reduction.

GEOLOGICAL SOCIETY OF LONDON:

425 TRANSACTIONS of the above; a complete set from the commencement in 1817 to 1856, FIRST SERIES, 5 vols. 1817-21, *complete*—SECOND SERIES, Vols. 1 to 7, 1824-56, *complete*—together 12 vols. 4to. *several hundred Geological Maps and plates, half bound russia*, £18. 18s 1811-56

426 PROCEEDINGS, 4 vols. 1826-45—QUARTERLY JOURNAL, Vols. I-XVII. Part 4, being Nos. 1 to 68 inclusive, 1845 to November 1861—together 9 vols. *hf. calf*, and 49 Nos. 8vo. *many plates*, A COMPLETE SET, (pub. at above £14. 12s) *rare*, £12. 1834-61
Sets completed at reasonable terms. Of the "Proceedings," the fourth volume is out of print; of the Quarterly Journal several of the early numbers.

427 PROCEEDINGS, from 1826 to 1842; Nos. 1-90, 93-96, 98, 100, 103—Abstracts of the Proceedings, 1856-9, Nos. 1-31.—3 vols. 8vo. *cloth*, and 29 Nos. 25s 1834-59
The Proceedings were published from 1826 to 1845, Vol. I. 4s 6d; Vol. II. 2s 6d, and III. 2s 6d; Vol. IV. out of print, only imperfect, to be had at the Society.

428 CLASSIFIED INDEX to the Transactions, Journal, &c. by Ormerod, *new*, 5s

GEOLOGICAL SOCIETY OF FRANCE:

428*MÉMOIRES, Vol. I. II. part 1, in 3 parts, 4to. *coloured plates*, 20s *Paris*, 1833-35

429 GESCHICHTE der KÜNSTE und WISSENSCHAFTEN seit der Wiederherstellung derselben bis an das Ende des achtzehnten Jahr-hunderts, A COMPLETE SET, *bound in* 44 vols. 8vo. (pub. at £26. 8s 6d) *half calf, contents lettered*, £3. 10s
Göttingen, 1796-1808

32   B. QUARITCH, 15 PICCADILLY, LONDON.

Contents: Cultur und Literatur des neueren Europa von Eichorn, 2 vols.; Zeichnende Künste von Fiorillo, 5 vols.; Poesie und Beredsamkeit von Bouterwek, 9 vols.; Studium der classichen Literatur von Heeren, 2 vols.; Historische Forschung und Kunst, von Wachler, 2 vols.; Neuere Philosophie von Buhle, 6 vols.; Mathematik, von Kastner, 4 vols.; Kriegskunst, von Hoyer, 2 vols.; Physik von Fischer, 8 vols. *plates*; Chemie von Gmelin, 3 vols.; Technologie, von Poppe, 3 vols.; Christlichen Moral von Stäudlin, 1 vol.; Praktische Theologie, von Ammon, Vol. I.; Schriftererklärung, von Meyer, 5 vols.

430 GESTA DEI PER FRANCOS, sive Orientalium Expeditionum et Regni Francorum Hierosolimitani Historia (per Bongars), 2 vols.—Marini Sanuti, Liber Secretorum Fidelium Crucis super Terræ Sanctæ recuperatione, quo et Terræ Sanctæ historia et geographia ab origine continentur, 1 vol.—together 3 vols. in 1, stout folio, *plan and plates, fine clean copy, on ordinary paper, as usual discoloured, old calf, rebacked, gilt edges*, £3.   *Hanoviæ*, 1611
431 —— the same, FINE PAPER, folio, *half calf*, £4.   1611
432 —— another copy, on FINE PAPER, folio, *vellum*, £5.   1611
Fine paper copies are very rare.

CONTENTS:

(Petavii et Cambdeni) Gesta Francorum
Roberti Monachi Historia Hierosolymitana
Baldrici Historia Ierosolimitana
Raimondus de Agiles
Albertus Aquensis
Fulcherii Peregrinantes Franci
Gauterii Bella Antiochena
Guiberti Abbatis et alii auctoris Gesta Dei per Francos

Willermi Tyrensis Historia
Jacobus de Vitriaco
Historia Hierosolimitana auctoris incerti
Regum et Principum Epistolæ
Oliverius Coloniensis de captione Damiatæ
Innocentii IV. Bulla
De Ludovico Rege Francorum
Sanuti Torselli liber Secretorum Fidelium crucis
Sanuti Epistolæ

The above comprise all the contemporary chronicles relative to the Crusades and the History of the Christian Empire of Jerusalem.
The curious plans by Sanuto, which he presented to Pope John XXII. in 1321, after having travelled through various countries, one of them being a Map of the then known world, in a circular form, with Jerusalem as its centre—give this work a peculiar interest in relation to the history of early geography.

GOETTINGEN ACADEMY:

433 COMMENTARII Societatis Regiæ Scientiarum Gottingensis, 1751-54, 4 vols.—Novi Commentarii, 1769-76, 7 vols.—Commentationes, 1778-99, 14 vols.—together 25 vols. 4to. *plates, half bound*, £2.   *Gottingae*, 1752-1800
This rare collection contains many valuable Physical, Mathematical, Philological, Historical. and Archæological Treatises by Haller, Hollman, Gesner, Michaelis, Kaestner, Wismuth, Blumenbach, Gatterer, Meiners, Tyschen, Lichtenberg, Heyne, and others.

434 GRÆVII Thesaurus Antiquitatum et Historiarum Italiæ collectus curâ et studio J. G. Grævii, et ad finem perductus à P. Burmanno, 9 vols. in 30 parts, divided into 16 vols. 1704-23; Thesaurus Antiquitatum Siciliæ, Sardiniæ, Corsicæ, etc. curâ J. G. Grævii, cum præfationibus, P. Burmanni, 15 vols. in 8, 1723-25; together 24 vols. folio, *fine frontispieces, portrait, and a profusion of interesting plates, fine copy, in old calf gilt*, £10.   *Lugd. Bat.* 1704-25
Priced, 1829, Longman, £25.. J. Bohn. £18. 18s, 1830, Payne and Foss, £25. 4s, 1835, Thorpe, £25. and £21.. 1842, £12. 12s, 1855, Köhler in Leipzig, 120 Thalers; Fetched, 1854, Puttick's, £12. 15s.
A vast compilation of all the writers upon the history and antiquities of Italy and its adjacent islands, forming a storehouse of learning nowhere else attainable; and from which the information contained in all the works since published has been derived. It is an indispensable book for a respectable library.

GRONINGEN ACADEMY:

435 Acta Secularia Academiæ Groninganæ, 1814—Annales, 1815-37, 22 vols.; 23 vols. 4to. *sd*. £2.   *Groningæ*, 1814-39

HAKLUYT SOCIETY:

436 PUBLICATIONS of the HAKLUYT SOCIETY, from the commencement in 1847 to 1860, 27 vols. 8vo. *many maps and plates, new in cloth, printed for subscribers only*, £12.   1847-60

CONTENTS:

Hawkins' (Sir Richd.) Observations in his Voiage into the South Sea in 1593, 1622; edited by Capt. C. R. Bethune   1847
Columbus, Select Letters, with other original documents relating to his Four Voyages, translated and edited by R. H. Major   1847
Ralegh's Discoverie of Guiana in 1595, 1596; edited by Sir R. N. Schomburgk, *map*   1848
Sir Francis Drake, his Voyage, 1595, by Thos. Maynarde, edited from the original MSS. by W. D. Cooley   1849
Rundall (Thos.) Narrative of Voyages towards the North-West in search of a Passage to Cathay and India, 1496 to 1631, *3 maps*   1849
Strachey (Wm.) Historie of Travaile into Virginia Britannia, edited from the MS. by R. H. Major, *map, facsimiles and 5 plates*   1849
Hakluyt (Rd.) Divers Voyages touching the discovery of America and the Islands adjacent, 1582; edited by J. Winter Jones, *facsimile and 2 maps*   1850
Rundall's Collection of early Documents on Japan   1850

Coat's Geography of Hudson's Bay, edited by Jno. Barrow   1851
Hakluyt (Rd.) Discovery and Conquest of Terra Florida by Don Ferdinando de Soto, 1611; edited by W. B. Rye, *map*   1851
Herberstein, Rerum Moscovitarum Commentarii: Notes upon Russia, translated and edited by R. H. Major, 2 vols. *2 facsimile maps and 4 plates*
De Veer (Gerrit) Three Voyages by the North-East to China, 1594-6, edited by C. T. Beke   1852
Mendoza (Juan Gonzalez de) Historie of China, transl. by Parke, 1588; edited by R. G. Staunton, 2 vols. 1853-4
D'Orléans (Pierre Joseph) History of the Tartar Conquerors of China, *Paris*, 1688; transl. and edited by the Earl of Ellesmere   1854
Fletcher (Francis) The World encompassed by Sir Francis Drake; edited by W. S. W. Vaux, *map*   1854
White (Adam) Collection of early Documents on Spitzbergen and Greenland   1855
Middleton (Sir Hen.) Voyage to Bantam and the Maluco

PUBLICATIONS OF LEARNED SOCIETIES, ETC.

Islands, 1606; ed. by B. Corney, *map and 5 plates* 1855
Bond (Edw A.) Russia at the Close of the 16th Century 1856
Benzoni (Girolamo) History of the New World; Travels, 1541-56, *Venice*, 1572. translated and edited by Adml. W. H. Smyth, *facsimiles of old woodcuts* 1857
Major (R. H.) India in the 15th Century 1857
Champlain, Voyage to the West Indies, 1599-1602; transl. by A. Wilmere, edited by N. Shaw, 4 *coloured and* 4 *plain facsimiles* 1859
Expeditions into the Valley of the Amazons, 1539, 1540, 1639; transl. and edited by C. R. Markham 1859
Gonzalez de Clavijo, Embassy to the Court of Timour at Samarcand, 1403-6, by R. Markham, *map* 1859
Hudson (Hen *the Navigator*) by G M Asher, 2 *maps* 1860
Early Voyages to Terra Australis, now called Australia, edited by R. H. Major, *maps* 1859

Besides the above set, I have several of the volumes, which will be sold separately.

437 HARLEIAN MISCELLANY, a Collection of scarce and curious Pamphlets and Tracts, in Manuscript and Print, found in the late Earl of Oxford's library, with historical Notes by Malham, 12 vols. 8vo. *green morocco extra, gilt edges*, £5. 10s   1808-11

Priced, 1831, Longman, £6. 6s; 1836, Bryant, £6. 6s; 1843, £5. 15s 6d; 1847, £5. 10s.
"I hardly know any one collection or set of volumes likely to be productive of more varied entertainment. From my own experience I can assert that the pleasing and instructive variety contained in it, has cheered the languor of sickness and enlivened the gloom of solitude."—*Dibdin*.
"This valuable political, historical, and antiquarian work, an indispensable auxiliary in the illustration of the Literature, Manners, &c. of the British, contains between 600 and 700 rare and curious tracts."—*Lowndes*.

438 HERTHA: Zeitschrift fur Erd- Völker und Staatenkunde, besorgt von H. Berghaus und K. F. V. Hoffmann, Vols. 1 to 13, 8vo. *portraits, maps and plates, half calf,* 30s   *Stuttgart,* 1825-9

A valuable periodical for recent geographical information, containing articles by A. v. Humboldt, H. Berghaus, Klaproth, Martens, K. v. Raumer, Martius, etc. Priced, 1850, Vols. 1-13, t.3. 3s.

439 HISTOIRE LITTERAIRE DE LA FRANCE, par les Bénédictins de St. Maur, Continuation par des membres de l'Académie des Inscriptions (Pastoret, Brial, Ginguené, Daunou, etc.), Vols. I.-XII. *old calf gilt;* Vols. XIII.-XXIII. *half calf gilt;* together 23 vols. 4to. *a fine set,* £21.   *Paris,* 1733-1856

Tom. 1. Les Gaules avant Jesus Christ, I. au IVe Siècles
2. Ve siècle
2. VIe et VIIe Siècles.
4, 5. VIIIe et IXe Siècles
6. Xe Siècle
7, 8, XIe Siècle
9-15. XIIe Siècle
16-23. XIIIe Siècle

Priced, 1847, Vols. I.—XIX, £25.

440 —— la même, Tome XV. stout 4to. *full of interesting matter, sd.* 6s   1820
"Dom. Rivet de la Grange was the principal author of the Literary History of France, of which he edited the first nine volumes. This is a most valuable and learned work, to which we have not as yet any sufficiently good parallel in England. All the authors of France, with their works, are there classed and passed in review; and this too with a display of learning and candour infinitely creditable to the writers. Many brethren of the Benedictine order contributed to the work."—*H. L. Jones*.

441 HOFMANNI (J.) LEXICON Universale, Historiam sacram et profanam, Chronologiam, etc. omnis aevi omniumque gentium explanans, 4 vols. folio, *best edition, vellum,* £2. 2s   *Lugd. Bat.* 1698.

Priced, 1840 and 1848, Payne and Foss, vellum, £3. 5s. "I heard a man of great learning declare, that whenever he could not recollect his knowledge, he opened Hoffman's Lexicon, where he was sure to find what he had lost."—*D'Israeli*. Dr. Parr used to recommend it strongly, as the "*Encyclopædia of the Ancient World*," and Chalmers says—"It is a most useful book of reference, which should find a place in every learned library."

441*INDIA REVIEW of works on SCIENCE, and Journal of Foreign Science and the Arts, embracing Mineralogy, Geology, Natural History, Physics, etc. 1837 to 1838, 3 vols. 8vo. *no title pages, numerous lithographic views, scientific plates and maps, and authentic portraits, no where else to be found, will be sold not subject to collation, boards, edges cut,* EXCESSIVELY RARE, *the only copy I have ever seen,* £4. 10s   *Calcutta,* 1837-38

An exceedingly valuable periodical, containing learned critiques on the Scientific and Geographical publications of that time, with many original contributions, amongst which may be mentioned Mr. Clelland's Report on the Physical Condition of the Assam Tea Plant; Roxburgh's Flora Indica; Papers on the Sugar Cane; Cayley on Ballooning; Sykes on the Geology of the Dekhan; and many other interesting articles.

442 INDO-CHINESE GLEANER, Nos. 14—18, being from October 1820 to October 1821 inclusive, in 1 vol. large 8vo. *extremely rare and curious, uncut,* 10s   *Malacca,* 1820-21

INSTITUTO DI CORRESPONDENZA ARCHEOLOGICA DI ROMA:
8vo. Series.

443 ANNALI DELL' INSTITUTO, from the beginning in 1829 to 1861, Vols. I—XXXIII. (wanting vols. 19, 22, 23, 26-28) in 41 vols. or parts, *several hundred plates, unbound*   *Roma e Parigi,* 1829-61

BULLETTINO DEGLI ANNALI, from the beginning in 1829 to 1861, Vols. I—XXXIII. (wanting 1847, 50, 51, 54, 55) in 30 vols. or parts, *plates*   *Roma,* 1829-61

REPERTORIO UNIVERSALE, Vol. I. 1834-43, *containing the Indexes continued from the Annali, sd.*   *Roma,* 1848

Imperial Folio Series:

MONUMENTI INEDITI, pubblicati sotto la direzione di GERHARD e PANOFKA, Vol. I. *containing Plates* 1—60, *Paris*, 1829-33—Vol. II. *containing Plates* 1—60,

Roma e Parigi, 1834-38—Vol. III. *containing Plates* 1—60 (wants Title and Plates 37—48) *Roma e Parigi*, 1839-43—Vol. IV. *containing Plates* 1—60 (*with* 24 *bis*) *Roma e Parigi*, 1844-48—Vol. V. *containing Plates* 1—60 (wanting 13—24), *Roma*, 1849-53—Vol. VI. (wanting Title) *containing Plates* 1—60 (*with* 27 *bis*), *Roma*, 1857-61; together 6 vols. *with* 338 *fine plates, unbound* 1829-61

Folio Series.

MONUMENTI, ANNALI E BULLETTINI, Vol. I. *containing Plates* 1—40 (1 *and* 2 *are photographs frequently wanting*), *with Text, Roma*, 1854—Vol. II. *containing Plates* 1—25, *with Text, Gotha*, 1855—Vol. III. *containing Plates* 1—30, *with Text, Lipsia*, 1856; together 4 vols. in 3, 95 *plates, unbound* 1854-56
In all 56 vols. in 72 parts, 8vo., 6 vols. impl. folio, and 3 vols. in 4, folio, *containing upwards of* 800 *Plates, the Earl of Aberdeen's copy*, £25. 1829-61

IRISH ARCHAEOLOGICAL (and CELTIC) SOCIETY:

444 PUBLICATIONS of the above, printed at the University Press, Dublin, a complete set, 20 vols. sm. 4to. (cost to subscribers, £22.) *cloth*, £12. *Dublin*, 1841-62

The following is a list of the Publications, and the prices at which they are sold separately:—

1. Tracts relating to Ireland, Vol. I. *Irish and English*, 15s — 1841
2. Grace, Kilkenniensis, Annales Hiberniae, ed. Butler, 8s — 1842
3. Cath Muighi Rath, edited by O'Donovan, *Irish and English*, 10s — 1842
4. Tracts relating to Ireland, Vol. II. 10s — 1842
5. Tribes of Hy-Many, *map, Irish and English*, by O'Donovan, 12s — 1843
6. Book of Obits of Christ Church, Dublin, by Crosthwaite and Todd, 12s — 1843
7. Registrum Ecclesiæ omnium sanctorum juxta Dublin, ed. Butler, 7s — 1844
8. Tribes and Customs of Hy-Fiachrach, *Irish and English*, by O'Donovan, 15s — 1844
9. O'Flaherty's H-Iar Connacht, A.D. 1684, by Hardiman, 15s — 1845
10. Miscellany of the Society, Vol. I. *Irish and English*, 8s — 1846
11. Irish Version of Nennius, *Irish and English*, by Todd, 15s — 1847
12. Annals of Ireland by Clyn and Dowling, edited by Ross, 8s — 1847
13. Macariae Excidium, by O'Kelly, *Irish and English*, 20s — 1850
14. Colton's (Archbishop) Visitation of Derry, 10s — 1851
15. Petty's History of the Down Survey, by Larcom, 15s — 1852
16. Hymns of the Ancient Church, Fasc. I. *Irish and English*, by Todd, 15s — 1855
17. Adamnan's Life of Columba, by Reeves, *a thick volume*, £2. — 1857
18. Annals of Ireland, fragments from ancient sources, *Irish and English*, by O'Donovan, 12s 6d — 1860
19. Irish Glosses: a Mediæval Tract, by Stokes, 12s 6d — 1860
20. Topographical Poems, *Irish and English*, by O'Donovan, 20s — 1862

IRISH ACADEMY:

445 TRANSACTIONS of the Royal Irish Academy, Vol. XXI. part 2, XXII. parts 2, 4, 6; 4 parts, 4to. *containing besides others, nine articles by Dr. Hincks on Assyrian and Egyptian inscriptions, plates of facsimiles, etc.* 35s *Dublin*, 1848-55

446 WILDE, Catalogue of the Antiquities in the Museum of the Royal Irish Academy, Vol. I. Stone, Earthen and Vegetable Materials, 8vo. *engravings, bds.* 5s *Dublin*, 1857

447 —— Vol. II. Animal Materials and Bronze, 8vo. *cuts*, 7s 1861

448 JOHN BULL (The) Weekly Newspaper, from the beginning in Dec. 17, 1820, to March 31, 1860, with the Titles and Indexes, 39 vols. folio, and 13 Nos. (pub. at £51. 11s unbound), *half calf, a fine clean set, from the library of the late Mr. J. C. Webber, of Woburn Place*, £12. 1820-60

An uninterrupted set of this famous Periodical from its commencement to the present. The early volumes contain the Wit and Humour both in Verse and Prose of THEODORE HOOK. The first two or three volumes containing his celebrated attacks on QUEEN CAROLINE are extremely scarce. They are also notorious for the slanders they contain and actions they occasioned.

449 JOURNAL DES SAVANTS, de 1836 jusqu'à 1856, 21 vols. royal 4to. (pub. at £37. 16s) *half bound calf neat*, £10. *Paris, Imprimerie Royale*, 1836-56

Containing contributions from Frenchmen, the most eminent in literature and science during the present century. "The *Journal des Savans* is one of the oldest publications of this class in Europe. After a lapse of 22 years, it has recommenced under the auspices of Government. M. Daunou, who is the principal Editor, has enriched it with some excellent articles on History. The names of Silvestre de Sacy, Abel Rémusat de Chéry, celebrated orientalists, are also on the list of contributors, as well as those of Cuvier, Raynouard, Gay-Lussac, etc."
Revue Ency. Vol. II. p. 400.

450 JOURNAL ASIATIQUE, ou Recueil de Memoires relatifs à l'Histoire, à la Philosophie, aux Sciences, à la Litterature et aux Langues des Peuples Orientaux, par Chézy, Klaproth, Abel-Remusat, St. Martin, Silvestre de Sacy, etc. FIRST SERIES, Vols. I—XI and Index, *complete*, 1822-1827; SECOND SERIES, Vols. I—XVI *complete*, 1828-1836; THIRD SERIES, Vols. I—XIV *complete in* 7, and 4to. atlas to Vol. IX, 1836-42; FOURTH SERIES, Vols. I—XX in 15, *complete*, 1843-52; FIFTH SERIES, Vols. I to XII and Nos. 49-57, *sd.* 1853-60— in all 54 vols. *half calf*, and 10 Numbers, 8vo. *many plates, Professor H. H. Wilson's copy*, £24 *Paris*, 1822-60

PUBLICATIONS OF LEARNED SOCIETIES, ETC. 35

451 JOURNAL ASIATIQUE, First Series, 11 vols. 1822-27; Second Series, 16 vols. 1828-36; Third Series, Vols. I—VIII. XI. XIV. 1836-42; Fourth Series, Vols. I.—XX. 1843—1852; Fifth Series, Nos. 1—59, 1853-60—together the Five Series, as described, 55 vols. 8vo. *half calf, the remainder in numbers, Professor Quatremere's copy,* £15   *Paris,* 1822-60

452 JOURNAL ASIATIQUE, a third set, incomplete, as follows: First Series, 11 vols. *complete;* Second Series, Nos. 1-42, 44, 45, 48, 54, 59, 93, 94; Third Series, Nos. 7, 8, 13, 14, Extrait 1839, 63, 73, 74; Fourth Series, Vols. I—IV, VII, XII, XVIII; Fifth Series, Vols. V—VIII.—together 18 vols. *half bound, the remainder in parts,* £6. 10s   *Paris,* 1822-56

453 JOURNAL OF THE INDIAN ARCHIPELAGO, and Eastern Asia, from the beginning in 1847 to December, 1852, Vols. I—VI. (wanting No. 3 of Vol. VI.) 8vo. *containing important matter on the races and languages of Eastern Asia, with Ethnological and Geographical plates, sd. rare,* £6. 10s   *Singapore,* 1847-51

454 JOURNAL OF SCIENCE AND THE ARTS, edited at the Royal Institution of Great Britain from 1816 to June 1830 inclusive, 29 vols. 8vo. *hf. rus. neat,* £2. 5s   Priced, 1834, £7. 17s 6d,; 1848, Longmans, vols. 1-27, £3. 3s.   1816-30

KILKENNY ARCHÆOLOGICAL SOCIETY:

455 TRANSACTIONS of the above—First Series, *complete,* 1849-55, 3 vols.—New Series, Vols. 1 to 3, 1856 to July, 1861—together 5 vols. *half morocco, uncut,* and 7 parts, sd. royal 8vo. *with a profusion of plates and woodcuts of Seals, Coins, Antiquities,* £4. 18s   *Dublin,* 1853-61

456 —— the same, Transactions and Proceedings, for 1852 to September 1855, in 11 parts, royal 8vo. *plates and cuts, sd.* 20s   *Dublin,* 1853-55

457 KITTO (Dr.) Journal of Sacred Literature, 2nd Series, 14 parts, 1851-55—Journal of Sacred Literature and Biblical Record, edited by Dr. Burgess, being the 3rd Series, 15 parts, 1855-58—together 29 parts, 8vo. (pub. at £7. 5s) *clean and uncut,* £2. 2s   1851-58

458 KLAPROTH's Asiatisches Magazin, 2 vols. 8vo. *all published, maps, and plates of Inscriptions, Coins, etc. bds.* 9s   *Weimar,* 1802

459 —— Magasin Asiatique, Nos. 1, 2, 3, 8vo. *map, sd.* 4s   *Paris,* 1825-26

LANCASHIRE AND CHESHIRE HISTORIC SOCIETY:

460 PROCEEDINGS, PAPERS, and TRANSACTIONS, Vol. I—XII. 8vo. *numerous plates of Antiquities* (pub. at £6. 6s) £4. 4s   *Liverpool,* 1849-60

461 —— the same, Vols. I—X. 8vo. *half green morocco, gilt tops, a very nice set,* £4. 15s   1849-58

462 LANGEBEK (J.) Suhm, Engelstoft et Werlauff, SCRIPTORES RERUM DANICARUM medii Ævi, partim hactenus inediti partim emendatius editi, 8 vols. folio, *plates and facsimiles, half calf,* £8.   *Hafniæ,* 1772-1834

A work of considerable importance both for English and Danish History.
Priced, 1837, Black, £10. 10s; 1847, H. Bohn, £8. 18s 6d and £13. 13s: all the volumes are out of print.
"All preceding collections of *Northern Antiquities* were exceeded equally in splendour, utility, and extent, by the meritorious labours of LANGEBEK, whose collection has now become a work of uncommon occurrence. The editor was doubtless the *Bouquet* of Denmark. It is said that the present venerable and learned Dr. Thorkelin, principal librarian of the Royal Library at Copenhagen, seldom pronounces the name of Langebek, without passing his hand across his eyes, or placing it on his heart. This is as it should be."—*Dibdin's Lib. Comp.*

463 LEIBNITII Opera Omnia nunc primum collecta, in classes distributa, præfationibus et indicibus exornata, studio L. Dutens, 6 vols. 4to. *plates, best edition, half calf neat,* £3. 10s   *Genevæ,* 1768
Collection très recherchée.—*Brunet.*

464 —— Scriptores, rerum Brunsvicensium illustrationi inservientes, omnes reformatione priores, chronica Ostfaliæ, res Longobardiæ et Guelforum, etc. 3 vols. folio, *russia,* 36s   *Hanov.* 1707-11

Priced, 1840, Payne and Foss, £5. 5s. This collection contains more than 150 writers, with a general Index. Some official decrees of George II. as Archduke of Brunswick, are bound up at the end of the third volume.

LEIPZIG TRANSACTIONS:

465 ACTA ERUDITORUM ab anno 1682 ad annum 1731, 50 vols. in 38, 1682-1731—Nova Acta ab anno 1732 ad annum 1776, 45 vols. in 22, 1732-82—Supplementa ad Acta, 10 vols. 1692-1734—Ad Nova Acta Supplementa, 8 vols. in 4, 1735-57—Indices ab anno 1682 ad annum 1741, 6 vols. 1693-1745, *numerous plates of science, art, antiquities, etc.*—together 119 vols. in 80, small stout 4to. *fine uniform set in vellum,* £10.   *Lipsiæ,* 1682-1745

Priced, 1847, H. Bohn, £25. Sold at Sotheby's in Feb. 1819, for £12. 12s.
A very interesting and valuable collection, containing an infinity of dissertations, essays, etc. on all subjects,

36   B. QUARITCH, 15 PICCADILLY, LONDON.

and by the most learned scholars. "De Bure says that the Acta Eruditorum is regarded as the best journal up to the time of its conclusion, and still preserves its credit in the literary world." He adds, "that it is to be wished that it had always served as a model for the periodical works which followed it."

466 MISCELLANEA LIPSIENSIA ad Incrementum Rei Litterariæ, 12 vols. in 3, *plates, Lipsiæ,* 1716-23 —Miscellanea Lipsiensia Nova, 9 vols. *ib.* 1742-52—together 21 vols. in 12, 12mo. *vellum*, 20s *Lips.* 1716-52
With autograph signature and notes of L. Kulenkamp.

LEYDEN ACADEMY:
467 ANNALES Academiae Lugduno-Batavae, 1815-37, 22 vols. 4to. *plates, bds.* 20s
Lugduni Batavorum, 1817-28

LIEGE ROYAL SOCIETY:
468 MÉMOIRES de la Societé Royale des Sciences de Liège, 8 vols. in 11, large 8vo. *plates and* 4*to. atlas, sd.* £3. *Liege,* 1843 55

LINCOLNSHIRE TOPOGRAPHICAL SOCIETY:
469 SELECTION of Papers relative to the county of Lincoln, read 1841-42, small 4to. *plates, interesting details on English domestic life in the Middle ages, cloth,* 12s
Lincoln, 1843

LINNÆAN SOCIETY:
470 TRANSACTIONS of the Linnean Society from the commencement in 1791 to 1833, Vols. 1 to 16, 4to. *many plates, half russia, neat,* £5.   1791-1833
The completion of the set supplied at about half price.
Many separate volumes and parts now in stock, are offered at a reduced rate for the completion of sets.
471 PROCEEDINGS, parts 1—10 (1856-58); Supplements to Vols. IV. and V. Zoology and Botany (1860); and Nos. 18, 19—together 14 parts, 8vo. (pub. at £2. 12s) *sd.* 36s   1856-61

LISBON ACADEMY:
472 MEMORIAS, HISTORIA e MEMORIAS, MEMORIAS dos Socios e dos Correspondentes da ACADEMIA REAL das SCIENCIAS de LISBOA, desde 1780 até 1837, Vols. I—XI, sm. folio, *plates and tables, hf. calf, uncut,* £5. 10s   *Lisboa,* 1797-1837
Priced, 1845, Bossange, 180 fr.; 1847, 11 vols. sd. £7. 17s 6d.
473 ——— Memorias de Litteratura Portugueza, 8 vols. in 4, stout smallest 4to. *half calf,* £2.   1792-1812
Priced, 1841, Vols. I—VI, £2. 2s; 1845, £3. 5s; 1848, Barrois, 90 fr.

Tom. I. Sobre os Povos (primeiros habitantes de Portugal); Juizes de Fora; Chronica do Algarve; Decadas ineditas de Couto; Moedas do Reino e conquistas, etc. etc.
II. Sobre a escrita dos Diplomas e papeis publicos; Litteratura Sagrada dos Judeos Portuguezes; Historia da Legislaçao de Portugal; etc. etc.
III. Apontamentos para a Historia Civil e Litteraria de Portugal; Antiguidades das Caldas de Vizela; Espirito da Lingua Portugueza; Litteratura sagrada dos Judeos Portuguezes; Jurisprudencia dos Morgados.
IV. Sobre a Lingua Portugueza; Elocuçao e estylo de Camoes e outros; Litteratura sagrada dos Judeos; Ensaio sobre as Palavras de que se servirao os Escritores dos Seculos XV. e XVI.
V. Filologia Portugueza; Ruinas do Mosteiro de Castro
de Avelaas, Monumento e Inscripçao Lapidar; Marinhas de Portugal, Codices Manuscritos do Mosteiro de Alcobaça; Quattro Inscripçoes Arabicas; Antiguidades do Mosteiro do Salvador de Vayrao; etc.
VI. Legislaçao Portugueza; Juizos dos primeiros seculos da Monarquia; Leis Antigas; Estado civil da Lusitania desde os Povos do Norte até os Arabes.
VII. Defeza de Camoes; Algunas Ediçoes Biblicas em lingua Portugueza, as Obras de Ferreira de Almeida; Historia da Legislaçao de Portugal; Chronologia dos Reis Mouras das Espanhas; Vidas e escritos de Mello e Nunes; Corregedores das Comarcas; Bibliotheca Lusitana Anti-Rabbinica; etc.
VIII. Origens da Typografia em Portugal no Seculo XV.; Typografia Portugueza do Sec. XVI.; Mathematicos Portuguezes.

474 LONDON AND EDINBURGH PHILOSOPHICAL MAGAZINE and JOURNAL of SCIENCE, conducted by SIR DAVID BREWSTER, R. Taylor, and R. Phillips, from the beginning of this new and united series in July 1832 to June 1850, Vols. I—XXXVI. 8vo. *numerous plates, neatly hf. bd. in calf,* £5.   1832-50
475 LONDON GAZETTE. GAZETTE EXTRAORDINARY, a remarkable and complete collection from 1797 to 1830, bound in 1 vol. folio, *hf. calf,* 30s   1797-1830
476 ——— Gazette, a not entirely complete set from 1842 to 1860, in Nos. to be sold separately for the completion of sets.
477 MADRAS JOURNAL of Literature and Science, edited by Morris, Cole and Brown, from the beginning in 1833, Vols. I.—XII. or Parts 1—29 inclusive, 12 vols. 8vo. QUITE COMPLETE, *with numerous plates of Hindoo Mythology, Antiquities, Geography, Natural History, some of the latter finely coloured, hf. russia neat,* £10.; *or a fine tall copy,* 12 vols. in 11, 8vo. *almost uncut, hf. russia,* £10. 10s   *Madras,* 1834-40

A valuable periodical, with many essays by learned Orientalists upon the Languages and History of the East, especially of the Indian Peninsula; and including an important contribution to comparative Philology, by the Rev. B. Schmid, entitled "An Essay on the Relationship of Languages and Nations."

478 MADRAS QUARTERLY JOURNAL of MEDICAL Science in all its branches, from the beginning in July 1860 to July 1862, Nos. I—IX. (wanting VI.) 8vo. *plates, sd.* 32s   1860-62

PUBLICATIONS OF LEARNED SOCIETIES, ETC.

MADRID ACADEMY:
479 MEMORIAS de la Real Academia de la Historia, 4 vols. 4to. *plates, Spanish calf neat*, 36s *Madrid*, 1796-1805
Containing, amongst other interesting information, Luzan y Ulloa sobre el origen y patria primitiva de los Godos; Ulloa sobre la Monarquia Goda; Hermosilla y Cornide, ruinas de Talavera la vieja; Ulloa, Cronologia para la historia de Espana; Cornide, Antigüedades de Cabeza; Marina, Antigüedades Hispano-hebreas; Traggia, reinado de D. Ramiro II.; Arnao, Ximenes, Falero, Impugnacion de Munda y Certima Celtibericas.

MAITLAND CLUB:
480 HAMILTON's Descriptions of the Sheriffdoms of Lanark and Renfrew (1710), with notes and appendices, 4to. *several plates of Antiquities, hf. morocco, gilt top,* 25s *Glasgow*, 1831
481 MALTE-BRUN, Annales des Voyages, de la Geographie, et de l'Histoire, avec des mémoires historiques sur l'origine, la Langue, les mœurs, etc. des peuples, et une table générale, 25 vols. 1809-14—EYRIÈS et MALTE-BRUN, Nouvelles Annales des Voyages, Vols. I—XXX. 1819-26; together 55 vols. 8vo. *several hundred maps and plates, the first thirty-seven vols. neatly hf. bd. calf, the next in green cloth,* £4. 16s *Paris*, 1809-26
482 —— EYRIÈS et MALTE-BRUN, Nouvelles Annales des Voyages, Vols. I—XII. in 14 vols. 8vo. *numerous maps and plates, cloth,* 18s 1819-21
483 MARTIN'S (Benjamin) Miscellaneous Correspondence, containing a variety of Subjects, Natural and Civil History, Geography, Mathematics, Poetry, Monthly occurrences, Catalogues of new books, etc. 1755-63, 4 vols. 8vo. *many plates of Natural History, the Mathematical and Physical Sciences, woodcuts, music, etc. hf. bd.* 36s 1759-64
A curious monthly magazine, with all the political home and foreign news of the time.

MASSACHUSETT'S HISTORICAL SOCIETY:
484 COLLECTIONS of the MASSACHUSETTS HISTORICAL SOCIETY, 1792-1823, FIRST AND SECOND SERIES, *complete*, 20 vols. in 10, 8vo. *all of the original issue, calf neat, from Southey's Library, with his autograph,* £5. 15s *Boston, N. E.* 1806-23
485 —— the same, THIRD SERIES, Vols. 8, 9, 10; FOURTH SERIES, Vols. 1, 2, 3— together 6 vols. large 8vo. *bds.* £2. *Boston*, 1843-56
486 MATTHÆI PARIS (*Monachi Albanensis, Angli*, 1259) Opera: Historia Major, cum Rogeri Wendoveri, Rishangeri, authorisque Chronicisque MSS. collata, cui accesserunt Vitæ Offarum et XXIII Abbatum S. Albani, &c., cum Variis Lectionibus, Glossario et Indicibus, editore W. Wats; folio, *full length portrait by T. Cecill, calf neat,* 20s; or *fine clean copy in vellum,* 25s 1640-39
Priced, 1837-48, Payne and Foss, mor. £3. 3s; 1840, Jas. Bohn, mor. £3. 15s. Fetched, Heath's copy, £1. 11s; Fesch, £1. 11s 6d. LARGE PAPER, fetched, Dent's, old mor. £13. 13s; Sykes, £7. 10s; Duke of Grafton's, £6
"*I think I have never read a more honest historian.*"—*Sharon Turner.*
487 MATTHÆI WESTMONASTERIENSIS Flores Historiarum, præcipue de Rebus Britannicis, ab exordio mundi ad annum 1307; accedit Florentii Wigornensis Chronicon ab Initio Mundi ad Annum 1118; cum Continuatione; folio, BEST EDITION, *fine copy in vellum,* 30s *Francofurti*, 1601
Priced by Thorpe £3. 15s; Payne and Foss, £4. 4s; Heath's copy sold for £3. 4s.
488 MAUND'S Botanic Garden, or Magazine of Hardy Flower Plants cultivated in Great Britain, parts 49-216, small 4to. 169 *coloured plates, with text,* (pub. at £12. 12s) *sd.* 25s *Jan.* 1829—*Dec.* 1842
489 MECHANICS' MAGAZINE, from the beginning, in August 30, 1823, to July 3, 1852, 57 vols. 8vo. *numerous engravings, neatly half bound calf, uniform,* £9. 1823-52
Such a fine clean set of this valuable Magazine is of uncommon occurrence. It comprises notices of all the Scientific improvements and discoveries of the present age, with biographical and literary notices, etc. An indispensable book for a country library or literary institute.
490 —— NEW SERIES, from the beginning in January 1859 to September 1861, Parts 1—33 (Vols. I. to VI. part 3), 4to. *numerous illustrations,* (pub. at 43s 6d) *sd.* 32s 1859-61
491 MELANGES tirés d'une Grand Bibliothèque, par Messieurs Paulmy et Coulant D'Orville, 64 vols. 8vo. *half bound,* £2. 16s *Paris*, 1799-1787
Les premiers volumes de ces Melanges renferment les extraits d'un grand nombre d'ouvrages Français antérieurs au 17e siècle; et sous ce rapport ils ne sont pas sans intérêt pour les personnes qui veulent connaître notre ancienne littérature; malheureusement les derniers volumes de l'ouvrage n'ont pas a beaucoup près la même mérite que le commencement; et c'est ce qui fait que cette volumineuse collection est peu recherchée.—*Brunet.*

MEMOIRES SUR L'HISTOIRE DE LA FRANCE:
492 PETITOT, Collection Complete des Memoires sur la France, PREMIÈRE SÉRIE, depuis le règne de Philippe Auguste jusqu'au commencement du XVIIe Siècle Avec des notices sur chaque ouvrage, 52 vols. *Paris*, 1819-26—PETITOT

et MONMERQUE, Collection complete des Memoires sur l'Histoire de France, SECONDE SÉRIE, depuis l'avènement de Henri IV. jusqu'à la Paix de Paris en 1763, avec des notices sur chaque ouvrage, 79 vols. *Paris*, 1820-29—together 131 vols. 8vo. (pub. at £40. unbound), *hf. bd. calf, clean set*, £27. *Paris*, 1819-29

493 PETITOT. Or separately, SECONDE SÉRIE, Vols. I—LXXVIII, (including XXI *bis* and Table Générale) wanting LV—LX, 73 vols. 8vo. *sd.* £9. 1820-29

The usual price of complete sets in 79 vols. is £20.

This valuable series of Memoirs has now become scarce,

Contents of the First Series:—

Tom.	Tom.	Tom.
1. Villehardouin	16. Chevalier de Fleurange	35. Henri, Duc de Bouillon
2. Joinville	Louis de Savoye	Guill. S. de Tavannes
3. Auteurs Arabes sur St. Louis	17, 18, 19. Martin de Bellay	36. Comte de Cheverny
4, 5. Bertrand du Guesclin	20, 21, 22. Blaise du Montluc	Hurault Ev. de Chartres
6, 7. Christine de Pisan	23, 24, 25. Gaspar, S. de Tavannes	37. Marguerite de Valois
Jean de Bourcicaut	26, 27, 28. Sire de Vieilleville	J. A. de Thou
Pierre de Fenin	28, 29, 30. Baron Duvillars	38. Jean de Choisnin
Mémoires sur Jean d'Arc	31, 32. François de Rabutin	Mat. Merle
Comte de Richemonte	32. Bern. de Salignac	38—43. P. Cayet, Chron. Novennaire
Florent d'Illiers	Gaspar de Coligny	43. Seigneur de St. Auban
9, 10. Ollivier de la Marche	Claude de la Chastre	44. Villeroy
11. Jacques du Clerc	Guil. de Rochechouart	Duc d'Angoulême
11, 12, 13. Philippe de Comines	33. Mich. de Castelnau	45—49. P. de l'Estolle
13, 14. Jean de Troyes	34. Joan de Mergy	49. J. Gillot
14. Guillaume de Villeneuve	Fr. de la None	C. Groutard
Bouchet, Mem de la Tremoille	Achille Gamon	M. Marillac
15, 16. Chevalier Bayard	Jean Philippe	50, 51. Fontenay Mareuil
		52. Table Générale

Contents of the Second Series:—

Tom.	Tom.	Tom.
1—9 Duc de Sully (Economies Royales)	40—43. Mademoiselle de Montpensier	58, 59. M. de * * *
10, 11. Cardinal Richelieu	44—46. Cardinal de Retz	59. Pierre de la Porte
11—15. President Jeanin	47. Guy Joly	60—63. Omer Talon
16. Maréchal d'Estrées	Claude Joly	63. Abbé de Choisy
16, 17. Pontchartrain	48. Conrart	64. Chevalier Temple
	Père Berthod	64, 65. Mme. de la Fayette
18, 19. Duc de Rohan	49, 50. Marquis de Montglat	65, 66. Mar. Duc de Berwick
19, 21. Bassompierre	51. De la Chartre	66. Madame de Caylus
21*—30. Cardinal Richelieu	50, 51. Rochefoucauld	67, 68. Marquis de Torcy
31. Gaston. Duc d'Orleans	52. Gourville	68—74. Maréchal de Villars
31, 32 Sieur de Pontis	53, 54. Pierre Lenet	71—74. Duc de Noailles
33, 44. Arnauld d'Andilly	53, 54. Comte de Montresor	74, 75. Comte Forbin
34. Abbé Arnauld	Fontrailles	75. Duguay-Trouin
Duchesse de Nemours	55, 56. Duc de Guise	76, 77. Duclos
35, 36. Compte de Brienne	56, 57. Marechal de Gramont	77. Madame de Stael
36—40. Madame de Motteville	58. Maréchal de Plessis	78. Table Générale

494 COLLECTION (NOUVELLE) DES MEMOIRES, pour servir à l'HISTOIRE DE FRANCE, depuis le XIIIme siècle jusqu'à la fin du XVIIme, précédés de Notices pour caractériser chaque auteur des Mémoires et son époque ; suivis de l'analyse des Documents historiques qui s'y rapportent, par MM. MICHAUD et POUJOULAT. Collection terminée, 33 vols. royal 8vo. *double columns, neatly half bound, calf gilt, contents lettered*, £17. 10s *Paris*, 1850

Contents:

Villehardouin	F. de Rabutin	Dubois	Claude Joly
Henri de Valenciennes	Saulx-Tavannes	P. V. Cayet	Turenne
Joinville	B. de Salignac	Pierre de l'Estoile	Le Duc d'York
Du Guesclin	G. de Coligny	Sully	Montpensier
Christ. de Pisan	La Chastre	Marbault	Rochefoucauld
J. J. Ursius	Rochechouart	Jeannin	Choisy
Pucelle d'Orleans	Castelnau	Fontenay-Mareuil	Duc de Guise
Richemont	J. de Mergey	Duc de Rohan	Grammont
Florent d'Illiers	F. de la Noue	Bassompierre	Du Plessis
O. de La Marche	Boyvin de Villars	D'Estrées	Mad. de La Fayette
P. de Comines	Marguerite de Valois	Pontis	Berwick
Jean de Troyes	Duc de Bouillon	Richelieu	Mad de Caylus
G. de Villeneuve	Duc d'Angoulême	Arnauld d'Andilly	Villars
De la Tremoille	Villeroy	L'Abbé Arnauld	Forbin
Bayard	De Thou	Gaston, Duc d'Orleans	Duguay-Trouin
Louis de Savoye	J. Gillot	Nemours	Noailles
Du Bellay	M Merle	Motteville	Duclos
Duc de Guise	Saint Auban	Cardinal de Retz	Madame de Stael, and many others
Condé	Louise Bourgeois	Guy Joly	
B. de Montluc			

ACADEMIE CELTIQUE ET SOCIETE DES ANTIQUAIRES:

495 MÉMOIRES DE L'ACADEMIE CELTIQUE, ou recherches sur les Antiquités Celtiques, Gauloises et Françoises (par MM. Lavallée, Cambry, Eloi Johanneau, Dulaure, Mangourit, Alex. Menoir, Pougens, Legonidec, Lerouge, Baudouin de Maisonblanche, etc. etc.) 5 vols. *plates*, 8vo. *calf gilt* Paris, 1807-10

L'Académie Celtique a été réorganisée sous le nom de *Soc été des Antiquaires de France*.

PUBLICATIONS OF LEARNED SOCIETIES, ETC. 39

496 MÉMOIRES et dissertations sur les ANTIQUITÉS NATIONALES et etrangères, publiés par la SOCIÉTÉ ROYALE DES ANTIQUAIRES DE FRANCE, 10 vols. 1817-34 — Nouvelle série, 10 vols. 1836-50—Troisième série, Vol. I. 1852—together 21 vols. 8vo. *plates, cf. ext.* with impl. 4to. Atlas of 17 plates, *hf. cf. gt.*   *Paris*, 1817-52
—— the above 2 lots in 27 vols. sold together for £8. 10s   1807-52

497 MERCURIO PERUANO de Historia, Literatura, y Noticias publicas que da a luz la Sociedad Academica de Amantes de Lima, 12 vols. sm. 4to. *vellum*, £12.
    Lima, 1791-95
   The above interesting collection of Periodical Writings is of the greatest rarity. Thorpe, in one of his Catalogues, states that a gentleman had assured him he could meet with but one copy in his travels through Spain, for which he was asked upwards of £30.
   It is generally found defective, and copies vary to a considerable degree. The above copy is no exception to this rule, although it is more nearly perfect than most others; it wants Nos. 303, 4, in Vol. IX. which are very frequently absent. Some Nos. have been omitted, while the pagination remains correct; and sometimes there are two with the same No., although the text runs on correctly. The last part of Vol. XI is number 382, yet the first of Vol. XII. receives the number 583, from which the numeration proceeds to the end (No. 611), although nothing is deficient. The periodical seems to have been produced under great difficulties and discouragements; it is said to have been suppressed by the Spanish government, which is not unlikely, as the enlightened opinions which the French Revolution had first set afloat were winning popularity amongst the educated youth of Spanish Peru. There is a sort of indignant bitterness in the title of the last volume which is stated to be "dado a luz por uno de los individuos de la Sociedad"

498 MEURSII (Jo.) OPERA OMNIA, ex recensione Johannis Lamii; 12 vols. roy. folio, *plates of Greek and Roman Antiquities, hf. vell. uncut*, £5. 5s   *Florent.* 1741-61
   Priced, 1824, Weigel, 80 thalers, afterwards 65 thalers; Thorpe, £25.; 1836, Thorpe, £16. 16s; 1837 and 1840 Payne and Foss, vellum, £12 12s; Thorpe, vellum, £12. 12s; 1840, Jas. Bohn, £12. 12s; 1841, £15. 15s; 1844, F. Macpherson, hf. bd. £8. 8s; 1854. I sold a copy for £7.; Sir Mark Sykes' copy fetched, £17. 5s; Parr's £14. 10s; Pinelli's £10. For a detailed List of Contents see No 5595 of the Catalogue of the London Library.
   Meursius' works form a desirable Supplement to the Collection of Antiquities published by Grævius and Gronovius.

499 MICROSCOPIC JOURNAL, and Structural Record, for 1841 and 1842, 2 vols. —Physiological Journal, Vol. I. in 1 vol. *half calf*— Quarterly Journal of Microscopical Science, including Transactions of the Microscopical Society of London, edited by Lankester and Busk, Nos. 1-12, and New Series, No. I. 1853 to January 1861, 8vo. *several hundred plates and woodcuts*, £7. 10s   1853-1861
   Complete sets are scarce. Nos. 2, 17, 22 and 26 of the Quarterly Journal, are out of print.

500 MONITEUR (le) GAZETTE NATIONALE ou le MONITEUR universel, No. 1, January 1, 1790, to June 30, 1790, with the SUPPLEMENTS, forming 1 vol. folio, *hf. bd. from Lord Auckland's library*, EXTREMELY RARE, £3. 3s   *Paris*, 1790
   Evidently missing to a set. Lord Auckland lent this volume probably to some friend who never returned it.

MOSCOW ACADEMY:

501 MÉMOIRES de la Société Impériale des Naturalistes de Moscou, Tom. I, II, IV, V, VII-X, XVII, XVIII, XIX, pt. 1, 4to. 158 *plates of Natural History, etc. mostly coloured*, 1811-60; Commentationes Societatis Physico-Medicæ apud Universitatem Caes. Mosquensem, Vol. 2, pars 1, 1817 : together 12 vols. 4to. *bds. very scarce*, £8. 8s   *Moscou*, 1811-60

502 BULLETIN de la Société Impériale des Naturalistes de Moscou redigé par Renard, depuis 1830 jusqu'a 1860, No. 1 ; some numbers wanting : in all 99 parts, large 8vo. *several hundred plates, some coloured, sd.* £20.   *Moscou*, 1837-57
   Collation - 1830, Nos. 1, 2; 1832, Nos. 1, 2, 3; 1833, Vol. VI.; 1834, Vol. VII.; 1835, Vol. VIII.; 1837, Nos. 1-8; 1838; Nos. 1-4: 1839 wanting; 1840 complete; 1841, Nos. 1-4; 1842, Nos. 1-4; 1843-45, complete; 1846, Nos. 3, 4; 1847, 1848, 1849 complete; 1850, Nos. 2, 3, 4; 1851-59 complete; 1860, No. 1. Missing parts supplied new for 8s each. Odd numbers in stock offered for 4s each.

MUNICH ACADEMY:

503 NEUE PHILOSOPHISCHE ABHANDLUNGEN der Baierischen Akademie der Wissenschaften, Band 1—7, (1778-97, *consecutive*): Denkschriften der K. Akademie der Wissenschaften zu München, Band 1—9 (für 1808-24) *consecutive*; Abhandlungen der Mathematisch-Physikalischen Klasse der K. Bayerischen Akademie der Wissenschaften, Band 1—5, part 2 (1829-48), *wanting Band 4 pt. 3, and Band 5 pt.* 1; Abhandlungen der historischen Classe, Band 3, *pt.* 2, 1842 ; 4to. *numerous folding plates, many of them coloured*, nineteen vols. *cloth bds.* and four parts *sd.* £5.   *München und Sulzbach*, 1778-1848
   The early volumes of this important series are very rare.

504 MURATORII (L. A.) RERUM ITALICARUM SCRIPTORES ab anno 500 ad annum 1500, quorum potissima pars nunc primùm in lucem prodit, cum præfationibus, notis, Indice, etc. Vols. I.—XXIV. in 27 vols. folio, *frontispieces, vignettes, maps, facsimiles of Mediæval Charters, etc. stamped vellum, gilt backs, a fine set*, £25.   *Mediolani*, 1723-38

505 MURATORI, delle Antichità Estensi ed Italiane, 2 vols. folio, *full length portrait of George I. to whom the book is dedicated, fine copy in vellum*, VERY RARE, £3. 10s *Modena, stamperia ducale*, 1717-40
   This copy belonged to the Bibliotheca del Consiglio di Stato "Regno d'Italia."
506 MURATORII (L. A.) Novus Thesaurus veterum Inscriptionum in præcipuis earumdem collectionibus hactenus prætermissarum, 4 vols. folio, *plates, sd.* 32s ; or, *a fine copy in vellum*, £2. *Mediolani*, 1739
   "In all his works Muratori proves himself a diligent and laborious writer, who aspires above the prejudices of a Catholic Priest. He was born in the year 1672, and died in the year 1750, after passing near sixty years in the libraries of Milan and Modena."—*Gibbon.*
507 NEW ENGLAND MAGAZINE, by J. T. and E. Buckingham, from the commencement in July 1831 to June 1835, 8 vols. 8vo. *ports. hf. cf. gt.* 36s *Boston*, 1831-35
   An interesting periodical containing valuable Biographies, Historical, Philological and Literary Notices, Original Communications, etc.
508 NEW ENGLAND HISTORICAL and GENEALOGICAL REGISTER, published under the direction of the New England Historic-Genealogical Society, FIRST SERIES, COMPLETE, 10 vols. 8vo. *numerous fine portraits, plates, facsimiles, etc. half calf*, RARE, £8. 10s *Boston*, 1847-56
509 —— The same, Vols. I.—IX. 8vo. *new in cloth*, £6. *Boston*, 1847-55
   Including papers on the early Records of the State, facsimile signatures of the first settlers; tracing the families of New England to their European progenitors: a very interesting periodical.
510 NICERON, MEMOIRES pour servir à l'histoire des HOMMES ILLUSTRES dans la Republique des Lettres, avec un Catalogue Raisonné de leurs Ouvrages et quelques Notices par le P. Oudin, J. B. Michault, et l'Abbé Goujet, 43 vols. in 44, 12mo. *veau fauve, fine copy, from Drury's and Dr. Hawtrey's libraries*, £8. 8s *Paris*, 1729-45
   The above copy has Vol. X. pt. 2, which is often wanting.
511 NICHOLS (John) Bibliotheca Topographica Britannica, the 52 parts forming 8 thick vols. 4to. *portrait, maps, genealogical tables and about* 250 *plates, bright gilt calf, very fine copy, from Miss Currer's library*, £21. 1780-90
   Priced, 1827, J. Bohn, 45l.; 1829, 32l.; 1840, 24l.; 1859, 21l.
   An extremely valuable and rare collection of English topography, the *fifty-two* parts of which are very rarely found together. *A similar copy sold at Nassau's sale for* 44l. 2s. *and at Dr. Heath's for* 47l.

NEW HAMPSHIRE HISTORICAL SOCIETY:
512 COLLECTIONS of the NEW HAMPSHIRE HISTORICAL SOCIETY, Vols. I.—VI. wanting III. 5 vols. 8vo. *three in bds. uncut, two in cloth, rare*, £2. 16s *Concord*, 1824
   Containing a variety of interesting matter relative to the early settlement, the conflicts with the Indians, the wars of the last century, original letters of Washington (with facsimile signature), Hancock and others, in connection with the War of Independence; exciting episodes of the adventures of the Borderers amongst the Red Men, etc.

NORDISKE OLDSKRIFT SELSKAB: Publications of the Royal Society of Northern Antiquaries.
513 NORDISK TIDSSKRIFT for Oldkyndighed (Historical and Philological Transactions), 3 vols. *bound*, 1832-36—MEMOIRES de la Société, 1836-49, 5 vols. *sd.* 1838-52—ANNALER for Nordisk Oldkyndighed, 1836-43, 1850-57, in 12 vols. *four bound, eight unbound*, 1837-57—ANTIQUARISK TIDSSKRIFT: Bulletin de la Société, 1843-57, 5 vols. in 9 parts, *unbound*, 1845-59—together 25 vols. 8vo. *numerous fine plates of Antiquities, Runic and Cuneiform inscriptions, etc. seven vols. in cf. extra, the remainder in* 22 *Nos. unbound*, £12. *Copenhagen*, 1832-59
   Sets completed.

Collectiones Historiae Populorum Septentrionalium, ed. Societas Regia Antiquariorum Septentrionalium:
514 FORNMANNA SÖGUR, eptir gömlum Handritum utgefnar ad tilhlutun hins Norræna Fornfræda Felags, 12 vols. *with facsimiles* 1825-37
   OLDNORDISKE SAGAER, udgivne i oversættelse, 12 vols. 1826-37
   SCRIPTA HISTORICA ISLANDORUM, de rebus gestis veterum Borealium, *Latine*, 12 vols. 1828-46
   NORDISKE FORTIDS SAGAER, efter den udgivne gamle Nordiske Grundskrift, af Rafn, 3 vols. 1829-30
   ISLENDINGA SÖGUR, eptir gömlum Handritum, 2 vols. 1829-30
   Together 41 vols. 8vo. FINE PAPER, *calf extra, a fine set, from Miss Currer's library*, £21. *Kjöbenhavn*, 1825-46
515 ANTIQUITATES AMERICANAE, sive Scriptores Septentrionales Rerum Ante-Columbianarum in America, edidit Soc. R. Antiq. Septemtr. impl. 4to. *maps and plates, russia, gilt edges*, 32s *Hafniae*, 1837

516 EGILSSON (Sveinbjörn) Lexicon Poeticum antiquæ linguæ Septentrionalis, cum praefatione historicâ et criticâ et Indice Siglorum, stout roy. 8vo. lii. *and* 934 *pp. double columns, sd.* 30*s* *Hafniæ,* 1860

517 SAGA Jatvardar Konungs hins helga, *facsimile,* 1852—Vestiges d'Asserbo et de Söborg, decouverts par Fred. VII. de Danemark, *plates,* 1855—RAFN, Antiquités de l'Orient, monuments Runographiques; Inscription Runique du Pirée, 1856; 4 parts 8vo. *sd.* 15*s* 1852-56

NORTHUMBERLAND (THE DUKE OF) PUBLICATIONS:

518 SMYTH'S ÆDES HARTWELLIANÆ; or Notices of the Manor and Mansion of Hartwell, Co. Bucks (Dr. Lee's Residence), large 4to. *plates, and upwards of* 50 *illustrations on wood and stone,* PRIVATELY PRINTED, *cloth,* £2. 16*s* 1851

Chapter I. Details respecting the Parish and Manor of Hartwell; II. The successive Lords of Hartwell, from the Conquest; III. The Apartments, Paintings, Library, Museum, Numismata and Egyptian Antiquities; IV. The Hartwell Observatory, the Transit Room, the Meteorological Department, etc.; with an Appendix and numerous Plates of Egyptian Antiquities, Monumental, Heraldic, Numismatic and Astronomical Illustrations, etc. and valuable Meteorological Observations.

519 SMYTH'S descriptive Catalogue of Roman Family Coins, belonging to the DUKE OF NORTHUMBERLAND, royal 4to. *cloth, privately printed,* £2. 10*s* 1856
A very well executed and excellent work.

520 NOTES AND QUERIES, a Medium of intercommunication for Literary Men, Artists, Antiquaries, Genealogists, etc. A COMPLETE SET, from the commencement, Nov. 3, 1849, to September, 1861, being Series I. 12 vols. *with Index;* Series II. 11 vols.—together 23 vols. and Index, sm. 4to. twenty vols. *neatly half bound calf, the rest in* 21 *parts,* £7. 10*s* 1849-61

"Notes and Queries is become now an established institution, being possessed of that great element of immortality, an individual character and purpose. When a man, or a book, or a periodical, has no strictly individual course, but is like fifty or a hundred, or a thousand other new books or periodicals, he or it may live and prosper doubtless, but the time will also come when he or it must die. There may be three score and ten years for a man, three score and ten months for a journal, three score and ten weeks for a book; but the time still comes soon when each must go hence and be seen no more. Force of individual character is the *sal sapientum*, the turner of base metal into gold, the preserving salt that is alone able to save from decay whatever perishable thing it touches. This Notes and Queries has; and because it has this, we may boldly predict that it shall be savoury in the mouths of generations yet to come. Literary men, centuries after we are gone, will be taking in their Notes and Queries; and the books that shall be hereafter, will be made the richer for the odd and interesting and important Notes they furnish to the authors who contribute Queries for the sake of getting them."—*Examiner*, 28th July, 1855.

521 NUMISMATIC JOURNAL, CHRONICLE, and Numismatic Society's Proceedings, from the beginning in 1836: Journal, Nos. 1-7, 1836-37; Chronicle, Nos. 1-75, or Vols. I.-XIX.—together 82 Nos. 8vo. *numerous plates,* £12. 12*s* 1836-57
Several numbers in stock for the completion of sets; also parts of the "Proceedings."

522 ORIENTAL Magazine and Calcutta Review, 2 vols. 8vo. *hf. rus.* 5*s* *Calcutta,* 1823
523 ORIENTAL MAGAZINE, Quarterly, Vol. I. (March and June 1824), 8vo. *half russia,* 5*s* *Calcutta,* 1824

ORIENTAL TRANSLATION FUND:

524 PUBLICATIONS OF THE ORIENTAL TRANSLATION FUND, LARGE PAPER SUBSCRIPTION COPY, 69 distinct works, forming 50 vols. impl. 4to. 45 vols. impl. 8vo. in all 95 vols. *with many maps and plates* (subscription price and original cost £304. 10*s*) *clean and new,* offered to the public at £75. 7*s*, now at £42. 1829-59
The following is a List of the works, and the *reduced* prices at which they can be supplied separately:

525 IBN BATUTA, Travels, by Lee, 4to. 10*s* 1829
526 JAHANGUEIR, Memoirs, by Price, 4to. 5*s* 1829
527 MACARIUS, Travels of, translated by Belfour, 9 parts in 7, 4to. £2. 2*s* 1829-37
528 HAN KOONG TSEW; or, the Sorrows of Han, by Davis, 4to. 2*s* 6*d* 1829
529 NEAMET ULLAH; History of the Afghans, by Dorn, 4to. 12*s* 1829-37
530 The FORTUNATE Union, from the Chinese, by Davis, 2 vols. 8vo. 12*s* 6*d* 1829
531 YAKKUN NATTANNAWA, a Cingalese Poem, transl. by Callaway, 8vo. 6*s* 1829
532 HATIM TAI, the Adventures of, from the Persian, by Forbes, 4to. 6*s* 1830
533 ALI HAZIN, the Life of, by Himself, translated by Belfour, 8vo. 5*s* 1830
534 ALI HAZIN, the Life of, by Himself, edited in Persian, by Belfour, 8vo. 5*s* 1831
535 MEMOIRS of a Malayan Family, from the Original, by Marsden, 8vo. 2*s* 1830
536 HISTORY of the War in Bosnia, 1737, 38, and 39, by Fraser, 8vo. 2*s* 1830
537 MULFUZAT TIMURY; Autobiog. Memoirs of Timur, by Stuart, 4to. 6*s* 1830
538 The HISTORY of Vartan, by Neumann, 4to. 3*s* 1830
539 The LIFE of Hafiz ul Mulk, by Elliott, 8vo. 3*s* 1834
540 MISCELLANEOUS Translations, 2 vols. 8vo. 12*s* 1831-34

541 HAJI KHALIFEH's Maritime Wars of the Turks, part 1, 4to. 2s 6d   1832
542 TRANSLATIONS from the Chinese and Armenian, by Neumann, 8vo. 10s   1831
543 The ALGEBRA of Mohammed Ben Musa, Arab. and Engl. by Rosen, 8vo. 6s 1831
544 The GEOGRAPHICAL Works of Sadik Isfahani, 8vo. 8s   1832
545 FIRDUSI. Shah Nameh, by Atkinson, 8vo. 12s
546 TEZKEREH AL VAKIAT; Memoirs of the Moghul Emperor Humayun, 4to. 3s 1832
547 SIYAR-UL-MUTAKHERIN; the Mahomedan Power in India, by Briggs, Vol. I. 5s 1832
548 HOEI LAN KI; or, l'Histoire du Cercle de Craie, par Julien, 8vo. 5s   1832
549 SAN KOKF TSOU RAN TO SETS; Aperçu général des Trois Royaumes, par Klaproth, 8vo. *with the plates in 4to.*—together 2 vols. 9s   1832
550 ANNALS of the Turkish Empire, by Fraser, Vol. I. 4to. 7s   1832
551 KALIDASÆ Raghuvansa Carmen. Sanskritè et Latinè, Ed. Stenzler, 4to. 18s 1832
552 CUSTOMS of the Women of Persia, by Atkinson, 8vo. 4s   1832
553 MIRKHOND. History of the Early Kings of Persia, by Shea, 8vo. 6s   1832
554 TUHFAT-UL MUJAHIDIN; History of the Mohammedans in Malabar, by Rowlandson, 8vo. 4s   1833
555 ALFIYYA; ou, Grammaire Arabe, par De Sacy, 8vo. 6s 6d   *Paris*, 1834
556 EVLIYA EFENDI, Travels in Europe, Asia, and Africa, from the Turkish, by Von Hammer, Parts I. and II. 4to. 20s   1834-50
557 A DESCRIPTION of the Burmese Empire, by Sangermano, by Tandy, 4to. 10s 1834
558 ESSAY on the Architecture of the Hindus, by Ram Raz, 4to. 10s   1834
559 ANNALES des Empereurs du Japon, traduites par Isaac Titsingh, 4to. £1. 1s 1835
560 DIDASCALIA; or, Apostolical Constitutions of the Abyssinian Church, 4to. 6s 1834
561 HARIVANSA; ou, Histoire de la Famille de Hari, traduit sur l'Original Sanscrit, par Langlois, 2 tomes in 3 vols. 4to. £2. 16s   1835-36
562 Les AVENTURES de Kamrup, par de Tassy, 8vo. 4s   1834
563 CHRONICLES of Rabbi Joseph Ben Joshua Ben Meir, the Sphardi, from the Hebrew, by Bialloblotzy, 2 vols. 8vo. £1.   1837
564 HISTORY of Gujarat, by Bird, 8vo. 8s   1835
565 LE LIVRE des Recompenses et des Peines, par Julien, 8vo. 17s   1835
566 HAJI KHALFÆ Lexicon Encyclopædicum et Bibliographicum, edidit Fluegel, 7 vols. complete, 4to. £5. 5s   *Leipzig*, 1835-60
This extremely valuable work is now offered at a great reduction; the former price was £10. 10s.
567 CHRONIQUE d'Abou-djafar Mohammed Tabari, Livr. 1, 4to. 7s   1836
568 LAILI AND MAJNUN, 8vo. 4s 6d   1836
569 The HISTORY of the Temple of Jerusalem, by Reynolds, 8vo. 12s   1836
570 The SANKHYA KARIKA; or, the Sankya Philosophy, by Colebrooke, 4to. 10s 6d 1837
571 MAKRIZI, Histoire des Sultans Mamlouks de l'Égypte, I. and II. 4to. 18s   1837
572 RIG Veda Sanhita, Sanskritè et Latinè, edidit Rosen, 4to. 18s   1837
573 KUMARA Sambhava, Sanskritè et Latinè, edidit Stenzler, 4to. 10s 6d   1838
574 PRACTICAL Philosophy of the Muhammadan People, by Thompson, 8vo. 8s   1839
575 GARCIN DE TASSY. Histoire de la Littérature Hindoui et Hindoustani, Tomes I. et II. 8vo. £1. 4s   1839-47
576 VISHNU PURANA; a System of Hindu Mythology and Tradition, translated from the Original Sanscrit, by H. H. Wilson, 4to. *very rare*, £2. 2s   1840
577 AL-MAKKARI. The History of the Mohammedan Dynasties in Spain, translated by Gayangos, 2 vols. 4to. £3. 3s   1840
578 EL-MAS'UDI's Historical Encyclopædia, from the Arabic, by Sprenger, Vol. I. 8vo. 6s   1841
579 SAMA VEDA. Translation of the Sanhitá of the Sama Veda, by Stevenson, 8vo. 7s   1841
580 SPECIMENS of the Popular Poetry of Persia, by Chodzko, 8vo. 12s 6d   1842
581 IBN KHALLIKAN'S Biographical Dictionary, by Mac Guckin de Slane, Vols. I. II. and Vol. III. part 1, 4to. £2. 2s   1842
582 HISTORY of Hyder Naik, from a Persian MS. by Miles, 8vo. 10s   1842
583 The DABISTAN; or, School of Manners, from the Persian, by Shea and Troyer, 3 vols. 8vo. 18s   1844
584 HISTORY of the Reign of Tipu Sultan, translated by Miles, 8vo. 8s 6d   1844
585 OUSELEY's Biographical Notices of Persian Poets, by Reynolds, 8vo. 6s   1846
586 The KALPA Sutra, and Nava Tatva, by Stevenson, 8vo. 6s   1848
587 The APOSTOLIC Constitutions, in Coptic and English, by Tattam, 8vo. 8s   1849
588 MAKAMAT; or, Rhetorical Anecdotes of Abu'l Kasem al Hariri, of Basra, translated by Preston, 8vo. 12s   185

PUBLICATIONS OF LEARNED SOCIETIES, ETC. 43

589 KALIDASA. The birth of the War God, from the Sanskrit, by Griffith, 8vo. 4s 1853
590 POEMS of the Huzailis, in Arabic, by Kosegarten, Vol. I. 4to. £1. 1s   1854
591 SPICILEGIUM Syriacum, translated by Cureton, 8vo. 9s   1855
VOYAGES DES PELERINS BOUDDHISTES:
592 HISTOIRE de la Vie de Hiouen-Thsang, 8vo. 7s 6d   1853
593 MEMOIRES sur les Contrées Occidentales, 2 vols. 8vo. 25s   1857-59
594 KITAB-I-YAMINI : Early Conquerors of Hindustan, by Reynolds, 8vo. 12s 6d 1858

PALÆONTOGRAPHICAL SOCIETY:
595 MONOGRAPHS of the PALÆONTOGRAPHICAL SOCIETY, complete from the beginning in 1847 to 1854, 32 parts in 9 vols. 4to. 389 *plates, sewed*, £8. 8s   1848-55
CONTENTS: Crag Mollusca, by Wood, 3 parts; Fossil Reptilia, by Owen, 5 parts; Entomostraca of the Cretaceous formation, by Jones; Permian Fossils, by King; Eocene Mollusca, by Edwards, 3 parts; British Fossil Corals, by Milne Edwards and Haime, 5 parts; Mollusca from the Great Oolite, by Morris and Lycett, 3 parts; British Brachiopoda, by Davidson, 6 parts; Fossil Lepadidæ, by Darwin; Echinodermata, by Forbes; Fossil Mollusca, by Sharpe, 2 parts; Fossil Balanidæ and Verrucidæ, by Darwin.
These publications are unrivalled in the Scientific Literature of Europe, and are sought after by the Savants of all countries; for this reason copies readily sell at the original subscription price. If published in the regular way of business the price would at least be double.

596 PALÆONTOGRAPHICA: Beiträge zur Naturgeschichte der Vorwelt, herausgegeben von DUNKER und MEYER, Vols. I.—VI. large 4to. 227 *plates, bds.* £6. 6s   *Cassel*, 1851-58
597 PALAMEDE (Le) Revue mensuelle des ECHECS et autres Jeux, 7 vols. 8vo. *portraits and Chess Problems*, (pub. at 144 fr.) *sd*. 35s   *Paris*, 1842-47
598 PENNY CYCLOPÆDIA (The) of the Society for the Diffusion of Useful Knowledge, 27 vols.—Supplement, A.—Z. 2 vols.—together 29 vols. impl. 8vo. *original edition, many thousand woodcuts, hf. calf neat*, £5.   1833-46
The best English Cyclopædia at a moderate price; the articles have been written by the best scholars of the time.

PERCY SOCIETY:
599 PUBLICATIONS of the PERCY SOCIETY: Reprints of Early English Poetry, Ballads, and Popular Literature of the Middle Ages, edited from original Manuscripts and scarce Publications, 30 vols. sm. 8vo. *with the suppressed tract of* " Quippes for a Newfangled Gentlewoman," *in vol*. 30, *having the indecent words printed at length; only 12 copies of which were reserved, half morocco extra, top edges gilt, contents lettered, a very handsome set*, £17. 10s   1840-52
Only 250 copies of these Publications were issued for subscribers, and as the Society has broken up, COMPLETE copies have become scarce.

600 **PENNSYLVANIA HISTORICAL SOCIETY, 1845-46:** containing reprints of Denton's New York, 1670; Senter's Journal of a secret expedition against Quebec, 1775: Townsend, on the Battle of Brandywine, 1777, 8vo. *plan and plates, cloth*, 6s   *Philadelphia*, 1845-46
601 CONTRIBUTIONS to American History, roy. 8vo. *cloth*, 7s 6d   *ib*. 1858
602 PENNSYLVANIA: The REGISTER of Pennsylvania, devoted to the preservation of Facts and Documents, etc. respecting the State of Pennsylvania, edited by S. HAZARD, Vols. I.—XVI., Jan. 1828—Jan. 1836; royal 8vo. *half calf, very rare*, £4.   *ib*. 1828-36
Trübner's Guide mentions 15 vols. only, *i. e*. from 1828 to July, 1835.

603 PERTZ, MONUMENTA GERMANIÆ HISTORICA, inde ab anno Christi 500 usque ad annum 1500 auspiciis societatis aperiendis fontibus rerum germanicarum medii ævi, edidit Geor. Henr. Pertz; Vols. I.—XIV. XVI. and XVII.—together 16 vols. and a part, large folio, LARGE PAPER, *plates of Charters, good sound copy, in half vellum, uncut, fine set*, £63.   *Hannover*, 1816-61
Vol. 15 is not yet published
The work consists of two Series: Scriptores, Vols. I.—XII., XVI. XVII.; and Leges, Vols. I. II., III parts.
An "*uncut*" LARGE PAPER copy is not only very scarce but also very desirable, as the early volumes are only met with bound, and usually much cut down.
Of this valuable and stupendous publication very few copies were printed, and they occur rarely for sale. Vols. 5, 6, and 7 are out of print; complete sets sell therefore beyond the publishing price.

604 —— another copy, Vols. I.—VIII. *five whole bound, one half bound calf, two in bds*. £21.   1816-44
This is the scarce portion, the continuation can be supplied new.

605 PERTZ, MONUMENTA. Vol. IV. folio, *rare*, £2. 10s   1837
606 PETERMANN'S GEOGRAPHICAL JOURNAL. Mittheilungen aus Perthes' Geographischer Anstalt über wichtige neue Erforschungen auf dem Gesammtge-

biete der Geographie, Vols. I—V. with the "Erganzungsheft" of Vol. VI., in 38 parts, 4to. *numerous maps, many coloured, (pub. at upwards of 20 Thalers)* 36s *Gotha*, 1855-60

PHILOLOGICAL SOCIETY:

607 PROCEEDINGS OF THE PHILOLOGICAL SOCIETY for 1842-53, 6 vols. 8vo. (subscription price 15 guineas)—TRANSACTIONS of the Philological Society, 1854-61, 7 vols. *(pub. at £7. 7s)*—together 13 vols. 8vo. £8. 10s   1842-61
Several numbers in stock, to be sold separately for the completion of sets.
I am happy to inform my customers that the Philological Transactions are now completed to the end of 1861. The 1858 vol. contains a collection of Early English Poems and Lives of Saints, 1250-1450, edited by F. G. Furnivall, The 1860-1861 volumes contain a new edition of the Middle-Cornish Passion of Christ (badly edited by D. G. Gillers, 1826), and a new Early English Play of the Sacrament, the first Drama not founded on a subject from the Scriptures or Lives of the Saints Both these are edited by Mr. Stokes, the editor of Cormac's Glossary. These two vols. therefore appeal to a larger class of readers than the ordinary vols. For this year the Society has also issued the *Libri Cura Cocorum*, edited by Mr. R. Morris, a collection of Early English Recipes for Potages, Sauces, Roast and Baked Meats, and Peticures, in verse. It is a very interesting brochure.

608 JOURNAL of CLASSICAL and SACRED PHILOLOGY, Vol. I. 8vo. *containing valuable articles by Donaldson, Dr. Todd (T. C. Dublin), Bubington, Major, etc. new in cloth,* 5s   *Camb.* 1854

609 PIERER'S UNIVERSAL LEXIKON: der Wissenschaften, Künste und Gewerbe, 34 vols. in 17, royal 8vo. *double columns, second improved edition,* with oblong sm. folio ATLAS, *half bound morocco,* £3. 16s   *Altenburg,* 1840-46
The most complete Encyclopædia in existence, edited by 220 learned and practical Men of Germany.

610 PORTFOLIO (The) or a Collection of State Papers, illustrative of the History of our Times, Nos. 1 to 45, being Vols. I—V. and VI. pts. 1—4, 8vo. *the first four volumes bd. in hf. calf, the remainder in 12 parts,* £2. 10s   1836-37
611 ——— the same, Nos. 1—38, 8vo. *sd.* 36s   1836-37
Vol. III. contains a curious "intercepted caricature" upon the political state of Europe in 1836.

QUEBEC LITERARY AND HISTORICAL SOCIETY:

612 TRANSACTIONS of the above, 1824-29, Vols. I. and II. 8vo. 12 *plates, bds. rare,* 30s   *Quebec,* 1829-31
Vol. II pp. 194-198, contains a GRAMMAR OF THE HURON LANGUAGE.

613 QUERARD, La FRANCE LITTERAIRE, ou Dictionnaire Bibliographique des Savants, Historiens, et Gens de Lettre de la France ainsi que des Littérateurs étrangers qui ont écrit en Francais, plus particulièrement pendant les XVIIIe et XIXe siècles, 10 vols. large 8vo. LARGE PAPER, *hf. bd. red morocco, gilt edges, from Miss Currer's library,* £8. 8s   *Paris,* 1827-43
614 ——— the same, 10 vols. 1827-43—La LITTÉRATURE FRANÇAISE contemporaine, continuation de la FRANCE LITTÉRAIRE, jusqu'à 1849, 6 vols. 1842-57—together 16 vols. 8vo. *hf. blue morocco extra, gilt tops, uncut,* A HANDSOME SET OF BOOKS, £10. 10s   *Paris,* 1827-57
Jusqu'à présent, il n'a pas encore paru d'ouvrage bibliographique aussi complet, ni aussi utile aux libraires et a tous ceux qui s'occupent de bibliographie, que le livre de M. Quérard; dans le Journal des Savants, M. Daunou en a fait plusieurs fois l'éloge; on ne saurait trop le recommander aux libraires, aux bibliothécaires et bibliophiles, à qui il s'adresse particulierement, et sans lequel il leur est impossible de remplir convenablement les devoirs de leur profession. C'est dans le but de leur être utiles que les éditeurs ont entrepris un pareil Répertoire, qui manquait totalement à la France.

RAY SOCIETY:

615 PUBLICATIONS, a complete set, in 8vo.

Reports on the progress of Zoology and Botany	1845	Darwin. Monograph of Cirripedia, 2 vols.	1851-54
Steenstrup on the Alterations of Generations	1845	Leighton on Angiocarpous Lichens	1851
Memorials of John Ray	1846	Botanical and Physiological Memoirs	1853
Reports and Papers on Botany	1846	In folio:	
Meyen, Botanical Geography	1846	Burmeister on the Organization of Trilobites, by P. Bell and Forbes	1846
Reports on Zoology	1847		
Oken, Elements of Physiophilosophy	1847	Forbes (Prof.) Monograph of the British Naked-Eyed Medusæ, &c. *plates*	1848
Correspondence of John Ray	1848		
Agassiz, Catalogue of Books, &c. on Zoology and Geology, 4 vols.	1848-54	Alder and Hancock, Nudibranchiate Mollusca, 7 parts, *many plates*	1845-55
Reports and Papers on Botany, by Henfrey	1849	Allman, Fresh Water Polyzoa	1856
Baird on British Entomostraca	1850	Williamson's Recent Foraminifera, *plates*	1857

In all 18 vols. 8vo. and 11 vols. folio, £12. 10s   1845-57
Sold separately:

616 ALDER and HANCOCK'S Monograph of the British NUDIBRANCHIATE MOLLUSCA, complete in 7 Parts, folio, 82 *plates, most of them* BEAUTIFULLY COLOURED, *(pub. at* £9. 12s*)* £5. 15s   1845-55
One of the most elaborate scientific publications produced in Europe; highly esteemed and sought after by Continental Savants. The early parts are out of print, but are in stock, and can be supplied by me.

617 ALLMAN'S Monograph of all the known species of the Fresh Water Polyzoa, folio, *coloured plates, bds.* 20s   1856

PUBLICATIONS OF LEARNED SOCIETIES, ETC.

618 BURMEISTER, the Organization of TRILOBITES, deduced from their living affinities, edited from the German by Bell and Forbes, folio, 4 *plates, bds.* 10s   1846
619 FORBES (E.) Monograph of the British Naked-eyed Medusæ, with figures of all the species, folio, 13 *finely coloured plates, bds.* 25s   1848

RECORD COMMISSION PUBLICATIONS:

620 DOMESDAY BOOK; seu Liber Censualis Willelmi I. Regis Angliae inter Archivos regni in domo Westmonasterii asservatus, 2 vols. 1783—Indices and General Introduction to Domesday, 1 vol. 1816—Additamenta ex Codice Antiquissimo Inquisitio Eliensis, Liber Winton, Boldon Book et Indices. 1 vol. 1816 —together 4 vols. royal folio, LARGE PAPER, *facsimiles, bound*   1783-1816

When the latter volumes, titles, indexes, etc. were put forth, but a very limited number were printed on Large Paper, and the early vols. being all of that description, too frequently present a most unsightly combination. The vols. here are all, as they should be, uniform in size, and the copy possesses the leaf in the "Exon Domesday," which, when the work was about to be printed, was discovered to have been abstracted; not very long ago, after many years of absence, this leaf was accidentally found, miles away, among some family papers, and then printed. In every way this is a very desirable copy of "the most valuable piece of antiquity possessed by any nation."
Almost every page of Dugdale's Baronage may be referred to as evidence of the importance of this census to the Genealogist.
"The Domesday Book of William the Conqueror is unquestionably the most valuable record of property possessed by any nation in Europe, whether we consider the extent, the variety or the importance of the information it contains. In this inestimable survey, the various manors are arranged under the names of the tenants in Capite, who were those who held of the King as the supreme lord of all the lands in England: thus exhibiting in the clearest manner the original distribution of property, at the time of the Conquest, throughout the kingdom; and presenting us with a view, which is nearly complete, of all the persons who, in the first twenty years after the Conquest, formed the Barons of England—the progenitors of those who, in subsequent times, were the active agents in wresting from King John the great Charter of our Liberties."—*Munford's Domesday Book of Norfolk.*

621 ROTULI Litterarum Clausarum in Turri Londinensi asservati, accurante T. D. Hardy, 2 vols. large folio, *cloth,* 30s   1833-44
622 ROTULI Litterarum Patentium in Turri Londinensi asservati, Vol. I. pars I. large folio, *cloth,* 15s   1835
623 ROTULI Chartarum in Turri Londinensi asservati, Vol. I. pars I. large folio, *cloth,* 15s   1837
624 ANCIENT LAWS and Institutes of ENGLAND under the Anglo-Saxon Kings, from Æthelbirht to Cnut, with an English Translation of the Saxon; the Laws of Edward the Confessor, William the Conqueror, and Henry I.; also Monumenta Ecclesiastica Anglicana, 7th—10th Century; and the ancient Latin version of the Anglo-Saxon Laws, with Glossary, etc. folio, *cloth,* 35s   1840
625 —— The same, 2 vols. royal 8vo. *cloth,* 32s   1840
626 ANCIENT LAWS and Institutes of WALES, with an English Translation of the Welsh Text, some Latin Transcripts, Indices and Glossary, folio, *cl.* £2.   1841
627 —— the same, 2 vols. royal 8vo. *cloth,* 36s   1841
628 DOCUMENTS illustrative of English history in the XIII—XIV. Centuries, from the Exchequer records, edited by H. COLE, folio, *cloth,* (*only 250 copies printed, at* £2. 5s 6d) 20s   1844
629 CALENDAR OF STATE PAPERS, DOMESTIC SERIES, preserved in the State Paper department of the Record Office, from 1547-1628, 7 vols. impl. 8vo. *cloth,* £4.   1856-59
Including:—Lemon's Reigns of Edward VI. Mary, Elizabeth, 1547-1580, 1 vol.
Green's Reign of James I. 1603-1610, 1 vol.
—— James I. 1611-1625, 3 vols.
Bruce's Charles I. 1725-28, 2 vols.

630 COOPER (C. P.) Account of the most important Public Records of Great Britain and the Publications of the Record Commission, 2 vols. 8vo. *hf. cf. gt.* £2. 16s 1832
Very scarce, only 250 copies having been printed, most of which were given to public libraries.

631 —— Proposal for the erection of a General Record Office, 8vo. *plan, cloth,* 3s 6d   1832
632 —— Papers relative to the project of building a General Record Office, 8vo. 3 *large folding plates, cloth,* 2s 6d   1835
633 REES'S CYCLOPÆDIA: or UNIVERSAL DICTIONARY of the Arts, Science, History, Biography, and Literature, 45 vols. 4to. *including the six vols. of plates, a complete set, half calf,* £5. 5s   1819
A stupendous and still valuable work, the most complete English Encyclopædia; cost the former proprietor nearly 100 guineas.

634 REEVE (Lovell Aug.) CONCHOLOGIA ICONICA, or Illustrations of the Shells of Molluscous Animals, Vol. I.—VIII. IX. parts 1, 2; with the Supplement to the Conus and Murex, 4to. 1159 *beautifully coloured plates, pub. at about* £73, *four vols. bound in cloth, the remainder unbound, Subscriber's copy,* £45.   1846-55

635 RETROSPECTIVE REVIEW, complete from the commencement in 1820 to its close in 1828, 16 vols. 8vo. (*published at* £10. 4s *in Nos.*) *hf. calf gilt,* £6. 6s   1820-28
   The First Series, 14 vols. 1820-26; the Second Series, edited by (Sir) N. Harris Nicolas. 1827-28. Priced, 1847, H. Bohn, bds. 6l.; hf. bd. 6l. 10s; calf extra, 8l. 8s: 1846, White, calf extra, 8l. 8s. It fetched, 1858, Puttick's, calf gilt, 9l.; 1851, Sotheby's, bds. 6l. 8s 6d.
   A valuable storehouse of learned reviews of good old books in the departments of Early English Literature, History, Travels, &c. It is to be regretted that the Scholars of England do not gather under a competent editor, and bring out as the result of their studies a similar periodical.

RHEINLAENDISCHER VEREIN:

636 JAHRBÜCHER des Vereins von Alterthumsfreunden im RHEINLANDE, Vols. 1-24, and Index, in 8 vols. 8vo. *plates of Roman Antiquities,* bds. £2. 16s   1842-57
   Ces annales contiennent des mémoires fort importants concernant l'archéologie classique et chrétienne. Le livre est publié aux frais de la société.

637 REVUE NUMISMATIQUE, PUBLIÉE PAR CARTIER ET L. DE LA SAUSSAYE, du 1er Janvier 1836 à Novembre 1858 incl. et la TABLE des 20 premiers volumes, in 109 vols. and parts, large 8vo. QUITE COMPLETE, *many plates and engravings,* VERY RARE, £18.   *Par.* 1836-58

638 —— Another set, *from the beginning in* 1836 to 1852, 17 vols. 8vo. *many plates,* sd. £12.   1836-52
                           Many odd parts in stock; sets completed.

639 REVUE de la NUMISMATIQUE BELGE, Vols. I.—IV. 8vo. 64 *plates,* sd. 9s
                                                                               Bruxelles, 1842-48

640 REVUE DES DEUX MONDES, du 1er Juillet 1851 au 1er Septembre 1859, an incomplete set in 101 Nos. large 8vo. sd. £2. 10s   *Paris,* 1851-59

ROXBURGHE CLUB:

641 ALEXANDER ROMANCE. The alliterative ROMANCE of ALEXANDER, from the unique manuscript in the Ashmolean Museum, edited by the Rev. J. Stevenson, *in old English, with a* GLOSSARY, 4to. *half morocco, uncut* £2. 2s   1849

642 THE AYENBITE of INWYT, written in the dialect of the County of Kent, by Dan Michel, of Northgate, in the year 1340, now first printed from the autograph MS. in the British Museum, edited with a Glossary by Rev. Jos. Stevenson, 4to. *printed for the* 40 *members, half morocco, uncut,* £3. 10s   1855

ROYAL INSTITUTION:

643 PROCEEDINGS, Vol. I. 1851-54, 8vo. *discourses by Faraday, Murchison, Owen, Lyell, Forbes, etc. cloth,* 7s 6d   1854

ROYAL SOCIETY:

644 PHILOSOPHICAL TRANSACTIONS OF THE ROYAL SOCIETY of London, AT LARGE, from the commencement in 1655 to 1844, with INDEXES to Vols. 1 to 110—R. Hook's Lectures—and Parsons' Crounian Lectures—together 141 vols. 4to. *many plates, russia,* A REMARKABLY FINE SET, £116.   1654-1844
   The difficulty of obtaining original editions of the early volumes, in any state, and especially in good condition, is well known. Hence the possession of a copy of the Transactions at large is a great rarity, even in public libraries'
   The continuation from 1845 to 1862 is in stock, and can be supplied at a much reduced price.

645 —— another set, 1665 to 1733 abridged, 7 vols. in 8; at Large, 1765-89, with Index of Vols. 1-70, 26 vols. in 30; 1791 to 1861 *to be sold separately* 1732-1861

645* PHILOSOPHICAL TRANSACTIONS OF THE ROYAL SOCIETY. The following Parts are in stock, and can be supplied as follows:

		£. s. d.	Offered at			£. s. d.	Offered at			£. s. d.	Offered at
1830	Part I.	1 10 0	0 15 0	1841	Part II.	1 10 0	0 16 0	1851	Part II.	2 10 0	1 5 0
——	,, II.	1 10 0	0 15 0	1842	,, I.	0 16 0	0 8 0	1852	,, I.	1 0 0	0 5 0
1831	,, I.	1 10 0	0 15 0	——	,, II.	1 2 0	0 11 0	——	,, II.	2 5 0	0 15 0
——	,, II.	1 12 0	0 16 0	1843	,, I.	1 10 0	0 5 0	1853	,, I.	0 18 0	0 6 0
1832	,, I.	1 1 0	0 11 0	——	,, II.	1 10 0	0 15 0	——	,, II.	0 12 0	0 4 0
——	,, II.	2 0 0	1 0 0	1844	,, I.	0 10 0	0 6 0	——	,, III.	1 2 0	0 8 0
1833	,, I.	1 1 0	0 11 0	——	,, II.	1 10 0	0 10 0	1854	,, I.	0 12 0	0 4 0
——	,, II.	2 18 0	1 9 0	1845	,, I.	0 16 0	0 4 0	——	,, II.	0 16 0	0 8 0
1834	,, I.	0 17 0	0 10 0	——	,, II.	1 0 0	0 10 0	1855	,, I.	0 16 0	0 8 0
——	,, II.	2 2 0	1 1 0	1846	,, I.	0 7 6	0 4 0	——	,, II.	1 6 0	0 13 0
1835	,, I.	1 2 0	0 11 0	——	,, II.	1 2 0	0 17 6	1856	,, I.	2 0 0	1 0 0
——	,, II.	0 14 0	0 8 0	——	,, III.	1 12 0	0 16 0	——	,, II.	1 4 0	0 12 0
1836	,, I.	1 10 0	0 15 0	——	,, IV.	1 12 0	0 16 0	——	,, III.	1 4 0	0 12 0
——	,, II.	2 0 0	1 1 0	1847	,, I.	0 14 0	0 7 0	1857	,, I.	1 8 0	0 14 0
1837	,, I.	1 8 0	0 18 0	——	,, II.	0 16 0	0 8 0	——	,, II.	1 4 0	0 12 0
——	,, II.	1 8 0	0 14 0	1848	,, I.	1 0 0	0 5 0	——	,, III.	1 2 0	0 11 0
1838	,, I.	0 13 0	0 7 0	——	,, II.	0 14 0	9 7 0	1858	,, I.	1 8 0	0 14 0
——	,, II.	1 8 0	0 15 0	1849	,, I.	1 0 0	0 10 0	——	,, II.	3 0 0	1 0 0
1839	,, I.	0 18 0	0 10 0	——	,, II.	2 5 0	1 2 6	1859	,, I.	2 10 0	1 8 0
——	,, II.	1 1 6	0 12 0	1850	,, I.	1 10 0	0 8 0	——	,, II.	2 5 0	1 10 0
1840	,, I.	0 18 0	0 6 0	——	,, II.	3 5 0	1 12 6	1860	,, I.	0 16 0	0 12 0
——	,, II.	2 5 0	1 3 0	1851	,, I.	2 10 0	0 15 0	——	,, II.	2 1 6	1 1 0
1841	,, I.	0 10 0	0 5 0								

PUBLICATIONS OF LEARNED SOCIETIES, ETC.

346 ABSTRACT of the Papers printed in the Philosophical Transactions of the Royal Society of London, from 1800 to 1830 inclusive, 2 vols. 8vo. *bds. 7s 6d* 1832-33
347 PROCEEDINGS of the Royal Society, Nos. 1-36 inclusive, 8vo. *sd. 36s* 1854-59
    The above contains all the papers read before the Society between 1854 and 1859.
348 TABLE des Mémoires de la Société Royale de Londres, 1665-1735, par M. de Bremond, sm. 4to. *calf, 5s* Paris, 1739

ROYAL SOCIETY OF LITERATURE:

349 TRANSACTIONS of the ROYAL SOCIETY of LITERATURE of the United Kingdom, 3 vols. in 6 parts 4to. *First Series complete, plates* (pub. at £9. 19s 6d), *bds.* 30s ; *or hf. green morocco, neat,* 36s 1827-29
350 —— the same, SECOND SERIES, Vols. I. to VI. 8vo. *many plates, two vols. in cloth, and 12 parts uncut,* £3. 1843-59
351 RYMER (Tho.) FŒDERA, CONVENTIONES, LITERÆ, et cujuscunque generis Acta Publica, inter Reges Angliæ et alios Imperatores, Reges, Pontifices, Principes, vel Communitates, ab anno 1101 ad nostra tempora ; collata et emendata studio G. Holmes, 10 vols. folio, *plates of Charters, etc. fine copy in half vellum,* £13. *Hagæ Com.* 1745

Priced, 1840, Leslie, 14*l.* 14s ; Payne and Foss, 18*l.* 18s ; J. Bohn, 18*l.* 18s ; fetched, 1857, Sotheby's, 13*l.*
 " —— a third, and by much the best edition, as having a complete and useful Index to the work was published at the Hague."—*Dibdin.*
 " An invaluable work, and as such it is esteemed both at home and abroad. It is equally interesting to the Antiquarian and Historian. Whoever wishes to write such a history of Great Britain as will do honour to himself and justice to his country must go to Rymer for his materials."— *Clarke's Bibliog. Dict.*
 " Rymer's Fœdera, with the Statutes of the Realm, the Rolls of Parliament, and Wilkins' Concilia, form an outline map of English mediæval history."—*English Review, No.* 2.
 The " Index Rerum præcipuarum in novis tomis Fœderum," which was added to this edition, and makes it by far the best, is marked by the most extreme minuteness and accuracy ; forming the fourth part of Vol. X., and consisting of 332 close pages, with treble columns.

SAINT PETERSBURGH ACADEMY:

652 PETROPOLITANÆ ACADEMIÆ Scientiarum Commentarii, ab anno 1726 ad annum 1746, 14 vols. *Petropoli,* 1728-51—Novi Commentarii, pro annis 1747-75, 20 vols. *ib.* 1750-76—Acta, pro annis, 1777-82, 12 parts in 6 vols. *ib.* 1778-86—Nova Acta, pro annis 1783-98, 15 vols. *ib.* 1783-1806—Mémoires de l'Académie Impériale des Sciences de St. Petersbourg, avec l'Histoire de l'Académie, pour les années 1803-20, 9 vols. *ib.* 1809-24—Memoirs written in the Russian Language, 5 vols. *ib.* 1808-19—Transactions of the Academy, written in Russian, 2 vols. in 1, *ib.* 1821-23—together 70 vols. 4to. *numerous plates, half russia, a fine set,* VERY RARE, £32. *Petrop.* 1728-1824
    This was a presentation copy to the Horticultural Society, from the Emperor Alexander.
653 —— another set, Commentarii Academiæ Scientiarum Imperialis Petropolitanæ, Vols. 1—14, 1726-46—Nova Acta Academiæ, cum historia ejusdem ad annum 1783, Vols. 1—15, *vol.* 13 *wanting,* 1783-1798—Mémoires de l'Académie Impériale des Sciences de St. Petersbourg, avec son histoire, 1803-6, Vols. 1-5, 1809-15—together 33 vols. 4to. *plates, hf. bd. scarce,* £10. 10s *St. Pet.* 1728-1815
    Talleyrand's copy, 94 vols. fetched 43*l.* 1s.
654 MÉMOIRES de l'Académie Impériale des Sciences de Saint Petersbourg, roy. 4to. *with many plates, facsimiles and diagrams :*
    Recueil des Actes de la Séance Publique, 1834, 1836-7, 1840, 1843-4—together 6 vols. *St. Petersbourg,* 1834-45
    Mémoires, 6me Série : Sciences Mathématiques et Physiques, Tomes 4, 5, et 7, *in 9 parts* *ib.* 1850-4
    —— 6me Série, Sciences Naturelles, Tome 5, pts. 1-4, VI. pts. 1-6, *in 7 parts* *ib.* 1846-9
    Bulletin Scientifique, Tomes I.-X. *Vol. VI. wants Nos.* 9 *and* 10   *ib.* 1836-42
    Bulletin de la Classe Physico-Mathématique, Tomes I.-IV., IX. *Nos.* 17-24, XI.-XVI.   *ib.* 1843-58
        Sold separately, Tomes XII.—XV.
    Memoires par Divers Savans, Tome VII.   *ib.* 1854
    Bulletin de la Classe Historico-Philologique, Tomes XI.-XIII.   *ib.* 1854-6
    Bulletin de l'Académie Impériale des Sciences, Tome I. *in* 6 *parts*   1860
    —— the above Series as described, £8.   1834-1860

SAINT PETERSBURG ARCHÆOLOGICAL AND NUMISMATIC SOCIETY:

655 MEMOIRES de la SOCIÉTÉ D'ARCHÉOLOGIE et de NUMISMATIQUE de St. Pétersbourg, avec les Bulletins, publiés par le Baron de KÖHNE, Vols. I.-VI. 8vo. 123 *plates of Coins, hf. calf,* £2. 10s *St. Petersb.* 1847-52

SAINT PETERSBURG GEOGRAPHICAL SOCIETY:

656 Transactions of the Imperial Russian Geographical Society, edited by Milioutin, from the beginning in 1849 to 1853, Nos. 1-9—Memoirs, Nos. 1-5; together 14 parts in 13, roy. 8vo. *in Russian, maps, sd.* 36s   *ib.* 1849-53

657 SATURDAY REVIEW (The) from its commencement to the end of last year, 12 vols. folio, Vols. I.-X. *bound in cloth, the remainder in* 52 *numbers,* £2. 2s 1855-61
A very desirable set of this remarkable literary and political journal.

658 SAVILE, Rerum Anglicarum Scriptores post Bedam præcipui: Willielmi Malmesburiensis, Henrici Huntindoniensis, Rogeri Hovedeni, Ethelwerdi et Ingulphi historiae, chronica et annales, cum tabulis chronologicis, folio, BEST EDITION, *fine copy in russia extra, from Miss Currer's library,* 32s   *Londini,* 1596
Priced, 1840, £3. 3s; 1844, £4. 4s.
This edition is more accurately printed than the Frankfort edition of 1601.
"William of Malmesbury has left us a work superior in composition to the annalists of the age, and to any preceding historian since the classical authors."—*Sharon Turner.*

659 SCOTS MAGAZINE, with which is incorporated the Edinburgh Magazine and Literary Miscellany, A COMPLETE SET *from the commencement in* 1739 *to its completion, June,* 1826, 97 vols. 8vo. *a fine set in calf,* £10.   *Edinb.* 1739-1826
One of the oldest and most valuable literary Periodicals published in the United Kingdom.

660 SEMANARIO ERUDITO, que comprehende varias obras ineditas, criticas, morales, instructivas, politicas, historicas, satiricas, y jocosas de nuestros majores autores antiguos y modernos, dadas a luz por Don Antonio Valladares de Sotomayor, Vols. I.-XXXIV. sm. 4to. (*wanting Vol.* 32) *Span. calf,* 30s *Madr.* 1787-91
A complete body of Spanish learning. "We are indebted to Senor Valladares for having published in this collection several treatises and other works, which until then had only existed in manuscript."—*Salva.*

SHAKESPEARE SOCIETY:

661 A complete Collection of the valuable Dramatic Works, and Reprints of Rare Pieces illustrative of the Drama during the Period of Shakespeare, issued to the Members of the Club, edited by Collier, Halliwell, Cunningham, Dyce, and others, a COMPLETE SET, 19 vols. 8vo. *half green morocco, gilt tops, uncut, contents lettered,* £9. 15s   1853
The Shakespeare Society being now dissolved, and the few complete sets of their publications dispersed, the present is a favourable opportunity for acquiring them at a moderate price. They consist of nearly Fifty different works illustrative of Shakespeare and the Literature of his time, comprising Old Plays, Poems, Curious Tracts, Memoirs, &c. either now printed for the first time, or difficult to be procured from their rarity, edited by eminent literary men.

    SILLIMAN—*See* American Journal.

SKANDINAVISKE LITTERATUR-SELSKABS:

662 Skrifter, 21 vols. in 11, 12mo. *plates and tables, hf. cf.* 30s   *Kjöbenhavn,* 1805-26
The writers of this valuable periodical include the most distinguished names in Northern literature—Finn Magnusen, Rask, Nyerup, Müller, Möller, Molbech, and others; and their contributions embrace the widest range of knowledge, historical, antiquarian, scientific and philological.
Fetched, 1819, Knight's sale, £3. 4s.

663 SMITH (C. Roach) COLLECTANEA ANTIQUA; Etchings and Notices of Ancient Remains illustrative of the Habits, Customs and History of Past Ages, 5 vols. 8vo. *nearly* 300 *Archæological Plates and Etchings, many of which are coloured, Mr. Walter Hawkins' copy, the first vol. bound in calf, the remainder unbound, rare,* £7. 7s   *Printed for subscribers only,* 1848-61
A complete copy of this extremely valuable publication.

664 —— Collectanea Antiqua, Vols. I—IV. 8vo. *neatly half bound calf, M. E. Onslow's copy,* £6.   1848-57
Vols. I. to IV. fetched, 1861, Sotheby's, £9.

665 —— An imperfect copy, No. 12, 1848; Vol. III. parts 1—4; Vol. IV. parts 1—4; Vols. V. parts 1—2; 1853-58—11 numbers, 8vo. *many plates, Mr. F. Hobler's copy,* £2. 12s 6d   1848-58
Printed for the subscribers and not published. "Mr. Roach Smith has brought to his task a thorough and familiar acquaintance with the writings of Roman and Greek authors, which enables him to interpret at a glance the significance of isolated and otherwise inscrutable facts and allusions. But besides these acquirements he possesses an enthusiastic spirit which has neither been daunted by opposition, nor chilled by indifference; and to this we owe the results recorded in his splendid volume. How many thanks are due from all historical and antiquarian enquirers to Mr. Roach Smith for his public-spirited labours! Fortunately, he needs no other memorial than this his greatest work, to attest his labours and his services"—*Leicester Chronicle.*

666 Smith (C. R.) Catalogue of his Museum of London Antiquities, *plates and cuts,* 8vo. *half morocco,* 20s   *Printed for subscribers only,* 1854

667 —— Illustrations of Roman London, 4to. *frontispiece, and* 41 *plates of Roman Antiquities, Tesselated Pavements, Statues, Edifices, etc. some of them coloured, half calf, printed for the subscribers and not published,* 35s   1859

668 SMITH'S Dictionary of Greek and Roman Biography and Mythology, 3 stout vols. 8vo. *illustrated by numerous engravings on wood,* (pub. at £5. 15s 6d) *cloth,* £4. 4s   1849-50

686 TANNERI BIBLIOTHECA BRITANNICO-HIBERNICA, sive de scriptoribus qui in Anglia, Scotia et Hibernia, ad sæculi XVII., initium floruerunt literarum ordine juxta familiarum nomina dispositis, commentariis edidit D. WILKINSON, folio, *fine portraits by Vertue, calf,* VERY RARE, £8. 8s   1748

A very learned Dictionary of the Early British Authors, with a list of their works, and the references where, and in which collections they can be found. Originally this valuable work was published at 25s; it has been steadily rising, and in 1856 an uncut copy fetched £11.

SYRO-EGYPTIAN SOCIETY OF LONDON:

687 ORIGINAL PAPERS, Vol. I. parts 1 and 2 (all published), 8vo. *with Barker's Memoir on Syria, the Prospectus and Reports from the beginning to* 1860, *several MS. letters and Mems. to and by W. Hawkins, Esq. a Member; and also* "Hieroglyphic Inscriptions from original Monuments," No. 1, folio, 6 *large plates,* 10s   1845-60

688 —— Original Papers, Vol. I. pts. 1, 2, 8vo. (all published), 5s   1845-50

689 THEATRICAL OBSERVER; and Daily Bills of the Play; Nos. 136-7025, from April 1829 to June 1844, in 16 vols. *neatly half bound calf, extremely scarce*, £4. 4s   1829-44

The above periodical contains critiques on the various performances at Covent Garden, Drury Lane, the Haymarket, and other Theatres. Having been published in Penny numbers, it is very rare, and the present copy is the only one ever offered for sale. Collectors of broadsides and chapbook Literature can testify to the extreme difficulty of procuring ephemeral publications issued at low prices.

690 THEOLOGISCHE STUDIEN und KRITIKEN: eine Zeitschrift für das gesammte Gebiet der Theologie, in Verbindung mit Gieseler, Lücke und Nitzsch, herausgegeben von C. ULLMANN und F. W. C. UMBREIT, 1828-48; mit Register, 1828-37; 22 vols. 8vo. (pub. at £10. 10s) *cloth,* £8.   *Hamb.* 1828-48

Priced, 1856, Schmidt in Halle, 60 thalers.

TOPOGRAPHICAL DEPARTMENT OF THE WAR OFFICE:

Publications issued under the direction of Colonel SIR HENRY JAMES:

DOMESDAY BOOK, or the Great Survey of England of William the Conqueror, A.D. 1086, photo-zincographed by Her Majesty's command at the Ordnance Survey Office, Southampton, Colonel Sir H. James, Director.

The following Counties have been published, each forming a separate vol. impl. 4to. *cloth:*

691 CORNWALL, Facsimile of the part relating to, 8s	1861	701 BEDFORDSHIRE, 8s	1862
692 MIDDLESEX, Facsimile, 8s	1861	702 STAFFORDSHIRE, 8s	1862
693 —— Literal extension of the Latin text, in modern type, with translation, indexes, and notes, 8s	1862	703 HEREFORDSHIRE, 8s	1862
		704 DORSETSHIRE, 8s	1862
		705 SOMERSETSHIRE, 10s	1862
		706 LEICESTERSHIRE and Rutland, 8s	1862
694 SUSSEX, Facsimile of the part relating to, 10s	1862	707 DEVONSHIRE, 10s	1862
		708 WORCESTERSHIRE, 8s	1862
695 SURREY, Facsimile, 8s	1862	709 GLOUCESTERSHIRE, 8s	1862
696 —— Literal extension and translation, 14s	1862	710 DERBYSHIRE, 8s	1862
		711 CAMBRIDGESHIRE, 10s	1862
697 HAMPSHIRE, Facsimile of the part relating to, 10s	1862	712 WILTSHIRE, 10s	1862
698 —— Extension and translation, 7s 6d	1862	CHESHIRE, including part of Lancashire, was also published, but the issue is now exhausted, and the stones have been destroyed. A liberal price will be given for copies.	
699 WARWICKSHIRE, Facsimile, 8s	1862		
700 SHROPSHIRE, 8s	1862		

For the complete work, in 4 vols. folio—see "RECORD COMMISSION."

Historical Atlas of Ireland:

713 NOWELL (DEAN) Two Ancient Maps of Ireland (ca. 1566) $\frac{1}{1,152,000}$ and $\frac{1}{3,648,000}$, facsimiled from the original MS. in the British Museum, coloured round the margins, *on a single sheet,* 1s 6d   1862

714 —— Copy of portion of an ANCIENT MANUSCRIPT in the British Museum, by Lawrence Nowell, Dean of Lichfield, who died in 1576; *being the text to illustrate the above Maps*, folio *of* 20 *pp. lithographed, sewed*, 1s   1862

Containing an authentic description of Ireland, from the time of Henry II., and giving the princes and chiefs, with details of their troops, resources, etc.

715 VIEW of the SIEGE of ENNISKILLEN, 1592, taken from McGuire by Captain Dowdall, facsimile from the original plan "made and dun by John Thomas, Solder," *a very curious plan on a large sheet, representing an episode of Elizabeth's Wars in Ireland, plain,* 2s 6d; *or coloured*, 11s   1862

716 ATLAS OF ULSTER, executed about the year 1690, in 31 Maps, each on a sheet measuring 28 in. by 22, *plain, an extremely important series of Maps,* 31s 1862
—— the same, VERY CAREFULLY COLOURED, £7. 8s 1862
1. A Generalle description of Ulster; 2. Tyrone; 3. Tyrconnelle; 4 and 5.*Baronie of Knockninnie: 6. Clancally; 7. Ciawley; 8. Maghery Steffanah; 9. Mahhery Boy; 10. Lurgh and Cole Mackernan; 11 and 12. Donganon; 13 and 14. Loghinisholin; 15 and 16. Strabane; 17. Omey; 18. Clogher; 19. Loghtie; 20. Tollagh Garvie; 21. Clanchy; 22. Castle Rahin; 23. Clonmahowne; 24. Tollachconeo; 25. Tollaghaghe; 26. Orier; 27. Fues; 28 and 29 Oneilan; 30. Ardmagh; 31. Toghrany.
These Maps possess much interest, as exhibiting the titles from the Crown of the landed proprietary of the present day in Ulster.

☞ The above Maps and text, bound together in 1 vol. large folio, *half bound, the maps plain*, £2. 16s; or, *the maps coloured*, £9.

717 TRESOR de Numismatique et de Glyptique, ou Recueil général de Médailles, Monnaies, Pierres gravées, Bas-Reliefs, etc. tant anciennes que modernes, gravé d'après le procédé de M. Achille Collas, avec un Texte par C. Lenormant, 253 livraisons complete, in 20 vols. large folio, *with numerous beautiful engravings of Coins, Medals, Gems, Seals, Bas-Reliefs, Busts, Marbles, Arms, Furniture, Bijouterie, and other Ornaments in Metal and Ivory,* (pub. at £67. in parts) *half calf neat*, £20. Paris, 1834-54
A complete Set of one of the most interesting and magnificent Works ever published, now daily becoming scarcer, its importance to the Coin-Collector and Virtuoso rendering it almost indispensable as a Book of Reference. This valuable publication is thus divided:—

I. MONUMENTS ANTIQUES.
1. Numismatique complete des Rois Grecs 1849
2. Iconographie des Empereurs Romains et de leurs Familles 1843
3. Nouvelle Galerie Mythologique 1850
4. Bas-Reliefs du Parthénon et du Temple de Phigalie 1834

II. MONUMENTS DU MOYEN-AGE ET DE L'HISTOIRE MODERNE.
1. Histoire de l'Art monétaire chez les Modernes, ou Choix des Monnaies du Moyen-Age et aux Epoques plus récentes 1846
2. Collection des Médailles coulées et ciselées en Italie aux XIVe et XVe Siècles 1834
3. Choix de Médailles executées en Allemagne aux XVIe et XVIIe Siècles 1834
4. Historique des Médailles des Papes 1839

5. Choix des plus belles Médailles Françaises depuis Charles VII. jusqu'à Louis XVI. 2 vols. in 1 1834-36
6. Sceaux des Rois et Reines d'Angleterre 1835
7. Sceaux des Rois et Reines de France 1834
8. Sceaux des Grands Feudataires de la Couronne de France 1834
9. Sceaux des Communes, Communantés, Evêques, Abbés, et Barons 1837
10. Recueil général de Bas-Reliefs et d'Ornements, ou Mélanges Typoglyphiques, Ivoires, Meubles, Armes, Bijoux, 2 vols. in 1 1836-39

III. MONUMENTS DE L'HISTOIRE CONTEMPORAINE.
1. Médailles de la Revolution Française 1836
2 Collection des Medailles de l'Empire Français et de l'Empereur Napoléon 1840

TURIN ACADEMY:

718 MISCELLANEA philosophico-mathematica Societatis privatæ Taurinensis, 1759-73, 5 vols. *half russia*—MEMOIRES de l'Académie Royale des Sciences de Turin, années 1784-1800, 6 vols. *bds.*—Mémoires de l'Academie des Sciences, Littérature et Beaux-Arts, années 1792-1812, 10 vols. *sewed* ("Science," 5 vols. et "Littérature," 5 vols.)—MEMORIE della Reale Academia delle Scienze di Torino, 1813-35, Vols. 22-39, *sewed*—together 39 vols. 4to. *many plates, rare,* £18. 18s 1759-1836
A very valuable collection, containing most important Mathematical Memoirs, by Lagrange, Plana, Bidone, &c.

719 —— Memorie della Reale Academia delle Scienze di Torino, Serie Seconda, Tomo IX.—XVI. 8 very stout vols. impl. 4to. *many plates, sewed,* £14.
Torino, 1848-57
The Turin Academy was first established in 1759; the title of the Transactions was changed repeatedly till 1814, when an Italian title was adopted. In 1813, a new Series began with volume 22, and from that volume the Transactions have been continued to the present time. The great importance and value of the many excellent Mathematical papers is well known.

720 TWYSDENI (Rogeri) Historiæ Anglicanæ Scriptores X ex vetustis MSS. nunc primum in lucem editi: adjectis variis Lectionibus, Glossario, Indiceque copioso, 2 vols. in 1, folio, FINE PAPER, *vellum or calf*, £4. 10s 1652
A very important collection of Early English Chronicles, viz.:—
I. Simon Dunelmiensis. II. Joannes Prior Hagustaldensis. III. Richardus Prior Hagustaldensis. IV. Ailredus Abbas Rievallensis. V. Radulphus de Diceto. VI. Joannes Brompton. VII. Gervasius Dorobornensis. VIII. Thomas Stubbs. IX. Guil Thorn. X. Henricus Knighton —The learned and ample glossary appended to this admirable collection was prepared by the famous WILLIAM SOMNER. Hearne tells us that even the Puritans themselves, affecting to be *Mæcenases*, with Cromwell at their head, displayed something like a patriotic ardour in purchasing copies of this work as soon as it appeared."—*Dibdin.*
Collation: it has to be stated that there exist no pp. 2297 to 2310.
Priced, 1843, Payne and Foss, vellum, £6. 6s; 1849, Rodd, russia, £6. and £6. 10s; at Col. Stanley's sale a copy fetched £13. 10s.—LARGE PAPER copies were priced, 1829, Thorpe, £14. 14s; 1832, Payne and Foss, £9. 9s

UNITED SERVICE INSTITUTION:

721 JOURNAL of the Royal United Service Institution, 3 vols. in 12 parts, 8vo. valuable articles on Military History, the Rifled Ordnance, etc. *plates and cuts, sd.* 24s
1857-60

722 UNIVERSAL HISTORY, Ancient and Modern: Ancient, 18 vols., Modern, 42; together 60 vols. 8vo. SECOND AND BEST EDITION, *maps and plates, fine copy in the original full calf gilt,* £8. 8s 1779-84
Priced, 1834, J. Bohn, 20*l*.; 1836, Arch, 14*l*. 14s; 1845, Rodwell, 10*l*. 10s; 1846, 9*l*. 9s; 1847 and 1849, 10*l*. 10s.

PUBLICATIONS OF LEARNED SOCIETIES, ETC. 49

669 SMITH'S Dictionary of Greek and Roman Antiquities, stout 8vo. *of 100 pages, illustrated by nearly five hundred engravings on wood, second improved and enlarged edition,* (pub. at £2. 2s) *cloth,* 33s 1859
670 ―― Dictionary of Greek and Roman Antiquities, 2 stout vols. 8vo. (pub. at £4.) *cloth,* £3. 5s 1856-57
671 ―― the above, together 6 vols. 8vo. (pub. at £11. 17s 6d) *new in cloth,* £8. 18s 6d 1856-61
672 ―― the same, 6 vols. 8vo. *new in strong whole morocco, gilt edges,* £12. 5s 1856
These valuable Dictionaries are indispensable to every library.

SMITHSONIAN INSTITUTION:
673 SMITHSONIAN Contributions to Knowledge, 11 vols. impl. 4to. *numerous fine plates, uncut,* £9. 9s
Washington, privately printed for the Smithsonian Institution, 1848-60
Amongst these valuable papers may be mentioned the following:—Squier and Davis, Ancient Monuments of the Mississippi Valley; Agassiz, Classification of Insects from Embryological data; Bailey's Microscopical Observations in South Carolina, Georgia and Florida; Girard, Natural History of the Fresh Water Fishes of North America; Harvey's History of the Marine Algae of North America; Gray, Plantae Wrightianae Texano-Neo-Mexicanae; Rigg's Dictionary of the Dacota language; Leidy, a Flora and Fauna within Living Animals; Torrey, Plantae Fremontiae; Leidy, Ancient Fauna of Nebraska; Lapham, Antiquities of Wisconsin; Haven, Archæology of the United States; Mayer's Observations on Mexican History and Archæology; Bowen's Yoruba Grammar and Dictionary: and several other important contributions, most of them accompanied with accurate illustrations.

SOCIETE DES ANTIQUARIES DE FRANCE.—See MEMOIRES.
SOCIETE DE GEOGRAPHIE:
674 RECUEIL de Voyages et de Memoires, 6 vols. 4to. *bound,* £6.   *Paris,* 1824-40
Contains the Voyages of Marco Paulo, Edrisi, etc. with Vocabularies of African languages, etc.
675 ―― Vol. I.: Voyages de Marco Polo, avec variantes, par Maltebrun, 1824— Vol. II.: Traductions de l'Arabe, Itinéraires, Monumens du pays arrosé par l'Ohio, Antiquités de l'Amerique, 2 parts, *with 18 plates,* 1827—2 vols. 4to. *half morocco, uncut,* 30s   *Paris,* 1824-27
676 ―― Marco Polo, 1 vol. 4to. *calf, rare,* 20s   1824

SOCIETY OF ARTS:
677 TRANSACTIONS, 1846-48, 2 parts, square 8vo. 52 *plates, several of them (Mosaics, specimens of Bookbinding, &c.) coloured and illuminated,* 10s   1847-49

SOCIETY (HISTORICAL) OF SCIENCE:
678 POPULAR Treatises on Science, during the Middle Ages, in Anglo-Saxon, Anglo-Norman, and English, edited by Wright, 8vo. *sd.* 7s 6d   1841

SOMERSETSHIRE ARCHÆOLOGICAL AND NATURAL HISTORY SOCIETY:
679 PROCEEDINGS at the general, quarterly, and annual meetings, held during the years 1849 to 1858, Vols. I—VIII. in 7, 8vo. *numerous plates and etchings, some in colours,* £2. 10s   *Taunton,* 1851-59
A very interesting collection of papers upon the local antiquities and Natural History of Somersetshire. Four of the vols. are half bound calf, three in boards.
680 SOMERS'S TRACTS: a Collection of SCARCE AND VALUABLE TRACTS on the most interesting and entertaining subjects, but chiefly such as relate to the History and Constitution of these Kingdoms, selected from an infinite number in print and manuscript, in the Royal, Cotton, Sion, and other public as well as private libraries, particularly that of the late LORD SOMERS, SECOND AND BEST EDITION, revised, augmented, and arranged by WALTER SCOTT, 13 vols. roy. 4to. (pub. at £42. in bds.) *a beautiful copy in russia extra, marbled edges,* £21.   1809-15
Priced by Payne and Foss, £31. 10s; Bernal's copy, 1855, fetched £21.
"Lord Somers' *Collection of Tracts* is, in truth, a splendid and lasting monument of the judgment and patriotism of that great man. This reprint, under the editorship of Sir Walter Scott, has the advantage of having the pieces arranged chronologically, and according to their subject-matter. The additional pieces are denoted by an asterisk. In no collection of the least historial pretence let these *Tracts* be found wanting."—*Dibdin.*

SPALDING CLUB:
681 PASSAGES from the Diary of General Patrick Gordon, 1635-99, 4to. *portrait, cloth,* 7s 6d   *Aberdeen,* 1859
682 STATISTICAL SOCIETY'S JOURNAL, Vols. XVI. (*wanting pt.* 3) XVII. (*wanting pt.* 3) XVIII. and XX. pt. 1, with general Index to Vols. I.-XV. 12 parts, 8vo. 10s   1853-57

STOCKHOLM ACADEMY:
683 KONGL. VETENSKAPS-Academiens Handlingar, for 1830, 1831, 1832, 1834, 4 vols. 8vo. *plates of Nat. History, uncut,* 10s   1831-34

E

SURTEES' SOCIETY:

684 PUBLICATIONS of the SURTEES SOCIETY, a set from the commencement, 40 vols. 8vo. *all consecutive* (pub. at £32. 5s) *cloth*, £25. 1835-61.
The following will be sold separately, with the allowance usual on new books.

CONTENTS:

1. Reginaldi Libellus de Admirandis Beati Cuthberti Virtutibus, 15s 1835
2. Durham Wills and Inventories, 15s 1835
3. The Towneley Mysteries; or Miracle Plays, 15s 1836
4. Testamenta Eboracensia, Vol. I. 15s 1836
5. Sanctuarium Dunelm. et Beverlac.; or, Registers of the Sanctuaries of Durham and Beverley, 15s 1837
6. The Charters, &c. of the Priory of Finchale, 15s 1837
7. The Catalogues of the Old Monastic Library at Durham, &c. 10s 1838
8. Miscellaneous Biography, the Lives of King Oswald and SS. Cuthbert and Eata, 10s 1838
9. The Three Historians of Durham, Coldingham, Graystanes, and Chambre, &c. 15s 1839
10. The Ritual of the Church of Durham, Latin and Saxon, 15s 1840
11. Jordan Fantosme's Anglo-Norman Chronicle of War between England and Scotland in 1173-4, 15s 1840
12. The Correspondence, Inventories, &c. of the Priory of Coldingham, 15s 1841
13. The Liber Vitæ of the Monastery of Durham, 10s 1841
14. The Correspondence of R. Bowes, Esq. Elizabeth's Ambassador to Scotland, 15s 1842
15. A Description of the Monuments, Rites, and Customs of the Church of Durham prior to the Dissolution, 10s 1842
16. The Anglo-Saxon and Early English Psalter, Vol. I. 15s 1843
17. The Correspondence of Matthew Hutton, Archbishop of York, 15s 1843
18. The Accounts of the Bursar of the Monastery of Durham, from 1530 to 1534, 15s 1844
19. The Anglo-Saxon and Early English Psalter, Vol. II. 15s 1844
20. The Life and Miracles of St. Godric, of Finchale, by Reginald, 15s 1845
21. Depositions, &c. from the Ecclesiastical Court of Durham, 15s 1845
22. Ecclesiastical Pro. of Bp. Barnes, 25s 1850
23. Latin Hymns of the Anglo-Saxon Church, 16s 1851
24. Memoir of Robert Surtees. *Out of print* 1852
25. Boldon Buke, a Survey of the See of Durham, 10s 6d 1852
26. Wills and Inventories from the Archdeaconry of Richmond, 14s 1853
27. Pontifical of Egbert, Archbishop of York, 723-766, 11s 1853
28. Lindisfarne and Rushworth Gospels, 14s 1854
29. Inventories of the Benedictine Houses of Jarrow and Monk Wearmouth, 12s 1854
30. Testamenta Eboracensia, Vol. 2, 25s 1855
31. Obituary Roll of Ebchester and Burnley, 12s 1856
32. Bishop Hatfield's Survey, 15s 1856
33. Rural Economy in Yorkshire in 1641 12s
34. Acts of the High Commission Court of Durham, 14s 1857
35. Fabric Rolls of York Minster, 25s 1858
36. Dugdale's Visitation of Yorke, 1665-66, 30s 1859
37. Miscellanea, 15s 1858
38. Wills and Inventories from the Registry at Durham, part 2, 12s 1860
39. The Lindisfarne and Rushworth Gospels, part 2, 10s 1861
40. Depositions from the Castle of York, relating to Offences in the Northern Counties in the 17th Century, 15s 1861

"Next to the *English Historical* we feel disposed to rank the Surtees, both on account of the liberality of its constitution and the general value of its books. If a portion of these possess only a local interest, we must remember that the society was organised for local purposes, and with a restricted sphere of action; and we are willing to connive at a few 'Wills,' 'Inventories,' and similar dry bones of ancient literature, in consideration of the sterling value of other publications. Not to dwell upon Reginald's account of St. Cuthbert, the collection of Durham historians, and other works, the importance of which is obvious at once, we could specify the Towneley Mysteries, the Durham Ritual, and the Anglo-Saxon and Northumbrian Psalters, as monuments, each unique in its kind, and furnishing materials for the elucidation of our northern dialects, both of the Saxon and mediæval period, which it would be vain to search for elsewhere. Even the 'Liber Vitæ,' or list of benefactors to the shrine of St. Cuthbert, possesses an interest far beyond what might have been expected from a mere catalogue of names. The initiated may there distinctly trace the changes of the original stock of Northern Angles, caused by successive infusions of Scandinavian, West Saxon, and Norman blood, till all become blended in that current of English nomenclature, which to this very day bears the plain impress of all."—*Garnett's Essays*, p. 116.

685 TANNER'S (Bp.) NOTITIA MONASTICA: or an Account of all Abbies, Priories, and Houses of Friers, formerly in England and Wales; and also of all the Colleges and Hospitals founded before 1540; a new edition with many additions, by J. NASMITH, folio, *portrait by Vertue, and plates of Arms, very neat in old calf*, £5. 10s *Cambridge*, 1787

BEST EDITION of this valuable and useful book.

In addition to the separate Index of each vol. Vol. 56 contains a General Index to the entire modern part; and Vols. 57-60 are supplementary, containing the history of the British isles.
"Consult the volumes of the Universal History, where you will find, either in the text or references, every historical information which can well be required."—*Prof. Smyth's Lectures on Modern History.*
"A library in itself, and an honour to the British press."—*Hale's Chronology.*

UPSALA ACADEMY:
723 NOVA ACTA Regiae Societatis Scientiarum Upsaliensis, Series III. Vols. I. II. 4to. *plates, sd.* 36s   *Upsal.* 1855-58

UTRECHT ACADEMY:
724 ANNALES ACADEMIÆ RHENO TRAJECTINÆ, 1816-1837, and Supplement to 1815-16, together 22 vols. 8vo. *sewed, uncut,* 27s   *Trajecti ad Rhenum,* 1818-37
725 VALLANCEY (Col. Charles) Collectanea de Rebus Hibernicis: Essays, &c. (chiefly from original MSS.) on the History and Antiquities of Ireland, Vols. I.—V., wanting No. 11 in Vol. II. 8vo. *portrait and plates,* 36s   1770-1804

These volumes are of great literary merit, and much sought after, in spite of Mr. Petrie's opinion, who says: "It is a difficult and rather unpleasant task to follow a writer so rambling in his reasonings, and so obscure in his style; his hypotheses are of a visionary nature." Mr. Petrie's account of the Round Towers differs materially from that given by Vallancey in his sixth volume. Vallancey advocates a similar view to that of O'Brien. Altogether the collection is well worth the attention of every Celtic and Irish Scholar.

726 VAPEREAU, Dictionnaire universel des CONTEMPORAINS, contenant toutes les personnes notables de la France et des pays étrangers, *complete,* A—Z, stout royal 8vo. 1802 pp. *half green morocco,* 21s   *Paris,* 1858

WARTON CLUB:
727 HISTORY of Fulk Fitz Warine, an outlawed Baron in the Reign of King John, by Wright, *Old French and English,* sm. 8vo. *sd.* 7s 6d   1855
728 LATIN Themes of Mary Queen of Scots, edited from her own MS. by A. de Montaiglon, sm. 8vo. *sd.* 5s   1855
729 VESTPHALEN (J.) MONUMENTA INEDITA Rerum Germanicarum praecipue Cimbricarum et Megapolensium, quibus varia Antiquitatum, Historiarum, Legum Juriumque Germaniæ, Holsatiae, etc. argumenta illustrantur, 4 vols. thick folio, *illustrated with numerous curious plates of Idols, Inscriptions, Monuments, Costumes, Arms, Portraits, &c. a good copy, half bound, uncut,* 36s; or *vellum,* £3.   *Lips.* 1739-45

WELSH MANUSCRIPT SOCIETY:
730 LIBER LANDAVENSIS, Llyfr Teilo, or Ancient Register of the Cathedral Church of Llandaff, in Latin, with English Translation and Notes, by Rev. W. J. Rees, roy. 8vo. *facsimiles, cloth, scarce,* 35s   *Llandovery,* 1840
731 IOLO MANUSCRIPTS. A Selection of ancient Welsh Manuscripts in Prose and Verse, from the Collection made by E. Williams, Iolo Morganwg, with English Translations and Notes by his Son Taliesin Williams ab Iolo, roy. 8vo. *plate, cloth,* 30s   *Llandovery,* 1848
732 HERALDIC VISITATIONS of Wales and its Marches, temp. Elizabeth and James I., edited by the late Sir Samuel Rush Meyrick, 2 vols. impl. 4to. *cloth,* £10.

Only 240 copies of this work were printed, which were all engaged by subscribers; it is therefore out of print and extremely scarce.

733 REES (W. J.) Lives of the CAMBRO-BRITISH SAINTS of the Fifth and immediate succeeding Centuries, royal 8vo. *frontispiece and facsimiles, cloth,* 27s   *Llandovery, Welsh MS. Soc.* 1853
734 DOSPARTH EDEYRN DAVOD AUR: ANCIENT WELSH GRAMMAR, compiled in the 13th Century by Edeyrn the Golden-tongued; with y Pum Llyfr Kerddwriaeth or Rules of Welsh Poetry, and translation and notes by the Rev. J. Williams Ab Ithel, 8vo. *(price to non-members £2. 2s) cl.* 25s   *Llandovery,* 1856
735 MEDDYGON MYDDFAI, MEDICAL PRACTICE of Rhiwallon and his Sons; with the Llyn-y-Fan, or Legend of the Lady of the Lake; edited by Williams Ab Ithel, with notes and translations by John Pughe, 8vo. *cloth,* 16s   1862
736 WILSON'S Historical, traditionary, and imaginative Tales of the Borders and of Scotland, 6 vols. 4to. *pictures of life on the Borders and in the North of England, one of the most interesting periodicals ever published, and a fitting companion to the works of Scott and Hogg, cloth,* £2. 16s   *Edinburgh,* 1835-40
737 ZEITSCHRIFT für die KUNDE des MORGENLANDES, herausgegeben von Ewald, Gabelentz, Kosegarten, Lassen, Neumann, Rödiger, und Rückert, vols. I.-VII. 8vo. *sd.* £2. 16s; or, *calf gilt,* £4.   *Göttingen u. Bonn.* 1837-50
738 ZEITSCHRIFT der DEUTSCHEN MORGENLÄNDISCHEN GESELLSCHAFT, Vols. I.—XIII.; Register zu I.—X, and Jahresberichte 1845 and 1846; 8vo. Vols. I.—XII. *calf gilt, the remainder in 5 parts, sd.* £6. 15s   *Leipzig,* 1847-59

Both from Professor Wilson's library.

739 —— the same, Vol. I. —X, pt. 4, 8vo. *facsimiles, sd.* £6.   *Leipzig,* 1848-56

740 ZOOLOGICAL JOURNAL, conducted by Bell, the Sowerbys, &c. parts II. to XIX. *wanting Nos.* 10 *and* 14, 73 *plates, some* COLOURED, 1824-31—Supplementary Plates, parts I. and III. 23 *plates, some* COLOURED, 1825-40, together 18 parts, 8vo. (pub. at £9. 19s) *sd.* 36s   1824-31

ZOOLOGICAL SOCIETY OF LONDON:

741 PROCEEDINGS of the COMMITTEE of Science and Correspondence of the Zoological Society of London, 1830-31, 2 vols. 8vo. (pub. at 12s) *cl. rare*, 10s 1832

742 PROCEEDINGS of the ZOOLOGICAL SOCIETY of London, 28 vols. 8vo. (pub. each at 6s, making £8. 8s) *cloth*, £6. 10s   1833-60

743 PROCEEDINGS of the ZOOLOGICAL SOCIETY of London, WITH ILLUSTRATIONS, from the commencement, 13 vols. 8vo. COMPLETE, *with* 442 COLOURED PLATES, (pub. at £20. 4s) *cloth, uncut*, £16. 16s   1848-60

744 TRANSACTIONS of the ZOOLOGICAL SOCIETY of London, 3 vols. and of Vol. IV. 6 parts, impl. 4to. *many* COLOURED *plates of Mammals, Birds, Fish, Insects, &c.* (pub. at £20: 13s) £15. 15s   1835-60

The above valuable work consists of contributions from the most eminent naturalists, among whom may be mentioned Yarrell, Bennett, Hope, Owen, Gould, Curtis, Rüppell, Bell, Cuvier, etc.

Contents of the set:			£. s. d.	Contents of the set:			£. s. d.
Vol. I., containing 59 Plates		.	4 18 0	Vol. IV., Part 3, containing 5 Plates			0 8 0
Vol. II.,	71	„ .	5 6 6	„ 4,	„	12 „	1 4 0
Vol. III.,	73	„ .	4 11 0	„ 5,	„	11 „	1 4 0
Vol. IV., Part 1.	8	„ .	0 12 6	„ 6,	„	10 „	1 4 0
„ 2.	17	„ .	1 5 0	Sets completed at a reasonable reduction.			

745 ZOOLOGICAL Society's Gardens and Menagerie delineated, Vol. I. Quadrupeds, Vol. II. Birds, 2 vols. *fine woodcuts, cloth*, 1831—TOWER MENAGERIE, or Natural History of the Animals contained in that Establishment, with Anecdotes, 1 vol. *woodcuts by Harvey, half morocco*, 1829—together, 3 vols. 8vo. 20s   1829-31

746 ZOOLOGIST (The), A Popular Monthly Magazine of Natural History, 1854 March, to 1856 January, 1858 November to March 1859, 1860 January to November, in 39 Nos. 8vo. *sd.* 20s   1854-60

DIRECTORIES, CALENDARS, PEERAGES.

The introduction of this Class is an entirely new feature in Booksellers' Catalogues. Gentlemen engaged upon statistical or historical Researches are constantly enquiring after such supposed "useless" volumes in Public Libraries, and miss them there to their regret.

747 ALMANACH de GOTHA, 1829-59—Gräfliches und Freiherrliches Taschenbuch, 1842-61—16mo. *various volumes, portraits and plates, to be sold separately*

748 ARMY LIST, published by the War Office, containing a List of the Officers of the Army and Royal Marines, from 1781 to 1853, (wanting 1783, 1785-89, 91-93, 1802, 4, 5, 7, and 1827)—together 58 vols. 8vo. *morocco, calf, and half calf, a valuable Military Directory for upwards of seventy years*, £5.   1781-1853

749 BANK OF ENGLAND. Names and Descriptions of the Proprietors of unclaimed Stock, 1780-90, 8vo. *bd. uncut, rare*, 12s   1791

750 BANKRUPT REGISTER, The Merchant and Traders Magazine, and Perry's Bankrupt and Insolvent Gazette, from January 1826 to December, 1855, with Indexes to each volume, 30 vols. 12mo. *half bd.* £5. 15s   1826-55

751 CAMBRIDGE UNIVERSITY CALENDAR for 1801, 1831-36, 1839, 41, 45 and 1854, together 11 vols. 12mo. (*pub at about 6s a volume*) 25s   Cambridge, 1801-54

752 CANADA Directory for 1857-58, containing names of the principal inhabitants in the Cities, Towns, and Villages, etc. stout roy. 8vo. *large folding Map*, 1544 pp. *double columns, cloth*, 10s   Montreal, 1858

754 CEYLON Calendar and Almanac, and Compendium of useful information, for 1837, 1841, 1843-47, 7 vols. 8vo. *map, with lists of Native Headmen and Kandyan Chiefs, Tables of Roads, etc. bound, scarce*, 35s   Colombo, 1837-47

755 CLERGY LIST, from 1842 to 1859, (wanting 1857-58) 16 vols. 8vo. (pub. at £7. 10s) *cloth*, 32s   1842-59

756 COURT GUIDES. BOYLE'S, for 1812 to 1858—ROBSON'S, for 1836 to 1843—at 1s each

757 DIETRICHSEN and HANNAY's Almanack, Book of General Information, etc. for 1841, 1847, 1849-61, 15 Nos. 8vo. 7s 6d   1841-61

758 DUBLIN DIRECTORY, for 1824, 1833, 1836, 1837, 1839, 1841-55, together 20 vols. 12mo. and 8vo. *not all of uniform publication, bd.* 36s   Dublin, 1824-55

759 EAST INDIA REGISTER and Army List, containing complete lists of the Company's servants, civil, military, and marine, with their appointments, com-

piled by Mason and Owen, and Clark, from 1795 to 1858 inclusive (wanting 1796-97, 1800-3, 1807, 15, 17-18)—together 89 vols. 12mo. *including variations issued in the same years, morocco,* £6. 1795-1858

760 —— another set, 1821-54 (wanting 1825, 35, 38, 51-53) together 36 vols. *including variations,* 12mo. *morocco,* 18s 1821-54

761 ELWICK's BANKRUPT Directory, from 1820 to 1843, alphabetically arranged, in 1 vol. 8vo. *cloth,* 7s 6d 1843

762 HAMBURGISCHES und ALTONAISCHES Adressbücher für 1855, 2 vols. in 1, roy. 8vo. *cloth,* 5s *Hamb. und Alt.* 1855

763 **INDIA.** PRINSEP's General Register of the BENGAL Establishment, 1790-1842, with a list of the Governors General, by Ramchunder Doss, large 8vo. *half calf,* 10s *Calcutta,* 1844

764 BENGAL and CALCUTTA Directory for 1809, 1812, 1815, 1827, 1829, 1837, 1839, 1845, 8 vols. 8vo. *wormed and injured, a few pages wanting,* 10s *Calcutta,* 1809-45

765 DODWELL and MILES, Alphabetical List of the MADRAS Civil Servants, 1780-1839, with lists of Governors General and East India Directors, royal 8vo. (pub. at 31s 6d) *cloth,* 7s 6d 1839

766 —— List of Bombay Civil Servants, 1780-1839—List of Madras Civil Servants, 1780-1839—List of Bengal Civil Servants, 1780-1838—together 3 vols. imp. 8vo. (pub. at £6. 6s) *cloth,* 20s 1839

767 —— Alphabetical List of the Officers and Medical Officers of the Indian Army, 1760-1837, and 1764-1838, 2 vols. royal 8vo. (pub. at £2. 17s) *cloth,* 25s 1838-39

768 —— List of the Officers of the Madras Army from 1760 to 1837, royal 8vo. *cloth,* 3s 6d 1838

769 LAW LIST. Clarke's New Law List for 1809, 14, 16, 18, 21, 26-40 (wanting 1838), 19 vols.; Stevens and Norton's Law List, 1841-57 (wanting 1856) 16 vols. —together 35 vols. 12mo. *bd.* £2. 1809-57

770 LIVERPOOL Directory for 1790, by Gore, 12mo. *hf. bd. rare,* 12s *Liverp.* 1790
The population of Liverpool at that time is stated at 55,000.

771 LONDON DIRECTORIES for 1760, 63 (*with map*), 1765, 68, 79, 80, 84, 88, 90, 1800, 1802, 1805-7, 10, 17-19, 1824-29, 31-36, 39-56; together 46 vols. 12mo. and large 8vo. *not all uniform publications,* £5. 1760-1856

772 LONDON and PROVINCIAL MEDICAL DIRECTORY, for 1846-56, 11 vols. 12mo. *containing a vast quantity of information,* (pub. at about £4. 10s) *cl.* 15s 1847-56

773 PHILADELPHIA Directory and Register for 1820, by Whitely, 12mo. *bd. scarce,* 10s *Philadelphia,* 1820

774 ROYAL KALENDAR and RIDER's BRITISH MERLIN, for 1762, 1774, 1775, 1788, 1789, 1792-1801, 1806, 1809-17, 1819-35, 1837-48, 1850, 53, 55, 56; together 66 vols. 12mo. *including many variations, corrected to later dates in various years, and several synchronical volumes of the* IMPERIAL KALENDAR, *morocco,* £4. 10s 1762-1856

Most of the volumes have bound up with them, the "Companion," and the Index, and a few are accompanied by the East India Calendar, and by Ridgway's Peerage, with plates of the Heraldic bearings.

775 SOUTH SEA HOUSE. List of Proprietors of Annuities, transferable in 1837, and unpaid in 1842, 8vo. *bds.* 10s 1842
Inserted at the end is a List of "Proprietors of unclaimed dividends of East India Stock, 1823."

776 WASHINGTON. National Calendar, and Annals of the UNITED STATES, from the beginning in 1820 to 1836, by Force, 15 vols. 12mo. *no volumes were published for* 1825, 6, 7), *bound, rare,* £2. 16s *Washington,* 1820-36

777 WALFORD'S County Families of the United Kingdom, or royal manual of the Titled and Untitled Aristocracy, with notices of descent, birth, marriage, education, appointments, etc. stout 8vo. *hf. morocco gilt,* 21s 1860

RELIGIOUS WORSHIPS, PHILOSOPHICAL SECTS, SECRET ASSOCIATIONS, ETC.

778 BRUCKERI (Jac.) Historia critica Philosophiæ, a mundi incunabulis ad nostram usque ætatem, 6 vols. 4to. *sized paper, portrait, vellum,* £2. 2s *Lipsiæ,* 1742-67
Still the standard book for the best view of all the ancient systems of philosophy of the East and West, and descending also to Bacon, Hobbes, Descartes, and the moderns
Priced, 1839, Thorpe, £3. 13s 6d; 1844, £3. 3s; 1844, Longman, £2. 18s; 1847, £3. 3s; 1848, Payne and Foss, £5. 5s.

779 BUHLE (John Gottl.) Lehrbuch der Geschichte der Philosophie, und einer kritischen Literatur derselben, 9 vols. 12mo. *cloth,* 10s 6d *Gottingen,* 1796-1804

780 CREUZER, Religions de l'Antiquité, par Guigniaut, 8 vols. 8vo. *many plates, uncut*, £2.   *Paris*, 1825-41
    The above imperfect set consists of Tome I. 1, Planches I., Tome I. 2, Tome II. 1, II. 2, première Section, III. 1, III. 2, première Section, Planches et Explications, III.—in all 8 vols.
781 DEL RIO (Martini) Disquisitiones Magicæ, superstitionum confutatio, stout sm. 4to. *engraved emblematic frontispiece, curious, stamped binding*, 10s 6d Colon. 1679
782 DESCARTES, Œuvres, publiées par V. Cousin, 11 vols. 8vo. *plates, half calf*, £3. 16s   *Paris*, 1824-26
783 DRUMMOND'S (Sir W.) Origines, or Remarks on the Origin of several Empires, States, and Cities, 4 vols. 8vo. *cloth*, 32s ; *calf gilt*, £2. 2s   1824-29
    In this valuable work, the successful endeavour of the author is to throw light upon the dark and earlier annals of ancient nations, and to dispel the mists of fable and tradition through which the events and characters of former time loom in exaggerated distortion before the eyes of the present.
784 DUPUIS, Origine de tous les Cultes, ou Religion universelle, avec sa vie par Auguis, 7 vols. 8vo. with 4to Atlas *of* 24 *curious plates, comprising the Symbols of the Ancient Religions, calf neat*, 36s   *Paris*, 1822
    An Atheistical work, which resolves the system of our belief into zodiacal symbols.
    Dupuis collected every passage which could make the resemblance of Christianity and the Oriental religious systems more marked, and concluded that Christianity was only an emanation of the philosophical school which had flourished in the East long before its divine founder appeared.
785 FABER'S ORIGIN of Pagan Idolatry, ascertained from historical testimony and circumstantial evidence, 3 vols. 4to. £6. 6s   1816
    This rare and important work represents all the religious Systems of Antiquity.
786 HEGEL (G. W. F.) Werke, vollständige Ausgabe durch ein Verein von Freunden des Verewigten Marheineke, Schulze, etc. 18 vols. in 10, 8vo. *hf. morocco*, £5. 10s   Priced, 1850, £8.   *Berlin*, 1832-40
787 KANT'S (Immanuel) Werke, sorgfältig revidirte Gesammtausgabe, mit Vorrede von Hartenstein, nebst einer sammlung von Briefen und öffentlichen Erklärungen und einem chronologischen Verzeichnisse Schriften Kant's, 10 vols. 8vo. *portrait and facsimile, fine copy, half calf*, £2.   *Leip*. 1838-9
788 MACKAY (Charles) Memoirs of Extraordinary Popular Delusions, 3 vols. 8vo. (pub. at £2. 12s 6d) *portraits, hf. calf neat*, 27s   1841
789 (MARTIN) Explication de divers Monumens singuliers, qui ont rapport à la Religion des plus anciens peuples, sm. 4to. *plates, hf. bd.* 15s   *Paris*, 1739
    A learned work, treating on the Zend, Druidic, and other religions as well as those of Egypt, Greece, and Rome, with descriptions of talismans and other singular relics.
790 MAURY (Alfred) Essai sur les Légendes Pieuses du Moyen-Age, 1843—Hallucinations Hypnagogiques—Recherches sur la Religion et Culte des populations primitives de la Grèce, 1855—in 1 vol. 8vo. *hf. bd.* 6s 6d   *ib.* 1843-55
791 ———— Histoire des Religions de la Grèce Antique, 3 vols. 8vo. *cloth, uncut*, 20s   *ib.* 1857-59
792 ———— la Magie et l'Astrologie dans l'Antiquité, et du Moyen Age, les Superstitions Païennes qui se sont perpétuées jusqu'à nos jours, 8vo. *sd. new*, 7s *ib.* 1860
793 MONBODDO (Lord) Antient Metaphysics, or the Science of Universals, with an appendix examining the principles of Sir Isaac Newton's philosophy, 6 vols. in 3. 4to. *fine copy in russia ext. from Miss Currer's library*, 35s   *Edinb*. 1779-99
    Priced, 1839, Longman, £3. 3s; fetched, 1860, Sotheby's, £2. 10s.
    Fine copy of a celebrated work by the creator of a vast and astonishing, though paradoxical system, which won from Herder the highest testimony to the genius of Lord Monboddo. Endowed with wonderful learning and talent, he yet holds such opinions as that of considering the ourang-outang a degraded form of the human species, a belief in the existence of syrens, etc. He maintained that all imaginable objects, however odd or monstrous, had their archetypes in nature; an assertion to which Johnson retorted that he believed it, since nature had produced a Monboddo.
794 MONTFAUCON, L'ANTIQUITÉ EXPLIQUÉE et représentée en figures 1719, 10 vols.—SUPPLÉMENT au livre de l'Antiquité expliquée, 5 vols. 1734— together 15 vols. folio, LARGE PAPER, *with upwards of* 900 *plates, comprising many thousand engravings of all the Roman, Greek, Egyptian, Arabic, Syriac, Spanish, and Gaulish Antiquities, illustrating chiefly the Public and Private Life of the* GREEKS *and* ROMANS, *their* RELIGIOUS WORSHIP, *Wars, Arts, etc. fine copy in old calf gilt*, £10. 10s   *Paris*, 1719-34
    A work still unsurpassed in utility: of great importance to Classical Scholars and Artists.
795 O'BRIEN (Henry) on the Round Towers of Ireland, or the Mysteries of Freemasonry, of Sabaism, and of Budhism unveiled, 8vo. *cuts, cloth, clean copy*, 36s   1834
    Very rare. "In O'Brien's work on the Round Towers of Ireland may be found much curious matter; and a good deal of light is thrown on the Horrors of Serpent or Boodhist Worship. It is, however, a wild and irreverent book, and by no means to be recommended to the general reader, independently of the nature of its details."
    "Proofs drawn from every possible branch of human learning."—*Spectator*.
796 O'BRIEN's Phœnician Ireland, translated from the Latin of J. L. Villanueva, with introduction, 8vo. *map and facsimiles, cloth*, 6s   1833

RELIGIOUS WORSHIPS, PHILOSOPHICAL SECTS, ETC. 57

797 ROLLE, Recherche sur le Culte de Bacchus, 3 vols. 8vo. *sd.* 18*s* Paris, 1824
798 SAINTE-CROIX, Recherches sur les Mysterès du Paganisme, secondé edition, par De Sacy—VILLOISON de Veterum Mysteriis; 2 vols. 8vo. *plates, vellum, a curious work*, 15*s* *ib.* 1817
799 SAINTINE, la Mythologie du Rhin, roy. 8vo. *with a profusion of bold and singular woodcut illustrations by* DORE, *hf. calf neat, gilt top, uncut*, 20*s* Paris, 1862
  A curious work, partaking of the grand and the grotesque; and in which the superstitions of the Rhine are traced back to the Scandinavian and the Sanscrit mythologies, as well as touching on the Celtic religious traditions, and the romantic legends of the middle ages.
800 SALVERTE, des Sciences Occultes, ou essai sur la Magie, les Prodiges et les Miracles, 2 vols. 8vo. *half calf*, 14*s* 1829
801 TOLAND's Theological and Philological Works, (with his Life), 7 parts in 1 vol. 8vo. *calf*, 5*s* 1718-32
802 —— Collection of several pieces, with Memoirs, 2 vols. in 1, 8vo. *calf*, 5*s* 1726
  Vol. I. contains "The History of the Druids," with comparative Vocabulary. Toland's infidel writings are curious.
803 **BRAHMINICAL:** COLEBROOKE'S (H. T.) Miscellaneous Essays, 2 vols. 8vo. BEST EDITION, *numerous facsimiles from early Indian MSS. and Inscriptions, rare*, £3. 3*s* 1837
804 —— the same, new edition of all the important Vedantic papers, 8vo. *cloth*, (pub. at 10*s* 6*d*) 9*s* 1858
  A rich assemblage of materials for the History and explanation of the Vedas.
805 COLEMAN'S (C.) MYTHOLOGY of the Hindus, 4to. *with* 39 *plates, illustrative of the principal Hindu Deities, cloth, rare*, £2. 12*s* 6*d* 1832
806 MAURICE'S Indian Antiquities, 7 vols. 8vo. *numerous plates, chiefly illustrative of the Ancient Worships of India, calf*, 25*s*; *or calf gilt*, 36*s* 1800
  A very curious work, containing Dissertations relative to the ancient Geographical divisions, the pure system of primeval theology, the grand Code of civil laws, the original code of Government, the widely-extended commerce, and the various and profound literature, of Hindostan: compared throughout with the religion, laws, government, and literature of Persia, Egypt, and Greece, the whole intended as introductory to the history of Hindostan, upon a comprehensive scale.
807 MOOR'S (E.) HINDU PANTHEON, royal 4to. 451 *pages of text, and* 105 *plates, in outline, of Hindoo Deities, hf. calf*, £5. 5*s* 1810
  A valuable work, now scarce. Priced, 1847, Allen, £7. 7*s*; Klaproth's copy fetched 158 fr.
808 —— Plates illustrating the HINDU PANTHEON, edited with brief DESCRIPTIVE INDEX, by the Rev. A. P. Moor, royal 4to. 104 *plates, with short descriptions, cloth, gilt edges*, 30*s* 1861
  Before this reprint of the Plates, the old edition could not be procured under six guineas. These plates form a valuable pictorial companion to Wilson's Vishu Purana, the Rig-Veda, and other Mythological works of India.
309 MOOR's Oriental Fragments, post 8vo. *plates of Coins, Seals, etc. cloth*, 4*s* 1834
  Includes: SANSCRIT NAMES in Ireland, Greece, Africa, America, New Zealand: articles on Comparative Mythology, etc.
310 MÜLLER'S (Max) History of the Ancient Sanscrit Literature so far as it illustrates the primitive religion of the Brahmans, 8vo. *cloth*, 18*s* 1859
811 WARD'S (Rev. W.) View of the History, Literature and Religion of the HINDOOS: including a minute description of their Manners and Customs, and translations from their principal works, 4 vols. 8vo. *calf gilt*, 32*s* 1817-20
812 —— The same, 3 vols. 8vo. *bds.* 27*s* 1822
813 WILSON'S (H. H.) WORKS, Vols. I. II., Essays and Lectures chiefly on the Religion of the Hindoos, collected and edited by Dr. R. ROST, 2 vols. 8vo. *all yet published (at* 21*s) new in cloth*, 18*s* 1862
814 DUPERRON (Anquetil) OUPNEK'HAT, *i. e.* Secretum tagendum: Opus ipsa in India rarissimum, continens antiquam et arcanam Doctrinam e quatuor sacris Indorum Libris, RAK BEID, DJEDJR BEID, SAM BEID, ATHRBAN BEID, e Persico in Latinum conversum et notis illustratum, 2 vols. 4to. *half russia*, 25*s*; *or calf gilt*, 30*s* Argent, 1801-2
815 RAMMOHUN ROY'S Translation of the principal Books, Passages and Texts of the Veds, 8vo. *cloth*, 10*s* 1832
816 —— the same, 8vo. *Italian vellum extra*, 12*s* 1832
  With this latter copy are bound up Cicero on the Nature of the Gods, translated by Francklin, and Outram on Sacrifices, translated by Allen.
817 RIG-VEDA-SANHITA. A Collection of Ancient Hindu Hymns, constituting the first Ashtaka, or Book of the Rig-Veda, translated from the Sanskrit by H. H. WILSON, Vols. I. II. III. 8vo. *cloth*, £2. 10*s* 1850-57
  The first volume is entirely OUT OF PRINT.
818 RIG-VEDA-SANHITA, Sanskritè et Latine, edidit Rosen, 4to. *cloth*, 18*s* 1837
819 RIGVEDA, ou libre des Hymnes, traduit du Sanscrit, par M. LANGLOIS, Vols. 3 and 4, 8vo. 15*s* Paris, 1850-51
820 SAMA VEDA. Translation of the Sanhita of the Sama Veda by Stevenson, 8vo. *bds. uncut*, 6*s* 6*d* 1842

821 VISHNU PURANA, a system of HINDU MYTHOLOGY and tradition, translated from the original Sanscrit, and illustrated by notes derived chiefly from other Puránas, by H. H. WILSON, 4to. xcii and 704 pp. *cl. rare*, £2. 2s 1840
Published by the Oriental Translation Fund, but now completely out of print. The "Vishnu Purana" embodies the real doctrine of the INDIAN SCRIPTURE, the "Unity of the Deity."

822 **BUDDHISM:** CUNNINGHAM'S (A.) Bhilsa Topes; or Buddhist Monuments of Central India, comprising a sketch of the History of Buddhism, 8vo. *plates* (pub. at 30s), *half calf gilt*, 25s 1854

823 FOE KOUE KI, ou relation des royaumes Bouddhiques, traduit du Chinois et commenté par Remusat, revu par Klaproth et Landresse, impl. 4to. *sd.* 12s
Paris, 1836

824 FORBES (Major) Eleven Years in Ceylon, its history and antiquities, 2 vols. 8vo. 15 *plates and cuts* (pub. at 21s) *cloth*, 8s 6d 1843
Containing much matter relative to the Buddist and Brahminical religions.

825 HODGSON'S (B. H.) Illustrations of the Literature and Relation of the BUDDHISTS, 8vo. *plates of facsimiles, Inscriptions, etc. cloth*, 12s *Serampore*, 1841

826 MAHAWANSO, the first Twenty Chapters, in Roman characters, by TURNOUR, with translation and prefatory Essay on Pali Buddhistical Literature, 8vo. *bds. uncut*, 7s 6d *Ceylon*, 1836

827 MAHAWANSO, in Roman Characters, with the translation subjoined, and an Essay on Páli Buddhistical Literature by TURNOUR, Vol. 1 (*all published*), 4to. *bds.* 18s *Ceylon*, 1837

828 MAHAWANSI, Raja-Ratnácari and Raja-Vali, forming the Sacred and Historical Books of Ceylon, with a collection of Tracts illustrative of Buddhism, translated from the Singhalese by Upham, 3 vols. 8vo. (pub. at £2. 2s) *bds.* 12s 1833

829 ——— Another copy, 3 vols. *hf. calf gilt*, 21s 1833

830 SAINT HILIARE, du Bouddhisme, 8vo. *cloth, uncut*, 4s *Paris*, 1855

831 TYTLER'S Inquiry into the origin and principles of Budaic Sabism, 4to. 4 *Mythological plates, hf. calf, rare*, 25s *Calcutta*, 1817

832 **CABIRISM:** FABER'S Mysteries of the CABIRI, or the Great Gods of Phenicia, Samothrace, Egypt, Troas, Greece, Italy and Crete, 2 vols. 8vo. *bds. uncut*, 16s *Oxford*, 1803

833 PICTET, du Culte des Cabires chez les anciens Irlandais, 8vo. *half calf neat, gilt top, uncut, rare*, 9s *Génève*, 1824
A work of deep learning, illustrated from the heathen Mythology of ancient Ireland.

834 **CONFUCIAN PHILOSOPHY:** CONFUCIUS Sinarum Philosophus sive Scientia Sinensis, Latine, a Couplet aliisque, cum Tabulâ Chronologicâ ab anno A. C. 2952 ad 1683 P. C. 2 vols. in 1, folio, *old calf*, 10s *Paris*, 1686-87

835 ABRÉGÉ HISTORIQUE des principaux traits de la vie de Confucius, small folio, 24 *plates by Helman after Chinese drawings, with engraved text, calf*, 7s 6d
Paris, ca. 1788

836 CHOU-KING, un des livres sacrés des Chinois, recueilli par Confucius, traduit par Gaubil, avec des notes par De Guignes et notice de l'Y-King, 4to. *plates, old calf gilt*, 18s *Paris*, 1770

837 ——— CONFUCII Chi-King, sive liber Carminum, Latine, à Lacharme et MOHL, 8vo. *bds. uncut*, 5s *Stuttgart*, 1830

838 Y-KING, antiquissimus Sinarum liber, ex Latina interpretatione Regis aliorumque, edidit MOHL, 2 vols. sm. 8vo. *plates, sd. uncut*, 10s *Stuttg.* 1834-39

839 LI KI, ou Mémorial des Rites. Chinois et Français, traduit pour la première fois, et accompagné de notes et commentaires, par CALLERY, large 4to. *bds.* 24s
Turin, 1853

840 LIVRES CLASSIQUES de l'Empire de la Chine, en Français, recueillis par Noel, 7 vols. 16mo. *sd. uncut*, 10s *Paris*, 1784-86

841 MENG TSEU vel Mencium inter Sinenses philosophos Confucio proximum, Sinice et Latine, edidit Julien, cum notis, etc. 3 vols. in 2, large 8vo. *Fine Paper, sd. uncut*, 21s *Lut. Paris*, 1824-29

842 PAUTHIER, Confucius et Mencius, les quatre livres de la Chine, traduits par Pauthier, 12mo. *bds.* 2s 6d *Paris*, 1841

843 **CULDEES:** JAMIESON (Dr. John) Historical Account of the ANCIENT CULDEES of Iona, and of their Settlements in Scotland, England, and Ireland, 4to. *frontispiece, half russia, rare*, £2. 16s *Edinb.* 1811

844 **DRUIDS:** DAVIES' Celtic Researches, on the Origin, Traditions, and Languages of the Ancient Britons; with Introductory Sketches on Primitive Society, royal 8vo. *bds.* 10s 1804

845 ——— Mythology and Rites of the British Druids, ascertained by national docu-

RELIGIOUS WORSHIPS, PHILOSOPHICAL SECTS, ETC. 59

ments, with an appendix of ancient poems and extracts, and remarks on Ancient British coins, royal 8vo. *half calf neat*, 10s   1809
"Davies, of Olverton, whose Celtic Researches and Mythology of the Druids are full of that curious information which is preserved nowhere but in the Welsh remains."—SOUTHEY, *Qy. Review*, v. 59, p. 254.

846 SACHEVERELL's Account of the Isle of Man, its inhabitants, Language, etc. with a Voyage to I-Columb-Kill, an account of the ancient Druids, etc. 12mo. *calf neat*, 7s   1702

847 STACKHOUSE'S Copies of Drawings illustrative of a course of lectures on the Architectural and other remains of Britain, Part I.; Ancient or Pagan Britain, 2 nos. in 1 vol. 4to. *40 plates of Stone Pillars, Cromlechs, Circles, Tumuli, etc. half calf, rare*, 20s   ca. 1820

848 STUKELEY (Dr. W.) Itinerarium Curiosum : or an account of the Antiquitys and remarkable Curiositys in Nature or Art, observ'd in Travels thro' Great Britain, folio, FIRST EDITION, *with 100 plates of English celebrated ancient Sites; Roman and Celtic Remains and Ruins, etc. fine copy in russia, gilt*, £2. 16s 1724
A facsimile reprint edition appeared about 1810.

849 —— the same, 1724—STONEHENGE, a Temple restor'd to the British Druids, *portrait and 35 plates*, 1740—ABURY, a Temple of the British Druids, *volume the second, 40 plates*, 1743—together 3 vols. folio, *176 curious plates, not quite uniform, in old calf gilt*, AN ORIGINAL COPY, £6. 6s   1724-43
The Stonehenge and Abury were reprinted *circa* 1835. Priced, 1825, Thorpe, the original edition, "Stonehenge and Abury," only, £14. 14s; 1828, Payne and Foss, £14. 14s; 1855, Baker's copy fetched £5. 7s 6d.

850 —— Itinerarium Curiosum : or an Account of the Antiquities and remarkable Curiosities in Nature or Art, observed in Travels through Great Britain, SECOND EDITION, *with large additions*, 2 vols. in 1, folio, *bds.* £4.   1776
The Centuria I. (or Vol. I) contains the Itinerarium, with the 100 plates of the first edition of 1724, and an additional plate of the "Solar Eclipse, 1724;" Centuria II. (or Vol. II.) the following unpublished works: The Brill, pp. 1-16; Iter Boreale, pp. 17-78; Ricardi Monachi de Situ Britanniæ, pp. 78-108; Richard of Cirencester, pp. 109-150; Carolus Bertram, pp. 151-168; The Weddings, pp. 169-178; Indices, 6 leaves; plates 1-102, 75 leaves; and Map of Roman Britain.
A long account of this most interesting work will be found in Savage's Librarian, together with a biographical sketch of the author, Vol. 2, pp. 145-180. Sold in Mr. Dent's sale for £11. 11s, in the Duke of Roxburghe's for £16. 10s, in Dr. Heath's for £16. 16s, and at King and Lochee's, in 1806, for £21.; 1855, Baker, £5. 2s 6d; 1856, Lane, with the Stonehenge and Abury, £11. 15s
"Stukeley, the most zealous of English Antiquaries."—*Palgrave's Commonwealth*, p. 349.

851 **DRUZES**: CHURCHILL'S (Col.) MOUNT LEBANON : a Ten Years' Residence, from 1842 to 1852 ; describing the Manners, Customs, and Religion of its Inhabitants, with a full and correct account of the Druze Religion, and containing Historical Records of the Mountain Tribes, from Personal Intercourse with their Chiefs and other Authentic Sources, by Colonel Churchill, Staff Officer on the British Expedition to Syria, *third edition*, 3 vols. 8vo. *with a large folding Map of the Mountain Range of the Lebanon, portraits and views*, 1853—Vol. IV. The DRUZES and the MARONITES under the Turkish Rule, 1862—together 4 vols. 8vo. with a General Index to the 4 vols. *printed uniformly*, (pub. at 35s) *cloth*, 21s   1853-62
The second volume contains an elaborate EXPOSÉ OF THE DRUZE RELIGION, its History, Doctrines, and Administration, based upon original Druze Manuscripts.

852 **EGYPTIANS (ANCIENT)**: BUNSEN, Egypt's Place in Universal history, translated by Cottrell, 4 vols. 8vo. *including an Egyptian Grammar and Dictionary, with plates of Egyptian Divinities, Hieroglyphical writing, etc.* (pub. at £5. 8s) *new in cl.* £4. 10s   1828-60

853 BURTON'S Excerpta Hieroglyphica, or Exact Copies of various Hieroglyphical Inscriptions and Sculptured Monuments still existing in Egypt and Nubia, and at Mount Sinai, etc. 4 parts, complete in 1 vol. oblong folio, *containing 62 most curious plates*, PRIVATELY PRINTED, *half bound, rare*, £3. 10s *Cairo*, 1825-37

854 JABLONSKI (J. E.) Pantheon Ægyptiorum de Diis, Religione et Theologia Ægyptiorum, 3 vols. in 1, 8vo. *green calf gilt*, 10s   *Francof.* 1750

855 —— Opuscula, quibus Lingua et Antiquitas Aegyptiorum, difficilia librorum sacrorum loca, etc. illustrantur, ed. Te Water, 4 vols. 8vo. *half calf neat*, 20s
Lugd. Bat. 1804-13

856 KIRCHERI Oedipus aegyptiacus h. e. universalis hieroglyphicae veterum instauratio, 3 stout vols. folio, *one sheet in MS., plates of Hieroglyphics and Egyptian Superstitions, old calf*, £2. 2s   *Romæ*, 1652-54

857 —— the same, 3 vols. in 4, folio, COMPLETE, *plates, calf*, £4.   1652-54
This learned work embodies all the then existing knowledge about Egypt: priced, 1834, J. Bohn, £4. 14s 6d.

858 LACOUR, les Hiéroglyphes Egyptiennes, 8vo. *plates, calf gilt*, 10s   *Bord.* 1821

859 LANDSEER'S Sabæan Researches; on the engraved Hieroglyphics of Chaldæa, Egypt, and Canaan, 4to. *plates of Babylonian Cylinders*, 12s   1836

859 *LENOIR, Nouvelle explication des Hiéroglyphes : des anciennes Allégories sacrées des Egyptiens, et des figures symboliques et sacrées des Egyptiens et des Grecs, 2 parts in 3 vols. 8vo. 74 *plates, half bound*, 10s *Paris*, 1809-10

860 PIGNORII vetustissimæ tabulæ æneæ Ægyptiorum (Mensæ Isiacæ) explicatio, antiquissimarum Superstitionum origines, etc. cum auctario de veteribus Æmuletis, sm. 4to. *plates, vellum*, 5s *Venetiis*, 1605

861 WILKINSON'S Manners and Customs of the Ancient Egyptians, their Private Life, Government, Laws, Arts, Religion, and History, BOTH SERIES, 6 vols. 8vo. *with* 600 *plates and cuts, illustrative of their Paintings, Monuments, Sculptures, etc. some in* COLOURS, *calf gilt*, £5. 5s 1837-41

862 **FREEMASONRY**: MANUAL de los Masones libres del Rio de la Plata, 8vo. *morocco*, 7s 6d *Buenos Aires*, 1856

863 DESAGULIERS (Dep. Grand-Master) Constitutions of the Freemasons, for the use of the Lodges, with Songs and Choruses, 4to. *frontispiece and Music, old calf*, 12s 1723

864 **GERMANS (Ancient)**: GRIMM'S Deutsche Mythologie, dritte Ausgabe, 3 vols. 8vo. *interleaved, half calf neat*, 21s *Göttingen*, 1854

865 PIGOTT's Manual of Scandinavian Mythology, an account of the two Eddas and the religion of Odin, with translations from Oehlenschlager, introduction, and appendix on the Sagas and superstitions, 8vo. *cloth*, 6s 6d 1839

866 **LAPPS AND FINNS**: LEEMIUS (Canutus) de Lapponibus Finmarchiæ, eorumque linguâ, vitâ et Religione pristinâ, cum Gunneri notis, et Jessens tractatu de Finnorum religione paganâ, *Danice et Latine*, 2 vols. in 1, 4to. 99 *very curious plates, calf*, 35s *Kiöbenhavn*, 1767

867 **MEXICANS (Ancient)**: POPOL VUH ; Le Livre Sacré et les Mythes de l'Antiquité Américaine avec les livres héroiques et historiques des Quichés, ouvrage original des Indigenes de Guatémala, *Quiche et Français*, avec des notes philologiques, un commentaire des peuples anciens de l'Amérique, etc. par Brasseur de Bourbourg, roy. 8vo. *frontispiece, sd*. 20s *Paris*, 1861
The GREAT BOOK of the MEXICANS, with a French translation: prefixed is a valuable and very learned introduction on the History and Mythology of the Ancient Mexicans.

868 **MOHAMMEDANS**: KORAN (Al) of Mahomet, translated out of Arabique into French, and now newly Englished, sq. 8vo. *bd*. 10s 1649
The first English translation.

869 ———— translated from Arabic into English with explanatory notes, by G. SALE, 2 vols. 8vo. *calf gilt*, 16s 1825

870 FORSTER (Rev. Chas.) Mahometanism unveiled, an inquiry in which that Archheresy, its diffusion and continuance, are examined on a new principle, tending to confirm the evidences, and aid the propagation of the Christian Faith, 2 vols. 8vo. *calf gilt, rare*, £2. 10s 1829
"The reader will find the subject of the Ishmaelitish descent of the Arabians treated in a clear and convincing manner by Mr. Forster in his learned and valuable work, Mahometanism Unveiled."—*Quarterly Review*.

871 **MOSAIC DOCTRINE**: CONJECTURES sur les Mémoires originaux dont Moyse s'est servi pour composer la Genese, 12mo. *old calf, very rare*, 12s *Bruxelles*, 1753
Bishop Colenso was here forestalled by 100 years.

872 **PARSEES**: ZEND-AVESTA, ouvrage de ZOROASTRE, contenant les idées theologiques, physiques et morales de ce législateur; les cérémonies du culte religieux qu'il a établi, et plusieurs traités importans sur l'ancienne histoire des Perses; traduit sur l'original Zend, avec des remarques, deux Vocabulaires, etc. par *Anquetil du Perron*, 3 vols. in 2, 4to. *plates, old calf gilt*, £3. 5s : or 3 vols. 4to. *vellum*, £3. 10s *Paris*, 1771
For Reviews of this elaborate work, see: Journal des Savans, 1771, Dec. : 1772, Mars et Mai.
"The immortal Anquetil-Duperron," as he is styled by the Biographie Universelle dared, while yet a boy in years, to undertake a work which Hyde had meditated but found himself incapable of accomplishing. Enrolling himself as a private soldier, to conquer the obstacles which prevented his freedom of action, he went in that capacity to India, studied the Zend, Pehlvi, Parsee, and Sanscrit, translated and collated with extraordinary care from a vast number of copies, the Gheber fragments of the Zend-Avesta ; and at the end of eight years, returned with 180 MSS. which he presented to the Royal Library. The fruit of these labors was this translation of the Zend-Avesta, the work of the famous Zoroaster, that philosopher whose mythical existence has never yet been clearly fixed in the records of history. It is said that £30,000 were offered by the English Government for the MS. translation, and refused.

873 ZEND-AVESTA, or the religious book of the Zorastians, edited and interpreted by Westergaard, Vol. I. pt. 4, the text of the Vendidad, 4to. *sd*. 4s *Copenh*. 1854

874 AVESTA die Heiligen schriften der Parsen, übersetzt von Spiegel, Vol. I : der Vendidad, 8vo. *sd*. 4s *Leipzig*, 1852

875 VENDIDAD SADE ; die heiligen Schriften Zoroasters : Yacna, Vispered und Vendidad, herausg. mit Glossar (in Römischen Schriften) von Brokhaus, roy. 8vo. 10s *Leipzig*, 1850

RELIGIOUS WORSHIPS, PHILOSOPHICAL SECTS, ETC.   61

876 DESATIR or sacred writings of the ancient Persian prophets, with Commentary and Glossary, *Persian, English and Glossary*, 2 vols. large 8vo. *half calf*, 32s ; or 2 vols. in 1, roy. 8vo. *hf. morocco, uncut*, 32s   Bombay, 1818
877 HAUG'S (M.) Essays on the Sacred Language, Writings, and Religion of the PARSEES, 8vo. *cloth*, 24s   Bombay, 1862
    A work of the greatest interest to all students of the Zend-Avesta, and the Religion of Zoroaster; pages 42-119 contain a GRAMMAR OF THE ZEND LANGUAGE, the Zend works in Roman letters.
878 HYDE (T.) HISTORIA RELIGIONIS VETERUM PERSARUM, eorumque Magorum ; Zoroastris Vita, ejusque et aliorum Vaticinia de Messiah ; Primitivæ Opiniones de Deo ; Originale Orientalis Sibyllæ Mysterium ; Zoroastris liber Sad-der, Latine ; cum speciminibus linguæ veteris, etc. 4to. *best edition, plates, calf*, 30s ; or, *half bound, uncut*, 32s ; or, *a fine copy in old calf neat*, 35s   Oxon. 1760
    Hibbert's copy fetched 3l. 3s ; Stanley's 4l. 10s. "The most learned work upon the religion of the ancient Persians which has appeared."—*Butler*. "A work of profound and various erudition, abounding with many new lights on the most curious and interesting subjects, filled with authentic testimonies which none but himself could bring to public view, and with many ingenious conjectures concerning the Theology, History, and learning of the Eastern Nations. This work has now become exceedingly scarce."—*Chalmers*. "Full of learned researches."—*Heeren*.
879 WILSON (John) The PARSI RELIGION, as contained in the Zand-Avastá, and propounded and defended by the Zoroastrians of India and Persia, 8vo. *cloth*, RARE, 24s   Bombay, 1843
    This author, whose profound learning is everywhere apparent in his work, was drawn into a controversy with the educated native upholders of the ancient creed he wrote upon. He was thus necessitated to study his subject deeply ; and to pass in review all that had already appeared concerning the Parsees. The Appendix contains Eastwick's translation concerning the Zartusht-Namah, the Sifat i Sirozah, etc.
880 **PHŒNICIANS**: SANCHUNIATHON, Analyse de, par Grotefend, *Paris*, 1836—Sanchuniathon's Phönizische Geschichte, übersetzt, *Lübeck*, 1837—Sanchoniathonis fragmenta de Cosmogonia et Theologia Phoenicum, Graece et Latine, ab Orellio, *Lipsiæ*, 1826—3 vols. in 1, 8vo. *facsimile, bds.* 6s 6d   1826-37
881 **POLYNESIANS**: GREY (Sir George) POLYNESIAN MYTHOLOGY and Ancient Traditional History of the New Zealand Race, post 8vo. 14 *illustrations*, (pub. at 10s 6d) *cloth*, 7s   1855
882 **PRIAPEIAN WORSHIP**: [DULAURE] des Divinités Génératrices, ou du Culte du Phallus chez les anciens et les modernes, 8vo. *a curious work, hf. russia neat*, 35s   Paris, 1805
    " L'on y trouvera le rapprochement d'un grand nombre de traits épars dans une immensité de livres peu communs dont l'ensemble offrira une face nouvelle."—*Preface*.
883 LE POIS, Discours sur les Medailles et Gravcures antiques, small 4to. *fine portrait, numerous engravings of Medals and some large woodcuts, including one of Priapus on page* 146, *fine tall copy*, 20s   Paris, 1579
884 POLIPHILI HYPNEROTOMACHIA, ubi humana omnia non nisi Somnium esse docet, atque obiter plurima scitu sanc quam digna commemorat (per Franciscum Colonna), folio, 170 *exquisitely beautiful woodcuts, none of which are mutilated, with the scarce leaf of "Errata," a very fine copy in calf extra, gilt edges*, £15. 15s   Venet. ALDUS, 1499
    Priced, Payne and Foss, 1858, on paper, 24l ; fetched Sir M. Sykes', 21l ; Hibbert's, 17l 15s.
    The extremely beautiful woodcuts, which adorn this very rare and desirable volume, are now generally attributed to Giovanni Bellino, the master of Titian and Giorgione. Formerly they were considered as the designs of RAPHAEL. The author has preserved his name in the first letter of each chapter which, being put together, form the line " Poliam frater Franciscus Columnas peramavit."
    In this Hypnerotomachia he deplores the death or loss of his mistress. He was a Dominican at Venice, having entered that order soon after 1467, and died there, upwards of eighty years old, in July, 1525.
    See Dibdin's Bibliotheca Spenceriana, iv. 145-65, where it is designated, " One of the most desirable volumes in the library of a collector, while it presents us with the most perfect specimen of the press of Aldus, and of the tastefulness of wood engraving in the fifteenth century."
885 POLIPHILE. (COLONNA) Hypnerotomachie, ou Discours du Songe de Poliphile, déduisant comme Amour le combat, à l'occasion de Polia, traduit de langage Italien (par Beroalde de Verville), folio, 197 *fine woodcuts, old calf gilt, rebacked*, £5.   Paris, Kerver, 1561
    Priced, 1860, Duquesne, Gand, 140 fr. ; fetched, 1858, Sotheby's, 5l.
    Des trois éditions de cette traduction, celle ci est la plus recherchée. Elle est augmentée d'un avertissement de J. Gohory.
    "It is not generally known that Goujon re-drew the embellishments of Beroalde de Verville's translation of the Polifilo, and that these, beautiful as they are in the Aldine edition, acquired new grace from the French artist."
            Sir F. Palgrave, in Turner's Letters from Normandy, I. p. 201.
SERPENT WORSHIP: It is a singular fact that in the religions of almost all nations the form of the Serpent is found, as a symbol of Divinity, good or evil ; even in that disputed point of Jewish and Christian doctrine,—the shape in which the tempter first appeared,—popular belief has always inclined to the idea of the Serpent. This is a subject to employ the full powers of speculative thought.

886 DEANE's Worship of the Serpent traced throughout the world, 8vo. *plates, half calf neat, gilt top, uncut,* 24s 1830
A very learned but singular work, devoted to prove that the worship of the serpent was universal; and examining the religions of Babylon, Persia, Hindustan, China, Mexico, Britain, Scandinavia, Italy, Illyricum, Thrace, Greece, Asia Minor and Phoenicia Scythia and Africa.

887 SEVERINUS (M. A.) VIPERA PYTHIA, id est de Viperae natura, Venemo, Medicina experimenta nova, sm. 4to. *allegorical frontispiece, showing the emblematical uses of Serpents, and several other plates explanative of Serpent Worship, calf,* 28s
Patav. 1851

888 SUFEES: THOLUCK, Ssufismus sive Theosophia Persarum pantheistica, e MSS. Persicis, Arabicis, Turcicis, eruta, 12mo. *bds.* 5s Berol. 1821

889 THUGGEE: ILLUSTRATIONS of the history and practices of the Thugs, 8vo. (pub. at 15s) *cloth,* 5s 1851

890 SLEEMAN'S Report on the Depredations committed by the THUG GANGS of Upper and Central India, 8vo. *map and tables, cloth, rare,* 15s *Calcutta,* 1840

THEOLOGY, ECCLESIASTICAL HISTORY.

The Hebrew Books are contained in the Catalogue of "Oriental Literature."

891 ANABAPTISTS.—HISTORIA Fanaticorum, oder Relation der Alten Anabaptisten und neuen Quäkern, aus dem Englischen übersetz Von Figken—Edicta wider die Schwärmer—Widertäufferischer Geist, Bericht was Jammer, etc. die Schwärmer gestifftet haben, *with* 4 *plates of Anabaptist enormities, and* 18 *portraits, including Socinus and Spinosa*—Die Quedlinburgischen Ertz-Schwermers Kratzensteins Geschichte: 4 vols. in 1, folio, *vellum,* £2. 16s
Franckf. und Cöthen, 1701

892 APPIANI (P. A. DELLA COMP. DI GESÙ) Vita di S. Emidio Vescovo d'Ascoli, e Martire, 4to. *portrait, the Dedication Copy to Pope Clement XI. bound in red* MOROCCO, *gilt edges, having the Papal arms in gold on the sides,* 18s *Koma,* 1702

893 AQUINAS. Encipit SECUNDA SECŪDÆ DOCTOR. STI. THOME DE AQNO de fide et eius obiecto quod est veritat. suma (sic in initio MS.) (In fine.) Hoc opus preclarū seda sc̄de bti Thome de Aquino alma in urbe Moguntia inclite nacōis Germanice artificiosa quadam adinvencōne imprimendi c̄summatu per Petrū Schoiffher de Gernhheim, MCCCCLXVII. large folio, black letter, *the initials painted in, ff.* 252 *and* 6, *hf. vellum,* £21. Moguntiæ, Schoiffher, 1467
A magnificent copy, with rough leaves and very large margins, of one of the earliest books with a date.

894 BARONIUS.—PAGI Critica Historico-Chronologica in Annales Ecclesiasticos BARONII, in qua narratio defenditur, illustratur, suppletur, ordo temporum corrigitur, &c. 4 vols. folio, *port.* LARGE PAPER, *calf,* £2. 2s *Antverp. et Colon.* 1727
Small paper copies generally fetch from £2. 10s to £2. 15s.
"The most important work which has ever appeared on ecclesiastical chronology."—DOWLING.

895 BATTHYAN (Ign. Comit. de, Episcopi Transyl.) Leges Ecclesiasticæ regni Hungariæ et provinciarum adjacentium, 3 vols. large folio, *engravings of Seals, &c. large paper, hf. calf, uncut,* 10s *Albæ Carolinæ et Claudiopoli,* 1785-1827

896 BECON (Thomas) Worckes, Parts 2 and 3, *imperfect*, in 1 stout volume, small folio, black letter, *portrait of Becon, and elegant separate titles to the numerous works, calf,* £2. London, John Day, 1560-64
The second part begins with folio 7, the third part ends with folio 516, two out of about thirty works of the great Reformer are therefore here imperfect. The volume was bound in 1712, and the birth of Bernard Burningham is recorded as having occurred in the same year.
Probably the scarcest of the works of the Old Reformers. to find complete and in good state. Rodd marked a very imperfect copy, 1840-44, £3. 8s. A fine copy, nearly perfect, 3 parts, last leaf of part 3 wanting, and some leaves slightly punctured by a worm, morocco, fetched, 1858, at Sotheby's, £7.

897 BOCHARTI Opera omnia: Phaleg, Chanaan et Hierozoicon, sive de Animalibus Scripturae, edidit Relandus, 3 vols. folio, *best edition, maps, old calf gilt,* 20s; or, *fine copy in vellum,* 25s Lugd. Bat. 1712
"Bonne edition de ces savants ouvrage. Celle de 1692 est moins belle et moins correcte."—BRUNET.

898 —— Hierozoicon, sive de Animalibus Scripturæ, recensuit Rosenmüller, 3 vols. 4to. *old calf neat,* 28s Lips. 1793-96

899 BOSSUET, Oeuvres choisies, par Sauvigny, 10 vols. 8vo. *calf,* 28s *Nismes,* 1784-90
Contents: Vol. l, Histoire; Vols. 2 and 3, Histoire des Variations; Vol. 4, Exposition de la doctrine Catholique; Vol. 5, Oraisons; Vol. 6, Elevations a Dieu; Vol. 7, Philosophie; Vol. 8. Politique; Vols. 9 and 10, Avertissemens aux Protestans.

900 —— Œuvres complètes, avec une Histoire de Bossuet par le Cardinal de Bausset, et Table générale, 12 vols. impl. 8vo. *double columns, finely printed, portrait, sd.* £3. 10s Paris, 1845-6

901 —— Histoire des Variations des Eglises Protestantes, 4 vols. 12mo. *calf,* 6s
Paris, 1747
The Sermons of Bossuet place him incontestably in the first line of Preachers; and even leave it open to argument whether he be not the first in that line. Bourdaloue and Massillon alone can dispute his pre-eminence.
C. BUTLER.

THEOLOGY, ECCLESIASTICAL HISTORY. 63

902 BOURDALOUE, Oeuvres complètes, nouvelle edition augmentée d'une notice sur sa vie et ses ouvrages, 16 vols. 8vo. *port. calf gilt*, £2. 10s *Versailles*, 1812

903 BROWN (E.) FASCICULUS RERUM expetendarum et fugiendarum, quorum pars magna nunc è MSS. Codd. in lucem prodit, 2 vols. fol. LARGE PAPER, *fine copy, red* MOROCCO EXTRA, *Harleian tooling*, RARE, £6. *Lond.* 1690

The articles contained in these volumes principally relate to the Reformation. Among them are :—Gulil. Wodfordi contra Johannem Wicklefum doctissimæ Decertationes - Articuli Wiclefi damnati per Concil. Constant. Ænas Sylvius, de Orig. Wiclefitarum, &c.—Grossetest [Episc. Lincolniensis] Opuscula inedita.— Ric. Archiep. Armaghii Defens. Curatorum, &c.—Episto. et Tract. Stephani Gardineri, Barnesii, Sampsonii, et aliorum, &c. &c.

904 BUNYAN'S Pilgrim's Progress, with Original Notes by the Rev. Thomas Scott, square 8vo. *portrait and Stothard's beautiful plates and vignettes, blue morocco, gilt edges, 32s* 1840

905 CALMET, Dictionnaire historique, critique, chronologique, geographique, et litteral de la BIBLE, 4 vols. folio, 300 *fine plates, old calf gilt*, £2. 5s *Paris*, 1730
Ouvrage fort estimé, 80 à 100 fr. La premiere edition, 1722, est moins recherchée.— BRUNET.

906 [CAMUS] Remarques sur un traité du pouvoir des Privilegiez d'entendre les Confessions, 12mo. *old calf gilt*, 6s 1642

907 [CARPENTER (John)] Schelomonocham, or King Solomon his solace, containing his Politie, his true Repentance, and his Salvation, sm. 4to. **black letter**, *title with engraved border of figures, including Diana and Acteon, limp vellum, remarkably fine copy*, £2. *London, John Windet*, 1606

"Dedicated to King James According to the title, this was 'first presented to the King's most excellente Majestie, and afterwards published.' On the second preliminary leaf is an acrostic poem in English of 30 lines. The work is not mentioned by any bibliographer."

908 CHAP de RASTIGNAC, Accord de la Revelation et de la Raison contre le Divorce, 8vo. *beautiful copy in the original French red morocco, gilt edges, with the Cardinal's arms on the sides*, 20s *Paris*, 1790

909 CHARLES I. Sylloge variorum Tractatum quibus Caroli innocentia illustratur, &c. sm. 4to. *bd.* 7s 6d 1648-49

910 CHOICE FRUITS: Law's Free Will Offering, 1747—Extracts from Law's Spirit of Prayer, and Address to the Clergy—in 1 vol. 12mo. *russia extra, gilt edges*, 15s 1747

911 **CHRISTIAN ART.** ARINGHI Roma Subterranea novissima in qua post BOSIUM, antiqua Christianorum et praecipue Martyrum Coemeteria, monimenta, epitaphia, inscriptiones, illustrantur, 2 vols. large folio, *numerous plates of Inscriptions, Monuments, etc. vellum*, £2. 10s *Romae*, 1651

"Edition plus ample et beaucoup meilleure que la premiere."— BURNET.

912 CIAMPINI OPERA, editio novissima, caeteris correctior et auctior; accesserunt Opuscula et auctoris vita: I. II. Vetera Monumenta, in quibus Musiva Opera, sacrarum profanarumque Ædium structura ac antiqui Ritus illustrantur, 2 vols. —De Sacris Aedificiis a Constantino Magno constructis, &c. 1 vol.—together 3 vols. folio, BEST EDITION, LARGE PAPER, *numerous plates of* EARLY CHRISTIAN ART AND ANTIQUITIES, *fine copy, old Italian calf gilt*, £3. *Romæ*, 1747

The first edition appeared, 3 vols. folio, 1690-93, and was priced, 1824, Rivington's £3. 3s 6d and £4. 4s. The third volume is often wanting.

913 CHRISTIAN OBSERVER, conducted by Members of the Established Church, from the beginning in 1802 to 1841 inclusive, 40 vols. 8vo. *uniform in hf. calf*, £2. 5s 1802-41

914 CHRYSOSTOMI (Sancti Joannis) Opera Omnia, *Graece et Latine*, nova Interpretatione, Præfationibus, Notis, variis lectionibus, illustrata et nova Vita, Appendicibus, Onomastico, Indicibus, locupletata studio Montfaucon, 13 vols. large folio, *portrait, best edition, original French calf, gilt backs, carmine edges*, £23. *Paris*, 1718-38

Priced, 1830, Thorpe, half russia, £31. 10s; 1832, Payne and Foss, £31. 10s; 1834, Stewart, £31. 10s and another time, £25. or in calf, £30. ; 1848, Payne and Foss, with holes in the title, vellum, £26. 5s; vellum, £25.
"We recommend the writings of *Chrysostom* to the perusal of those who have time, and whose care of souls will admit of it. *Barrow*, it is said, had read every line of them, and one might also fancy it, from the clearness and volubility of his style. Nor are his works of use only to the *Divine*,—the *Historian* will find much in them to notice; and the scattered allusions in his writings to customs, usages, &c. will yield fruits which have never yet been fully gathered."

915 CHRYSOSTOMI Homiliae sex, Graece, ab HARMARO, 16mo. *title mounted, hf. bound*, 5s *Oxonii*, 1586

916 CIACONII Vitæ et Res Gestæ Pontificum Romanorum, et Cardinalium, 2 vols. in 1, roy. folio, *portraits and plates of Heraldic Insignia of all the Popes and Cardinals, calf*, 25s *Romæ*, 1630

917 COCHLÆUS. Septiceps Lutherus, ubique sibi contrarius, à Cocleo, sm. 4to. *curious woodcut title, bds.* 10s *Lyps.* 1529

918 COMBEFIS, Bibliothecæ Græcorum Patrum Auctarium novissimum, Gr. et Lat. 2 vols. in 1, folio, *old orange morocco, gilt edges,* LOUIS XVIth's COPY, *the sides and back covered with the crowned " L" and fleurs-de-Lys intermingled, in gold, and having the Royal Arms, within a wreath, as centres,* 36s *Parisiis,* 1672

919 DEBREYNE, Œuvres Médico-Theologiques : Pensées sur la Matérialisme moderne—Etude de la Mort—La Théologie morale—Physiologie humaine avec un code d'Hygiène pratique—Mœchialogie, des péchés contre les 6e et 9e commandements, 5 vols. 8vo. *hf. morocco,* 24s *Paris,* 1844-46

920 DEVOCIONES y Exercicios en que se deve ocupar un Christiano, 16mo. *calf,* 7s 6d *Bruselas,* 1660

921 DONNE (Dr. John, *Deane of St. Paul's*) Eighty Sermons, 1640—Fifty Sermons, 1649, 2 vols. folio, *old calf, uniform,* 32s 1640-59
Rare. The first volume only was priced, 1841, Rodd, with a portrait by Merian, calf, £3. The two volumes fetched, 1854, Pickering's, old calf, £2. 3s.

922 DU MONSTIER NEUSTRIA PIA, seu de omnibus et singulis Abbatiis et Prioratibus totius NORMANIÆ, folio, a *remarkably fine tall copy, old calf gilt,* £4. *Rothomagi,* 1663
" Recherché et peu commun."—BRUNET. Since Brunet wrote this, the work has become still scarcer, and has risen proportionately in price. This interesting historical volume is of great importance to the scholar, particularly for the Norman period of English history.

923 ECCLESIASTICAL DISCIPLINE : An humble Motion unto the Right Honorable LL. of hir Majesties Privie Counsell, wherein is considered how necessarie it were that the Ecclesiastical discipline were reformed, smallest 4to. 112 pp. *purple morocco,* 16s 1590
A rare and curious little work against Papists.

924 FABRICII Lux Evangelii, Notitia Propagatorum per orbem totum, cum Juliani Imp. Epistoliis, sm. 4to. *calf,* 7s 6d *Hamburghi,* 1731

925 FLEURY (Cardinal) Histoire Ecclesiastique, avec la Continuation jusqu'en 1595, par Fabre et Goujet, 36 vols. 1691-1738—Table Generale des Matières par Rondet, 1 vol. 1774—together 37 vols. 4to. *neat in old French calf, gilt backs,* £4. 15s *Paris,* 1691-1744
Edition la plus estimée.

926 —— Histoire du Christianisme (Ecclésiastique) augmentée de l'histoire du XVe siècle, et continuée jusqu'à la fin du XVIIIe siècle par Vidal, avec table générale, 6 vols. royal 8vo. *double columns, sd.* 20s *Paris,* 1836-7
"Fleury's History of the Church is the best that has been written."—VOLTAIRE.

927 FOX'S ACTS and MONUMENTS of matters most speciall and memorable, happening in the Church ; with an Universal History, wherein is set forth the whole Race and Course of the Church, with the Bloody Times, Horrible Troubles, and great Persecutions against the true Martyrs of Christ, 3 vols. royal folio, *portraits and plates,* LARGE PAPER, *good copy, old calf, well preserved,* £4. 1684
NINTH AND BEST EDITION. Priced, SMALL PAPER: Ives and Swan, £4. 4s; 1834, Straker, £6. 6s and £6. 16s 6d; 1843, J. Bohn, £8. 18s 6d.
LARGE PAPER: Priced, Ives and Swan, stained, £7.; 1829, Howell, £12. 12s; 1831, Straker, £8. 18s 6d and £9. 19s 6d; 1837, Arch. £12. 12s; 1840, Jas. Bohn, £15. 15s; 1840, Payne and Foss, £10. 10s; 1855-56, Lasbury £6. 6s. Fetched, 1856, Williams's, £21.

928 FORTALITIUM Fidei contra Judeos, Sarracenos aliosque (ab Alphonso de Spina), 12mo. *fine copy in limp vellum, scarce,* 7s *Lugduni,* 1511

929 FUNERAL SERMONS. A Collection of 18 in 1 vol. sm. 4to. *hf. cf.* 20s 1657-1663
Most of these Sermons, published anterior to the Great Fire, are very scarce. Some of them contain Poems in English and Latin by graduates of Oxford and Cambridge.

930 GARDEN of SPIRITUAL FLOWERS, planted by Ri. Ro., Will. Per., Ri. Gree., M. M., and Geo. Web., 2 parts in 1 vol. 18mo. *title surrounded by an Arabesque woodcut border, purple morocco, gilt edges, fine copy,* RARE, 30s 1622
I found no trace of this interesting volume of ascetic reflections. The spirit of the moral advice is excellent and in some instances very plain spoken. Richard Rogers and George Webbe appear to have been the principal contributors.

931 GENESTE's Parallel Histories of Judah and Israel, 2 vols. roy. 8vo. (pub. at £1. 11s 6d) *cloth,* 12s 1843

932 GERDESII Historia Reformationis, sive Annales Evangelii Sæc. XVI. Doctrinæque Reformatæ, 4 vols. 4to. *numerous portraits of the Reformers, including Englishmen, vellum,* 15s *Groning.* 1744-52
Priced, 1837, Thorpe, £2. 12s 6d.

933 GERUNG VON MEMMINGEN, Ain Kurtze Underweysung wei man Got allain beychten sol, sm. 4to. *beautiful woodcut border, hf. bd.* 10s 1523
An extremely powerful Tract against Auricular Confession.

THEOLOGY, ECCLESIASTICAL HISTORY. 65

934 GESENIUS, der Prophet Jesaia, übersetzt, mit philologisch-kritischen und historischen Commentar, 4 parts in 3 vols. *hf. calf*, 20s   *Leip.* 1821-29
935 GIESELER, Lehrbuch der Kirchengeschichte und der Dogmengeschichte, 6 vols. in 8, 8vo. *third edition*, (pub. at £3. 4s 6d) *cloth*, 25s   *Bonn*, 1831-55
936 GONTERY, la PIERRE DE TOUCHE, pour desabuser les esprits trompez soubs couleur de Reformation, 1614 — Correction fraternelle, *Bourdeaus*, 1615—in one vol. stout 12mo. *fine copies, vellum, rare*, 9s   1614-15
937 GLAIRE, les Livres Saints vengés, ou la vérité historique et divine des Testaments, 2 vols. 8vo. *cloth*, 7s 6d   *Paris*, 1845
938 GUION (Madame de la Mothe) Discours Chrétiens et spirituels, 2 vols. 8vo. *Paris*, 1790—Lettres, avec la correspondance secrette de Fénélon, et quelques anecdotes curieuses, Vols. 3-5, 12mo. *Londres*, 1768—together 5 vols. *calf extra*, 21s   1768-90
939 HAAG, La France Protestante, ou Vies des Protestants Français, avec une notice sur le Protestantisme en France, 9 vols. in 5, royal 8vo. *in form of a Dictionary, half morocco*, £3. 16s   *Paris*, 1846-59
    A valuable work, full of historical, literary, and bibliographical information.
940 HALL (Bishop). Plaine and Familiar Explication of all the hard texts of the whole divine Scripture by Jos. Exon, 2 vols. in 1, folio, *engraved title*, FIRST EDITION, *calf*, 12s   1633-2
941 HALL'S (P.) RELIQUIÆ LITURGICÆ; Documents connected with the Liturgy, exhibiting the Substitutes, Alterations, etc. 5 vols.—FRAGMENTA LITURGICA; Documents in illustration of the order of Public Worship, 7 vols.—together 12 vols. 12mo. *cloth*, 30s   *Bath*, 1847-48
    A very interesting production, consisting of reprints of early prayer-books, and other liturgical literature.
943 HAROLDUS. Beati Thuribii Alphonsi Mogroveii Archiepiscopi Limensis Vita exemplaris, per Fr. Franciscum Haroldum, Hibernum Limericensem, sm. 4to. *portrait, and with corrections, probably by the author himself, fine copy, in russia extra, gilt edges, by Clarke and Bedford, scarce*, 36s   *Romæ*, 1680
    Such is the extreme rarity of the above volume, that the author (an Irishman) appears to have been unknown to all bibliographers.
944 HARVEY (Gul. W.) Ecclesiæ Anglicanæ Vindex Catholicus, sive articulorum Ecclesiæ Angl. cum scriptis Patrum collatio, 3 vols. 8vo. (pub. at £2. 14s) *hf. morocco*, 36s   *Cantab.* 1841-43
945 HENRION, Histoire generale de l'Eglise, depuis les Apotres jusqu'à Gregoire XVI., le fonds emprunté à Berault-Bercastel, enrichie des meilleurs historiens et continuée jusqu'à nos jours, 12 vols. 8vo. *calf*, £2.   *Paris*, 1839
    A History of the Roman Catholic Church of Europe. Priced, 1845, Bossange, Paris, sd. £2.18s.
945*HIERONYMI (D.) EPISTOLÆ, LIBRI CONTRA HÆRETICOS et Commentaria in quatuor Prophetas Majores, in Ecclesiasten et in duodecim Prophetas Minores, vita Hieronymi, etc. à Mariano Victorio, 5 vols. in 4, folio, *red morocco, super extra, silk linings, gilt edges*, £3. 16s   *Romæ, Paul Manut.* 1565-71
946 HISTOIRE de l'Edit de NANTES, contenant les choses remarquables avant et après sa publication, jusques à present, 5 vols. 4to. *calf neat*, 18s   *Delft*, 1693-5
947 HOWARDE (Henry) Defensative against the POYSON of supposed PROPHESIES, not hitherto confuted, which being grounded upon old paynted books, expositions of dreames, oracles, etc. have been causes of great disorder, sq. 8vo. *old calf, curious*, 25s   *London*, 1583
948 HUSS (Joh.) DE ECCLESIA: De Causa Boemica, Paulus Constantius, sm. 4to. *with a few old MS. notes, hf. calf*, 12s   (? *Tiguri*, 1525)
949 IGNATIAN EPISTLES. Corpus Ignatianum, a complete collection, in Syriac, Greek, and Latin, by Cureton, roy. 8vo. *facsimiles, cloth*, 16s   1849
950 JEWEL (*Bishoppe of Sarisburie*) A Replie unto M. Hardinges Answeare: by perusing whereof the discrete Reader may see the weake, and unstable groundes of the Romaine Religion, folio. *fine tall copy with many rough leaves, original calf, with a dragon and E. S. (Episcop. Sar.) on the sides*, VERY RARE, £3. 10s
    London, in Fleetstreate, at the signe of the Black Oliphante, Henry Wykes, 1566
    Collation: Title; 'Unto the Christian Reader,' 2 leaves; 'An Answeare to Mr. Hardinge's Preface,' 5 leaves; Table, 17 leaves; 'Faults escaped,' 1 leaf; pp. 1-641, containing 27 articles, viz. "of private Masse, of Communion under both kindes, of Praiers in a strange tongue, of the Supremacie, of Real Presence, of being in many places, of Elevation, of Adoration, of the Canopie, of Accidents without subjecte, of dividing the Sacrament, of Figure, Signe, etc., of pluralitie of Masses, of Adoration of Images, of Reading the Scriptures, of Consecration under Silence, of the Sacrifice, of Receiving the Communion for others, of Application, of Opus operatum, of Lorde and God, of remaining under the Accidents, whether a Mouse, etc., of Individuum Vagum, whether the Fourmes of the Sacramente, of Hidinge and Cooveringe, of Ignorance;" 'An Answeare to M. Hardinge's Conclusion,' 5 leaves.

F

951 JEWELL'S (John) Works, newly set forth, with amendment of divers quotations, and a brief discourse of his life, stout folio, *corners of the first few leaves stained, otherwise a good copy in old calf neat, rare*, 30s 1611
Priced, 1824, Thorpe, £6 16s 6d; 1846, Stewart, £5. 18s.

952 Kardec (Allan) Œuvres Mystiques: Le Livre des Esprits, écrit sous la dictée d'esprits superieurs—Manifestations Spirites—Qu'est-ce que le Spiritisme— Livre des esprits, seconde édition entièrement refondue, 4 vols. 8vo. and 12mo. *sd. very curious*, 7s 6d   Paris, 1857-60

953 KELLY'S Lectures on the Book of Revelation, 8vo. *cloth*, 5s   1861

954 Kempis de Imitatione Christi ad fidem Autographi 1441, ed. Lambinet, 12mo. *plates, veau fauve extra, gilt edges*, 7s 6d   Paris, 1810

955 KENNETT'S (W.) Parochial Antiquities attempted in the History of Ambrosden, Burcester, and other adjacent parts in the Counties of Oxford and Bucks, 2 vols. 4to. *portrait and plates, calf gilt*, £2.   Oxford, 1818
Hibbert's copy, 1829, fetched £3. 11s.

956 Krafft, Historie vom Exorcismo, 12mo. *calf, curious*, 5s   Hamburg, 1750

957 KITTO (Dr.) Journal of Sacred Literature, 2nd Series, 14 parts, 1851-55—Journal of Sacred Literature and Biblical Record, edited by Dr. Burgess, being the 3rd Series, 15 parts, 1855-58—together 29 parts, 8vo. (pub. at £7. 5s) *clean and uncut*, £2. 2s   1851-58

958 Laderchius de sacris Basilicis Marcellini presbyteri et Petri exorcistae de urbe, 4to. *vellum*, 7s 6d   Romae, 1705

959 LAUD'S (Archbishop) Speech delivered in the Starr-Chamber, on the xiv of June mdxxxvii. at the Censure of John Bastwick, Henry Burton, and William Prinn, concerning pretended Innovations in the Church—Dow (Chris.) Innovations unjustly charged upon the present Church and State, an answer to Burton's libellous Pamphlet—in 1 vol. sm. 4to. *bds. uncut*, 36s   1637
Two very rare and curious tracts; of the first, only twenty copies were printed.

960 (La Peyrere) Præadamitæ, sive exercitatio super Paulum ad Romanos, sm. 4to. *vellum, morocco backs*, 10s   1645
First and anonymous edition of this famous work, which created so much confusion, and was suppressed.

961 LE VALOIS (Père) Œuvres spirituelles, contenant lettres sur la nécessité de la Retraite, sur les Mystères de la Sainte Vierge, etc. 3 vols. 12mo. *beautiful copy in rich old blue morocco extra*, 30s   Paris, 1758

962 Leydeckeri Historia Ecclesiæ Africanæ, sm. 4to. *vellum*, 7s 6d   Ultraj. 1690

963 MABILLON et Germain, Museum Italicum, seu Collectio Veterum Scriptorum, ex Bibliothecis Italicis, 2 vols. 4to. *many plates of Middle-Age Art from MSS. &c.* very fine copy *in old* French red morocco, *gilt edges, the Arms of Card. Le Tellier on the sides*, £5. 5s   Lut. Par. 1687-89

964 —— the same, 2 vols. 4to. *bound*, 9s   1724

965 Mabillon Vetera Analecta, varia fragmenta scriptorum ecclesiasticorum inedita, 2 vols. in 1, stout sm. 8vo. *calf*, 10s   Lut. Par. 1675-83

966 Maitland's Essays on subjects connected with the Reformation in England, 8vo. 590 pp. *calf gilt*, 12s   1849

967 MACMAHON (Hugonis, Armacani totius Hiberniæ Primatis) Jus Primatiale Armacanum, in Archiepiscopos, Episcopos, et universum Clerum Hiberniæ, etiam Prosecutio ejusdem Argumenti contra Anonymum, sm. 4to. *with both the leaves of errata, russia, very neat*, extremely rare, 32s   1728
Few copies possess the second errata; Thorpe says he never saw another but the one he had, 1842, priced £5. 5s.
See Carte's Ormond, vol. II. p. 27.

968 Mason, of the Consecration of the Bishops in the Church of England, sm. folio, *first edition, clean copy, calf, scarce*, 6s   1613

969 MASSILLON, Œuvres, 13 vols. *portrait, hf. calf gilt*, £2. 10s   Par. 1810
"Edition à la fois belle, correcte et imprimée sur beau papier."—Brunet.

970 MASSILLON, Œuvres complètes, 13 vols. *portrait, unbound*, 15s   ib. 1822-25

971 MATTER, Histoire Critique du Gnosticisme, et de son influence sur les sectes religieuses et philosophiques des six premiers siècles de l'ère chrétienne, 3 vols. 8vo. *sd.* 12s 6d   Paris, 1843

972 MILMAN (Dean) History of Latin Christianity, including that of the Popes, 6 vols. 8vo. (pub. at £3. 12s) *new in cloth*, £2. 18s   1857
"One of the most remarkable works of the present age, in which the author reviews, with curious erudition, and in a profoundly philosophical spirit, the various changes that have taken place in the Roman hierarchy; and while he fully exposes the manifold errors and corruptions of the system, he shows throughout that enlightened charity, which is the most precious of Christian graces, as unhappily the rarest."—Prescott's Philip the Second.

THEOLOGY, ECCLESIASTICAL HISTORY.

973 MORAVIANS. Acta Fratrum Unitatis in Angliâ, 1749: Report of the Committee on the Petition of the Moravian Churches, etc. sm. folio, *calf, 7s 6d* 1749

974 MONASTIER, Histoire de l'Eglise Vaudoise, et des Vaudois en Piémont, 2 vols. 8vo. *sd. 7s 6d* *Toulouse*, 1847

975 MOSHEIM'S Ecclesiastical History, from the birth of Christ to the beginning of the 18th century, translated from the Latin by Maclaine, 6 vols. 8vo. *calf gilt*, 20s 1825

976 MURPHY (Ant. Conaciensis) Theologia Dogmatica adversus Atheos, Libertinos, Judæos, caeterosque Infideles et Hetherodoxos, 4 vols. in 2, sm. 4to. *bd. rare*, 30s *Pragæ*, 1753

977 NEANDER'S Allgemeine Geschichte der Christlichen Religion und Kirche (bis zum Baseler Konzil), 6 vols. in 11, 1825-52; Geschichte der Pflanzung und Leitung der christlichen Kirche durch die Apostel, 2 vols. in 1, *map*, 1838; Leben Jesu Christi, 1839—together 14 vols. in 13, 8vo. (pub. at £4. 4s) *calf neat*, £2. 10s *Hamburg*, 1825-52

978 NEUES THEOLOGISCHES JOURNAL, herausgegeben von Hänlein, Ammon, Gabler, und andern, 28 vols. 12mo. *half bound*, 20s *Nürnberg*, 1793-1810

979 O'BRIEN (Ant.) de Divina Revelatione seu naturali ac revelatâ Religione, accedunt Theses Theologicæ Francisci Kirwan et Jacobi O'Kelly, 2 vols. sm. 4to. *bd. rare*, 30s *Pragæ*, 1759-62

980 OLSHAUSEN, Biblischer Commentar über sämmtliche Schriften des Neuen Testaments, mit Continuation von Ebrard und Wiesinger, 5 vols. in 9, 8vo. *seven volumes calf extra, two sewed*, £2. 12s *Königsberg*, 1837-50

981 PALLAVICINO (Sforza) Istoria del Concilio di Trento, 3 vols. sm. 4to. PORTRAIT, *French calf gilt*, 20s *Milano*, 1745
A compendious and very elegantly written history, which, being in the Roman Catholic interest, is always opposed to the smaller work of Sarpi by those who study both sides of the question.

982 PARKER (Mat.) de Antiquitate Britannicæ Ecclesiæ et Privilegiis Ecclesiæ Cantuar. cum Archiepiscopis ejusdem LXX, e 21 exemplarium 1572 excusorum sibique discrepantium collatione, recensuit Drake, folio, *fine portrait by Vertue, plates of Tombs, Arms, &c. calf*, 16s 1729

983 PARKER (Sam.) Reasons for abrogating the Test, 12mo. *calf, rare*, 18s *Holyrood House*, 1688

984 PATRUM APOSTOLICORUM, SS. Barnabæ, Hermæ, Clementis, Ignatii, Polycarpi, Opera Genuina, cum Ignatii Epistolis, *Gr. et Lat.* curâ R. Russel, 2 vols. large 8vo. LARGE THICK PAPER, *in the original calf, very scarce*, £3. 16s
The Rev. Theod. Williams' copy fetched £6. 15s. 1746

985 PATRUM APOSTOLICORUM, Scripta genuina Græca, Græce et Latine, ed. Horneman, 3 parts in 1 vol. sm. 4to. *hf. russia*, 7s 6d *Hauniæ*, 1828-29

986 PERKINS' (William, *of the Universitie of Cambridge*) Workes, 3 vols. folio, *with curious tables of the order of the causes of Salvation and Damnation, half calf*, 25s 1612-31
"The works of Perkins (a distinguished Puritan who died in 1602) are distinguished for their piety, learning, extensive knowledge of the Scriptures, and strong Calvinistic argumentation."—ORME'S BIBLIOTHECA BIBLICA.

987 POCOCKE'S THEOLOGICAL WORKS, containing the "Porta Mosis" *in English and Hebrew*, and *English* commentaries on Hosea, Joel, Micah, etc. 2 vols. folio, *portrait, fine copy in old calf neat*, 20s 1740

988 POPES. Essai historique sur la puissance temporelle des Papes, 2 vols. 8vo. *calf neat*, 6s *Paris*, 1818

989 POWELL (Vavasor) Common Prayer Book no Divine Service; or xxvii Reasons against any Humane Liturgies or Common-Prayer-Books, smallest 4to. *title, 4 preliminary leaves, and 44 pp. hf. bound, scarce*, 25s 1661
Anthony Wood says, "Vavasor Powell was an Anabaptist and a man of an infamous character, a Field-Preacher, and a great stickler against King Charles 1st. He died in the Fleet Prison, 27th Oct. 1670, and was buried in the Dissenters' burial ground by Bunhill Fields."

990 RAYSII, Hierogazophylacium Belgicum, 18mo. *vellum, very scarce*, 7s *Duaci*, 1628

991 REGGIUS Kemnathensis de statu Ecclesiae Britannicae hodierno, sq. 8vo. *bds.* 6s *Dantisci*, 1647

992 REYNERI, Apostolatus Benedictinorum in Anglia, de Antiquitate Ordinis S. Benedicti in Anglia, cum APPENDICE copiosa Instrumentorum venerandæ vetustatis, 2 vols. in 1, folio, *frontispiece, containing small portraits, vellum, scarce*, 32s *Duaci*, 1626
Priced with the Appendix, 1826-30, Payne and Foss, £2. 12s 6d; 1837-48, Payne and Foss, £2. 2s; 1857, mor. £2. 12s 6d; 1858, russia ext. £6. 16s 6d. The Towneley copy sold for £3 10s.
"The chief of our historians of this order (Benedictines)."—NICHOLSON.

993 RIBADENEYRA, Flos Sanctorum de las Vidas de los Santos, aumentado por Nieremberg, Garcia y Guerrero, 3 vols. folio, *calf*, £2. 5*s* *Barcelona*, 1790
Considered by Palomino to be absolutely indispensable to every Spanish artist, as being to modern Papal hagiography what Lemprière is to ancient Pagan mythology."—*Ford's Handbook*.

994 ROBINSON'S Scripture Characters, or practical improvement of the principal Histories in the Old and New Testament, 4 vols. large 8vo. *tree-marbled calf gilt*, 30*s* 1793

995 ROSENMUELLER (E. F. C.) Scholia in VETUS TESTAMENTUM, XI parts in 23 vols. 8vo. COMPLETE (sells £12. unbound), *calf neat*, £8. 8*s* *Lips*. 1821-35
Contents: Pentateuchus, 3 vols.; Jesajae Vaticinia, 3 vols.; Psalmi, 3 vols.; Jobus, 1 vol.; Ezechiel, 2 vols.; Prophetæ minores, 4 vols.; Jeremiæ Vaticinia et Threni, 2 vols.; Proverbia, Eccles. et Canticus, 2 vols.; Daniel, 1 vol.; Libri histor. Jos., Judices, Ruth, 2 vols.

996 STE. CATHERINE de Sienne, Histoire, par Malan, 2 vols 8vo. *hf. mor*. 7*s* 6*d* 1846

997 SANTA CATHARINA DA SIENA, Epistole et Orationi, con la sua vita et capitoli in sua laude, sm. 4to. *portrait, the pages of sheet P transposed in printing, vellum, with some rough leaves*, VERY RARE, £2. 12*s* *Vinetia, Toresano*, 1548
Fetched, 1856, Hodgson's, £3. 10*s*.
In this copy the leaves 113, 114, 119, and 120, are not printed in smaller type than the rest of the books, as is stated by Molini in Florence to be the case with all that had passed through his hands. Renouard and Brunet do not mention the typographical error by which, in the above copy, those leaves (portion of sheet P) are misplaced in printing. From these circumstances, I conclude that the copies generally met with contain those leaves reprinted, while the above belongs to the original issue.

998 SALVADOR, Loi de Moise ou système religieux et politique des Hébreux, 8vo. *hf. calf*, 7*s* *Paris*, 1822

999 —— STRAUSS et GIBBON; Guillon, Examen critique de leurs Doctrines sur Jesus-Christ, 2 vols. 8vo. 900 pp. *sd*. 5*s* *Paris*, 1841

1000 SANDERUS, de origine ac progressu Schismatis Anglicani, ed. Ribadeneira, 12mo. *vellum*, 10*s* *Coloniae Agrip*. 1610
Containing a list of Englishmen martyred for religion, 1580-5.

1001 SANDERS, les trois livres contenants l'origine et progrez du Scisme d'Angleterre, augmentez par Rishton, 16mo. *bds*. 12*s* 1587

1002 SARPI (Fra Paolo) Historia del Concilio Tridentino, di Soave, sm. folio, *large paper, stained, vellum*, 12*s* *Londra*, 1619
Edition originale, recherchée.—BRUNET.

1003 —— Historia del Concilio Tridentino, sm. 4to. *vellum*, 8*s* *Geneva*, 1660

1004 SCHMALTZII (Valentini) Catechismus der Leute die in Poln, Littauen, etc. affirmiren dass Niemand anders denn der Vater der einige Gott sey, sm. 4to. *a neat MS. copy of this rare Socinian Catechism printed at Rackaw*, 1612, *vellum*, 20*s* *ca.* 1680

1005 SCHEUCHZER, PHYSIQUE SACRÉE, ou Histoire Naturelle de la Bible, traduite du Latin, 8 vols. folio, *fine impressions of the 750 plates, very fine copy in old red morocco, gilt leaves*, £12. *Amst*. 1732-37
Priced, 1825, Thorpe, morocco, £31. 10*s*; 1837, Payne and Foss, morocco, £24.
A most beautiful picture book of the Bible, containing 750 fine plates of scenes recorded in the Holy Scriptures, of Trees, Plants, Animals, Fossils, etc.

1006 SCHULTENS, OPERA: Proverbia Salomonis, *Hebraice et Latine*—Liber Jobi, *Hebraice et Latine*—Origines Hebraeae—Opera Minora—together 5 vols. 4to. *a nice copy in old calf gilt*, 30*s* *Lugd. Bat.* 1737-69
"Schultens' works show profound learning and just criticism."—*Chalmers*.

1007 SCHROECKH (J. M.) Christliche Kirchengeschichte, bis zu 1517, mit dem Allgemeinen Register, 35 vols. *portrait*—Christliche Kirchengeschichte seit der Reformation, bis 1648, 10 vols.—together 45 vols. bound in 28, 8vo. *calf*, £3.
Leip. 1772-1812
Priced, 1830, Black and Armstrong, 35 vols. £11 11*s*; fetched, 1832, Sotheby's, £5. 7*s* 6*d*.
The best compendious Church History, according to PROTESTANT views, still unsurpassed by any work of similar extent. Of late it has become scarce.

1008 SHARROCK, Judicia de variis Incontinentiæ speciebus, Adulterio, Polygamia, et Concubinatu, etc. 12mo. *vellum*, 7*s* 6*d* *Oxon*. 1662

1009 SLEIDAN (Jean) Histoire de la Reformation, ou Memoires sur l'état de la Religion sous l'Empire de Charles V, traduite par Courrayer, avec des notes, 3 vols. 4to. *hf. calf*, 21*s* *La Haye*, 1767

1010 SOCINI (Fausti) Opera Omnia, exegetica et didactica atque polemica, 2 vols. in 1, stout folio, 1656 pp. *double columns, in the original hogskin, two figures with inscriptions stamped in gold on the sides, rare*, 36*s* *Irenopoli*, 1656
Priced formerly, 3*l*. 3*s*.

1011 STRAUSS, das Leben Jesu, 2 vols stout 8vo. *second edition*, 8*s* 6*d* *Tübingen*, 1837

1012 —— Vie de Jésus, ou examen critique de son histoire, traduit par Littré, 4 parts in 2 vols. 8vo. *cloth*, 10*s* *Paris*, 1839-40

THEOLOGY, ECCLESIASTICAL HISTORY. 69

1013 STRAUS-DÜRCKHEIM, Théologie de la Nature, 3 vols. 8vo. *plates slightly stained, sd. 7s 6d*   *Paris*, 1852

1014 STRYPE (J.) HISTORICAL AND BIOGRAPHICAL WORKS, viz.—
Ecclesiastical Memorials of the Reformation under King Henry VIII., King Edward VI., and Queen Mary I., 3 vols. *portrait*   1721
Annals of the Reformation during the first XII Years of Queen Elizabeth's Happy Reign, 4 vols.   1725
Lives of Archbishops Cranmer, Grindal, Parker, and Whitgift, 4 vols. *portraits, some added*   1694, 1710, 1711, 1718
Life of Sir Thomas Smith, Secretary of State to Edward VI. and Queen Elizabeth, 1 vol. 8vo. *portrait*   1698
Life of Aylmer, Bishop of London, 1 vol. 8vo. *portrait*   1701
The GENERAL INDEX to Strype's Works, compiled by the Rev. R. T. Laurence, 2 vols. in 1, 8vo.   1828
Together 15 vols. viz.—in folio 11, in 8vo. 4, FINE SERIES, *calf*, £10. 10s.
Priced, 1824, J. Bohn, russia, 42l.; 1824, Rivington, russia, 52l. 10s.

1015 SUICERI (J. C.) THESAURUS ECCLESIASTICUS, è Patribus Græcis exhibens quæcunque Phrases, Rita, Dogmata, Hæreses, et hujus modi alia spectant, 2 vols. folio, EDITIO OPTIMA, *fine copy in calf*, £3. 8s   *Amst. Wetsten.*, 1728
"This is the best edition of a most valuable work; which, though indispensably necessary for understanding the writings of the Greek Fathers, incidentally contains many illustrations of Scripture. It is said to have caused the learned author 20 years labour."—*Horne.*

1016 SYNODORUM ACTA. Gelasii commentarius actorum Niceni Consilii, Balforeo interprete; Compendium universalium Synodorum, Latine à Sculteto, 1604—Acta Synodi Ephesi habitae, *Graece*, 1591—3 vols. in 1, folio, *a fine fresh copy in the original hogskin binding, with a Bishop's Arms stamped in black on the side, rare,* 15s   (? *Heidelberg*) 1591-1604

1017 TAYLOR (Jeremy) Whole Works, with Life and critical Examination of his Writings by Bishop Heber, 15 vols. 8vo. *portrait, calf*, £4. 4s   1822

1018 ——— Whole Works, with Life by Heber, revised and corrected by Eden, in 10 vols. 8vo. *portrait*, (*pub. at* £5. 5s *in bds.*) *calf*, £5.   1852-54
"We will venture to assert that there is in any one of the prose folios of Jeremy Taylor more fancy and original imagery, more brilliant conceptions and glowing expressions, more new figures and new applications of old figures; more, in short, of the body of the soul of poetry, than in all the odes and epics that have since been produced in Europe."—*Edinburgh Review.*

1019 TESTAMENT of the Twelve Patriarchs, the Sons of Jacob, translated by Grosthead, and now Englished, 18mo. 13 *rude woodcuts, including title, rather soiled, calf antique, rare,* 10s   1686

1020 THEOLOGISCHE STUDIEN und KRITIKEN: eine Zeitschrift für das gesammte Gebiet der Theologie, heraus. von ULLMANN und UMBREIT, mit Register, 22 vols. 8vo. (*pub. at* £10. 10s) *cloth,* £8.   *Hamb.* 1828-48

1021 THOMASSIN, Ancienne et nouvelle Discipline de l'Eglise, touchant les benefices et les beneficiers, 3 vols. folio, *old calf gilt, fine copy,* 32s   *Paris,* 1725

1022 TYMME's Silver Watch Bell, the sound whereof is able to win the profane worldling, 18mo. 𝔅lack letter, *calf neat, rare,* 12s   *London, Knight,* 1611
"This rare book is beautifully written; its author was a man of great genius."—*MS. Note of Mr. Spence.*

1023 ULLMANN's Reformers before the Reformation, translated by Menzies, 2 vols. 8vo. *cloth, 7s 6d*   *Edinb.* 1855

1024 WALKER's Virtuous Woman, a Sermon, preached at Felsted, 1678, at the Funeral of MARY, Countess Dowager of WARWICK, 12mo. with Genealogical Notices, *half calf, rare,* 6s   1678

1025 WALCHII Bibliotheca Theologica Selecta, litterariis Adnotationibus instructa, 4 thick vols. 8vo. *calf,* 16s   *Jenæ,* 1757-65
"A very valuable and copious Catalogue raisonné of Foreign Theology, in which the merits and demerits of Commentators are discussed."—*Horne.*

1026 WARD (Hugo) S. Rumoldi, Martyris incliti, *Archiepiscopi Dubliniensis,* Acta, Martyrium, Liturgia antiqua et Patria, per Hugonem Vardæum *Hibernum* collecta, et a T. Sirino edita, small 4to. *with the Genealogia Alexandri (often deficient), in old calf, scarce,* £2.   *Lovanii,* 1662
Priced by Payne and Foss, 1948, 3l. 3s. Containing much curious matter relative to Irish history not elsewhere obtainable.—"This is the most interesting, as well as the most rare, of the different Lives of the Irish Saints."—*Bibliotheca Grenvilliana.*

1027 WESSENBERG, die grossen Kirchenversammlungen des 15ten und 16ten Jahrhunderts, 4 vols. 8vo. *hf. calf,* 10s   *Constanz,* 1840

1028 WHARTONI (Henr.) ANGLIA SACRA: sive collectio Historiarum partim antiquitùs partim recenter scriptarum, de Archiepiscopis Angliæ à prima Fidei Christianæ susceptione ad Ann. 1540, 2 vols. folio, LARGE PAPER, *old calf, rebacked, from Archbp. Tenison's library*, £5. 15s *Lond.* 1691
Large Paper copies are rare. A very full catalogue of the writers is prefixed to each volume.

1029 WHITGIFT's Life, by Sir George PAULE, sq. 12mo. *portrait, calf, clean copy,* 6s
1612

1030 (WILLIAMS) the Baptistery, or the way of Eternal Life, 8vo. *with 32 curious plates, red morocco, edges gilt and gauffré, rare,* 32s *Oxford,* 1846

1031 WILLIS (Browne) SURVEY OF THE CATHEDRALS of York, Durham, Carlisle, Chester, Man, Litchfield, Hereford, Worcester, Gloucester, Bristol, Lincoln, Ely, Oxford, Peterborough. Canterbury, Rochester, London, Winchester. Chichester, Norwich, Salisbury, Wells, Exeter, St. David's, Landaff, Bangor, and St. Asaph, 3 vols.—PAROCHIALE ANGLICANUM, 1 vol.; together, 4 vols. in 3, 4to. *with portrait of Willis and some other additional plates, besides the original* 32, *old calf,* £3. 5s 1742 (1727-33)

1032 WILSON'S Lands of the Bible visited and described, 2 vols. 8vo. *with map, plates, and cuts,* (pub. at 36s) *cloth,* 20s *Edinb.* 1847

1033 ZUINGLII amica Exegesis, id est, Expositio Eucharistiae negocii, sm. 4to. *the printer's device, frogs climbing a tree, and " Christof Frosch over zuo Zurich," half morocco,* 7s *s. l. e. a.* (Zurich, Froschover ? 1527)

1034 **INQUISITION.**—PEREIRA, Narrative of his persecution by the Inquisition, 2 vols. 8vo. *portrait, hf. calf,* 6s
1811

1035 DISCUSION del proyecto de decreto sobre la Inquisicion, square 8vo. 694 pp. *sewed,* 5s *Cadiz,* 1813

1036 LLORENTE, Histoire critique de l'Inquisition d'Espagne jusqu' à Ferdinand VII, traduite par Pellier, 4 vols. 8vo. *hf. calf gilt,* 20s *Paris,* 1817
"The great storehouse from which are to be drawn more well authenticated facts relating to the subject than can be found in all other sources put together."—TICKNOR I. 415.

1037 **JESUITS.**—APOLOGIE de l'Institut des Jesuites, 12mo. *calf,* 5s 1763

1038 EXTRAITS des Assertions dangereuses et pernicieuses des Jesuites, 3 vols. 12mo. *calf,* 6s *Amst.* 1763

1039 POLITIQUE des Jesuites, 12mo. *old calf, rare,* 5s *Londres,* 1688

1040 RELATIONS DES JESUITES, contenant ce qui s'est passé de plus remarquable dans les Missions des Pères de la Compagnie de Jésus dans la Nouvelle France, ouvrage publié sous les auspices du Gouvernment Canadien, 1611-72, 3 vols. stout royal 8vo. *double columns, containing reprints of the journals and letters of the Missionaries in* CANADA, *during a most interesting period, calf gilt,* £4. 4s
Quebec, 1858

1041 RIBADENERA, Vie d'Ignace Loyola, 12mo. *vellum,* 6s *Arras,* 1607

1042 **JEWS.**—BROWN's (W.) Antiquities of the Jews, 2 vols. 8vo. *cloth,* 5s 1826

1043 CARBEN (Victor Von). Hier inne wirt gelesen wie Her Victor von Carben, welicher eyn Rabi der Juden gewest ist zu Christlichen glawbn komen, *Nuremberg, H. Höltzel,* 1508—DER JUDENBENEDICITE wie sy gott den heren loben und im umb die speytz dancken, *curious woodcuts, Collen, H. Gutschaiff*—in 1 vol. 4to. *original oak boards, a portion of an ancient musical manuscript having curious figures for notes, is pasted on the boards,* 15s
The first is an interesting tract on the conversion of Victor von Carben from Judaism to Christianity; the second tract, having on the title, in French, 'Qui bien leur feroit rayson,' treats on the prayers and ceremonies of the Jews before meals.

1044 DEPPING, les Juifs dans le Moyen Age, 8vo. *cloth,* 6s *Paris,* 1845

1045 JOST, Geschichte der Israeliten seit der Zeit der Maccabäer bis auf unsre Tage, 9 vols. in 5, 8vo. *new, in cloth,* 32s *Berl.* 1820-28

1046 STEHELINS Rabbinical Literature; or the Traditions of the Jews contained in the Talmud and other mystical writings, and their opinions concerning Messiah; with Buxtorf's account of their religious customs and ceremonies, and a Preliminary Inquiry into the origin, &c. of these traditions, 2 vols. sm. 8vo. *half calf neat,* RARE, £2. 1748

1047 TOVEY'S (D'Blossiers) ANGLIA JUDAICA; or, the History and Antiquities of the Jews in England, 4to. *plate, hf. bd. morocco, uncut,* 32s *Oxford,* 1738
Fetched, 1855, Bernal's copy, £2.

1048 WOTTON'S Miscellaneous Discourses, relating to the Traditions and Usages of the Scribes and Pharisees in Christ's time; on the MISNA, Shabbath, and Eruvin, 2 vols. sm. 8vo. *old calf, very neat, very rare,* £2. 2s 1718

HORAE, MISSALS, OFFICIA, PASSIONALES, and EARLY LITURGICAL LITERATURE, in all LANGUAGES.

1049 **Armenian.** HYMNS of the Armenian Church, in Armenian, stout 12mo. *ornamental initials, and numerous curious woodcuts, original stamped binding, well preserved, rare,* 36s (? *Rome*) 1702

1050 **Basque.** Guiristinoen Doctrina Laburra haur ga tei irakhasteco Piarres de Lavieuxville, 12mo. *olive morocco, gilt edges, very rare,* £3. *Bayonan,* 1757

1051 **Brazilian.** BERNARDO DE NANTES, Catechismo Indico da Lingua Kariris, crescentado de varias Praticas Doutrinaes e Moraes, adaptadas do capacidade dos INDIOS DO BRAZIL, 12mo. *veau fauve, gilt edges, by Vogel, beautiful copy, very rare,* £5. *Lisboa,* 1709

1052 **Croatian.** CROATIAN HOMILIES. Kurtze auszlegung über die Sonntags unnd der fürnembsten Fest Evangelia durch das gantz Jar, *jetzt erstlich in Crobatischer Sprach mit Crobatischen Buchstaben getruckt,* sm. 4to. *woodcut initials, very fine copy in old calf, gauffré edges, portraits of the three editors stamped on the sides,* RARE, £2. 16s *Tubingen,* 1562

The end of the German preface is signed by the editors; Primus Truber *Creiner,* Antonius *Dalmata,* Stephanus *Consul Histrianus.*

1053 BREVIARIUM Romanum SLAVONICO idiomate jussu Innocentii PP. XI. editum, stout sm. 4to. *printed in red and black in the Croatian Glogolitic character (charactere Sancti Hieronymi), clean copy in vellum,* £2.
Romae, Prop. fidei, 1688

1054 **English.** ARTICLES whereupon it was agreed by the Archbishoppes and Bishoppes and the whole cleargie, in the Convocation at London in the yere 1562, for the avoiding of the diversities of opinions, and for the stablishyng of consent touching true religion, put foorth by the Queenes authoritie, smallest 4to. *title surrounded by an elegant woodcut border,* 28 pp. *very beautiful copy, purple morocco,* £3. 3s
Imprinted at London in Paules Churchyard, by Richard Jugge and John Cawood, printers to the Queenes Majestie, 1571

The first edition was printed by R. Grafton, 1553; a copy of it fetched, 1857, Sotheby's £5. 10s. The above ENGLISH Edition is extremely rare; I traced the sale of no copy, nor does Lowndes quote the sale of one. The LATIN Edition, printed in the same year by John Day, is of frequent occurrence.

1055 ARTICLES of the CHURCH: Sparrow's Collection of Articles, Injunctions, Canons, with other Publick Records of the Church, chiefly in the times of Edward VI., Elizabeth, James I. and Charles I.—in 1 vol. *many in* Black letter, sm. 4to. *plate of Arms, calf,* 20s 1675

1056 CERTAYNE SERMONS or HOMILIES appoynted by the Kynges Maiestie to be declared and redde, by all persones, Vicars, or Curates, every Sondaye in their Churches, where they have cure, smallest 4to. *second issue of the* FIRST EDITION, Black letter, *very fine copy, with the large device, purple morocco extra, gilt edges,* £8. 8s
Imprinted at London the xxi *daye of June, in the seconde yere of the reigne of our sovereigne lorde kyng Edward the VI.: By Richard Grafton, printer to his moste royall Majestie. In the yere of our Lorde,* 1548

This, the first book of our Homilies, was written by Archbishop Cranmer. The issue of 1548 corresponds with that of 1547; both contain sheets A—Z in fours. The entire copy, including the last leaf, containing the Colophon, and on the reverse the large device, is in beautiful preservation.
The issue by R. Grafton, dated 1547, fetched, 1857, at Sotheby's, £7. 10s. The present copy is marked higher on account of its finer condition. Lowndes ignores the issue of 1548. I have been unable to trace the sale of a copy.

1057 CERTAINE SERMONS or HOMILIES appoynted to be read in Churches, in the time of the late Queene Elizabeth of famous memory, and now thought fit to be reprinted by authority from the Kings most excellent maiesty, the first and second tome in 1 vol. folio, *tall, clean and sound copy, in the original calf binding,* 36s *London, the date neatly altered to* 1600,? 1639

1058 A FORME OF COMMON PRAYER, together with an order of Fasting, smallest 4to. *purple* MOROCCO *extra, gilt edges, fine copy,* £2. 12s
Lond. R. Barker, and the assignes of John Bill, 1636
" The Prayers are to be read every Wednesday during this Visitation Set forth by his Maiesties Authority."

1059 COMMON PRAYER, BOOK OF, and Administration of the Sacraments, and other Rites of the Church of England, 1639—Psalmes in English Meeter, with apt Notes, *for the Company of Stationers,* 1640—in 1 vol. small 4to. Black letter, *in fair preservation, calf,* 20s 1639-40

1060 COMMON PRAYER, THE BOOK OF, and Administration of the Sacraments, and other Rites and Ceremonies according to the use of the Church of England, with the Psalter or Psalms of David, and the Form of Ordaining Bishops, &c. folio, *very beautiful title, engraved by Williamson, the text printed in Black Letter, and entirely surrounded by carefully ruled double lines,* ROYAL COPY, *in the original old blue* MOROCCO, *elaborately tooled sides, paintings of flowers and the Royal Coat of Arms on the gilt edges; a magnificent volume, in excellent preservation,* £8. 8s *London, printed by his M printers, cum privilegio,* 1669
From the Library of Charles II., with the autograph of Rupert Clarke on the margin of the title.

1061 LITURGIA, seu liber precum communium et Sacramentorum, 16mo. *old morocco,* 6s   *Lond.* 1681

1062 LITURGIA Inglesa, o Libro del Rezado publico, de la administracion de los Sacramentos, y otros Ritos de la Yglesia de Ingalaterra, sm. 4to. *old calf*, 20s; or *old blue mor. gilt edges, Arms on sides*, 32s *Augusta Trinob.* CIƆ.IƆI.IXIIV.
⁎ This first translation of the English Liturgy into Spanish, and which is hardly known, was made by Thomas Carrascon, (a Spanish friar who embraced the Protestant religion,) at the command of King James, who rewarded his labours by making him a canon of Hereford Cathedral.

1063 PETITION FOR PEACE : with the REFORMATION of the LITURGY, as it was presented to the Right Reverend Bishops, by the DIVINES appointed by his Majesties Commission to treat with them about the ALTERATION of it, sm. 4to. 95 pp. *purple morocco, gilt edges,* £2. 10s   *London*, 1661
Without the name of the printer, or any of the names of the Petitioners. Ending: "To him BE Glory for ever. Amen."

1064 PETITION FOR PEACE, *a new edition, the words of the title and of the book the same as the above, but differently put into type,* sm. 4to. 101 pp. ending: To him BEE Glory for ever. Amen." *a splendid copy in purple* MOROCCO *extra,* UNCUT, £5.   *London, printed* A.D. 1661
Both editions are very rare, they are not mentioned in Lowndes; I have met with no trace of the sale of a copy. Appended to the last copy is " A true and perfect copy of the whole disputation at the Savoy, etc. printed in the year 1662," 4 *leaves*

1065 PRIMER set furth by the kinges majestie and his Clergie, to be taught, learned and red, sm. 8vo. 𝔅𝔩𝔞𝔠𝔨 𝔩𝔢𝔱𝔱𝔢𝔯, *calf, with some rough leaves*, 18s
1546 : Reprinted without any alteration, (? 1590)

1066 **French.** CODICES Sacramentorum nongentis annis vetustiores, nimirum Libri 3 Sacramentorum Romanæ Ecclesiæ, Missale Gothicum, sive Gallicanum Vetus, Missale Francorum, Missale Gallicanum Vetus, cura Thomasii, sm. 4to. *old calf gilt,* 21s   *Romæ*, 1680

1067 **Gaelic** Book of Common Prayer with the Psalter, 8vo. *bd.* 5s   *Edinb.* 1794

1068 CONFESSION OF FAITH, Catechisms by the Assembly of Divines at Westminster, with the assistance of the Church of Scotland, *in the Gaelic language*, 16mo. *bd. rare,* 9s   *Edinb.* 1727

1069 **German (Low)** KERCKENORDENINGE : Wo ydt mit Christlyker Lere, vorrekinge der Sacramente, Ordination der Denere des Evangelii, ordentlyken Ceremonien, in den Kerchen Visitation, Consistorio unde Scholen, im Hertochdome tho Mockenlenborch, &c. geholden wert, sm. 4to. *large coat-of-arms on the back of the title, with musical notes to the portions chanted by the priest, fine copy, calf gilt,* £2.   *Gedrucket tho Rostock, by Ludowich Dietz,* 1557
" Interesting as a monument of the Symbolism of the early Lutheran Church, and of the language of Lower Saxony bearing great affinity to old English."

1070 **Guarani.** RUYZ (Padre Antonio) Catecismo de la lingua Guarani, *Guarani y Castellano*, 16mo. *limp vellum, very rare,* £3. 10s   *Madrid*, 1640

1071 **Irish.** STAPLETON (Theobaldi) Catechismus seu doctrina Christiana Latino-Hibernica, cum Modo perutili legendi linguam Hibernicam, sm. 4to. *Latin and Irish, green morocco, very rare,* 35s   *Bruxellis*, 1639

1072 **Jewish.** FORM OF PRAYERS according to the Custom of the Polish and German Jews, *Hebrew and English,* translated into English by David Levy, carefully revised, corrected and illustrated (by Lyon), 7 vols. roy. 8vo. *roan gilt,* £2. 5s   *H. Abrahams,* 5609 (1848)

1073 **Mexican.** PARADES, Catecismo Mexicano, que contiene toda la Doctrina Christiana con todas sus Declaraciones, dispusolo primeramente en Castellano el Padre Geronymo de Ripalda, literalmente lo traduxo del Castellano en proprio Idioma Mexicano el padre Ignacio de Paredes, con otras cosas, 12mo. RARE, *fine copy, red Turkey morocco, gilt edges, by Fr. Bedford.* £5. 5s
En Mexico, en la Imprenta de la Bibliotheca Mexicana, 1758
Extremely rare, I can not trace the sale of one copy.

1074 **Mohawk.** Book of Common Prayer, Collects, &c. *English and Mohawk, by Nelles and Hill, 8vo. bd. 18s* Hamilton, (*U. S.*) 1842
1075 **Romaic.** LITURGIA BELGICA, *Romaice :* Tōn ekklēsiōn tēs Belgikēs Christianikē didaskalia kai Taxis, 4to. LARGE PAPER, *the whole in Modern Greek, vellum,* 20s Lugd. Bat. Elzev. 1648
1076 COMMON PRAYER and Psalter, 18mo. *cloth,* 5s Bagster
1077 **Russian.** KULCZYNSKI, Specimen Ecclesiæ Ruthenicæ cum sede Romanâ unitæ, de Archiespisc. Kiov. Metropolitisque etc. large 8vo. *sd.* 7s 6d
(*Romæ*, 1732), *Paris*, 1860
1078 **MISSALE** BENEDICTINE religionis Monachorum cenobii Mellicensis, folio, *rubric initials, headings, and directions, in the original oak boards, rare,* £2. 2s Nurnberge, Georgius Stöchs de Sulczpach, ca. 1500
1078*MISSALE CHALDAICUM, ex decreto Congregationis de propaganda fide editum, folio, *in Syriac characters, hf. morocco,* 15s Romæ, 1767
1079 MISSALE mixtum, secundum regulam Beati Isidori dictum MOZARABES, cum præfat. notis et Appendice, ab Alexandro Lesleo, 2 parts in 1 vol. 4to. *fine copy in vellum, rare,* £2. 2s Priced, 1834, £3. 3s. Romæ, 1755
1080 MISSALE ROMANUM ex decreto concilii Tridentini restitutum et Pii V jussu editum folio, *with many quaint woodcuts, leaves* 128-130 *and* 265 *have been badly used, deficiencies of the corners have been replaced by inferior facsimile, otherwise the volume is in fair condition ; its feature however is its* SPLENDID OLD VENE-TIAN CALF BINDING, *the centre of the two sides being in the Indented Venetian style, which preserves the rich gilding, consisting of the Passion of Christ, and the Evangelists, with gold borders on the outer side of the corner, gilt gauffré and painted edges,* £6. Venetiis, 1576
An interesting specimen of the Venetian binding of the period.
1081 MISSALE ROMANUM ex decreto Sacrosancti Concilii Tridentini restitutum, Pii V. Pont. Max. jussu editum, stout 8vo. *with Music, plate of the Crucifixion, Ascension, etc. old black morocco, with clasps, gilt edges,* 12s Antverpiae, 1711
1082 MISSALE ad usum insignis ecclesie TRAJECTESIS, una cū eiusdē ecclie cōsuetudinibus ac observātiis, ad vetustiorū, excplariū veritatem recognitus, folio, BLACK LETTER, *woodcut border round the title, illustrative of the life of Christ, with numerous other fine woodcuts, two leaves of the Canon Missae, with a very fine woodcut of the Crucifixion, full size of the page, are on vellum, with several leaves of Music, in sound condition throughout, old stamped calf,* £2. 18s
Antverpiæ, 1527
1083 **PASSIONALE, Dutch.** PASSIONAEL, ende is geheyten in Latijn Aurea Legenda dat beduyt in Duytsche dye gulden legende, folio, 𝔅lack letter, *the initial letters painted in, fine copy in the original oak boards, covered with stamped leather,* 36s Goude, in Hollant, Gheraert Leeu, 1480
Priced, 1839, Thorpe, old mor. 4l 5s; 1841-2, Thorpe, old mor. 3l 13s 6d.
"This extremely rare edition, which has apparently escaped the researches of nearly all bibliographers, is a fine and early specimen of printing at Gouda by Gerard Leeu; who, after the year 1484, settled himself at Antwerp."
1084 PASSIONAEL (dat) WINTER STUCK ; eñ is gehietē in latijn Aurea Legeda ; dat beduut in Duytsce : die guldē legende, 4to. 𝔅lack letter, *numerous large, curious, and rude woodcuts, the Crucifixion, Adoration of the Magi, Murder of the Innocents, Saints, Bishops, etc. Dutch calf gilt,* £2 Delfft in Holland, 1487
1085 PASSIONAEL. Dit es d'levē ons liefs heeren Jhesu Cristi, met addicien van schoonen moralen eñ geestelikē leeringhen eñ devoten meditacien, sm. folio, *woodcut on the title and a profusion through the book, plain ; with painted initials, original oak boards covered with stamped calf, very rare,* £6. 10s
Antwerpen int Huys vā Delft Henrick Eckert vā Homberch, 1503
1086 **Low German.** PASSIONAEL, "Hyr hevet sik an dat samer deel der hilghen levent unde to deme erstē male van deme levē hilgē lerer Sūte Ambrosi' de bischoppe." On the verso of fol. 180 " Hyr endiget sik dat sommer deel. . . On fol. 181 "Hyr hevet sik an dat Winter del." At the end " Hyr endiget sik der hilligē levent dat een seer nutte speeghel is der minschen. . ." 2 parts in 1, stout large folio (15½ inches by 11), 420 *leaves,* 𝔅lack letter, *Rubric initials, numerous woodcuts, in the original oak binding, partly uncut,* £17. 10s (? Lübeck, 1470)
A very beautiful copy of a work in the Low Saxon dialect, unknown to most bibliographers. Hain cites a copy, wanting, as he states the two leaves of table ; but which also wanted the Register that is to be found in this copy (misplaced between ff. 402-3), and the existence of which he was not aware of. He attributes the work to the concluding portion of the fifteenth century ; but it is considered to be nearly thirty years earlier.
This enormous volume, filled with very curious wood-engravings, is, without contradiction, one of the most interesting monuments of Ancient German typography.

1087 PASSIONAEL. Hyr hevet syk an dat Passionael: Unde dat Levend der Hylghen: unde to deme ersten dat Samer deel—*In fine*: Hyr endighet sik dat passionael efte der hyllighen levendt mit velen nyen merckliken historien, ... uth deme latine in dat dudesck ghebracht uñ gedrukket dorch dat beevel uñ kunst Steffani Arndes inwaner uñ borgher der keyserlike stat Lubeck, int yar unses herë MCCCCXCII up dē dach sunte Elizabeth, stout folio, 418 *leaves, with many quaint* WOODCUTS, *though rude, but very good impressions, most probably used here for the first time, all the cuts entirely free from color, singularly fine sound copy, calf,* VERY RARE, £9. 9s *Lübeck, Arnd*, 1492

An early edition of the Passionale in Low German; for reviews see Panzer's Annalen, page 194; von Seelen Select. litterar. p. 632; Suhl's Verzeichniss, p. 55; Helmst. Biblioth. Bruns Bietr. zur krit Bearb. p. 177; Goetze merkwürdigkeiten Band 2 p. 463.—Goetz ridicules the contents of this work, but he adds, that he must praise the Low German translator for occasionally doubting the truth of these stories. This edition contains several ORIGINAL Legends, extremely fabulous, not contained in the Latin and High German editions.

1088 PSALTERIUM, *Latine, Incipit:* [B] eatus vir qui nō abiit in cōsilio ipiorū. *In fine*, Finit psalteriū impressū per Fridericū Crewsner de Nurenberga, Laus deo Clementissimo, stout sm. 4to. 162 *leaves, thick paper, bold gothic type,* 19 *lines to a full page, remarkably well preserved in the original impressed binding, the Virgin and child stamped in gold on the sides, with clasps,* £8. 8s   ca. 1472

EXTREMELY RARE. The first letter illuminated in gold and colours, the other initials painted in, with the musical notes added in manuscript. Various prayers, Litanies, etc. in a handwriting of the 15th century are added on the fly-leaves at the commencement and the end. This copy agrees with Panzer's collation.
Priced, 1847, Thorpe, £10. 10s.
It seems to me doubtful, whether this volume was really printed at Nürnberg; the little variety of type used makes it appear rather to have been produced at some small monastery, "per F. Crewsner *de* Nurenberga."

1089 SUMMA JOHANNIS, FIRST EDITION, in *Low German*, sm. folio, *very fine copy, in old calf, not mentioned by Scheller,* £5.   *Lubek, S. Arndes*, 1487

COLLATION: Table of contents, 8 *leaves*; the book commencing: Hir hevet sik an de vorrede disses bokes genomet Suma Johannis, welker de eerwerdige vader lezemester Johannes van Vryborgh prediker ordens to latine ghemaket unde uth deme hylligen decret boke getoge hefft. Unde van latine in dat dudesche gemaket dorch einen hochgelerden doctore geheten brod. Bartold, *sheets* A—S (in 8 eight) T in 10 *leaves.* "This version in the language of Lower Saxony is very rare and highly interesting in a philological point of view. The colophon is curious: Here ends itself Summa Joannis which is taken out of the holy book of Decretals, which is most useful to the instruction of the people to their soul's happiness."—*Singer's MS. note.*

1090 VIE (la) de nostre Seigneur Jesu Christ, par figures, selon le texte des quattre Evangelistes, avec toutes les Evangiles, Epistres et Propheties de toute l'année, "par grace et privilege de la Majesté Imperiale," 12mo. lettres gothiques, *several hundred fine woodcuts by an eminent French artist, olive morocco extra, gilt edges,* £2.

The volume ends "Le jour dedacesse, Apoca XXI a;" the colophon being apparently wanting. The prologue is signed "Escript dempres *Gand, aux Chartreus, les xxv de Decembre l'am MDXXXVII.*

BIBLES AND TESTAMENTS.

1091 BIBLIA SACRA POLYGLOTTA, complectentia Textus Originales, Hebraicum, (cum Pentateucho Samaritano), Chaldaicum, Graecum, versionesque antiquas, Samaritanam, Graecam, Chaldaicam, Syriacam, Arabicam, Æthiopicam Persicam, et Vulgatam Latinam, cum omnium Translationibus Latinis, et apparatu, appendicibus, tabulis, &c. edidit Brianus WALTONUS, 6 vols. *fine portrait by Lombart, engraved title and other plates by Hollar,* ROYAL COPY, *Lond.* 1657—E. CASTELLI, Lexicon Heptaglotton, Heb. Chald. Syr. Sam. Æthiop. Arab. et Pers. cum omnium Grammaticis, 2 vols. *portrait by Faithorne, ib.* 1699—together 8 vols. royal folio, *fine copy, in the original old English blue morocco, full gilt back, sides tooled with gold lines, ruled with red lines throughout,* £30.   1657-69

Priced, 1831, Thorpe, with both prefaces, £45; 1831, Payne and Foss, vellum, £36.; 1837, Payne and Foss, with the Royal dedication, mor. £52. 10s, russia, £42. By auction a copy sold in 1855, with the dedication to Charles II., and the reprint, morocco, £35.
"This Polyglot is of the utmost importance to a critic, not only on account of the extracts which it contains from a variety of important MSS., but particularly on account of the Oriental versions, from which he must collect various readings of the New Testament. Though several of the MSS. which are quoted in the Polyglot have since that time been more accurately collated, and no one would now have recourse to that edition for the reading of the Codex Alexandrinus or Cantabrigiensis; yet some of the MSS. which Usher had collected, have never since been examined, Mill and Wetstein have inserted those readings in their collections as they found them in the Polyglot. Now, as errors of the press are unavoidable, especially in a work like Wetstein's, it is necessary to have a recourse to the Polyglot whenever a doubt arises in regard to the accuracy of a quotation by Mill or Wetstein, in order to see whether these MSS. which were collated for the London Polyglot, have the readings in question or not."
BP. MARSH'S MICHÆLIS

1092 BIBLIA SACRA POLYGLOTTA, Textus Archetypos Versionesque præcipuas ab Ecclesia antiquitùs receptas necnon versiones recentiores complectentia; accedunt Prolegomena in Textuum Archetyporum Versionumque antiquarum

BIBLES AND TESTAMENTS. 75

Crisin literalem, auctore Samuele LEE, large stout folio, *a beautiful copy in blue morocco extra, gilt leaves, rare*, £11. 10s *Londini, Bagster*, 1831
An excellent Polyglot edition of the Bible, in *Hebrew, Greek, Latin, English, French, German, Italian and Spanish*, now very scarce. At the end of the volume are, Variae lectiones in versionem septuaginta virorum, Novum Testamentum Græcum, Pentateuchum Hebræo-Samaritanum, and the whole of the New Testament *in Syriac*.

1093 PSALTERIUM in *quatuor* linguis Hebræa, Græca, Chaldæa et Latina, edidit Potkenus, sm. folio, *calf gilt*, 36s *Coloniæ*, 1518
The version called Chaldee on the title, is Ethiopic, that language being supposed in Potken's time to be the true Chaldee, while the language called Chaldee was considered to be simply a corrupt colloquial dialect.—See Dibdin's Bibl. Spencer, vii. p. 196.
Edition beaucoup plus rare que celle de Gênes. Vend. £4. 4s, Pinelli.—BRUNET.

1094 JONAH, The Book of, in four Semitic versions, Chaldee, Syriac, Aethiopic, and Arabic, with Glossaries, by Wright, 8vo. (pub. at 7s 6d) *cloth*, 4s 6d 1857
1095 **Akra.** Gospels of Matthew and John, 12mo. *calf*, 3s 6d ? 1844
1096 **Amharic.** Bible: Old Testament, from the beginning, Sign. B—6 G; New Testament, *B—*SS. edited by Platt, 4to. *no title, calf neat*, 7s 6d (? 1850)
1097 **Anglo-Saxon.** HEPTATEUCHUS, Job, et Evangelium Nicodemi, *Anglo-Saxonice*, Historiæ Judith Fragmentum, *Dano-Saxonice*, edidit E. Thwaites, 8vo. *frontispiece, a fine copy, calf*, 12s *Oxon.* 1698
In this work it was Aelfric's object to furnish his countrymen with a translation of those parts of the Scripture only which he conceived to be most important for them to know; and in the execution of his purpose, although he has sometimes given an accurate verbal translation of the passages he has selected from Holy Writ, yet he has for the most part stated, in his own words, only the substance of the precepts inculcated, and the history recorded by the inspired penman.

1098 PSALTERIUM Davidis Latino-Saxonicum Vetus à J. SPELMANNO editum, sm. 4to. FINE COPY, *formerly Sir W. Dugdale's, from Miss Currer's library, in blue morocco, extra gilt edges*, £4. *Lond.* 1640
Upon the title is written "Ex dono Henrici Spelmanni Equitis;" and underneath "N.B. This is Sir Wm. Dugdale's Writing, E.R M." (Edward Rowe Mores.)

1099 PSALMORUM Versio antiqua Latina, cum Paraphrasi *Anglo-Saxonica*, partim metrice, ed. Thorpe, 8vo. *facsimile, hf. calf*, 7s 6d *Oxonii*, 1835
1100 HALGAN GODSPEL (Da) on Englisc: the Anglo-Saxon version of the Holy Gospels, edited from the original MSS. by Benjamin Thorpe, 12mo. (pub. at 12s) *cloth*, 6s 1842
1101 **Arabic.** BIBLIA Sacra Arabica Sacræ Congregationis de Propaganda fide jussu edita ad usum Ecclesiarum Orientalium, additis e regione Bibliis Latinis Vulgatis (ed. Sergius Risius), 3 vols. folio, *hf. vellum*, 25s *Romæ*, 1671
Priced, 1828, Payne and Foss, £3. 6s; 1837, Dolman, £4. 14s 6d; 1832, Dondé-Dupré, 88 fr. and 90 fr.; 1823 1840, 1848, Payne and Foss, £5. 5s. Described by Clément, in the "Bibliothèque Curieuse," and by Van Praet.

1102 **Armenian.** Bible, 4 vols. 12mo. *hf. bound* 10s *Venice*, 1805
1103 **Berber.** St. Luc, 12 Chapitres de, en langue Berbère, 8vo. *calf*, 2s 6d 1833
1104 **Bohemian.** BIBLIA SACRA, Starcho y Noweho Zakona, stout 8vo. *calf*, 5s 1831
1105 Nowy Zakonwnowe de Tesstiny prekozeny: *Bohemian Testament*, 18mo. *fine copy in red morocco, gilt edges*, 25s *Wytissteny*, 1596
1106 **Breton.** TESTAMENT NEVEZ, Brezounek, gant LE GONIDEC, 12mo. *calf*, 3s 6d *Angoulem*, 1827
1107 TESTAMENT NEVEZ, 12mo. *half bound*, 5s *Brest*, 1847
1108 **Burmese.** The New Testament, 8vo. *calf*, 7s 6d *Maulmein*, 1837
1109 **Caffir.** Old Testament, Genesis to Joshua, 8vo. *bds.* 10s *Emkangiso*, 1857
1110 **Chaldee.** Gospels in Syriac characters, 4to. *calf*, 5s ? 1840
1111 **Chinese.** Old and New Testaments in Chinese, translated by Marshman, 2 vols. impl. 8vo. *first edition, calf neat*, 15s *Serampore*, 1817-22
1112 GOSPEL of St. John, according to the dialect of Shanghai, in the Roman Character, with Vocabulary, by Prof. Summers, 12mo. *hf. calf*, 5s 1853
1113 **Coptic.** PSALTERIUM cum Cantico Mosis, etc. ed. Tuki, Coptice et Arabice, sm. 4to. *hf. russia*, 7s 6d *Romæ*, 1744
1114 NOVUM TESTAMENTUM Ægyptium vulgo Copticum, *Coptice et Latine*, ed. Wilkins, 4to. *calf*, 12s *Oxon.* 1716
1115 **Cotta.** The Old Testament, stout 8vo. *no title, sd. uncut*, 5s ? *Colombo*, 1830
1116 **Danish.** Bibelen eller den hellige Skrift, 8vo. *calf*, 5s 1855
1117 PSALME-BOG, Samling af gamle og nye Psalmer, high 16mo. *Danish red morocco, a curious specimen of binding*, 10s *Kiöbenhavn*, 1780

1118 **Dutch.** BIBLE mit horen Boecken ende elc Boeck mit alle sijne capitalen bi enē notabelen Meester wel overgheset ende wel naerstelic gecorrigeert ende wel ghespelt, 2 vols. in 1, stout sm. folio, EDITIO PRINCEPS, litt. goth. *the prologue, which is frequently wanting, inlaid: otherwise a very fine sound and perfect copy, the initials painted in, the first illuminated, in the original oak boards, covered with stamped calf, in fine preservation,* VERY RARE, £7. 16s

Delft, Jacob Jacobsoen, Mauritius Yemantszoen, 1477

Priced, 1837, Payne and Foss, £10. 10s.; the Crevenna copy fetched 224 fr.; Dr. Hawtrey's £8. This is not only the first book printed at Delft, but is also the first edition of the Bible in Dutch. It only contains the Old Testament (without the Psalter) including the Apocrypha. The Psalter and New Testament were not printed till some years later.

Dr. Cotton calls it a book of high rarity, and states that a copy is preserved in the University Library of Leyden. Dr. Dibdin likewise remarks, that as the FIRST impression of the Dutch Bible, it cannot fail to be interesting to every owner of a copy of it.

1119 BIBEL (De): Oude ende Nyeuwe Testament, folio, *woodcut title and numerous rude woodcuts, oak boards,* 12s *Antwerpen,* 1560

A Roman Catholic version, containing the Apocryphal books in their usual place. The Colophon of the Old Testament is dated 1553, and that of the New 1560.

1120 BIJBEL, volgens het Besluit van de Synode 1618-19, 8vo. *calf,* 5s   1846

1121 **ENGLISH.** BIBLE, THE GREAT. The Byble in Englyshe, that is to saye the content of all the holy Scrypture, bothe of ye olde and newe testament, stout folio, *a copy of Cromwell's Bible, commonly called the first edition of Cranmer's, not perfect, very tall copy, in the original binding, excessively rare,* £48. *Fynisshed in Apryll Anno* MCCCCCXXXIX.

A most desirable copy for completion by facsimile; Mr. Harris would be glad to receive the commission. The title and five succeeding preliminary pages, and also the title preceding the third book of Esdras, are wanting. The first couple of leaves, and the last two, as also a few in the middle of the book, are injured and defective; but the greater portion of the work is in good condition. The titles and woodcuts of the "Great Bible" are considered superb, and have been attributed to Hans Holbein; the type is large and beautiful, and the paper excellent.

The extreme rarity of the above Bible may be imagined when it is stated that Gardner's copy fetched 12*l*.

1122 BYBLE, nowe lately with greate industry and diligence recognized (by EDMUND BECKE after TAVERNER's recognition, with prologues to the New Testament by WILLIAM TINDALE), folio, in gothic type, 65 *lines to a full page,* 3 *titles with four woodcuts to each, numerous engravings and ornamental initials; wanting a corner of a leaf in the Kalendar, title to the Old Testament, in place of which the title to the New Testament is put, one leaf Ecclesiasticus* viii., *one leaf at Baruch* ii., *and from Revelations* xvii. *to the end ; otherwise a fair copy, old calf,* £8. 8s   *London, by John Daye and William Seres,* 1549

The FIRST complete English BIBLE printed during the reign of Edward VI.; it is Taverner's edition, by Becke. Very rare; even imperfect copies seldom occur for sale. Priced, complete, 1853, Thorpe, original binding, £31. 10s.; 1847, Thorpe, russia, £52. 10s. Fetched, 1854, Gardner's sale, original binding, £40. Mended copies: fetched, 1857, at Stevens' sale, bottom of the title restored by Harris, morocco, £22.; 1854; Pickering's, title and leaf mended in the margins, morocco, £16. The value has considerably risen within the last few years.

Collation of the present copy: Title of the Old Testament supplied by the Title of the New Testament; the Kalendar, 2 leaves; 'An exhortation' and 'the summe and content of all the holy Scriptures,' 1 leaf; Dedication to 'Prince Edward the sixt' by Edmunde Becke,' and 'A description and successe,' 2 leaves; 'To the Christen Readers,' a column, and 'A table of the principall matters in the Byble,' 23 leaves; 'The suppatacion,' 1 page; 'Prologe' and 'Regyster,' 2 leaves: Genesis, Deuteron. fol. 1-lxxxviii.; woodcut title to seconde part and Joshua, fol. i-cxliii.; woodcut title to the 'thyrd part and Psalter to Malachy,' fol. i-cxlv., at the first psalm occurs the largest woodcut in the book, being about half the size of the page; 'the Apocripha,' with a woodcut title, fol. i-lxxvi.; the title to 'the Newe Testament' is, as before stated, placed at the commencement; Uuillia Tindale unto the Christen Reader, followed by the New Testament as far as chapter xvi. of the Revelation of St. John,' folio i-cxviii.

The woodcuts are all different, and on one of them is an engraver's mark, J. F. The two largest are one at the reverse of title of the Psalms, the other at folio xlix of Esaie, the latter of which is ink-marked.

See Cotton, Ames by Dibdin, and Lewis

1123 BYBLE (The) whych is all the holy Scripture (MATTHEWE'S VERSION, published by EDMUNDE BECKE, with Tyndale's prologues), sm. folio, black letter, *imperfect in the preliminary matter, poor copy, cut close, some leaves at the beginning and several at the end much injured, in the original sheep binding,* 18s   1549

This excessively rare edition of the Holy Scriptures was published by Becke, with considerable alterations from Matthewe's translation. Priced, 1836, Thorpe, £21.; another time, £18. 18s: fetched, 1858, Sotheby's, £26. Imperfect, priced, 1836, Jno. Arch, £6. 6s; 1857, £2. 12s 6d.

The above copy wants the title and 19 preliminary leaves. It begins with Tyndale's Address to the Reader. It further wants a leaf in Genesis, a leaf in Exodus, the last leaf of Deuteronomy, and a leaf of the Psalms.

1124 BIBLE (THE HOLY), containing the Old Testament and the New (and the Apocrypha), appointed to be read in Churches, large folio, black letter, *the title rather soiled, and the margins of the six leaves of the Kalendar stained, otherwise a tall and fine copy, with good margins, in the original old rough calf binding,* £8.   *London, by Robert Barker, printer to the Queenes most excellent Maiestie, Anno* 1602

A very scarce edition of ARCHBISHOP PARKER'S VERSION, with his prologues, generally known as the BISHOP'S BIBLE. A copy fetched, 1854, Gardner's sale, russia, £9. 10s. Collation: Title, with a broad and finely engraved border with figures of the four Evangelists and the 12 Apostles, emblem of lamb slain on a block, and heraldic signs

BIBLES AND TESTAMENTS.

of the twelve tribes; Kalendar, 6 leaves; 'An Almanacke,' 1 page; Archbishop's Cranmer's Prologue, 6 pages; 'The whole Scripture,' 3 pp.; 'Table of the Genealogie of Adam passing by the Patriarches,' etc. 'in lineall descent to Christ,' 6 leaves, on the reverse of the last is a large woodcut, nearly the size of the page, of Adam and Eve in Eden, Genesis—Malachias, leaves numbered 1–314; Title to the Apocrypha with an engraved border differing from the first title; leaves numbered 316–393; Title to 'the Newe Testament,' with border differing from the former two; 'The description of the Holy Land,' 1 leaf, followed by the New Testament, leaves numbered 395–496.

1125 THE BIBLE, translated according to the Ebrew and Greeke, and conferred with the best translations in divers Languages, with a Concordance and Metrical Psalter, small 4to. *woodcut titles and music*, black letter, *belonged in 1628 to the Ffriend family, old calf*, 30s   London, Robert Barker, 1608-10

1126 BIBLE; that is, the Holy Scriptures contained in the Old and New Testament (and Apocrypha), black letter, *with 34 genealogical tables by J. S(peed), a 'description of Canaan,' and large map; on the reverse of the third leaf is a large woodcut of Adam and Eve in Eden; numerous woodcuts in the text*, London, Robert Barker, 1616—The BOOKE OF COMMON PRAYER, *with the Psalter, small black and roman letter*, Lond. Robt. Barker, 1616—BOOKE OF PSALMS in English meetre by STERNHOLD, HOPKINS, and others, *with apt notes to sing them*, 1634—3 vols. in 1, sm. folio, *the title to the Common Prayer soiled, otherwise fine copies, dark blue morocco, old style*, £5.   1616-24

A scarce edition of the GENEVAN VERSION, or Breeches Bible, with Tomson's revised New Testament; No. 123 of Lea Wilson's Collection. This is the last edition of the once most popular version, then long maintained popularity no doubt being due to the notes, it was afterwards entirely superseded by the Royal or authorised version. Priced, 1843, Payne and Foss, mor. gt. £7. 7s; Bindley's copy sold for £7. 10s. The Book of Common Prayer, not mentioned by Lowndes, is also scarce.

1127 BIBLE (the Holy), with the whole Book of Psalmes in English meeter, 3 vols. in 1, 12mo. *old English red morocco extra*, 25s   Robert Barker, ? 1618 or 1632

The dates upon the three title pages have been erased, but this must be the edition of 1618 or 1632.

1128 BIBLE (Holy), the Old and New Testament, 2 vols. 18mo. *pocket edition, engraved title, a good sound copy in vellum*, 18s   Cambridge, R. Daniel, 1648

1857, Utterson's copy fetched £2. 19s.

1129 BIBLE (The Holy), containing the Old Testament and the New, and the Psalms in English metre by Sternhold and Hopkins—together 3 vols. in 1, small 8vo. *title engraved by Vaughan, fine copy in old English red morocco, tooled back and sides, gilt edges, in beautiful preservation*, 32s   Cambridge, John Field, 1661

Sold in Hollis' sale for £3. 13s 6d. A rare edition, containing an important substitution in the Acts, chap. vi. verso 3, where, instead of 'we may appoint,' is 'ye may appoint.'

1130 BIBLE (The Holy), containing the Old Testament and Apocrypha, *engraved title page*, Cambridge, Hayes, 1677—New Testament, *ib.* Field, 1666—Book of Common Prayer, *ib. id.* 1666—Psalms in English Metre, *ib. id.* 1666—4 vols. in 1, small 4to. *old blue morocco, with borders of gold on the sides, and the initials C. F. (Charlotte Finch), inlaid in the centre, edges stamped and partly gilt, a fine specimen of old English binding*, £2. 2s   1666-77

1131 BIBLE (Holy), THE AUTHORISED VERSION, royal folio, *most beautifully printed by Baskerville, with a large clear type, fine clean copy, red* MOROCCO, *richly gilt sides*, £7   Cambridge, John Baskerville, 1763

This is one of the most beautiful books ever printed. Sold in the Duke of Roxburghe's sale for £10. 15s, Dr. Heath's for £9., and Rev. T. Williams's for £8. 10s.

1132 BIBLE (the Holy) containing the Old and New Testament and Apocrypha, printed from the first edition (compared with others) of the present translation, with notes by Thomas WILSON, Bp. of Sodor and Man, and various Renderings collected by CRUTTWELL, 3 vols. impl. 4to. *very fine copy in old English blue* MOROCCO, *joints, gilt edges*, £2.   Bath, 1785

This edition contains a Translation of the Apocryphal Third Book of Maccabees, which had not appeared in any English Bibles since Becke's edition of 1551. The text and marginal references are printed with equal beauty and correctness.

1133 HOLY BIBLE, containing the Old Testament and the New, with the APOCRYPHA, 5 vols. large 8vo. *hf. calf*, 16s   Reeves, 1802

1134 HOLY BIBLE, with Notes explanatory and practical, by D'OYLEY and MANT, 3 vols. royal 4to. LARGE PAPER, *maps and many fine plates, after Paintings by the great Masters, a superb copy in rich blue* MOROCCO EXTRA, *broad borders of gold, gilt edges*, £3. 16s   Oxford, 1817

D'Oyley and Mant's is the best "Family Bible;" even biblical Scholars will consult it profitably.

1135 HOLY BIBLE, containing the Old and New Testaments, 4to. *dark brown* MOROCCO, *blind tooling on the sides, gilt edges*, 22s   Oxford, 1824

1136 HOLY BIBLE, with commentary and critical Notes by ADAM CLARKE, LL.D. 8 vols. royal 4to. *portrait and maps, half calf, uncut*, £3. 5s   1825-17

Copies seldom occur for sale of this learned commentator's edition; 1853, Hurt's copy, calf, fetched £5.

1137 PICTORIAL BIBLE, being the Old and New Testaments according to the Authorized version, with original notes, by KITTO, 3 vols. impl. 8vo. *Knight's Pictorial edition, many hundred fine woodcuts, hf. calf neat, uncut*, 36s 1836

1138 BIBLIA, the Bible, that is, the HOLY SCRIPTURES, faithfully and truly translated by MYLES COVERDALE, Bishop of Exeter, 1535, stout 4to. *woodcut title*, (pub. at 35s) *cloth*, 25s 1535; *reprinted*, 1838

1139 BIBLE (Holy), containing the Old and New Testament, with the Apocryphal Books in the earliest English Versions made from the Latin Vulgate, by John WYCLIFFE and his followers, edited by the Rev. Josiah Forshall and SIR FREDERIC MADDEN, *the two versions printed in parallel columns and the notes underneath, cloth*, £5.; *or antique calf, red edges*, £6. 15s *Oxford University Press*, 1850

  It is astonishing, considering the widely spread Bible Worship in England and America, that the above scholarly edition of the really FIRST ENGLISH BIBLE should be so much neglected, both by the religious world and by Philologists.

  All the known Manuscripts (170 in number) of the English translations of the Old and New Testament by Wycliffe and his followers have here been most carefully collated by the first Palæographer in England, and an accurate text of TWO VERSIONS has thus been obtained. This publication is the best issued for years from the Oxford University press,—England should be proud of this LITERARY MONUMENT, a glorious Inheritance of the Middle Ages.

  The ample critical notes and various readings will prove of great interest to Saxon and English Scholars.

  The previously existing editions of the New Testament, 1731, 1810, 1848, were all printed from one Manuscript only; their value is very slender.

1140 NEW TESTAMENT, published in 1526, *the first translation* from the Greek by Tyndale, reprinted verbatim, with a Memoir by Offor, sm. 8vo. *portrait, cloth*, 8s 1836

1141 NEW TESTAMENT, translated by the English College at Rhemes; set forth the SECOND TIME by the same College returned to Doway, with New Table of Heretical Corruptions, and annotations augmented, 4to. *very fine copy, purple* MOROCCO, *gilt edges, scarce*, £3. 5s *Antwerp, Daniel Verv̄liet*, 1600

  The second edition is as scarce as the first.

1142 NEW TESTAMENT, conferred diligently with the Greeke, sm. 4to. *the inner marginal notes of five leaves injured, ruled throughout, old English blue morocco,* 12s *Robert Barker*, 1606

1143 NEW TESTAMENT, newly translated from the original Greek, 12mo. *calf, rare,* 12s *Robert Barker*, 1642

  At the end of this Testament is an epitome of the Scriptures, by Questions and Answers.

1144 ANDERSON'S Annals of the English Bible, 2 vols. 8vo. *portrait*, (pub. at 30s) *cloth*, 15s *Pickering*, 1845

1145 COTTON'S Editions of the Bible and parts thereof, in English, from 1505 to 1850, with Appendix, 8vo. *second enlarged edition, cloth*, 7s *Oxford*, 1852

1146 GILL'S Exposition of the Old and New Testaments, the origin of mankind, etc. 6 vols. stout roy. 8vo. *cloth*, £2. 16s 1852

1147 LEWIS' History of the translations of the Bible and New Testament into English; with a list of editions of the Bible, from 1526 to the present, 8vo. *plates, bds.* 5s 1818

1148 WILSON (Lea) Account of EDITIONS OF BIBLES, Testaments, Psalms, and other Books of the Holy Scriptures, in English, in his Collection, 4to. *vellum, uncut*, PRIVATELY PRINTED, *and none for sale, very scarce*, £10. 1845

  The extreme care taken by the late Mr. Wilson in the compilation of this will always render it a valuable book of reference for collations, &c. The number of copies printed was very small; some say 50, others, 120; nearly all were given to public libraries. It is in consequence gradually rising in price.

  As some irregularity occurs in the paging, the following collation is given: Title with coat of arms on reverse; Preface, 3 leaves; pp. 1-135; Appendix, pp. 129*-136*; then pp. 137-352, including Index.

1149 **Esquimaux.** PENTATEUCH, Psalms of David, and the New Testament in the Esquimaux language, 3 vols. 12mo. *bd.* 6s 1830-41

1150 TESTAMENTETAK, 12mo. *calf*, 5s 1840

1151 IMGERUTIT attorekset illagektunnut Labradorĕmetunnut, 12mo. the Moravian Hymn-Book in the Esquimaux language, 882 *Hymns, cl.* 10s *Lœbaume*, ? 1840

1152 **Ethiopic.** PSALMORUM Liber et (16) alia Cantica Biblica, *Æthiopice*; et Alphabetum seu potius Syllabarium Linguarum Chaldæarum (Æthiopicarum); impressum ingenio et impensis Joannis POTKEN, 4to. *fine woodcut on the first leaf, very fine copy in red morocco, gilt edges*, RARE, £3. 16s *Romae*, 1513

  The first book printed in the Æthiopic character.

  Priced, 1827, Thorpe, £5. 5s, and 1841-2, £4. 4s; 1837-40, Payne and Foss, £4. 4s.

1153 PSALTERIUM Davidis, *Æthiopice et Latine*, cum notis, etc. curâ LUDOLPHI, sm. 4to. *calf*, 7s 6d *Franc.* 1701

1154 PSALTERIUM Davidis, Æthiopice, 4to. *calf*, 5s 1815

1155 NOVUM TESTAMENTUM, Aethiopice, edidit Platt, sm. 4to. *calf*, 7s 6d 1830

BIBLES AND TESTAMENTS. 79

1156 **Feejee** New Testament, 12mo. *calf, 5s* 1853
1157 **Finnish.** Biblia eli Pyha Raamattu, Wanha ja Uusi Testamenti, 8vo. *calf,*
5s *St. Pietarborisa*, 1817
1158 BIBLIA, Wanha ja Uusi Testamenti, 8vo. *calf,* 10s *Stockholma*, 1838
1159 **FRENCH. BIBLE FRANCAISE.** Les Paraboles de Salomon, les Prophetes, et les Machabees, (par Le Febvre d'Estaples), folio, *triple woodcuts of the chapter headings, and woodcut initials, bd.* £2. 10s (? *Anvers*, 1528, or 1534)
The edition of 1534, of Le Fevre's Bible, which was originally brought out irregularly and in different portions in consequence of the persecution he endured, is extremely rare, having been rigorously suppressed.
Collation: The first page is blank; the second is headed "Le Prologue," under which there is a woodcut, the upper portion being a curious representation of the Trinity, with the names of the Evangelists; then follows the prologue "Pour inciter tous bos chresties etc." finishing on the page. The "Paraboles de Salomon" then begin on the second leaf, numbered "Fueillet 1," and the numeration proceeds to the last leaf, where the second book of "Machabees" ends, numbered "Fueillet cxliiii," the subscription on the verso of which is "Sensuit le nouveau testament," etc.

1160 LA SAINTE BIBLE, avec les livres des Machabées, folio, *fine woodcuts, vellum*, 30s *Lyon, J. de Tournes*, 1554
A Protestant version, executed under the revision of the Genevan pastors, and richly adorned with vignettes.
1161 BIBLE (la) qui est toute la Saincte escriture du vieil et nouveau testament, stout 12mo. *engraved title, old calf, gilt edges, fine copy*, 10s *Rochelle*, 1616
1162 BIBLE, LA SAINTE, les Psaumes en vers François, le Catéchisme, etc. revus par les Pasteurs de Geneve, 3 vols. in 1, stout folio, *with the Apocrypha, and the Music of the Psalms, bd. in sealskin, gilt edges*, 15s *Geneve*, 1712
1163 BIBLE (La Sainte) traduite sur les Textes originaux avec les differences de la Vulgate, 12mo. *a very scarce edition, King Louis Philippe's copy, in old French red morocco, gilt edges*, 27s *Cologne*, 1739
1164 BIBLE (La Sainte) traduite en François sur la Vulgate, avec les livres de l'Apocryphe, par Le Maistre de Saci, *ornée de 300 figures gravées d'après les dessins de Marillier*, 12 vols. large 8vo. *half calf, uncut*, £2. 6s *Paris*, 1789
The last volume contains "Dictionnaire de la Géographie sacrée."
1165 BIBLE, d'après l'édition de Ostervald, 4to. *calf extra, gilt edges*, 7s *Lausanne*, 1822
1166 PSALMORUM versio antiqua Gallica, e Cod. MS. (Saec. XIII) in Bibl. Bodl., cum aliis monumentis pervetustis, ed. Michel, 8vo. *facsimile, cloth, only a limited number of copies printed*, 7s 6d *Oxon.* 1860
1167 NOUVEAU TESTAMENT, reveu par les Pasteurs et Professeurs de l'Eglise de Genève—Les Pseaumes de David en Rime Françoise par Clement Marot et Theodore de Beze, les Prieres Ecclesiastiques, le Catéchisme, &c. *with the Tunes*, 2 vols. in 1, 4to. *a magnificent specimen of old red* MOROCCO, *gilt edges, having the sides and back completely covered with elaborate and minute gold tooling by Le Gascon*, £3. 10s *Charenton, P. des Hayes*, (? 1650)
1168 **French and Latin.** BIBLE (La Sainte) en *latin* et en *françois*, avec des notes, 4 vols. folio, *illustrated with a fine series of several hundred large* ENGRAVINGS *by Picart, Hoet, Houbraken, Pool, etc. with explanations under each plate in* SIX LANGUAGES, *La Haye, Hondt*, 1728, *old calf gilt*, £3. *Paris*, 1715
Cost the late J. J. de Hochepied Baron Larpent 200 francs.
1169 LE NOUVEAU TESTAMENT, en latin et françois, 16mo. *calf*, 8s *Rob. Estienne*, 1552
1170 **Gaelic.** BIOBLA Naomtha, Sein Tiomna agus an Tiomna Nuadh, re Bedel agus O'Domhnuill, 2 vols. in 1, stout 12mo. *the Irish version transferred into Roman characters for the use of the Scottish Gaels, a fine copy in old red morocco, gilt edges, by Roger Payne, from Miss Currer's library*, £2. 10s
Lunnduin, 1690
1170*LEABHRAICHE an T-SEANN TIOMNAIDH, 4 vols. 8vo. *Fine Paper, hf. bd. uncut*, 36s *Dunn-Eidin*, 1783-1801
1171 **GERMAN.** BIBEL TEUTSCH, der ander Tayl, (*Proverbs to Revelations*) stout folio, *the first edition of the rare Otmar Bible, slightly differing from the second*, 1518, *with numerous rude and curious woodcuts, in the original oak bds.* 25s *Augspurg, Hans Otmar*, 1507
1172 NAW TESTAMENT (das) nach lawt der Christlichē Kirchen bewertē Text corrigirt uñ zu recht gebracht (von Jeron. Emser), folio, *with numerous fine large woodcuts by Lucas Cranach, those in the Revelations full size of the page, stamped hogskin, rare*, £2. 10s *Dresden, Stöckel*, 1527
A Roman Catholic version executed in opposition to Luther's. With it are bound up RICIUS de Celesti Agriculturâ, *Aug. Vind.* 1541; and CHRYSOSTOMI sermones de Job, etc. *Lips.* 1538.
1173 BIBEL oder die ganze Heilige Schrift, royal 8vo. *brown morocco, gilt edges*, 5s
Cöln, 1851

1174 **Low German or Saxon.** BIBLIA DUDESCH, vor alle andere Bibeln lutterer uñ klarer na rechtem warem dudeschem uñ sessischer sprake, 2 vols. folio, *many bold woodcuts* (the same as those in the Cologne Bible), *remarkably fine copy, stamped hogskin, with clasps*, £9. 9s
Halberstad (date on woodcut-frontispiece, 1520) 1522
Carefully described by GOEZE, in his "Historie der gedruckten Niedersächsischen Bibeln von 1470-1621," 4to. *Halle*, 1675, pp. 95-105. Goeze mentions (pages 104-5) that this Bible is very scarce, even more so than the Lübeck edition; he never saw any other copy beyond his own; he thinks that Luther's version, appearing shortly after the present, must have injured its sale to that extent, that a large portion of the entire edition may have got used as waste paper. Goeze concludes by calling this edition "A JEWEL," the sight of which must always be pleasant to a connoisseur of Literary treasures.

1175 BIBLIA: Dat ys de gantze Hillige Schrift vordüdtschet dorch D. Marti. Luth. uth der lesten Correctur mercklick vorbetert unde mit grotē vlyte corrigert, (mit Bugenhagens und Dietrichs Summarien), 2 vols. stout folio, BLACK LETTER, *numerous large woodcuts by Lucas Cranach and others, fine copy in the original stamped pigskin, dated* 1546, *with brass corners,* £6.
Magdeborch dorch Hans Walther, 1545
This is the last edition of the Bible in the Low-German dialect revised by Luther. For a long and accurate description of it see Goezens Versuch einer Historie der gedruckten niedersächsischen Bibeln, pp. 275-295.

1176 BIBLIA dat ys de gantze Hillige Schrift, *Düdesch,* d. M. Luther, fol. *woodcuts, russia, good copy, rare,* £3. 3s *Magdeborch,* 1578

1177 BIBLIA, dat ys de gantze Hillige Schrifft, *Sassisch,* Dr. M. Luther's, stout sm. 4to. *with the Apocrypha, the last leaf damaged and mounted, stamped sheep,* 16s
Wittemberch, 1599-1600

1178 PSALTER eertyts door Joannem Bugenhagen in Latyn beschreven, door Bucerum wt Hebreeuscher Spraken verduytscht, ende seer schoon wtgelecht, sm. folio, *printed in three different kinds of* BLACK LETTER, *fine copy in vellum,* £2. *Geneve door Petrum Stephanum van Gendt (circa* 1570)
Rare, mentioned neither by Brunet, Ebert, Goeze nor Walch.

1179 NYE TESTAMENT Jhesu Christi, dorch Luther, mit vlyte vordüdeschet, mit schönen Figuren, Summarien unde Concordantien, vormals yn *Sassischer* Sprake nicht geseen, stout small 4to. *many woodcuts, original stamped binding,* 36s *Wittemberch, dorch Georgen Rhuwen (in fine, Rhawen) Erven,* 1562
In this edition of the New Testament is Luther's address to his friends and foes, not to find fault with it; at the end of the preface is Luther's severe judgment of the Epistle of St. James, which has been left out afterwards. There is also wanting in this edition the verse 1st St. John, v. 7, "For there are three, etc."

1180 NYE TESTAMENT Lutheri, mit Figuren, Summarien unde Concordantien, 12mo. *numerous woodcuts, vellum,* 18s *Wittemberg,* 1613

1181 **Gothic** BIBLE, GRAMMAR and VOCABULARY; Massman's Unfilas. Die Heiligen Schriften alten und neuen Bundes in Gothischer Sprache, *Gothic,* with the *Greek* and *Latin* text on opposite pages, with notes, a Glossary, a Grammar, and an historical Introduction, 8vo. xcii and 812 pp. (pub. at 14s) sd. 8s 6d
Stuttgart, 1857
To the Anglo-Saxon and good English scholar the above work will prove of great utility and interest.

1182 ULFILAS Gothische Bibelübersetzung, *Gothisch und Lateinisch,* mit Sprachlehre und Glossar, von Fulda und Reinwald, herausg. von Zahn, 4to. *hf. calf,* 15s *Weissenfels,* 1805

1183 **Gothic and Anglo-Saxon.** Evangeliorum IV, Versiones perantiquæ duæ, Gothica et Anglo-Saxonica, ediderunt Junius et Mareschallus, cum Glossario Gothico, etc. 2 vols. in 1, small 4to. *vellum,* 10s *Amst.,* 1684

1184 —— the same, 1665—CAEDMONIS Paraphrasis poetica Genesios, etc. *Anglo-Saxonica, without plates,* 1655—2 vols. in 1, sm. 4to. *vel.* 14s *Dordrechti,* 1655-65
The Amsterdam edition of 1684 is the same as the Dordrecht edition of 1665, with a new title.
Priced, 1832 and 1840, Payne and Foss, £2. 10s; Large Paper, 1848, Payne and Foss, £4. 4s: fetched, 1857, Conybeare's, 38s—See *Dibdin's Bibl. Spencer. V.* p. 120.

1185 ULPHILÆ partium ineditarum specimen, à Maio, 4to. *facsim.* 3s 6d *Mediol.* 1819

1186 EVANGELIUM JOHANNIS, in *Gothischer* Sprache, mit GLOSSAR von Massmann, 4to. *facsimile, hf. bd.* 7s *München,* 1834

1187 **Greek.** BIBLIA Theias dēladē Graphēs Palaias te kai Neas, *Græce,* (juxta Septuaginta) curâ Andr. Asulani, 3 vols. in 1, folio, *very fine and large copy in pigskin, from Miss Currer's library,* £12. 12s *Venet. Aldus,* 1518
The Rev. Th. Williams' copy, much inferior to the above, fetched £14.
In this rare and beautiful edition, the text of the Septuagint was published for the first time, as the Complutensian edition, although printed in 1516, did not appear till 1520. It is a fine specimen of the Greek typography of Aldus, and is very correctly executed with a beautiful character. Copies in a fine perfect state, like the present, are very rare. There is a variation in this copy at folio 240, where the heading appears Σοφια Σολομωντος instead of Σιραχ. See Renouard, Brunet, Horne's Introduction, Bibliotheca Sussexiana, etc.

BIBLES AND TESTAMENTS.

1188 DIVINAE SCRIPTURAE, nempe Veteris ac Novi Testamenti omnia, *Graece*, a viro doctissimo, (Fr. Junio aut. Fr. Sylburgio) recognita, folio, *vellum, a bargain, 7s* *Francof.* 1597

1189 BIBLIA GRAECA: Vetus Testamentum, secundum LXX. Gr. et Lat. cum Scholiis Romanae editionis, in singula capita distributis, omnia de exemplari Romano fidelissime et studiosissime expressa; accedit NOVUM TESTAMENTUM, studio J. Morini, 3 vols. folio, *fine copy, calf gilt*, 30s *Paris*, 1628

"In great request, not only for the neatness and correctness of the execution, but also for the learned notes." *Hartwell Horne.*

1190 VETUS TESTAMENTUM, Graece ex Versione Septuaginta juxta exemp. Vatican. sm. 4to. LARGE PAPER, *calf extra, gilt edges*, 12s *Lond.* 1653

1191 BIBLIA GRAECA, ex versione LXX ad editionem Grabe edita et criticis dissertationibus illustrata, à Breitingero, 4 vols. 4to. *calf gilt*, 25s *Tiguri*, 1730-33

In a recent number of the Gentleman's Magazine, the above is recommended as the best edition of the Septuagint.

1192 VETUS TESTAMENTUM Graecum, curis HOLMES et PARSONS, 5 vols. in 3, large folio, (pub. at £25. *in sheets*), *calf neat*, £7. *Oxon.* 1798-1827

The Dean of Peterborough's copy, in calf, fetched, 1853, £11. 10s.

1193 VETUS TESTAMENTUM, Graece e Codice MS. ALEXANDRINO, qui Londini in Bibliotheca Musei Britannici asservatur, Typis ad similitudinem ipsius Codicis Scripturae fideliter descriptum, cura et labore H. H. BABER, 3 vols. impl. folio, (pub. at £18. 18s) *bds.* £7. 7s 1816-21

Priced, 1834, Straker, £14. 14s; 1837 and 1840, Payne and Foss, russia, £26. 5s; Dr. Hawtrey's copy fetched, 1853, £13 15s. The edition was confined to 250 copies Woide's edition of the "NEW TESTAMENT" of the same Codex, bound uniformly, should be bought with this the "Old Testament."

1194 VETUS TESTAMENTUM Graecum sec. Septuaginta, ed. Van Ess, 8vo. *bd.* 7s 1835
1195 VETUS TESTAMENTUM Graece juxta LXX, ed. Tischendorf, 2 vols. 8vo. 10s 1850
1196 VETUS TESTAMENTUM, secundum LXX Interpretes, curante Van Ess, 8vo. *hf. purple morocco*, 10s *Lipsiae*, 1855

1197 THE VATICAN CODEX: Η ΠΑΛΑΙΑ ΚΑΙ Η ΚΑΙΝΗ ΔΙΑΘΗΚΗ: Vetus et Novum Testamentum ex antiquissimo Codice Vaticano edidit Angelus MAIUS S. R. E. Card. 5 vols. royal 4to. *with two facsimiles from the Codex*, (pub. at £10. 10s sewed) *newly whole bound* MOROCCO, *gilt edges*, £8. 8s *Romae*, 1857
1198 ——— the same, LARGE PAPER, 5 vols. impl. 4to. *neat, in vellum*, £10. 10s 1857

The great importance of this "Authorized Vatican edition" of the Septuagint and New Testament rests upon the fact, that the CODEX VATICANUS, from which this edition is said to be a faithful typographical reproduction, is the OLDEST MANUSCRIPT EXTANT OF THE HOLY SCRIPTURES. All Biblical critics must therefore consult this edition, to elucidate difficult passages and the various readings of the later manuscripts. Though it may be regretted, that the Vatican did not follow the example set by the British Museum in their facsimile-publication of the Codex Alexandrinus by Baber and Woide, and produced a similar edition of the Vatican Codex, the work in its present form has the advantage, that it can be read by such Greek Scholars, who would have been unable to make out either the original MS. or a facsimile edition.
"To Public Libraries *this* edition is indispensable; Protestants must refer to it, Catholics consider it the ONLY AUTHENTIC EDITION."

1199 PSALTERIUM Graecum, e Codice MS. Alexandrino Musei Britann. cura Baber, royal folio, *half calf*, 5s ; *calf*, 7s 1812
1200 DANIEL secundum Septuaginta ex tetraplis Origenis, sm. 4to. *bds.* 7s 6d *Gött.* 1774
1201 APOCRYPHA: Bibliorum Pars Graeca, quae Hebraicè non invenitur, sm. 4to. *good copy, limp vellum*, 5s *Antv. Plantin*, 1584
1202 NOVUM TESTAMENTUM Graecum, 12mo. *fine tall copy, old calf, rebacked*, 20s *Lutetiae, R. Stephanus*, 1546

This is the first of the celebrated O Mirificam editions. Fetched in Col. Stanley's sale £8. 8s; 1853, Dr. Hawtrey's, mor. £2. 3s.

1203 NOVUM TESTAMENTUM Graecum, 16mo. *fine copy in old French red* MOROCCO, *gilt edges*, 18s *Amst. Elsev.* 1678
1204 NOVUM TESTAMENTUM GRAECUM, cum lectionibus variantibus et notis, studio J. MILII, editio secunda, ex recensione L. KUSTERI, large folio, LARGE PAPER, *very fine copy, old red morocco, gilt edges*, £3. 12s *Lips.* 1723

A very handsome book; priced, 1832, Payne and Foss, £4. See Dibdin's Biblioth. Spencer, V. p. 105.

1205 NOVUM TESTAMENTUM Graecum, cum variis lect. etc. ed. G. D. T. M. D (Gerardus de Maestricht), *editio optima*, 12mo. *frontispiece and maps, blue morocco, gilt edges*, 10s *Amst. Wetsten.* 1735
1206 NOVUM TESTAMENTUM, Gr. edit. receptae, cum lect. var. necnon commentario pleniore ex scriptoribus veteribus Hebraeis, Graecis et Latinis Histo-

riam et vim verborum illustrante, operâ et studio J. J. WETSTENII, 2 vols. folio, half bound, calf, £4. 10s   *Amst.* 1751

"'.No sound critic should be without this invaluable work."—HALES.
|Priced, 1822, £10. 10s; 1840, £7. 17s 6d; 1840, morocco, £12. 12s; 1831, £8. 8s. Sir Mark Sykes's copy fetched £8. 5s; Roscoe's, £7. Purton Cooper's copy, russia, 1855, £5 10s; 1853, C. Turner's copy, £5.

1207 NOVUM TESTAMENTUM Græcum, e Cod. MS. ALEXANDRINO descriptum a C. G. WOIDE, cum Appendice, royal folio, *fine copy, russia, gilt, edges*, £5. 5s 1786

1208 QUATUOR EVANGELIA, Graece, cum variantibus lectionibus Codd. Vaticanæ, Barberinæ, Laurentianæ, Vindobonensis, Escurialensis, Hauniensis, etc. edidit BIRCH, stout folio, LARGE PAPER, *very fine copy in vellum extra, from Miss Currer's library*, £4. 4s   *Havniæ*, 1788

Very rare on Large Paper. See Bibl. Spenceriana, V. p. 121.

1209 CODEX THEODORI BEZAE Cantabrigiensis, Evangelia et Apostolorum Acta complectens, quadratis literis, Graeco-Latinus, ed. Kipling, 2 vols. royal folio, *a beautiful edition, printed so as to resemble a MS. with types cut expressly for this edition*, hf russia, £3. 10s   *Cantab.* 1793

Only 250 copies were printed; Meerman's copy fetched 70 flor.; Sir M. Sykes' £5. 7s; the Placentia copy, 120 fr.

1210 NOVUM TESTAMENTUM Græce, ex recensione GRIESBACHII, cum selecta Lectionum Varietate, 4 vols. in 2, folio, *4 fine plates, after the Old Masters, proofs before letters, Large vellum paper*, hf. blue morocco, £3. 5s   *Lipsiae*,1803-7

Printed with a beautiful type cast expressly for the work. The subscription price in paris was 250 francs.
Priced, 1829, J. Bohn, mor. £8. 8s; 1832 and 1848, Payne and Foss, russia, £7. 7s; 1848, Longman's, mor. £5.
See Dibdin's *Bibl. Spencer.* V. p. 107.

1211 NEW TESTAMENT, with English Notes, critical, philological, and explanatory, 3 vols. 8vo. (pub. at £2. 5s) bds. 7s   *Valpy*, 1836

1212 NEW TESTAMENT, with English notes, by Bloomfield, 2 vols. 8vo. hf. cf. 12s 1839

1213 NOVUM TESTAMENTUM Graece, ed. Tischendorf, sm. 8vo. *blue morocco, gilt edges*, 10s   *Lips.* 1839

1214 GREEK TESTAMENT: critically revised text, various readings, marginal references, prolegomena, and commentary, by Dean ALFORD, complete in 4 vols. divided into 5, 8vo. (pub. at £5. 2s) *new in cloth*, £4. 4s   1859-62

1215 BENGELII Gnomon Novi Testamenti, editio tertia à Steudel, 2 vols. 8vo. *half morocco, neat*, 18s   *Tubingæ*, 1850

1216 —— Idem, nova editio, à Bengelio et Steudel, stout roy. 8vo. *printed on writing paper*, (pub. at 18s), *new in cloth*, 10s; hf. morocco, 12s   1862

Bengel's excellent work is so well known and appreciated, that it needs no recommendation.

1217 BLANCHINI (Jos.) Vindiciae Canonicarum Scripturarum vulgatae latinae editionis, seu vetera sacrorum bibliorum fragmenta, juxta graecam vulgatam, et hexaplarem, latinam antiquam italam nunc primum edita, stout folio, *with facsimiles of Greek MSS.* hf. calf neat, *rare*, 36s   *Romae*, 1740

Appended is "Psalterium duplex cum Canticis juxta vulgatam græcam lxx seniorum et antiquam latinam italam versionem," the Greek in Roman letters.

1218 BRUDER, Concordantiae omnium vocum Novi Testamenti primum à Schmidio, nunc auctæ et emendatæ, 4to. hf. morocco, 30s   *Lips.* 1853

1219 ROBINSON'S Greek and English Lexicon of the New Testament, 8vo. 918 pp. double columns, hf. russia, 7s   1839

1220 TROMMII (A.) Concordantiæ Græcæ LXX Interpretum, 2 vols. folio, *fine copy, old calf gilt*, 36s   *Amst.* 1718

1221 —— the same, LARGE PAPER, 2 vols. large folio, *calf gilt, marbled edges, fine copy*, £2. 16s   1718

Very rare in this Large Paper state. This is a Concordance of the *Alexandrine* copy of the *Greek* Septuagint, with the corresponding Hebrew words. The Index of the second volume furnishes a valuable *Hebrew-Greek* Lexicon, by giving the *Hebrew* words with their various renderings in *Greek*. For methodical and judicious arrangement, it is, perhaps, the best Concordance published in any language; and it is particularly useful as a key to the *Alexandrine* Greek, which is the basis of the *Evangelical*.—DR. HALES.

1222 SCHLEUSNER, Novus Thesaurus Philologico-criticus, sive Lexicon VETERIS TESTAMENTI, 5 vols. in 3, 1820-21—Novum Lexicon Græco-Latinum in NOVUM TESTAMENTUM, 2 vols. 1819—together 7 vols. in 5, 8vo. hf. russia, £2. 16s
Lipsiae, 1819-21

1223 **HEBREW.** BIBLIA HEBRAICA, edidit Bomberg, sm. thick 4to. *calf, good sound copy*, 20s   Editio rarissima.   *Venetiis*, 1521

1224 BIBLIA HEBRAICA, cum commentariis David Kimchi, à Vatablo recognita, 24 parts in 3 vols. sm.folio, LARGE PAPER, *fine clean copy, in the criginal stamped hogskin, Melancthon's copy*, £10.   *Parisiis, Rob. Stephanus*, 1539-44

1225 BIBLIA HEBRAICA, cum notis Hebraicis et Latinis, ex recensione Jablonski, 4to. LARGE PAPER, *beautifully printed, with a few MS. notes, old calf gilt*, 15s
Berolini, 1699

BIBLES AND TESTAMENTS.

1226 BIBLIA HEBRAICA, eleganti et majusculâ characterum formâ, authore E.
Huttero; et ejusdem Cubus Alphabeticus sanctæ Hebrææ Linguæ, folio, *a good
copy*, £2. 16s *Hamburgi*, 1587-8
"The plan of this work is both ingenious and useful. All the *Servile* Letters are *hollow* and white, the rest *solid* and black; by which the radicals are at once seen. If any radical letter be wanting, it is added above the word, exactly over the place where it should be inserted. This lessens the labour of the student, for he discovers at first view the root for which he is to search his Lexicon. But in this also the indefatigable Hutter affords him the readiest assistance on the most easy terms, by his curious invention which he calls '*Cubus Alphabeticus Sanct. Hebr. Ling.*'"—DR. CLARKE.

1226*BIBLIA sacra Hebraea, stout sm. 8vo. *calf*, 7s *Amst.* 1661
1227 BIBLIA HEBRAICA, cum variis lectionibus a KENNICOTTO et de ROSSI, stout sm. 4to. *ruled with red ink, red morocco*, 25s *Lips.* 1793
1227*VETUS TESTAMENTUM Hebraicum (*sine punctis*), cum variis lectionibus ed. Kennicott, 2 vols. large folio, *calf*, £2. 16s *Oxon.* 1776-80
One of the most laborious, and certainly the most splendid effort of modern times for the advancement of Biblical literature. Kennicott compared all the Hebrew MSS. in Europe to obtain the above correct version.

1228 BIBLE HÉBRAIQUE, 2 vols. 12mo. *beautifully printed, calf*, 5s *Paris,* 1808
1228*Rabbinical Hebrew. BIBLIA HEBRAICA cum utraque Masora, Targo, necnon commentar. Rabbinorum, ed. BOMBERG, editio nova, 4 vols. large folio, *bds.* £4. *Venezia, P. and L. Bragadin,* 1617-18
This edition is said to have undergone the censure of the Inquisition.

1229 BIBLIA HEBRAICA ET CHALDAICA, cum Masoris, commentariis Jarchi, Kimchi, etc. studio BUXTORFII, 4 vols. in 2, large folio, FINE PAPER, *in the original stamped binding*, £4. *Basileae,* 1620
Cette édition est estimée des Hébraïsants qui la préfèrent même à celles de Bomberg, à cause des variantes qu'elle contient.—BRUNET.

1229*BIBLIA MAGNA HEBRAICA, EDITIO RABBINICA, (Mikra Gedoola), cum utrâque Masora et Targis Hebraice, 4 vols. royal folio, *a beautiful copy in the original russia covered wooden binding*, VERY RARE, £14. 14s *Amst.* 1724-27
1230 —— eadem, 4 vols. large folio, *almost as fine a copy as the above, wanting two preliminary leaves, one in Vol. I, the other in Vol. IV, but the text complete, russia,* £9. 9s 1724-27
"EDITION regardée comme la plus ample et la MEILLEURE DE TOUTES LES BIBLES RABBINIQUES. Elle a pour base les éditions de Bomberg, et renferme non seulement tout ce que celles-ci contiennent, mais encore les variantes de Buxtorf, avec les remarques ajoutées par l'éditeur."—BRUNET.

1230*BUXTORFII (J.) Lexicon Chaldaicum Talmudicum et Rabbinicum stout folio, *vellum, a good copy,* £2. *Basil.* 1639-40
A most important work, the fruit of 30 years' labour, containing all the Chaldee, Talmudical and Rabbinical words, in the Chaldee Paraphrases of the Old Testament, both the Talmuds and the Cabbalistic Writers.

1231 FUERST, Veteris Testamenti Concordantiæ Hebraicæ atque Chaldaicæ, cum Lexico duplici, stout folio, (pub at £4. 4s, sd.) *calf*, £2. 16s. *Lips.* 1840
The best and most complete Concordance to the Old Testament, comprising every Hebrew and Chaldee word : with a modern Hebrew and a Latin Index, &c
"This is a noble monument of German learning and industry, the accuracy and typographical execution of which reflect the highest honour on the author, as well as on the printer and publisher."

1232 **Hebrew and French.** LA BIBLE, traduction nouvelle, l'Hébreu en regard, avec des notes, les variantes, etc. par Cohen, 5 vols. 8vo. *containing the* PENTATEUCH, *cloth, uncut,* 12s *Paris,* 1831-34

1233 **Hebrew and German:** Die Heilige Schrift : the *Hebrew* text, with an improved *German* version, by COHEN, bound in 4 vols. 8vo. *Fine Paper, calf gilt,* 28s *Hamburg,* 1824

1234 **Hebrew and Latin.** BIBLIA HEBRAICA, cum interlineari Interpretatione Latinâ Xantis Pagnini Lucensis, cum Parte quæ Hebraice non reperitur, item Testamento Novo Græce cum vulgata interpretatione, curâ Montani, 5 vols. 8vo. *vellum, morocco backs,* 32s *Plantin. Raphelengii, (Lugd. Bat.)* 1613
Of this interlinear version it has been said, that if the Hebrew text of any particular book were lost, it might be restored by its help.

1235 LIBER JOBI, metrice divisus, *Hebraice et Latine* à Schultens, cum notis, ed. Grey, 8vo. *old red morocco, gilt edges,* 10s 6d 1742
1236 **Hebrew-Chaldee.** Genesis et Exodus, sm. 4to. *cf.* 5s (? *Constantinople,* 1700)
1237 BARTOLOCCI BIBLIOTHECA MAGNA RABBINICA, de Scriptoribus et Scriptis Hebr. et Talmud.; et Jos. IMBONATI Bibliotheca Latino-Hebraica, 5 vols. folio, *fine copy, old calf gilt, rare,* £5. 15s *Romæ,* 1675-94
"Of great use in biblical criticism."—CLARKE'S BIBLIOG. DICT.
"Le recueil le plus complet qu'on ait en extraits des livres des rabbins, tant manuscrits qu'imprimés."—BIOGRAPHIE UNIVERSELLE. This is considered superior to Wolf's Bibliotheca, inasmuch as it contains many original dissertations on Hebrew criticism.

1238 CALASII Concordantiæ Sacrorum Bibliorum Hebraicorum, edidit Romaine, 4 vols. large folio, *best edition, hf. calf, uncut,* £3. *Lond.* 1747-49
"This work is infinitely useful. In it the Hebrew passages are translated into Latin, ranged in two columns; and in the margin are the differences of the Vulgate and the Septuagint. In the beginning of every article we see all the significations disposed in order; and at the end, the combination of the Hebrew with other languages."—CALMET.

1239 ENGLISHMAN'S HEBREW and CHALDEE Concordance of the Old Testament, an attempt at verbal connexion between the Original and the translation, with Indexes, 2 stout vols. royal 8vo. (pub. at £3. 13s 6d) *cloth, a most valuable and useful book*, £2. 8s 1843

1240 GESENIUS, Hebrew and English Lexicon of the Old Testament and Biblical Chaldee, translated by Robinson, stout large 8vo. 1144 pp. double cols. *morocco gilt*, 25s 1844

1241 WILSON'S Bible Student's Guide to the Old Testament, by reference to the original Hebrew, 4to. (pub. at £2. 2s) *cloth*, 16s 1850

1242 **Illyrian.** Biblia Sacra Veteris Foederis Sixti V. et Clementis VIII. jussu in idioma Slavino-Illyricum dialecti Bosnensis traducta, *Illyrice et Latine*, 6 vols. 8vo. *with one of the Apocryphal books, viz.* Maccabees, sd. 25s *Budimi*, 1831

1243 **Irish.** Old Testament: Sein Tiomna, le BEDEL, thick 4to. *first edition, calf*, 16s *London*, 1685

1244 NEW TESTAMENT: Tiomna Nuadh, re O'Domhuill, 4to. *second edition, no preface, calf*, 16s *Lunnduin*, 1681

1245 —— the same, sm. 4to. *with the Preface in English and Irish, hf. mor.* 30s 1681

1246 **Italian.** BIBBIA, cioè, il Vecchio et il Nuovo Testamento, translati in lingua Italiana da Giovanni Diodati, 4to. *fine tall copy in vellum*, 25s 1607

FIRST EDITION of the most esteemed Protestant translation of the Bible into the Italian language. Of the merits of the translation, and the opinions of the Critics upon its elegance and its accuracy, and of the labours and talents of the Author, see *Bibliotheca Sussexiana*, Vol. II. pp. 185 and 201, where this copy is described. Also *Dibdin, Bibl. Spencer.* V. p. 85.

1247 BIBLIA SACRA, tradotta e commentata da Diodati, con l'aggiunta de' Sacri Salmi, in Rime, folio, *with a frontispiece dated* 1640, *tall copy in the original smooth morocco*, RARE, 36s *Geneva, G. Chouet*, 1641

The second edition of this the most highly-esteemed Protestant translation. The Apocrypha is placed at the end of the New Testament. Priced, 1845, with MS. notes by Queen Charlotte, mor. gt. £7. 17s 6d; 1858, Asher, Berlin, with MS. musical notes to the Psalms, 200 fr.; Large Paper, Thorpe, mor. gt. £7. 7s. See Dibdin's Biblioth. Spencer. V. p. 85.

1248 BIBLIA (La Sacra) in lingua Italiana, da Mattia d'Erberg, folio, *old calf*, 28s *Norimbergo, spese del autore*, 1712

An edition privately printed, in which the Apocryphal books are intermixed with the other holy books according to the caprice of the editor.

1249 **Italian and Latin.** VECCHIO TESTAMENTO, secondo la Volgata, tradotto in Lingua Italiana e con Annotazioni illustrato, da Martini, 17 vols. 8vo. *Italian gilt binding*, 20s *Torino*, 1776-81

"La meilleure de toutes les traductions Italiennes du texte sacré."—BRUNET.

1250 **LATIN.** BIBLIA SACRA LATINA, continens Vetus Testamentum et Libros Apocryphicos, in 1 stout volume, sm. folio, all the CAPITALS filled in by hand and illuminated, *a superb copy of this fine early Monument of Typography*, UNCUT *throughout, with very ample contemporary MS. notes, partly on the margins, partly interleaved, original hogskin binding*, £7. 10s

Sine anno, loco aut typographo, (sed COLONIÆ, typis UDALRICI ZELL, 1470)

The copy belonged, in 1553, to Brother Herman de Affelin.

COLLATION:—Vol. I. 345 leaves, the last blank; Vol. II. 198 leaves, the last blank, ending with "Explicit liber se 'dus Machabeorum." Printed upon stout paper, with a watermark 3¼ inches long, a cross on a kind of trident, in double columns of 42 lines, the printed page measuring 8 inches, the leaf rather more than 11½ inches by 8¾. Without signatures, numerals, catchwords, head-lines, or any indication of the printer, but according to Masch and Meermann the FIRST edition of Ulric Zell's Latin Bible. This copy has neither the Tabula of 28 leaves, nor the New Testament. Pettigrew's description does not absolutely tally with the above copy, there is a variation between it and the facsimile (Bibl. Suss. Vol. I. part 2, plate IV. No. 2); the Duke of Sussex's was probably U. Zell's SECOND edition.

1251 BIBLIORUM SACRORUM LATINÆ VERSIONES ANTIQUÆ SEU VETUS ITALICA, cum Vulgatâ Latinâ et cum textu Græco comparata, accedunt Præfationes, Observationes, ac notæ D. Petri Sabbatier, 3 vols. folio, *fine copy in calf gilt*, £6. 6s *Paris (Didot)*, 1751

"Rare et recherché."—BRUNET.

1252 BIBLIA Sacra juxta Vulgatum repurgata, adhibita fontium auctoritate a Joanne Benedicto Parisiensi, folio, *with the various readings, fine copy, ruled throughout with red ink, old calf gilt, Arms on sides*, 36s *Paris*, 1549

1253 VETUS TESTAMENTUM secundum LXX, *Latine* redditum et ex auctoritate SIXTI V. editum, cum Indice Dictionum et Loquutionum Hebraicarum, Graecarum, Latinarum, thick folio, *remarkably fine copy, overlapping vellum*, £8. 8s *Romae, in aedibus Populi Romani, apud Georgium Ferrarium*, 1588

An important edition, from which the suppressed one of 1590 was made. See Dibdin's Bibl. Spencer. VII. p. 51. "On the reverse of the title is the order of the books, which terminates with the III. Maccabees. This is succeeded by an address of Cardinal Caraffa to Pope Sixtus V.; a Preface to the reader; and the Papal privilege and approbation. The Bible is printed in a large Roman letter, and Scholia, from ancient versions and fathers, are ap-

BIBLES AND TESTAMENTS. 85

ended to each chapter. The sources whence these are derived are distinguished in the Greek edition of 1587, from which this translation has been made with great fidelity by Nobilius. It was executed under the auspices of Pope Ixtus V.; and Nobilius, we learn from the preface of Morinus, was assisted in the labour by Antony Agellius, Laelius, alveda, and Peter Morin. This edition is rare, and highly esteemed."

PETTIGREW'S BIBL. SUSSEX, Vol. I. part 2, p. 446.

254 BIBLIA LATINA, Vulgatæ Editionis, 6 vols. 8vo. *a pretty copy, red morocco, gilt edges, rare,* 20s Cologne, *(Leyde, Elzevir)* 1679
255 BIBLIA SACRA, Latine, cum Vatabli et variorum annotationibus, interpretatio duplex, vetus et nova, 2 vols. folio, LARGE PAPER, *fine clean copy in French calf gilt, scarce,* 30s Paris, 1729
256 PSALMORUM Liber, cum Canticis et Hymnis, jussu Reginæ Matris, 18mo. *plates, Large paper, very scarce, last leaf a beautiful facsimile, fine copy in old blue morocco, gilt edges, by De Rome, with the Arms of the Rev. Theodore Williams,* 21s Paris, 1586
    This edition is elegantly printed in large letter, and was executed at the expense of the Queen-Mother for resents only.
257 EVANGELIARUM QUADRUPLEX LATINAE VERSIONIS ANTIQUAE seu veteris Italicae, nunc primum in lucem editum ex Codicibus Manuscriptis, sub auspiciis Johannis V. Regis Lusitaniae, a J. BLANCHINO, 2 vols. stout folio, *numerous fine* FACSIMILES *from ancient MSS. Codices of the Scriptures, chiefly European, hf. calf, uncut,* £2. 10s Romae, 1749
258 —— the same, 2 vols. in 3, folio, (a smaller size, but) THICK PAPER, *old calf,* £2. 16s 1749
259 NOVI TESTAMENTI editio postrema per Erasmum, stout 12mo. *fine woodcuts, old stamped calf,* 6s Tiguri, 1554
260 JAMES (J.) Bellum Papale, sive concordia discors Sixti V. et Clementis VIII.; circa Hieronymianam editionem, sm. 4to. *bd. rare,* 10s London, 1600
261 —— another edition, 16mo. *vellum,* 6s 1678
    "Rare obvius et infrequens liber."
262 **Lettish.** BIHBELE tahs Wezzas un Jaunas Derribus, stout 8vo. *calf, clasps,* 7s Rihga, 1794
263 BIHBELE tahs Wezzas un Jaunas Derribus, stout 8vo. *with the Apocrypha, cf.* 5s Jelgawa, 1807
264 **Magyar.** SZENT Biblia, Karoli Gaspar, 12mo. *half morocco,* 7s Ultrajektomban, 1794
265 BIBLIA, Istennek o es Uj Testamentomaban, stout 8vo. *calf,* 5s Löszegen, 1840
266 NEW TESTAMENT. A mi urunk Jesus Christusnak Ui Testamentoma, fordittatett Caroli Gaspar, 12mo. *old black morocco, gilt edges,* 10s ? 1750
267 **Malay.** Vetus et Novum Testamentum *Malaice,* cura Jo. Willmet, 3 vols. royal 8vo. *morocco super extra, gilt edges, a superb presentation copy,* 9s Harlemi, 1820-24
268 EVANGELIA daan Berboatan : Gospels and Acts, sm. 4to. *calf,* 10s Oxford, 1677
269 **Maltese.** GIOVANNI (San) Il Vangelo tradotto in Lingua *Italiana e·Maltese,* 8vo. *bds.* 4s 1822
270 **Maltese and Latin.** Quatuor Evangelia, et Actus Apostolorum, *Melitice et Latine,* ed. Jowett, 8vo. *cloth,* 8s 1829
271 **Mantchu.** The Old Testament and St. Matthew, *in Mantchu,* 9 vols. 4to. *stitched,* 7s ? 1830
272 **Manx.** Yn Vible Casherick, 2 vols. in 1, 8vo. *calf,* 6s 1819
273 **Marathi.** The Old Testament in the Mahrathi Language, impl. 8vo. *bd.* 6s Bombay, 1853
274 **Mongolian.** OLD TESTAMENT, by R. Yuille, bound up with a rival translation of Genesis by some other English Missionary in Siberia, 2 vols. in 1, 4to. *bd.* 15s Selenginsk, Siberia, 1830
275 THE GENESIS, separately, translated by R. Yuille, 4to. *bd.* 2s—or Large Paper, 6s ib. 1830
276 **Negro-English.** Da Njoe Testament, translated into the Negro-English language, by the Missionaries of the Unitas Fratrum, 8vo. *calf,* 20s 1829
277 **New Zealand.** Genesis, now first translated into the New Zealand Language, 12mo. 6s Purewa, 1845
278 JUDGES to PSALMS, 12mo. *calf,* 5s Ranana, 1855
279 NEW TESTAMENT, 12mo. *calf,* 5s ib. 1841
280 **Persian.** The Pentateuch in Persian, 4to. *hf. russia,* 5s Calcutta, 1828

1281 **Rarotonga.** Bibilia, Koreromotu Taito e Ou, stout 8vo. *calf*, 5*s*   1851
1282 TESTAMENT. Te Korero-motiu, 12mo, *bound*, 5*s*   *Londona*
1283 **Romaic.** BIBLE and Testament, in Modern Greek, 8vo. *cf.* 4*s* *Oxon.* 1850
1284 PALAIA DIATHĒKĒ kata tous LXX, ek tou Alexandrinou Cŏdĕkos, 4 vols. 8vo. *cloth*, 15*s*   *Athēnēsi*, 1843-50
1285 **Romaic and Greek.** KAINĒ DIATHĒKĒ diglōttos, antiprosōpōs, to prōtotypon kai hē Metaphrasis eis haplēn dialekton, dia Maximou tou Kallioupolitou, 2 vols. 4to. *vellum*, 30*s*   (*Genevæ*), 1638
   "Edition rare."—BRUNET. See Dibdin's Bibl. Spenceriana.
1286 **ROMANSCH d'Engadina Bassa.** LA SACRA BIBLIA tradutta in lingua Rumanscha d'Engadina Bassa, 4 vols. in 1, stout folio, *with the Apocryphal Books at the end, curious woodcut title containing several compartments of figures, wanting pp. 9-10 in Genesis, and a few leaves towards the end mended, in the original stamped binding, very rare*, £5.   *Scuol, (Schuls) Jacob Dorta*, 1679
1287 DA LA BIBLIA ilg secuond Cudasch : EXODUS, mis in la usitada lingua da Engadina Bassa, tras Joan Pitschen, Salutz, 12mo. *wanting the first leaf of preface, bd. very rare*, 30*s*   *Scuol, Dorta*, 1662
1288 NOUF TESTAMAINT, in Rumansch d'Engadina Bassa, 8vo. *sd.* 7*s* 6*d*   *Basel*, 1812
1289 **Romansch de la Ligia Grischa.** LA S. BIBLA, quei ei : tut la Soinchia Scartira, ner Veder a Nief Testament, cun ils cudischs Apocryphs, messa giu ent ilg languaig Rumonsch de la Ligia Grischa, 3 vols. in 1, folio, FINE PAPER, *massively bound, in blue morocco super extra, by Clarke*, EXTREMELY RARE, £12.   *Coira*, 1717-18
   Priced, 1840, Payne and Foss, £12. 12*s.* It has been sold as high as twenty guineas in ordinary condition.
   This version, made for the use of the Protestants of the Grison country, and printed under the patronage of George I. of England, is rarely to be found in fine condition. In the second vol. sheets N, O, P, Q, are printed on smaller paper of rather a finer quality, and probably intended to match, as in two other copies these sheets are similar to this. This copy has not the dedication to George I., which was inserted only in the copies intended for England.
1290 NIEF TESTAMENT, editiun nova da Carisch, 8vo. *with a list of Romansch versions since* 1560, *half bound*, 7*s* 6*d*   *Quera*, 1856
1291 **Samaritan.** PENTATEUCHUS Hebræo-Samaritanus charactere Hebræo-Chaldaico editus à Blayney, 8vo. *calf*, 5*s*   *Oxonii*, 1790
1292 **Sechuana** Bible. Bibela ea Boitsepho, Kabo I, *Genesis to Kings*, 8vo. *cloth*, 18*s*   *Kuruman*, 1853
1293 NEW TESTAMENT, 12mo. *calf*, 5*s*   1840
1294 **Slavonic.** Biblia, Vetchago i Novago Zaveta, stout 8vo. *calf, gilt edges*, 5*s*   (? *St. Peters.* 1820)
1295 SLAVONIC Bible, 4to. *calf*, 7*s*   (? *ib.* 1840)
1296 PSALTER, sm. 4to. *massive old calf, fine copy*, 9*s*   (? 1700)
1297 **Singhalese.** The Holy Bible, 3 vols. 4to. *whole bound*, 10*s*   *Colombo*, 1819
1298 NEW TESTAMENT. Evangelium, etc. in de Singaleesche Tale overgebragt, door Fybrants en Philipez, 4to. *curious sealskin binding, rare*, 16*s*   *Colombo*, 1772-80
1299 **SPANISH.** BIBLIA, trasladada en Español (por Cassiodoro de Reyna), sm. 4to. *in the original gilt calf, rebacked and repaired, some of the preliminary pages, and a few at the end a little weak and slightly wormed, gilt edges*, 28*s*; —or another copy, *in old red morocco gilt, rebacked, quite clean and fair throughout*, 36*s*   (*Basile*), 1569
   Dr. Hawtrey's copy fetched, 1853, mor. £2. 16*s.*
   This edition of the Protestant Translation, on account of which Cassiodore de Reyna was burnt by the Inquisition, is generally known from the device on the title, as the "Bible de l'Ours;" and when republished in 1602, by Cyprian de Vatora, it had already become so rare that no copies could be obtained.
1300 BIBLIA del Vieio y Nuevo Testamento, conferida con los Textos Hebreos y Griegos, por Cypriano de Valera, sm. folio, *old calf*, 10*s*   *Amst.* 1602
   Priced, 1837, Thorpe, mor. £2. 12*s* 6*d*: Marquis of Lansdowne's copy fetched, mor. £1. 9*s.*
1301 BIBLIA en lengua Española traduzida de la verdad Hebrayca, con privilegio del Duque de Ferrara, folio, *engraved title, original stamped binding*, 7*s* 6*d*   *Amsterdam*, G. Ioost, 5606—*in fine*, 5390, *i. e.* 1630
1302 TESTAMENTO NUEVO, de nuestro Señor Jesu Christo, 16mo. *fine copy, Spanish cf. rare*, 20*s*   (? *Geneva*) *Ricardo del Campo*, 1596
   The preface speaks of the "pobres y ignorantes Moriscos," for whom this edition was intended.
1303 Los CUATRO EVANJELIOS traducidos al Español, con notas por RULE, sm. 4to. *bds.* 7*s*   *Gibraltar*, 1841
1304 **Swedish.** BIBELEN, Gamla och Nya Testamentet, 8vo. *calf*, 6*s*   *Stockholm*, 1853

BIBLES AND TESTAMENTS.

1305 **SYRIAC.** Novum Testamentum Syriace, Ferdinandi Rom. Imperatoris jussu, characteribus et linguâ Syrâ, Scriptorio prelo diligenter expressum, curâ Widmanstadii, small 4to. *beautifully printed with silver type, the Syriac title black with red vowel points, woodcuts, tall copy in russia*, £2. 2s
Viennæ Austr. Cymbermannus, 1555
1306 ———— idem, sm. 4to. *the Syriac title printed in red with vowel points black, very tall copy in old red morocco extra, rebacked,* £2. 10s 1555
1307 ———— idem, sm. 4to. *Syriac title black with red points, limp vellum,* 20s
Zymmerman, 1562 (1555)
1308 ———— idem, *black title, with red points, Viennæ,* 1555-62—Syriacæ linguæ prima Elementa, quibus adjecta sunt Christianæ Religionis solennes quotidianæque Precationes, *ib.* 1555—in 1 vol. small 4to. *vellum, singularly fine copy of this choice and rare book,* £4. 1555-62

An elegant edition, and the first book published in Syriac, of which 1000 copies were printed at the expense of the Emperor Ferdinand the First. Half the edition was sent away to the Antioch and Maronite patriarchs. Widmanstad was assisted in this edition by Moses of Mardin, and Postel. The former was sent by Ignatius, patriarch of the Maronite Christians, to Pope Julius III. in 1552, to acknowledge the supremacy of the Roman pontiff over the Syrian church.
"It is impossible for anything to be more elegant, or better proportioned," says Père Simon, "than the character of this edition."
Few copies exactly resemble each other; and the discrepancies have been but unsatisfactorily accounted for by all the bibliographers. Ebert and Brunet differ upon the subject; in some respects the above copies agree with the former, and in others with the latter. The first two agree with each other in all respects except the ink in which the Syriac title is printed; and the latter two are also like each other, but have not the dedication to King Maximilian and some other preliminary matter before the Epistles of St. Paul, which exist in the former. This dedication appears to be wanting in most copies, as well as the dedications to the Archdukes Ferdinand and Charles, which have never been met with in any known copy. A very exact description is given in Denis, *die Merkwürdigkeiten der Garellischen Bibliothek,* pp. 285-90. See also Le Long, Müller, Maittaire, Bibliothèque de Sacy, Ebert, Brunet, etc.

1309 NOVUM TESTAMENTUM, ed. Gutbirius, 1663—Gutbirii Lexicon Syriacum, 1667, 12mo. *morocco,* 6s *Hamburgi,* 1663-7
1310 CODEX SYRIACO-HEXAPLARIS: Liber quartus Regum e Cod. Parisiensi, Jesaias, duodecim Prophetæ Minores, Proverbia, Jobus, Canticus, Ecclesiastes, e Cod. Mediolanensi, *Syriace* edidit Middeldorpf, 2 vols. in 1, 4to. *fine paper* (originally pub. at £2. 14s) *half calf,* 21s *Berol.* 1835
1311 NOVUM TESTAMENTUM, Syriace et Latine, curâ Leusden et Schaaf, cum variis lectionibus, 4to. *calf,* 10s *Lugd. Bat.* 1708
1312 NOVUM TESTAMENTUM, Syriace et Latine, à Leusden et Schaaf—SCHAAF, LEXICON Syriacum—2 vols. 4to. *hf. russia;* or *vellum,* 36s *Lugd. Bat.* 1717
1313 EVANGELIORUM Sacrorum et Actuum Apostolorum Epistolarumque versio Syriaco-Philoxena, ex Codd. Ridleianis nunc primùm edita cum interpretatione et notis, à White, 4 vols. in 2, 4to. *bds.* 20s *Oxon.* 1778-99
1314 NEW TESTAMENT in Syriac, 4to. *calf,* 5s ? 1840
1315 **Tamul.** Old and New Testament in Tamil, 4 vols. 8vo. *calf,* 7s *Madras,* 1827
1316 BIBLE, 2 vols. in 1, stout 8vo. *calf,* 6s 6d ? 1840
1317 NEW TESTAMENT in Malabar, 8vo. *calf,* 5s ? *Madras,* 1820
1318 **Tartar** Testament, 8vo. *in Arabic characters, calf,* 5s 1818
1319 **Tonga** New Testament, 12mo. *with MS. Vocabulary, calf,* 3s 6d 1852
1320 **Welsh.** Y BIBL CYSSEGR-LAN; sef yr Hen Destament a'r Newydd, thick folio, 𝔅lack letter, *a few leaves tender, the last two leaves a modern reprint, old calf,* £2. 8s 1620
Second edition of the Welsh Bible.

1320*BIBL CYSSEGR-LAN, 12mo. *calf,* 5s *Caer Grawnt,* 1826
1321 BIBL CYSSEGR-LAN, Hen Destament a'r Newydd, stout 4to. *with the Apocrypha, calf neat,* 10s 6d *Llundain,* 1857
1322 COMMON Prayer: Gwasanaeth Cyhoedd Eglwys Loegr, 8vo. *hf. bd.* 6s 1755
1323 WILLIAMS' Concordance: Mynegeir Ysgrythurol, 4to. *calf,* 5s *Caerfyrd.* 1773
1324 **Wendish.** BIBLIA, Tu Je Use Suetu Pismu Stariga inu Noviga Testamentà, Slovenski tolmazhena, skusi Juria Dalmatina; Bibel, das ist, die gantze heilige Schrift Windisch durch Georg Dalmatinum, 3 vols. in 1, folio, *numerous woodcuts, very tall copy in the original stamped binding,* £3. 10s
Wittemberg, 1584

A corner of the title slightly injured, and the seven first leaves supplied from an inferior copy.
Dr. Hawtrey's copy fetched, 1853, £6. 12s 6d. This is an excessively rare volume, having been rigidly suppressed, and most of the copies burnt.

1325 BIBLIA, Stareho a Noweho Sakona, small 8vo. *with the Apocrypha, hogskin*, 7s
Budeschini, 1742
1326 ADLER, Bibliotheca Biblica Würtenbergensium Ducis olim Lorckiana, sm. 4to.
bds. 16s   Fetched, 1856, Sotheby's 27s.   *Altonæ*, 1787
1327 LE LONG et BOERNERI Bibliotheca Sacra continuata ab. A. G. MASCH, 6 *Parts in* 2 *vols.* 4to. *best edition, calf gilt, very neat*, 32s   *Halæ*, 1778-90
" Ce qui a paru de cette édition fait vivement regretter la suite."—BRUNET.
Contents: Vol. I. Bibliography of all the Editions of the Bible in Hebrew; Vol. II. The Oriental Versions; Vol. III. The Greek Versions; Vol. IV. V. The Latin Versions.

CLASSICS, GREEK AND LATIN PHILOLOGY.
Ancient History, Topography of Greece and Rome, Byzantine Historians, Ancient Worships, Etc.
Ancient Art, see Catalogue of " Fine Arts."

1328 ACTUARII Opera, de actionibus et spiritus animalis affectibus, de Urinis, methodo medendi, etc. stout 12mo. *red morocco extra, gilt edges, the Aldine device on the title, rare*, 15s   *Parisiis*, 1556
Priced, 1833, Thorpe, £2. 2s.
1329 AELIANUS de naturâ Animalium, ed. Jacobs, 2 vols. 8vo. *bds.* 10s   *Jenæ*, 1832
1330 ÆSCHYLI Tragœdiæ sex, 12mo. *the margins of some leaves cut out, old red morocco*, 10s   *Paris*, 1552
1331 AMMIANI MARCELLINI rerum gestarum qui supersunt libri, à Gronovio, 4to. *portrait, russia neat*, 12s   *Lugd. Bat.* 1693
1332 ANACRÉON, Odes, en *Français, Grec*, et *Latin*, par Gail, 4to. *with the Music, calf, gilt edges*, 12s   *Paris*, 1799
1333 ANTHOLOGIA Epigrammatōn, seu Florilegium diversorum Epigrammatum veterum, cura H. Stephani, 4to. *old* MOROCCO, *gilt backs*, 12s   *Paris*, 1566
1334 ANTHOLOGIA GRÆCA, cum versione latinâ Hugonis Grotii, edita ab Hieronymo de Bosch, 3 vols.—DE BOSCH, Observationes et notæ in Anthologiam Græcam quibus accedunt Salmasii notae ineditae, 1 vol.—De Bosch Poemata, 1 vol.—together 5 vols. folio, LARGEST PAPER, *a superb copy, russia extra, gilt edges*, £7. 10s   *Ultrajecti*, 1795-1810
Previously sold for £21.
1335 ANTHOLOGIA GRÆCA, sive Poetarum Graecorum Lusus, *Gr.* ex recensione Brunckii, indices et comment. adjecit Jacobs, 13 vols. 8vo. (pub. at £5. *sd.*) *calf, very neat*, £3. 10s   *Lipsiæ*, 1794-1814
The Dean of Peterborough's copy fetched £3. 12s; Fynes Clinton's copy in russia fetched £7.; priced, 1835, Thorpe, £5. 15s 6d; 1840, Jas. Bohn, calf, £6. 6s; 1843, Payne and Foss, fine paper, russia, £8. 8s.
1336 ANTHOLOGIA GRÆCA ad fidem Codicis Parisini, curavit et annotationem criticam adjecit Jacobs, 4 vols. in 3, 8vo. *calf neat*, 36s   *Lips.* 1813-17
1337 APIANI (Petri) et Bapt. AMANTII Inscriptiones Sacrosanctæ Vetustatis non Romanæ sed totius Orbis, terra marique conquisitæ, sm. folio, *printed within woodcut borders and containing several hundred illustrations of Ancient Art, stamped black morocco, gilt edges, rare*, 30s   *Ingolstadii*, 1534
Priced Payne and Foss, £2. 2s. "Devenu fort rare."—BRUNET. This work was printed in the house of the author, and is dedicated to Raymond Fugger.
1338 APOLLONII RHODII Argonautica, cum Scholiis, *Græce*, cura G. Asulani, 12mo. *old red morocco*, 24s ; *or a very fine tall copy, ruled, French red* MOROCCO, *broad borders of gold, silk linings, gilt edges, from the McCarthy collection*, £3.   *Venetiis, Aldus*, 1521
" Cette edition est belle et très-rare."—RENOUARD. Priced, 1824, Thorpe, £3. 13s 6d; 1830, Payne and Foss, £4. 4s, another, £5. 5s; Heber's copy fetched £8. 8s; Heath's, £3. 16s.
1339 APOLLONII RHODII Argonautica cum Scholiis Græce, cum notis ed. Wellauer, 2 vols. in 1, 8vo. *red morocco, uncut, top edges gilt*, 14s   *Lipsiæ*, 1828
1340 APOLLONII Sophistæ Lexicon Græcum Iliadis et Odysseæ ed. Villoison, 2 vols. 4to. *calf*, 7s 6d   *Lut. Paris*, 1773
1341 APULEII Opera omnia, cum notis var. curante Oudendorpio ed. Ruhnkenius, 3 vols. 4to. *half calf, uncut*, 32s   *Lugd. Bat.* 1786-1823
Previously priced £3. 5s; 1840, Payne and Foss, £5. 5s; 1827, Black, £6.; 1853, Dr. Hawtrey's copy in morocco I sold for £3. 16s.
1342 ———— the same, LARGE PAPER, 3 vols. royal 4to. *a beautiful copy, in blue* MOROCCO *extra, gilt edges*, £6. 15s   1786-1823
Priced, 1829, J Bohn, mor. £12. 12s; 1832 and 1840, russia, £8. 8s.
" There is good reasons to congratulate the classical world on the appearance of this *masterly performance ;*

CLASSICS, GREEK AND LATIN PHILOLOGY, &c. 89

which had long been expected, and of which the execution *has even surpassed all expectation*." "The most complete and best edition of the works of Apuleius."—*Brunet*. Copies of this edition are rare, owing to the great length of time (nearly 40 years) between the publication of the first and latter volumes.

1343 ARCHIMEDIS Opera nonnulla Latine a Commandino Urbinate, folio, *diagrams, old calf*, 6s ; or, *vellum*, 10s   *Venet. Ald.* 1558
1344 —— Opera, Græce et Latine, cum commentariis per Rivaltium, folio, *diagrams, calf*, 7s 6d   *Paris*, 1615
1345 ARCHIMEDIS quæ supersunt omnia, cum Eutocii Ascalonitæ Commentariis, Græce et Latine ex recensione Torelli, cum variantibus, royal folio, EDITIO OPTIMA, LARGE PAPER, *frontispiece by Burghers, fine copy, calf*, 15s   *Oxon.* 1792

Priced, 1824, Rivington, £3. 3s

1346 ARISTIDES, Græce, ex recensione Dindorfii, 3 vols. 8vo. *calf gilt*, 18s   *Lips.* 1829
1347 —— idem, 3 vols. 8vo. FINE PAPER, *hf. red morocco, gilt edges*, 32s   *ib.* 1829
1348 ARISTOPHANIS Comoediae auctoritate libri praeclarissimi saeculi decimi emendatæ a Philippo Invernizio, 13 vols. 8vo. *calf gilt*, £2. 5s   *Lips.* 1794-1826
1349 —— eædem, 13 vols. stout 8vo. THICK PAPER, *bds. uncut*, £2. 16s *Lips.* 1794-1826
1350 —— Comoediae cum scholiis et varietate lectionis, recensuit Becker, *Græce ac Latine*, 5 vols. 8vo. *calf, uncut*, 16s   1829
1351 —— Comœdiæ, Græce, cum notulis H. A. Holden, *interleaved* in 2 vols. 8vo. with Dr. Hawtrey's autograph notes, *hf. red morocco*, 12s   *Cantabrigiæ*, 1848
1352 —— the Acharnanians and Knights, in English, (by Frere), sm. 4to. *each page surrounded by lines, presentation copy to Dr. Hawtrey, bds.* 30s

UNPUBLISHED, *printed at the Government Press, Malta*, 1839

1353 ARISTOTELIS et THEOPHRASTI Scripta quædam, *Græce*, 12mo. *Louis XVth's copy in old French green morocco, gilt edges, with his cypher on the back, the binding by Padeloup, with his ticket*, 36s   *Paris, H. Stephanus*, 1557
1354 ARISTOTELIS Opera Omnia, Græce et Latine, edidit Im. Bekker; cum Scholiis Græcis C. A. Brandis; edidit Academia Regia Borussica, 4 vols. 4to. *sd. new*, £2. 2s   *Berol.* 1831-36

The edition on ordinary paper is published at 24 Thalers; that on fine paper at 32 Thalers.

1355 —— de Animalibus historiæ, *Graece et Latine*, textum recensuit, Scaligeri versionem recognovit, commentariosque adjecit Schneider, 4 vols. 8vo. *fine paper, calf gilt*, 36s   *Lipsiae*, 1811

"Le nom de l'éditeur atteste le merite de cette édition."—BRUNET.

1356 —— Histoire des Animaux, avec la traduction Françoise, par Camus, *Grec et Français*, 2 vols. 4to. *calf*, 10s   *Paris*, 1783
1357 ARISTOTE, Politique de, traduite par St.-Hilaire, *Grec et Français*, 2 vols. 8vo. *calf neat*, 7s   *Paris*, 1837
1358 AMMONII HERMIÆ in prædicamenta Aristotelis commentarius cum Aristotelis vita, *Græce*, 12mo. *bds.* 5s   *Venet. Ald.* 1546
1359 ARRIANI Expeditio Alexandri et Historia Indica, Gr. et Lat. ed. Raphelius, cum notis, Indice, et Photii Eclogis, a Schotto, st. 8vo. *calf neat*, 8s *Amst.* 1757
1360 —— the same, Large Paper, 8vo. *fine copy in calf extra, gilt edges, bound by Bozérian*, 21s   1757
1361 —— Expeditio Alexandri, et Indica, Græce et Latine à Vulcanio, ed. Blancardus, 2 vols. sm. 8vo. *maps, etc. russia*, 7s 6d   *ib.* 1768
1362 —— translated by Rooke, roy. 8vo. *map, hf. russia*, 5s   1812
1363 ARTEMIDORUS de Somniorum interpretatione ; et de Insomniis quod Synesii nomine circumfertur, 12mo. *fine copy in old red morocco extra, gilt edges*, 24s   *Venetiis*, 1518

"PREMIERE EDITION, très rare."—RENOUARD. Thuanus's copy, at Prince Soubise's sale, produced 54 fr., Mons. d'Hangard's the like sum; Count M'Carthy's 112 fr.

1364 ATHÉNÉE, Banquet des Savants, traduit tant sur les textes imprimés que sur plusieurs manuscrits, par Jean-Baptiste Lefebvre de Villebrune, 5 vols. 4to. *calf neat*, 20s ; *or beautifully bound in French calf extra*, 30s   *Paris*, 1788-9
1365 —— the same, 5 vols. 4to. *with new engraved title, 1792, and 42 beautiful engravings by Picart, on 34 plates, after the designs of Barbier, hf. russia*, £3. 3s

Paris, 1788-92

1366 ATHENAEI Naucratitae Deipnosophistarum libri quindecim ex optimis codicibus nunc primum collatis, *Graece et Latine*, ed. SCHWEIGHAEUSER, 14 vols. 8vo. *fine copy in russia*, £3.   *Argent.* 1801-7

"But of all the philologists of ancient Greece, Athenæus is probably the most amusing and instructive ; and there is hardly any work of which the incomplete state in which it is left is more to be regretted, than the *Deipno-*

sophistæ (The Banquet of the Wise Men) of this curious Philogogist. It may be only essential to remark, that the *first* edition of Athenæus was put forth by *Aldus* in 1514, Gr. folio; and that the *best* editions are those by Casaubon and Schweighæuser."—DIBDIN.

1367 AUGUSTÆ HISTORIÆ SCRIPTORES. Nervæ et Trajani atque Adriani vitæ ex Dione, Merula interprete; Heliogabalus ad meretrices; Egnatius de Cæsaribus; Aristides Smyrnæus de laudibus Romæ: Conflagratio Vesevii montis, cum aliis opusculis, Latinè curâ Egnatii, 12mo. *old red morocco, gilt edges*, 21s
Venetiis, 1519

1367* —— the same, *a very tall fine copy*, 12mo. *olive morocco, ornamental tooling on back and sides*, £2. 2s 1519
Priced, 1840, J. Bohn, £2.; Payne and Foss, £3. 3s. Renouard's copy fetched £1. 18s.; Libri, 1859, £1. 11s. "Edition plus ample que la précédente; souvent confondue avec le Suetone et autres historien, 1516 et 1521."—BRUNET.

1368 AUGUSTAE Historiae Scriptores sex, 2 vols. stout 12mo. *calf*, 7s *Lugd. Bat.* 1671
1369 AULI GELLII Noctes Atticæ, cum notis indicibusque, ed. Lion, 2 vols. 8vo. *calf extra*, 9s *Gottingae*, 1824
1370 BENFEY'S Griechisches Wurzel-Lexikon, THICK PAPER, 2 vols. stout 8vo. *bds.* 16s   A valuable Dictionary of Comparative Philology.   *Berlin*, 1839-42
1371 BERGIER (N.) Histoire des Grands Chemins de l'Empire Romain, 2 vols. 4to. LARGE PAPER, *portraits and plates, calf*, 21s   *Bruxelles*, 1728
1372 BYZANTINE HISTORIANS. Corpus Scriptorum Historiæ Byzantinæ, *Graece et Latine*, cum notis, editio copiosior, operâ Niehbuhrii, Im. Bekkeri, Schopeni, Dindorfi aliorumque, Vols. I-XLVIII, (*all published*), 8vo. (pub. at 147 Thalers) *sd*. £10. 10s   *Bonnæ*, 1828-55

CONTENTS: Agathias; Cantacuzenus; Leo Diaconus, Theodosius: Nicephorus Greg.; Con. Porphyrogenitus; Syncellus et Niceph.; Dexippus, Eunapius, Priscus, etc.; Malalas; Chron. Pasch.; Procopius; Ducas; Theophylactus Simoc., Genesius; Nicetas Chon.; Pachymeres; Cinnamus, Niceph. Bry.; Glycas; Merobaudes et Corippus; Const. Manasses, Joel, Acropolita; Zosimus; J. Lydus; Silentiarius, etc.; Theophanes, etc.; Cedrenus; Phrantzes, Codinus, A. Comnena, Ephraemius, Zonaras, Leo Gram., Chalcocondylas, M. Attaliota, etc. etc.

1373 BODE (Dr. G. H.) Geschichte der Hellenischen Dichtkunst: Epik, Lyrik und Dramatik, 5 vols. 8vo. *calf*, 30s   *Leipzig*, 1838-40
1374 BOECKHIUS ET FRANZIUS, Corpus Inscriptionum Græcarum, 3 vols. roy. folio, (pub. at £10. 4s.) *sewed*, £4. 10s; or *hf. calf, uncut*, £6. 15s *Berol*. 1828-53
Clinton's copy, wanting a part, fetched £7 5s.
"This collection of all the known Greek Inscriptions, arranged according to Towns to which they relate, is executed with judgment and learning, and supplies a great desideratum in ancient historical literature."—HEEREN.

1375 BUTTMANN's Lexilogus; or, a critical examination of Greek words and passages, principally from Homer and Hesiod, translated, with notes, by Fishlake, 8vo. (pub. at 18s) *bds*. 6s; *calf neat*, 7s 6d   1836
1375* —— Mythologus, oder gesammelte Abhandlungen über die Sagen des Alterthums, 2 vols. 8vo. *hf. olive morocco*, 7s 6d   *Berlin*, 1828-29
1376 CÆSAR de Bello Gallico et Civili, Alexandrino, etc. ed. Hunter, 2 vols. 8vo. *maps, etc. russia*, 5s   *Cupri*, 1809
1377 —— les Commentaires, *Latin et Français*, avec des notes, un coup d'œil sur les Gaulois, les institutions militaires Romaines, la vie de César, etc. par Le Deist de Botidoux, 5 vols. 8vo. *map, calf neat*, Dr. Hawtrey's copy, £2. 2s
Paris, 1809
1378 EDMONDS' Observations upon Cæsar's Commentaries, setting forth the Practice of ye Art Militarie in the time of the Romaine Empire, folio, *engraved title, portrait*, 6 *maps and plates, tall clean copy, original calf*, 25s   1604
1379 CÆSAR'S Commentaries translated into English; with a Discourse on the Roman Art of War, by Duncan, folio, *portrait, maps, plans, and fine plates,* including the Buffalo (*a small corner torn from it*), *good copy in calf*, 20s   1753
An excellent translation, highly esteemed; the book generally fetches from £3. to £4.

1380 CANINA, Indicazione topografica di ROMA ANTICA, 1 vol. 8vo. *and large folding plan of Rome in case*, roy. 8vo. *cloth*, 10s   *Roma*, 1850
1381 CELSI de Medicina libri VIII, ex recensione et cum notis Targæ, 2 vols. 8vo. *hf. morocco*, 10s   *Argent*. 1806
1382 CHALCONDYLÆ Erotemata, sive Institutiones Grammaticæ, *Græce*, cum Moschopulo de Nominum ac verborum Syntaxi, 12mo. *very fine copy, red morocco extra, gilt edges, rare*, 16s   *Basil*. 1546
1383 CHAMPAGNY, les Césars, jusqu'à Néron, avec un tableau du monde Romain, etc. 2 vols. 8vo. *calf gilt*, Dr. Hawtrey's copy, 14s   *Paris*, 1853

CLASSICS, GREEK AND LATIN PHILOLOGY, ETC. 91

1384 CHRYSOLORÆ Erotemata; de formatione Temporum ex Chalcondylâ; Gaza de constructione; de anomalis verbis; de encliticis, etc. *Græce et Latine*, smallest 4to. *mor. gilt edges, extremely rare*, £5. 5s   *Compluti, A. G. Brocarius*, 1514
Priced, Thorpe, 1833, £21.; 1836, £10. 10s.; fetched, 1857, Sotheby's, £6.; Heber's fetched £7. 17s 6d.
The first Greek book printed in Spain, and much rarer than even the editio princeps of Milan. It is a volume of the greatest interest and rarity, and is printed with the same characters as those used in the celebrated Polyglott Bible of Alcala, and has Cardinal Ximenes' Arms on the title. On the last leaf but one is a letter in Greek from Demetrius Ducas, the editor, in which he says, that he was summoned to Spain by Cardinal Ximenes for the publication of books to facilitate the study of the Greek language.
1385 —— Erotemata, Chalcondylas, Gaza, etc. *Græce*, 12mo. PRESENTATION COPY TO GROLIER, "Ex dono et liberalitate D. Martini Buceri ex Libris Capitonis et Oecolampadii," *with autograph notes by these distinguished scholars, and the signature of Grosley (the celebrated Grolier), bds. rare*, 15s   *Venetiis, Ald.* 1512
1386 —— Erotemata, *Græce*, 12mo. *fine copy, blue morocco, joints, gilt edges*, 32s
Venetiis, Aldus, 1517
"Cette edition contient de plus que celle de 1512, *les Distiques de Caton*, mis en Grec, et *les Erotemata de Guarini*."—BRUNET.
1387 —— Erotemata, *Græce*, 12mo. *red mor. gilt edges*, 10s   *Venetiis, Sabio*, 1548
A very scarce edition, with the Preface of Aldus.
1388 CHRYSOSTOMI (Dio.) Orationes LXXX, cum varietate lectionum, et indice, stout 12mo. *fine tall copy in vellum*, 12s   *Venetiis, Turrisanus*, 1551?
"Cette edition rare est la première de cet auteur; vend. 2 liv. Pinelli, 51 fr. Larcher, 27 fr. Chardin, 1 liv. 6 sh. Butler."—BRUNET.
1389 CICERONIS Opera, cum delectu commentariorum, ed. Olivetus, 9 vols. 4to. *old calf gilt*, 35s   *Paris*, 1740-42
1390 —— Opera omnia, ex recensione Ernesti, cum ejusdem notis et Clave Ciceroniana, 8 vols. 8vo. *calf*, 22s   *Halis*, 1774
1391 —— OPERA QUÆ SUPERSUNT OMNIA, ac deperditorum Fragmenta, cum varietate Lambiniana MDLXVI., Grævio-Garatoniana, Ernestiana, Beckiana, Schuetziana, ac præstantissimarum cujusque libri editionum integra, edidit Orellius, 7 vols.—Scholia, 2 vols.—Onomasticon Tullianum et Fasti Consul. et triumph. Rom. 3 vols.—together 12 vols. impl. 8vo. *best edition, fine copy in calf gilt, contents lettered, scarce*, £6.   *Turici*, 1826-37
Priced, 1843-53, unbound, £6. 6s.; 1844, White, cf. gt £8. 8s.
1392 NIZOLII Lexicon Ciceronianum, 3 vols. 8vo. *best edition, bds.* £2.   1820
1393 CLAUDIANI Opera, diligentissime castigata, à F. Asulano, 12mo. *old blue morocco extra*, 25s   *Venetiis*, 1523
Priced, 1824, Thorpe, £2. 12s 6d; 1840, Payne and Foss, £2. 2s; Renouard's copy fetched £1. 12s; Sir Mark Sykes's, £2. 1s. The only Aldine edition of Claudian, and very rare in fine condition.
1394 CLINTON'S Fasti Hellenici: Chronology of Greece, 3 vols. 4to. (pub. at £4.) *bds.* £2.   1834-51
1395 —— Fasti Romani: Chronology of Rome, 2 vols. and Appendix, 4to. (pub. at £3. 8s 6d) *bds.* £2. 12s 6d   1845-50
1396 CLUVERII Geographia Antiqua; Germania, Italia, et Sicilia, 4 vols. folio, *portrait and maps, fine copy in hf. vellum*, 30s   *Lugd. Bat. Elzevir*, 1619-31
"I have already remarked his prodigious mass of materials. In speaking of the meanest village all the learning of antiquity and the middle ages occur to his memory."—GIBBON.
Priced, 1824, John Bohn, £9. 9s and £15. 15s; 1840, John Bohn, £4. 14s 6d; 1840, Payne and Foss, £8. 8s.
1397 COMICORUM GRÆCORUM FRAGMENTA: Historia critica Comicorum Græcorum; Poetae Comoediae Antiquae; Comoediae Mediae; Comoediae Modernae; collegit et disposuit Meineke, 4 vols. in 5, 8vo. *neat in vellum, gilt backs*, £2. 10s; or *calf gilt, by Hayday*, £3.   *Berolini*, 1839-41
1398 —— the same work, now completed, 5 vols. in 7, 8vo. *sd. new*, £2. 8s 1839-57
1399 CONSTANTINI PORPHYROGENNETÆ Opera, *Græce et Latine*, à Meursio, sm. 8vo. *old red morocco, gilt edges*, 10s   *Lugd. Bat. Elzevir*, 1617
1400 CORNELIUS NEPOS. Æmilii Probi seu Cornelii Nepotis liber de Vita excellentium Imperatorum, a Lambino, sm. 4to. *a fine copy, in old orange morocco, gilt edges, the sides covered by elaborate gold tooling, with arms in centre, French binding of the XVIIth century*, 28s   *Lutetiæ, Benenatus*, 1569
1401 CORPUS GRAMMATICORUM LATINORUM Veterum, collegit, auxit, recensuit ac potiorem lectionis varietatem adjecit Lindemann, 4 vols. in 3, 4to. *cloth, uncut*, 22s   *Lips.* 1831-40
1402 CORY'S Ancient Fragments of the Phoenician, Chaldaean, Egyptian, Tyrian, Carthaginian, and other writers, with an introductory dissertation, *second edition*, 8vo. *cloth*, RARE, 32s   1832
1403 COUSIN, Histoire de Constantinople, depuis Justin jusqu'à la fin de l'Empire, 8 vols. 12mo. *old calf*, 12s; or *vellum*, 12s   *Paris*, 1685
"Cette traduction abrégée des historiens Byzantins, n'est pas fort estimée, mais on n'en a pas de meilleure. Plus recherchée que l'in 4to."—BRUNET.

1404 CREUZER (F.) Deutsche Schriften, neue und verbesserte Auflage, 12 vols. in 10, 8vo. *many plates, hf. morocco, gilt tops, uncut,* £4.   *Leipz. und Darmst.* 1836-54
    Contents: I.—IV. Symbolik und Mythologie der Griechen; V.—VII. Archæologie der alten Kunst; VIII. Kunst der Griechen; IX. Griechische und Römische Literatur; X.—XII. Römische Geschichte; Leben; Classische Philologie.

1405 ——— Religions de l'Antiquité, par Guigniaut, imperfect, 8 vols. £2   1825-41

1406 CREVIER, Histoire des Empereurs Romains depuis Auguste jusqu'à Constantine, 12 vols. in 11, 12mo. *maps, neat in old calf gilt,* 20s   *Paris,* 1749-55
    Priced, 1840, Jas. Bohn, 36s.

1407 CTESIÆ Operum reliquiae, ed. Bachr, *vellum extra,* 12s   *Francof.* 1824

1408 CURTIUS, Geschichte des Wegebaus bei den Griechen, 4to. 7s   *Berlin,* 1855

1409 DAMMII Lexicon Græcum etymologicum et reale, ed. Duncan, stout 4to. 1128 pages, (pub. at £4. 14s 6d) *calf gilt,* 5s   *Glasg.* 1824

1410 D'ANVILLE's Ancient Geography, translated, 2 vols. 8vo. *maps, calf,* 5s   1810

1411 DAUNOU (C. F.) Cours d'Études Historiques, pub. par Taillandier, 20 vols. 8vo. *brown morocco,* £2. 16s   *Paris,* 1842-9

  Tom. 1. Examen et Choix de Faits
    Critique de l'Histoire
  2. Usages de l'Histoire
    Classification des Faits
    Geographie
  3, 4. Chronologie technique

    Chronologie litigieuse
    Chronologie positive
  7. Exposition des Faits
    Art d'écrire l'histoire
  8, 9 Herodote
  10. Thucydide

  11. Xenophon
  12. Polybe
    Diodore de Sicile
  13 to 19. Histoire Romaine
  20. Recherches sur les systèmes philosophiques: Table des Matières.

1412 DEMOSTHENIS Opera omnia, *Graece*, edidit Reiske, editio correctior curante Schæfero, cum prefatione de editionibus, cumque apparatu critico et indicibus, 9 vols. 8vo. *uncut,* 16s   *Lips.* 1822-23

1413 DÉMOSTHÈNE et ESCHINE, Œuvres complètes, *en Grec et en Français*, par Auger et Planche, 10 vols. 8vo. *fine portrait, calf neat,* 25s   *Paris,* 1819-21

1414 ULPIANI Commentarioli in Orationes Demosthenis, cum enarrationibus et Arpocrationis dictionario rhetorum, *Graece*, ab Asulano, folio, *fine copy in russia, gilt edges,* 32s   *Venetiis,* 1527
    Priced, 1840, Payne and Foss, £2. 5s: Meerman's copy fetched 21 florins.

1415 DIODORI SICULI Bibliotheca Historica, à Rhodomano et Wesselingio, *Graece et Latine,* 2 vols. fol. *frontispiece and fine portrait of Wesseling, hf. bound, uncut,* 16s   *Amst.* 1746

1416 ——— Bibliotheca Historica, *Gr. et Lat.* cum notis variorum et Wesselingii, 11 vols. 8vo. FINE PAPER, *calf gilt,* £2. 18s; or *smooth russia extra, gilt edges, a very choice copy,* £5.   *Biponti et Argentorati,* 1793-1807
  Cost the late Mr. Fynes Clinton, £12. 12s. "It was the wish of Dr. Harwood that a commodious edition of this entertaining Greek writer might be given to the world. The present beautiful and judicious work seems to have realized this wish."

1417 ——— Bibliotheca historica, *Graece*, ex recensione Dindorfii, 5 vols. in 4, 8vo. *half calf,* 25s   *Lips.* 1828

1418 DIOGENES LAERTIUS de vitis, dogmatibus et apophthegmatibus Philosophorum, *Graece et Latine,* cum notis Casauboni, etc. ed. Meibomius, 2 vols. 4to. *Editio optima, numerous portraits, vellum, gilt edges,* 25s   *Amst.* 1692
  Priced, 1844, £2. 5s. "Not only a very elegant and beautiful work, but by far the most critical and perfect edition. The Historia Mulierum Philosopharum, by Menage, and copious indexes are subjoined."—DIBDIN.

1419 DIONIS CASSII Historiae Romanae quae supersunt, *Graece et Latine,* 2 vols. folio, *2 portraits, beautiful copy in old calf gilt,* £2. 10s   *Hamburgi,* 1750-52

1420 DIONYSII HALICARNASSENSIS OPERA OMNIA, *Graece et Latine,* cum annotationibus Stephani, Sylburgii, Porti, Casauboni, Fulvii Ursini, Hudsoni, Valesii, et Reiske, 6 vols. 8vo. *hf. calf,* 21s; or *calf gilt,* 25s   *Lipsiæ,* 1774-77

1421 ——— idem, 6 vols. 8vo. *very strongly whole bound in vellum,* £2. 2s   1774-77
  Priced, 1844, White, £3. 5s. Fetched, Sir M. M. Sykes', russia, £4. 18s.
  "In his edition of this author, Reiske has shewn mature judgment and profound grammatical knowledge, and by his successful emendation of the text has removed many difficulties."—FUHRMANN.

1422 DENYS D'HALICARNASSE, Antiquités Romaines, traduites par Bellanger, 6 vols. in 3, 8vo. *calf gilt,* 12s   *Paris,* 1800

1423 DIONYSIUS PERIEGETES, *Gr. et Lat.* cum commentariis et Bernhardy, 2 vols. in 1, 8vo. *russia gilt,* 5s   *Lips.* 1828

1424 D'ORVILLE, Sicula, quibus Siciliæ Veteris rudera, illustrantur—Numismata Sicula à Burmanno, 2 vols. in 1, folio, *portrait, and many plates of Antiquities and Coins, prize vellum,* 14s   *Amst.* 1764
    Ouvrage fort estimé.   Priced, 1840, Payne and Foss, £3.

CLASSICS, GREEK AND LATIN PHILOLOGY, ETC. 93

1425 DRUMANN (W.) Geschichte Roms in seinem Uebergange von der Republikanischen zur Monarchischen Verfassung, oder Pompejus, Caesar, Cicero und ihre Zeitgenossen, nach Geschlechtern und mit Genealogischen Tabellen, 6 vols. 8vo. (cost £3. 10s) *hf. calf gilt,* 30s *Königsberg,* 1834-44
A masterpiece of historical research, comprising the biographies of all the great Roman Statesmen and Warriors from about 300 years before Christ to the establishment of the Imperial Monarchy: and especially treating of the momentous period of transition in which an Empire gradually rose upon the growing greatness of an Oligarchy. The valuable genealogical tables give it a particular interest as showing the progression of the aristocratic element.

1426 DUCANGE (*C. du Presne*) Glossarium ad Scriptores Mediæ et Infimæ Græcitatis acced. Appendices, 2 vols. in 1, folio, *rare,* £3. 16s *Lugd.* 1688
"Livre très recherché, et devenu peu commun, 80-100 francs."—Brunet.
This, "the *Greek* Ducange," has become a very rare book, and its price has constantly risen, the above being the only edition.

1427 DUCANGE. Glossarium Mediæ et Infimæ Latinitatis, conditum a Carlo Dufresne domino Ducange, auctum a monachis ordinis S. Benedicti, cum supplementi integris D. P. Carpentieri, et additamentis Adelungii et aliorum, digessit G. A. L. Henschel, 7 vols.—Glossarium Latino-germanicum mediæ et infimæ ætatis, ed. Diefenbach, 1 vol. *Francof.* 1857—together 8 vols. 4to. *hf. morocco, neat* £13. 16s *Paris,* 1840-50-57
Cette nouvelle édition remplace avec avantage et à un prix plus modique l'ancienne édition de Ducange revue par les Bénédictins, et celle du supplément de D. Carpentier, devenue de jour en jour plus chère, elle a été revue et augmentée par M. Henschel. d'apres les travaux postérieurs.
"Without the Glossary of Ducange nothing can be done satisfactorily in the study of history previous to the sixteenth century: we can hardly decipher a single parchment without having recourse to these pages."—H. L. Jones.
A very useful work to all engaged in Antiquarian studies, giving full particulars about Mediæval Ceremonies Customs, Laws, etc. containing also obsolete Technical Terms of every kind.

1428 DUNLOP'S History of Roman Literature from its earliest period to, and during the Augustan Age, with Appendix, 3 vols. 8vo. *calf gilt,* £2. 16s 1823-28
1429 Eichwald's Alte Geographie des Caspischen Meeres, des Kaukasus und Süd-Russlands, 8vo. *maps and plates, hf. calf,* 5s 6d *Berlin,* 1838
1430 Engelmann, Bibliotheca Scriptorum Classicorum Græcorum et Latinorum, 8vo. 48 and 508 pp. *a valuable bibliography, with prices, hf. calf neat,* 6s *Leipsic,* 1848
1431 EPICTETI Enchiridion, Cebetis Tabula, Prodici Hercules, et Cleanthis Hymnus, *Græce et Latine,* 12mo. charta maxima, *morocco, joints inside, by C. Lewis; from the libraries of the Rev. Theodore Williams and Miss Currer,* 35s *Glasguæ, Foulis,* 1744
1432 —— Opera et Fragmenta: viz. Dissertationes, Enchiridion, Fragmenta, cum Simplicii Commentario, Notis, Indicibusque, *Gr. et Lat.* ed. Schweighæuser, 6 vols. 8vo. fine paper, *hf. morocco, gilt top, uncut,* 32s *Lipsiæ,* 1799-1800
Priced, 1848, Payne and Foss, calf extra, £5. 5s; 1854, Heath, calf gilt, £3. 3s; by Klincksieck, Paris, papier d'Hollande, cartonné, 72 fr.; 1855, Heussner, Bruxelles, br. 36 fr. Large Paper, 1840, Payne and Foss, russia, £6. 6s.

1433 EPISTOLAE Basilii, Libanii, Chionis, Aeschinis et Isocratis, Phalaridis, Bruti, Apollonii, Juliani; Demosthenis, Platonis, Aristotelis, Philippi, Alexandri, et aliorum, 2 vols. in 1, stout sm. 4to. editio princeps, *very fine copy in red russia neat, gilt edges, very rare,* £2. 16s *Venetiis,* 1499
Priced, 1830, Thorpe, £5. 15s 6d; Pickering, £4. 4s; 1855, Tross, 135 fr.; 1857, Asher, 60 fr.; 1858, Butsch in Augsburg, a wormed copy, 28 flor.; fetched at Hibbert's sale £3 3s, Sir M. Sykes' £3. 3s, Dr. Heath's £3. 15s, Sotheby's, in May, 1815, £4 4s, Caillard's 130 fr.; Libri sale, 1859, £6. 6s.
This edition is printed '*cum privilegio;*' one of the earliest so published, and it is believed the first by Aldus.

Etruscan Antiquities.—See Grotefend, Lanzi, Micali, etc. *Also under Class* Fine Arts.

1434 EUCLIDIS Elementa, Graece, edidit Grynaeus, folio, editio princeps, *calf,* 16s Rare; Johnson's copy fetched, £3. *Basileæ, Hervagius,* 1533

1435 —— Elementorum sex priores libri, recogniti à Melder, 16mo. *diagrams, bds. uncut, fine copy,* 20s *Lugd. Bat. Elzevir,* 1673
1436 —— Œuvres de, *en Grec, en Latin, et en Français,* par Peyrard, 3 vols. 4to. *hf. bd. morocco, uncut,* £2. 10s *Paris,* 1814
1437 —— les memes, 3 vols. roy. 4to. papier velin, *in red morocco extra, silk linings, by Bozérian,* £5. *Paris,* 1814-18
1438 EURIPIDIS Tragœdia et fragmenta, *Græce et Latine,* recensuit Matthiæ, 9 vols. 8vo. *best edition, calf gilt,* 25s *Lipsiæ,* 1813-29
1439 FABRETTI Glossarium Italicum in quo omnia vocabula continentur ex Umbricis Sabinis Oscis Volscis Etruscis caeterisque quae supersunt collecta, 4 fasciculi, A—IG, roy. 4to. 16 *plates of Inscriptions, and numerous cuts of Coins, sd.* 15s *Aug. Taurinorum,* 1859

1440 FACCIOLATI Totius Latinitatis Lexicon, opera Forcellini; edidit, Anglicam interpretationém in locum Italicæ substituit BAILEY, 2 stout vols. impl. 4to. (pub. at £6. 16s 6d) 2700 pp. *treble columns, calf, very neat*, £3. 1828

1441 FETES et COURTISANES de la Grèce, comprenant la Chronique Religieuse, Mœurs Publiques, Chronique Scandaleuse, et Mœurs Privées, 4 vols. 8vo. *with plates by Garnerey, and engraved Music, calf neat*, 15s *Paris*, 1801

1442 FLORUS (L. Annæus). Salmasius addidit Lucium Ampelium nunquam antehac editum, 16mo. FINE COPY, *green morocco, gilt edges*, 9s *Lugd. Bat. Elzevir*, 1638

1443 FOEMINARUM novem illustrium Fragmenta: Sapphus, Erinnae, etc. Fragmenta et Elogia, *Gr. et Lat.* ed. Wolfius, *Hamburgi*, 1735—MULIERUM GRÆCUM Fragmenta et Elogia, cura Wolfii, *Gottingæ*, 1739—Prolegomena ad Nov. Test. Græc. Amst. 1730—4 vols. in 2, 4to. *uniform, calf gilt, fine copy*, 25s 1730-39
A rare collection, cost its former owner £3. 10s.

1444 FORBIGER'S Handbuch der alten Geographie mit historischer Einleitung, 3 vols. large 8vo. *Maps and Tables* (pub. at £3. unbound) *hf. calf*, 20s; or roy. 8vo. *half green morocco, neat*, 36s *Leip.* 1842-48

1445 FRONTINI Opera, ed. Societas Bipontina, 8vo. *half vellum*, 4s *Biponti*, 1788

1446 FRONTINI Strategematica, cum notis variorum, curante Oudendorpio, 8vo. *frontispiece, fine paper*, BEST EDITION, *russia extra, gilt edges*, 12s *Lugd. Batav.* 1779
Priced, 1840, J. Bohn, 27s.

1447 GELL'S (Sir W.) Topography of ROME and its vicinity, 2 vols. roy. 8vo. LARGE PAPER, *woodcuts, with large map in separate case, cloth*, 25s 1834

1448 GEOGRAPHI GRÆCI MINORES, *Græce et Latine*, ed. Müller, 2 vols. roy. 8vo. *with Atlas of 29 coloured maps, sd. new*, £2. 5s *Paris*, 1855-61

1449 GEOPONICORUM, sive de Re Rustica lib. XX, *Gr. et Lat.* notulas et Indices adjecit Needham, 8vo. *fine copy in rich old red morocco extra, gilt edges, by De Rome*, £2. 2s *Cantab.* 1704

1450 GERMANICI CÆSARIS Reliquiæ, ex recensione Orellii, edente Giles, 8vo. *a beautiful copy, red* MOROCCO *extra, gilt edges, with richly gilt borders*, 14s 1838

1451 GLADSTONE'S (W. E.) Studies on HOMER and the Homeric Age, 3 vols. 8vo. *cloth, out of print*, £2. *Oxford*, 1858

1452 GLOSSARIUM EROTICUM linguæ latinæ, sive Theogoniæ Legum et morum nuptialium apud Romanos explanatio nova, auctore P. P. 8vo. 15s *Paris*, 1826

1453 GNOMICI POETÆ GRÆCI, *Graece et Latine*, cum notis, ed. Brunck, *very fine copy, old green morocco, gilt edges, by De Rome*, 30s *Argent.* 1784

1454 GRÆVII THESAURUS ANTIQUITATUM ET HISTORIARUM ITALIÆ collectus curâ et studio J. G. Grævii, et ad finem perductus à P. Burmanno, 9 vols. in 30 parts, divided into 16 vols. 1704-23; Thesaurus Antiquitatum Siciliæ, Sardiniæ, Corsicæ, etc. curâ J. G. Grævii, cum præfationibus, P. Burmanni, 15 vols. in 8, 1723-25; together 24 vols. folio, *fine frontispieces, portrait, and a profusion of interesting plates, fine copy, in old cf. gilt*, £10. *Lugd. Bat.* 1704-25

1455 —— Thesaurus Antiquitatum ROMANARUM, congestus à Grævio, 12 vols. *Traj. ad Rhen.* 1694-99—SALLENGRE, Novus Thesaurus Antiquitatum Romanarum, 3 vols. *Hag. Com.* 1706—PITISCI Lexicon Antiquitatum Romanarum, 2 vols. *Leovard.* 1713; together 17 vols. folio, *fine frontispieces, maps and plates, old calf gilt, from Miss Currer's library*, £2 10s 1694-1713
Sallengre, alone, which is one of the rarest Supplements to Grævius, was priced, 1825, by Thorpe, £5. 5s.;

1456 GROTE'S HISTORY OF GREECE, 12 vols. 8vo. (pub. at £9. 12s), *with portrait, maps and Index, cloth*, £7. 10s 1846-56

1457 —— the same, new edition, complete in 8 vols. 8vo. *portrait and maps*, (pub. at £5. 12s) *cloth*, £4. 9s 1863
" A great literary undertaking, equally notable whether we regard it as an accession to what is of standard value in our language, or as an honourable monument of what English scholarship can do."—ATHENÆUM.

1458 GROTEFEND, Rudimenta Linguæ Oscæ et linguæ Umbricæ, ex inscriptionibus antiquis, 4to. *facsimiles and alphabets, hf. morocco*, 15s *Hannov.* 1839

1459 GRUTERI Corpus Inscriptionum totius Orbis Romanae ex recens. et cum annot. Grævii, 2 vols. folio, *many plates of Roman Antiquities, fine copy in vellum*, £4. 4s *Amst.* 1707
Priced, 1832, Payne and Foss, £3. 10s; 1855, Tross, 130 fr.; Heath's £4. 6s. LARGE PAPER: 1844, Macpherson, £7. 7s; the Duke of Grafton's copy, £3. 15s; Askew's, £4.
An excellent work for Classical Scholars, giving amongst the artistic regulations, those of the various Worships.

1460 GUARNACCI, Origini Italiche, 3 vols. sm. 4to. *with 26 plates of early Italian, chiefly Etruscan Art, vellum*, 10s *Roma*, 1785-87

CLASSICS, GREEK AND LATIN PHILOLOGY, ETC. 95

1461 GUARINI Erotemata, *Graece*, cum multis additamentis et commentariis, 16mo.
calf neat, 21s *Ferrariæ, Mazochus*, 1509
Edition très rare, et rendue célèbre par les Dissertations qu'elle a occasionnées à differens Bibliographes.

1462 HARDT'S Catalogus Codicum Manuscriptorum Græcorum Bibliothecæ Regiæ Bavaricæ, 5 vols. 4to. LARGE PAPER, *bds.* 32s *Monachii*, 1806
Priced, 1845, Rodd, £2. 12s 6d; 1847, H. Bohn, calf, £5. 5s.

1463 HEEREN'S HISTORISCHE WERKE, 15 vols. 8vo. *maps, etc.* (pub. at £7. *sewed*), *fine copy in calf extra, from Dr. Hawtrey's library*, £4. 4s. *Göttingen*, 1821-26
Complete copies are scarce.

1464 —— Historical Works, translated from the German: Political History of Ancient Greece; Manual of Ancient History; Reflections on the Carthaginians and Ethiopians; the Egyptians, the Persians, Babylonians, Phoenicians and Scythians, the Indians; Historical Treatises; European States and Colonies; together 10 vols. 8vo. *calf extra*, £4. 5s *Oxford*, 1829-34

1465 —— another edition, in 9 vols. 8vo. *cloth*, £3. *Oxford*, 1834-46

1466 HEINECCII Antiquitatum Romanarum Syntagma, ed. Haubold, stout 8vo. *bds.* 6s *Franc.* 1822

1467 HELWING's Geschichte des Achäischen Bundes, 8vo. *blue mor.* 5s *Lemgo*, 1859

1468 HERODIANI historiæ, *Græce et Latine*, interprete Politiano, curâ Asulani, 12mo. *fine tall copy in blue morocco extra, edges very slightly cut, several rough leaves*, 24s *Venetiis*, 1524
Priced, 1840, Payne and Foss, £2. 2s; fetched, 1857, Sotheby's, £1. 14s.

1469 HERODOTUS, textum ad Gaisfordii editionem recognovit, perpetua Creuzeri et sua annotatione instruxit, tabulas indicesque adjecit Baehr, 4 vols. 8vo. *half russia*, 18s; *calf gilt*, 21s *Lipsiae*, 1830-35

1470 —— A new English version, edited with Notes and Appendices, illustrating the history and geography of Herodotus, by G. RAWLINSON, assisted by Col. Sir H. RAWLINSON and Sir G. J. WILKINSON, 4 vols. 8vo. *maps and illustrations*, (pub. at £3. 12s) *cloth, new and clean*, £2. 12s 1858-60
Sir Henry Rawlinson's recent Assyrian discoveries must direct the attention of all Biblical and Classical Scholars to these volumes, which constitute the best edition, with all the latest discoveries and illustrations, of the Father of History.
The above is a copy of the genuine edition, printed in larger type, and better arranged than the later one, in which the references to the Index are hastily and incorrectly changed, and the type and getting up of the work inferior to this.

1471 BOBRIK, Geographie des Herodot, 8vo. *the atlas of twelve maps bound up with the text, hf. morocco gilt, uncut*, 7s 6d *Königsberg*, 1838

1472 HESIODI Theogonia, *Graece*, ed. Van Lennep, 8vo. *bds.* 5s *Amst.* 1843

1473 HESYCHII LEXICON, *Graece*, cum notis variorum et J. Alberti, 2 vols. large folio, *fine portrait of Alberti, by Houbraken, very fine copy in Dutch vellum, from the Rev. J. Mitford's library*, £2. *Lugd. Bat.* 1746-66

1474 HIEROCLES in aurea Pythagareorum carmina, *Graece et Latine*, à Curterio, ed. princ. 16mo. *vellum*, 6s *Paris*, 1583

1475 HIPPOCRATIS Opera omnia, *Graece et Latine*, ed. Van der Linden, 2 vols. stout sm. 8vo. *vellum*, 20s *Lugd. Bat.* 1665

1476 —— Opera omnia, *Graece et Latine*, cum notis, etc. ed. Kühn, 3 vols. stout 8v. *calf neat*, 24s *Lips.* 1825

1477 —— Coacæ Praenotiones, *Graece et Latine*, à Foesio et Jonstono, 16mo. red MOROCCO *extra, gilt edges*, 25s *Amst. Elzevir*, 1660

1478 HOMERI Opera omnia, *Graece*, ex recensione Demetrii Chalcondylæ, cum Herodoti Plutarchique vitis Homeri, et Dionis Chrysostomi dissertatione, EDITIO PRINCEPS, 2 vols. folio, *the first leaf of Vol. I. inlaid, but otherwise* A FINE TALL AND PURE COPY, *old russia gilt, from Miss Currer's library*, VERY RARE, £70. *Florent. Bernardus Nerlius*, 1488
Priced, 1843, Payne and Foss, £84.: 1848, £75.; Heath's copy fetched £94. 10s; Willett's £88.; 1853, Dr Hawtrey's £70.
"Splendour, rarity, value, truly exquisite."—DIBDIN. On no edition of any classic have bibliographers been more eloquent or bestowed a greater share of praise than on this most magnificent and esteemed work, without exception the most beautiful book the Greek press produced in the fifteenth century."—Moss.

1479 HOMERI Opera: Ilias, Ploutarchou kai Herodotou Bioi Homērou, Odusseia, Batrachomuomachia, Humnoi, in 2 vols. 12mo. *fine copy in calf gilt, gilt edges*, £5. 5s *Venet.* 1504
Cette première édition Aldine se trouve difficilement en bon état. Vendu, 60 fl. Crevenna, £6. 15s, Butler. BRUNET.

1480 HOMERI Ilias et Odyssea, cum SCHOLIIS GRÆCIS opera Micylli et Camerarii; accedunt Porphyrii Quæstiones et de Antro Nympharum *Graece*, 2 vols. in 1, small folio, *ruled, with numerous* MANUSCRIPT NOTES *in a beautiful Greek character*, 15s *Basiliæ, Hervag.* 1541

1481 HOMERI Ilias, Odyssea, Batrachomyomachia, Hymni, cum multiplici lectione, vitâque Homeri à Herodoto, Plutarcho et Dione Chrysostomo, *omnia Graece*, curâ Francini, 2 vols. 12mo. *very fine copy in red morocco extra, gilt and gauffré edges*, £2. 10s *Venetiis, Junta*, 1537
Priced, 1830, Payne and Foss, £5. 5s; 1832, £3. 3s
Of this rare edition, *said* to contain 56 leaves of Various Readings, Heyne has observed, "*Nec tamen usquam illa (Multiplex Lectio) conspicitur;*" though from the publications of Renouard and Dibdin, we should expect them in the 56 separately numbered leaves, at the end of the Odyssey. These, however, consist only of the Biographical Notices. In his new edition, Renouard acknowledges his error, and places the non-existence of these Var. Lect. beyond doubt. In the Bibl. Saraz, this edition is termed "*omnium præstantissima et in maximo pretio.*"

1482 HOMERI OPERA OMNIA cum Commentariis EUSTATHII, Archiep. Thessalonicensis, *Graece*, EDITIO PRINCEPS, 4 vols. folio, *very fine, clean, and sound copy, red morocco, gt. edges*, £9. 9s *Romæ, ap. Ant. Bladum*, (TYPIS ALDINIS,) 1542-50
"Edition belle et très-rare de cet ouvrage estimé des savans."—BRUNET. Nic. Majoranus thus speaks of the merits of Eustathius:—"Interpres iste Homeri doctissimus, philosophus acutissimus, theologus religiosissimus qui sensus abditos eruit, speciem omnem deformitatis abstergit, arcana sapientiæ et pietatis aperit. Imprimisque id agit, nequam totius philosophiæ partem artificiis poeticis occultatam ignoremus. Incredibile est memoratu, quantas opes Græcæ eloquentiæ, quantos Thesauros omnium disciplinarum expromit" Mr. Moss also calls it "a very rare and beautiful edition, and held in very great esteem by the curious." Dr. Heath's copy sold for £68. 5s; Professor Porson's for £55.; and the Duke of Roxburghe's for £42.

1483 HOMERI Opera omnia, ex recensione et cum notis S. CLARKII, 5 vols. 8vo. *neat*, £2. 2s *Glasguae*, 1814

1484 SCHAUFELBERGERI Nova Clavis Homerica, cum Camerarii, Clarkii, Ernesti, etc. annotationibus et scholiis prefatione Breitingeri, etc. 8 vols. 8vo. *Fine Paper, calf gilt*, 18s *Turici*, 1761-68
" Rare et très recherché."—BRUNET.

1485 HOMER, a burlesque translation of, 2 vols. 8vo. *numerous very humourous plates, calf gilt*, 25s 1797
A work full of humour, by Thomas Brydges, but which often transgresses the bounds of decency.—LOWNDES.

1486 HORATIUS FLACCUS, recensuit Orellius, cum varietate lectionis, notis et interpretatione, 2 vols. 8vo. *calf gilt*, 20s *Turici*, 1837-38

1487 —— Opera, cura H. H. MILMAN, sq. 8vo. *beautifully printed on Fine Paper, with graceful borderings, head and tail pieces*, (pub. at 42s) *Spanish calf extra, gilt edges*, 20s 1853

1488 —— ad codd. Sec. IX et X exactum, commentarii critico et exegetico illustratum edidit Ritter, 2 vols. 8vo. (*sd. new*, 23s) *russia gilt*, 15s *Lips*. 1856-57

1489 HORACE, Odes, Epodes, Carmen Seculare, Satires, Epistles and Art of Poetry, in Latin and English, with critical notes, by Francis, 4 vols. 8vo. *old smooth calf*, 18s 1743-53

1490 HORACIO Flacco, *in Latino*, con la Declaracion Magistral en lengua Castellana por Villen de Biedma, folio, *fine tall copy, formerly Count Hoym's, in old gilt "veau fauve," having his Arms stamped in gold on sides*, £3. *Granada*, 1599

1491 INSCRIPTIONUM LATINARUM selectarum amplissima collectio ad illustrationem Romanæ Antiquitatis, disciplinæ, etc. ed. Orellius et Henzen, 3 vols. roy. 8vo. *sd. new*, £2. 2s. *Turici*, 1828-60

1492 INSCRIPTIONES Regni Neapolitani Latinæ, folio, *sd. new*, £3. 10s. 1852

1493 **Itineraria.** VETERA ROMANORUM ITINERARIA, sive, Antonini Itinerarium, etc. ed. WESSELING, 4to. *vellum*, 18s., or *green morocco, gt. edges*, 30s *Amst*. 1735
" A most excellent edition of one of the most useful works we have on the Geography of Greece."—*Gibbon*.
" Wesseling was one of the *idle learned*, but he possessed a kind of knowledge not useless even to a historian of Greece."—*Thirlwall*.

1494 RECUEIL des Itineraires Anciens : Itineraire d'Antonin, la Table de Peutinger et des Periples Grecs, par Lapie, et Fortia d'Urban, 4to. with large folio Atlas, *sd*. 15s. *Paris*, 1845

1495 JACOBITZ und SEILER, Handwörterbuch der Griechischen Sprache, 3 vols. roy. 8vo. *double cols. russia extra*, 32s *Leipzig*, 1839-46

1496 JAHRBÜCHER (Neue) für Philologie und Pædagogik oder Kritische Bibliothek für Schul. und Unterrichtswesen, von Seebode und Jahn, Vols. I.-XVIII., 1831-36, with Supplement, Vols. I.-VI. 1831-37 ; together 22 vols. 8vo. *eleven vols. hf. calf, the remainder in 44 nos.* £2. 16s *Leipzig*, 1831-37

1497 JAMBLICHUS de Mysteriis Ægyptiorum, Chaldæorum, Assyriorum, cum Procli, Porphyrii, Synesii, Pselli et aliorum Opusculis de Dæmonibus, etc. omnia Latinè, small folio, FIRST EDITION, *old red morocco extra, gilt edges, by De Rome, rare*, £2. 2s *Venetiis*, 1497
Priced, 1834, Leslie, £2. 2s; 1835, Techener, 60 fr.; 1848, Payne and Foss, £3. 13s 6d.

CLASSICS, GREEK AND LATIN PHILOLOGY, ETC. 97

1498 JAMBLICHUS de Mysteriis, Ægyptiorum, Chaldæorum, Assyriorum, Proclus, etc. folio, *fine copy in calf neat, gilt edges*, 18s   *Venet. Ald.* 1516

1499 JOSEPHI OPERA OMNIA, Gr. et Lat. cum Notis et Nova Versione Hudsoni; acced. notæ Variorum, etc. cura Havercampi, BEST EDITION, 2 vols. folio, *very fine copy, vellum*, £2. 2s   *Amst.* 1726

1500 ——— the same, LARGE PAPER, 2 vols. royal folio, EDITIO OPTIMA, *vellum*, £2. 18s
    Amst. 1726

<small>Priced, 1829, Longman's, vellum, £9. 9s; 1837 and 1840, Payne and Foss, mor. £14. 14s; 1844, White, vell. ex. £4. 10s; 1857, vell. £4. 4s; the Devonshire duplicate fetched £4. 1s. "This is usually considered the Editio Optima. The typographical execution is beautiful."—*Horne*.</small>

1501 JOSEPHI OPERA OMNIA, *Gr. et Lat.* ad editionem Havercampi cum Oxoniensi Hudsoni collatam, curavit Oberthür, 3 vols. in 6, 8vo. *calf,* 18s   *Lips.* 1782-85

1502 ——— the same, 3 vols. 8vo. *old olive morocco extra, gilt edges*, £2.   1782-85

1503 ——— Opera, ed. Richter, 6 vols. in 3, 12mo. *bds.* 5s   *Lips.* 1826

1504 JUSTIN. Trogi Pompei historiæ, ab Justino—Æmylii Probi (Cornelii Nepotis) imperatorum vitæ, ab Asulano, 2 vols. in 1, 12mo. *red morocco, gilt edges, the anchor in gold on both sides*, 18s   *Venetiis,* 1522
<small>Priced, 1824, Thorpe, £2. 12s 6d; fetched, 1857, Sotheby's, £1. 12s "Edition rare."—*Brunet*.</small>

1505 JUVENALIS Satiræ, ad codd. Parismos, cum lectionum varietate, notis, etc. ed. Achaintre, 2 vols. 8vo. *calf extra*, 10s   *Paris.* 1810

1506 JUVENAL and PERSIUS, Satires of, translated into English Verse by GIFFORD, 2 vols. 8vo. *bds.* 10s   1817

1507 KIEPERT (H.) Topographisch-historischer Atlas von Hellas und den Hellenischen Colonien, atlas folio, 24 *beautifully engraved and very correct Maps, coloured*, 19s   *Berlin,* 1851
<small>The reader of Grote's and Thirlwall's Histories should have this valuable Atlas at his side.</small>

1508 KLAUSEN, Aeneas und die Penaten; die Italischen Volksreligionen unter dem Einfluss der Griechischen, 2 vols. 8vo. *plates of Coins, etc. calf extra*, 16s
    Hamburg, 1839-40

1509 KOPP, PALÆOGRAPHIA CRITICA, 4 vols. 4to. (pub. at £16. 16s) £3. 10s 1817-19

1510 LABOULAYE, Essai sur les Lois Criminelles des Romains, 8vo. *calf gilt*, 5s   1845

1511 LACTANTIUS Firmianus de Divinis Institutionibus, folio, *the initials of each book painted and illuminated, fine large copy in old russia gilt (ancient Harleian binding)*, VERY RARE, £21.
    Rome, Sweynheym et Pannarts, in domo Petri de Maximo, MCCCCLXVIII

<small>The first book printed in Italy is known to have been the "Lactantius," which appeared at Subiaco in 1465. In speaking of the edition of 1468, the one now occupying our attention, and which is one of the first works printed at Rome, M. Brunet says:—"An edition as rare, but less precious than that of 1465." This copy, having the large initials in gold and colours, is very fine and very large in the margins, which renders it a regular folio instead of a *small folio*, as described by Brunet.
This copy, having a few slight wormholes at the beginning and end, contains 219 leaves, 218 printed (as announced by M. Brunet), and a blank at the commencement, on which is a long manuscript note, dated 1482, notifying the donation and deposition of the book, and requesting the reader's prayers.
One fact seems to have passed hitherto unnoticed, which is, that at the end of the volume are to be found various pieces of poetry taken from Ovid, &c. and amongst these *the description* of the Phœnix commencing —
"[C]lossi per li gram saui se confessa," given by Dante in the "Divina Commedia." These lines, which are wanting in the "Lactantius" of 1465, appeared here prior to the editions of Dante printed at Foligno and Jesi. This volume being the third book printed at Rome and the seventh printed in Italy, and all the works printed before this in Italy ("Donatus," "Lactantius," "Cicero de Oratore," "Augustinus de Civitate Dei," "Ciceronis Epistolæ ad Familiares," and "Turrecremata") being in Latin, without one word in Italian, the conclusion is that this is undoubtedly the first printed book in which Italian occurs; and it is very remarkable that with verses of Dante printing in Italian should have commenced. This is a curious fact which we do not remember to have met anywhere mentioned.</small>

1512 LACTANTII Opera, cum Tertulliani Apologetico, 12mo, *fine copy in old red morocco, gilt leaves*, 14s   *Venet.* 1535
<small>Priced, 1834, Pickering, £5. 5s; 1848, Payne and Foss, £3. 3s: Renouard's copy fetched £3. 12s. "Très bonne édition, bien supérieure à celle de 1515."—*Renouard*.</small>

1513 LANGLOIS, Voyage dans la Cilicie et dans les Montagnes du Taurus, pendant les années 1852-53, royal 8vo. *map, portrait, and* 28 *plates of Classical Antiquities, etc. half calf, uncut, gilt top*, 16s   *Paris,* 1861

1514 LANZI, Saggio di Lingua ETRUSCA e di altre antiche d'Italia, 3 vols. 8vo. *best edition, portraits and plates of early Italian Inscriptions and Art, sd.* 15s ; *hf. calf gilt*, 32s ; or, *fine copy in calf extra*, 36s   *Firenze,* 1824-5
<small>"The Etruscan dialect, the characters of which are the same as those of the Umbrian and Oscan dialects, had not been identified and made out with certainty till within the last fifty years: for the inscribed monuments of these people being rare and scanty, it has been a work of time, as well as of great industry and sagacity, to draw any well-established conclusions from them."—*Cramer's Ancient Italy*.</small>

1515 LASCARIS, Institutiones Universæ, cum plurimis auctariis, *Graece et Latine*, sm. 4to. *fine copy, morocco extra*, 32s   *Ferrariæ, Maciochius,* 1510

H

1516 LEAKE (Col.) Travels in the Morea, 3 vols. 8vo. *map, plans, and plates* (pub. at £2. 5s), *cloth*, 15s 1830
1517 —— Travels in NORTHERN GREECE, 4 vols. 8vo. *maps and plates, cloth*, £2. 10s 1835
    The most authentic book on the Epirus, Macedonia, Illyria, Thessaly, etc. unrivalled in exactness.
1518 LETRONNE, Fragments des Poemes geographiques de Scymnus et du faux Dicéarque, 8vo, *hf. calf*, 7s 6d *Paris*, 1840
1519 LEWIS (Sir George C.) Historical Survey of the Astronomy of the Ancients, 8vo. (pub. at 15s), *cloth*, 10s 1862
1520 LEXICON Græco-Latinum, cui ad summum locupletato etiam Etymologiæ vocum accesserunt, folio, *title within a broad woodcut border of emblematic figures, old red morocco, gilt edges, arms on sides*, 15s *Basileæ, Valder*. 1541
1521 LIDDELL'S History of Rome, from the earliest times to the establishment of the Empire, 2 vols. 8vo. (pub. at 25s) *cloth*, 17s 1855
1522 LIVII Historiarum libri ex recensione Gronovii, 3 vols. 16mo. *green morccco extra, gilt edges, a very pretty book*, £2. 2s *Lugd. Bat. Elzevir*, 1654-3
1523 —— Historiarum libri quot extant, ex recensione Gronovii, 16mo. *frontispiece, very fine tall copy in old red morocco, gilt edges, from Dr. Hawtrey's library*, 30s *Amst. Elzevir*, 1678
1524 —— Historiæ, à Drakenborchio, cum Streinnio de gentibus Romanis et Ernesti Glossario, 6 vols. sm. 8vo. *russia*, 7s 6d *Oxon*. 1800
1525 LIVII Historiarum ab urbe condita libri qui supersunt omnes, cum notis variorum curante Drakenborch, acc. Supplementa Freinshemii, 7 vols. 4to. EDITIO OPTIMA, *fine portrait by Houbraken and plates, hf. bd. neat, uncut*, £2. 10s ; or *fine copy in Dutch vellum*, £3. *Lugd. Bat.* 1738-48
    Priced, 1823, Deighton, £12. 12s ; 1834. Pickering, £10. 10s ; Porson's copy fetched £12. 17s.
    "The labours of Drakenborch have entitled his edition to a superiority over every preceding one. Ernesti, Harles, and the Bipont editors are unanimous in their approbation of this truly Critical Production.—*Dibdin.*
1526 LIVII Historiæ, curâ Twiss, 4 vols. 8vo. (pub. at £1. 18s) *cloth*, 6s *Oxonii*, 1840-41
1527 LOBECK, Pathologiae Græci Sermonis elementi, 8vo. *calf*, 7s 6d *Reg. Boruss.* 1853
1528 LONGI Pastoralia de Daphni et Chloe, *Graece*, ed. Dutens, 1776— Amours Pastorales, *en Français*, par Amyot, 1731—2 vols. in 1, 12mo. *fine copies in old blue morocco, gilt edges*, 12s *Paris*, 1731-76
1529 —— Pastoralia, *Graece et Latine*, cum notis, ed. Villoison, 8vo. *vel.* 5s 1778
1530 LUCANI (M. Annæi) Pharsalia, cum vitâ suâ, Genethliaco ex Stacio, etc. folio, *fine large and pure copy, massively bound in green morocco extra, gilt edges*, £21.
    sine notâ loci, typogr. aut anni, sed circa 1475
    VERY RARE. COLLATION:—M. Annei Lucani vita ex commentario antiquiss, 2 pages; ex dimidiato codice particula ad poetae huius vitam pertinens sumpta, 1 page : Martialis, Genethliacon, etc. 5 pages; Text, 232 pp.— *See Hain, Brunet, Dibdin, and other Bibliographers for a description of this edition.*
1531 LUCANI Pharsalia, cum notis ed. Burmannus, 4to. *vellum*, 5s *Leidae*, 1740
1532 LUCIANI Opera, cum nova versione ac notis Hemsterhusii et Gesneri, *Graece et Latine*, 4 vols. 4to. *hf. calf*, 21s *Amst*. 1743
1533 LUCRETIUS, de rerum naturâ, 12mo. *fine copy in blue morocco extra, gilt gauffré edges, sides ornamented with gold tooling and anchor*, 30s *Ven. Ald.* 1515
    Priced, 1840, Payne and Foss, £2. 2s ; 1848, £3. 3s.
1534 —— De Rerum Natura lib. VI., cum notis Variorum, cura Havercampi, 2 vols. 4to. *plates, vellum*, 25s *Lugd. Bat.* 1725
1535 LUCRETIUS CARUS of the Nature of Things, in English verse by Creech, 2 vols. sm. 8vo. *calf*, 9s 1714-15
1536 MACROBII in Somnium Scipionis ex Cicerone explanatio ; et Saturnalia, cum Censorino de die natali, 12mo. *calf*, 25s *Ven. Ald.* 1528
    Heber's copy fetched £3. 1s.
1537 MANILII Astronomicōn libri 5, *Lat. et Gallice*, à Pingré, 2 vols. 8vo. *calf*, 5s *Paris*, 1786
1538 MANNERT (K.) Geographie der Griechen und Römer, aus ihren Schriften dargestellt, 10 vols. in 14, 8vo. *maps* (pub. at £5. 16s) *calf gilt*, £2. 10s *Nürnberg*, 1799-1825
1539 —— the same, 10 vols in 14, 8vo. *hf. calf gilt*, £2. 2s *Leipzig*, 1802-29
    The most extensive, and one of the best works ever published upon Ancient Geography.
1540 MANSO'S SPARTA, Geschichte und Verfassung dieses Staates, 3 vols. 8vo. *neatly hf. bound*, 10s 6d *; or calf gilt*, 14s *Leip.* 1800-5
    An excellent work of special history, with exact Chronological and Genealogical information ; full of profound research into Grecian Antiquities.

CLASSICS, GREEK AND LATIN PHILOLOGY, ETC. 99

1541 MANUTII (Aldi, Pauli filii) Orthographiæ ratio ex libris, etc. cum Aldo avo de vocalibus diphthongisque, 12mo. *calf, 7s* *Venet. Ald.* 1566
  The best of all the Aldine editions. A copy at Sir M. Sykes' sale fetched £6. 12s 6d.

1542 —— Grammaticæ Institutiones et de vitiatâ vocalium ac diphthongorum prolatione, 12mo. *woodcut portrait of Aldus on title, some old MS. notes, calf gilt, gilt edges*, 12s *Ven. Ald.* 1575

1543 —— de Quæsitis per epistolam, lib. III. 12mo. *old red morocco extra, gilt edges*, 6s *Ven.* 1576

1544 MARCIEN d'Héraclée Periple, epitome d'Artemidore, etc. *Gr. et Lat.* par Miller, 8vo. *map, sd.* 6s *Paris*, 1839

1545 MARTIALIS Epigrammata, 12mo. *old edition, mor. gilt edges*, 25s *Ven.* 1517
  Sir Mark Sykes' copy fetched £2. 8s.

1546 —— Epigrammata, cum Calderini commentariis, animadver. Heraldi, varietate lectionum, etc. 2 vols. sm 4to. *fine copy in old yellow morocco extra, gilt edges, from the Lamoignon Collection*, £2. 2s *Paris*, 1601
  Formerly priced £3. 3s.

1547 —— Epigrammata, Paraphrasi et notis variorum ad usum Delphini, interpretatus est Collesso, et Numismatibus exornavit Smids, 8vo. *plates of coins, fine copy in old red morocco, gilt edges*, 36s *Amst.* 1701
  "Edition recherchée."—*Brunet.* The coins are sometimes wanting.

1548 —— Epigrammata, 2 vols. 16mo. *old calf gilt*, 6s 6d *Paris, Barbou*, 1754
1549 —— Epigrammes, *Latines et Françoises*, 3 vols. 8vo. *calf*, 12s *Paphos*, (1807)
1550 —— Epigrammes, *Latines et Françoises*, traduction nouvelle par Simon, avec des notes, publiée par Simon et Auguis, 3 vols. 8vo. *hf. bd. neat*, 16s *Par.* 1819
  A very interesting feature in this edition is the insertion (besides the translation) of all the best imitations in French of the Epigrams, since Marot's time, several hundred in number.

1551 MATTHIAE's Greek Grammar, by Bloomfield, 2 vols. 8vo. *calf gilt*, 6s 1818
1552 MAXIMIANI ETRUSCI Elegiæ sex, curante Giles, 8vo. *only 100 copies printed, blue* MOROCCO *super extra, gilt edges*, 10s 1838
1553 MICALI, l'Italia avanti il dominio dei Romani, 4 vols. 8vo.—Antichi Monumenti d'Italia, folio, *map and 70 plates of Etruscan, Oscan, Umbrian, etc. Antiquities, Coins, Bronzes, etc. hf. bd. vellum neat*, 30s ; or, *calf extra*, 32s *Firenze*, 1810-21
  First edition of the text, with the augmented Atlas of the second edition. There were only 60 plates in the first.

1554 —— Storia degli Antichi Popoli Italiani, 3 vols. 8vo. *with impl. folio atlas, comprising* 120 *beautiful plates of Antiquities, Bronzes, Coins, Medals, &c. hf. calf gilt*, 35s *Firenze*, 1832-33
  The Archæological labours of Micali have thrown a considerable light upon the early history of Italy. Sir William Betham says, "Micali is the most philosophical, candid, and intelligent, as well as the most recent Italian writer on the origin of the ancient People of Italy ; he exposes the fabrications and falsifications of the Greeks and Romans, as well as the dreaming abilities of Passeri, Lanzi and Gori, with considerable effect."—*Etruria Celtica.*

1555 MEDICÆ ARTIS PRINCIPES, post Hippocratem et Galenum, Græci Latinitate donati, et Latini, 5 vols. in 2, folio, *curious cuts illustrative of surgical operations, etc. good copy in vellum*, 36s *Parisiis, Stephanus*, 1567
  Priced, 1831, bound by De Rome, £6. 6s ; 1848, Payne and Foss, red morocco, £5. 5s ; Evans' copy fetched £4. 9s ; Didot's, fine copy in morocco, 137 fr. "Collection estimée et difficile à trouver bien conditionnée."—*Brunet.*

1556 MINUCII Felicis Octavius, ex recensione Davisii, 12mo. *the Duke of Grafton's copy, in old yellow morocco gilt*, 21s *Glasg. Foulis*, 1750
1557 MITFORD'S History of Greece, 10 vols. 8vo. *hf. calf gilt*, 24s 1820
1558 MOMMSEN'S Römische Geschichte, zweite Auflage, 3 vols. sm. 8vo. *with military map, cloth*, 15s *Berlin*, 1854-56
1559 MONTFAUCONI Palæographia Græca, sive de Ortu et Progressu Literarum Græcarum, et de variis Scriptionis Græc. generibus, itemque de Abbreviationibus, folio, *plates of facsimiles of Inscriptions, Monuments, &c. bds.* 2 *leaves MSS. uncut*, 20s ; or *calf*, 32s *Paris*, 1708
1560 MORCELLI Opera Epigraphica : de Stylo Inscriptionum Latinarum, 3 vols.— Inscriptiones, commentariis subjectis—Parergon Inscriptionum novissimarum, *Pataviae*, 1818—Lexicon Epigraphicum Morcellianum, 4 vols. *Bononiæ*, 1835— together 9 vols. sm. folio, *fine copy in vellum*, £8. 8s 1818-35
1561 —— Opera Epigraphica, 5 vols. impl. 4to. *calf gilt*, £2. 10s *Patavii*, 1818-23
  There is no writer upon the subject of Inscriptions worthy of being compared with Morcellus: this new edition of his charming works is very much improved."—*Dr. Parr.*

1562 Moss, Manual of Classical Bibliography, 2 vols. 8vo. (pub. at 30s) *hf. vellum gilt*, 8s 1837

H 2

1563 MOVER'S Untersuchungen über die Religion und die Gottheiten der Phönizier : die Phönizier und das Phönizische Alterthum, Vols. I—III. part 1, 8vo. *three hf. calf, and a part*, 32s *Bonn u. Berlin*, 1841-56

1564 MÜLLER (K. O.) Denkmäler der alten Kunst, nach der Auswahl und Anordnung von Müller, gezeichnet und radirt von Oesterley, 2 vols. oblong 4to. 149 *fine plates, comprising several thousand objects of Ancient Art, hf. red morocco, gilt edges*, £2. *Göttingen*, 1832

1565 —— Geschichten Hellenischer Stämme und Städte : die Dorier; die Etrusker ; Orchomenos und die Minyer, 4 vols. 8vo. *maps, hf. calf*, 22s *Breslau*, 1824-28

1566 —— Griechische Literatur, bis Alexander, 2 vols. 8vo. *sd.* 4s *Breslau*, 1841

1567 —— History of the Doric Race, translated by Tufnell and (Sir) G. C. Lewis, 2 vols. 8vo. *maps, calf gilt*, 15s *Oxf.* 1830

1568 MURE'S Critical History of the Language and Literature of Antient GREECE, second edition, 5 vols. 8vo. (pub. at £3. 9s) *new in cloth*, £2. 12s 1854-5

1569 MUSICAE ANTIQUAE AUCTORES septem, *Graece et Latine*, ed. MEIBOMIUS, 2 vols. in 1, stout sm. 4to. £2. 10s *Amst.* 1652

1570 **Mythology.** BANIER (l'Abbé) la Mythologie et les Fables expliquées par l'Histoire, 3 vols. 4to. *fine copy in old red morocco, gilt edges, from Miss Currer's library*, £2. 12s *Paris*, 1738-40
Priced, 1848, Payne and Foss, £4. 4s.

1571 NIEBUHR'S Römische Geschichte, 3 vols. 8vo. *half calf*, 10s *Berlin*, 1827-32

1572 —— fourth edition, 3 vols. 8vo. *hf. calf*, 20s ; *or calf extra*, 22s *Berlin*, 1832-36

1573 —— historische und philologische Vorträge : Römische Geschichte bis zum Untergang des abendländischen Reichs, 3 vols.—Alte Geschichte nach Justin's Folge, 3 vols.—Vorträge über alte Länder und Völkerkunde, 1 vol. 1851— together 7 vols. 8vo. *hf. bd. red morocco, from Dr. Hawtrey's library*, £2. 16s *Berlin*, 1846-51

1574 —— VORTRÄGE über alte Geschichte, Vols. I. II. 8vo. *cloth*, 6s *Berlin*, 1847

1575 —— Vorträge über Römische Geschichte, 3 vols. 8vo. *sd.* 7s 6d *ib.* 1848

"Apart from any thought of Greek or Roman history, it is good mental exercise to read not seldom in such books as these, which give health to the wits by putting them in contact with robust and active intellect. To the jaded mind a few chapters of Niebuhr come with a bracing influence, like that of sea air on the jaded body. We are very glad, therefore, to bid hearty welcome to a first-rate English version of these lectures upon ancient history —worthy companions to the lectures upon ancient Rome."—*Examiner.*

1576 NONII MARCELLI Compendiosa Doctrina ad filium de Proprietate Sermonum, folio, *fine large copy with the scarce blank leaf a 1, russia extra, gilt edges, an admirable specimen of early printing*, 36s *Venet. Jenson*, 1476
Priced, 1832-48, Payne and Foss, mor. £2. 2s 6d; Sir M. Sykes, £6. 15s.

1577 OPPIANUS de Venatione, *Gr. ac Lat.* cum commentario à Bodino, 8vo. *fine copy, vellum, rare*, 10s *Paris*, 1549-55

1578 ORATORES GRÆCI, cum versione Lat. et not. var. cura Reiskii, 12 vols. 8vo. £2. 10s *Lips.* 1770-73
The most correct edition of the Greek Orators.

1579 REISKII Indices Graecitatis in Oratores Atticos, emend. MITCHELL, 2 vols. 8vo. *bds.* 9s ; *calf gilt*, 12s *Oxon.* 1828

1580 OROSII adversus Paganos historiae, cum animadversionibus ed. HAVERCAMPUS, 4to. *numerous cuts of Coins, vellum gilt*, 18s 6d *Lugd. Bat.* 1767

1582 ORPHICA, *Græce et Latine*, cum notis STEPHANI, etc. ed. Hermannus, stout 8vo. *russia, gilt edges, or hf. red morocco gilt, uncut*, 12s *Lips.* 1805
"Edition la plus ample de ce recueil."—BRUNET.

1583 OVIDII Opera, ed. Burmannus, 3 vols. 24mo. *vellum*, 8s *Amst.* 1714

1584 —— OPERA OMNIA, cum notis variorum et P. Burmanni, 4 vols. 4to. *fine frontispieces, best edition, fine copy, half calf, uncut; or Dutch vellum*, 32s *Amst.* 1727

1585 —— Opera, e textu Burmanni, cum notis Harlesii, Gierigii, Lemairi aliorumque, 5 vols. 8vo. *calf gilt*, 32s *Oxon.* 1825-26

1586 OVIDIO, Le Metamorfosi, ridotte da Anguillara in ottava rima, con le Annotationi di Horologgi e gli Argomenti di Turchi, sm. 4to. *engraved title and several plates by Giacomo Francho, fine copy in* OLD RED MOROCCO, *gilt edges*, 30s *Vinegia, Giunti*, 1584
Hibbert's copy, 1829, fetched 35s.

1587 PANVINII (ONUPHRII) de Ludis Circensibus libri II. et de Trumphis liber unus, folio, *engraved title and numerous very large plates of Games, Processions, Coins, etc. vellum*, 10s *Venet.* 1600

CLASSICS, GREEK AND LATIN PHILOLOGY, ETC.

1588 PAULY (A.) Encyclopædie der klassischen Alterthumswissenschaft, fortgesetzt von Walz und Teuffel, complete, 6 vols. in 7, 8vo. (pub. £10. 5s 6d) *neatly half bd. calf,* £6. 16s *Stuttgart,* 1839-52
First-class Philologists will do well to possess, besides Smith's Dictionaries, the above valuable Encyclopædia of Classic Learning.

1589 PAUSANIAE Græciæ descriptio, *Grec et Français,* par CLAVIER, 6 vols. in 3, 8vo. *calf extra,* 20s *Paris,* 1814-23

1590 ——— Græciæ descriptio, *Graece et Latine,* cum notis, ed. Siebelis, 5 vols. 8vo. *map, calf extra,* £2. 2s *Lipsiæ,* 1822-28

1591 PERSIUS. Geschichte des Textes des Persius von Hauthal, 2 vols. 1837—Satirae, cum scholiis antiquis, ed. Jahn—and several other editions of Persius—in 2 vols. stout 8vo. *half calf,* 7s 6d *Leipz.* 1837-43

1592 ——— Satiræ, atque Lucilii Fragmenta, ed. Achaintre, 8vo. FINE PAPER, *morocco extra, gilt edges,* 10s *Parisiis,* 1812

1593 PEUTINGERIANA TABULA ITINERARIA quæ in Augusta Bibliotheca Vindobonensi nunc servatur, adcurate exscripta, à F. C. de Scheyb, roy. folio, LARGE PAPER, *bds. only* 100 *copies were printed,* £2. 16s *Vindob.* 1753
Priced, 1831, £3. 3s. "Belle édition, savante et utile."—RENOUARD.

1594 ——— Tabula Itineraria Peutingeriana, primum aeri incisa 1753, denuo cum Codice Vindoboni collata, cum Mannerti introductione, studio Academiae literarum Monacensis, atlas 4to. *the* 12 *maps on coloured paper, hf. morocco,* £2. 12s *Lipsiæ,* 1824

1595 ——— Tabula Itineraria militaris Romana antiqua Theodosiana, primus in Italia edidit Podocatharus Christianopulos, folio, 2 *palaeographic plates and* 12 *maps, half bound, uncut,* £2. 5s *Aesii in Piceno,* 1809
This is an accurate facsimile of the famous Peutingerian or Theodosian Map, one of the most extraordinary remains of antiquity, and perhaps unique of its kind. The original, which is preserved in the public library of Vienna, and esteemed its greatest ornament, is about 24 feet long and 14 inches broad. It is a rude sort of map, on which not only the different cities, rivers, &c. are pointed out by their names, but the objects also are distinguished, and the roads and military routes traced out by lines: it is supposed to have been made at Constantinople, about A D. 393. See *Fabricii Bibl. Antiquaria, Horsley's Britannia Romana,* p. 507, &c.

1596 PHAEDRI Fabulae Aesopiae, cum notis variorum et Burmanni, stout 8vo. *russia extra, gilt edges,* 12s *Lugd. Bat.* 1745

1597 ——— Fabulae, curante Burmanno, cum notis, sm. 8vo. *fine copy in red morocco, gilt edges,* 9s *Amst.* 1698

1598 PHILONIS JUDAEI Opera Omnia, *Graece et Latine,* ad editionem Mangey, collatis MSS., ed. Pfeiffer, 5 vols. 8vo. *calf,* 20s *Erlangae,* 1785-1820

1599 ——— Opera omnia, textus editus ad fidem optimarum editionum, 8 vols. 12mo. *bds.* 12s *Lips.* 1828-30

1600 PHILOSTRATI (Flavii) quae supersunt, Ph. Junioris Heroica, etc. ed. Kayser, 4to. *sd.* 10s *Turici,* 1846

1601 PHILOSTRATI Heroica, ad fidem manuscriptorum, *Graece et Latine,* cura Boissonade, 8vo. *russia extra,* 7s *Paris.* 1806

1602 PHOTII MYRIOBIBLON sive Bibliotheca librorum, Graece et Latine, ab Hoeschelio et Schotto, folio, BEST EDITION, *calf,* 9s *Rothomagi,* 1653

1603 ——— the same, large folio, FINE PAPER, *vellum,* 32s *id.* 1653

1604 PINDARI Olympia, Pythia, Nemea, Isthmia; Callimachi Hymni; Dionysius de Situ Orbis; Lycophronis Alexandra, *omnia Graecè, a beautiful and clean copy, in rich old red morocco extra, gilt edges, by Derome,* £2. 16s *Aldus,* 1513
Priced, Thorpe, £4. 4s.; sold in De Cotte's sale for 100 francs; in M. d'O——'s for 160 francs; in Dr. Heath's, for £2. 10s; and in Sir M. Sykes' for £3. 10s. Mr. Gardiner's copy fetched, 1854, Sotheby's, £4.
EDITIO PRINCEPS of *Pindar, Dionysius,* and of *Lycophron,* but not of *Callimachus.* A full account of this book is given by Mr. Dibdin, in the Bibliotheca Spenceriana, Vol. II. pp. 238-9. "The preface of this edition is extremely interesting. After giving a sketch of the war that had ravaged Italy, and suspended his typographical labours, Aldus takes a view of what he had already done in the cause of literature, and meditates on his probable future efforts. From a part of this preface, we learn that Aldus had already exercised the art of printing twenty years, which proves that he began about the year 1493." It is a valuable document of Aldine history. Renouard is elaborate in his notice of it; he calls it a "rare édition, et fort belle."

1605 PINDARI OPERA, *Graece et Latine,* textum in genuina metra restituit, recensuit, annotationem criticam, scholia, commentarium et Indices adjecit Boeckhius, 3 vols. 4to. (pub. at £6. 12s) *half russia, uncut,* £2. 10s; or *calf extra,* £2. 16s *Lips.* 1811-21
"The most rich, full, and complete of all the editions of Pindar. No man ever set to work more thoroughly and in earnest than did Boeckhius in the task here under consideration. A rigid examination of all the more ancient and celebrated impressions has been instituted, and a number of MSS. of more or less importance, but generally of a superior class, have been consulted for the first time."—DIBDIN.

1606 PLACENTINII Epitome Graecae Palaeographiae, 4to. *hf. bd.* 6s *Rom.* 1735

1607 PLATONIS Opera, quæ supersunt, *Græce,* cum variis lectionibus recognovit
God. Stallbaum, 13 vols. 8vo. *bds.* 25*s* *Lipsiæ,* 1821-5
Fetched, 1854, Sotheby, £2. 10*s*.

1608 —— Opera omnia, editio auctior, in 12 vols. 8vo. *cloth,* £4. 4*s* *Gothæ,* 1832-60
This forms the best edition of the works of Plato. It consists of the text edited by Ast, with Stallbaum's notes.

1609 —— Opera quae feruntur omnia, *Græce,* recognoverunt Baiter, Orellius, et Winckelmann, cum varietate lectionum, 4to. (*sd.* 25*s*) *vellum,* 21*s* *Turici,* 1839

1610 PLAUTI Comoediae cum notis variorum et Gronovii, 3 vols. in 1, stout 8vo. *engraved title, calf gilt,* 7*s* 6*d* *Amst.* 1684

1611 —— Comoediae quae supersunt, recensuit Weise, 2 vols. 8vo. *hf. calf neat,* 8*s* *Lipsiæ,* 1837-38

1612 —— THEATRE DES LATINS : Plaute, *Latin et Français,* avec des dissertations, etc. par Levée et Le Monnier, 8 vols. 8vo. *calf neat,* 20*s* *Paris,* 1820

1613 HAMILTON on the Punic passages in Plautus, 4to. *sd.* 4*s* 6*d* *Dublin,* 1837

1614 PLINII SECUNDI (Caii) Naturalis Historiæ Libri XXXVII, ex recensione Johannis Andreæ Episcopi Aleriensis cum ejusdem ad Paulum II. epistola, stout royal folio, *a very large and fine copy, with about 40 large initials, finely drawn and painted in gold and colours (after the twenty-first by a different artist, who has drawn figures on the margins), in Old English morocco, with broad borders of gold, and having ornamented centres of sides in rich gilding,* £25.
Venetiis, N. Jenson, 1472

Dr. Askew's copy fetched £23.; Royer's, 572 francs.
A truly splendid volume, called "The Glory of Jenson's Press." Dr. Dibdin, in the Bibl. Spenc. says that the present is "more beautiful and magnificent even than either of the preceding editions."—"Bibliographers have not failed to describe, in glowing language, the beauty and value of this impression, which is probably, considering its bulk, the chef-d'œuvre of the celebrated artist who executed it."
If there be one book more than another which, of its kind and extent, may be said to be A MIRACLE OF ART in the early annals of printing, it may be pronounced to be the volume now under consideration. The elegance of the Roman type, the regularity of the press work, the strength and tint of the paper, the breadth of the margins, and the quantity of text which each page exhibits, afford altogether A PERFECT PICTURE OF ANCIENT TYPOGRAPHY.

1615 PLINII Naturalis Historia, cum notis variorum, ed. Franzius, 10 vols. sm. 8vo. *bds.* 20*s* *Lips.* 1778-91

1616 —— eadem, cum commentariis criticis et indicibus, ed. Sillig, 8 vols. 8vo. *new,* £4. 16*s* *Hamb. et Gothæ,* 1851-57

1617 PLINE, Histoire Naturelle, *Latine et Francaise,* traduction nouvelle par Ajasson de Grandsagne, annotée par Brongniart, Cuvier, etc. 20 vols. in 10, 8vo. *hf. calf gilt,* £3. 3*s* Cost new £7.; priced, 1850, £4. *Paris,* 1829-33

1618 PLOTINI Opera omnia, *Græce et Latine;* vita à Porphyrio; cum Ficini commentariis, annotationem addidit Wyttenbach, indices Moser, ed. Creuzer, 3 vols. 4to. (originally pub. at £6.) *cloth, new,* 25*s* *Oxon.* 1835

1619 PLUTARCHI quæ supersunt Opera omnia, *Græce et Latine,* principibus ex editionibus castigavit, variorum et suis annotationibus instruxit J. J. REISKE, 12 vols. 8vo. *portrait of Reiske, engravings of heads,* (pub. at £8. 8*s*) *calf,* 35*s*; or *russia gilt,* £2. 8*s* *Lipsiæ,* 1774-82

1620 PLUTARCHI quæ supersunt omnia cum adnotationibus variorum, opera HUTTEN, 14 vols. 8vo. *sized paper, hf. morocco neat,* 36*s*; or *a fine tall copy in half blue* MOROCCO *gilt, uncut,* £4. *Tubingae,* 1791-1804
Fetched, Drury, morocco, £6.; Dean of Peterborough's, £4. 12*s*.
This edition presents us with the most accurate text that has yet been published, and is accompanied with the valuable remarks of the editor, and a selection of the notes of preceding annotators.—FUHRMANN.

1621 PLUTARCHI Vitæ Illustrium Virorum e Græco in Latinum versæ, 2 vols. in 1, folio, *a very fine copy,* ORIGINAL BINDING, *neatly rebacked,* £2.
Venet. per Jo. Rig. de Monteferrato, 1491
The first leaf of each volume is printed within an elegant border, and has a spirited woodcut.

1622 PLUTARCHI MORALIA, *Gr. et Lat.* cura D. Wyttenbach, cum Indice Graecitatis, 8 vols. royal 4to. *calf extra,* £4. 15*s* *Oxonii,* 1795-1830
Published at £15. 13*s* 6*d*. Of Vol. VII. (Animadvers. Vol. II.) only one part was ever published, 1821. The binding of this set has cost £5.

1623 PLUTARCH'S Lives, translated from the original Greek, with notes critical and historical, and a life of Plutarch by J. and W. Langhorne, LARGE PAPER, 6 vols. roy. 8vo. *calf gilt,* 25*s*; or *a very beautiful copy, tree-marbled calf extra,* £2. 16*s* 1801

1624 POETARUM TRAGICORUM Græcorum (Æschyli, Sophoclis, Euripidis, Thespidis, etc.), fragmenta collegit Wagner, 3 vols. 8vo. *calf gilt,* 18*s* *Vratisl.* 1852-48

CLASSICS, GREEK AND LATIN PHILOLOGY, ETC. 103

1625 POETÆ CHRISTIANI VETERES, Græcè et Latinè (Prudentius, Prosper Aquitanicus, Johannes Damascenus, Cosmas, Sedulius, Juvencus, Arator, Proba Falconia, Lactantius, Gregorius Nazianzenus, NONNUS, etc.) 4 vols. sm. 4to. *fine copy in French blue morocco extra, gilt edges, by Motet*, £12.   *Venet.* 1501-4
Priced, Thorpe, £15. 15s; 1828, £25.; 1829, J. Bohn, £31. 10s; 1831, H. Bohn, £15. 15s; 1835, Thorpe, £15. 15s; 1836, £14. 14s; 1839, £18. 18s; 1840, J. Bohn, £18. 18s; 1843, Hearne, £21; Payne and Foss, £12. 12s; 1836, £15. 15s; Sir Mark Sykes' copy fetched £26. 15s 6d; Roscoe's, £18. 7s 6d; Hibbert's, £17. 5s; Bishop Butler's, £12. 12s.
Emphatically and justly termed by Renouard, COLLECTION INFINIMENT RARE ET PRÉCIEUSE. This copy is quite complete according to his collation, including not only the extremely rare volume of Nonni Panopolitanæ Paraphrasis Evangelii secundum Joannem, but the four leaves in the third volume which are generally wanting. That volume also contains the Greek text of the first six chapters of St. John's Gospel, so that this work contains the first printed portion of the New Testament.
Dr. Dibdin says these are amongst "the very rarest of the Aldine publications to be found in a perfect state." This is complete according to the description given by Renouard, Annales des Aldes, pages 24 and 26. This is the first work in which the Device of the Anchor is made use of, and is often priced from £12. to £20.

1626 POETAE MINORES GRAECI, praecipua Lectionis varietate et Indicibus locupletissimis instruxit Gaisford, 4 vols. in 3, 8vo. *hf. calf neat*, 30s   *Oxonii*, 1814-20
1627 POETÆ MINORES GRAECI, ed. Gaisford; editio aucta, 5 vols. 8vo. *calf gilt*, 21s
Lips. 1823
Contents: Theocritus, Bion, Moschus, Hesiodus, Theognis, Archilochus, Solon, Simonides, Mimnermus, Callinus, Tyrtaeus, Phocylides, Naumachius, Panyasis, Rhianus, Euenus, Indices et Scholia. "Collection fort estimée. Les deux premier volumes renferment les textes; le 3e contient les Scholia in Hesiodum, et le 4e les Scholia in Theocritum, 72 fr."—BRUNET. "A highly esteemed collection."—LOWNDES.

1628 POETÆ LATINI VETERES, ad optimarum editionum fidem expressi, 2 vols. in 1, very stout 8vo. (1550 *pages, double columns*), *very handsomely and correctly printed, sewed, scarce*, 12s 6d   *Florentiæ*, 1829
This edition contains 30 authors, and has the verses marked for convenience of reference. The works of Plautus, Terence, and Seneca, which are wanting in the editions of London and Frankfort, are included in this.

1629 POETÆ LATINI MINORES; sive GRATII Falisci Cyngeticon, NEMESIANI Cyngeticon, CALPURNII Eclogæ, etc., à P. BURMANNO, 2 vols. 4to. 16s *Leidae*, 1731
Porson's copy fetched £2. 3s.

1630 —— the same, LARGE PAPER, 2 vols. roy. 4to. *a beautiful copy in blue* MOROCCO, *gilt edges*, £4. 15s   1731
Hibbert's copy fetched £5. 7s 6d.

1631 POETAE LATINI MINORES, curavit WERNSDORF, 8 parts in 6 vols. 8vo. *calf*, £3. 3s
Altenburgi, 1780-90
Drury's copy fetched £4. 13s; 1855, Lord Rothesay's, £3. 13s 6d. Copies on FINE PAPER fetched: 1857, 10 vols. russia, £7. 10s, and sold (by me) for £8.   Contents:—Tom 1. Carmina de Venatione, Aucupio, et Piscatu.   2. Bucolica et Idyllia.   3. Satyrici, Elegiæ et Lyricæ.   4. Carmina Heroica,   5. Carmina Geographica.   6. Carmina de re hortensi et villatica; item amatoria et ludicra.

1632 POLYÆNI Strategemata, *Gr. et Lat.* ed. Maasvicius, 8vo. *bd.* 5s *Lugd. Bat.* 1690
1633 POLYBII Historia, *Græce et Latine*, recensuit, emendatiore interpretatione, varietate Lectionis, adnotationibus et indicibus illustravit Schweighæuser, 9 vols.—Supplementum continens Æneæ Tactici Commentarium de Toleranda Obsidione, *Graece et Latine*, ab Orellio, 1 vol. 1818—together 10 vols. 8vo. FINE PAPER, *fine copy in calf gilt*, £2. 10s   *Lips.* 1789-1818
An incomparable edition, and justly called the EDITIO OPTIMA of Polybius.

1634 POLYBII Historiæ, *Græce et Lat.* ed. Schweighäuser, cum Lexico, nova editio, 5 vols. 8vo. (*pub. at* £4.) *half calf neat*, 28s   *Oxon.* 1823-22
1635 POLYBIUS, *Græce*, ex recensione Im. Bekkeri, 2 vols. 8vo. *calf gilt*, 10s   1844
1636 PTOLEMÆI omnia quæ extant Opera, præter Geographiam, curâ Schrekhenfuchsio, cum commentationibus, sm. folio, *diagrams, calf*, 9s 6d   *Basil.* 1558
" Edition très estimée."—BRUNET.

1637 —— de GEOGRAPHIA libri VIII. *Græce*, sm. 4to. *first edition, hf. bd. scarce, a very tall copy*, 18s   *Basileæ, Froben.* 1533
1638 PRUDENTII Opera, recensita notisque illustrata à Weitzio, 2 vols. in 1, stout sm. 8vo. *fine copy, beautifully bound in olive morocco, with joints, gilt edges, by Clarke, from Rev. T. Williams's and Miss Currer's libraries*, £2. 2s *Hanov.* 1613
1639 PTOLEMAEI (Claudii) Cosmographia, *Latine*, sm. folio, 152 *leaves, a fine tall and clean copy, the first of the initial letters illuminated in gold and colours, the others rubricated, neat, in old vellum*, £2. 2s
Vicenciae, Hermanus Leuilapis Coloniensis, 1475
FIRST EDITION. On account of the superior quality of the type and paper, this is a desirable specimen of early printing. Priced, 1829, Longman, £5. 5s. Fetched, Nicol's sale, £4. 1s; Althorpe's, £3. 5s.

1640 PTHOLOMEI GEOGRAPHIA, editio secunda, folio, *with the scarce and very curious* FIRST SET OF 27 MAPS *ever published, first leaf of text in MS. bd.* £3.
Rome, arte ac impensis Petri de Turre, anno MCCCCLXXXX.

1641 PTOLEMAEUS, auctus, restitutus, emaculatus, roy. folio, *numerous large maps, hf. bd. 9s* *Argentorati*, 1520

1642 —— GEOGRAPHIA, Lat. cum Neotericor. perlustrationibus, edidit L. Phrisius, large folio, 49 *maps and many woodcuts, remarkably fine copy in stamped hogskin*, £2.   *Argent. Grieninger*, 1522
This is a remarkable edition, as containing the passage respecting Palestine (on the third map of Africa) which afforded one of the pretexts for the condemnation of Servetus, as it was unjustly alleged, at the period of his trial, to have been first printed by him in his edition of 1535.

1643 PTOLEMÆI Geographicæ enarrationis libri octo, ex Pirckeymheri tralatione, *Latine*, à Villanovano (Serveto) recogniti, large folio, *numerous woodcut borders, vignettes and* 50 *maps, tall copy in calf,* 20s   *Lugd.* 1535
"Edition assez rare et célèbre à cause du nom de son éditeur."—BRUNET.

1644 PTOLEMÆI Magna Constructio, id est Coelestium motuum pertractatio, cum Theonis commentario, Græce, folio, *first edition, with some MS. notes on the Chronology, otherwise a fine copy, in old calf, rare,* 14s   *Basil.* 1538
Heath's copy fetched £3. 3s. Theon's commentary is often wanting.

1645 PTOLEMÆI Theatrum Geographiæ Veteris, I: Geographia, *Gr. et Lat.* ad codices Palatinos, opera BERTII—II: Itineraria Antonini, Provinciæ Romanæ, Civitates Gallicæ, Itinerarium a Burdigala Hierosolymam; TABULA PEUTINGE-RIANA, cum notis Velseri; Ortelii Tabulæ aliquot—in 1 vol. large folio, *two engraved titles and numerous carefully engraved maps, very fine copy, old calf neat,* £3. 12s   *Amst. Elzevir,* 1618-19
It is difficult to obtain a fine large copy of this, THE BEST EDITION, of Ptolemy's Geography. Copies fetched, Dent's, mor. £8. 12s 6d; Hibbert's, russia, £6. 6s; Edwards's, hogskin, £8. 8s; Dr. Sumner's, russia, £6. 10s. Cropped copies sell low.

1646 PUTSCHIUS. GRAMMATICÆ LATINÆ Auctores Antiqui opera et studio Heliæ Putschii, quorum aliquot nunquam antehac editi, reliqui ex MSS. Codicibus ita augentur et emendantur ut nunc primum prodire videantur, 2 vols. in 1, sm. 4to. *vellum,* £2. 2s   *Hanov.* 1605

1647 —— the same, *a fine copy in calf,* or in *vellum,* £3. 3s   1605
Priced, morocco, 1840, Payne and Foss, £7.
See a long analysis of this very valuable work in the Bibliotheca Ernesti, vol. 3, p. 393.
This important collection contains more than thirty ancient Grammarians, viz. Charisius, Diomedes, Priscianus, Probus, Magno, P. Diaconus, Phocas, Asper, Donatus, Servius, Sergius Cledonius, Victorinus, Augustinus, Consentius, Alcuinus, Eutyches, Fronto, Vel. Longus, Caper, Scaurus, Agroetius, Cassiodorus, Beda, Terentianus, Victorinus, Plotius, Cæsius, Bassus, Fortunatianus, Rufinus, Censorinus, Macrobius, Incerti.

1648 QUINTILIEN de l'Institution de l'Orateur, avec sa vie et des notes, etc. stout sm. 4to. *calf, arms on the sides, rare,* 5s   *Paris,* 1663

1649 QUINTI CALABRI Derelicta ab Homero; TRYPHIODORI Excidium Trojæ; CO-LUTHI Raptus Helenæ, *omnia Graece,* 12mo. *editio Princeps, fine tall copy, in the original calf,* 14s   *Venet. Aid.* (circa 1505)
Priced, 1840, Payne and Foss, £1 16s; another copy in morocco, £3. 13s 6d; 1840, James Bohn, £1. 1s; 1842, Thorpe, £1. 1s. Fetched 1856, Sotheby's, £3. 13s; 1857, Sotheby, £1. 8s; 1858, Sotheby, £1. 16s.

1650 QUINTUS CURTIUS RUFUS de Rebus gestis Alexandri Magni, 18mo. *fine copy, with Autograph of* "ANT. AUG. RENOUARD, 1795," *red morocco, silk linings, vellum fly-leaves, gilt edges, by De Rome le Jeune,* 25s *Lugd. Gryphius,* 1547

1651 REICHARDI Orbis Terrarum Antiquus, cum Thesauro topographico etc. folio, *printed on bluish paper, bds. uncut, rare,* 20s   *Norimb.* 1824
Containing the ancient and modern names of places in parallel columns.

1652 RHETORES GRÆCI ex codicibus Florentinis, Mediol., Monac., etc. auctiores edidit, *Graece,* annotationibus indicibusque locupletavit Walz, 9 vols. in 10, 8vo. (*cost sewed* £7. 15s) *calf gilt, very neat,* £3. 10s   *Stuttg.* 1832-36

1653 RIDDLE'S copious Latin English Lexicon, founded on the German-Latin Dictionaries of W. Freund, stout 4to. *second edition, calf gilt,* 22s   1851

1654 ROSE, Inscriptiones Græcæ vetustissimæ, cum observationibus, etc. 8vo. *numerous plates of facsimiles, calf,* 10s   *Cantab.* 1825

1655 RUSTICÆ REI SCRIPTORES.—Libri de Re Rusticâ, Cato, Terentius Varro, J. M. Columella, Palladius, etc. 8vo. *fine copy in russia gilt,* 18s; *or a very large copy in the original binding, clasps,* 25s   *Venetiis,* 1514
Priced, 1835, Techener, 60 fr.; the Fonthill copy fetched £4. 13s.

1656 —— alia editio, 8vo. *red morocco,* 12s   *Venet. Aldus,* 1533

1657 —— veteres Latini: Cato, Varro, Columella, Palladius, etc. cum notis et Lexico, ed. Gesner, 2 vols. 4to. *hf. morocco neat, uncut,* 22s   *Lips.* 1773-74

1658 SAINTE-CROIX, Recherches sur les Mystères du Paganisme, seconde édition, par De Sacy—VILLOISON de Veterum Mysteriis, 3 vols. in 2, 8vo. *plates, hf. calf gilt,* 18s   *Paris,* 1817

1659 SALLUSTII Opera quae supersunt, cum notis et indice, ed. Kritzius, 3 vols. 8vo. *calf gilt,* 20s   *Lipsiæ,* 1828-53

CLASSICS, GREEK AND LATIN PHILOLOGY, ETC. 105

1660 SANCHUNIATHONIS, Historiae Phoeniciae, *Gr. et Lat.* à Wagenfeld, *Bremen* 1837—Analyse de Sanchuniathon, traduite par Lebas, *Paris*, 1836—2 vols. in 1, 8vo. *hf. calf, 7s 6d* 1836-37
1661 SCAPULAE Lexicon Graeco Latinum, cum indicibus auctis et correctis, et lexico etymologico, stout folio, *fine copy in russia*, 20s *Oxon*, 1820
1662 SCRIPTORES Latini Rei Metricæ, ed. Gaisford, 8vo. *calf extra, gilt edges*, 6s 1837
1663 SENECAE Opera, cum Lipsii, Gronovii aliorumque commentariis, 3 vols. stout sm. 8vo. *vellum*, 16s *Amst. Elzevir*, 1672
"By far the most beautiful and correct edition of Seneca."—HARWOOD.
1664 ———— Opera omnia, ed. Lipsius et Gronovius, 4 vols. 16mo. *calf gilt*, 16s *Lugd. Bat. Elzevir*, 1649
1665 SEXTI Philosophi Pyrrhoniarum Hypotypōseōn libri III. *Latine*, à Stephano, sm. 8vo. *morocco, gilt edges*, 10s 6d *H. Stephanus*, 1562
1666 SEXTUS POMPEIUS FESTUS de Verborum significatione cum Pauli epitome, à Muellero, oblong 4to. *calf neat*, 12s *Lips.* 1839
1667 SILII ITALICI Punica (ed. Heber, æt. 18) 2 vols. 8vo. *an elegant edition, in red morocco extra, gilt edges, from Miss Currer's library*, 12s *Bulmer*, 1792
1668 SILLIG's Dictionary of the Artists of Antiquity, by Williams, with Pliny Nat. Hist. 34-36, 8vo. *cloth*, 5s 1837
1669 SLUITER, Lectiones Andocideæ, cum Valckenaerii et Luzacii notis, 8vo. *calf extra*, 5s *Lugd. Bat.* 1804
1670 SMITH'S DICTIONARY of Greek and Roman BIOGRAPHY and MYTHOLOGY, 3 stout vols. 8vo. *illustrated by numerous engravings on wood* (pub. at £5. 15s 6d) *cloth*, £4. 4s 1861-58
1671 ———— Dictionary of Greek and Roman ANTIQUITIES, stout 8vo. of 1100 *pages, illustrated by nearly five hundred engravings on wood, second improved and enlarged edition* (pub. at £2. 2s), *cloth*, 33s 1859
1672 ———— Dictionary of Greek and Roman GEOGRAPHY, 2 stout vols. 8vo. (pub. at £4.) *cloth*, £3. 5s 1856-57
1673 ———— the above, together 6 vols. 8vo. (pub. at £11. 17s 6d) last edition, *new in cloth*, £8. 18s 6d 1856-61
1674 ———— the same, 6 vols. 8vo. *new in strong whole morocco, gilt edges*, £12. 5s 1856
1675 SOLINI Collectanea sive Polyhistor, à Reyhero, 12mo. *calf*, 5s *Gothae*, 1665
1676 SOPHOCLIS quæ extant omnia cum veterum grammaticorum scholiis, *Graece et Latine*, ed. BRUNCK, 2 vols. royal 4to. *fine copy in red* MOROCCO, *gilt edges*, £2. *Argent.* 1786
"Edition belle, correcte, et fort estimée. Vendue 95 fr. Larcher."—BRUNET.
1677 ———— Tragedies, *in Greek*, with critical notes, by Mitchell, 2 vols. 8vo. (pub. at 28s) *calf*, 14s *Oxford*, 1844
1678 ———— Tragoediae, *Graece*, cum notis recensuit Wunderus, 2 vols. 8vo. *calf extra*, 18s *Gothae*, 1848
1679 ———— Trachineæ, *Graece*, à Wundero, 8vo. *interleaved, half vellum*, 5s 1850
1680 ———— Ajax, commentario perpetuo illustravit Lobeck, *editio secunda*, 8vo. *sd.* 4s *Lips.* 1835
1681 COMMENTARII in septem Tragedias Sophoclis, opus rarissimum in Gymnasio Mediceo a Leone Decimo recognitum, *Graece*, 8vo. *first edition, large and fine copy in French calf, gilt leaves*, 25s *Romae*, 1518
Priced, 1830, Payne and Foss, morocco, £4. 4s; 1840 and 1848, £2. 12s 6d; 1840, Rodd, £2 12s 6d. Fetched, Sir M. Sykes. £2. 18s; Roscoe's, £2. 12s; LARGE PAPER, the Duke of Grafton's, £4. 10s.
1682 SPENCE'S (Joseph) POLYMETIS; or, an Enquiry concerning the Agreement between the Works of the Roman Poets and the Remains of the ANCIENT ARTISTS; being an Attempt to illustrate them mutually from one another, folio, FIRST AND BEST EDITION, *fine portrait by Vertue, and* 41 *plates, early impressions, including the Caricature portrait of Provost Cooke, represented as a Pedagogue with the head of an ass, afterwards suppressed, fine copy, russia, super extra, gilt edges*, £2. 12s 6d *Dodsley*, 1747
Priced, 1822, Thorpe, £5. 15s 6d; 1820, J. Bohn, £6. 6s; 1840, £4. 14s 6d.
1683 SPRUNER'S Atlas Antiquus, folio, 27 *large coloured maps*, (pub. at 24s) *cloth*, 20s *Gothae*, 1850
1684 STAHR's Torso; Kunst, Künstler, und Kunstwerke der Alten, 2 vols. 8vo. *half calf gilt*, 10s 6d *Braunschweig*, 1854-55
1685 STATII Opera, cum notis variorum, cura Veenhusen, 8vo. *a fine copy in red* MOROCCO, *gilt edges*, 18s *Lugd. Bat.* 1671

1686 STEPHANUS de Urbibus, Græce et Latine à Pinedo, cum Gronovii additionibus, folio, *old calf gilt, 7s 6d* *Amst.* 1678
1687 —— the same, folio, *presentation copy, vellum gilt, 8s* *ib.* 1678
1688 —— idem, restitutus, editus, et commentario illustratus à BERKELIO, folio, *vellum, 7s 6d* *Lugd. Bat.* 1694
1689 STEPHANI (H.) THESAURUS LINGUÆ GRÆCÆ, cum Indice, Glossariis, et Appendice Scotti, editio nova, auctior et emendatior, curâ VALPY, complete in 8 vols. folio, *fine copy, whole bd. calf gilt*, £6. 15s 1815-28
Published at £44. 10s; LARGE PAPER at £105.; 1854, Gardner's copy, *russia*, fetched £15. 10s. The gradual downfall in the price of this great publication shows the change of the studies in England from classical pursuits to other branches of literature.
1690 —— idem, auctus ordineque alphabetico digestus, tertio ediderunt Hase et Dindorf, parts 1—63, folio, *sd. new*, £25. *Paris*, 1831-62
Three more parts at 12s each will complete this important work.
1691 STOBÆI Florilegium, Græce et Latine, edidit Gaisford, 4 vols. 8vo. *calf gilt, 32s* *Oxon.* 1822
1692 STRABONIS Rerum Geographicum libri XVII, *Græce et Latine*, editio Casauboni, Morellii, etc. curante Almeloveen, 2 vols. folio, *best edition, fine copy in old calf gilt, 20s* *Amst.* 1707
Priced, 1834, J. Bohn, £3. 3s; the Fonthill copy fetched £5.; Gough's, £4. 6s.
1693 STRABONIS RERUM GEOGRAPHICARUM Libri XVII, *Græce et Latine*, ad optimos codices manuscriptos recensuit, varietate lectionis, adnotationibusque illustravit, Xylandri versionem emendavit Siebenkees, 7 vols. 8vo. *calf neat*, £2. 2s; or *calf gilt*, £3. 10s *Lipsiæ*, 1796-1818
A Thick Paper copy was priced by Payne and Foss, 1848, £14. 14s.
The first six volumes contain the Text, various readings, and Latin Translation. The seventh volume contains Casaubon's Commentary on the first three books (cum notis variorum) edited by Friedemann. This has never been continued.
1694 —— Rerum Geographicarum libri XVII, *Gr. et Lat.* ed. Falconer, cum notis variorum, *maps*, 2 vols. large folio, *calf gilt, 32s* *Oxon.* 1807
" This is considered the most valuable and most ample edition of Strabo."—*Dibdin.*
1695 STRABONIS Geographica, recensuit, commentario critico instruxit Kramer, 3 vols. 8vo. (*cost sd.* 38s) *calf gilt*, 36s *Berol.* 1844-52
1696 STRABON, GÉOGRAPHIE, traduite du Grec en Français par M. M. de la Porte du Theil, Coray et Letronne, avec des Notes et une Introduction par Gosselin, 5 vols. atlas 4to. LARGE VELLUM PAPER, *half red morocco, uncut, by Koehler, very rare*, £12. 10s *Paris*, 1805-19
Payne and Foss priced a copy, 1841, £25.; 1836, Bossange, £25. " Ce livre a été tiré à une cinquantaine d'exemplaires en Grand Papier Velin, qui n'ont pas été livré au commerce."—*Brunet.*
This is perhaps one of the finest books ever published on large paper. The copies on this paper were taken off by order of Napoleon, who presented them to the most celebrated literary characters of his time. It is believed that there are only two other copies in this country, which are in private collections.
1697 SUETONII Opera cum Commentario Beroaldi, folio, *fine copy, blue morocco, silk linings, gilt edges*, 32s *Bononiae*, 1493
1698 SUIDÆ Lexicon Græcum, folio, FIRST EDITION, *fine copy*, having the "Διαλογος Στεφανου του Μελανος (*a Dialogue omitted in all the subsequent editions) the first page of the work within* BEAUTIFULLY ILLUMINATED BORDERS, *and the Initial letters painted in colours, old red morocco, rare*, £3. 16s
Mediolani, Chalcondylus, Bissolus, Mangius, 1499
This copy is enriched with many most valuable Manuscript additions and corrections in Greek.
1699 TACITI Opera, recensuit Lallemand, 3 vols. 18mo. *frontispieces and vignettes by Eisen, calf, gilt edges*, 6s *Paris, Barbou*, 1760
1700 —— Opera omnia, recognovit Brotier, cum notis, supplementis, etc. 5 vols. roy. 8vo. *Large Paper, fine copy, calf extra*, 16s *Valpy*, 1812
"Brotier's supplement is executed with great elegance, and equal ability."—*Murphy.*
1701 —— Opera, ex recensione Ernesti, curavit Oberlinus, 4 vols. 8vo. *calf gilt*, 18s 1825
1702 —— Opera Omnia ad fidem Codd. Mediceorum ab Baitero excussorum recensuit Orellius, 2 vols. roy. 8vo. *sewed*, 10s 6d *Turici*, 1848
1703 TAYLOR's Pythagorean Fragments, *in English*, 8vo. *cloth*, 4s *Chiswick*, 1822
1704 TERENTII Comœdiæ, 4to. *calf extra, gilt edges*, 14s *Privately printed*, 1854
1705 —— Comœdiæ VI, ex recens. Lindenbrogii, cum notis variorum et Zeunii, 2 vols. 8vo. *vellum extra*, 10s 6d *Lond.* 1820
1706 THEOGNIS restitutus; in English verse, with comments, (by Frere) sm. 4to. *privately printed, cloth, presentation copy to Dr. Hawtrey*, 21s *Malta*, 1842
1707 THEOPHRASTUS de Historia Plantarum, *Græcè et Latinè*, ed. Bodaeus à Stapel, cum notis Scaligeri et Constantini, stout folio, *several hundred woodcuts, fine copy, vellum*, 14s *Amst.* 1644

CLASSICS, GREEK AND LATIN PHILOLOGY, ETC. 107

1708 THEOPHRASTUS de Historia Plantarum, *Græce*, curante Stackhouse, 2 vols. sm. 8vo. *portrait and plates, calf gilt, 9s* Oxonii, 1813

1709 THESAURUS Cornucopiæ et Horti Adonidis, *Graece* (curantibus Guarino, Antenoreo, Bolzanio, Politiano et Aldo Manutio), EDITIO PRINCEPS, folio, *fine copy in red morocco, gilt edges, the Roxburghe arms on sides, very rare,* £2. 10s
Venetiis, Ald. 1496
Priced, 1824, Thorpe, £5. 15s 6d; 1826, Payne and Foss £9. 9s and £7. 7s; 1830, £6. 6s; 1831, £2. 12s 6d; 1833, Thorpe, £3. 3s; 1834, £4. 4s; 1858, Lilly, £6. 6s; fetched at Roxburghe sale, £7. 10s; Duke of Devonshire's, £5. 10s; Sir Mark Sykes', £3. 10s; Roscoe's, £4. 15s; Renouard's, £2. 6s; Drury's, £2. 10s
"This publication is a collection of grammatical tracts, selected with incredible labour from the remains of *thirty-four ancient grammarians*. The work is justly considered as one of the finest productions of the Aldine press."—*Roscoe.*

1710 THUCYDIDES de Bello Peloponnesiaco, *Graece et Latine*, ad editionem Wasse et Dukeri expressus cum variis lectionibus, 6 vols. 8vo. *fine set in old russia, gilt edges,* 18s Biponti, 1788

1711 —— Historia, *Graece*, cum notis variorum et Indicibus, edidit Poppo, in 11 vols. 8vo. FINE PAPER, *calf gilt,* £2. 10s Lips. 1821-40

1712 —— De Bello Peloponnesiaco, *Græce*, cum notis, etc. ed. Goeller, 2 vols. in 1, 8vo. *portr. and map, hf. calf,* 5s 1835

1713 UKERT, Geographie der Griechen und Römer, bis auf Ptolemäus, Vols. I—III. pt. 1. in 4 vols. 8vo. *several maps, hf. calf neat,* 20s Weimar, 1816-43
Vol. III. part 2 completes the work.

1714 VACHEROT, Histoire de l'Ecole d'Alexandrie, 2 vols. 8vo. *sd.* 5s Paris, 1846

1715 VALERII FLACCI Argonautica, Jo. Bapt. Pii Carmen ex quarto Argonauticon Apollonii, Orphei Argonautica, 12mo. *fine copy in blue morocco extra, gilt gauffré edges, the anchor stamped in gold on sides,* 36s Venetiis, 1523
Priced, 1840, J. Bohn, £6. 6s; fetched £1. 19s; Libri sale, 1859, £9.
"In this edition Asulanus has shown himself a scholar of no common erudition."

1716 VALERII MAXIMI Dictorum factorumque memorabilium libri novem, 16mo. *a curious specimen of old stamped binding,* 7s Mogunt. 1544

1717 VALERIUS MAXIMUS, 18mo. *hf. bd. uncut,* 5s Amst. Elzevir, 1671

1718 BURGO (Dionysii de) Declaratio VALERII MAXIMI, smallest folio, the MAC-CARTHY CHOICE COPY, *in green morocco, with borders of gold on the sides, gilt edges, almost uncut, very rare,* £6. *sine ullâ notâ, circa* 1470
Sir Mark Sykes's copy fetched £5.; priced, 1826, Baynes, £8. 8s.
This work consists of 369 leaves, with 36 lines in a full page. It is in that small Roman type, known by the peculiarly formed letter R, by some attributed to Mentelin.
Dibdin writes that "neither Fabricius nor Ernesti were aware of the Commentary of D. de Burgo being IN PRINT, and Ossinger was equally ignorant of its existence. Maittaire is the only Bibliographer, before Braun, who notices it." However, the defect of preceding Bibliographers is amply supplied by the accurate description given by Dibdin in the Bibliotheca Spenceriana.

1719 VEGETIUS. VEGETII aliorumque de Re Militari libri; Frontini Opera, a Scriverio, 1606-7—CATANEUS de Arte bellica, 1600—in 1 vol. stout sm. 4to. *numerous cuts, vellum,* 10s Lugd. 1600-7

1720 —— Veteres de Re Militari Scriptores; Vegetius, Frontinus, Aelianus, Modestus Polybius, Aeneas, etc. cum notis Scriverii aliorumque, stout 8vo. *plates, old russia, or vellum,* 5s Vesaliæ, 1670

1721 VENATICÆ REI SCRIPTORES. Poetæ Latini Rei Venaticæ Scriptores et Bucolici Antiqui, cum notis variorum, curâ Kempheri, 4to. *frontispiece and vignettes, calf,* 6s Lugd. Bat. 1728

1722 —— the same, LARGE PAPER, impl. 4to. *fine impressions of the plates, red* MOROCCO *extra, uncut,* A SPLENDID COPY, £4. 10s 1728
Priced, 1837-40, Payne and Foss, old binding, £5. 5s. Fetched, Drury's, mor. £4. Contents: Gratius Faliscus, M. A. O. Nemesianus, T. Calpurnius Siculus, Cajus de Canibus Britannicis.

1723 VIRGILII Opera, cum Servii Commentariis et Indice, castigationibus varietatibusque lectionis, per Pierium, folio, *fine copy, old green* MOROCCO, *broad border of gold, gilt edges,* 27s Paris, R. Stephan. 1532
Sir John St. Aubyn's copy fetched £2. 18s. "Cette édition est belle et mérite d'être recherchée."—*Brunet.*

1724 —— OPERA cum commentariis Servii, Philargyrii, Pierii; accedunt Heinsii aliorumque notæ nunc primum editæ, cum animadversionibus BURMANNORUM, 4 vols. roy. 4to. LARGE PAPER, *fine copy in old calf gilt, elegant gold borders on sides,* £3. 10s Amstel. 1746
Large Paper copies are scarce; one was priced, 1825, Thorpe, £12. 12s; 1832, Payne and Foss, vellum, £6. 6s. The above was Lord Haberton's copy, who paid £12. 12s for it.
"Of this celebrated edition," says Dr. Dibdin, "so well known to the classical world, it would be useless to present the reader with a formal account of the voluminous contents. Ernesti has highly extolled it, calling it '*omnium principem et canonem Virgilii*.' Some copies are struck off ON LARGE PAPER, which bring a considerable price."—*Introd. to the Classics.*

1725 VIRGILIUS, VARIETATE LECTIONIS ET PERPETUA Adnotatione illustratus à HEYNE, cum Indicibus, editio aucta, 6 vols. 8vo. FINE PAPER, *ornamented with*

204 *beautiful* VIGNETTES *designed by* FIORILLO, *engraved by Geyser, and with a bust of Heyne, calf gilt,* Lord Calthorpe's copy, £3. *Lips.* 1800

Priced 1832, Payne and Foss, £10. 10s; in 1848, £6. 6s and £8. 8s; 1850, Jas. Bohn, £6. 6s.
ON VELLUM PAPER, priced, 1848, Payne and Foss, mor. £12. 12s; fetched, 1854, Sotheby's, morocco, £6. 10s.
"The most beautiful publication of a Latin Classic that the German press has ever produced." "The Leipzig edition of 1800 is the last and most complete edition of Heyne. The first four volumes contain the regular works of Virgil; the fifth the 'Carmina Minora,' Life of Virgil, and account of MSS. and editions; the sixth volume has two copious indexes, viz. Verborum, et nominum, an index to the notes and commentaries, explanations of the plates and vignettes, and seven pages of 'supplenda emendanda.' It contains also many new excursus and emendations."—*Dibdin.*

1726 VIRGILIUS, illustratus a Heyne, curavit WAGNER, 5 vols. in 4, 8vo. *calf gilt*, 30s
Lips. 1830

1727 VIRGIL's Works, in English prose, with the *Latin* text, order, and notes, by Davidson, 2 vols. 8vo. *calf gilt*, 5s *Dublin*, 1811

1728 VIRGILE, Œuvres, en *Francais,* en *Espagnol,* en *Italien,* en *Anglais,* et en *Allemand,* EDITION POLYGLOTTE, roy. 8vo. *hf. bd. uncut*, 18s; or *calf extra, gilt edges*, 21s *Paris*, 1838

1729 VOCABULARIUS Fructuosus omni ætati perutilis ex Papia, Britone, Catholicon, Alano, Ysidoro, aliisque quamplurimis Magistris collectus, qui alio nomine Brevilogus nuncupatur, folio, *remarkably fine copy, russia extra, very rare,* £4. 10s (*Coloniae, per Conradum de Hoemborch,* 1470)

A noble specimen of typography in the infancy of the art; printed without signatures, pagination, catchwords, or colophon. The capitals filled in by hand with red ink. Not mentioned by Brunet nor Hain.

1730 VOSSII (G. J.) Etymologicon Linguæ LATINÆ, accedunt Mazochii Etymologiæ et Tyrrhenicæ voces, 2 vols. folio, BEST EDITION, *vellum*, 10s *Neap.* 1762-8

1731 WACHSMUTH, Hellenische Alterthums-Kunde, 4 vols. 8vo. *cf.* 10s *Halle*, 1826-30

1732 WALCKENAER, Geographie ancienne des Gaules, avec analyse des Itinéraires anciens, 2 vols. 8vo. with folio Atlas of 9 Maps, *hf. calf*, 18s *Paris*, 1839

1733 WELCKER, die Griechischen Tragödien mit Rücksicht auf den epischen Cyclus, 3 vols. 8vo. *cloth, uncut*, 18s *Bonn*, 1839-41

1734 WOLFII Anecdota Græca ex Codicibus MS. Græce et Latine, 4 vols. 12mo. *calf gilt*, 12s *Hamb.* 1722-24

1735 WYTTENBACHII Opuscula varii argumenti, Oratoria, Historica, Critica, 2 vols. in 4, 8vo. LARGE PAPER, *calf extra*, 24s *Lugd. Bat.* 1821

Priced, 1848, Payne and Foss, £3. 3s.

1736 XENOPHONTIS OPERA, *Graece et Latine,* castigatius tertiò editæ, operâ Leunclavii Amelburni; cum Porti et F. Porti notis, &c. large folio, LARGE PAPER, *very fine copy in blue* MOROCCO, *gilt leaves, by Simier*, £4.
Lutetiae Parisiorum, Typis Regiis, 1625

"Belle edition, dont les exemplaires sont rares et recherchés en Gr. Pap."—*Brunet.*
Priced, 1824, Thorpe, £6. 6s; 1829, mor. £7. 7s; 1837-40, Payne and Foss, £5. 5s and £8.8s, 1848, £5. 5s. Copies fetched De Cotte, 350 fr.; Dent, £6. 18s; Hibbert, £6. 6s; Didot, 260, fr.; the Fonthill, £9. 9s; 1856, at Sotheby's, mor. £5.

1736*XENOPHONTIS Scripta, *Graece,* commentariis illustrata à Weiske, 6 vols. sm. 8vo. *hf. bd.* 10s *Lips.* 1798-1804

1737 XENOPHONTIS Opera quæ extant, ex libr. script. fide et virorum doct. coniect. recensuit et interp. est J. O. Schneider, 6 vols. 8vo. £2. *Lipsiae*, 1838

1738 GEMISTUS PLETHO de iis quæ post pugnam ad Mantineam gesta sunt— Herodiani a Marci principatu historiarum libri octo—Narratiunculæ in Thucydidem—*omnia Graecè,* 3 parts in 1, folio, *old French citron morocco extra, gilt edges*, £2. 2s *Venetiis*, 1503

Priced, 1827, Thorpe, £6. 6s; 1830, Payne and Foss, £2. 2s; fetched at Sir M. Sykes' sale, £2. 4s.
This work is the necessary supplement of Thucydides and Xenophon.

1738*PAPE, Handwörterbuch der Griechischen Sprache, 3 vols. large 8vo. *hf. bd.* 10s *Braunschweig*, 1842

LATIN MISCELLANIES.

Including Mediaeval Latin Writers, Mystical Literature, Astrology, Satires, etc.

1739 ACCIPITRARIÆ REI SCRIPTORES, nunc primum editi, accessit Kunosophion: Demetrii Hierakosophion, Orneosophion, *Gr. et Lat.*; Michaelis Orneosophion *Gr.*; Kunosophion, *Gr. et Lat.*; Aquilæ Symmachi Epistola, Catalanice, etc.; Thuanus de re Accipitraria, et Fracastorii Alcon, *Latin*; in 1 vol. sm. 4to. *fine copy in calf gilt, with a crown on the back, from Miss Currer's library*, 15s *Paris. Morel.* 1612

Recueil recherché et dont les exemplaires sont rares.—BRUNET.

1740 ADAMSON, Ta tōn Mousōn Eisodia: the Muses' welcome to the high and mightie Prince James, at his happie returne to his old and native Kingdome of Scotland, after 13 years' absence, in 1617—Ta tōn Mousōn Exodia : Planctus Musarum in Jacobi recessu; 2 vols. in 1, folio, *portrait of the King, in the original stamped and gilt calf, rare*, £3. 16s *Edinburgh*, 1618
Priced, 1827, Thorpe, £8. 8s; 1840, J. Bohn, £4. 4s; Constable's copy fetched £7. ; Bindley's £6. 2s 6d; Perry's £5. 15s 6d ; Archbishop Tenison's for about £17.
A most interesting volume, describing his Majesty's progress throughout, in verse and prose, with the speeches spoken at the several towns and gentlemen's seats, whom his majesty honoured with his presence, with names of the persons who delivered them at each place, and comprising some of the best specimens in Latin and English, of the principal Scotish poets of the day ; including, Alexander Hume, John Gell, WILLIAM DRUMMOND of Hawthornden, Thomas Hope, Henry Charteris, etc.

1741 ASCHAMI (Rog.) Epistolae, small 8vo. *best edition, frontispiece containing 12 portraits, etc. calf, 7s* *Oxoniae*, 1703
Williams's copy fetched, £1. 7s; LARGE PAPER, Dent's copy, £2. 2s.

1742 BALTHASARIS DE VIAS Sylvae Regiae, sm. 4to. *engraved title, fine copy in old calf gilt*, 10s *Paris*, 1623

1743 BILFINGERI de Origine et permissione Mali commentatio philosophica, 12mo. *old red morocco extra*, 12s *Tubingae*, 1743

1744 BOISSARDI Poemata, 16mo. *vellum*, 10s *Metis*, 1689-87

1745 BOTFIELD (*Beriah*) Præfationes et Epistolæ Editionibus principibus Auctorum veterum præpositæ—*Also with the title :* " Prefaces to the first editions of the Greek and Roman Classics and the Sacred Scriptures, London, Bohn, 1861," 4to. *half morocco, uncut*, £4. 4s *Cantabrigiæ*, 1861
A most important contribution to the Literature of Bibliography. Mr. Botfield's INTRODUCTION, pp. i—lxxvi. written in English, conveys to the reader the clearest notion of the History and Uncertainty of the Early *Manuscript* Literature and its transition to the relatively speaking much more critical and certain *Printed* Literature.
The PREFACES extend from page 1—666 ; the INDEX editorum, from p. 667—674. Some of the Prefaces are in Greek, all have been reprinted with scrupulous accuracy.

1746 (BOUCHER). De Justa Abdicatione Henrici III. e Francorum Regno, sm. 8vo. *fine copy in old French morocco, gilt edges, rare*, 30s *Lugd.* 1589
This interesting volume contains some curious particulars relative to England and Scotland, and a severe attack upon monarchical right divine. It was ordered to be burnt. See De Bure and Peignot.

1747 BRUNUS (Jord.) de Umbris Idearum—Ars Memoriæ, *woodcuts*, Cantus Circæus ad memoriæ praxim Judiciariam ordinatus ; in 1 vol. 12mo. *fine copy in old red morocco, gilt leaves*, £2. *Paris*, 1582

1748 CASAUBONI (Isaaci) EPHEMERIDES, cum praefatione et notis, edente Russell, 2 vols. 8vo. *morocco extra, blind tooled, gilt edges*, 30s *Oxon.* 1850

1749 CHYMICA VANNUS, reconditorium Sapientiæ numinis mundi magni, sq. 8vo. *old calf, very curious*, 9s *Amst.* 1666

1750 CRINITI de honesta disciplina, etc. Poemata, 16mo. *red morocco*, 6s *Lugduni*, 1561

1751 CURTII Virorum illustr. ex ordine Eremit. Augustini elogia, sm. 4to. *numerous portraits, fine impressions, vellum*, 32s *Antv.* 1636

1752 DAMIANI A GOES Opuscula, de Aethiopibus, Lapponibus, Bello Cambaico, etc. sq. 8vo. *hf. bound*, 7s *Lovan.* 1544

1753 DELEPIERRE (O.) Macaroneana, ou Mélanges de Literature Macaronique des différents Peuples de l'Europe, 8vo. VELLUM PAPER, *red morocco extra, gilt edges*, £2. *Paris*, 1852

1754 DISSERTATIONUM LUDICRARUM et Amœnitatum Scriptores, 16mo. *very fine copy in old red morocco extra, gilt edges*, 25s *Lugd. Bat.* 1638

1755 EPIGRAMMATUM Delectus, cum Proverbiis Latinis, Græcis, Hispanis, Italis, 16mo. *fine copy, old smooth morocco extra, by Deseuil*, 30s *Paris*, 1659

1756 EPISTOLÆ OBSCUORUM VIRORUM, sq. 16mo. *cloth*, 5s *Lips.* 1858

1757 ERASMI ROTERODAMI OPERA omnia emendatiora et auctiora ex recensione Joannis Clerici, cum Indice generali, 11 vols. folio, BEST EDITION, *very neat, in Dutch vellum gilt, from Miss Currer's library*, £10. 10s *Lugd. Bat.* 1703-6
Priced, 1840, Payne and Foss, £15. 15s.

1758 —— Adagiorum chiliades quatuor cum sesquicenturiâ cura H. Stephani, folio, *the text very neatly ruled with red lines, calf*, 10s *R. Stephanus*, 1558
Later editions were mutilated.

1759 —— Colloquia, cum notis variorum et Indice, curante Schrevelio, sm. 8vo. *vellum*, 5s *Amst.* 1693

1760 —— Morias Encomion—MORI Utopia, 2 vols. in 1, 12mo. *frontispiece, a pretty book, French calf, gilt edges*, 7s 6d *Lond., Paris. Barbou*, 1777

1761 FRACASTORII Opera omnia ; Homocentrica, Dies Critici, Sympathia Syphilidis, etc. 4to. *calf*, 8s *Venet. Junt.* 1555

1762 FRISCHLINI Opera Poetica, Comoediae et Tragoediæ, 12mo. *red morocco extra, gilt edges*, 10s *Argentorati*, 1583-85

1763 GALTHERI (Philippi) ALEXANDREIS nunc primum in Gallia Gallicisque characteribus edita, sm. 4to. 84 *leaves in Script-type*, (*Lettres de Civilité*) VERY RARE, *fine copy, blue morocco, gilt edges*, £2. 10s   *Lugduni, Granjon,* 1558

1764 GRIBALDUS de Jure Fisci, 16mo. *fine copy in olive morocco, gilt edges, by Clarke, rare*, 12s   *Venetiis,* 1551

    The printer's name subscribed at the end is Dominicus Llilius, but Renouard says, "Je pense que cet opuscule a été imprimé chez les fils d'Alde pour Dom. Lilius."

1765 GWYDONIS DE COLUMPNA, Hystoria Troyana, sm. 4to. FIRST EDITION *with a date, initials and capitals coloured, fine large copy, vellum, very scarce*, £2.   *Coloniæ, Arnold Therhurne,* 1477

    This celebrated romance was written in 1287, in England, the author having accompanied Edward I, on his return from the Crusades.

1766 HARDT, Opuscula varia, in all 35 curious Greek and Latin works by this learned writer, including the Arabia Graeca, 2 vols. 12mo. *bds.* 5s   *Helmst.* 1712-18

1767 ——— Aenigmata prisci orbis, Jonas in Luce, folio, 792 pp. *vellum*, 10s   *ib.* 1723

    "This very curious book, notwithstanding Waterland's censure, contains an infinite quantity of interesting research."—MS. NOTE BY SINGER.

1768 HERMETIS TRISMEGISTI Tractatus aureus, de Lapidis Philosophici secreto, 16mo. *cuts, vellum*, 7s   *Lipsiae,* 1610

1769 HROTSVITHA, (*religieuse Allemande du* X^e *siècle*) Théatre, *Latin et Français*, avec une introduction et des notes, par Magnin, 8vo. *hf. calf*, 14s *Paris,* 1845

1770 HUTTEN (Ulrichi ab) Opera omnia (Latina et Germanica) ed. Münch, 5 vols. sm. 8vo. *hf. bd.* 21s   *Berolini,* 1821-25

1771 ——— de Vita sua Epistola, cum Burckhardi commentario, etc. 2 vols. 12mo. *portraits, calf gilt*, 7s 6d   *Wolfenbutteli,* 1717

1772 INDAGINE (J. ab) Introductiones apotelesmaticae in Physiognomiam, Astrologiam naturalem, etc. 12mo. *cuts, old calf*, 7s   *Aug. Triboc.* 1663

1773 ISSELT de Bello Coloniensi, 12mo. *curious cuts of Sieges and Battles, half morocco extra*, 12s   *Colon. Agripp.* 1584

1774 JANI PANNONII (Sec. XVI) Poemata ac Opuscula, 2 vols. 8vo. LARGE PAPER, *hf. calf, uncut*, 25s   *Traj. ad Rhen.* 1784

1775 JOANNIS SECUNDI Opera omnia, cum notis adhuc ineditis Burmanni cura P. Bosscha, 2 vols. 8vo. *portrait*, THICK PAPER, *fine copy, red Turkey* MOROCCO *extra, gilt edges, by Smith*, £2. 18s   *Lugd. Bat.* 1821

1776 LACINII Pretiosa Margarita novella, cum collectaneis ex Alberto Magno, etc. 12mo. *cuts, old calf, rare*, 7s   *Venet.* 1546

1777 LONGOLII Epistolæ, item Riccius de Imitatione, 18mo. *fine copy, choice old French red morocco, gilt edges*, 9s   *Lugd.* 1563

1778 LULLII (Raymundi) Opera quae ad suam Artem memoriae pertinent, cum J. Bruni, Corn. Agrippæ aliorumque comment. indice, et Alstedii Clavi Artis Lullianæ, 2 vols. in 1, very stout 12mo. *curious diagrams, vellum*, 14s *Argent.* 1609

1779 MARY QUEEN OF SCOTS. JEBB (SAM.) DE VITA et rebus gestis MARIÆ, Scotorum Reginæ, Autores XVI, 2 vols. folio, *portrait by Vertue, calf, rare*, 21s   *Lond.* 1725

    Priced, 1840, Payne and Foss, 36s; the Fonthill copy fetched, £2. 5s; comprising Chambre, Leslie, Blackwood, Barnstaple, Buchanan, Cone, Castelnan, etc.

1780 SUMMARIUM de morte Mariæ Stuartæ, cum responsionibus Reginæ Angliæ et Sententia mortis, operâ Rom. Scoti—Maria Stuarta Martyr Ecclesiae, innocens à caede Darleana, Vindice Barnestapolio; in 1 vol. 16mo. *olive morocco extra, gilt edges*, £2.   *Coloniae,* 1627

1781 MERLINI COCAII [THEOPHILI FOLENGI] Poetæ Macaronicorum Opus, per Lodolam redactus: Zanitonella, Phantasiæ, Moschææ facetus liber, Epistolae et Epigrammata, 16mo. *numerous woodcuts, old red morocco extra, gilt edges*, £2. 10s   *Tusculani, Lac. Benac.* 1521

    A very rare edition, printed with a singular type, between the Roman and Italic.

1782 ——— alia editio, 16mo. *russia, very neat*, 9s   *Venet.* 1585

1783 ——— Folengi (Theoph.) Opus Macaronicum, cum notis illustratum, et VOCABULARIO Vernaculo, Etrusco et Latino, 2 vols. 4to. *portrait and vignettes, hf. bd.* 18s   *Amst.* 1768-71

1784 MILTONI Ars Logica, cum Rami vitâ, 12mo. *calf*, 5s   1672

1785 NIPHUS (Augustinus) de Pulchro, et Amore (de voluptario amore, etc.) sm. 4to. CLVIII *leaves printed in a curious italic type, vellum*, 21s *s. l.* (*Venice*) *A.B.* 1526

    Very rare. The only editions Brunet mentions are those of Lugd. Batav. 1641 and 1646. On the colophon stands "Niphani Novembris, MDXXIX," but the permission is dated "die vii. Decembris, MDXXX."

LATIN MISCELLANIES, ETC.

1786 PARSONS (Robert). Elizabethæ Angliæ Reginæ sævissimum in Catholicos Edictum, promulgatum Londini, 29 Nov. 1591, cum Responsione, qua sævitia, mendacia et fraudes deteguntur, per Philopatrum, smallest 4to. *fine copy, morocco elegant, gilt edges*, £2. *Romæ*, 1593

Very rare, Lowndes quotes the sale of no copy.

1787 PETRARCHAE (Trans.) Opera quæ extant omnia; adjecimus ejusdem authoris, quae Hetrusco sermone scripsit carmina sive Rythmos, folio, *hf. calf*, 20s
Basileæ, 1581

Best edition. Vol. 4. contains "I Sonetti e le Canzoni et i Triomphi."

1788 PETAVII (Dionysii) Opus de Doctrinâ Temporum, cum Præfatione et Dissertatione de LXX hebdomadibus Joan. Harduini, 3 vols. folio, *portrait, old calf neat*, 24s *Antwerpiæ*, 1703

Heath's copy fetched £3. 9s. A work of incredible labour and compass. The Jesuits learning is copious and correct, his latinity is pure, his method clear, his argument profound and well connected, but he is the slave of the Fathers."—GIBBON.

1789 PEUCERUS de praecipuis Divinationum generibus, Astrologiâ, Magiâ, Somniis, Oraculis, etc. stout 12mo. *vellum*, 7s *Servestae*, 1591

1790 PHILALETHES [L. Moulin] Rerum nuper in Scotia gestarum historia, 16mo. *calf*, 10s *Dantisci*, 1641

1791 PHYSIOPHILI Specimen Monachologiae methodo Linnaeana, 4to. *3 plates of the Garments of all the Monastic Orders, a singular satirical work, hf. bd.* 9s
Aug. Vind. 1783

1792 POLITIANI Omnia Opera, et alia quædam lectu digna, folio, *fine copy in red morocco, gilt edges by Roger Payne*, £3. 16s *Venetiis*, 1498

Priced, 1824, Thorpe, £4. 4s; 1830, Payne and Foss, £5. 5s; Pickering, £5. 5s; 1840, J. Bohn. £5. 5s; Steeven's copy fetched £9. 9s; Pinelli's £8. 8s; Sir M. Sykes, £7. 17s 6d; Askew, £5. 12s 6d; Drury's, £5. 5s; Duke of Grafton, £5. "The only edition in which the conspiracy of the Pazzi is narrated. There is probably no production of the Aldine press which exceeds the present in beauty of type and of printing. The paper is also of a mellow and pleasing tint."—BIBLIOTHECA SPENCERIANA.

1793 PONTANI (Joannis Joviani) Opera omnia, 3 vols. 8vo. *with the Charon complete, of which most copies were destroyed by order of the Inquisition, russia gilt, edges little cut, scarce*, 36s *Venetiis*, 1518-19

Fetched, 1858, without the Charron, £2. 2s; 1860, £2. 5s: Heber's copy fetched £2. 18s.
Vol. II. leaves 63-67, contains the famous Dialogue between Charron and several ghosts, in which the vices and licentiousness of churchmen are coarsely but powerfully painted, by fictitious episodes.

1794 SANNAZARI Opera latine scripta, cura Broukhusii cum notis Vlamingii, 8vo. *red morocco*, 14s *Amst.* 1728

"This contains, at page 201, the celebrated epigram 'De Mirabili Urbe Venetiis,' for the writing of which the Venetian Senate awarded him four hundred gold pieces."

1795 SAULII Carmina selecta—Opus anagrammaticum, in 1 vol. 8vo. *portrait of the Doge Giustiniani of Genoa, vellum*, 6s *Neap.* 1646

1796 SCALIGERI (Jos.) Opus de emendatione Temporum cum veterum Græcorum fragmentis, stout folio, *old calf*, 10s *Lugd. Bat.* 1598

1797 SCALIGER (J. C.) de Causis Linguae Latinae, 4to. *Horne Tooke's copy, calf neat*, 6s *Lugd.* 1540

1798 SCHURMAN (Annæ Mariæ a) Opuscula Hebræa, Græca, Latina, Gallica, prosaica et metrica, 16mo. *second edition, beautiful portrait of this learned lady, designed and engraved by herself, fine copy, morocco extra*, 21s *Lugd. Bat.* 1650

1799 —— eadem, 12mo. *third edition, with an additional portrait by Kilian inserted, whole blue morocco extra, edges uncut*, 30s *Traj. ad Rhen.* 1652

1800 SPINOZÆ Opera quæ extant omnia, 2 vols. 8vo. *portrait, hf. bd.* 15s *Jenæ*, 1802-3

1801 SPRENGER (J.) Malleus maleficarum, 16mo. *old calf*, 6s *Venet.* 1576

1802 STRACCHÆ de Mercaturâ seu Mercatore tractatus, 16mo. *vellum, very rare*, 7s 6d
Venet. (*Ald.* 1553)

Priced, 1830, Payne and Foss, £4. 4s; Thorpe, £3. 13s 6.1; 1835, £2. 2s; Renouard's copy fetched £2. 16s.
"Ce volume est rare."—BRUNET.—The above copy is of the still scarcer issue, without the date.

1803 SULPITII SEVERI Opera omnia quae extant, 16mo. *frontisp. morocco extra, gilt edges*, 20s *Lugd. Bat.* 1643

1804 THUANI Historiarum sui temporis libri CXXXVIII, accedunt ejusdem de Vita sua Commentarii et Rigaltii continuatio, curavit BUCKLEY, 7 vols. folio, BEST EDITION, LARGE PAPER, *fine copy, old calf gilt*, £2. *Lond.* 1733

LARGE PAPER copies were priced: 1837, Payne and Foss, £24.; 1848, £12. 12s; 1856, Lilly, £6. 6s. Copies sold by auction: Sykes', £22 1s; the Duke of Grafton's, £13. 13s; Talleyrand's, £10. 10s; 1854, Dr. Hawtrey's, £7. 15s; 1854, Gardner's, £4.; 1858, at Sotheby's, mor. £13. 5s

1805 VELSERI Rerum Augustanar. Vindelicar. libri VIII., sm. folio, *frontispiece and plates of Antiquities, chiefly Roman, vellum*, 21s *Venet.* 1594

1806 VIDAE, *Cremonensis Albae Episcopi*, Opera omnia, 4 vols. 8vo. *portrait, old calf neat*, 7s 6d *Oxon.* 1722-33
1807 ——— POEMATA, cum dialogis, curâ Russel, 2 vols. 12mo. *calf*, 7s 6d 1732
1808 VINCENTII BELUACENSIS Liber Gratiæ, Laudes Virginis Mariæ, Liber de S. Johanne Evangelista, Tractatus de Eruditione Filiorum Regalium et Consolatio super Morte Amici, folio, *the initial letters painted in, fine copy in old French citron morocco, gilt edges*, VERY SCARCE, 36s *Basileae, J. de Amerbach*, 1481
  Fetched, Feb. 1816, in Marsh's sale at Christie's £6. 6s.
1809 VINEIS (Petri de, *Secretary to the Emperor Frederic II*.) Epistolæ, cum Schardio de fide Pontificum erga Imperatores, 2 vols. in 1, stout 16mo. FIRST EDITION, *scarce, old calf. Caumartin arms*, 10s *Basileae*, 1566
1810 WECKERI de Secretis libri XVII, ex variis authoribus collecti, very stout 12mo. *limp vellum*, 7s 6d *Basil.* 1582
1811 ——— Idem, tertiùm jam aucti, stout 12mo. *original stamped binding*, 18s *ib.* 1592
1812 [WISHEART (G.)] de Rebus sub JACOBO MONTISROSARUM MARCHIONE in anno 1644 et duobus sequent. gestis, 12mo. *blue morocco, gilt edges, very rare*, 36s (? *Paris*,) 1647
  This is the book so much admired for its elegant Latinity, which was hung in derision from Montrose's neck at his execution. It was printed at various times in English, but the original Latin is very rare.
1813 WOLFII (Joh.) Lectionum Memorabilium et Reconditarum Centenarii XVI, cum Indice absolutissimo à Linsio cognomine Hagendorn, (*added loose*), 2 vols. folio, *engraved titles, portrait of the author, and numerous curious woodcuts including figures of monsters, representations of extraordinary Phenomena, etc.; original edition, with the best impressions of the woodcuts, nice clean copy, in the original stamped binding*, 36s *Lavingæ*, 1600-8
  Sold at the Roxburgh sale for £6. 16s 6d. The Index is very frequently wanting. This prodigious repertory appears never to have received that accurate and minute description to which its contents give it so decided a claim. The compiler, Wolfius, is said to have been employed on it during the greater part of his life, diligently transcribing from more than three thousand authors, chiefly Protestant, all the Anecdotes, Historiettes, Memorable Events, Sketches, Epigrams, Remarkable Prophecies, and an indescribable variety of other matters, which seemed worthy of insertion. Many of these relate to eminent Englishmen, and are probably extracted from some of our publications of the fifteenth century, with which the editor may have become acquainted during his residence in this country, as Ambassador from the Electors Palatine.

BIBLIOGRAPHY, LITERARY HISTORY, TYPOGRAPHY.

1814 ADLER's biblischkritische Reise nach Rom, *Altona*, 1783—Geschichte der Königl. Paris.Bibliothek, *Quedl.* 1778, etc. 3 vols. in 1, 12mo. *bds.* 5s 1778-83
1815 ADRIAN, Catalogus codicum MSS. Bibliothecae Academicae Gissensis, 4to. *facsimiles, sd.* 5s ; *bds.* 7s 6d *Francof.* 1840
1816 ALCOBATIÆ (in Lusitaniâ) BIBLIOTHECÆ INDEX Codicum, (MSS.) sm. folio, *Large Fine Paper, two facsimiles, old red morocco gilt, Royal Arms of Portugal on sides*, 32s *Olisipone*, 1775
1817 ALEGAMBE, Bibliotheca Scriptorum Societatis Jesu, post Catalogum Ribadeneirae concinnata cum Catalogo religiosorum Soc. Jesu pro fide interemptorum, folio, *vellum*, 10s *Antverp.* 1643
  Including the names and works of many Englishmen and Irishmen.
1818 AMSTERDAM ACADEMY. Catalogus van de Boekerij, Vol. I. in 2 parts, *all yet published*, 8vo. 636 pp. *bds.* 5s *Amst.* 1858-60
  Comprises the Transactions of Learned Societies.
1819 ANTONIO (Nic.) Bibliotheca Hispana, vetus et nova, sive Hispani Scriptores qui ab Octaviani Augusti ævo ad 1684 floruerunt, curante Franc. Perezio Bayerio, 4 vols. fol. *calf*, £2. ; *fine copy in Spanish calf*, £4. 10s *Matriti*, 1778
  An invaluable body of information concerning Spanish books and authors. It must be considered as the keystone of every Spanish library. Dr. Dibdin in his "Library Companion," regrets its rarity, and values the small paper at £12. 12s
  "An excellent edition, the BIBLIOTHECA VETUS being enriched with notes by Perez Bayer, a learned Valencian, the BIBLIOTHECA NOVA receiving additions from Antonio's own manuscripts, that bring down his notices of Spanish writers to the time of his death in 1684. In the earlier portion, embracing the names of about 1300 authors, little remains to be desired. The latter portion contains notices of nearly 8000 writers,—it is a monument of industry, firmness, and fidelity. The two, taken together, constitute their author, beyond all reasonable question, the father and founder of the literary history of his country.'—TICKNOR, I. 128.
1820 AUDIFFREDI. Catalogus Historico-Criticus Romanarum editionum Sæculi XV, 4to. *calf*, 6s *Romæ*, 1783
1821 BARBIER et DESESSARTS, Nouvelle Bibliothèque d'un Homme de Gout, 5 vols. 8vo. *hf. bound*, 7s *Paris*, 1808-10
1822 BARBIER, Dictionnaire des Ouvrages ANONYMES et PSEUDONYMES, en Francais et Latin, avec les noms des Auteurs, Traducteurs et Editeurs, des notes

historiques et critiques, 4 vols. 8vo. *containing* 23,647 *titles, hf. calf, rare,*
£2. 12s 6d *Paris*, 1822-27
Priced, FINE PAPER, 1848, calf, £4. 14s 6d. "An admirably well-executed work."—DIBDIN.
"Notre Histoire littéraire n'a jamais rassemblé plus de documents curieux que dans les Anonymes de M. Barbier."—NODIER.
"Ouvrage le plus considérable, le plus détaillé, et le plus instructif, qui ait paru sur les anonymes. Il n'est pas possible de répandre plus d'erudition dans un ouvrage de cette nature; les notes nombreuses et savantes annoncent des recherches immenses."—PEIGNOT.

1823 BAUER, Bibliotheca Librorum rariorum universalis, *cum* 2 *Supplementis,* 7 vols. 12mo. 36s *Nürnberg*, 1770-91
1824 —— idem, *cum Supplemento,* 6 vols. 12mo. *calf,* 10s *ib.* 1770-4
1825 BAUMGARTEN'S Nachrichten von einer Hallischen Bibliothek, 8 vols. 1748-51—Nachrichten von merkwürdigen Büchern, 12 vols. 1752-58—together 20 vols. 12mo. *Vol. XII. of the latter contains a General Index to both works, old calf gilt,* 36s *Halle,* 1748-58
1826 BAYLE, Dictionnaire historique et critique; 5me edition par Des Maizeaux, 4 vols. folio, *an excellent copy in russia,* £2. 8s *Amst.* 1740
1827 —— Dictionnaire historique et critique; nouvelle édition, augmentée de notes extraites de Chaufepié, Joly, Marchand, etc. 16 vols. 8vo. £5. 15s *Paris,* 1820
"Bayle was a man of immense but desultory reading; of a subtle understanding, invincible patience, and not less indomitable industry, The notes are the grand field in which Bayle delighted to pour forth his knowledge; and I believe that his 'Life of Nero' furnished a Greek quotation at a late state trial. If sceptical, he was peaceably disposed, although constantly assailed. Even his 'magnum opus,' the Dictionary, was criticised before it appeared. Jurieu, Saurin, and Le Clerc were unable to ruffle the calmness of his temper, or embitter the sweetness of his retirement. He told Des Maizeaux, that from twenty to forty, he worked fourteen hours a day—and, in fact, he never knew what leisure was."—*Dibdin's Library Companion.*

1828 BELOE'S (Rev. W.) Anecdotes of Literature and Scarce Books, 6 vols. 8vo. *calf,* £2. 1807-12
1829 —— The Sexagenarian; or the Recollections of a Literary Life, 2 vols. 8vo. *calf gilt,* 21s 1817
The names are filled in by Alexander Chalmers, from Sir F. Freeling's copy.

1830 BENEDICTINES. Histoire littéraire de la Congrégation de St. Maur, sm. 4to. *calf,* 15s *Bruxelles,* 1770
1831 BERNARD (Aug. membre de la Société des Antiquaires) de l'Origine et des Débuts de l'Imprimerie en Europe, 2 vols. 8vo. 13 *plates of facsimiles, papier vergé,* (pub. at 20 fr.) *new sd.* 10s; or, *hf. morocco, uncut,* 18s *Paris,* 1853
1832 BIBLIOTHECA ANGLO-POETICA: Descriptive Catalogue of a Collection of rare Old Poetry, formed by Park and Hill, on sale by Longmans, roy. 8vo. *woodcut frontispieces, portraits and initials, calf extra,* 24s 1815
1833 BIOGRAPHICAL DICTIONARY of the Society for the diffusion of Useful Knowledge, 4 vols. in 7, A—Azz, 8vo. *cloth,* 14s 1842-44
1834 BIOGRAPHE UNIVERSELLE, ancienne et moderne, ouvrage entièrement neuf, 52 vols. 8vo. *sd.* £4. 10s; or 52 vols. 8vo. FINE PAPER, *the genuine book, cloth lettered,* £6. *Paris, Michaud,* 1811-28
1835 BISCIONII Bibliothecae Ebraicæ Græcae Florentinae Mediceo-Laurentianae Catalogus, 2 vols. 8vo. *vellum,* 6s *Florent.* 1757
1836 BLANDFORD Library: Catalogus Librorum in Bibliotheca Blandfordiensi repertorum, 9 fasc.; Librorum nuper additorum, 1814; in 1 vol. fol. THICK PAPER, *references to the library shelves neatly written in, russia, gilt edges, with the Marquis of Blandford's arms,* "*White Knights' Library*" *on sides,* 26s *Privately printed,* 1812-14
1837 BLAUSUS, Kentniss seltener und merkwürdiger Bücher, 2 vols. in 1, 12mo. *sd.* 750 *pp.* 10s 1753
1838 BODLEIAN LIBRARY. CATALOGUS Codicum Manuscriptorum ARABICORUM, confecit Nicholl, roy. fol. *bds.* 7s 6d 1821
1839 CATALOGUE of Early English Poetry and works illustrating the Drama, collectedby Malone, folio, *hf. calf,* 7s 6d *Oxford,* 1836
1840 CATALOGUS LIBRORUM IMPRESSORUM Bibliothecæ Bodleianæ in Academiâ Oxoniensi, 3 vols. 1843—Catalogus impressorum librorum quibus aucta est Bibl. Bodl. 1851—4 vols. folio, (pub. at £5.) *cloth, new,* £4. *Oxonii,* 1843-51
1841 —— ejusdem Tomus IV: Impressorum librorum quibus aucta est Bibl. Bodl. 1835-47, folio, (pub. at 25s) *cloth,* 21s 1851
1842 BOUTERWEK'S Geschichte der Poesie und Beredsamkeit, in Italien, Spanien, Portugal, Frankreich, England und Deutschland, XIII—XVIII Jahrhund. 12 vols. in 6, 8vo. (pub. at 21 thalers) *hf. calf,* 21s *Gött.* 1801-19
Contents: Vol. 1, 2, Einleitung; Italienische Poesie: 3, 4, Spanische und Portuguesische Poesie; 5, 6, Französische Poesie; 7, 8, ENGLISCHE POESIE; 9-11, Deutsche Poesie; 12, Syst. und Namen-Register.

1843 BOUTOURLIN (Comte de) Catalogue de sa Bibliothèque (publié par ses fils), stout
roy. 8vo. *bds. 7s 6d* *Florence,* 1831
1844 BRITISH MUSEUM: CATALOGUE of the HARLEIAN MSS. now in the
British Museum, with Indexes, 3 vols. large folio, *calf gilt, fine copy,* 25s 1808
1845 BIBLIOTHECÆ REGIÆ Catalogus, 5 vols. *portraits*—Catalogue of the
Maps, Prints, Drawings, etc. presented by George IV.; together 6 vols. roy.
folio, *bds. uncut,* £4. 10s. 1820-29
1846 CATALOGUE of MSS. in the British Museum, New Series, Vol. I. parts
1, 2, 3, the ARUNDEL and BURNEY MANUSCRIPTS and INDEXES, 3 vols. folio,
facsimiles, (pub. at £3. 1s) *bds.* £2. 1834-40
1847 —— the same, Part I. The ARUNDEL MSS. *bds.* 10s 1834
1848 CATALOGUS Codicum ORIENTALIUM Musei Britannici, tres partes, in 4 vols.
royal folio, *facsimiles*, (pub. at £2. 10s) *bds.* £2. 1838-47
Contents; I. Codd. Syriaci et Carshunici; II. Arabici, 2 parts; III. Aethiopici. Sets completed.
1849 CATALOGUE of the Printed Books, Vol. I. A to Azz. sm. fol. *cloth,* 16s 1841
This volume contains 91 admirable rules for cataloguing. The article Academies supplies a valuable Bibliography of all the Transactions of Learned and Publishing Societies.
1850 CATALOGUE of the Manuscript Maps, Charts, and Plans, and of the Topographical Drawings in the British Museum, 2 vols. royal 8vo. (pub. at 20s) *cloth,*
15s 1844
1851 INDEX to the Additional MANUSCRIPTS, with those of the Egerton collection, preserved in the British Museum, and acquired in the years 1783-1835,
folio, *cloth, out of print,* £2. 2s 1849
1852 CATALOGUE of Additions to the Manuscripts in the British Museum in the
years 1841-45, stout royal 8vo. (pub. at 20s) *bds.* 15s 1850
1853 LIST of the BOOKS OF REFERENCE in the Reading Room of the British Museum, 8vo. *plans, cloth,* 7s 6d 1859
1854 GRAY (J. E.) Second Letter to the Earl of Ellesmere on the management of
the Library, 8vo. *sd. privately printed,* 7s 6d 1849
1855 BREITKOPF, Ursprung der Spielkarten, Einführung des Leinenpapieres, und
Anfang der Holzschneidekunst in Europa, 2 vols. *plates,* 1784-1801—Erfindung
der Buchdruckerkunst, 1779—Bibliographie und Bibliophilie, 1793—Exemplum
Typographiæ Sinicæ, 1789—in 1 vol. 4to. *calf gilt,* 27s *Leipzig,* 1779-1801
1856 BRUNET, Manuel du Libraire et de l'Amateur de Livres; avec la Table en
forme de Catalogue raisonné, 5 vols. 8vo. *the fourth,* AND LAST *complete edition,
cloth,* £2.; or, *hf. russia,* £2. 16s *Paris,* 1842-44
1856* —— le même, cinquième édition refondue et augmentée, Vols. I.-IV. Part I.
(A—Pom.) in 7 parts, royal 8vo. *each part published at 10 fr.; sd. complete as
far as issued,* £2. 19s 6d *ib.* 1860-62
1857 BRYDGES (Sir E.) BRITISH BIBLIOGRAPHER, with Communications from
Haslewood, Fry, Park, and others, 4 vols. 8vo. *portraits, scarce,* £5. 10s 1810-14
Only 250 copies printed. Important Critical and Bibliographical Reviews of Early English Poetry, Romances, and English Literature in general, whole works in many instances being reprinted.
1858 BRYDGES (Sir E.) CENSURA LITERARIA, containing Titles, Abstracts and
Opinions of OLD ENGLISH BOOKS, 10 vols. 8vo. SECOND AND BEST EDITION,
*the articles arranged under headings, and chronologically, calf extra, gilt edges,
very scarce,* £10. 5s 1811
An exceedingly valuable and interesting Bibliography of Old English Literature; in most cases the Prefaces and Extracts from the work are given, as well as a Review of their contents.
1859 —— Polyanthea Librorum vetustiorum Italicorum, Gall. Hisp. Angl. et Latinorum, 8vo. THICK PAPER, *hf. calf, gilt top, uncut, only* 75 *copies printed,* 20s
Genevæ, 1822
1860 BURCKHARD, Bibliotheca Augusta Wolffenbutteli, 4to. *vellum,* 5s *Lips.* 1744
1861 CAMUS, Notice d'un Livre imprimé à Bamberg en 1462, par Albert Pfister, 4to.
facsimile plates of the engravings, printing, water-marks, &c. bds. 5s *Paris,* 1799
1862 —— the same, LARGE PAPER, impl. 4to. *calf neat,* 16s 1799
1863 —— Mémoire sur la collection des Grands et Petits Voyages, et sur les Voyages de Thevenot, 4to. *hf. calf,* £1. 4s 1802
1864 CATALOGUE de la Bibliothèque du CONSEIL D'ETAT, 2 vols. in 1, folio, *bds.* 15s
Paris, (1803)
A remarkably well-executed Catalogue of a fine collection, printed apparently on Large Paper, with ample margins for additions. It comprises 10,051 articles in Classes—to 3,200 ANONYMOUS or PSEUDONYMOUS works the real or reputed authors are added.
1865 CELSII Bibliothecæ Regiæ Stockholmensis historia, 12mo. *calf,* 5s *Holm.* 1751
1866 CHALMERS'S Biographical Dictionary of the most eminent persons in every
nation, particularly the British and Irish, 32 vols. 8vo. *calf neat,* £5. 15s 1812-17

BIBLIOGRAPHY, LITERARY HISTORY, TYPOGRAPHY. 115

1867 CHARITIUS de viris eruditis Gedani ortis, sq. 8vo. *hf. bd. rare*, 4*s*   *Vittemb.* 1715
1868 CHRIST (Joh. Fr.) Catalogus Bibliothecæ suae, auctione publica vendita, 2 vols. 12mo. *fine paper, with prices, bds.* 3*s* 6*d*   *Lipsiæ*, 1757-8
1869 CICOGNA, Saggio di Bibliografia VENEZIANA, imp. 8vo. *portrait of Valmarana,* LARGE PAPER, *hf. calf, uncut*, 28*s*   *Venezia,* 1847
    An excellent classified catalogue of works printed at or relating to VENICE, with literary and bibliographical notes, and an Index.
1870 CLARKE's Bibliographical Miscellany: Origin of Printing, Writers on Bibliography, English Translations of the Classics, Works of Arabic and Persian writers, printed and MSS. etc. 2 vols. in 1, stout 12mo. *cloth,* 7*s* 6*d*   1806
1871 CLEMENT, Bibliothèque Curieuse, historique, et critique, ou Catalogue Raisonné des Livres difficiles à trouver, 9 vols. 4to. A—Hes, *all published, old calf,* 25*s*; or *a fine copy in old calf, gilt backs*, 35*s*   *Göttingen*, 1750-60
    " A *sine quâ non* with collectors; unconsciously dear."—DIBDIN.
    " Un répertoire utile où se trouvent des articles fort curieux que l'on chercherait vainement ailleurs."—BRUNET.
1872 CLEMMII Novae Amoenitates literariae, 8vo. *vellum*, 5*s*   *Stuttg.* 1764
1873 COURTIN, ENCYCLOPÉDIE MODERNE, ou Dictionnaire abrégé des Sciences, des Lettres et des Arts, avec indication des ouvrages où les divers sujets sont développés et approfondis, 26 vols. 8vo. *two of them containing the plates, sd.* a bargain, 18*s*   1824
    Priced, 1845, Bossange, 195 fr. Among the Contributors to this excellent Modern Encyclopædia may be remarked, Arnault, Azais, Jouy, Orfila, Tissot, Benjamin Constant, Lanjuinais, &c.
1874 CREVENNA, Catalogue raisonné de sa collection de livres, 6 vols. in 3, 4to. *hf. bound*, 36*s*   *Amstel.* 1775
    "Catalogue curieux, dont le 5e tome renferme diverses lettres inédites d'hommes célèbres du 16e et du 17e siècle. Vendu 55 fr. M'Carthy."—BRUNET. Priced, 1852, Payne and Foss, £3. 3*s*; 1837 and 1838, £3.
1875 —— Catalogue de M. Crevenna, (*Sale catalogue, with Supplement of prices*), 5 vols. 8vo. *sd.* 9*s*   *Amst.* 1789
1876 DARLING'S CYCLOPÆDIA BIBLIOGRAPHICA, a library manual of Theological and general Literature, stout impl. 8vo. 3328 *columns*, (pub. at £2. 12*s* 6*d*) *cloth*, 32*s*   1854
1877 DAVIS' Journey round the Library of a Bibliomaniac, or Notes concerning rare and curious books, 8vo. *bds.* 4*s* 6*d*   1821
1878 DE BURE, Bibliographie instructive, ou Traité de la connoissance des Livres Rares et singuliers, 7 vols. 8vo. *neat in russia*, 15*s*   *Paris*, 1763-68
1879 —— la même, 7 vols.—SUPPLEMENT à la Bibliographie instructive, ou Catalogue des livres de Gaignat, 2 vols.—together 9 vols. 8vo. *hf. bd.* 18*s*   1763-69
    The articles are chosen with discernment and the descriptions very exact.—BRUNET.
1880 — MERCIER, Lettres sur la Bibliographie instructive, 8vo. LARGE PAPER, *veau fauve, gilt edges*, 7*s* 6*d*   *Paris*, 1763
1881 DE BURE, et NYON, Catalogue des Livres de la Bibliothèque du Duc de La Vallière, 1e partie, 3 vols. with the Supplement, containing the prices, etc. 1 vol.; 2e partie, 6 vols.—together 10 vols. 8vo. *calf*, 20*s*   *Paris*, 1783-84
1882 DELEPIERRE, Macaronéana, ou Mélanges de Littérature Macaronique, 8vo. *sd.* 8*s* 6*d*   1852
1883 —— the same, VELLUM PAPER, 8vo. *morocco extra*, £2.   1852
1884 DENIS (M.) CODICES Manuscripti Theologici Bibliothecae Palatinae Vindobonensis Latinæ aliarumque Occidentis linguarum, 6 vols. fol. *plates of facsimiles, calf,* £3. 10*s*   *Vindob.* 1793-1802
    Ouvrage très estimé des Bibliographes.—BRUNET.
1885 LAMBECII, Commentaria de Bibliotheca Caesarea Vindobonensi, 8 vols.— KOLLARII Supplementorum lib. primus, 1 vol.—together, 9 vols. folio, *facsimiles, calf,* £4.   *ib.* 1766-90
    " Cet ouvrage n'a pas été terminé, ce que nous en possédons fait regretter vivement la suite."—BRUNET.
1886 NESSEL, Breviarium et Supplementum Lambecii: Catalogus omnium Codd. MSS. Graecorum necnon Orientalium Biblioth. Vindobonensis, 2 vols. folio, *numerous plates of facsimiles, calf*, 36*s*   *Vind.* 1690
    These three celebrated works are full of interesting *Opuscula* from unpublished manuscripts, and, containing a great number of *facsimiles* of Oriental, Greek, and Latin early manuscripts, form one of the most magnificent monuments ever erected to diplomatic and philological studies.
    The above three numbers forming one set, uniformly bound in calf, will be *sold together for* £8.
1887 DENIS, die Merkwürdigkeiten der Garellischen Bibliothek, 4to. *hf. bound, an interesting Bibliography*, 6*s*   1780
1888 DENT (John) Sale Catalogue of his splendid, curious and extensive Library, 2 parts, *with prices and names*—Sale Catalogue of Dent's Coins, 3 parts in 1 vol. 8vo. *hf. morocco, uncut*, 32*s*   1827
1889 —— the same, roy. 8vo. *with names and prices, and a MS. letter of J. H. Burn, bookseller*, 1827, *inserted, concerning the library*, 25*s*   1827

1890 DE-ROSSI, Libri di Letteratura Ebraica ed Orientale, 8vo. *sd.* 10*s Parma*, 1812
1891 DIBDIN'S TYPOGRAPHICAL ANTIQUITIES of England, Scotland, and Ireland, begun by Ames, augmented by Herbert, and now greatly enlarged, 4 vols. 4to. *ports. facsimiles, and numerous engravings on wood,* (pub. at £14. 14*s*) £7. 15*s*
1810-19
1892 ——— the same, Vol. I.: CAXTON'S PUBLICATIONS, 4to. *portrait of Ames, plates and cuts, bds.* 20*s*
1810
1893 ——— the same, Vol. IV. 4to. *portraits,* (pub. at £3. 13*s* 6*d*) *bds.* 15*s* 1819
Contains the publications of R. Wolfe, John Day, W. Seres, R. Jugge, R. Walley, G. Lynne, J. Cawood, R. Tottell, T. Marshe, etc.
1894 ——— BIBLIOGRAPHICAL DECAMERON, or Ten Days pleasant Discourse upon Illuminated Manuscripts and subjects connected with Early Engraving, Typography and Bibliography, 3 vols. royal 8vo. *with a beautifully engraved series of* WOODCUTS *and* COPPER-PLATES *of* PORTRAITS, *Illuminations, etc. bds.* £8. 15*s*
1817
1895 ——— Bibliographical, Antiquarian, and Picturesque Tour in FRANCE and GERMANY, 3 vols. stout roy. 8vo. *numerous fine plates, vignettes, facsimiles, etc. olive* MOROCCO *extra, gilt edges*, £10. 10*s*
1821
1896 ——— Bibliographical, Antiquarian, and Picturesque Tour in the Northern Counties of England, and in Scotland, 2 vols. royal 8vo. *upwards of* 100 *plates, facsimiles of early portraits, prints, etc. uncut,* £3. 10*s*
1838
1897 ——— LIBRARY COMPANION, or the young man's guide and the old man's comfort, in the choice of a library, *second edition,* stout 8vo. *green morocco, gilt edges,* 27*s*
1825
1898 ——— Reminiscences of a Literary Life, with INDEX, 3 vols. 8vo. *plates of Portraits, Autographs, facsimiles, etc. bds.* 28*s*
1836
1899 DICTIONNAIRE BIBLIOGRAPHIQUE, historique et critique de LIVRES RARES, avec le Supplement, 4 vols. 8vo. *hf. bound, uncut,* 16*s Paris*, 1802
1900 DICTIONNAIRE GÉNÉRAL de BIOGRAPHIE et d'Histoire, de Mythologie, de Géographie ancienne et moderne comparé, des antiquités et des institutions Grecques, Romaines, Françaises et étrangères, par Dezobry et Bachelet, 2 vols. roy. 8vo. *hf. morocco,* 32*s Paris*, 1857
1901 DRYANDER (Jonas) Catalogus Bibliothecæ Historico-Naturalis Josephi Banks, Baroneti, 5 vols. in 9, 8vo. *interleaved, hf. calf,* £2. 10*s* 1798-1800
Priced, 1825, Thorpe, £8. 18*s* 6*d*; 1830, Payne and Foss, £6. 6*s*; 1830, Longman, £4. 10*s*; 1842, Nattali, £4. 14*s* 6*d.*
A singularly well made Catalogue, in classified order, giving careful calculations of the number of pages and plates of each work.
1902 DUPRAT, Histoire de l'Imprimerie Impériale de France, roy. 8vo. *numerous specimens of Types in all languages, etc. hf. calf neat, gilt top, uncut,* 12*s Paris*, 1861
1903 EBERT'S allgemeines Bibliographisches Lexikon, 2 vols. in 1, 4to. *sized paper, hf. calf,* 18*s Leipzig*, 1821
1904 ENGELMANN, Bibliotheca Geographica, stout 8vo. 1225 *pp. a valuable Bibliography of Geographical works from the middle of the last century to the present, with prices, hf. calf,* 10*s Leipzig*, 1858
1905 ——— Bibliotheca Historico-Naturalis, der Bücher in 1700-1846 erschienenen, Vol. I, 8vo. *with prices, cloth,* 10*s ib.* 1846
1906 ——— Supplement-Band: Bibliotheca Zoologica, enthaltend die in Periodischen Werken aufgenommenen, und die von 1846-60 erschienenen Schriften, 2 vols. stout 8vo. *with prices, cloth,* 20*s ib.* 1861
"These catalogues are considered indispensable by every Zoologist."—*J. H Gray.*
1907 ——— Bibliotheca Philologica, of Grammars, Dictionaries, etc. for the study of Greek and Latin, 8vo. *sd.* 3*s* 6*d* 1853
1908 ——— Bibliotheca Scriptorum Classicorum, editions of the Greek and Latin Classics, etc. that have appeared up to the end of 1846, 8vo. *cloth,* 5*s ; hf. calf,* 6*s*
1847
1909 FABRICII (J. A.) Bibliotheca Græca, sive, Notitia Scriptorum veterum Græcorum quorumcumque Monumenta integra aut fragmenta extant, &c. variorum curis emendatior atque auctior, curante HARLES, 12 vols. 4to. BEST EDITION, *hf. calf,* £4. 10*s Hamb.* 1790-1809
Priced, 1835, £14. 14*s* ; 1836, unbound, £8. 8*s.*
1910 FALKENSTEIN'S Geschichte der Buchdruckerkunst in ihrer Entstehung und Ausbildung, Verzeichniss der Drucker bis 1500, etc. 4to. *upwards of* 40 *facsimiles, some coloured, of the early productions of Typography, modern types, etc. cloth,* 18*s ;* or *hf. morocco, uncut, gilt top,* 24*s Leipzig*, 1840
1911 FIRMIAN. Bibliotheca Firmiana sive Thesaurus librorum (impress. MSS. etc.) quem Comes C. a Firmian collegit, 7 vols. large 4to. *bd. uncut,* 21*s Mediol.* 1783

1912 FLÖGEL's Geschichte der Komischen Litteratur, 4 vols. 8vo. *plates, hf. calf*, 12s
Leignitz und Leipz. 1784-87
1913 FRANCKII Catalogi Bibliothecae BUNAVIANAE Tomi tres, 7 vols. in 4, stout sm. 4to. COMPLETE, *with references to reviews in learned Transactions, a valuable catalogue, vellum*, 30s *Lipsiæ*, 1750-56
"This Catalogue may be considered as a monument of bibliographical industry; it is becoming scarce, and fetches a high price on the continent."
1914 FRERE, Manuel du Bibliographe Normand, des ouvrages relatifs à la Normandie depuis l'origine de l'Imprimerie, avec des notes biographiques et l'histoire de l'Imprimerie en Normandie, 2 vols. roy. 8vo. 1135 *pp. double columns, sd.* 34s
Rouen, 1858-60
1915 FREYTAG, Analecta Litteraria de Libris rarioribus, stout 12mo. *vel.* 18s *Lips.* 1750
1916 GAMBA, Bibliografia delle Novelle Italiane, 8vo. *giving the prices fetched at sales, sd.* 10s *Firenze*, 1835
1917 GEORGI (T.) Allgemeines Europäisches Bücher-Lexicon (Universal Dictionary of Books printed in Europe from 1500 to 1757, with the date, size, price, and number of sheets or pages of each), 8 vols. in 5, folio, (including three Supplements), *hf. bd. scarce*, £2. 2s *Leipzig*, 1742-58
Priced, 1829, Treuttel, £3.; 1841, £3. 3s; 1847, £2. 2s; 1856, Tross, 55 fr.; Weigel in Leipsic, 18 thalers.
This laborious work contains the titles of more books than any other bibliographical work ever published.
Le cinquième volume contient la seule bibliographie qui donne les livres français des derniers siècles imprimés dans les Pays-Bas et à Cologne.
1918 GIRARDOT, Catalogue des MSS. de la Bibliothèque des Bourges, roy. 4to. 164 pp. *executed in lithography, with facsimiles, sd. only 90 copies printed*, 12s 1859
1919 GOEZEN'S Historie der gedruckten Niedersächsischen Bibeln, 1470-1621, *Halle*, 1775—Verzeichniss seiner Samml. seltener und merkwürdiger Bibeln in verschiedenen Sprachen mit kritischen und liter. Anmerkungen, 1777—PALM, Historie der deutschen Bibel-Uebersetzung Lutheri, 1517-34, herausg. von Goezen, 1772—together 3 vols. 4to. *hf. calf neat, gilt tops, uncut, contents lettered*, 25s *Halle*, 1772-77
1920 ——— Verzeichniss seiner Sammlung seltener Bibeln in verschiedenen Sprachen, 4to. *hf. calf*, 12s *Halle*, 1777
1921 GORII Symbolæ Litterariæ, Opuscula varia, philologica, scientifica, antiquaria, signa, lapides, numismata, Gemmas, etc. Medii Ævi complectentes, 10 vols. in 5, 8vo. *numerous plates of Antiquities, Coins, &c.* 32s *Florentiæ*, 1748-52
1922 GRAESSE, Lehrbuch einer allgemeinen Literärgeschichte aller bekannten Völker; Band I. Völker der alten Welt, 2 Abtheilungen; Band II. Völker des Mittelalters, 3 Abtheilungen in 5 vols. (Vol. 6 wanting) together 7 vols. 8vo. *calf gilt*, 30s *Dresd. und Leip.* 1837-42
1923 BIBLIOTHECA GRENVILLIANA, Bibliographical Notices of the Library of the Right Hon. Thomas Grenville, by Payne and Foss, 1842, 3 vols. royal 8vo. *cloth, uncut, very rare, Vols. I. and II. are out of print, only a few copies were published*, £8. 1842-48
1924 GUIGARD, Bibliotheque Heraldique de la France, 8vo. 527 *pp. double columns, a valuable Bibliography of works on Heraldry, chiefly French, sd.* 14s *Paris*, 1861
1925 HAENEL, Catalogi Libr. Manuscriptorum, qui in Biblioth. Galliæ, Helvetiæ, Belgii, Britanniæ Magnæ, Hispaniæ, Lusitaniæ asservantur, 4to. *calf*, 27s 1830
1926 HAIN (L.) Repertorium Bibliographicum, in quo libri omnes ab Arte Typographica inventa usque ad MD, typis expressi ordine alphabetico enumerantur, 4 vols. 8vo. *Fine Paper*, (pub. at £5. 5s) *interleaved, russia*, 32s *Stuttg.* 1826-38
The object of this work is similar to Panzeri Annales, but the arrangement being alphabetical is more convenient.
1927 HALLAM'S Introduction to the Literature of Europe in the XV, XVI, and XVII Centuries, 3 vols. 8vo. *second edition*, (pub. at 36s) *calf gilt*, 25s 1843
1928 HASSLER, Ulm's Buchdrucker Kunst: die Buchdrucker-Geschichte Ulm's, mit Beiträgen zur Culturgeschichte, und zur Geschichte der Holzschneidekunst, 4to. *illuminated frontispiece, and 8 plates of Facsimiles and Woodcuts from Early Printed Books, bds.* 7s *Ulm*, 1840
1928*——— the same, 1840—Explicatio monumenti Typographici antiquissimi nuper reperti, cum supplementis ad historiam, 1840—in 1 vol. 4to. *bds.* 9s *Ulm*, 1840
Containing specimens and descriptions of some of the most interesting Monuments of Early Typography.
1929 HAYM, Biblioteca Italiana, notizia de' Libri rari Italiani, 4 parts in 2 vols. 8vo. *calf neat*, 10s *Milano*, 1803
1930 HISTOIRE de l'Invention de l'Imprimerie par les monuments, folio, *illuminated portrait of Guttenberg, and facsimiles of the earliest specimens of printing*, 50 *pp. sd.* 10s *Paris*, 1840

1931 HEBER (R.) BIBLIOTHECA HEBERIANA, Catalogue of the Library of the late Rich. Heber, COMPLETE, 13 parts, bound in 4 vols. 8vo. WITH PRICES and purchasers' names to each article, hf. calf gilt, gilt tops, uncut, £3. 16s 1834-37
1857, Fetched at Sotheby's, £4. 19s.
The most extensive, extraordinary, and valuable collection of books brought together by any single individual. The total amount the books realized was more than 50,000 pounds.

1932 HOFMANNI Lexicon Universale, Historiam, Chronologiam, Mythologiam, etc. omnis aevi explanans, 4 vols. folio, best edition, vel. £2. 2s Lugd. Bat. 1698

1933 HOLMES (John, of Retford) Descriptive Catalogue of the Books in his Library, the whole series, with Supplements and Indexes, complete, 5 vols. in 2, 8vo. portrait, hf. morocco, gilt tops, £2. 12s 6d Norwich, 1828-37
A catalogue, with copious notes, of a fine collection, especially rich in Early English Literature. Collation: Vol. I. portrait, title, 2 prelim. leaves, pp. 1-310, Errata; Vol II. title, 3 prelim. leaves, pp. 1-286, Errata; Vol. III. plate of library, title, 3 prelim. leaves, pp. 1-295; Vol. IV. 2 prelim. leaves, pp. 1-224, including Index; Supplement, title, 2 prelim. leaves, pp. 1-84.

1934 HOLTROP, Catalogus librorum Saec. XV impressorum, in Bibliotheca Regia Hagana asservatorum, 8vo. sd. 7s Hagae, 1856

1935 HORNE (T. H.) Introduction to Bibliography, 2 vols. 8vo. engravings and plates of facsimiles, bd. 10s 1814

1936 HUNTER'S Three Catalogues; the Contents of the Red Book of the Exchequer, of the Dodsworth MSS. in the Bodleian, and of the MSS. in the Library of Lincoln's Inn, 8vo. only 100 copies printed, 15s 1838

1937 INDEX Librorum prohibitorum ac expurgandorum novissimus, 2 vols. folio, the genuine edition, vellum, scarce, 20s Matriti, 1747

1938 INDEX librorum prohibitorum, Benedicti XIV jussu editus, sm. 8vo. calf, 5s 1770

1939 IRIARTE (J.) Regiae Bibliothecae Matritensis Codices GRAECI MSS. Vol. I. all published, folio, russia gilt, 25s Matriti, 1769

1940 JANOZKI, Nachricht von den in der Hochgräfl.—Zaluskischen Bibliothek raren Polnischen Büchern, 4 vols. in 1, 8vo. portraits, hf. calf, 12s Dresd. 1747-53

1941 KENSINGTON MUSEUM, Classified Catalogue of the Educational Division, 8vo. sd. 2s 6d 1862

1942 KIPPIS, BIOGRAPHIA BRITANNICA; or the Lives of the most eminent persons who have flourished in Great Britain and Ireland from the earliest ages to the present time, Vols. 1-5 (A-F), all published, folio, second edition, hf. bd. quite uncut, 36s 1778-93
This valuable work was never completed. It contains the lives of Bacon, Barclay, Barrington, Bedell, Bentinck, Casaubon, Cook, Digby, Doddridge, and many other eminent men.

1943 LABORDE, Débuts de l'Imprimerie à Strasbourg, roy. 8vo. facsimiles, sd. rare, 7s 6d Paris, 1840

1943*——— Débuts de l'Imprimerie à Mayence et à Bamberg, ou description des Lettres d'Indulgence de Nicolas V, imprimées en 1454, large 4to. 9 plates of Facsimiles, with woodcuts, bds. very rare, 30s Paris, 1840

1944 LACKINGTON (the Bookseller), Memoirs, by himself, 8vo. uncastrated edition, portrait, hf. calf, 5s 1794

1945 LACROIX DU MAINE et DU VERDIER, Bibliotheques Françoises, nouvelle edition augmentée par La Monnoye, Bouhier, Falconnet, et Juvigny, 6 vols. 4to. old calf gilt, 36s Paris, 1772-73
"Ouvrage très précieux pour l'histoire littéraire de la France antérieurement à la fin du 16e siècle."—BRUNET.

1946 LE LONG, Bibliotheque Historique de la France, contenant le Catalogue de tous les Ouvrages imprimés et Manuscrits qui traitent de ce Royaume; augmentée par Fontette, 5 vols. folio, a beautiful copy from Miss Currer's library, in old French calf extra, with Arms on sides, £10. 10s Paris, 1768-78

1947 LE LONG et BOEHNERI Bibliotheca Sacra, cum notis à Masch, 5 vols. in 4, 4to. bds. 15s Halae, 1778-90

1948 LENGLET DU FRESNOY, Méthode pour étudier l'Histoire, avec un Catalogue des principaux Historiens, 15 vols. 12mo. calf, 15s Paris, 1772

1949 LIBRI'S Sale Catalogues, August 1-15th, 1859, April 25th to July 26th, 1861, July 1862, in 4 parts, roy. 8vo. facsimiles, sd. 12s 1859-62

1950 ——— MONUMENTS INEDITS ou peu connus, qui se rapportent à l'Histoire des Arts du Dessin, considérés dans leur application à l'Ornement des Livres, folio, the text in French and English, with 60 facsimile plates in gold and colours of Illuminated MSS., Ornamental Bookbinding, and other specimens of Art, ranging from the sixth to the sixteenth century, (pub. at £9. 9s) in portfolio, £8. 8s Londres, 1862

BIBLIOGRAPHY, LITERARY HISTORY, TYPOGRAPHY. 119

1951 LINCOLN'S INN LIBRARY:
    a Catalogue of the Printed Books, with an account of the MSS. roy. 8vo. cloth, 6*s*   1835
    b Hunter's Catalogue of the MSS. (Historical and Legal, formerly collected by Sir Matthew Hale, Maynard and others, with descriptions), roy. 8vo. cloth, 7*s* 6*d*   1838
    c Specimen of a Catalogue of the Books on Foreign Law, presented by C. Purton Cooper: Spanish Law, roy. 8vo. *cloth,* 7*s* 6*d*   1847
    d Catalogue of Books on Foreign Law, founded on Cooper's Collection, Vol. I.: Laws and Jurisprudence of France, with *Index,* roy. 8vo. xvi and 436 pp. *hf. morocco,* 12*s*   1849

1951*LONDON INSTITUTION. Catalogue of the Library of the London Institution, systematically classed, with Indexes of Subjects, Authors, and Books, 4 vols. roy. 8vo. *cloth, (not published)* £2. 10*s*   1835-52
    Interesting for giving the contents of large sets of books, or publications of learned societies.

1952 MACHADO (D. Barbosa) Bibliotheca Lusitana, Vol. I. folio, *uncut,* 20*s*   1741
    "Machado Bibliotheca Lusitana is the great authority on all matters of fact in Portuguese literary history. It is one of the amplest and most important works of literary Biography and Bibliography ever published; but, unhappily, it is also one of the rarest, a large part of the impression having been destroyed in the fire that followed the great earthquake at Lisbon in 1755."—Ticknor, III. p. 151.

1953 MAITLAND (Rev. S. R.) List of some of the Early Printed Books in the Archiepiscopal Library at Lambeth, 8vo. *cloth, rare,* £2. 2*s*   1843
1954 ——— Index of such English Books printed before the year MDC as are now in the Archiepiscopal Library at Lambeth, 8vo. *cloth,* 7*s* 6*d*   1845
1955 Majansii Specimen Bibliothecæ, catalogus operum Hispanorum, sm. 4to. *with an Index, calf,* 7*s* 6*d*   *Hannov.* 1753
1956 Manne, Nouveau Dictionnaire des Ouvrages Anonymes et Pseudonymes, nouvelle édition, 8vo. 406 *pp. double columns, sd.* 7*s* 6*d*   *Lyon,* 1862
1957 Marsand, Scoperta d'una ediz. del Decamerone del Sec. XV, 4to. *facsimile, bds.* 3*s* 6*d*   *Venez.* 1815
1958 Marsden. Bibliotheca Marsdeniana, or Catalogue of Books and Manuscripts collected for a General Comparison of Languages, and the study of Oriental literature, etc. 4to. *bds. not printed for sale,* 7*s*   1827
1959 MARTIN'S Bibliographical Catalogue of Books, privately printed; including those of the Bannatyne, Maitland and Roxburghe Clubs, and of the Private Presses of Lee Priory, Strawberry Hill, etc. 8vo. *front. etc. cloth,* 20*s*.   1834
1960 ——— the same, large paper, 2 vols. impl. 8vo. first edition, *with the Works of Printing Societies, frontispiece plain and coloured, cloth,* £2.   1834
    The Large Paper issue matches in size and forms a companion to Dibdin's Bibliotheca Spenceriana.

1961 Martin's Bibliographical Catalogue of Privately Printed Books, 8vo. *second edition, cloth,* 17*s* 6*d*   1854
1962 Meerman, de l'Invention de l'Imprimerie, 8vo. *bds.* 4*s* 6*d*   *Paris,* 1809
1963 MEUSELII Bibliotheca Historica, post Struvium et Buderum, nunc amplificata et emendata; accedunt Indices, 11 vols. in 22, 8vo. *sd.* 18*s*   *Lips.* 1782-1804
1964 ——— the same, fine paper, 22 vols. 8vo. *German bds.* 25*s;* or, in 11 vols. *hf. bd.* 32*s*   *ib.* 1782-1804
    Priced, 1840, Jas. Bohn, £5. 5*s*; fetched, 1854, Dr. Hawtrey's, £3. 4*s*; Mitford's, £3. 18*s*. This useful and valuable work, the best of its class, is the fruit of great industry. It contains a most extensive enumeration of works relating to history, geography, statistics, etc. arranged with considerable care.

1965 Mirabeau, Catalogue des livres de sa Bibliothèque, 8vo. *the prices added in MS. calf, rare,* 5*s*   *Paris,* 1791
1966 Moeller, Catalogus librorum MSS. et impressorum in Bibliotheca Gothana asservatorum, Vol. I. *(all published),* 4to. *cold. plates, hf. calf,* 12*s*   *Gotha,* 1826
1967 MONTFAUCON, Bibliotheca Bibliothecarum Manuscriptorum Nova, ubi describuntur quae innumeris Bibl. continentur, 2 vols. folio, *calf,* 25*s*   *Paris,* 1739
1968 Moreni, Bibliografia Storico-Ragionata della Toscana o sia Catalogo degli Scrittori che l'hanno illustrata, 2 vols. 4to. *sd.* 15*s*   *Firenze,* 1805
1969 MOULE'S Bibliotheca Heraldica Magnae Britanniae: an Analytical Catalogue of Books on Genealogy, Heraldry, Nobility, Knighthood, etc. and a Supplement of Foreign Genealogical Works, roy. 4to. (pub. at 36*s*) *portrait, calf,* 24*s*   1822
1970 MURR'S Journal zur Kunst-Geschichte und zur allgemeinen Litteratur, 17 vols. 12mo. *plates, German bds.* 21*s*   *Nürnberg,* 1775-89
    A very valuable and learned repository of Antiquarian, Artistic, Philological and Literary Treatises, positively indispensable to a public library; and containing the most varied information upon all branches of Literature and Art.

1971 MURR, Memorabilia Bibliothecarum publicarum NORIMBERGENSIUM et Universitatis Altdorfinæ, 3 vols. 8vo. *several facsimiles of MSS., Autographs, Early Printing, etc. bds.* 15s *Norimb.* 1786-91

1972 NICERON, MEMOIRES pour servir à l'histoire des HOMMES ILLUSTRES dans la Republique des Lettres, avec un Catalogue Raisonné de leurs Ouvrages, et quelques Notices par Oudin, Michault, et Goujet, 43 vols. in 44, 12mo. *veau fauve, fine copy, from Drury's and Dr. Hawtrey's libraries,* £8.8s *Paris,* 1729-45
The above copy has Vol. X. pt. 2, which is often wanting.

1973 —— Tomes I.-XXXII. 12mo. *old calf gilt,* 18s 1729-35

1974 NICHOLS, LITERARY ANECDOTES of the Eighteenth Century, 9 vols. 1812-15—Illustrations of the LITERARY HISTORY of the Eighteenth Century, 8 vols. 1817-58—together 17 vols. 8vo. *numerous portraits and plates,* (pub. at more than £25. in bds.) *tree-marbled calf extra, by* RIVIERE, A VERY FINE UNIFORM SET, £13.13s 1812-58

1975 NODIER, Description raisonnée d'une Collection de Livres, 8vo. *sd.* 5s 1844

1976 OETTINGER, Bibliographie Bibliographique ou Dictionnaire de 26,000 ouvrages anciens et moderns relatifs à l'histoire des hommes célèbres, roy. 8vo. 788 *pp. double columns, cloth,* 12s 6d *Leipzic,* 1850
An indispensable supplement to the Biographie Universelle and all other biographical dictionaries, being a dictionary of biographical works arranged in chronological order under the subjects.

1977 OLIVEIRA, Diagnosis typographica, 8vo. *sd.* 5s *Lisboa,* 1804
Instructions for the Compositors of the Royal Printing-Establishment at Lisbon.

1978 OSMONT, Dictionnaire typographique, historique, etc. des Livres Rares, 2 vols. 8vo. *old calf gilt,* 6s *Paris,* 1768

1979 **Oxford University.** BLACK, Catalogue of the Manuscripts, bequeathed by Elias ASHMOLE. Windsor Herald, also additional MSS. 4to. *cloth,* 24s *Oxford,* 1845

1980 TAYLOR INSTITUTION, Oxford, Catalogue of the Library of the, 8vo. *cloth, new,* 2s 6d *ib.* 1861

1981 PAEILE, Essai sur l'Invention de l'Imprimerie, 8vo. *sd.* 5s *Paris,* 1859

1982 PANIZZI, Bibliographical Notices of early Editions of the Orlando Inamorato and Furioso, 8vo. *port. cloth,* 10s 1831
24 copies only have been taken off for private distribution from the edition of the Orlando.

1982*PANZER, ANNALES TYPOGRAPHICI, ab Artis inventae origine ad annum 1536, 11 vols. 4to. *hf. bd.* £7. 10s *Norimbergae,* 1793-1803
The most elaborate and trustworthy record yet published of the early history of printing; it comes down to the year 1536, though the title-page of the first volume limits it to the fifteenth century. Panzer's great compilation consists of eleven volumes, published at intervals in the course of eleven years,—the first in 1793, the last in 1803. At first the author proposed to carry his Annals no further than the year 1500, and he achieved his purpose in five volumes; he then extended his design, and carried the work up to 1536 in six volumes more. There is, it may be remarked, one serious defect in Panzer's arrangements. While he inserted books in every other European language —Swedish, Dutch, Bohemian, &c.—he systematically omitted all those in German, because they were included, or intended to be included, in a separate work, the 'Annalen der ältern deutschen Litteratur,'—which he unfortunately did not live to bring down further than the year 1526.

1983 PANZER'S Annalen der ältern Deutschen Litteratur, von Erfindung der Buchdruckerkunst bis MDXX, *Nürn.* 1788—Zusätze, bis MDXX, *Leip.* 1802—Annalen von 1521-26, *Nürnb.* 1805, 3 vols. in 2, small 4to. 30s 1788-1805

1984 —— Zusätze zu den Annalen der älteren Deutchen Litteratur, 4to. *sd.* 6s *Leipzig,* 1802

1985 PAQUOT, Memoires pour l'Histoire Littéraire des Pays-Bas, de la Principauté de Liege, et des contrées voisines, 18 vols. 8vo. *fine paper, sd.* 25s *Louv.* 1763-70
"Cet ouvrage se distingue par des details intéressants et une certaine exactitude."—BRUNET.

1986 PEEL (Sir Robert) Bibliotheca Hibernicana, descriptive Catalogue of a select Irish library, (by W. Shaw Mason) 8vo. *facsimile and portrait, bds. presentation copy to the Duke of Buckingham, privately printed,* 50 *copies only,* 18s *Dub.* 1823

1987 QUÉRARD, La FRANCE LITTÉRAIRE, ou Dictionnaire Bibliographique des Savants, Historiens, et Gens de Lettre de la France ainsi que des Littérateurs étrangers qui ont écrit en Francaise, plus particulièrement pendant les XVIIIe et XIXe siècles, 10 vols. large 8vo. LARGE PAPER, *hf. bd. red morocco, gilt edges, from Miss Currer's library,* £8. 8s *Paris,* 1827-43

1988 —— the same, 5 vols. in 9 parts, A—Lion, 8vo. *sd.* 18s *ib.* 1827-33

1989 —— the same, 10 vols. 1827-43—La LITTÉRATURE FRANÇAISE contemporaine, continuation de la FRANCE LITTÉRAIRE, jusqu'à 1849, 6 vols. 1842-57—together 16 vols. 8vo. *hf. blue morocco extra, gilt tops, uncut,* A HANDSOME SET OF BOOKS, £10. 10s *ib.* 1827-57

BIBLIOGRAPHY, LITERARY HISTORY, TYPOGRAPHY. 121

1990 PETTIGREW'S Bibliotheca Sussexiana, a descriptive Catalogue, with historical and biographical notices, of the MSS. and printed Books in the library of the Duke of Sussex, 2 vols. in 3, impl. 8vo. *portrait and several plates of facsimiles, two hf. bd. one in bds.* 30s   1827-39

1991 —— the same, 3 vols. impl. 8vo. *bds.* 36s   1827-39

1992 REIFFENBERG (le Baron de) Le BIBLIOPHILE BELGE, 9 vols.—Seconde Série, Bulletin du Bibliophile Belge, Vol. I.; together 10 vols. 8vo. *portrait of C. Nodier, and numerous facsimiles of early printing, typographical marks, etc. hf. calf gilt*, £2. 18s   Bruxelles, 1845-54
An extremely valuable Bibliography and Literary History, numbering some of the most learned men of Europe amongst its contributors. It also reviews the current bibliographical publications of the day, upon whatever subject or in whatever language.

1993 REINWALD, Catalogue annuel de la Librairie Française, pour 1858-61, 8vo. 12s   Paris, 1858-61

1994 REPORT from the Select Committee on PUBLIC LIBRARIES, with proceedings, minutes, and Appendix, and Index, 1849—Report from the Select Committee on Arts and Manufactures, with Index, etc. 1836—2 vols. in 1, stout folio, *half calf gilt, plans,* 10s 6d   1836-49

1995 RENOUARD, Catalogue de la Bibliothèque d'un Amateur, avec des notes, 4 vols. 8vo. *half calf, uncut,* 10s   Paris, 1819
A most useful catalogue of an extensive collection of rare and curious books. M.§Renouard was well skilled in bibliography.

1996 —— Bibliotheca Aldina, an extensive assemblage of the productions of the Aldine press, 2 parts in 1, 8vo. *with the prices and purchasers' names, hf. calf, gilt top, uncut, very rare,* 15s   1828-34

1997 —— Annales de l'Imprimerie des ALDE, stout 8vo. *portraits, half calf, gilt top, uncut,* 21s   Paris, 1834
"Renouard, in his description of the Aldine press is without a rival."—BELOE'S ANECDOTES.

1998 —— Catalogue de sa Bibliothèque, avec Indice, (pour la vente), 8vo. 4s   1854

1999 RICH, Bibliotheca Americana Nova: Catalogue of Books relating to America, in various languages, Vol. II. *containing all the books printed from* 1801 to 1844, 1846—Supplement to Part I.—Additions and Corrections, 1701-1800, 1841: 8vo. *cloth,* 25s   1841-5
The same price will be given by B. Q. for the first volume.

2000 —— Bibliotheca Americana Nova, Vol. II. 1801-44, 8vo. *printed on one side only, cloth,* 16s   1846

2001 ROSE'S Biographical Dictionary, 12 vols. 8vo. *double columns, calf gilt, very neat,* £4. 15s   1857

2002 RUDDIMAN and GOODALL, Catalogue of the Library of the Faculty of Advocates, Edinburgh, 3 vols. folio, *without the Appendix, a fine copy, in calf gilt, from Miss Currer's library,* 25s   Edinb. 1742-1807
An exact Catalogue of a fine collection of more than 30,000 vols. and many MSS.

2003 SACY (Silvestre de) Catalogue de sa Bibliothèque, 3 vols. 8vo. *a most valuable Catalogue of one of the best Oriental Libraries ever collected, sd.* 16s   1842-47

2004 —— the same, Vol, I, 8vo. *sd.* 5s   1842

2005 —— the same, Vol. III. 8vo. *sd.* 10s   1847

2006 SAINTE PALAIE, Histoire Littéraire des Troubadours, extraits, etc. 3 vols. 12mo. *half calf neat,* 3s 6d   Paris, 1774

2007 —— Memoires sur l'ancienne Chevalerie, 3 vols. 12mo. *calf,* 5s   ib. 1781

2008 SALE CATALOGUES. See Christine, Crevenna, Dent, Gribner, Mirabeau, Renouard, Turgot, Willett.

2009 LIST of the Catalogues of the Libraries sold by auction by Messrs. Baker, Leigh and Sotheby, 1744-1816, 8vo. *hf. bd.* 3s 6d   1818

2010 SANTANDER (De la Serna) Catalogue des Livres de sa Bibliothèque, avec des notes bibliographiques et litteraires, 5 vols. 8vo. *with 5 folding plates of Water Marks, half calf,* 18s   Brux. 1803

2011 —— la même, 5 vols. 8vo. *a fine copy, in calf neat, from Miss Currer's library,* 20s   1803
This Library was sold off in Paris in 1809. "An extensive collection of interesting works. This catalogue, which is rarely seen in our own country, is well worth a place in any library."—DIBDIN'S BIBLIOMANIA, p. 127. "C'est un des meilleurs ouvrages en ce genre, les Notices bibliographiques sont très bien faites."—PEIGNOT.

2012 —— Dictionnaire Bibliographique choisi du siècle, avec un Essai sur l'Origine de l'Imprimerie et une notice des Imprimeurs, 3 vols. 8vo. *fine paper. sd.* 16s   Brux. 1805-7

2013 —— another copy, 3 vols. 8vo. *cf.* 18s   1805-7
Priced, 1840, Payne and Foss, £1. 7s; Roscoe's copy fetched £1. 15s.

2014 SANDERI. Bibliotheca Belgica Manuscripta; Elenchus Codicum MSS. in Belgii Bibliothecis adhuc latentium, 2 vols. in 1, sm. 4to. *vell.* 25s *Insulis*, 1641-44
2015 SAVAGE'S Practical Hints on Decorative Printing, atlas 4to. LARGE PAPER, *with all the numerous plates, coloured and plain, exhibiting all the varieties of Book Decorations, and Method of Printing in Colours, with Descriptive Letterpress, and titles in gold* (pub. at £11. 11s) *hf. bd.* red mor. uncut, 27s 1822
2016 SAVÉRIEN, Histoire des Philosophes modernes, 8 vols. 12mo. *frontispieces, and about* 50 PORTRAITS *by François, including Hobbes, Bacon, Locke, Erasmus, Bayle, Spinosa, Descartes, Newton, Leibnitz, Boyle, etc. old cf. gt.* 25s *Paris*, 1773
2017 SAXII, Historia literario-typographica MEDIOLANENSIS, cum Appendice Epistolarum et Catalogo codicum Mediolani impressorum 1465-1500, large folio, *vellum*, 30s *Med.* 1745
2018 SCHIADÆ et Kappii Arcana Bibl. Synod. Moscuensis sacra, *Lips.* 1724—Beyeri Arcana Bibl. Dresdens, *Dresd.* 1738—Eckhard de Cod. Græc. N. T. quo usus est Lutherus, 1722, etc. in 1 vol. 12mo. *hf. vellum*, 7s 6d 1722-46
2019 SCHELHORN, Amoenitates Literariæ, quibusvariæ observationes, scripta anecdota, et rariora opuscula exhibentur, 14 vols. in 4, 12mo. *vellum*, 21s *Franc. et Lips.* 1725-31
A repertory of curious information on the most recondite subjects.
2020 SCHELLER'S Bücherkunde der Sassisch-Niederdeutschen Sprache, 8vo. *bds.* 10s *Braunschweig*, 1826
2021 SCHRÖDER, Incunabula Artis Typographicæ in Suecia, 4to *sd.* 10s *Upsal.* 1842;
2022 SEEMILLER, Bibliothecæ Academ. Ingolstad. Incunabula Typographica, seu Libr₂ ante MD impressi, cum Indice, 4 parts in 2 vols. 4to. 9s *Ingolst.* 1787-9
2023 SMITH (J. *British Consul at Venice*). Paschalii Bibliotheca Smithiana, sm. 4to *halfbound*, 16s *Venetiis*, 1755
Particularly valuable on account of the Addenda, containing "Prefationes et Epistolæ voluminibus editis appositae ante annum MCCCC."
2024 SOTHEBY (S. Leigh) PRINCIPIA TYPOGRAPHICA: the BLOCK-BOOKS, or, Xylographic Delineations of Scripture History, issued in Holland, Flanders and Germany, during THE FIFTEENTH CENTURY, exemplified in connexion with the Origin of Printing, with Notices on the Paper-Marks of the period, 3 vols. impl. 4to. *illustrated with* 120 *large engravings, some in colours, in exact similitude of the very rare Original Block-Books, hf. mor. uncut*, £9. 9s 1858
Only 215 copies of this work, out of the 250 printed were sold. The remainder have been presented to Public Libraries and otherwise specially reserved, but not for sale.
2025 STEPHENS, Brittiska och Fransyska Handskrifterna uti Kongl. Biblioth. i Stockholm, 8vo. *sd.* 5s *Stockh.* 1848
2026 STEVENS' Historical Nuggets: Bibliotheca Americana, account of rare books relating to America, 2 vols. 12mo. *a Bookseller's Catalogue with prices, cloth,* £3. 3s 1862
2027 STIRLING, Books relating to Proverbs, Emblems, Apopthegms, Epitaphs, and Ana, 8vo. *an elegant Catalogue, privately printed, hf. mor.* 25s 1860
2027*STOCKMEYER und REBER, Beiträge zur BASLER Buchdruckergeschichte, herausg. von der Histor. Gesellschaft, roy. 8vo. *with facsimiles, cloth*, 7s 6d *Basel*, 1840
2028 TOULOUSE ACADEMY. Histoire et Memoires de l'Académie Royale des Sciences, Inscriptions, et Belles Lettres de Toulouse, 4 vols. 4to. *plates of Archæology, Natural History, etc. hf. bd.* 20s *Toulouse*, 1782-90
2029 TRÜBNER'S Bibliographical Guide to American Literature, during the last forty years, 8vo. *hf. bd.* 12s 1859
2030 TURGOT, Catalogue de sa Bibliothèque, 8vo. *the prices marked in MS. calf*, 5s *Paris*, 1744
2031 **Types.** BROGIOTTUS. Indice de Caratteri con l'inventori e nomi di essi, nella STAMPA VATICANA e Camerale, 8vo. *vellum*, 25s *Roma*, 1628
Containing Specimens of Types in the European and Oriental languages, of all descriptions, and including several pages of Musical notes.
2032 VANDERHAEGHEN, Bibliographie Gantoise, Recherches sur la vie et les travaux des Imprimeurs de Gand (1483-1850), dans les XVe, XVIe, XVIIe. et XVIIIe Siècles, Vols. I. II. III. large 8vo. *numerous facsimiles of Typographical Marks, sd.* 20s *Gand*, 1858-61
Only 250 copies were printed; the work will be finished in five vols. "C'est une étude sérieuse, raisonnée, approfondie, parsemée de faits piquants, d'aperçus ingénieux, de documents curieux, sur les publications de nos anciens typographes."
2033 VASSALLO (Dr. Cesare) Catalogo dei libri nella pubblica Biblioteca di MALTA, 4 vols. in 1, royal 8vo. *half calf*, 24s *Valletta*, 1843-44
A carefully classified Catalogue of an excellent and very useful library.

BIBLIOGRAPHY, LITERARY HISTORY, TOPOGRAPHY. 123

2034 VAN PRAET, Catalogue des livres imprimés sur vélin de la Bibliothéque du Roi, 5 vols. in 4, *Paris*, 1822; Tom. VI. Supplement, 1828—Catalogue des livres imprimés sur vélin qui se trouvent dans les bibliothéques tant publiques que particulières, pour servir de suite au catalogue des livres de la Bibliothèque du Roi, 3 vols. in 1, *Paris*, 1824; Tom. IV. Supplement, 1828—together 10 vols. in 7, 8vo. *calf*, £4. 5s *Paris*, 1822-28
Only 200 copies were printed. Priced, 1840, Jas. Bohn, £5. 15s 6d. "L'importance et la grande valeur des livres décrits, l'exactitude rigoreuse des descriptions, et les anecdotes intéressantes que le savant rédacteur a su y répandre, nous font regarder ce catalogue comme un des plus curieux qui existent."—*Brunet*.

2035 VATER's Litteratur der Grammatiken, Lexika, und Wörtersammlungen aller Sprachen, von Jülg, 8vo. *sd.* 5s 6d *Berlin*, 1847

2036 VERARD. Renouvier, Gravures en Bois dans les livres d'Anthoine Verard, 1485-1512, 8vo. *sd. only 200 printed*, 7s *Paris*, 1859

2037 VINCENT's Classified Catalogue of the Library of the ROYAL INSTITUTION, with Indexes of Authors and Subjects, and list of Historical Pamphlets, stout 8vo. 928 *pp. half bound*, 7s 1857

2038 WALCHII, Bibliotheca Theologica, cum litterariis adnotationibus, 4 vols. 8vo. *calf or vellum*, 16s *Jenæ*, 1757-65
"All who are conversant with sacred literature have borne testimony to the correctness and research of Walch."—*Horne*.

2039 WATT'S Bibliotheca Britannica, or General Index to British and Foreign Literature, including an account of upwards of 40,000 Authors, as well as the Works they have written, 2 parts (Authors, and Subjects) in 4 vols. 4to. (pub. at £11. 11s) *half calf*, £4. 10s; or, *in calf gilt*, £5. 5s *Edinb.* 1824
"Let me not forget to notice that wonderful work of Dr. Watt, both father and son FELL VICTIMS to their zeal in its completion; such a concentration of labour was hardly ever beheld; and it should never fail to be the LIBRARY COMPANION of all collectors."—*Dibdin*.

2040 WILLETT. Catalogue of the Library at Merly, sold at Sotheby's, December 1813, 8vo. *prices and purchasers' names added in MS. hf. bd.* 5s 1813

2041 WILSON. Bibles, Testaments, Psalms and other Books of the Holy Scriptures, in English, in the Collection of Lea Wilson, sm. 4to. *vellum, uncut, rare*, £10. *Privately printed*, 1845

2042 WOLFII (J. C.) Bibliotheca Hebræa, sive notitia Auctorum Hebraeorum cujuscunque ætatis, et Scriptorum, Hebraicè, vel conversorum, cum Gaffarelli Indice Codicum Cabbalistic. MSS. 4 vols. stout sm. 4to. *vel. rare*, £2.16s *Hamb.* 1715-33

2043 —— Monumenta Typographica, 2 vols. stout 12mo. *hf. vellum*, 6s; or, *russia neat*, 10s *Hamb.* 1740

2044 WOOD (Anthony a) ATHENÆ OXONIENSES: An exact History of all the Writers and Bishops who have had their Education in the University of Oxford; to which are added the Fasti, or Annals of the said University; new edition with additions, and a Continuation by Dr. Bliss, 4 vols. royal 4to. (pub. at £15. 15s in bds.) *calf gilt*, £10. 1813
"More care, attention, accuracy, and valuable enlargement, from an inexhaustible stock of materials (some of them contemporaneous) has rarely been witnessed, than in the editorial labours of Dr. Bliss."

2045 WRANGHAM (Archd.) Catalogue of the English Portion of his Library, 8vo. *cloth, only 70 copies printed, unpublished*, 12s *Malton*, 1826

2046 YOUNG (Sir C.) Catalogue of the Arundel Manuscripts in the College of Arms, roy. 8vo. *not published, bds.* 14s 1829

2047 ZAPF, Reisen in einige Klöster Schwabens, durch den Scharzwald, und in die Schweiz, 4to. 13 *plates of Facsimiles from MSS. etc. bds.* 7s 6d *Erlangen*, 1786

2047*—— Aelteste Buchdrukergeschichte Schwabens, 8vo. *fine paper, half bound*, 7s 6d *Ulm*, 1791

2048 ZEDLER'S Universal Lexicon aller Wissenschafften und Künste, welche bishero durch menschlichen Verstand und Witz erfunden worden, A-Z, 64 vols.—Supplement, A-Caq, 4 vols.—together 68 vols. folio, complete, *vellum neat, contents lettered on each volume, a good and clean copy throughout, a bargain*, £14.
Halle und Leipz. Zedler, 1732-54
This voluminous and highly valuable Encyclopædia, well known and appreciated in Germany, is but seldom found in this country. It is the grandest and most complete Encyclopædia ever published, and contains the entire range of human knowledge, the arts and sciences, discoveries and inventions, technical terms, &c. up to the time of its publication. Sir Frederick Madden, the Keeper of the MSS. British Museum, speaks in the highest terms of praise of this stupendous work. Mr. Cogswell, the eminent librarian of the Astor Library, New York, also extols its great utility.
To Public Libraries such a work is indispensable, since it forms the very Key to all Human Knowledge and to all Learning, previous to its publication.
"Of all Encyclopædias the best, containing the whole range of the Human Knowledge gathered with great care into one body."—*Meusel*.
"Ausim contendere, difficile esse, in uno volumine toto invenire errores tot, quot in Lexico illo Gallorum Encyclopædico (Diderot and D'Alembert, Encyclopédie), sunt in una pagina. Mille quæstiones incidere, quæ bre viter et sufficienter ex illo (Zedler) possint decidi. Et indicati sunt fontes, unde, si cujus intersit, peti possunt plura. Ad

hoc utilissimum est in Bibliotheca magna, ubi statim ad manus sunt libri indicati, et ubi plures fontes invenias. Neminem temere frustra demittet, quidquid ibi quæras ; et ubique relegat ad Fontes, quos habuerint auctores. Nempe ille materiam infinitam ex libris innumerabilibus redegit in ordinem. Est Index generalis omnium fere Librorum "— *Gesner, Erud. Univ.* tom. I. p. 515.

2049 ZELTNERI, Correctorum in Typographiis Eruditorum Centuria, 12mo. *containing lives of* MYLES COVERDALE, *P. Manuzio, Erasmus, Melancthon, Plantin, Servetus, H. Stephens, &c. calf gilt,* 9s   Norimb. 1716

2050 ZENO (Apostolo) Biblioteca di Fontanini, 2 vols. sm. 4to. *cloth,* 15s *Parma,* 1803
"The favourite among Italian Bibliographers."—*Dibdin.*

2051 LONDON CORPORATION Library, Alphabetical Index to the Catalogue of the, 8vo. *bds.* 3s 6d   1846

GAMES, SPORTS, EXERCISES.

2052 BLAINE'S ENCYCLOPÆDIA OF RURAL SPORTS, Complete Account, Historical, Practical, and Descriptive, of Hunting, Shooting, Fishing, Racing, &c. 8vo. *with above* 600 *woodcut illustrations, including* 20 *from Designs by* JOHN LEECH, (pub. at 42s) *new,* 35s

2053 LEHMANNI Tractatus de variis Ludendi generibus, sm. 4to. *hf. morocco, uncut,* 7s 6d   Budissæ, 1680

2054 BOOK OF SAINT ALBANS. The Book containing the treatises of Hawking, Hunting, Coat-Armour, Fishing, and Blasing of Arms [by Dame Juliana Berners], *cuts of arms, &c.* Reprinted in black and red type, after Wynkyn de Worde's Edition, of 1496, with an Introduction by Joseph Haslewood, Esq. folio, *calf,* £6. 6s   1810

2055 [COX], the Gentleman's Recreation : Hunting, Hawking, Fowling, Fishing, thick 8vo. *fifth edition, plates, calf,* 9s   1707

2056 —— the same, *sixth edition,* 8vo. *frontispiece and 3 folding plates, calf neat, the back symbolically tooled,* 10s   1721
This latter copy has the folding sheet of music, giving easy directions for Blowing the Horn, which is often wanting. The Appendix contains choice receipts for the cure of several maladies.

2057 STRUTT'S Sports and Pastimes of the People of England, from the earliest period to the present, new edition, with Index, by Hone, 8vo. 140 *curious woodcuts, after ancient paintings, bds.* 7s 6d   1830

2058 WEYDTWERGK. Vögel zufahen mit Raubvögeln, Netzen, etc. ; Wildt fahen mit Netzen, Stricken, etc. ; Fisch zufahen mit Netzen, Reusen, etc. und wie man alles darzu dienlich bereytten, auffzichen, halten uñ machen sol, jetz new gemehrt, *Franckfurt am Meyn,* 1531—TAPPII (Eberhardi) Waidwerck und Federspiel, von der Häbichen unnd Falcken, *Strassburg, Cammer Lander,* 1542 ; in 1 vol. smallest 4to. *curious woodcuts, bds. uncut, extremely rare,* £3. 3s   1531-42

2059 **ANGLING.** TAYLOR (Sam.) Angling in all its branches, *with list of Artificial Flies, etc.* 8vo. *bds.* 5s   1800

2060 WALTON AND COTTON'S COMPLETE ANGLER, with original Memoirs and Notes by Sir HARRIS NICOLAS, 2 vols. impl. 8vo. PICKERING'S SPLENDID EDITION, *with* 61 *plates, portraits and vignettes, by Stothard, Inskipp, etc.* (pub. at £10. 10s), *calf gilt,* £4. ; *or, a very fine copy, calf extra, gilt edges,* £5.   1836

2061 CAIRNIE'S Essay on Curling and Artificial Pond-Making, 8vo. *plates, a curious work on North British Sports, bds.* 5s   Glasgow, 1833

2062 FRANCK'S Northern Memoirs, with the contemplative and practical Angler, 1658, 8vo. *calf neat,* 6s   Edinb. 1821

2063 HERBERT, Frank Forester's Fish and Fishing of the United States and British North America, 8vo. *woodcuts of fishes,* (pub. at 16s) *cloth,* 7s 6d   1849

2064 **Bird Fancying.** The Bird-Fancier's Delight, observations and directions on the taking, breeding, and teaching of Singing Birds, 12mo. *calf,* 7s 6d   1714

2065 **CARDS.** BREITKOPF, Ursprung der Spielkarten, etc. Theil 1. : Die Spielkarten und das Leinenpapier, sm. 4to. 14 *plates, hf. calf,* 7s   Leipz. 1784

2066 MURNER (Thomæ) Logica Memorativa : Chartiludium Logice, sive totius dialectice memoria, sm. 4to. *numerous woodcuts, very rare,* £7. 7s   Argent. 1509
A singular work, in which Murner attempted to teach logic by means of a game of cards ; thereby acquiring the name of a sorcerer.— See SINGER'S HISTORY, pp 211, 216.

2067 SINGER'S (S. W.) Researches into the History of PLAYING CARDS ; with Illustrations of the Origin of Printing and Engraving on Wood, 4to. *with many singularly curious Engravings from early Prints, Paintings on Wood and Ivory, Packs of Cards, &c. illustrative of Mediaeval Art,* red MOROCCO *extra, gilt edges,* £5. 5s   1816
"It is seldom that the public have seen a more beautifully planned and executed work than the present. The

facsimile engravings upon wood cannot be surpassed. The entire impression is limited to 250 copies, so that, when the intrinsic work and extrinsic beauty be considered, the curious will not fail to secure copies whenever they make their appearance."—DIBDIN'S DECAMERON, vol. ii. p. 399.

2068 GEOGRAPHICAL Playing Cards, German or Dutch, 32 (wanting the titles) 5*s*
ca. 1700

2069 GERMAN PLAYING CARDS, 49, *twelve being Court Cards, spiritedly designed, representing the heroes of the Greek Revolution, with their names,* bound in a vol. 24mo. *brown morocco,* 12*s* *ca.* 1829

2070 JOLLIVET, l'excellent Jeu du Tricque-Trac, très doux esbat és nobles compagnies—Académie ou Maison des Jeux, Picquet, etc. *Paris,* 1604—2 vols. in 1, 12mo. *limp vellum, rare,* 28*s*

2071 POPISH PLOT. Twenty curiously designed Cards, illustrative of the Popish Plot, *among which are, Mr. Dugdale in Staffordshire reading letters; Argyle receiving a wound on his head; the Duke of Monmouth beheaded on Tower Hill; Pitts whipt through every town in Dorsetshire; etc. with inscriptions under,* RARE, 28*s* *circa* 1690

2072 Rouse's Doctrine of Chances, or the Theory of Gaming made easy, 8vo. *bd.* 5*s*
s. a. (? 1810)

2073 **CHESS.** ALEXANDRE, Encyclopédie des Echecs, roy. 4to. *text in French, German, Italian, and English, sd.* 6*s* *Paris,* 1837

2074 —— Collection des plus beaux Problemes d'Echecs, plus de 2000, roy. 8vo. *sd.* 7*s* 6*d* *Paris,* 1846

2075 AUTOMATON CHESS PLAYER. Inanimate Reason, by Windisch, 1784—Observations on the Automaton, 1819—Attempt to analyse the Automaton Chess Player, 1821—3 *Tracts on Kempelen's celebrated exhibition,* 8vo. *with plates,* 7*s* 6*d* 1784-1821

2076 BILGUER's Handbuch des Schachspiels, herausg. von Lasa, royal 8vo. *hf. morocco,* 5*s* *Berlin,* 1852

2077 CAXTON'S Game of Chess, a facsimile reproduction of the first work printed in England, from the copy in the British Museum, 4to. 23 *woodcuts, printed on antique paper, new in cloth,* ONLY 80 COPIES PRINTED, 20*s* 1862
Preceded by an introduction, a List of the works ascribed to Caxton, list of the places and persons where and by whom printing was practised in the time of Caxton, and a Synopsis of characters used.

2078 CESSOLE (Giacobo da), Opera nuova nella quale se insegna il regimento e costumi delli huomini et delle doñe etc. sopra il giuoco degli Scacchi, 12mo. 56 *leaves, red morocco extra,* £3. 3*s* *Vineggia, Bindoni e Pasini,* 1534
Questa traduzione è diversa da quella di Firenze, 1493.—HAYM.

2079 DAMIANO PORTUGHESE, Libro da imparare giocare a Scachi, et de belissimi Partiti, revisti et recorretti, con somma diligentia emendati da molti famosissimi Giocatori, in lingua Spagnola et Taliana, 16mo. *woodcut on title and numerous diagrams,* FINE COPY, RARE, *yellow morocco extra, by Clarke and Bedford,* £3. 16*s* *without date, (ca.* 1510
Fetched at the Townley sale, £4. 10*s*.

2080 FORBES' History of Chess, from its Invention in India to its Establishment in Europe, 8vo. *new in cloth,* 9*s* 6*d* 1860

2081 FRONDES CADUCÆ; The Buke of ye Chess, script. per manū Jhōis Sloane, 4to. black letter, *with rubric headings, hf. mor. uncut,* 18*s* *Auchinleck Press,* 1818
Edited by Sir Alexander Boswell, and only 40 copies printed for private circulation.

2082 Giuoco incomparabile degli Scacchi, opera d'autore Modenese, 3 parts in 1 vol. 8vo. *hf. calf, gilt top, uncut,* 7*s* 6*d* *Venezia,* 1812

2083 GIUOCHO DEGLI SCACCHI. Volgarizzamento del libro de' Costumi e degli offizii de' Nobili sopra il Giuoco degli Scacchi di J. da Cessole, tratto da un Codice Magliabechiano da Pietro Marocco, 8vo. *with very curious facsimiles, engraved after the Drawings of the Early MS. showing the Mediaeval Traders, Officials, etc. at their customary occupations, hf. morocco,* 6*s* *Milano,* 1829
Doubly interesting, as one of the earliest Chess-books, and as an attractive picture of Mediaeval Manners and Customs. Privately printed at the expense of the learned editor.

2084 HYDE, De Ludis Orientalibus: Historia Shahiludii, Nerdiludii, cum aliis Arabum, Pers. Ind. Chin. etc. Ludis, 3 vols. in 1, 12mo. *plates, vel. rare,* 10*s* *Oxon.* 1694

2085 PALAMEDE (Le) Revue mensuelle des ECHECS et autres Jeux, 7 vols. 8vo. *portraits and Chess Problems,* (pub. at 108 fr.) *sd.* 35*s* *Paris,* 1842-47

2086 TWISS' Miscellanies, 2 vols.—CHESS, 2 vols.—together 4 vols. in 2, 8vo. *plates, hf. calf, uniform,* 15*s* 1787-1805

2087 **COOKERY.** CARVING and SERVING: A Collection of Engravings of Birds, Fish, Fruit, &c. showing the Methods of carving and of sending Dishes to

Table, with fantastic Designs for Fruit and Pastry, 4to. *consisting of coats of arms and* 31 *plates, calf, very rare,* £2. 5s *(? Lyon, Arnoullet,* 1541)

"Livre fort excellent de Cuisine, très utile et profitable, contenant en soy la manière d'habiller touttes Viandes, avec la manière de servir Banquets et Festins, par le grand Escuyer de Cuisine, Lyon, Olivier Arnouillet, 1541. *Très rare et presque introuvable.* V. Catal. de Filheul, 1779, p. 107."—*MS. note.*

2088 SCAPPI (Bartolemeo) Opera, in sei libri, sm. 4to. *numerous curious illustrations of Kitchen utensils, Cooking operations, etc. vellum,* £2. 2s *Venetia,* 1598

The author of this very curious book was the "Cuoco secreto di Papa Pio V."

2089 **HORSEMANSHIP.** ALESANDRO (Giuseppe, Duca di Peschio Canciano) Pietra Paragone de' Cavalieri, con regole di Cavalcare, norme circa la professione di Spada, insegnamenti d'altri esercizii d'Armi e Cavalereschi, il modo di curare l'infermità de' Cavalli, etc. folio, 26 *portraits, and about* 100 *plates of Bridles, Bits, Equestrian exercises, Animals of the Chase, etc. vellum,* £2. 10s

"Ouvrage peu commun."—BRUNET. *Napoli,* 1711

2090 FIASCHI, la Singolar Maniera dell' imbrigliare, atteggiare e ferrare Cavalli, infermità de' Cavalli e rimedii, sm. 4to. *upwards of* 60 *curious Woodcuts, nearly all the full size of the page, representing Bridles, Bits, Horseshoes, and Horsetraining, with the Music of the movements, limp vell. rare,* 20s *Venezia,* 1598

2091 GREY (Thomas de) Compleat Horse-Man and expert Ferrier, sm. 4to. *equestrian portrait of James, Marquis Hamilton, calf,* 14s 1670

2092 NEWCASTLE (Duke of) Méthode et Invention nouvelle de dresser les Chevaux, royal folio, *frontispiece dated* 1658, *and* 42 *large and beautiful engravings after Diepenbeke of Horsemanship, portraits, etc. very slightly stained, old calf gilt,* £2. 1737

2092*SAUNIER (Gaspard de) L'ART DE LA CAVALERIE, ou la manière de devenir bon Ecuyer, par des règles à dresser les Chevaux pour le Manège, la Guerre, la Chasse, la Promenade, le Tournois, etc. folio, 27 *large plates of Equestrian Exercises, Bridles, etc. calf,* 25s *Paris,* 1756

2093 **HUNTING, FALCONRY,** etc. ARGOTE DE MOLINA, libro de la Monteria, que mando escrevir el Rey Don Alonso de Castillo y de Leon, ultimo deste nombre, folio, *numerous woodcuts of hunting, hf. calf,* £3. 5s *Sevilla,* 1582

Salva marks a copy of this book £4. 4s, 1824; Thorpe, £8. 18s 6d; 1830, Payne and Foss, £4. 4s; 1861, Ford's copy I sold for £5.

2094 CARCANO (Sforzino) tre libri degli Uccelli da Preda, con la vera cognitione dell' Arte de' Struccieri et il modo d'ammaestrare tutti gli Augelli di rapina, et un Trattato de' Cani, 12mo. *woodcut initials, limp vellum, rare,* 36s *Venetia,* 1586

2095 DICTIONNAIRE théorique et pratique de CHASSE et de Pesche, 2 vols. 12mo. *hf. bd. gilt,* 12s *Paris,* 1769

2096 FOUILLOUX (Jacques du) La Venerie, précédée de Notes Biographiques, et une Notice Bibliographique, roy. 8vo. *with about* 50 *curious woodcuts, facsimiles of those that appeared in the early editions, the Music of the Hunting Cries, and a Glossary of terms, calf gilt, gauffred edges,* 21s *Angers,* 1844

2097 FREEMAN and SALVIN'S FALCONRY, its claims, history and practice, with remarks on training the Otter and Cormorant, post 8vo. *woodcuts, cloth,* 9s 1859

2098 LATHAM (Symon), LATHAM'S FALCONRY, or the Faulcon's Lure and Cure, in two Books, 2 parts in 1 vol. smallest 4to. *curious woodcuts, green morocco extra, by Bedford, rare,* £3. 15s *Lond. Tho. Harper,* 1633

2099 RAIMONDI (Eugenio) delle Caccie libri IV, col libro vº della Villa, sm. 4to. *plates, limp vell. somewhat stained, very rare,* £2. 10s *(Napoli, Scoriggio,* 1626)

Copies of this edition, which is the best and most complete, are found to differ from each other. The above is of the rare issue in which there is no date on the title, and the last page is blank.

2100 SCHLEGEL (H.) et VERSTER VAN WULVERHORST, Traité de Fauconnerie, atlas folio, 92 pp. of text, *with* 17 *large plates of the noble Sport of Falconry, designed by the celebrated Sonderland and M. Wolf, consisting of frontispiece, two grand Views, two plates of Instruments and Implements,* COLOURED, *and* 12 *large splendidly* COLOURED *plates of Falcons,* (pub. at £8. 8s) in a portfolio, *a splendid work,* £5. *Leyden,* 1853

With a very carefully made CATALOGUE RAISONNÉ of all the works relating to Falconry in Greek, Latin, French, the Romance Dialects, Italian, Portuguese, German, Dutch, Spanish, Swedish, Russian, Japanese, Chinese, Arabic, Persian, Turkish.

2101 SEBRIGHT (Sir J. S.) On Hawking, 8vo. *inserted are Extracts from Strutt's Sports and Pastimes, MS. Poem on Hawking, plates, and a drawing, hf. bd.* 12s 1828

2102 SPORTSMAN'S CABINET, or a Delineation of the Dogs used in the Sports of the Field, and the Canine Race in general, 2 vols. 4to. 28 *engravings of every breed by* JOHN SCOTT, *vignettes by Bewick, &c. fine impressions,* (pub. at £7. 7s) *calf,* 12s 1803-4

2103 THUANUS. Il Falconiere di Tuano, con Ucellatura a Vischio di BARGEO, Latino ed Italiano da Bergantini, 4to. *printed on coarse tinted paper, vellum, scarce,* 18*s*   *Venezia,* 1735

2104 TURBERVILLE'S (George) THE NOBLE ART OF VENERIE OR HUNTING, collected for the pleasure of all Noblemen and Gentlemen, out of the best Authors, reduced into such termes as are used in this noble Realme, *slightly imperfect at the end*—Booke of Falconrie, or Hawking, for the delight of all Noblemen and Gentlemen, collected out of the best Authors, Italians and Frenchmen; and some English Practises concerning Falconrie, *no title*—2 vols. in 1, sm. 4to. black letter, *fine large woodcuts of animals and hunting groups, the latter curious for the costume; the margins cut close, and in some places slightly injured, old calf,* £2.   *London, Purfoot,* 1611
Priced, 1826, Baynes, vell. £6. 6*s*; 1828, Thorpe, mor. £4. 14*s* 6*d*; 1834-40, Thorpe, with other prints, mor. £4. 4*s*; 1840, Jas. Bohn, mor. £4. 14*s* 6*d.* Fetched, 1856, Bland's, mor. ext. £4. 12*s*; 1857, Utterson's, mor. £4. 16*s*; 1858, Haward's, mor. ext. £5 10*s.* The Booke of Hunting contains a good deal of Turberville's Poetry. The Booke of Falconrie has the Commendation of Hawking, and the Epilogue in verse.

2105 VYNER'S Notitia Venatica; a treatise on Fox Hunting, roy. 8vo. *lithographs, cloth,* 5*s*   1841

2106 WILLIAMSON'S (Capt. Thos.) ORIENTAL FIELD SPORTS, a complete description of the Wild Sports of the East, exhibiting the Natural History of the Elephant, Tiger, Wolf, &c., feathered Game, Fishes, and Serpents, 2 vols. roy. 4to. 40 *coloured plates,* (pub. at £10. 10*s*) *red mor. extra, gilt edges,* 32*s*   1819

2107 **Swimming.** DYGBEIUS (Everardns) de Arte Natandi, sm. 4to. *many curious woodcuts of Swimming and Diving, limp vellum,* 32*s*   *Lond.* 1587

2108 **Sword Exercise and Fencing:** HOPE'S New Method of Fencing, the Art of Fighting with Back-Sword, Sheering-Sword, Small Sword, and Sword and Pistol, sm. 4to. *calf,* 7*s*   *Edinb.* 1714

2109 —— Vindication of the Art of Self-Defence, with proposal for a Court of Honour, 12mo. *large plate, calf,* 5*s*   1729

2110 [PUTEO (Paris de)] Duello, libro de Re, Imperatori, Principi, Signori, Gentil'homini, continente Disfide, Cōcordie, Pace, Casi accadenti, etc. 12mo. *vellum,* 14*s*   *Venetia,* 1525

2111 RADA (F. L. de) Nobleza de la ESPADA, cuyo esplendor se espresa en tres libros, segun Ciencia, Arte y Esperiencia, 3 vols. in 2, folio, *engraved title-page, and more than* 60 *plates, fine copy, vellum,* £2. 16*s*   *Madrid,* 1705
RARE: not mentioned by Brunet nor Salva.
The most ample and elaborate work on fencing and sword play which has appeared.

2112 **Wrestling and Leaping.** PETTER (N. *Ringmeister*) der Künstliche Ringer, oder Anleitung zu der fürtrefflichen Ringe-Kunst, 4to. *upwards of* 70 *spirited engravings of every kind of Wrestling, engraved by Romeyn de Hooge, vellum,* 27*s*   *Amsterdam,* 1674

2113 TUCCARO, Trois Dialogues de l'Exercice de Sauter et Voltiger en l'Air, 4to. *with upwards of* 80 *curious woodcuts of Vaulting and Tumbling, fine copy, red morocco extra,* £2. 12*s*   *Paris,* 1599
"Livre assez rare; vend. 70 frs. Mac-Carthy."—BRUNET.

MUSIC AND SONGS.

2114 ANTIPHONARIUM et GRADUALE ROMANUM, juxta Brev. Concilii Trid. et Pii V. authoritate editum, cum Cantu Gregoriano accuratè notato, 2 vols. 8vo. *calf,* 20*s*   *Lut. Paris,* 1723-34

2115 BAINI, Memorie della Vita e delle Opere di PALESTRINA, Il Principe della Musica, 2 vols. 4to. *portrait, hf. calf,* 20*s*   *Roma,* 1828

2116 BASQUE SONGS. IZTUETA (De F.) Eus caldon anciña ancinaco ta are lendabibico etorquien Dantza on iritci pozcarri gaitzic gabecoen Soñu gogoangarriac beren itz neurtu edo VERSOAQUIN, sm. folio, *title, dedication, part of preface, and* 35 *pages of engraved music, with the words, the inner margins of which have been mended, hf. bd. extremely rare,* £2. 10*s*   *Donostian,* 1826

2117 —— *a neatly written Manuscript copy of the above, with all the preface, quite perfect throughout,* sm. folio, *hf. bd.* 25*s*

2118 ANCIENT CONCERTS, Word Books for the Years 1785 to 1845, *some wanting,* 37 vols. 12mo. *bound, the early volumes are very scarce,* 20*s*   1785-1845

2119 BURNEY, General History of Music from the earliest Ages, 4 vols. 4to. *plates after Bartolozzi, very fine copy in the original gilt russia, backs emblematically tooled,* £4. 15*s*   1776
" Dr. Burney gave dignity to the character of the musician by joining with it that of the scholar and philosopher."—SIR W. JONES.

2120 ESTWICK, Usefulness of Church Music, a sermon, sq. 8vo. 22 *pp. sd. very rare,*
7s 6d 1696
2121 EXIMENO, Origine e Regole della Musica, 4to. *hf. bd. uncut,* 6s Roma, 1774
2122 FERRIOL Y BOXERAUS, Reglas utiles para los aficionados a DANZAR, provechoso divertimiento de los que gustan tocar instrumentos, y polyticas advertencias a todo genero de personas, 18mo. *rude woodcuts of the figures and steps, with the Music, very fine copy in limp vellum, scarce,* £2. Capoa, 1745
Collation: Title; Dedication, 2 leaves; Carta de Aprobacion, 1 leaf; Prologo, Erratas, etc. 6 leaves; Reglas a danzar, pp. 1-264; Music and steps, 8 folding woodcut leaves; Text contd. pp. 281-294; Contradanza, wrongly paged, pp. 87-90; Tabla, pp. 299-302.
2123 FETIS, BIOGRAPHIE universelle des MUSICIENS et Bibliographie générale de la Musique, 8 vols. roy. 8vo. *with a historical introduction and several plates of Music, containing Ancient Melodies of all nations, etc. original edition, hf. bd.* £2.; or *hf. green mor. gilt top, uncut, contents lettered,* £2. 12s Brux. 1837-44
A very excellent work; both the Lives and Lists of Works of the Musicians are extensive and elaborate.
2124 FEUILLET et DEZAIS, Chorégraphie, ou l'Art de Décrire la Dance, par figures, etc. 1763—Recueils de Dances composées par Feuillet et Pecour, 1709—3 vols. in 1, sm. 4to. 247 *pages, engraved throughout, showing the figures of the Dances, with the Tunes, a scarce book, bds.* 18s Paris, 1709-63
2125 FUX (Jo. Jos.) Gradus ad Parnassum, Manuductio ad Compositionem, folio, *original and best edition, frontispiece, calf gilt,* 9s Viennæ Aust. 1725
2126 GEORGE, Crown Prince (now King) of HANOVER. Ideen über die Eigenschaften der Musik, *the Author's signature on title-page, an interesting autograph letter from Rev. R. W. Jelf (the Prince's former tutor) to Dr. Hawtrey inserted, blue morocco, gilt edges,* 7s 6d Hannover, 1839
2127 GERBERTUS (Mart.) de Cantu et Musica sacra, a primâ ecclesiæ ætate usque ad praesens tempus, 2 vols. 4to. *plates of facsimiles of old Music, calf gilt,* £2. 14s
San-Blas, 1774
Ouvrage recherché et tres-important pour l'histoire de la musique au moyen-âge.
2128 GERBERTI SCRIPTORES Ecclesiastici de MUSICA SACRA, ex variis Italiae, Galliae et Germaniae Codd. MSS. collecti, 3 vols. 4to. *calf, very neat,* £3. 10s
San-Blas, 1784
2129 GOETHE'S Lieder, Oden, Balladen und Romanzen, mit Musik von Reichardt, 4 parts in 1 vol. oblong 4to. *hf. morocco,* 12s Leipzig, 1809
2130 GUNN'S Historical Enquiry respecting the Harp in the Highlands, from the earliest times, 4to. *Large Paper, plates, russia gilt,* 10s 6d Edinb. 1807
2131 HAWKINS' (Sir John) General History of the Science and Practice of Music, 5 vols. 4to. *with* 51 *portraits, and numerous engravings of Musical Instruments, many pieces of old Music, &c. a beautiful copy in old English calf gilt,* £5. 5s 1776
A very esteemed work. Harward's copy fetched, 1858, at Sotheby's, £6. 7s 6d.
2132 JONES (Edw.) Musical and Poetical Relicks of the WELSH BARDS, and History of the Bards and Druids, with an account of their Music, Poetry and musical Instruments, *Welsh and English, with the Music,* impl. 4to. *fronts. bds.* 20s 1794
2133 ——— the Bardic Museum of primitive British literature, impl. 4to. *Welsh and English, with* 26 *engraved pp. of Music, frontispiece, hf. bd. rare,* 20s 1802
"Forming a second volume to the Musical and Poetical Relicks."

2134 HAGEN (F. H. von der) MINNESINGER, DEUTSCHE LIEDERDICHTER des XII, XIII und XIV Jahrhunderts, aus allen bekanntesten Handschriften und früheren Drucken gesammelt und berichtigt, 4 vols. in 3, 4to. *with the Music, bds.* 30s; or, FINE PAPER, *bds.* £2. Leipzig, 1838
2135 ——— the same, VELLUM PAPER, 4 vols. in 3, 4to. *calf extra, gilt edges,* £4. 10s
2136 HANDEL'S (G. F.) Works; Oratorios, Duettos, Cantatas, &c. Dr. Arnold's edition, IN FULL SCORE, 24 vols. folio, *beautiful portraits, a fine set in calf, gilt backs, contents lettered,* £7. 1789
CONTENTS:—Vol. 1, Athalia; Vol. 2, Theodora; Vol. 3, Messiah; Vol. 4, Te Deums; Vol. 5, Jubilate, Te Deum laudamus; Vol. 6, Sosarme, Water Music, &c.; Vol. 7, Semele; Vol. 8, Acis and Galatea; Vol. 9, Teseo; Vol. 10, Hercules; Vol. 11, Triumph of Time and Truth; Vol. 12, Deborah; Vol 13, Jephthah; Vol. 14, Esther and Susanna; Vol. 15, Letters and Sonatas; Vol. 16, Concertos; Vol. 17, Masque and Alexander Balus; Vol. 18, Trios, Cantatas, and La Resurrezione; Vol. 19, Anthems; Vol. 20, Anthems; Vol. 21, Agrippina; Vol. 22, L'Allegro Il Penseroso, ed il Moderato; Vol. 23, Concertos, &c. for the Organ, Hautboy, &c.; Vol. 24, Thirteen Chamber Duettos, and Twelve Cantatas.
2137 HARDIMAN'S Irish Minstrelsy, or Bardic Remains of Ireland, *in Irish,* with *English* poetical translations, and extensive notes, 2 vols. 8vo. *portrait of Carolan, hf. morocco,* £2. 2s 1831
2138 HEINICHEN, der General-Bass in der Composition, sm. 4to. 980 pp. *Music, hf. vellum,* 6s 6d Dresd. 1728

2139 HOGG'S JACOBITE RELICS OF SCOTLAND, being the Songs, Airs, and Legends of the Adherents of the House of Stuart, *with the Music*, BOTH SERIES, COMPLETE, 2 vols. 8vo. *bds.* £2. 10s; or, CALF EXTRA, *gilt edges, very scarce*, £2. 16s *Edinb.* 1819-21
2140 —— the same, FIRST SERIES, 1 vol. 8vo. *hf. calf gilt*, 25s 1819

The Second Series is not so scarce as this the FIRST. "James Hogg, miraculous James Hogg, with his bright fancies, and quaint thoughts, his genial humour, and his true-souled naturalness."—*Irish Quarterly.*

2141 JACOB's National Psalmody, harmonized, with chants, etc. impl. 8vo. 200 *pp. of engraved Music, bds.* 7s 6d ? 1830
2142 KIRCHERI (Athanasii) Musurgia sive Ars magna Consoni et Dissoni, quâ universa sonorum doctrina et musicæ scientia traditur, et admirandae vires Consoni et Dissoni in Mundo, Natura et omni pene facultate demonstrantur, 2 vols. in 1, very stout folio, *with frontispieces and upwards of* 30 *large plates and cuts of Music, Machinery, Mathematics, etc. vellum, very fine copy*, 32s *Romæ,* 1650

This work, says Dr. Burney, which undoubtedly contains many curious and amusing portions, is however disgraced by the author's credulity and ill-founded assertions. The author has been truly called "Vir immensae quidem, sed indigestae eruditionis." Yet with all its imperfections, the Musurgia contains much curious and useful information.

2143 LA BORDE, Essai sur la Musique, 4 vols. 4to. *upwards of* 200 *very fine* PLATES *of Musical Instruments and Performances, many engraved pages of Songs with the Music, and celebrated Airs of all Countries, superb copy in the original French red* MOROCCO *extra, gilt backs and sides, a beautiful copy*, £4. 10s
Paris, 1780

Priced, 1831, H. Bohn, £5. 15s.

2144 LAMBRANZI (G.) Deliciæ Theatrales: Nuova e Curiosa Scuola de' BALLI THEATRALI, sm. folio, *a series of fifty plates, illustrative of the Pantomimic Dances of different Nations, with the Postures, Music, &c.; also a frontispiece containing a portrait of Lambranzi*, FINE IMPRESSIONS, *fine copy, beautifully bound in red morocco, gilt edges by Petit, very scarce*, £3. 3s *Norimb.* 1716

Fetched, at Bernal's sale, £3. 10s.

2145 MACE (Tho.) Musick's Monument, or a Remembrancer of the best Practical Musick, both Divine and Civil, that has ever been known to have been in the World, sm. folio, *with a fine impression of the rare portrait by Faithorne, old calf rebacked, fine copy, from Miss Currer's library*, 32s 1676

Priced, 1856, £2. 2s. "A most delectable book."—BURNEY.

2146 MANFREDINI, Difesa della Musica Moderna, *Bologna,* 1788—Regole Armoniche *Venez.* 1797—Riccati sopra il Contrappunto, *Castel Franco,* 1762—in 1 vol. 8vo. *hf. bd.* 12s 1762-97
2147 MARTINI Storia della Musica, 3 vols. 4to. *folding plates and tables, very neat in calf, rare,* £2. 6s; or, *hf. morocco, uncut,* £2. 2s *Bologna,* 1757-81

A classical and very elaborate work.

2148 —— Esemplare o sia saggio practico di Contrappunto sopra il Canto Fermo, 2 vols. in 1, sm. folio, *vellum,* 18s *Bologna,* 1774-75
2149 MARX, Musikalische Kompositionslehre praktisch-theoretisch, 4 vols. 8vo. *sd.* 24s *Leipzig,* 1847-52
2150 MEIBOMIUS, Antiquae Musicae Auctores septem, et Martianus Capella de Musica, *Graece et Latine,* 2 vols. in 1, 4to. *folding diagrams,* £2. 10s *Amstel.* 1652
2151 PENNA (Lorenzo) li Primi Albori Musicali per li Principianti della Musica Figurata: Canto Figurato, Contrapunto e l'Organo ò Clavicembalo, sm. 4to. *portrait, large woodcut of the hand and scale at p.* 9, *bds. uncut,* 32s; or, *calf extra, gilt edges, the Duke of Marlborough's copy,* 36s *Bologna,* 1696

Best edition of this rare and curious work, containing the author's last additions. See Burney's History, iii. 539.

2152 PSALTER, or Psalms of David, printed as they are to be sung in Churches, sm. 4to. Black letter, *rubric initials, with the Music noted in black on red lines, each page surrounded by a woodcut border, bds. uncut,* 7s 6d 1843
2153 RANZ DE VACHES. Recueil de Ranz de Vaches et Chansons nationales de la Suisse, oblong 4to. *Preface, Index, frontispiece, and* 100 *pp. of engraved Music, the Songs chiefly in Swiss German patois, half calf neat,* 18s *Bern,* 1826
2154 RECUEIL de CANTATES, Françoises et Italiennes, Airs Serieux et à Boire, oblong 4to. *with the musical notes, calf, good sound copy,* 7s *Amst.* 1726
2155 RIMBAULT's Bibliotheca Madrigaliana; Musical and Poetical Works (1600-1700), in England, 8vo. *cloth,* 3s 1847

K

2156 STADEN. Operum Musicorum Posthumorum pars I. Cantus I. II. III. IV. Tenor I, II, Bassus et Bassus generalis, *five parts complete*, folio, *vellum, rare*, 25s
Norimb. 1643
A valuable and interesting memorial of old Instrumental music, of rich harmony and peculiar modulation. This work is not mentioned by Fétis.

2157 TARTINI, Principj dell' Armonia Musicale, sm. 4to. *sd.* 5s   *Padova*, 1767
2158 THOMSON, (W.) Orpheus Caledonius, or a Collection of the best Scotch Songs, set to Musick, folio, *engraved, fine copy in old calf, gilt edges*, 15s   ? 1725
2159 TIBALDI, Sonate a tre, due Violini e Violone ò Organo, 6 parts bound in 1 vol. 4to. *engraved titles, original gilt vellum*, 20s   *Roma*, 1704
I believe the above work to be the only example where engraved plates and the moveable type have been used conjointly.

2160 TOMMASEO, Canti Popolari Toscani, Corsi, Illirici, Greci, con opuscolo originale, 4 vols. 8vo. *plates, half calf neat*, 36s   *Venezia*, 1841-42
2161 UHLAND'S Alte Hoch- und Niederdeutsche Volkslieder, 2 vols. 8vo. *hf. calf, neat*, 18s   *Stutt. und Tübing.* 1844-45
2162 VILLOTEAU, Recherches sur l'analogie de la Musique, avec les arts qui ont pour objet l'imitation du langage, 2 vols. royal 8vo. *2 plates and 4 folding tables*, VELLUM PAPER, *fine copy, hf. mor. uncut, very scarce*, 32s   *Paris, Impr. Imp.* 1807
"Renouard purchased the whole of the remaining copies of this book in 1812, and destroyed all but 163 copies, including 33 *on vellum paper*, of which class this is the copy he reserved for himself. He justly observes that the book is not one which is susceptible of extensive sale, and that it is probably as little read by Musicians as Meibomius's curious collection of Antiquæ Musicæ Auctores."—*W. S. Singer's MS. Note*, 1840.

2163 VOCAL MUSIC, or the Songster's Companion, a new and choice collection of Songs, Cantatas, *with the Music*, 2 vols. 16mo. *old calf*, 7s 6d   ca. 1720
2164 WILLEM'S (J. F.) Oude Vlaemsche Liederen: Flemish Songs, *with the Music*, royal 8vo. *hf. morocco*, 12s   *Gent*, 1848
—— the same, impl. 8vo. *Large and thick Paper, half calf uncut, a handsome book*, 36s   1834
Only a few copies were printed on Thick paper.

2165 ZARLINO (G.) tutte l'Opere: Istitutioni e Dimostrationi Harmoniche; con Sopplimenti Musicali, 4 vols. in 2, folio, *cuts, fine copy in limp vellum, rare*, £2. 10s   *Venetia*, 1588-89
There appears to have been no title published to the second volume. Fetched, 1858, Puttick, £4. 10s.

2166 —— Istitutioni Harmoniche, *Venetia*, 1558—ARON, Toscanello in Musica, con la gionta, *Vineggia*, 1539—2 vols. in 1, sm. folio, *Music and Diagrams, vellum, gilt edges*, £2. 10s   1539-58

POLITICAL ECONOMY, JURISPRUDENCE, DIPLOMACY.

2167 ALDRIDGE's Goldsmith's Repository, on the Assaying of Metals, Rules for finding the value of Bullion, 8vo. *half calf, rare*, 10s   1789
2168 ASSIZE OF BREAD. Here beginneth the Booke, named the Assise of Breade, what it ought to weygh, after the price of a Quarter of Wheate. And also the Assyse of Ale, with all maner of Woode and Cole, Lath, Boord, and Tymber, and the Weyght of Butter and Cheese, very small 4to. 𝕭lack letter, *4 very curious woodcuts on the title, and 4 small woodcuts of loaves of bread on nearly every page, a very fine copy in* RED MOROCCO EXTRA *by Bedford*, VERY RARE, £4. 15s   *London, Hugh Jackson, s. a.* (? 1605)
Collation: Title, 1 leaf; The Ordinance of the Realme, and Assize of Breade, A. II to D. 4, in all 16 pages.

2169 POWEL (John) Assize of Bread and other Assizes of Weights and Measures, sm. 4to. *64 small curious woodcuts in squares, four at the head of each page in the table of weights, with quaint couplets over each, hf. bd. uncnt*, 25s   1714
2170 AZUNI, Dizionario della Giurisprudenza Mercantile, 4 vols. 4to. *hf. bd.* 7s 6d
Nizza, 1786-88
2171 BALDASSERONI, delle Assicurazioni Maritime, 5 vols. 4to. *sd.* 20s *Fir.* 1801-4
2172 BANKRUPT REGISTERS. The Merchant and Traders Magazine, and Perry's Bankrupt and Insolvent Gazette, from January 1826 to December 1855, with Indexes to each volume, 30 vols. 12mo. *hf. bd.* £5. 15s   1826-55
2173 PERRY'S Bankrupt and Insolvent Weekly Gazette, a complete Register of English, Scotch, and Irish Bankrupts, etc. from 1852 to 1858 inclusive, 7 vols. 4to. *half bd.* £2. 16s   1852-58
2174 BAUDRILLART, Bodin et son temps, théories politiques au XV. Siec. 8vo. *sd.* 5s
Paris, 1853

POLITICAL ECONOMY, JURISPRUDENCE. DIPLOMACY. 131

2175 BAVOUX, des Conflits ou Empiètement de l'Autorité administrative sur le pouvoir judiciaire, 2 vols. 4to. *sd. 7s 6d* *Paris*, 1828
2176 BENTHAM'S (Jeremy) WORKS, now first collected; under the superintendence of his executor, John Bowring, 22 parts forming 11 vols. large 8vo. *portrait*, (pub. at £9. 18s) *cloth*, £5. 5s 1838-43
2177 ——— the same, Vols. XIX-XXII, containing Memoirs of Bentham by Bowring, General Index, and Introduction by Burton, 4 vols. large 8vo. *portrait, cloth*, 15s 1842-43
2178 ——— Fragment on Government, with a Critique on Blackstone's Commentaries, 8vo. *calf neat*, 10s 1786
2179 ——— Plan of Parliamentary Reform, 8vo. *bds*. 5s 1817
2180 ——— Elements of the Art of Packing as applied to Special Juries, 8vo. *bds*.5s 1821
2181 ——— Introduction to the principles of Morals and Legislation, 2 vols. 8vo. *portrait, bds. 7s 6d* 1823
2182 ——— Traité de Législation, par Dumont, nouvelle édition, 8vo. (pub. at 10s) *cloth, new*, 8s 6d 1862
2183 BURTON's Benthamiana, select extracts, sm. 8vo. *portrait, cloth*, 6s 1843

"In Jeremy Bentham (says a great critic) the world has lost the great teacher and patriot of his time; the man who has exercised, and is exercising over the fortunes of mankind, the widest and most durable influence."
"A knowledge of Bentham's works (says another) is a key which unlocks all the mysteries of social as well as political government."
Quotations from the above edition in 22 vols. are not accepted as final by Bentham's disciples, but the separate works are considered authorities.

2184 BERROYER et LAURIERE, Bibliothèque des Coutumes, 4to. *calf*, 5s *Paris*, 1699
2185 CODE HENRY, (Loi Civile, Penale, Militaire, etc.) stout sm. 8vo. *half vellum*, 7s 6d *Cap Henry, (ca.* 1780)

France and the French are disguised under the name of Hayti and the Haytians.

2186 CODES (Les Six) avec la Charte constitutionelle et ses Lois, stout 8vo. *calf neat*, 6s *Paris*, 1828
2187 CODES (Les Neuf) la Charte nouvelle de 1830, etc. stout 12mo. *calf*, 5s *ib.* 1833
2188 CÓDIGO Penal Español, 8vo. *sd.* 5s *Madrid*, 1822
2189 CORPUS JURIS CIVILIS Romani, cum notis Gothofredi, Modii, et Van Leeuwen indicibus, historia et chronologia, 2 vols. in 1, stout roy. 4to. *calf*, 15s *Lipsiæ*, 1740
2190 CORPUS JURIS CIVILIS, recensuit Gebauer et Spangenberg, 2 vols. 1776-97
—JUSTINIANI Authenticæ seu Novellæ Constitutiones, Gr. et Lat. ab Hombergk et Spangenberg, 1797—3 vols. large 4to. *hf. bd. uncut*, 30s *Gott.* 1776-97
"Edition collationée sur les meilleurs textes, tant MSS. qu' imprimés."—*Brunet.*
2191 CORPUS JURIS CIVILIS, curâ Beck, 2 vols. 4to. *hf. bd.* 20s *Lipsiae*, 1829-31
2192 COMMERCIAL Relations of the United States with other Countries, reported by Edmund Flagg, 5 vols. 4to. *cloth*, £4. 1856-57

These volumes contain the reports of the Navigation and Commerce between the United States, South America, the East Indies, Africa, and the different countries of Europe, annually given to the President of the United States.

2193 COWELL's Interpreter, the true meaning of such Words as are mentioned in the Law Writers or Statutes, sq. 8vo. *old calf, 7s 6d* 1637
2194 CRAGII (Thomæ de Riccarton) Jus Feudale, operâ Jacobi Bailie, folio, *calf,* 7s 6d *Edin.* 1732
2195 DAVYS (Sr. John) primer Report des Cases en Ley en Ireland, fol. *calf*, 12s 1628
The first reports of Irish judgments ever made public.
2196 DOCTRINA Placitandi, ou l'art et science de Bon Pleading, *in Norman-English*, 2 vols. sm. 4to. *calf*, 5s *London*, 1677
2197 DOUBLEDAY's True Law of Population, 8vo. *cloth*, 3s 6d 1843
2198 DUPONT-WHITE, l'Individu et l'Etat, 8vo. *sd.* 5s *Paris*, 1857
2199 ECONOMISTICI ITALIANI: Scrittori classici Italiani di Economia politica, con notizie degli Autori; Parte Antica, 7 vols.—Parte Moderna, 41 vols.—Supplimento ed Indici, 2 vols.—together 50 vols. 8vo. *hf. cf.* £6. *Milano*, 1803-16
Priced, 1832, Thorpe, £15.
"The Italians have a great many Economical works, especially with reference to money. The best of these works were published in a chronological Series (the above), a publication which does honour to Italy."—*McCulloch.*

2200 EMERIGON, Traité des Assurances et des Contrats à la Grosse, 2 vols. 4to. *calf*, 10s *Marseille*, 1783
"A very valuable and important work."—*McCulloch.*
2201 FISHERIES. Method of curing White Herrings and all White Fish, 1750—Considerations upon the White Herring and Cod Fisheries, 1749—in 1 vol. 8vo. *hf. morocco, uncut*, RARE, 9s 1749-50

K 2

2202 Fraser's Review of the Domestic Fisheries of Great Britain and Ireland, 4to. map, (pub. at 18s) bds. 10s *Edinb.* 1818
2203 FLASSAN, Histoire générale et raisonnée de la Diplomatie Française, ou de la Politique de la France, 7 vols. 8vo. *calf gilt*, 24s *Paris*, 1811
2204 GIOJA, Nuovo Prospetto delle Scienze Economiche, Idee teoriche e pratiche d'Amministrazione privata e pubblica, 6 vols. 1815-17—Seconda Serie: Trattato del Merito e delle Ricompense, 2 vols.—together, 8 vols. 4to. *original edition, sd. uncut*, 30s *Milano*, 1815-19
2205 Heineccii Antiquitates Germanicae jurisprudentiam patriam illustrantes, 3 vols. 8vo. *half vellum*, 7s 6d *Hafniae*, 1772-73
2206 HIGGINS' Observations and Advices for the improvement of the Manufacture of Muscovado Sugar and Rum, 3 parts in 2 vols. 8vo. *plates of implements, half russia, extremely rare*, 18s *St. Jago de la Vega*, 1797-1801
Printed at a town, formerly the capital of Jamaica.
2207 HOUARD, Traités sur les Coutumes Anglo-Normandes, publiés en Angleterre, depuis le onzième, jusqu'au quatorzième siècle, 4 vols. 4to. *very fine copy, half bound morocco, gilt tops, uncut*, £3. *Rouen*, 1776
Containing a Dissertation in which the Laws made under the Heptarchy are abstracted and compared, Extracts from Domesday Book, Laws of Hen. I. &c with notes explanatory and illustrative of the Laws and customs of England and France. "A valuable work."
2208 Hugo (Gustave) Histoire du Droit Romain, traduit par Jourdan, large 8vo. *sd.* 6s *Brux.* 1840
2209 KELHAM'S Dictionary of the Norman or Old French Language; added are the Laws of William the Conqueror, 8vo. *half calf*, 21s; *calf extra*, 30s 1779
2210 Keller über Litis Contestation, und Urtheil nach Römischem Recht, 8vo. *calf*, 5s *Zürich*, 1827
2211 KOCH, Histoire des Traités de Paix entre les Puissances de l'Europe, depuis la Paix de Westphalie, ouvrage entièrement refoudu, augmenté, et continué par Schoell, 15 vols. 8vo. *sd*. 30s; or, *calf gilt*, £2. 16s *Paris*, 1817-18
Priced, 1841, £7. 17s 6d; 1845, £6. 10s 6d.
"This work is not only valuable for its rich collection of facts, recorded with clearness and precision; but it is also distinguished for the most scrupulous impartiality, and that philosophical order which presents every event in the most interesting point of view."—*Barbier*.
2212 Landrecht (Allgemeines) für die Preussischen Staaten, mit Register, 5 vols. 8vo. *half bound*, 10s *Berlin*, 1832
2213 LEVI'S Annals of British Legislation; being a classified and analysed summary of Public Bills, Statutes, etc. Vols. I. to VIII., 1856—*May*, 1861, 6 vols. *cloth*, and 12 parts, impl. 8vo. 30s 1856-61
MACCULLOCH (J. R.) the Works of:
2214 Observations on the Duty on Sea-Borne Coal, and on the Peculiar Duties and Charges on Coal in the Port of London, 8vo. 7s 6d *London*, 1830
This tract preceded, and we believe promoted, the repeal of the duty on sea-borne coal.
2215 ———— Dictionary, Practical, Theoretical, and Historical, of Commerce, and Commercial Navigation, *maps and plans*, thick 8vo. new edition, with Supplement, corrected throughout and enlarged, (pub. at 50s) *cloth*, £2. 2s 1859
"Without exaggeration, one of the most wonderful compilations of the age. The power of continuous labour, the wide range of inquiry, and the power of artistical finish brought into play by this work, are probably unrivalled in the history of litterature."—Spectator.
2216 ———— Dictionary, Geographical, Statistical, and Historical, of the various Countries, places, and natural objects in the world, 2 vols. 8vo. *new edition, with Supplement*, (pub. at £3. 3s) 6 *large maps, cloth*, £2. 12s 6d 1854
2217 ———— Statistical Account of the British Empire, 2 vols. 8vo. (pub at £2. 2s) *cloth*, 25s 1847
2218 ———— Principles of Political Economy, 8vo. 10s 1825
2219 ———— Literature of Political Economy, a classified Catalogue with historical, critical, and biographical notices, 8vo. *cloth*, 7s 6d 1845
2220 ———— Treatise on the Principles and practical influence of Taxation and the Funding System, 8vo. 7s 6d 1845
2221 ———— Taxation, 8vo. *cloth, new*, *Edinb.* 1863
Orders received for this, the latest work of the great Political Economist. See also "Overstone," "Ricardo," and "Adam Smith."
2222 MARTENS, Recueil de Traitée d'Alliance, de Paix, de Commerce, de limites, et plusieurs autres actes servant a la connoissance des relations étrangères, 1761 à 1808, 8 vols. Gottingue, 1817-35—Nouveau Recueil, 1808 à 1835, 12 vols. in 14, Gottingue, 1817-37—Table generale, 1re partie, 1 vol. Gottingue, 1837—together 23 vols. 8vo. *calf*, £2. 12s 1817-37
Completed for about £8.
2223 MARTENS Précis du Droit des Gens moderne de l'Europe, 8vo. *hf. calf.* 5s *Gott.* 1821

POLITICAL ECONOMY, JURISPRUDENCE, DIPLOMACY. 133

2224 MEYER, Esprit, Origine et Progrès des Institutions Judiciaires de l'Europe, 6 vols. 8vo. *calf neat, 20s* *La Haye*, 1819
2225 MONTBRION, Dictionnaire du Commerce, de la Banque, et des Manufactures, 2 vols. royal 8vo. 1956 *pp. double cols. calf gilt*, 14*s* *Paris*, 1847
2226 NEUMANN, Recueil des Traités et Conventions conclus par l'AUTRICHE avec les puissances étrangéres, depuis 1763 jusqu' à nos jours, 6 vols. 8vo. *calf gilt*, £2. *Leipzig*, 1855-59
2227 NEISON's Contributions to Vital Statistics, 4to. *cloth*, 6*s* 1845
2228 OELRICH's volstaendige Sammlung alter und neuer Gesez-Bücher der kaiserlichen und des heil.-römischen reichsfreien Stadt Bremen, 4to. *calf*, 10*s* 1771
2228*OVERSTONE (Lord) Tracts and other publications on METALLIC and PAPER CURRENCY (edited by J. R. MCCULLOCH), stout 8vo. *cloth, presentation copy to Dr. Hawtrey, with the author's autograph, rare*, £2. 10*s* 1857
2229 PASTORET (le Marquis de) Histoire de la Législation, 11 vols. 8vo. *calf gilt*, £2. 10*s* *Paris*, 1817-37
A very learned work. Contents: 1. Legislation des Assyriens et Babyloniens, 2. des Egyptiens, 3, 4, des Hébreux, 5-9. Legislation Grecque, 10 des Carthaginois, 11. des Siciliens.
2230 PIANTANIDA, della Giurisprudenza Marittima-Commerciale, antica e moderna, 4 vols. 4to. *sewed*, 16*s* *Milano*, 1806
2231 PREVOST de St. Lucien, Moyens d'extirper l'Usure, 12mo. *calf*, 5*s* *Paris*, 1775
2232 PUFENDORF, of the Law of Nature and Nations, in English by Kennett, with Barbeyrac's notes, edited by Carew, folio, *calf*, 10*s* 1729
2233 PULLEIN, the Culture of Silk, its Practice and Improvement, 8vo. *cf. nt.* 5*s* 1758
2234 RASTELL (John) Abbreviamentum librorum legum Anglorum, sm. folio, Black letter, *calf*, 32*s* 1517
A very scarce Law Book in the Norman or Old French language. It is in 3 parts, in the first of which sheets D, F, and K have 6 leaves, P, 4, the others 8; IInd part, Sheet Q has 10 leaves.
2235 RICARDO's Works, with a notice of his Life and Writings by McCulloch, 8vo. *cloth*, 8*s* 6*d* 1846
2236 ROTTECK und Welcker's Staats-Lexikon, 12 vols. 8vo. *calf extra, fine copy*, £4. 5*s* A valuable Encyclopædia of Political Sciences. *Altona*, 1845-48
2237 SADLER's Law of Population, Vols. I.-II. *all published*, 8vo. (pub. at 30*s*) *bds.* 10*s* 1830
2238 SAINT VINCENT, and its dependencies, Laws, folio, *bd.* 5*s* *Bridgenorth*, 1811
2238*SANDARS, the Institutes of JUSTINIAN, Latin, with English translation, introduction and notes, 8vo. 606 pp. (pub. at 15*s*) *new in cloth*, 12*s* 6*d* 1858
2239 SAVIGNY, das Recht des Besitzes, 8vo. *hf. calf neat*, 5*s* *Giessen*, 1837
2240 SCHERER, Histoire du Commerce de toutes les Nations, traduite par Richelot et Vogel, 2 vols. 8vo. (pub. at 18 fr.) *sd.* 7*s* 6*d* 1857
2241 SENCKENBERG, Corpus Juris Feudalis Germanici, von Eisenhart, 8vo. *portrait, hf. bound*, 5*s* *Halle*, 1772
2242 SENEBIER, Traité des Changes et des Arbitrages, 4to. *sd.* 5*s* *Lausanne*, 1797
2243 SMITH'S (Adam) Inquiry into the nature and causes of the WEALTH OF NATIONS, with Life, etc. by J. R. MCCULLOCH, 4 vols. 8vo. BEST EDITION, *portrait, cloth*, 32*s*; or, *calf gilt*, £2. 10*s* *Edinb.* 1828
2244 SMITH (John) Chronicon Rusticum-Commerciale; or Memoirs of Wool, etc. 2 vols. 8vo. *first edition, old calf, fine clean copy*, 10*s* 1747
One of the most valuable works on the history of any branch of trade.—MCCULLOCH.
2245 SOUTH SEA COMPANY. Particular and Inventory of the Estate of Sir John Fellows, late Sub-Governor, and the other Directors, and how disposed of, 2 vols. folio, *old calf, rare*, 15*s* 1721
2246 SPAIN. Considerations sur les Finances d' Espagne, 18mo. *calf*, 5*s* *Dresde*, 1755
2247 SYMONDS' Papers on the Organization of the Civil Service, 8vo. *cloth, privately printed*, 7*s* 6*d* 1848
2248 TARGA, sopra la Contrattazione Marittima, 4to. *hf. bd.* 5*s* *Trieste*, 1805
2249 TOOKE (Thos.) History of Prices, and of the State of the Circulation, from 1793 to 1856 inclusive, 6 vols. 8vo. *cloth, very rare*, £6. 6*s* 1838-56
2250 —— the same, Vols. I, II, IV. 1793-1837, 1839-47, 3 vols. 8vo. *cloth*, £2. 18*s* 1838-48

Tooke's principles, confirmed as they have been by the events of the last three years, are steadily making way with reflecting men, and will probably, at no distant period, be universally regarded as forming the basis of all true monetary science."—MORNING CHRONICLE, 1847.

2251 TRAITÉS Publics de la Royale Maison de SAVOIE, avec les puissances étrangères depuis la Paix de Chateau-Cambresis, publiés par ordre du Roi, 5 vols. royal 4to. *hf. bound, uncut*, £2. *Turin*, 1836
2252 VATTEL, le Droit des Gens, 2 vols. 8vo. *sd.* 5*s* *Paris*, 1820

2253 WARNKÖNIG, Commentarii Juris Romani privati, 3 vols. 8vo. *half calf,* 15s
Leodii, 1825-29
2254 WHEATON, Histoire des progrès du Droit des Gens en Europe, large 8vo. *cloth, uncut,* 6s
Leipzig, 1841
2255 TRACTS, viz: STOCK'S Account of what passed at Killala in the summer of 1798—Authentic detail of an affair of Honour between W. Todd Jones, Esq. and Sir R. Musgrave—PAINE (T.) on the Cure of the Yellow Fever, and the means of preventing it, *scarce, Lond. Clio Rickman,* 1807—Manuscrit venu de Ste. Helene d'une maniere inconnue, 1817, *supposed to have been written by Bonaparte*—COPLESTON (Dr.) Letters to Sir R. Peel on the pernicious effects of a variable Standard of Value, *Oxford,* 1819—REMONSTRANCE to Murray respecting a recent publication, viz. Cain, a Mystery ; others on Coin, Bullion, and Banking, by HUSKISSON, MUSHET, RICARDO, TORRENS, TOOKE, LOYD, PALMER, etc. included in this Collection ; *neatly and uniformly bound in* 11 *vols. hf. calf gilt,* 36s
1798-1848

2256 POLITICAL ECONOMY TRACTS: a Collection of 31 scarce and valuable Tracts on Money, Lotteries, Taxes, Trade, Usury, etc. 8vo. and 4to. 21s
INCLUDING : 1694-1766

On Raising Money	? 1690	Ways and Means	1695	Collett's Tables	1731
Condition of France	1692	Angliæ Tutamen	1695	Duties of the Nation	1744
Jones's Vindication against the Athenian Mercury	1692	Considerations for Trade	1695	The Duties on Tea	1714
		Dissertations des Lotteries	1700	Reduction of Land-tax	1749
Advantages and Losses of England	1693	Considerations against the Continuance of the Bank	s. a.	The British Sugar-Colony Trade	1759
				Pinto, la Circulation et le Crédit	1771
Nevil Payne's letter, etc.	1693	Case of the Turkey Company and Italian Merchants	1720	Sir J. Graham's Coin and Currency	1827
History of the Taxes of France	1694				
Million-Act, Lottery-Act, and Bank	1693	Asgill on Gold and Silver	1720	And other valuable Tracts.	
		The National Debt	1727		

2257 **INDIAN LAW.** BEAUFORT'S Digest of the Criminal Law of Fort William, stout sm. 4to. *hf. bd.* 7s 6d
Calcutta, 1850
2258 BRIDGNELL'S Indian Commercial Tables of Weights, Measures, and Money, roy. 8vo. *hf. bd.* 10s
Calcutta, 1852
2259 COLEBROOKE'S Digest of the Regulations and Laws enacted for the Civil Government of the Presidency of BENGAL, in alphabetical order, with SUPPLEMENT containing a Collection of the Regulations anterior to 1793, 3 stout vols. folio, *calf, very scarce,* £3. 12s
Calcutta, 1807
2260 —— Two Treatises on the Hindu Law of Inheritance, 4to. *bd.* 12s *ib.* 1810
2261 HARINGTON, Analysis of the Laws and Regulations for the Civil Government of the British territories under the Presidency of Bengal, complete in 3 vols. stout folio, *calf, the* 1st *vol. in bds.* 30s
Calcutta, 1805-17
2262 HEDAYA, or Guide, a Commentary on the Mussulman Laws, translated by Chas. HAMILTON, Vols. 1, 2, 3, 4to. *bds.* 20s
1791
2263 MACNAGHTEN'S Considerations on the Hindu Law, as it is current in Bengal, 4to. *bds. scarce,* £2. 10s; or, *half russia,* £2. 12s 6d
Serampore, 1824
2264 —— Principles and precedents of Moohummudan Law (including the tenets of the Schia sectaries, etc.) *hf. russia,* £2. 10s
Calcutta, 1825
2265 MARSHMAN'S Guide to the Civil Law of the Presidency of Fort William, stout 4to. *hf. calf,* 6s
Serampore, 1848
2266 MISHCAT-UL-MASABIH, a collection of most authentic traditions regarding the actions and sayings of Mohammed, 2 vols. 4to. *hf. russia,* £2. 5s *Calc.* 1809
2267 MORLEY'S Analytical Digest of all the Reported Cases decided in the Supreme Courts of Judicature in India, in the Courts of the E. I. Company, and on Appeal from India by Her Majesty in Council, 2 vols. royal 8vo. (pub. at £8. 8s) *calf neat,* £3. 10s
1849-50
2268 —— Analytical Digest of Indian Cases, *new series,* vol. I. royal 8vo. *presentation copy,* (pub. at 50s) *cloth,* 30s
1852
2269 STRANGE'S Elements of Hindu Law, referable to Bitish judicature in India, 2 vols. royal 8vo. 20s
1825

2270 **Sudder Courts:**
A. REPORTS of Civil Causes adjudged by the Court of Sudur Udalut, for the Presidency of Bombay, 1800-24, 2 vols. folio, *hf. bd.* 36s
Bombay, 1824-5
B. CIRCULAR Orders of the Sudder Dewanny Adawlut, 1795-1852, with Index, by Carrau, 8vo. *hf. calf,* 7s 6d
Calcutta, 1853
C. CONSTRUCTIONS of the Regulations and Acts of the Sudder Dewanny Adawlut, 1798-1847, with Index, by Buckland, stout 8vo. *hf. calf,* 7s 6d *ib.* 1855

D. Decisions and Rules of Practice, 1792-1855, by Carrau, 2 vols. in 1, 8vo. *hf. calf*,
7*s* 6*d* *ib.* 1856
E. Index to the Select Reports, 8vo. *hf. calf*, 7*s* 6*d* *ib.* 1849
F. Reports of Summary Cases in the Presidency Sudder-Court, 1834-53, with Index,
by Carrau, 8vo. *hf. calf*, 7*s* 6*d* *ib.* 1853

MILITARY SCIENCES.

2271 AIDE-MÉMOIRE to the Military Sciences, framed from contributions by Officers and others connected with the services, originally edited by the Corps of Royal Engineers, second edition, enlarged, 3 vols. roy. 8vo. *nearly 350 engravings and several hundred woodcuts*, (pub. at £4. 10*s*) *new in cloth*, £3 15*s* 1862
Among the contributors to this important work are the most distinguished officers in the service, including Sir Henry James, Sir John Burgoyne, etc.
2272 Ambert, Esquisses historiques de l'Armée Francaise, impl. 8vo. *coloured plates, cloth,* 5*s* *Bruxelles*, 1841
2273 Armandi, Histoire militaire des Elephants, 8vo. *sd.* 4*s* *Paris*, 1843
2274 Barriffe's Military Discipline, or the Young Artilleryman, on the Musket and Pike, the Swedish Brigade, etc. sm. 4to. *portraits and plans, calf*, 12*s* 1643
2275 Beauchamp, Histoire de la Compagne de 1814, et de la Restauration, 2 vols. 8vo. *calf neat,* 5*s* *Paris*, 1815
2276 Beaujour, Voyage militaire dans l'Empire Othoman, 2 vols. 8vo. *without the maps, sd.* 5*s* *Paris*, 1829
2277 BEGBIE'S History of the Madras Artillery, and the East India Company's power in Southern India, 2 vols.—Migout on Gun Carriages; De Brack's Advance Posts of Light Cavalry, 2 vols.—4 vols. 8vo. *plates, calf,* 20*s*
Madras, 1842-53
2278 BOURRIENNE, Memoires sur Nàpoleon, le Directoire, le Consulat, l'Empire, la Restauration, 10 vols. 8vo. *hf. calf*, 12*s* *Paris*, 1829
2279 (BOUSMARD) Essai général de Fortification et de l'Attaque et Défense des places, 3 vols. 4to. *calf*, with folio Atlas *of 57 plates, hf. bd.* 12*s* *Berlin*, 1797-99
2280 ——— le Supplément, "Tentatives à faire pour perfectionneer de l'Art de Fortifier des Places," 1 vol. 4to. *calf*, 7*s* 6*d* *Paris*, 1804
2281 BRADDOCK'S Memoir on Gunpowder, with the principles of its Manufacture and Proof, 4to. *hf. bd. rare,* 20*s* *Madras*, 1829
2282 BULLETINS of the Campaigns, 1793-1815 (*no vol. was pub. for* 1802) 22 vols.—Bulletins of State Intelligence, 1816-17, 1823, 1827-32, 9 vols.; together 31 vols. 12mo. *hf. bd.* £2. 16*s* 1793-1832
2283 Chesney's Observations on the past and present stste of Fire-Arms, 8vo. (pub. at 12*s* 6*d*) *cloth,* 5*s* 1852
2284 Code Militaire, ou compilation des Ordonnances concernant les gens de guerre, 3 vols. 12mo. *old red morocco,* 10*s* *Paris*, 1728
2285 Connolly's History of the Corps of Royal Sappers and Miners, 2 vols. 8vo. 17 *coloured lithographs, hf. calf gilt,* 16*s* 1855
2286 Creasy's Fifteen Decisive Battles of the World, from Marathon to Waterloo, 8vo. *eighth edition, cloth,* 10*s* 1858
2287 Daniel, Histoire de la Milice Françoise, 2 vols. 4to. *with* 70 *plates of Arms, Armour, Warfare, etc. bd.* 10*s* *Amst.* 1724
2288 D'Antoni's Treatises on Gunpowder, Fire-Arms, and Artillery, 8vo. 9 *large plates to the Artillery, calf,* 9*s* 1789
2289 DELAISTRE, Science de l'Ingénieur, des Chemins, des Ponts, des Canaux et des Aqueducs, 3 vols. 4to. 56 *plates, hf. calf,* 20*s* *Lyon*, 1825
2290 De Luc, Passage des Alpes par Annibal, 8vo. *no map, hf. bd.* 5*s* *Genève*, 1818
2291 DRINKWATER'S History of the Siege of Gibraltar, with an account of that garrison, 4to. *numerous plans and plates, russia neat,* 18*s* 1786
2292 DUMONT et ROUSSET, Histoire Militaire du Prince Eugene de Savoye, du Prince et Duc de Marlborough, et du Prince de Nassau-Frise, Vols. I. and II. large folio, *numerous fine plates of Battles, Sieges, etc. old calf gilt,* 25*s*
La Haye, 1729
2293 Eguiluz, Milicia, Discurso y Regla Militar, sm. 4to. *diagrams, limp vellum,* 7*s* 6*d* *Madrid*, 1592
2294 Eugene de Savoye, Histoire de, 5 vols. 12mo. *plans, half red morocco,* 9*s*
Vienne, 1790

2295 EULER'S True Principles of Gunnery, translated, with explanations, by Brown, 4to. *Large Paper, plates, old red morocco, gilt edges,* 18s   1777
2296 **FIREWORKS** (Recreative and Military). Simienowicz, the Great Art of Artillery, translated by Shelvocke, folio, *plates of Fireworks and Fire-Arms, calf,* 20s   1729
2297 BIRINGUCCIO, Pirotechnia, nella quale si tratta delle Minere, e di quanto s'appartiene all' Arte della Fusione, ò Getto di Metalli, far Campane, Artegliere, Fuochi artificiati, &c. thick 16mo. *curious woodcuts, fine copy in vellum,* 12s
       Venetia, 1559
2298 FORTIFICATIONS de France. Plans (89) in Colours, of Fortified Towns and Cities in France and its Colonies, neatly executed, sm. 8vo. *old French red morocco, dentelle borders, gilt edges,* 21s   (1740)
2299 FOY (Général) Histoire de la Guerre de la Peninsule, sous Napoléon, 4 vols. 8vo. *folding table and facsimiles, hf. calf neat,* 10s   Paris, 1827
2300 Frederic le Grand: Tactique Prussienne, ou Systéme Militaire de la Prusse, 93 *plates and plans, calf gilt,* 7s   Paris, 1789
2301 Guibert, Oeuvres Militaires, 5 vols. 8vo. *numerous plans, calf, plundered from a French chateau in the march from Waterloo to Paris,* 12s   Paris, 1803
2302 —— Essai général de Tactique, 4to. *large plates, hf. bd. uncut,* 6s   1773
2303 Guischardt, Mémoires militaires sur les Grecs et les Romains, 2 vols. 4to. *numerous plates and plans of the great battles, calf neat,* 7s 6d   La Haye, 1758
2304 Historical Record of the East India Company's First Madras European Regiment, 8vo. *plates, cloth,* 8s   1843
2305 JOHNSTON (Keith) Plans of Countries, Battles, Sieges, and Sea Fights, illustrative of the History of Europe, from the French Revolution to Waterloo, with Vocabulary, crown 4to. 109 *plates.* (pub. at 31s 6d) new, 26s 6d   1862
2306 —— another edition, demy 4to. (pub. at £3. 3s) new, £2. 12s 6d   1862
2307 JOMINI, Histoire critique et militaire des Guerres de Frédéric II. 3 vols. 8vo. *calf neat,* 7s 6d   Paris, 1818
2308 —— Histoire critique et militaire des Guerres de la Revolution, 10 vols. 8vo. *no maps, bds.* 20s   1820-22
2309 Labaume, Relation de la Campagne de Russie, 8vo. *plates, cf.* 3s 6d   Paris, 1815
2310 McCLELLAN (*the Federal General*) Report of the Sec. of State communicating the report of Capt. McClellan, one of the officers sent to the Seat of War in Europe, 1855-56, 4to. *large plan of Sevastopol and several plates, cloth,* 15s
       Washington, 1857
2311 Macdougal's Campaigns of Hannibal, arranged and critically considered, sm. 8vo. *cloth,* 5s   1858
2312 —— the Theory of War, illustrated by examples, 12mo. *with description of the great battles of Napoleon, Moreau, Marlborough, Turenne, Condé, plates, cloth,* 7s 6d   1862
2313 MACHIAVEL (Nicholas) The Arte of Warre; set forth in English by Peter Withorne, sq. 12mo. *elaborate woodcut title and two woodcuts,* 𝕭lack letter *with neat MS. notes, in the autograph of G. Harvey, a very fine large copy in calf extra, by Bedford,* £2. 10s   1573
2314 MADRAS ARTILLERY. Repository Exercise, compiled by Colonel Frith—Proceedings of the Artillery Select Committee, 1824-32, 2 vols. folio, *lithographed, with* 125 *plates, containing an infinite number of fine sketches to illustrate valuable experiments and improvements in Artillery, half bd. not uniform,* 30s   Fort St. George, 1830-32
2315 MALLET On the Physical Conditions in the Construction of Artillery, the materials employed, and causes of the destruction of Cannon in service, royal 4to. 9 *large plates,* (pub. at 30s) *cloth,* 7s 6d   1856

A very important work, explaining the varied and perplexing forms of molecular structure of cast-iron wrought-iron and steel—it must prove valuable in practice not only to the Gun-Founder and Forgeman, but to the Civil and Mechanical Engineer generally, and to every scientific worker in metals.

2316 Mauvillon sur l'influence de la Poudre à Canon, 8vo. *hf. bd.* 6s   Dessau, 1782
2317 Moorsom's Historical Record of the 52nd Regiment (Oxfordshire Light Infantry), from 1755 to 1858, roy. 8vo. *portraits, coloured plates and plans, cloth,* 18s 1860
2318 Müffling, Aus meinem Leben, 8vo. *hf. cf. neat,* 5s   Berlin, 1851
2319 Muller's Elements of Mathematics: Attack and Defence of Fortifyed places; Practical Fortification; Treatise of Artillery—6 vols. 8vo. *plans and plates, calf,* 9s   1747-65

MILITARY SCIENCES.

2320 NAPIER'S History of the War in the Peninsula and in the South of France, 1807-17, 6 vols. 8vo. *numerous plates, calf gilt*, £4. 10s   1835-40
2321 NAPOLEON III., Etudes sur l'Artillerie, 4to. *sd. 5s*   *Paris*, 1846
2521*NETHERLANDS HISTORIAN (The) an exact relation of the late Warrs between Great Britain and the French King against the States Generall, 1671-74, stout 16mo. *numerous portraits and plans, calf, rare,* 10s   *Amst.* 1675
2322 NOTICE historique des Descentes dans les isles Britanniques, depuis Guillaume le Conquérant, 8vo. *map, hf. bd. 5s*   *Pas de Calais*, 1798
2323 POLYBE, Histoire de, nouvellement traduite par Thuillier, avec un Commentaire, etc. 6 vols. 4to. *numerous plans and plates, calf*, 12s   *Paris*, 1727-30
2324 —— Histoire avec le Supplement commentaire de De Folard, etc. 7 vols. 4to. *many plans, hf. bd.* 20s   *Amst.* 1774
2325 PUFENDORFUS de Rebus a Carolo Gustavo Sueciæ Rege gestis, 2 vols. folio, *with upwards of* 100 *plates of Portraits, Battles, Pageants, Sieges, and Views in Sweden, Norway, Denmark, and Poland, original and beautiful impressions, a very fine copy in russia, gilt edges,* 32s   *Norimb.* 1696
     A later edition appeared, Nürnberg, 1729, with inferior impressions of the plates.
2326 PUYSEGUR, Art de la Guerre, par principes et par règles, 2 vols. 4to. *numerous plans, calf*, 7s 6d   *Paris*, 1749
2327 ROCQUANCOURT, Cours d'Art et d'Histoire Militaires, 2 vols. large 8vo. *plates, cloth*, 7s 6d   *Bruxelles*, 1836-38
2328 ROYAL ENGINEERS. Papers on subjects connected with the duties of the Corps of Royal Engineers, 10 vols. 4to. *numerous maps, plans, and plates,* (pub. at £15. 2s) *cloth*, £2. 14s   1844-49
2329 SAXE (Maurice, Comte de) Mes Rêveries, ouvrage posthume, avec sa vie etc par Pérau, 2 vols. 4to. 83 *coloured plates, old calf gilt*, 15s   *Amst.* 1757
2330 SPECTATEUR (le) Militaire, recueil de Science, d'Art et Histoire Militaires, Vols. XXIV—XXX. 7 vols. 8vo. *maps and plates, hf. calf*, 12s   *Paris*, 1838-41
2331 STRADA (Famianus) de Bello Belgico, ab excessu Caroli V usque ad annum 1590, folio, BEST EDITION, *frontispieces, containing a Map of Holland within the form of the Belgian lion, and numerous fine plates by Baur, of Battles, Sieges, etc. old calf gilt*, 15s   *Romæ*, 1640-4
2332 —— History of the Low-Country Warres, in English by Stapylton, folio, *portraits, bound*, 7s 6d   1650
2333 SURIREY DE SAINT REMY, Mémoires d'artillerie, 2 vols. sm. 4to. *portrait and about* 170 *plates, calf gilt, very neat,* 36s   *Amst.* 1702
2334 SUTCLIFFE, Practice, proceedings, and Lawes of Arms, out of the doings of most valiant Captaines, sq. 8vo. *closely cut, calf,* 18s   1593
2335 TARLETON'S History of the Campaigns of 1780 and 1781, in the Southern Provinces of North America, 4to. *plans, calf gilt,* 24s   1787
2336 TURPIN DE CRISSÉ, Essai sur l'Art de la Guerre, 2 vols. 4to. *plans of military operations, a* SUPERB COPY *in pale olive* MOROCCO *extra, gilt edges, Arms on sides,* 18s   *Paris*, 1754
2337 VEGETIUS Renatus et alii Scriptores Antiqui de Re Militari, stout sm. 8vo. *old russia,* 10s   *Vesal. Cliv.* 1670
2338 WELLINGTON'S Despatches during his Campaigns in India, Denmark, Portugal, Spain, the Low Countries, and France, 1799-1818, by Gurwood, with General Index, 13 vols. 8vo. BEST EDITION, (pub. at £13. 10s) *calf*, £7. 15s   1837-39
2339 WELLINGTON'S Supplementary Despatches and Memoranda : India 1797-1805, edited by his son, the Duke of Wellington, Vols. 3 and 4, 8vo. (pub. at £2.) *cloth*, 18s   1859
2340 GURWOOD's Selections from the Wellington Despatches, 8vo. *hf. rus. gt.* 6s 1851
2341 WELLESLEY'S (*Marquess*) DESPATCHES, Minutes, and Correspondence during his administration in INDIA, 5 vols. 8vo. *portrait, maps, etc. calf gilt,* £3. 10s ; *or a very beautiful copy, calf extra, with the author's autograph,* £5.
     1836-37
2342 TRACTS on Military Affairs. 12 Tracts relating to the Campaigns in Flanders and Germany, etc. sm. 4to. 15s   1691-1704

Sawle on the last Campaign in Flanders 1691	History of Standing Armies in England 1698	Essay on the Militia 1701
D'Auvergne, the last Campaignes, 1692, and 1693, 2 parts 1693	Journal of the Siege of Barcelona 1698	German and French Journals of the late Campaign
Paris Relation of Landen 1693	Necessity of a Landforce, in peace 1698	Tallard's Account of Blenheim 1701
Letter from St. Germains 1697		Account of the last Campaigns 1704
		1704

NAVAL AFFAIRS.

2343 BAYFII Annotationes de Captivis in quibus tractatur de Re Navali, etc. sm. 4to. *large woodcuts, bd. curious,* 7s 6d *Paris,* 1536

2344 CRESCENTIO (Bartolomeo) Nautica Mediterranea, della fabrica delle Galee, Galeazze, e Galeoni, coi lor armamenti, l'error delle Charte, il Calendario Nautico, un Archibugio che tira senza fuoco, et un Portolano di tutti i porti, etc. 2 vols. in 1, sm. 4to. *large folding Chart, plans, cuts, and tables, limp vellum, rare,* £2. 10s *Roma,* 1602-7
   A copy fetched at the Libri sale, 1859, £2. 12s. This work describes all the Nautical Instruments then in use, the ordnance, etc. including a curious Air-gun.

2345 HARRIS on the effects of Lightning on Floating Bodies, 4to. *bds.* 7s 6d 1823

2346 JAL, Archéologie Navale, 2 vols. roy. 8vo. *numerous cuts, and Index of Nautical Expressions in various languages, cloth,* 10s *Paris,* 1840

2347 VOCABULARY of Sea Phrases and Terms of Art, used in Seamanship and Naval Architecture, 2 vols. 16mo. *calf gilt,* 7s 1799

2348 TRACTS on English NAVAL AFFAIRS, an interesting collection of 11, *all of them scarce,* £2.

Life of Arthur Earl of Torrington, with remarks on his Tryal (1690) 1691	Reflections upon Stephens' Relation of the Action between the Fleets, June 22-July 5 1691	Essay on England's Safety dependant on a formidable Navy 1702
Account by Admirals Ashby and Rooke of the Engagement between the Fleets 1691	Journal of the Brest Expedition by Lord Caermarthen, *plan* 1694	The English Navy 1702
The Great Sea-Fight with the French Fleet, Barfleur, May 19, 1692 1692	English Men-of-War taken 1696	Rooke's Voyage to the Mediterranean, with Description of Gibraltar 1704
	Great Britain's Groans: or, the Oppression of Loyal Seamen 1695	Review (A) of the late Engagement at Sea, with Remarks on Sir G. R(ooke) 1704

2349 TRACTS, a collection of, on Modern Naval and Maritime Affairs, 8vo. *the lot,* 7s 1825-56

ORIENTAL HISTORY AND POLYGLOTTS, TRANSACTIONS OF
THE ORIENTAL SOCIETIES OF EUROPE AND ASIA.

Translations from Oriental Languages have been inserted after their respective originals. For ORIENTAL BIBLES *see ante. Works on* Assyria, China, Egypt, India, Japan, *and* Turkey, *are grouped separately.*

2350 ADELUNG, Mithridates oder allgemeine Sprachenkunde, 4 vols. 8vo. *the "Lord's Prayer," in* 500 *Languages and Dialects, a bargain,* 16s ; *bd.* 21s *Berl.* 1806-17
   Vols. I and III, are devoted to the Asiatic and American languages, and the fourth contains the supplements by Vater and Humboldt.

2351 ALFRAGANI Elementa Astronomica, *Arab. et Lat.* à Golio, *Amst.* 1669—Peritsol, Itinera Mundi, *Hebr. et Lat.* et Bobovii Turcarum Liturgia, à Hyde, *Oxon.* 1690-91—Verbiest, Astronomia Europæa sub Imp. Tartaro Sinico Cam Hy, Diling. 1687 — Mentzel, Sylloge minutiar. Lexici Lat. Sin. characteristici, *Norimb.* 1685—5 vols. in 1, stout sq. 8vo. *vellum,* 10s 1669-91

2352 ALPHABETS. BALLHORN's Grammatography, a Manual of reference to the ALPHABETS of ANCIENT and MODERN LANGUAGES, impl. 8vo. 102 ALPHABETS, *with ample and valuable information on the nature and mechanism of each language, cloth,* 7s *London,* 1861

2353 —— the same, the 8th GERMAN edition, royal 8vo. *cloth,* 5s *Leipzig,* 1859

2354 AMERICAN ORIENTAL SOCIETY: JOURNAL of the above, 5 vols. 8vo. *plates of facsimiles, etc. in* 11 *parts, sd.* £3. 10s ; or 5 vols. *neatly half bound calf,* £4. 4s *Boston, New York, &c.* 1847-56
   This periodical contains learned articles by Burnouf, Lassen, Whitney, and other eminent Orientalists.

2355 ANNALS of Oriental Literature, 8vo. *hf. russia, rare,* 6s 1821
   Containing articles by Bopp, and translations from the Persian, and Sanscrit, Reviews of the Mahabharata, the Kamus, Edrisi's Africa, etc.

2356 ANTAR, a Bedoueen Romance, translated from the Arabic by Terrick Hamilton, 4 vols. sm. 8vo. *bds.* 10s ; *hf. calf,* 15s 1820
   A series of very interesting Eastern tales.

2357 ARABIAN NIGHTS' (The) Entertainments, a new translation from the Arabic, with copious notes by LANE, 3 vols. impl. 8vo. *genuine and* BEST EDITION, *first impressions of the* MANY HUNDRED WOODCUTS *by* Harvey, *cloth,* £2. 10s 1839

2358 THE THOUSAND AND ONE NIGHTS, by Lane, a new edition, edited by E. S. POOLE, 3 vols. 8vo. *woodcuts, cloth,* 25s 1859

ORIENTAL HISTORY AND POLYGLOTTS, ETC. 139

2360 **Armenia.** SAINT-MARTIN, Mémoires historiques et géographiques sur l'Armenie, avec l'histoire des princes Orpélians par Orpélian, *Armenien et Français*, etc. 2 vols. large 8vo. *cloth*, 28s *Paris*, 1819
2361 ASIATIC RESEARCHES, or Transactions of the Society instituted in England for inquiring into the History, the Antiquities, the Arts and Sciences, and Literature of Asia, A PERFECT UNMIXED SET, 20 vols. and Index, 1 vol.—together 21 vols. royal 4to. *many plates, calf gilt*, £30. *Calcutta*, 1788-1836
2362 ———— another set, 20 vols. and Index, 4to. *somewhat wormed, cloth, cut edges*, £18. *Calcutta*, 1788-1836
2363 **ASIATIC SOCIETY OF BENGAL: BENGAL JOURNAL.** JOURNAL OF THE ASIATIC SOCIETY OF BENGAL, *complete from the beginning to the present*, Nos. 1—284, forming 31 vols. 8vo. *with all the numerous plates and Tables of Contents, excessively rare both in India and Europe*, £36. *Calcutta*, 1832-62
2364 **ASIATIC SOCIETY OF GREAT BRITAIN AND IRELAND:** Transactions, *complete*, 3 stout vols. 4to. *plates of facsimiles, etc.* (pub. at £9. 7s) *sd.* 20s; or *hf. calf*, 24s 1827-35
Sets completed at a moderate rate.
2365 ASIATIC SOCIETY : Journal of the Royal Asiatic Society of Great Britain and Ireland, from the beginning to 1861, 8vo. *complete as far as published*, Vols. I.—XX. part 1, *many plates*, (pub. £11. 8s) *sd.* £10. 1834-62
Sets completed at moderate charges.
2366 ASIATIC MISCELLANY, consisting of Original productions, translations, extracts from curious publications, &c. 2 vols. 1785-86—New Asiatic Miscellany, Vol. I. 1789—3 vols. 4to. *hf. bound, not uniform*, 20s *Calcutta*, 1785-89
2367 **BATAVIAN ACADEMY TRANSACTIONS:** VERHANDELINGEN van het Bataviaasch Genootschap der Kunsten en Wetenschappen, Vol. I, III—IX, XII--XIV., with a separate vol. containing the "Javaansche Spraakkunst, door De Groot en Gericke," together 12 vols. 8vo. *plates, not uniform, Dr. Horsfield's copy, very rare*, £7. *Bataviæ*, 1771-1833
2368 BELNOS (S. C.) the Sundhya, or the Daily Prayers of the Brahmins illustrated, atlas folio, 24 *coloured plates, shewing the Attitudes, and different Signs and Figures performed by the Brahmins during their devotions*; with a descriptive text, *half morocco*, 36s 1851
Privately printed and sold to Subscribers only.
2369 BIRD (James) Historical Researches on the Origin and Principles of the Buddha and Jaina Religions; embracing the leading Tenets of their System, with Accounts of the Sculptures in the Caves of Western India, folio, 54 *plates of Buddhistic Monuments and Inscriptions, hf. bound*, 24s *Bombay*, 1847
2370 BOCHARTI Opera: Phaleg, Chanaan et Hierozoicon, ed. Relandus, 3 vols. folio, *best edition, maps, calf*, 20s; or, *fine copy in vellum*, 25s *Lugd. Bat.* 1712
2371 ———— Hierozoicon, sive de Animalibus Scripturæ, recensuit Rosenmüller, 3 vols. 4to. *old calf neat*, 28s *Lips.* 1793-96
2372 **BOMBAY GEOGRAPHICAL SOCIETY:** TRANSACTIONS and Proceedings of the Bombay Geographical Society, from the beginning, in 1836, to 1856, Vols. I.—XII. (XI. wanting) 11 vols. 8vo. nine vols. *hf. bound, edges cut, and two unbound*, £7. 10s *Bombay*, 1836-56
2373 **BOMBAY LITERARY SOCIETY** Transactions; translations from the Chinese, the Persian, etc. dissertations on Hindoo Mythology, Ethics, Antiquities, Mahomedan Mysticism, comparison of the Gipsy and Hindostanee languages, plan of a comparative Vocabulary of Indian Languages by Sir J. Mackintosh, on Cuneiform Inscriptions, etc. *numerous plates of Antiquities, facsimiles, etc.* 3 vols. 4to. *half russia*, £2. 16s 1819-20-23
2374 ———— the same, Vol. I, II, 4to. *plates, not uniform*, 25s 1819-20
2375 BRETON's Vocabulary of Medical and Technical terms in English, Arabic, Persian, Hindee and Sanscrit, 4to. *water stained, hf. bd.* 10s *Calcutta*, 1825
2376 BRYDGES (Sir H. J.) Dynasty of the Kajars, the reigning Royal Family of Persia, 8vo. *map and plates, cloth*, 9s 1833
2377 BURNOUF, Commentaire sur le YACNA, l'un des livres religieux des Parses, ouvrage contenant le text *Zend*, les Variantes des quatre manuscrits de la bibliothèque royale et la version *Sanscrite* inédite de Nériosengh, tome I. 4to. *all published*, £2. 16s *Paris*, 1833

2378 CALCUTTA JOURNAL, from 1818 to 1821, 14 vols.—Asiatic Department, 1821 to 1823, 7 vols.—together 21 vols. royal 4to. *maps and plates, not uniform, very rare*, £6. *Calcutta*, 1818-23
An important Indian periodical, almost unknown in Europe.

2379 CALCUTTA JOURNAL of Natural History, Nos. 11-16, 19-21, 8vo. *plates, sd.* 25s *Calcutta*, 1842-45

2380 CALCUTTA MAGAZINE and Miscellany, for 1814-15, 2 vols. 8vo. *hf. bd.* 20s *Calcutta*, 1814-15

2381 CALCUTTA REVIEW, from the beginning in 1844 to Dec. 1859, being Nos. 1—66 (without No. 39-40, intended for the Index), complete; together 33 vols. 8vo.—7 volumes neatly bound, *half calf, the remainder in quarterly parts, uncut*, £10. *Calcutta*, 1844-59

2382 CALCUTTA MEDICAL and PHYSICAL SOCIETY'S Transactions, 7 vols. 8vo. *bds.* £4. *Calcutta*, 1825-35

2383 CASTELLI (E.) LEXICON HEPTAGLOTTON: hebraicum, chaldaicum, syriacum, samaritanum, aethiopicum, arabicum et persicum, 2 vols. royal folio, *portrait, slightly stained, a good serviceable copy in old calf gilt*, £3. *London*, 1699

2384 CATALOGUE des MANUSCRITS et Xylographes Orientaux de la Bibliothèque Imp. publique de ST. PETERSBOURG, stout roy. 8vo. xliv. and 719 pp. *presentation copy, hf. morocco*, 30s *St. Pétersb.* 1852

2385 CATALOGUS Codicum Manuscriptorum ARABICORUM in Bibl. Bodleianâ, confecit Nicholl, royal fol. *bds.* 7s 6d 1821

2386 CATALOGUS Codicum ORIENTALIUM Musei Britannici, tres partes, in 4 vols. royal folio, *facsimiles*, (pub. at £2. 10s) *bds.* £2. 1838-47
Contents: I. Codd. Syriaci et Carshunici; II. Arabici, 2 parts; III. Aethiopici. Sets completed.

2387 CHÉNIER, Recherches sur les Maures, et histoire de Maroc, 3 vols. 8vo. *maps, hf. calf*, 6s *Paris*, 1787

2388 CHURCHILL'S (Col.) MOUNT LEBANON: a Ten Years' Residence, from 1842 to 1852; describing the Manners, Customs, and Religion of its Inhabitants, with a full and correct account of the Druze Religion, and containing Historical Records of the Mountain Tribes, from Personal Intercourse with their Chiefs and other Authentic Sources, by Colonel Churchill, Staff Officer on the British Expedition to Syria, *third edition*, 3 vols. 8vo. *with a large folding Map of the Mountain Range of the Lebanon, portraits and views*, 1853—Vol. IV. The DRUZES and the MARONITES under the Turkish Rule, 1862—together 4 vols. 8vo. with a General Index to the 4 vols. *printed uniformly*, (pub. at 35s) *cloth*, 21s 1853-62

2389 CHURCHILL'S DRUZES and MARONITES, under the Ottoman Turks, showing the policy of the Turkish government in Syria from its restoration to the Sultan in 1840 down to 1861; exposing the feelings and principles which have actuated the Druzes and Maronites during that period, and containing a correct account of the late civil war between those two sects, and of the MASSACRES IN THE LEBANON AND IN DAMASCUS; with comments on the French occupation, and on the proceedings of the European International Commission in Syria, by COLONEL CHURCHILL, *Author of Ten Years' Residence in Mount Lebanon*, 1 vol. 12mo. 296 pp. *cloth*, 5s 1862

2390 COLEBROOKE'S (H. T.) Miscellaneous Essays, 2 vols. 8vo. BEST EDITION, *numerous facsimiles from early Indian MSS. and Inscriptions, rare*, £2. 16s 1837

2391 —— the same, new edition of all the important Vedantic papers, 8vo. *cloth*, (pub. at 10s 6d) 8s 6d 1858
A rich assemblage of Materials for the History and explanation of the Vedas.

2392 COLEMAN'S (C.) MYTHOLOGY of the Hindus, 4to. *with* 39 *plates illustrative of the principal Hindu Deities, cloth, rare*, £2. 12s 6d 1832

2393 CRAWFORD'S History of the Indian Archipelago, 3 vols. *plates, hf. calf*, 24s 1820

2394 —— Journal of an Embassy to the Court of Ava, 1827, 4to. *map and plates, hf. bound*, 7s 6d 1859

2395 CUNNINGHAM'S LADÁK, physical, statistical and historical, with notices of surrounding countries, roy. 8vo. *large map and numerous fine plates, some coloured*, (pub. at 36s) *cloth*, 30s; or, *hf. calf neat*, 33s 1854

2396 —— the Bhilsa Topes: or Buddhist Monuments of Central India, comprising a sketch of the rise, progress and decline of Buddhism, 8vo. 33 *plates*, (pub. at 30s) *cloth*, 24s 1854

ORIENTAL HISTORY AND POLYGLOTTS, ETC. 141

2397 DE GUIGNES, Histoire Générale des Huns, des Turcs, des Mongols, et des autres Tartares Occidentaux, 5 vols. 4to. *French cf. gt. fine copy*, £4. 16s 1756-68

2398 D'HERBELOT, BIBLIOTHÈQUE ORIENTALE, avec les corrections et additions de Schultens, continuée par Visdelou et Galand, 4 vols. 4to. BEST EDITION, *very fine copy in calf, gilt edges, from Miss Currer's library*, £7. 7s *La Haye*, 1777-79

2398* —— the same, LARGE PAPER, 4 vols. roy. 4to. *old calf gilt*, £9. 9s 1777-79

2399 DIG-DURSHUN, Nos. 1—15, April 1818, to March 1820, in 1 vol. 8vo. *a periodical containing essays chiefly on Oriental subjects, hf. calf*, 10s *Calcutta*, 1818-20

2400 DORN'S Muhammedanische Quellen zur Geschichte der Küstenlænder des Kaspischen Meeres, Vols. I.-IV. 8vo. *containing the original Persian, Arabic, and Turkish texts, one vol. hf. red morocco, three sd.* 32s *St. Petersb.* 1850-58

2401 DOZY (R.) Recherches sur l'Histoire et la Littérature de l'Espagne pendant le Moyen Age; 2e édition augmentée, 2 vols. sm. 8vo. *sd.* 14s *Leyde*, 1860

2402 —— Histoire des Musulmans d'Espagne jusqu'à la conquête de l'Andalousie par les Almoravides (711—1110), 4 vols. small 8vo. *sd.* 24s *Leyde*, 1861

2403 DU JARRIC, Histoire des choses plus mémorables advenues tant ez Indes Orientales que autres païs, 2 vols. small 4to. *limp vellum*, 16s *Bourdeaus*, 1608-10

The third Vol. which appeared in 1614, is rarely found with the others.

2404 DUPERRON, OUPNEK'HAT, *i.e.* Secretum tegendum, continens arcanam Doctrinam e sacris Indorum Libris, RAK BEID, DJEDJR BEID, SAM BEID, ATHRBAN BEID, *Latine*, 2 vols. 4to. *hf. russia*, 25s ; or, *calf gilt*, 30s *Argent*. 1801-2

2405 EBN HAUKAL, Oriental Geography translated from the Arabic, by Ouseley, 4to. *map, hf. russia*, 7s 6d 1800

2406 ELLIS' MIRASI RIGHT, [Inheritance], with Documents in *Canarese, Telugu, Tamil, &c.* folio, *hf. calf*, 10s *Madras*, 1818

2407 ELPHINSTONE (Hon. M.) Account of CAUBUL and its Dependencies, 4to. *map and coloured plates, bds.* 7s 6d ; or, *hf. russia*, 10s 1815

2408 FALLMERAYER'S Geschichte des Kaiserthums von TRAPEZUNT, 4to. *hf. bd. a valuable work, based on information unknown to Gibbon*, 10s *München*, 1827

2409 FORBES' (Jas.) ORIENTAL MEMOIRS ; a Narrative of Seventeen Years' Residence in India, including Observations on parts of Africa and South America, and Journals of Four Indian Voyages, 4 vols. 4to. *with all the plates, a beautiful copy in calf extra*, £4. 1813

Priced, 1831, H. Bohn, *calf*, £0. 10s; 1834, Arch, £12. 12s; 1837, Arch, £10. 10s; 1843, J. Bohn, *russia*, £12. 12s; Rodwell, *morocco*, £12. 12s. "This is the original and only complete edition."

2410 FORSTER'S Mahometanism Unveiled, 2 vols. 8vo. *calf gilt*, £2. 10s 1829

2411 —— Historical Geography of Arabia, with Appendix containing translations of Hamyaritic Inscriptions, Alphabet and Glossary, 2 vols. 8vo. *maps and plates, cloth*, 18s ; *calf extra*, 28s 1844

2412 —— SINAI Photographed, or contemporary records of Israel in the Wilderness, folio, *portrait in photograph, and* 8 *photographs of Inscriptions, Sculptured Tablets, etc., Map, and* 6 *other plates, with a large folding Table entitled* "A HARMONY OF (45) PRIMEVAL ALPHABETS," *cloth, new, only* 250 *copies printed*, £3. 1862

"It would be unjust to deny the author credit for the persistency of his research, and his intense devotion to a favorite theme. His volume has an interest for the scholar, the antiquary, and the Christian. Upwards of a hundred inscriptions are given and explained by our author with minute and verbal decipherment."

Athenæum, Nov. 29, '62.

2413 GATE to the Hebrew, Arabic, and Syriac unlocked, 8vo. 24 *plates of Grammatical tables, cloth*, 5s 1828

2414 GAUBIL, Histoire de Gentchiscan et de la Dinastie des Mongous ses successeurs, tirée du Chinois, 4to. *uncut*, 15s *Paris*, 1739

A valuable adjunct to "Deguignes, Histoire des Huns, etc. 5 vols. 4to."

2415 GESCHICHTE der Araber vor Muhamed, 8vo. *chronol. tables, bds.* 5s *Berl.* 1836

2416 GRINDLAY'S (Capt.) Views in India, Scenery, Costume, and Architecture, chiefly on the Western side of India, atlas 4to *consisting of* 36 *most beautifully coloured plates, highly finished in imitation of drawings, with descriptive letter-press, original edition*, (pub. at £14. 14s) *hf. green morocco*, £2. 5s 1830

2417 HAMMER-PURGSTALL, Geschichte der Ilchane, das ist der Mongolen in Persien, 2 vols. in 3, large 8vo. *half calf*, 7s 6d *Darmstadt*, 1842-43

2418 —— Gemäldesaal der Lebens-Beschreibungen Moslimischer Herrscher der ersten sieben Jahrhunderte der Hidschret, 6 vols. 8vo. *frontispieces after MSS.* (pub. at 36s) *hf. morocco*, 16s *Leipzig*, 1837-39

2419 —— Ancient Alphabets and Hieroglyphic Characters explained, translated from the Arabic, sq. 8vo. *bds.* 5s 1806

2420 HAUG'S (M.) Essays on the Sacred Language, Writings, and Religion of the
Parsees, 8vo. *cloth*, 24s   *Bombay*, 1862
2421 HEDAYA (The) or Guide.; a Commentary on the Mussulman Laws; translated
by order of the Governor-General and Council of Bengal, by Charles Hamilton,
4 vols. 4to. *a fine clean copy in bds*. £4.   *Lond*. 1791
2423 HERODOTUS, a new English version, with Notes and Appendices, by G. Rawlinson, assisted by Col. Sir H. Rawlinson and Sir G. J. Wilkinson, 4 vols.
8vo. *maps and illustrations*, (pub at £3. 12s) *cloth, new and clean*, £2. 12s 1858-60
Based upon the recent Assyrian discoveries.
2424 Hodgson's Literature and Religion of the Buddhists, 8vo. *plates, cloth*, 12s
Serampore, 1841
2425 Hyakinth, Denkwürdigk. über die Mongolei, aus dem Russ. übersetzt von Borg,
8vo. *map and coloured plates, a valuable work, sd*. 7s 6d   *Berlin*, 1832
2426 HYDE (T.) Historia Religionis veterum Persarum, eorumque Magorum;
Zoroastris Vita, ejusque et aliorum Vaticinia de Messiah; Primitivæ Opiniones
de Deo; Originale Orientis Sibyllæ Mysterium; Zoroastris liber Sad-der,
Latine; cum Appendice, etc. 4to. *best edition, plates, calf*, 30s; *hf. bd. uncut*,
32s; or, *fine copy in old calf neat*, 35s   *Oxon*., 1760
2427 JONES (Sir W.) Works, with Life by Lord Teignmouth, 13 vols. 8vo. *calf gilt*,
£2.   Bernal's copy fetched, 1855, £5. 15s.   1807
2428 Jones (Sir W.) Memoirs of the Life, Writings, and Correspondence of, by Lord
Teignmouth, 4to. *portrait, russia neat*, 10s   1804
2429 JOURNAL of the Indian Archipelago, and Eastern Asia, from the beginning
in 1847 to December, 1852, Vols. I.—VI. (wanting No. 3 of Vol. VI.) 8vo.
*important articles on the races and languages of Eastern Asia, with plates, sd.
rare*, £6. 10s   *Singapore*, 1847-51
2430 KÆMPFERI, Amœnitates Exoticae, relationes rerum Persicarum et Ulterioris
Asiæ, stout sm. 4to. *many plates, calf neat*, 10s   *Lemgoviae*, 1712
2431 —— —— History of Japan, its Government, Temples, Palaces, Castles, etc. its
Natural History, Customs, Manufactures and Trade, translated by Scheuchzer,
with two Appendices, 2 vols. folio, 45 *plates, old calf*, £2. 2s   1727-28
Still the best book on Japan.
2432 KENNEDY'S (Lieut.-Col. Vans) Researches into the Origin and Affinity of
the principal Languages of Asia and Europe, 4to. *with* 11 *plates of Ancient
Alphabets and Inscriptions*, (pub. at £2. 12s 6d) *cloth, a bargain*, 10s   1828
2433 —— —— Researches into the Nature and Affinity of Ancient and Hindu Mythology, 4to. xx and 494 pp. (pub. at £2. 12s 6d) *cloth*, 20s   1831
2434 KLAPROTH (J.) Asia Polyglotta, 4to. 14 and 400 pp. *with the folio Atlas of
Languages, comprising* 59 *Tables of Vocabularies, map*, 20s   *Paris*, 1823
Rare; the only edition of this valuable work. Also issued by an unscrupulous publisher with a new title,
dated 1831.
2435 —— —— Mémoires relatifs à l'Asie; recherches philologiques sur l'Orient, 8vo.
with Formosan Vocabulary, map, plates, cloth, 7s   *Paris*, 1824
2436 —— —— Tableaux historiques de l'Asie, depuis la Monarchie de Cyrus jusqu'à
nos jours, accompagnés de Recherches Historiques et Ethnographiques, 4to.
and folio Atlas of 27 *coloured historical maps, sd*. 36s   *Paris*, 1826
2437 KORAN (Al) of Mahomet, translated out of Arabique into French, and now
newly Englished, sq. 8vo. *the first English translation, bd*. 10s   1649
2438 —— —— translated from Arabic into English with explanatory notes, by G. Sale,
2 vols. 8vo. *plates, calf neat*, 12s 6d   1821
2439 —— —— translated, the Suras in chronological order, with notes and index, by
Rodwell, sm. 8vo. (pub. at 10s 6d) *cloth, new*, 8s 9d   1861
2440 La Croix, History of Genghizcan the Great, 8vo. *map, calf gilt*, 10s   1722
2441 —— —— the same 8vo. *hf. calf*, 7s 6d   *Calcutta*, 1816
2442 Letellier, Vocabulaire Oriental: Français-Italien, Arabe, Turc, et Grec, oblong 8vo. *cloth*, 5s   *Paris*, 1838
2443 Lindsay, Observations on an Ancient Talisman brought from Syria, 4to. *a tract
with* 2 *plates, privately printed*, 3s 6d   *Cork*, 1855
2444 LUDOLFI Historia Ethiopica sive descriptio regni Habessinarum, 1681—
Commentarius geographicus, historicus et criticus, 1691 — 2 vols. folio, *portraits and plates, calf*, 20s; or, *a nice copy in old calf gilt*, 30s   *Francof*. 1681-91
2445 —— —— Commentarius ad historiam Aethiopicam, fol. *plates, vellum*, 7s   1691
The best work on Abyssinia: it gives an Account of the History, Literature, Natural History, Antiquities,
Religion, Chronology, Language, Proverbs, and everything curious relating to that country. The Commentary
forming the second volume is very scarce.

ORIENTAL HISTORY AND POLYGLOTTS, ETC. 143

2446 MACNAGHTEN'S Hindu Law, 4to. *bds.* £2. 10s; or, *hf. russia*, £2. 12s 6d
                              Serampore, 1824
2447 —— Moohummudan Law, 4to. *hf. russia*, £2. 10s   *Calcutta*, 1825
2448 —— Hindu and Mohammadan Law, edited by H. H. Wilson, sm. 8vo. *new in cloth,* 5s   186
2450 MADRAS Journal of Literature and Science, edited by Messrs. Cole and Brown, Vols. I.-XII. or Parts 1-29 inclusive, 8vo. QUITE COMPLETE, *with numerous plates of Hindoo Mythology, Antiquities, Geography, Natural History, half russia neat*, £10.   *Madras*, 1833-40
2451 MAFFEII Historia Indica, selectæ ex Indiâ Epistolae, etc. cum Ign. Loiolae Vita, folio, *fine clean copy, vellum*, 15s   *Colon. Agrip.* 1589
2452 MAHAVANSI, Raja-Ratnacari and Raja-Vali, the Sacred and Historical Books of Ceylon, etc. translated from the Singhalese by Upham, 3 vols. 8vo. (pub. at £2. 2s) *hf. calf gilt*, 21s   1833
2453 MALCOLM (Major-General Sir John) WORKS:
 a SKETCH of the SIKHS, roy. 8vo. *bds.* 7s   1812
 b MEMOIRS of Lord CLIVE, 3 vols. sm. folio, *original edition, lithographed, with some pencil corrections, hf. calf, rare*, 15s   (? 1827)
 c LIFE of Lord CLIVE, 3 vols. 8vo. *portrait and map, hf calf,* 25s ; *bds.* 30s   1836
 d HISTORY of PERSIA, 2 vols. impl. 4to. *map and plates, calf gilt*, 24s   1815
 e —— the same, 2 vols. 8vo. *new edition, hf. calf,* 30s; *uncut,* 36s   1829
 f POLITICAL History of INDIA, 1784-1823, 2 vols. *half calf*, 7s 6d   1826
 g MEMOIR of Central India, including Malwa, 2 vols. *maps, hf. calf,* 10s   1824
 h GOVERNMENT of India, *bds.* 5s   1833
2454 MARSDEN, NUMISMATA ORIENTALIA, 2 vols. in 1, 4to. *with 57 plates, hf. calf,* £6. 6s   1823-25
2455 —— the same, Vol. II. impl. 4to. 30 *plates, bds.* 25s   1825
2456 MASUDI's Fatemite Dynasty, by Nicholson, *Tübingen,* 1840; etc. in 1 vol. 8vo. *hf. calf,* 5s
2457 MEDICI, Grammaire Polyglotte, *Arabe, Persane, Turque et Tartare,* impl. 4to. *hf. bound,* 7s   *Venise,* 1844
2458 MELANGES ASIATIQUES, tirés du Bulletin Historico-Philologique de St. Petersbourg, 1849-56, Vols. I.-III. Pt. 5, roy. 8vo. *plates,* 2 vols. *hf. morocco gilt, and five parts,* £2.   *St. Petersburg,* 1852-9
2459 MENINSKI LEXICON ARABICO-PERSICO-TURCICUM, adjectâ ad singulas Voces et Phrases significatione Latinâ, ad usitatiores etiam Italicâ, recognitum et auctum, 4 vols. fol. *poor copy, a few leaves slightly damaged, bds. edges cut,* 36s *Vien.* 1780
2 46 —— the same, 4 vols. in 2, stout folio, *hf. calf,* £2. 5s   *ib.* 1780
Priced, SMALL PAPER, 1834, Straker, £11 11s, and £14. 14s; 1835, Dondé-Dupré, 450 fr.; 1841, Allen, £8. 8s; 1854, Maisonneuve, 375 fr. LARGE PAPER, Lee's copy in russia, which cost him £18. 18s, I sold, 1856, for £8. 8s; priced, 1835, D. Dupré, 550 fr.; Barrois, 340 fr.
2461 MENINSKI. Complementum Thesauri Linguarum Orientalium, seu Onomasticum Latino-Turcico-Arabico-Persicum, folio, *with the usual stains, old calf, rare,* 36s   *Viennae,* 1687
    This volume completes both editions, that of 1680 and 1780.

MENU LAWS—see *Sanscrit.*

2462 MINES de l'Orient, exploitées par une Société d'Amateurs (De Murr, Rosenmüller, Eichhorn, Klaproth, HAMMER, etc.) 24 parts, forming 6 vols. *plates and facsimiles,* (pub. at £8. 10s) *hf. calf, fine copy, from Professor Quartremere's library,* £4. 15s   *Viennae,* 1809-18
  Priced, 1847, £9. 9s; Klaproth's copy fetched 123 fr.; 1855, Earl of Munster's, £6. 6s.
2463 MISHCAT-UL-MASABIH; a Collection of the most authentic Traditions of the Actions and Sayings of Muhammed; exhibiting the manners and customs, civil, religious, and military policy of the Muslemàns; translated from the Arabic, by Capt. MATTHEWS, 2 vols. impl. 4to. *sd.* 20s; *calf neat,* £2. 2s   *Calcutta,* 1809-10
 These traditions constitute the second authority of Musselman law, and are considered as a *supplement to the Koran.* "The only complete work in the English language on these traditionary laws. It contains the most important and authentic traditions of Muhammed."—MILLS.
2464 MOOR'S (E.) HINDU PANTHEON, royal 4to. 451 *pp.* and 105 *plates of Hindoo Deities, hf. calf,* £5.; or *calf neat,* £6.   1810
  A valuable work, now scarce. Priced, 1847, Allen, £7. 7s; Klaproth's copy fetched 158 fr.
2465 —— the Plates, edited with DESCRIPTIVE INDEX, by the Rev. A. P. Moor, roy. 4to. 104 *plates, cloth, gilt edges,* 27s   1861

2466 MORLEY'S Catalogue of the Arabic and Persian MSS. of the Royal Asiatic Society, 8vo. *sd. 2s* 1854

2467 —— Description of a Planispheric Astrolabe, constructed for Shah Sultan Hussain Safawi, of Persia, now in the British Museum, with Notes illustrative and explanatory, atlas folio, 21 *large plates, comprising 61 engravings of Eastern and some European Astrolabes, bds. £4.* 1856
<small>Only 100 copies were printed, and these are now all either presented or sold. Besides the famous Persian Astrolabe specially described, the work contains also concise notices of twelve other Astrolabes, Eastern and European, hitherto undescribed.</small>

2468 MUIR'S Life of Mahomet, with introduction on the original sources, and the Pre-Islamite history of Arabia, Vols. III. and IV. 8vo. *maps,* (pub. at 21s) *new in cloth,* 15s 1861

2469 MUNRO. Gleig's Life of Sir Thos. Munro, late Governor of Madras, with Extracts from his Private Papers, etc. 3 vols. 8vo. *port. and map, cf. gt.* 25s 1830

2470 Norbergi Opuscula Academica, 3 vols. 12mo. *sd. 7s* *Lond. Goth.* 1817-19
<small>Valuable essays on the language, literature, etc. of the Eastern nations.</small>

2471 ORIENTAL TRANSLATION FUND Publications, Large Paper Subscription Copy, 69 distinct works, forming 50 vols. impl. 4to. 45 vols. impl. 8vo. in all 95 vols. *with many maps and plates* (subscription price and original cost £304. 10s) *clean and new,* offered to the public at £75. 7s, now at £42. 1829-59

2472 Pandurang Hàrì, or Memoirs of a Hindoo, 3 vols. 12mo. (pub. at 24s) *cl. 6s* 1826

2473 PERCEVAL (Caussin de) Essai sur l'Histoire des Arabes, 3 vols. 8vo. *Genealogical tables, hf. calf neat,* £2. 2s *Paris,* 1847-48

2474 Poems: Sir William Jones' Latin Poetry, with English Versions, etc. sm. 4to. *hf. bound, rare,* 5s *Calc.* 1800

2475 PRICE'S Mahommedan History, from the Arabian Legislator to the Emperor Akbar, and the Establishment of the Mogul Empire, from original Persian Authorities, 3 vols. 4to. *large coloured map of Asia,* (pub. at £7. 17s 6d) *bds.* 18s 1821
<small>Major Price spent twenty-four years in the East, and compiled the above work, which is the one faithfully representing Oriental Records and traditions.</small>

2476 RAWLINSON'S Five Great Monarchies of the Ancient Eastern World; History, Geography, and Antiquities of Chaldæa, Assyria, Babylon, Media, and Persia, 3 vols. Vol. I. Chaldaea and Assyria, 8vo. pp. 616, 230 *woodcuts,* (pub. at 16s) 13s 4d 1862

2477 Reinaud, Description des Monumens Musulmans du cabinet du Duc de Blacas, 2 vols. 8vo. *plates, sd. 6s* *Paris,* 1828

2478 —— Extraits des historiens Arabes relatifs aux Croisades, *Français,* stout 8vo. *sd.* 7s 6d 1829

2479 —— Relation des Voyages des Arabes et des Persans dans l'Inde et à la Chine, *Arabe et Français,* 2 vols. 16mo. *sd. 6s* 1845

2480 Relandi Dissertationes Miscellaneæ, 3 vols. 12mo. *vellum,* 10s 6d *Traj.* 1707-13
<small>Dissertations on the Paradise, the Red Sea, the Cabiri Gods, the Zend, the Talmud, Mohammed, Polynesian Languages, and one of 108 pp. on the Languages of America.</small>

2481 RÉMUSAT (Abel) Recherches sur les langues Tartares ou Mémoires sur différens points de la Grammaire et de la Littérature des Mandchous, des Mongols, des Oingours, et des Tibetains, Vol. I. 4to. *all published, boards, uncut, preface imperfect,* 16s *Paris,* 1820

2482 —— Papier Vélin, 4to. *half russia,* 36s 1820

2483 —— Nouveau Mélanges Asiatiques, 2 vols. 8vo. *calf neat,* 12s 6d *Paris,* 1829

2484 ROBERTS'S HOLY LAND, Syria, Idumea, and Arabia, with historical descriptions by Croly, 4 vols. atlas folio, 125 *magnificent plates,* coloured like the Original Drawings, *each plate mounted on cardboard, and fastened on guards,* 1842—Egypt and Nubia, from Drawings made on the spot by David Roberts, R.A., with historical descriptions by Brockedon, complete, 21 parts in 13, forming 3 vols. atlas folio, 123 plates most beautifully coloured to imitate the Original Drawings, *and mounted on cardboard* (pub. at £44. 2s), 1846-49—together 7 vols. atlas folio, complete (pub. at £88. 4s; cost of binding £20.), *half bound blue morocco, gilt edges, a most sumptuous set of books,* £75. 1842-49

2486 ROBERTS'S Sketches in the Holy Land, Syria, Idumea and Arabia, Egypt and Nubia, etc. complete, in 4 vols. atlas folio, *portrait and* 40 *beautiful and most attractive plates of all the Remains and sites famous in* Bible History, *the Chief Monuments of Art and Nature in Egypt, etc. executed in tints, an original subscriber's copy* (sold at £2.) *half bound,* morocco, *gilt edges,* £27. *Lond. F. G. Moon,* 1842-45

ORIENTAL HISTORY AND POLYGLOTTS, ETC. 145

2487 RUSSELL'S Natural History of Aleppo, *second enlarged edition*, 2 vols. 4to. *plates, half bound*, 10s 1794
2488 SACY (Silvestre de) Mémoires sur diverses Antiquités de la Perse, et sur les Médailles des Sassanides, avec l'Histoire de Mirkhond en Français, 4to. *plates, half russia neat*, 15s *Paris*, 1793
2489 SACY (Silvestre de) Catalogue de sa Bibliothèque, 3 vols. 8vo. *sewed*, 16s 1842-47
2490 ——— Miscellanies: Calendriers Grég., Russe, Musulman, etc.—Ouvrages de littérature Indienne—Le Kabous-Nameh, etc. 13 interesting tracts in 1 vol. 8vo. *calf*, 7s 6d 1810-13
2491 SAINCTYON (Sieur de) Histoire du Grand Tamerlan, 18mo. *fine copy in red morocco extra*, 7s *Amst.* 1678
2492 SAINT-MARTIN, sur la Carte de l'Asie centrale et de l'Inde, roy. 8vo. *map, sewed*, 4s 1858
2493 ——— Géographie et populations primitives du Nord-Ouest de l'Inde, 8vo. *sewed*, 7s *Paris*, 1859
2494 SCHINDLERI Lexicon Pentaglotton, Hebraicum, Chaldaicum, Syriacum, Talmudico-Rabbinicum et Arabicum, cum triplici Indice, folio, *calf*, 6s 1612
2495 SCHLEGEL, Indische Bibliothek, Vols. I.—III. Part 1, 8vo. 2 vols. *calf gilt, and a part*, 18s *Bohn*, 1823-30
2496 SPRENGER, Catalogue of the Arabic, Persian and Hindustany MSS. of the Libraries of the King of Oudh, Vol. I. Poetry, roy. 8vo. *sd.* 7s 6d *Calcutta*, 1854
2497 STEWART's Catalogue of the Oriental Library of TIPPOO SULTAN of Mysore, to which are prefixed ALL THE EXTRACTS FROM ORIENTAL MSS. WITH ENGLISH TRANSLATIONS, roy. 4to. (pub. at £4. 4s) 18s 1809
2498 SYRIA, the Holy Land, Asia Minor, etc. in a series of Views, drawn by BARTLETT, PURSER, etc. 3 vols. 4to. 121 PRETTY VIEWS, *proof impressions*, with descriptions by CARNE (pub. at £3. 8s), *half calf gilt*, 20s 1836
2499 TAMERLAN, proprement appellé Timour, ses Instituts, avec sa Vie par Langlès, 8vo. *portrait*, 5s; or *vellum*. 6s 6d *Paris*, 1787
2500 TORRES (Diego de) Relations des Cherifs, et des Royaumes de Marroc, Fez et Tarudant, etc. sm. 4to. *vellum*, 9s *Paris*, 1636
2501 TOTT (Baron de) Mémoire sur les Turcs et les Tartares, 2 vols. 4to. *plates, calf gilt*, 7s *Amst.* 1785
2502 TYTLER'S Origin and Principles of Budaic Sabism, 4to. 4 *Mythological plates,* VERY RARE, *half calf*, 25s *Calcutta*, 1817
2503 VALENTYN, Oud en Nieuw Oost-Indien, etc. A collection of Voyages to the East Indies, Japan, Moluccas, many Islands in the Eastern Seas, the Cape, etc. *in Dutch*, 5 vols. folio, *with a profusion of engravings of Natural History, Views, Portraits, etc. beautiful impressions, old calf, gilt backs, scarce*, £3. 10s *Dordrecht en Amst.* 1724-26
Containing a Geographical, Political, Ecclesiastical, and Natural History of all the countries in the East where the Dutch had settlements.
2504 WARREN'S KALA SANKALITA: Memoirs on the various modes in which the Nations of Southern India divide time, 4to. *half calf, scarce*, 30s *Madras*, 1825
2505 WILSON'S (H. H.) Descriptive Catalogue of MACKENZIE's Collection of ORIENTAL MANUSCRIPTS, etc. 2 vols. 4to. *half calf*, 21s *Calcutta*, 1828
2506 WILSON ARIANA ANTIQUA, Antiquities and Coins of Affghanistan, 4to. *map and 29 plates of Bactrian Coins, Antiquities, etc. cloth*, 36s 1841
This very learned and elaborate work was priced in a Numismatic Catalogue, 1854, £2. 12s 6d; at sales, copies usually fetch 2 guineas.
2507 WILSON (John) The PARSI RELIGION, as contained in the Zand-Avastá, and propounded by the Zoroastrians of India and Persia, 8vo. *cl.* 24s *Bombay*, 1843
2508 WÜSTENFELD Vergleichungs-Tabellen der Muhammedanischen und Christlichen Zeitrechnung, 4to. *fine paper, hf. calf*, 5s *Leipzig*, 1854
2509 ZEITSCHRIFT für die KUNDE des MORGENLANDES, herausgegeben von Ewald, Gabelentz, Kosegarten, Lassen, Neumann, Rödiger, und Rückert, Vols. I.—VII. 8vo. *sd.* £2. 16s; or, *calf gilt*, £4. *Göttingen u. Bonn*, 1837-50
2510 ——— der DEUTSCHEN MORGENLÄNDISCHEN GESELLSCHAFT, Vols. I.—XIII.; Register zu I.—X. and Jahresbericht 1845 and 1846; 8vo. Vols. I.—XII. *calf gilt, the remainder in 5 parts, sd.* £6. 15s *Leipzig*, 1847-59
Both from Professor Wilson's library.
2511 ——— the same, Vol. I.—X. pt. 4, 8vo. A COMPLETE SET, *facsimiles, sewed*, £5. *Leipzig*, 1848-56
Vol. V. No. 1, at present wanting, will be supplied.

2512 ZEND-AVESTA, ouvrage de ZOROASTRE, contenant ses idées théologiques, physiques et morales, le culte religieux qu'il a établi, et plusieurs traités sur l'ancienne histoire des Perses; traduit en Français, avec des remarques, etc. par *Anquetil du Perron*, 3 vols. in 2, 4to. *plates, old cf. gilt*, £3. 10s Paris, 1771

2513 ZENKER, Bibliotheca Orientalis, Manuel de Bibliographie Orientale, Vol. II. 8vo. *sewed*, 15s Leipzig, 1861

2514 **ASSYRIA.** BOTTA'S NINEVEH: Monument de Ninive découvert et décrit par Botta, mesuré et dessiné par Flandin, 5 vols. atlas folio, *with* 371 *magnificent plates of Architecture, Sculpture, and Inscriptions (formerly sold for* 80 *guineas), hf. bd. morocco, with emblematic tooling, gilt edges*, £28. 1849-50

Priced, 1857, in 90 livraisons, £65.; hf. morocco, £73. 10s. This magnificent work was published by order of the French Government, and under the direction of a committee of the Institute. Contents, Vols. I. and II. ARCHITECTURE AND SCULPTURE, 168 plates: Vols. III. and IV. INSCRIPTIONS, 203 plates; Vol. V. TEXT. " To Botta is due the merit of having found the first Assyrian monument."—*Layard*.

2515 LAYARD'S EXPEDITIONS TO ASSYRIA: The MONUMENTS of NINEVEH; being the FIRST SERIES of Illustrations of Sculptures, Bas-Reliefs, and other Remains of Art found among the Ruins of Nineveh, from Drawings made on the Spot, 100 *plates* (pub. at £10. 10s), 1846—The MONUMENTS OF NINEVEH, SECOND SERIES, consisting of Illustrations of the Sculptures, Bas-Reliefs, Vases, and Bronzes discovered during the Second Expedition, principally illustrative of the Wars and Exploits of Sennacherib, 71 *fine plates, some coloured*, (pub. at £10. 10s), 1853—the Two SERIES COMPLETE, 2 vols. impl. folio, 171 *plates*, (pub. at £21.) A GENUINE ORIGINAL COPY, *the first volume in a portfolio, the second hf. morocco*, £7. 1846-53

2516 LAYARD'S Nineveh and its Remains, 2 vols. 8vo. *plates and cuts*, (pub. at 36s) *cloth*, 18s; *calf*, 21s 1849

2517 **CHINA.** BIOT, Dictionnaire des Noms des Villes et Arrondissements dans l'Empire Chinois, *Chinois et Franç.* 8vo. *sd.* 6s; or *hf. russia*, 7s 6d Paris, 1842

2518 BAYERUS de Horis Sinicis et Cyclo Horario, 4to. *plates, sd.* 2s 6d Petr. 1735

2519 CHINESE REPOSITORY (on the History, Statistics, Language, etc. of China and the adjacent countries), from the beginning, Vols. I—XX., *a complete set*, with General Index, 21 vols. 8vo. *maps and plates, hf. calf*, £28. Canton, 1832-51

2520 —— the same, Vols. I—XV. XIX. XX. 8vo. *eleven vols. bound, and six in parts*, £18. 1832-51

An imperfect copy in stock, of which Numbers are sold separately.

2521 CONFUCIUS. Abrégé historique de sa vie, sm. folio, 24 *plates after Chinese drawings, calf*, 7s 6d Paris, ca. 1788

2522 DUHALDE, Description Geographique, historique, chronologique, politique, et phisique de l'Empire de la Chine, et de la Tartarie Chinoise, 4 vols. large stout folio, *numerous maps and plates, calf*, £2. 10s Paris, 1735

" Includes a vast mass of valuable materials."—*Murray*.

2523 —— la même, nouvelle edition, 4 vols. 4to. *with large folio Atlas of* 42 *maps, by D'Anville, old calf gilt, good copy*, 25s La Haye, 1736-37

2524 HAGER, Panthéon Chinois, 1806—MÉDAILLES Chinoises, et Numismatique, 1805 —2 vols. in 1, roy. 4to. *plates, hf. russia*, 18s Paris, 1805-6

2525 HAU KIOU CHOAAN, the pleasing history, translated, with a collection of CHINESE PROVERBS, and poetry, 4 vols. 12mo. *frontispieces, calf*, 7s 6d 1761

2526 HUC, Voyage dans la Tartarie, le Thibet et la Chine, 1844-46, 2 vols. 1854— L'Empire Chinois, 2 vols. 1854—together 4 vols. 8vo. *maps, half calf neat, uniform*, 16s 1853-54

2527 JULIEN, KING-TE-TCHIN-THAO-LOU, Histoire de la Porcelaine Chinoise, *en Français*, roy. 8vo. *map and* 14 *plates, presentation copy to Professor Wilson, sd.* 16s Paris, 1856

2528 KIRCHERI China monumentis quà sacris quà profanis illustrata, folio, *numerous fine plates and portraits, fine copy, vellum*, 6s 6d; or *vellum gilt*, 10s Amst. 1677

2529 MAGAILLANS, Nouvelle relation de la Chine, composée en l'année 1668, sm. 4to. *plan of Pekin, calf*, 15s Paris, 1668

2530 MAILLA, HISTOIRE générale de la Chine, ou Annales de cet empire traduites du Tong-Kien Kang-Mou, publiés par GROSIER, 12 vols.—Supplement: GROSIER, Description de la Chine, 1 vol.—together 13 vols. 4to. *no plates, bds. uncut*, 32s Paris, 1777-85

ORIENTAL HISTORY AND POLYGLOTTS, ETC. 147

2531 MARTINIUS (M.) Bellum Tartaricum, or Conquest of China, translated into English, 16mo. *portrait (by Cross), and map, russia, with joints, silk linings, rare,* 36s 1654
   The most graphic account of the Conquest of China by the Tartars
2532 MEMOIRES concernant l'Histoire, les Sciences, les Arts, les Mœurs, les Usages, etc. des Chinois, par les Missionaires de Pékin (Amyot, Bourgeois, Ko et Poiret) Vols. I-XIV, 14 vols. 4to. *numerous plates, a fine copy in old French calf gilt,* £5. *Paris,* 1776-89
   " Cette collection ne doit pas être confondue avec la plupart des relations des missionaires relatives à la Chine ; elle renferme des recherches et des observations précieuses sur des objets du plus grand intérêt: c'est incontestablement le meilleur ouvrage que les Jésuites aient publié sur la Chine."—*Boucher.*
2533 MORRISON'S View of China for Philological purposes, Chinese Chronology, Geography, Customs, etc. 4to. *bds. rare,* 10s 6d *Macao,* 1817
2534 MUELLERI Tractatus Sinici: Oratio dominica *Sinice;* Monumentum Sinicum, *cum musicâ, etc.;* Von der Sineser Schrifft und Druck ; Unschuld gegen Grebnitzen Beschuldig.; Kircheri epistolæ ; Beidavaci Hist. Sinensis, *Arab. et Lat.*; Commentatio alphabetica ; Basilicon Sinense ; etc. in 1 vol. sq. 8vo. *calf gilt, rare,* 28s 1674-89
2535 RICCI, Histoire de l'Expedition Chrestienne au Royaume de la Chine, entreprise par les Pères de la Compagnie de Jesus, traduite par Trigault, sm. 4to. *calf gilt,* 20s *Lille,* 1617
2536 RIPA, Storia della fondazione della congregazione de' Cinesi detta la Sagra Famiglia, 3 vols. 8vo. *half calf neat,* 24s *Napoli,* 1832
2537 STAUNTON, Account of an EMBASSY from the King of Great Britain to the Emperor of China ; including observations made and information obtained in travelling through that ancient Empire, with a relation of the Voyage undertaken on the occasion, taken chiefly from the papers of the EARL OF MACARTNEY, 2 vols. 4to. *with folio* ATLAS *of plates, russia, or calf gilt,* 25s 1797
2538 —— Notes of Proceedings and occurrences, during the British Embassy to PEKIN, in 1816, 8vo. *printed for private circulation, hf. russia, rare,* 20s 1824
2539 TA TSING LEU LEE ; the Fundamental Laws of China, translated by Staunton, roy. 4to. *half calf gilt,* 15s 1810
2540 VAN BRAAM, Ambassade de la Compagnie des Indes Orientales Hollandaises vers l'Empereur de la Chine, 1794-1795, avec la description de plusieurs parties de la Chine inconnues aux Européens, traduit par Saint Méry, 2 vols. 4to. *maps and plates, uncut, rare,* 12s *Philadelphie,* 1797-98
   Printed at Philadelphia, North America, and dedicated to George Washington, President of the United States.

2541 **EGYPT.** AHMAD BIN ABUBEKR, HIEROGLYPHICS explained ; with an account of the Egyptian priests, *Arabic and English* by HAMMER, sm. 4to. 6s 1806
2542 ALPINI (Prosperi) Medicina Aegyptiorum, etc. sm. 4to. *bds.* 5s *Lugd. Bat.* 1718
2543 —— idem, cum Veslingii notis, 2 vols. in 1, sm. 4to. *calf,* 6s *Patav.* 1740-38
2544 BELZONI'S Narrative of the Operations and Discoveries within the Pyramids, Tombs, etc. in Egypt and Nubia, 4to. *bds.* 10s 1820
2545 —— the same, 2 vols. 8vo. *third edition, plates, hf. bd.* 7s 6d 1822
2546 —— THE PLATES, illustrative of the Researches and Operations in Egypt and Nubia, atlas folio, 50 *finely coloured plates, bds. or hf. bd.* £2. 10s 1820-22
2547 BONOMI AND ARUNDALE, Gallery of Antiquities in the British Museum, with Descriptions by BIRCH, 2 parts in 1 vol. 192 *figures of interesting subjects, represented on 57 elaborate plates, many coloured,* (pub. at £2. 12s 6d) *gilt cloth, with Eyptian devices in gold on back and sides,* £1. 1844
   An interesting volume.
2548 BRUGSCH. Numerorum Demoticorum doctrina, impl. 4to. *plates, bds.* 5s 1849
2549 BUNSEN'S Aegypten's Stelle in der Weltsgeschichte, 3 vols. in 2, 8vo. *with* 53 *plates, hf. bd. calf,* 10s *Hamburg,* 1845
2550 BUNSEN, Egypt's Place in Universal history, translated by Cottrell, 4 vols. 8vo. *including an Egyptian Grammar and Dictionary, with plates of Egyptian Divinities, Hieroglyphical writing, etc.* (pub. at £5. 8s) *new in cl.* £4. 10s 1848-60
2551 BURTON'S Excerpta Hieroglyphica, or Exact Copies of various Hieroglyphical Inscriptions and Sculptured Monuments still existing in Egypt, and at Mount Sinai, &c. &c. 4 parts, complete in 1 vol. oblong folio, *containing* 62 *most curious plates,* PRIVATELY PRINTED, *hf. bd. very rare,* £3. 10s *Cairo,* 1825-37

L 2

2552 CHAMPOLLION le Jeune, Lettres sur le Musée Royal Egyptien de Turin, 2 vols. 8vo. *with sm. 4to. Atlas of* 16 *plates, sd.* 9s   *Paris,* 1824-26

2553 —— Précis du Système Hiéroglyphique des anciens Egyptiens, 2 vols. 8vo. 26 *plates of hieroglyphics, sd.* 16s   *Paris,* 1828

2554 CHAMPOLLION, GRAMMAIRE EGYPTIENNE, ou principes generaux de l'écriture sacrée Egyptienne appliquée a la representation de la langue parlée, 3 parts, folio, *sd.* £2. 12s   *Paris,* 1836-41

2555 DENON. VOYAGE DANS LA BASSE ET LA HAUTE EGYPTE, pendant les Campagnes du General Bonaparte, 2 vols. atlas folio, THE LARGE GOVERNMENT EDITION, *with* 141 *fine engravings of Antiquities, Views, Hieroglyphics, etc. containing above* 500 *subjects, fine copy, russia, gilt edges,* £3. 16s   1802
Hibbert's copy fetched £8. 8s; Dent's £13. 13s; White Knight's £14. 14s; Sir Mark Sykes's £10. 10s; Gough's £13. 2s 6d; the Fonthill copy £35. 14s; Edwards's £21.; Talleyrand's £26. 5s; 1858, Haward's £6. 17s 6d. The new edition, 1807, 2 vols. 4to. and Atlas of 100 plates, has no value.

2556 DENON, Voyages dans la Basse et la Haute Egypte, pendant les Campagnes de Bonaparte, 2 vols. 4to. *calf neat, and folio atlas of* 109 *plates of Views, Antiquities, Hieroglyphics, &c.* 18s   *Lond.* 1809

2557 EGYPTIAN SOCIETY: Miscellanea Aegyptiaca, 4to. *interesting articles on Egypt by Members of the Egyptian Society, cloth,* 6s   *Alexandria,* 1842

2558 [FELIX, Major] Notes on Hieroglyphics, small folio, *lithographed, plates of Phonetic Alphabets and Hieroglyphical Inscriptions, bds. very rare,* 25s (? 1830)

2559 —— the Original Manuscript of the above, folio, *curious drawings of Hieroglyphics, sd.* £2. 2s

2560 HAMMER. Rouleau de Papyrus publié par Fontana et expliqué par Hammer, oblong folio, *one large facsimile plate in nine folds each the size of the page,* 7s 6d   *Vienne,* 1822

2561 HIERATIC PAPYRI. Select Papyri in the Hieratic character from the collections of the British Museum, with Hawkins' Remarks, parts I. to III. royal folio, 168 *plates,* (pub. at £4. 7s) *bds.* £2. 12s   1841-44

2562 HIEROGLYPHICS, published by the Egyptian Society and the Royal Society of Literature, arranged by Thomas Young, impl. folio, *complete,* 98 *plates,* VERY RARE, £5. 15s   *London,* 1823, &c.
Of plates 81 to 98 only a few copies were taken off.

2563 JABLONSKI Pantheon Ægyptiorum, de Diis, Religione et Theologia Ægyptiorum, 3 vols. in 1, 8vo. *hf. calf gilt,* 10s   *Francof.* 1750

2564 —— Opuscula, quibus Lingua et Antiquitas Aegyptiorum, etc. illustrantur, ed. Te Water, 4 vols. 8vo. *hf. calf,* 20s   *Lugd. Bat.* 1804-13

2565 JOMARD, Mémoire sur le Système métrique des Anciens Egyptiens, folio, 308 *pp. with* 10 *Tables, sd.* 7s   *Paris,* 1817

2566 KIRCHERI OEDIPUS AEGYPTIACUS: universalis Hieroglyphicae veterum instauratio, 4 vols. folio, *plates of Hieroglyphics and Egyptian Superstitions, old calf,* £3. 10s   *Romæ,* 1652-54
This learned work embodies all the then existing knowledge about Egypt: priced, 1834, J. Bohn, £4. 14s 6d.

2567 LACOUR, les Hiéroglyphes Egyptiennes, 8vo. *plates, calf,* 10s   *Bord.* 1821

2568 LANE's Manners and Customs of the Modern Egyptians, 2 vols. post 8vo. *cuts, cloth,* 5s   1836

2569 LEBAS, l'Obelisque de Luxor, atlas 4to. *plates, hf. calf,* 7s   *Paris,* 1839

2570 LEEMANS, MONUMENS EGYPTIENS, du Musée d'Antiquités des Pays-Bas, à Leide, the ATLAS, roy. fol. 69 *plates, with* 8vo. *text, uncut,* RARE, £2. 10s 1839-45
Collation of the plates: SERIES I, Monumens de la Religion et de Culte public, *titles, &c.* 4 *leaves of text, plates* 1-15, 19-40, *mostly coloured, of Sculptures and Hieroglyphics;* SERIES II, Monumens civils, *plates* 1-14 *of Demotic Inscriptions, and* 8 *plates on* 4 *leaves of an apparently Demotic Greek Vocabulary;* SERIES III, Monumens funéraires, *plates* 1-10 *of Sculptures, plain.*

2571 —— Monumens Égyptiens à legendes royales, 8vo. 32 *plates, sd.* 4s *Leide,* 1838

2572 —— Papyrus Egyptien Démotique à Transcriptions Grecques du Musée d'Antiquités à Leyde, 2 vols. roy. folio, 22 *plates, the* 8vo. *text inlaid, to match in size, hf. calf,* 25s   *Leide,* 1839

2573 —— HORAPOLLINIS Niloi Hieroglyphica, *Græce et Lat.* ed. Leemans, 8vo. *coloured plates, calf,* 9s   *Amst.* 1835

2574 LENOIR, Nouvelle explication des Hiéroglyphes, 3 vols. 8vo. 74 *plates, hf. bound,* 10s   *Paris,* 1809-10

2575 NOLAN's Egyptian Chronology analysed, 8vo. *cloth,* 10s   1848

2576 NORDEN (F. L.) Voyage d'Egypte et de Nubie, (traduit du Danois en François par des Roches de Parthenais), 2 vols. in 1, royal folio, *original and best French edition, published by the Danish Government, portrait and* 160 *plates, fine copy, red morocco, gilt edges,* £2. *Copenhague,* 1755

Priced, 1832-40, Payne and Foss, £6. 6s; 1834, Arch, £6. 6s; the Duke of Devonshire's duplicate copy fetched £3. 16s; the Duke of Grafton's £4. 10s; Dent's £5. 2s 6d; LARGE PAPER, 1832, Payne and Foss, £12. 12s; Paris's copy fetched £14.

2577 QUATREMÈRE, Mémoires géogr. sur l'Egypte, 2 vols. 8vo. *hf. calf,* 12s *Paris,* 1811
2578 —— Sur la Langue et la Littérature de l'Egypte, 8vo. *calf extra,* 5s 1808
2579 RHIND, Thebes, its Tombs and their Tenants, ancient and modern, with a Record of Excavations in the Necropolis, roy. 8vo. *map and* 16 *illustrations,* (pub. at 18s) *sd. new,* 15s 1863
2580 ROSELLINI, I MONUMENTI DELL' EGITTO e della NUBIA, disegnati dalla Spedizione Scientifico-letteraria Toscana in Egitto, distribuiti in ordine di materie, interpretati ed illustrati, 3 vols. atlas folio, *containing about* 400 *large plates of Hieroglyphs, Egyptian Architecture, Sculpture and Paintings, many in colours,* with 9 vols. 8vo. of Text—together 12 vols. *newly hf. red mor. gilt tops, uncut, the backs emblematically tooled, a fine library set,* £30. *Pisa,* 1834-24

This magnificent work was published under the auspices of the Duke of Tuscany; owing to the very limited number printed, complete copies must soon become very scarce. Usually sold unbound at £40. L'auteur de cet important ouvrage, qui avait accompagné en Egypte Champollion le jeune, est mort à Pise le 4 Juin, 1843, après avoir publié les huit vol. in 8vo. de texte cités dans le Manuel, et 38 livr. de planches gr. in fol. Pour compléter l'ouvrage il ne manque que 19 planches dont il a laissé les dessins, et un vol de texte pour les monuments religieux dont il a laissé des matériaux qui sont suffisants pour le mettre en état d'être publié. Pourtant jusqu'ici rien n'a paru, et il y a tout à craindre que l'ouvrage devra rester imparfait."

2581 SAMS (J.) Objects of Antiquity from Ancient Egypt, folio, 34 *coloured plates, hf. calf, rare,* 15s 1839
2582 SHARPE's Triple Mummy Case of Aroeri-Ao, 4to. 8 *large coloured plates, bds.* 7s 6d *Syro-Egyptian Society,* 1858
2583 THILORIER, Examen des principaux Groupes Hiérogl. roy. 4to. 5s 1832
2584 VYSE (Colonel H.) Operations at the PYRAMIDS of GIZEH, in 1837, and account of a voyage into Upper Egypt, 3 vols. impl. 8vo. 127 *maps and plates, cloth,* £2. 8s 1840-42
2585 WILKINSON'S (Sir Gardner) Materia Hieroglyphica, part I. sq. 8vo. *with the stamp of the Royal Soc. of Edinb.* 7s *Malta,* 1828
2586 —— Extracts from several Hieroglyphical subjects found at Thebes and other parts of Egypt, with remarks, 8vo. *plates* 1, 4, 5, *and* 6 *of hieroglyphs,* 2 *and* 3 *were not published, very rare,* 6s *Malta,* 1830
2587 —— Topography of Thebes and general view of Egypt, 8vo. *numerous plates, calf gilt,* 18s 1835
2588 —— MANNERS AND CUSTOMS OF THE ANCIENT EGYPTIANS, including their Private Life, Government, Laws, Arts, Manufactures, Religion, Early History, and Agriculture, etc. derived from a comparison of the paintings, sculptures, and monuments still existing, with the accounts of ancient authors, BOTH SERIES, 6 vols. 8vo. BEST EDITION, *with* 600 *plates and cuts, illustrative of their Paintings, Monuments, Sculptures, etc. some in* COLOURS, *cf. gt. rare,* £5. 1837-41
2589 —— the same, SECOND SERIES, 2 vols.—Supplement containing INDEX, and 88 PLATES, *some coloured,* 1 vol.; together 3 vols. 8vo. *cloth,* 30s 1841
2590 —— Popular Account of the Ancient Egyptians, 2 vols. sm. 8vo. *many woodcuts, cloth,* 10s 1854
2591 —— Topographical Survey of Thebes, Tapé, Thaba, or Diospolis Magna, and the Pyramids of Geezeh, by Sir Gardiner Wilkinson, *in* 7 *large plates on six sheets, each* 34½ *in. by* 22½, 28s 1830
2592 —— Fragments of the Hieratic Papyrus at Turin, containing the Names of Egyptian Kings, *with the Hieratic Inscription at the back,* 8vo. *with the Atlas of the* 11 *Facsimile Hieratic Papyri of Kings, sewed, only a few copies privately printed, very rare,* 30s 1851

A very important publication, completing the learned works of the author, of Lepsius, Rosellini, &c. To all interested in Egyptian History a necessary work.

2593 —— Modern Egypt and Thebes, 2 vols. 8vo. *woodcuts and map,* 35s 1843
2594 YORKE and LEAKE's Remarks on some Egyptian Monuments in England, impl. 4to. 23 *plates, bds.* 7s *Royal Soc. of Literature,* 1826

2595 **INDIA.** AYEEN AKBERY. The Institutes of the Emperor Akber, translated by F. Gladwin, 3 vols. 4to. BEST EDITION, 36s   *Calcutta*, 1783-86
2596 —— the same, 2 vols. 4to. *half bound, uncut*, 12s   1800
2597 —— the same, 2 vols. 8vo. *calf gilt*, 7s   1800
    A description of the whole Indian Empire, written by order of the Emperor Akber. "Perhaps no book in the republic of letters contains so much information in so small a compass."—*Clarke.*

2598 BAPTIST MISSIONARY SOCIETY, Accounts relative to, 6 vols. 8vo. *portraits and maps, hf. calf,* 20s   *Clipstone*, 1800-17

2599 BABER. Memoirs of Zehir-ed-din Mohammed Baber, Emperor of Hindustan, written by himself originally in the Jaghati Turki; translated by John Leyden and Erskine, 4to. *map, hf. bd.* 28s; *or, bds. uncut,* £2.; *or, tree-marbled calf extra, gilt edges, back and sides finely tooled, rare,* £2. 10s   1826
    "One of the most instructive, and, to well prepared minds, one of the most interesting publications of the present age."—*Sir Jas. Mackintosh.*

2600 BAYLEY's Dorjé-Ling, roy. 8vo. *cloth,* 4s   *Calcutta*, 1838
2601 BENGAL and AGRA Annual Guide and Gazetteer for 1842, 2 vols. 8vo. *maps and plates* (pub. at £2.), *cloth,* 6s   *Calcutta*, 1841-42
2602 BENGAL: Remarks on the State of Husbandry and Commerce of Bengal, roy. 4to. *bd.* 5s   *Calcutta*, 1795
2603 BERNOULLI, Description de l'Inde, contenant la Géographie de l'Indoustan, TIEFFENTHALER; Recherches sur l'Inde, ANQUETIL DU PERRON; Carte Général par Rennell, avec des additions par Bernoulli, 3 vols. 4to. 64 *maps and plates, calf,* 16s   1786-88
2604 BOHLEN, das alte Indien, etc. 2 vols. 8vo. *hf. calf,* 7s   *Königsb.* 1830
2604*BOILEAU'S Narrative of a tour through the Western States of RAJWARA, with tables and memoranda, statistical, philological and geographical, large 4to. *several plates, parallel Vocabularies, etc. bds.* 28s   *Calcutta*, 1837
2605 BOMBAY PRESIDENCY: Selections from the Records of the Bombay Government, a collection of 46 vols. and parts, roy 8vo. *numerous maps and plans, bds.* £7   *Bombay*, 1855-58

CONTENTS.

Miscellaneous Information connected with the Petty States of Junjeera, Jowar, Poor, etc. etc. 1856
Miscellaneous Information connected with the Native States under the control of the Political Superintendent of Pohlunpoor 1856
Miscellaneous Information connected with the Province of Kattywar in Guzerat 1856
Miscellaneous Information connected with the Persian Gulf 1856
Reports of the Executive Engineers in the Southern, Central, and Northern Provinces of Bombay, 1856-58, 2 vols. 1858
Miscellaneous Information connected with the Mahee Kanta 1855

Memoir on the Sawunt Waree State—Report on the Portuguese Settlements in India 1855
Memoir and brief notes relative to the Kutch State 1855
Memoir on the Satara Territory, with the early history of its inhabitants 1857
Col. Walker's Reports on the Province of Kattywar 1856
Miscellaneous Information connected with the Petty States in the Rewa Kanta in Guzerat, 2 vols. 1856
Results of the Scrutiny by the Inam Commission of the lists of Deccan Suringams 1856
Proceedings adopted for the suppression of Infanticide in Kattywar, Part II. 1856
With numerous minor Reports on Salt, Excise, Canal Clearances, Railways, Thuggee, Dacoity, etc. etc.

2606 BRIGGS (*Secretary Bombay Municipality*) The Nizam, his History and Relations with the British Government, 2 vols. 8vo. *Portraits of the Nawab Salar Jung, the Nizam's Dewan, Col. Cuthbert Davidson, Plan of the Residency, showing the Works for the Defence at Hyderabad,* 1857, *and Map of the Nizam's Dominions, cloth, new,* £2. 2s   1861
    Of the entire edition of 750 copies, only 50 have been destined for sale in England.

2607 BRIGGS, Land Tax in India considered as a measure of Finance, 8vo. *bds.* 5s 1830
2608 BRITISH INDIA analyzed: the establishments of TIPPOO SULTAN, and of the conquerors of Hindostan, 3 vols. 8vo. *valuable, hf. bd.* 5s   1795
2609 BROWN's India Tracts: Jungle Terry districts, and History of the Sicks, 4to. *maps, bd.* 6s   1788
2610 BRUCE's Annals of the East India Company, from 1600 to 1708, 3 vols. 4to. *calf gilt,* 10s   1810
2611 BUDAON, Statistical Report of the district of, by Court, roy. 4to. 6s *Agra*, 1855
2612 CRAUFURD's Sketches on the History, religion, learning and manners of the Hindoos, 2 vols. 8vo. *cloth,* 7s 6d   1792
2613 COLEBROOKE'S Digest of the Regulations and Laws enacted for the Civil Government of the Presidency of BENGAL, in alphabetical order, with SUPPLEMENT containing a Collection of the Regulations anterior to 1793, 3 stout vols. folio, *calf, very scarce,* £3. 12s   *Calcutta*, 1807
2614 —— Two Treatises on the Hindu Law of Inheritance, 4to. *bd.* 12s   *ib.* 1810

ORIENTAL HISTORY AND POLYGLOTTS, ETC. 151

2615 DIXON'S Sketch of Mairwara, with an account of the Mairs, 4to. *maps, plans, and views, cloth, privately printed*, 21s 1850
2616 ———— Report on Ajmeer and Mairwara, 4to. *cloth*, 4s *Agra*, 1853
2617 DUFF'S History of the Mahrattas, 3 vols. 8vo. £4. 1836
   A most elaborate work, entirely based upon original documents, unpublished MSS., official Papers, &c. hidden in the palaces, temples, and private repositories of the natives.
   The History begins with the Conquest of the Deccan by the Mahommedans, A.D. 1000, and extends to the British possession in 1819.

2618 ELPHINSTONE'S History of India, 8vo. *fourth edition, with Index and map,* (*pub. at* 18s), *new, in cloth*, 15s
2619 FERISHTA'S History of Hindostan, translated from the Persian, with introduction and continuation by Dow, 3 vols. 8vo. LARGE PAPER, *map and plates, calf neat*, 9s 1803
2620 ———— History of the rise of the Mahomedan Power in India, till 1612, translated by J. BRIGGS, 4 vols. 8vo. *Genealogical Tables, hf. calf*, £2. 7s 1829
2621 FORBES' Oriental Memoirs, 4 vols. royal 4to. *many plates of Views and Costumes, and* NATURAL PRODUCTIONS *of the* EAST, *several of the latter* BRILLIANTLY COLOURED, *calf extra*, £4. 1813
2622 ———— the same, LARGE PAPER, 4 vols. impl. 4to. *an almost* UNIQUE COPY, *having* PROOF IMPRESSIONS *of the plates on* INDIA PAPER, *with many etchings, the Natural History carefully* COLOURED, *and an unpublished sheet, printed only for the large paper copies, at the close of which is an Autograph of Mr. Forbes; splendidly bound in olive* MOROCCO, *broad borders of gold, gilt and marbled edges*, £12. 12s 1813
   A superb work in the finest possible state, previously priced £20.

2623 FORBES' (A. K.) Râs Mâlâ; or Hindoo Annals of GOOZERAT, in Western India, 2 vols. 8vo. *numerous architectural illustrations, some coloured, cloth*, 20s 1856
2624 FRANCKLIN, on the Tenets and doctrines of the JEYNES and Boodhists, conjectured to be the Brachmanes of ancient India, 4to. *plates*, 12s 1827
2625 ———— Inquiry concerning Ancient PALIBOTHRA, 4 parts in 1 vol. 4to. 21 *plates and facsimiles, bd.* 9s 1815-22
2626 ———— Military Memoirs of General THOMAS, 4to. *plates, bd.* 4s *Calcutta*, 1803
2627 FRIEND OF INDIA, Quarterly Series, 3 vols. 8vo. *Professor Wilson's copy, hf. russia neat, rare and valuable*, 36s *Serampore*, 1821
   Contains Rammohun Roy's original dissertations on Christianity; interesting Essays on Hindoo Polytheism, the Indian Archipelago, the Vedic Literature, etc.

2628 HAMILTON'S East India Gazetteer, with Glossary, 2 vols. 8vo. *second edition, maps, bd.* 5s 1828
2629 ———— Description of Hindostan and the adjacent countries, 2 vols. 4to. *map, hf. russia*, 9s 1820
2630 HARINGTON, Analysis of the Laws and Regulations for the Civil Government of the British territories under the Presidency of Bengal, complete in 3 vols. stout folio, *calf, the 1st vol. in bds.* 30s *Calcutta*, 1805-17
2631 HART'S (Capt. P. D.) Architectural illustrations of the principal Mahometan Buildings of BEEJAPORE, executed under the direction of Bartle Frere, B.C.S. edited by James FERGUSON, impl. folio, 73 *large Photographs of Plans, Sections, etc. hf. red morocco, uncut*, £2. 16s 1859
2632 HOOGHLY River, Reports of the Committee on the, fol. 7 *maps, sd.* 6s *Calc.* 1854
2633 HOUGH, British Operations at Cabool, 1841-42, 8vo. *map, hf. russia*, 12s *ib.* 1849
2634 HUTCHINSON'S Allygurh Statistics, 4to. *numerous maps, cloth*, 7s 6d *Roorkee*, 1856
2635 JERVIS on the Weights and Measures of KONKUN, and the territories subject to Bombay, 8vo. *hf. calf*, 7s *Bombay*, 1829
2636 JONES on the Canal Irrigation of Rohilcund, etc. 4to. *maps, cl.* 10s *Roorkee*, 1855
2637 KENNET's Madras Commercial Ready Assistant, tables of the exchange current in the East Indies, folio, *hf. bound*, 10s *Madras*, 1833
2638 ———— Ready Computist, correct Interest, Exchange, and Merchandise Tables, 4 parts, folio, *bds.* 9s *Madras*, 1847-49
2639 LASSEN'S INDISCHE ALTERTHUMSKUNDE, 3 vols. 8vo. *maps*, £3. 10s 1847-58
   A most learned work on the Ancient History and Geography of India. Some parts are out of print.

2640 MALCOLM's Report of Malwa, 4to. *no title, calf*, 9s *Calcutta*, 1822
2641 MARTIN's History, Antiquities, Topography, and Statistics of EASTERN INDIA, 3 stout vols. 8vo. *maps and numerous plates, cloth*, 7s 1838

2642 MADRAS GOVERNMENT: Selections from the Records of the Madras Government, published by Authority, 68 vols. and parts, royal 8vo. and 10 vols. and parts, 4to. *with numerous plates and plans*, £4.   *Madras*, 1855-58

CONTENTS:

Royal 8vo.
Papers on the Supply of Madras with Water   1856
Report on Public Instruction in the Madras Presidency   1855
Reports on the Fibres of Southern India   1856
Report on the disturbances in Purla Kimedy, 2 vols. 1856
Papers relating to the Budget of Public Works   1857
Report on the Government Museums   1857

Papers relative to the Revenue Survey   1858
Papers relating to Public Works   1858
With many other minor Reports on Salt, Public Instruction, Home Government, Railways, etc.

4to.
Report on the Prisons of Madras   1859
Reports on the Railway Department for 1856, 1857 and 1858, 3 vols.   1855-58

2643 MAURICE (Rev. T.) Ancient and Modern History of Hindostan, 4 vols. 4to. *plates, calf, Professor Wilson's copy*, 32s   1795-1803

2644 —— Indian Antiquities, the ancient Geography, Theology, Government, Commerce, and Literature of Hindostan, 7 vols. 8vo. *numerous plates, calf*, 25s; or, *calf gilt*, 36s   1800

2645 MILLS' Report on the province of Assam, sm. folio, *hf. bd.* 10s   *Calcutta*, 1854

2646 MILL'S HISTORY OF BRITISH INDIA, with a Continuation from 1805 to 1835, and copious Notes and Illustrations, by Horace Hayman Wilson, Boden Professor of Sanscrit at Oxford, 9 vols. 8vo. *fourth edition*, £4. 10s   1840-48

2647 MONTGOMERY'S Statistical Report of CAWNPOOR, royal 4to. *maps, showing the smallest Hamlets in that District, cloth, privately printed*, 27s   *Cal.* 1849

A pattern volume of a good topographical work; the list of villages contains their names in Urdu and English, classifications of the Population, etc.

2648 —— Principles of Law for the guidance of Civil Justice Officers in the Punjab, sm. folio, *bd.* 16s   *Lahore*, 1854

2649 MOOHUMMUD'S History of Jounpoor, from the Persian, 8vo. *bd.* 6s   *Calc.* 1814

2650 MOORCROFT and TREBECK'S Travels in the Himalayan Provinces of Hindustan and the Punjab, in Ladakh, Kashmir, Bokhara, &c. edited by H. H. Wilson, 2 vols. 8vo. *map and plates, morocco*, 14s   1841

2651 MORLEY'S Analytical Digest of all the Reported Cases decided in the Supreme Courts of Judicature in India, in the Courts of the E. I. Company, and on Appeal from India by Her Majesty in Council, 2 vols. roy. 8vo. (pub. at £8. 8s) *calf neat*, £3. 10s   1849-50

2652 —— Analytical Digest of Indian Cases, *new series*, Vol. I. royal 8vo. *presentation copy*, (pub. at 50s) *cloth*, 30s   1852

2653 NAWAB of Surat, Papers relating to the inheritance, roy. 8vo. 5s   *Bombay*, 1853

2654 NEUMANN'S Geschichte des Englischen Reiches in Asien, 2 vols. 8vo. *sd.* 6s 1857

2655 NIMAR, Reports on the Province of, 4to. *maps, cloth*, 5s   *Roorkee*, 1856

2656 NORTON'S Rudimentals, Discourses on Government, &c. to the Natives of India, 8vo. *cloth*, 6s   *Madras*, 1841

2657 ORME (R.) History of the Military Transactions of the British Nation in Indostan, 3 vols. *maps*, 1803—HISTORICAL FRAGMENTS of the Mogul Empire, of the Morattoes, and of the English concerns in Indostan, *portrait*, 1 vol. 1805— together 4 vols. 4to. *a very nice copy in calf gilt*, £2. 16s   1803-5

This valuable historical work "occupies so vast a field that every future historian of modern India must unavoidably trench, in a greater or less degree, upon his premises."

2658 —— Historical Fragments of the Mogul Empire, Morattoes, English concerns, etc. 4to. *portrait and maps, hf. calf, scarce*, 10s   1805

2659 PRINSEP'S (Jas.) Essays on INDIAN ANTIQUITIES, historic, numismatic and paleographic, with his USEFUL TABLES illustrative of Indian history, coinage, weights, measures, etc. edited with Notes and additions by THOMAS, 2 stout vols. 8vo. 53 *plates of early Indian and Bactrian Coins and Antiquities*, (pub. at £2. 12s 6d) *cloth*, £2.   1858

Mr Edward Thomas, late of the Bengal Civil Service, deserves the thanks of all Oriental Scholars for this first collected edition of Prinsep; his notes and additional matter are very considerable. These volumes form a complete Chronology of India, based upon the most authentic records, viz. the Coins of all the rulers. The reproduction of the "Useful Tables" is a boon to all the possessors of the "Bengal Journal" to which they form a necessary adjunct.

2660 PUNJAB and North-Western Provinces, a Collection of Reports on Administration, Popular Education, Selections from Government Records, etc. 24 parts, 8vo. and 4to. 12s   *Agra, Lahore, etc.* 1856, etc.

2661 ROGER, la Porte ouverte, à la connoissance du Paganisme caché, la vie des Bramines, etc. 4to. *plates, calf*, 6s   *Amst.* 1670

ORIENTAL HISTORY AND POLYGLOTTS, ETC.

2662 SALSET. Antient Monuments of India, at Salset, etc. 4to. *plates, hf. bd.* 4s 1785
2663 SEIR-MUTAQHARIN, or View of Modern Times, from the year 1118 to the year 1195 of the Hidjrah, containing in general the Reigns of the Seven last Emperors of Hindostan, and in particular, an Account of the English Wars in Bengal, 3 vols. 4to. *fine copy in russia, or calf gilt,* £2. 2s   *Calcutta,* 1789
                                    Priced, 1839, £5. 5s.
2664 SHURREEF, Qanoon-e-Islam; Customs of the Moosulmans of India, their rites and ceremonies, translated by Herklots, with appendix and glossary, stout 8vo. 7 *plates,* (pub. at 16s) *bds.* 9s   1832
2665 SIKHS. PRINSEP's Sikh Power, and Life of Runjeet Singh, 8vo. *portrait, cloth,* 6s   *Calcutta,* 1834
2666 SMYTH's History of the Reigning Family of Lahore, the Jummoo Rajahs and the Seik Soldiers, 8vo. *map and plates,* 5s   *Calcutta,* 1847
2667 STRANGE'S Elements of Hindu Law, referable to British judicature in India, 2 vols. royal 8vo. 20s   1825
2668 **Sudder Court:** REPORTS of Civil Causes adjudged by the Court of Sudur Udalut, Bombay, 1800-24, 2 vols. folio, *hf. bound,* 36s   *Bombay,* 1824-5
2669 CONSTRUCTIONS, Lower and N.W. Prov. 1793-1856, 12mo. *cl.* 3s 6d   *Cal.* 1856
2670 CIRCULAR Orders, Calcutta, 1795-1855, 12mo. *cloth,* 3s 6d   *ib.* 1855
2671 SUMMARY Decisions, 12mo. *cloth,* 3s 6d   1855
2671*DECISIONS of the Sudder Dewanny Adawlut, Nos. 1 to 10, for 1857, and Nos. 3, 5, 6, 7, 8, 10, for 1858, 16 Nos. 8vo. *sd.* 20s   *Calcutta,* 1857-58
2672 TENNENT'S Ceylon, an account of the island, physical, historical, and topographical, its natural history, antiquities, etc. 2 vols. 8vo. *maps, plans, and cuts, hf. calf neat, gilt top, uncut,* 28s   1859
2673 THORNTON'S Gazetteer of the territories under the government of the East India Company, and of the native States on the continent of India, 4 vols. 8vo. *map,* (pub. at £4.) *cloth,* 36s   1854
2674 ———— Gazetteer of the countries adjacent to India on the North-West, Sinde, Afghanistan, Beloochistan, the Punjab, etc. 2 vols. 8vo. *map, cloth,* 8s   1844
2675 ———— Gazetteer of India, in one volume, stout 8vo. *map, cloth,* 17s   1857
2676 THUGS. SLEEMAN, Ramaseeana, VOCABULARY of the peculiar language used by the THUGS, with introduction on their system, and the measures for its suppression, 8vo. *plates, bds.* 14s   *Calcutta,* 1836
2677 ———— REPORT on the Depredations of the THUG GANGS, 8vo. *map and tables, cloth, rare,* 15s   *ib.* 1840
2678 ———— ILLUSTRATIONS of the History and Practices of the THUGS, 8vo. *cloth,* 5s   1851
2679 TIPPOO SULTAN's Select Letters to his Military Commanders, Governors, Agents, &c. translated by Kirkpatrick, 4to. (pub. at 21s) *hf. russia,* 5s   1811
2680 MACKENZIE's War with Tippoo Sultaun, 1789-92, with Appendices, 2 vols. 4to. *hf. calf, not uniform,* 6s   *Calcutta,* 1791-4
2681 TOD'S (Col. J.) ANNALS AND ANTIQUITIES OF RAJAST'HAN, or the Central and Western Rajpoot States of India (commonly called Rajpootana), 2 vols. impl. 4to. *above 50 extremely beautiful line engravings by Finden, and large folding maps,* (pub. at £9. 9s) *hf. russia,* £7. 15s   1829
2682 TWINING, on the Diseases of Bengal, 8vo. *cloth,* 5s   *Calcutta,* 1832
2683 WARD (W.) Account of the Writings, Religion, and Manners of the Hindoos, History, Literature, and Mythology of the Hindoos, with a description of their Manners and Customs, 4 vols. 8vo. *3rd edition, hf. bd.* 18s; or *cf. gt.* 25s 1817-20
2684 ———— the same, *fourth edition,* 3 vols. 8vo. *bds.* 24s   1822
2685 WEBER's Indische Skizzen, 8vo. *facsimile,* THICK PAPER, 4s   *Berlin,* 1857
2686 WELLESLEY'S (*Marquess*) DESPATCHES, Minutes and Correspondence during his administration in India, 5 vols. 8vo. *portrait, maps, etc. calf gilt,* £3. 10s; or *a very beautiful copy, calf extra, with the author's autograph,* £5   1836-37
2687 WILK'S (Lieut.-Col. Mark) Historical Sketches of the SOUTH OF INDIA, in an attempt to trace the History of Mysore, from the origin of the Hindoo Government to the extinction of the Mohammedan dynasty in 1799, 3 vols. 4to. *maps, hf. russia,* £2. 16s   1810-17
2688 ———— *a fine copy in bright calf gilt,* £3. 10s   1810-17

                     "A very valuable and authentic work."—LOWNDES.

2688*JAPAN. ALCOCK (Sir R.) The Capital of the Tycoon: a Narrative of a Three Years' Residence in Japan, 2 vols. 8vo. *with maps, coloured plates, and above* 100 *illustrations,* (pub. at £2. 2s) *cloth,* 35s 1863
"We have not previously had a book like this on Japan. As a narrative it is excellent; and as containing the results of large observation and close study among a strangely interesting people, it possesses an importance for all thinking readers."—*Athenæum, Feb.* 21, 1863.

2689 CHARLEVOIX Histoire et Description général du JAPON, ses productions, son Gouvernement, son Commerce, &c. avec les Fastes chronologiques de la decouverte du Nouveau Monde, 9 vols. 12mo. *folding map, numerous plates of Costume, Musical Instruments, and other Japanese curiosities, calf,* 21s *Paris,* 1736

2690 FISSCHER (J. F. Van Overmeer) Bijdrage tot de Kennis van het Japansche Rijk, roy. 4to. *plates of the Costume of the Japanese, &c. in brilliant colouring heightened with gold and silver, calf gilt,* £2. 2s *Amsterdam,* 1833

2691 FROIS de Rebus Japonicis, 12mo. sd. 7s *Moguntiæ,* 1599

2692 GLORIEUSE Mort de 9 Chrestiens Japponois, 12mo. vel. *curious,* 10s *Douay,* 1612

2693 HISTOIRE de ce qui s'est passé à Japon, 1625-27, 12mo. *vellum,* 10s *Paris,* 1633

2694 TITSINGH'S (M.) Illustrations of JAPAN, impl. 4to. *with* 13 *coloured plates after the Japanese, calf,* 36s 1822

2695 TRIGAUTIUS de Christianis apud Japonios triumphis, 1612-20, cum Raderi auctario, etc. sq. 8vo. *numerous plates, bd.* 24s *Monachi,* 1623

See General Alphabet "KAEMPFER."

2696 **PALESTINE.** GARCIA, Derechos de Tierra Santa, sq. 8vo. 5s 1814

2976 RELANDI (H.) Palæstina ex monumentis veteribus illustrata, 2 vols. in 1, sm. 4to. *maps and plates, vellum,* 8s 6d; or, *Miss Currer's copy in old calf gilt, with fine portrait of Reland inserted,* 10s *Trajecti,* 1714

2698 —— the same, LARGE PAPER, 2 vols. 4to. *maps and plates, fine copy in Dutch vellum, rare,* 25s *ib.* 1714
Priced, 1818, 3hs; 1831, morocco, £3. 3s; LARGE PAPER, Hibbert's copy, mor. fetched, £3. 5s. "One of the most valuable and elaborate works on Sacred Geography ever published."—ORME.

2699 **TURKEY.** D'OHSSON (Mouradja) Tableau général de l'Empire Othoman, comprenant le Legislation Mahométaine et l'histoire de cet Empire, 2 vols. roy. fol. 137 *fine plates, hf. bd. calf,* 36s *Paris,* 1787-90

2700 —— the same, with the scarce THIRD volume, 3 vols. impl. folio, 233 *plates, whole bound russia, borders, gilt edges, binding of first volume one side cracked,* £11. 1787-1820
The third volume is wanting to most copies. Col. Stanley's copy, 2 vols. only, fetched £29. 8s; Knight's, £15.

2701 GEORGIEVIZ, de Origine imperii Turcorum, cum libello de eorum moribus et praefatione Melanthonis, 12mo. 35 *woodcut portraits of the Turkish Sultans, specimens of Turkish and Slavonic, orange morocco, very rare,* 28s *Witeberg.* 1560
Meusel cites the edition of 1562 as the first.

2702 HAMMER (Joseph von) Geschichte des Osmanischen Reiches, aus unbenützten Handschriften und Archiven, 10 vols. 8vo. *maps, calf,* £2. 10s *Pesth,* 1827-35

2703 —— zweyte verbesserte Ausgabe, 4 vols. 8vo. *maps, hf. calf,* 25s *Pesth,* 1834-36

2704 —— Histoire de l'Empire Ottoman depuis son Origine jusqu'à nos jours, ouvrage puisé aux sources les plus authentiques et rédigé sur des Documents et des Manuscrits la plupart inconnus en Europe, 18 vols. 8vo. and folio atlas, 21 *maps and* 15 *plates, representing the principal Battles and Sieges of the Turks* (pub. at £6. 6s), £3. 3s *Paris,* 1835-51

2705 —— Constantinopolis und der Bosphorus, 2 vols. stout sm. 8vo. *large paper, half morocco,* 25s *Pesth,* 1822

2706 —— Geschichte der Chane der Krim unter Osmanischer Herrschaft, roy. 8vo. *finely printed on writing paper, hf. morocco,* 10s *Wien,* 1856

2707 KNOLLES' (Richard) Turkish History, from the original of that nation, to the growth of the Ottoman Empire, with Continuation by Sir P. Rycaut, 3 vols. folio, *numerous portraits, old calf neat,* 16s 1687-1700
"But none of our writers can, in my opinion, justly contest the superiority of Knolles, who, in his History of the Turks, has displayed all the excellences that narration can admit; his style, though somewhat obscured by time, and sometimes vitiated by false wit, is pure, nervous, elevated, and clear."—*Dr Johnson.*

2708 HISTOIRE DES TURCS: A scarce collection of Tracts containing valuable information with respect to Oriental History, extending from 1553-1615, 5 tracts in 1 vol. sm. 4to. *hf. bd,* 27s
CONTENTS: Villegaignon, la guerre de Malte, et de l'issue dicelle imputée aux françois, 1553—Postel, l'origine, loy et coustume des Tartares, Persiens, et autres Ismaelit 1560—l'ostel, de la Republique des Turcs, 1560—Postel, la tierce partie des Orientales histoires ou est expo ondition, puissance, et revenue de l'Empire Turquesque, *Pot.* 1560—Articles du traicté faict en 1604, entre Roy e Navarre et Sultan Amurat, *Paris,* 1615.

ORIENTAL MANUSCRIPTS.   155

2710 D'HERBELOT, Bibliothèque Orientale, avec le Supplement, 2 vols. in 1, folio,
     calf neat, 36s   *Maestricht*, 1776-80
2711 DAVIS, the Chinese, China, and its inhabitants, 2 vols. 12mo. *numerous woodcuts,
     cloth*, 5s   1840
2712 MEMORANDA on the Tombs of the Egyptians, on Mummies, etc. 8vo. *bds*. 4s 1822
2713 UPHAM'S History and Doctrine of BUDHISM, with notices of the Kappooism
     or Demon-Worship and Bali incantations of Ceylon, impl. 4to. 43 *plates from
     Singhalese designs, of Deities, etc. cloth*, 36s   1829

ORIENTAL MANUSCRIPTS.

2714 KORAN MUJEED. A most magnificent and valuable Arabic MS. stout fol.
     385 *leaves, measuring* 15 *inches by* 9¾, *most beautifully written in Ornamental,
     Black, Coloured, and Gold Arabic Letters, on the finest Khan Baligh paper, in
     Iranee characters; the top, middle, and bottom lines of each page are in gold and
     blue letters, the title pages and headings of each Soorah very richly illuminated
     in gold and colours; a few Prayers, finely illuminated, are added; on the back
     leaves are the* SEALS OF MOHAMED SHAH, PADSHAH, OR KING OF DELHI;
     MEER GHOLAM ALI KHAN TALPORE, KING OF SCINDE: *and inferior Princes
     to whom this book formerly belonged; bound in the native Persian style*, £60.

   This wonderful MS. was purchased at the sale of the confiscated Property of the late RUNJEET SINGH, and is of undoubted Antiquity. As the art of writing and ornamenting Oriental works has been much on the decline since this Koran was prepared, its value has much increased, and it could not be replaced. Each leaf is paged, but the no. 202 is accidentally omitted. Arabic Manuscripts executed by Persian Artists are preferred to all others, as it is in Persia only where Oriental Penmanship was carried on as an Art, and where the writers of MSS. ranked equal with the great Courtiers. Any Nobleman or Gentleman desirous of a really fine specimen of Persian Art should secure this volume.

2715 EVANGELIA IV., ARMENICE, *Manuscript on paper*, 18mo. *beautifully written,
     with* DRAWINGS *of the Evangelists, and numerous* ORNAMENTS, *executed in gold
     and colours*, £21.   *Sæc.* XVI.

   This beautiful Gem is covered with a rich cinque-cento binding of gilt silver, elaborately carved, having on the obverse side of the covers a representation of the Crucifixion, with the Heads of the Four Evangelists as corners; and on the reverse the Resurrection with the devices of the Evangelists as corners. The whole exhibits an exquisite specimen of Byzantine Art. It is enclosed in a silk bag, on which the Crucifix and other ornaments are worked in silver lace.

2716 CHINESE MYTHOLOGY. Fifty splendid large and well executed Native
     Drawings, illustrating the Mythology of the Chinese, *in brilliant colouring,
     each representation on Chinese paper, very nicely laid down on drawing paper of
     the first quality, ruled round with red and black, four lines, title in Manuscript
     by C. Proctor*, impl. folio, meas. 20 inches by 15, *green morocco extra, leather
     joints inside, double bands, by Staggemier*, £12. 12s

   English names are placed on many of the subjects. The destruction of works of Art has been so great lately in China, that it would be extremely difficult to obtain now, even at a high price, such a set of mythological Drawings.

2716* CHINESE COSTUME. A volume, atlas folio, *containing* 32 *large and beau-
     tiful Drawings, of Male and Female Figures, in the richest costumes, brilliantly
     coloured and executed in the most delicate and elaborate style of Chinese Art,
     olive morocco, gold borders, Chinese silk sides, gilt edges*, £15.   *Sæc.* XIX.
2717 CHINESE DRAWINGS. A volume, containing 72 Native Drawings (11 inches
     by 13), IN BRILLIANT COLOURS, GOLD AND SILVER, exhibiting the various
     Trades, Manufactures, Employments, Amusements, Sports and ordinary Occu-
     pations of the Celestial Empire, prefaced by a well written title by C. Proctor,
     the whole series very neatly edged and mounted, square fol. (size 12½ in. by 14),
     purple morocco extra, double bands, £12.

   This is really a beautiful specimen of Chinese Art; probably not surpassed by any similar collection of Drawings in England. The learned Sinologue Dr. Lockhart has assured me, that it would be extremely difficult to find in China now such an elaborately executed set of Drawings.

2718 CHINESE DRAWINGS: ENTOMOLOGY. 28 *Drawings beautifully executed
     in colours, comprising* 50 *figures of* BUTTERFLIES *and other* INSECTS, *with their*
     CATERPILLARS *and the* PLANTS *on which they feed, also* 8 *Drawings of* SILK-
     WORMS *in their several stages; all finished with the most scrupulous fidelity to
     nature, and at the same time with an attention to Art and colour, so wonderful as
     almost to deceive the eye into the belief of the actual existence of the figures
     depicted, hf. green morocco*, £7.

2719 **CHINESE BOTANY.** 49 BEAUTIFULLY COLOURED DRAWINGS *of* CHINESE PLANTS *in bloom, finished with the utmost care and delicacy, in which respect they may be considered along with the above as the perfection of Chinese imitative art, hf. green morocco,* £8.

The above, evidently executed at the same time, and by the same hands, form a Collection of Chinese Drawings unique as to their minuteness, fidelity to nature and beauty of execution, and as far as regards the first two volumes, unrivalled by those of an European or any other nation. In fact, at first sight, so striking is the artistic effect that no one would believe them to be anything but the most finished productions of European artists; on closer inspection, however, the peculiar minuteness of detail strikes the mind of the spectator that they are possibly of Chinese origin, which impression is confirmed by a complete examination.

Chinese Art has so much fallen off in modern times, that these Drawings may be considered as the very best specimens which could possibly be procured. Mr. Scarisbrick bought these volumes at a very high price.

2720 **HEBREW-ITALIAN.** PRECES ET PRÆCEPTA HEBRÆORUM, *Hebraice*, small 4to. *a beautiful specimen of Caligraphy, written in very elegant Romano-Jewish Characters, with points, and having the commencing words in* LETTERS OF GOLD, *surrounded by ornamental borders, painted in various colours, upon vellum, richly bound in green velvet, the sides and edges thereof protected with centres, (having a lion rampant and three stars, as arms, engraved thereon), corners and clasps of solid silver,* £35. *Sæc.* XV.

Illuminated Hebrew MSS. by Italian Artists are of very rare occurrence. This elegant specimen of Italian Art was a marriage gift, it is in the purest state of preservation. Some of the Prayers are intermixed with Benedictions in Italian, but written in Hebrew characters.

2721 LITURGIA HEBRAICA, cum punctis, small folio, Fine Manuscript of the XVIth Century, UPON VELLUM, *written in black ink, interspersed with red and green, one of the headings finished with green and gold, the margins of a few leaves ornamented with curious drawings, in fine preservation, bound in morocco, with joints, in a case,* £12. *Sæc.* XVI.

2722 HINDOO MYTHOLOGY. A FULL SERIES OF ALL THE DEITIES AND INCARNATIONS OF THE HINDOO RELIGION, with some PORTRAITS OF INDIAN AND PERSO-INDIAN PRINCES, together 111 EXQUISITE DRAWINGS, comprising about 250 subjects, the largest measuring 14 inches by 10, *carefully designed and executed in* RICH COLOURS AND GOLD, *by most accomplished Native Artists during the last Century, Persian and Sanscrit names above each Drawing, with unarranged English explanations made in India; all the Drawings mounted, and bound in 4 vols. folio, old blue morocco, gilt edges,* £55. (ca. 1750)

A Collection important for its artistic and Mythological value. The Hindoo Pantheon surpasses that of Greece by the extraordinary variety in the forms of its Gods, and by their still more wonderful achievements. The belief of the Hindoos in these Heroes of the Vedas is universal and likely to remain so, in spite of civilising and missionary efforts. To all students of the Vedantic philosophy the above collection will be highly instructive, it ought to find a resting place in some Public Library in England or on the Continent.

2723 **PERSIAN ART.** FIRDOUSI, SHAH NAMAH, 4to. *a Persian MS. beautifully written in a clear minute hand, in four columns, within gold lines, the headings in gold and coloured inks, with two splendidly illuminated Anwans, and 27* MINIATURES *coloured and gilt, some slightly injured, magnificently bound in whole red morocco super extra, inlaid with ornamental pieces of coloured leather, and exquisitely tooled, from the Earl of Aberdeen's library,* £12. 12s

Sæc. XVI.

Considering the constant destruction of Literary treasures in the East, the above is a very EARLY SPECIMEN OF PERSIAN ART.

2724 NIZAMI, SECANDER NAMEH; BURRY and BHURRY, etc.; a very richly decorated PERSIAN Manuscript, written within FILLETS OF GOLD, round each page, while between every line and column throughout the volume is an ornament also of gold, folio, WITH FORTY MINIATURE ILLUMINATIONS, *many the whole size of the page,* ALL BRILLIANTLY PAINTED AND FINISHED WITH GOLD, *green morocco,* £18. 18s

2725 SOZ GUDÁZ NAW'I (Songs of Burning Passion), large 8vo. *a Persian MS.* with 7 singularly curious ILLUMINATIONS OF THE FULL SIZE OF THE PAGE, *morocco,* £4. 4s (? 1750)

Of the numerous Oriental MSS. with illuminations which have passed through my hands, I never had one approaching the above in delicacy of design and softness of expression. The usual outré colouring is entirely avoided here; and the drawings possess even the mellowness of the European Camaïeu-gris style, so little expected in Eastern Art. The volume was brought from Persia by Sir Robert Campbell.

2726 **ARABIC.** AAMDATU'L ISLÁM: Traditions of Mohammed, *Arabic*, with *Persian* commentary, 8vo. *clear MS. somewhat wormed, hf. calf,* 7s 6d *Saec.* XVII.

2727 ABDOUNIYAH, Sharh ul-, a historical work, *in Arabic*, 12mo. *a neatly written MS. on 564 pages, slightly imperfect, hf. bd.* 20s *Sacc.* XVII.

2728 ABD UL FAKIRU 'L HAKIR: *Arabic and Turkish Miscellany, narrow sm. folio, 200 pp. neat MS. bd. 12s*   *A. H.* 1088
2729 ABU-JAAFAR AT-TUSI, Tahzib al-Ahkam, or first part of the Kutub-i Arbañ, or four great Collections of Shiah Traditions, folio, *neatly written,* 268 *leaves, hf. vellum,* 24s   *Saec. XVII.*
2730 ABU JAAFAR BABUWIYA ALKUMY, Kitabun Man la yahdhura al-Fakiat: the 4th or last of the Books which contain the authentic Traditions of the Shiya, 8vo. *exquisitely written,* 490 *pp. ruled in with double gold lines, old red morocco, gilt edges,* £2. 10s   *Saec.* XVI.
2731 ABU'L-ABBAS AHMED Ibn Yúsuf AL-DIMASHKI, Akhbar ud-Duwal: History of the World, from the earliest Times; with an Account of the Wonders of Sea and Land, *a neatly written Arabic MS. on* 500 *leaves, some mended,* stout sm. 4to. *bound,* 36s   *Sæc.* XVII.
    A very valuable Arabic manuscript, written about 250 years ago.
2732 ABUL ABBAS Ismail Ben Abbas, Akhbar min Millatu 'l-Yemen: History of Yemen, 8vo. 225 pp. neat transcript by Hunt, *hf. calf,* 7s 6d   *Sæc.* XIX.
2733 ABU 'LSEROOR, the History of Egypt from the earliest time to the XVIth Century, with the Genealogies of the later Kings, *in Arabic,* sm. 4to. 267 *leaves, in a peculiarly small and neat hand,* £2. 2s   *Copied about A. D.* 1580
2734 AHMED Ibn Yúsuf al-Shurreef, Nuzhat ul Sultan, or the favourite amusements of the Sultan, War against the Christians, 8vo. 312 pp. *beautifully written, neat oriental binding,* £3. 10s   *Sæc.* XV.
    Autograph MS. by the celebrated Ahmet, son of Yousef Ash Sharif of Broussa, who composed it for Mohammed II., the conqueror of Constantinople, in the year 863 A.H. In the year 1785, this manuscript belonged to a certain Ahmet Pascha, son of Ibrahim Nushed, and since the name of Sultan Mehemet the true owner of the book was very likely on the back of the first page, that page has been taken away to conceal the fact; but this does not injure the work, inasmuch as only the usual phrase: In the name of God, etc. is lost. The handwriting is splendid, and the whole of the book is executed in such a manner as to make it a fit present to a Great Prince. The author dedicates his work to the Sultan by a piece of poetry, the verses of which commence each by one letter of the sentence: *Sultan Mehemet may God grant him victory over his enemies.* Mr. Catafago, who has examined the Arabic Manuscripts of the British Museum and the Bibliothèque Imperiale in Paris, says, that he has never met with a more interesting Manuscript; he values it at £10.
2735 AJAYYIBU 'l-makdur fi Nawaib-i-TIMÚR: History of Timur, folio, *a beautifully written manuscipt on* 178 *leaves,* by Shahabuddin, *bd.* 20s   *Sæc.* XVI.
2736 AL-BEKRI, Fatahu 'l-Sabaat Al-Husún: 8vo. Capture of the Seven Castles, *Arabic Romance, clearly written,* 8vo. *bd.* 6s   *Sæc.* XVII.
2738 ALEPPO. Fadl Halib, 4to. *neatly written,* 194 *leaves, calf gilt,* 7s   *Sæc.* XVIII.
2739 ALFFIYAH, a neat and clean MS. of this celebrated Poetic Grammar by Ibn Malek, 8vo. *bd.* 5s   *Sæc.* XVIII.
2740 ALF LEILAH WA LEILAH *biltammam:* ARABIAN NIGHTS *complete, in Arabic, a distinctly written MS. on* 3578 *pp.* bound in 4 vols. sm. 4to. *native binding, from Lord Guildford's Library,* £4. 4s   *Sæec.* XVII.
2741 ―――― ARABIAN NIGHTS' Entertainment, in Arabic, COMPLETE, *a very neatly written MS. on* 3031 *pp. of charta bombycina,* 4 vols. 4to. £7. 10s   *Sæc.* XVIII.
2742 ―――― a portion, about the twelfth part, 8vo. *Hunt's transcript from a MS. in the B. M.,* 211 *pp. a drawing on title page, with notes, hf. calf,* 6s   *Sæc.* XIX.
2743 ―――― Two Hundred Nights, *Arabic MS.* Vol. I. 4to. *neatly written on very fine paper, bound,* 20s   *Saec.* XVII.
2744 ―――― *a portion containing* 7 *tales,* sq. 8vo. *an old but distinctly written MS. on* 219 *leaves, native binding,* 5s   *Saec.* XVII.
2745 ―――― sq. 8vo. *a neat MS. of* 7 *tales, on* 394 *pages, bound,* 5s 6d   *Saec.* XVIII.
2746 ALI BAHJATI 'L BALAGHATI, being the Sayings of the Khalif Aly on various subjects, *in Arabic,* 4to. *a beautifully written MS. on* 352 *pages, ruled in with gold and red and blue lines, the title illuminated in gold and colours, oriental binding,* £2. 2s   *Saec.* XVIII.
    Arabic MSS. of the Sayings of Ali are very rare. The above contains much more matter than the printed edition by Fleischer.
2747 ANTAR. Kitab Sirat Antar bin Shaddad, wa Májara'lah, Romance of Antar, Vols. I. II. sq. 8vo. *an early MS. bd.* 7s 6d   *Saec.* XVII.
2748 ARABSHAH (Ibn, *the author of Timur's Life*), FAKIHAT-UL-KHULIFA, the Fruit of the Khalifs, thick sq. 8vo. *Shaikh Ibrahim's copy, Arabic MS. very neatly written on* 472 *pages, in Neskhi, native binding,* £2.   *Saec.* XVIII.
2749 ARABIC-TURKISH DICTIONARY, sm. 4to. *bd.* 6s   *Const. A. H.* 934, (1527)
2750 ARABIC GRAMMAR: a connected Series of celebrated works on Grammar, in early MS., 8 vols. sq. 8vo. *a valuable collection, bd.* 12s   *Saec.* XVII.

2751 BEIZAWY (Al) Anwaru 'l-Tenzil: Commentary on the Koran, *in Arabic*, stout sm. folio, *a close but distinct MS.*, 594 *pp. on glazed paper, the first page illuminated, native binding*, £5. 10s *Saec.* XVI.

2751*BOKHARI (Sidi) Kitabu 'l-Hajj, sm. 4to. *Arabic MS. commentary on portion of the Koran, well written, native binding*, 20s *Sæc.* XVII.
Apparently from Northern Africa.

2752 DELAILU 'L KHEIRAT: the Canonical Prayer Book of the Mohammedans, 24mo. 268 *pp. prettily written in coloured inks, and the African character, native binding*, 15s *Saec.* XVII.

2753 FATHU 'L BAHNASA: Conquest of the City of Bahnasa, *i.e.* Central Egypt, sm. 8vo. *Hunt's transcript neatly and distinctly written, with the points, from a native MS. ruled with red lines, red morocco,* 20s 1846

2754 FARAYID WA KALAYID: Pearls and Necklaces, sq. 12mo. *a collection of* PROVERBS, *&c. well written, calf,* 5s *Saec.* XVII.

2755 GHITI UL-LOGHAT, an Arabic-Persian Lexicon, folio, *neatly written*, 646 *pp. bd.* 7s 6d 1696

2755*HAJJI KHALFAH, Kashf-ul-Zanún: Biographical Encyclopædia, thick fol. 1128 *pp. neatly written, bd.* £2. 5s *Saec.* XVIII.

2756 HALEBY (Al-) Alaalak Ulkhatirati; a Chronicle of Syria and Mesopotamia, folio, *a rare and valuable Manuscript in Arabic, beautifully written on* 272 *pages of glazed paper, native binding, in a case,* 25s *Saec.* XVII.
"This volume contains about half the work, all the first section and half of the second."—NOTE BY MR. HUNT.

2757 HALEBY, Multaka l' Abhur, 12mo. *an elegant MS.* 432 *pp. the first page illuminated, bd.* 5s *Saec.* XVIII.

2758 HAMASAH; or Ancient Arabian Poems, collected by Abu Temmam, with Notes and Versions, by Sir W. Jones, stout 4to. *transcript by Rev. G. Hunt, from an Arabic MS. in the library of the Royal Society, formerly belonging to Sir W. Jones, very carefully written, hf. cf. interleaved,* £2. 10s *Saec.* XIX.
At the commencement is a note by Mr. Hunt, who valued this MS. at £21. for its intrinsic worth and rarity.

2759 HAMASAH. Mujallid min Sharh-ul-Hamasa, impl. 8vo. *the greater portion of a celebrated commentary, clear well written MS. stained,* 36s *Saec.* XVI.

2761 HARIRI (Abu Mohammed Casen of Bassora) Al Makamat, folio, *neatly written,* 12s *Saec.* XVII.

2762 HAROUN ARRASHID, Kissat: Adventures of Haroun al Rashid, and other Tales, 4to. *clear MS. slightly imperfect, bd.* 9s *Saec.* XVIII.

2763 —— Waláatu 'l-Hirz al Wazir, the Vizier's Amulet, a story, etc. 24mo. 322 *pp. well written, native binding,* 6s *Saec.* XVII.

2764 HUNNEEFY, Khuzanet-al-Moofteen: the Treasure of Wisdom, folio, *beautifully written, calf neat,* £2. *Saec.* XVII.

2765 IBN HAJJI, (Takieddin ul Hamawi) Sharh-ul-Badiyiyat: on the Art of Versification, sm. folio, *finely written on* 328 *leaves, bound in a case,* £3. *Saec.* XIX.
This famous work is said to be "such a treasury of literature as almost to render all other books needless."

2766 IBN HASHAM, Sharh Malahat ul Arab, (Arabic Grammar), with another by Hariri, etc. 16mo. *a complete course of Arabic literature,* 7s 6d *Saec.* XVIII.

2767 IBN-I-FARIZ, *in Arabic*, (Uri Bodl. Cat. No. MCCXCVI.) folio, *neatly written transcript by Hunt, hf. calf,* 5s *Saec.* XIX.

2769 IBN KHALLIKAN, Wafayat ul Aayan: Biographical Dictionary, a learned and entertaining work in *elegant Arabic, very well written MS. on* 1032 *pages,* 2 vols. large 8vo. *bd.* 20s *Saec.* XVII.

2770 JELÁLEDDIN, Kitabu 'l-Zabarjadi, Tawarikhu l'-Osman Ghazy: Chronicles of the Ottoman Conquerors, sm. 4to. *a rare and important MS.* 225 *leaves, neatly written,* £2. 10s A. D. 1672
An important and very rare MS.

2772 KAIRUANI, Midkhal Ila Ilm ad-Din wa'd-Diyanah, *in Arabic*, sm. 4to. *finely written, oriental binding,* 5s

2773 KASAY, Kissas ul-Nabiyat: Histories of the Prophets, Vol. 1, sq. 8vo. *clear MS.* 390 *pp. hf. calf,* 7s 6d *Saec.* XVII.

2774 KHAMIS, Tarikhu 'l, a history of Mohammed, *in Arabic*, folio, *an early and well written MS.* 511 *pages, a few leaves stained, apparantly wanting the first leaf, native binding*, 20s *Saec.* XV.
2775 —— *a neatly written transcript by Hunt, from a MS. belonging to Mr. Bland of Randall's Park, Surrey,* 1187 *pages*, 3 vols. large sq. 8vo. *hf. cf.* 30s *Saec.* XIX.
2776 KHOOSAH, Ghwynatoot-talib: the perpetual Almanack according to Astronomical calculations, by Hassain Khoosah, folio, *very neat MS. in red and black*, 160 *leaves, oriental binding, clean and sound*, £3. *Saec.* XVII.
2777 KITABU 'L-ISTIBSAR FAMA IKHTILAF: The Second of the Four Collections of Traditions deemed authentic and authoritative, by the Shiya, sm. folio, *a precious and beautifully written MS.* 488 *pp. on glazed paper, enclosed by gold and coloured lines, native binding, stamped and gilt on the sides*, £5. *Saec.* XVI.

<small>The schisms and dissensions which took place among the Mohummudans, after the demise of their legislator and founder, especially the contest for the succession to the *Kalafut*, or pontificate which gave rise to the *Shiyah* or sectaries of *Alee*, have occasioned various differences and disagreements both in reading and interpreting the word of the *Koran*, and in admitting or rejecting the traditions which compose the oral law."—*Asiatic Researches.*</small>

2778 KITAB KEBRIT AHMAR: the Book of the Philosopher's Stone, a Sufic work, with another, in 1 vol. sq. 8vo. *neat MS. Arabic and Turkish, bd.* 7s 6d *Saec.* XVII.
2779 KITABU 'L KABAYIR (the Book of Mortal Sins) a work of Mohammedan Theology, thick sm. 4to. *cvrious old MS. on Charta Bombycina,* 760 pp. *original broken binding,* 20s *Saec.* XVII.
2780 KOLAM SAYYID AL MURSALEENA, a collection of Mohammedan Prayers, 8vo. *neatly written MS. on* 164 *pages, in a distinct Mograbin character, pointed throughout, bd.* 20s *Saec.* XVII.
2781 KORAN, folio, *an early and well written MS. in coloured inks, in the African character,* 188 *pp. imperfect, hf. calf,* 9s *Saec.* XVII.
2782 KORAN, Section VII: with some Prayers, 8vo. *a very old MS. on* 60 *pages, bd.* 5s *Saec.* XVI.
2783 KORAN, first part of, clear MS. with the Vowel points, stout 12mo. 552 *pages, native binding,* 12s *Saec.* XVIII.
2784 KORAN COMMENTARY. A most extensive and valuable Commentary, expounding, as is believed, according to the Doctrine of the Sect of Shiites, all the Soorahs of the Koran, 2 stout vols. folio. MS. *very beautifully written, Indian binding,* £4. 4s *Saec.* XVII.

<small>This MS. is "a famous work, by Hussain Vaez, surnamed Cashefi, containing the whole text of the Koran, with a literal translation, and an excellent commentary, both in *Persian.*"</small>

2785 KURRATU 'L-AYUN: a History of Yemen, stout sq. 8vo. *an early and plainly written Arabic MS. on* 800 *pages, native binding,* 25s *Saec.* XVII.

<small>Purchased at Mocha in 1805.</small>

2786 LUBAB-UL-TAAWYL: Pure Part of the Mystic Interpretation, 2 vols. folio, *fine MS. very distinctly written on* 1494 *pages, the titles beautifully illuminated, ruled in with red lines, native binding,* 20s *Saec.* XVIII.
2787 MAJMUA fi Adabayát: Miscellany of Elegant Literature, sq. 12mo. 162 pp. *bd.* 7s *Saec.* XVII.
2788 MAJMUA fi Ansabu 'l-Maluki wa 'l- Saadat: History of the Monarchs, 4to. *very old MS. of* 96 *pages, probably written when the Arabic character was in its infancy, native binding,* 10s 6d *Saec.* XIII.
2789 MAJMUA Shiár, a Collection of Arabian Poems from the best Poets, 8vo. 296 pp. AN EARLY MS. *bd.* 8s 6d *Saec.* XVII.
2790 MAKARIMU 'L-AKHLAK: Essay on the Moral Virtues from Mahomet's life, 4to. *a beautiful Arabic MS. on* 706 *pages, written at Mecca,* A.D. 1596, *half calf,* 20s *Saec.* XVI.
2791 MAKARIMU 'L-AKHLAK, with Commentary and Preface in *Persian*, folio, *very neat Arabic MS.* 626 *pp. ruled in with red lines, calf gilt,* £2. *Saec.* XVII.

<small>A beautiful and very valuable MS. previously priced £4. 14s 6d.</small>

2792 MEIDANI, Amthál: Arabic Proverbs, Vol. I. sq. 8vo. *in an extremely old MS.*; Vol. II. completing the work, is in folio, *a very clearly written Arabic MS.* dated 1183 A. H. 2 vols. *hf. bd.* 36s
2793 MOALLAKAT. Kasayid al Sabah, sm. 8vo. Hunt's neat transcript, sm. 8vo. 166 pp. *calf gilt,* 6s *Saec.* XIX.
2794 —— Sharh Kasáyid al Sabah, Vol. I. containing Commentary on Amrulkeis, Tarafih, and Zoheir, 4to. *transcript by Hunt,* 236 *pp. half calf,* 7s *Saec.* XIX.

2795 MOHAMMED BEN YAACOOB-EL-KALBINI, Tahzibu l'-Kafy: Rules, and Doctrines of the Mohammedan Religion Laws, &c. with Supplement containing the Genealogy of Mohammed, Treatises on the Annual Pilgrimages to his Tomb, and some Articles of the Law, &c. with the Supplement, 4 vols. folio, *a very neatly written Arabic MS. on 3084 pages, native binding*, £4. 10s Saec. XVII.
2796 MOHAMMED IBN-AL-HUSSAIN, Kafy fi Ulm al Hissab: Treatise on Arithmetic and Geometry, Land Surveying, &c. 4to. 240 pp. *hf. bd.* 20s Saec. XVII.
  A most valuable and scarce Arabic work; beautifully written in the Nashk character.
2797 MUSTATRIF MIN KULL FAZIN MUSTATRIFF, a Miscellany of Historical, Literary, Theological and other essays, high 4to. *an early and closely written Arabic MS. on 668 pages (Uri Bodl. Cat. No.* CCCLXXXIII), *bound in russia,* £2. 10s Saec. XVII.
2798 AL-MUSTATRIF: Account of the wonders of the World, *in Arabic,* folio, *beautifully written,* 172 *leaves, Oriental binding,* 22s Saec. XVII.
2799 MOTANABBI, Diwan, 8vo. *neat MS. of the celebrated Poet,* 310 *pp. ruled in with red lines,* 18s Saec. XVIII.
2800 MULLA JALAL. Sharh Hashiya 'l Mantik, 8vo. *very old MS. on Logic, mended, bd.* 7s Saec. XV.
2801 MUNTAKHAB UL LOGHÁT, sm. folio, *an early MS. of this valuable Lexicon, bd.* 12s Saec. XVI.
2802 MUJUMMAH UL BIAAN, fi tufsur ul KORÁN; a copious comment on the KORAN, by Abu 'l-Fazzul Al- Tabarsi, a learned and laborious writer, who flourished in the XIIth Century, *in Arabic, except the 1st page, containing an account of the author, which is in Persian,* large folio, *a splendidly written* MANUSCRIPT, *on* 1386 *pp., two pages* HIGHLY ILLUMINATED IN GOLD AND COLOURS, *ruled in with* GOLD *and blue lines, ornamental native binding, the sides painted in gold and colours,* A MAGNIFICENT VOLUME, £10. Saec. XVII.
  A beautiful specimen of Arabic penmanship, and also of Persian bibliopegistic art.
2803 PRAYERS: The book of prayers which are daily and continually read in the Mosques, folio, *an early Arabic manuscript written in the* AFRICAN *or western writing, imperfect, but the great number of prayers which it contains deserve a particular attention, in a portfolio,* 12s Saec. XVII.
2804 RAML: a work on Geomancy, sq. 8vo. *clear MS. in red and black, native binding,* 10s A. H. 1105
2805 RAWDAT-I-KHATIB Kasim; a work on the Science of Life, 8vo. *a fine Arabic MS. on charta bombycina, with illuminated heading, each page enclosed by gold lines, native binding, formerly in the possession of several persons of high rank in the East,* 36s A. H. 983 (1574)
2806 SAHIFATU 'L- KAMILR, the Prayers of the Mohammedan Church, 8vo. *a beautiful MS. in Arabic, with interlinear Persian commentary in red ink, on charta bombycina, the title and headings illuminated, each page enclosed by gold and coloured lines, native binding,* £2. 10s Saec. XVI.
  Taken in the sack of the Royal Palace at Delhi, 1858.
2807 SALAHEDDIN KHALIL BEN ABIK AL SAFADI, Kitabu l'- Lahán: Cantica Varia, Vol. I., Verses and Letters to Literati of his day, with their replies, stout sq. 8vo. *well written MS. enclosed by red and blue lines, cf.* 25s Saec. XVII.
  "Ibi et Poeticae Artis et sermonis Arabici elegantiae et eloquentiae Thesaurum invenias."—*Casiri Tom. I. p.* 80.
2808 SAYERAT AL HILIBIYYAT, the Life of Mohammed, Vol. III. sm. folio, *an early MS.* 450 *pp. first page mended, unbound,* 7s Saec. XVII.
2809 SEIF BEN DHI 'L-YEZEN (Al Soltán) Hikayat, sq. 8vo. *a complete copy of this celebrated Romance, beautifully written, the title illuminated in gold and colours, ruled in with red lines, neatly bound, gilt edges, intended for presentation to King Louis Philippe,* £3. 5s Constantinop. 1841
2810 —— the same, sm. folio, *neatly written Transcript,* 420 *pp. not completed, native binding,* 12s
2811 —— Al Safar al Awwal; the same Romance, Vol. I. stout sq. 8vo. 690 *pp. in the African character, pointed,* 18s Saec. XVIII.
  In Lane's Manners of the Egyptians we read of the great *scarcity* of copies of this work, that even fragments are with difficulty procured.
2812 SHARH SHARÁAT ul Islam: Explanations of the Musulman Laws, by Yacub Ibn Seyd Aly, sq. 8vo. *important and neat MS.* 458 *pp. bd.* 8s 6d Saec. XVI.
2813 SHAZURI ZAHAB. Sharh-i-Diwan Shazury, a commentary on the Shazury Zahab, by Al Kasim of Spain, 8vo. *native binding,* 12s *Aleppo,* (*A. H.* 1069) 1649

2814 SIBT IBN AL-JOWZY (Abu Modhafer) Mirat ul Zeman, (Mirror of the Time) Vol. II. in two Sections, 2 vols. sm. folio, *a neat transcript by Hunt, of this famous work on the lives of illustrious men, hf. calf gilt,* 25s   Saec. XIX.

2815 SIONITA (Gabriel) Bahs ul Matalib fi Annahu : Arabic Grammar, sq. 8vo. *neatly written MS.* 598 *pp. in good preservation, bd.* 12s   Alexandr. Saec. XVI.
    This book was taken out of the library of Buda, when that city was stormed on Sept. 2, 1686.—*MS. note.*

2816 SURAH UL-LOGHAT, high 4to. *a very useful Arabic Lexicon, with the vowels, points, etc. the meaning in Persian,* 1020 *pp. clear MS. last chapter imperfect, native binding,* 8s 6d   Saec. XVII.

2817 ——— sm. folio, 606 *pp. neatly written, margins wormed, bound,* 7s Saec. XVII.

2818 TAKSI : Mohammedan Ritual, sm. 4to. *old Arabic MS. not perfect,* 10s Sæc. XVI.

2819 TARIBU 'L-MAJALIS : Delight of Feasts, 8vo. *an early but beautifully written Arabic MS.* 262 *pp. enclosed with gold lines, native binding,* 6s   Saec. XVII.

2820 WASÁYAH, Kitab-ool. Commentary on the Mohammedan Law of Jurisprudence, an interesting MS. well written in the Talik character, sm. 4to. 552 pp. *native binding,* 14s   Sæc. XV.
    This volume was taken by a German trooper from a Turkish Pasha, two hundred years ago.

2821 ZUZENY, Sharh Saaba Muállakat. Commentary on the Seven Moallaka, with the Texts, royal 8vo. clear MS. 252 pp. *green roan,* 10s   Sæc. XVIII.
    It appears from the Kushf-ooz-Zanoon that the author of this Commentary died A.H. 465.

2822 **ASSYRIAN** INSCRIPTIONS : The Rubbings of all the Cuneiform Inscriptions at Susa, taken by W. K. Loftus, Esq., in 1850, in all 160 pieces, most distinctly executed upon a thick greyish paper, the lot, 30s
    The attention of Public Libraries is drawn to this lot.

2823 **BURMESE.** SUMANGALA-VILASINI : BURMESE MS. on 301 palm leaves, containing the second half (pp. 325-625) of a *Burmese* translation of the commentary called SUMANGALA-VILÂSINÎ on the SUTTAPÎTAKA, or moral portion of the sacred Scriptures of the Buddhists. The MS. was finished in September, 1801. The leaves measure 19 inches by 2½, they are all consecutive, and in excellent preservation, between two thick oak boards of the same size, *gilt all round,* £3. 10s

2824 **HEBREW.** AVICENNÆ Canon totius Medicinæ, stout 8vo. *extremely curious and interesting* MS. *comprising the Precepts of that greatest of all Mediaeval Physicians Avicenna* (980-1036), *translated from the Arabic into Hebrew, very legibly written without points, on paper and vellum, with autograph of Renaudot, hogskin, gilt edges,* £3. 5s   Saec. XVI.

2825 **HINDI.** BIHARI, *Hindi* Poem on the Amours of Chrisn and Radha among the Goupies, large stout 8vo. *a fine* MS. *written in a very bold character on* 930 *pages, ruld in with yellow, red and blue lines, native binding,* VERY RARE, £4. 15s   Saec. XVIII.
    "Poëme sur les Amours de Krishna et de Radha chez les Gopis, composé en Hindi par Bihari. Il consiste en 700 stances de deux vers rimés chacune, dans le mètre nommé Dohâ. Chaque stance est suivie d'un commentaire et d'une imitation étendue de l'idée exprimée dans la stance: cette imitation est aussi en vers mais dans un metre différent."—*Chézy.*

2826 **HINDUSTANI.** GUL-I-MAGHFARAT : The Rose of Forgiveness, an important MS. in *Urdu,* in the best hand-writing, and containing the Lamentations of the SHIITES, respecting their Martyrs, Aly, Hussein, Hassan, Kassem, &c. &c. folio, 107 *leaves, calf,* 36s   A.H. 1248 (A.D. 1832)
    The work is divided in Assemblies or Meetings, because of the anniversaries on which the Shiites assemble to lament for the martyrs of their faith. It has been printed at Calcutta, and translated into French by L'Abbé Bertrand.

2827 MEER JAFIR Zuta Alee, Kooleat, 8vo. a *Jest book, in Hindustani, neatly written,* 254 *pages, bd.* 6s   Saec. XVIII.

2828 SOUDA, Kulliat-i-, the complete Poetical Works, *Hindoostanee,* sm. folio, *well written,* 404 *leaves, native binding,* 15s   1820

2829 **MAHRATTI.** MAHARASHTRA Vyakarana, a Mahratti Grammar, folio, *an elegant* MS. *in the Devanagari character,* 199 *pages, calf,* 10s   Saec. XIX.

2830 **PALI.** The KAMMAVACHA, a code of Regulations concerning the admittance of novices to the Buddhist priesthood, chapters 1 and 4, a beautiful MS. *written on fourteen leaves of the Palmyra Tree, in the square Pali character, richly lacquered, gold ground, in fine condition,* 21 *inches long and* 4 *wide,* £3.

2831 KAMMAVACHA (the), Pali MS. on 17 palm leaves, elaborately PAINTED IN THE SQUARE PALI CHARACTER, contains the Pali original of chapters I. and VII. of the Kammavâchâ, *i.e.* the Buddhistic manual of rituals used at the consecration of priests, £4. 10*s*

*** The seventh chapter has not yet been edited.—A beautiful specimen of Pali Art, written in black on a gold ground, covered with profuse devices and other decorations; each leaf measures 20 inches by 3¼, preserved between two wooden boards, enriched with ornamentation gilt on a red ground.

2832 KAMMAVACHA (the), MS. on 15 palm leaves, of the same description and character as the former, containing the first and fourth chapters of the Kammavâchâ in the *Pali* original, £3. 10*s*

This is also a very beautiful specimen of Eastern Art, meas. 21 inches by 3¼, preserved between two richly gilt wooden boards.

2833 **PERSIAN.** ABU 'L-FAZL, Akber Nameh, or the History of Akbar, King of Delhi (1460), 2 vols. 4to. 604 *leaves, Vol. I. slightly wormed, original oriental binding, stamped and gilt,* 12*s* (*Written A.D.* 1653)

2834 —— AYAR I DANISH: the Touchstone of Learning (translation of Pilpay's Fables), sq. 8vo. *plain MS.* 584 *pp. roan,* 6*s* *A.H.* 1096, *A.D.* 1684

2835 AFSUS. Diwan-i-Afsus, 4to. *Persian poems, beautifully written in double columns,* 440 *pp. enclosed by gold and red lines, the first page wanting, native binding,* 22*s* Saec. XVIII.

2836 AGRA, Description and History of, imp. 8vo. *neat Persian MS. hf. morocco gilt,* 12*s* Saec. XIX.

2837 AHMED-I-KERMANI, Diwan, 12mo. *neatly written,* 5*s* Saec. XVIII.

2838 AJAYYIB-UL-BULDÁN: History and Geography of the World, folio, 960 pp. *fine MS. beautifully written, within ruled borders, russia,* £2. 2*s* Saec. XVII.

2839 AKHBAR. Muntakhab Akhbar: Select News Reports, 2 vols. one small, the other roy. 8vo. *Persian Newspapers published at Lucknow, narrating the deposition of the Vizir Ali, and other public matters, hf. calf,* 7*s* 6*d* *A.H.* 1199-1202

2840 ALF LAILA, Arabian Nights' Entertainment, *in Persian,* Vol. I. large 4to. *neatly written MS.* 918 *pp. glazed paper, cloth,* 16*s* Saec. XVIII.

2841 ANWAR-I-SUHAILY, stout 4to. *well written,* 782 *pp. hf. mor.* 15*s* Saec. XVII.

2843 —— the same, sm. folio, *well written,* 600 *pp. native binding,* 10*s* Saec. XVII.

2844 —— the same, sm. 4to. *very neatly written, within coloured lines, on tinted paper, bd.* 25*s* Saec. XVIII.

A handsome MS. probably from Northern Persia.

2845 ARFY, Diwan, 8vo. *small neat MS. enclosed by red lines,* 7*s* 6*d* Saec. XVII.

2846 AURUNGZEBE. Diwan-i-Aftáb; Poems by Shah Aulum, sm. 4to. *neat MS.* 122 *pp. bd.* 5*s* Saec. XVIII.

2847 BIHAR-I-DANISH: the Sea of Knowledge, 8vo. *neat and clear written MS. in the Taalik character, enclosed by coloured lines,* 10*s* 1820

2848 BAKI, Diwan wa Ghazliyat: Poems, in Persian, of the famous Poet Baki, (Saec. XIV.), 8vo. *very neat MS.* 216 *pp. ruled in with gold lines, two title pages illuminated, bd.* 7*s* 6*d* A. H. 1004 (1596)

2849 DABISTAN-I-MUZAHIB; School of Sects, folio, 461 *pp. neatly written. bd.* 25*s* Saec. XVIII.

2850 DEFTERHAYI MESNEWI wa Tabiani Mánoui: Narratives, Traditions, Sayings, etc. relative to Sufism, 4to. *beautiful MS. in four columns, doubly ruled with gold lines, the titles to each book highly* ILLUMINATED IN GOLD AND COLOURS, 771 *pp. native binding,* £2. 16*s* Saec. XVI.

2851 FARHANG-I-ISTALAHAT: Dictionary of Phrases, explained in Persian, stout sm. folio, *bd. from Professor Wilson's library,* £2. 10*s* A. H. 1099 (1687)

2852 FARHANG-I-RASHÍDI: a Persian Dictionary *in Persian,* by 'Abdu-l-Rashíd al-Husainí, folio, *neat MS.* 944 *pp. hf. bd.* 7*s* A. H. 1220

2853 FERIDEDDIN ATTAR, Majmáa Masnawiat: 12mo. 306 *pp. ruled in with gold lines, three illuminated titles, bd.* 7*s* Saec. XVII.

2854 FIRDAUSI, SHAH NAMAH; 4to. portion of this famous Epic, containing the Episodes of Isfendiyar and Sohrab, 420 *pp. quadr. columns, well written, bd.* 25*s* Saec. XVII.

2855 —— a volume roy. 8vo. *imperfect in the beginning and end, but containing a large proportion of the Shah Namah, beautifully written in quadr. columns, within gold lines,* 626 *pp. unbd.* 18*s* Saec. XVII.

ORIENTAL MANUSCRIPTS. 163

2856 GHARAIBU 'L-DUNYA; Wonders of the World, 8vo. *hf. calf, 6s*   A.H. 1083

2857 HAFIZ. DIWAN-i-Hafiz, sq. 8vo. *most beautifully written* MS. 398 *pp. three splendid illuminated anwáns, or titles, ornamented throughout in gold and colours, each ode decorated with corner-pieces of flowers, a leaf cut out and slits in others, native binding, stamped and gilt inside and outside,* 36s Saec. XVIII.

2858 —— DIWAN, 8vo. *beautifully written* MS. 386 *pp. ruled with gold lines, bd.* 15s   Saec. XVII.

2859 —— Diwan: Poems of Hafiz, 8vo. *very neat* MS. *ornamented with gold lines, bd. 7s*   Saec. XVIII.

2860 —— Ghazliyat: Odes of Hafiz, sq. 8vo. 160 *pp. double cols. bd.* 10s Saec. XVII.

2861 HAIDARI, Nishan: Memoirs of Hyder Ali, sq. 8vo. 328 *pp. bd. 7s 6d* Saec. 1806

2862 HAJJI MUSTAPHA, Bostán: the Garden, a poetical work, in imitation of Sadi's, 12mo. *neatly written, bd.* 5s   A. H. 1204

2863 HATIM TAÏ, Kissah, 12mo. *neatly written copy of this Romance, a few leaves lost at end, bd.* 5s   Saec. XVIII.

2864 HIKAYAT: Historical Stories, 8vo. 620 *pp. plainly written, bd.* 5s Saec. XVII.

2865 HOSSEINY (Abu 'l-Barakat) Gharar al-Durr (Ornaments of Pearls): a Life of Mohammed, sm. 4to. *neatly written, within gold lines, stained, bd. 7s 6d*   1589

2866 HUSSAIN, Akhbar Ahwal Abnáï-Rozgar: a History of India for 5000 years back, by Ghulam Hussain. 2 vols. folio, *an interesting* MS. 608 *and* 996 *pp. bd.* £3. 5s   1772

2867 IBN ABD'ULKURIM Shirazi, Tarikh-i-Daulat-i-Silsilah-i-Zand; History of the Zend and Kajar Dynasties, sq. 8vo. *neat* MS. 248 *pp, bd.* 24s Saec. XVIII.

2868 IBN AHMED, Nashk-ul-Azhar, fi Ajayyib-ul-Akthar: Flower-Odours from the Wonders of Countries, a celebrated historico-geographical work, *well written, bd.* 18s   Saec. XVIII.

2869 JAMI, Nafahat-ul-Uns: The Odours of Friendship, a Biographical Work, sm. folio, *the names of the subjects are in red,* 336 *leaves, hf. bd.* 32s A. 1169 (1755)

2870 —— SUHBET-UL-ABRAR: Society of the Just, a collection of Tales, *neatly written,* 308 *pp. bd.* 6s   Saec. XVIII.

2871 —— Yusuf wa Zulaikhá; roy. 8vo. *a fine* MS. *of this celebrated romantic poem, with illuminated frontispiece, gilt titles, gold ruled borders, and coloured patterns on the margin of every page,* 346 *pp. hf. russia,* 25s   Saec. XVI.

2872 —— Yusuf wa Zuleikha, sq. 8vo. 276 *pp. clearly written, bd.* 5s Saec. XVII.

2873 KANZ al Loghát; a well known Arabic and Persian Dictionary, sq. 8vo. *neat* MS. 660 *pp. bd.* 6s   Saec. XVII.

2874 KAZWINI, Nazhet-ul-Kulúb: a Geographical Dictionary, sm. folio, *very neatly written,* 226 *pp. bd.* 10s   Saec. XVII.

2875 KHILIYAT, sm. 8vo. *clear small* MS. *hf. morocco gilt,* 5s Saec. XVI.

2876 KHOSROU, Korán al-Saadin; 8vo. *neat* MS. 265 *pp. bd.* 6s Saec. XVII.

2877 KHOSRU. KULYAT AMIR KHOSRU: complete Works of this famous Indo-Persian Poet, 5 parts in 1 vol. imp. 8vo. *written in the finest style of elegance, the first two pages or Anwáns splendidly illuminated, and the four subsequent titles also illuminated, the text entirely inlaid, and bordered with gold and blue lines, an unblemished and beautiful* MS. *bound in purple morocco extra, gilt edges, from the libraries of Dr. Adam Clarke and Miss Currer,* £8. 8s Saec. XVII.
Cost Dr. Adam Clarke £10. 10s.

2878 —— Ayat Kitab Amir Khosru, roy. 8vo. 598 *pp. beautifully written, but some pages slightly defective and stained, each page enclosed by gold and blue lines, hf. calf neat,* 12s   Saec. XVIII.

2879 KHONDMIR, Tarikh-i-Abu 'l-Ghazy, wa Ajayibu 'l-Buldán: History of Abulghazy, and Wonders of Regions, sm. folio, 506 *pp. well written* MS. *bd.* 15s   Saec. XVII.
The two volumes added by Khondmir to his father's General History, the Rawzat ul-Safa.

2880 KISSAH SA HAZAR AZAR: Tales, folio, 310 *pp. bd.* 15s Saec. XIX.
Brought from Sheeraz.

2881 KISSAS-UL-AMBIA: Memoirs of the Prophets, 4to. 464 pp. bd. 7s   Saec. XVI.
2882 KORAN. Ayátu 'l-Koran: the most important verses of the Koran, in *Arabic*, with *Persian* commentaries, sq. 8vo. *neatly written, bd.* 5s   Saec. XVIII.
2883 TAWKIÁ IKHTAR: a Commentary on the Koran, sm. folio, *Persian and Arabic, illuminated title page, text within gold lines, bd.* 7s 6d   Saec. XIX.
2884 KUSHF UL LOGHAT: the Revealer of Words, a celebrated Persian and Arabic Dictionary, sm. stout folio, *very neatly written,* 1040 pp. *ruled in with red and blue lines, bd.* £2. 5s   A. H. 1017 (1608)
See Stewart's Catalogue, p. 131.
"The Kushf ul Loghat contains Persian words in common use, and such Arabic words as are most frequently found in the Persian language."—*Clarke's Bibliographical Misc.*
2885 LUBAB AL AKHBAR. Traditionary Sayings of Mohammed, sq. 8vo. *well written,* 146 pp. bd. 6s   Saec. XVI.
2886 MIFTEH-I-KULÚB; the Key of Hearts, sq. 8vo. 256 pp. bd. 5s   Saec. XIX.
2887 MIRKHOND, RAWZAT UL-SUFÁ, Jildha Awal wa Siwum: the Garden of Purity, Vols. I. and III. containing his Universal History from the Creation to the twelfth Imám of Ali's successors, (the absent Vol. II. contains the lives of Mohammed and the first four Khalifs) 2 vols. sm. folio, *neatly written,* 597 *and* 454 pp. *a leaf wanting in Vol. III. bd. not uniform,* 15s   Saec. XVII.
2888 MULLAL RUMI, JALÁLU-'L-DIN. MASNAWI, folio, 576 pp. *a fine MS. of this great Mystic Poem, in four columns, ruled in with red lines, bd. from Professor H. H. Wilson's library,* £3. 3s   A. H. 1101 (1689)
2889 ——— MASNAWI, another edition, folio, 513 pp. *quadrup. columns, neatly written, ruled in with red lines, and red headings, bd.* £2.   Saec. XVII.
2890 ——— MASNAWI, folio, *a beautifully small handwriting, in quadruple columns, bd.* £2. 16s   Saec. XVIII.
2891 ——— Masnawi, the first three parts, sm. folio, 298 pp. *neatly written in four columns, ruled in with red lines, margins wormed and mended, bd.* 24s   Saec. XVII.
"The author of this extraordinary work was the celebrated Moulavy Jelal addeen: he founded an order of dervishes in the city of Conyeh (Iconium) in Asiatic Turkey and died A. D. 1212. He was buried in the monastery, and his tomb was visited for many centuries by his devout countrymen, who consider his works as the effect of inspiration, and only inferior to the Koran."—*Major Stewart.*
2892 MUNTAKHUB UL LOGHÁT, by Abdool Rashid; a Dictionary of Arabic Words explained in *Persian,* sm. folio, *very neatly written,* 420 pp. bd. *a valuable MS.* 18s   A. H. 1126
A very useful dictionary, in much repute in Hindoostan.
2893 MUZHIR UL ATHAR: Revealer of Footsteps, a Poetical Work, by Khoja Kirmani, sm. 8vo. *finely written,* 274 pp. *ruled in with gold and blue lines, the first page illuminated, roan,* 10s   Saec. XVII.
2894 NAZIHATU 'L-ARWAH: Delight of Minds, roy. 8vo. *very neat MS.* 302 pp. bd. 6s   Saec. XVII.
2895 NEAMUT ULLA, GHAZULIAT: Odes, Elegies, and Poems, narrow folio, 488 pp. *beautifully written, slightly wormed, russia,* 14s   Saec. XVI.
2896 NEGARISTAN: the Picture Gallery, by Abu-'l-Barakat, a collection of political, historical, and moral Tales and Anecdotes, *beautifully written,* 698 pp. *calf,* 25s   A. H. 1070 (1660)
2897 ——— the same, 8vo. *neat MS.* 142 pp. *calf,* 5s   A. H. 1198
2898 NIZAMI, KULYÁT: Makhzen ul- Asrar; Khosrou wa Shirin; Leila wa Majnún; Haft Pigr; Iskander Namah; Asrar ul- Aashikin; 6 parts in 1 vol. sm. folio, 568 pp. *the two front pages gracefully adorned with floreated margins in gold, and an illuminated heading, with flowers of various hues, the pages of text in four columns, bordered by silver and coloured lines, bd.* £2. 5s   Saec. XIX.
2899 ——— Wamik wa Azrá (Lover and Maid); Leila wa Majnún; Khosru wa Shirin; 3 parts in 1 vol. 18mo. *a beautiful MS. of Nizami's Love Poems, written within gold borders, the three titles illuminated, bd. the covers elaborately painted with birds and flowers,* 36s   Saec. XIX.
2900 ——— ISKANDER NAMEH: or History of Alexander the Great, st. 4to. *neat MS. wormed,* 469 pp. bd. 7s   Saec. XVII.
2901 ——— Iskander Nameh. impl. 8vo. 400 pp. *very neatly written on thin paper, calf,* 5s   Saec. XVIII.
2902 ——— Iskander Nameh; 4to. 274 pp. *calf,* 7s 6d   Saec. XVII.
2903 ——— Khosrou wa Shirin, 12mo. *very neatly written, with illuminated title, and* 23 *drawings, bd. the covers gilt and painted,* £2. 2s   Saec. XVIII.
A curious specimen of AFGHAN ART; having been executed at *Herat.*

2953 ABDO-'L WAHID Al Marrekoshi, History of the Almohades, *Arabic*, with Notes by Dozy, roy. 8vo. *cloth, 9s* *Leyden*, 1847
2954 ABULFEDA, Takwimu 'l-Buldán, Géographie, texte *Arabe*, par Reinaud et M. G. de Slane, 1840—Traduite en *Français*, avec des notes par Reinaud, Vol. I. et II. 1re partie, (*all yet published*) *plates*, 1848—together 3 vols. 4to. *hf. calf, uncut*, £3. 10s *Paris*, 1840-48
2955 ——— Al-Towarikh al-Kadamat: Historia Ante-islamica, *Arabice et Latine*, cum notis, etc. ed. Fleischer, 4to. *sd. 6s* *Lips.* 1831
2956 ——— Zikr dyár Misr: descriptio Aegypti, *Arab. et Lat.* roy. 8vo. *sd. 5s* 1776
2957 ABU ISHAC EL FARESI (El Issthachri) Kitabu l'Akalym: Liber Climatum, *Arabice*, cum notis ed. Moeller, 4to. 126 *pp. in facsimile of a MS. with 16 coloured maps and designs on paper representing the original, bds.* 30s *Gothæ*, 1839
2958 ABU 'L FARAJ, Tarikh Mukhtasar Al Duwal: Historia Compendiosa Dynastiarum (Orientalium) usque ad tempora authoris, *Arab. et Lat.* a Pocockio, cum Supplemento, 2 vols. in 1, stout sm. 4to. *sound clean copy in calf,* 20s *Oxon.* 1663
2959 ABU ZACARIA JAHIA Ebn el Awam, Kitabu l'Falāhat: Libro de Agricultura, *Arab. y Espanol*, por Banqueri, con discurso preliminar y Catalogo de los nombres de Plantes, *slightly stained*, 2 vols. folio, *calf,* 30s *Madrid*, 1802
Priced, 1824. Thorpe, mor. £5. 5s.
Ouvrage interessant non-seulement comme production d'un écrivain Arabe Espagnol, mais encore parce qu'il ait voir l'état avancé de l'agriculture sous les Maures.
2960 ABU ZAKARIYA YAHYA el Nawawi, Biographical Dictionary, *in Arabic*, by Wüstenfeld, roy. 8vo. *sd. 8s* *Gött.* 1842-47
2961 ALF LEILAH WA LEILAH: Book of the Thousand Nights and One Night, commonly known as the "Arabian Nights' Entertainments," now, for the first time, published complete in the Original Arabic, from an Egyptian MS. brought to India by the late Major Turner Macan, editor of the "Shah Nameh," edited by Sir W. H. Macnaghten, 4 vols. roy. 8vo. (pub. at £6.) *sd.* £2. 16s *Calc.* 1832-42
The Calcutta edition of the Arabian Nights, as edited by Macnaghten from an Egyptian MS. is much richer than Habicht's edition from a Tunis MS. and is therefore preferred as the best.
The above edition of the Arabian Nights will be found a most useful book for the practical study of the Modern Arabic Language.
2962 ALF LEILAH: Contes Inédits des Mille et Une Nuits, extraits de l'Arabe par HAMMER, *en Français*, par Trébutien, 3 vols. 8vo. *green calf,* 24s *Paris*, 1828
2963 ALFIYYA (Mille Règles) Grammaire Arabe par Ibn Malec, *Arabe et Franç.* par De Sacy, roy. 8vo. *cloth,* 6s 6d *O. T. F.* 1833
2964 ALNASAFI, Pillar of the Creed of the Sunnites, etc. *Arabic*, by Cureton, roy. 8vo. *cloth, 5s* 1843
2965 AMTHAAL UL-ARAB: ARABUM PROVERBIA, vocalibus instruxit, Latiné vertit, commentario illustravit et edidit G. W. Freytag; insunt à Meidanio collecta Proverbia, commentatio, indices tres et Addenda, 4 parts in 3 vols. 8vo. 2900 pp. (pub. at £4. 14s 6d) *sd.* 35s; or *hf. calf, uncut*, £2. 5s *Bonnae*, 1838-43
2966 ——— the same, VELLUM PAPER, 4 vols. 8vo. *blue morocco, gilt tops, very rare,* £6. 15s 1838-43
Containing Meidani's Collection of Proverbs, and others, the text with vowel points, and a close translation; the grammatical and historical commentaries of Meidani upon the Proverbs; extracts from the works of Scharef-Aldin, Samaschari, and other writers, with additional notes by the learned editor; an Arabic and a Latin Index; and a treatise upon Arabic proverbs, and those authors who have written upon them.
2967 ARABSHAH, Akhbar Timur: Vita Timuri, vulgo Tamerlanis, *Arab.* à Golio, sq. 8vo. *bd.* 7s 6d *Lugd. Bat.* 1636
2968 ——— Vitae et rerum gestarum Timuri vulgò Tamerlanis, historia, *Arabice et Latine*, cum. annott. ed. MANGER, 2 vols. in 3, sm. 4to. *hf. calf, gilt top, uncut*, £3. 10s *Leovardiæ*, 1767-72
2969 ATHANASIOU Patriarchou Ierosolymôn Psychophelés Biblos. Homilies of the Patriarch Athanasius, according to the Eastern Orthodox Church, in *Arabic*, with a preface in *Arabic and Modern Greek* by the Patriarch CHRYSANTHUS, folio, *large woodcuts and vignettes*, 421 pp. *calf,* £2. *Aleppo*, 1711
This book is a model of Christian Arabic eloquence, every sermon containing many interesting anecdotes.
2970 BEIDHAWII Commentarius in Coranum, *Arabice*, edidit H. O. Fleischer, 2 vols. 4to. £2. 16s *Lipsiæ*, 1846-48
2971 BLED DE BRAINE, Cours de langue Arabe, 8vo. *hf. calf,* 4s; or, *calf gilt,* 6s 1846
2972 BOHA-EDDIN, Siratu 'l-Sultán Al-Malik Al-Nasir Salah-Eddin: Bohadini Vita et res gestae SULTANI SALADINI: necnon excerpta ex historiis Abulfedae,

etc. *Arabice et Latine,* cum commmentariis, etc. ed. Schultens, folio, *neatly bd.*
9s *Lugd. Bat.* 1732
Copies dated 1755 have merely a new title. "Bohadinus was secretary to the Sultan, and has inserted an interesting journal of Saladin's watchful and wary accompaniment of Richard's progress."—TURNER.

2973 BOHLEN, de poeta Motenabbio, 8vo. *hf. bound, 4s*   *Bonnae,* ? 1830
2973*BOKHARI (Abu Abdallah Mohammed Ibn Ismaïl al Jaffer) al Jami' ul Sahih: Recueil de Traditions Mahométanes, *en Arabe,* publié par Krehl, Vol. I. *(all yet published),* 4to. *bds.* 30s   *Leide,* 1862
2974 BURCKHARDT'S ARABIC PROVERBS, or the Manners and Customs of the Modern Egyptians, illustrated from their Proverbial Sayings, 4to. *calf,* £3. 3s   1830
2975 BUSSY, l'Idiôme d'Alger, avec dictionnaire, *Franç.-Arabe et Arabe-Fr.* 8vo. *hf. calf,* 6s   *Alger,* 1847
2976 CANES, Diccionario Español Latino-Arabigo, para facilitar el estudio de la lengua arabiga a los que viajaren ó contraten en Africa y Levante, etc. 3 vols. folio, *a very careful and highly esteemed work, bds. uncut,* 18s   *Madrid,* 1787
"Cet ouvrage est particulierement destiné aux personnes, qui ont besoin d'apprendre à parler et à écrire la angue arabe."—*Caussin de Perceval fils.*

2977 CANES, Gramatica Arabigo-Española, sm. 4to. *red morocco,* 4s   1776
2978 CARLYLE's Specimens of Arabian Poetry, with some account of the authors, *Arabic and English,* 4to. *calf,* 5s   *Camb.* 1796
2979 CASIRI Bibliotheca Arabico-Hispana Escurialensis, sive Librorum omnium MSS. quos Arabice compositos Bibliotheca Escurialensis complectitur recensio, 2 vols. folio, *bds. uncut,* 24s ; or, 2 vols. in 1 folio, *hf. cf. nt.* 28s *Matriti,* 1760-70
This valuable work was printed at the expense of the king of Spain, and very few copies were worked off, besides those intended for presents.

2980 CASPARI, Grammatica Arabica, cum Chrestomathiâ et Lexico, 8vo. *bds.* 6s   1848
2981 CATAFAGO'S Arabic Dictionary: an Arabic-English and English-Arabic Dictionary, by Joseph Catafago, Esq., *of Aleppo, Syria,* 2 vols. sm. 8vo. Vol. I. xii. and 316 pp. Vol. II. viii. and 744 *pp. double columns, much matter compressed into a small space, all the Arabic words with the pronunciation in Roman letters,* (pub. at £2.) *cloth,* 30s   1858
2982 —— the same, 8vo. LARGE PAPER, (pub. at £3. 3s) *hf. morocco,* 36s   1858
2983 DOZY, Dictionnaire détaillé des noms des Vêtements chez les Arabes, 4to. LARGE PAPER, *hf. morocco gilt,* 20s   *Amst.* 1845
2984 ——— Catalogus Codd. Orient. Bibl. Acad. Lugd. Bat. 2 vols. 8vo. *extracts from Arabic MSS. sd.* 18s   *Lugd. Bat.* 1851
2985 —— Notices sur quelques MSS. Arabes, *in Arabic,* 8vo. *cloth,* 6s   1847-51
2986 EDRISII Geographia, *Arabice,* sm. 4to. *sd.* 4s   *Romae,* 1592
2987 —— Geographia Nubiensis, *Latinè,* à G. Sionita et J. Hesronita, sm. 4to. *calf,* 7s 6d   *Paris,* 1619
2988 —— the above two works, *Arabic* text, and *Latin* translation, bound in 1 vol. sq. 8vo. *calf neat,* 14s   1592-1619
2989 —— Africa, *Lat.* curavit Hartmann, 8vo. *sd.* 5s   *Gott.* 1795
2990 —— Géographie de, en Français, par Jaubert, tome II. 4to. 12s   *Paris,* 1840
2991 ELLIOTT'S Bibliographical Index to the Historians of Modern India, Vol. I. 8vo. *bds.* 20s   *Calcutta,* 1849
2992 ELMACINUS. El-Makin, Tarikhu 'l-Muslumin: Historia Saracenica, *Arab. et Lat.* operâ Erpenii, folio, *vellum, bd.* 10s   *Lug. Bat.* 1625
2993 ERPENII Grammatica Arabica, cum fabulis Lokmani, &c. à Schultens, sq. 8vo. *hf. bd.* 6s   *Lug. Bat.* 1767
2994 —— the same, without Lokman, sq. 8vo. *bd.* 4s   1770
2995 EUCLID. Kitab tahrir Usúl: Euclid's Elements, by Nasir Eddin Al-Toussy, *in Arabic, first edition,* folio, 453 pp. *Diagrams, neatly bound,* 15s   *Rome,* 1593
2996 EUTYCHII *(Patriarchæ Alexandrini)* Annales, *Arabice et Latine,* curâ Pocockii, 2 vols. in 1, stout sm. 4to. *fine copy in vellum,* £2. 10s   *Oxon.* 1658
2997 —— the same, *with fine portrait of John Selden, old calf neat, from Abp. Tenison's Library, scarce,* £2. 10s   1659
"Eutychius has handed down in his Annals some curious traditional notices of the early history of his church, and has communicated much important contemporary information."—*Dowling.*

2998 FARHAT *(Germanos Maronite)* Dictionnaire Arabe, augmenté par R. de Dahdah, 4to. (pub at £5. 5s) £3. 10s   *Marseilles,* 1849
This valuable and rare Dictionary is a new edition of the KAMOOS, with all the useless matter left out, and many words, particularly those occuring in Christian works, added.

2999 FARIS' Arabic and English Exercises and Dialogues, 8vo. 10s (*Malta,* 1840)

2904 PERSIAN, ARABIC, and HINDI Vocabulary, 8vo. 258 pp. 6s   Saec. XIX.
2905 PROVERBS, with *English* translations, collected by Hunt,—Sadi, Pend Namah, in 1 vol. 12mo. *neatly written, hf. cf. 6s*   Saec. XIX.
2906 RISÁLAT SARF, sq. 8vo. *a valuable Persian treatise on Arabic Grammar, bd. 7s*   Saec. XVI.
2907 SÁDI, Kulyát afsa Al-Mutakkihin Sheykh Sádi: the complete Works, thick 8vo. 1048 pp. *beautifully written within gold lines, russ.25s*   A. H. 1009 (1600)
2908 —— Kulyát: complete Works, folio, 960 pp. *well written in a bold hand, calf,* 32s   " A valuable manuscript."—*Captain Cator.*   A. H. 1263
2909 —— Bostan: the Garden, 12mo. *very neat MS. of this great Poem, bd. gilt covers, 7s*   A. H. 1241
2910 SAHAB-HUZERAT, Basatien noos Salàteen: History of *Dekkan,* high 4to. 173 leaves, bd. 5s   Saec. XVII.
2911 SAIB, DIWAN: the Poems of Sahib, or Sahaib, stout high 4to. *well written MS. in double columns,* 670 pp. *hf. calf,* £2. 5s   Saec. XVIII.
2912 SAKI Musta'id Khan, Maásiri 'Alamgiri: History of Aurangzib, 4to. *neat MS.* 712 pp. bd. 6s   A. H. 1182, A. D. 1768
2913 SHEHABY Tarrassul, sm. 8vo. *a curious work on Calligraphy, with examples, calf,* 6s   Saec. XVI.
2914 SUWAL WA JAWAB: a religious treatise in question and answer, 8vo. 110 pp. *neatly written, bd. 7s*   Saec. XVII.
2915 TABAKÁTI AKBAR SHAH: a general History of India to the reign of Akbar, by Khojah Nizámu-l-dín Ahmad Ben Muhammad Mukim al Harawi, st. 4to. *very neat MS.* 970 pp. *ruled in with blue and yellow lines, first page illuminated, bd.* £2. 5s   Saec. XVIII.
2916 TABARI, Abu Jaffer Mohammed, TARIKH PISR JORAIR: Universal History, from the Creation to 300 A. H. translated from the Arabic, and continued to A. H. 487, by the Vizir Abdulgani, folio, *a well written MS.* 1176 pp. bd. £3. 5s   Saec. XVI.

Tabari was born A. H. 224, died A. H. 310. This Persian translation is considered more valuable than the Arabic original, from its numerous and curious additions.

2917 TÁBIR NAMAH. Tábir-i-Ruyat (Explanations of Dreams), sm. folio, *a very early and curious MS. neatly written on glazed paper, bd.* £2. 16s A.H. 808 (1405)
Written in Arabic characters.
2918 TABSIRAT U'L AWAMINI: the Enlightener of the Illiterate, on the Sects of Islam, and on Philosophy, Magism, Judaism, and Christianity, 4to. *neat* MS. 376 pp. bd. 12s   A. H. 1139
2919 TARIKH ASHAM: History of the Expedition against Assam, A. D. 1662, 4to. *beautiful MS. ruled with gold and coloured lines,* 206 pp. *the first illuminated, bd.* 12s   Saec. XVII.
2920 TARIKHI KHANI MUÁLLI NISHÁN: Chronicles of the Kings of KHORASSAN of the Abbas dynasty, folio, *neat MS.* 820 pp. *two pages beautifully ornamented in gold and colours, a valuable MS. native binding,* £2. 12s Saec. XIX.
2921 TÁRÍKHI KASHMIR: History of Kashmir, by Naráyan Kúl 'Ajiz, 4to. *very neat MS.* 178 pp. bd. 6s   1817
2922 TARIKH-I-SHAMSHIR-KHANI: History of the Sabre-Lords, 4to. *fine* MS. 380 pp. *in good condition, roan,* 10s   1772
2923 TARK CHIHAL WEIK: Art of the KNIFE and DAGGER—MOORCROFT's Observations in his Travels, taken down by his Moonshee, in 1 vol. 4to. *neatly written Persian MS. on* 298 *pages, bd.* 10s   1819
2924 TIMOUR. MALFÁZÁT-I-TIMURI: or Memoirs of Timur, translated into *Persian,* by Abu Tálib Husaini, revised by Muhammad Afzal Bukhári, folio, *very neat MS.* 734 pp. *ruled in, calf,* 6s   Saec. XVI.
2925 TOZAK-I-TIMURIYA; Institutes of Tamerlane, 8vo. 554 pp. 6s   Saec. XVII.
2926 TUHFHAT-UL-MUMININ: Persian Materia Medica, folio, *neatly written,* 431 pp. *ruled in, wormed in a few places, bd.* 10s   Saec. XVII.
2926* —— another copy, folio, 560 pp. bd. 9s   Saec. XVII.
2927 TUHFAT-UL-SALATIN (a Present for Kings): Selections from Persian Poets, 4to. *a very neat MS.* 528 pp. *slightly stained, old green morocco,* 32s *ib.* XVIII.
Presented by Prince Goolam Mohummud to Colonel White, Superintendent of the affairs of Mysore Princes.
2928 VOCABULARY of Figurative Expressions, with their meanings, and the authorities, folio, *all in Persian, hf. bd. 7s 6d*   ca. 1800

2929 ZAFAR Namah; History of Timur by Sharaf-ad-Din 'Ali Yazdi, 4to. *beautifully written*, 758 *pp. bd.* 28s *Saec.* XVII.
  Khondamir considers his work as *pre-eminent above all other Histories in the Persian Language for beauty of style*. It was completed A.H. 828 (A.D. 1424).
2930 Zelali, Mahmud wa Ayaz, and other Poems, 8vo. 640 pp. *neatly written, with illuminated titles, bd.* 10s *Saec.* XVII.
2931 ZINAT-AL-KULUB: Cyclopædia of Astronomy, Natural History, Anatomy, Geography, &c. 4to. 360 *pp. closely written, bd.* 30s *Saec.* XVI.
  This MS. contains some very curious information. The author frequently quotes the Ajaib-al-Makhlukat.
2932 ZINAT-ul-TAWARIKH: Beauty of Chronicles, Vol. II. folio. *a finely written MS*. 584 *pp. in good condition, a valuable historical work, bd.* 30s *Saec.* XVIII.
2933 **PUNJABI, or SIKH.** ADI GRANTH, the great Sacred Book of the Sikhs, sq. folio, 33 *leaves containing table of contents, and* 648 *leaves of text, the two front and two concluding pages richly and elegantly illuminated, all the text enclosed within margins of gold and coloured lines, written in the Gurumukhi character, native binding, a fine specimen of Sikh art*, £20. *Saec.* XVII.
2934 Adi Granth, a more recent copy, without the table, in the Gurumukhi character, stout folio, 467 *leaves, native binding*, £5. 1874 (1817)
2935 DASAMA PADSHAH KA GRANTH: one of the Sacred Books, which shares with the Adi Granth the chief veneration of the Sikhs, stout oblong sm. folio, 10 *leaves of table, and* 798 *leaves of text, native binding,* £2. 10s *Saec.* XVIII.
  The second portion of this MS. is the Vichitranâtak of Gurda Govind, the tenth Patriarch of the Sikhs.
2936 ——— another Sikh MS. probably one of the works of Guru Govind, in the Gurumukhi character, stout oblong 12mo. 552 *leaves, bd.* 25s *Saec.* XVIII.
2937 **SANSCRIT.** ADHYATMA RAMAYANA: a Poem on the adventures of Ramah (one of the incarnations of Vishnu) attributed to Vyasa Deva; a different work from the larger and more celebrated one of Valmiki, high folio, 332 *pp. clearly written, calf extra, ornamental sides*, £3. *Sæc.* XVII.
2938 Munk, Catalogue des MSS. Sanskrits de la Bibl. de Paris, 8vo. 190*pp. neat MS. hf. bd.* 10s 1844
2939 Sanscrit MSS., a bundle of long strips folded, about 300 leaves, 8vo. *cheap*, 6s
2940 **TIBETAN.** Klaproth (Julius) Tibetanisches Wörter-Verzeichniss; Vocabularium Tartaricum, etc. 8vo. 106 *pp. bds.* 12s *Sæc.* XIX.
  In the autograph of this eminent Philologist. Some pages are in that of Bayer the celebrated Orientalist.
2941 **TURKISH.** Abul-Hassan-Ismael, Halwiyat-i-Sultáni, st. sm. 4to. 868 *pp. bd.* 7s (A.H. 1144, A.D. 1731
2942 ALF LAILA, Terjamat, a volume containing 600 Nights, sm. folio, *very excellent handwriting, fine preservation, bound*, £2. 10s *Saec.* XVI.
2943 DESTUR AL KATIB: The Secretary's Model, roy. 8vo. *an interesting early Turkish MS. neatly written on glazed paper, containing numerous Historical Letters and State Papers, as guides to composition for Ministers, Government Secretaries, etc.* 25s A.H. 867 (1462)
2945 Hikyayat. Forty two Tales, *the last apparently wanting two leaves*, sq. 8vo. *clear MS. bd.* 5s *Saec.* XVII.
2946 Jirrah Namah: Treatise on Anatomy, Surgery, and Medicine, sq. 8vo. *clear MS. bd.* 5s *Saec.* XVII.
2947 Moham. Catechism, sm. 8vo. 144 *pp. ruled with gold lines, bd.* 5s A.H. 970

ORIENTAL LITERATURE AND TRANSLATIONS.

2948 **AMHARIC.** Isenberg's Amharic Grammar, roy. 8vo. *bds.* 10s 6d 1842
2949 ISENBERG'S Dictionary, Amharic-English and English-Amharic, 3 vols. in 1, 4to. 434 *double cols. cloth*, 25s 1841
2950 LUDOLFI Lexicon Amharico-Latinum, et Grammatica linguæ Amharicæ, 2 vols. folio, *sd.* 24s *Francof.* 1698
2951 **ARABIC.** Abdollatiphi Compend. Memorabil. Aegypti, *Arab.* à White, 8vo. *sd.* 5s *Tub.* 1789
2952 Abd-Allatif, Relation de l'Egypte, traduit de l'Arabe par S. de Sacy, 4to. 16s *Paris*, 1810

ORIENTAL BOOKS.

3000 FARIS' ARABIC GRAMMAR: a Practical Grammar of the Arabic Grammar of the Arabic Language, with Interlineal Reading Lessons, Dialogues, and Vocabulary, by FARIS EL-SHIDIAC, a Native of Mount Lebanon, Syria: formerly Professor of Arabic at the University of Malta; Translator of the whole Bible into Arabic ; Author of " An English Grammar for Arabs," and of the Arabic work called " the Fariyac," 1 vol. 12mo. (pub. at 5s) *cloth*, 4s 1856

3001 FATA Durr mukhtar fi Sharh, Tanwir ul Absar: a Treatise on Mohammedan Law, *in Arabic*, roy. 8vo. 1085 pp. *bd*. 15s *Calcutta*, 1827

3002 FLORES Grammat. Arabici idiomatis, ab Agapito à Valle Flemmarum, 8vo. *sd.* 5s *Romæ*, 1845

3003 FREYTAGII Lexicon Arabico-Latinum, præsertim ex Djeuharii Firuzabadiique et aliorum Arabum operibus desumtum, adhibitis Golii quoque et aliorum libris, confectum; accedit Index Vocum Latinarum locupletissimus, 4 vols. 4to. (pub. at £5. 5s) *calf neat*, £3. 3s *Halis*, 1830-37

3004 —— Lexicon Arabico-Latinum in usum tironum, 4to. (pub. at 36s *sd.*) *cloth*, 15s ; *vellum*, 21s *Halis*, 1837

3005 FUTAWA ALEMGIRI: a Collection of Opinions and Precepts of Mohammedan Law, compiled by Sheikh Nizam and other learned Men, by command of the Emperor Aurungzeb Alemgir, *in Arabic*, 6 vols. roy. 4to. (pub. at £9.) *hf. russia*, £6. *Calcutta*, 1828-35

3006 —— the same, Vols. 3, 4, 5, roy. 4to. *sd*. 36s 1831-34

3007 FUTAWA QAZEE KHAN on the Institutes of Aboo Huneefa, *in Arabic, lithographed*, 4 vols. 8vo. *sd*. 12s 6d *Calcutta*, 1835

3008 GERMANI (D.) Fabrica linguæ Arabicæ, a Dictionary, Italian, Latin, and Arabic, folio, 1238 pp. *double columns, vellum*, 10s *Romæ*, 1639

3009 GHAIAT UL-BAYAN, a Grammar in Arabic, *being the original of Professor Lumsden's*, roy. 4to. *calf gilt, rare*, 25s *Calcutta*, 1836

3010 GIGGEI Thesaurus Linguæ Arabicæ, 4 vols. folio, *vel.* or *calf*, 25s *Mediol*. 1632

"This excellent work is a translation of the KAMOOS, which, being entirely written in Arabic, few but proficients in the language can derive any benefit from, and on this account the work *of Giggeus is particularly valuable.*"—*Clarke*. "Quoiqu'en grande partie effacé par les lexiques Arabes qui l'ont suivi, cet ouvrage renferme un assez grand nombre d'interprétations que jusqu'à ces derniers temps on eût cherché vainement ailleurs; vend. 80 fr. Soubise; 130 fr. Langlès; 76 fr. Debure; 36 fr. br. en 1840."—*Brunet*.

3011 GOLII Lexicon Arabico-Latinum, cum Indice Latino-Arabico, fol. *title supplied in MS. neatly bd.* 21s ; or, *a fine copy in calf or vellum*, £3. *Lugd. Bat. Elz*. 1653

3012 —— the same, *with numerous valuable MSS. additions by the Rev. G. Hunt,* folio, *hf. calf*. £2. 10s 1653

"This is an invaluable work, and the best on the subject ever published."—*Clarke*. "Ce dictionnaire est un livre classique indispensable à tous ceux qui étudient et meme qui savent l'Arabe."—*Bibl. Elzev*. Golius' Arabic Lexicon is preferred by many Arabic Scholars to Freytag.

"A work much esteemed and sought after, not only by the learned who use it, but also by the curious; which renders the price very considerable in commerce, where copies are with difficulty found."—*De Bure*.

3013 HAJJI KHALFAH, Kashf ul-Zanún án Asamy 'l-Kutub wa 'l-Fanún: Lexicon Bibliographicum et Encyclopædicum, *Arab. et Lat.* edidit Fluegel cum notis Indice, etc. 7 vols 4to. *complete, cloth*, £5. 5s *Leipzig*, 1835-60
The former price was £10. 10s.

3014 HAMASA. ASHAAR AL-HAMASAH: HAMASÆ CARMINA, *Arabice*, cum Tebrisii scholiis primum edidit, Indicibus instruxit, versione *Latinâ*, et commentario illustravit Freytag, 3 vols. in 2, 4to. (pub. at £5. 5s) *uncut*, £3. 10s ; or, *hf. calf*, £4. *Bonnæ*, 1828-51

3015 HAMZAE Ispahanensis Annales, ed Gottwaldt. *Arab. et Lat.* 2 vols. in 1, 12mo. *bds*. 5s 1844-48

3016 HAMMER-PURGSTALL, LITERATURGESCHICHTE DER ARABER, 7 stout vols. impl. 8vo. (pub. at £8. 8s *sd*.) *hf, calf, uncut*, £6. 6s *Wien*, 1850-56

A book of the most stupendous learning and assiduity, containing the complete History of the Arabian Literature from the earliest to the present times, 9915 Biographies, with quotations from the works of each author.

3017 HARIRI (Sheykh Ibn Mohammed Al-Kasim) Kitabu 'l-MAKAMAT: Les Séances, *en Arabe*, avec un commentaire, etc. par DE SACY, sm. folio, *best edition of this entertaining work, red mor. extra, gilt edges,* £4 16s *Paris*, 1822

3018 —— Loghátu 'l-Makamat: Arabic and Persian Dictionnary to Hariri, by Jaun Alee (Supplement to the Calcutta edition), roy. 4to. *bd*. 10s *Calcutta*, 1814

HANDJÉRI, Dictionnaire. *See post under* TURKISH.

3019 HERBIN, Principes de la langue Arabe moderne, suivis de Proverbes Arabes, roy. 4to. 11 *plates of writing, calf gilt*, 5s *Paris*, 1803

3020 HIDAYAH, with its Commentary, the KIFAYAH, *in Arabic*, by Hukeem Moulvee Abdool Mujeed, Vol. I. 4to. *cloth*, 32s *Calcutta*, 1834

3021 HIDAYAH, with its Commentary, the KIFAYAH, *in Arabic*, by Hukeem
Moulvee Abdool Mujeed, Vol. III. 4to. 20s *Calcutta*, 1831
3022 —— the same, Vol. IV. 4to. sd. 12s *ib.* 1833
For translation, *see* General Alphabet, *ante*.
3023 INAYAH, a Commentary on the Hidayah, compiled by Mohummud Akmuloodeen, Ibn Muhmood, Ahmudonil Hunufee, edited in *Arabic* by Ramdhun Sen, 4 vols. 4to. (pub. at £6.) sd. £4. *Calcutta*, 1830-37
3024 —— the same, Vols. 3 and 4, 4to. sd. 30s 1830-34
3025 HUMBERT, Anthologie Arabe, sm. 8vo. *hf. morocco*, 10s *Paris*, 1819
3026 —— Arabica Chrestomathia, Vol. I. Arabicum textum complectens, 8vo. 348 pp. sd. 7s 6d *Paris*, 1834
3027 IBN-ADHÁRI, Al-Bayano 'l-Mogrib: Histoire de l'Afrique et de l'Espagne, *Arabe et Français*, par Dozy, 2 vols. 8vo. *hf. calf*, 15s *Leyde*, 1848-51
3028 IBN BATOUTAH, Tohfat-ul-Nuzzar; Voyages, *texte Arabe et Français*, par Defrémery et Sanguinetti, 4 vols. 8vo. *sd. calf gilt*, 36s *Paris*, 1853
3029 IBN DOREIDI Poemation, *Arab. et Lat.* cum scholiis Chaluwiae et Lachumaei, ed. Aggæus Haima, 4to. LARGE PAPER, *calf*, 10s *Franeq.* 1773
3030 IBN JUBAIR, Rahilat: Travels, *in Arabic*, by Wright, 8vo. sd. 10s *Leyden*, 1852
3031 IBN KHALDUN, Akhbar Al-Franj: De Expeditionibus Francorum, *Arab. et Lat.* ed. Tornberg, 4to. sd. 6s 6d *; or calf*, 7s 6d *Upsaliae*, 1840
3032 KALILA WA DIMNA. Calila et Dimna, ou Fables de BIDPAI, *en Arabe*, avec la Moallaka de Lébid, *en Arabe et Français*, par Silvestre de Sacy, 4to. sd. 15s*; hf. bd.* 18s; or *calf extra*, 21s *Paris*, 1816
3033 KAMOOS, or THE OCEAN; AN ARABIC DICTIONARY, by Mujd-ood deen Moohummud-oobno Yakoob of Feerozabad, collated with many MS. copies, and corrected by Shykh Ahmudoobno Shirwanee, in the Arabic department of Fort William, 2 vols. folio. £10. 10s. *Calcutta*, 1817
  No copy has been sold by auction for years. The Kamoos is the best Arabic Dictionary, explained in Arabic, every word with the vowel points.
3034 KAZIMIRSKI DICTIONNAIRE ARABE FRANÇAIS contenant toutes les racines de la langue ARABE, leurs dérivés, tant dans l'idiome vulgaire que dans l'idiome littéral, ainsi que les dialectes D'ALGER et de MAROC, 2 stout vols. roy. 8vo. 1638 pp. *double columns, uncut*, £4. 4s 1846-60
3035 KORAN. ALCORANI textus universus, *Arabice et Latine*, cum prodromo, notis, etc. ed. MARRACCIUS, 2 vols. folio. *calf*, 36s *Patavii*, 1698
3036 KORAN, *Arabic*, with vowel points, edited by Flügel, 4to. bd. 12s *Leipsig*, 1841
3037 CORANUS, *Arabice*, Flügelianum textum recognitum curavit Redslob, 8vo. *red morocco*, 18s *Lips.* 1837
3038 —— the same, THICK PAPER, 8vo. bds. 15s 1837
3039 —— Concordantiae Corani, ad literarum ordinem et verborum radices, 4to. bds. 12s. *Lips.* 1842
3040 KORAN *in Arabic*, with Commentary, folio, 478 pp. *and* 6 pp. *Tables, beautiful edition, with the vowel points, hf. bd. very rare*, 36s *Kazan*, 1816
3041 —— another, very similar edition *in Arabic*, with all the vowel points, folio, 478 pp. and 6 pp. *of Tables, red morocco, gilt edges*, 38s ? *Kazan, ca.* 1830
  There is a variation in some matters of typography in these two editions.
3042 —— *in Arabic*, with Interlineary Version in *Hindustani*, and two *Persian* Commentaries, the Tafsiri Hosseini and the Tafsiri Abbasi, on the margins, 2 vols. impl. 4to. *calf*, £2. 5s *Calcutta*, 1837
3043 —— *in Arabic*, with *Persian* Commentary, Vol. I. 4to. 940 pp. *lithographed, the Arabic text in the centre of each page boldly executed, with the vowel points, the Persian commentary around it in smaller letters, sd.* 28s (? *Calcutta*, 1850)
3044 —— *in Arabic*, with the Commentary of Zamakhshari, entitled the Kashshaf, by Lees, Vol. I. impl. 4to. sd. 14s *Calcutta*, 1856
  Printed for presents only.
3045 NUJUMU 'L-FÚRKAN,. An Arabic Dictionary to the Koran, sq. 8vo. *hf. bd.* 6s
? *Calcutta*, 1824
For translations of the Koran, *see* General Alphabet, *ante*.
3046 KOSEGARTENII Chrestomathia Arabica, 8vo. *with all the vowel points and a good Lexicon, bd.* 9s. *Lips.* 1828
3047 —— the same, FINE PAPER, large 8vo. *hf. calf neat*, 14s 1828

3048 LAFUENTE Y ALCANTARA, Catalogo de los Codd. Arabigos adquiridos en Tetuan, impl. 8vo. *sd*. 5*s* *Madrid*, 1862
3049 LANE'S ARABIC-ENGLISH DICTIONARY, to be completed in 6 vols. 4to. *orders received* 1863

His Grace the Duke of Northumberland has most munificently agreed to pay the £10,000 required for the publication of this gigantic undertaking. The price of the work will therefore be considerably under the usual publishing rates.

3050 LUMSDEN'S ARABIC GRAMMAR, Vol. I. *all published*, st. fol. *bd*. 20*s* *ib*. 1823

The best Arabic Grammar, explained in English.

3051 MAKKARI (Al.) Analectes sur l'Histoire et la Littérature des ARABES D'ESPAGNE par Al-Makkari, publiés en *Arabe*, par MM. Dozy, Dugat, Krehl et Wright, avec Introduction, 2 vols. 4to. 210 and 1878 pp. (pub. at 60 florins) *cloth*, £3. 16*s* *Leyde*, 1855-61

A very important work, just completed.

3052 MARASID-AL-ITTILAA, Lexicon Geographicum, *Arabice*, ed. Juynboll, fascic. 3, 4, 5, 6, 8vo. *sd*. 25*s* *Lugd. Bat.* 1851-53
3053 MARCEL, Vocabulaire Français-Arabe (d'Afrique), 8vo. 4*s* *Paris*, 1837
3054 MIUT AMIL and Shurhoo Miut Amil, two Treatises on Arabic Syntax, with Annotations, Stories, and Citations, &c. by Lockett, roy. 4to. *Arabic and English, bds*. 8*s* *Calcutta*, 1814
3056 MOELLER, Catalogus Librorum Bibl. Gothanæ, Tom. I. (all publ.) Codices MSS. Arabici, 4to. *coloured facsim. hf. bd*. 12*s* *Gothæ*, 1826
3057 MOONTUKHUB-OOL-LOGHAUT: a Dictionary of Arabic Words, with Persian translation, according to the Kamoos, etc. by Molovee Daud, 4to. *calf*, 18*s* *Calcutta*, 1808
3058 PERCEVAL (C. de) Grammaire Arabe vulgaire, 8vo. *hf. bd*. 4*s* *Paris*, 1833
3059 POCOCKE, Specimen historiae Arabum; Abul-Faraj; cum historia ex Abul-feda à De Sacy, ed. White, *Arab. et Lat*. sm. 4to. *portrait, bds*. 6*s* *Oxonii*, 1806
3060 QUATREMÈRE, Notice d'un Manuscrit Arabe, contenant la description de l'Afrique, 4to. *hf. morocco*, 7*s* *Paris*, 1831
3061 ROORDA, Grammatica Arabica, cum Chrestomathiâ et Lexico à Cool, 8vo. *hf. bd*. 5*s* *Lugd. Bat.* 1835
3062 ROSENMÜLLERI Institutiones Linguae Arabicae; sententiæ et narrationes, cum Glossario et Appendice, 8vo. *hf. russia*, 7*s* 6*d* 1818
3063 SACY (S. de) GRAMMAIRE ARABE, 2 vols. 8vo. *plates, sd*. 15*s*; *hf. calf*, 20*s*; or, *in green morocco, gilt edges*, 32*s* *Paris*, 1810
3064 —— GRAMMAIRE ARABE, à l'usage des élèves de l'école spéciale des langues orientales vivantes, SECONDE ÉDITION, corrigée et augmentée, à laquelle on a joint un traité de la prosodie et de la métrique des Arabes, 2 vols. stout 8vo. 1345 pp. 8 *plates and numerous tables*, £5. 10*s* *Paris, Impr. Roy.* 1831
3065 —— Chrestomathie Arabe, extraits de divers Ecrivains Arabes, *Arabe et Français*, 3 vols. 8vo. *sd*. 15*s*; *bound*, 20*s* *Paris*, 1806
3066 —— la même, SECONDE ÉDITION, corrigée et augmentée, 3 vols. 8vo. £3. 10*s* *Paris*, 1826-27
3067 —— A collection of 34 Tracts, by or relating to this celebrated Orientalist, in an 8vo. case, 25*s* 1800-40

Including, Les Ismaélis et les Nosairis de Syrie, par Rousseau—Itinéraire en Perse par Bagdad, 1813—Notice de Abd-Allatif—Correspondance entre Tamerlan et Charles VI. 1812—Poéme d'Uweissi, 1811—Mémoire sur les Samaritains, 1812—L'Egypte, par Quatremère, 1811—Sur les traductions d'Ouvrages Orientales, 1810—Funérailles de Remusat, Chézy, et St. Martin, 1833—Vie et Ouvrages de Chézy, 1835—Traduction des livres Saints, 1824—Notice du Livre de Kabous, 1811—Les Assassins, 1809—Notice du Numophylacium de Fraehn, 1813—Vie de A. Rémusat, 1834—Mesures des Musulmans, *Paris*, 1799—Notice de la Bibliotheca Arabica, de Schnurrer, 1811—Operations Militaires des Wahabis—Notice de la description de la Chorasmie, par Alexandrides, 1807—Art de traduire les Anciens, par Carrega, 1809.

3068 SCHNURRER, Bibliotheca Arabica, 8vo. *calf*, 4*s* *Halæ*, 1811
3069 SHARASTANI (Muhammad Al-) Kitabu 'l-Milal wa 'l-Nihil: Book of the Religious and Philosophical Sects, *in Arabic*, edited by Cureton, 2 vols. roy. 8vo. (pub. at 30*s*) *cloth*, 20*s* *Or. Text Soc.* 1842-6
3070 SOORAH (The) an *Arabic* Dictionary explained in *Persian*, by Jumal, being a translation of a celebrated Arabic Dictionary entitled the Sihah, revised according to the Qamoos, etc. 2 vols. roy. 4to. *bd. or bds*. 15*s* *Calcutta*, 1812-15
3071 —— the same, another edition, enlarged by Abdool Mojeed, impl. 4to. *presentation copy from the editor to Prof. Wilson, hf. bd*. £2. 2*s* *Cal.* 1830

3072 TABARI, Abu Dschaferi Mohammed, Tarikh Al-Malouk: Annales Regum, *Arabice et Latine*, edidit Kosegarten, 3 vols. 4to. 36s 1831-53
3073 TORNBERG, Annales Regum Mauritaniæ, ab Abi Zer vel Abd el Halim conscripti, Vol. I. *Arabic text*, in 2 parts, 4to. *sd*. 10s Upsal, 1843
3074 WILKEN, De Bellis Cruciatorum ex Abulfeda, 4to. *hf. calf*, 5s Gottingae, 1798
3075 WILLMET, Lexicon Arabicum-Latinum in Coranum, Haririum et vitam Timuri, 4to. *hf. calf*, 7s 6d; *calf neat*, 10s Lugd. Bat. 1784

"Ouvrage estimé."—*Brunet.* A good Dictionary for Classical Arabic.

3076 WRIGHT'S Grammar of the Arabic Language, translated from the German of Caspari, with additions, 8vo. (pub. at 15s) *new in cloth*, 12s 6d 1862
3077 WUESTENFELD'S Genealogische Tabellen der Arabischen Stämme und Familien mit Register, 2 vols. 8vo. 47 *large folding Genealogical tables, half morocco*, 18s Göttingen, 1852-53
3078 ZAMACHSHARY. Samachscharii Lexicon Arabicum Persicum, ed. Wetzstein, cum indicibus, 4to. *bds*. 10s 6d Lips. 1850
3079 ——— Kitabu 'l- Jibal, wa 'l-Makanat, wa 'l-Mayat, Lexicon Geographicum, *Arab.* curâ Juynboll, 8vo. *hf. calf*, 5s Lugd. Bat. 1856
3080 **ARMENIAN.** AUCHER and BRAND'S Armenian-English and English-Armenian Dictionary, 2 vols. roy. 8vo. *calf*, 36s Venice, 1821-5
3081 ——— Dictionnaire Francais-Armenien-Turc, roy. 8vo. *the Turkish in Armenian characters, hf. morocco, uncut*, 10s; or, *calf gilt*, 12s Venise, 1840
3082 ——— Armenian-English Grammar, sm. 8vo. *hf. bd*. 2s 6d Venice, 1819
3083 ——— the same, 2nd edition, 8vo. *hf. bound*, 5s ib. 1832
3084 BELLAUD, Essai sur la langue Arménienne, 8vo. *sd*. 3s Paris, 1812
3085 EUSEBII PAMPHILI, Chronicon bipartitum, *Armeniace, Latine, et Graece*, cum notis, etc. à AUCHER, roy. folio, *bds*. 12s Venetiis, 1818
3086 GALANI Grammatica linguae literalis Armenicæ, cum Dictionario, sm. 4to. *calf*, 7s 6d Romæ, 1645
3087 GRAMMAR in Armenian, with copious extracts from the literature, 2 vols. in 1, 8vo. 770 pp. *calf neat, gilt edges*, 12s Venice, 1852
3088 ——— another Grammar, 8vo. 308 pp. *bds*. 5s ib. 1846
3089 KEMPIS, Imitatio Christi, in *Armenian*, 12mo. *hf. bd*. 5s Romæ, 1705
3090 MOSIS CHORENENSIS Historia Armenae Nationis, etc. *Armen*. stout 12mo. 6s 1695
3091 MOSIS CHORENENSIS Historia Armeniaca, *Armenice et Latine*, cum notis Whistoni, 4to. *map*, 30s 1736
3092 SCHROEDER, Thesaurus linguae Armenicae, sm. 4to. *vell*. or *calf*, 7s 6d *Amst*. 1711

The Picture Letters, or Grotesque Capitals, after originals in early MSS. are beautifully engraved; Callot must have taken his ideas from them.

3093 SOMAL, Storia Letteraria di Armenia, 8vo. *hf. calf*, 5s Venezia, 1829
3094 ——— Quadro della Storia, 1829—Liturgia Armena, *Arm. e Lat*. da Avedichan, 1826—in 1 vol. 8vo. *cloth*, 6s 1826-29
3095 VILLOTTE, Dictionarium Latino-Armenicum, cum tabulâ chronologicâ Regum et Patriarchum, folio, *calf*, 12s Romæ, 1714
3096 **ASSYRIAN.** BENFEY, die Persischen Keilinschriften, mit Uebersetz. und Glossar, 8vo. *sd*. 2s Leipz. 1847
3097 BURNOUF, Mémoires sur deux Inscriptions Cunéiformes trouvées près d'Hamadan, 4to. *plates, hf. calf*, 7s 6d Paris, 1836
3098 CULLIMORE'S Oriental Cylinders, 1, 2, 3, 4, impl. 8vo. 32 *plates, containing engravings of* 174 *Babylonian Cylinders or Seals, cloth, rare*, 15s 1842
3099 LAYARD, Inscriptions in the Cuneiform Character, from Assyrian Monuments, royal folio, 98 *leaves of Inscriptions, bds*. 18s B. M. publ. 1851
3100 LICHTENSTEIN, Palæographia Assyrio-Persica, 4to. *plates*, 3s 6d Helmst. 1803
3101 LÖWENSTERN, Déchiffrement de l'Ecriture Assyr. à Khorsabad, roy. 8vo. *plates, sd*. 3s 6d 1843
3102 RAWLINSON and NORRIS'S Selection from the Historical Inscriptions of Chaldaea, Assyria, and Babylonia, large folio, 70 *lithographic plates*, with descriptions, *bds*. 18s British Museum pub. 1861
3103 WESTERGAARD, Sakiske Art af Akhaemenidernes Kileskrift, 4to. *bds*. 6s Kjöb.1854
3104 ASSYRIAN TRACTS, a curious collection of 7, 8vo. the lot, 4s 1815-36

See also "ASSYRIA" ante.

ORIENTAL BOOKS.   173

3105 **Berber.** VENTURE DE PARADIS, Grammaire et dictionnaire abrégés de la Langue Berbère, revus par Jaubert, 4to. *sd.* 10*s*   *Paris*, 1844
Burmese. *See* INDIAN LANGUAGES.
3106 **CHINESE.** BAZIN, Principes du Chinois vulgaire, 8vo. *hf. bd.* 3*s* 6*d* *Par.* 1845
3107 BAYERI (Th. S.) Museum Sinicum, linguam et literaturam explicans, 2 vols. in 1, stout 12mo. *calf,* 7*s* 6*d*   *Petrop.* 1730
  Including an engraved "Lexicon Sinicum," in which some MSS. notes are added.
3107*BUDDHIST PRAYERS, in Chinese, narrow sm. folio, *two curious figures of Buddha, bds.* 15*s*   *Saec.* XIX.
3108 CALLERY, Systema phoneticum scripturæ Sinicæ; Dictionnaire chinois-latin-français, 2 vols. in 1, royal 8vo. *calf, a Scholar's copy, with MSS. additions, calf,* £2.   *Macao,* 1841
3109 —— Dictionnaire Encyclopédique de la langue Chinoise, Tome I, roy. 8vo. 36 *and* 212 *pp. double cols. bds.* 5*s*   *Macao, Paris,* 1845
3110 CHINESE CLASSICS, *Chinese and English,* with notes, prolegomena, and indexes, by Legge, Vols. I, II : Confucian Analects, the Great Learning, and the Doctrine of the Mean ; and the Works of Mencius, 2 vols. stout roy. 8vo. *cf. morocco,* £2. 5*s*   To be completed in seven vols.   *Hong Kong,* 1861
3111 CHINESE DICTIONARY, *in Chinese,* 12mo. *half morocco,* 9*s*   *Saec.* XVIII.
3112 CONFUCIUS. Le CHOU KING, un des livres sacrés des Chinois, qui renferme leur ancienne Histoire, leur Gouvernement, etc. traduit par GAUBIL, avec des notes par De GUIGNES, 4to. *plates, calf,* 18*s*   1770
3113 —— Chi-King, liber Carminum, *Lat.* à MOHL, 8vo. *bds.* 5*s*   *Stuttg.* 1830
3114 —— Ta Hio, *Chin. Franç. et Lat.* par Pauthier, roy. 8vo. *bds.* 5*s* *Paris,* 1832
3115 CONFUCIUS, sive Scientia Sinensis, *Lat.* a Couplet aliisque, 2 vols. in 1, folio, *old calf,* 10*s*   *Paris,* 1686-87
3116 DE GUIGNES, Dictionnaire Chinois, Français et Latin, 1813 — KLAPROTH, Supplément, 1819—2 vols. roy. folio, *containing together* 1344 *pp. a bargain,* 18*s*   *Paris,* 1813-19
  The immense size of this valuable work is the only reason that it bears so low a price in commerce.

3117 —— Lettre de Pekin, sur la langue Chinoise, etc. 4to. 29 *plates,* 3*s* 6*d*   1773
3118 DU PONCEAU, on the Chinese system of Writing, with Cochinchinese Vocabularies, roy. 8vo. *bds.* 6*s*   *Philadelphia,* 1838
3119 E TSUNG KIN LEEN : the Medical Profession's Golden Mirror, a celebrated Treatise on Medicine, 38 vols. roy. 8vo. *(wanting vols.* 12, 14, 17), *with several hun-very curious cuts, in* 4 *blue cases, wormed,* 25*s*
  Compiled by order of the Emperor Keen Lung. One hundred persons were employed for four years upon it. All the existing treatises on Medicine were collected by the Government for the purpose of being examined by the editors of this work, in order that it might be made as complete as possible. It is, perhaps, the most complete epitome of Chinese Medical Science extant.
3120 FOE KOUE KI, relation des royaumes Bouddhiques, *en Français,* commentée par RÉMUSAT, ouvrage complété et augmenté par KLAPROTH et Landresse, roy. 4to. *sd.* 12*s* 6*d*   *Paris,* 1836
3121 GONCALVES, Diccionario China-Portuguez e Portuguez-China, 3 vols. in 2, stout sm. 4to. 2028 *pp. double columns, half calf neat,* £3. 3*s*   *Macao,* 1831-33
3122 HAGER, Monument de Yu, la plus ancienne inscription de la Chine, large folio, 32 *plates of ancient characters, etc. sd.* 7*s* 6*d*   *Paris,* 1802
3123 HWEI YANG YIN KWO LUH, 8vo. *full of singular woodcuts, chiefly representing tortures inflicted by Demons, of a most grotesque character, sd.* 10*s* *Saec.* XVIII.
3124 LIFE OF CHRIST, CHINESE BLOCK BOOK, impl. 8vo. *with* 51 *large woodcuts, almost the size of the page, executed in the European style by native artists, an extraordinary specimen of Chinese Art, in old red morocco extra, from the libraries of Sir Mark Sykes and Miss Currer,* £8. 8*s*   *Saec.* XVII.
  Evidently promulgated by the Jesuits to obtain Christian converts. This volume must be ranked with the Mediæval Block Books issued in Germany and the Low Countries for a similar purpose.
  The European humour is shown on one of the plates by a Dwarf teazing a Monkey.
3125 JULIEN, Exercices de Syntaxe et de Lexigraphie Chinoise, 8vo. *sd.* 5*s* 6*d*   1842
3126 KL(APROTH), Chrestomathie Chinoise, 4to. 202 *lithographed pages of Chinese, sd.* 10*s*   *Paris, Soc. Asiat.* 1833
3127 LAO-TSEU, Livre de la Voie et de la Vertu, *Chin. et Franç.* par Julien, 8vo. *sd.* 8*s* 6*d*   *Paris,* 1842
3128 LIE-SIEN-CHUEN, 8vo. *curious woodcuts, sd.* 9*s*   *Saec.* XIX.

3129 MARSHMAN'S Dissertation on the characters and sounds of the Chinese Language, 4to. *folding tables of the Elements, cloth, very rare,* 20s *Serampore,* 1809
3130 —— Chinese Grammar, with a dissertation on the Characters and Colloquial Medium, and Appendix of the Ta-Hyoh, *Chinese and English,* 4to. £2. *Serampore,* 1814
3131 MEDHURST (W. H.) Chinese-English and English-Chinese Dictionary, containing all the words of the Chinese Imperial Dictionary, arranged according to Radicals, 4 vols. 8vo. £10. *Batavia,* 1842, *and Shanghae,* 1847

Most copies are very much stained. The whole edition consisted of 500 copies, now all dispersed.

3132 (MEDHURST) Translation of a Comparative Vocabulary, Chinese, Corean, and Japanese, with the Thousand Character Classic, *Chinese and Corean,* and indexes, 8vo. *half calf,* 36s *Batavia,* 1835
3133 MENG TSEU vel Mencium inter Sinenses philosophos Confucio proximum, *Sinice et Lat.* edidit Julien, cum notis, etc. 3 vols. in 2, large 8vo. *sd.* 18s; or *half calf gilt,* 24s *Lut. Paris,* 1824-29
3134 MING KE TSANG TUNG, History of the Ming Dynasty, *in Chinese,* 6 vols. high 4to. *complete,* 15s (1800)

The Ming dynasty was overthrown in 1644. The Rebels profess to aim at its re-establishment.

3135 MORRISON'S Chinese Grammar, 4to. *bds.* 30s *Serampore,* 1815
3136 —— Dictionary of the Chinese Language, divided into 3 parts, I. Chinese and English, arranged according to the Radicals, 3 vols.: II. Chinese and English, arranged alphabetically, 2 vols.; III. English and Chinese, 1 vol.—forming together 6 vols. roy. 4to. *bds.* £9. 9s; or 6 vols. in 4, *two leaves wanting in a volume, calf,* £7. 7s *Macao,* 1815-22
3137 —— the same, parts I, Vols. 1, 2; and III, in 3 vols. roy. 4to. *bds.* £2. 16s

These volumes comprise the Chinese-English, two out of three vols. (arranged according to the Radicals) and English Chinese Alphabets.

Priced, 1847, bds. £14.; Bunsen's copy, calf, I bought for £14. 15s; Earl of Munster's copy, calf, fetched, 1855, £12. 15s. This laborious production includes all the famous characters comprised in the Chinese Dictionary in 32 volumes, folio, published in 1761. It has already become a rare book, the number printed having been comparatively small. The type is no longer extant, and cannot be reproduced but at great cost; and the patient, self-denying labour requisite for a new edition, mere pecuniary outlay cannot command.

3138 MORRISON'S Translations; Davis, San-Yu-Low, 8vo. *bds.* 2s 6d *Canton,* 1815
3139 —— Chinese Miscellany, consisting of extracts in the native character, with translations and philological remarks, large 4to. *plates, bds.* 7s 6d 1825
3140 —— Vocabulary of the Canton Dialect, *complete,* 3 parts in 2 vols. 8vo. *bds. rare,* 36s *Macao,* 1828

A Vocabulary English-Chinese and Chinese English; and Chinese Words and Phrases.

3141 —— the same, Part III: Chinese Words and Phrases, 8vo. *scarce,* 18s 1828
3142 NATURAL HISTORY,—a work in Chinese, in 9 parts, roy. 8vo. *with numerous illustrations, a few coloured, of Birds, Flowers, Plants, etc. sd.* 12s ? 1810
3143 PAUTHIER, l'Inscription syro-chinoise de Si-Ngan-Fou, monument nestorien de 781 A.D., 8vo. 2s 6d *Paris,* 1858
3144 —— Vindiciae Sinicae, roy. 8vo. *sd.* 2s 1842
3145 REMUSAT, Elémens de la GRAMMAIRE CHINOISE, ou principes généraux du Kow-Wen ou style antique, et du Kouan-Hoa, c'est a dire, la langue commune généralement usitée dans l'Empire Chinoise, 8vo. *plates, original edition, hf. bd.* 7s 6d *Paris,* 1822
3146 —— the same, 8vo. *last edition, sd.* 12s *Paris,* 1857
3147 ROCHET, Manuel pratique de la langue Chinoise Vulgaire, avec Vocabulaire, roy. 8vo. *calf gilt, Dr. Hawtrey's copy,.* 10s *Paris,* 1846
3148 SAU SHIN KI, or San Kiao Yuen Lin Shing Ti Fuh, 3 vols. in 1, 12mo. *numerous woodcuts, sd.* 7s 6d 1820
3149 SCHOTT, Vocabularium Sinicum, 4to. *hf. morocco,* 7s 6d *Berol.* 1844
3150 SACRED AND HISTORICAL BOOKS of the Chinese, I KING, 1 vol.—SHI KING, 3 vols.—SHU KING, 2 vols.—LI KI, 5 vols.—CHUN TSIU, 2 vols.—*in Chinese,* together 13 vols. roy. 8vo. *enclosed in mahogany case,* £3. 10s *ca.* 1825
3150*THE FOUR BOOKS of Confucius and his disciples, Ta Hio, Chung Yung, 1 vol.—Lun Yu, 2 vols.—Mang Tszi, 3 vols.—*in Chinese,* together 6 vols. roy. 8vo. *with illustrations, enclosed in mahogany case,* £2. 16s *ca.* 1825
3151 SZE SHOO: the Four Books, in Chinese, 6 vols. high 4to. 5s ? 1820
3151* —— the same, 5 vols. in 2, 8vo. *hf. calf,* 15s ? 1830

ORIENTAL BOOKS. 175

3152 SUMMERS (Professor) Handbook of the Chinese Language, Parts I and II: Grammar and Chrestomathy, 8vo. 48 *lithographed pages of Chinese extracts, the Chrestomathy chiefly in Roman characters*, (*pub. at* 28*s*) *hf. morocco, new*, 23*s* 6*d*
Oxford, 1863
3153 —— Chinese Grammar, with Dialogues and Vocabulary, 12mo. *shortly to be published* *Quaritch,* 1863

This will form an excellent Manual for the learner, to initiate him in the knowledge of Chinese. Such a work has not before been attempted; all other Chinese Grammars, being attended with abstruse difficulties, unremoved by any preparation, while this little handbook resembles rather the elementary works of European languages.

3154 TA TSING LEU LE: Laws of the Tartar dynasty, *in Chinese*, 24 vols. (wanting XXIII) in 2 cases, impl. 8vo. 5*s* ? 1800
3155 WARS of the Three Kingdoms, an historical Novel, 20 vols. in 2 cases, 12mo. *chinese style*, 7*s* 6*d* (? 1800)
3156 XUE WUN: an Explanation of the ANCIENT CHINESE CHARACTERS, *in Chinese*, 6 vols. royal 8vo. *sd.* 36*s* *ca.* 1800
3157 YIH TUNG CHE: Statistical Account of the Chinese Empire, *in Chinese*, 36 vols. *sd.* £2. 5*s* ? 1800
3158 **Chinese and Mantchou.** TSEU SSE, l'Invariable Milieu, *Chinois, Mandchou, Lat. et Franç.*, par Rémusat, 4to. *half morocco,* 12*s* 6*d* *Paris,* 1817
3159 **CIRCASSIAN.** LOEWE's Dictionary, English-Circassian-Turkish, and Circassian-English-Turkish, 8vo. (pub. at 21*s*) *sd.* 10*s* 1851
3160 **COCHIN-CHINESE.** ALEXANDRI DE RHODES Dictionarium Annamiticum Lusitanum et Latinum, cum Indice Latino, sm. 4to. *hf. russ.* 7*s* 6*d Romæ,*1651
3161 PIGNEAUX ET TABERD, Dictionarum Anamitico-Latinum et Latino-Anamiticum, 2 vols. 4to. *uncut,* £2. *Fredericnagori (Serampore),* 1838
3162 JABLONSKI Glossarium Vocum Aegyptiarum cum Tewateri auctario, Spicilegio, etc. folio, *hf, bd,* 5*s* (*ex. nov. ed.* Steph. *Thesaur.*)
3163 **COPTIC.** MACDONALD (W. B. *of Rammerscales*) Coptic Grammar, for self-tuition, 8vo. *title, preface, and* 54 *pp. lithographed, sd.* 2*s* *Edinb.* 1856
3164 PEYRON, Lexicon linguae Copticae, 4to. 470 pp. *bds.* 24*s* *Taurini,* 1835
3164*—— Grammatica linguæ Copticæ, cum additamentis ad Lexicon, roy. 8vo. *sd.* 5*s*: *hf. calf,* 6*s* 6*d* *Taurini,* 1841
3165 ROSSII (Ig.) Etymologiae Aegyptiacae, 4to. *calf gilt,* 36*s* *Romae,* 1808
3166 SPOHN de Lingua et literis veterum Aegyptiorum, 4to. 12 *large plates of Hieroglyphics, calf gilt,* 8*s* *Lips.* 1825
3167 TATTAM'S Grammar of the Egyptian Language, of the Coptic and Sahidic dialects, 8vo. *bds.* 5*s* 1830
3168 —— the same, with Appendix of a Dictionary of the ancient Egyptian, lithographed in the Enchorial character, by Young, 8vo. *bds.* 12*s* 1830
3169 —— Lexicon Aegyptiaco-Latinum, cum indice vocum Latinarum, stout 8vo. *cloth,* 27*s* *Oxonii,* 1835

☞ For Hieroglyphics see ante, under "Egypt."

3170 YOUNG's Recent Discoveries in Hieroglyphical Literature and Egyptian Antiquities, 8vo. *bds.* 5*s* 1823
3171 —— Memoir, with Catalogue of his Works; DICTIONARY of the Ancient Egyptian, 2 parts in 1 vol. 8vo. *port. cloth,* 7*s* 6*d* 1831
3172 ZOËGA, Catalogus Codicum Copticorum MSS. in Museo Borgiano Velitris asservatorum, folio, including copious extracts and translations, 663 pp. 7 *plates of facsimiles, sd.* 25*s* *Romæ,* 1810
3173 **ETHIOPIC.** HARTMANNI Grammatica Aethiop. sq. 8vo. *hf. bd.* 5*s* 1707
3174 LUDOLFI (J.) GRAMMATICA Aethiopica, accedit prosodia, cum appendicibus, folio, VERY RARE, £2. 10*s* *Francofurti,* 1702
3175 —— Lexicon AETHIOPICO-LATINUM, cum Grammatica, etc. ed. Wanslebius, 4to. *bd.* 12*s* *Lond.* 1661
3176 —— the same, second edition, folio, *very rare,* £2. 16*s* *Francof.* 1699
3177 PSALTERUM DAVIDIS, *Ethiop. et Lat.* curâ LUDOLFI, sm. 4to. *bd.* 7*s* *Franc.* 1701
3178 WEMMERS, Lexicon Aethiopicum, cum institutionibus linguae et indice, sm. 4to. *calf,* 10*s* *Romae,* 1639
3179 **GEORGIAN.** BROSSET, Mémoires inédits sur la Géorgie, including a Grammar, extracts and translations, 8vo. *hf. russia,* 7*s* 6*d* *ca.* 1840

3180 KLAPROTH, Vocabulaire et Grammaire de la langue Géorgienne, 8vo. *hf. calf,* 7s 6d *Paris,* 1827
3181 SAMOUTCHITEL: Russian-Georgian Grammar and Lexicon, 4to. *bds.* 6s 1820
3182 TCHOUBINOFF, Dictionnaire Géorgien-Russe-Français, 4to. 22 and 736 pp. *double columns, hf. calf neat,* 32s *St. Petersb.* 1840
3183 **HEBREW, CHALDEE, SYRIAC.** ABEN EZRA's Margolioth Tobah, folio, *plate of astronomical diagrams, stamped calf, rare,* 10s *Amst.* 1721
3184 ABUL-PHARAGII sive Bar Hebræi Chronicon Syriacum, Syriace et Lat. vertit, notisque illustravit Bruns, edidit Kirsh, 2 vols. 4to. £2. 10s *Lips.* 1789
3185 ABUL-PHARAGIUS. Bar-Hebræi Chronici Syriaci specimen, à Bernstein, 4to. *bds.* 5s *Lips.* 1822
3186 AMBROSII Introductio in Chald. Syriac, Armen. et 10 alias linguas, sq. 8vo. *half bd.* 10s *Romae,* 1539-52
3186*ANECDOTA SYRIACA, edidit Land, Vol. I. (all yet published) 4to. *the Syriac texts at the end,* 28 *Lithographed Facsimiles of Ancient MSS. and Palimpsests,* 12s 6d *Lugd. Bat.* 1862
3187 AQUIN, L'Examen du Monde: Sentences des Hebreux: et leurs Modes d'interpreter la Bible, 8vo. *Hebr. et Franc., slightly wormed, vellum,* 7s *Paris,* 1629
3188 ATHANASIUS, Festal Letters of, discovered in an ancient *Syriac* version, and edited by Cureton, roy. 8vo. *cloth,* 9s 1848
3189 AVENARII Lexicon Ebraicum, folio, *stamped calf,* 6s *Witeberg.* 1568
3190 BAAL AKEDAH: Akedath Jitzchak, *in Hebvew,* 5 vols. in 2, stout 8vo. *half calf,* 25s *Pressburg,* 1849
3191 BARTOLOCCI (Jul.) BIBLIOTHECA MAGNA RABBINICA, de Scriptoribus et Scriptis Hebr. et Talmud.; et Jos. IMBONATI Bibliotheca Latino-Hebraica, folio, *old calf gilt,* £5. 15s *Romæ,* 1675-94
3192 BECKII Paraphrasis Chaldaica, Lib. 2¹ Chronicorum, e Cod. antiquo, *Chald. et Lat.* cum notis, sq. 8vo. *half bd.* 7s *Aug. Vind.* 1683
3193 BERNARD's Creed and Ethics of the Jews, in selections from the Yad Hachazakah of Maimonides, *Heb. and English,* with Notes, etc. 8vo. (pub. at 21s) *bds.* 12s *Cambridge,* 1832
3194 BERNSTEIN and KIRSCH's SYRIAC CHRESTOMATHY and LEXICON. Vol. I. KIRSCHII Chrestomathia, 226 pp. Syriac Text; Vol. II. BERNSTENII Lexicon Syriacum, 582 pp. 2 vols. in 1, 8vo. (pub. at 14s) *cloth,* 7s 6d; or in 2 vols. *half russia,* 10s 6d *Lips.* 1832-6
The best work for learning the Syriac Language. The Chrestomathy contains: Fabellae Ludicrae; Historica ex Bar-Hebraei Chronico Syriaco, et ex Actis Sanctorum; Biblica et Poetica. The Lexicon contains every word likely to be wanted, and is nearly as ample as Castell's.
3195 BERTRAMI Comparatio Grammaticæ Hebraicae et Aramicae, dialectorumque Aramicarum, 4to. *vellum, fine copy,* 6s (*Lugduni?*) 1574
3196 BIBLIA HEBRAICA, eleganti et majusculâ characterum forma, authore E. Huttero; et ejusdem Cubus Alphabeticus sanctæ Hebræ Linguæ, 2 vols. folio, *calf, a good copy,* £2. 2s *Hamburgi,* 1857-8
3197 BRESHITH RABBAH, with Samuel Jafeh's Commentary, "Jefeh Thoar," *in Hebrew,* stout sm. folio, *bd.* 15s *Fürth,* 1691
The type of this work was partly set up by a woman.
3198 BUSERA, Berith Abraham, *in Hebrew,* 4to. *bd.* 10s *Leghorn,* 1790
3199 BUXTORFII Concordantiae Bibliorum Hebraicæ cum Lexico et Masora, royal folio, *vellum,* 18s *Bas.* 1632
3200 ―― Lexicon Chaldaicum Talmudicum et Rabbinicum, thick folio, *vellum, a good copy,* £2. *Basil.* 1639
3201 ―― de Abbrev. Hebr. Talmudi recensio, etc. 12mo. *hf. bd.* 7s 6d 1708
3202 ―― Synagoga Judaica, *Heb, et Lat.* 12mo. *vellum,* 5s *Basil,* 1641
3203 CALASIO (Marius de) Concordantiæ Sacrorum Bibliorum Hebraicorum, edidit Gul. Romaine, 4 vols. large folio, *best edition, hf. calf, uncut,* £3. 10s 1747-49
3204 CASTELLI Lexicon Syriacum adnotavit Michaelis, 2 vols. in 1, sm. 4to. *hf. russia,* 21s *Goettingae,* 1788
3205 CELLARII Horae Samaritanae, excerp. Pentateuchi, *Samar. et Lat.* cum Glossario, etc. sq. 8vo. *vellum,* 9s *Franc.* 1705
3206 CONFORTE, liber Kore Ha-Dorot, *hebraice,* ed. Cassel, 4to. 3s 6d 1846
3207 DE ROSSI, Dizionario storico degli autori Ebrei e delle loro opere, 2 vols. in 1, 8vo. *half calf,* 25s *Parma,* 1802
3208 ―― Introduzione alla Sacra Scrittura, 8vo. *sd.* 7s 6d *ib.* 1817

ORIENTAL BOOKS.

3210 DUKES, zur Kenntniss der Neuhebräischen religiösen Poesie, 8vo. 5s 1842
3211 —— Rabbinische Blumenlese: Sprüche des Sirach, Talmud, Sprichwörter, *Hebr. Chald. und Deutsch*, mit Glossar. etc. 8vo. *cloth*, 5s 6d *Leipz*. 1844
3212 EISENMENGER's Entdecktes Judenthum, mit Register der Hebräischen Bücher, 2 vols. in 1, stout sq. 8vo. 2154 pp. *vellum*, 14s *Königsb*. 1711
3213 ELOH BANI HANEURIM: Hebrew Poems, sq. 8vo. *some with Italian transl. bds.* 9s 1768
3214 ENGLISHMAN'S HEBREW and CHALDEE CONCORDANCE of the Old Testament, 2 vols. royal 8vo. (pub. £3. 13s 6d), *cloth*, £2. 8s 1843
3215 EUSEBIUS, History of the Martyrs in Palestine, *Syriac and Eng.* with notes by Cureton, royal 8vo. *cloth*, 6s 1861
3216 FAGII Perush, exegesis dicaionum Hebraicarum, in 4 capp. Geneseos, 4to. *sd.* 5s *Isnæ*, 1542
3217 FACSIMILES of the Hebrew MSS. at the Synagogue, K'ae-fung-foo, sq. 8vo. *sd.* 6s *Shanghae*, 1851
3218 FORSTERI Dictionarium Hebraicum, fol. *stamped binding*, 6s *Basil*. 1564
   This copy has many passages underlined and marked through by the Jesuits.
3219 FORSTER, Israelitish Authorship of the Sinaitic Inscriptions, 8vo. *cl.* 3s 6d 1856
3220 FUERST, Veteris Testamenti Concordantiæ Hebraicæ atque Chaldaicæ, cum Lexico duplici, stout folio, (pub. at £4. 4s *sd.*) £2. 16s *Lips*. 1840
3221 GESENIUS, Hebräische Grammatik, 8vo. *bds.* 3s 6d *Halle*, 1831
3222 —— Thesaurus philologicus Linguae Hebraeae et Chaldaeae Veteris Testamenti, 3 vols. 4to. *half bound calf*, £2. 16s *Lipsiae*, 1835-42
   The best Hebrew Dictionary extant.
3223 —— Hebrew and Chaldee Lexicon to the Old Testament, with additions by Tregelles, stout sm. 4to. (pub. at 28s 6d) 24s 1846
3224 —— Hebrew Lexicon of the Old Testament, translated by Robinson, stout large 8vo. *russia extra*, 25s 1844
3225 GUARIN, Grammatica Hebraica et Chaldaica cum Indicibus, 2 vols. 4to. *calf*, 15s *Lut. Par*. 1724-6
3226 HAHN ET SIEFFERT, Chrestomathia Syriaca, Ephraemi carmina, 8vo. *hf. bd.* 5s 1825
3227 HOFFMANNI Grammatica Syriaca, 4to. *hf. calf*, 12s *Halae*, 1827
3228 HOLLOWAY's Originals, physical and theological; Essay towards a discovery of descriptive ideas from the Roots in words, 2 vols. 8vo. *Large Paper*, *half bd. uncut*, 12s *Oxford*, 1751
3229 IGNATIAN EPISTLES: Corpus Ignatianum, a complete Collection of the Ignatian Epistles, genuine, interpolated and spurious, *Syriac, Greek, and Latin*, with *English* translation of the Syriac text, notes and introduction by CURETON, roy. 8vo. 2 *facsimiles, cloth*, 18s 1849
3230 JEWISH PRAYERS. Form of Prayers according to the Custom of the Polish and German Jews, Heb. and English, translated into English by David Levy, carefully revised, corrected and illustrated (by Isaac L. Lyon), 7 vols. roy. 8vo. *roan gilt*, £2. 10s *H. Abrahams*, (5609) 1849
3231 KABBALA DENUDATA seu Doctrina Hebraeorum transcendentalis et metaphysica atque theologica, opus antiquissimae Philosophiae Barbaricae variis speciminibus refertissimun (ex Hebraeo Latine reddita a C. Knorr von Rosenroth), 3 vols. in 2, stout sm 4to. *without the Adumbratio*, 70 pp. *but with the rare* 'Porta Coelorum,' 255 pp.; 17 *plates, vellum*, £2. 16s *Sulzbaci*, 1677-84
   One of the most singular and complete works on the Kabala, and much in request, not only on account of its rarity, but for the information it contains on that mysterious science. These copies contain the 'Liber, seu Porta Cœlorum,' which Brunet says is so rarely found with it. "This work is very difficult to be obtained complete with the piece of 70 pages, entitled, 'Adumbratio Kabbalæ Christianæ,' which ought to be at the end of the last volume; it is yet much rarer, with a treatise of 192 pages, intitled, Liber seu Porta Cœlorum,' &c.—BRUNET.
   Collation of a complete copy: Frontispiece; Title; 17 preliminary leaves; pp. 3-740. Apparatus in Librum Sohar pars secunda, half-title; pp. 3-312; Adumbratio Kabbalae Christianae, id est Syncatabasis Hebraizans, Francof. 1684, 70 pp; Apparatus in libr. Sohar, Pars 3tia. et 4ta. quarum prior est. . . Porta cœlorum, 192 pp. followed by 'Appartus in libr. Sohar, Pars 4ta.' a half-title and pp. 195-255; this last part includes 16 folding plates. Tomus Secundus: Plate, 'Cancrinus'; Title; pp. 1-598; half-title, 'Partis secundae Tractatus quartus'; pp. 3-478.
3232 LANDAU, Erstlinge, ein Almanach für Freunde der hebräischen und biblischen Literatur, *in Hebrew*, 12 vols. 12mo. *hf. bd.* £2. *Wien*, 1820-24
   Contains Hebrew Poetry and valuable articles on Rabbinical and Biblical literature.
3233 LEVI (D.) Lingua Sacra, in three parts. Part I. Hebrew Grammar—II. Hebrew-English Dictionary—III. Terms and Phrases—together 5 vols. 8vo. *calf*, 18s 1803
3234 LINDO's Hebrew-English and English-Hebrew Dictionary, 8vo. *hf. calf*, 5s 1846

3235 MAIMONIDES, MISCHNA TORA, Yad Hachazakah, 4 vols. in 2, folio, *calf, from Archdeacon Tenison's library*, £3. 16s *Amsterdam*, 5461
With a dedication in Spanish, signed, IMANUEL ATHIAS.
3236 —— MORA NEBOCHIM, *Hebraice*, cum commentariis Hebr. Jesnitz, folio, *bd. good copy*, 36s 1742
3237 —— de Idolatria, *Hebr. et Lat.* à Vossio, *Amst.* 1641—Seldenus de Calendario Judaico, *Lond.* 1644, sm. 4to. *vellum*, 6s 1641-44
3238 MARINI Thesaurus linguae sanctae, 3 vols. in 1, st. fol. *port. calf*, 6s *Venet.* 1593
3239 MICHAELIS, Supplementa ad Lexica Hebraica, 6 parts in 3 vols. sm. 4to. *hf. bd.* 9s *Gottingae*, 1792
3241 MISCHNA, sive totius Hebraeorum Juris, Rituum, Antiquitatum, ac Legum oralium systema, cum clarissimorum Rabbinorum Maimonidis et Bartenoræ Commentariis integris, *Hebraice et Latine*, ed. G. Surenhusius, 6 vols. folio, plates, *hf. bound*, £2. 10s *Amst.* 1678-1703
3242 MISCHNA, oder der Text des Talmuds, übersetzt von Rabe, mit Anmerkungen, etc. 6 vols. in 3 4to. *bd.* 15s *Onolzbach*, 1760-63
3243 MISSALE CHALDAICUM, ex decreto Congr. de Prop. Fide editum, folio, *in Syriac characters, hf. bound*, 15s *Romae*, 1767
3244 Mosis Almosnini Tephilah Lemosheh, *Hebr.* sq. 8vo. *vellum*, 15s *Salonich*, 1563
3245 MUNSTERI (Seb.) Kalendarium Hebraicum, smallest 4to. *vellum*, 6s *Basil.* 1527
3246 NORBERG, Lexicon Codicis Nasaræi cui nomen Adamus, *Syriaco-Latinum*, 4to. *sd.* 16s *Lond. Gothorum*, 1816
3247 OPPENHEIMERI Collectio Davidis, Catalogus Bibliothecæ Hebrææ librorum impress. et MSS. stout 12mo. *sd.* 10s; or, *hf. bd.* 12s *Hamb.* 1826
A valuable Catalogue of Hebrew books.
3248 PASSIONEI Lexicon Hebraico-Chaldaico-Latino-Biblicum, 2 vols. folio, *portrait, fine copy, vellum*, 16s *Avenione*, 1765
"The arrangement of this Lexicon renders it of easy reference. The entire words, the roots, and the Latin interpretation being placed in parallel columns."
3249 PETHACHIA, Voyages dans le XII. S. *hébr. et franç.* par Carmoly, 8vo. 5s 1831
3250 POCOCKE'S THEOLOGICAL WORKS, containing his "Porta Mosis" *in English and Hebrew*, and *English* commentaries on Hosea, Joel, Micha, etc. 2 vols. fol. *portrait, calf*, 20s 1740
3251 RABBINORUM VETERUM commentarii: Modi Exponendi Pentat. *Par.* 1620—Targum Jonathani, *Paris*, 1556—In Prov. Salom. *Med.* 1620; in 1 vol. sm. 4to. *calf*, 12s 1556-1620
3252 RELANDI Analecta rabbinica, comprehendentia libellos quosdam singulares et alia quæ ad lectionem et interpretationem rabbinicorum faciunt, 12mo. *portrait, calf*, 10s *Trajecti*, 1723
3253 REUCHLIN de Rudimentis Hebraicis, *Basil*, 1537—Pagnini Enchiridion Vocab. Haruch, Thargum, etc. *Romae*, 1523; 2 vols. in 1, sm. fol. *bd.* 10s 1523-37
3254 SCHAAF, Lexicon Syriacum concordantiale, Novum Testamentum Syriacum, 2 vols. 4to. *a fine copy, well bound*, 36s *Lugd. Batav.* 1717
3255 SCHŒTTGENII HORÆ HEBRAICÆ et TALMUDICÆ in Novum Testamentum, 2 vols. sm. 4to. *calf*, £2. 18s *Dresdae*, 1733-42
3256 SEPHER AEMANAH: Liber Fidei, *Hebr. et Lat.* à Fagio, sm. 4to. *vellum*, 10s 1542
3257 SEPHER KODESH, a Key to the Hieratic Cypher of the Scriptures, 8vo. *plates, cloth, rare*, 6s *Privately printed, Jersey, ca.* 1840
3258 SEPHER PENE ARIE, *in Hebrew*, sm. folio, *bd.* 10s *Amsterdam, ca.* 1680
3259 STEHELIN'S Rabbinical Literature: or the Traditions of the Jews contained in the Talmud and other mystical writings, customs and ceremonies, origin, &c. of these traditions, 2 vols. sm. 8vo. *hf. calf*, £2. 5s 1748
3260 TALMUD. The Treatises Baba Bathra (*wanting title*) and Sanhedrin, with Rashi's Commentary and the Tosephtoth (Additamenta); MAIMONIDES on the Mishna, sm. folio *old russia*, 18s *Amsterdam, Bendenisti*, 5405 (A.D. 1645)
3261 TARGUMS. Etheridge's Targums of Onkelos and Jonathan Ben Uzziel on the Pentateuch: with the Fragments of the Jerusalem Targum, from the Chaldee: Genesis and Exodus, post 8vo. pp. 590, *cloth*, 8s 6d 1862
The first attempt to translate into English the Targums or ancient Aramaic paraphrases on the books of the Old Testament. The translation is literal, and made directly from the Chaldee.
3262 THOMASSINI Glossarium universale Hebraicum, folio, *port. hf bd.* 6s *Par.* 1697
3263 UHLEMANN, Institutiones Linguae Samaritanae, cum Chrestomathia et Lexico, 8vo. *hf. calf*, 10s *Lips.* 1837

3264 WOLFII (J. C.) Bibliotheca Hebræa, Auctorum Hebraeorum cujusque ætatis, Gaffarelli index Cod. Cabbalisticorum MSS. 4 vols. stout sm. 4to. *vellum, rare,* £2. 16s *Hamb.* 1715-33

3265 WOTTON'S Miscellaneous Discourses on the Scribes and Pharisees, the MISNA, Shabbath, and Eruvin, 2 vols. sm. 8vo. *old calf neat rare,* £2. 2s 1718

3266 YALHUT SHAMANA; an excellent Commentary on the Bible, by Rabb: Abram Samuel, thick folio, *engraved title, the text in the Rabbinical letters, without points, fine sound copy in russsia,* 36s *Amst.* (? 1680)

3267 YECHIYA Perushim, or Commentaries on the Hagiographa, *in Hebrew,* folio, *the margin of twenty leaves slightly wormed,* 15s *Bologna,* 1528

3268 **INDIAN LANGUAGES.** CALDWELL'S Comparative Grammar of the Dravidian or South-Indian Family of Languages, 8vo. 528 pp. *a work of profound learning, cloth,* 20s 1856

3269 DRUMMOND's Illustrations of the Grammatical parts of Guzeratee, Mahratta and English, sm. folio, *wants a leaf, hf. bd.* 7s 6d *Bombay,* 1808

3270 **BENGALI.** BAITAL PACHISI in *Bengalee,* 8vo. *hf. bd.* 5s ? 1810

3271 CAREY (W.) Dictionary of the Bengalee Language, (Bengali-English), 2 vols. in 3, 4to. £3. *Serampore,* 1825

3272 —— Dictionary of the Bengalee Language, abridged from the 4to. dictionary, (Bengali-English and English-Bengali), 2 vols. 8vo. *cloth,* 20s *ib.* 1839-40

3273 —— Bengalee Grammar, 8vo. *bds.* 5s *ib.* 1818

3274 FORSTER's English-Bengalee and Bengalee-English Vocabulary, 2 vols. 4to. *hf. russia,* 7s 6d *Calcutta,* 1799-1802

3275 HAUGHTON'S Rudiments of Bengali Grammar, 4to. *bd. rare,* 28s 1821

3276 —— Bengali-English Glossary, to the Tota-Itihas, the Batris Singhasan, Krishna Chandra, the Purusha-Parikhya and the Hitopadesa, 4to. (pub. at 30s) *bds.* 6s 1825

3277 —— Bengali and Sanscrit Dictionary explained in English, and adapted for Students of either Language ; to which is added an Index, serving as a reversed Dictionary, stout 4to. (pub. at £7. 7s) 30s 1833

Haughton's works are the best for learning the Bengali Language.

3278 SANSCRIT AND BENGALI Opuscula, etc.: Bytal Puchisi, *in English;* Pooroos Purikhya, *Sanscr. and Engl.;* Vidvun Moda Taranginee, *Sanscr. and Engl.;* and several others, in 1 vol. 8vo. 10s *Calcutta, etc.* 1830-34

3279 **Burmese.** HOUGH'S (G. H.) English and Burman Vocabulary, preceded by a GRAMMAR, obl. 8vo. *hf. bd.* 15s *Serampore,* 1825

3280 LANE's English Burmese Dictionary, 4to. *hf. calf,* £2. *ib.* 1841

3281 LATTER'S Grammar of the Language of Burmah, 4to. *bds.* 25s *Calcutta,* 1845

3282 **Canarese.** REEVES (William) Dictionary, English and Carnataca, and Carnataca and English, 2 parts in 4 vols. roy. 4to. *calf,* £6. 6s *Madras,* 1824-32

3282*Gujarati. CLARKSON's Gujaráti Grammar, 4to. 25s *Bombay,* 1847

3283 **HINDOSTANI** (*Brij Bakha, Hindee, Hindui, Urdu, Dakhni, etc.*) HINDEE and HINDOSTANEE SELECTIONS, with the Rudiments of Hindustanee and Bruj Bhakha Grammar, Prem Sagur in *Hindee*—Khuree Bola and English Vocabulary and Grammar—Betal Pucheesee, Selections from the Bhuktú Mal, the Rektus, the Ramayunu—Hindee Songs—Extracts from the Bagh-o-Buhar, Gooli Bukawulee, Araishi Mahfil, Ukhlaq Hindee, Sukontala, etc. in 2 vols. 4to. about 1500 pp. *hf. calf,* £2. 10s *Calcutta,* 1830

This work was originally compiled for the use of the Interpreters to the Native Corps of the Bengal Army.

3284 PRICE'S Hindee and Hindoostanee Selections, with Rudiments of Hindoostanee and BRUJ BHAKHA Grammar, 2 vols. roy. 4to. *hf. russ.* 21s *Calc.* 1827

3285 TASSY (Garcin de) Histoire de la Littérature Hindoui et Hindoustani, avec Extraits, etc. Vols. I, II, (all publ.) roy. 8vo. 20s 1839-47

3286 **Brij Bhakha.** RAJNEETI; or tales of the Hindoos, *in Brij Bakha,* 8vo. *cloth,* 10s *Calcutta,* 1809

3287 —— the same, 8vo. *cloth,* 6s *ib.* 1827

3288 **Hindee.** BAITÁL PACHÍSI; or, Twenty-five Tales of a Demon, a new edition of the *Hindi* Text, carefully revised, with the words expressed in the Hindústáni character immediately under the corresponding word in the Nágarí, and with a perfectly literal word-for-word *English interlinear translation,* accompanied by

N 2

a free translation in English at the foot of each page, and Explanatory Notes, by W. B. Barker, edited by D. B. Eastwick, roy. 8vo. *cloth*, 18s *Hertford*, 1855

All the Vowel-points are inserted, and every means adopted to smooth the path of the learner; and it is hoped that by the aid of this book ALONE, a competent knowledge of Hindústáni may be acquired with ease in the course of two or three months.

3289 BAITAL PACHISI, or the 25 Tales of a Demon, a new and corrected edition, *Hindee*, with a Vocabulary, 8vo. 7s 6d   1861
3290 BALLANTYNE's Hindi and Braj Bhákhá Grammar, 4to. *cloth*, 4s   1839
3291 PREM SAGUR; or the History of Krishnu, *in Hindee*, by Lullu Lal, with a vocabulary K'huree Bolee and English, royal 4to. *hf. russia*, 12s   *Calcutta*, 1825
3292 PREM SAGÁR; or the Ocean of Love, literally *translated* from the Hindi of Lallú Lal by Eastwick, 4to. (pub. at 21s) *bds*. 10s 6d   1851
3293 ZAMAYANEE, the *Sanskrit* Epos on the Adventures of Zama, *in Hindi*, 4to. *calf*, 10s   *Calcutta*, (? 1820)
3294 **Hindui.** PREM SAGUR, translated into *Hinduvee* by Lulloo Lal, roy. 4to. *calf*, 14s   *Calc.* 1810
3295 KRICHNA et sa Doctrine, par PAVIE, 8vo. *sd*. 5s   *Paris*, 1852
3296 **Urdu.** ARAISH I MUHFIL: a History of the Hindoo Princes of Dehlee, by Ulee Ufsos, *in Hindustani*, roy. 4to. *hf. morocco*, 12s   *Calcutta*, 1808
3297 BÁGH O BUHAR: Tale of the Four Durwesh, *in English*, by Meer Ummun, sq. 8vo. *calf, cut close*, 6s   *Calcutta*, 1813
3298 BAGH O BAHAR, consisting of entertaining Tales, *in Hindustani*, by Mir Amman of Dihli, *fourth edition*, carefully corrected, the Vowel points and Punctuation marked throughout, with Vocabulary, by Forbes, roy. 8vo. (pub. at 12s 6d) *new in cloth*, 10s   1860
3299 ——— or the Tales of the Four Darveshes, *in English*, by Forbes, 8vo. *cloth*, 7s   1857
3300 DOBBIE's (Capt. R. S.) Pocket Dictionary of English and Hindustani, fcap. 8vo. (pub. at 8s) *cloth*, 2s 6d   1847
3301 EASTWICK'S GRAMMAR of the HINDUSTANI Language, to which are added Selections for Reading, new edition, enlarged with a Vocabulary, Dialogues, 12 facsimiles of Persian and Devanagari Writing, etc. by the Rev. G. Small, 8vo. (pub. at 10s) *cloth*, 5s   1858
3302 ENGLISH and HINDUSTANI Student's Assistant, Idiomatical Exercises, Dialogues, 12mo. *cloth*, 3s 6d   *Calc.* 1837
3303 FALLON's English-Hind. Law and Commerc. Dictionary, roy. 8vo. *sd*. 9s *Calc.* 1858
3304 FIELD EXERCISE, Catechetical explanation, *in Hindoostanee*, *Persian character*, 8vo. *cloth*, 5s   *Calcutta*, 1847
3305 ——— the same, *Nagree character*, 8vo. *cloth*, 5s   1847
3306 FORBES' Grammar of the Hindustani language, in the Oriental and Roman character, with extracts and vocabulary, 8vo. *cloth*, 10s   1862
3307 GOOLI BUKAWULEE, a Tale in *Hindustani*, edited by Gilchrist, roy. 4to. *hf. bd.* 6s   *Calcutta*, 1804
3308 ——— Muzhubi Ishq, *in Ordoo*, by Ufsos and Gilchrist, revised, by Roebuck, 8vo. *bds*. 7s   *ib.* 1815
3309 GRAMATICA Indostana, sm. 8vo. with Portuguese and Hind. vocabularies, phrases, etc. *all Roman character, bd. very rare and curious*, 12s   *Roma*, 1778
3310 HUNTER'S Hindoostanee and English Dictionary, originally compiled by Capt. J. Taylor, 2 vols. roy. 4to. *bds*. 16s; 4to. *calf*, 18s; or, *a fine copy*, 2 vols. roy. 4to. *calf gilt*, 28s   *Calcutta*, 1808
3311 ——— the same, abridged by Smyth, large 8vo. *neatly bd.* 12s   1820
3311*IKWANU-S-SAFA, *in Hindustani*, by Ikram Ali, new edition, by Forbes and Rieu, roy. 8vo. (pub. at 12s 6d) *cloth*, 10s 6d   1861
3312 KHIRUD UFROZ, *in Hindustanee*, translated by Hufeez Ood-deen Uhmud from the Ayar Danish of Ubool Fuzl, revised by Roebuck, 2 vols. large 8vo. *hf. bd.* 5s   *Calcutta*, 1815
3313 KHIRAD-AFROZ: the Illuminator of the Understanding; the Hindustani Text, with Notes by Eastwick, 4to. (pub. at £1. 11s 6d) *cloth*, 22s; or, *in hf. morocco neat*, 24s   *Hertford*, 1857
3314 KORAN. Quran: Abdul Qadir ká tarjuma zubán i Urdu men, *Urdu, Roman character*, 8vo. *bds. rare*, 12s   *Iláhábád*, 1844

3315 SHAKESPEARE'S Dictionary, Hindustani and English, and English and Hindustani, the latter being entirely new, *fourth (the last) edition, greatly enlarged,* stout 4to. (pub. at £5. 5s) *bound,* 25s   1849
3316 SHAKESPEARE'S Grammar of the Hindustani Language, to which is added a Grammar of the Dakhni, *sixth edition* (the last), royal 8vo. *facsimiles,* (pub. at 14s) *cloth,* 6s   1855
3317 SHAKESPEARE's Muntakhabat-I-Hindi, Selections in Hindustani, with verbal Translations or Vocabularies, and a Grammatical Analysis of some parts, Vol. I. *sixth edition, bds.* 1852 ; Vol. II. *fourth edition, half calf,* 1844—2 vols. 4to. (pub. at £2. 2s) 5s   1844-52
3318 THOMPSON'S (J. T.) Oordoo and English Dictionary, arranged according to the English alphabet, roy. 8vo. *cloth,* 22s   Serampore, 1838

    A Hindustani Dictionary, having the Hindustani words, first in Roman, then in Arabic and Devanagari characters, explained in English.

3319 ——— English-Oordoo Dictionary, in Roman characters, with the accentuation, sq. 16mo. 235 pp. *double cols. cloth,* 7s   *Calc.* 1845
3320 YATES, Introduction to the Hindustani language, 3 parts in 1, 8vo. 432 pp. *half calf,* 7s 6d   *Calc.* 1845

    Grammar, 87 pp.; Reading Lessons, 179 pp.; Vocabulary, 164 pp. double columns.

3321 TUQUEE. KOOLIYAT MEER TUQEE : the Poems of Meer Mohummud Tuqee, comprising the whole of his numerous and celebrated compositions in the *Oordoo* Language, published under the patronage of the College of Fort William, stout roy. 4to. *a good sound copy.* 18s   *Calcutta,* 1811
3322 **Mahratti.** BHAGAVAT GHITA, *Sanscrit,* with five-fold poetical translation into *Mahratti,* thick sqr. 8vo. *lithographed, calf,* 18s   *Bombay,* 1842
3323 CAPON's Guide to the acquirement of the Maratha language, sm. 4to. *selections, dialogues, etc. in the Maratha and Roman character, with interlinear translation, lithographed, hf. bound,* 12s   *Bombay,* 1830
3324 CAREY's Mahratta-English Dictionary, 8vo. 652 pp. *no title, hf. calf,* 5s   1810
3325 ESOP's FABLES, in *Murathee,* sq. 8vo. *numerous very curious cuts, calf,* 12s 1840
3326 KENNEDY'S (Lieut.-Col. Vans) Dictionary, Maratha-English and English-Maratha, 2 parts in 1, small folio, *bd.* 7s ; or, *neatly hf. bd.* 12s   *Bombay,* 1824
3327 MARATHI-ENGLISH Vocabulary, 8vo. 159 pp. *double cols. cloth,* 5s *Bombay,* 1851
3328 MOLESWORTH'S Dictionary, Marathee-English and English-Marathee, compiled for the Government of Bombay, by Capt. James T. Molesworth, assisted by Lieutenants T. and G. Candy, 2 vols. 4to. *bd.* £3. 10s   *Bom.* 1833-47
3329 WILSON's Idiomatical exercises, 12mo. *cloth,* 4s 6d   *Bombay,* 1851
3330 **Malayalim.** PEET'S Grammar of the Malayalim language, as spoken in the principalities of Travancore and Cochin, and the districts of North and South Malabar, 20s   *Cottayam,* 1841
3331 **Manipuri.** GORDON's Dictionary in *English, Bengali, and Manipuri,* 8vo. *cloth,* 21s   *Calcutta,* 1851
3332 **Orissa.** SUTTON's Oriya Dictionary, Vol. I. Grammar and an English-Oriya Dictionary, royal 8vo. *cloth,* 16s   *Cuttack,* 1841
3333 **Punjabee.** CAREY's Grammar of the Punjabee language, 8vo. *bds.* 9s 1812
3334 STARKEY'S Dictionary, English and PUNJABEE, Grammar and Dialogues, 8vo. *cloth, rare,* 25s   *Calcutta,* 1849
3335 **Sindhi.** STACK's English-Sindhi Dictionary, 8vo. 231 pp. *double cols. cloth,* 15s   *Bombay,* 1849
3336 **Singhalese.** BIBLE, Vol. II. sqr. 8vo. pp. 671-1183, *sd.* 5s ?*Colombo,* 1814
3337 CHATER's Grammar of the Cingalese language, 8vo. 141 pp. *bds.* 15s *Colombo,* 1815
3338 ——— Introduction to Reading, 12mo. 105 pp. *dialogues, Singhalese and English, bd.* 7s 6d   *Colombo,* 1819
3339 ORDO Salutis in usum catechetarum, *in Singhalese,* 18mo. *bd.* 10s *Trangamb.* 1730
3340 SIDATH SANGARAWA, a Grammar of the Singalese language, translated into English, with introduction, notes and appendices, stout 8vo. *two plates wanting, bd. rare,* 20s   *Colombo,* 1852
3341 **Tamul.** BESCHII Grammatica Latino-Tamulica, sm. 4to. *hf. bd.* 5s   1813
3342 BLIN, Dictionnaire Français-Tamoul et Tamoul-Français, obl. 8vo. *sd.* 7s *Par.* 1831
3343 COMMON PRAYER and Psalter, in *Tamul,* 8vo. *wonderful type, bound,* 7s 6d   1818

3344 HOOLE, Dureisani-Tamil-Puttagam : part of the Common Prayer, with Grammar and Vocabulary, 8vo. *roan, 4s* 1859
3345 HYMNS in Tamil, *with Music*, 8vo. *bds. 4s* Madras, 1853
3346 KAIVALJANAVANITA, a Vedanta poem, *Tamil and English*, with Glossary, Notes, and Grammar; and comparative tables of Dravida languages, by Grant, 8vo. *cloth, 15s* Leipz. 1855
3347 RHENIUS, Tamil Grammar, with appendix, 8vo. *half calf, 18s* Madras, 1846
3348 ROTTLER'S Dictionary of the Tamil and English Languages, revised by Taylor and Vencatachala, parts 1 and 3, 4to. *rare, 30s* 1834-37
3349 SCHULTZE, Hymnologia Damulica, 12mo. 160 *Hymns metrically rendered from the German, half morocco*, 12s Tranqueb. 1723
3350 TAYLOR, ORIENTAL HISTORICAL Manuscripts, in the *Tamil* language, translated with annotations, 2 vols. 4to. *bds. 9s* Madras, 1835
3350*WINSLOW'S Tamil-English Dictionary of High and Low Tamil, stout 4to. 976 *pp. doub. cols. bds. new*, £3. 13s 6d Madras, 1862
3351 ZIEGENBALG, Grammatica Damulica, sm. 4to. *bd. 3s 6d* Halae, 1716

3352 **Telugu.** BROWNE'S TELUGU-English and English-Telugu Dictionary, 2 stout vols. royal 8vo. £6. 6s Madras, 1852-53
3353 ——— Dictionary, English and Telugu, stout royal 8vo. 8, xxx, and 1392 pp. *cloth, 30s* Madras, 1852
3354 CAMBELL'S Grammar of the Teloogoo Language, third edition, sm. 4to. *hf. bd. 25s* Madras, 1849

3354***JAKOUT.** BOEHTLINGK, die Sprache dar Jakuten (Siberia) : Grammatik, Text und Wörterbuch, *Jakout and German*, impl. 4to. 14s Petersb. 1851

3355 **JAPANESE.** ALCOCK (Rutherford) Elements of Japanese Grammar, 4to. *with lithographed table of characters, sd. 18s* Shangai, 1861
3356 MEDHURST, English-Japanese and Japanese-English Vocabulary, compiled from native works, *sd.* 18s Batavia, 1830
3357 ——— Translation of a Comparative Vocabulary of Chinese, Corean, and Japanese, with an English-Corean Index, and the Thousand Character Classics, 8vo. 36s Batavia, 1835
3358 ROSNY (Leon de) Introduction à l'étude de la Langue JAPONAISE, 8vo. *with 7 lithographic plates, sd.* 9s Paris, 1857
3359 SIEBOLD, Isagoge in Bibliothecam Japonicam et studium Literarum Japonicarum, impl. 4to. *half calf,* 10s 6d Lugd. Bat. 1841
3360 SIN ZOO ZI LIN GJŎK BEN : Literarum Ideographicarum Thesaurus, sive omnes Literae Sinensium, Pronuntiatione Japonica adscripta, opus Japonicum, ed. SIEBOLD, impl. 4to. *only 100 copies printed, bds.* £2. Lugd. Bat. 1834

3361 **Javanese.** CORNETS DE GROOT, Javaansche Spraakkunst, med Leesboek door Gericke, ed Woordenboek door Roorda, 2 vols. 8vo. *bds.* 12s Amst. 1843
3362 HANGLING DARMO, *Javaansch* door Winter, 4to. *bds.* 5s Batavia, 1853

3363 **MALAY.** CRAWFORD'S Grammar and Dictionary of the Malay Language, 2 vols. 8vo. *the Malay in Roman letters* (pub. at 36s) *cloth,* 21s 1852
3364 HAEX, Dictionarium Malaico-Latinum et Latino-Malaicum, sm. 4to. *hf. morocco, uncut, rare,* 12s Romae, 1631
3365 HOWISON's Dictionary and Grammar of the Malay Tongue, as spoken in Malacca, Sumatra, Java, Borneo, Pulo Pinang, etc. in 2 parts, Malay-English and English Malay, *with the pronunciation*, in 1 vol. 4to. *map, cloth*, 10s 1801
  The Malay in this Dictionary is a different Dialect from that of Marsden.
3366 MARSDEN'S Malayan-English and English-Malayan DICTIONARY, and Malayan Grammar, 2 vols. 4to. *bds.* 30s 1812
3366*——— the same, *half morocco, or calf,* 36s 1812

3367 **MALTESE.** FALZON, Dizionario Maltese-Italiano-Inglese, con una Espozione Grammaticale, 8vo. *hf. bd.* 15s Malta, 1845
2368 VASSALLI, Lexicon Melitense-Latino-Italum, 4to. 44, *and* 681 *pp. double columns, hf. bd.* 16s Romae, 1796
3369 ——— Grammatica della Lingua Maltese, 8vo. *second edition, bd.* 3s 6d 1827
3370 ——— l'istesso, 1827—Motti, Aforismi e Proverbii, 1828—2 vols. in 1, 8vo. *bds. 6s* Malta, 1827-8
3371 VELLA's Maltese Grammar, 12mo. *hf. calf,* 4s Leghorn, 1831

3372 **MANTCHOU**: AMYOT, Dictionnaire Tartare-Mantchou Française, avec des additions et l'Alphabet, par LANGLÈS, 3 vols. 4to. *with English and French MS. corrections, hf. calf,* 32s *Paris,* 1789-90
3373 AMYOT.—Le même, précédé de la Grammaire Tartare-Mantchou d'Amyot, etc. 4 vols. in 2, 4to. *calf,* £2. *Paris,* 1787-90
3374 GABELENTZ, Grammaire Mandchoue, 8vo. *hf. bd.* 6s 1832
3375 **Mongolian.** GOSPELS of Matthew and John, and Acts, narrow sm. folio, *bd.* 5s *St. Pet.* (1840)
3375*SCHMIDT, Geschichte der Ost-Mongolen und ihres Fürstenhauses, *Mongol. und Deutsch,* mit Anmerk. 4to. *hf. calf,* 14s *St. Petersb.* 1829
3376 ——— Grammatik der Mongolischen Sprache, 4to. *facsimiles, hf. cf.* 9s *ib.* 1831
3377 YUILLE, Mongolian Grammar, *in Mongolian,* 4to. *bds.* 7s 6d (Siberia), 1837
See also *Tatar.*
3378 **PALI.** BURNOUF ET LASSEN, sur le Pali, 8vo. (*Grammar, etc.*) 6 *plates,* 7s *Paris,* 1826
3379 CLOUGH's Pali Grammar and Vocabulary, 8vo. 30s *Colom.* 1824
3380 MAHAWANSO, in Roman Characters, with the translation, and an Essay on Páli Literature, by TURNOUR, Vol. 1 *(all published),* 4to. *bds.* 18s *Ceylon,* 1837
3381* ——— the same, Caps. I—XX, with transl. and the prefat. Essay, 8vo. *bds.* 7s 6d *ib.* 1836
3381 **PERSIAN.** ANWAR-I-SUHAILY: a paraphrase in Persian, of the FABLES of PILPAI, by Hussein Váiz Hashify, stout sm. folio, *lithog. hf. calf,* 16s; or *a beautiful copy in russia, joints, gold borders, gilt edges,* 25s *Bombay,* 1828
The best and most complete edition of this famous collection of Persian Stories.
3382 ——— The same, 2 vols. 8vo. *lithographed, hf. calf,* 12s *Bombay,* 1834
3383 ——— an edition, lithographed, sm. folio, 332 *pp. with numerous curious cuts, bd.* 20s *ib.* 1261 (1845)
3384 ANVAR-I SUHELI, or Lights of Canopus, the Persian version of Bidpai's Fables, *Persian,* edited by Ouseley, 4to. (pub. at £1. 11s 6d) *bds.* 26s *Hertford,* 1851
3385 ——— the same, royal 4to. LARGE PAPER, *half morocco,* 30s 1851
3386 ANVAR-I SUHAILI; or the Lights of Canopus; being the celebrated work of Husain Và'z u'l Háshifii, translated for the first time into English prose and verse (on the same principles as the author's translations of the 'Gulistan'), with an elaborate Preface and copious Notes, by E. B. Eastwick, royal 8vo. (pub. at £2. 2s) *cloth,* 18s 1854
"The most excellent book in the language is, in my opinion, the collection of tales and fables called "Anvari Suhaili, by Husain Va'iz, who took the celebrated work of Bidpai for his text, and has comprised all the wisdom of the Eastern nations in fourteen beautiful chapters."—*W. Scott.*

3387 BAHARI-UL-ANWAR: History of Hassan, the twelfth Iman, *in Persian,* folio, 467 *pp. lithogr. bd.* 14s 1268 (1851)
3388 BLEECK'S PERSIAN GRAMMAR: a Grammar of the Persian Language, containing Dialogues, Reading Lessons, and a Vocabulary, by A. H. Bleeck, 12mo. 288 *pp.* (pub. at 7s 6d) *cloth,* 5s 1857
3389 BOORHANI QATIU, a Dictionary of the Persian Language explained in Persian, alphabetically arranged according to the European System, with a Grammar prefixed, by Moohummud Hoosuen Ibni Khuluf Oot-Tubreezee, poetically styled Boorhan, with Appendix by T. Roebuck, sm. folio, *stained, hf calf,* 30s *Calcutta,* 1818
3390 ——— the same, folio, LARGE PAPER, *hf. blue Turkey morocco,* £4. 4s; or *a very fine sound copy, hf. russia,* £6. *Calcutta,* 1818
☞ Only 30 copies printed on Large Paper. Its usual selling price for *small paper* copies in 4to. is five guineas.
The above Dictionary, which is alphabetically arranged according to the System of European Lexicons, comprises the whole of the words, phrases, and metaphors, in the Furhungi Juhangeiree, the Mujmool Foors of Soorooree, the Soormue Sooluemanee, and the Suhah ood Udwiyn, together with many words and terms from the Greek, Syriac, Arabic, Turkish, and other languages.
"The Boorhani Qatiu is the most copious and easily consulted of all the Persian Lexicons at this time extant; and it has always been censidered as a standard work, which every Persian scholar ought to possess."—*Lumsden.*

3391 BORHAN KATIA', Farhang, 2 vols. folio, *lithogr. hf. bound,* £2. 10s 1832
3392 DABISTAN-I-MUZAHIB; School of Sects, *in Persian,* 4to. *bd.* 14s 1836
3393 ——— another edition, sm. folio, 334 *pp. bd.* 10s *Bombay,* 1262 (1846)
3394 DESATIR, or sacred writings of the ancient Persian prophets, with Commentary and Glossary, *Ancient Persian, Modern Persian, and English,* 2 vols. 1, in *hf. morocco,* 32s *Bombay,* 1818

3395 FERISHTA (Mahomed Kasim) TARIKH-I-FERISHTA; History of the Mohammedan Power in India till the year 1612, *in Persian*, edited by J. BRIGGS, 2 vols. folio, *lithogr. hf. bd.* £4.; or *hf. citron morocco,* £4. 16s Bombay, 1832
This the original edition contains many passages abridged or left out in the English translation, 4 vols. 8vo.

3396 FIRDOUSEE, Shah Namah, an Heroic Poem, containing the History of Persia from Kioomurs to Yesdejird; that is, from the earliest times to the conquest of that Empire by the Arabs, by Abool Kasim Firdousee; carefully collated with the oldest and best MSS., and illustrated with a copious Glossary of obsolete words and obscure idioms; with an introduction and Life of the Author, in English and Persian, and an Appendix containing the interpolated Episodes, &c. found in different MSS. by Turner Macan, 4 vols. roy. 8vo. bd. £4.; *hf. russia gilt,* £5.; or *green morocco, gilt edges,* £6. 6s Calcutta, 1829

3397 ——— the same, Vols. I, II, IV, in 2 vols. roy. 8vo. *not uniform,* £2. 1829
Contains an English and Persian preface, a Life of Firdousee, and the complete text.
" La première rédaction critique de Firdousi qui ait été entreprise par un Européen. M. Macan était plus propre que personne à remplir cette tâche, car il connaissait parfaitement la littérature persane et avait passé la plus grande partie de sa vie dans la meilleure société des provinces septentrionales de l'Inde."—*Mohl.*

3398 FIRDUSI, Shah Namah, 1103 *pp.*—Hikayat lamahakat Shah Namah, 101 *pp.* —Fahrsat, 31 *pp.*—sm. folio, *with a profusion of curious* ILLUSTRATIONS, *some the full size of the page,* 1235 *pp. lithographed in quadruple columns, a most complete edition, containing the entire Text with introduction, Appendix of the interpolated Episodes, and Index, red mor. super extra,* £5. 10s Bombay, 1846
Ce poeme embrasse toute l'histoire d'un grand empire, l'ouvrage national par excellence.
" The Persian soldiery," says Mr. Binning, "when about to engage in combat, are accustomed to sing aloud certain passages of the Sháhnámah, which practice has the effect of inspiring them to absolute fury, as the verses of Homer did the warriors of Greece, or as the Runic lays of the Skalds were wont to animate the fierce Berserkars of Norway."

3399 FIRDUSI. Farhangisarúr-i-Sultani: the Shah Namah abridged in prose, sm. folio, 312 *pp. lithogr. bd.* 12s ca. 1850

3400 GLADWIN'S PERSIAN MOONSHEE; Grammar; the Pundnameh of Sady, specimens of Arabic Stories, Lives of the Philosophers, Kowayed us Sultanet Shahjehan, part of St. Matthew, dialogues, etc. *in Persian and English,* 3 parts in 1, 4to. *bd.* 20s 1801

3401 GULISTAN IRAM; Poems and Tales, sm. 8vo. *curious plates, bds.* 6s 1270 (1853)

3402 HAFIZ, Diwán: Works, with an Account of his Life and Writings, *all Persian,* sm. fol. *hf. russia, scarce,* £2. Calcutta, 1791

3403 HAFT KULZUM, or the Seven Seas, a Dictionary and Grammar of the Persian Language, by his late Majesty the King of Oude, 7 vols. in 3, roy. folio, (pub. at £25.) *hf. bd. russia,* £4. 4s; or 7 vols. in 2, *calf neat,* £4. 15s Lucknow, 1822
Priced, 1830, Parbury, £30.; 1833, Allen, £30.; 1834, Thorpe, £25.; 1836, Thorpe, a fine presentation copy, £35.; 1841, Madden, £15. 15s.; 1859, Maisonneuve, 250 fr. This splendid book was printed at the royal press in the city of Lucknow. The first six volumes contain the Dictionary, the seventh the Grammar. Dr. Sprenger examined the MSS. at Lucknow, and speaks as follows of the remaining copies of the above:—"At the end of the hall there are bags full of books completely destroyed by white ants. Even new books have not been spared by these destructive insects; nearly the whole of the edition of the 'Taj alloghát' has been destroyed, and most of the remaining copies of the 'Haft Qulzum' have had the same fate."

HANDJÉRI, Dictionnaire.—*See post, under* TURKISH.

3404 HATIFY, Laili u Majnún, *in Persian,* edited by Sir William Jones, roy. 8vo. *printed to resemble a MS. within double lines of vermilion and gold, four illuminated Anwáns, with borders of flowers painted upon gold, the leaves powdered with gold, Eastern ornamental binding,* £2. 5s Calcutta, M. Cantopher, 1788

3405 JOHNSON'S Dictionary of Persian, Arabic and English, stout impl. 4to. 4to. 1240 *pp. treble columns,* (pub. at £4.) *cloth,* £3. 5s London, 1852

3406 JONES' Persian Grammar, by Lee, *9th edition,* 4to. 6 *plates of specimens* (pub. at 21s) *hf. bd,* 6s 1828

3407 KHAZANAT UL ILM, a Course of Mathematics, *Persian,* roy. 4to. *diagrams, sd.* 10s Calcutta, 1837

3408 KHONDMIR. Geschichte Tabaristan's und der Serbedare, *Pers. und Deutsch,* von Dorn, roy. 4to. *hf. calf,* 6s St. Petersb. 1850

3409 LUMSDEN'S (M.) Grammar of the Persian Language; comprising a Portion of the Elements of Arabic Inflection; together with some Observations on the Structure of either Language, considered with reference to the Principles of General Grammar, by M. Lumsden, LL.D. 2 vols. fol. *bd.* 15s; or *hf. cf. neat,* 20s 1810

3410 MIRÁT-I-SEKANDERY: a famous historical work, *in Persian,* sm. folio, 457 *pp. lithogr. hf. bd.* 7s 6d (? Bombay) 1831

3411 MIRKHOND, Kaftar dar Kazayat Atabekán: History of the Atábeks of Syria and Persia, *Persian*, by Morley, roy. 8vo. *plates of coins, cloth*, 9s   1848
3412 MULLAL RUMI, Mathnawi: a celebrated Mystic Poem, sm. folio, 202 *pp. in* 4 *cols. lithogr. bd.* 25s   *A. H.* 1263 (1846)
3413 MUNAKIB UL HAÏDARI: a Miscellany, addressed to the King of Oude; Extracts from *Persian* Authors, sm. folio, 230 pp. *bd.* 10s   *A. H.* 1235
3414 NIZAMI, SEKANDER NAMAH, *Persian, an excellent critical edition*, sm. folio, 342 pp. *lithographed, Eastern binding*, 32s   Bombay, 1843
3415 PERSIAN CLASSICS. Selections from the most esteemed Persian Writers: Akhlaki Mushini—Leily o Majnoon—Behari Danish—Zuleikha—Abul Fuzl, Insha—Sadi Diwán—Akhlaki Jallali—Sabat ul Abrar—Jami, Rokati—Sekander Namah; in 2 vols. large 4to. lithogr. *hf. morocco gilt*, 36s   Calcutta, 1828
3416 RAMDHUN SEN, English and Persian Dictionary, impl. 8vo. *bds.* 25s   *Calc.* 1833
3417 RICHARDSON'S Persian Arabic and English, and English Persian Arabic Dictionary, with a dissertation on the Languages, Literature, and manners of Eastern nations, 3 vols. stout folio, *the title and opening pages of dissertation in Vol. I. slightly injured and inlaid*, 36s   Oxford, 1777-80
3418 RICHARDSON'S DICTIONARY: Arabic and Persian Dictionary, explained in Eng. and English-Arabic-Persian Dictionary, 2 vols. royal 4to. *hf. bd. russia neat*, £5. 5s   1806-10
3419 ——— English-Persian and Arabic Dictionary, with additions and improvements by Wilkins, Vol. II. royal 4to. *bd. uncut, rare*, £3.   London, 1810
    "The "English Persian" part is exceedingly rare, not having been reprinted.
3420 ROUSSEAU'S Persian Vocabulary, 8vo. *hf. bound*, 5s   1802
3420*SADI, Gulistan, *Persian and English*, by Gladwin, 2 vols. 4to. *hf. bd.* 18s   Calcutta, 1806
3421 ——— Gulistan, in *Persian*, large 8vo. 379 *pp. bds.* 12s   *A. H.* 1249 (1833)
3422 ——— Gulistan, a complete analysis of the entire text, *Persian and English*, roy. 8vo. two translations, one being literal, word for word, by Anderson, 592 pp. *cloth*, 30s   Calcutta, 1861
3423 ——— Gulistan, in *English*, with Preface and Life, by Eastwick, 8vo. *bd. rare*, 25s   Hertford, 1852
3424 ——— Bostan, with a compendious Commentary and Dictionary of hard words, all in *Persian*, 4to. *lithographed, bds.* 12s; or *hf. russia neat*, 16s   Calc. 1828
3425 SPLIETH, Grammatica Persica, roy. 8vo. *in Persian, sd.* 5s   Halis, 1846
3422* ——— the same, new edition, *Perian*, by Johnson, 4to. *cloth*, 15s   Hertford, 1863
3426 STEWART'S Original and Modern Persian Letters, *Persian and English*, with analysis of the Shekesteh Alphabet, 4to. 24 *lithographs of Oriental Writing*, (pub. at £2. 2s) *calf gilt*, 10s   1825
3427 TOOTI NAMEH, or tales of a Parrot, *Persian and English*, roy. 8vo. *calf gilt, gilt edges*, 10s   1801
3428 TUCKER'S (W. T.) Pocket Dictionary of English and Persian, fcap. 8vo. *with the pronunciation*, (pub. 7s) *cloth*, 2s 6d   1850
3429 **PHOENICIAN.** GESENIUS, Scripturae linguaeque Phoeniciae monumenta quotquot supersunt, 3 parts in 2, 4to. 48 *plates, bds.* 20s   Lips. 1837
3430 ——— Paläographische Studien über phönizische und punische Schrift, 4to. 6 *plates, with several pencil marks in elucidation of the text, sd.* 4s   Leipzig, 1835
3431 **PUSHTU.** DORN'S Chrestomathy of the Pushtu or Afghan Language, with an Afghan and English Glossary, impl. 4to. *hf. rus. uncut*, 30s Peterb. 1847
3432 RAVERTY'S Grammar of the Pukhto, Pushto, or language of the Afghans, with examples, translations, and remarks on the language, literature and descent of the Afghans, 4to. *cloth*, 21s   1860
3433 **SANSCRIT.** ADELUNG, Bibliotheca Sanscrita: Literatur der Sanskrit-Sprache, 8vo. *second much improved edition, bds.* 8s   St. Petersburg, 1837
3434 AMERA COSHA. COSHA, or Dictionary of the Sanscrit Language, by Amera Sinha, *Sanscrit and English*, by Colebrooke, roy. 4to. *hf. calf*, 32s Seramp. 1808
3434*BALLANTYNE'S First Lessons in Sanscrit Grammar, introduction to the Hitopadesa, Lessons and Vocabulary, 8vo. *cloth*, 5s   1862
3435 BHAGAVAD-GITA, or the sacred lay: a colloquy between Krishna and Arjuna, *in Sanskrit*, with Vocabulary, by THOMSON, sq. sm. 8vo. (pub. at 9s) *cloth*, 5s 1855
3436 ——— the same, *in English*, by Thomson, with copious Notes, sq. sm. 8vo. (pub. at 12s) *cloth*, 7s   1855

3437 BHARTRIHARIS Sententiæ et Carmen Chauri eroticum, *Sanscr. et Lat.* cum notis, à Bohlen, 4to. *sd. 6s*; or, *thick paper, bds. gilt edges,* 9s *Berolini,* 1833
3438 BÖHTLINGK, Sanskrit-Chrestomathie, 8vo. Extracts from the Mahabharata, Ramayana, Manu, Vedas, etc. 451 pp. *hf. calf,* 15s *St. Petersb.* 1845
3439 BÖHTLINGK und ROTH, Sanskrit-Wörterbuch, herausg. von der Kaiserlichen Akademie der Wissenschaften, Vols. I, II. roy. 4to. £2. 2s *St. Petersb.* 1855-61
3440 BOPP, Grammatica critica linguae Sanscritæ, altera emendata editio, sm. 4to. *calf gilt,* 12s *Berolini,* 1832
3441 —— Glossarium Sanscritum, sm. 4to. 216 *pp. double cols. calf,* 6s *Berol.* 1830
3442 —— Glossarium Sanscritum, in quo omnes Radices et Vocabula usitatissima explicantur et cum Vocabulis graecis, latinis, germanicis, lithuanicis, Slavicis, Celticis comparantur, 4to. £2. *ib.* 1847
3443 BRIJ BILUS, or Boundless Licentiousness in Brij with 16,000 Women, an erotic work in *Sanscrit* verse, with ample commentary in prose, thick 8vo. *hf. bound, rare,* 24s *Calcutta* (? 1820)

With numerous English pencil memoranda in elucidation of the text.

3444 CHHÁNDOGYA UPANISHAD, with the commentary of Sankara Achárya, and the gloss of Ananda Giri, *Sanscrit,* by Röer, 8vo. *calf,* 12s *Calcutta,* 1850
3445 DASA KUMARA CHARITA (the), or adventures of Ten Princes, by Sri Dandi, *Sanscrit,* by Wilson, impl. 8vo. *cloth,* 10s *S. Or. T.* 1846
3446 DESGRANGES, Grammaire Sanscrite, 2 vols. 4to. *hf. calf,* 25s *Paris,* 1845-57
3447 FORSTER'S Essay on the Principles of Sanscrit Grammar, part I, (all published) impl. 4to. xxii and 700 pp. *bds.* 12s *Calcutta,* 1810
3448 GILDEMEISTER, Bibliotheca Sanscrita, 8vo. *sd.* 4s *Bonnae,* 1847
3449 HITOPADESA, the *Sanskrit* Text, with a Grammatical Analysis, alphabetically arranged, and an English Index of Words, serving the purpose of a reversed Dictionary, by Francis Johnson, Professor of Sanskrit at the East India College, 4to. (pub. at 31s 6d) *bds. new,* 26s 1847
3450 —— the same, in English, by Johnson, 4to. (pub. at 10s 6d) *bd.* 9s 1848
3451 HEETOPADES of Veeshnoo-Sarma, *in English,* by Wilkins, 8vo. *calf,* 6s 1777
3452 KALIDASA'S Cakuntala, *Sanskrit und Deutsch,* mit Anmerkungen, von Bœhtlink, impl. 8vo. *hf. purple morocco extra,* 16s *Bonn,* 1846
3453 KALIDÁSA, Sakuntalá, or Sakuntala recognized by the Ring, a *Sanskrit* Drama, by Kálidása; the Devanágarí Recension of the Text, now for the first time edited in England, with literal English Translation of all the Metrical passages, schemes of the Metres, and copious Critical and Explanatory Notes, by Monier Williams, M.A., royal 8vo. (pub. at 31s 6d) *cloth,* 18s 1853
3454 —— SAKUNTALA; or Sakuntalá recognized by the Ring; a Sanskrit Drama, translated into *English* prose and verse by Williams, *second edition,* 4to. 300 pp. *printed in the highest style of art,* with original designs on wood, head and tail pieces and borders in gold and colours, (pub. at £2. 2s) *fancy cloth richly gilt, gilt edges,* 36s; or, *in morocco super extra, sides richly gilt, gilt edges,* £2. 16s
1855
3455 —— a cheap edition of the above, the text the same, but without illuminations, 8vo. *cloth,* 5s 1856
3456 —— the Mégha Dúta, or Cloud Messenger, *Sanscrit and English,* with Vocabulary, by Wilson, impl. 8vo. *2nd edition, cloth,* 7s 1843
3457 LASSEN, Anthologia Sanscritica, cum Glossario, sm. 8vo. *calf,* 6s *Bonnae,* 1828
3458 MAHÁBHÁRATA (The), an Epic Poem, by the celebrated Veda vyása Rishi, printed in the Bengalee character from the best MSS. edited by learned Pandites of Calcutta, 4 vols. 4to. *sd.* £6. 6s *Calcutta,* 1834-39
3459 MAHABHARATA, Johnson's selections from the, royal 8vo. *bds.* 5s 1842
3460 DILUVIUM, cum 3 aliis episodiis, *Sanscr.* à Bopp, sm. 4to. *sd.* 5s *Berol.* 1829
3461 NALOPAKHYANAM, Story of Nalus, *Sanscr. and English* (by Milman), with Vocabulary and Introduction by Williams, large 8vo. *cloth,* 10s 1860
3462 MANAVA-DHERMA-SASTRA, or the Ordinances of Menu, according to the Gloss of Calluca, comprising the Indian System of Duties, religious and civil, translated by Sir W. Jones, new edition, with notes by Haughton, *in Sanscrit and English,* 2 vols. 4to. (pub. at £4. 4s) £2. 16s 1825

3463 MANAVA-Dharma-Sastra. Lois de Manou, *en Sanscrit*, avec des notes, etc. par Deslongchamps, 8vo. (pub. at 18s) *sd. 7s*; *hf. russia, 9s* *Paris*, 1830
3464 —— Lois de Manou, *en Français*, avec des notes, par Deslongchamps, 8vo. *sd. 7s 6d* *Paris*, 1833
3465 MÜLLER'S (Max) History of the Ancient Sanscrit Literature, so far as it illustrates the primitive religion of the Brahmans, 8vo. *cloth*, 18s 1859
Of this work it is but faint praise to say that it is the most remarkable effort of genius combined with erudition that our age has produced.—*Pantheon*, May 10, 1862.
3466 Mricchakatika, curriculum figlinum Sudrakae, *Sanscr.* ed. Stenzler, impl. 8vo. *sd.* 10s *Bonnae*, 1846
3467 Muir's Original Sanskrit Texts on the origin and progress of the Religion and Institutions of India, 3 vols. 8vo. *cloth, rare*, £2. 5s 1858-61
3468 NAISHADHA-CHARITA : or Adventures of Nala Raja of Naishadha, by Sri Harsha of Cashmir, *in Sanskrit*, pt. 1, with Commentary, thick 8vo. *sd.* 25s ; *cloth*, 27s *Calcutta*, 1836
3469 Neeti Sunkhulun, Collection of the Sanskrit Slokas [Aphorisms], *Sanscr. and English*, by Krishen Bahadur, 8vo. *hf. calf*, 9s *Serampore*, 1831
3470 PANINI-SUTRA-VITRI, or the Grammatical Aphorisms of Panini, in Sanscrit, 2 vols. sqr. 8vo. *calf, scarce*, £2. 5s ; *sd. uncut*, £2. 10s *Calcutta*, 1810
3471 —— Grammatische Regeln, herausgegeben von Böhtlingk, *in Sanskrit*, 2 vols. 8vo. *bds.* 24s *Bonn*, 1839-40
3472 PANINI : his place in Sanskrit Literature, by Goldstücker, impl. 8vo. xvi. and 268 pp. *cloth*, 12s 1861
3473 Prakrita-Prakasa ; or the Prákrit Grammar of Vararuchi, with the Commentary (Manoramá) of Bhámaha, by Edward Byles Cowell, roy. 8vo. 230 pp. (pub. at 21s) *bds.* 12s 1854
3474 PURANAS. Ancient Indian Literature: Sheev, Brehme Vivertte, and Arthe Prekash Shastre Pooranas, *English*, in 1 vol. 4to. *hf. bound*, 9s 1809
3475 BHAGAVAT PURANA, *in Sanscrit*, lithographed and printed on tinted paper in imitation of the original MSS. 457 sheets, sm. fol. *very rare*, £3. 16s (? 1848)
3475*—— the same, sm. folio, *wanting a sheet*, £1. 16s
3476 Purana Sangraha, collection of the Puranas, No. 1. Markandeya Purana, *Sanscr. and Engl.* by Banerjea, 8vo. *sd.* 3s 6d *Calc.* 1851
3477 SABDA KALPA DRUMA, an Encyclopedical Lexicon, *in Sanscrit*, by Radhakanta Deva, Vols. I.—V. roy. 4to. *hf. russia, with photographic portrait of Raja Radha Kant Bahadoor, extremely rare in this country, Professor Wilson's copy*, £22. *Calcutta*, 1833-50

The unintermittent labours of more than a quarter of a century have at last come to a successful close. The author has already achieved his reputation, as well among the Pandits of Hindustan, as the Savants of Europe. His Sanskrit Encyclopædia stands foremost among the contributions which the present or any preceding century has rendered to Sanskrit learning. The utility of such a voluminous compendium of the arts and sciences has been fully appreciated, and its author has received more than a solitary mark of acknowledgment from the Oriental scholars of the day. It would be rather curious to inspect the numberless testimonies of approbation which Native and Mahrátta, English and German, have competed with each other in offering to his merits; nor is the labour undeserving of even a higher tribute. The Rája has spent the brightest part of his mortal existence in the hope of living an immortal life for generations to come, and reared an imperishable monument for himself. It can be stated that our Encyclopedist is always in his element on Puránic, Tantric, and on all subjects connected with the modern literature of the Bráhmans, to which he has done ample justice. The work is not very full in the technicalities of the medical science, of the different systems of philosophy and of the Vedas ; but we hope the Rájá will supply these deficiencies in the supplement he promises; and in that expectation, strongly recommend to his notice Yaska's Nirukta, every page of which will supply him with new matter; the first page of the Nighantu contains at least a hundred words not to be met with in his Lexicon.

3478 VALMEEKI'S Ramayuna, *in Sanscrit and English*, by Carey and Marshman, Vol. II. roy. 4to. *a very fine copy in bds. rare*, £2. 10s *Serampore*, 1808
3479 VALMICIS Ramayana, id est Carmen Epicum de Ramæ rebus gestis *Sanskrite et Latine*, edidit Schlegel, Vols. I. II. pt. 1, in 3 vols. large 8vo. (*all published*) *thick paper, presentation copy, with the learned editor's autograph inscription, bds.* 36s *Bon.* 1829-38
3480 —— Ramayuna in English, by Carey and Marshman, Vol. I. 8vo. *cloth, all published*, 12s 1808
3481 —— Muerte de Yachnadatta, *Sanscrito y Espanol*, con notas, por Eguilaz Yungas, imp. 8vo. *sd.* 10s *Granada*, 1861
3482 Vedanta Sara, Elements of Theology, with commentary in *Sanscrit*, 8vo. *hf. russia*, 6s *Cal.* 1829
3483 VEDAS. Rammohun Roy's translation of the principal Books, Passages and Texts of the Veds, 8vo. *cloth*, 10s 1832

3484 RIG-VEDA-SANHITA: the Sacred Hymns of the Brahmans, together with the Commentary of Sayanacharya, in Sanskrit, edited by Max Müller, 3 vols. very stout royal 4to. (pub. at £7. 10s) *cloth*, £5. 10s   1849-56

3485 RIG-VEDA-SANHITA. A Collection of Ancient Hindu Hymns, constituting the first Ashtaka, or Book of the Rig-Veda, translated from the Sanskrit by H. H. WILSON, Vols. I. II. III. 8vo. *cloth*, RARE, £3. 10s   1850-57
    The first volume is entirely OUT OF PRINT.

3486 RIGVEDA, ou livre des Hymnes, traduit du Sanscrit, par M. LANGLOIS, Vols. 3 and 4, 8vo. 12s   *Paris*, 1850-51

3487 SAMA VEDA, SANHITA of the, *in Sanscrit*, by Stevenson and H. H. Wilson, roy. 8vo. *cloth*, 5s   *S. O. T.* 1843

3488 —— Hymnen des Sama Veda, *Sansk.* von Benfey, roy. 8vo. *hf. cf.* 7s 6d 1848

3489 VOPADEVA's Mugdhabodha, *Sanskrit*, mit Wörterverzeichniss, von Böhtlingk, 8vo. *sd.* 10s   *St. Petersb.* 1847

3490 WESTERGAARD, RADICES Linguæ SANSCRITÆ, copia exemplorum illustratae, 4to. *hf. russia*, 20s   *Bonnae*, 1841

3491 WILLIAMS (Monier) ENGLISH AND SANSKRIT DICTIONARY, 4to. (pub. at £3. 3s) £2. 10s   *London*, 1851

3492 —— Grammar of the Sanscrit Language, with a Selection from the Institutes of Menu, roy. 8vo. *second edition, cloth*, 10s 6d   *Oxford*, 1857

3493 WILSON'S Dictionary, Sanscrit and English, translated, amended, and enlarged from an original compilation prepared by learned Natives, 4to. £5.   *Calc.* 1819

3494 WILSON's Sanscrit and English Dictionary, *second edition, greatly enlarged*, roy. 4to. *calf*, £12.   1832
    The high price of Wilson's Dictionary has to be ascribed to the slow progress of Professor Goldstücker's proposed new edition. The few parts published (No. 5, early in March, 1863, and the 6th advertised) are of no practical use to students.

3495 WILSON's Select Specimens of the Theatre of the Hindoos, translated from the *Sanscrit, second edition*, 2 vols. 8vo. *calf gilt*, 16s   1835

3496 WILSON's Sanscrit Grammar, 8vo. *second edition, hf. calf*, 16s   1847

3497 YATES'S Dictionary in Sanscrit and English, 8vo. *hf. bd.* £2. 8s *Calcutta*, 1846

3498 —— Sanscrit Grammar, 8vo. *bds.* 9s   *Calcutta*, 1820

3499 **SIAMESE.** LOW'S Grammar of the Thai or SIAMESE language, 4to. *with 7 lithographs of specimens, bds.* 7s 6d   *Calcutta*, 1828

3500 PALLEGOIX, Grammatica Linguæ Thai, 4to. *hf. bd. rare*, 36s *Bangkok*, 1850

3501 —— Siamese Dictionary; Dictionarium Linguæ Thaï, sive Siamensis, interpretatione latina, gallica, et Anglica illustratum, auctore D. J. B. Pallegoix, episcopo Mallensi, vicario apostolico Siamensi, stout folio, *the Siamese in native and Roman Letters, explained in French and English*, £3. 3s   *Paris*, 1854

3502 **TATAR.** ABULGHASI Bahadür Chani, Historia Mongolorum et Tatarorum, *Tatarice (charac. Arab.)* curâ Fraehnii, large folio, *hf. calf*, £2.   *Casani*, 1825
    Printed at the expense of Count Nicholas Romanzoff.

3503 CASTREN'S NORDISCHE REISEN und FORSCHUNGEN, herausg. von Schiefner: Reiseberichte und Briefe, 1838-49, 2 vols. 1853-56—Ostjakische Sprachlehre, 1849—Finnische Mythologie, 1853—Samojedische Grammatik, 1854—Wörterverzeichniss aus den Samojed. Sprachen, 1855—Ethnolog. Vorles. über die Altaischen Völker, 1837—Koibalische und Karagassische Sprachlehre, 1857—Burjätische Sprachlehre nebst Wörterverzeichniss, 1857—in all, 9 vols. roy. 8vo. *uniform in green cloth*, £3. 15s   *St. Petersb.* 1849-57

3504 CASTREN, Grammatica Syrjaena, 8vo. *cloth*, 5s ; *calf gilt*, 6s 6d *Helsingfor.* 1844

3505 GIGANOFF, Slovar Rossüsko-Tatarski, 4to. 682 *pp. hf. bd.* 25s *St. Petersb.* 1804

3506 SCHIEFNER, über die Thusch-Sprache, oder die Khistische Mundart, roy. folio, *hf. bound*, 9s   *St. Petersb.* 1858

3507 SCHOTT über die Tatarischen Sprachen, 4to. *hf. morocco*, 7s 6d *Berlin*, 1831

3508 SJÖGREN, Wohnsitze und Verhältnisse der Jatwägen, roy. 4to. *hf. bound*, 7s 6d   *St. Petersb.* 1858

3509 STRAHLENBERG's Description of Russia, Siberia, and Great Tartary, with Polyglot table of 32 Tartarian Dialects and Kalmuck-Mungalian Vocabulary, sm. 4to. *calf*, 10s   1738

3510 WIEDEMANN, Tscheremissische Grammatik, 8vo. *sd.* 3s   *Reval*, 1847

3511 —— Syrjänische Grammatik, 8vo. *sd.* 3s   *ib.* 1847

3512 —— Wotjakische Grammatik, 8vo. *cloth*, 7s   *ib.* 1851

3513 **TIBETAN.** Foucaux, Parabole de l'Enfant Egaré (Chap. IV. du Lotus la Bonne Foi) *Sanscrit, Tibétain, et Français,* 8vo. THICK PAPER, *sd. 7s Paris,* 1854
3514 Foucaux, Grammaire de la Langue Tibetaine, 8vo. *presentation copy, with author's autograph inscription, sd. 5s ; hf. morocco,* 6s 6d *Paris,* 1858
3515 GEORGII Alphabetum Tibetanum, cum disquisitione de vario litterarum ac regionis nomine, gentis origine, moribus, etc. stout 4to. 94 *and* 820 *pp. plates of the Llama Idolatry, calf,* 21s *Romae,* 1762
3516 KOEROES, Dictionary, Tibetan and English, prepared with the assistance of the Bandè Sangs-Rgyas Phun-Tshogs, a learned Láma, 4to. *cl.* 25s *Calcut.* 1834
3517 —— Grammar of the Tibetan Language, 4to. *calf gilt,* 16s *ib.* 1834
3518 —— the same, Grammar and Dictionary, in 1 vol. 4to. *calf neat,* 36s *ib.* 1834
3519 RGYA TCH'ER ROL PA, ou Développement des Jeux, contenant l'Histoire du Bouddha Cakya-Mouni *en Tibétain et Français,* par Foucaux, 2 vols. in 1, 4to. *hf. calf gilt,* £2. *Paris,* 1847-48
3520 SCHRŒTER, Dictionary of the Bhotanta, or Boutan Language, edited by Marshman, with a GRAMMAR, 4to. *calf,* 36s *Serampore,* 1826

This language is spoken in the region on the Himalaya Mountains, usually called Chinese Tartary, extending in a line of 1000 miles of border land, between the Languages of India derived from the Sanscrit, and the language spoken throughout Tartary.

3521 **TURKISH.** ALF LEILAH VE LEILAH, Terjemah: the Arabian Nights *in Turkish,* in 2 vols. roy. 8vo. *bd.* 30s (*Constant. ca.* 1830)
3522 BARKER's Turkish Grammar, Dialogues and Vocabulary, a practical Guide to the acquisition of the Turkish Language, 1 vol. 12mo. 166 pp. (pub. at 4s) *cloth,* 2s 6d 1854
3523 BARKER's Reading Book, with a Grammar and Vocabulary, the pronunciation given, 8vo. (pub. at 14s) *cloth,* 4s 1854
3524 BIANCHI, Dictionnaire Turc-Français et Français-Turc, 4 stout vols. 8vo. *half calf,* £3.; *calf gilt,* £3. 16s *Paris,* 1835-47
3525 —— Vocabulaire Turc-Français et Français-Turc, st. 8vo. *hf. bd.* 6s *Par.* 1831
3526 CLARKE (Hyde) Help to memory in learning Turkish, 12mo. 14 pp. *containing the most useful words and phrases, English and Tnrkish, cloth,* 1s *Const.* 1862
3527 —— Guide de la Conversation en Français et en Turc, ob. roy. 8vo. 2s 6d 1839
3528 —— seconde edition, oblong 8vo. *sd.* 4s 1852
3529 FARHANG-I-SHAOURY: Thesaurus Linguæ Persicæ et Turcicæ, Persian-Turkish Dictionary, by Ibrahim Effendi Monteferrica, 2 vols. sm. folio, *fine copy, French calf, from Miss Currer's library,* £2. 10s *Constant. A. H.* 1155 (1742)
3530 GHARIB HIKAYAT ASHIK: "A Strange Story," *Turkish Romance,* sm. 4to. *curious lithographs of a sentimental character, bd. rare,* 10s *Const.* 1274 (1857)

The first Turkish artistic production met with by me.

3531 GULSHEN-I-MAARIF: History of the Ottoman Empire, *in Turkish,* 2 vols. stout sm. 4to. 2540 pp. *bd.* 18s *Const. ca.* 1830
3532 GUNJINAH HIKMET: Treasury of Wisdom, sq. 8vo. 184 *pp.* 5s *Const.* 1256
3533 GUZEL-OGLOU, Dialogues Français-Turcs, 8vo. 404 pp. *hf. bd.* 5s *Const.* 1852
3534 HANDJERI (A.) Dictionnaire Français-ARABE-PERSAN et TURC, 3 vols. in 2, 4to. (pub. at about £7.7s) *bds.* £3. *Moscou,* 1840-41

One Alphabet, beginning with French; a valuable companion to the Dictionaries of Johnson for *Persian,* Golius or Freytag for *Arabic,* and Meininski for *Turkish.*

3535 KAMOOS Abul-Kemel Es-Seid Ahmed Aassim, El-Okeanus, al bessit fi Terjamat il-Kamus, an ARABIC DICTIONARY, explained in *Turkish,* 2 vols. folio, 1900 pp. *bd.* £2. 16s *Scutari, A. H.* 1230-33 (1815-17)
3536 MALLOUF, Dictionnaire Français-Turc, thick 12mo. 912 pp. *hf. mor.* 5s *Par.* 1856
3537 —— Dialogues Turcs-Français, obl. 12mo. *hf. calf,* 4s *Smyrne,* 1854
3538 MENINSKI, Grammatica Turcica, cum praeceptis linguae Arab. et Persicæ, etc. fol. *calf,* 5s *Vien.* 1680

For the "DICTIONARY," see General Oriental Literature.

3539 REDHOUSE'S English and Turkish Dictionary, in 2 parts: Part I. English and Turkish. Part II. Turkish-English; in which the Turkish words are represented in the Oriental character, as well as their correct pronunciation and accentuation shewn in English letters, by J. W. Redhouse, F.R.S.A., *Member of the Imperial Academy of Science of Constantinople, &c. &c.* in 1 stout vol. sm. sq. 8vo. xxvi. and 1151 pp. (pub. at £2.) *cloth,* 30s 1857

3540 REDHOUSE'S ENGLISH-TURKISH LEXICON, showing in TURKISH, the literal, incidental, figurative, colloquial, and technical significations of the ENGLISH TERMS ; preceded by a sketch of English Etymology, royal 8vo. xvi. and 828 pp. *printed with very small but singularly clear types, both the English and the Turkish,* (pub. at 24s) *half bound red morocco, new,* 20s   1861

3541 REDHOUSE, Grammaire de la Langue Ottomane, large 8vo. *cloth,* 9s   Paris, 1846

3542 RHASIS (G.) Vocabulaire Française-Turc, 4to. 327 *pp. doub. cols. with the pronunc. in Roman letter, bd.* 7s 6d   St. Petersb. 1828

3543 SHARHI PENDI ATTAR : explanations of the poem of Attar, *Turkish,* by Murad, 8vo. 367 pp. *bd.* 6s   Const. A. H. 1252

3544 ZEND. ZENDAVESTA : Zend text of the Vendidad, by Westergaard, 4to. *sd.* 4s   Cop. 1854

3545 AVESTA, *Deutsch,* von Spiegel, Vol. I : Vendidad, 8vo. *sd.* 4s   Leip. 1852

3546 VENDIDAD SADE : Yacna, Vispered und Vendidad, Zend. (Röm. Schrift.) mit Glossar von Brockhaus, roy. 8vo. 10s   Leipz. 1850

SEE *ante,* General Alphabet " HAUG," " HYDE," and " ZEND AVESTA."

AFRICAN LANGUAGES.

3547 BAIKIE on the Hausa and Fulfulde languages, sm. 8vo. *sd.* 2s 6d   1861

3548 DIALOGUES, and portion of the N. T. *English, Arabic, Haussa, and Bornu,* obl. sm. folio, 116 pp. *lithographed, sd.* 7s 6d ; *hf. calf,* 9s   1853

3549 KOELLE, POLYGLOTTA AFRICANA, a Vocabulary of nearly 300 Words and Phrases in more than 100 African Languages, roy. folio, 24 *and* 187 *pp. tabularly arranged, cloth,* 21s   1854

3550 OUTLINE of a Vocabulary of the languages of Western and Central Africa, obl. 16mo. 213 *pp. cloth,* 5s   1841

3551 **Bunda.** CANNECATTIM, Diccionario da LINGUA BUNDA ou Angolense, Bunda-Portugueza-Latina, sm. 4to. 720 *pp. treble cols. mor.* 36s *Lisboa, Imp. Reg.* 1804

3552 **Haussa.** SCHÖN'S Vocabulary, Haussa-English and English-Haussa, with Grammar, 8vo. *cloth,* 6s   1843

3553 **Kaffir.** BOYCE'S Grammar of the Kaffir Language, *third edition,* augmented by Davis, sm. 8vo. *cloth,* 7s   1863

3554 **Secuana.** CASALIS, Etudes sur la Langue Séchuana, 8vo. *sd.* 5s *Par.* 1841

3555 **Sherbro** and English Church Catechism, 12mo. *hf. bd.* 6s   1824

3556 **Susoo** GRAMMAR and VOCABULARY, 8vo. *bds. rare,* 20s   Edinb. 1802

3557 SPELLING Book for the Susoos, and Catechism, *Susoo and English,* 12mo. *bds. very rare,* 32s   ib. 1802

3558 **Towarek.** Grammatical Sketch of the Temahuq or Towarek, 8vo. *cloth,* 2s 6d   1862

3559 **Wolof.** DARD, Dictionnaire Français-Wolof-Bambara, et Wolof-Français, 8vo. *hf. calf,* 5s   Paris, 1825

AMERICAN LANGUAGES.

3560 AMERICAN ETHNOLOGICAL SOCIETY'S Transactions, 2 vols. 8vo. *sd. rare,* 30s   New York, 1845-48
Comprises valuable Papers, including VOCABULARIES of the MEXICAN NATIONS.

3561 LUDEWIG's Literature of American Aboriginal languages, edited by Trübner, 8vo. *cloth,* 7s   1858

3562 PICKERING on a uniform orthography for the Indian languages of North America, 4to. *sd. rare,* 9s   Cambridge, U. S. 1820

3563 **Abnaki.** AMERICAN ACADEMY of Arts and Sciences, Memoirs, Vol. I, containing RASLES, Abnaki Dictionary, with notes by Pickering, 4to. *cloth,* 20s
Cambridge, U. S. 1833

3564 **Aruwack.** GESCHICHTE unsers Herrn Jesu Christi, *translated into the Aruwack dialect,* 8vo. *calf,* RARE, *unmentioned by Rich,* 25s   Philadelphia, 1799

3565 **Aymara.** TORRES RUBIO (Diego de) Arte de la lengua Aymara, 12mo. *Title, Approbacion, and last* 9 *leaves in neat MS. limp vell. very rare,* £3.   Lima, 1616-17
Besides a Grammar of the Aymara language, it contains Vocabularies Spanish-Aymara and Aymara-Spanish, Preparations for Confession, Forms of Matrimony and extreme Unction, all having the Aymara and Spanish in opposite columns. Collation: Title and leaves numbered 2-52 ; Vocabulario (*Espanol-Aymara*) 21 leaves unnumbered ; Confessionario, Orden para administrar, 18 leaves numbered 1-17 ; Vocabulario Aymara, Prologo, 1 leaf ; Vocabulario Aymara (*-Espanol*), Letania de N. Senora, Acto de contricion, en Aymara, 16 leaves.

3566 **Brazilian.** DENIS, Fête Brésilienne à Rouen, 1550, avec un fragment sur la Théogonie, et des poesies, *en langue Tupique*, 8vo. *plate, sd. 7s 6d Paris,* 1851

3567 BERNARDO DE NANTES, Katecismo Indico da Lingua Kariris, adaptado ao Genio dos Indios do Brasil, 12mo. *calf extra*, VERY RARE, £5. *Lisboa,* 1709

3568 **Caraibe.** RAYMOND BRETON, Dictionnaire Caraibe-Français, meslé de quantité de Remarques historiques pour l'esclaircissement de la Langue, 1664—Dictionnaire Français Caraibe, 1666—Catechisme Caraibe, avec une Traduction Française, 1664—3 vols. in 1, 16mo. *calf*, RARE, £5. 15s *Aux.* 1664-66

A lexicographical production of extreme rarity. The author, a Dominican, was sub-prior of the Monastery of Preaching Friars at Blainville; and one of the first four French Missionaries deputed to the Island of Gardeloupe, now called Guadeloup, and the Caribbee Islands in America. The same learned Missionary wrote a Caribbee Grammar, published 1667.

3569 **Chilian.** FEBRES (A.) Arte de la Lengua general del Reyno de Chile, con Dialogo Chileno-Hispano curioso, la Doctrina Christiana, *Chilena y Castellana,* Vocabulario Hispano-Chileno y Calepino Chileno-Hispano, stout 12mo. 683 pp. *limp vellum*, EXCESSIVELY RARE, £5. 15s *Lima,* 1765

3570 **Dakota.** RIGGS' Dakota Grammar and Dictionary, collected by the members of the Dakota Mission, roy. 4to. *cloth,* 21s *Washington,* 1852
The Dakota language is that spoken by the Sioux Indians.

3571 **Delaware.** Collection of Hymns in the Delaware Language, for the Christian Indians, 12mo. *hf. bd.* RARE, *unmentioned by Rich,* 32s *Philadelphia,* 1803

3572 ZEISBERGER's Grammar of the Lenni Lenape, or Delaware Indians, by Duponceau, sm. 4to. *hf. bd.* 9s (*U. S.*) 1816-17

3573 **Greenlandish.** FABRICIUS, Grönlandsk Grammatica end Ordbog; *Greenlandish-Danish* Grammar and Dictionary, 2 vols. 12mo. *interleaved, hf. bd.* 20s *Kiöb.* 1801-4

3574 **Guarani.** RUYZ (Antonio) Catecismo de la Lengua Guarani, *Guarani y Espanol,* 16mo. *limp vellum,* OF EXTREME RARITY, *not mentioned by Brunet,* £3. 10s *Madrid,* 1640

3575 **Huron.** SAGARD (Gabriel) Dictionnaire de la langue Huronne, necessaire à traiter avec les Sauvages du pays, 16mo. *title and preface,* 12 *pp. Dictionary,* 66 *pp. hf. bound,* £2 *Paris,* 1632

3576 **Kechua (Ancient Peruvian).** TSCHUDI, die Kechua Sprache; Sprachlehre, Sprachproben, und Wörterbuch, 3 vols. in 2, *hf. cf. uncut,* 25s *Wien,* 1853

3577 **Mexican, Aztec, Quichua, Othomite.** BUSCHMANN, die Völker und Sprachen Neu Mexico's und der westseite des Britischen Nord-Amerika's, 4to. *bds.* 16s *Berlin,* 1858

3578 —— der Athapaskische Sprachstamm, 4to. *bds.* 16s 1856

3579 EVANGELIARIUM, EPISTOLARIUM ET LECTIONARIUM AZTECUM, sive Mexicanum, ex Antiquo Codice Mexicano, nuper reperto, depromptum cum præfatione, interpretatione, adnotationibus, Glossario edidit BERNARDINUS BIONDELLI, folio, pp. 574, *only 400 copies printed, on stout writing paper, bds.* £5. 15s *Mediolani,* 1858

The very interesting Codex, of which the above is a careful reprint, was discovered in Mexico by Beltrami in the year 1826, and came into the hands of the present editor by purchase from the heirs. It is composed in the purest and most elegant Nahuatl that was ever written, by Bernardino Sahagun, a Spanish Monk of the Franciscan order, with the assistance of two Scions of royalty in Anahuac, one the son of Montezuma, the other the son of the Prince of Tezcuco—and purports to be a "postilla" on the Gospels and Epistles. Sahagun arrived at Mexico in the year 1529, and lived and laboured with great success in that country for fully sixty years. Of his many works in and on the Nahuatl language, the above is the only one which has been saved from perdition. Mr. Biondelli has accompanied Sahagun's text by a Latin version, has added a copious Vocabulary, Nahuatl and Latin, and by his introductory observations, has thrown considerable light not alone upon the Nahuatl language, its affinity to other families of languages, its grammatical peculiarities, but also upon the traditions, institutions, and monuments of the Aztecs—thus forming a complete treasury of everything appertaining to the ancient Aztecs. Altogether this is a volume which cannot be dispensed with by the student in linguistics.

3580 NAXERA de lingua Othomitorum, 4to. *sd.* 4s *Phil.* 1835

3581 PAREDES. Catecismo Mexicano, que contiene toda la Doctrina Christiana con todas sus Declaraciones, dispusolo en Castellano Geronymo de Ripalda, literalmente lo traduxo en Idioma Mexicano Ignacio de Paredes, 12mo. RARE, *fine copy, red Turkey morocco, gilt edges, by Fr. Bedford,* £5. 5s
En Mexico, en la Imprenta de la Bibliotheca Mexicana, 1758
Extremely rare, I cannot trace the sale of one copy.

3582 POPOL VUH, le Livre sacré et les Mythes de l'Antiquité Américaine, avec les Livres héroïques et historiques des Quichés; ouvrage original des Indigènes de Guatémala, *texte Quiché* et traduction *française* en regard, accompagné de

notes philologiques et d'un commentaire sur la Mythologie et les migrations des peuples anciens de l'Amérique, etc. comparé sur les documents originaux et inédits, par BRASSEUR de BOURBOURG, 8vo. CCLXXX and 368 pp. *sd.* 20*s*
Paris, 1861

The GREAT BOOK of the MEXICANS, with a French translation; prefixed is a valuable and very learned introduction on the History and Mythology of the Ancient Mexicans.

3583 BRASSEUR DE BOURBOURG, Gramatica de la lengua Quiche: Grammaire de la langue Quichée, espagnole-française, mise en parallèle avec ses deux dialectes, Cakchiquel et Tzutuhil, tirée des manuscrits des meilleurs auteurs guatémaliens, avec des notes philologiques, un vocabulaire Quiché et un Essai sur la poésie, la musique, la danse et l'art dramatique des Mexicains et des Guatémaltèques avant la conquête, et le Rabipal Achi drame indigène, sa musique, *quiché et français*, royal 8vo. *plates, sd.* 21*s*   *Paris,* 1862

Ces deux beaux ouvrages forment aussi les deux premiers volumes de la Collection des documents dans les langues indigènes pour servir à l'étude de l'histoire et de la philosophie de l'Amérique ancienne.

3584 **Mosquito.** HENDERSON's Moskito (Honduras) Grammar, 8vo. *bound,* 12*s*
New York, 1846
3585 **Moxa.** MARBAN (Pedro) Arte della Lengua Moxa, con su Vocabulario y Catechismo, 12mo. *vell. fine copy,* £5.   *Ciudad de los Reyes* (*Lima*), 1702

Collation: Title, dedication, etc. 16 pp.; Arte de la Lengua Moxa, fol. 1-117; Vocabulario de la Lengua Moxa, fol. 118-664; Cathecismo menor en Lengua Espanola y Moxa, fol. 1-142; Algunas advertencias tocantes al valor del Matrimonio entre los Indios recien convertidos, 2 pp.; Cartilla y Doctrina cristiana en Lengua Moxa, 20 pp.; Declaracion, fol. 163-202; Indice, 2 pp.

POLYNESIAN AND AUSTRALIAN LANGUAGES.

3586 **Australian and Tasmanian.** GREY's Vocabulary of the Dialects of South-Western Australia, 16mo. 2*s* 6*d*   1841
3587 GREY (Sir George) Journal of an Expedition from Auckland to Taranaki, 1849-50, *New Zealand and English*, 12mo. *cloth, rare,* 7*s*   *Auckland,* 1851
3588 SHÜRMANN's Parnkalla Vocabulary, with grammar, 8vo. *calf gilt,* 16*s Adel.* 1844
3589 TEICHELMANN and Schürmann, Grammar, Vocabulary, and Phraseology of the Aboriginal Language of South Australia, 8vo. *scarce,* 10*s*   *Adelaide,* 1840
3590 THRELKELD's Key to the structure of the Aboriginal language of Hunter's River, Lake Macquarie, etc. New South Wales, 8vo. *bds. rare,* 12*s Sydney,* 1850
3591 WILLIAMS's New Zealand and English Dictionary, and Grammar, sm. 8vo. *bds.* 7*s*   *Paihia,* 1844
3592 **Javanese, Kawi, Macassar,** etc. RAFFLES'S (Sir Stamford) HISTORY OF JAVA, 2 vols. 4to. *large map and* 65 *plates, some coloured,* (pub. at £6. 6*s*) *half bound,* £2. 16*s*   1817
3593 HUMBOLDT, über die KAWI-SPRACHE auf der Insel Java; nebst Einleitung über die Verschiedenheit des menschlichen Sprachbaues und ihren Einfluss auf die geistige Entwicklung des Menschengeschlechts, 3 vols. 4to. *bds.* £2. 10*s*; or, *hf. green morocco, neat,* £3. 10*s*   *Berlin,* 1836-40
3594 MATTHES, Makassaarsche Spraakkunst, large 8vo. *cl.* 7*s Amst.* (*Makassar*) 1858
3595 **Philippine Islands.** DOMINGO DE LOS SANTOS, Vocabulario de la Lengua Tagala, sm. folio, *printed on silk paper, vellum, rare, from Professor Wilson's copy,* £5. 15*s*   *Manilla,* 1794

My last copy I sold for £8.; the new edition of the above is a careless reprint.

3596 DOUTREMAN, Pedagogo Christiano, y Cadvha Nga Bahin sa, con sa Binisaya, stout 16mo. 493 *leaves, somewhat wormed about the middle of the book, limp vel. rare,* 28*s*   *Manila,* 1751
3597 EZGUERRA, Arte de la lengua Bisaya, de la Provincia de Leyte, sm. 4to. *limp vellum, very rare,* £4. 4*s*   *Manila,* 1747
3598 SANTOS (Domingo de los) Vocabulario de la Lengua Tagala, sm. folio, *limp vellum, very rare,* £4. 4*s*   (*Manilla*) *Imprenta nueva de Dayot, por Oliva,* 1835
3599 TOTANES (Sebastian de) Arte de la Lengua Tacala y Manual Tagalog, para la administracion de los Santos Sacramentos, 2 vols. in 1, smallest 4to. *fine copy, printed on paper manufactured from silk, vellum, extremely rare,* £2. 10*s*
Sampaloc, extra Manila, 1796
3600 —— Arte de la Lengua Tagala, y Manual Tagalog, 2 vols. in 1, sm. 4to. *limp vellum,* 20*s*
Manila, 1850

NEW BOOKS AT REDUCED PRICES.

3601 **Tahitian, Hawaian, Marquesan,** etc. BIBILIA, the Bible, *in Tahitian*, 8vo.
calf, 5s 1838
3602 BUSCHMANN, Apercu de la langue des Iles Marquises, Taitienne, avec Vocabulaire par HUMBOLDT, 8vo. *sd. 3s 6d* *Berlin,* 1843
3603 CHAMISSO über die Hawaiische Sprache, 4to. *hf. morocco,* 7s 6d *Leipz.* 1837
3604 MOSBLECH, Vocab. Océanien-Franç. et Franç.-Océan. (*Marquises, Sandwich, etc.*)
12mo. *hf. calf,* 5s *Paris,* 1843

POLYGLOTTS, COMPARATIVE GRAMMAR.

3605 A. B. C. Buch in Hundert Sprachen, 1743—Orationes Dominicæ fere 100, 1740
—2 vols in 1, 12mo. *plates, bds.* 7s 6d *Leipzig,* 1740-43
3606 ADELUNG, Mithridates oder allgemeine Sprachenkunde, 4 vols. in 5, 8vo.
contains the "Lord's Prayer" in 500 *Languages and Dialects, sewed,* 16s ; or
bound, 21s *Berlin,* 1806-17
3607 —— the same, 4 vols. 8vo. *calf extra,* £2. 2s 1806-17

    A History of all the known Languages and Dialects, with an account of the books printed in or relating to them, and above 500 different specimens, consisting chiefly of the Lord's Prayer. Divided as follows : Vol. I. Asiatic Languages, 1806—II. European Languages, 1809—III. part I, African Languages, 1812—III. part 2, American Languages, 1813—III. part 3, American Languages, continued, 1816—IV. Supplement, by *Vater ; Humboldt's* Supplement on the Basque Language; Vater's Nachträge zum III. Bande, 1817.
    "Adelung's Mithridates contain specimens of all the known Languages of the world; a work as classical to the comparative philologist as Blackstone's Commentaries are to the Lawyer."—*Latham.*
    "Le Mithridate, quoique parsemé d'erreurs graves, n'est pas moins pour cela un des ouvrages les plus savans et un de ceux qui honorent le plus le siècle qui l'a vu naitre."—*Balbi.*

3608 BALBI (Adr.) ATLAS ETHNOGRAPHIQUE du Globe, ou Classification des Peuples anciens et modernes d'après leurs Langues ; précede d'un coup d'œil sur l'Histoire de la Langue Sclave, et sur la marche de la Littérature en Russie, impl. folio, *with about* 700 *Vocabularies*—Introduction à l'Atlas Ethnographique, Tome 1, 8vo. 32s *Paris,* 1826
3609 —— Atlas Ethnographique, impl. folio, *without the introd. bds.* 20s 1826

    This work consists of Charts classifying languages according to ethnographic kingdoms, which are followed by comparative tables of elementary words in every known language; the introduction contains a vast collection of valuable and interesting information on the general principles of the science.

3610 ALPHABETS. BALLHORN's Grammatography, a Manual of reference to the ALPHABETS of ANCIENT and MODERN LANGUAGES, impl. 8vo. 102 ALPHABETS, *with ample and valuable information on the nature and mechanism of each language, cloth,* 7s *London,* 1861
3611 —— the same, GERMAN edition, roy. 8vo. 70 *alphabets, cloth,* 5s *Leipz.* 1859

    This compact manual of alphabets includes the following Languages: Persian, Median and Assyrian Cuneiform; Oldest Symbols, (Hieroglyphic, Hieratic, Demotic, Phenician, Numidian, Ancient Hebrew, Aramaic, Estragelo, Palmyrian, Cufic, Ancient Greek, Ancient Italian, Etrurian); Hebrew; Rabbinical; German Rabbinical; Hebrew Cursive; Samaritan; Syriac; Arabic; Arabic Double-letter; Ethiopic; Ethiopic and Amharic; Turkish; Persian; Afghan; Coptic ; Chinese; Japanese; Sanscrit; Tamul; Zend; Burmese; Carnatic; Guzerati; Telingi; Bengalese; Bugi (Celebes Island) ; Javanese; Thibetan; Mongolian; Mandchu ; Armenian; Georgian; Greek, Greek Abbreviated; Modern Greek; Cyrillian; Glagolitic; Croatic-Glagolitic; Russian; Russian Cursive; Servian; Illyrian; Wallachian; Polish; Wendish; Bohemian; Hungarian; Lettish; Danish; Swedish; Anglo-Saxon; Irish; Gothic; Runic; German.

3612 BERGHAUS, Physikalischer Atlas : Meteorologie, Hydrologie, Geologie, Erdmagnetismus, Pflanzengeographie, Thiergeographie, Anthropographie, und Ethnographie, 8 parts in 1 vol. fol. 93 *col. maps,* £3. 10s *Gotha,* 1852
3613 —— the same, Parts 7, 8, Anthropographie and Ethnographie, *with the corresponding* 23 *coloured maps,* in 1 vol. folio, *bds.* 10s 1852
3614 BIONDELLI, Studii Linguistici, 8vo. *hf. cf. neat,* 7s. *Milano,* 1856
3615 BONAPARTE'S (Prince Louis Lucien) Works and Publications. Universal European Polyglott Dictionary: Specimen Lexici Comparativi omnium Linguarum Europaearum, opera et studio Ludovici Luciani Bonaparte, sm. folio, 56 pp. *sd.* 12s *Privately printed, Florentiae,* 1847
3616 PARABOLA DE SEMINATORE ex Matthæo in LXXII Europaeas Linguas ac Dialectos versa, et Romanis characteribus expressa, 8vo. *printed on stout paper, each version separately, many letters expressly cast for this work,* 30s *Londini,* 1857
3617 LANGUE BASQUE et LANGUES FINNOISES, 4to. 46*pp. and* 4 *tables, sd.* 21s 1862
3618 CATALOGUES des ouvrages de Linguistique Européenne, édités par le Prince L. L. Bonaparte, 2 vols. 16mo. 7s 6d 1858

o

3619 BOPP, Vergleichende Grammatik des Sanskrit, Zend, Griechischen, Lateinischen, Litthauischen, Altslawischen, Gothischen und Deutschen Sprachen, 6 parts in 1 vol. sm. 4to. BEST EDITION, *in russia, gilt edges, rare*, £2. 10s; *or calf gilt*, £2. 5s
Berlin, 1833

3620 —— Comparative Grammar of the Sanscrit, Zend, Greek, Latin, Lithuanian, Gothic, German, and Sclavonic Languages, translated from the German by Lieut. Eastwick, conducted through the press by H. H. Wilson, 3 vols. 8vo. complete, (pub. at £3. 7s 6d) *cloth*, 35s
1862

Professor Bopp gives numerous and undeniable proofs of the close connexion which subsists between the sacred language of the Indus and the languages of Greece and Rome, the Celtic, Teutonic, and Sclavonic nations. "A work which will form for ever the safe and solid foundation of comparative philology."—*Max Müller*.

3621 BOPP GLOSSARIUM SANSCRITUM, in quo omnes Radices et Vocabula usitatissima explicantur et cum Vocabulis graecis, latinis, germanicis, lithuanicis, Slavicis, Celticis comparantur, 4to. 36s
Berlin, 1847

3622 —— Vocalismus oder sprachvergleichende Kritiken über Grimm's Deutsche Grammatik und Graff's althochdeutschen Sprachschatz, 8vo. *sd.* 5s; *hf. cf.* 7s 1836

3623 (CHAMBERLAYNE) Oratio Dominica plus 100 linguis expressa, sm. 4to. including *American, Asiatic, and African, calf*, 7s 6d
1713

3624 DICTIONARIUM Lat., Ital., Dalmatisch, Böhmisch, Polnisch, Teutsch, Ungarisch, obl. sm. 4to. *first a parallel Dictionary of all, afterwards each language rendered separately in Latin, title and part of preface wanting, bd.* 15s *Prague*, 1605

3625 DIEFFENBACH, Lexicon Comparativum Linguarum Indo-Germanicarum; Vergleichendes Woerterbuch der Gothischen Sprache, mit Berücksichtigung der Romanischen, Lithauisch-Slavischen und Keltischen Sprachen, und Zuziehung der Finnischen Familie, 2 vols. in 1, stout 8vo. 1320 pp. (pub. at 36s) *hf. morocco*, 25s
Frankfurt, 1851

"Whoever may desire to trace Etymology will do well to consult Dieffenbach."—*S. W. Singer*.

3626 DUPRAT, Essai sur les Races de l'Afrique Septentr. 8vo. *hf. cf.* 5s 6d *Paris*, 1845

3627 EICHHOFF, Parallèle des Langues de l'Europe et de l'Inde, royal 4to. *half russia gilt*, 20s
Paris, 1836

One of the indispensable works for the study of Comparative Grammar.

3628 FORSTER, the one Primeval Language, traced through Ancient Inscriptions in alphabetical characters of lost Powers from the four Continents, 3 vols. 8vo. with *Chart of Harmony of Primeval Alphabets*, (pub. at £3. 3s) *cl.* 25s 1851-7

3629 FOX [George, *the Quaker*] John STUBBS and Benj. FURLEY. A Battle-door for Teachers and Professors to learn Singular and Plural; You to Many and Thou to One (in many Languages), sm. folio, *original title imperfect, one reprinted added, original calf*, RARE, 35s
1660

This copy has the rare extra slip of "Errors" pasted on the leaf of Errata. Amongst the "many languages" besides the Oriental, are the Saxon, Welsh, Mence, Cornish, Bohemian, Slavonian, Polonian, Lithuanian, etc.

3630 FRY (Edmund) Pantographia: accurate copies of all the known Alphabets in the World, impl. 8vo. *bds.* 5s; *or, calf gilt*, 7s 6d
1799

3631 HERVAS, Catalogo delle Lingue conosciute—Origine ed Armonia degl' Idiomi— Aritmetica delle nazioni—Vocabolario Polígloto, con prolegom. sopra piu di 150 Lingue—Saggio pratico, con l'Orazione Dominicale in piu di 300 Lingue— —5 vols in 2, 4to. *hf. bd.* £2. 16s
Cesena, 1784-87

3632 —— Catalogo de las Lenguas de las Naciones conocidas y Numeracion, Division, y Clases de estas, segun la diversidad de sus Idiomas y Dialectos, 6 vols. sm. 4to. *sd.* £2. 15s
Madrid, 1800-5

A learned work, similar to Adelung's Mithridates. Contents: Vol. I. Lenguas y Naciones Americanas. Vol. II. Lenguas y Naciones de las Islas de los mares pacifico e indiano austral y oriental, y del continente de Asia. III. IV. V. VI. Lenguas y Naciones Europeas. "The Abbé *Hervas* published his Catalogue of Tongues and Arithmetic of Nations, part of a large and remarkable work, the "Saggio del Universo.' His data he collected by means of an almost unlimited correspondence with the Jesuit missionaries of the Propaganda."—*Latham*.
The works of Hervas are; Catalogo delle Lingue; Vocabolario Polyglotta; Trattado delle Grammatiche; Arithmetico delle Nazione conosciute.
"Ouvrages qui, malgré beaucoup de défauts et d'erreurs, dûs en partie à l'epoque où ils furent redigés et en partie au manque d'une saine critique dans le choix des matériaux, n'en contiennent pas moins de trésors précieux pour l'histoire et la science des langues, surtout à l'égard de celles du Nouveau Monde."—*Balbi*.

3634 HOLTZMANN, Kelten und Germanen, sq. 8vo. *cloth*, 5s
Stuttgart, 1855

3635 JAMIESON (J.) Hermes Scythicus, the radical affinities of the Greek and Latin to the Gothic, 8vo. (pub. at 12s) *hf. calf*, 6s
Edinb. 1814

POLYGLOTTS, COMPARATIVE GRAMMAR.

636 KENNEDY'S (Lieut.-Col. Vans) Researches into the Origin and Affinity of the principal Languages of Asia and Europe, 4to. *with 11 plates of Ancient Alphabets and Inscriptions*, (pub. at £2. 12s 6d) *cloth, a bargain*, 10s 1828
637 —— Researches into the Nature and Affinity of Ancient and Hindu Mythology, 4to. (pub. at £2. 12s 6d) *cloth*, 20s 1831
638 LATHAM'S Native Tribes of the Russian Empire, 8vo. *specimens of languages, large colored Map, etc. cloth*, 5s 1854
639 —— Elements of Comparative Philology, stout 8vo. 774 pp. (*pub. at* 21s) *cloth*, 16s 6d 1862
640 LINDSAY (J. B.) Lord's Prayer in 50 languages, native and Roman characters, 8vo. *cloth*, 6s *Dundee*, 1846
641 MARCEL, Oratio Dominica 150 linguis versa, propriis cujusque characteribus expressa, roy. 4to. *bds.* 21s *Parisiis*, 1805
642 MEIDINGER'S vergleichendes etymologisches Wörterbuch der Gothisch-Teutonischen Mundarten, (Alt Goth., Alt und neu Hoch Deutsch, Alt Sächisch, Niederländ., Angelsäch., Engl., Island., Schwed., Dän.) 8vo. *bds.* 10s *Frankf.* 1833
643 MERIAN, Principes de l'etude comparative des Langues, avec Klaproth sur les Langues Sémitiques, 8vo. *sd.* 3s 6d *Paris*, 1828
644 MINSHEU, Ductor in Linguas. The Guide into (Eleven) Tongues, viz. English, British, or Welsh, Low Dutch, High Dutch, French, Italian, Spanish, Portugueze, Latin, Greek, Hebrew, etc. folio, *hf. calf*, 16s 1617
Best edition of this curious old Polyglott, the 2nd edition omits the Welsh and Portugueze.
646 MINSHEU'S Guide into Tongues; their agreement one with another, also their Etymologies, *in nine languages*, viz. *English, Low Dutch, High Dutch, French, Italian, Spanish, Latin, Greek, Hebrew, etc.* folio, *calf*, 10s 1627
647 MUELLER (Max) Lectures on the Science of Language, delivered at the Royal Institution, in 1861, *third edition*, 8vo. (pub. at 12s) *new in cloth*, 10s 1862
The best recent work on the Science of Language.
648 NEMNICH'S allgemeines Polyglotten-Lexicon der Naturgeschichte, 8 parts in 3 vols. sm. 4to. a Latin Alphabet with polyglott explanations, and also separate alphabets German, English, Portuguese, French, Italian, Spanish, Dutch, Swedish, and Danish Norse and Icelandic, *hf. calf*, 21s *Hamburg*, 1793-98
649 —— Neues Waaren-Lexikon in Zwölf Sprachen, *German, English, Dutch, Danish, Swedish, Russian, French, Italian, Spanish, Portuguese, Modern-Greek and Latin*. 3 vols. sm. 4to. *hf. calf gilt*, 9s *Hamburg*, 1821
650 NOTT AND GLIDDON, Indigenous Race of the Earth, with monographs on Philology, Cranioscopy, Palaeontology, etc. by Maury, Pulsky and Meigs, stout large 8vo. *plates and cuts, cloth*, 24s *Philadelphia*, 1857
651 PARSONS (Jas.) Remains of Japhet, being historical enquiries into the Affinity and Origin of the European Languages, 4to. *plates of Alphabets, hf. bd.* 7s 6d; *or a fine copy, calf*, 10s 1767
Interesting on account of the author's knowledge of the Celtic Languages. Pp. 278-309, contain a history of Ish and Welsh Words, showing their affinity.
652 **PHILOLOGICAL SOCIETY:** PROCEEDINGS OF THE PHILOLOGICAL SOCIETY for 1842-53, 6 vols. 8vo. (subscription price 15 guineas)— TRANSACTIONS of the Philological Society, 1854-61, 7 vols. (*pub. at* £7. 7s)— together 13 vols. 8vo. £8. 10s 1842-61
653 POTT'S Etymologische Forschungen auf dem Gebiete der Indo-Germanischen Sprachen, unter Berücksichtigung ihrer Hauptformen, Sankrit, Zend. Pers., Griech.-Latein., Littau.-Slawisch, German., und Keltisch, 2 vols. 8vo. *sd.* 30s *Lemgo and Detmold*, 1859-61
654 PRICHARD'S (J. C.) Researches into the Physical History of Mankind, 4th edition, 5 vols. 8vo. (pub. £4. 2s 6d) *coloured, plates, cloth*, £3. 3s 1841-47
655 PRICHARD'S Natural History of Man, and Inquiries into modifying Influences on the different Tribes of the Human Family, *fourth edition*, enlarged by Norris, 2 vols. roy. 8vo. 62 *coloured plates of the Races of the Earth, and* 100 *woodcuts*, (pub. at 38s) *morocco back*, 28s 1855
656 PRICHARD'S Six Ethnographical Maps, *coloured*, with letterpress, illustrating the "Natural History of Man" and "Researches," atlas folio, (pub. at 21s) 14s 1843

3657 REEHORST's Mariner's and Merchant's Polyglot Technical Dictionary, obl. 8vo.
 upwards of 10,000 *words in English, Dutch, German, Danish, Swedish, French,
 Ital., Spanish, Portug., and Russian, cloth,* 10s 1850
3658 SCHLÖZER's Allgemeine Nordische Geschichte, Einleitung zur Kenntniss aller
 Skandinav. Finn. Slav. Lettischen und Sibirischen Völker, 4to. *maps, calf
 gilt,* 7s A very valuable book. *Halle,* 1771
3659 SCHMELLER'S Akademische Abhandlungen : Nothwendigkeit eines ethno-
 graph. Gesammtnamens—Quantität im Bayrisch. und oberdeutschen Dialek-
 ten, etc.— Ueber Wolfram von Eschenbach—Versbau in der alliterirenden
 Poesie—München,1397-1403—EpistolaRoscelini ad Abaelardum-AlemansNach-
 richten über die Entdeckungen der Portugiesen Handschriftliche Seekarten—
 Endung *ez* (*es*) Spani. und portug. Familiennamen- -Raphael Sanzio—10 *tracts*,
 in 1 vol. 4to. *hf. morocco,* 14s 1833-45
3660 VATER's Litteratur der Grammatiken, Lexika und Wörtersammlungen aller
 Sprachen der Erde von Jülg, 8vo. *hf. bd.* 5s *Berlin,* 1847
3661 WHITER (W.) Etymologicon Universale, or Universal Etymological Dictionary on a New Plan, 3 vols. 4to. *calf extra,* 32s *Cambridge,* 1822-5
3662 WINNING's Manual of comparative Philology, Affinity of the Indo-European
 Languages, 8vo. *cloth,* 6s 1838
3663 **ALBANIAN.** LECCE (F. M. da) Osservazioni grammaticali nella Lingua Alba-
 nese, sm. 4to. *hf. bound,* 7s *Roma,* 1716
3664 HAHN (J. G. von) Albanesische Studien : 1, Ethnograhpisch-Historisches ;
 2, Beitraege zu einer Grammatik des Toskischen, und Albanesische Sprachproben ; 3, Albanesisch-Deutsches Lexicon—1 thick vol. 4to. *map, facsimile,
 &c.* (pub at £1. 10s) *sd.* 18s *Jena,* 1854
3665 XYLANDER, Sprache der Albanesen oder Schkipetaren, 8vo. *hf. calf,* 3s 6d 1829
3666 **BASQUE.** ALPHABET of the primitive language of Spain, roy. 8vo. *bds.* 7s 6d
 Boston, 1829
3667 ASTARLOA, Apologia de la Lengua Bascongada, ó Ensayo de su Perfeccion y
 Antiguedad sobre todas las que se conocen, sm. 4to. 452 pp. *cf.* 6s *Madrid,* 1803
 Priced, 1831, Bohn, 24s. A very learned antiquarian and philological work, proving the antiquity and isolated position of the Basque Language.
3668 AXULAR (Pedro de) Gueroco guero edo Gueroco luçamendutam ibiltceac ;
 Meditations on Sin, *in the Basque language;* 12mo. 623 pp. and 8 pp. of Index :
 the margins cut close, and the references in some places cut into, a hole in leaf
 127, *vellum, extremely rare,* £3. 3s *Bordelen, C. Milanges, s. a.*
 This volume is without a date on the title, but at end of each of the three approbations is found the date 1642. An edition dated Bordelen, C. Milanges, 1643, fetched at Libri's sale, where it was called 'the first edition, unknown to Brunet,' mor. £13.
 "L'un des livres basques les plus rares et les plus estimés."
 "Seconde éditione d'un ouvrage basque devenu rare, et qui est remarquable par le ton de philosophie hardie qui y règne. Dans une approbation, datée de St. Jean de Luz, 25 Décembre 1642, ce livre est ainsi désigné: 'Librum de poenitentia non differenda;' mais son titre peut se rendre en français par ces mots: 'Meditations sur le péché ou sur la lumière.'"—BRUNET.
BONAPARTE (Prince L. L.) Publications :
 3669 APOCALIPSIS de San Juan, *Vascuence Vizcaino,* por Uriarte, 16mo.
 51 *copies printed,* 27s 1857
 3670 PRODROMUS evangelii Matthæi octupli : oratio dominica, Hispanicè, Gallicè et
 omnibus *dialectis Vasconicis* versa, 4to. 1s 6d 1857
 3671 DIALOGUES BASQUES: Guipuscoans, Biscaïens, Labourdins, Souletins,
 par Iturriaga, Uriarte, Duvoisin, et Inchauspe, avec deux traductions Espagnole et Française, 8vo. *sd.* 27s 1857
 3672 APOCALYPSE de Saint Jean, en *Basque Souletin,* par Inchauspe, 16mo.
 50 *copies printed,* 27s *Londres,* 1858
 3673 VERBE BASQUE (Le) par l'Abbé Inchauspe, publié par le Prince L. L.
 Bonaparte, 4to. £3. 7s *Bayonne,* 1858
 3674 CANTICUM Canticorum Salomonis, 3 *Vasconicis dialectis Hispaniæ* versum ab
 Uriarte et L. L. Bonaparte, 4to. 15s 1858
 3675 CANTIQUE des Cantiques de Solomon, en *Basque Labourdin,* par Duvoisin,
 16mo. 4s 6d 1859
 3676 ——— en *Basque Guipuscoan,* 16mo. *sd.* 4s 6d 1862
 3677 ——— en *Basque Biscayen central* de Bilbao, de Marquina, par Uriarte, avec
 dictionnaire par L. L. Bonaparte, 16mo. 10s 6d 1863

BONAPARTE (Prince L. L.) Publications—*continued.*
3678 CANTICUM trium puerorum in 7 *dialectos Vasconicas* versum, 4to. 4s 6d 1858
3679 —— idem, in 11 *dial. Vasc.* à L. L. Bonaparte, *new phonetic types*, 4to. 7s 6d 1858
3680 EVANGELIO segun San Mateo, traducido al Vascuence, *dialecto Guipuzcoano,* por Uriarte, 8vo. *only 25 copies printed,* 27s 1858
3681 APOCALIPSIS de San Juan, traducido al *Vascuence, dialecto Guipuzcoano,* por Uriarte, 16mo. *only 50 copies printed,* £2. 14s 1858
3682 DOCTRINA Cristiana, en el *Vascuence de Llodio,* provincia de Alava, 32mo. *50 copies printed,* 27s 1858
3683 —— la misma, *in Vascuence* Vizcaino, de Marquina, Bermes, Arratia, Contro y Ochandiano, 4to. £2. 1863
3684 BIBLIA, edo Testament Duvoisin Kapitainak, etc. : Bible, traduit en *Basque,* dialecte du *Labourd,* large 8vo. *when completed,* £10. 1859
3685 BIBLIA edo Testamentu: the Bible in the *Guipuscoan dialect* of Basque, by Uriarte, L. L. Bonaparte and Azpiazu, 8vo. *not yet completed,* £10. 1859
3686 RUTH, le Livre de, traduit en *Basque Labourdin,* par Duvoisin, 32mo. 4s 6d 1860
3687 PROFECIA de Jonas, en Vasc. Navar. de Elizondo, Baztan, por Echenique, 16mo. *sd.* 4s 6d 1863
3687* —— Basque de la Basse Navarre, de Cize, par Casenave, 16mo. 4s 6d. 1863
688 CHAHO, Voyage en Navarre pendant l'insurrection des Basques, (1830-35) 8vo. *plates, sd.* 3s 6d ; or, *hf. calf,* 5s *Paris,* 1836
689 DISSERTATION, sur la Langue Basque, 8vo. *hf. calf, uncut,* 10s *Bayonne ?* 1832
690 ERRO, Observaciones filosoficas en favor del Alfabeto primitivo, 8vo. *calf,* 20s *Pamplona,* 1807
691 —— El Mundo Primitivo o Examen filosófico de la Antiguedad y Cultura de la Nacion Bascongada, Tom. I. *(all published)* 8vo. *neatly bd.* 10s *Madrid,* 1815
692 HARRIET, Gramatica Escuaraz eta Francesez : Dictionnaire Basque-Franç. et Franç.-Basque ; Remarques sur la langue Basque, in 1 vol. 12mo. 512 *pp. calf rare,* 36s *Bayonan,* 1741
693 HIRIART, Introduction aux langues Basque et Francaise, 12mo. *bds.* 5s *Bay.* 1840
694 KEMPIS, Jesu-Christoren Imitacionea, 16mo. *calf,* 7s *Bayonne,* 1825
695 LARRAMENDI, Arte de la Lengua Bascongada, 12mo. *vel.* 9s *Salamanca,* 1729
696 —— de la Antiguedad y universalidad del Bascuenze en España, 16mo. *vellum, rare,* 12s *Salamanca,* 1728
Collation : preliminary matter, 229 pp. Dictionary, 828 pp. Supplement, 8 pp. Errata, 8 pp.
697 LARRAMENDI, Diccionario Trilingue del Castellano, Bascuence, y Latin, 2 vols. folio, *very fine copy, calf gilt, rare,* £6. *San Sebastian,* 1728
698 —— Diccionario, nueva edicion publicada por Zuazua, 2 vols. in 1, roy. 4to. *half morocco, uncut,* 36s *San Sebastian,* 1853
The only Basque Dictionary;—of great importance to the Linguist. Larramendi spent all his life in the imposition of this grand work; no other Basque Dictionary has been printed since; copies sold formerly for upwards of £20.; 1843, Salva, 200 fr.
"Cet ouvrage est un des plus importants pour les personnes qui se livrent à l'etude du basque, et nous dirons toute assurance que c'est le plus difficile à rencontrer de tous ceux qui sortirent des presses espagnoles pendant siècle dernier."—SALVA.
699 LÉCLUSE, Grammaire et Vocabulaire Basque, 2 parts in 1 vol. 8vo. *hf. bd. uncut, rare,* 16s *Toulouse,* 1826
700 LIZARRAGAC, Urteco igande guztietaraco platicac Edo Itzaldiac, 8vo. *Basque Sermons, sd.* 5s *Donost.* 1846
701 MICHEL *(Franc.)* le PAYS BASQUE, sa population, sa Langue, ses Moeurs, sa Littérature et sa Classique, 8vo. 548 pp. *sd.* 5s. 1857
702 OIHENART, Proverbes et Poésies Basques, sm. 8vo. *hf. cf.* 21s *Bordeaux,* 1847
703 SALABERRY, Vocabulaire de mots Basques Bas-Navarrais, 12mo. 2s *Bay.* 1857
704 SORREGUIETA, Semana Hispano-Bascongada, la unica de la Europa, y la mas antigua del orbe, con supplementos de Etimologias Bascongadas, etc.—MONUMENTOS del BASCUENCE--2 vols. in 1, sm. 4to. *calf,* 12s *Pamplona,* 1804
Salva calls this work one of the scarcest and most curious relating to the Bicayan language and antiquities.
705 YRIZAR y Moya, l'Eusqucre et ses Erderes, la Langue Basque et ses dérivés, 5 vols. 8vo. *sd.* 5s *Paris,* 1841
706 YZTUETA, Guipuzcoaco Provinciaren Condaira edo Historia, 8vo. *sewed,* 7s 1847
707 **CELTIC.** BOPP, die Celtischen Sprachen in ihr. Verhältnisse zum Sanskrit, Zend, Griech., Latein., German., Litthan., and Slawischen, 4to. *sd. very rare,* 15s *Berlin,* 1839

3708 CELTIC HEXAPLA: the Song of Solomon in all the living dialects of the *Gaelic and Cambrian languages*, (in English, Irish, Gaelic, Manx, French, Welsh, Breton, Vannetais), 4to. 20s *Prince L. L. Bonaparte*, 1858

3709 HUGHES, Horae Britannicae, or studies in Ancient British History, and on the Antiquities of Great Britain, 2 vols. 8vo. *treating on all Celtic languages and races, hf. calf, uncut,* (the second volume is scarce) 27s   1818-19

3710 JONES' (Rowland) Origin of Languages and Nations, etymologically, etc. defined in an English, Celtic, Greek, Latin Lexicon, 8vo. *hf. calf*, 7s   1764

3711 LHUYD'S (E.) Archæologia Britannica, the Languages, Histories, and Customs of the original Inhabitants of Great Britain from collections and observations in Wales, Cornwall, Bas-Bretagne, Ireland and Scotland, Vol. I. fol. *fine tall copy, calf,* £2. 2s   *Oxf.* 1707

No more was ever published. It contains: I. Comparative Etymology—II. Comparative Vocabulary of the Original Languages of Britain and Ireland—III and IV. Armoric Grammar and Vocabulary by Manoir—V. Welsh Words omitted in Dr Davies's Dictionary—VI. Cornish Grammar- VII. Antiquâ Britanniæ Linguâ Scriptorum Catalogus—VIII. British Etymologicon, by Parry—IX. Introduction to the Irish language—X. Focloir; an Irish-English Dictionary—XI. Catalogue of Irish MSS.

3712 MACLEAN'S History of the Celtic language, 12mo. *cloth*, 3s   1840

3713 PRICHARD'S Eastern Origin of the Celtic Nations proved by a comparison of their Dialects with the Sanscrit, Greek, Latin and Teutonic Languages, forming a Supplement to Researches into the Physical History of Mankind, by James Cowles Prichard, M.D., F.R.S., edited with many additions, *and brought down to the present state of philological learning*, by R. G. LATHAM, M.A., F.R.S., 8vo. 408 pp. (pub. at 16s) *cloth*, 7s 6d   1857

3714 SPECIMEN of an Etimological Vocabulary, to retrieve the ancient Celtic, 8vo. *calf*, 6s   1768

3715 ZEUSS, Grammatica Celtica, e Monumentis Vetustis tam Hibernicæ Linguæ quam Britannicæ Dialecti Cambricæ, Cornicæ, Armoricæ, nec non e Gallicæ priscæ reliquiis, 2 vols. 8vo. 1167 pp. *new* 24s; *hf. cf. gilt top*, 28s *Lipsiae*, 1854

The most learned Celtic Polyglott hitherto published. It is really astonishing what immense stores of Philological research are treasured up in these two volumes.

3716 **Breton.** [ARMERYE] Dictionnaire Français-Breton, de Vannes, sm. 8vo. *calf*, 6s   *Leide*, 1744

3717 BUHÉ, Sant Isidor Patron el Labourision, 16mo. *hf. mor. uncut*, 5s *Guénèt*, 1808

3718 DELAPORTE, Recherches sur la Bretagne, 2 vols. sm. 8vo. *cloth*, 6s *Rennes*, 1819

3719 HISTOÉRIEU ag er Scritur, 18mo. *bd.* 3s   *Guénet*, 1792

3720 KEMPIS. Imitation Jesus-Christ, gat Zoparz, 12mo. *cf. rare*, 15s *Quemper*, 1743

2721 LEPELLETIER, Dictionnaire de Langue Bretonne, ou l'on voit son antiquité et son affinité avec les anciennes langues et l'étymologie de plusieurs mots des autres langues, folio, *fine copy in hogskin*, £3.   *Paris*, 1752

"An excellent Dictionary of the old Breton language: Lepelletier was one of the most learned Scholars in Celtic matters that Brittany has produced."—H. L. JONES.

3722 LEGONIDEC, Grammaire Celto-Bretonne, 8vo. *calf*, 9s; *cf. gt.* 10s 6d *Paris*, 1807

3723 LEGONIDEC Dictionnaire Breton-Français et Français-Breton, avec la Grammaire Celto-Bretonne; enrichi des mots Gallois et Gaëls correspondants au Breton, etc. par Villemarqué, 2 vols. 4to. *sd. uncut*, 32s   *Saint Brieuc*, 1847-50

An excellent Dictionary, indispensable to every Celtic student, and offered at a moderate price.

3724 MIORCEC DE KERDANET, Notices sur les Littérateurs, Poëtes, Troubadours, Historiens, etc. de la Bretagne, 12mo. *hf. calf*, 6s   *Brest*, 1818

3725 ROSTRENEN, Dictionnaire François-Celtique, ou François-Breton, 4to. 978 pp. *double cols, cf.* 10s; *fine copy in old cf. gt. Arms on sides, rare*, 21s *Rennes*, 1732

3726 VILLEMARQÉ, BARZAZ-BREIZ, Chants Populaires de la Bretagne, *Breton et Franç.* avec des Mélodies originales, *quatrième edition augmentée*, 2 vols. 12mo. 970 *pp. text, and* 56 *pp. music, sd,* 5s   *Paris*, 1846

3727 —— Poèmes des Bardes Bretons du VI. Siècle, *Breton et Franç.* 8vo. *sewed*, 10s   *Paris*, 1850

3728 **Cornish.** JORDAN'S Creation of the World, with Noah's Flood, written 1611, *Cornish and English* by Keigwin, ed. by Gilbert, 8vo. *hf. bd.* 10s   1827

3729 MOUNT CALVARY, *in Cornish*, with Keigwin's *English* translation, 1628, edited by Gilbert, 8vo. *hf. bd.* 10s   1826

3730 NORRIS. The Ancient Cornish Drama, edited and translated by Edwin Norris, with Grammar, Vocabulary etc. 2 vols. 8vo. (pub. at 21s) *cloth*, 18s   1859

3731 PRYCE'S Archaeologia Cornu-Britannica, an Essay to preserve the Ancient Cornish Language, with Grammar and Vocabulary, 4to. *cf.* 30s *Sherborne*, 1790
Bound up with Wotton's View of Hickes' Thesaurus, 1735.

3732 WILLIAMS' Lexicon Cornu-Britannicum, a Dictionary Cornish and English, with the synonyms in Welsh, Armoric, Irish, Gaelic, and Manx, Part I (*all yet pubd.*) 4to. *sd.* 15s *Llandovery*, 1862

3733 **Gaelic.** MEDICINA EST QUE CORPUS VEL TUETUR VEL RESTAURAT, etc. An ancient Gaelic MS., *in the Irish character, and with rudely executed* INITIALS, *some in red and green, of that grotesque character, and elaborate interlacements, by which early Irish MSS. are distinguished,* two parts, containing in the first a HERBAL, specifying in alphabetical order the names and virtues of Simples: the second being a Treatise divided into chapters upon the nature and symptoms of Diseases, small 4to. 118 *leaves, bd. recently come from the Highlands of Scotland,* £25. *ca. See.* XIV.

The extraordinary rarity of Highland MSS. is well known; but to meet with such a specimen as the above, ENTIRELY IN THE IRISH CHARACTER, and of a period so remote, is something unprecedented. Philologists and Celtic scholars should examine this monument of the ancient Gaelic language; it will be a curious study to discover how far there existed in early times a divergence between the Irish and the Scotch dialects. Apart from its wonderful rarity, the intrinsic merit of the MS will consist chiefly in its philological value, although there is also an interest in any work which conveys the opinions of a remote age, and a segregated race, upon the Art of Healing and the Medicinal merits of Botany. Each chapter or section begins with a Latin heading or phrase, also in the Irish character, explained and developed in Gaelic. The division which begins with the heading given above is the more ancient portion of the MS.; the remainder is probably somewhat later, and on the first few leaves of this part are some marginal notes, correcting or explaining the old abbreviations or orthography, such as "flor chiann" for "farcan," and "petroselinum" for "pet. sidinu." In one place the note is English, in a handwriting of the Elizabethan period, written over "Afodillus etc." thus: "Daffadil, Thistil or sea holm not ramps." At the divisions of the sections, there are prayers, and verses, etc.; in one of which occurs the name *McEvan* —"Chuir McIebhin san Dan." In another place appears the name of "Ealadhnoir I-Coinnidh," who is perhaps the same lady who returns thanks to God on another page, in mingled Latin and Gaelic, for her recovery from a disease of the eyes, "septies canit. ilinga mea." Elsewhere there is a Genealogical list of names, of the family of the Mac Donnells or Macdonalds, running down an entire page. Altogether, it may be confidently asserted that such an article as this never before appeared in any bookseller's catalogue.

3734 APOCRIPHA, chum na *Gaelic Albannaich*, le Alasdair Macgriogair, 8vo. the first edition of the Apocrypha in Gaelic, £2. *Prince L. L. Bonaparte*, 1860

3735 ARMSTRONG'S Gaelic-English and English-Gaelic Dictionary, with Gaelic Grammar, 4to. (*pub. at* £3. 13s 6d) *bds.* 16s; or *hf. calf*, 20s 1825

3736 BIBLE. Sean Tiomnadh, 2 vols. 12mo. *second edition, corrected by Ross, calf*, 10s *Edin.* 1807

3737 BUCHANAN'S Defence of the Scots Highlanders, 8vo. *bds.* 7s 6d 1794

3738 BUNIAIN, Sealleana Fhlaimheanais agus Ifrinn, le Munro, 16mo. *bds.* 2s 6d 1825

3739 CAMPBELL, Nuadh Orain Ghailach, 16mo. *bds.* 3s 6d *Cork*, 1798

3740 CAMPBELL, Smuaintean Cudthromacha, le Macphairlain, 16mo. *bds.* 3s 6d (1798)

3741 CAMPBELL'S Popular Tales of the West Highlands, orally collected, *Gaelic and English*, with notes, 2 vols. 12mo. *cloth*, 10s 1860

3742 CLARSACH nam Beann, (Gaelic Songs), 18mo. 3s 6d *Dun Eidinn*, 1838

3743 CONFESSION OF FAITH, translated into *Irish*, by the Synod of Argyle, 3 vols. in 1, 16mo. *rare*, 9s *Edin.* 1727

3744 CUAIRTEAR NAN GLEANN, 1840-43, Vols. I. and III. 8vo. *a monthly literary periodical in Gaelic, bds.* 7s 6d *Glasgow*, 1841-43

3745 CURRIE'S Gaelic Grammar, 12mo. *bds.* 3s 6d *Edinb.* 1828

3746 COCHRUINNEACHA Dhan, Orain, etc. Poems collected in the Highlands, 12mo. *bds.* 3s 6d *Inbhirneis*, 1821

3747 DICTIONARIUM SCOTO-CELTICUM, a Dictionary of the Gaelic Language, compiled by the Highland Society, *Gaelic, English and Latin*, 2 vols. 4to. (*pub. at* £7. 7s) *cloth*, 36s *Edinb.* 1828

3748 DEWAR, Laoidhean, o' n Scrioptur, 16mo. *hf. bd.* 2s 6d 1806

3749 FORBES' Double Grammar of English and Gaelic, 12mo. *cloth*, 4s *Edinb.* 1843

3750 GILLIES, Sean Dain agus Orain Ghaidhealach, 12mo. *hf. bd.* 7s 6d *Perth*, 1786

3751 GRANT'S Thoughts on the Origin and descent of the Gael, 8vo. *hf. cf.* 7s 6d 1814

3752 GRANND, Dain Spioradail, 12mo. *bds.* 3s 6d *Elgin*, 1827

3753 MACALASTAIR, Orain, Marbhrannan, agus Duanagan, 12mo. *bds.* 3s 6d 1829

3754 MACALPINE'S Pronouncing Gaelic Dictionary, with a Grammar, 12mo. *pp.* 53 *and* 281 *pp. doub. cols. cloth*, 5s *Edin.* 1845

3755 MACDOMHNUILL, Orain Ghaidhealach, le Tuairneir, 12mo. *bd.* 5s *Glasgow*, 1809

3756 MACFARLAN, Gaelic-English Vocabulary, 8vo. *half calf*, 5s   *Edinb.* 1795
3757 ——— Poems, with the third ILIAD etc. in Gaelic, 12mo. *bd.* 6s   *Ed.* 1813
3758 MACGHRIGAIR, Orain Ghaelach, 12mo. *bd.* 5s   *Edinb.* 1801
3759 MACKINTOSH's Gaelic Proverbs, *Gaelic and Engl.* 12mo. *sd.* 7s 6d ; or *hf. calf gilt*, 8s 6d   *Ed.* 1819
3760 MACLEOD, an Teachdaire Gaelach, 1829-31, 2 vols. in 1, 8vo. *a literary periodical*, *bds.* 7s 6d   *Glasgow*, 1830-31
3761 MACLEOD (Norman) and Dewar, Dictionary Gaelic-English and English-Gaelic, stout 8vo. 1005 *pp. doub. cols. calf*, 12s   *Glasgow*, 1831
3762 MACLEOD, Orain Nuadh Ghaelach, 8vo. *hf. calf*, 7s 6d   *Inbhirn.* 1811
3763 MACKENZIE, Report of the Committee of the Highland Society of Scotland on the Poems of Ossian ; Appendix, *with specimens of the Poems in Gaelic and English;* Account of Gaelic MSS. 8vo. 3 *facsimiles*, 9s   *Edinb.* 1805
3764 MUNRO's Grammar of the Scottish Gaelic, 16mo. *bd.* 3s   *Edin.* 1835
3765 ——— second edition, 18mo. *bd.* 4s   *ib.* 1843
3766 ORAIN Gaidhealach, cochruin. nuadh, 12mo. *bd.* 3s 6d   *Inbhirn.* 1806
3767 OSSIAN'S POEMS, *Gaelic and Latin*, by Macfarlane, with a dissertation by Sir John Sinclair, a translation from the Italian of the Abbe Cesarotti's Controversy, with Notes, &c., by J. M. Arthur, published under the sanction of the Highland Society, 3 vols. impl. 8vo. *plates*, LARGE AND THICK PAPER, *old red morocco, gilt edges*, £3. 3s   1807
3768 ——— The Poems of Ossian, Orrann, Ulin, and other Bards, collected by H. and J. M'Callum, *in Gaelic and English*, 8vo. *bds.* 4s 6d   *Montrose*, 1816
3769 ——— the Poems of Ossian by MACPHERSON, 2 vols. 8vo. *calf*, 7s 6d   1790
3770 ——— Some of Ossian's Lesser Poems, in English, with prelim. discourse, by McDonald, 8vo. *bds.* 7s   *Liverpool*, 1805
3771 ——— Phingaléis, *Latine* à Macdonald, large 8vo. *calf gilt*, 5s   *Ed.* 1820
3772 DAVIES' Claims of Ossian, an Essay on the Scottish and Irish Poems under that name, royal 8vo. *hf. calf*, 9s   *Swansea*, 1825
3773 GRAHAM's Essay on the Poems of Ossian, with Richardson on the Mythology, including Temora, book 7, *Gaelic* and English, 8vo. *bds.* 10s   *Ed.* 1807
3774 TRACTS on Ossian, various, in 1 vol. 8vo. *cloth*, 3s 6d   1760-1825
3775 REID's Bibliotheca Scoto-Celtica, of all the books printed in Gaelic, with biograph. notices, 8vo. *bds.* 9s   *Glasgow*, 1832
3776 Ros (Uilleam) Orain Ghaelach, le McChoinnich, 12mo. *cloth*, 5s   *Glasg.* 1824
3777 SHAW's Analysis of the Gaelic language, 8vo. *calf*, 3s 6d   *Ed.* 1778
3778 SKENE (W. F.) the Highlanders of Scotland, their origin, history, and antiquities, 2 vols. 8vo. *bds.* 12s   1836
3779 SMITH's Galic Antiquities, a history of the Druids, etc. with a collection of Ancient Poems, 4to. *hf. calf*, 8s   *Edin.* 1780
3780 STEWART (A. and D.) Collection of the Works of the Highland Bards, *Gaelic*, with Glossary, 8vo. *bd.* 7s ; *calf neat*, 9s   *Duneidin*, 1804
3781 ——— Gaelic Grammar, 8vo. *bd.* 2s 6d   1801
3782 **Irish.** BETHAM's Irish Antiquarian Researches, 2 vols. in 1, 8vo. 12 *facsimiles of MS. calf gilt*, 18s   *Dublin*, 1826
3783 ——— Etruria-Celtica ; Etruscan Literature and Antiquities, 2 vols. 8vo. *facsimiles, cloth*, 10s   *Dublin*, 1842
3784 BROOKE'S (Miss) Reliques of Irish Poetry, *English and Irish*, and an Irish tale, 8vo. *green morocco, gilt edges*, 18s   *Dublin*, 1816
3785 CELTIC SOCIETY's PUBLICATIONS (The)), Founded MDCCXLV. The Complete Series of 6 vols. royal 8vo. *portraits* (sold to subscribers for £7.) clean copy in *cloth*, £2. 2s   1847-53
    Amalgamated with the Irish Archæological Society.
3786 CONEY's Irish-English Dictionary, 8vo. 382 *pp. calf*, 6s   *Dublin*, 1849
3787 DUBLIN GAELIC Society's Transactions, vol. I. 8vo. *containing the celebrated Story of Deirdse, Irish and English, with extracts from Keating, notes, dissertations*, etc. *bds.* 5s ; *hf. bd.* 7s   *Dublin*, 1808
3788 HARDIMAN'S Irish Minstrelsy, or Bardic Remains of Ireland, *Irish and English*, with extensive notes, 2 vols. 8vo. *portrait of Carolan, hf. morocco*, £2. 2s   1831

EUROPEAN PHILOLOGY.

3789 IRISH ARCHÆOLOGICAL (and Celtic) Society's Publications, printed at the University Press, Dublin, a complete set, 19 vols. 4to. (cost to subscribers, £22.) *cloth*, £11. 10s — *Dublin*, 1841-62
3790 Mason (Monck) Irish Grammar, 12mo. *bds*. 2s — *Dublin*, 1842
3791 Meigcrath, Dánta, etc. *in MS*. sq. 8vo. *hf. bd.* 12s — *Atha-Cliath*, 1847
3792 Molloy Grammatica Latino-Hibernica, 12mo. rare, *calf neat*, 15s *Romæ*, 1677
    At the end of this curious and uncommon volume are some poems in Latin and Irish.
3793 —— Lucerna Fidelium, 18mo. *all in Irish, sd.* 5s — *ib.* 1676
3794 O'Brien, Focalóir Gaoidhilge-Sax Bhéarla : Irish-English Dictionary, 4to. *bd.* 20s — *Paris*, 1768
3795 —— Focalóir Gaoidhilge, 1768—MAC CUIRTIN, English-Irish Dictionary, Focloir Bearla Gaoidheilge, 1732, 2 vols. 4to. remarkably fine copies, *uniform in old russia gilt, rare*, £2. 10s — *Paris*, 1732-68
3796 O'Connor's Gaelic (Irish) Grammar, 12mo. *hf. bd.* 5s — *Dublin*, 1808
3797 O'Hodhasa (O'Hussey), Bonabhentúra, Teagasg Criosdaidhe, 12mo. 259 *pp. all in the Irish character, morocco, gilt and gauffred edges*, 12s 6d *Romæ*, 1707
3798 O'Reilly, Sanas Gaoidhilge Sagsbhearla : Irish-English Dictionary, with the Supplement and a compendious Irish Grammar, 4to. *bds.* 30s — *Dublin*, 1817
3799 OSSIANIC SOCIETY (of Dublin) Transactions, from the beginning, Vols. I.-VI. 8vo. *cloth*, 32s — *Dublin*, 1853-61
    Containing works of early Irish Literature, edited with transactions and notes by O'Kearney, Connellan, O'Grady, and other well known scholars.
3800 Walsh's Reliques of Irish Jacobite Poetry, *Irish and English*, Part 1, 8vo. *sd.* 3s 6d — *Dublin*, 1844
3801 Pictet, Culte des Cabires chez les Irlandais, 8vo. *hf. calf,* 9s — *Génève*, 1824
3802 **Manx.** Church Catechism. Principles of Christianity, etc. *in Manx and English*, by Thomas Bishop of Sodor, sm. 8vo. *bd.* 10s — *Liverpool*, 1761
3803 Cregeen (*Archibald*) Dictionary of the Manks Language, with the corresponding words or explanations in English; interspersed with many Gaelic Proverbs, 8vo. 12s — *Douglas*, 1835
3804 Kelly (J.) Practical Grammar of the Antient Gaelic, or Language of the Isle of Mann, usually called Manks, 4to. *hf. cf.* 32s; or *hf. calf very neat*, 36s 1804
3805 **Welsh.** Aneurin, the Gododin, trans. by Probert, etc. sm. 8vo. *bds.* 5s 1820
3806 BOXHORNII Origines Gallicae in quibus Gallorum origines, antiquitates, mores, lingua, etc. illustrantur ; cum Lexico Britannico-Latino, Adagiis Druidum, etc. sm. 4to. *fine copy, calf*, 20s — *Amst.* 1654
3807 DAVIES (J.) Antiquae Linguae Britannicæ nunc vulgo dictæ Cambro Britannicæ, et Linguæ Latinæ, Dictionarium duplex; accesserunt Adagia Britannica, high 4to. *Welsh-Latin and Latin-Welsh, calf*, £2. 2s — *Lond.* 1632
3808 —— the same, sm. fol. *no title, poor copy, hf. bd.* 18s 1632
    "A most elaborate and excellent work."—Nicholson.
3809 —— Antiquae Linguae Britannicae, dictae Cambro-Britannicae, Cymraecae vel Cambricae, Rudimenta, 16mo. *old calf*, 10s — *Lond.* 1621
3810 Davies' (Robt.) Welsh Grammar, *all Welsh*, 12mo. *hf. bd.* 2s — *Chester*, 1808
3811 —— Icithadur neu Ramadeg Cymraeg, 12mo. *cloth*, 3s 6d — *Dinbych*, 1848
3812 Evans (E.) Specimens of the Antient Welsh Bards, *Welsh and English*, with notes, etc. 4to. *calf gilt*, 18s 1746
3813 Evans's English-Welsh Vocabulary, with Welsh Grammar by Richards, 12mo. *bds.* 2s 6d — *Merthyr*,? 1810
3814 Jones, Blodeu-Gerdd Cymry, 12mo. *collection of Welsh Poems, hf. bd.* 5s 1823
3815 JONES (J. M.) Gramadeg Cymreig Ymarferol : a practical Welsh Grammar, *a plain MS. on 192 pages, with a drawing of Beaumaris, Llanidloes*, 1847— Hughes' (Hugh) Welsh Grammar, *legible MS. on 184 leaves, Caernarfon*, 1846 —together 2 vols. 4to. *hf. bd.* 36s 1846-47
    Two rival Welsh Grammars; at the end of one vol. is a sharp critique on the merits of the two productions. Both are evidently very valuable works.
3816 Llywarç Hen's Elegies, etc. *Welsh and Engl.* by Owen, 1792—Cymmrodorion, or Metropolitan Cambrian Institution, Transactions, Vol. I. 1822—2 vols. in 1, 8vo. *hf. calf*, 12s 1792-1822

3817 MABINOGION (The), from the Llyfr Coch o Hergest, and other ancient Welsh Manuscripts, with an English translation and notes, by LADY CHARLOTTE GUEST, 7 parts, forming 3 vols. royal 8vo. *numerous woodcuts and facsimiles of old Welsh and other MSS. uncut, sd. £4. 10s* 1838-49

3818 —— the same, 3 vols. royal 8vo. *hf. green mor. gilt top, uncut,* £5. 15s 1838-49
"We must not forget the services rendered to her country by Lady Charlotte Guest, whose Mabinogion is an inestimable treasure. There are the favourite topics of the most celebrated troubadours of mediaeval Europe to be found in all their primitive beauty and simplicity; and without any disparagement to Sir Thomas Mallory or Mr. Tennyson, few can have any notion of the primitive beauty of these old tales till they read them in 'The Mabinogion.'"—*Athenæum,* No. 1814, Aug. 2, 1862.

3819 MILTON, COLL GWYNFA, cyfieithiad gan Idrison, 8vo. Paradise Lost *in Welsh,* by Pughe, *bds.* 5s 1819

3820 MYVRIAN ARCHÆOLOGY OF WALES, collected out of ancient Manuscripts, 3 large vols. 8vo. 3 vols. 8vo. *half calf, a fair copy,* £12. 1801-7

3821 —— the same, 3 vols. 8vo. *fine copy in old russia,* £16. 16s 1801-7

3822 —— Vol. I. the scarcest portion of the work, roy. 8vo. *bds.* £5. 1801
"Of all the labourers in the field of Celtic antiquities, none deserves more honourable remembrance than Owen Jones, the poor peasant of Myvyr, who, unassisted by patronage, devoted his life to the preservation of the literature of his country. He came up to London, a poor boy, engaged as a clerk in some city establishment, and, after forty years of self-denial, with the accumulations of his scanty earnings, published the Myvyrian Archaeology, at his own cost, in 1801 and 1807. It was a work which might have been done by a king, an institution, or a society of the noble and the learned; but it was accomplished, and scrupulously accomplished, by a poor Welsh peasant."—*Athenæum,* No. 1814, Aug. 2, 1862.

3823 OWEN (William) WELSH and ENGLISH DICTIONARY, compiled from the Laws, History, Poetry, Bardism, Proverbs, with quotations, 1793—Welsh Grammar, 1803—3 vols. in 2, 8vo. *calf,* 28s 1793-1803

3824 —— Welsh Grammar, roy. 8vo. *calf,* 5s 1803

3825 —— Welsh and English Dictionary, 12mo. *bds.* 4s 1826

3826 PUGHE (W. OWEN) Dictionary of the Welsh Language, explained in English, to which is prefixed a Welsh Grammar, *second edition,* 2 vols. royal 8vo. *cloth,* £3. *Denbigh,* 1832
This is the second and improved edition of Owen's work, the author having changed his name.

3827 RICHARDS' Welsh-English Dictionary, with Grammar and Proverbs, 8vo. *bds.* 9s *Bristol,* 1753

3828 RICHARDS's Welsh Grammar, 12mo. *sd.* 2s *Merthyr,* 1839

3829 ROBERTS' Welsh Interpreter, oblong 12mo. *cloth,* 2s 1831

3830 ROWLAND's Welsh Grammar, sm. 8vo. *cloth,* 4s 1857

3831 SPURRELL'S WELSH DICTIONARY, *second edition;* An English-Welsh Pronouncing Dictionary, 1 vol.—A Welsh-English Dictionary, 1 vol.—the 2 vols. in 1, 16mo. *cloth,* 7s 6d 1861

3832 SPURRELL's Grammar of the Welsh Language, 12mo. *second edition, cloth,* 3s 1853

3833 STEPHENS' Literature of the Kymry; an Essay on the History of the Language and Literature of Wales, from Gruffydd ab Kynan (1080,) to Gruffydd Llwyd (1322;) with specimens of Ancient Welsh Poetry, etc. 8vo. (pub. at 12s 6d) *cloth,* 10s 6d *Llandovery,* 1849

3834 TALHAIARN, Gwaith, Works in Welsh and English, 12mo. *cloth,* 5s 1855

3835 THOMAS, Corph y Gainge, *Welsh Poems,* 16mo. *hf. bd.* 10s *Caernarvon,* 1834

3836 TURNER's Vindication of the Genuineness of ANEURIN, TALIESSIN, Llywarch Hen, and Merdhin, with Specimens of the Poems, 8vo. *bds.* 10s 1803

3837 **Welsh MSS. Society.** LIBER LANDAVENSIS, Llyfr Teilo, or the ancient register of the Cathedral Church of Llandaff, by Rev. W. J. Rees, roy. 8vo. Latin and English, plate, *cloth,* 28s 1840

3838 —— IOLO MANUSCRIPTS; a selection of Ancient Welsh MSS. from the collection of Iolo Morganwg, edited by Taliesin Williams, *Welsh and English,* roy. 8vo. plate, *cloth,* 28s 1848

3839 MEDDYGON MYDDFAI: the Physicians of Myddfai, *Welsh and Engl.* by Pughe and Williams ab Ithel, etc. 8vo. *cloth,* 16s 6d *Llandovery,* 1840

3840 WILLIAMS (Archdeacon) Gomer, an Analysis of the Language and Knowledge of the Ancient Kymry, 2 vols. 8vo. *cloth,* 10s 6d 1854

3841 **GERMANIC.** SPENER, Notitia Germaniae Antiquae, stout 4to. *map, sd.* 7s 6d *Halae,* 1717

3842 **Anglo-Saxon.** AELFRIC SOCIETY'S PUBLICATIONS, *the Complete Series,* the Homilies of Ælfric, parts 1-10—Poetry of the Codex Vercellensis, 2 parts—The Dialogues of Salomon and Saturn, 3 parts, edited by J. M. Kemble; together 15 parts, 8vo. £2. 10s 1843-48

3843 ANCIENT LAWS and Institutes of ENGLAND, comprising Laws enacted under the Anglo-Saxon Kings, from Ethelbirht to Cnut, with an English Translation of the Saxon; the Laws called Edward the Confessor's; the Laws of William the Conqueror, and those ascribed to Henry the First; also Monumenta Ecclesiastica Anglicana, from the 7th to the 10th century; and the Ancient Latin version of the Anglo-Saxon Laws, with a compendious Glossary, etc. 2 vols. roy. 8vo. 36s   1840

3844 BEDÆ Opera. Historia Ecclesiastica Gentis Anglorum; Eadem à *Rege Aluredo Anglo-Saxonicè* reddita; Vita S. Cudbercti; Historia Abbatum Wiramuth. et Gyruensium; Epistola ad Ecgberctum; de Locis sanctis; Martyrologium, cum auctuario Flori, etc.; Vita Felicis etc. Curâ et studio Johan. Smith, folio, *best edition, plates, old calf, good copy,* £2. 10s   *Cantabr.* 1722

Priced, 1829, Thorpe, mor. £7. 17s 6d; 1842, Stewart, £4. 10s. Large Paper, Rodd, £6. 10s.

3845 BENSON, Vocabularium Anglo-Saxonicum, lex. Somneri auctius, 8vo. *cf.* 5s 1701

3846 BEOWULF. Poems of Beowulf, the Travellers' Song, and the Battle of Finnes-Burh, *Anglo-Saxon and English,* with historical Preface, Glossary, and Philological Notes, by John Mitchell Kemble, 2 vols. 12mo, *calf gilt, binding not quite uniform,* £2. 12s   1833-37

3847 ——— The Anglo-Saxon Poems of, with a literal translation, notes, glossary, &c. by Thorpe, 8vo. *cloth,* 7s 6d   *Oxf.* 1855

3848 BOETHIUS de Consolatione philosophiae, King Alfred's *Anglo-Saxon* version, with *English* translation by Cardale, 8vo. *bds.* 20s   1829

3849 BOSWORTH'S (Rev. Dr. J) Dictionary of the Anglo-Saxon Language, with a Preface on the Origin and Connection of the Germanic Tongues, a Map of Languages, and the Essentials of Anglo-Saxon Grammar, roy. 8vo. BEST EDITION, *cloth,* £2. 15s   1838

3850 ——— Origin of the English, Germanic, and Scandinavian Languages and Nations, etc. roy. 8vo. *with map of Europ. languages, cloth,* 16s   1848

3851 ——— COMPENDIOUS ANGLO-SAXON and English Dictionary, 8vo. *cloth,* 10s 1852

3852 CÆDMON'S Metrical Paraphrase of parts of the Holy Scriptures, *Anglo-Saxon and English,* with notes by Thorpe, roy. 8vo. *hf. calf,* 12s   *Soc. Antiq.* 1832

3853 CODEX EXONIENSIS: a collection of Anglo-Saxon Poetry, from a MS. in the Library of the Dean and Chapter of Exeter, with an English Translation by Thorpe, roy. 8vo. XIV. and 546 pp. 21s   *Soc. Antiquaries,* 1842

3854 CONYBEARE's Illustrations of Anglo-Saxon Poetry, 4to. LARGE PAPER, *presentation copy, bds. scarce.* 30s   1826

3855 ELSTOB, Ancient English-Saxon Homily on the Birth-day of St. Gregory, *Anglo-Saxon and English,* with notes, 8vo. *calf, fine copy,* 7s 6d   1709

3856 GOSPELS. Halgan Godspel on Englisc, *Anglo-Saxon,* by Thorpe, sm. 8vo. (pub. at 12s) *cloth,* 6s   1842

3857 HENSHALL, Gothic Gospel of St. Matthew, 4th Century, with the corresponding Saxon, from the Durham book, 8th Century, with English trans. 8vo. 6s 1807

3858 ——— Yldestan Radchenistres Gewitnessa, etc. 8vo. *bds.* 5s   1807

3859 HEPTATEUCHUS, liber Job, et Evangelium Nicodemi, *Anglo-Saxonice,* ed. Thwaites, 8vo. *calf, fine copy,* 10s   *Oxon.* 1698

3860 HICKESII LINGUARUM VETT. SEPTENTRIONALIUM (*Anglo-Saxon, Moeso-Goth. Franco-Theotisc. Island.*) Thesaurus Grammatico-Criticus et Archæologicus, 3 vols. in 2, folio, *facsimiles and plates of Anglo-Saxon coins, old calf,* £4. 10s   *Oxon.* 1703-5

3861 ——— the same, 3 vols. folio, *new calf gilt,* £5. 15s   1703-5

Sold in Horne Tooke's sale for £14. 10s, and in Willett's for £12. 12s; priced, 1836, Thorpe, £8. 8s; 1840 and 1848, Payne and Foss, £12. 12s.

"This work has had so many just praises given to it at home and abroad, that few English readers can be strangers to its contents."—NICOLSON. Many valuable portions of this grand work are taken from original Saxon MSS. now lost. An indispensable work for consultation to the student of Anglo-Saxon Literature, containing Icelandic, Anglo-Saxon and Gothic Grammars and Dictionaries; also valuable Anglo-Saxon fragments. "Hickes displays throughout great erudition, unwearied industry, and sometimes successful investigation; it is enriched with numerous engravings of Ancient Monuments, Runic inscriptions, various documents, and specimens of Poetry that are not elsewhere to be found in print."—RASK.

3862 INGRAM on Anglo-Saxon Literature, 1807; HENSHALL, Saxon and English Languages, 1798; ALFRED's Will, *Anglo-Saxon and English,* 1788; PEGGE's Anglo-Saxon Remains, *plate of coins,* 1756; etc., in 1 vol. 4to. *hf. cf.* 9s   1756-1807

3863 JUNII Etymologicum Anglicanum, edidit accessionibus multis E. Lye, cum vita Auctoris et Grammatica Anglo-Saxonica, folio, *portrait from Vandyke by Vertue, calf,* 20s *Oxon.* 1743

3864 —— the same, LARGE PAPER, *a very fine copy in russia, gilt edges,* £4. 4s 1743

"Ouvrage très recherché, mais difficile à trouver, 60 à 30 fr. Vend. 4 liv. 4 sh. Heber; en Gr. Pap. 6 liv. Sykes; 41 flor. Meerman."—*Brunet.* A valuable comparative and etymological Dictionary. "A work of uncommon erudition and vast merit."—*Clarke.*

3865 KLIPSTEIN, Anglo-Saxon Grammar, sm. 8vo. *cloth,* 6s *New York,* 1848

3866 LAYAMON'S BRUT: or Chronicle of Britain, a Poetical *Semi-Saxon* Paraphrase of the Brut of Wace, with a literal translation, notes, and a Grammatical Glossary by Sir Frederick Madden, 3 vols. roy. 8vo. *facsimile, bds.* £2. 1847

"A highly important publication. The entire Poem is now placed within reach of those who have neither opportunity nor inclination to grapple with the obscurities of MSS.; and this has now been done under a very careful eye, and with a rich accompaniment of elucidations."—*Garnett's Essays,* p. 128.

3867 MÜLLER, Collectanea Anglo-Saxonica, cum Vocabularia, 12mo. *bd.* 2s 6d 1835

3868 ORMULUM (The), now first edited from the original MS. in the Bodleian, with notes and Glossary, by White, 2 vols. 8vo. *plates of facsimiles,* (pub. at 21s), *cloth, new,* 17s 6d *Oxford,* 1852

3869 OROSIUS' Compendious History of the World, *King Alfred's Anglo-Saxon Version, with English translation by Bosworth,* roy. 8vo. *lxiv,* 133, *and* 198 pp. 14 *plates of facsimiles, MS. and coloured map of the world, according to Orosius and Alfred,* (pub. at 16s) *cloth,* 12s 1859

3870 RASK'S Grammar of the Anglo-Saxon Tongue, with Praxis; enlarged and improved by the Author, edited by B. Thorpe, 8vo. *plates,* 16s *Copenhagen,* 1830

3871 —— Angelsaksisk Sproglaere, 8vo. *bds.* 2s 6d *Stockholm,* 1817

3872 SAXON CHRONICLE (The), *Anglo-Saxon and English,* with notes, critical and explanatory, chronological, topographical, and glossarial Indices, and a Grammar, by INGRAM, 4to. *map and plates, bds.* £2. 5s 1823

3873 SAXON CHRONICLE dissected, with a Review of the Saxon Annalists, Appendix, Glossary, etc. sm. 8vo. *bds.* 10s 1830

3874 SOMNERI (Gul.) Dictionarum Saxonico-Latino-Anglicum, voces phrasesque præcipuas Anglo-Saxonicas cum Latinâ et Anglicâ interpretatione complectens; Ælfrici Abbatis Grammatica Latino-Saxonica, cum Glossario suo ejusdem generis, folio, *hf. calf,* £2. *Oxon.* 1659

Fetched, Parr's sale, £5. 10s; Perry's, russia, £5. 5s; 1819, Sotheby's, £6; 1856, Sotheby's, £6. "A work highly deserving of mention, which bears honourable witness to the learning and industry of its author. The Grammar of Aelfric is a relic, curious in itself, and valuable to the student."—*Rask.*

3875 THORPE's Analecta Anglo-Saxonica, selections from various authors, (Aelfric, Aelfred, Layamon, the Ormulum, etc.) with notes and Glossary, sm. 8vo. *cloth,* 6s 1846

3876 WACKERBARTH, Music and the Anglo-Saxons, an account of the Anglo-Saxon Orchestra, with remarks on the Church Music of the 19th century, 8vo. *facsimiles, cloth,* 2s 6d 1837

3877 **Teutonic.** ADELUNG, Altdeutsche Gedichte welche aus der Heidelberg. Bibliothek in die Vatikanische gekommen sind, 2 vols. 12mo. *sd.* 5s 6d; *hf. cf.* 7s *Königsberg,* 1796

3878 ANZEIGER für Kunde des deutschen Mittelalters, herausg. von Aufsess und Mone, Vols. I—III, in 1 vol. 4to. *plates, bds.* 10s 1832-34

3879 BÄRMANN's Groote-Höög- un Häwel-Book, 12mo. 370 pp. *Poems in the Hamburg vulgar dialect, cloth,* 5s 1827

3880 BONER's Fabeln aus den Zeiten der Minnesinger, 12mo. *with Glossary of* 78 pp. *calf,* 4s *Zürich,* 1757

3881 —— der Edelstein, Gedicht mit Wörterbuche, von Benecke, 8vo. *calf gilt,* 6s *Berlin,* 1816

Best edition of this old German Fabulist, with a valuable Glossary.

3882 BORNEMANN's Gedichte in Plattdeutscher Mundart, 8vo. *portrait, gilt,* 5s 1827

3883 BREMISCH-Niedersächsisches Wörterbuch, worin alle in ganz Nieder-Sachsen gebräuchlichen Mundarten, nebst veralteten Wörtern und Redensarten, ebenfalls unbekannte Dialekte erkläret sind, 5 vols. 12mo. *hf. bd.* 35s *Brem.* 1767-71

3884 BÜSCHING, der Deutschen Leben, Kunst und Wissen in Mittelalter, 2 vols. 12mo. *plates, cloth,* 5s *Breslau,* 1817-19

EUROPEAN PHILOLOGY. 205

3885 CHRIEMHILDEN Rache, und die Klage; 2 Heldengedichte aus d. schwäb. Zeitpunkte, mit Glossarium, sm. 4to. *sd. 3s*   *Zyrich,* 1757

3886 DÄHNERT's Platt-Deutsches Wörterbuch, nach der Pommerschen und Rüg. Mundart, sm. 4to. *bds. with autograph of Coleridge,* 10s   *Stralsund,* 1781

3887 DETMAR, Chronik des Franciscaner Lesemeisters Detmar, mit Ergänzungen, von Grautoff, *in Low German,* 2 vols. 8vo. *cloth,* 6s   *Hamburg,* 1829-20

3888 DOCEN's Geschichte der teutschen Literatur, 2 vols. in 1, sm. 8vo. *cloth,* 4s 1807

3889 FRANKFURT. GELEHRTENVEREIN für Deutsche Sprache, Abhandlungen, 3 vols. in 1, 8vo. *facsimiles of gothic writing, cloth,* 10s   *Frank.* 1818-21
   A valuable work, especially for the old German language.

3890 GOTTFRIED's VON STRASSBURG Werke, (Tristan und Isolde, Minnelieder, etc.) mit Einleitung und Wörterbuch, von Von der Hagen, 2 vols. in 1, 8vo. *hf. cf.* 14s   *Breslau,* 1823
   Gottfried of Strasburg was one of the Minnesingers in the XIIIth Century.

3891 TRISTAN, mit der Fortsetzung Ulrichs von Turheim, herausg. von Groote, 4to. *with Glossary of old German, facsimile, etc. hf. calf,* 9s   *Berlin,* 1821

3892 GRAFF, ALTHOCHDEUTSCHER SPRACHSCHATZ, oder Wörterbuch der althochdeutschen Sprache (Dictionary of the Old German Language, with references to the Greek and Latin, Oriental, Northern, and other Languages,) 6 vols.—Massman's Vollständiger Index zu Graff's Althochdeutschen Sprachschatze, 1 vol.—together 7 vols. 4to. *hf. bd.* £2. *2s; or, hf. cf. nt.* £2. 10s   *Berl.* 1834-46
   This Dictionary contains all the old German words used before the 12th century, compared with the present High German, the Indian Dialects, the Greek, Latin, Old Prussian, Gothic, Anglo-Saxon, Old Dutch, Icelandic, Sanscrit, &c. and shewing the roots which the High and Low German, the English, the Dutch, the Danish, and the Swedish Languages have in common.

3893 GRIMM'S (J.) Deutsche Grammatik, 4 vols. 8vo. £2. 10s   *Goettingen,* 1822-37

3894 —— Deutsche Mythologie, 2e Ausgabe, 2 vols. 8vo. *calf gilt,* 20s *Götting.* 1844

3895 —— the same, 3rd edition, *interleaved,* 3 vols. 8vo. *hf. calf,* 21s   *ib.* 1854

3896 —— Deutsche Rechtsalterthümer, 8vo. 971 pp. *with Index of Words, philological notes, etc. bds.* 9s   *Göttingen,* 1854

3897 HAGEN (F. H. von der) und BÜSCHING, Deutsche Gedichte des Mittelalters, 2 vols. 4to. *facsimiles, bound,* 15s   *Berlin,* 1808-20
   Containing: Einleitung, König Rother, Herzog Ernst, Wigamur, der Heilige George, Salomon und Morolf, das Helden Buch, Biterolf und Deitlieb, etc. etc. with notes.

3898 HAGEN und Büsching, Geschichte der Deutschen Poesie, von der ältesten Zeit, 8vo. *bds.* 6s   *Berlin,* 1812

3899 HAGEN (F. H. von der) MINNESINGER, DEUTSCHE LIEDERDICHTER des XII. XIII. und XIV. Jahrhunderts, aus allen bekannten Handschriften und früheren Drucken gesammelt und berichtigt, 4 vols. in 3, 4to. *with the Music, bds.* 30s; *or,* FINE PAPER, *bds.* £2.   *Leipzig,* 1838

3900 —— the same, VELLUM PAPER, 4 vols. in 3, 4to. £2. 16s
   The grandest collection of the German POETICAL ROMANCES and Lyrical Effusions of the Middle Ages.

3900*—— Narrenbuch, mit Anhang, 12mo. *hf.-mor.* 6s   *Halle,* 1811

3901 HAGEN (G.) Reimchronik der Stadt Cöln, mit Wörterbuch, etc. von Groote, 8vo. *hf. calf,* 2s 6d   *Cöln,* 1834

3902 HARTMAN's Iwein der Riter, von Benecke, *Old German,* 12mo. *sd.* 2s 6d   1827

3903 HATTEMER, Denkmahle des Mittelalters; St. Gallen's Altteutsche Sprachschätze, 3 vols. impl. 8vo. *5 plates of facsimiles, bds.* 30s   *St. Gallen,* 1844-49
   A most valuable contribution to literature. The ancient Glosses are of the greatest antiquity.

3904 HOFSTAETER, Altdeutsche Gedichte, 2 vols. in 1, stout 8vo. *cloth,* 4s *Wien,* 1811

3905 KILIANI (*Cornelii Dufflaei*) Etymologicum Teutonicæ Linguæ sive Dictionarium Teutonico-Latinum, præcipuas Teutonicæ Linguæ dictiones et phrases, Latine interpretatas, et cum aliis Linguis collatas complectens; curante Hasselto Arnhemiensi, qui et suas adnotationes adjecit, 2 vols. in 1, 4to. *hf. bd. best edition, uncut,* 25s; *or,* 2 vols. *calf gilt,* 28s   *Traj. Bat.* 1777

3906 KINDERLING's Geschichte der Nieder-Sächs. oder Plattdeutschen Sprache, 8vo. *bds.* 4s.   *Magd.* 1800

3907 LAMPRECHT, Alexander, Gedicht des XIIen Jahrhunderts, Urtext und Übersetzung, nebst Einleitung, Erläuterungen, etc. von Weisman, 2 vols. 12mo. *old Teut. and German, hf. mor.* 6s   *Frankf.* 1850

3908 MAILATH und Köffinger, KOLOCZAER Codex altdeutcher Gedichte, 8vo. *bds.* 2s; *cf. gt.* 3s   *Pesth,* 1817

3909 MANESSEN'S Sammlung von (CXL) Minnesingern aus dem Schwæb. Zeitpuncte, herausg. von Bodmer, 2 vols. *Zyrich*, 1758-59—Retzer's Nachlese zu Sineds Liedern, *Wien*, 1784—3 vols. in 1, sm. 4to. *hf. bd.* 18s   1758-84
A most valuable collection of these poems.

3910 MASSMAN, DEUTSCHE GEDICHTE des XII Jahrhund. etc. von Massmann, 2 vols. 1837—Gedichte des XII und XIII Jahrhund. von Hahn, 1840—3 vols. in 1, 8vo. *hf. calf gilt*, 5s   1837-40

3911 MEIGERIUS de Panurgia Lamiarum, Strigum ac Veneficarum, cohortisque Magicae Cacodaemonia, dat ys: Nödige und nutte Underrichtinge, etc. in *Low German*, sq. 8vo. *calf neat*, 32s   *Hamborch*, 1587

3912 MICHÆLER, Tabulæ parallelæ antiquiss. Dialectorum, Teutonicarum, Mœso-Goth. Anglo-Sax. Runicæ, Islandicæ, etc. thick 12mo. *bds.* 10s *Oeniponte*, 1776

3913 NIBELUNGEN LIED, *Altdeutsch*, von Hagen, mit Wörterb. 8vo. 3s 6d *Bresl.* 1820

3914 NIBELUNGEN NOTH und die Klage, herausg. von Lachmann, *Altdeutsch*, 8vo. 4s 6d   *Berlin*, 1841

3915 NIEBELUNGEN LIED, übertsetzt von Marbach, roy. 4to. *printed within ornamental woodcut borders, and with numerous large and beautiful illustrations by Bendemann and Hübner, bds.* 20s   *Leipzig*, 1840

3916 NIBELUNGEN NOTH, bearbeitet von Pfizer, 4to. *numerous beautiful woodcut vignettes and illustrations by Carolsfeld and Neureuther, cloth*, 18s *Stuttg.* 1843

3917 OELRICHS Sammlung alter und neuer Gesez-Bücher der Stadt Bremen, aus original Handschriften, *Alt-Niedersächsisch*, stout 4to. *plates of facsimiles, calf*, 16s   *Bremen*, 1771

3918 PARÆNETICORUM VETERUM pars I. *(all published)* in qua producuntur Columbanus, Tyrol Rex Scotorum *(cum effig.)* Winsbekius, Winsbekia, etc. cum notis Goldasti, sm. 4to. *vellum*, 12s   *Insulae, lac. Acron.* 1604

OLD GERMAN Poems, with valuable philological notes.

3919 REINEKE de Vos mit dem Koker, *in Low German*, sm. 4to. *reprint of the edition of* 1498, *hf. cf. uncut*, 7s; or *smallest* 4to. *calf extra*, 10s *Wulffenbüttel*, 1711

3920 REYNIKE VOSS de Olde, nyge gedrücket, erlüchtet und vorbetert, thick 12mo. *the Poem and commentary both in Low German, fine copy in old elegantly stamped calf binding of the period, rare*, 30s   *Franckfort*, 1575

3921 SCHERZII Glossarium Germanicum Medii Ævi, potissimum Dialecti Suevicæ; edidit, illustravit, supplevit Oberlinus, 2 vols. folio, *calf*, 30s *Argent.* 1781-84
"Ouvrage le plus ample pour étudier les anciennes dialectes dont a été formée la langue allemande. C'est une suite au *Glossarium linguæ francicæ*, du Thesaurus de Schilter."—*Brunet*.

3922 SCHILTERI THESAURUS ANTIQUITATUM TEUTONICARUM, Ecclesiasticarum, Civilium, Litterariarum: Monumenta Francica, Alemannica, Saxonica, Biblica, Ecclesiastica, et Civilia, cum Glossario Teutonico non Linguæ solum inservituro sed et Antiquitatibus abundanti, 3 vols. folio, *facsimiles in Ornaments in Ancient MSS. vellum*, £2.; or, *a fine copy*, £2. 10s   *Ulmæ*, 1727-28
"Schilteri Thesaurus Teutonicus est un recueil rempli de documents précieux pour l'histoire civile et littéraire de l'Allemagne à l'époque Carlovingienne; Vendu 125 fr."—*Brunet.*
A most valuable collection of the earliest monuments of the Northern Languages in Europe, containing the works of OTFRID, NOTKER, WILLERAN, an ANGLO-SAXON List of the Gospels for Sundays and Festivals, FRANCIC LAWS, Rhythmus Antiquus de CAROLO MAGNO, &c. The third volume is entirely occupied by the valuable GLOSSARY.
"The Thesaurus of Schilter is a real mine of Francic Literature. The text is founded on a careful collation of all the MSS. to which he could obtain access, and these are highly valuable for their antiquity and correctness."
—*Warton's English Poetry by Price*.

3923 SCHMELLER, Evangelii Matthaei versio *Francica* Saec. IX, nec non *Gothica* Saec. IV, 8vo. *bds.* 2s 6d   *Stuttg.* 1827

3924 —— —— Bayerisches Wörterbuch, Sammlung von Wörtern und Ausdrücken in den lebenden Mundarten der ältern Provincial-Litteratur, etc. 4 vols. in 2, 8vo. *calf neat*, £2.   *Stuttgart*, 1827-37

3925 SCHMIDT, Westerwäldisches Idiotikon, 12mo. *cloth*, 3s *Hadamar*, 1800

3926 SCHMID, Schwäbisches Idiotikon, 8vo. *sd.* 4s.   *Berlin*, (? 1820)

3927 SCHUEREN (Gherard van der) Teuthonista of Duytschlender, uitgegeven door Boonzager, met Vorrede van Clignett, 4to. *sd.* 18s; or, *hf. russia, interleaved, only 180 copies printed*, 21s   *Leyden*, 1804
A reprint of the first or German-Latin part of a very rare Old German and Latin Vocabulary printed at Cologne, 1477, the last copy of which fetched at Singer's sale £26.; not long ago Mr. Q placed a very fine copy in the library of his Highness Prince Louis Lucien Bonaparte. Besides being carefully edited, this reprint has the advantages of a preface and a bibliographical list of Old German Vocabularies of the XV and XVI centuries.

3927 *SCHÜTZE, Holtseinisches Idiotikon, oder Sammlung plattdeutscher, alter und neugebildeter Worte, Wortformen, Redensarten, Volkwitzes, Sprichwörter, und aus dem Sprachschatze Sitten, Gebräuche, Spiele, etc. der Holsteiner, nebst Einleitung, 4 vols. in 1, stout sm. 8vo. *calf*, 18s; or, 4 vols. in 2, *hf. morocco, gilt tops*, 24s *Hamb.* 1800-6

A valuable Glossary of Low German, comprising a collection of Ancient and Modern Low German Words, Idioms, Witticisms, Proverbs, Nursery and other Rhymes, Anecdotes, and Expressions illustrating the Manners, Customs, Games, and Festivals of the Holsteiners.

3928 STAUFFENBERG, der Ritter von, ein *altdeutsches* Gedicht, von Engelhardt, 8vo. *22 coloured facsimiles, calf*, 10s *Strassb.* 1823

Very few copies were printed and those only for subscribers.

3929 SUHM, Symbolae ad Literaturam Teut. Antiquiorem, 4to. *old German poems and Theotisc glossaries, sd.* 5s *Havniae*, 1787

3930 SUMMA JOHANNIS, FIRST EDITION, in *Low German*, sm. folio, *very fine copy in old calf, not mentioned by Schiller*, £4. 10s *Lubek, St. Arndes*, 1487

Collation: Table of contents, 8 leaves; the book commencing: Hir hevet sik an de vorrede disses bokes genomet Suma Johannis, welker de eerwerdige vader lezemeister Johannes van Vryborgh prediker ordens to latine ghemaket unde uth deme hylligen decret boke getoge hefft. Unde van latine in dat dudesche gemaket dorch einen hochgelerden doctore geheten brod. Bartolo, sheets A—S (in 8 eight) T in 10 leaves. "This version in the language of Lower Saxony is very rare and highly interesting in a philological point of view."—*Singer's MS. note.*

3931 UHLAND (L.) Alte hoch- und niederdeutsche Volkslieder, 2 vols. 8vo. *hf. calf neat*, 18s *Stuttgart*, 1844-45

3932 VOCABULARIUS EX QUO (Latino-Teutonicus). *Colophon :* Presens hoc opusculum non stili aut penne suffragio sz nova artificiosaqz invencione quadā ad eusebiā dei īdustrie zwollis est cōsūmatu (*consummatum*) sub anno Nativitatis. M. cccc. lxxix feria quinta ante festū Nativitatis domini, sm. stout 4to. 230 *leaves of 25 lines each, the initial letters rubricated, some contemporary hand has scrawled figures on about a dozen leaves, in other respects a fine, sound and clean copy, in the original stamped pigskin binding*, £6. 10s *Zwollis*, 1479

An excessively rare Vocabulary, Latin-Low-German; priced, 1833, Thorpe, russia, £10. 10s. Bound up with the above is a High-German-Latin Vocabulary. "Vocabularius incipiens teutonicum ante latinum;" 188 leaves, apparently wanting the last one, black letter, without date or name of place. Zwoll is a fortified town in the province of Overyssel. Printing was introduced here in 1479, by Johannes de Vollhoe and Petrus Os de Breda. Panzer names, as the first book, Bonaventuræ Sermones de Tempore et de Sanctis; the present is the fourth produced at that press.

"This very rare and curious Vocabulary is the first Latino Teutonic Glossary printed in the Netherlands. It is designated as the Vocabularius 'Ex Quo' from the first words of the preface, from which it appears to have been intended for the use of poor scholars: "Ut eo facilius sacram scripturam litteraliter intelligere possent."

"This edition is valuable not only as a typographical curiosity, being one of the first books printed at Zwoll, see the very curious colophon, but from the explanation being in the Plattdeutsch and having a strong resemblance to some of our old English Vocabularies."

"It is of more importance to the English Philologer than any other old Vocabulary except the Teuthonist of Van Schueren, and affords elucidations of some of our old English words which are not to be found in that valuable work."

3933 VULCANIUS de Literis et Linguâ Getarum, etc. cum speciminibus variarum linguarum, 12mo. *Vocabularies of several languages including Basque, Gipsey, Icelandic, etc. bd.* 5s *Lugd. Bat.* 1697

3934 WACHTERI GLOSSARIUM GERMANICUM, continens origines et antiquitates totius Linguae Germanicae, folio, *sound copy, calf or vellum*, 25s; or, *fine copy, calf gilt*, 36s *Lips.* 1737

3935 WEBER'S Illustrations of Northern Antiquities, with additions by Jamieson and Sir Walter Scott, impl. 4to. (pub. at £3. 3s) *hf. morocco*, 15s; or, *calf gilt*, 24s *Edinburgh*, 1814

A valuable work, comprising translations from the earlier Teutonic and Scandinavian Romances, the Book of Heroes, and Nibelungen, with Tales from the Old German, Danish, Swedish and Icelandic.

3936 WILHELM der Heilige von Oranse, von Turheim und Eschilbach, durch Casparson, 2 vols. in 1, 4to. *calf*, 4s *Cassel*, 1781-84

3937 WILLERAMI in Canticum Canticorum Paraphrasis, *veteri Lingua Francica, etc.* cum explic. Belg. et Notis, 1598—Junii Observationes in Willeramum, 1655; 12mo. *vellum*, 7s 1598-1655

3938 WIRNT VON GRAVENBERCH, WIGALOIS der Ritter mit dem Rade, herausg. mit Anmerk. und Wörterbuch, von Benecke, 12mo. 3s *Berlin*, 1819

3939 —— the same, 12mo. FINE PAPER, *hf. morocco*, 6s 1819

A Romance of the Round Table in the Middle High German Dialect.

3940 ZEUSS, die Deutschen und die Nachbarstämme, 8vo. viii and 780 pp. *hf. calf*, 10s *München*, 1837

A learned Ethnological work, giving an ample account of Ancient Tribes and Races of Europe.

3941 ZIEMANN's Mittelhochdeutsches Wörterbuch, nebst Grammatischer Einleitung, 8vo. *pp. 16 and 720, doub. cols. hf. bd. neat*, 10s 6d *Quedlin.* 1838

3942 **Dutch, Flemish, Frisic.** AHN's Grammar of the Dutch Language, small 8vo. *cloth*, 4s 1854

3943 ANONYMI Idea Languæ Belgicæ, à Van Driel, 8vo. 4s *Lug. Bat.* 1783
3944 ASEGA-BUCH, *Alt-friesisch und Deutsch,* mit Anmerk. von WIARDA, 4to. *hf. calf,* 7s *Berlin,* 1805
3945 BENDSEN, die Nord-friesische Sprache nach der Moringer Mundart, zur Vergleich. mit den verwandten Sprachen, von VRIES, 8vo. *sd.* 7s 6d *Leide,* 1860
3946 DEUTSCH-HOLLÄNDISCHES und Holländ.-Deutsches Wörterbuch, 2 vols. 12mo. *calf neat,* 10s *Zütphen,* 1819-23
3947 HEELU, Chronique de la Bataille de Woeringen (1288), publiée par Willems, st. 4to. *original Flemish, with Introduction, Notes, Glossary, etc. portrait, and Genealogical Table, hf. bd.* 9s. *Brux.* 1836
3948 HOFFMANN (von Fallersleben) Horae Belgicae, partes I—V et VII, 8vo. *facsimiles, boards,* 10s *Vratils.* 1830-45
3949 —— the same, parts 1, 2, 6, 7 and 10, *second ed. (except 6 which is of the first)* in 2 vols. sm. 8vo. *hf. mor.* 12s *Breslau,* 1838-54

A valuable collection of Dutch Poems; the seventh part contains a "Glossarium Belgicum."

3950 HOLTROP'S English-Dutch and Dutch-English Dictionary, 2 vols. stout 8vo. *hf. bd.* 15s *Dordr.* 1789-1801
3951 —— the same, revised by Stevenson, 2 vols. 8vo. *hf. calf,* 20s *Amst.* 1823-24
3952 LENNEP (J. van) Romantische Werken: de Pleegzoon, Ferdinand Huyck, de Roos van Dekama, Elizabeth Musch, Onze Voorouders, Vier Verspreide Verhalen, 14 vols. 12mo. *frontispieces, new in cloth,* £2. 16s *Rotterdam,* 1859-60
3953 JAGER'S Taalkundig Magazijn, of gemengde Bijdragen tot de Kennis der Nederduitsche Taal, 4 vols. 8vo. *hf. calf gilt, uncut,* £2. *Rotterdam,* 1835-42
A valuable collection of Philological Dissertations.
3954 KAUSLER'S Denkmäler Altniederländischer Sprache und Litteratur nach ungedruckten Quellen: Reim Chronik von Flandern; Altniederländische Gedichte XIII—XV. Jahrhunderts, 2 vols. 8vo. *bds.* 24s *Tübingen,* 1840-44
3955 MELIS STOKE, Hollandse Jaarboeken of Rijm-Kronijk, door Alkemade, folio, 34 *fine portraits page size, and* 2 *other plates, vellum,* 20s *Leyden,* 1699
3956 —— Rijmkronijk, med historie-, oudheid-, en Taalkundige Aanmerkingen door Huydecoper, 3 vols. 8vo. *vellum,* 10s *Leyden,* 1772
3957 MONE's Uebersicht der Niederländischen Volks-Literatur älterer Zeit, 8vo. *cloth,* 5s *Tübingen,* 1838
3958 OLINGER, Dictionnaire Hollandais-Français et Français-Hollandais, 2 vols. stout roy. 8vo. 836 *and* 1185 *pp. treble cols. sd.* 9s *Bruxelles,* 1828
3959 OUDE FRIESCHE WETTEN, 2 vols. in 1, 4to. *Ancient Laws, Old Frisic and Dutch, hf. bd.* 7s 6d *Campen,* 1782
3960 OUTZEN's GLOSSARIUM DER FRIESISCHEN SPRACHE, besonders in nordfriesischer Mundart, zur Vergleichung mit den verwandten German. und nordischen Sprachen, sm. 4to. *hf. calf neat,* 12s *Kopenhagen,* 1837
3961 PLANTINI Thesaurus Theutonicæ linguæ; Thresor du langage Bas-Alman, dict vulgairement Flameng, traduict en *François* et en *Latin,* 4to. nearly 600 pp. *double columns, very choice copy in old calf gilt,* 25s *Ant. Plantin,* 1573
L'auteur de ce dictionnaire estimé, recherché et rare, est le fameux imprimeur Christophe Plantin.
3962 REDERIJCK-KUNST, in Rijm, Redenkaveling ende Letter-kunst, 1587—Twe-Spraack van de Letterkunst, 1584—in 1 vol. 12mo. *vell.* 5s *Leyden,* 1584-87
3963 REINAERT DE VOS, episch Fabeldicht, XII, XIIIe Eeuw, met Aenmerkingen, van Willems, roy. 8vo. *plates and facsim. hf. mor. uncut,* 14s *Gent,* 1850
3964 SEWEL'S Dutch-English and English-Dutch Dictionary, to which are prefixed an English and a Dutch Grammar, augmented by Buys, 2 vols. 4to. *hf. bd.* 10s; *or, calf,* 12s. *Amst.* 1766
3965 ULENSPIEGEL (Thyl) het leven, 18mo. *rude cuts, hf. bd.* 4s *Gend, s. a.* (1810)
3966 VANDER-MILII Lingua Belgica, acc. quaedam ad omnes linguas pertinentia, sm. 4to. *hf. bd.* 5s *Lugd. Bat.* 1612
3967 VAN DER PYL, Dutch Grammar, with a great number of Exercises, 8vo. *hf. calf neat,* 7s 6d; *calf,* 9s *Rott.* 1819
3968 VERHAAL van veele Diefstallen, sq. 8vo. *History of Burglars and Robbers,* 13 *portraits and* 4 *plates, calf,* 10s *Amst.* 1710
3969 VLAERDINGS REDENRYCK-BERGH, sm. 4to. very curious *Miracle-Plays, with woodcuts, in the frontisp. Our Saviour performing on the Bass-Viol, hf. bd.* 10s *Amst.* 1617

3970 WASSENBERGH, Taalkundige Bijdragen tot den Frieschen Tongval, 2 vols. in 1, 8vo. *hf. vel. 6s* *Franeker*, 1806
Containing the Idioticon Frisicum, the Dissertation on Frisian Names, Friesche Gedichten, &c.
3971 WEILAND, Nederduitsch Taalkundig Woordenboek, 11 vols. in 6, 8vo. *calf gilt*, £2. 16s Previously priced, £5. 5s. *Amst.* 1799-1811
3972 WIARDA, Altfriesisches Wörterbuch, 518 *pp.*—Geschichte der alten Fries. Sprache, 2 vols. in 1, 8vo. *hf. calf, 7s* *Aurich,* 1784-86
3973 WILLEM'S (J. F.) Oude Vlaemsche Liederen: Flemish Songs, *with the Music,* royal 8vo. *hf. morocco,* 12s *Gent,* 1848
3974 —— the same, impl. 8vo. *Large and thick Paper, half calf uncut, a handsome book,* 36s Only a few copies were printed on Thick paper. 1834

3975 **SCANDINAVIAN LANGUAGES:** BAGGESEN, der Dänische Staat mit den Herzogthümern, 8vo. *hf. mor. 5s.* *Kop.* 1845
3976 BARTHOLINI Antiquitates Danicae et de causis contemptæ a Danis Mortis, sm. 4to. *portrait, vellum,* 16s *Hafniæ,* 1690
3977 BIRCHERODII Disquisitiones Antiquitatum Daniæ Gentilis, 7 parts in 1 vol sm. 4to. *vellum, rare,* 12s *Havniae,* 1701
3978 CELSII Bibliothecae Upsaliensis Historia, 8vo. *hf. calf, 7s 6d* *Upsal,* 1745
3979 DAHLMANN's Geschichte von Dännemark, 3 vols. 8vo. *sd. 6s* *Hamburg,* 1840-43
3980 DALINS (Olof) Geschichte des Reichs Schweden, durch Benzelstierna und Dähnert, 3 vols. in 4, sm. 4to. *hf. bd. 9s* *Greifswald,* 1756-63
3981 GRAABERG di Hemsö, Saggio istorico su gli Scaldi, 8vo. *calf gilt, 7s* *Pisa,* 1811
3982 IHRE, GLOSSARIUM SUIO-GOTHICUM, in quo tam hodierno usu frequentata Vocabula, quam in ævi medii scriptis obvia, explicantur, et ex Dialectis Mœso-Gothica, Anglo-Saxonica, Anglica hodierna, Alemannica, Islandica, ceterisque Gothicis et Celticis illustrantur, 2 vols. in 1, folio, *scarce,* £3. 3s. *Upsalæ,* 1769
With the following autograph note on title-page: "Francis Palgrave his book, bought during the continental blockade at the price of £7. 7s—" Drury's copy fetched £6. 10s. "Ouvrage très estimé."—BRUNET. "One of the best Dictionaries of any language in Europe; it is indeed a masterpiece of criticism and erudition."—BOUCHER. Highly praised by Jamieson in his Scottish Dictionary.
3983 IHRE, Fragmenta versionis Ulphilanae, *Goth. et Lat.* cum dissert. philologicis, sq. 8vo. *hf. bd. 5s* *Ups.* 1763
3984 LOCCENII Antiquitates Suio-Gothicæ—Rugman, Gaumlu Laugum, *Islandicè*— Loccenii Lexicon Juris Sueo-Gothici, 3 vols. in 1, 12mo. *vellum,* 10s *Ups.* 1665-70
3985 MAGNI Historia de omnibus Gothorum Sueonumque Regibus, sm. stout folio, *many quaint wood engravings and woodcut initial letters, original edition, with good impressions, very fine clean copy in the original limp vellum,* 36s *Romæ,* 1554

NORDISKE OLDSKRIFT SELSKAB: Publications of the Royal Society of Northern Antiquaries.

3986 NORDISK TIDSSKRIFT for Oldkyndighed (Historical and Philological Transactions), 3 vols. *bound,* 1832-36—MEMOIRES de la Société, 1836-49, 5 vols. *sd.* 1838-52—ANNALER for Nordisk Oldkyndighed, 1836-43, 1850-57, in 12 vols. *four bound, eight unbound,* 1837-57—ANTIQUARISK TIDSSKRIFT: Bulletin de la Société, 1843-57, 5 vols. in 9 parts, *unbound,* 1845-59—together 25 vols. 8vo. *numerous fine plates of Antiquities, Runic and Cuneiform inscriptions, etc. seven volumes in calf extra, the remainder in 22 Nos.,* £12. *Copenhagen,* 1832-59

Sets completed.

Collectiones Historiae Populorum Septentrionalium, ed. Societas Regia Antiquariorum Septentrionalium:

3987 FORNMANNA SÖGUR, eptir gömlum Handritum utgefnar ad tilhlutun hins Norræna Fornfræda Felags, 12 vols. *with facsimiles* 1825-37
OLDNORDISKE SAGAER, udgivne i oversættelse, 12 vols. 1826-37
SCRIPTA HISTORICA ISLANDORUM, de rebus gestis veterum Borealium, *Latine,* 12 vols. 1828-46
NORDISKE FORTIDS SAGAER, efter den udgivne gamle Nordiske Grundskrift, af Rafn, 3 vols. 1829-30
ISLENDINGA SÖGUR, eptir gömlum Handritum, 2 vols. 1829-30
Together 41 vols. 8vo. FINE PAPER, *calf extra, a fine set, from Miss Currer's library,* £21. *Kjöbenhavn,* 1825-46

3988 ANTIQUITATES AMERICANAE, sive Scriptores Septentrionales Rerum Ante-Columbianarum in America, edidit Soc. R. Antiq. Septemtr. impl. 4to. *maps and plates, russia, gilt edges*, 32s — *Hafniae*, 1837

3989 MALLET's Northern Antiquities; the customs, religion and laws of the Ancient Danes, Saxons, etc., with translations of the Edda, etc., 2 vols. 8vo. *cf.* 6s — 1770

3990 MARMIER, Littérature en Danemark et en Suede, 8vo. *sd.* 2s 6d — 1839

3991 OLAUS LE GRAND, Histoire des Pays Septentrionaus, 18mo. *curious cuts, calf,* 6s — *Anvers,* 1561

3992 PETERSEN, det Danske, Norske og Svenske Sprogs Historie, 2 vols. 12mo. *hf. calf,* 9s — *Kjöb.* 1831

3993 PIGOTT's Manual of Scandinavian Mythology, 12mo. *cloth,* 6s 6d — 1839

3994 STIERNHÖÖK de Jure Sueonum et Gothorum vetusto libri 2, de judiciis, judicibus, causis civilibus, criminalibus etc. sq. 8vo. *calf,* 7s 6d — *Holmiae,* 1672

3995 THORKELIN, Diplomatarium Arna-Magnaeanum, exhibens Monumenta Diplomatica, historiam atque jura Daniae, Norvegicae etc. illustrantia, 2 vols. in 1, sm. 4to. *hf. morocco, uncut,* 21s — *Hauniae,* 1786

3996 TORFAEI Series Dynastarum et Regum Daniae, 1702—TORFAEANA sive notae in Seriem Regum, 1777—2 vols. sm. 4to. *ports. bd.* 10s — *Hafn.* 1702-77

3997 —— HISTORIA RERUM NORVEGICARUM; in qua praeter Norvegiae descriptionem primordia gentis, instituta, mores, incrementa, genealogia, chronologia, etc. continentur, 4 vols. folio, *Chronolol. Tables, &c. vellum,* £4. — *Haf.* 1711

3998 VERELII Historia Suio-Gothica, sm. 4to. *portr. hf. bd.* 4s — *Holm.* 1730

3999 (WILD) Sueciae Historia Pragmatica, Jus Publicum, sm. 4to. *cf.* 9s — *Holm.* 1731

4000 PRIOR, ANCIENT DANISH Ballads, translated from the originals, 3 vols. 8vo. *cloth,* 18s — 1860

The introduction and notes are of interest to the Scandinavian Scholar; the spirited Poems will be attractive to the general reader.

4001 **Danish.** BAY'S Danish Dictionary, 2 vols. 12mo. 1807—with Schneider's Danish Grammar, 3 vols. *hf. calf,* 12s — 1807

4002 BAY, Engelsk-Dansk Ordbog, 2 vols. 8vo. *hf. bd.* 14s — *Kjöb.* 1806

4003 DANSKE MAGAZIN, af et til det Danske Sprogs og Histories Forbedring Selskab, 6 vols. in 2, sm. 4to. *cuts of Coins, &c. hf. cf.* 18s — *Kiöb.* 1745-52

4004 FERRALL and REPP's Danish-English Dictionary, 1845—Rosing's English-Danish Dictionary, 1853, 2 vols. 12mo. *sd.* 12s — *Kopenhagen,* 1845-53

4005 GRIMM, Altdänische Heldenlieder und Märchen, 8vo. *calf,* 12s *Heidelb.* 1811

4006 HEIBERG, Skrifter af Forfatteren til en Hverdags-Historie, 4 vols. 12mo. *half calf neat,* 15s — *Kjöb.* 1849

4007 HERTHEDAL ved Leyre i Siaeland, og gamle Dannemark, sm. 4to. 5s — 1745

4008 HOLBERGS samtlige Comoedier, med Anmoerkninger ved Boye, 8vo. *cloth* 10s; *hf. morocco,* 12s — *Kiöb.* 1843

4009 INGEMANN'S samlede Skrifter: Dramatiske Digte, 6 vols.; Digte og Romaner, 12 vols.; Eventyr og Fortvellinger, 8 vols.; Romanzer og Sange, 8 vols. together 34 vols. in 19, 12mo. *a pretty set of those celebrated works in hf. calf, gilt backs,* £3. 3s — *Kjöb.* 1843-45

4010 JOMSVIKINGA SAGA og Knytlinga, *Dansk,* af Rafn, 8vo. *sd.* 7s 6d — *Kiöb.* 1829

4011 JUDSKE LOWBOG, stout sm. 4to. *with the various additions,* Black letter, *portraits of the Kings of Denmark, calf, gilt edges,* 12s — *Kiöbenhaffn,* 1642-44

4012 LANGEBEK, Trende Skalde Digte, sm. 4to. *bds.* 4s — *Kjöb.* 1772

4013 LÖKKE, Modersmaalets Formlaere, 8vo. *Fine Paper, hf. calf,* 6s. — *Krist.* 1855

4014 MOLBECH, Dansk Ordbog med Sprogbrug, Talemaader og Exempler, 2 vols. 8vo. *calf gilt,* 36s — *Kiöbenhavn,* 1833

4015 MÜLLERS Sagabibliothek, med Anmoerkninger og indledende Afhandlinger, 3 vols. 12mo. *the best work on the Sagas, thick paper, sd.* £2. — *Kiöb.* 1817-20

4015* —— Undersögelse af Danmarks og Norges Sagnhistorie, sm. 4to. 7s — 1823

4016 NYERUP's Almindelig Morskabslœsning, *extracts from the old romances,* etc. *Kjöb.* 1816—BRUDER RAUSCH, was wunders er getriben hat, von Endlicher, *Old German and Danish,* only 50 copies printed, *Wien,* 1835, in 1 vol. 12mo. *hf. mor.* 20s — *Kjöb.* 1816

4017 OEHLENSCHLÄGERS Poetiske Skrifter, 2 vols. 12mo. *calf gilt*, 9s   *Kiöb.* 1805
4018 PAUS, Samling af gamle Norske Love; Hagens og Magni Gule-Tings-Lov, og Bye-Lov, etc. oversatte med Anmœrk. 2 vols. sm. 4to. 7s   *Kiöb.* 1751-52
4020 RAHBEL og NYERUP, Den Danske Digtekunsts Middelalder, 2 vols. in 1, st. 12mo. *cloth*, 5s   *Kjöb.* 1805-8
4021 RASK's Danish Grammar, by Repp. 8vo. *second edition, sd.* 5s   *Cop.* 1846
4022 RESEN, Christians II. Danske Lov-Böger, sm. 4to. 𝕭lack letter, *blue morocco, gilt edges*, 12s   *Kiöb.* 1684
4023 SUHM, Samlinger til den Danske Historie, 6 vols. in 2, sm. 4to. *a collection by Suhm and Sandvig of miscellaneous and rare tracts on Danish History and Antiquities, hf. bd.* 21s   *Kjöb.* 1779-84
4024 UGELSPEGEL, Tiile, Underlig historie, 12mo. *rude cuts, bds.* 6s   *Kiöb.* 1786
4025 WEYLLE, Glossarium Juridicum Danico-Norvegicum, det er, Alle gamle Danske oc Norske Glosers rette Forklaring, st. sm. 4to. *hf. bd.* 6s; *calf,* 9s   *Kiöb.* 1652
4026 WIWET, Forsög til Fortoelning om moerkvoerdige Danske og Norske Sager, 2 vols. 12mo. *hf. calf,* 5s   *Kiöb.* 1774-75
4027 WOLFF, Dansk og Engelsk Ordbog: Danish-English Dictionary, 4to. 546 *pp. treb. cols. hf. bd.* 9s; *calf*, 12s   1779

4028 **Icelandic, Old Norse.** ASLAK BOLTS Jordebog, af Munch, 8vo. *in Icelandic, sd.* 4s   *Christ.* 1852
4029 BIÖRNER, Nordiska Kämpa Dater; continens Regum, etc. in Orbe Hyperboreo antiquo res gestas, folio, *comprising all the most important Northern Sagas, in Icelandic, Swedish, and Latin, four leaves wanting in Ragnar Lodbrok, calf gilt*, 20s   *Stockholm*, 1737
4030 CORPUS JURIS SUEO-GOTORUM Antiqui: Westgöta och Östgöta-Lagen, udgifven af Collin och Schlyter, 2 vols. 4to. *in the Old Norse, with introductions and notes, hf. calf,* 32s   *Stockholm*, 1827-30
4031 DIETRICHS Altnordisches Lesebuch, mit Grammatik und Glossar, 8vo. *hf. calf,* 5s   *Leipz.* 1843
4032 EDDA SAEMUNDAR hinns Froda; Edda Rhythmica seu antiquior, vulgo Saemundina dicta, Pars I, Odae Mythologicae, 1787; II, Odae Mythico-Historicae, 1818; III, Völuspa, Havamal, et Rigsmal, omnia *Island. et Latine*, cum notis et glossariis—together 3 vols. 4to. £5. 5s   *Hafniae*, 1787-1828
                  Priced, 1841, £6. 6s; 1848, £7.; 1849, £6. 6s.
4033 EDDA SAEMUNDI aliàs Woluspa, philosophia antiquissima Norvego-Danica, *Isl. et Lat.* cum notis, à Resenio, sq. 16mo. *vellum, rare,* 27s   *Haffn.* 1673
4034 EDDA SAEMUNDAR hinns Froda: carmina vetera Scaldorum, *Island.* à Rask, 1818—Altnordische Sagen und Lieder, *Island.* durch Hagen, *s. a.*—in 1 vol. 8vo. *hf. morocco*, 18s   1818
4035 EDDA, *Deutsch*, nebst Einleitung über Nord. Poesie, etc. von Rühs, 8vo. *calf gilt*, 5s 6d   *Berlin*, 1812
4036 EDDA de Saemund. Poëmes Islandais, Voluspa, Vafthrudnismal, Lokasenna, *Isl. et Franç.* avec Glossaire, par Bergmann, 8vo. *hf. calf*, 10s   *Paris*, 1838
EDDA Snorronis—*See* Snorro.
4037 EINARI, Sciagraphia Historiae literariae Islandicae autorum et scriptorum, 8vo. *bd. uncut*, 6s   *Havn.* 1777
4038 ERICI Regis Lex Siellandica: Sjellandske Lov, *Isl. og Dansk*, af Kolderup-Rosenvinge, 4to. *hf. calf*, 7s 6d   *Kiöb.* 1821
4039 FAEREYINGA SAGA eller Faeroeboernes Historie, af Rafn, impl. 8vo. *in Icelandic, Faeroëse, and Danish, with coloured facsimile, sd.* 10s; *calf gilt*, 12s   *Kjöb.* 1832
4040 FAGRSKINNA, Norsk Konge-Saga, af Munch og Unger, roy. 8vo. *text with notes, etc. cloth*, 5s   *Christiania*, 1847
4041 GOTHLAND. Guta-Lagh: der Insel Gothland altes Rechtsbuch, *Alt.-Nord. und Alt- und Neu-Deutsch*, von Schildener, 4to. *bds.* 6s   *Greifswald*, 1818
4042 GRÁGÁS, Codex Juris Islandorum antiquissimus, *Island. et Lat.* cum comment. Schlegelii, etc., ed. Monrad, Thorlacius, Werlauff, Müller, Finn Magnussen, 2 vols. 4to. *bds.* 30s   *Havniae*, 1829
4043 GUDMUNDI ANDREAE Lexicon Islandicum, sive linguae Gothicae Runae dictionarium, à Resenio, sm. 4to. *ports.* 270 *pp. doub. cols.* 12s   *Havn.* 1683

4044 GUNNLAUGI SAGA: Sagan af Gunnlaugi Ormstungu ok Skalld-Rafni, sive Gunnlaugi Vermilinguis et Rafnis Poetæ Vita *Island. et Lat.* cum notis et dissertationibus (de Lingua Islandica, etc.) 4to. FINE PAPER, *plates, hf. bd.* 15s; *calf gilt*, 18s *Hafniæ*, 1775
4045 —— the same, FINE PAPER, 1775—EGILS-SAGA, *Island. et Lat.* 1809—2 vols. in 1, sm. 4to. *plates, hf. morocco*, 22s *Hafniæ*, 1775-1809
4046 HERVARAR SAGA ok Heidrekskongs, *Island. et Lat.* cum notis, etc. ed Biörno et Suhm, sm. 4to. *hf. bd.* 9s *Hafniæ*, 1785
4047 —— the same, 1785—Viga-Glums Saga, *Isl. et Lat.* à Thorkelin—in 1 vol. sm. 4to. *hf. bd. uncut*, 16s *Hafn.* 1785-87
4048 HIRD-SKRAA, *gamle Norsk og Dansk*, med Forklaring, etc. af Dolmer og Hvitfild, sq. 8vo. *hf. bd. rare*, 10s *Kiöb.* 1666
4049 —— Jus Aulicum antiquum Norvagicum, cum Witherlags-Roett, *Island. Dan. et Lat.* à Resenio, sq. 8vo. 729 *pp. bds.* 7s 6d *Haff.* 1673
4050 HALDERSONII Lexicon Islandico-Latino-Danicum, curâ Raskii, cum præfatione P. E. Mulleri, 2 vols. in 1, sm. 4to. £2. 15s *Havniæ*, 1814
4051 ISLANDS LANDNAMABOK, hoc est liber Originum Islandiae, *Island. et Lat.* 4to. *russia gilt*, 21s *Havniae*, 1774
4052 JOHNSTONE, Antiquitates Celto-Scandicæ, ex Snorrone, etc. *Island. et Lat.*— Antiquitates Celto-Normannicæ, *Isl. et Lat.*; Chronicle of the Man and the Isles, 2 vols. in 1, 4to. *calf*, 16s *Havniæ*, 1786
4053 KARLAMAGNUS Saga ok Kappa Hans, *Norsk*, af Unger, roy. 8vo. *hf. calf neat, uncut*, 10s *Christiania*, 1860
4054 KONGS-SKUGG-SIO. Speculum Regale, *Islandice, Dan. et Lat.* edidit et notis illustravit Einersen, thick 4to. *calf*, 18s; or *hf. bd. uncut*, 21s *Sorõe*, 1768

Like most similar productions of the ancient Icelanders, this Chronicle carefully preserves the remembrance of every remarkable event that happened among their neighbours, the Norwegians, Danes, Swedes, Greenlanders, and others. Its peculiar value, however, consists in the very curious and circumstantial account which it gives of the STATE OF IRELAND IN THE ELEVENTH CENTURY—its Saints and their Miracles—and the manners and customs of the inhabitants.

4055 KONGE SPEILET et philosophisk-Didaktisk Skrift, *Islandisk*, 8vo. *cloth*, 5s 1848
4056 KORMAKS SAGA, *Island. et Lat.* ed Rask, Rafn, etc. *hf. calf*, 9s *Hfn.* 1832
4057 MAGNUS, Norregs Kongur, Lok-Bok Islendinga, 12mo. *hf. russ.* 7s 6d *Hool.* 1709
4058 MAGNUS Konongs Laga-Bæters Gula-Things-Laug; Jus Commune Norvegicum, *Island. Dan. et Lat.* 4to. *facsimiles, Fine Paper, hf. calf*, 18s *Havniæ*, 1817
4059 MILTON's Paradisar Missir, *islenzku*, Thorlakssyni, 8vo. *morocco back*, 8s 1828
4060 NIALS SAGA, *Latine*, cum Glossario, à Thorkelin, 1809—Sagan af Niali, *Island.* af Olavius, 1772—2 vols. in 1, sm. 4to. *hf. calf*, 24s *Havn.* 1772-1809
4061 NYERUP, over Nordens Aeldste Poesi, 12mo. *bds.* 2s *Kjöb.* 1798
4062 OLAF TRYGGVESÖNS Saga, *Island.* ved Munk, 8vo. *sd.* 4s *Christ.* 1853
4063 ORKNEYINGA SAGA, sive Historia Orcadensium, a prima Orcadum per Norvegos occupatione; SAGA HINS HELGA MAGNUSAR, *Island. et Lat.* ed. Jonæus, 4to. *calf, rare*, 27s *Hafniæ*, 1780
4064 RASK, Bejledning til det Islandske Sprog, 12mo. 3s *Kjöb.* 1811
4065 —— Anvisning till Isländskan Fornspraaket, 8vo. *hf. russ.* 7s 6d *Stockh.* 1818
4066 —— Grammar of the Icelandic or Old Norse Tongue, translated from the Swedish, by Dasent, 8vo. *hf. calf*, 16s 1843
4067 SNORRE STURLUSONS Heims-Kringla, Nordlänske Konunga Sagor, *Island. Dan. et Lat.*, ed. Peringskiöld, folio, *old red morocco gilt, stamped with the arms of Louis XIV*, 21s *Stockh.* 1697
4068 SNORRE STURLESON'S HEIMSKRINGLA; Historia Regum Norvegicorum, nova editio aucta, *Islandice, Danice et Latine*, opera G. Schöning, 6 vols. folio, *maps*, etc. *hf. bound, uncut*, £6. 6s *Hauniae*, 1777-1826
4069 —— THE HEIMSKRINGLA; or Chronicles of the Kings of Norway, translated from the Icelandic, with a preliminary dissertation, 3 vols. 8vo. (pub. at 36s) *cloth*, 14s 1844
4070 —— Yferborna Atlingars Edda, *Island. Suec. et Lat.* ed. Göransson, sm. 4to. *hf. bound*, 7s *Upsala*, (? 1780)
4071 —— Edda, samt Skalda, *Isländsk*, af Rask, och *Svensk*, 2 vols. in 1, 8vo. *bds.* 10s *Stockh.* 1818-19
4072 —— Saga Olafs Konungs ens Helga af Munch, 8vo. *facsimile*, 7s *Christ.* 1853

EUROPEAN PHILOLOGY. 213

4073 SVERRIS, Noregs Konungs, Saga, *Island. Dan. et Lat.* ediderunt Thorlacius et Werlauff, folio, FINE PAPER, *hf. bound*, 20s *Havniæ*, 1813
4074 THORLÄKSSONAR Islenzk Ljödabök, 2 vols. 12mo. *Poetical Translations from the English, German, Danish, and other languages, bds*. 18s *Kaupmannahöfn*, 1842-3
4075 TRAUTVETTER's Schlüssel zur Edda, 12mo. *hf. bd.* 5s *Berlin*, 1815
Bound up with "Hagen's Edda-Lieder und Irmin."
4076 VATNSDÆLA SAGA ok Saga af Finnboga, *Isl. ok Dan.* af Werlauff, *Kjöb.* 1812—CARL IX, och Gustaf Adolphs Chrönikor, *Stockh.* 1759, etc. in 1 vol. st. sm. 4to. 1350 pp. *hf. morocco*, 10s 1759-1812
"La Vatnsdaela- Saga nous présente une image vive et vraie des moeurs islandaises au Xe S."—DEPPING.
4077 VERELII Manuductio ad Runographiam Scandicam antiquam, *numerous curious woodcuts of Runic inscriptions*, 1653—Hervarar Saga, *Island. et Suec.* cum notis Verelii, *woodcuts*, 1672—in 1 vol. folio, *hf. bound*, 16s *Upsal.* 1672-75
Lord Walpole's copy, with an additional manuscript page on Runic Inscriptions.
4078 VERELIUS, Gothrici et Rolfi historia *Isl. et Suec.* 1664 — Monumenta lapidum Runicorum, 48 *woodcuts, page size*—in 1 vol. 12mo. *hf. bd.* 7s 6d *Upsal.* 1664
4079 WILKINA SAGA, sive Historia Wilkinensium, Theoderici Veronensis, ac Niflungorum; continens Regum atque Heroum quorundam Gothicorum Res gestas, per Russiam, Poloniam, Hungariam, Italiam, Burgundiam, Hispaniam, etc. *Islandice, Suecice, et Latine*, edidit J. Peringskiold, fol. *genealogical tables, hf. bound calf, rare*, £2. 2s *Stockh.* 1715
"Cet ouvrage, qui est très curieux, est rare hors du royaume de Suede.'—DU FRESNOY.

4080 **Swedish.** ATTERBOM, Svenska Siare och Skalder, 4 vols. sm. 8vo. *hf. bound*, 10s *Upsala*, 1841-47
4081 BJÖRNER, de Orthographia linguae Suiogothicâ, Runicâ et vulgari, sm. 4to. *sd.* 7s *Stockh.* 1742
4082 —— Svea Rikens Haevda Aelder, sm. 4to. *bds.* 5s *ib.* 1748
4083 BRUZELIUS, Sweriges Historia, sm. 8vo. *hf. bound*, 9s *Lund*, 1830
4084 DELEN'S English Swedish Dictionary; Engelskt och Suenskt Lexicon, 4to. *Stockholm*, 1806-7—WIDEGREN, Svenskt och Engelskt Lexicon; Swedish-English Lexicon, *Stockholm*, 1788—2 vols. 4to. *the two Alphabets complete, hf. calf*, £2. 10s 1788-1807
4085 EENBERG, Beskrifning om Upsala och des Antiquiteter, med Relation om sidste Branden, narrow 12mo. *calf*, 7s 6d *Upsala*, 1703-4
4086 HADORPHIUS, Twä GAMBLA SWENSKE RIJM KRÖNIKOR, then förre kort, och innehåller Sextijo twä Swea och Götha Konungar, 2 vols. in 1, stout sm. 4to. THICK PAPER, *beautiful copy, old calf, gilt edges*, RARE, £3. *Stockholm*, 1674-6
A rare volume, containing two Ancient Swedish Chronicles, the one in Rhyme, and the other in Prose.
4087 KELLGREN's samlade Skrifter, 3 vols. sm. 8vo. *Swedish Tragedies, etc. portrait, half calf*, 10s *Stockholm*, 1811
4088 KUNUNGA ok HÖFDINGDA Styrilse; Regum Principumque Institutio, *Suecicè et Lat.* a Scheffero, folio, *hf. vellum*, 12s *Holmiæ*, 1669
4089 —— the same, *Large Paper*, folio, *vellum*, 18s *ib.* 1669
4090 LIDEN, Historiola litteraria Poetarum Suecan., sq. 8vo. *bds.* 5s *Upsal.* 1764-65
4091 MAY's Swedish Grammar, 8vo. *hf. calf*, 6s *Stockh.* 1854
4092 SERENIUS' English-Swedish Dictionary, *second edition, with additions*, 4to. *calf*, 7s 6d *Nykoping*, 1757
4093 SPEGEL, Glossarium Suio-gothicum, eller Swensk-Ordabok, sm. 4to. *with English, French, Danish, Latin, German, Dutch, Italian and Anglo-Saxon equivalents, calf gilt*, 16s *Lund.* 1712
4094 STAGNELII samlade Skrifter, af Hammarsköld, 3 vols. 8vo. *hf. calf*, 10s *Stock.* 1830
4095 SVENSKA FOLK-SAGOR och Safventyr, Vol. I.—Samlingar utgifna af Svenska Fornskrift-Sällskapet, Vol. I. pt. II.; Vol. II. parts 1-4; Vol. III. parts 1 and 3; Vol. IV. parts, 1, 2, 3, and 5; Vol. V. parts 1 and 2; Vol. VI. part 1—together 17 pts. 8vo. *the lot*, 18s *Stockholm*, 1844-48
4096 SVENSKA FOLK-WISOR utgifne af Geijer och Afzelius, 3 vols. sm. 8vo. *no music, hf. red morocco, uncut*, 18s *Stockholm*, 1814
4097 SVERIKES RIKES LAGH-BÖKER: Landz, Stadz, Vplandz, Wästgötha, Oestgötha, Söderman, Wästmanna, och Helsing-Lagh, 10 vols. in 1, st. folio, *original calf, clasps, very rare*, 25s *Stockholm*, 1663-66

4098 TEGNER's Frithiof's Saga, 8vo. *in Swedish, plates, hf. calf*, 7s 6d   *Stock.* 1831
4099 WARMHOLTZ, Bibliotheca Historica Sueo-Gothica, 2 vols. in 1, 8vo. *a valuable Bibliography in Swedish, of works upon Sweden, hf. bd.* 12s   *Stockholm,* 1782
4100 WESTE, DICTIONNAIRE SUÉDOIS-Francois et François-Suédois, 4 vols. 8vo. *hf. bd.* £2. 10s   *Stockholm,* 1795-1807
4101 —— Dictionnaire Suédois-francois; being the most useful part separately, 2 vols. 8vo. *hf. bd.* 30s   1807
The best Swedish Dictionary.

ROMANCE LANGUAGES.
Patois of France, and Poetry of the Troubadours.

The " Italian Dialects" will follow the Italian Books, the " Spanish Dialects," Catalan, Limousin, etc. the Spanish Books.

4102 SISMONDI, de la Littérature du Midi de l'Europe, 4 vols. 8vo. *bd.* 10s *Paris,* 1813
4103 ANCIENS (LES) POETES DE LA FRANCE, publiés sous les auspices du Ministre de l'Instruction publique, et par Guessard. etc.: Doon de Mayence; Gaufrey; Fierabras; Parise la Duchesse; Huon de Bordeaux; Aye d'Avignon; Gui de Nanteuil; Gaydon, 6 vols. stout 12mo. *cloth,* 21s   *Paris, typ. Elz.* 1859
4104 ANCIEN THEATRE FRANCOIS; ou Ouvrages Dramatiques, les plus remarquables depuis les Mystères jusqu'a Corneille, publié par Viollet le Duc, avec Glossaire, 10 vols. 12mo. *whole blue morocco, edges uncut, top edges gilt,* £5. 10s   *Paris, typ. Elzev. chez P. Jannet,* 1854
4105 BASSELIN (Olivier) Vaux-de-Vire, suivis d'anciennes Poésies Normandes, etc. avec des notes par Du Bois, 8vo. *calf extra,* 9s   *Caen,* 1821
4106 BERONIE, Dictionnaire du Patois du Bas-Limousin, 4to. *hf. bd.* 6s *Tulle,* (? 1825)
4107 BRUCE-WHYTE, Histoire des Langues Romanes et de leur littérature jusqu'au XIV siècle, 3 vols. roy. 8vo. *hf. calf,* 28s   *Paris,* 1841
A work of great learning, with extracts and translations, etc.
4108 BRUNET, Notice de quelques ouvrages en Patois du Midi, 12mo. 4s 6d   1840
4109 CHANSON D'ANTIOCHE, composée au XII Siècle par le Pelerin Richard; renouvellée sous Philippe Auguste, par Graindor de Douay, publiée pour la première fois par Paulin Paris, 2 vols. 8vo. *sd.*12s ; *or, blue morocco, gilt edges,* 24s   *Paris,* 1848
4110 CHARLEMAGNE, an Anglo-Norman Poem of the 12th century, now first published with glossarial Index by Michel, 12mo. *cold. facsimile, hf. bd uncut,* 6s   1836
4111 CHRONIQUES Anglo-Normandes, par Michel, Vol. I. 8vo. *hf. mor.* 6s *Douen,* 1836
4112 DE LA RUE (Abbé) Essais Historiques sur les Bardes, les Jongleurs et les Trouveres, Normands et Anglo-Normands, 3 vols. 8vo. *hf. calf gilt,* 24s   *Caen,* 1834
4113 DICTIONNAIRE de la Provence, et du Comté-Venaissin, 2 vols. 4to. *old calf gilt,* 18s   *Marseille,* 1785
4114 DICTIONNAIRE Rouchi-Français, 18mo. *hf. morocco, uncut,* 5s *Valenciennes,* 1826
4115 DIEZ, Grammatik der Romanischen Sprache, 3 vols. 8vo. *the best Grammar of the Romance Language, sd.* 21s   *Bonn,* 1856-60
4116 —— Etymologisches Wörterbuch der Romanischen Sprachen, vermehrte Ausgabe, 2 vols. *including all the Romance languages,* 8vo. *sd.* 13s 6d *Bonn,* 1861-62
4117 **Documents inedits**: BENOIT, (Siecle XII.) Chroniques des Ducs de Normandie, avec Glossaire, par Michel, 3 vols. 4to. *cloth,* 30s   *Paris,* 1836-44
4118 DINAUX, les Trouvères Brabançons, Hainuyers, Liégeois, et Namurois, large 8vo. 40 and 717 pp. *sd.* 8s 6d   *Brux.* 1863
4119 DOCTRINA PLACITANDI, ou l'Art de Bon Pleading, sm. 4to. *Norman-English Law language, calf,* 7s 6d   1677
4120 DYER (Jacques, Chief Justice) Reports des divers matters touchant mults points en le Reynes de Hen. 8, Edw. 6, Mar. et Eliz. folio, 10s   1688
4121 EUSTACHE LE MOINE, Roman de, publié par Michel, roy. 8vo. *facsimile, hf. morocco, only* 110 *copies printed,* 7s 6d   *Par.* 1834
4122 FIERABRAS, Roman von, *Provenzalisch,* von Bekker, 4to. *hf. bd.* 8s *Berlin,* 1829

EUROPEAN PHILOLOGY. 215

4123 (Francois) Dictionnaire Roman, Walon, Celtique et Tudesque, par un Bénédictin de Vannes, 4to. LARGE PAPER, *calf gilt*, 18*s* *Bouillon*, 1777
4124 ——— Vocabulaire Austrasien, 8vo. *hf. russ.* 4*s* *Metz*, 1773
4125 Froissart, le premier livre des Chroniques, texte inédit, par Kervyn de Lettenhove, roy. 8vo. *sd.* 6*s* *Brux.* 1863
4126 Gascounades (las) Poesies Patoises, 12mo. 101 *pp. sd.* 3*s* *Dax, ca.* 1846
4127 Goudelin, las Obros, e Diccionnari Moundino-Franç. 12mo. *calf,* 5*s* 1700
4128 Guernsey. Rimes Guernesiaises par un Catelan, 8vo. *cloth,* 10*s* *ca.* 1850
4129 Guillaume d'Orange, chansons de Geste, des XIe et XII. siècles, publié par Jonckbloet, 2 vols. 8vo. *sd.* 18*s* 1854
4130 Hécart, Dictionnaire Rouchi-Français, 8vo. 496 *pp. hf. calf,* 12*s* *Valenc.* 1834
4131 HONNORAT, Dictionnaire Provençal-Francais, ou Dictionnaire de la Langue d'Oc, Ancienne et Moderne, contenant pres de 100,000 mots, suivi d'un Vocabulaire Français-Provençal, 4 vols. 4to. *hf. morocco,* £2. 10*sDigne,* 1846-48
4132 HORN et RIMENHILD, Recueil des Poëmes relatifs a leurs Aventures, en François, en Anglois ou en Ecossois, XIII—XVI Siècles, publié par Michel, 4to. *facsimiles, cloth,* 25*s* *Par.* 1845
Privately printed for the members of the Bannatyne Club.
4133 JASMIN, las Pappillotos, 3 vols. 8vo. *the Poems of this celebrated Coiffeur-Poet, French and Provençal, portrait, calf extra, gilt edges,* £2. 12*s* 6*d Agen,* 1842-51
4134 Jubinal, Lettres à Salvandy, sur quelques MS. de la Bibli. de la Haye, large 8vo. *sd.* 5*s* 1846
4135 ——— Mystères Inédits du XV siècle, publiés pour la première fois, 2 vols. 8vo. *facsimile, hf. calf,* 12*s* *Paris,* 1837
4136 LA FONTAINE, Fables causidos, 8vo. *in Gascon with a Dictionary, portrait, old calf gilt,* 7*s* 6*d* *Bayonne,* 1776
4137 Lewis (Sir G. C.) on the Origin and Formation of the Romance Languages, 8vo. *cloth,* 7*s* 6*d* *Oxford,* 1835
4138 LORRIS ET MEUNG, ROMMANT DE LA ROSE, nouvellement reveu et corrigé oultre les precedentes impressions, 12mo. 𝔤𝔬𝔱𝔥𝔦𝔠 𝔩𝔢𝔱𝔱𝔢𝔯, *woodcuts, old calf,* £4. *Paris,* 1538
Priced, 1829, £4. 4*s*; recently, £6. 6*s*; fetched, 1860, £4. 4*s*: Dr. Hawtrey's copy, £4. 14*s* 6*d*
A very rare and highly esteemed edition of this celebrated poetical romance.
4139 ——— the same, 3 vols. 12mo. *Vol.* 1 *wanting title, calf,* 5*s* *Paris,* 1735
4140 Miral Moundi, 12mo. *avec poems with Dictionary, calf,* 4*s* 6*d* *Toulouso,* 1801
4141 Marie de France, (Poëte du XIII Siècle) Poésies de, publiées par Roquefort, 2 vols. 8vo. *sd.* 7*s* 6*d* *Paris,* 1819
4142 Oberlin, sur le Patois Lorrain du Ban de la Roche, fief d'Alsace, avec une Grammaire et un Glossaire, 12mo. *bds.* 7*s* *Stras.* 1775
4143 Olivet (Fabre d'), le Troubadour, Poésies Occitaniques du XIII Siècle, traduites, 2 vols. 8vo. *calf,* 7*s* 6*d* *Paris,* 1804
4144 Paris (Paulin) le Romancero Français, sm. 8vo. *bds.* 7*s* 6*d* *Paris,* 1833
4145 Parnasse Occitanien, choix de poesies des Troubadours, (par Rochegude)— (Rochegude) Essai d'un Glossaire Occitanien—2 vols. 8vo. *blue calf extra, gilt edges,* 7*s* 6*d* *Toulouse,* 1819
4146 RAYNOUARD, Choix des Poésies originales des Troubadours, contenant une Grammaire Romane, Dissertation sur les Cours d'Amour, Poésies, Biographies des Troubadours, et la Grammaire comparée des Langues de l'Europe Latine, dans leurs rapports avec la Langue des Troubadours, 6 vols. 8vo. *calf gilt, fine copy, scarce,* £8. 8*s* *Paris,* 1816-21
Contents:—Vol. 1. Grammaire Romane—II. Sur les Troubabours; les Cours d'Amour; Monuments de la Langue Romane avant ces Poètes—III. Piéces Amoureuses, 1090-1260—IV. Tensons, Complaintes, sur les Croisades, Sirventes—V. Biographie des Troubadours—VI. Grammaire comparée des Langues de l'Europe Latine, dans leur rapports avec la Langue des Troubadours. Copies on Papier Vélin were priced, 1845, Bossange, mor. £12. 12*s*; 1849, mor. £14. 14*s*.
4147 Raynouard, Grammaire Romane, ou Grammaire de la langue des Troubadours, 851 *pp. sd. rare,* 16*s; calf,* 20*s* *Paris,* 1816
This work must not be confounded with the following.
4148 ——— Grammaire comparee des langues de l'Europe Latine, 1821—Schlegel sur la Langue et la Littérature Provençales, *scarce,* 1818—2 vols. in 1, 8vo. *hf. calf,* 12*s* *Paris,* 1818-21

4149 RAYNOUARD, Lexique Roman, ou Dictionnaire de la Langue des Troubadours, comparée avec les autres Langues de l'Europe Latine, précédé de nouvelles Recherches historiques et philologiques, d'un Resumé de la Grammaire Romane et d'un Nouveau Choix des Poésies originales des Troubadours, 6 vols. 8vo. (pub. at £5. 5s sd.) *half morocco, uncut*, £4. *Par.* 1838-44

"Les travaux de Mr. Raynouard sont destinés à remplir une grande lacune dans l'histoire littéraire du moyen age. L'érudition de Mr. R. est aussi étendue que solide; mais ce qui est bien plus admirable encore, c'est la critique lumineuse, la methode vraiment philosophique qu'il apporte dans toutes ses recherches."—Schlegel.

4150 ROMAN de Mahomet, et livre de la Loi au Sarrazin—Roman du Comte de Poitiers—Lais d' Ignaurès, et du Trot—par Reinaud et Michel, et autres, 8vo. 3 vols. in 1, *illuminated facsimiles, hf. bd.* 14s; or, *calf gilt*, 17s 6d *Par.* 1831-32

4151 ROMAN DE LA VIOLETTE ou de Gerard de Nevers, en Vers du XIII Siècle, par Gibert de Montreuil, publié pour la première fois par F. Michel, 8vo. *several facsimiles, a double set, plain and coloured some illuminated, citron morocco extra, the back inlaid with pieces of cold. leather, gilt edges*, £4. 10s 1834
Only 250 copies printed.

4152 ROMANS DES DOUZE PAIRS DE FRANCE: — ROMANS de Parise la Duchesse, publié par Martonne, 8vo. *bds.* 7s 6d; or, *hf. morocco*, 9s 1836

4153 ROMANS de Raoul de Cambrai et de Bernier, publié par Le Glay, 8vo. *half morocco, uncut*, 9s 1840

4154 ROMAN DU RENART, publié d'après les MSS. de la Bibliothèque du Roi des XIIIe, XIVe, et XVe siècles, par Méon, etc. 4 vols. 1826—Suppléments, variantes, et corrections, publié d'après les manuscrits de la Bibliothèque du roi et de la Bibliothèque de l'Arsenal, par Chabaille, 1 vol. 1835—together 5 vols. roy. 8vo. LARGE VELLUM PAPER, WITH PROOF PLATES *before the numbers and etchings, hf. morocco gilt*, £4. 10s *Paris*, 1826-32

The best edition of this extraordinary Mediæval Romance in "Old French." The fourth volume contains "Renard le Nouvel" with Musical accompaniments.

4155 RENARD, les Romans du, analysés par Bothe, 8vo. *hf. russia gilt*, 12s *Paris*, 1845
4156 ROQUEFORT, Glossaire de la langue Romane, avec le Supplément, et des dissertations, 3 vols. 8vo. *frontispiece and facsimile, calf gilt*, £2. 16s *Paris*, 1808-20
4157 SAINT-SURIN, l'Hotel de Cluny au moyen-age, et autres poésies, 8vo. 6s 1835
4158 S(AUVAGE), Dictionnaire Languedocien-François, avec un recueil de Proverbes et de dictons Languedociens et Provençaux, 2 vols. 8vo. *calf neat*, 16s; or 1 vol. *calf extra, gilt edges*, 20s *Nismes*, 1785
4159 SERVENTOIS et Sottes Chansons, *Poems of the XIII-XIV. Centuries, with Glossary, few copies printed, hf. morocco*, 10s *Valenciennes*, 1833
4160 TRISTAN, recueil des Poëmes relatifs à ses aventures composés *en François, et Anglo-Normand, et en Grec*, dans les XII et XIII siècles, publié par Michel, 3 vols. 12mo. (pub. at £2.) *cloth*, 28s 1835-39
4161 WACE, le Roman de Rou et des Ducs de Normandie, publié pour la première fois d'après les manuscrits, par Pluquet, 2 vols. *facsimiles, sd.* 28s; or, *hf. calf*, 32s *Rouen*, 1824
4162 —— Roman de Brut, avec commentaire, glossaire, etc. par Le Roux de Lincy, 2 vols. 8vo. *facsimiles, cloth*, 18s; or, *hf. calf, uniform with the Roman de Rou*, 24s *Rouen*, 1836-38
4163 —— Description des MSS. 2 parts, 8vo. *facsim. being the introductory dissertation, sd.* 2s 1836
4164 PLUQUET, Notice sur la Vie et les Ecrits de Wace, impl. 8vo. 3s *Rouen*, 1824
4165 **Romansch.** Carisch, Grammatische Formenlehre der Deutschen und Rhäto-romanischen Sprache, 8vo. *sd.* 3s 6d *Chur.* 1852
4166 Cipariu, Gramateca limbei Romane, 8vo. *sd.* 3s 6d *Blasiu*, 1855
4167 Conradi, Deutsch-Romanische Grammatik, 8vo. *with Vocabularies, extracts, in both dialects*, etc. *bds.* 5s *Zurich*, 1820
4168 **Wallachian.** Blazewicz, Grammatik der Dacoromanischen Sprache, 8vo. *bds.* 5s *Lemberg*, 1844
4169 Iszer, Walachisch-Deutsches Wörterbuch, 8vo. *hf. calf*, 7s 6d *Kronstadt*, 1850
4170 Stanley (Hon. H.) Rouman-Anthology, being a collection of the National Ballads of Moldavia and Wallachia, with translations, 8vo. *morocco extra, gilt edges*, 15s *Hertford*, 1856

4171 **ROMAIC, or Modern Greek.** Agglikē Gram. sm. 8vo. *cloth*, 3s 6d   1839
4172 BUZANTIOU (Skarl. D.) Lexicon Ellénikon-Gallikon kai Gallikon-Ellenikon, 2 vols. in 1, imp. 8vo. 394 and 239 pp. *treble cols. bds*. 20s   *Athénésin*, 1846
4173 CORPE'S Introduction to Neo-Hellenic or Modern Greek; containing a Guide to its Pronunciation and an Epitome of its Grammar, 12mo. vi and 152 pp. with an Appendix of 24 pp. *cloth*, 5s   *Printed for the Author*, 1851
"The (increasing commerce of Greece, and the probability that a new and valuable literature will shortly adorn the land of Eschylus and Thucydides, render a book like the present particularly acceptable. It is concise, clear, and satisfactory."—*Westminster Review*.

4174 DAVID, Parallélismos tés Ellén. kai Graik. Glóssés, 8vo. *hf. bd*. 3s 6d   1820
4175 ―― Modern Greek Grammar, by Winnock, 8vo. 5s   1825
4176 ELLĒNISMOS, tomos prōtos: Grammatikē, 8vo. 750 pp. a Grammar of *Classical Greek, hf. vellum*, 7s   *Leipsiai*, 1835
4177 EGCHEIRIDION Gallograikikon: Guide de conversation, 12mo. *hf. cf*. 3s 6d   1832
4178 FAURIEL (C.) Chants populaires de la Grèce moderne, en vers *grecs* et prose *française*, avec des notes, 2 vols. 8vo. *hf. calf neat*, £2.   *Paris*, 1824-25
The first volume is *very rare*, the second can easily be procured.
4179 ―― the same, wanting title to Vol. I. 2 vols. *hf. calf*, 28s   1824-25
4180 FONTENELLE. Omiliai peri Plēthuos Kosmōn, para Kodrikā, stout 8vo. *calf*, 7s 6d   *Vienné*, 1794
4181 KOMAS, Hellêno-Rōssiko-Gallikon Lexikon, 2 vols. in 1, 4to. 548 pp. *double cols. hf. calf*, 16s   *Moscha*, 1811
4182 KŌNSTANTINOS, peri tēs Suggeneias tēs Slavono-Rossikēs Glossēs pros tēn Ellēnikēn, 3 vols. 8vo. *on the affinity of the Sclavonic and Hellenic, in Greek and Russian, sd*. 12s   *Petroupolei*, 1828
4183 KOUMA, Lexikon dia tous meletôntas ta ton palaiôn Ellênôn suggrammata, kata to Ellênogermanikon tou Reimerou, 2 vols. 4to. *fine copy, in russia extra, gilt edges*, £2. 16s   *Vienné*, 1827
4184 LOWNDES'S Modern Greek-English and English-Modern-Greek Dictionary, 2 vols. 8vo. *hf. morocco*, £3. 15s   *Corfu*, 1827-37
4185 ―― English-Modern-Greek Lexicon, 8vo. *being the rare volume, the bottom part of a few leaves injured by a nail, bds.*; or, another copy, *title inlaid, hf. calf*, 30s   *Corfu*, 1827
4186 MACRI'S Modern Greek Interpreter, being Dialogues in Modern Greek, English and Italian; prefixed is a Grammar of the Modern Greek Language, sq. 16mo. *hf. bd*. 2s   *Corfu*, 1825
An indispensable volume for travellers in the Levant, Ionian Islands, Turkey, Greece, etc.
4187 MARCELLUS, Chants du peuple en Grèce, *Grec et Français, hf. cf*. 15s   *Par*. 1851
4188 PANDŌRA, suggramma periodikon, suntaktai Ragkavēs, Papparregopoulos, etc. Vols. I., II., 4to. a fortnightly literary periodical, from April 1850, to April 1852, *calf extra, gilt edges*, 12s   *Athenais*, 1850-52
4189 POLYMERÈ Lexicon Anglo Ellēnikon, 8vo. *hf. calf*, 12s   *Ermoupolei*, 1854
4190 RAGGOU-VANSA, kai GITA, metaphr. ek ton Brachman. para Galanou, kai Tupadou, 2 vols. in. 1, 8vo. *present. copy to Prof. Wilson, calf*, 15s   *Ath*. 1850-48
4191 ROBERTSON'S Modern Greek Grammar, with Extracts, 12mo. *calf*, 4s   1818
4192 SHERIDAN'S Songs of Greece, in English verse, 8vo. *hf. calf*, 7s 6d.   1825
4193 STAGEIRITOU Ogugia, ē Archaiologia, periechousa ton archaiotatōn Ethnōn ten Istorian, etc. 5 vols. sm. 8vo. *calf gilt*, 27s   *Vienne*, 1815-20
4194 SOPHOCLES, Romaic or Modern Greek Grammar, sm. 8vo. *hf. bd*. 7s 6d   1858
4195 THEOCHAROPOULOS, Grammaire Grecque universelle, ancienne et moderne, part 1: Lexicologie, 8vo. *sd*. 5s   *Paris*, 1830
4196 ―― Dialogues, etc. *French, English, and Greek*, 12mo. *calf gilt*, 4s 6d   1828
4197 THOMA, Methode de la langue Grecque-Vulgaire, sm. 8vo. *Greek, French, Latin, and Italian, calf*, 4s   *Paris*, 1709
4198 TRIKOUPE (Spuridōnos) Istoria tēs Ellēnikēs Epanastaseôs: History of the Hellenic Revolution, 1821-26, 4 vols. 8vo. (pub. at £2. 8s) *sd*.£2. *Londinō*,1853-7-6
4199 XENOU, Erôis tes Ellenikēs Epanastaseôs, Skenai en Elladi, 1821-28, 2 vols. 8vo. *cloth*, 10s   *Londinô*, 1861

SARMATIAN LANGUAGES.

Comprising, I. Lithuanian and Lettish; and II. the Sclavonic Languages, viz. Bohemian, Croatian, Illyrian, Polish, Russian, Slovenish, and Wendish.

4200 DOBROWSKY, Slovanka: zur Kenntniss der alten und neuen Slaw. Literatur, der Sprachkunde nach allen Mundarten, 8vo. *hf. bd. 9s*   *Prag.* 1814
4201 KOHLII Introductio in historiam et rem literariam Slavorum, 12mo. *bd. 7s*   1729
4202 RADIUS, Languages of the Slavonic nations, 12mo. *cloth, 2s 6d*   1853
4203 SCHAFARICK's Slawische Alterthümer, von Aehrenfeld und Wuttke, 2 vols. 8vo. *hf. calf,* 14s   *Leips.* 1843-44
4204 **Bohemian.** CEBUSKY, Böhmische Grammatik, 8vo. 3s 6d   *Wien,* 1854
4205 DOBROWSKY, Geschichte der Böhmischen Sprache, 8vo. *facsim. 5s Prag.* 1818
4206 JUNGMANN, Slownjk Cesko-Nemecky, *Bohemian-Latin-German Dictionary,* COMPLETE, A-Z, 5 vols. 4to. *neatly hf. bd. rare,* £5. 5s   *Praze,* 1835-39
     This is the great Bohemian Dictionary published by the Royal Academy of Prague.
4207 KNJZKA: Büchlein in Behmisch und Deutsch, wie ein Behem Deutsch und ein Deutscher Behemisch lesen etc. lernen soll, 12mo. *vell.* 12s   *Prag.* 1595
4208 RESCHELII (T.) Dictionarium Latino-Bohemicum, stout sm. 4to. *fine copy in the original stamped pigskin, very scarce,* 24s   *Olomucii,* 1560
4209 **Croatian.** RELKOVICH, Slavonisch- und Deutsche Grammatik, mit Wörterbuch etc. 12mo. *calf,* 9s   *Agram,* 1767
4210 **Illyrian.** DELLA BELLA (Ardelio) Dizionario Italiano-Latino-Illirico, con Gramatica etc. 2 vols. in 1, sm. 4to. *hf. bd.* 18s   *Ragusa,* 1785
4211 STULLI Lexicon Latino-Italico-Illyricum, ditissimum ac locupletissimum, cum Proverbiis, etc. 2 vols. 4to. *Budae,* 1801—Lexicon Illyrico-Italico-Latinum, *Ragusae,* 1806, 2 vols.—together 4 vols. *hf. calf, rare,* £5.   1801-6
4212 —— Lexicon Latino-Illiricum, 2 vols. 4to. *hf. russia,* 16s   *Budae,* 1801-6
4213 VOLTIGGI, Ricsoslovnik (Wörterbuch) Illiricskoga, Italianskoga i Nimacskoga, stout 8vo. *Illyrian-Italian-German, hf. morocco,* 12s   *U. Becsu (Vienna),* 1802
4214 **Lithuanian.** MIELCKE, Littauisch-Deutsches und Deutsch-Littauisches Wörterbuch, mit Spruchwörtern, etc. vermehret, 2 vols. in 1, stout 12mo. *Fine Paper, hf. calf,* 20s   *Königsberg,* 1800
Lusatian.—See Wendish.
4215 **Polish.** BANDTKE's Slownik dokladny: Polnisch-Deutsches Wörterbuch, stout 8vo. 1032 pp. *Bresl.* 1806—Moszczenski, Deutsches und Polnisches Wörterbuch, 8vo. *Leipzig,* 1791—together 2 vols. 8vo. *hf. bd.* 15s   1791-1806
4216 CNAPII (Gregorii) Thesaurus Polono-Latino-Græcus; Polonorum, Roxolanorum, Sclavonum, Boëmorum usui accommodatum, 3 vols. in 1, thick folio, *old calf, rare,* 21s   *Cracoviæ,* 1643
4217 —— Synonyma seu Dictionarium Polono-Latinum, 12mo. *citron morocco, gilt edges,* 30s   *Calissii,* 1698
     Lord Rothesay's copy fetched, 1855, £2. 5s.
4218 JORDAN, Polnisch-Deutsches und Deutsch-Poln. Wörterbuch, 16mo. *bd.* 3s 6d
4220 MRONGOVIUS, Polnisch-Deutsches und Deutsch-Polnisches Wörterbuch, 2 vols. 4to. 1430 pp. *double cols. hf. calf,* 25s   *Königsberg,* 1835-37
4221 POHL, Polnische Grammatik, 8vo. 3s   *Breslau,* 1849
4222 SCHMIDT, Dictionnaire Polonais-Franç. et Franç- Polonais, 16mo. *bd.* 3s 6d
4223 **Russian.** BACMEISTER's Russische Bibliothek zur Kenntniss des gegenwärt. Zustandes der Literatur in Russland, 11 vols. 12mo. *calf,* 32s   *St. Pet.* 1772-86
4224 FENELON, Contes et Fables, *Russe et Franç.* 12mo. *hf. bd.* 5s   1815
4225 GRAMMATIN'S English and Russian Dictionary, 2 vols. in 1, 4to. *hf. bd. rare,* 30s   *Moscow,* 1808
4226 HEARD's Practical Grammar of the Russian Language, with the Key, 12mo. *half calf,* 7s   *St. Petersb.* 1827
4227 —— Russian Grammar and Key, 1827—Vater, Grammaire Polonaise, *Halle,* 1807—3 vols. in 1, 12mo. *calf,* 10s   1807-27
4228 HEYM, Dictionnaire portatif Russe-Française et Allemand, 4 vols. 16mo. *the 3 Alphabets complete, calf neat,* 12s   *Riga,* 1804-5
4229 —— GEIMOFF Rossiisko- Phrantzuzsko-Niemetskii Slovar, vo Sviatneim: Heym's Russian-French-German Dictionary, new edition, stout sq. 12mo. *half calf,* 10s   *Leipzig,* 1835

4230 KARAMSIN, Istoriya Gosudarstva Rossiiskago: History of the Russian Empire, 12 vols. 8vo. *volume 6 wanting, hf. bd. 20s* *Santkpeterburg*, 1830-31
4231 —— the same, complete, 12 vols. 8vo. *sd. £2. 15s* *ib.* 1833
4232 KOVALEVSKI, Buddiiska Kosmologia, 8vo. *5s* *Kazan*, 1837
4233 PUSHKAREFF, Putevolitel po Sanktpeterburg, 8vo. *sd. 5s* 1843
4234 REIFF'S PARALLEL DICTIONARIES of Russian, French, German and English, with Grammars, 4 vols. sq. 12mo. *four Alphabets, sd. 36s Karlsru, etc.* 1860-62
4235 —— Grammaire Russe, 8vo. *hf. bd. 5s* *St. Petersb.* 1821
4236 —— la meme, nouvelle édition, 8vo. *sd. 6s* 1851
4237 SCHMIDT's Russisch - Deutsches und Deutsch-Russisches Wörterbuch, 2 stout vols. sq. 16mo. 1912 pp. *double cols. hf. calf*, 10s *Moskwa*, 1839
4238 SCHTANOFF, English-Russian Dictionary, stout sm. 8vo. *bd.* 10s *Sanktpeterb.* 1784
4239 SVININA, Kartinei Rossii, izdannei Delacroa, sm. 4to. *numerous plates of scenery, costume etc.* 10s *Riga*, 1840
4240 TATISTCHEW, Dictionnaire complet François-Russe, *seconde édition*, impl. 4to. *hf. bd.* 20s *Moscow*, 1827
4241 —— seconde edition, 2 stout vols. 8vo. *bd.* 10s *St. Petersb.* 1798
4242 **Servian.** SWÖTLIKA, Vocabularium Latino-Serbicum, 12mo. *bd.* 10s *Buda*, 1721
4243 **Slovenish (Modern).** BERNOLAK Schlowakische Grammatik, 8vo. *4s Ofen*, 1817
4244 (KOPITAR) Grammatik der Slav. Sprache in Krain, etc. 12mo. *bds. 5s Laib.* 1800
Pp. 385-460 comprise a valuable Bibliography of Early Slavonic publications.
4245 MURKO's Slowenisch-Deutsches und Deutsch-Slowenisches Wörterbuch, 2 vols. sm. 8vo. *calf*, 15s *Grätz*, 1833
4246 —— Slowenische Sprachlehre, 8vo. *hf. calf*, 4s *ib.* 1832
The Slovenish Dialect is spoken in Styria, Carinthia, Carniolia, and the Western Districts of Hungary.
4247 **Slavonic (Old) The Church Language:** DOBROWSKI, Institutiones Linguæ Slavicae dialecti veteris, 8vo. *calf gilt*, 15s *Vindob.* 1822
4247*BOUKVAR YAZEIKA: a Slavonic Primer, 12mo. *stated by a MS. note to be the earliest printed book in the language, wanting apparently the last leaf, bds.* 10s 1636
4248 BREVIARIUM ROMANUM Slavonico Idiomate jussu Innocentii XI editum, thick sm. 4to. *very rare, vellum*, £2. 2s *Romæ*, 1688
Printed in the characters commonly called "SAINT JEROME," with the Rubrics in red. This copy belonged to Cardinal Albani, and has the impression of his signet on title-page.
4249 LITURGY, in the Old Church language, 12mo. *woodcuts, original binding stamped with figures in gold, edges gilt and gauffré*, 18s *ca.* 1745
4250 SLOVAR Tserkovno-Slavyenskago i Russkago Yazeika, Imperator. Akadem., 4 vols. in 2, stout roy. 4to. *a Dictionary of the Church Slavonic explained in Russian, hf. bound*, 36s *Sanktpeter*, 1847
4251 **Wendish.** GUTSMAN, Deutsch-Windisches Wörterbuch, 4to. *bds.* 12s. 1789
4252 SCHMIGOZ, Windische Sprachlehre, 8vo. *bds.* 7s *Grätz*, 1812
4253 SCHNEIDER's Wendische Grammatik, Kathol. Dialect. 8vo. *5s Budissin*, 1853

UGRIAN LANGUAGES.

Comprising Hungarian, Finnish, Lapponic, etc.

4255 **Hungarian.** BASFI und BENKÖ, Nationallieder der Magyaren, *German*, 12mo. *half calf*, 5s 1852
4256 BEREGSZASZI Aehnlichkeit der Hungarischen Sprache mit den Morgenländischen, 4to. 216 pp. *bds. rare*, 20s *Leipzig*, 1796
A rare work, shewing the affinity of the Hungarian, Bohemian, Albanian, Gipsy, and European languages, with the Hebrew, Arabic, Persian, Hindustani, Calmuc, and Tartar.
4257 BLOCH, Ungarische Grammatik, 8vo. *bds.* 3s 6d *Pesth*, 1842
4258 CSINK's Grammar of the Hungarian Language, with exercises, Selections and Vocabularies, a Historical sketch of Hungarian Literature, etc. stout 12mo. *nearly* 600 pp. *cloth*, 5s 1853
4259 DANKOVSZKY, Lexicon Magyaricon (Magyaro-Latino-Germanicum) critico-etymologicum, stout 8vo. 1000 pp. *hf. calf*, 20s *Presburg*, 1833
4260 KALMAR, Prodromus Idiomatis Scythico-Mogorico-Chuno- (seu Hunno-) Avarici, 8vo. *calf*, 7s *Posonii*, 1770

4261 SARTORIUS, Magyar Lelki Ora (Spirituale Horologium) tall 12mo. *original binding*, 10s *Vitemb.* 1730
4262 WEKEY's Hungarian Grammar, 12mo. *cloth*, 3s 6d 1852
4263 **Finnish.** EUREN, Finsk Spraaklära, sm. 8vo. *hf. morocco*, 7s *Abo*, 1849
4264 IDMAN (Nils) Recherches sur l'Ancien Peuple Finois, traduit par Gênet, 12mo. FINE PAPER, *calf gilt*, 7s 6d *Strasbourg*, 1778
4265 JUSLENII Fennici Lexici tentamen, Fennico-Latino-Suecicum, sm. 4to. *hf. calf, rare*, 20s *Stockholm*, 1745
4266 LÉOUZON LE DUC, la Finlande, avec le Kalewala complet, *en Francois*, 8vo. *hf. calf*, 10s *Paris*, 1845
4267 RENVALL, Lexicon Linguae Finnicae, cum interpretatione latina et germanica, 2 vols. in 1, 4to. *hf. calf, rare*, 36s *Aboae*, 1826
4268 Uusi suomenkielinen Wirsikirja, tall 12mo. *old calf*, 7s *Stockholm*, 1779
4269 VHAEL, Grammatica Fennica, 12mo. 4 *leaves and* 109 *pp. clean copy, hf. calf, rare*, 12s *Aboae*, 1733
4270 **Lapponic.** FIELLSTRÖM, Grammatica Lapponica, 12mo. *sd.* 5s *Holmiae*, 1738
4271 GANANDER (Hen.) Grammatica Lapponica, 12mo. 6s *Holmiæ*, 1743
4272 IHRE, Lexicon Lapponicum, Lapp.-Suec.-Latinum, cum Indice Suec.-Lapponico, necnon Grammaticâ Lapponicâ à Lindahl et Oehrling, 4to. *hf. bd.* 25s *Holm.* 1780
4273 STOCKFLETH. Norsk-Lappisk Ordbog, stout 8vo. *hf. cf. nt.* 14s *Christiania*, 1852
4274 **Wotisk.** AHLQUIST, Wotisk Grammatik jemte Spraakprof och Ordförteckning, 4to. *with a Vocabulary referring to the cognate words in Finnish, Esthonian, Lapp, Russian, etc. hf. calf*, 12s *Helsingfor.* 1856
Tatar. See under *Oriental Philology.*
4275 **Gipsey and Slang.** SUNDT, Beretning om Fanteeller Landstrygerfolket i Norge, *with Glossary of Norwegian Gipsey Slang*, sm. 8vo. 10s *Christ.* 1850
4276 BIONDELLI, Studii sulle Lingue Furbesche, 12mo. *sd.* 5s *Milano*, 1846

NATURAL HISTORY, SCIENCES, MATHEMATICS.

4279 ABEL, Œuvres complètes, avec des notes et développements par Holmboe, 2 vols. in 1, 4to. *hf. calf*, £2. 6s *Christiania*, 1839
La seule édition des œuvres de ce grand Mathématicien.
ACADEMIE DES SCIENCES [DE PARIS].
4280 MÉMOIRES DE L'INSTITUT: Mathématiques et Physiques, 1806-15, 14 vols. in 19—Mémoires par Divers Savans, Tomes I, II *(all pub.)*—Littérature et Beaux-Arts, Tomes I—V—Sciences Morales, I—V—Rapports, 1810; together 27 vols. in 32 1798-1811
MÉMOIRES DE L'ACADÈMIE ROYALE des Sciences, du commencement en 1816, Vols. I—XIX, XXI—XXIV, XXVII, part 1, 1818-54, 56—Mémoires par Divers Savants, Tome I—XIV, 1827-1856—Comptes Rendus, 1835, Nos. 1-22, etc. *wanting No.* 18, *a very rare volume*, 1835—Tomes VI—XVII, 1838-43—Tome XXVI, 1848 1er. semestre—Comptes Rendus, Supplément, Tome I—Recueil des Discours, 1820-39, 2 vols.; together 55 vols. 1818-56
MÉMOIRES DE L'ACADÈMIE ROYALE des Sciences Morales et politiques, Tomes I.-X—Savants-Etrangers, I, III, 13 vols. 1837-55
MÉMOIRES DE L'INSTITUT NATIONAL:
Academie des Inscriptions, XVIII, XIX, XX, part 2, XXI, XXIII, part 2—Mémoires par divers Savants, 1e serie, II-V—2e serie, I, III; together 11 vols. 1843-59 Together 103 vols. 4to. (pub. at about £120.) *sewed*, £52. 1798-1859
4281 HISTOIRE de L'ACADEMIE ROYALE des SCIENCES, from the commencement in 1699 to 1772 *(wanting* 1747*)*—Table, 1699-1734, *Amsterdam*, 1741—Table, 1681-90, 1709—Discours, Tables générales, 1731-70, *Paris*, 1747-74—Suite des Mémoires, 1718, 1727, 1740—Memoires donnés à l'Academie, par Fontaine—Gallon, Machines et Inventions, 1666-1734—Ouvrages adoptez—Memoires pour l'Histoire naturelle, *La Haye*, 1731—Mathematique et Physique; in all 94 vols. 4to. *many plates, uniform in old French calf*, £10. 1692-1775

NATURAL HISTORY, SCIENCES, MATHEMATICS. 221

4282 HISTOIRE et Memoires de l'Academie des Sciences, Années 1699-1744, 46 vols. 12mo. *many plates, calf,* 20s *Amsterdam,* 1706-51
4283 ACHARII Lichenographia Universalis, stout 4to. 14 *coloured plates, sd.* 16s; or *calf,* 21s *Gott.* 1810
4284 ACOSTA (Chr.) Tractado de las Drogas y medicinas de las Indias Orientales, FIRST EDITION, sq. 8vo. *numerous woodcuts, calf, fair copy,* 25s *Burgos,* 1578
4285 ADAMS's Essays on the Microscope, with a history of Insects, stout 4to. with obl. 4to. atlas of 32 *plates of Microscopic Instruments, Animalculae, &c.* 2 vols. *bds.* 7s 1798
4286 AGASSIZ, Recherches sur les POISSONS FOSSILES, comprenant la description d'environ 1000 espèces qui n'existent plus, une nouvelle classification des Poissons, exprimant leurs rapports avec la série des formations, leur développement, etc. 5 vols. roy. 4to. of Text, *and folio Atlases of* 394 *plates,* in 3 vols.—together 10 vols. in 8, *hf. cf. uncut,* £24. *Neuchatel,* 1833-45
4287 ——— the same, in 7 vols. *a fine copy in calf gilt, from the library of Dr. Traill,* £27. 1833-35

TEXT.				
The text of this work was never completed. The entire collation is as follows:—		Vol. V. Part 1		pp. 1—122
		——— 2		pp. 1—160
Vol. I.	pp. xii and 1 to 40, Feuilleton additionel, pp. 130	PLATES.		
		Vol. I. complete	. . .	10
Vol. II. Part 1	pp. 310	II. complete	. . .	149
——— 2	pp. xii. and 336	III. complete	. . .	83
Vol. III.	pp. viii. and 390	IV. complete	. . .	61
Vol. IV.	pp. xv. 296	V. complete	. . .	91
				— 394

4288 AGASSIZ, Monographie des Poissons Fossiles du Vieux Grès Rouge ou Système Devonien (old Red Sandstone) des Iles Britanniques et de Russie, roy. 4to. with roy. folio *of* 43 *plates,* (A-F, and 1-33) *calf,* £4. 4s *Neuchatel,* 1843-44
4289 ——— Essay on Classification, 2 parts, roy. 4to. *sd.* 10s (*Boston,* 1857)
4290 ——— the same, with Index, 8vo. *cloth,* 10s *London,* 1859
<small>A text book of reference for the student, in which he may find notices of all that has been accomplished in the various departments of Natural History.</small>

4291 AGASSIZ, Etudes sur les Glaciers, *Atlas only,* folio, 32 *plates, hf. bd.* 24s 1840
4292 ——— Monographie d'Echinodermes. Anatomie du genre Echinus, plates 1 to 9 —Anatomie des Echinodermes, CLXVI to CXCIV; pages 1-28 of Text; plates XL to XLIII, 12s (*ca.* 1842)
4294 AGRICOLÆ (Georgii) de Re Metallica libri XII, quibus Officia, Instrumenta, Machinæ ac omnia ad Metallicam spectantia describuntur et per effigies, adjunctis Latinis Germanicisque appellationibus, ob oculos ponuntur; cum libro de Animantibus Subterraneis, folio, LARGE PAPER, *with several hundred large and fine woodcuts of Mining Operations, Tools, Machinery, etc.* old *calf, from the Old Electoral Library of Bavaria, very fine copy,* £2. 16s *Basiliæ,* 1556
4295 ——— de Re Metallica, et Animantibus Subterraneis, alia editio, folio, *woodcuts, vellum,* 20s *Basil,* 1561
4296 ——— de Re Metallica, et Animantibus subterraneis, de Subterraneis, de effluentibus ex terra, de Fossilibus, etc. folio, *woodcuts, hf. vellum,* 18s *Basil.* 1617
4297 AGRICULTURAL and Horticultural Society of India, Transactions, Vols. I.—VII. 8vo. *cloth,* 25s *Calcutta,* 1838-49
<small>Vol. 8 completing the Series appeared 1841.</small>

4298 ALDROVANDI (Ulyssis) Opera omnia: Ornithologia, 3 vols. 1599-1640-1603—de Insectis, 1638—Animalia exanguia, mollia, crustacea, etc. 1642—Pisces et Cetae, 1638—Quadrupedes solidipedes, 1639—Quadrupedes Bisulci, 1642—Quadrupedes digitati, 1637—Serpentes et Dracones, 1640—Monstrorum historia cum paralip. hist. omnium Animalium, 1642—Musaeum Metallicum, 1648—Dendrologia naturalis, 1668—together 13 vols. folio, *several hundred woodcuts, calf,* £6. 10s *Bononiae,* 1599-1668
4299 ALTENA, Species Batrachiorum, 4to. 4 *plates, hf. russia,* 6s *Lugd. Bat.* 1829
4300 AMERICAN ACADEMY. Transactions of the American Philosophical Society, Philadelphia, Vols. I.-IV. 1769 to 1799, *plates, Philidelphia,* 1771-99—Memoirs of the American Academy of Arts and Sciences, Vol. 1, 1780-3, *plates, Boston,* 1785—together 5 vols. 4to. *bd.* £2. 10s 1771-99
<small>The American Philosophical Society was the first, and the American Academy the second Literary Society in America. They received original contributions from Franklin, Priestley, and the most eminent men of the time.</small>

4301 AMERICAN ACADEMY of Arts and Sciences, Memoirs, *New Series*, Vols. I.-IV pt. 1, V, VI part 1, *plates*, £7.   *Cambridge, U. S.* 1833-57

4302 AMERICAN JOURNAL of Science and Arts, conducted by Profesor SILLIMAN, B. Silliman, Jr., and James D. Dana, SECOND SERIES, May 1846 to November 1860, being Vols. I to XXX, 8vo. *numerous plates, hf. bd. green morocco,* £10. 10s   *New Haven,* 1846-60

The First Series consists of 50 vols. and extends from 1818-45.

4303 **AMSTERDAM ACADEMY TRANSACTIONS.** Koninklijk-Nederlandsche Instituut van Wetenschappen, Letterkunde en Schoone Kunsten.
JAARBOEKEN der Wetenschappen en Kunsten, 1806-7, 3 vols. in 1, 4to.   1809-10
Eerste Klasse: VERHANDELINGEN, 7 vols. 1812-25 — NIEUWE VERHANDELINGEN, 13 vols. 1827-48 — VERHANDELIGEN, Derde Reeks, 5 vols. 1849-52 — together 25 vols. 4to. *a complete series of the Transactions of the First Class from the beginning to* 1852   1812-52
VERSLAG van de Werkzaamheden der Erste Klasse, 4to.   1809-16
KRAIJENHOFF, Précis des Operations Géodesiques et Astronomiques en Hollande, 4to.   1827
Tweede Klasse: VERHANDELINGEN, 8 vols. in 7, 4to.   1818-43
NIEUWE REEKS van Verhandelingen, 2 vols. roy. 8vo.   1850-51
MAERLANT, Spiegel Historiael of Rijm Kronik, met Aanteekeningen van Clignett en Winkel, 4 vols.—AANTEEKENINGEN door HALBERTSMA, 1 vol.—5 vols. roy. 8vo. *the old Dutch text, with extensive philological commentaries*   1784-51

The first two vols. were published at Leyden in 1784-5; Vol. III. was brought out by the Institute in 1812; and the fourth and fifth in 1849-51.

WOORDENBOEK op de Werken van HOOFT, 4 vols. roy. 8vo.   1825-38
Derde Klasse: GEDENKSCHRIFTEN, Hedendaagsche Talen, 5 vols. 4to. 1817-36
COMMENTATIONES LATINAE, 6 vols. 4to.   1818-36
FRETS en HOLTIUS, Prijsverhandelingen, 4to.   1822
Vierde Klasse: KIESEWELTER en FÉTIS Verhandelingen (les mérites des Néerlandais, aux XIV-XVI Siècles) 4to. 73 *pp. of engraved music*   1829
ALGEMEENE VERGADERINGEN, Processen-Verbaal, 1808-29, in 3 vols. 4to. 1808-29
OPENBARE VERGADERINGEN, Verslagen van de 1e, 2e, 4e Klasse, 1817-39, 1817-40, 1817-41, 6 vols. 4to.   1817-41
VERSLAGEN en MEDEDEELINGEN, 1841-46—JAARBOEKEN, 1847-51, in 8 vols. roy. 8vo.   1841-51
BESCHOUWINGEN, 8vo.   1849
Together 57 vols. 4to. and 20 vols. roy. 8vo. all uniformly *half bound, green morocco, gilt,* £15. 15s   *Amst. Haag, Leyden, etc.* 1784-1852

4304 AMSTERDAM ACADEMY: VERHANDELINGEN, Vols. 1—6, in 5 vols·—Verhandelingen der eerste Klasse van het Instituut, 3de Reeks, Deelen 4, 5, 1851-2; together 8 vols. in 6, 4to. *plates, three in cloth, three sd.* £3.   1851-58

4305 —— the same, Vols. 1.—VI. 4to. *plates, sewed,* £2. 10s   1854-58

4306 VERSLAGEN en Mededeelingen: NATUURKUNDE, Vols. I.—VII. 1853-58—LETTERKUNDE, Vols. I.—III, 1855-58—together 10 vols. 8vo. *plates,* £3. 1853-58

4307 AFDEELING NATUURKUNDE, 7 vols. in 4, stout 8vo. *plates, cloth,* £3.   1853-58

4308 ANNALEN DER PHYSIK und CHEMIE, herausgegeben zu Berlin von J. C. Poggendorff, Bände 82-111, (der ganzen Folge, 158-187) *numerous plates, twenty-four vols. half bound, edges cut, and six vols. bds. uncut,* together 30 vols. 8vo. *numerous plates,* £6. 10s   *Leipzig,* 1851-60

4309 ANNALES DES MINES: JOURNAL DES MINES, from the beginning in 1793 to Jan. 1812, Nos. 1-181, being Vols. I. to XXXI, 1. 8vo. *numerous plates, twelve vols. hf. bd. six in bds. the rest in parts,* £5.   *Paris,* 1793-1812

4310 ANNALES DES MINES ou Recueil de Mémoires sur l'Exploitation des Mines et sur les Sciences et les Arts qui s'y rapportent, redigés par les Ingénieurs des Mines; *quatrième série,* Vols. 9 to 20, 12 vols. 1846-1851—*Cinquième série,* Vols. 1 to 8, 1852-55—Lois, Décrets, Arrets et autres Actes concernant les Mines et Usines, cinquième série, 4 vols. 1852-55—together 24 vols. 8vo. *numerous folding maps and plates,* 10 vols. *half calf,* 14 *in cloth all uniformly lettered and gilt,* £8. 10s   *Paris,* 1846-55

NATURAL HISTORY, SCIENCES, MATHEMATICS.

4311 ANNALS of PHILOSOPHY, or Magazine of Chemistry, Mineralogy, Mechanics, Natural History, Agriculture, and the Arts, edited by Dr. Thomson, 16 vols.—New Series, The ANNALS of PHILOSOPHY, 12 vols.: together 28 vols. 8vo. 151 *plates*, (*pub. at £21.*) *bds. uncut*, £2.; or *half russia*, £2. 10s 1813-26

4312 ANSTED's Geology, introductory, descriptive, and practical, 2 vols. 8vo. *numerous woodcuts, cloth*, 28s 1844

4313 ARAGO, Œuvres complétes, publiées par Barral, avec introduction par Humboldt: Notices Biographiques, 3 vols.—Notices Scientifiques 5 vols.—Voyages Scientifiques, 1 vol.—Mémoires Scientifiques, 2 vols.—Mélanges, 1 vol.—Astronomie Populaire, 4 vols.—Tables, 1 vol.—together 17 vols. 8vo. *plates, half calf neat*, £5. *Paris*, 1854-59

4314 ARCHIMEDE, Vita, Invenzioni, e Scritti di, da Mazzuchelli, 4to. *plates, half morocco*, 10s *Brescia*, 1737

4315 ARGELANDER, Observationes Astronomicæ in specula Universit. Litter. Fennicæ Aboae, 1824-28, factæ, 3 vols. in 1, folio, *hf. bd. uncut*, 16s *Helsingfors*, 1830-32

4316 —— Astronomische Beobachtungen zu Bonn, Vol. I. Durchmusterung des nördl. Himmels, 45-80 Grad, 1841-44, 4to. *sd*. 6s *Bonn*, 1846

4317 ASTRONOMICAL SOCIETY'S MEMOIRS, complete from the commencement of the series in 1821 to 1857, Vols. I—XXVI. in 31 divisions, large 4to. *numerous plates*, (*pub. at about £50.*) *unbound*, £18. 1822-58

4318 —— another set, Vols. I—IX. in 7 vols. 4to. *plates, hf. calf*, £6. 1822-36

4319 AUDUBON and BACHMAN's Viviparous Quadrupeds of North America, TEXT, 3 vols. impl. 8vo. *with plates*, 124, 151-155, *these completing the large folio series, cloth*, £6. 6s *New York, J. J. Audubon*, 1846-54

4320 AUDUBON'S ORNITHOLOGICAL BIOGRAPHY; or an Account of the Habits of the Birds of the United States of America: accompanied by Descriptions of the Objects represented in the Work entitled "THE BIRDS OF AMERICA," 5 vols. impl. 8vo. *cuts, cloth*, £6. 1831-39

4321 AUDUBON. QUADRUPEDS OF NORTH AMERICA, part of Vol. III. atlas folio, plates 106-115, 124, 126, 127, 128, 139-150, *being 35 plates most exquisitely coloured*, £3. 10s *New York*, 1848

4322 AUSTRIAN IMPERIAL ACADEMY OF SCIENCES; *published as follows* Denkschriften der kaiserlichen Akademie der Wissenschaften: MATHEMATISCH-NATURWISSENSCHAFTLICHE CLASSE: Band I—VII, and IX, large 4to. *coloured plates*, 1850-55—PHILOSOPHISCH-HISTORISCHE CLASSE: Band I—VI, and VIII, large 4to. *plates*, 1850-57—SITZUNGSBERICHTE: MATHEMATISCH-NATURWISSEN-SCHAFTLICHE CLASSE, Vol. I—XXIV (1850, no Aug. Sept.) 8vo. 1849-57—PHILOSOPHISCH-HISTORISCHE CLASSE, Vols.I—XVII, XXI, part 3, XXII, XXIII. (1849, no Aug. Sept.; 1850, no Aug. Sept.) 8vo. 1848-59—this series, folio, 4to. and 8vo. together, £25. 1848-59

4323 ARCHIV für Kunde österreichischer Geschichts-Quellen, 1848-1849, parts 1 to 5, Jahrgänge 1849-1857, being vols. I—XV part I, XVII parts 1 and 2, and XVIII part 1, 8vo. *numerous plates*, £3. 10s 1848-57

4324 FONTES RERUM AUSTRIACARUM: Erste Abtheilung: Scriptores, Band I.; Zweite Abtheilung: Diplomataria et Acta, Band II—X, XIII, XV, 12 vols. 8vo. £2. 10s 1850-57

4325 AVICENNAE liber Canonis, de Medicinis cordialibus, de removendis nocumentis in regimine sanitatis, de Syrupoacetoso, *Lat.* ab Alpago, fol. *bd.* 10s *Venet.*1582

4326 —— Canon Medicinae, de viribus cordis, de Removendis nocumentis, de Syrupo acetoso cum notis, ed. Paulinus, 2 vols. folio, *enlarged edition, engraved title, of which a corner torn off, mounted, bd.* 12s *Venet.* 1595

4327 BAILEY (F.) Account of the Rev. John FLAMSTEED, the first Astronomer Royal, compiled from his own Manuscripts, &c. with his British Catalogue of Stars, stout 4to. *bds. scarce*, £3. 3s *printed by order of the Admiralty*, 1835

4328 BAUER, Illustrationes FLORAE NOVAE HOLLANDIAE sive Icones generum quae descripsit Brown, royal fol. 15 *plates*, £2. 2s *Lond. Auctor*, 1813

4329 —— the same, *with coloured plates, bd. extremely rare*, £5. 15s 1813

A most beautiful work, its rarity is extreme. Suppressed by the late Mr. Brown.

4330 BARBUT, Genres des Insectes de Linné, échantillons d'insectes d'Angleterre, 4to. *French and English, port. and 22 coloured plates, hf. bd. 16s* 1781

4331 BARBA (A. A.) Arte de los Metales, en que se enseña el verdadero beneficio de los de Oro, y Plata por Azogue, con Carillo su las antiguas Minas de Espana, sq. 8vo. *numerous woodcuts, vellum, 27s* Madrid, 1729

4332 BARREME, Livre facile pour aprendre l'Arithmetique sans maistre, 12mo. *calf, 6s* Paris, 1672

4333 BARTOLI, Modo di Misvrare le Distantie, sm. 4to. *elegantly designed woodcut title, and diagrams, vellum, 6s* Venetia, 1564

4334 BARTON (W. C. P.) Flora of North America, 3 vols. 4to. 106 *coloured plates, hf. calf, £2. 10s; or hf. green morocco, gilt tops, uncut, £3. 3s* Philadel. 1821-3

4335 BATAVIAN ACADEMY TRANSACTIONS: Verhandlingen van het Bataviaasch Genootschap der Konsten en Wetenschappen, Vol. I, III—IX, XII—XIV., 12 vols. 8vo. *plates, not uniform, Dr. Horsfield's copy, very rare, £7.* 1771-1833

4336 BATEMAN (J.) THE ORCHIDACEÆ OF MEXICO AND GUATEMALA, fol. A MAGNIFICENT WORK, THE PLATES EXQUISITELY COLOURED, *hf. green morocco, £21.* 1843

4337 BEAGLE VOYAGE: Zoology of the Voyage of H.M.S. Beagle, under the command of Capt. Fitzroy R.N. during the years 1832 and 1836, edited and superintended by Charles Darwin, Esq. *Naturalist to the Expedition,* complete in 19 parts, bound in 3 vols. impl. 4to. *containing 165 plates of fossils, mammals, birds, fishes, reptiles, etc. those of the mammalia and birds beautifully coloured* (pub. at £8. 15s in parts) £7. 7s 1839-43

In 1856 Yarrell's copy fetched £7. 10s.
FOSSIL MAMMALIA. By Richard Owen, Esq., F.R.S. Professor of Anatomy and Physiology of the Royal College of Surgeons, London. With a Geological Introduction, by Charles Darwin, Esq.
MAMMALIA. By George R. Waterhouse, Curator of the Zoological Society of London, etc.
BIRDS. By John Gould, with a Notice of their Habits and Ranges, by Charles Darwin.
FISH. By the Rev. Leonard Jenyns.
REPTILES. By Thomas Bell.

4338 BEDFORD (Duke of). HOOKER (Sir W. J.) Letter on the late Duke of Bedford's Services rendered to Botany and Horticulture, impl. 8vo. *with a coloured plate of the Willow-leaved Bedfordia, bds. 10s* Glasgow, 1840

4339 BEECHEY. Zoology of Captain Beechey's Voyage, compiled from the Collections and Notes of Captain Beechey, and the Scientific Gentlemen who accompanied the Expedition—the Mammalia, by Dr. Richardson; Ornithology, by N. A. Vigors, Esq.; Fishes, by G. T. Lay, Esq; and E. T. Bennett, Esq.; Crustacea, by Richard Owen, Esq.; Reptiles, by John Edward Gray, Esq.; Shells, by W. Sowerby, Esq.; and Geology, by the Rev. Dr. Buckland, 4to. *illustrated by 47 plates, containing many hundred figures,* BEAUTIFULLY COLOURED, *by Sowerby,* (pub. at £5. 5s) *cloth bds. £3. 3s* 1839

4340 BELL'S History of British Quadrupeds, including the Cetacea, 8vo. *nearly 200 fine woodcuts, cloth, 24s* 1837

4341 —— the same, roy. 8vo. LARGE PAPER, *hf. morocco, gilt edges, from Miss Currer's library, £3.* 1837

4342 —— History of British Reptiles, roy. 8vo. LARGE PAPER, *numerous fine woodcuts, hf. red morocco, gilt edges, from Miss Currer's library, 21s* 1839

4343 —— History of Quadrupeds, 1837—History of Reptiles, 1839, 2 vols. in 1, stout 8vo. *calf gilt, uncut, 35s* 1837-39

4344*—— the same, LARGE PAPER, roy. 8vo. *hf. russia gilt, 30s* 1853

4344 —— History of the British Stalk-eyed Crustacea, 8vo. 174 *woodcuts, calf neat, gilt edges, 24s* 1853

4345 BENNETT'S Selections of Rare and Curious Fishes found upon the coast of CEYLON, from drawings made on the island, roy. 4to. 30 *beautiful plates, coloured from life, cloth, 36s* Printed for the author, 1851

4346 BENNETT (Dr. G.) Wanderings in New South Wales, Batavia, Pedir Coast, Singapore, and China, being the Journal of a NATURALIST, 1833-34, 2 vols. 8vo. *plates, calf neat, 18s* 1834

4347 BENTLEY's Historical View of Hindu Astronomy, ancient and modern, with remarks on Chinese, 4to. *plates, 18s* Calcutta, 1823

NATURAL HISTORY, SCIENCES, MATHEMATICS.

4348 BERLINER Astronomisches Jahbruch, von Encke, 1831-43, 1850-56, together 20 vols. 8vo. (pub. at about 66 thalers) *twelve hf. bd. eight unbound, 25s* 1829-53

    A collection, important for the memoirs of practical Astronomy inserted by the editor. A set of 26 vols. priced, 1858, Friedländer, 32 thalers.

4349 BERLIN ACADEMY: STERNKARTEN. Cataloge zu den 24 Stunden der Akademischen Sternkarten, bearbeitet von verschiedenen Astronomen, (Bradley, Piazzi, Lalande, und Bessel, etc.) 24 parts in 1 vol. impl. 4to. with large folio *atlas of 25 maps, hf. morocco,* £3. *10s*   *Berlin,* 1858-59

4350 BERNOUILLI Opera omnia, 4 vols. sm. 4to. *portraits and numerous mathematical plates. old calf gilt,* 15s   *Lausannae,* 1742

4351 BERZELIUS Lehrbuch der Chemie, übersetzt von Woehler, 10 vols. in 6, 8vo. *4th ed. plates, half calf neat,* 30s   *Dresden,* 1835-51

    " A man of astonishing industry, unrivalled in his command of chemical resources."—HERSCHELL.

4352 BESSEL'S Astronomische Beobachtungen auf der Sternwarte in Königsberg, Abtheilung I—XVI, Nov. 1813 bis December 1831, bound in 6 vols. folio, *half calf,* £2. *16s*   *Königsberg,* 1815-35

    Priced, 1855-58, Friedländer in Berlin, 25 Abth. 50 thalers; Abth. 1-24 and 29, Asher, 160 francs.

4353 BETTINI Aerarium Philosophiae Mathematicae, 3 stout vols. sm. 4to. *frontispiece and numerous woodcuts, original stamped binding,* 24s   *Bononiae,* 1648

    At the end of Vol. III. is a supplement, de Sandalio, Cithara, Microcosmo, Arcu, Tympano, with plates.

4354 —— Recreationes Mathematicae, folio, *woodcuts, bds.* 12s   *ib.* 1659

4355 BEWICK (T.) General History of Quadrupeds, *second edition, upwards of 200 woodcuts, calf, back emblematically gilt,* 31s   *Newcastle,* 1791

4355* —— the same, seventh edition, 8vo, *hf. cf.* 20s   1820

4356 —— History of British Birds, 2 vols. royal 8vo. *first edition,* LARGE PAPER, *about 300 beautiful cuts, calf neat,* £7. *7s*   1797-1804

4357 —— the same, LARGE PAPER, Vol. I only, roy. 8vo. *bds.* £2. *2s*   1797

4358 —— the same, sixth edition, enlarged, 2 vols. 8vo. about 300 *beautiful woodcuts,* £2. *2s*   *Newcastle,* 1826

    " Open the work where ye will, only look at the Bird, his attitude, his eye—is he not alive? I actually and ardently aver, that I have gazed till I have readily imagined motion, aye colour! * * * Each Bird, too, has his character most physiognomically marked * * * * The moral habits of each are as distinctly marked as had he painted portraits of individuals for Lavater."—*From a very interesting account of Bewick and his method of Working by* J. F. M. DOVASTON, *in* LOUDON'S *Mag. of Nat. Hist., Vols.* 2 *and* 3.

4359 BIGELOW'S American Medical Botany, 3 vols. royal 8vo. *with 60 coloured plates, hf. bd.* £3.   *Boston, U. S.* 1817-20

4360 —— Florula Bostoniensis; the Plants of Boston, roy. 8vo. *bds.* 6s   1814

4361 BIOT, Traité élémentaire d'Astronomie Physique, troisième edition augmentée, 4 vols. 8vo. and 4to. ATLAS *of* 81 *plates, hf. calf.* 25s   *Paris,* 1831-47

    " One of the most profound, perspicuous, and lucid writers on Physical subjects."—ATHENÆUM, No. 1525.

4362 BLANCO, Flora de Filipinas, 8vo. 2*nd impression,* lix. and 619 *pp. hf. bound,* 25s   *Manila,* 1845

4363 BLOCH (M. E.) Ichthyologie, ou Histoire Naturelle, Générale, et Particulière, des Poissons, 12 vols. in 6, royal folio, LARGE PAPER, *with* 432 *beautifully* COLOURED *engravings of Fish, quite perfect, an original copy, the plates elaborately* COLOURED *and heightened with* SILVER, *a fine copy in hf. green morocco, gilt edges,* £37. *16s*   *Berlin,* 1785-97

    Still the best work on Fishes, as far as the plates are concerned.

    Copies very seldom occur in a perfect state in this country, owing to an accident which destroyed the greater portion of the last six volumes, immediately after their publication.

    " Bloch was a Jewish physician, settled in Berlin ; and his Ichthyology, in 12 folio parts, containing no less than 432 coloured plates, was such an undertaking as no one would have courage to prosecute in these days, unless with the determination of submitting to a large pecuniary sacrifice. It is without doubt the most complete work, in regard to figures, that has ever been published. Both his characters and his descriptions are excellent. One only regrets that a work so essential to every ichthyologist, is, of necessity, so expensive."—SWAINSON.

4364 BLOCH, Ichthyologie ou Histoire Naturelle des Poissons, 4 vols. 8vo. 521 *finely coloured plates, hf. calf gilt,* £3.   *Berlin, chez l'auteur,*1796

4565 BLUME et Fischer, Flora Javae, nec non insularum adjacentium, fasc. 1-42, large folio, *with* 257 *finely coloured plates, in parts,* £15.   *Bruxellis,* 1827-51

    All that has yet been published of this great work. There is no text published to plate 94. Lecanopteris Carnosa, nor to plates 15 to 28, Loranthus formosus, etc. Priced, 1856, Williams and Norgate, £20.; Weigel in Leipsic, 120 Thalers.

4366 BLUME (C. L.) RUMPHIA, sive commentationes botanicæ imprimis de plantis Indiæ Orientalis, tum penitus incognitis, tum quæ in libris Rheedii, Rumphii, Roxburghii, Wallichii et aliorum recens. 4 vols. in 2, royal folio, *complete* 214 *coloured plates* (pub. at £25.) *hf. calf, uncut*, £18. 18s   *Leydæ et Brux.* 1835-48
A most important publication, copies seldom occur for sale in England.
4367 —— the same, wanting in Vol. I, plates 55, 57-63, 66 ; in Vol. II, 71-75, 80-82, 85, £10.   1835-48
4368 BOISDUVAL, Species général des LÉPIDOPTÈRES, Vol. 1, 8vo. 24 *finely coloured plates, hf. calf*, 12s   *Paris*, 1836
4369 BOETII Opera omnia, EDITIO PRIMA, folio, litt. goth. *bds.* 16s   *Venet.* 1491
Containing the three treatises *De Arithmetica, De Musica,* and *De Geometria,* besides the other works.
4370 —— Introductio in Arithmeticam, *woodcut title, and fine large woodcut at the end,* 1503—Artificialis Introductio in Ethicos Aristotelis, 1502—in 1 vol. sm. folio, *overlapping vellum,* 14s   *Paris*, 1502-3
4371 BOJANUS, Anatome Testudinis Europaeae, large folio, 31 *plates, russia, rare,* 36s   *Vilnae,* 1819-21
4372 Boot, Gemmarum et Lapidum historia, 12mo. *cuts, hf. bd.* 7s 6d   *Lug. Bat.* 1636
4373 BONN AND BRESLAU ACADEMY : VERHANDLUNGEN der Kaiserlichen Leop. Carol. Akademie : Nova Acta Physico-Medica Academiæ Cæsareæ Leopoldino-Carolinæ naturae curiosorum, Vols. X. part 2 ; XVI. 2 ; XVII. 1, 2, and Supplement ; XVIII. 2, and 2 Supplements ; XIX. 1, 2, and 2 Supplements ; XX. 1, 2 ; XXI. 1, 2 ; XXII. Supplement ; XXIII. 1, 2, and Supplement ; XXIV. 1 ; XXV. 1, 2 ; XXVI. 1 ; in 24 vols. or *parts,* large 4to. *numerous plates, many coloured, sd.* £10.   *Vrastisl. et Bonn.* 1821-57
4374 SCHULTZ, Cyclose des Lebenssaftes in den Pflanzen, 4to. 33 *plates,* 7s 6d   1841
4375 LEHMANN, Revisio Potentillarum, large 4to. *with* 64 *plates,* 16s   1856
4376 BORELLUS de vero Telescopi Inventore, cum omnium Conspiciliorum historia, sq. 8vo. *cuts, vellum,* 7s 6d   *Hagae,* 1655
4377 BORGNIS Traité complet de Mecanique, appliquée aux arts, contenant les theories pour diriger l'invention et l'emploi de toutes les espèces de Machines, 9 vols. 4to. 249 *plates by Girard and Adam, hf. calf,* £4.   *Paris,* 1818-21
Priced, 1845, by Bossange, Paris, 220 fr.
4378 BORGO (Luca Pacioli di) SUMMA de ARITHMETICA, Geometria, Proportioni, et Proportionalita, sm. folio, *title and dedication within a deep woodcut border, diagrams,* GOTHIC LETTER, *bds. uncut, rare,* £2. 10s ; or *a fine copy, on* THICK PAPER, *original calf, rebacked,* £4. 4s *Tusculano, su la riva dil laco Benac.* 1567
4379 BORGO (Pietro) Libro de Abacho, sm. 4to. *vellum, rare,* 20s *Venet. Lenus,* 1567
4380 BOTANICAL TRACTS : A valuable Collection of 38 Modern Tracts and minor works, relating to the Science of Botany, *with numerous plates,* bound in 3 vols. 4to. *half calf, from the library of Prof. Henfrey, F.R.S.* £2. 16s
Including: Bischoff, Naturgeschichte der Salvinie, 3 plates, 1826—Bischoff, die Cryptogamischen Gewächse, 7 plates, 1828—Bischoff, Bemerkungen über die Liebermoose, 5 plates, 1835—Lindenberg, Monographie der Riccieen, 19 COLOURED *plates,* 1836—Mettenius, zur Kenntniss der Rhizocarpeen, 3 plates 1846—Meyen, zur Physiologie und Systematik der Algen, 4 *coloured plates,* 1828—Duchartre, sur la Clandestine d'Europe, 8 plates, 1847—Güthe Mittheilungen aus der Pflanzenwelt, 2 plates, 1821—Henslow on a Monstrosity of the common Mignionette, 2 plates, 1833—Henslow on the Examination of a Hybrid Digitalis, 4 plates, 1831, and many other valuable works.
4381 BOWDICH's Analysis of the Natural Classifications of Mammalia, 15 *plates*—Introduction to Cuvier's Ornithology, 253 *engravings,* in 1 vol. 8vo. *half calf,* 8s   *Paris,* 1821
4382 BRAVARDIN [*Bradwardine*] Geometria Speculativa, cum tractatu de Quadratura Circuli, 4to. *woodcuts, bds.* 32s   *Paris, J. Petit,* 1511
4383 BREHM, Beiträge zur Völgelkunde in Beschreibungen neu entdeckter und seltener deutscher Vögel, 3 vols. 8vo. *plates, hf. mor.* 18s   *Neustadt,* 1820-22
4383*BRITISH ASSOCIATION. Reports of the British Association for the Promotion of Science, from the commencement in 1831 to 1861, 30 vols. 8vo. *numerous engravings, many coloured,* (pub. £22. 6s) *bds.* £10. 10s ; *cf. nt.* £15. 1833-61
A repository of the deepest and most varied learning. Odd volumes can be supplied at a reduction.
BRITISH MUSEUM NATURAL HISTORY CATALOGUES. *See ante* page 25.
4384 BRONN, Naturhistorisch-öconomische Reisen (Schweitz, Italien, und Sudfrankreich), 1824-27, 2 vols. 8vo. 1340 pp. 12 *plates of Geology, hf. calf,* 6s   1826-31
4385 BROTERI Phytographia Lusitaniae seu rariorum Stirpium descriptiones, Vol. I. folio, 82 *plates, hf. calf,* 10s   *Olisip.* 1816
4386 BRUSSELS ACADEMY. Bulletins de l'Académie Royale de Bruxelles (de Belgique), 1835-50, Tomes 2-4, 6-11, pt. 1, (*tome* 9 *wanting No.* 3), 12 pt. 2, 14 pt. 2—17 pt. 1 ; 20 vols. 8vo. *plates of Antiquities, Natural History,* £3.   1835-40

NATURAL HISTORY, SCIENCES, MATHEMATICS.

4387 BUCH, Physicalische Beschreibung der Canarischen Inseln, roy. 4to. *with impl. folio atlas of* 12 *engravings, and maps on* 8 *plates, bds.* £2. *Berlin,* 1825
4388 —— the same, without Atlas, large 4to. *hf. calf neat,* 24s 1825
   The large Atlas is very rare. A map of Teneriffe and one of Great Canary, mentioned in the Index as not then ready, seem never to have been published.
4389 BUCKLAND'S Reliquiæ Diluvianæ; or Observations on the Organic Remains in caves, fissures, and diluvial gravel, attesting an universal deluge, 4to. 27 *plates, some coloured, calf gilt,* 18s 1824
4390 —— Geology and Mineralogy considered with reference to Natural Theology, 2 vols. 8vo. 87 *plates,* (pub. at 35s) *cloth,* 18s *Bridgewater Treatises,* 1839
4391 BUFFON, DAUBENTON et LACÉPÈDE, Histoire Naturelle générale et particulière, 38 vols. 4to. *numerous plates, old calf gilt,* £7. 10s *Paris,* 1749-89
   Contents: I, Hist. naturelle générale, 15 vols.—II, Supplément, 7 vols.—III, Oiseaux, 9 vols.—IV, Minéraux, 5 vols—V, Ovipares et Serpens, par de Lacépède, 2 vols. Sold, 1856, mor. £9. 5s. Priced, 1841, Wood, coloured plates, £38.
4392 BULLIARD et VENTENAT, Herbier de la France, contenant : l'Histoire des Plantes Vénéneuses de la France, *uncut,* 1784; l'Histoire des Champignons de la France, 4 vols. 4to. *hf. calf neat,* 1809-12; et Dictionnaire de Botanique, *uncut,* 1812—together 6 vols. *with* 474 *finely coloured plates,* 4 vols. 4to. *hf. calf neat,* 2 folio. *sd. uncut,* £3. 5s *Paris,* 1785-1812
4393 CALCUTTA MEDICAL and PHYSICAL SOCIETY'S Transactions, 7 vols. 8vo. *plates, clean set in boards, very rare,* £4. 4s *Calcutta,* 1825-35
   The above Transactions contain valuable papers by the best scientific men in India.
4394 CALDERINI, Modo d'usar il Bossolo per pigliar piante de luoghi, 12mo. *woodcuts, vell.* 6s *Milano,* 1598
4395 CAMBRIDGE OBSERVATORY. Astronomical Observations made at the Observatory of Cambridge, by G. B. AIRY and Rev. James CHALLIS, for the years 1828-1845, Vols. I-XVI, roy. 4to. *twelve vols. hf. bd. and four in bds. presentation copy to Professor Schumacher,* £4. *Cambridge,* 1829-50
4396 CAMBRIDGE MATHEMATICAL JOURNAL, edited by R. L. Ellis, SERIES I, 4 vols. 1839-45—CAMBRIDGE AND DUBLIN MATHEMATICAL JOURNAL, edited by W. Thomson, Vols. 1 to 7, 1846-52—together 11 vols. 4 vols. *half calf, the remainder unbound,* £7. 15s *Cambridge,* 1839-52
4397 CAMBRIDGE PHILOSOPHICAL SOCIETY'S TRANSACTIONS, Vols. 1 and 2, 4to. *half calf,* 36s *Cambridge,* 1822-27
4398 —— the same, Vol. 5, Parts 2 and 3, 4to. *sd.* 20s 1834-35
4399 —— the same, Vol. 8, Part 5, 4to. *sd.* 12s 1849
4400 CANGIAMILA (*in Sicilia Inquisitor*) Embryologia sacra, sive de officio Sacerdotum, Medicorum, etc. circa aeternam Parvulorum in utero existentium salutem, sm. folio, *plate, vellum, curious and rare,* 12s *Panormi,* 1758
   Religious insanity was never carried further than in this work.
4400*CAVENDISH SOCIETY'S Publications from the beginning, *complete,* 25 vols. 8vo. *cloth,* and 1 vol. sm. 4to. *bds.* (*cost to subscribers,* £15. 15s) £10. 10s 1848-62

A complete set, consists of

Graham's Chemical Reports
Gmelin's Handbook of Chemistry, translated by Watts, Vols. I-XV.
Wilson's Life of Cavendish
Lehmann's Physiological Chemistry, 3 vols.

Funke's Atlas to Lehmann, sm. 4to.
Bischoff's Chemical and Physical Geology, 3 vols.
Henry's Life of Dalton
Laurent's Chemical Method

Making together 26 vols. of which Graham's Reports and the first vol. of Lehmann are out of print, and others becoming scarce. I can supply the scarce vol. of Dalton's Life separately for 10 .

4401 CATESBY'S NATURAL HISTORY OF CAROLINA, FLORIDA, and the BAHAMA ISLANDS; ORIGINAL and BEST EDITION: WITH THE SUPPLEMENT, 2 vols. impl. folio, *map and* 220 *beautifully* COLOURED PLATES *of American Birds, Animals, Fishes, Insects, Plants, &c. Sir Hans* SLOANE'S *copy, turned out from the British Museum, old red morocco, gilt edges,* £7. 7s 1731-43
   Priced, 1834, £14. 14s; 1857, £13. 13s; 1837, P. and Foss, £15. 15s Fetched in the Merly sale, £44. 2s; Dr. Askew's £25 ; Col. Stanley's, £34. 13s. The subsequent editions have the plates executed in an inferior colouring.
4402 CAVALERIO, Geometria Indivisibilibus continuorum, sm. 4to. *diagrams, best edition, vellum,* 25s *Bononiæ,* 1653
   Ouvrage célèbre dans l'histoire de géométrie.—BRUNET

4403 CAVANILLES, Dissertationes Botanicae Monadelphiae Classis, 10 parts in 3 vols. 4to. x and 433 pp. of text, 296 plates, calf gilt, £2. 16s   Matriti, 1785-90
Priced, 1847, £5. 5s.   "On en trouve peu d'exemplaires complets."--BRUNET.

4404 CENOMANUS, de Arboribus Coniferis, etc. sm. 4to. *woodcuts of Pines, vellum, rare,* 9s
Paris. 1553

4405 CEVA de Lineis rectis se sectantibus, sm. 4to. 10 *plates, bd.* 7s 6d   Mediol. 1678

4406 CHENU (Dr.) ENCYCLOPÉDIE D'HISTOIRE NATURELLE, d'après les travaux des Naturalistes les plus éminens : Buffon, Daubenton, Lacépède, G. et F. Cuvier, St. Hilaire, Latreille, de Jussieu, Brongniart, &c.—Oiseaux, 6 parts, and Index—Coléoptères, 2 parts—Quadrumanes, 1 part—Carnassiers, 2 parts—Botanique, 2 parts, and Index—Papillons, 1 part—Papillons Nocturnes, 1 part—Rongeurs et Pachydermes, Ruminants, &c. 2 parts—Reptiles et Poissons, and Index—Crustacés, Mollusques, et Zoophytes, 1 part—Tables Générales de Lépidoptères et Mammifères, 2 parts—together 24 parts, in 8 vols. high 4to. *an immense profusion of woodcuts, strongly half bound red morocco, uncut,* £10.   Paris, 1851-58
The cheapest modern set of works on Natural History. The woodcuts are very creditable.

4407 CHINESE ORNITHOLOGY : A collection of 100 NATIVE DRAWINGS of Birds, in 1 vol. atlas folio, *large and elegant designs, beautifully coloured, forming a fine specimen of Chinese Art, the name of each bird added at foot in Chinese characters, richly bound in green morocco super extra, with sides and linings of Chinese silk worked with coloured figures,* £16. 16s   ca. 1820

4408 CIVIL ENGINEER and ARCHITECT'S JOURNAL, from the beginning in October 1837 to October 1861, Vols. I. to XXIV. 4to. *numerous plates and cuts, nineteen vols. bound in cloth, the remainder in* 58 *parts,* £12.   1837-61
A similar set, unbound, recently priced in a bookseller's catalogue £15. 15s.

4409 CHRISTIAN, Traité de Mécanique, 3 vols. 4to. *plates, calf gilt,* 12s   Paris, 1822-25

4410 CLAVII Algebra, sq. 8vo. *bd.* 6s   Aurel. Allobr. 1609

4411 CLEGG on the Manufacture and Distribution of Coal Gas, 4to. 19 *plates and numerous woodcuts,* (pub. at 28s) *cloth,* 14s   1841

4412 CLERCK, Natural History of Swedish Spiders, (? 1795)—ALBIN on English Spiders, (? 1795)—in 1 vol. 4to. 28 *coloured plates, no title,* 10s   (? 1795)

4413 COLEBROOKE (*Sir Henry Thomas*), ALGEBRA, with ARITHMETIC and MENSURATION, translated from the Sanscrit of BRAHMEGUPTA and BHASCARA, 4to. viii, lxxxiv, and 378 pp. (pub. at £3. 3s) *cloth,* 25s   1817

4414 CRAMER et STOLL, PAPILLONS EXOTIQUES des trois Parties du Monde, l'Asie, l'Afrique, et l'Amérique, avec le SUPPLÉMENT, 5 vols. 442 *plates,* 1779-91—STOLL, Réprésentation des Cigales, des Punaises, des Spectres, des Mantes, des Sauterelles, des Grillons, et des Blattes, 4 vols. in 3, 120 *plates,* 1788-1813—VOET, Catalogue Systématique des Coléoptères, avec l'explication en *Français, en Latin, et en Hollandais,* 4 vols. in 2, 105 *plates*—together 13 vols. in 10, roy. 4to. 667 *beautifully coloured plates, containing several thousand impressions, every one* RETOUCHED IN COLOURS *by an artist,* UNIQUE COPY, *in Dutch calf extra, gilt edges,* £42.   Amst. et La Haye, 1779-1806
This fine copy is from the library of Miss Currer, and originally that of Raye de Breukelerwaert, who has written on the fly-leaves "EXEMPLAIRE CHOISI dont les objets ont été repeints sur les Originaux de mon Cabinet."

4415 CLOQUET, Anatomie des Vers Intestinaux, 4to. 8 *large plates, hf. russia,* 6s   1842

4416 CONNELL's Differential and Integral Calculus, 8vo. *cloth,* 5s   1844

4417 CONYBEARE and PHILLIPS, Outlines of the Geology of England and Wales, part 1, *all published,* sm. 8vo. *plates, calf, scarce,* 12s   1822

4418 COPENHAGEN ACADEMY TRANSACTIONS. Det Kongelige Danske Videnskabernes Selskabs Philosophiske og Historiske Afhandlinger, Deel I-V, 1823-36—Naturvidenskabelige og Mathematiske Afhandlinger, 12 vols. *complete series,* 1824-46—*Femte Række,* Naturvidenskabelig og Mathematisk Afdeling, Bind I-III, 1849-53 : together 20 vols. 4to. *upwards of* 250 *plates, bds.* £6.   1823-53

4419 ———— Det kongelige Danske Videnskabernes Selskabs naturvidenskabelige og mathematiske Afhandlinger, Vols. I-VIII, 4to. *many plates, bds.* £2.   1824-41

4420 CORNWALL ROYAL GEOLOGICAL SOCIETY, Transactions, Vols. I-IV, 8vo. *map and plates, two vols. calf, and two in bds. rare,* £2. 16s   Penzance, 1818-32

4421 CORSI, Catalogo d' una collezione di Pietre di Decorazione, con Supplemento, 8vo. *green morocco,* 7s   Roma, 1825-27

4422 ———— delle Pietre Antiche, 8vo. *a valuable work, sd.* 7s 6d   Roma, 1845

NATURAL HISTORY, SCIENCES, MATHEMATICS. 229

4423 COSSALI, Origine, transporto in Italia, e primi progressi dell' Algebra, storia critica con nuove disquisizioni analitiche e metafisiche, 2 vols. roy. 4to. *plates, sd.* 18*s*; or *hf. russia neat*, 25*s* *Parma, Reale, Tipogr.* 1797-9
4424 COSSARD's History of Astronomy, 4to. *diagrams, calf,* 5*s* 1767
4425 CRIVELLI, Elementi d'Arithmetica, 8vo. *vellum,* 6*s* *Venezia,* 1728
4426 CURTIS (J.) Guide to an arrangement of British Insects, Catalogue of all the named species in Great Britain and Ireland, 8vo. *cloth,* 7*s* 1829
4427 CURTIS (John) BRITISH ENTOMOLOGY, or illustrations and descriptions of the genera of Insects found in Great Britain and Ireland, complete in 16 vols. roy. 8vo. *with* 770 *coloured plates,* (pub. at £43. 16*s*) *a very fine original copy,* £16. 16*s* 1823-40
4428 CURTIS'S BOTANICAL MAGAZINE, from the commencement in 1786 to December, 1860, COMPLETE SET 1786-1860

CONTENTS:

SERIES I. Vols. 1--53; *plates,* 1—2704, with text; Index, 1 vol. [1786] 1793-1826
The last volume (53) ends also Dr. John SIMS' Series, called the NEW SERIES.
SERIES II. conducted by S. Curtis and Sir W. J. Hooker, Vols. 54—70; or New Series, Vols. I.—XVII.; *plates,* 2705—4131, with text and Index to the Second Series—17 vols. 1827-44
SERIES III. by Sir W. J. Hooker, Vols. 71—86, or Third Series, I—XVI.; *plates,* 4132—5248, with text 1845-1860
This, the scarcest portion, was published at 2 guineas per volume, making 32 guineas.
Together, the 3 Series, *hf. bd. uncut,* £55. 1786-1860
A fine complete set of Curtis's Magazine is seldom offered for sale Sets completed.
4429 CURTIS (W.) BOTANICAL MAGAZINE: ENGLISH and LATIN GENERAL INDEXES to the Plants contained in the seventeen volumes of the New or SECOND SERIES (being from Vols. LIV to LXX, inclusive of the whole work) of the Botanical Magazine, royal 8vo. *sd.* £2. 1862
I can also offer the text of the SECOND SERIES, and many of the plates on advantageous terms.
4430 CUVIER, le Règne Animal distribué d'après son organisation, pour servir de base a l'hist. naturelle des Animaux, 4 vols. 8vo. 15 *plates, hf. cf.* 15*s* *Paris,* 1817
4431 ——— nouvelle édition augmentée, 5 vols. 8vo. 20 *plates, hf. calf,* 12*s* 1829
4432 CUVIER, LE RÈGNE ANIMAL distribué d'après son organisation, pour servir de base à l'histoire naturelle des Animaux et d'introduction à l'Anatomie Comparée; nouvelle édition accompagnée de planches gravées, représentant les types de tous les genres, les caractères distinctifs des divers groupes, etc. etc. publiée par une réunion d'élèves de Cuvier; MM. *Audouin, Blanchard, Deshayes, de Quatrefages, d'Orbigny, Duvernoy, Laurillard, Milne Edwards, Roulin et Valenciennes,* 11 volumes de texte et 11 atlas, 22 vols. in 20, impl. 8vo. (small folio), *with* 993 *beautifully coloured plates* (pub. at £65.), *hf. morocco, gilt tops, uncut, a handsome set of books,* £36. *Paris,* 1848-49

ANALYSIS OF EACH DIVISION.	No. of Plates.	Price.		
1. Les Mammifères et les Races Humaines avec Atlas, par Milne Edwards, Laurillard et Roulin	121	7	15	0
2. Les Oiseaux avec Atlas, par A. d'Orbigny	102	6	15	0
3. Les Reptiles avec Atlas, par Duvernoy	46	3	5	0
4. Poissons avec Atlas, par Valenciennes	122	8	0	0
5. Les Mollusques avec Atlas, par Deshayes	152	9	15	0
6. Les Insectes avec Atlas, par Audouin, Blanchard et Milne Edwards	202	13	15	0
7. Les Arachnides avec Atlas, par Dugès et Milne Edwards	31	2	5	0
8. Les Crustacés avec Atlas, par Milne Edwards	87	5	15	0
9. Les Annélides avec Atlas, par Milne Edwards et de Quatrefages	30	2	0	0
10. Les Zoophytes avec Atlas, par Milne Edwards et Blanchard	100	6	5	0
The work complete	993	65	10	0

4433 CUVIER, ANIMAL KINGDOM, translated with additional descriptions, by E. GRIFFTH, Pidgeon, and others, with classified index, 16 vols. roy. 8vo. *several hundred* COLOURED PLATES, LARGE PAPER, *hf. green morocco, top edges gilt,* £21. 1827-35
A beautiful copy, from Miss Currer's library.
4434 ——— Recherches sur les OSSEMENS FOSSILES, ou l'on rétablit les caractères de plusieurs animaux dont les révolutions du globe ont détruit les espèces, 10 vols. 8vo. and 2 vols. 4to. *best edition,* 278 *plates,* £2. 10*s* *Paris,* 1836
4435 ——— Histoire des Progrés des Sciences Naturelles, depuis 1789 jusqu'a ce jour, 4 vols. 8vo. *calf gilt,* 21*s* *Paris,* 1829
4435*——— the same, nouvelle edition, complétée par M. de Saint Agy, 5 vols. in 2, 8vo. *hf. bd.* 15*s* 1841

4436 CUVIER, des Dents des Mammifères considerées comme caractères zoologiques. stout 8vo. 103 *plates, bds.* 21*s*   *Strasb.* 1825
4437 CUVIER, et VALENCIENNES, Histoire naturelle des POISSONS, (ouvrage contenant plus de 5000 espèces de ces animaux, distribués conformément à leurs rapports d'organisation, avec des observations sur leur anatomie, et des recherches sur leur nomenclature ancienne et moderne), 22 vols. 8vo. 650 *plates*, (*pub. at* 297 *fr.*) *hf. calf neat, Dr. Traill's copy*, £10. 10*s*   *Paris*, 1828-49
4438 —— the same, 22 vols. 8vo. PAPIER VELIN, *with* COLORED PLATES, (*pub. at* 616 *francs*) *hf. bd.* £17. 10*s*   *Paris*, 1828-49
4439 CUVIER et BRONGNIART, Géographie mineralogique des Environs de PARIS, 4to. *map and plate, sd.* 5*s*   *Paris*, 1811
4440 D'ALEMBERT, OPUSCULES MATHÉMATIQUES, ou Mémoires sur différens sujets de Géométrie, de Mechanique, d'Optique, d'Astronomie, etc. 8 vols. sm. 4to. *plates, calf gilt*, £5.   *Paris*, 1761-80
    Dr. Hutton's copy, vellum, fetched £7. 7*s.*
4441 —— Traité de l'Equilibre et du Mouvement des Fluides, sm. 4to. 10 *plates, French calf gilt*, 9*s*   *ib.* 1744
4442 —— Réflexions sur la cause generale des Vents, sm. 4to. 2 *plates, calf,* 9*s*   1747
4443 —— Memoires sur différens sujets de Mathematiques, 8vo. *plates, old French red morocco extra, gilt edges*, 10*s*   1748
4444 —— Recherches sur la Précession des Equinoxes, et sur la nutation de l'axe de la terre, dans le système Newtonien, sm. 4to. 4 *plates, calf,* 10*s*   1749
4445 —— Essai d'une nouvelle théorie de la Résistance des Fluides, sm. 4to. 2 *plates, calf gilt*, 10*s*   1752
4446 —— Recherches sur differens points importans du Système du Monde, 3 vols. sm. 4to. 6 *plates, fine copy in old French calf extra, gilt edges*, £2. 2*s*   1754-56
4447 —— Élémens de MUSIQUE théorique et pratique, 8vo. 10 *plates, hf. bd. uncut,* 15*s*   *Lyon*, 1779
4448 —— Traité de DYNAMIQUE, sm. 4to. *plates, old calf gilt*, 10*s*   1743
4449 —— le même, seconde edition augmentée, sm. 4to. *calf gilt*, 12*s*   1796

"D'Alembert's name will remain to the end of the world among those who, in the loftiest subjects of enquiry, have extended and enlarged the boundaries of knowledge."—*Alison.*

4450 DARWIN on the contrivances by which Orchids are fertilised, sm. 8vo. *cuts, cloth, new*, 7*s* 6*d*   1862
4450*DALYELL (Sir J. G.) the Powers of the Creator displayed in the Creation; or observations on life amidst the various forms of the HUMBLER TRIBES of animated nature, 2 vols. 4to. 116 *finely* COLOURED *plates of living subjects* (pub. at £8. 8*s*) *bds.* £3. 16*s*   *Van Voorst*, 1851-53
4451 —— the same, 2 vols.—Supplement, 27 *plates*, 1 vol.—together 3 vols. 4to. 143 *col. plates* (pub. at £10. 10*s*) *bds.* £6.   1851-58
4451*DE CANDOLLE, Prodromus Systematis Naturalis Regni Vegetabilis, 14 vols. in 16, 8vo. COMPLETE (pub. at 204 *fr.*) *cloth, double lettered*, £6. 6*s Paris*, 1824-58
4452 —— the same, Vols. I-IV, 8vo, *hf. russia*, 25*s*   *ib.* 1824-30
4453 —— Regni Vegetabilis Systema naturale, Vols. I, II, (*all published*), 8vo. *calf gilt*, 6*s*   *ib.* 1818
4454 —— Organographie Végétale, pour servir d'introduction à la Physiologie, 2 vols.—Physiologie Vegetale, ou exposition des fonctions des Végétaux, 3 vols. —together 5 vols. 8vo. 60 *plates*, (*pub. at* 38 *fr.*) *calf gilt*, 12*s*   *ib.* 1827-32
4455 —— Vegetable Organography, translated by Kingdon, 2 vols. 8vo. 23 *plates*, (*pub. at* 15*s*) *cloth*, 6*s*   1841
4456 (DE L'HOPITAL) Analyse des Infiniment Petits, sm. 4to. *calf*, 10*s* 6*d Paris*, 1696
4457 DELAMBRE, ASTRONOMIE: Histoire de l'Astronomie Ancienne, 2 vols. 1817— —Astronomie Moderne, 2 vols. 1821—Astronomie du moyen-age, 1 vol. 1819 —together 5 vols. 4to. *plates, bds. scarce*, £4. 10*s*   *Paris*, 1819-21
4458 DE LA RIVE, Traité d'Electricité théorique et appliquée, 3 vols. stout 8vo. 447 *woodcuts, sd.* 21*s*   *Paris*, 1854-58
4459 DE MORGAN, Arithmetical Books from the invention of printing to the present, 8vo. *a valuable bibliography, cloth*, 2*s* 6*d*   1847
4460 DESCRIPTION des ARTS et MÉTIERS, faite ou approuvée par M. M. de l'Académie Royale des Sciences, bound in 24 vols. folio, *several hundred excellent plates, halfcalf, contents lettered*, £7. 10*s*   *Paris*, 1761-89
    This work is a collection of practical Treatises on the various Arts and Manufactures, and minute Descriptions of the Implements and Processes, accompanied with admirable illustrations.

NATURAL HISTORY, SCIENCES, MATHEMATICS. 231

4461 DESMAREST, Considérations sur la Classe des Crustacés, stout 8vo. 56 *plates of* 140 *species, bds.* 18*s* *Paris*, 1825
4462 DESNOUES et GUGLIELMINI (*Professeurs de Bologne et de Padoue*) Lettres sur différentes nouvelles Decouvertes, sm. 8vo. *plates, rare and curious,* 7*s* *Rome,* 1706
4463 DEUSINGII de vero Systemate Mundi dissert. mathemat. sq. 8vo. *diagrams, vellum,* 5*s* *Amst. Elzev.* 1643
4464 DIARIAN REPOSITORY, or Mathematical Register, 4to. *hf. calf, curious,* 5*s* 1774
4465 DICTIONNAIRE (Nouveau) D'HISTOIRE NATURELLE, appliquée aux Arts, à l'Agriculture, à l'Economie Rurale et Domestique, à la Médicine, etc. par une Société de Naturalistes et d'Agriculteurs ; Nouvelle Edition, presqu' entièrement refondue et considerablement augmentée, avec des Figures tirées des trois Règnes de la Nature, 36 volumes, 8vo. and 1 vol. *with several hundred plates, calf neat,* £4. 10*s* *Paris,* 1816-19
4466 DILLENII Historia MUSCORUM ; in qua circiter 600 species describuntur, cum Appendice, etc. 4to. 85 *plates, half calf,* 18*s* *Oxon.* 1811
Scarce, only 250 copies printed.
4467 DILLWYN'S BRITISH CONFERVÆ; or coloured Figures and Descriptions of British Plants, referred by Botanists to the Genus Conferva; 4to. 115 *tinted plates,* (pub. at £5. 9*s*) *bds.* 25*s* 1809
4468 —— the same, *the plates* COLOURED, *hf. russia,* £2. 16*s* 1809
4469 —— Hortus Collinsonianus, royal 8vo. *presentation copy, with autograph inscription, bds.* 5*s* *Swansea, privately printed,* 1845
4470 —— Memoranda relating to Coleopterous Insects found in the neighbourhood of Swansea, large 8vo. *cloth, privately printed,* 7*s* 6*d* *Swansea,* 1829
4471 —— Review of References to the Hortus Malabaricus, 8vo. *privately printed.* 10*s* *ib.* 1830
4472 DIOPHANTI ALEXANDRINI Arithmetica, et de Numeris, cum commentariis Bacheti et de Fermat, *Graece et Lat,* fol. *calf,* 20*s* *Tolosæ,* 1670
4473 DIXON'S (F.) GEOLOGY and Fossils of the Tertiary and Cretaceous Formations of SUSSEX, royal 4to. 41 *plates, some coloured, new in cloth,* 25*s* 1850
A valuable and useful work ; the Geologist will find in its pages, or accurate plates, a helping guide in the course of his investigations.
4474 DONOVAN'S (E.) Natural History of BRITISH INSECTS in their several states, with the periods of their transformations, their food, economy, &c. and the History of such minute Insects as require investigation by the Microscope, 16 vols. 8vo. *complete with* 576 *finely coloured plates of Insects, their Chrysalides, and Caterpillars, and the plants on which they feed, calf gilt,* £9. 1792-1813
4475 —— Natural History of BRITISH SHELLS, figures and descriptions of all the species hitherto discovered, in the Linnean manner, 5 vols. royal 8vo. 180 *beautifully coloured plates, an original copy* (pub. at £7. 15*s*), *hf. bd. uncut,* £2. 5*s* 1804
4476 D'ORBIGNY, Dictionnaire universel d'Histoire Naturelle, résumant et complétant tous les faits présentés par les Encyclopédies, avec la description des êtres et des divers phénomènes de la nature par Arago, Audouin, Brongniart, Duponchel, Saint-Hilaire, Milne Edwards, etc. 13 vols. *of Text and* 3 *vols. of Atlas, containing* 288 *fine* COLOURED *plates,* together 16 vols. royal 8vo. *hf. red morocco,* £12. *Paris,* 1861
4477 DRAPARNAUD, Histoire Naturelle des Mollusques terrestres et fluviatiles de la France, avec le COMPLÉMENT, par Michaud, 2 vols. 4to. 16 *plates, sd.* 15*s*; or in 1 vol. *hf. morocco, gilt top, uncut,* 20*s* *Paris,* 1805-31
4478 DRURY'S (D.) Illustrations of Natural History, 3 vols. impl. 4to. *text in English and French, upwards of* 600 *figures of* EXOTIC INSECTS, *engraved on* 150 *plates, original* COLOURED *copy,* 3 vols. 4to. (pub. at £15. 15*s*) *hf. bd. uncut,* £2. 16*s* 1770-82
With an Index to Volumes II. and III. ; to the first none was published. "Drury's work has not been surpassed in beauty and accuracy of execution by any of the sumptuous efforts of the present day."
4479 DRURY (H.) the USEFUL PLANTS of INDIA, alphabetically arranged, with botanical descriptions, and notices of their values, 8vo. *cloth,* 21*s* *Madras,* 1858
4480 DRYANDER (James) Catalogus Bibliothecæ Historico-Naturalis Josephi Banks, Baroneti, 5 vols. in 9, 8vo. *hf. calf,* £2. 10*s* 1798-1800
4481 DUFRÉNOY, Traité de Mineralogie, 3 vols. *plates, with Atlas of* 224 *plates,* together 4 vols. 8vo. *calf extra,* 36*s* *Paris,* 1844-45
4482 DUGES, Recherches sur l'Ostéologie et la Myologie des Batraciens, 4to. 20 *plates, calf,* 10*s* *Paris,* 1834

4483 DUNKER, Index Molluscorum in itinere ad Guineam collectorum à Tams, 4to. 9 *cold. plates of nearly* 300 *specimens, cloth*, 12s 6d   *Cassel*, 1853

4484 DUPONCHEL, Catalogue méthodique des Lepidoptères d'Europe, stout 8vo. *interleaved hf. calf*, 12s   *Paris*, 1844
The above contains a general Index to the great work of "Godart et Duponchel sur les Lépidoptères de France."

4485 EAST INDIA Company Museum: Catalogue of the Mammalia, 1851—Catalogue of the Birds, by Horsfield and Moore. 2 vols. 1854-58—Catalogue of the Lepidopterous Insects by the same, Vol. I. 1857—together 4 vols. 8vo. *cloth*, £2. 5s   1851-58

4486 EDINBURGH ROYAL SOCIETY'S TRANSACTIONS, from the commencement in 1798 to 1857, 21 vols. 4to. *numerous plates*, 20 vols. *handsomely bound in calf gilt, the last in 4 parts, a fine set and now very scarce*, £21.   *Edinb*. 1788-1858

4487 EDWARDS (Geo.) NATURAL HISTORY of UNCOMMON BIRDS, and of some other rare and undescribed animals, *with the list of subscribers*, 4 vols.; GLEANINGS of NATURAL HISTORY, 3 vols.; together 7 vols. roy. 4to. 362 PLATES FINELY COLOURED *by the* AUTHOR, *uniform in old calf gilt*, £7. 7s.   1743-64
Dr. GEORGE SHAW'S COPY, who has latinized the names of each figured representation, and written it very neatly on each plate.
Priced, 1828, Payne and Foss, £31. 10s: 1831, Egerton, £24.; 1843, Bohn, £14. 14s. Fetched, Hibbert's copy, £20; and copies have frequently brought much higher prices at sales.
"Edwards was remarkably exact in his descriptions, and sufficiently so in his figures, that no zoological library, especially one for reference, should be without his volumes. His works are assuredly the most valuable, on general Ornithology, that have ever appeared in England."—SWAINSON.

4488 EHRENBERG'S Infusoria: Die Infusions-Thierchen als volkommene Organismen, in 2 vols. royal folio, *with* 64 *very finely* COLOURED *plates*, (pub. at £18.) *bds. rare*, £12.   *Leipzig*, 1838
The grandest publication of its kind; copies are getting already very scarce.
"It should be recollected that Ehrenberg, with a thirty-shilling microscope, produced his great work on the Infusoria: a work with which British microscopy has nothing to compare, although it has spent thousands of pounds annually on its instruments."—DR. LANKESTER'S SCHLEIDEN'S BOTANY, p. 580.

4489 EHRENBERG, Organisation, Systematik und Geographisches Verhältniss der Infusionsthierchen, folio, 8 *coloured plates, bds*. 15s   *Berlin*, 1830

4090 ENCYCLOPÆDIA BRITANNICA, or Dictionary of Arts, Sciences, and General Literature, seventh edition, 21 vols. 4to. *numerous engravings, strongly half bound calf, a bargain*, £9. 9s   *Edinb*. 1842

4191 ENCYCLOPÆDIA METROPOLITANA: MIXED SCIENCES, 4 vols. 4to. containing—Vol. I. Mechanics, Pneumatics, Optics, Astronomy, Magnetism, &c.—Vol. II. Electricity, Heat, Light, Chemistry, Sound, &c.—Vol. III. Meteorology, Architecture, Fine Arts, &c.—Vol. IV. Agriculture, Political Economy, Naval Architecture, Geology, &c. *numerous plates, hf. calf*, 28s   1829-36

4492 ENDLICHER (St.) Genera plantarum, secundum ordines naturales disposita, cum Supplemento primo et Indice, stout roy. 8vo. (pub. at £3. 16s 6d, *sd.) cloth*, £2. 5s   *Vindebonæ*, 1836-40

4493 ENDLICHER'S Paradisus Vindobonensis: Abbildungen seltener und schönblühender Pflanzen der Wiener und anderer Gärten und Museen, von Hartinger und Seeman, Vol. I. impl. folio, *text in German and English, with* 80 *beautiful plates, carefully coloured (pub. at* 112 *Thalers)*, £9.   *Wien*, 1860-62

4494 ENTOMOLOGICAL SOCIETY'S TRANSACTIONS, Vols. I.-IV. 1836-47, *calf gilt*—PROCEEDINGS, 1833-46, 2 vols. *half calf*—NEW SERIES, Vol. I. pts. 1—3; Vol. II. pts. 1, 5, and 6; Vol. III. pts. 1-7; Vol. IV. pts. 1-7; Vol. V. pts. 1 and 2—together 6 vols. and 22 parts, 8vo. *numerous beautifully coloured plates of Insects*, £7. 10s   1833-52

4495 ENTOMOLOGICAL MAGAZINE, from the beginning in 1832 to 1838, 5 vols. 8vo. *plates, some coloured, cloth*, £3. 10s   1832-8
With the last vol. is bound up "Walker's Monographia Chalciditum." This periodical contains interesting articles by Westwood, Newman, Curtis, Walker, Halliday, and others.

4496 ENGELMANN, Bibliotheca Historico-Naturalis, der Bücher in 1700-1846 erschienenen, Vol. I. 8vo. *with prices, sd*. 10s   *Leipzig*, 1846

4497 ——— Supplement-Band: Bibliotheca Zoologica, enthaltende die in Periodischen Werken aufgenommenen, und die von 1846-60 erschienenen Schriften, 2 vols. stout 8vo. *with prices, sd*. 20s   *ib*. 1861
"These catalogues are considered indispensable by every Zoologist."—J. H. GRAY.

4498 ESCHSCHOLTZ, Zoologischer Atlas, descriptions and figures of new species of Animals discovered by Kotzebue in his second Journey round the World, 4 parts, folio, COMPLETE, 20 COLOURED *plates of Mammals, Birds, Shells, etc. sd. a valuable work*, 12s   *Berlin*, 1829-31

4499 ESPER (E. J. C.) EUROPEAN AND EXOTIC BUTTERFLIES. Die Schmetterlinge in Abbildungen nach der Natur, mit Beschreibungen (The Lepidopterous Insects of Europe figured from Nature, with Descriptions), complete, *with the Supplements*, in 11 vols. (Text, 5 vols. in 6; Supplements, 1 vol.; Plates, 5 vols.) sm. 4to. *an original copy, plates finely coloured, bd. rare*, £10. 10s *Erlangen*, 1777-94

An admirable work, in which Esper has also figured many of the Caterpillars and the Plants on which they feed.

COLLATION.	Plates.	Pages.	COLLATION.	Plates.	Pages.
TAGFALTER.			EULEN.		
1. Theil. 1. Bd. Tab. I—XXIV.	24 ⎫		4. Theil. 1. Bd. Tab. LXXX.—CXVII. Noct.		
„ XXV—L. Suppl. I—	⎬	1—388	1—38.	38 ⎫	
XXVI.	26 ⎭		„ CXVII. A. Noct. 38a.	1	
2. Bd. „ LI.—XCIII. Cont. I—	⎫		„ CXVIII.—CXXV. Noct.		
XLIII.	43 ⎬	1—190	39—46.	8 ⎬	1—372
„ XCIV.—CXIII Cont.	1 ⎫	1—120	„ CXXV. B. Noct. 46b.	1	
49—78	30 ⎭	1—48	„ CXXV. C. Noct. 46c.	1	
DÆMMRUNGSFALTER.			„ XCIX. Noct. 20. B.	1	
2 Theil. „ I.—XVIII.	18 ⎫		„ CV. Noct. 26. B.	1 ⎭	
XIX.—XXV. Suppl.	⎬	1—196	2 Bd. „ CXXVI.—CXCVIII.	373—698	
I.—VII.	7 ⎭		Noct. 47—119.	73 ⎰ 1—85	
„ XXVI.—XLVII. Cont.	⎰ 197—234				
1—22.	22 ⎱ 1—52		SPINNER.		
SPINNER.			5 Theil. „ I.—LII.	52	1—276
3 Theil. „ I VI.	6 ⎫				
„ VI. A.	⎬	1—396		441	
„ VII.—LXXIX.	73 ⎭			Register—16	
„ LXXX.—XCIV. Cont.	⎰				
I.—XV.	15 ⎱ 1—104				

N.B Die Tafeln d. 1. Theiles 2. Band XCIV. Cont. 49 u. folg. sind. unrichtig bezeichnet. Es sollte heissen: Tab. XCIV. Cont. 44. u folg. Die im Texte zu Tab. CXXIII. Tom. I. erwähnten Zusätze, so wie die Tafeln des I. Theils 2. Band CXXIV.—CXXVI. sind nicht erschienen. Die Tafeln das IV. Theils I. Band LXXX. Noct. 1 u. folg. sind unrichtig bezeichnet, anstatt: Tab. I. Noct. 1 u. folg.; eben so CXCVIII. Noct. 49 anstatt; Tab. CXCVIII. Noct. 119. Der Text zu der Tafel des V. Theils XLIX. fig. 2—5 und zu den folgenden drei Tafeln ist nicht erschienen.

4500 ESPER'S ZOOPHYTES: Pflanzenthiere in Abbildungen nach der Natur mit Farben erleuchtet, 3 vols.—Fortsetzungen, Vol. I.—together 4 vols. in 2 of Text, with 3 vols. *containing* 442 COLOURED *plates, (being the illustrations to the entire work)* in all 7 vols. in 5, 4to. *hf. cf. gt. back*, £6. 10s *Nürnberg*, 1788-1830

Published complete, 431 plates, 1788-1806, at 76 Thalers ; priced, 1847, described as having 442 plates, £7. 7s Collation.—Vol. I. Title, Vorbericht, 5 leaves; Text, pp. 1 to 320. Plates, Isis, 1 to 4; Madrepora, 1 to 31, with 21 a; Millepora, 1 to 17; Cellepora, 1 to 6.
Vol. II. Title, Text, pp. 1 to 303. Plates, Gorgonia, 1 to 39; Antipathes, 1 to 9; Spongia, 1 to 49, with 7a and 21a.
Fortsetzungen, Vol. I. Title, half-title, Text, pp. 1 to 230. Plates, Madrepora, 32 to 83; Millepora, 18 to 28; Cellepora, 7 to 11; Gorgon, 39a to 50; Antipath. 10 to 13; Spong. 50 to 62.
Fortsetzungen, Vol. II. Half-title, Text, pp. 1 to 44. Plates, Isis, 9 to 11; Antipath. 14; Madrep. 84 to 87; Petrificata, 1 to 5; Spong. 63 to 70; Gorg. 51 to 55; Alcyon, 1 to 25; Pennatula, 1 to 8; Tubularia, 1 to 27; Corallina, 1 to 12; Flustra, 1 to 35; Sertular, 1 to 7; Vortie, 1 to 7.

4501 EUCLIDES, los seis libros primeros de la Geometria traduzidos por çamorano, *Madrid*, 1576—Perspectiva y Especularia, traduz. por Onderiz, *Sevilla*, 1585, 2 vols. in 1, sm. 4to. *diagrams, vellum*, 10s 1576-85

4502 EUCLIDIS Liber Elementorum, *Latine*, folio, FIRST EDITION, *beautiful capitals, many hundred diagrams, very fine copy, with early MS. notes, in the original limp vellum*, 30s *Venet. Ratdolt*, 1482

Première édition de cette version, et en même temps un des plus anciens livres imprimés ou se trouvent des figures de mathématiques,—BRUNET.

See also ante, page 93

4503 EULERI, Institutiones Calculi Differentialis, cum ejus usu in analysi finitimorum ac doctrina serierum, (ed. Sperionius) stout 4to. *calf*, 27s *Ticini*, 1787

4504 —— de causa physicâ Electricitatis, etc. 4to. *sd*. 5s *Petrop*. (1755)

4505 EYTON'S (T. C.) Monograph of the Anatidæ, or DUCK TRIBE, (including the Geese and Swans), 4to. *with* 24 *plates, (of which* 6 *are coloured,) and upwards of* 70 *woodcuts of Bills and Feet*, (pub. at £4.) *cloth bds*. £2. 10s 1838

4506 FABRI Strapulensis in Arithmetica Boethi epitome, 18mo. *vellum*, 7s *Basil*. 1553

4507 FABRICII Genera Insectorum, *Chilonii*, 1776—Species Insect. 2 vols. *Hamb*. 1781 —Mantissa Insect. 2 vols. *Hafn*. 1787, 5 vols. 8vo. *bd*. 7s 1776-87

4508 FALCONER and CAUTLEY's Fauna Antiqua Sivalensis, or the Fossil Zoology of the Sewalik Hills in the North of India, Parts 1 to 9, roy. folio, *numerous plates, sd.* with the Letter-press description to Part 1, roy. 8vo. *all yet issued*, (pub. at £9. 9s) *sd*. £5 1846-9

4509 FÉE, Essai sur les Cryptogames des Ecorces Exotiques officinales, 2 vols. large 4to. 43 *plates, mostly coloured*, 25s *Paris*, 1824-37

Contents: pp. 1-168, plate, 1-34; 2me. partie, supplément et revision, pp. 1-180, plates, 35-43.

4510 FERMAT, Varia Opera Mathematica, cum selectis ejusdem Epistolis de rebus ad Mathematicas disciplinas, aut Physicam pertinentibus, folio, *numerous diagrams, sd.* 30s *Tolosae*, 1679 (*Berlin*, 1861)

The original edition of Fermat Opera Varia, having become so scarce, the French Academy determined to reprint it, but not having done so, Mr. Friedländer the enterprising German publisher, has brought out an exact facsimile of the original by a new process invented by him.

4511 FERUSSAC, Histoire naturelle générale et particuliere des Mollusques Terrestres et Fluviatiles, œuvre posthume, continué et publié par le Baron d'Audebard de Ferrusac fils, 2 vols. large folio, GRAND PAPIER, 162 *very finely* COLOURED *plates*, (pub. at £63. and now reduced to £24.) *hf. bound russia*, £8. *Paris* 1819, *etc.*

Collation of the Plates: Planches 1-54, 56-71, 73-75, 77-82, 91-92, 101, 103-105, 108-10, 112-15, 117, 121, 125-128, 131-33, 135-36, 140-141, 147-48, 153, 155, 159, 163. 4 A, 7 A, 8 A-E, 9 A-B, 11 A, 21 A-B, 24 A, 25 A-B, 27 A, 28 B, 32 A-B, 39 A-B, 46 A, 49 A, 50 A, 51 A, 53 A, 51 A-B, 56 A-B, 58 A, 63 A, 66*, 69 A, 73 A, 75 A-B, 124 B, 131 A-B, 141 A, 142 B, 145 B. Fossils, 5 plates.

4512 FICHTEL et MOLL, Testacea Microscopica aliaque minuta ex generibus Argonauta et Nautilus, roy. 4to. LARGE PAPER, 24 COLOURED PLATES, *red morocco, super extra, gilt edges,* £2. 2s *Viennae*, 1798

4513 FIGUIER, Œuvres scientifiques: L'Alchimie et les Alchimistes, 1 vol.—L'Année Scientifique, 1857-60, 5 vols.—Principales Découvertes scientifiques, 4 vols.—together 10 vols. 8vo. *maps, cuts, etc. cloth,* 25s *Paris*, 1857-60

4514 **Fireworks.** BIRINGUCCIO, Pirotechnia, delle diversità delle Minere, della Fusione, ò Getto di Metalli, etc. sq. 8vo. *curious woodcuts, fine copy in vellum,* RARE, 14s *Venetia*, 1558

4515 ——— the same, another edition, thick 16mo. *curious woodcuts, vellum,* 12s 1559

4516 PYROTECHNICAL Discourses by KUNKEL, Stahl, and Fritschius, sm. 8vo. *old calf,* 6s 1730

4517 TRAITÉ des Feux d'Artifice pour le Spectacle, 8vo. *frontispiece and* 13 *folded plates, calf,* 6s *Paris*, 1747

4518 FITZROY (Admiral) the Weather Book, a manual of practical Meteorology, stout 8vo. 15 *plates with numerous meteorologial illustrations,* (pub. at 15s) *cloth,* 12s 6d 1863

Admiral Fitzroy's method is one of the highest practical utility, and should be studied.

4519 FISCHER et Meyer, Sertum Petropolitanum, seu Icones Plantarum in Horto Botanico Imperiali florentium, 10 *coloured plates*—Construction d'une Serre de Palmiers, *plan,* imp. folio, 12s *St. Petersb.* 1846

4520 FISCHER (G.) Zoognosia tabulis synopticis illustrata, Vol. I, 4to. Vols. II and III, 8vo. *hf. bd.* 7s 6d *Mosquae*, 1813-14

4521 FISCHER de Waldheim, Bibliographia Palœonthologica, 8vo. *sd.* 6s *Mosquae*, 1834

4522 FLORA DANICA. Icones Plantarum sponte nascentium in Regnis Daniæ et Norwegiæ, etc. editae ab Auctoribus, G. C. Œder, O. F. Müller, M. Vahl, J. W. Hornemann, et Liebmann, Fasc. I. ad XXXII. in 11 vols. folio, FINE PAPER, *with* 1920 *accurately* COLOURED PLATES, *presentation copy from H. M. the King of Denmark, F. II. S., to the Horticultural Society,* 10 *vols. calf, gilt edges, the eleventh volume in boards,* £25. *Havniæ*, 1766-1827

4523 ——— another set, fasciculi 1—43, or Vols. I.—XIV., 2580 *cloured plates,* 1766-1852—Supplementum, fasc. 1, cura, F. M. Liebmann, 60 *coloured plates,* 1853 —together 44 fasciculi, folio, 2640 FINELY COLOURED PLATES, (pub. at 800 Rixdalers) *fourteen volumes, hf. morocco, the remainder in parts,* £42. *ib.* 1766-1853

4524 FLORA DANICA, Vols. I—XI, or fasc. 1 to 22, folio, *containing plates* 1—1920, *very accurately* COLOURED, *wanting plates* 301, 302, *and the titles to V, VII, XI, unbound,* £5. *ib.* 1766-1827

Though the advertiser has succeeded in obtaining these two sets of the "FLORA DANICA," on fine paper, with COLOURED plates, he declares complete sets to be of the VERY RAREST OCCURRENCE in England or elsewhere. Copies with plain plates are easily obtained in Copenhagen, at 315 Rixdalers; the early volumes of coloured copies, on Fine Paper, are out of print, and of the new parts only the exact number wanted for the subscribers are executed. The "Flora Danica" is the most beautiful work of its kind published; it includes also every kind of FUNGI, omitted in Sowerby's English Botany. It may further be stated that there is scarcely any difference between the Flora of Denmark and that of Great Britain.

4525 HORNEMANN, Nomenclatura Floræ Danicæ emendata, 8vo. *fine paper, hf. calf,* 20s *Hafniæ*, 1827

4526 FORSKAAL, Flora Aegyptiaco-Arabica; Descriptiones Animalium in Oriente observatorum, etc.; edente Niebuhr, 2 vols. in 1, 4to. *maps, calf,* 15s *Haun.* 1775

NATURAL HISTORY, SCIENCES, MATHEMATICS. 235

4527 FORBES (E.) History of British Star-Fishes, and other animals of the Class Echinodermata, roy. 8vo. LARGE PAPER, *numerous woodcuts and elegant vignettes, hf. green morocco, gilt edges, very neat*, 30s 1841

4528 FORBES and HANLEY'S History of BRITISH MOLLUSCA, and their Shells, 4 vols. royal 8vo. 198 *very finely coloured plates of the animals and their shells,* (pub. at £13. in parts) *calf extra, gilt edges, by Hayday, Miss Currer's copy,* £11. 11s *Van Voorst*, 1853

4529 FORSTER, Florula Insularum Australium, 8vo *bds*. 5s *Gott*. 1786

4530 FRASER (Louis) Zoologia Typica, or Figures of new and rare Mammals and Birds, described in the Proceedings or exhibited in the collections of the ZOOLOGICAL SOCIETY OF LONDON, complete in 14 parts, impl. 4to. *with* 70 *large and finely* COLOURED *plates of* MAMMALS, BIRDS, *and a few plants,* (pub. at £7. 9s 6d) £5. *London, published by the Author*, 1849

4531 FREND'S Evening Amusements, or the Beauty of the Heavens displayed, 18 vols. in 9, *an annual publication of Astronomical Science, maps and numerous plates, calf,* 20s 1804-21

4532 FRIES (Eliae) Systema Mycologicum sistens Fungos hucusque cognitos, 3 vols. 12mo. *calf,* 15s *Gryphiswaldiae*, 1821

4533 FRISCH'S (J. L.) Vorstellung der Vögel Deutschlandes und beyläufig auch einiger Fremden, in Kupfer gebracht von F. H. Frisch (Representation of the Birds of Germany, and occasionally of some Exotic Birds), folio, 241 COLOURED *plates of* BIRDS, *with their names in German, Latin, and French, accompanied by text and an Index, a beautiful copy in russia*, £4. 10s *Berlin*, 1763

The colouring of the plates is very artistically done; the Birds are mostly life size.

4534 FRITZSCHE über den Pollen, 4to. 13 *coloured plates, bds.* 7s 6d *St. Petersb*. 1857
4535 FRISII, Arithmetica practica, 12mo. *mended, bds*. 7s *Witebergae*, 1547
4536 FUESSLY, Archives de l'Histoire des Insectes, 4to. 50 *cold. plates, hf. calf,* 7s 1794
4537 GAERTNER de Fructibus et Seminibus Plantarum, 2 vols. 1788—Supplementum Carpologiae, 1805—3 vols. 4to. 225 *plates, bd. Dr. Traill's copy,* £2. 2s; or together, *calf gilt*, £2. 16s *Stutgardiae*, 1788-1805
4538 GALEOTTI, Constitution Géognostique de Brabant, 4to. *plates, sd.* 5s 1838
4539 GALILEO GALILEI, OPERE, 2 vols. stout sm. 4to. *many cuts*, EDIZIONE PRIMA, *vellum,* 20s *Bologna,* 1656
4540 —— the same, THICK PAPER, *extremely rare, only one other copy known, calf, gilt edges,* £4. 16s 1656
4541 —— OPERE, accresciute di molte cose inedite, 4 vols. sm. 4to. *portrait and cuts, calf,* 20s *Padova*, 1744
4542 GALILEI (GALILEO) OPERE, PRIMA EDIZIONE COMPLETA, condotta sugli autentici manoscritti palatini (per cura di Eugenio Alberi), 16 vols. roy. 8vo. *including Galileo's correspondence,* LARGE PAPER, *portrait and numerous plates, sd. uncut*, £6. 6s *Firenze,* 1842-56

Many of the works of Galileo circulated extensively during his lifetime in MS., and were never printed. These have been collected from various parts of Europe, and are printed for the first time in this edition, verifying its claim to the title of *prima edizione completa.*
"Cette édition comprend tout ce que l'on connaissait déjà d'écrits de Galilée imprimés, plus une quantité de morceaux inédits qui constituent le tiers de la collection, parmi lesquels la correspondance de Galilée avec les savants de son temps, composée de près de 1600 lettres contenues en six volumes. Il s'y trouve aussi une quantité d'autres pièces qui se rapportent aux œuvres et à la vie de Galilée, ce qui constitue un corps d'ouvrage qui laisse bien en arrière toutes les précédentes editions des œuvres de ce grand homme."—*Brunet.*

4543 GALILEO, Discorsi e Dimostrazioni Matematiche, sq. 8vo. *bd*. 18s *Leida*, 1638
4544 GALILEO, the System of the World, in four dialogues, Inglished by Thomas Salisbury, folio, *calf, rare,* 24s 1661
4545 GARDINER (William) ILLUSTRATIONS of BRITISH BOTANY, and the natural method of arrangement, 3 vols. folio, *consisting of upwards of* 200 *carefully laid down* SPECIMENS OF PLANTS, *with MS. tables of contents, and the names to every Plant, Flower, or Moss, chiefly after Hooker, written under each, hf. bd.* £2. 5s *Dundee,* 1850

I have seldom seen flowers more delicately laid down. The arrangement is as follows: Vol. I, Vasculares, Exogens and Endogens, Flowering Plants; Vol. II. British Ferns and their Allies; Vol. III. Cellulares, Musci, Lichenes, Algae and Zoophyta.

4545*GAUSS, Theoria Motus; Theory of the Motion of the Heavenly Bodies moving about the Sun, in Conic Sections, translated by Davis, 4to. *plates, cloth,* 20s *Boston, U. S.* 1857

4546 GEINITZ, Grundriss der Versteinerungskunde, stout imp. 8vo. 28 *Plates of Fossils, Remains of Antediluvian Animals, etc. hf. calf*, 24s   *Dresden*, 1846

4546*GEMS. FEUCHTWANGER's Treatise on Gems, their practical and scientific value, 8vo. *cloth*, 5s   *New York*, 1838

4547 GEOFFROY, Histoire des Insectes, 2 vols. 4to. 22 COLOURED *plates, calf*, 12s 1799

4548 GEOLOGICAL SOCIETY'S TRANSACTIONS; a complete set from the commencement in 1817 to 1856, FIRST SERIES, 5 vols. 1817-21, *complete*—SECOND SERIES, Vols. 1 to 7, 1824-56, *complete*—together 12 vols. 4to. *several hundred Geological Maps and plates, hf. calf neat,* £18. 18s   1811-56

4549 PROCEEDINGS, 4 vols. 1826-45—QUARTERLY JOURNAL, Vols. I-XVII. Part 4, being Nos. 1 to 68 inclusive, 1845 to November 1861—together 9 vols. *hf. calf,* and 49 Nos. 8vo. *many plates*, A COMPLETE SET, (pub. at above £14. 12s) *rare*, £12.   1826-61

Sets completed at reasonable terms. Of the "Proceedings," the fourth volume is out of print; of the Quarterly Journal several of the early numbers.

4550 GEOLOGICAL SOCIETY OF FRANCE: Mémoires de la Société Géologique de France, Vols. I, II pt. 1, in 3 parts, 4to. *coloured plates, sd.* 20s   *Paris*, 1833-35

4551 GERARDE'S (John) Herball, or general Historie of Plants, very much enlarged and amended by Thomas Johnson, folio, *frontispiece, containing the portrait, by Payne, with several hundred woodcuts, fine copy in calf neat, from Miss Currer's library,* £2. 2s   1636

Praised and constantly quoted by Sir James Smith, in his *English Flora*; and Dr. G. Johnston, in the Preface to his excellent *Berwick Flora*, calls it "A book in which the botanical student will find much matter of amusement, and sometimes an excellence of description rare even in modern works, though expressed in a quaint manner and antiquated style."

Many remedial compounds mentioned by Gerarde, which modern enlightenment has treated as ridiculous, are now resuming their old importance.

4552 GHENT. ANNALES DE LA SOCIÉTÉ ROYALE d'Agriculture et de Botanique de Gand, 5 vols. impl. 8vo. *several hundred* COLOURED *plates, hf. calf,* £3. 3s 1845-49

4553 GILBERTI (*Colcestriensis*) de Magnete, magneticisque corporibus, et de magno Magnete tellure Physiologia nova, sm. folio, *numerous woodcuts, hf. bd. rare,* 12s   *Londini*, 1600

4554 —— idem Tractatus, sive Physiologia Nova emendatius edita à Lochman, sm. 4to. *plates and cuts, margins somewhat injured*, 15s   *Sedini*, 1628

A rare and important work for the history of early magnetical discovery, containing many curious original experiments. "Galilei calls the author a great man, and is envious of his great magnetic discoveries."

4555 GIRALT, Ensayo de una Flora Fanerogámica Gallega, 8vo. 16s   *Santiago*, 1852

4556 GODARD et DUPONCHEL, Histoire naturelle des LÉPIDOPTÈRES ou Papillons de France: Diurnes, 2 vols.—Crepusculaires, 1 vol.—Nocturnes, 8 vols. in 10—Supplément, 4 vols. — Monographie des Zygénides, 1 vol. — Catalogue méthodique des Lepidoptères, 1 vol.—together 17 vols. in 19, 8vo. 560 *coloured plates,* (*pub. at 807 fr. sd.*) *half calf neat,* £15.   *Paris*, 1821-44

COLLATION OF THE PLATES.		SUPPLEMENT.	
Planche explicative	1	Diurnes	50
Diurnes: Vol. I.	39	Crepusculaire	12
—— plates redesigned	6	Nocturnes	90
Vol II.	28	Monographie des Zygénides	8
Crepusculaires, Plates 13-22	12		
Nocturnes	314		Total 560

4557 GOEPPERT, über Steinkohlen, 4to. 23 *geological plates*, 14s   *Leiden*, 1848

4558 GORDON and GLENDINNING, the Pinetum, being a synopsis of all the Coniferous Plants at present known, with descriptions, history and synonymes, 8vo. xxii and 353 pp. (pub. at 15s) *cloth*, 12s   1858

The descriptions of the Genera are comprehensive though concise; and each species is accompanied by all its synonyms, with the authorities for them. Care has also been taken to furnish such information respecting habits, value, products, etc. as are likely to be required by the planter or cultivator.

4559 GÖTTINGEN ACADEMY: Commentarii Societatis Regiæ Scientiarum Gottingensis, 1751-54, 4 vols.—Novi Commentarii, 1769-76, 7 vols.—Commentationes, 1778-99, 14 vols.—together 25 vols. 4to. *plates, hf. bd.* £2. *Gottingae*, 1752-1800

4560 GOLDFUSS, Petrefacta Germaniæ: Abbildungen und Beschreibung der Petrefacten Deutschlands und der angrenzenden Länder, 4to. *text in German and Latin, with Supplement, and folio Atlas of about* 200 *Plates, second edition,* (*pub. at 70 thalers*) £8. 10s   *Leipzig*, 1862

NATURAL HISTORY, SCIENCES, MATHEMATICS.

4561 GOULD'S (John) BIRDS OF EUROPE, COMPLETE, 5 vols. impl. folio, 449 *superbly coloured plates, an original beautiful* SUBSCRIBER'S COPY, (*out of print*) £110. 1837
"Of the five volumes of which the work on the birds of Europe consists, the first comprises the raptorial order or birds of prey, namely, vultures, (of which three species are found in southern Europe), the eagles, hawks, and owls. The second and third are devoted to the insessorial, or perching birds, an extensive order, composed of groups varying in habits and manners, in powers of flight and in the nature of their food. Some, like the swallow, take their insect prey on the wing, some search for it on the ground, some on the bark or among the foliage of the trees; others are exclusively berry-feeders, and others feed upon insects and their larvæ, together with grain and fruits. The rasorial (or gallinaceous) and the grallatorial (or wading) orders are comprehended in the fourth volume, and the natatorial (or swimming) order occupies the fifth.

4561* GOULD'S BIRDS OF AUSTRALIA, complete in 7 vols. atlas folio, *with* 600 *plates, most* CAREFULLY COLOURED, (pub. in 36 parts at three guineas, making £113. 8s; cost of binding, £17. 10s, total, £130. 18s) *half bound, green morocco, Miss Currer's subscription copy*, £115. 1848
This great work will soon be out of print, as very few copies remain in the hands of the author, who sells them in boards at £115. cash.

4562 ———— BIRDS OF AUSTRALIA, SUPPLEMENT, Parts I, II, III, impl. folio, 49 *finely col. plates, with descriptions,* (pub. at £9. 9s) *bds.* £6. 6s 1851-59

4563 ———— MAMMALS OF AUSTRALIA, Parts I.-XII. impl. folio, 180 *beautifully* COLOURED *plates* (pub. at £37. 16s) *Mr. Bell's original subscription copy in parts,* £25. 1845-60
One more part will complete the work; the price of which will then be raised.

4564 ———— BIRDS OF GREAT BRITAIN, the author's latest work, Parts I, II, impl. fol. 30 *beautifully coloured plates,* £6. 6s 1862-63
It cannot at present be stated in how many parts the work will be completed, but it is expected to finish it in eight or nine years.

4565 ———— A Century of Birds from the Himalaya Mountains, impl. folio, 80 *coloured plates, pub.* at £14. 14s, *out of print* 1832

4566 ———— BIRDS of ASIA, Parts 1—15, impl. folio, *pub. at* £47. 5s (*the number of parts in which this work will be concluded, cannot yet be determined*) 1850-62

4567 ———— MONOGRAPH of the TROCHILIDÆ, or family of HUMMING BIRDS, 25 parts forming 5 vols. imp. folio, *coloured plates, published at* £78. 15s 1850-61

4568 ———— Monograph of the Ramphastidae, or family of Toucans, imp. folio, 34 *colored plates, pub.* at £7.

4569 ———— Ramphastidae, second edition, with additions, *plates redrawn, pub. at* £12. 12s

4570 ———— Monograph of the Trogonidae, or family of Trogons, imp. folio, 36 *coloured plates, pub.* at £8. 1838

4571 ———— Trogonidae, second edition, Part I (to be completed in 4 parts) impl. fol. *all the plates redrawn, with additions, pub. at* £3. 3s

4572 ———— Monograph of the Odontophorinae, or Partridges of America, imp. folio, *coloured plates, pub. at* £8. 8s 1844-50

4573 GRAY (John Edw.) ILLUSTRATIONS OF INDIAN ZOOLOGY, consisting of coloured plates of new or hitherto unfigured Animals from the Collection of Major-General HARDWICKE, 20 parts in 2 vols. roy. folio, 202 *beautifully* COLOURED *plates* (pub. at £21. *sewed*) £16. 16s 1830-34
A beautiful work, a necessary companion to the labours of Geoffroy St. Hilaire and Cuvier.

☞ Sets completed, at the rate of 1s. and 2s. per plate.

4574 GRAY (G. R.) THE GENERA OF BIRDS, comprising their generic characters, a notice of the Habits of each Genus, and an extensive List of Species referred to their several Genera, 50 parts forming 3 vols. folio, with Appendix and Index, *illustrated by about* 350 *superb plates,* THE BIRDS FULLY COLOURED, *the details plain, by D. W. Mitchell,* (subscription price, £26. 5s, now selling for £31. 10s) £25. 1844-49

4575 ———— the same, *wanting the plates to Accipitres,* 1-15, *plain and coloured,* 3 vols. folio, *hf. red morocco,* £16. 16s 1844-49
The scientific merit of Gray's text, and the artistic beauty of Mitchell's plates, render the above a most desirable work for any library. Very few copies ever turn up under the present price of 30 guineas; it is the most Scientific work on Ornithology published in Great Britain, more complete, and as accurate as the costly works of Gould.

4576 GREG and LETTSOM, Manual of the Mineralogy of Great Britain and Ireland, 8vo. (pub. at 15s) *cloth,* 9s 1858

4577 GREVILLE'S SCOTTISH CRYPTOGAMIC FLORA, or coloured figures and descriptions of Cryptogamic plants belonging to the order FUNGI: and intended chiefly to serve as a continuation of English Botany, 6 vols. large 8vo. 360 COLOURED *plates of* FUNGI, *etc. original copy in hf. green morocco, gilt edges,* £6. 6s *Edinburgh,* 1823-28

4578 GREGORY's Treatise on Mechanics, theoretical, practical and descriptive, 3 vols. 8vo. " a work of great use," 63 *large plates, half calf*, 7s 6d   1826

4580 GREVIN (Jacques) Deux livres des VENINS, des bestes venimeuses, theriaques, poisons et contrepoisons, sm. 4to. *curious woodcuts, vell. rare*, 27s Anvers, 1568

4581 GRIFFITH and HENFREY's Micrographic Dictionary, a guide to the investigation of the nature of Microscopic objects, stout 8vo. 41 *plates, some coloured, and* 816 *woodcuts* (pub. at 45s) *cloth*, 25s   1826

4582 GRIFFITH'S (W.) Indian Botanical Works, arranged by John Maclelland: Posthumous Papers, bequeathed to the Hon. East India Company.
A. 8vo. Text: Journal of Travels in Assam, Burma, Bootan, Affghanistan, etc. *portrait of Griffith, and* 16 *plates, Calcutta*, 1847—Vol. II. Itinerary Notes of Plants collected in the Khasyah and Bootan Mountains and in Affghanistan, 1837-41, *map, and* 3 *plates*, 1848—Notulae ad Plantas Asiaticas; part 1, Development of Organs in Phanerogamous Plants, 1847—Notulae, part 2, on the higher Cryptogamous Plants, 1849 — Notulae, part 3, Monocotyledonous Plants, 1851 — Notulae, part 4, Dicotyledonous Plants, 1854 — Calcutta Journal of Natural History, Nos. 17, 18, containing the Palms of British East India, and the Cryptogamous Plants of Roxburghe, by Griffiths, 1844
B. 4to. Plates: Icones Plantarum Asiaticarum, part 1, Development of Organs in Phanerogamous Plants, 62 *coloured plates*, 1847; part 2, Cryptogamous Plants, 1849, *plates*, 63-138; part 3, Monocotyledonous Plants, 1851, *plates* 139-174, 243-359; part 4, Dicotyledonous Plants, 1854, *plates* 360-661
C. folio, Plates: Palms of British East India, *complete*, 1 vol. royal folio, *plates* 775-242 B
The 3 series complete—together 6 vols. 8vo. 4 vols. 4to. and 1 vol. folio, *bds*.
A COMPLETE SET, £10.   *Calcutta*, 1848-54

4583 ——— the same, quite perfect, but without the two numbers of the Calcutta Journal, £8. 8s   1848-54
Many odd parts of these works float about the market, complete sets however are very scarce, as some of the parts were printed in a small number only.

4584 GRONINGEN ACADEMY. Annales Academiæ Groninganæ, 1815 to 1837; Acta Saecularia Groninganae, 1814—together 23 vols. 4to. *uncut*, £2.   1814-39

4585 GUNNERI Flora Norvegica, 2 parts in 1 vol. sm. folio, 12 *plates, bd*. 12s
Nidrosiae (Tronheim, in the North of Norway), 1766-72

4586 GYLLENHALL, Insecta Suecica, Classis I.: Coleoptera sive Eleuterata, 3 vols. 8vo. *calf*, 14s   *Scaris*, 1808-13

4587 HALDEMAN'S Monograph of the Freshwater Univalve Mollusca of the United States, including notices of species in other parts of North America, complete as far as published, 8 Nos. in 1 vol. roy. 8vo. 39 *finely* COLOURED *plates, rare in this country, hf. calf, uncut*, £2. 12s   *Phil*. 1842

4588 HALLER, Bibliotheca Botanica, 2 vols. 4to. *calf gilt*, 10s   *Lond*. 1771
A very useful and most carefully written Bibliography of all Botanical Works.

4589 HARRIS (MOSES) THE AURELIAN; or Natural History of English Insects, namely, Moths and Butterflies, together with the plants on which they feed, roy. folio, LARGE PAPER, 44 *plates, containing* 400 *figures of Moths, Butterflies, etc. beautifully coloured, calf*, 20s   *Printed for the Author*, 1766

4590 ——— Exposition of English Insects, described and arranged according to the Linnan System, imp. 4to. *text in French and English, frontispiece and* 51 *coloured plates*, " a beautiful work in great estimation," *hf. bd*. 28s   1782

4591 HARRIS' (T. W.) Treatise on some of the insects injurious to Vegetation, new edition, enlarged and improved, with engravings drawn from nature under the supervision of Agassiz, by Flint, 8vo. 8 *coloured plates, containing several specimens, and numerous woodcuts, cloth, new*, 20s   *Boston*, 1862

4592 ——— the same, large 8vo. *plates beautifully coloured* (pub. at £2. 2s) *new in cloth*, 32s   *Boston*, 1862

4593 HARRIS'S (Captain W.) GAME AND WILD ANIMALS OF SOUTHERN AFRICA, delineated from Life in their Native Haunts, during a Hunting Expedition from the Cape Colony as far as the Tropic of Capricorn, in the years 1836 and 1837, with Sketches of the Field Sports, large impl. fol. *containing* 30 *highly interesting and beautifully* COLOURED ENGRAVINGS, *and* 30 *vignettes of Heads, Skins, &c*. (pub. at £10. 10s in bds.) *whole bound in green* MOROCCO *extra, gilt edges, by* HERING, *an original copy from Mr. Richardson's library*, £5. 5s
Published for the proprietor, 1840
A sumptuous volume, a companion to Gould's works.

NATURAL HISTORY, SCIENCES, MATHEMATICS.

4594 HARVEY'S (W. H.) PHYCOLOGIA BRITTANICA, or, a history of British Sea-Weeds, containing coloured figures and descriptions of all the species of Algae inhabiting the shores of the British Islands, 4 vols, roy. 8vo. 360 *beautifully coloured plates arranged systematically according to the synopsis* (pub. at £7. 17s 6d) *cloth, uncut*, £6. 1846-51

4595 HARVEY's Manual of British Algæ, 8vo. *woodcuts, cloth, 7s 6d Van Voorst*, 1841

4596 HASSALL'S History of the British Fresh-Water Algæ, including the Desmideæ and Diotomaceæ, 2 vols. 8vo. (pub. at 45s) 103 *tinted plates, cloth*, 36s 1845

4597 HASSKARL, Catalogus Plantarum in horto botanico Bogoriensi cultarum alter, 8vo. *bds. 7s* *Bataviae*, 1844

4598 HAWORTH, Lepidoptera Britannica, sistens Digestionem novam Insectorum quæ in Magna Britannia reperiuntur, 4 parts, 8vo. complete, *bds.* 30s 1803-28
Very few copies of this valuable work exist complete. Collation: Parts 1-4 have xxxv. and 610 pp. To the first part are appended: Miscellanea naturalia, sive dissertationes sex, 206 pages.

4599 HAYES (W.) PORTRAITS OF RARE AND CURIOUS BIRDS, with their Descriptions, from the Menagery of OSTERLY PARK, 2 vols. in 1, roy. 4to. AN ORIGINAL COPY, 100 *plates beautifully coloured, russia extra, with arms of the Duke of Roxburghe on sides*, £3. 16s 1794-99
Priced, 1827, Greenland, £7. 7s; 1840, Longman, £6. 6s. Evans' copy fetched £5. 5s. Copies are seldom met with more than 80 plates.

4600 HENDERSON'S (Alex.) History of Ancient and Modern WINES, 4to. *beautiful woodcuts* (pub. at £2. 2s) *hf. morocco, uncut,* 30s 1824
1829, Hibbert's copy fetched £2. 2s.

4601 HENNAH's Account of the Lime Rocks of Plymouth, impl. 8vo. *plates, bds.* 7s 6d *Plymouth, ca.* 1826

4602 HERBAL. The great Herball newly corrected. In fine, Thus endeth the grete herball with hys tables, sm. folio, 𝕭lack letter, *double columns, title within a woodcut border, a fine tall copy, some of the leaves being uncut, in the original stamped old calf binding,* RARE, £2. *Londini in edibus Thome Gybson*, 1539
Collation: Title within a woodcut border, on the back of which is "the prenter to the reder," 1 leaf; Table after the latyn names, 3 leaves; A 1 to Cc 6, in fours, except Cc, which has six.

4603 HERBAL. EARLY LOW GERMAN. ORTUS SANITATIS. Hiir hevet an de lustighe und nochlighe GAERDE DER SUNTHEIT, in *Low German*, smallest folio, *printed in* gothic letter, *many curious woodcuts, vellum*, £4. *Lubeck, Arnd*, 1492
Valuable to Philologists; many English popular names for Plants and Flowers, will find here their synonyms.

4604 HERBST (J. F. W.) Versuch einer Naturgeschichte der KRABBEN und KREBSE; the Natural History of Crabs and Crawfish, with a systematic description of their Species, 3 vols. 4to. *portrait and* 62 *large* COLOURED *plates* (pub. at £11. 5s) *hf. russia, an original copy*, £4. *Zurich*, 1782; *Berlin*, 1796-99
Without a title to the third volume.

4605 HERMANN, Mémoire Aptérologique, par Hammer, folio, 9 *coloured plates of Aptera, hf. russia*, 20s *Strasbourg*, 1804

4606 HERNANDEZ (Fr.) Rerum Medicarum Novæ Hispaniæ Thesaurus, cum notis Terentii, Fabri, &c. cumque hist. Animalium et Mineralium libro unico, in 1 vol. folio, *numerous cuts of American Plants, Quadrupeds, Birds, etc. title inlaid, fine copy in calf, rebacked; or in old red morocco, gilt edges*, £4. *Romæ*, 1651

4607 HERONE, Spiritali, ridotti in lingua volgare da Giorgi, sq. 8vo. *numerous woodcuts, vellum*, 9s *Urbino*, 1592

4608 HERRMANNSEN Indicis generum Malacozoorum primordia, Fasc. 1 to 6, 8vo. *sd.* 6s *Cassel*, 1846-47

4609 HEUFLER, Flora Cryptogama vallis Arpasch, Carpat. Transylv. imp. folio, 7 *fine plates by the nature-printing process*, 10s *Viennae*, 1853

4610 HEWITSON'S BRITISH OOLOGY, being Illustrations of the Eggs of British Birds, 2 vols. roy. 8vo. 128 PLATES FINELY COLOURED, *green morocco extra, gilt edges, from Miss Currer's library*, £4. *Newcastle-on-Tyne, n. d.* (1831-8)
Priced, 1847, £5. 5s.

4611 HISTORY of Fossil Fuel, the Collieries, and Coal Trade, 8vo. *cuts, cloth*, 6s 1841

4612 HOLMES on the Coal Mines of Durham and Northumberland, 8vo. *plates, bds.* 5s 1816

4613 HOLMSKIOLD, Fungi Danici: Clavariae, Ramariaeque, etc. imp. *Lat. et Dan.* folio, *fine paper, with* 32 COLOURED *plates, bds.* 20s *Hauniae*, 1790

4614 HOOKER'S (J. D.) FLORA ANTARCTICA: the Botany of the Antarctic Voyage of H.M.S. EREBUS and TERROR, 1839-1843, 25 parts complete, royal 4to. *illustrated with* 198 *beautifully coloured plates*, £9. 9s 1844-47

4615 —— RHODODENDRONS of SIKKIM-HIMALAYA; being an Account of the Rhododendrons recently discovered in the Mountains of Eastern Himalaya, edited by Sir W. Hooker, impl. folio, *with* 30 *large* COLOURED *plates by W. Fitch*, (pub. at £3. 16s in parts) *hf. green morocco*, £3. 1849

4616 HOOKER (Sir W. J.) BRITISH JUNGERMANNIÆ, being a History, with coloured figures of each species of the Genus, and Microscopical Analyses of the parts, royal 4to. 88 *finely coloured plates, calf gilt*, RARE, £6. 1816

4617 —— MUSCI EXOTICI, containing the Figures and Descriptions of Foreign Mosses, and other Cryptogamic Subjects, 2 vols. 4to. 152 *remarkably well co-*LOURED *plates, hf. calf, presentation copy from the author to Dr. Horsfield, with the latter's autograph, rare*, £3. 10s 1818-20

Priced, small paper, plates uncoloured, 1855, cloth, £2. 5s; Large Paper, coloured plates, 1840, J. Boh¹, unbound, £7. 7s.
Collation of the plates: 1-12, 25-96, 121-176; with 12 additional plates, Nos. 49-60.

4618 —— FILICES EXOTICAE, or Coloured Figures and Descriptions of Exotic Ferns, chiefly of such as are cultivated in the Royal Gardens at Kew, roy. 4to. 100 *beautifully coloured plates by* FITCH (pub. at £6. 11s, unbound) *hf. green morocco, gilt edges*, £5. 5s 1859
The most magnificent work on Foreign Ferns that has yet appeared.

4619 HOPE (Hen. Philip) Catalogue of his Collection of PEARLS and PRECIOUS STONES, arranged and described by B. HERTZ, atlas, 44 *plates, cloth, probably the author's copy, numerous MS. references*, 25s 1839
Fetched, 1854, Loscombe, £2. 5s.

4620 HORSFIELD'S (Dr. T.) PLANTÆ JAVANICÆ RARIORES descriptæ, iconibusque illustratæ, quas in insulâ JAVA, 1802-18, legit et investigavit Thomas Horsfield, e siccis descriptiones elaboravit BENNETT; observationes structuram respicientes, adjecit ROBERTUS BROWN, atlas 4to. *large map, and* 50 *beautifully coloured plates* (pub. at £8. 8s) *half morocco*, £4. 1838-52

4621 —— Zoological Researches in Java and the neighbouring Islands, 4to. 65 *finely coloured plates, and* 7 *of Anatomy* (pub. at £8. 8s) *rare*, £4. 15s 1824

4622 —— Descriptive Catalogue of the LEPIDOPTEROUS INSECTS in the Museum of the East India Company, illustrated by Figures of New Species and of the Metamorphosis of Indian Lepidoptera, with introductory observations, parts I. and II. *(all published)*, 8 *plates by Curtis and Newton, finely coloured*, (pub. at £4. 4s) 1828-9 —MACLEAY'S Annulosa Javanica, No. 1, *all published, one plate, containing* 9 *figures* (pub. at 10s 6d)—together, 3 parts in 1 vol. roy. 4to. *hf. morocco*, 30s 1828-9

4623 —— Catalogue of the Lepidopterous Insects in the Museum of the East India Company, Vol. I. 8vo. 18 *coloured plates, cloth*, 10s 1857

4624 —— Catalogue of Birds in the E.I.C. Museum, Vol. I. 8vo. 7s 6d 1854

4625 HORTUS INDICUS MALABARICUS, continens Regni Malabarici omnis generis Plantas rariores, adornatus per H. Van Reede Van Drakestein et J. Casearium; commentariis illustravit Arnoldus Syen, 12 vols. in 6, large folio, *comprising* 794 *folding plates, the name of each Plant in Latin, Tamul, Sanscrit, and Arabic, sound copy in old gilt russia*, £12. 12s; or, *old calf gilt*, £15. Amst. 1678-1703

Mr. A. B. Lambert paid Edwards, the bookseller, £47. 5s for a copy; none has occurred in London sales for many years. Priced, 1854, Müller in Amsterdam, 325 florins,
Ouvrage estimé et recherché dont les exemplaires sont rares Vendu avec la *Flora Malabarica*, petite brochure, 1061 liv. à l'hôtel de Bullion, en 1786; 721 liv. chez le duc de la Vallière, en 1784; mais ordin. 500 à 600 liv.

4626 HUGHES' Natural History of Barbadoes, roy. folio, LARGE PAPER, *map and* 29 *plates, calf*, 20s 1750

4627 HUMPHREYS and WESTWOOD, British Moths and their Transformations, 2 vols.—British BUTTERFLIES and their Transformations—together, 3 vols. 4to. *best edition*, 166 *beautifully coloured plates*, (pub. at £7. 8s), *cloth*, £4. 1848-51
The alphabetical list of the English names of Moths does not exist.

4628 HUTTON'S Tracts on Mathematical and Philosophical Subjects, the Theory of Bridges, the Force of Gunpowder, the Practice of Artillery, etc. 3 vols. 8vo. *calf neat*, 18s 1812

4629 IDELER, Ursprung und Bedeutung der Sternnamen, 8vo. *hf. bd.* 5s 6d *Berlin*, 1809

NATURAL HISTORY, SCIENCES, MATHEMATICS. 243

4672 LEIPZIG TRANSACTIONS. Acta Eruditorum ab anno 1682 ad annum 1731, 50 vols. in 38, 1682-1731—Nova Acta, 1732-76, 45 vols. in 22, 1732-82—Supplementa, 10 vols. 1692-1734—Ad Nova Acta Supplementa, 8 vols. in 4, 1735-57—Indices, 1682-1741, 6 vols. 1693-1745—together 119 vols. in 80, sm. st. 4to. *numerous plates, fine uniform set in vellum*, £10. *Lipsiæ*, 1682-1782

4673 Le Seur et Jacquier, Calcul Intégral, 2 vols. 4to. *plates, calf*, 12s *Paris*, 1768

4674 LESSON, Ouvrages de : Histoire Naturelle des Oiseaux-Mouches, 1 vol. 8vo. *grand-raisin accompagné de 86 planches coloriées*—Histoire Naturelle des Colibris, suivie d'un supplément à l'Histoire naturelle des oiseaux-mouches, 1 vol. 8vo. *grand-raisin, accompagné de 66 planches coloriées*, (dont Colibris, 40 *planches*, et le Supplément des Oiseaux-Mouches, 26 *planches*)—Histoire Naturelle des Trochilidées, suivie d'un index, dans laquelle sont décrites et classées méthodiquement toutes les races et espèces du genre *Trochilus*, 1 vol. 8vo. *grand-raisin, accompagné de 66 planches coloriées*, vellum paper, divided into 4 vols. royal 8vo. 218 *beautifully coloured plates*, (pub. at 440 fr. in parts) *hf. bound red morocco, gilt tops, uncut*, £8. 15s *Paris*, 1840

4675 ——— Illustrations de Zoologie, ou recueil de figures d'Animaux peintes d'après nature, 8vo. (pub. at £2. 10s) 60 *coloured plates, hf. morocco*, 30s *Paris*, 1831

4676 ——— Histoire naturelle des Colibris, avec Supplément a l'histoire des Oiseaux-Mouches, 8vo. 64 *coloured plates*, (pub. at about 36s) *the margins of the last 10 leaves slightly wormed, hf. calf*, 28s *Paris*, (1837)

4677 ——— Histoire des Zoophytes : Acalèphes, 8vo. 12 *plates, hf. calf*, 15s *ib*. 1843

4678 LEWIN'S (W.) Papilios of Great Britain, systematically arranged, accurately engraved, and painted from Nature, with the Natural History of each Species, in English and French, 46 *plates accurately and delicately coloured under the author's inspection, calf*, 25s 1795

4679 LEWIN (J. W.) *late of Paramatta, New South Wales*, Natural History of the Birds of New South Wales, collected, engraved, and faithfully painted after nature, folio, fine paper, 26 brilliantly coloured plates, *russia gilt*, £2. 12s 6d 1805

" Admirable figures, full of truth and nature; accompanied by valuable observations on the habits and economy of the Birds."—*Swainson*. "According to the first ornithologists of the day, these plates are of permanent value."—*Wood*.

4680 LEYDEN Academy Transactions : Annales Academiae Lugduno-Batavae, 1815-37, 22 vols. 4to. *plates, bds.* 20s *Lugd. Bat.* 1817-38

4681 LIEGE. Mémoires de la Société Royale des Sciences de Liège, 8 vols. in 11, large 8vo. *plates and* 4to. *atlas, sd.* £3. *Liege*, 1843-55

4682 (LINDLEY), Icones Plantarum spontè Chinâ nascentium ; è Bibliotheca Braamianâ excerptæ, roy. folio, 30 *finely coloured plates of Chinese flowers in bloom*, (pub. at £3. 3s) *cloth*, 15s 1821
Priced, 1847, £1. 11s 6d.

4683 LINDLEY and Hutton's Fossil Flora, complete in 24 parts, 8vo. *many plates, sd.* £5. 15s 1831-37

4684 LINNEAN SOCIETY'S TRANSACTIONS, from the commencement in 1791 to 1833, Vol. I. to XVI, 4to. *hf. russia*, £5. 1791-1833
The reduced charge which the Society now make for Vols. I-XX, is £20.
The completion of the set supplied at about half price. Many separate volumes and parts now in stock, are offered at a reduced price for the completion of sets.

4685 LINNEAN SOCIETY'S Proceedings, part 1—10 (1856-58); Supplements to Vols. IV. and V. Zoology and Botany (1860); and Nos. 18, 19—together 14 parts, 8vo. (pub. at £2. 12s) *sd.* 36s 1856-61

4686 Linnaei Systema Naturæ per regna tria, ed. à Gmelin, 3 vols. in 8, sm. 8vo. *calf*, 12s *Lugd*. 1789-96

4687 LIONVILLE, Journal de Mathématiques Pures et Appliquées, Recueil mensuel de Mémoires sur les diverses parties des Mathématiques, Vols. I-XIII, 4to. *plates* (pub. at 330 fr.) *nine vols. in cloth, the remainder sd. an extremely valuable and rare scientific periodical*, £10. 10s *Paris*, 1836-48
Priced, 1855, Friedländer in Berlin, Vols. I-XIX, 125 thalers; 1856, Vols I-XIX, £20.; 1859, Weber in Berlin, Vols. I-XX, 125 thalers.

4688 LISBON ACADEMY. Memorias, Historia e Memorias, Memorias dos Socios a dos Correspondentes da Academia Real das Sciencias de Lisboa, desde 1780 teé 1837, Vols. I—XI, sm. folio, *plates and tables, hf. calf, uncut*, £5. 10s *Lisboa*, 1797-1837

4689 LISTER (M.) Historia Conchyliorum et Tabularum Anatomicarum, editio altera, recensuit et Indicibus auxit G. Huddesford, folio, *with* 1079 *plates, fine copy, hf. bd.* 25*s*   *Oxonii*, 1770-1823
With the above will be sold "Dillwyn's Index, *Oxon.* 1823."
Priced, 1836, £5. 15*s*. 6*d*; 1836, £5.; 1837-1840, £4. 4*s*; 1841, £6. 16*s* 6*d*.
"It contains his general system, or synopsis, of conchology, and is enriched with no less than 1079 plates or figures of shells; among which several represent with great accuracy, the internal structures of the animals themselves: most of these figures are so accurate, and all are so characteristic, that even to this day they are indispensable to the conchologist, and this remarkable volume forms one of the most valuable and standard works in this department of Zoology."—SWAINSON.

4690 LOUDON'S (J. C.) Arboretum et Fruticetum Britannicum, or the Trees and Shrubs of Britain, 8 vols. 8vo. *four with text and four with above* 400 *plates of Trees, and upwards of* 2500 *beautiful woodcuts of Trees and Shrubs*, (pub. at £10.) *hf. green morocco*, £4. 10*s*   1838

4691 —— Encyclopædia of Trees and Shrubs, being the Arboretum abridged, stout 8vo. 2000 *woodcuts* (pub. at £2. 10*s*) *cloth*, 25*s*   1842

4691* —— Suburban Horticulturist; the Culture of the Kitchen, Fruit and Forcing Garden, 8vo. *cuts*, (pub. at 15*s*) *cloth*, 7*s*   1842

4692 LOUREIRO, Flora Cochin-Chinensis, cum Plantis in Sinensi imperio, Africa Orientali, Indiaque observatis, 2 vols. 4to. *calf*, 16*s*   *Ulyssipone*, 1790

4693 LOW'S Illustrations of the Breeds of the Domestic Animals of the British Islands, 2 vols. in 1, atlas 4to. 56 *most beautifully* COLOURED PLATES *of Horses, Oxen, Sheep, Goats, and Hogs, drawn by Nicholson*, (pub. at £16. 16*s*.) *hf. morocco extra, gilt edges*, £5. 15*s*   1842

4694 LOWE, Primitiae Faunae et Florae Maderæ et Portus Sancti, 4to. 4 *plates*, 7*s* 6*d*   *Cambr.* 1831

4695 LUCAS, Histoire Naturelle des Crustacés, des Arachnides et des Myriapodes, 8vo. 46 *plates, hf. calf*, 20*s*   *Paris*, 1840

4696 LUND, Brasiliens uddöde Dyrskabning, 1842— Brasiliens Dyreverden, Part I, II, IV, 26 *plates*, 13 *coloured*, 1838-42; in 1 vol. 4to. *hf. bd.* 6*s*   *Kiöbenh.* 1839-42

4697 LYELL'S (Sir Charles) Geological Evidences of the Antiquity of Man, with remarks on theories of the origin of species by variation, 8vo. *plate and woodcuts, cloth*, 12*s*   1863

4698 LYONET, Traité anatomique de la CHENILLE qui ronge le Bois de Saule, 4to. *plate of the apparatus and beautiful impressions of the* 18 *anatomical plates, very fine copy, calf gilt*, 25*s*   *La Haye*, 1760

4699 —— le même, avec une explication des planches, et une description des outils de l'auteur, 4to. 18 *plates, calf gilt*, 30*s*   1762
The plates in this book were entirely the work of Lyonet himself, who for that purpose acquired the Arts of design and engraving, having been unable to find an artist capable for the task.

4700 M'DONALD'S Dictionary of Gardening, 2 vols. 4to. 60 *coloured plates by Edwards, red morocco, gilt edges*, (pub. at £5. 5*s*) 12*s*   1807

4701 MACGILLIVRAY'S (Wm.) Natural History of Dee Side and Braemar, edited by Dr. Lankester, 8vo. *Geological map of the district, and woodcut engravings from drawings by the author, Viscountess Canning, &c. privately printed at the expense of Her Majesty, cloth*, £4. 4*s*   1855
Yarrell's copy fetched, in 1857, £7.

4702 MADRAS JOURNAL of Literature and Science, edited by Morris, Cole and Brown, from the beginning in 1833, Vols. I.—XII. or Parts 1—29 inclusive, 12 vols. 8vo. QUITE COMPLETE, *numerous plates, some of those on Natural History coloured, hf. russia neat*, £10.; or *a fine tall copy*, 12 vols. in 11, 8vo. *half russia, almost uncut*, £10. 10*s*   *Madras*, 1834-40

4703 MADRAS QUARTERLY JOURNAL OF MEDICAL Science, from July 1860 to July 1862, Nos. I—IX. (wanting VI.) 8vo. *plates, sd.* 32*s*   1860-62

4704 MAMMATT'S GEOLOGICAL FACTS and practical Observations, to elucidate the Formation of the Ashby Coal-Field, roy. 4to. *map, profiles, sections of Strata, and* 102 *coloured plates of Vegetable Fossils, hf. calf gilt*, 36*s*   1836
"A splendid volume, with many able and judicious remarks."—*Fairholme's Geology.*

4705 MANDEY'S Mechanic Powers, with a treatise of Circular motion, sq. 8vo. *plates, bds.* 12*s*   1709

4706 MANGETI Bibliotheca Scriptorum Medicorum veterum et recentiorum, 4 vols. in 2, stout folio, *several portraits, old calf*, 15*s*   *Genevæ*, 1731
Priced, 1840, Payne and Foss, £3. 3*s*.

4707 MANTELL'S Pictorial Atlas of Fossil Remains, 4to. 74 *coloured plates*, (pub. at £2. 5*s*) *cloth*, 24*s*   1850

NATURAL HISTORY, SCIENCES, MATHEMATICS. 241

4630 JACKSON's Geological and Agricultural survey of Rhode-Island, roy. 8vo. *plates*,
6s *Providence*, 1840
4631 JACOBÆUS de Ranis, acc. Bartholinus de Nervorum usu, 12mo. *plates, calf, rare*,
6s *Paris*, 1676
4632 JAMESON's Mineralogical Travels through the Hebrides, Orkney and Shetland Islands, and Mainland of Scotland, 2 vols. 4to. *maps and plates, fine copy in gilt russia*, 12s *Edinburgh*, 1813
4632*JARDINE'S (Sir W.) NATURALIST'S LIBRARY, a complete set, 40 vols. 12mo. *portraits, vignettes, and upwards of a thousand plates, hf. calf, contents lettered,*
AN ORIGINAL COPY, £7. 10s *Edinburgh*, 1843
CONTENTS:—Mammalia, 13 vols.; Ornithology, 14 vols.; Entomology, 7 vols.; Ichthyology, 6 vols
By far the best and completest history and illustration of animated nature that has ever appeared. It is in every sense of the word a NATURALIST'S LIBRARY, embracing the result of the labours of all the great natural historians brought down to the latest period.
" We could hardly have thought that any new periodical would have obtained our approbation so entirely as the 'Naturalist's Library;' but the price is so low, the coloured plates so elegant, and their descriptions so scientific and correct, that we cannot withhold our warmest praise. It is a perfect bijou, and as valuable as pretty." *Literary Gazette.*
"This book is, perhaps, the most beautiful, and the cheapest series ever offered to the public."—*Athenæum.*

4633 JEAN (A.) Arithmetique au Miroir, 12mo. *vellum*, 5s (*Paris*), 1649
4634 JEFFREYS, British Conchology, Vol. I.: LAND AND FRESHWATER SHELLS, sm. 8vo. *frontispiece and* 8 *plates, cloth, new*, 10s 6d 1862
4635 JERDON'S (T. C.) Illustrations of INDIAN ORNITHOLOGY, COMPLETE, 4 parts in 1 vol. roy 4to. LARGE PAPER, 50 SUPERBLY COLOURED *plates of new, unfigured and interesting species of Birds, from the South of India, originally issued to subscribers at* 25 *rupees, now out of print* *Madras*, 1845-47
The following numbers are in stock, and will be sold separately, viz. Small Paper, No. 3, plates 26 to 40, pub. at 6 rupees, 12s; LARGE PAPER, No. 2, plates 13 to 25, pub. at 6 rupees, 12s; No. 3, plates 26 to 39, pub. at 8 rupees, 16s; No. 4, plates 41 to 50, pub. at 5 rupees, 10s.
4636 —— The BIRDS of INDIA, a Natural History of all the Birds known to inhabit continental India: with Descriptions of the Species, Genera, &c. of such families as are not found in India, making it a Manual of Ornithology specially adapted for India, Vol. I. 8vo. *cloth*, 21s *Calcutta*, 1862
To be completed in two volumes.
4637 JOHNSTON (George) History of the British Sponges and Lithophytes, 8vo. *cuts and* 25 *tinted plates (pub. in bds. at* 30s*), calf gilt*, 24s 1842
4638 —— History of the British Zoophytes, 2 vols. 8vo. *numerous cuts and* 74 *plates,* (pub. at 42s) *cloth*, 30s 1847
4639 JONES (T. Rymer) Outline of the Organisation of the Animal Kingdom, and Manual of Comparative Anatomy, stout 8vo. 400 *woodcuts,* (pub. at 31s 6d) *cloth,* 21s *Van Voorst*, 1855
4640 JORDANUS de Ponderositate Nicolai Tartaleae, *Ven.* 1565—Archimedes de Insistentibus Aquae, *Ven.* 1565—Wickner, Tabula Ascensionum Obliq. *Tubing.* 1561 —3 vols. in 1, sq. 8vo. *vellum, rare*, 7s 6d 1561-65
4641 JOURNAL DES SAVANTS, de 1836 jusqu'à 1856, 21 vols. roy. 4to (pub. at £37. 16s) *hf. calf neat*, £10. *Paris*, 1836-56
4642 JURINE, Nouvelle Methode de classer les Hyménoptères, 4to. 14 *plates, mostly coloured, bds.* 10s *Genève*, 1807
4643 KAEMPFER, Icones Plantarum in Japonia collectarum, folio, 59 *plates*, 7s 1791
4644 KAUP, das Thierreich in seinen Hauptformen, 3 vols. 8vo. *with above* 200 *woodcuts, including nearly* 100 *engravings of Birds, bds.* 7s 6d *Darmst.* 1835-6
4645 KELAART, Prodromus Faunae Zeylanicæ: Contributions to the Zoology of Ceylon, 8vo. *cloth*, and Appendix, 10s *Ceylon*, 1852
4646 KIRBY, Freeman's Life of, 8vo. *valuable scientific information, cloth*, 7s 1852
4647 KJÆRBOELLING, Ornithologia Danica: Danmarks Fugle, 8vo. *with folio Atlas of* 96 *coloured plates, comprising* 600 *engravings of the Birds of Denmark. Sweden, Norway, Iceland, and the Färoe Islands*, £3. 3s *Kiöb.* 1852
4648 KLEINII Opera Omnia, *arranged and bound in* 5 vols. 4to. *many hundred fine plates of Natural History, hf. calf, uniform,* £2. 5s *Lipsiæ*, 1751-1778
Contents: Vol. I, Quadrupedum Historia Naturalis; Tentamen Herpetologiae; Historia Avium—Vol. II, Ova Avium; De lapidibus Macrocosmi; De Terris et Mineralibus; Circa Plantarum Marinarum fabricam, Testarum Tubulorum Marinorum—Vol. III, Stemmata Avium; Dubia ad class de Quadrupp.; Dispositio Echinodermatum; Nomenclator Lithologicus—Vol. IV, De auditu Piscium; Historia naturalis Piscium—Vol. V, Naturalis dispositio Echinodermatum.
4649 —— Tubuli Marini, 1731—Tetracologica, 1753—and others in 1 vol. 4to. *plates, hf. calf*, 10s 1731-53

R

4650 KLUEGEL, Mathematisches Wörterbuch, 5 vols.—Supplement, 2 vols.—together 7 vols. 8vo. *calf gilt*, £2. 2s   Leipzig, 1803-36

4651 KNORR et WALCH, Recueil des Monumens des Catastrophes que le Globe a essuyées, contenant des Petrifactions, etc. avec Tables systématiques et alphabetiques, 4 vols. folio, *portrait and 272 plates, hf. calf*, £5.   Nurem. 1768-77
    An excellent, original, and very cheap copy of this grand work; priced, 1822, £21.; 1843, £31. 10s; 1832 and 1840, £14. 14s; 1847, £13. 13s, in russia, £16. 16s.
    This, which is the most splendid work on the remains of the Organic World that has ever been published, contains a vast collection of Fossil Shells, Fish, Vegetable and Mineral Impressions, &c. drawn of the natural size, and coloured with the greatest possible accuracy.

4652 KNORR Deliciae Naturæ: Délices Physiques Choisies, ou Choix de tout ce que les trois Règnes de la Naturo renferment de plus digne des Recherches d'un Amateur curieux pour former un Cabinet, 2 vols. in 1, roy. folio, LARGE PAPER, 91 *large very finely coloured plates of Birds, Mammals, Amphibia, Shells, Crabs, Fossils, Minerals, etc. the Text in German and French, green morocco, gilt edges*, £2. 6s   Nürnberg, 1764-76-67
    The Fonthill copy fetched £6. 16s 6d; North's, £7. 7s; Hodges', £14. 3s 6d; Col. Stanley's, £15. 15s. Priced, 1845, £6, 6s; 1848, £6. 6s; 1829, £12.

4653 KOOP's Historical Account of the Substances used to describe events and convey ideas, with Appendix, imp. 8vo. LARGE PAPER, *printed on paper made from straw, morocco*, 20s   1800

4654 ——— the same, 8vo. *on paper made from old printed paper, hf. bd.* 7s 6d   1801

4655 KREBS, Beschreibung und Abbildung der sämmtlichen Holzarten, welche in mittlern und nördlichen Deutschland wild wachsen, imp. 4to. 145 *coloured plates*, (pub. *sewed* at 37½ Thalers), *hf. calf*, £2. 10s   Braunschweig, 1826

4657 LACROIX (S. F.) Traité du Calcul Différentiel et du Calcul Intégral, 3 vols. 4to. *seconde (la dernière) édition, plates, sd.* £2. 10s; or *calf nt.* £3. 5s Paris, 1810-19

4658 LADY's Diary for 1752 *(the year in which the style was altered)* 12mo. *hf. bd.* 6s 1752

4659 LAMARCK, Histoire Naturelle des Animaux sans vertèbres; deuxième edition, par Deshayes et Milne Edwards, 11 vols. 8vo. (pub. at £4. 8s *sewed*) *hf. calf*, £3.   Paris, 1835-45

4660 LAMBERT. DON's Account of the Lambertian Herbarium, atlas folio, being part of Lambert's Genus Pinus, Vol. II, *plate, bds.* 10s   1824

4661 LANDEN's Mathematical Memoirs, 2 vols. 1780-89—Mathematical Lucubrations, 1755; etc. 7 vols. in 2, 4to. *being the complete works of this eminent Mathematician, bds.* 12s   1755-89

4662 LANDSEER'S (Thos.) Characteristic Sketches of Animals, drawn from the Life, with descriptive Notices by Barrow, impl. 4to. 64 *beautiful plans and vignettes*, PROOFS ON INDIA PAPER, (pub. at £4. 16s) *bds.* £2. 10s   1832

4663 LEACH'S (Wm. E.) Zoological Miscellany, being descriptions of new, or interesting Animals, illustrated with coloured figures by NODDER, 4 vols. in 2, royal 8vo. 150 *coloured plates, bds.* VERY RARE, £3. 16s   1814-17

4664 ——— the same, Illustrations without Text, *wanting plates* 120, 139, in 1 vol. 8vo. *hf. bd.* 35s   1814-17

4664*——— Synopsis of the Mollusca of Great Britain, 8vo. 13 *plates, cloth*, 7s 1852

4665 LEBINOM, Risunki Sanktpeterburgskoi Phlora: St. Petersburg Flora, *in Russian*, 8vo. 100 *coloured plates, the names in Latin and Russian, hf. bd. rare*, 12s   St. Pet. 1836

4666 LEDEBOUR (C. F.) Icones Plantarum novarum imperfecte cognitarum, floram Rossicam, imprimis Altaicam illustrantes, 5 vols. roy. folio, 500 *coloured plates, hf. green* MOROCCO, *gilt tops, uncut*, £15.   Rigae, 1829-34
    This grand work was published by order of the Russian Government, and at their expense. Publishe at 416 thalers, coloured, and 318 thalers, plain plates.

4667 ——— Flora Rossica, sive enumeratio Plantarum in totius Imperii Rossici provinciis observatarum, 2 st. vols. 8vo. *map, hf. calf*, 18s   Stuttgart, 1842

4668 LEGENDRE, Théorie des Nombres, 4to. *seconde édition, sd.* 7s   Paris, 1808

4669 LEIBNITII Opera omnia nunc primum collecta, præfationibus et indicibus exornata a Dutens, 6 vols. 4to. *plates, best edition, hf. calf*, £3. 10s Genevæ, 1768

4670 ——— Mathematische Schriften von Gerhardt, 2 vols. in 1, 8vo. *Large Paper, hf. calf, uncut*, 7s   Berlin, 1849-50

4671 LEIGHTON's Flora of Shropshire, 8vo. *plates* (pub. at 24s) *cloth*, 9s   1841

4708 MARGARITA PHILOSOPHICA, philosophiae principia ab Orontio Fineo aucta, sm. 4to. *curious woodcut titles and other engravings, top margins slightly stained, good copy, vellum*, 12s [See also *Reisch*] *Basileæ*, 1535

This curious book may be regarded as the cyclopædia of scientific knowledge of its time, and must have been highly popular. "If the number were sufficient of those who wish to take their notions of liberal education in Europe before the Reformation from original sources, a reprint of the *Margarita Philosophica* would be made. The diversity of the matters which it treats, stamp it as the best book for such a purpose."—*De Morgan.*

4709 MARKREE CATALOGUE of Stars near the Ecliptic, observed at Markree, 1848-54, hitherto unpublished, by Cooper, 4 vols. roy. 8vo. *cloth*, 24s *Dublin*, 1851-54

4710 MARSCHALL à BIEBERSTEIN, Flora Taurico-Caucasica, cum Supplemento, 3 vols. 8vo. *bd.* 15s *Charkouiæ*, 1808-19

4711 MARTELLI, Chiave del Calendario Gregoriano, 18mo. *hf. morocco*, 18s *Lione*, 1583

4712 MARTYN'S (T.) UNIVERSAL CONCHOLOGIST, exhibiting the Figure of every known Shell, accurately drawn and painted after Nature; with a new systematic arrangement, *English and French*, 4 vols. atlas 4to. *two plates of Medals, and* 161 *plates, comprising* 322 *figures of* SHELLS MOST EXQUISITELY COLOURED *by the author himself, and mounted on stout blue paper, very fine copy in red* MOROCCO EXTRA, £15. 1784

Very rare, when complete; Vols. 3 and 4 are rarely met with. Priced, complete, 1841, J. Bohn, £18. 18s; 1847, H. G. Bohn, £18. 18s; 1841, H. Bohn, £24.

4713 —— ARANEI, or Natural History of Spiders, including the principal parts of Albin's Work on English Spiders, and the whole of Clerck's publication on Swedish Spiders, revised and enlarged, impl. 4to. 28 *plates, comprising numerous beautifully coloured figures, very fine copy in blue morocco super extra, gilt edges,* £3. 3s 1793

Priced, 1824, Rivington, £4. 4s; 1839, Longman, *hf. bound*, £3. 10s; 1847, £3. 13s 6d.

4714 MARTIN (W.) Petrifacta Derbiensia, figures and descriptions of Petrifactions collected in Derbyshire, with the Systematical Arrangement, 4to. 52 *coloured plates, bds.* 16s Priced, 1841, Bohn, £2. 5s. *Wigan*, 1809

4715 MASERES (Fr.) SCRIPTORES LOGARITHMICI; or a collection of several curious tracts on the Nature and Construction of Logarithms, 6 vols. 4to. (pub. at £12. 10s 6d in bds.) *calf neat*, £3. 1791-1807

4716 MAUNOIR, la Porrette et Monte Catini, (Bains Ital.) 8vo. 5s *Florence*, 1848

4717 MECHANICS' MAGAZINE, from the beginning, August 1823, to July 1852, 57 vols. 8vo. *numerous engravings, neat in hf. calf,* £9. 1823-52

4718 —— NEW SERIES, from the beginning, January 1859 to Sept. 1861, Parts 1—33 (Vols. I to VI, part 3), 4to. *numerous illustrations, sd.* 32s 1859-61

4719 MEDICÆ ARTIS PRINCIPES, post Hippocratem et Galenum, Græci, Latinitate donati, et Latini, 5 vols. in 2, folio, *curious cuts, illustrative of surgical operations, vellum*, 20s *Parisiis, Stephanus,* 1567

Priced, 1831, bound by De Rome, £6. 6s; 1848, Payne and Foss, red morocco, £5. 5s; Evans' copy fetched £4. 9s; Didot's fine copy in morocco, 137 fr.

An important collection of the Medical and Empirical writers of Ancient Greece and Rome. To Antiquaries who wish to have the sources of many Mediæval superstitions these volumes will prove attractive.

CONTENTS:—

Greek Writers.		*Latin Writers.*
Actuarius	Ruffus Ephesius	Celsus
N. Myrepsus	P. Aegineta	Scrib. Largus
Aretaeus	Aëtius	Marc. Empiricus
	Al. Trallianus	Fragmenta

" Collection estimée et difficile à trouver bien conditionnée."—BRUNET.

4720 MEIDINGER, Icones Piscium Austriæ indigenorum, roy. folio, 30 *finely coloured plates, bds.* 10s *Viennae*, 1785-88
Priced, 1836, £1. 15s.

4721 MENABENI, del Grand' Animale o Gran Bestia, Cervo e Lupo, 16mo. 6s 1585

4722 MERIAN'S (M. S.) INSECTS: Dissertatio de Generatione et Metamorphosibus Insectorum Surinamensium, atlas folio, 72 *accurately executed and richly coloured* DRAWINGS, *the Insects most beautifully represented, with the plants on which they feed, a very superior copy, frontispiece, title-page and dedication heightened with gold, russia extra, gilt edges, by Mackinlay,* £5. *Amst.* 1719

4724 MESMES (J. P. de) Les Institutions Astronomiques, contenans les principaux fondemens et premieres causes des cours et movemens celestes, folio, *fine copy in overlapping vellum*, 20s *Paris, M. de Vascosan*, 1557

4725 MEYEN, ueber die neuesten Fortschritte der Anatomie und Physiologie der Gewächse, 4to. 21 *plates, calf*, 8s *Haarlem*, 1836

4726 ——— Neues System der Pflanzen-Physiologie, 3 vols. 8vo. *plates, neatly bound*, 6s *Berlin*, 1837-39

4727 MEYER'S (H. L.) ILLUSTRATIONS OF BRITISH BIRDS and their Eggs, 4 vols. impl. 4to. *with 328 large and very beautifully coloured engravings*, (pub. at £56. 16s) in parts, *morocco, gilt leaves*, £21. [1835-41]
A genuine subscriber's copy, much preferable to a *second* 4to. ISSUE made recently. Priced, 1856, £30.
This beautiful work comprises accurate figures both of migratory and indigenous birds, and in most instances both male and female, accompanied by their eggs and by curious or rare nests.

4728 ——— ILLUSTRATIONS OF BRITISH BIRDS and their Eggs, SECOND EDITION, 7 vols. large 8vo. *with 322 coloured plates, with descriptive letterpress*, (pub. at £18. 10s) *hf. morocco*, £10. 1842-50
A *second* issue of this second edition appeared in 1857.

4729 MEYER (H. von) PALÆONTOGRAPHICA: Beiträge zur Naturgeschichte der Vorwelt, herausg. von DUNKER und MEYER, Vols. I—VI, large 4to. 227 *plates, bds.* £6. *Cassel*, 1851-58

4730 ——— FAUNA DER VORWELT: Fossile Säugethiere, Vögel, und Reptilien, 12 *plates*—Die Saurier des Muschelkalkes, 70 *plates*—Saurier aus dem Kupferschiefer, 9 *plates*—Reptilen aus dem lithographischen Schiefer des Jura, 21 *plates*; 4 parts, folio, 112 *plates, some double* (published at 73 Thalers), *uncut*, £7. 15s *Frankfurt a. M.* 1845-59

4731 MICHAUX, Histoire des Chênes de l'Amérique, 36 *plates, Papier Vélin, hf. russia,* 12s *Paris*, 1801
Fetched, 1859, Sotheby's, ordinary paper, £1. 7s.

4732 MICROSCOPIC JOURNAL, and Structural Record, for 1841 and 1842, 2 vols. in 1, *cloth*—Microscopical Society's Transactions, Vol. I. pts. 1, 2, 1842-44—QUARTERLY JOURNAL of Microscopical Science, including Transactions of the Microscopical Society of London, edited by Lankester and Busk, Nos. 1—33, (wanting Nos. 10, 14) and New Series, No. I—VIII, from October 1852, to October 1862, *two vols. hf. calf, the rest in parts*; 8vo. *several hundred plates and woodcuts*, £8. 8s 1853-1862
Complete sets are scarce. Nos. 2, 17, 22, and 26 of the Quarterly Journal, are out of print.

4733 MILLER'S (J. S.) Natural History of the Crinoidea or Lily-shaped Animals, with Observations on the Genera Asteria, Euryale, Comatula, and Marsupites, roy. 4to. 50 *coloured plates, bds.* 32s; or *hf. calf,* 36s *Bristol*, 1821
Priced, 1824, Wood, £2. 12s 6d; 1843, Jas. Bohn, £2. 8s.

4734 MILNE EDWARDS, Histoire naturelle des Crustacés, 4 vols. 8vo. *including Atlas of 42 plates, some coloured,* (pub. at 43 fr.) *hf. calf,* 16s 1834

4735 MILNE EDWARDS, QUATREFAGES, et BLANCHARD, Recherches Anatomiques et Zoologiques, faites pendant un voyage sur les côtes de la Sicile, et de la France, 3 vols. roy. 4to. 83 *plates, many coloured, the inner margin of a few pages and plates in Vol. I. slightly wormed, hf. calf,* £4. 4s *Paris,* (ca. 1840)
Collation of Plates: 1-28; 10-13; 1-26; Classification, 1; and 1-25.

4736 **Mines.** ANNUAIRE du Journal des Mines de Russie, 1835-42, 9 vols. 8vo. *plates, some coloured, sd.* 25s *S. Peterb.* 1840-45

4737 ABBOTT'S Essay on the Mines of England, 8vo. *bds. privately printed,* 10s 1833

4738 MIQUEL, Flora van Nederlandsch Indie, Vol. I, parts 1-6, Vol. I. second division (tweede Afdeeling) parts 1, 2; Vol. II, parts 1-6; Vol. III. parts 1-3—together 17 parts, large 8vo. *plates, sd.* 36s *Amst.* 1855-59

4739 MOIGNO, Leçons de Calcul Différentiel et de Calcul Intégral, redigées d'après Cauchy, 2 vols. 8vo. *russia gilt, very scarce,* £2. 10s *Paris,* 1840-44

4740 MONTAGU'S (G.) TESTACEA BRITANNICA, or Natural History of British Shells, Marine, Land, and Fresh Water, systematically arranged, with Supplement, 3 vols. 4to. *Fine Paper, with copious valuable additions in MS. by* DR. GOODALL, *including numerous tracings, etc. calf neat,* £3. 10s 1803-8
Priced, 1855, hf. morocco, £4. 4s.

4741 MONTUCLA (J. F.) Histoire des Mathématiques, depuis leur origine jusqu'à nos jours; tableau et développement des découvertes, vies et contestations des Mathématiciens, etc. 4 vols. 4to. *portrait and plates, hf. bd.* £4. 10s; or *calf,* £5. *Paris,* 1799-1802
The best and only complete History of the Mathematical Sciences.

NATURAL HISTORY, SCIENCES, MATHEMATICS. 247

4742 Moon's (Al.) Catalogue of the Indigenous and Exotic Plants growing in Ceylon, Singhalese and English, impl. 4to. bd. 7s *Colombo*, 1824
4743 MOORE (Thomas) and LINDLEY, the FERNS of Great Britain and Ireland, NATURE-PRINTED by Henry BRADBURY, impl. folio, 51 *large coloured plates, hf. green morocco, very neat, gilt edges*, £8. 8s 1855
4744 MORLAND (Sir S.) Description and Use of Two Arithmetick Instruments, 16mo. *portrait and plates, calf, scarce*, 9s 1673
4745 MORLAND, Elévation des Eaux par Machines, Huit Problèmes de Méchanique, etc. 4to. *numerous plates, calf*, 7s 6d *Paris*, 1685
4746 MORLEY (W. H.) Description of a Planispheric ASTROLABE, constructed for Shah Sultan Hussain Safawi, King of Persia, now in the British Museum, with Notes, etc. atlas folio, 21 *large plates, comprising* 61 *engravings, only* 100 *copies printed, bds*. £4. 1856
4747 MOSCOW ACADEMY: Mémoires de la Société Impériale des Naturalistes de Moscou, Tom. I, II, IV, V, VII-X, XVII, XVIII, XIX, pt. 1, 4to. 158 *plates, mostly coloured*, 1811-60; Commentationes Societatis Physico-Medicae, Vol. 2, pars 1, 1817; together 12 vols. 4to. *very scarce*, £8. 8s *Moscou*, 1811-60
4748 BULLETIN de la Société Impériale des Naturalistes de Moscou redigé par Renard, depuis 1829 jusqu'a 1860, A COMPLETE SET from the commencement, about 150 parts, large 8vo. *several hundred plates, many finely* COLOURED, *complete sets are extremely rare*, £35. *Moscou*, 1830-60
Parts supplied new for 8s. each; odd numbers in stock offered for 4s each.
4749 MOULE (Th.) Heraldry of Fish, notices of the principal families bearing Fish in their Arms, 8vo. *numerous heraldic woodcuts, cloth*, 12s 1842
4750 MÜLLER (Joh. Mahler) die vorzüglichsten Sing-Vögel Teutschlands, mit ihren Nestern und Eyern, 4to. 25 *coloured plates, hf. morocco*, 9s *Nürnberg*, 1800
4751 MURCHISON'S SILURIAN SYSTEM, founded on Geological Researches, in various Counties of England and Wales, with Descriptions of the Coal Fields and Overlying Formations, 2 vols. roy. 4to. *geological maps, engravings, and plates of Fossils; without the large map*, (pub. at £8. 8s) *sd*. £3. 16s 1839
4752 —— Siluria, the history of the oldest Fossiliferous Rocks and their foundations, stout 8vo. *third edition, map*, 41 *plates and numerous cuts, cloth*, 32s 1859
4753 —— GEOLOGY of RUSSIA in Europe and the Ural Mountains, by R. Murchison, E. de Verneuil, and Count A. von Keyserling; Vol. I.Geology: Vol. II. Paléontologie (*in French*), 2 vols. roy. 4to. *with* 7 *Maps and Geological Sections*, 12 *Views, and* 50 *plates of Fossil Remains, chiefly Shells, with numerous woodcuts*, (pub. at £8. 8s) *cloth bds*. £5. 15s 1845
Contents: Vol. I. Geology, with Views, plates of Corals and 7 large Maps. Vol. II. Palæontology, 50 plates.
4754 NAIERA (Ant. de) Sūma Astrologica, para enseñar pronosticos de los tiempos, y conocer la fertilidad, o esterilidad del Año, sm. 4to. *vellum, rare*, 10s *Lisb*. 1632
4755 NEMNICH'S Natural History Polyglott: Allgemeines Polyglotten-Lexicon der Naturgeschichte; *a Latin Alphabet*, explained in German, Danish, Swedish, English, French, Italian, Spanish, Portuguese, and occasionally Japanese, Chinese, Cochinchinese, Hungarian, Bohemian, Greenlandish, Finnish, etc. 4 parts—Wörterbuch der Naturgeschichte, consisting of Polyglott Alphabets, *beginning* with German, English, Portuguese, French, Italian, Spanish, Dutch, Swedish, Danish, Norwegian and Icelandic, *explained* in Latin, 9 parts, together 13 parts in 6 vols. sm. 4to. *complete, bds*. 15s, or *hf. bd*. 24s *Hamburg*, 1793, etc.
Priced, 1824. W. Wood, hf. russia, £5. 5s and £4. 14s 6d; 1841, W. Wood, bd. £3. 15s; 1847, Nattali, £2. 4s.
A work indispensable to Naturalists.
4756 NEPERI (*Lord Napier*) Mirifici Logarithmorum Canonis descriptio, sq. 8vo. *woodcut title, fine copy in limp vellum, gilt edges, rare*, 25s *Edinb*. 1614
4757 NEWMAN'S History of British Ferns, 8vo. *numerous cuts*, (pub. at 18s) *cloth*, 10s *Van Voorst*, 1854
4758 —— the Entomologist, Nos. I-XXVI (November 1840 to December 1842) in 1 vol. 8vo. *plates, cloth*, 14s *Van Voorst*, 1840-42
4759 NEWTON (Isaaci) Opera quae exstant omnia, commentariis illustrabat Horsley, 5 vols. 4to. *first title mended, calf*, £6. 6s 1779-85
Copies have generally fetched from £8. to £10.
4760 NEW YORK. THE NATURAL HISTORY OF NEW YORK, published by the authority of the State of New York, viz.:—
ZOOLOGY. Mammalia, Ornithology, Reptiles, Fishes, Mollusca and Crustacea, by J. E. de Kay, 5 vols. 329 *plates*

BOTANY, by John Torrey, M.D. 2 vols. 161 *plates*
MINERALOGY, by L. C. Beck, M.D. 8 *plates*
GEOLOGY, by W. W. Mather, E. Emmons, L. Vanuxem, and J. Hall, 4 vols. 71 *plates*
PALÆONTOLOGY, by J. Hall, 2 vols. 173 *plates*
AGRICULTURE, by E. Emmons, 5 vols. 223 *plates*
Together 19 vols. royal 4to. WITH 965 PLATES, *most of which are* BEAUTIFULLY COLOURED, *after nature*, (pub. at £32.) *cloth*, £25.   New York, 1842-51
Many of the volumes are out of print, and complete sets are rarely met with.

4761 NICOLS (Thos.) A Lapidary, or the History of Pretious Stones, with cautions for those that deal with them, sq. 12mo. *old calf*, 9s   Cambridge, 1652
4762 NOCCA et BALBIS, Flora Ticinensis, 2 vols. 4to. 28 *plates*, *hf. bd*. 20s   Tic. 1816-21
4763 NOZEMAN en HOUTTUYN, NEDERLANDSCHE VOGELEN: Natural History of the Birds of the Netherlands, in Dutch, 5 vols. royal folio, *containing 250 large engravings of Birds, with their Nests and Eggs, beautifully coloured by Christian and J. C. Sepp, calf extra, a fine copy*, £18. 18s   Amst. 1770-1829
"Ouvrage bien éxecuté, et dont on trouve peu d'exemplaires complets."—BRUNET.
Priced, complete, 5 vols. 1770-1829, 250 plates, 1832 and 1839, £35.: 1836, £31. 10s; 1844, £31. 10s.

4764 O'BRIEN's Treatise on Calico-Printing, 2 vols. in 1, 12mo. *bds*. 10s   1792
4765 OLIVIER (M.) ENTOMOLOGIE, OU HISTOIRE NATURELLE DES COLÉOPTÈRES, 6 vols. 4to. 363 *plates*, FINELY COLOURED, *hf. bd*. RARE, £15.   Paris, 1799-1808
The most complete and best work on Beetles.

4766 OPPEL, Analysis Triangulorum, sm. folio, *plates*, *hf. bd*. 10s   Dresdae, 1746
4767 OWEN (David Dale) Report of a Geological Survey of Wisconsin, Iowa, and Minnesota, and incidentally of a portion of Nebraska Territory, roy. 4to. *numerous woodcuts*, with Illustrations *consisting of large map and 46 plates, those of Strata coloured, many of them very large, and folding, a very valuable work, executed by authority of Congress*, (pub. at £3.) *cloth*, 36s   Philadelphia, 1852
4768 ——— Report on the Mineral Lands of the United States, 8vo. *numerous coloured geological plates, hf. bd*. 6s   (Washington), 1840
4769 OWEN (Richard) History of British Fossil Mammals and Birds, 8vo. 237 *woodcuts* (pub. at 31s 6d), *cloth*, 25s   Van Voorst, 1846
4770 ——— On Parthenogenesis, 8vo. *cloth*, 5s   1849
4771 ——— On the Nature of Limbs, 8vo. *plates, cloth, rare*, 9s   1849
4772 ——— Lectures on the COMPARATIVE ANATOMY and Physiology of the INVERTEBRATE ANIMALS; delivered at the Royal College of Surgeons, 2nd edition, 8vo. *numerous woodcuts* (pub. at 21s) *cloth*, 17s   1855
4773 PALEONTOGRAPHICAL SOCIETY'S PUBLICATIONS, *a complete set from the beginning in 1848 to 1858*, 13 vols. 4to. *many hundred plates* (price to subscribers, £13. 13s) *clean and uncut*, £11. 15s   1848-60
4774 PALMSTRUCH och VENUS, Suensk Botanik, Vols. I—VI, part 6, roy. 8vo. 396 *coloured plates, with text*, 18s   Stockholm, 1802-10
4775 PALSTERCAMP (A. de Bylandt) Théorie des Volcans, 3 vols. 8vo. *and large folio Atlas of* 16 *plates, sd*. 21s   Paris, 1835-36
4775*PAPPI ALEXANDRINI, Mathematicae Collectiones, *Latine*, à Federico Commandrino, cum comment. sm. folio, *fine copy, calf gilt*, 36s   Bonon. 1660
4776 ——— the same, 1660—APOLLONII Pergaei Conica, et ARCHIMEDIS Assumpta, *Lat*. ab Ecchellense et Borello, *Florent*. 1661—in 1 vol. folio, *diagrams, calf*, 25s   1660-61
4777 PAULI AEGINETAE Opus de Re Medicâ, *Latine*, à Guintherio Andernaco, folio, *vellum*, 7s 6d   Parisiis, 1532
4778 PEARSON'S PRACTICAL ASTRONOMY, containing tables to facilitate the reduction of celestial observations, with descriptions of the various Instruments and methods of using them, 2 stout vols. and 2 parts, roy. 4to. 31 *plates, bds*. £6. 15s; or in 2 vols. *hf. calf*, £7. 7s   1824-29
4779 PERCHERON, Bibliographie Entomologique, des ouvrages entomologiques depuis les temps les plus réculés jusqu'à 1834, et les Monographes et Mémoires contenus dans les Recueils Français et étrangers, ouvrages périodiques des Sociétés, table Chronologique, etc. 2 vols. 8vo. *sd*. 6s   Paris, 1837
4780 ——— the same, 2 vols. in 1, 8vo. *hf. morocco*, 10s   1837
A masterpiece of Bibliography—of the greatest use to all Entomologists.

NATURAL HISTORY, SCIENCES, MATHEMATICS. 249

4781 PERCY's METALLURGY : the Art of extracting Metals from their Ores and adapting them to various purposes of Manufacture : Slags, Fuel, Fire Clays, &c. Copper, Zinc, and Brass, 8vo. *numerous cuts,* 16s 1861

4782 PILLER et MITTERPACHER, Iter per Poseganam Sclavoniae provinciam, 1782, 4to. LARGE PAPER, 16 *plates, those of Insects coloured, calf,* 14s *Budæ,* 1783

4783 PISO (Gul.) de Indiae utriusque Re Naturali et medicâ, 5 vols. in 1, folio, *many woodcuts of Natural History, vellum,* 20s *Amst. Elzevir,* 1658
With a Chilian Vocabulary.

4784 PLUMIER, Traité des Fougères de l'Amerique, large folio, 172 *plates of* FERNS, large folio, *old calf,* RARE, £2. 16s *Paris,* 1705

4785 ——— Description des Plantes de l'Amérique, folio, 108 *plates,* 30s 1693

4786 POMODORO, Geometrica Prattica, folio, first edition, *engraved title with a Cardinal's arms, plates, fine copy, vellum, rare, not mentioned by Brunet nor by De Morgan,* 10s *Roma,* 1599

4787 PONTOPPIDAN'S Natural History of Norway, folio, 291 pp., *map and* 28 *curious plates of Scenery, Natural History, including the famous Sea Serpent, etc. fine copy in old russia, from Miss Currer's library,* 32s 1755

4788 PRICHARD'S (J. C.) Researches into the Physical History of Mankind, 5 vols. 8vo. (pub. £4. 2s 6d) *coloured plates, cloth,* £3. 3s 1841-47
Dr. Prichard in his Researches has shown, "that to execute such a design as his we must combine the knowledge of the physiological laws of nature with the traditions of history and the philosophical comparison of languages. Mr. Lyell quotes Dr. Prichard's books more frequently than any other."—*Whewell's E. Ind. Sc. III.* 483.

4789 PRITZEL, Thesaurus Literaturae Botanicae omnium gentium 15,000 operum recensens, 4to. *interleaved, hf. calf,* £2. 10s *Lipsiae,* 1851

4790 PURBACCHII Theoricae novae Planetarum, cum scholiis ab Reinholdo, 12mo. *numerous cuts, margin of the first three leaves slightly wormed, otherwise a remarkably fine clean copy, vellum,* 12s *Parisiis,* 1553

4791 QUER, Flora Española ò Historia de las Plantas, que ce crian en España, con la continuacion por Gomez de Ortega, 6 vols. 4to. *with* 196 *plates, fine copy in Spanish calf,* £2. 16s *Madrid, Ibarra,* 1762-84
A complete copy of this standard work, and Supplement. Priced, 1828, £6. 6s ; Pappenheim's copy sold 100 fr.

4792 RACCOLTA (Nuova) d'Autori, che trattano del MOTO dell' ACQUE, 7 vols. sm. 4to. *plates, vellum, fine copy,* 24s *Parma,* 1766-68
A standard collection of Italian authors on Hydraulics, Waterworks, Canals, Embanking, &c.

4793 RAY SOCIETY'S PUBLICATIONS, a complete set, in 8vo. in all 18 vols. 8vo. *cloth,* and 11 vols. folio, £12. 10s 1845-57

CONTENTS:

Reports on the Progress of Zoology and Botany	1845	Darwin. Monograph of Cirripedia, 2 vols.	1851-54
Steenstrup on the Alterations of Generations	1845	Leighton on Angiocarpous Lichens	1851
Memorials of John Ray	1846	Botanical and Physiological Memoirs	1853
Reports and Papers on Botany	1846	In folio:	
Meyen, Botanical Geography	1846	Burmeister on the Organisation of Trilobites, by P. Bell and Forbes	1846
Report on Zoology	1847		
Oken, Elements of Physiophilosophy	1847	Forbes (Prof.) Monograph of the British Naked-Eyed Medusæ, &c. *plates*	1848
Correspondence of John Ray	1848		
Agassiz, Catalogue of Books, &c. on Zoology and Geology, 4 vols.	1848-54	Alder and Hancock, Nudibranchiate Mollusca, 7 parts, *many plates*	1845-55
Reports and Papers on Botany, by Henfrey	1849	Allman, Fresh Water Polyzoa	1856
Baird on British Entomostraca	1850	Williamson's Recent Foraminifera, *plates*	1857

4794 AGASSIZ, Bibliographia Zoologiae et Geologiae: a general Catalogue of all Books, Tracts and Memoirs on Zoology and Geology, enlarged by Strickland, 4 vols. 8vo. *cloth,* £2. 10s 1848-54

4795 ALDER and HANCOCK, Monograph of the British NUDIBRANCHIATE MOLLUSCA, complete in 7 parts, impl. 4to. 82 *plates, most of them beautifully* COLOURED, *bds.* £5. 15s ; *hf. green morocco,* £4. 15s 1845-55
One of the most elaborate scientific publications produced in Europe; highly esteemed and sought after by Continental Savants. The early parts are out of print, but are in stock and can be supplied by me.

4796 ALLMAN'S Monograph of all the known species of the Fresh Water Polyzoa, fol. *coloured plates, bds.* 20s 1856

4797 BLACKWALL's History of the Spiders of Great Britain and Ireland, Part I. 4to. 12 *coloured plates, bds.* £1. 5s 1861

4798 BURMEISTER, Organization of Trilobites, folio, 6 *plates, bds.* 10s 1846

4799 CARPENTER, Parker and Jones, Introduction to the Study of the Foraminifera, imp. 4to. *woodcuts and* 22 *plates, bds.* £1. 11s 6d 1862

4800 FORBES (E.) Monograph of the British Naked-eyed Medusæ, with figures of all the species, folio, 13 *finely coloured plates, bds.* 25s 1848

4801 HUXLEY (Professor) Oceanic Hydrozoa, description of the Calycophoridæ and Physophoridæ observed during the voyage of the Rattlesnake, 1846-50, imp. folio, 12 *plates, bds.* £1. 5*s* 1859

4802 REAUMUR, Memoires pour servir a l'Histoire des Insectes, 6 vols. stout sm. 4to. *with 267 plates, containing many thousand engravings of Butterflies, Moths, &c. with their Chrysalides and Caterpillars, also the Plants on which they feed, French calf,* £2. ; *or a fine copy, neat, in old Dutch calf gilt, with the autograph of H.R.H. the Princess Eliza,* £2. 12*s* 6*d*   *Paris,* 1734-42
Priced, 1824, Wood, £6. 6*s*; 1829, John Bohn, russia, £7. 10*s*; 1829, Longman, £3. 3*s*; 1831, Bohn, veau fauve, £3. 13*s* 6*d*; 1836, Jas. Bohn, £3. 13*s* 6*d* and £4. 4*s*; 1840, Payne and Foss, blue morocco, £7. 7*s*; 1847, H. G. Bohn, £3. 3*s*; 1848, Payne and Foss, morocco, £7. 7*s*; Willett's copy fetched £5. 15*s* 6*d*.
"A volume, indeed, would scarcely suffice to do justice to the pre-eminent merits of Reaumur. I must therefore content myself with observing, that in judgment and ingenuity, in patient assiduity, in elegance of language, and felicity of illustration, he has rarely, if ever, been equalled. Every subject was thoroughly investigated, in the true spirit of philosophical inquiry. Everywhere you see him the same unprejudiced observer, attached to no system, anxious only for the truth, and the advancement of true science."—*Kirby and Spence, Entomology, Vol.* iv. *p.* 454.

4803 REEVE'S CONCHOLOGIA ICONICA, or Illustrations of the Shells of Molluscous Animals, Vol. I—VIII, IX, parts 1, 2; with the Supplement to the Conus and Murex, 4to. 1159 *beautifully coloured plates, pub. at about* £73, *four vols. in cloth, the rest unbound, Subscriber's copy,* £45.   1846-55

4804 ——— Land and Freshwater Mollusks of the British Isles, 8vo. *woodcuts and portrait of Draparnaud* (pub. at 10*s* 6*d*), *cloth, new,* 8*s* 9*d*   1863

4805 REGIOMONTANI Fundamenta Operationum *Neuburg,* 1557—Joachimi Rhetici Doctrina Triangulorum, *Basil.*—COPERNICUS de Revolutionibus Orbium cœlest. *Basil.* 1566—in 1 vol. sm. folio, *calf neat,* 12*s*   1557-66

4806 REISCH, Margarita Filosofica nella quale si trattano tutte le dottrine comprese nella Ciclopedia dagli antichi, sm. 4to. *treating of all the Arts and Sciences, curious cuts, vellum,* 30*s* [See also *Margarita*]   *Venet.* 1600

4807 RICCATI (V.) et H. Saladini Institutiones Analyticæ, 2 vols. in 3, 4to. *plates, bds. scarce,* £1.   *Bononiæ,* 1765-67

4808 RICCATI (Conte G.) delle Corde ovvero Fibre elastiche Schediasmi Fisico-matematici, 4to. *plates, uncut,* 10*s*   *Bologna,* 1767
A scarce work, celebrated in the history of mathematical Acoustics.

4809 RICHARD, Mémoire sur les Conifères et les Cycadées, terminé par A. Richard, *Lat. et Franç.* imp. 4to. PAPIER VÉLIN, 30 *plates* (pub. at 85 fr.) *sd.* 25*s*   1826

4810 RICHARDSON'S (John), Wm. SWAINSON, and Rev. W. KIRBY, FAUNA BOREALI-AMERICANA, or Zoology of North America, containing descriptions of the Subjects collected in the late Northern Expeditions under Sir John Franklin, (Quadrupeds, 28 plates ; Birds, 50 plates ; Fishes, 24 plates ; Insects, 8 plates :) published under the Authority of the Right Hon. the Secretary of State for Colonial Affairs, 4 vols. 4to. 110 *plates, most of them beautifully coloured, half russia* (pub. at £9. 9*s*) £6. 6*s*   1829-36
Priced, 1841, Bohn, £9. 9*s*; 1847, £7. 7*s*; fetched, 1846, Steevens', £6. 6*s*.
"We cannot speak in too high terms of admiration with regard to that splendid national production, the *Fauna Boreali-Americana*. It is undoubtedly the best work of its kind that has ever appeared, and will, we expect, long remain so."—*Neville Wood.*

4811 RISSO et POITEAU, Histoire Naturelle des Orangers, impl. 4to, *with* 109 BEAUTIFULLY COLOURED PLATES *of Orange and Lemon Plants, &c., in Flower and Fruit* (pub. at 216 *francs, unbound), hf. russia neat, a fine copy from Miss Currer's library,* £3. 10*s*   *Paris,* 1818

4812 ROCHEL Plantæ Banatus (Temeswar. Hungariæ) rariores, folio, *fine paper,* 2 *maps and* 40 *plates, hf. bd.* 16*s*   *Pestini,* 1828

4813 ROESEL'S INSECTEN-BELUSTIGUNG, monätlich-herausgegeben, mit der BEYTRÄGE VON KLEEMAN, in 4 vols. stout sm. 4to. *frontispieces, and* 400 *plates of Butterflies, Caterpillars, etc. beautifully coloured, hf. bd.* £5.   *Nürnberg,* 1746-61
Priced, 1840, Wood, £15. 15*s*; in 1860, I sold a copy for £5. 5*s*.
COLLATION: Vol. I. Pages 64, 60, 64, 312, 48 and 48; Plates, coloured, 10, 10, 8, 63, 13 and 17.—Vol. II. Pages 24, 72, 28, 16, 32, 76, 200, 64 and 52; Plates 2, 9, 3, 6, 4, 17, 30, 13 and 10.— Vol. III. Pages 624; Plates 101.—Vol. IV. Pages 48 (Life of Roesel, with portrait) and 264; Plates 40; Supplement by Kleeman, 376 pp. and 44 plates.

4814 ——— KLEEMANN'S Beyträge, *separately,* sm. 4to. 44 *coloured plates, hf. calf,* 14*s*   (*ib.* 1761)

4815 ROESEL historia naturalis Ranaram nostratium, large folio, 24 *coloured plates of Frogs and their Anatomy, each with a key-plate, the text in Latin and German, fine copy in russia extra,* 25*s*   *Nürnb.* 1758
Priced, 1840, £3. 15*s*.

4816 RONDELETIUS de Piscibus Marinis, folio, *with several hundred woodcuts of Fishes, including two very curious representations* of the "Monk Fish" and the "Bishop Fish," *fine copy in old French calf extra*, by DE ROME, *from the library of Marshal Masséna*, £2. 2s *Lugduni*, 1554-55

4817 RONDELET, Histoire des Poissons, traduite de Latin, par Joubert, 2 vols. in 1, sm. folio, *portrait and fine woodcuts, Vol. I, which contains the Marine Fishes, has the same woodcuts as the Latin work above, hf.* morocco, 25s *Lion*, 1558

"With all its defects, this early specimen of ichthyology has great and even extraordinary merit in the excellency of the woodcuts copiously introduced in its pages; they are bold and accurate, and in general so characteristic that nearly all the species may at once be identified."—SWAINSON.

4818 ROSCOE'S (W.) MONANDRIAN PLANTS of the Order of Scitamineæ, chiefly drawn from living specimens in the Botanic Garden at Liverpool; arranged according to the System of Linnæus, with Descriptions and Observations, complete, atlas folio, *containing* 112 *very large and finely coloured plates, half green morocco, uncut*, £5. 15s *Liverpool*, 1828

Priced, 1847, unbound, £15. 15s; half mor. £16. 16s. A very limited number of copies of this beautiful work was printed by subscription.

4819 ROSSII Fauna Etrusca, sistens Insecta in provinciis Florentina et Pisana collecta, 2 vols. in 1, 4to. *frontispieces and* 10 *coloured plates, old French calf gilt*, 25s *Liburni*, 1790

4820 —— Mantissa Insectorum exhibens species nuper in Etruriâ collectas, 4to. 8 *coloured plates, hf. morocco*, 18s *Pisis*, 1792

4821 ROXBURGH'S Flora Indica; or descriptions of Indian Plants, new edition by Carey, 3 vols. 8vo. (pub. at £3. 12s) *bds*. £3. 10s *Seramp*. 1832

4823 —— the same, Vols. I, II, 8vo. *bds*. 30s 1832

4824 ROXBURGH'S Plants of the Coast of Coromandel, Vol. III. parts 3, 4, atlas folio, *coloured plates* 251 *to* 300 (pub. at £6. 6s) *bds. rare*, £2. 16s 1819

4825 ROYAL SOCIETY. PHILOSOPHICAL TRANSACTIONS of the Royal Society of London, at large, from the commencement in 1665 to 1844, with Indexes to Vols. 1 to 110—R. Hook's Lectures,—and Parsons' Crounian Lectures—together 141 vols. 4to. *many plates, russia, a remarkably fine set*, £116. 1654-1844

The difficulty of obtaining original editions of the early volumes, in any state, and especially in good condition, is well known. Hence the possession of a copy of the Transactions at large is a great rarity, even in public libraries. The continuation from 1845 to 1862 is in stock and can be supplied at a much reduced price.

4826 ROYAL SOCIETY. Philosophical Transactions of the Royal Society of London, from 1828 to 1860, part I.—together 71 parts, 4to. (pub. at £93. 17s) *uncut*, £30. 1828-60

A considerable number of early volumes and recent parts are constantly kept in stock. Sets completed on reasonable terms.

4827 ROYAL SOCIETY'S PROCEEDINGS, NOS. 1-51 inclusive, 8vo. *sd*. £2. 10s 1854-62

The above contains all the papers read before the Society between 1854 and 1862.

4828 RUEPPELL'S Atlas zu der Reise im nördlichen Afrika, Erste Abtheilung: ZOOLOGIE, herausg. von der Senckenberg. naturforschenden Gesellschaft, 5 parts in 1 vol. stout atlas 4to. 118 *plates, mostly coloured* (pub. at 43¼ Thalers) *bds*. £4. 4s *Frankfurt*, 1826-28

COLLATION: I. Säugethiere, von Cretzschmar, 30 plates; II. Vögel, von Cretzschmar, 36 plates; III. Reptilien, von Heyden, 5 plates; IV. Fischer des rothen Meers, 35 plates; V. Neue Wirbellose Thiere, des R. Meers, 12 plates.

4829 RUMPHII (G. E.) Herbarium Amboinense, complectens Arbores, Frutices, Herbas, Plantas terrestres et aquaticas, quæ in Amboina et adjacentibus Insulis reperiuntur; item varia Insectorum Animaliumque genera, *Belgice et Latine*, ed. Burmann, cum Auctario, 7 vols. in 6, large folio, *nearly* 700 *fine engravings, fine copy in old gilt russia*, £5. 15s *Amst*. 1741-56

Plate 70 in Vol. V. was not published. Priced, 1840, £7.: 1854, 62 fl. "Rumphius' account of plants contains many which are not peculiar to the little Island of Amboyna, and embraces their names and synonyms, their botanical description, their flowering seasons, their habitats, their uses, and the mode of culture of such as are objects of cultivation. He was evidently a man of talents, sound sense, and indefatigable industry."—CRAWFURD.

4830 RUMPHIUS, d'Amboinsche Rariteitkamer of eene bescryvinge van allerhande Schaalvisschen, folio, *portrait of Rumphius and* 60 *plates of* SHELLS *and Fossils, fine copy in Dutch calf*, 20s *Amst*. 1705

4831 RUSSELL (Dr. P.) Account of Indian Serpents, 46 *plates*, 1796—CONTINUATION, part 1, containing Preface, 11 pp. and Plates 1-10, 1801—together 2 vols. roy. folio, *with* 56 *coloured plates, bds*. VERY RARE, £4. 1796-1801

4832 —— Descriptions and Figures of 200 Fishes, collected at Vizagapatam, on the Coast of Coromandel, 2 vols. roy. folio, 171 *plates, numbered* 1 *to* 208, *hf. bd*. £4. 4s 1803

Psiced. 1840, W. Wood, £5. 10s; 1841, Allen, £8. 8s. Plates, 17, 33, 34, 36, 55, 164, 200, 201, 202, 205, 206, as stated in the letterpress, were not published.

4833 SACROBUSTO (Joan. de) Sphera, cum Commentis Esculani, Capuani, Fabri Stapulensis, etc. folio, GOTHIC LETTER, *diagrams, hf. morocco*, 16s   *Venet*. 1518

4834 SAGRA (Ramon de la) Historia Fisica, Politica, y Natural de la Isla de CUBA, bound in 7 vols. folio, *coloured plates, half roan*, (pub. at near 1000 francs) *as described below*, £10.   *Paris*, 1838-42

CONTENTS :

HISTORIA FISICA y Politica, Introduccion, Geographia, Clima, Poblacion, Agricultura, Comercio Maritimo, Rentas y Gastos, Fuerza Armada, Appendice 2 vols. 79 and 302 pp. and 207 pp. *with* 10 *maps*.
BOTANICA, Plantas Vasculares. por Richard; Text, pp. 1—116; plates, 1—56, plain, wanting 24, 40, 51, 52, 53, 54—Plantas Cellulares, Text, pp. 1—152, Plates, 1—20, *coloured*, in one volume, *no title*.
FORAMINIFERAS, por D'ORBIGNY; text, title, half title, pp.

1—180, Plates, 1—12, *some coloured* — MAMMIFEROS Text, half title, pp. 1—39, Plates, 1—8, *coloured*, in one volume.
AVES, por D'ORBIGNY; Text, title, pp. 1—220, Plates, 1—32, *beautifully coloured*.
REPTILES, por COCTEAU y BIBRON; Text, title, half title, pp 1—142. Tabla, 1 p., Plates, 1—30, *finely coloured*.
MOLUSCOS, Text, pp. 1—216, Plates, 1—22, *finely coloured*, wanting 10, 11, 12.

4835 SAINT PETERSBURGH ACADEMY: PETROPOLITANÆ ACADEMIÆ Scientiarum Commentarii, 1726 ad 1746, 14 vols. 1728-51 — Novi Commentarii, 1747-75, 20 vols. 1750-76 — Acta, 1777-82, 12 parts in 6 vols. 1778-86 — Nova Acta, 1783-98, 15 vols. 1783-1806 — Memoires de l'Académie, 1803-20, 9 vols. 1803-24 — Memoirs, *in Russian*, 5 vols. 1808-19 — Transactions, *in Russian*, 2 vols. in 1, 1821-23 — together 70 vols. 4to. *numerous plates, hf. russia, a fine set*, VERY RARE, £36.   *Petrop*. 1728-1824

4836 SALERNE, l'Histoire Naturelle éclaircie dans l'Ornithologie, 4to. 31 *plates of Birds, fine copy in old calf*, 15s   *Paris*, 1767

4837 SAMOULLE, The Entomologist's Useful Compendium; 8vo. *a double set of* 12 *plates, plain and coloured, hf. calf*, 10s   1819

4838 SAUSSURE, Monographie des Guêpes Sociales, impl. 8vo. pp. 1-240 *(appendix not complete), plates* 2-14, 17-18, 20-24, 27-29; *altogether* 23 *plates, many coloured, in case*, 12s   *Paris*, 1853

4839 SAY (T.) American Entomology, or Descriptions of the Insects of North America, 3 vols. 8vo. *beautifully coloured plates, hf. citron morocco, gilt edges, by Mackenzie, from Miss Currer's library, scarce*, £3. 15s   *Philadelphia*, 1824-28

4840 —— American Conchology, descriptions of the Shells of North America, 8vo. 60 *coloured plates, hf. bd.* 32s   *New Harmony, Indiana*, 1830

4841 SCHÆFFERI Icones Insectorum circa Ratisbonam indigenorum, 3 vols. roy. 4to. 280 *coloured plates*, LARGE PAPER, *old calf extra*, £3.   *Ratisb*. 1766

Marked, an early coloured copy, £7. 15s.   Priced, 1824, £6. 6s; 1856, 28 thalers; 1859, 25 thalers; 1840, Jas. Bohn, £5. 5s; H. Bohn, 1847, £4. 4s and £5. 5s.

4842 SCHAEFFER'S Versuche und Muster ohne alle Lumpen papier zu machen, 2 parts in 1 vol. sq. 8vo. 5 *coloured plates, and* 33 *specimens of various Papers, calf*, 20s   *Regensburg*, 1765

4843 —— Sämtliche Papier Versuche, zwote Auflage; Versuche und Muster Papier zu machen, 2 vols.—Neue Versuche und Pflanzenreich zum Papiermachen, etc. zu gebrauchen, 4 vols.—together 6 vols. in 2, sq. sm. 8vo. 13 *plates, chiefly coloured, and* 81 *specimens of Papers, calf, Miss Currer's copy*, £2. 2s   *ib*. 1772

Priced, in a bookseller's catalogue, £4.

4844 SCHELLENBERG Genres des Mouches Diptères, *French and German*, 8vo. 42 *finely coloured plates, with a MS. Index added, bds.* 21s   *Zuric*, 1803

4845 SCHEUCHZER, PHYSIQUE SACRÉE, ou Histoire Naturelle de la Bible, traduite du Latin, 8 vols. folio, *fine impressions of the* 750 *plates, very fine copy in old red morocco, gilt leaves*, £12.   *Amst*. 1732-37

Priced, 1825, Thorpe, *morocco*, £31. 10s; 1837, Payne and Foss, *morocco*, £23.

A most beautiful picture book of the Bible, containing 750 fine plates of scenes recorded in the Holy Scriptures, of Trees, Animals, Fossils, etc.

4846 SCHINZ, Beschreibung und Abbildung der Künstlichen Nester und Eyer der Vögel, impl. 4to. 74 *coloured plates of Birds, their Nests and Eggs, German bds. uncut*, 32s   Priced, 1841, £4. 10s.   *Zürich*, 1830

4847 SCHLEGEL (H.) Essai sur la Physionomie des Serpens, 2 vols. 8vo. with folio Atlas, *containing* 21 *plates and* 3 *maps, hf. morocco*, 20s   *La Haye*, 1837

4848 SCHOENHERR, SYNONYMIA INSECTORUM; Genera et species Curculionidum, cum synonymia hujus familiae; species hactenus minus cognitae a Gyllenhal, Bohemau aliisque illustratae, 8 vols. in 16, stout 8vo. £4. 10s   *Paris*, 1833-45

4849 —— Synonymia Insectorum, Tom. I.: Eleutherata oder Käfer, with Appendix, in 4 vols. 8vo. 6 *coloured plates of Beetles, bds.* 12s   *Stockholm*, 1806-17

4966 WILSON'S (James) ILLUSTRATIONS of ZOOLOGY, being Representations of New, Rare, or Remarkable Subjects of the Animal Kingdom, drawn and coloured after Nature, with historical and descriptive details, folio, *comprising 36 beautiful plates* (pub. at £7. 7s) *green morocco, gilt edges*, £4. 15s *Edinb.* 1831

4967 WISE on the Hindu System of Medicine, 8vo. *cloth, 7s* *Calcutta,* 1845

4968 WOOD'S Index Testaceologicus or Catalogue of Shells, bound in 2 vols. sm. 8vo. *a double set of* 38 *plates, coloured and plain, containing* 2300 *figures* (pub. at £6. 17s 6d) *calf neat,* 35s 1825

4969 ——— INDEX ENTOMOLOGICUS, a complete illustrated Catalogue of the Lepidopterous Insects of Great Britain, roy. 8vo. 59 *beautifully coloured plates, containing* 1944 *figures*, (pub. at £12. 4s) *calf gilt, uncut,* £6. 1839-54
The above edition is an original copy, to which the supplement has been added.

4970 YARRELL'S History of British Birds, FIRST EDITION, second corrected issue, 3 vols. 1843—Supplement, 1845—bound in 3 vols. 8vo. *calf gilt*, £4. 14s 1843-45

4971 ——— the same, 3 vols. 8vo. *calf gilt, uncut*, £5. 15s 1843
The above edition is eagerly sought after by amateurs of beautiful woodcuts, on account of the excellence of the early impressions.

4972 ——— the same, *third edition*, 3 vols. 8vo. *containing* 550 *illustrations, new cloth*, £4. 19s 6d 1856

4973 ——— History of BRITISH FISHES, *first edition*, 2 vols. 1836—The Supplement, by Yarrell, 2 pts. in 1 vol. 1839—together 3 vols. 8vo. *about* 400 *superb woodcuts*, (pub. at £3. 3s and 5s) *cloth,* £2. 16s 1836-39

4974 ——— the Supplement, by Sir J. Richardson, *with a portrait and memoir*, 1 vol. *cloth*, 12s 6d 1860
"The wood engravings to Yarrell's works by Thompson as far exceed those of Bewick, as finished line engraving does etching."— SPECTATOR, July 15, 1837.

4975 Yo SAN FI ROK, l'Art d'élever les Vers à Soie au Japon par Ouekari Morikouni, *Français, par* Bonafous et Hoffmann, 4to. 50 *plates after the original Japanese drawings, bds.* 12s 6d *Paris,* 1848

4976 YOUATT, the Horse, with treatise of Draught, 8vo. *numerous woodcuts, cloth*, 12s 1853

4977 YOUNG'S (G.) and BIRD, Geological Survey of the Yorkshire Coast, 4to. *front.* 2 *charts, and* 17 *coloured plates,* (pub. at 42s) *bds.* 30s *Whitby,* 1828

4978 YOUNG'S (T.) Lectures on Natural Philosophy and the Mechanical Arts, 2 vols. 4to. 57 *plates, fine copy, pale* RUSSIA EXTRA, *gilt edges, by Hayday, scarce,* £2. 10s 1807
Priced, 1836, £5. 15s 6d; 1847, bds. £4. 4s.

4979 ZACH (Freyherr Fr. von) Monatliche Correspondenz zur Beförderung der Erd- und Himmels-Kunde, Januar 1800 bis December 1813, 28 vols. 8vo. *portrait and diagrams, hf. calf neat, rare*, £4. 10s *Gotha,* 1800-13

4980 ——— Tabulæ Motuum Solis, cum Supplemento, stout 4to. *fine paper, hf. bd.* 6s *Gothæ,* 1792-1804

4981 ——— l'Attraction des Montagnes, 2 vols. 8vo. *plates, calf*, 6s *Avignon,* 1814

4982 ZAHN, Oculus Artificialis Teledioptricus, sive Telescopium ex abditis rerum naturalium novâ methodo protractum, folio, *plates of Optical Instruments, calf, fine copy,* 15s *Norimb.* 1702

4983 ZETTERSTEDT, Insecta Lapponica, cum Indice, 4to. *hf. mor.* 10s *Lips.* 1840

4984 ZIMMERMAN, Specimen Zoologiae Geographicae, 4to. *map, cf.* 6s *Lugd. Bat.* 1777

4985 ZOOLOGICAL SOCIETY's Publications for 1863, consisting of 3 parts of Proceedings, with upwards of 40 plates neatly coloured, and one or more parts of Transactions, with from 10 to 15 plates, 28s 1863

4986 ZUCHETTA, Prima parte della Arithmetica, folio, *portrait on the title, and of C. Papa on the dedication, limp vellum*, 16s *Brescia,* 1600
This scarce work is quoted only in his Index by Professor de Morgan, who apparently was not able to find a copy to give the title.

4987 BRITISH ASSOCIATION. Reports of the British Association for the Promotion of Science, from the commencement in 1831 to 1861, 30 vols. 8vo. *numerous engravings, many coloured*, (pub. £22. 6s) *bds.* £10. 10s ; *cf. nt.* £15. 1833-61
A set of 23 vols. only priced, 1857, £10. 10s. A repository of the deepest and most varied learning. Odd volumes can be supplied at a reduction.

4988 PAPPI ALEXANDRINI, Mathematicae Collectiones, *Latine*, à Federico Commandrino, cum commentariis, sm. folio, *fine copy, in tree-marbled calf gilt*, 36s *Bonon.* 1660

4989 **GAMES AND SPORTS.** ARCUSSIA (Charles, Seigneur d'Esparron) la Fauconnerie, avec une instruction pour traitter les Autours, 12mo. wanting pp. 131-32, 10 *plates of Falcons, limp vellum, very rare,* £2. *Paris,* 1599

4990 BERJEAU, Varieties of Dogs, as found in old Sculpture, Pictures, Engravings and Books, showing how long many of the breeds now existing have been known, sq. 8vo. 52 *plates, containing upwards of* 100 *specimens, some very grotesque, new in cloth,* 10s 6d 1863

4991 BLOME (R.) GENTLEMAN'S RECREATION, in two parts; the first being an Encyclopædia of Arts and Sciences; the second of HORSEMANSHIP, HAWKING, HUNTING, FOWLING, and FISHING, with a treatise of Cock Fighting, large folio, *frontispiece and about* 100 *plates, calf, Lord Macaulay's copy,* £4. 4s 1686
A copy fetched, 1858, at Sotheby's, *russia,* £4. 10s.

4992 BOOK OF SAINT ALBANS. The Book containing the treatises of Hawking, Hunting, Coat-Armour, Fishing, and Blasing of Arms [by DAME JULIANA BERNERS], reprinted in black and red type, after Wynkyn de Worde's Edition of 1496, with Introduction, biographical and bibliographical notices, by Haslewood, folio, imp. 8vo. *numerous curious woodcuts, including many coats of Arms, &c. hf. bd. uncut,* £8. 8s 1810

4993 CORSINI (Accursio) Apologetico della Caccia, ove dopò narrati i vitij da scrittori rimproverati scopronsi le sue virtu, etc. sm. 4to. *limp vel.* 25s *Bergamo,* 1626

4994 ESPINAR (M. de) Arte de BALLESTERIA, y Monteria, escrita con metodo, par escusar la fatiga que ocasiona la ignorancia, sq. 8vo. *fine copy, plates of Hunting, etc.* 24s *Madrid,* 1644
FIRST EDITION, RARE, Priced, 1826, Salva, L. P., £3 3s. "Volume peu commun."—*Brunet.*

4995 STRADANI VENATIONES Ferarum, Avium, Piscium; Pugnæ Pestiariorum, et Mutuæ Bestiarum, obl. folio, *frontispiece and* 87 *large engravings of all kinds of Hunting, engraved by Collaert, Galle, &c. early and very fine impressions of the plates, old calf,* £2. 12s 6d (*Antv.* 1578)

4996 —— Venationis omne genus, Aucupii Piscatusque, obl. sm. folio, *another and varying edition of the above work,* 44 *plates* (1-44) *calf,* 18s 1578
A copy with the entire series of 104 plates priced, 1856, Foss, 100 fr.

4997 ATTI della RIUNIONE degli SCIENZIATI ITALIANI, tenuti in Pisa, Torino, Firenze, Padova, Lucca, Milano, e Napoli, dalla prima istituzione nel 1839 sino al 1845, coi Diarij delle III-VII Riunioni (*none was published for the first and second years*) 1841-45, together 12 vols. in 13, roy. 4to. *plates, a vast repertory of Literary and Scientific articles, corresponding exactly to the British Association Reports, very neatly hf. bd.* £5. *Pisa, etc. Napoli,* 1840-46

4998 ALDROVANDI (Ulyssis) Opera: Ornithologia, 3 vols. 1599-1645—de Insectis, 1638—Animalia exanguia, mollia, crustacea, etc. 1642—Pisces et Cetac, 1638—Quadrupedes solidipedes, 1639—Quadrupedes Bisulci, 1642—Quadrupedes digitati, 1645—Serpentes et Dracones, 1640—Monstrorum historia cum paralip. hist. omnium Animalium, 1642—together 11 vols. folio, *several hundred woodcuts, fine copies in old blue* MOROCCO, *gilt edges,* £10. 10s *Bononiae,* 1599-1645

4999 ARCHIMEDIS Opera quae extant, novis demonstrationibus illustrata per D. Rivaltium à Flurantia, folio, *numerous woodcuts, old calf,* 7s 6d; or *a fine copy in the original stamped bdg.* 12s *Paris,* 1615

4999*BELON (P.) Histoire de la Nature des Oyseaux, 7 Books in 1 vol. sm. folio, *about* 100 *fine woodcuts,* 4 *pp. in MS., vellum,* 10s *Paris,* 1555

5000 BEWICK'S (Thos.) History of QUADRUPEDS, FIRST EDITION, 8vo. *upwards of* 200 *cuts, fine impressions, hf. green morocco,* £2. 12s *Newcastle,* 1790

5000*BLONDEL (F.) Thermarum Aquisgranensium, et Porcetanarum elucidatio et Thaumaturgia, sq. 8vo. *portrait and curious engravings representing Vapour, Shower, and other Baths, bd. rare,* 7s *Aquisgr.* (*Aix la Chapelle*) 1688

5001 BUC'HOZ, Herbier ou Collection des Plantes Médicinales de la Chine, d'après un MS. peint et unique dans la Bibliotheque de l'Empereur de la Chine, roy. folio, consisting of 100 FINELY COLOURED *plates, subscribed "peint à la Chine," no text ever published, bds.* 36s *Paris,* 1781

5001*BURMEISTER, Genera Insectorum, Vol. I: Rhynchota, in 10 parts, roy. 8vo. 40 *finely coloured plates,* (*pub. at* 10 *Thalers*) 10s *Berol.* 1840-46

5002 CAMUS, Cours de Mathématique, trois parties: Arithmétique, Géometrie, Méchanique Statique, 4 vols. 8vo. *numerous diagrams, calf,* 15s *Paris,* 1749-52
Mentioned in De Bure as very rare.

4850 SCHOEPFF, Historia Testudinum, impl. 4to. 31 *cold. plates, hf. bd.* 15s *Erlang.*1792
4851 SCHOTTI Cursus Mathematicus sive encyclopaedia Mathematicarum disciplinarum fol. *curious frontispiece studded with diagrams, representing the Copernican System, hogskin,* 12s *Herbipoli,* 1661
4852 SCHOUW, Grundzüge einer allgemeinen Pflanzengeographie, 8vo. 528 pp. *calf; with oblong folio Atlas of 22 coloured plates, hf. morocco,* 6s *Berlin,* 1825
4853 SCHUBERT Astronomie Théorique, 3 vols. 4to. *plates, calf,* 30s *St. Pet.* 1822
4854 SCHUMACHER (C. F.) Nouveau Système des Habitations des Vers Testacés, 4to. 22 *plates, hf. bd.* 15s *Copenhague,* 1817
4855 SCHUMACHER'S (H. C.) Astronomische Nachrichten, Vols. XXVI-XXXIX, mit Ergänzungsheft, 4to. *in numbers* (pub. at 90 Thalers) £3. *Altona,* 1847-54

A rare and valuable periodical publication. Some of the titles are wanting, but the text is complete from No. 01 to 926.

4856 SCLATER'S Catalogue of a collection of American Birds, 8vo. 20 *coloured plates, new cloth,* 25s 1862
4857 SÉDILLOT, Memoires sur les Instruments Astronomiques des Arabes, 4to. 36 *plates, a very learned work, hf. calf,* 24s 1841
4858 SELBY'S ILLUSTRATIONS OF BRITISH ORNITHOLOGY: LAND AND WATER BIRDS, *a most magnificent work of* BRITISH BIRDS, containing an exact and faithful representation, in their full natural size, of all the known species found in Great Britain, 383 *Figures in* 228 *beautifully* COLOURED PLATES, 2 vols. elephant folio, (published at £105.)—The letterpress descriptions, 2 vols. —together, 4 vols. *hf. calf, a picked copy, chosen by the author for Miss Currer, who paid* £94. 10s *for it,* £36. 1833-34

The grandest work on Ornithology published in this country, the same for British Birds that Audubon's is for the birds of America. Every figure, excepting in a very few instances of extremely large birds, is of the full natural size, beautifully and accurately drawn, with all the spirit of life.
"Every individual of the Falcon and Owl Families would make A PERFECT PICTURE OF ITSELF, so beautifully and correctly are they executed: THEY HAVE CERTAINLY NEVER BEEN EQUALLED, EVEN BY GOULD AND AUDUBON."
Ornithologist's Text Book.
"It would be impossible to improve on any of the *Raptores,* which for fidelity, boldness, and spirit, are unequalled—every feather is distinct, yet beautifully blended."—*Wood's Ornithological Guide.*
"What a splendid work! This is the kind of ornamental furniture, in which we, were we men of fortune, would delight. The tables in our passages, galleries, parlours, boudoirs, and drawing-rooms should groan—no, not groan—but smile, with suitably-bound volumes of Natural History, on the opening of any one of which, would suddenly gleam before us some rich and rare, bright and beauteous, minute or mighty production of the great mother —Nature. What a treasure, for instance, during a rainy afternoon in the country, is such a gloriously illuminated work as this of Mr. Selby, to a small party uncertain in what spirit they shall woo the hours.—It is, without doubt, the most splendid of the kind ever published in Britain. It is needless to say anything of the style of colouring— let a pure and steady light stream on the plumage of these phantom-birds, bright as the realities in the woods and on the mountains, and we shall beguile ourselves away into their solitary forest haunts. Was there ever, for instance, such a descriptive dream of a coloured engraving of the Cushat, Quest, or Ringdove, dreamt before?"
Blackwood's Magazine.

4859 SELBY's History of British Forest Trees, indigenous and introduced, 8vo. *nearly* 200 *fine woodcuts,* (pub. at 28s) *cloth,* 22s 1842
4860 SELLII Historia naturalis Teredinis seu Xylophagi marini, 4to. *coloured plates, vellum,* 6s *Traj.* 1733
4861 SEPP's Nederlandsche Insecten, 3 parts in 1 vol. 26 *coloured plates of Dutch Lepidoptera, hf. russia,* 14s *Amst.* 1762
4862 SERPENTS. 44 large HINDOO DRAWINGS, accurately figured and coloured, of various Indian Serpents, with the native names appended, roy. folio. *the actual skin of a Serpent* 43 *inches long inserted separately in the book, bd.* £2. *ca.* 1800
4863 SERPENT WORSHIP. GESNERI Hist. Animalium: Carroni Serpentum natura, etc. 2 vols. in 1, folio, *woodcuts, hf. bd. a curious book,* 7s 6d *Franc.* 1612
4864 SIBBALD (Sir R.) Scotia Illustrata, sive Prodomus Historiæ Naturalis Scotiæ, folio, 22 *plates in* 20, *including the rare portrait of Boyd, vell.* 10s *Edinb.* 1784
4865 —— the same, LARGE PAPER, roy. folio, ORIGINAL EDITION, 22 *plates of Plants, Birds, Fishes, &c. calf neat,* 30s 1683-84

Priced, LARGE PAPER, Constable, £3. 10s; 1827, Thorpe, £4. 14s 6d. The plate by De Leu, containing the portrait of Alexander Boyd, is often wanting. Sir Robert Sibbald, says Bp. Nicholson, was one of the greatest ornaments of his country and profession which this age has produced.

4866 SIEBOLD, FAUNA JAPONICA, sive descriptio Animalium in Japonia collectorum, conjunctis studiis Temminck, Schlegel, et De Haan; CRUSTACEA, elaborante DE HAAN, atlas folio, 70 *large plates, hf. russia,* £4. *Lugd. Bat.* 1850

4867 SIEBOLD (C. T. E.) True Parthenogenesis in Moths and Bees, by Dallas, 8vo. *cloth*, 5s 1857
4868 SMITH'S (And.) Illustrations of the ZOOLOGY OF SOUTH AFRICA, 28 parts, impl. 4to. COMPLETE, 280 *finely* COLOURED PLATES, *with text*, (pub. at £18. but now entirely out of print) in parts, uncut, £12. 12s *London*, 1838-1849

<small>Odd parts in stock. In 1856 Yarrell's copy fetched £13. This valuable work is arranged as follows. Mammalia, 53 plates—Aves, 113 plates—Reptilia, 78 plates—Pisces, 31 plates—Invertebratæ, 4 plates—total, 280 plates.</small>

4869 SMITH (Sir J. E.) Coloured Figures of imperfectly described or unknown Plants, atlas folio, 18 *finely coloured plates, with descriptions in Latin and English, without a title page, half russia,* uncut, SCARCE, 20s 1790
4870 —— Introduction to Botany, by Hooker, 8vo. 36 *plates*, (pub. at 16s) 9s 1833
4871 SMITH (R.) Compleat System of Opticks, with the Remarks, etc. very stout sm. 4to. *numerous plates, calf,* 25s *Cambridge*, 1738
4872 SMITHSONIAN INSTITUTION. Smithsonian Contributions to Knowledge, 11 vols. impl. 4to. *numerous fine plates,* uncut, £9. 9s *Washington*, 1848-60

I can sell separately the following portions:

4873 GRAY (Asa) Plantae Wrightianae Texano-Neo Mexicanae, a collection of plants by Wright, 2 parts, roy. 4to. 14 *plates, sd.* 12s 1853
4874 LEIDY's Flora and Fauna within living Animals, roy. 4to. *plates*, 5s 1851
4875 TORREY'S Plantae Fremontianae, 10 *plates*—Darlington Californica, 1 *plate*—Batis Maritima, 1 *plate*—3 parts, roy. 4to. 5s 1853
4876 SMITHSONIAN Miscellaneous Collections: Meteorological Tables, Observations, etc.; Catalogues of Coleoptera, of Reptiles, etc. 8 parts 8vo. 10s 1850-58
4877 SONNERAT, Voyage à la Nouvelle Guinée, 4to. 120 *plates of Natural History, cf.* 12s *Paris*, 1776
4878 SOWERBY'S (G. B.) Thesaurus Conchyliorum, or Figures and Descriptions of Shells, part I to XX, imp. 8vo. 235 *plates finely finished in colours*, (pub. at £25.) sd. £14. 14s 1842-59
4879 —— Genera of Recent and Fossil Shells, Nos. XXXVIII—XLII, 5 parts, 8vo. 36 *coloured plates*, 15s *ca.* 1822
4880 SOWERBY (James) English Botany, or Coloured Figures of British Plants, with their essential Characters, Synonymes, and Places of Growth, described by Sir James E. Smith, with general Index, 36 vols. in 23, large 8vo. complete, ORIGINAL AND BEST EDITION *containing* 2592 *coloured plates*, (pub. at £55. 8s 6d) *hf. russia*, £24. *Lond.* 1790-1814

<small>A most desirable set, this being an original copy, without any mixture whatever of the later impressions; and having besides the peculiar advantage of being arranged systematically in classes, thereby facilitating the use and study of the work to no ordinary degree.
This fine work contains every English Plant and every Flower, truthfully delineated after nature, with a precise description. Original sets, like the above, are more accurately coloured than others.</small>

4881 —— the Supplement by HOOKER, Babington, etc. separately, 4 vols. roy. 8vo. *plates*, 2593-2960, *with text*, £10. 1831-49
4882 SOWERBY'S (J.) British Mineralogy, or coloured figures intended to elucidate the Mineralogy of Great Britain, 5 vols. 8vo. 550 *plates, beautifully coloured*, (pub. in Nos. at £17. 5s) *calf gilt*, £8. 8s 1804-11
4883 —— Exotic Mineralogy: or coloured figures of Foreign Minerals, as a Supplement to British Mineralogy, 2 vols. roy. 8vo. 169 *finely coloured plates, fine clean copy, in bds.* uncut, £5. 1811-17

<small>The latter parts of both of these valuable works are out of print, and the plates have been sold for old copper.</small>

4884 SPRENGEL. LINNAEI Systema Vegetabilium, curante Sprengel, 4 vols. in 5, 8vo. *calf*, 25s 1825
4885 SPRY'S British Coleoptera Delineated, consisting of Figures and Descriptions of all the Genera of British Beetles, edited by Shuckard, 8vo. *with* 94 *plates, comprising* 638 *figures of Beetles, beautifully and most accurately drawn*, (pub. at £2. 2s) *cloth*, 12s 1861
4886 —— the same, 8vo. *the plates* COLOURED, *cloth gilt*, £2. 12s 1861

<small>The most perfect work yet published in this department of British Entomology.</small>

4887 STEPHENS' Systematic Catalogue of British Insects, being an attempt to arrange all the hitherto discovered Indigenous Insects, stout 8vo. (pub. at 27s) *bds.* 12s 1829

NATURAL HISTORY, SCIENCES, MATHEMATICS. 255

4888 STEPHENS' (J. F.) Illustrations of British Entomology, or a Synopsis of Indigenous Insects; their generic and specific Distinctions; with an account of their Metamorphoses, Localities, Food and Economy; (all the known British Species, arranged in two great Classes of *Haustellata* and *Manibulata*), 86 parts, forming 12 vols. bound in 9, 8vo. (*Haustellata*, 4 vols.; *Mandibulata*, 7 vols.; Suppl. 1 vol.) 100 *beautifully* COLOURED *plates, comprising numerous figures*, (pub. at £21.) *hf. bd.* £6. 6s   1828-46

    This work gives in a systematic form, descriptions of all the insects hitherto detected in Great Britain and Ireland; with coloured figures of some of the rarer and more interesting species. It embraces an acccount of a far greater number of species than has hitherto appeared in the indigenous Fauna of any country.

4889 STANDISH, LEPIDOPTERA BRITANNICA: A Series of upwards of 1000 exquisitely coloured Drawings of the rarer MOTHS and BUTTERFLIES to be found in ENGLAND, remarkably accurate in drawing and colour, A BEAUTIFUL VOLUME, imp. 4to. (leaves 1-8, 1-19, 1-218,) *green morocco super extra, gilt edges*, £21.
                                                                                      ca. 1840

    An extremely important volume of great scientific merit and of perfect artistic beauty. On the page opposite the Drawings is a neatly written tabular form giving:

No. of plates.	The LATIN NAMES.	Numbers on each sheet.	The ENGLISH NAMES.	The Genus.

4890 STERNBERG, Essai d'un Exposé Géognostico-Botanique de la FLORE du MONDE PRIMITIF, traduit par Bray, 6 parts in 1 vol. folio, 90 *coloured plates*, (I-LXI, A-E, I-XXVI) pub. 44 Thal. *hf. calf gilt*, RARE, £7. 7s *Ratisb.*, 1820-33
                              Priced, 1841, Bohn, £10.; 1847, £7. 7s.

4891 STEUART'S Account of the PEARL FISHERIES of Ceylon. 4to. *map and chart, bds.* 12s   *Ceylon, Cotta*, 1843
                With Steuart's MSS. Report to Sir Benj. Hawes.

4892 STEUDEL, Nomenclator Botanicus, seu Synonymia Plantarum Universalis, 2 vols. impl. 8vo. *hf. calf*, 28s   *Stuttgart*, 1841

4893 STOFLERINI Elucidatio fabricae ususque ASTROLABII, acc. Abacus Regionum et Calendarium Romanum, 1518-1579, sm. folio, *numerous woodcuts of Astrolabes, etc. good sound copy, vellum*, £2. 2s   *Oppenheym*, 1518-24

4894 —— Eadem, 12mo. *woodcuts, a scarce edition*, 10s   *Paris*, 1570

4895 STOLL, Répresentation des Spectres, des Mantes, des Sauterelles, des Grillons, des Criquets, et des Blattes, *Holland. et Franç.* Divisions 1, 3, 4, 4to. 36 *finely coloured plates, hf. bd.* 18s   *Amst.* 1787

4896 STRICKLAND's Ornithological Synonyms, edited by Sir W. Jardine, Accipitres, 8vo. (pub. at 12s 6d) *cloth*, 7s   1855

4897 **Sun Dials.** ROIZ, Libro de Reloges Solares, sq. 8vo. *numerous diagrams, vellum, rare*, 10s   *Valencia*, 1575

4898 SWAINSON, Geography and Classification of Animals—Natural History of Quadrupeds, 2 vols. 12mo. *many cuts, calf gilt*, 7s   1836

4899 SWAINSON'S ZOOLOGICAL ILLUSTRATIONS; or, original figures and descriptions of new, rare, or interesting Animals, selected chiefly from the Classes of Ornithology, Entomology, and Couchology, 1st Series 3 vols. 2nd Series 3 vols.—together 6 vols. royal 8vo. 318 *beautifully* COLOURED *plates*, (pub. at £16. 16s) *half mor. gilt edges*, £6. 6s   1820-33

4900 SWALLOW'S First and Second Annual Reports of the Geological Society of Missouri, large 8vo. *coloured maps and plates, cloth*, 16s   *Jefferson City*, 1855

4901 SWEET'S GERANIACEÆ, or Natural order of Gerania, with directions for their treatment, complete, 5 vols. roy. 8vo. 500 *finely coloured plates*, (pub. at £19.) *an original copy from the Horticultural Society, hf. calf*, £4. 10s   1820-30
                Priced 1847, Bohn, hf. calf, £10. 10s. and mor. £13. 13s.

4902 TACQUET, Opera Mathematica, a Veterani, st. folio, with the two scarce works at end, *many plates, vellum*, 9s   *Antv.* 1669

4903 TARTAGLIA, General Trattato di Numeri, et Misure, 6 parts in 3 vols. sm. folio, *woodcut portrait and diagrams, vellum, scarce*, £3. 10s   *Vinegia*, 1556-60
    A celebrated work, dedicated "al molto nobile et egregio Signor il Signor Ricardo Ventvorth (Wentworth) Gentil' huomo Inglese." Of this enormous book, I may say that it wants a volume to describe it.—*De Morgan.* Tres curieux par les details des querelles de l'auteur avec Cardan.—*Montucla.*

4904 —— Nova Scientia, Sopra gli tiri delle Artiglierie, etc.—Regola di solevare Navi, in 1 vol. sq. 8vo. *numerous curious woodcuts, not subject to collation, bds.* 10s   *Vinegia*, 1518-62

4905 TEMMINCK ET MEIFFREN LAUGIER DE CHARTROUZE, Nouveau Recueil de Planches Coloriees d'Oiseaux, pour servir de suite et de complément aux planches enluminées de BUFFON, 5 vols. impl. 4to. *complete*, 600 *plates*, BEAUTIFULLY COLOURED, *fine tall copy, hf. calf*, £36. *Paris*, 1838

A SPLENDID WORK, published at £65. The Index to the above is incorrectly made, not mentioning plates 124, 201, 345, 354, 360, 381 and 519; and other plates are mentioned in duplicate.

4906 TEMMINCK, Verhandelingen over de Natuurlijke Geschiedenis der Nederlandsche overzeesche Bezittengen, door de leden der natuurkundige Commissie in INDIE en andere Schrijvers: ZOOLOGIE, BOTANIE, LAND EN VOLKENKUNDE, 3 vols. folio, 165 *beautifully* COLOURED *plates of Mammals, Birds, Fishes, Reptiles, Insects, and Plants, maps, plates of Scenery, Human Figures, Implements, etc. hf. morocco, rare*, £15. *Leiden*, 1839-44

Of this valuable work, only a few copies were printed at the expense of the Dutch Government. The Mammalia were done by Sal. Müller; the Birds by Schlegel; the Insects by Haan; the Botany by Korthals.

4907 TEMMINCK, Manuel d'Ornothologie, seconde edition augmentée, 3 vols. 8vo. *sd*. 10s *Paris*, 1820

4908 TENORE FLORA NAPOLITANA, ossia descrizione della piante del regno di Napoli, 3 vols. roy. fol. of Text, and 3 vols. imp. folio, *comprising* 128 *coloured plates, of which Nos*. 121, 123, 124, 126 *and* 127 *are wanting, bds. uncut, presentation copy from the author to the Horticultural Society, scarce*, £8. *Nap*.1811-38

A magnificent publication, which cost to subscribers 1500 francs. This copy has the quarto Tract entitled "Ad Floræ Neapolitanæ Prodromum Appendix quinta, Neapoli, 1826."

4909 —— Geographie Physique et Botanique de Naples, 8vo. *maps, hf. calf,* 8s 1827
4910 —— Crochi della Flora Napolitana, 4to. 4 *coloured plates*, 1826—Catalogo degli Alberi ed Arbusti, 8vo. 1827—Syncarpia e Donzellia, 4to. 2 *coloured plates*, 1840—Macria, 4to. 1847—Cipressi, 4to. 2 *plates*, 1853—Pianta Conifera, 4to. 2 *plates*, 1853—Platani, 4to. 1856—together 7 tracts, 8vo. and 4to. *presented by the author to the Horticultural Society*, 16s *Napoli*, 1826-56
4911 TERQUEM, Bulletin de Bibliographie, d'Histoire, et Biographie Mathematiques, 3 vols. 8vo. *sd*. 10s *Paris*, 1855-57
4912 TEXEDA, Suma de Arithmetica pratica, sq. 12mo. 64 *leaves, curious woodcut title defective, diagrams, rare*, 30s *Valladolid*, 1546
4913 THUNBERG, Dissertationes Academicae, 3 vols. 12mo. *plates, calf*, 7s 1799-1801
4914 TITFORD'S Sketches towards a Hortus Botanicus Americanus, with Glossary and Index, large 4to. *frontispiece and* 17 *finely coloured plates, rare, containing about* 200 *specimens of Plants, Fruits, Flowers, etc. calf neat*, 28s 1811
4915 TODD'S (R. B.) Cyclopaedia of ANATOMY and PHYSIOLOGY, *complete*, with Supplement, 5 vols. stout roy. 8vo. *several hundred woodcuts*, (pub. at £10. 10s) *calf gilt*. £5. 1836-59
4916 TORREY (J.) Flora of the State of New York, 3 vols. roy. 4to. *the text interleaved*, 161 *plates, an autograph letter of the author prefixed, hf. mor*. £2. 10s *Albany, U. S*. 1843
4917 TORRICELLII Opera Geometrica: de Sphæra, et Solidis Sphæralibus. sq. 8vo. *vellum*, 16s *Florentiæ*, 1644
4918 TRAITE de la Lumiere, etc. 2 vols. in 1, sq. 8vo. *diagrams, calf*, 5s *Leide*, 1690
4919 TREMBLEY, Mémoires pour servir a l'histoire d'un genre de Polypes d'eau douce, 4to. *vignettes and* 13 *plates, old calf*, 12s *Leide*, 1744
4920 TRIMENS Rhopalocera Africae Australis, a Catalogue of South African Butterflies, Part I. *(all yet pubd.)* 8vo. *plate*, 7s 6d *Cape Town*, 1862
4921 TUOMEY'S Report on the Geology of South Carolina, 4to. *frontispiece, maps, and woodcuts, calf*, 25s *Colombia, S.C*. 1848
4922 TURIN ACADEMY: MISCELLANEA Philosophico-Mathematica Societatis privatae Taurinensis, 5 vols, *very scarce*, 1759-73—MÉMOIRES de l'Academie des Sciences, 1784-1800, 6 vols. 1786-1801—MÉMOIRES de l'Academie des Sciences, de Litérature et des Beaux Arts, 1801-1810—SCIENCES PHYSIQUES et Mathematiques, 5 vols.—LITERATURE et Beaux Arts, 5 vols. 1803-13—MÉMOIRES de l'Académie Royale des Sciences, 1813-14, 1 vol. 1816—MEMORIE della Reale Academia delle Scienze, 18 vols. 1818-38—MEMORIE SERIE SECONDA, Tomo I, 1839—together 41 vols. 4to. *numerous plates, those of Natural History* COLORED, *uniform, hf. calf extra*, £25. *Turin*, 1759-1839
4923 —— Memorie della Reale Academia delle Scienze di Torino, Serie Seconda, Tomo IX.-XVI. 8 *very stout vols.impl. 4to. many plates, sd*. £15. *Torino*, 1848-57

NATURAL HISTORY, SCIENCES, MATHEMATICS. 257

4924 TURNER (Dawson) Muscologiæ Hibernicæ Spicilegium sm. 8vo. 16 *coloured plates, crimson morocco extra, gilt edges*, 10s   1804

4225 —— NATURAL HISTORY OF FUCI, or Sea Weeds, being correct Figures and Descriptions of the Plants referred by Botanists to the Genus Fucus, *Latin and English*, 4 vols. roy. 4to. 458 *coloured plates, containing accurate representations of Marine Plants*, £8. 8s   1808-19

4926 —— the same, LARGE PAPER, 4 vols. in 2, folio, *binding broken, russia*, £15.   1808-19

One of 25 copies printed on a folio size (and of these only 12 had the plates coloured); in it are inserted original drawings of *Fucus Membranaceus* by the late Dr. Mohr of Kiel, and of *Fucus Buccinalis*, the true Linnæan plant, and different from what is figured in this work, by Sir W. J. Hooker, together with a portrait of the author from a private lithographic drawing on stone, by Miss H. S. Turner.

4927 TURTON'S Manual of the Land and Freshwater Shells of the British Islands, by Gray, sm. 8vo. 12 *coloured plates*, (pub. 15s) *cloth*, 7s   1840

4928 TWILT, Toet-Steen van d'Algebra Spetiosa, *bound up with other curious works on Geometry and Arithmetic, etc.* in 1 vol. stout sq. 8vo. vel. 7s 6d   Amst. 1669, *etc.*

4929 TYNDALL (J.) Heat considered as a means of Motion, 8vo. *woodcuts*, (pub. at 9s 6d) *cloth, new*, 8s   1863

4930 UIBELAKER, System des Karlsbader Sinters, folio, FINE PAPER, 39 *coloured plates of Mineralogy, bds*. 12s   *Erlangen*, 1786

4931 VAUCHER, Histoire des Conferves d'eau douce, sm. 4to. 17 *plates, bds*. 10s   1803

4932 VERATI, Storia del Magnetismo Animale, 4 vols. 8vo. *sd.* 9s   *Firenze*, 1845-6

4933 VIETAE Opera Mathematica, cum notis, etc. ed. Schooten, sm. folio, *diagrams, calf gilt*, 7s 6d; or *vellum*, 10s   *Lugd. Bat.* 1646
"Belle édition."—BRUNET.

4934 VILLE, Recherches sur la Végétation, large 8vo. *photographs, hf. cf.* 5s   1857

4935 VOET (J. E.) Catalogus systematicus Coleopterorum, 2 vols. 4to. *with 105 plates, containing several hundred figures of Insects*, FINELY COLOURED, *the descriptions in Latin, French, and Dutch, hf. bd. uncut*, £3. 10s   *Hagæ*, 1806

Priced, 1855, Artaria in Mannheim, 36 florins.

See also CRAMER.

4936 VOIGT, Hortus Suburbanus Calcuttensis: a Catalogue of Plants cultivated at the E. I. Co.'s Botanical Garden, Calcutta, by Griffith, roy. 8vo. *cl.* 32s *Cal.* 1845

4937 VOLTA (Conte A.) Elogio da Mocchetti, roy. 8vo. 6s   *Como*, 1833

4938 WALDSTEIN et Kitaibel, Descriptiones et Icones Plantarum Rariorum HUN-GARIÆ, 3 vols. roy. folio, *complete, containing* 280 FINELY COLOURED *plates*, (pub. at £78. 15s) *hf. bound*, £12.   *Viennæ*, 1802

This work is very rare in England and even in Germany; nearly all the copies I have noticed are imperfect. Priced, 1836, £25.; 1855, 120 thalers.

4939 WALLICH, PLANTÆ ASIATICÆ RARIORES, or Descriptions and Figures of a select number of unpublished East Indian Plants, 3 vols. impl. fol. *containing* 300 *most beautifully coloured plates, hf. morocco, full gilt backs, gilt tops, uncut*, £16. 16s   1830-32

Each part, containing 25 plates, was published at 2 guineas; the work was completed in 21 parts. The finest and most beautiful of all the Botanical works published in this or any other country. There were only 250 copies issued for the original Subscribers.

4940 WALLICH, Nipal Plants: Tentamen Florae Napalensis illustratae, folio, pp. 1-64, *plates*, COLOURED, 1-50, *very rare*, £2.   (*Calcutta*), 1826

4941 WALLIS, Opera Mathematica, etiam Opera quædam Miscellanea, 4 vols. in 3, stout folio, *a portrait in each, old calf*, 36   *Oxonii*, 1693-9

The Commercium Epistolicum contains several letters of Fermat, Frenicle. &c. on the theory of numbers, never re-printed, and which are not to be found in *Fermat's Opera Varia*. The second volume contains a collection of Greek works (by Ptolemy, Porphyrius, &c.) on music.

4942 WARREN (J. C.) Description of a Skeleton of the Mastodon Giganteus of North America, roy. 4to. 29 *plates, cloth*, £2.   *Boston*, 1855

4943 WARREN'S (Col. J.) KALA SANKALITA: a Collection of Memoirs on the various modes in which the Nations of Southern India divide time, 4to. *hf. calf, scarce*, 30s   *Madras*, 1825

4944 **WATCHMAKING.** BERTHOUD, Essai sur l'Horlogerie, relativement à l'usage civil, à l'astronomie et a la navigation, et de la Mesure du temps, 2 vols. —Supplement, 1 vol.—together 3 vols. 4to. *plates, shewing the mechanism of Watches and Chronometers, calf, rare*, 36s   *Paris*, 1763-87

4945 —— Horloges Marines, 4to. 27 *plates, exhibiting the mechanism of chronometers, calf*, 15s   1773

4946 DUBOIS, Histoire de l'Horlogerie depuis son origine avec Recherches sur la Mesure de temps dans l'antiquité, 4to. *numerous woodcuts, and several fine plates by* SEBÉ, *some heightened with gold, calf extra*, £2. 10s   *Paris*, 1849
The best and most practical work on Clockmaking.

4947 FLEURIEU, Voyage fait par ordre du Roi 1768-69, pour éprouver en mer les Horloges Marines, inventés par Berthoud, 2 vols. 4to. *charts of the Atlantic and Western Isles. calf gilt*, 15s   *Paris*, 1773

4948 GEISSLER, der Uhrmacher, oder Lehrbegrif der Uhrmacherkunst, 10 vols. in 5, small 4to. *numerous plates, hf. bd.* 12s   *Leipzig*, 1793-99

4949 THIOUT, Traité de l'Horlogerie mechanique et pratique, 2 vols. 4to. 91 *plates illustrating the mechanism of watches, calf,* 12s   *Paris*, 1741

4950 WATERHOUSE'S (C. R.) Natural History of the MAMMALIA, 2 vols. stout large 8vo. 44 *fine steel engravings and numerous woodcuts,* (pub. at £2. 18s) *cloth*, 38s   1846-8

4951 WATSON (P. W.) DENDROLOGIA BRITANNICA, or Trees and Shrubs that will live in the open air of Britain throughout the year, 2 vols. roy. 8vo. 172 *coloured plates,* (pub. at £5. 5s) *bds.* £3.; or *hf. russia, uncut,* RARE, £3. 10s   1825

4952 WEBER de Aure Animalium Aquatilium, 4to. 10 *plates, hf. rus.* 7s 6d *Lips.* 1820

4953 WESTWOOD'S Introduction to the MODERN CLASSIFICATION OF INSECTS; comprising an Account of the Habits and Transformations of the different Families; a Synopsis of all the British, and the more remarkable Foreign Genera, 2 vols. 8vo. *above* 150 *woodcuts, comprising about* 2500 *figures,* (pub. at £2. 5s) *cloth,* 15s 6d; or *hf. calf,* 18s   1839-40

"A careful and judicious digest of rare and extensive learning, of elaborate and deep research. It is impossible to read these interesting pages, and compare the text with the numerous cuts, executed from the author's own drawings, without feeling a profound respect for the invincible industry which has collected so immense a mass of information."—*Entomological Magazine.*

4954 WHEWELL'S History of the Inductive Sciences, 3 vols. 1837—Philosophy of the Inductive Sciences, 3 vols. 1837—Philosophy of the Inductive Sciences, 2 vols. 1840—together 5 vols. 8vo. (pub. at £3. 12s) *uniformly bound in calf extra, by White,* £2. 10s   1837-40

4955 WIGHT (R.) *Surgeon to the Madras Establishment,* ICONES PLANTARUM INDIÆ ORIENTALIS, or Figures of Indian Plants, 6 vols. with the scarce INDEX, roy. 4to. 2101 *plates,* (pub. at £27. 10s) *neat in hf. calf,* £21.   *Madras,* 1838-56

4956 —— Vol. I. 4to. 289 *plates, with the descriptions pasted on them, title in MS. hf. morocco,* 23s   1838

4957 —— Vol. IV. 4to. *with* 452 *plates,* (pub. at £6.) £3. 19s   1848-50

4958 —— Vol. V. 4to. *with* 299 *plates,* (pub. at £4.) £2. 18s   1851

4959 —— Vol. VI. 4to. *with* 181 *plates,* (pub. at £2. 10s) £2. 7s   1853

4960 —— GENERAL INDEX of the Plants described and figured in Dr. Wright's work, entitled "Icones Plantarum Indiae Orientalis," 4to. 66 *pp. wanting to many copies, sd.* £2.   *Madras,* 1856

4961 WIKSTROM (J. E.) Conspectus Litteraturæ Botanicae in Suecia, 8vo. *cloth, an excellent bibliography,* 6s 6d   *Holmiae,* 1831

4962 (WILKIN, G.) le Monde dans la LUNE, provant que la Lune peut estre un Monde, et la Terre une Planette, par Montagne, 12mo. *old hogskin, rare,* 12s *Rouen,* 1655

4963 WILKIN (J.) Mathematical Magick, 12mo. *portrait and cuts, calf, a curious book,* 7s   1680

4964 WILLDENOW Hortus Berolinensis, sive Icones Plantarum rariorum, in horto regio botanico excultarum, large folio, 110 *finely coloured plates,* (pub. at 38 Thalers) 20s   *Berl.* 1816

4965 WILSON AND BONAPARTE, AMERICAN ORNITHOLOGY, or Natural History of the Birds of the United States; with continuation by Prince Charles Lucien Bonaparte, new edition, completed by the insertion of above 100 Birds omitted in the original, with Notes, and the Author's Life, by Sir William Jardine, 3 vols. 8vo. *portrait by Wilson, and* 97 BEAUTIFULLY COLOURED *plates exhibiting* 363 *figures, hf. morocco,* £6. 5s   1832

American Ornithology has uniformly presented a highly interesting subject of investigation to Naturalists, even when the means of gratifying their curiosity were difficult of attainment. Wilson's invaluable work removed the obstacles to this attractive study, and conferred on him an imperishable renown. His ardent and perspicuous mind enabled him to exhibit the truths he discovered, in *warm and captivating* language; while the faithfulness of his delineations shew the accuracy of his pencil.

WORKS ON NATURAL HISTORY. 261

5003 CARDANI OPERA OMNIA, aucta, et emendata curâ Caroli Sponii, 10 vols. folio, *fine clean copy, in old calf, gilt backs, scarce,* £4. 4s *Lugduni,* 1663
Priced, Thorpe, £6. 6s.
5004 CHASLES, Recherches de Géométrie Pure sur les lignes et les surfaces du second degré, 1829 — Propriétés générales des Cônes du 2e degré, 1830— Coniques Sphériques, 1831—3 vols. in 1, 4to. *bds.* 36s *Bruxelles,* 1829-31
5005 ———— Aperçu historique sur l' Origine et le développement des Méthodes en Géométrie, suivi d'un Mémoire de Geometrie, stout 4to. *hf. bd. out of print, and* EXTREMELY RARE, £6. 10s *Bruxelles,* 1837
5005*CASTELLUS de Hyaena Odorifera, 16mo. *old blue morocco, gilt edges,* 5s *Fran.* 1668
5006 CURIEUSE KUNST und WERCK-SCHUL, I: Feuer-Kunst, stout sq. 8vo. 1414 *pp. frontispiece and woodcuts, vellum,* 12s *Nürnberg,* 1705
A curious work, in five books: Metallurgy; Pottery; Earthenware; etc. Glass Manufactures; Precious Stones; Chemical and Medicinal Secrets.
5006*CURTIS' BRITISH ENTOMOLOGY, roy. 8vo. *a set of the illustrations, without text, not quite complete, but containing* 706 *plates, upwards of* 400 *being* BEAUTIFULLY COLOURED, £6. 1823-40
5007 DISCIPLINAE MATHEMATICAE in quibus se exercuit—directore Ciermans, sm. folio, *engraved title, and numerous plates representing Machinery and Scientific operations, etc. vellum, rare,* 21s *Lovanii,* 1639
5008 DONOVAN'S EXOTIC INSECTS. HARRIS' Exposition of English Insects, 15 *plates,* 1782—DONOVAN's Insects of CHINA, 50 *plates,* 1798; of INDIA and the Indian Islands, 58 *plates,* 1800; of NEW HOLLAND, New Zealand, New Guinea, Otaheite, and other Islands in the Indian, Southern and Pacific Oceans, 42 *plates,* 1805--together 4 vols. roy. 4to. *with* 201 FINELY COLOURED *plates, uniformly bound in green morocco extra, (pub. at* £19. 16s) *broad borders of gold, gilt edges,* £10. 1782-1805
5009 ENTOMOLOGIST's Weekly Intelligencer, complete from the beginning in April 1856 to its termination in Sept. 1861, Vols. I-X—The Substitute, (*continuation of the Intelligencer*) Nos. 1-11, 13-20 -- together 280 Nos. 8vo. and sm. 8vo. *out of print and rare,* £2. 10s 1656-62
5010 ENTOMOLOGICAL SOCIETY'S TRANSACTIONS and Proceedings, First Series, 5 vols. 1836-49—NEW SERIES, Vols. I; II; III, pts. 1-7; IV, pts, 1-7; V, pts. 1, 2, 1850-59—together 10 vols. 8vo. *numerous beautifully coloured plates, seven vols. very neat in hf. calf gilt, and* 16 *parts,* £10. 1833-59
5011 ENTOMOLOGICAL MAGAZINE, from the beginning in 1832 to 1838, 5 vols. 8vo. *plates, some coloured, cloth, uncut,* £3. 10s 1832-8
This periodical numbered among its contributors the most eminent Entomologists of the day, including Curtis, Westwood, Newman, Walker, Halliday, and others.
5012 EUCLIDIS Elementorum libri xv, *Graece,* 12mo. *second edition, calf, very rare,* 18s *Romae,* 1545
Priced, Thorpe, £2. 12s 6d; the above copy is bound up with several rare early works, Psellus, Ptolemy, etc. upon Geometry and Arithmetic.
5013 FINEI (Orontii) de Solaribus Horologiis et Quadrantibus libri quatuor, sm. 4to. *numerous woodcuts and diagrams, fine copy in vellum neat, rare,* 15s *Paris.* 1560
5014 GALILEI (GALILEO) OPERE, PRIMA EDIZIONE COMPLETA, condotta sugli autentici manoscritti palatini (per cura di Eugenio Alberi), col SUPPLEMENTO, 17 vols. large 8vo. *including Galileo's correspondence, about* 1600 *letters, portrait and numerous plates, sd. uncut,* £5. *Firenze,* 1842-56
5015 GEER (Charles de) Memoires pour servir à l' HISTOIRE DES INSECTES, 7 vols. in 8, stout 4to. *portrait and* 238 *fine plates containing several thousand figures, a very fine copy in old French marbled calf extra, gilt edges, very rare,* £12. 12s *Stockholm,* 1752-78
Priced, 1824, Wood, £18. 18s; 1830, £21.; Hibbert's copy fetched £15. 15s
"Cet ouvrage, un des meilleurs que nous ayons sur cette partie de l'histoire naturelle, est fort recherché et difficile à trouver. Le premier volume surtout est fort rare parceque l'auteur, mécontent de son peu de succès, détruisit, dit-on, une partie de l'édition."—BRUNET.
5016 GOULD'S BIRDS OF ASIA, Parts 1—14, imp. folio, *with* 231 *large and beautifully coloured plates, (pub. at* £44. 2s) *bds.* £33. 1850-62
A magnificent work, containing the finest specimens of Mr. Gould's artistic power and scientific knowledge.
5916*HISTOIRE UNIVERSELLE de tous les OYSEAUX de l' Univers, 3 vols. in 1, stout roy. folio, *neat old MS. in a Flemish hand,* 747 *pp. bound in old blue morocco, gilt edges,* £2. 2s *ca.* 1690
Containing a curious chapter "Du vray Dieu ayant des Ailes."
5017 HORSFIELD's Catalogue of the Birds in the Museum of the East India Company, 2 vols. 8vo. *cloth,* 15s 1854-58

5018 HUEBNER'S Sammlung EUROPÄISCHER SCHMETTERLINGE, nebst Fortsetzung von Geyer, 9 vols. in 4, 1805-41—GESCHICHTE Europäischer Schmetterlinge, nebst Fortsetzung, 9 vols. in 4 divisions, 1805-41—together 18 vols. 4to. *containing* 701 *and* 432 *beautifully coloured plates, divided as below; with* 1 *vol. containing portion of the text to both works* (*pp.* 1-194 *and* 1-32) £18. *Augsb.* 1806-41

DIVISION OF PLATES.

	Sammlung.	Geschichte.
Papiliones	1—181	1— 56
Sphinges	1— 35	1— 29
Bombyces	1— 70	1— 73
Noctuae	1—157	1—136
Geometrae	1—105	1— 82
Pyralides	1— 30	1— 11
Tortices	1— 47	1— 16
Tineae	1— 69	1— 24
Alucitae	1— 7	1— 4

88 plates in the Sammlung, and 16 plates in the Geschichte, are wanting to make the set of plates complete. The two works were published at 350 and 200 Thalers. The former priced, 1856, £23. 10s; the latter, £13. 10s; the latter priced by Falks, in Leipzig, 90 Thalers.

5018*HUTTON'S Philosophical and Mathematical DICTIONARY, 2 vols. 4to. *best edition, plates and diagrams,* (pub. at £6. 6s) *hf. calf,* 25s 1815
Priced, 1847, £2. 12s 6d.

5019 KNOX, Game Birds and Wild Fowl, their friends and foes, sm. 8vo. *frontispiece, cloth,* 7s 1850

5019*LIBRI, Histoire des Sciences Mathématiques depuis la Renaissance, Vols. I.-IV, 8vo. *all published, diagrams, sd.* 30s *Paris,* 1838-41

5020 LINNAEA ENTOMOLOGICA, Zeitschrift herausgegeben von dem Entomologischen Vereine in Stettin, Vols. I-XI, 8vo. 40 *plates,* (pub. at 22 *Thalers, sd.*) *eight vols. hf. calf gilt, three sd.* £3. 10s *Berlin,* 1846-57

5021 LINNEAN SOCIETY'S Proceedings from the commencement in November 1838 to May 1862: Proceedings, 1838-55, 2 vols.—Journal of the Proceedings, 6 Nos. 1-23, or Vols. I.-VI, with the 6 Supplements—together 8 vols. 8vo. (*pub. at about* £5.) in Nos. £2. 16s 1838-62

5022 MACLEAY'S Horæ Entomologicæ, or Essays on the Annulose Animals, Vol. I, parts 1, 2 (*all pub.*), in 1 vol. 8vo. 3 *plates, half calf neat, rare,* £2. 16s 1819-21

5023 MAGASIN DE ZOOLOGIE, publié par Guérin-Méneville, from the beginning in 1831 to 1849, the INSECTS only: First Series, 278 plates (wanting No. 22), 1831-38; Second Series, 152 plates (wanting Livraison 39, text and 3 plates), 1839-49—together 19 vols. sm. 8vo. *with* 330 *finely coloured plates* (*pub. at about* 270 *fr.*), *unbd.* £2. 10s *Paris,* 1831-49

5024 MARSHAM, Entomologia Britannica, Vol. I: Coleoptera, 8vo. *all pub. half calf neat,* 12s 1802

5024*MEYER'S ILLUSTRATIONS OF BRITISH BIRDS and their Eggs, SECOND EDITION, 7 vols. large 8vo. *with* 322 FINELY COLOURED *plates* (pub. at £18. 10s), *hf. green morocco, gilt edges,* £7. 7s 1842-50
A *second* issue of this second edition appeared in 1857, with inferior coloring in the plates.

5025 MORRIS (Rev. F. O.) History of BRITISH BIRDS, with an illustration of each species, 6 vols. roy. 8vo. 358 *finely cold. plates* (pub. at £5. 2s), £3. 10s 1851-57
A copy fetched at Foster's, 1858, £6.

5026 MULSANT, Opuscules Entomologiques, 4 parts or vols. roy. 8vo. *plates, sd.* 20s *Paris,* 1852-53

5027 OLIVIER, ENTOMOLOGIE, OU HISTOIRE NATURELLE DES INSECTES, avec leurs caractères generiques et spécifiques, leur description, leur Synonymie, etc.: COLÉOPTERES, 6 vols. stout 4to. 363 *plates,* FINELY COLOURED, *hf. bd.* £15.; or *a fine tall copy,* 6 *vols. roy.* 4to. *bds. uncut, with the plates bound separately in* 4 *vols. green* MOROCCO *extra, gilt edges,* £15. *Paris,* 1789-1800
The best and most complete work upon Beetles which has yet appeared.

5028 PANZER's Kritische Revision der Insekten-Faune Deutschlands, 2 vols. 12mo. 2 *coloured plates, bds.* 5s. *Nürnb.* 1805-6

5029 —— Index Entomologicus, Pars 1 (*all pub.*): Eleutherata, 12mo. 3s 6d 1813

5030 PISONIS Historia Naturalis Brasiliae, in quâ non tantùm Plantae et Animalia sed et indigenarum morbi, ingenia, et mores describuntur, folio, *upwards of* 500 *woodcuts, calf,* 20s *Amst.* 1648

5031 QUEBEC LITERARY and HISTORICAL SOCIETY's Transactions, Vol. I, 8vo. *plates of Natural History, bds. rare,* 15s *Quebec,* 1829

WORKS ON NATURAL HISTORY. 263

5032 RAII (Johannis) Historia Plantarum Generalis, species hactenus editas aliasque inventas complectens, cum Lexico Botanico, etc. 3 vols. folio, *portrait, old calf gilt*, 25s 1693

5033 RALF'S British Desmidieae, roy. 8vo. 35 *coloured plates, cloth*, £2. 2s 1848

5034 RATZEBURG, die FORST-INSEKTEN, oder Abbildung und Beschreibung der in den Wäldern Preussens und der Nachbarstaaten als schädlich oder nützlich bekannt gewordenen Insecten, 3 vols. 53 *plates, many coloured, and woodcuts*, 1829-44—DIE ICHNEUMONEN der Forst-Insecten, ein Anhang zur Abbild. der Forst-Insecten, 3 vols. 7 *plates, and several woodcuts*, 1844-52—together 6 vols. 4to. *three in russia extra, gilt edges, and three in bds*. £7. 7s Berlin, 1729-52

5035 REGIOMONTANI (Joannis) Epytoma in Almagestum Ptolomei, sm. folio, *numerous diagrams, fine large copy, hf. bd*. RARE, 20s
(*Venetia*), *Johannes Hamman de Landoia, dictus Hertzog*, 1496

A work of uncommon scarcity, the sole edition printed in the XVth Century; I cannot trace the sale of one copy during the last forty years. Hain gives an exact collation, but Brunet and Panzer were ignorant of it.

5036 REISCH MARGARITA PHILOSOPHICA nova, sq. 8vo. *a profusion of curious and large woodcuts, largely relating to Music, a tall copy in the original stamped binding, almost uncut, with numerous rough leaves*, 15s Argent. 1512

"Ouvrage singulier et fort bien exécute, avec des figures en bois remarquables."—*Brunet.* "This work has exercised a great influence upon the spreading of mathematical and physical knowledge, and Chasles has proved the importance of Reisch's Encyclopædia for the History of Mathematical Sciences."—*A. Von Humboldt.* A work in twelve books, comprising a distinct treatise on all the seven liberal sciences."—*Burney.*

5037 ROESEL'S INSECTEN-BELUSTIGUNG, monatlich-herausgegeben, mit der BEYTRÄGE VON KLEEMAN, in 5 vols. stout sm. 4to. *frontispieces and* 376 *plates of Butterflies, Caterpillars, etc.* BEAUTIFULLY COLOURED, *calf neat*, £2. 16s
Nürnberg, 1746-61

Priced, 1840, Wood, £15. 15s ; in 1860, I sold a copy for £5. 5s.
COLLATION: Vol. I. Pages 64, 60, 64, 312, 48 and 48; Plates, coloured, 10, 10, 8, 63, 13 and 17.—Vol. II. Pages 24, 72, 38, 16, 32, 76, 200, 64 and 52; Plates 2, 9, 3, 6, 4, 17, 30, 13 and 10—Vol. III. Pages 624 ; Plates 101.—Vol. IV. Pages 48 (Life of Roesel, with portrait and 264 ; Plates 40; Supplement by Kleeman, 376 pp. and 44 plates.

5038 ROSCOE'S (W.) MONANDRIAN PLANTS of the Order of Scitamineæ, atlas folio, containing 112 *very large and finely* COLOURED PLATES, *green morocco, super extra, gilt edges*, £5. 5s Liverpool, 1828

5039 RUMPHII HERBARIUM AMBOINENSE, complectens Arbores, Frutices, Herbas, Plantas terrestres et aquaticas, quæ in Amboina et adjacentibus Insulis reperiuntur; item varia Insectorum Animaliumque genera, *Belgice et Latine*, ed. Burmann, 6 vols. roy. folio, LARGE PAPER, 666 *fine engravings, fine copy in old calf gilt*, £4. Amst. 1741
"Vendu, Gr. Pap. Patu de Mello, m. r. 200 fr."—BRUNET.

5040 SEPP'S (J. G.) DUTCH INSECTS: Beschouwing der Wonderen Gods in de minstgeachte Schepzelen, of NEDERLANDSCHE INSECTEN, Vols. I-VI, and VII pp. 1-84, 4to. 319 BEAUTIFULLY COLOURED PLATES (*pub. at* 200 *Thalers*) *three vols. hf. bd. uncut, two vols. bds. the rest unbound*, £7. 10s Amsterdam, 1762-1854

"Entomology, in the following year, was enriched with the most inimitable delineations of insects which this or any age has produced ; and which form the plates to that beautiful work by Sepp, (in Dutch) on the insects of the Low Countries. This publication came out in numbers, and perfect sets are now exceedingly rare: those portions we possess, relate exclusively to the Lepidoptera, every species being delineated, in all its several transformations, from the egg to the perfect insect : the drawing of the subjects is chaste, elegant, and cannot be excelled for accuracy ; while the style of engraving is admirably suited to express all the softness of the original drawings. These plates, in fact, have never been equalled, far less excelled, by any in modern times."—SWAINSON.
Vols. I-IV, priced, 1835, £22. 12s ; Vols. I-V, priced, 1843, £15. 15s ; Vols. I-V, and part of VI, priced, 1847, £12. 12s; Vols. I-IV, priced, 1855, Artaria in Mannheim, 120 fl.; a set similar to the above, priced, 1855, Friedlaender in Berlin, 68 Thalers.

5041 SOLIER, Essai sur les Collaptérides de la tribu des Blapsites, roy. 8vo. 15 *plates*, 7s 6d Turin, 1848

5042 SOCIÉTÉ ENTOMOLOGIQUE DE LA FRANCE, Annales, a complete set from the beginning to 1862, PREMIÈRE SERIE, 11 vols. 1832-42—DEUXIÈME SÉRIE, 10 vols. 1843-52—TROISIÈME SÉRIE, 8 vols. 1853-60—QUATRIÈME SÉRIE, Vols. I and II, pt. 1, 1861-62—together 31 vols. 8vo. 463 *plates, many of them finely coloured, (pub. at* 730 *fr.*) *twenty-one vols. in cloth bds. one vol. hf. calf, the remainder in one vol. and* 29 *parts, sd.* VERY RARE, £24. Paris, 1832-62

5043 SPRY and SHUCKARD British Coleoptera delineated, figures of all the genera of British Beetles, 8vo. 8 *plates* (*pub. at* 42s) *cloth*, 18s 1861

5044 STAINTON, ZELLER, and DOUGLAS, Natural History of TINEINA, in English, French, German, and Latin, 7 vols. 8vo. *numerous finely coloured plates (pub. at £4. 7s 6d) cloth*, £3. 10s 1855-62
   The first series is to be completed in 10 volumes.
5045 STURM (Jacob) Deutschland's Fauna in Abbildungen nach der Natur mit Beschreibungen, fortgesetzt von J. H. C. F. Sturm, V_e. Abtheilung, DIE INSEKTEN: KÄFER, Vols. I-XXIII, 12mo. 424 *finely coloured plates (pub. at* 65 Thalers) nine vols. *in bds. the rest unbd*. £5. 10s *Nürnberg*, 1805-57
   Vols. I-XXII, priced, 1856, Friedländer, in Berlin, 40 Thalers; a set similar to the above priced, 1860, Schmidt in Halle, 40 Thalers; Kœhler in Leipzig, 40 Thalers.
5046 STURM's Verzeichniss meiner Insecten-Sammlung, part 1 (*all published*) 8vo. 4 *coloured plates, bds*. 3s 6d *Nürnberg*, 1800
5047 ——— Catalog der KAEFER-Sammlung, 8vo. 6 *finely coloured plates, bds*. 7s 6d *Nürnberg*, 1843
5048 VENEZIA E LE SUE LAGUNE, 3 vols. stout impl. 8vo. *maps and many views of the principal buildings, bds.* £2. 16s *Venezia*, 1847
   This grand historical, statistical, and SCIENTIFIC work on Venice was privately printed by the Town Council of Venice, and given to the Members of the Scientific Society, on holding their ninth meeting in their town.
   The work contains the civil and political History of the Republic, the history of all the artists Venice produced, and an extensive description of their works, also the physical, and natural history of the Venetian territories.
5049 VITALIS (J. B.) Cours élémentaire de Teinture sur Laine, Soie, Lin, Chanvre et Coton, et sur l'Art d'imprimer les Toiles, 8vo. *hf. bd. neat*, 7s *Rouen*, 1827
5050 WALKER'S Insecta Saundersiana, or characters of undescribed Insects in the collection of W. W. Saunders: Diptera, 4 parts; Homoptera, 1; together 5 parts, 8vo. *plates*, 20s 1850-58
5051 WOOD'S Index Entomologicus. WESTWOOD'S New Supplement, an illustrated Catalogue of the Lepidopterous Insects of Great Britain, roy. 8vo. 5 *coloured plates*, (*pub. at* 12s 6d) *bds*. 10s 1854
5052 ZOOLOGICAL JOURNAL, by Bell, Children, Sowerby, Horsfield, Kirby, Yarrell, Vigors, &c. in 5 vols. 8vo. (*cost* £11. 5s *in parts*) 97 *coloured plates, calf neat*, £5. 1825-35
5053 ENTOMOLOGICAL TRACTS, a collection of about 70 Opuscula and Minor Works upon Entomology, *with numerous coloured plates, including many valuable MSS. memoranda of Mr. Curtis, the lot a bargain*, £3. 1820, etc.
5054 ——— Treatises on COLEOPTERA, etc. A volume, stout 4to. containing Dalman, Analecta Entomologica, 4 *plates*, Erlang. 1793; Kirby on Herbst, *coloured plates;* Kirby on Insects, 5 *coloured plates;* Leach on Meloe, 2 *coloured plates;* Francillon's Rare Scarabaeus, *coloured plate*, etc. *bds*. 36s 1793-1823

GEOGRAPHY, VOYAGES, TRAVELS.

5055 ACERBI's Travels through Sweden, Finland, and Lapland, 1798-99, 2 vols. 4to *port. and* 70 *plates, those of Natural History coloured*, (pub. at £5. 5s *in bds.*) *calf*, 9s 1802
5056 ALDRETE (B.) Varias Antiguedades de España, Africa y otras Provincias, sm. 4to. *frontispiece, fine tall copy, Dutch vellum*, 25s *Amberes*, 1614
   A very learned and curious work, full of important and profound researches.
5057 Alpine Club, Passes, and Glaciers—a Series of Excursions, 8vo. *coloured plates*, etc. *cloth*, 10s 1859
5058 ALVAREZ, Historiale Description de l'Ethiopie, 16mo. *first edition of the French translation, good copy in old calf, scarce*, 27s *Anvers, Plantin*, 1558
   The work by Alvarez, who was secretary to the embassy, deserves particular notice, as the first detailed narrative of travels in that country, and as he visited the southern provinces of Amhara, Shoa, and Angot, which have not been since reached until very recently.
5059 AMBOYNA. True Relation of the cruel and barbarous proceedings against the English by the Netherlandish Governor, 1632—Remonstrance of the Directors—Acts of the Processe against the English—Catalogue of Damages, 1664—Stubbs' Justification of the present War, 1673—and other pieces in 2 vols. sm. 8vo. *curious plates*, 25s 1632-73
5060 AMICO ET STATELLA, Lexicon Topographicum Siculum, 2 vols. in 4, sm. 4to. *plates, vellum*, 15s *Panormi (et Catan.)* 1757-59
5061 APIANO (Pedro) Cosmographia, añadida por Gemma Frisio, con l'Anillo Astronomico, y descripcion de las Indias, sm. 4to. *woodcuts, including several curious diagrams, with moveable pieces, bd*. 28s *Anvers*, 1575

GEOGRAPHY, VOYAGES, TRAVELS.

5062 ARUNDELL's Discoveries in Asia Minor, 2 vols. 8vo. *map and several plates, bds*, 10s 1834

5063 AZUNI, Dissertation sur l'origine de la Boussole, 8vo. *hf. calf neat*, 7s 6d 1809

5064 AVRIL (*Soc. Jes.*) Voyage en divers etats d'Europe et d'Asie, 12mo. *plates, vellum,* 6s *Paris,* 1692-3

5065 BARROS (Joao de) da ASIA; dos feitos, que os Portugueses fizeram no descubrimento e conquista dos mares e terras do Oriente, 9 tom.—DIEGO DE COUTO, da Asia, 15 tom.—together 24 vols. 12mo. *maps and portrait, old calf,* £3.; *or a fine copy in calf gilt from Dr. Hawtrey's library,* £8. 8s *Lisboa,* 1778-88
<small>The best account of the Early Discoveries of the Portuguese in Asia.
Priced, 1824, Rivington and Cochraue, £8. 8s; 1840, Payne and Foss, mor. £12. 12s. Fetched, Langlès, 133 fr. Collation, Decades I.—IV. by Barros, 8 vols.; Life of Barros, and Index, 1 vol. Another Fourth Decade, and Decades, V.—XII. by Couto, 15 vols. including Index to Couto.</small>

5066 BARROW, Travels in the Interior of Southern Africa, 1797-98, 2 vols. 4to. *plates, fine copy, russia,* 12s 1801-4

5067 —— Travels in CHINA, 4to. *coloured plates, russia neat*, 7s 6d 1804

5068 —— Voyage to Cochin China, 1792-93, with account of a Journey to Southern Africa, 4to. *numerous coloured plates, calf gilt,* 7s 6d 1806

5069 BARTH (H.) Travels and Discoveries in North and Central Africa, 1849-55, 5 vols. 8vo. *maps, woodcuts, and plates,* (pub. at £5. 5s) *bds.* 36s 1857-58

5070 —— Reisen in Nord- und Central- Afrika, 1849-55, 5 vols. 8vo. *maps and plates, cloth,* £2. 5s *Gotha,* 1857-58
<small>Vol. V. contains a Temàshight Vocabulary.</small>

5071 BARTHEMA. LUDOVICI PATRITII Romani Novum Itinerarivm Æthiopiæ, Ægipti, utriusque Arabiae, Persidis, Siriæ ac Indiæ intra et extra Gangem, interprete Archangelo Madrignano, sm. folio, *first Latin edition,* FINE COPY, *old red mor. gilt edges,* RARE, £6. 15s (*Milani*) *auspitiis Bernardini Carvaial* (1511)
<small>The first Latin edition, as described by bibliographers, is "de la dernière rareté." Hibbert purchased this copy June 22, 1818, at Sotheby's, for £11. 18s. Another copy sold in the White Knight's sale for £18. 7s 6d. "Livre peu commun et fort recherché."—BRUNET.</small>

5072 BARTHEMA. Die Ritterlich und lobwürdig Reisz des gestrengen und über all ander weyt erfarnen Ritters und Landtfarers Herren Ludowico Vartoman von Bolonia, sagend von Egypto, Syria, Arabia, Persia, India und Ethiopia, &c. sm. 4to. *with 49 curious woodcuts,* black letter, *fine copy,* VERY SCARCE, £3. 3s *Straszburg, Johann. Knobloch,* 1516
<small>Panzer and Brunet mentions an edition printed at Augsburg in 1515, and Panzer another by Knobloch at Strasburg, in 1815, but not this of 1516. The popularity of the work must have been great to call forth three editions within a few months. The Author's adventures were extraordinary, and his Tales respecting Amours, Wedding Customs, and similar subjects, are told with humour, sometimes bordering on indecency. See especially Book II, Chapt. 7; Book III, Chapt. 19, 25, 51, 74; Book IV, Chapt. 3, &c. &c.
"Ce voyage est singulierement recherché à cause de son ancienneté, on y trouve les monumens moins dégradés par le temps, et la barbarie des Mussulmans. Les peuples qui se sont beaucoup plus melangés encore depuis, y ont une physionomie differente de celle qu'ils ont de nos jours. La naïveté du style donne un certain charme à la narration, et garantit la véracité du voyageur."—BOUCHER DE LA RICHARDERIE.</small>

5073 BARTHEMA, Uitnemende en Zeerwonderlijke Zee-en-Land Reise, sq. 8vo. *engraved title, containing portrait of the author and 4 plates, vellum,* 12s *Utrecht,* 1654

5074 —— the same, another edition, *portrait and 4 plates, vellum,* 12s *ib.* 1655
<small>This last edition differs slightly from that of 1654. There is no dedication to the edition of 1655, and the paging runs from p. 1 to 136, while in that of 1654 the paging commmences in each part.</small>

5075 BEHAIM. GHILLANY's Geschichte des Seefahrers Martin Behaim; mit Abhandlung über die ältesten Karten des Neuen Continents, von Humboldt, atlas 4to. *with portrait, plates of Behaim's Globes, and of the 3 oldest maps of* AMERICA, *bds.* 25s *Nürnberg,* 1853

5076 BERBRUGGER, ALGERIE historique, pittoresque et monumentale. Recueil de vues, monuments, combats, cérémonies, costumes et portraits dessinés dans les provinces d'Alger, Oran, Bone et Constantine, avec texte historique et descriptif des localités, mœurs, usages, jeux et divertissements de ses habitants, 5 parts in 3 vols. atlas folio, *beautifully illuminated title,* 149 *fine plates in tints, comprising Views, Antiquities, Costume, Battle Pieces, etc. the Botany in colours, and* 21 *vignettes, hf. morocco,* £7. 7s 1843
<small>A fine and very sumptuous work; a Supplement treats on the Coins of Algiers, with engravings of them. Published at 20 guineas. Fetched, 1853, Pickering's, £11. 11s, 1854, vellum paper, Sotheby's £8. Part I. Province of ALGIERS, contains 2 maps, 10 vignettes, and 54 large tinted plates. Part II. Province of ORAN, 2 vignettes and 33 plates.—Part III. Province of BONE, 1 vignette and 19 plates.—Par. IV. Province of CONSTANTINE, 7 vignettes and 16 plates. –Part V. Races, Money and Flora of Algeria, 17 plates, the 10 plates of Flora beautifully coloured.</small>

5076*BERGERON, Voyages faits principalement en Asie dans les XII.—XV. Siècle, par B. de Tudele, Marc Paul, Mandeville, etc. par Bergeron, 2 vols. 4to. *maps, bds. 7s 6d;* or *calf,* 10s *La Haye,* 1735
Priced, 1848, Payne and Foss, £2. 2s.

5077 BERNIER, Voyages, contenant la description des Etats du Grand Mogol, de l'Hindoustan, de Kachemire, 2 vols. 12mo. *maps and plates, old red morocco, gilt edges,* 27s *Amst.* 1699
" Edition recherchée de cette excellente relation."—BRUNET.

5078 BERLINGERI (Francesco) Septe Giornate della Geographia (in terza Rima) large folio, *with all the* 31 MAPS *engraved on copper, excessively rare, some leaves damaged, etc. sold not subject to collation, a tall copy in bds.* £4.
Firenze, Nicolo Todesco, (circa 1480)
Priced, 1837 and 1840, by Payne and Foss, with the title and register, mor. £16. 16s; in 1848, by the same, £21.; sold by auction, 1847, at Paris, 461 fr.
Francisco Berlinghieri, a Florentine, contributed greatly to the study of Italian Poetry by this popular work on Geography. It must have been published about the year 1480, as the Duke of Urbino, to whom it is dedicated, died in 1482. Perfect copies are of rare occurrence.

5079 BERTII Breviarium totius Orbis Terrarum, 18mo. *vellum,* 5s *Franc. de Bry.* 1627

5080 BERYTE (de Bisschop) Reis uit Frankryk naar China, 1683—Derde Zee-getogt (Willems van West-Zanen) na de Oost-Indien, 1648—Kort Verhael van Macassar, 1666-69—3 vols. in 1, 8vo. *many plates, vellum, rare,* 36s *Amst.* 1648-83

5081 BISCHOFF und MOELLER, Vergleichendes Wörterbuch der alten, mittleren, und neuen Geographie, 8vo. *a valuable book, hf. calf,* 8s *Gotha,* 1829

5082 BLUME (C. L.) de Indische Bij, Deel I. 8vo. iv. and 664 pp. *bds.* 5s *Leyden,* 1843

5083 BOSWELL's Account of Corsica, 8vo. *folding map, old calf gilt,* 5s *Glasgow,* 1768

5084 BOUCHER DE LA RICHARDERIE, Bibliothèque universelle des Voyages, avec des Extraits, 6 vols. 8vo. *hf. bd.* 12s *Paris,* 1808
Priced, 1824, Rivingtons, £2. 2s; 1846, Payne and Foss, £3. 3s.

5085 BREVE Relatione de' Veaggi di tre Vescovi Francesi in Cina, Cocincina, e Tonchino, 12mo. *vellum,* 7s 6d *Roma,* 1669

5086 BRONIOVII Tartariæ descriptio, item Transylvaniæ ac Moldaviæ, etc. descriptio à Reichersdorff, item Wernherus de admirandis Hungariæ aquis, sm. folio, CURIOUS MAPS, *calf neat, good copy,* £2. *Colon. Agr.* 1595

5087 BROSSES (Chas. de) Terra Australis Cognita: or Voyages to the Southern Hemisphere, in the XVII-XVIII centuries, by Callander, 3 vols. 8vo. *map, calf,* 18s *Edinburgh,* 1766

5088 BRUCE'S Travels to discover the Source of the Nile, 5 vols. large 4to. *first and best edition, fine impressions of the plates, calf, good copy,* 25s; or, *a fine tall copy,* roy. 4to. *in old russia,* 30s 1790
Priced, 1829, morocco, £7. 7s.

5089 BURCHELL'S (W. J.) Travels in the Interior of Southern Africa, 2 vols. 4to. *finely coloured plates, map separate,* (pub. at £9. 9s) *calf gilt,* £3. 10s 1822-24
An original copy; the colouring of the plates is much superior to those subsequently issued.

5090 BURCKHARDT'S (J. L.) TRAVELS: Travels in Syria and the Holy Land, 1822—Travels in Nubia, 1819—Travels in Arabia, *very scare,* 1829—Notes on the Bedouins and Wahabys, 1830—Arabic Proverbs, or Manners and Customs of the Modern Egyptians, 1830, *rare*—5 vols. 4to. *maps and plates, tall copies, uniform in calf extra, gilt edges,* A MAGNIFICENT COPY, £15. 1819-22-29-30
Collation of the Arabia: xvi. and 478 pp.; 5 maps, viz., Map of Hedjaz, Plan of Mekka, Plan of Arafat, Plan of Wady Muda, Plan of Medina.

5091 —— Travels in Syria and the Holy Land, 4to. *portrait and maps, hf. calf,* 30s; or *bds.* £2. 2s 1822

5092 —— Notes on the Bedouins and Wahabys, collected during his Travels in the East, 4to. *hf. calf gilt,* £2. 2s; or *bds.* £2. 10s 1830
"What can I say of the late Sheik Burckhardt, who was so well acquainted with the language and manners of these people, that none of them suspected him to be an European! His account of the tribes in these countries is so minutely correct, that little or nothing remains for observation in modern Egypt and Nubia."—*Belzoni.*
"Few travellers have done more for geography than this author: antiquities, manners, customs, &c. were examined and investigated by him with a success which could only have been insured by such zeal, perseverance, and judgment, as he evidently possessed."—*Stevenson.*

5093 BURNES's Travels into Bokhara, being the account of a Journey from India to Cabool, Tartary, and Persia, 3 vols. 18mo. *map and plates, calf gilt,* 9s 1835

5094 BURNEY'S (Capt. Jas.) Chronological History of the Discoveries in the South Sea, or Pacific Ocean; with a History of the Buccaneers of America, 5 vols. imp. 4to. *maps and charts, calf gilt,* £2. 1803-17

"A masterly digest of the voyages in the South Sea, displaying rare union of nautical science and literary research."—*Quarterly Review.*

Contents: Vol. 1. Earliest discoveries by Europeans to Sir F. Drake's Voyage in 1579. Vol. 2. from 1579 to 1620. Vol. 3. from 1620 to 1688. Vol. 4. from 1688 to 1723, including history of the Buccaneers. Vol. 5. to 1764—General Index.

5096 CAILLIAUD (F.) Voyage à Méroé, au Fleuve Blanc, au-delà de Fâzoql dans le Midi de Sennâr, à Syouah et dans cinq autres Oasis, 4 vols. 8vo. *and atlases of plates bound in 1 vol.* impl. folio, (pub. at £10. 10s) *calf gilt,* or *hf. morocco, uncut,* £3. *Paris*, 1823-27

"The name of Caillaud has for the last ten years stood high among the explainers of Egyptian antiquities, and the zealous devotees of African Discovery. The work now before us presents us with the results of his second visit to Egypt, and of his journeys to the Oasis and adjacent countries during that period, although more than five years have elapsed between his return to France and the entire completion of the present work, (a circumstance that need not excite surprise, considering that the graphic portion contains no less than 150 engravings). The public has reason to be satisfied that the task of editing his researches and discoveries has in this instance fallen into the author's own hands."—*Foreign Quarterly Review.*

5097 CAMPOMANES, Antigüedad maritima de Cartago, con el Periplo de Hannon, sq. 8vo. *a learned work on the ancient Geography of Africa, sd.* 7s *Madrid*, 1756

5098 CAMUS, Mémoire sur les Grands et Petits Voyages, et les Voyages de Thevenot, 4to. *the best bibliography for De Bry and Thevenot, bds.* 20s *Paris*, 1802

5099 CASTANHEDA (Fernão Lopez de) Livro Primeiro da Historia do Descobrimento e Conquista da India pelos Portuguesos, 𝔟𝔩𝔞𝔠𝔨 𝔩𝔢𝔱𝔱𝔢𝔯, *wanting title*, 1554 —Livro segundo, 1552—Livro terceiro, *imperfect at end*, 1552; 3 vols. in 1, fol. *woodcuts, vellum, very rare,* 36s *Coimbra*, 1554-52

Lord Rothesay's copy; Heber's copy in 6 vols. fetched £19.; Books 1 and 2 fetched at Nichols' sale £2. 9s.

5100 CAUCASUS, Mémoires sur les pays entre la Mer Noire et la Mer Caspienne, 3 parts, *large map and Barbié's map* (1793) *added*, 1797—D'Anville, Mer Caspienne, *map*, 1777—in 1 vol. 4to. *hf. bd. rare,* 14s *Paris*, 1777-97

5101 —— Mémoires sur les pays entre la Mer Noire et Caspienne, 4to. *map, calf,* 8s 1797

Comprises the Vocabulary of the Caucasian Dialects, viz. *Abkhas, Altikesek, Cudan, Cabardien, Ossetien, Dugorian, Kisti, Ingoushi,* and *Georgian.*

5102 CHARDIN (Jean) Voyages en Perse et autres lieux de l'Orient, nouvelle édition augmentée du Couronnement de Soliman III, et de passages qui ne se trouvent point dans les éditions précédentes, 4 vols. 4to. BEST EDITION, *portrait and plates, fine copy in calf, gilt edges,* 30s *Amst.* 1735

Marked by James Bohn £4. 4s. Fetched, 1855, Sotheby's *morocco,* £4. 8s.

5103 CLARKE (E. D.) Travels in various Countries of Europe, Asia, and Africa, 6 vols. roy. 4to. LARGE PAPER, *maps, portraits, and beautiful plates, fine impressions,* (pub. at £30. 5s *in bds.*) *fine copy in russia, gilt edges,* Hanrott's copy, £4. 4s 1810-23

The Dean of Peterboro's copy fetched, 1853, £7. Priced, 1840, Jas. Bohn, *russia,* £14.; 1843, John Bohn, *calf,* £12.; 1848, Payne and Foss, *russia,* £14. 14s.

5104 —— Travels in various countries of Europe, Asia, and Africa, 11 vols. 1816-24 —Life, 2 vols. 1825—together 13 vols. 8vo. *portraits and maps, calf,* 36s 1816-25

"The most instructive and engaging travels ever published in this country."—*Lowndes.*

"The splendour and celebrity of all travels performed by Englishmen have been exceeded by that of the late and deeply lamented Dr. Edward Clarke. Upon the whole, if Humboldt be the first, Clarke is the second traveller of his age."—*Dibdin.*

5105 COLONIAL INTELLIGENCER; or Aborigines' Friend, 1847-52, 4 vols. 8vo. *three volumes cloth and one in nos.* 10s 1847-52

5106 CRANTZ, History of Greenland, description of the Country and its inhabitants, 2 vols. 8vo. *maps and plates, calf,* 12s 1767

5107 —— the same, with continuation and notes, 2 vols. 8vo. (pub. at £1. 1s) *bds.* 7s 6d 1820

5108 CRAWFORD'S History of the Indian Archipelago, 3 vols. 8vo. *plates, half calf neat,* 24s 1820

5109 CRESCENTIO (Bartolomeo) Nautica Mediterranea et un Portolano, sm. 4to. *numerous plates, including a curious representation of a Pneumatic Arquebuss, vellum,* £2. 10s *Roma*, 1607

5110 CUNNINGHAM, Two Years in New South Wales, 2 vols. 12mo. *map, hf. calf,* 6s 1827

5111 DAMIANI A GOES Fides, religio, moresque Aethiopum sub imperio Preciosi Joannis (vulgo Presbyteri) degentium, cum enarratione confoederationis inter Aethiopum imperatores et reges Lusitaniae initae; Deploratio Lappianae gentis, etc. 12mo. *veau fauve extra,* 20s *Parisiis*, 1541

5112 DAMPIER'S Collection of Voyages, *fourth edition*, 4 vols. 8vo. *numerous maps and plates, old calf gilt*, 20s 1699-1703-9

5113 —— Collection of Voyoges, by Dampier, Wafer, Funnell, Cowley, Sharp, Woods, and Roberts, BEST EDITION, 4 vols. sm. 8vo. *clean copy, fine impressions of the numerous maps and plates, old calf gilt, scarce*, £2. 10s 1729
Hibberts' copy fetched £4. 9s; Bernal's, at Sotheby's, 1855, calf extra, £5. 12s 6d.
"To this work, written in the style of a plain blunt sailor, and *full of correct information*, particularly relative to the numerous Islands in the Pacific Ocean, Cook, Byron, and others have been greatly indebted."—LOWNDES.

5114 D'ANVILLE, Analyse géographique de l'Italie, 4to. *maps, calf*, 6s 1744
5115 —— Italie, 1744—Eclaircissemens sur la carte de l'Inde, 1753—2 vols. in 1, 4to. *calf*, 7s 6d 1744-53
5116 —— Notice de l'Ancienne Gaule, 4to. *coloured map, calf*, 5s Paris, 1760
5117 —— Memoires sur l'Egypte, et la Mer Rouge, 4to. *maps, calf gilt*, 10s 1766
5118 —— Mesures Itinéraires, anciennes et modernes, 8vo. *calf*, 3s 1769
5119 —— Etats en Europe après la chute de l'Empire Romain, 4to. *bds.* 5s 1771
5120 —— l'Empire de Russie—l'Empire Turc—in 1 vol. 16mo. *bds.* 5s 1772
5121 —— Antiquité Geographique de l'Inde et d'autres contrées de la Haute Asie, 4to. *maps, half calf*, 6s 1775
5122 —— Memoire sur la Chine, sm. 8vo. *calf gilt*, 5s 1776
5123 —— L'Euphrate et le Tigre, 4to. *map, hf. russia, neat*, 6s 6d 1779
5124 DAVY's Interior of Ceylon, and its Inhabitants, 4to. *map and plates* (pub. £3. 13s 6d), *hf. bd.* 6s 1821
Priced, 1840, 30s; Bernal's copy in calf fetched, 1855, 30s.

5125 DAULIER DES LANDES, Beautez de la Perse, Description de ce qu'il y a de plus curieux dans ce Royaume; avec une Relation de quelques avantures maritimes, [par Louis Marot] sq. 8vo. *frontispiece, map, and 17 plates, fine copy in vellum, scarce*, 32s Paris, 1673

5126 DAUMAS le Sahara Algérien, 8vo. *hf. red morocco*, 5s Paris, 1845

DE BRY'S VOYAGES, sets completed, improved, and variations supplied; the following parts are in stock at present:

5127 **LATIN.** GRANDS VOYAGES: AMERICA. Part I, Virginia, second edition, no date; Part II, second edition, 1591; Part IV, second edition, 1594; Part V, second edition, 1595; Part VI, second edition, 1596-1617; Part VII, first edition, 1599; Part VII, second edition, ("Pars V") 1625; Part VIII, second edition, 1625; Part IX, second edition, 1633; Part X, 1619; Part XI, 1619; Appendix to Part XI, 1620.

5128 PETITS VOYAGES: INDIA ORIENTALIS. Part I, Congo, 1598; Part II, 1599; Part III, 1601; Part IV, 1601; Part V, 1601; Part VI, 1604: Part VII, 1606; Part VIII, 1607; Part IX, *no title*, 1612; Part X, 1613.

5129 **GERMAN.** GRANDS VOYAGES: AMERICA. Part IV, (1594); V, (1595); VI, 1597; VII, 1597; VIII, 1599; Additamentum, 1600; IX, 1601; all first editions.

5130 —— PETITS VOYAGES: Africa and India. Part I, 1609; II, 1613; III, first edition, 1599.

5131 GERMAN DE BRY, Collation of the First Edition of the: Grands Voyages (West Indies and America, 14 parts, 1590-1630)—PETITS VOYAGES (Africa and the East Indies), 13 parts, 1597-1628. ONE SHEET, of the same size as the "Grands Voyages," 6 columns, 21s *Privately printed*, 1860
This careful collation is by a Nobleman, and conducted through the press by the advertiser. The collation is the most correct ever made, stating the contents and date of every part, the number of preliminary leaves, maps, plates, printed and black leaves.

5132 GOTTFRIED (J. L. *i.e.* ABELIN) Historia Antipodum: Newe Welt und Americanische Historien, inhaltende warhafftige und vollkommene Beschreibungen aller West-Indianischen Landschafften, etc. 3 parts in 1 vol. folio, *folding map of the whole continent of America,* 1 *of Virginia,* 2 *other separate maps the size of the page,* 3 *folding plates of views, many curious engravings finely executed by* MATTHEW MERIAN; *some leaves at the end slightly wormed, otherwise a good copy, vellum,* £2. 16s *Frankfurt-am-Meyn*, 1631
The plates in this volume are exactly those used in the Grands Voyages by the DE BRYS, they represent the peculiar ceremonies and habits of the Savages, as well as the cruelties perpetrated by them; the wonderful feats performed both by the natives and Spaniards, such as choking crocodiles, chaining dragons, and the like; also extraordinary monsters, serpents with wings, being half human and half birds, animals with heads, &c.

GEOGRAPHY, VOYAGES, TRAVELS. 269

5133 **DUTCH.** DE BRY ABRIDGEMENT: GOTTFRIED (J. L.) [*Abelin*] Voyagien door Francoisen, Deenen, Italiaanen, Hoogduytsen, Portuguysen, Spaniaarden, Engelsen en andere vreemde Volkeren gedaan na Oost- en West Indien, 8 vols. folio, *many maps and curious plates in the style of De Bry, fine copy, Dutch calf gilt*, £5. *Leyden, Vander Aa*, 1706-7
Fetched, 8 vols. in 4, Fonthill sale, £9. 9s. " Collection curieuse, pas commune en France."—BRUNET.

5134 **FRENCH.** Petits Voyages. Premier Livre de l'Histoire de la Navigation aux Indes Orientales, 1609—Second Livre, Journal ou Comptoir, contenant Voyage fait par les huit navires d'Amsterdam, en 1598, *with a Vocabulary, French, Malay and Javanese*, 1609—Description du penible Voyage fait, par Olivier du Nort, pour descouvrir les Costes de Cica, Chili et Peru, 1598-1601, 1610—Description du riche Royaume d'Or de Gunea (Guinea) aultrement de Mina, *with Vocabulary Guneis-French, ib.* 1605—LE VER, Description de trois Voyages, au Nord par derriere Norwege et Tartarie vers China et Catay, 1600—together 5 vols. in 1, fol. *numerous maps and engravings, fine copy in old Dutch calf, gilt back*, £6. *Amst. Nicolas*, 1600-10

5135 D'AUTEROCHE (Chappe) Voyage en Sibérie, 1761, contenant les moeurs, les usages des Russes, et l'etat actuel de cette puissance, etc. 2 vols. in 3, LARGE PAPER, 53 *beautiful plates; with the Atlas of* 31 *large maps;* together 4 vols. folio, *a very fine copy in old French calf gilt*, 30s *Paris*, 1768
Priced, 1818, Longmans, £12. 12s. Fetched, 1813, Col. Stanley's, at Evans's, morocco, £26. 15s. The Atlas contains the map No. 10. "Carte des Vosges," which having appeared some time after the others, is frequently wanting.

5136 DELLA VALLE, VIAGGI divisi in tre parti: la Turchia, la Persia, e l'India, 3 parts in 4 vols. sm. 4to. *first edition, vellum*, £2. 2s *Roma*, 1650-63

5137 —— the same, 1650-63—Funerale di Sitti M. Gioerida della Valle, (*his Mesopotamian wife whose body he brought to bury in Rome*) *portrait and plate*, 1627, in 4 vols. sm. 4to. *calf*, £2. 10s 1627-63
Priced, 1824, Rivington, £10. 10s; 1840, Payne and Foss, £8. 8s. North's copy fetched, russia, £5. 2s 6d; Marquis of Lansdowne's, £3. 13s 6d; Mead's £3. 15s. "La premiere edition, 1650, est plus belle que celle de 1662-63.—BRUNET.

5138 DENHAM and CLAPPERTON, Travels and Discoveries in Northern and Central Africa, 2 vols. 8vo. *map and plates, calf gilt*, 10s 1828

5139 [DESHAYES de Courmesnin] Voyage de Levant, en 1621, sm. 4to. *folding plates,* (*title mounted and date altered to* 1632) *old calf neat*, 16s *Paris*, 1629
"Relation interessante, où l'on remarque surtout une bonne description de Jerusalem."—BRUNET.

5140 DICCIONARIO Geografico-Historico de España por la real Academia de la Historia, Seccion I; El Reyno de Navarra, Señorio de Viscaya, y provincias de Alava y Guipuzocn, 2 vols. 4to. *hf. bd.* 10s *Madrid*, 1802
The best historical Gazetteer of the Basque Provinces.

5141 DIEFFENBACH's Travels in New Zealand, its Geography, Geology, Botany, and Natural History, 2 vols. 8vo. *with a New Zealand Grammar and Dictionary, plates,* (pub. £1. 4s) *cloth*, 12s 1843
"Incomparably the best work on New Zealand that has yet appeared."

5142 D'OHSSON, Peuples du Caucase, dans le Xe siécle, ou Voyage d'ABOUEL-CASSIM, 8vo. *hf. calf*, 4s 6d *Paris*, 1828

5142*DRAKE (Sir Francis) Le Voyage curieux faict autour du Monde par François Drach augmenté de la seconde partie (par Louvencourt de Vauchelles), 12mo. *vellum*, RARE, 32s *Paris*, 1641

5143 [DUCOS] (Baron) Itinéraire et Souvenirs d'Angleterre et d'Ecosse, 1814-26, 4 vols. roy. 8vo. *maps and plates, vellum paper, half morocco extra*, £2. 2s *Paris*, 1828
Cet ouvrage n'a été tiré qu'à 200 exemplaires pour la circulation privée. L'Auteur est le Baron Ducos ancien ministre de France.

5144 ECHARD's Gazetteer's or Newsman's Interpreter, a Geographical Index of Europe, 12mo. *calf*, 5s 1751

5145 ELLIS'S Polynesian Researches in the South Sea Islands, 2 vols. 8vo. *cuts and plates, bds.* 9s 1829

5146 ELPHINSTONE's Account of Caubul and its dependencies, 2 vols. 8vo. *revised edition, map and plates, cloth*, 10s 1839

5147 FARA (J. F.) de Chorographiâ Sardiniæ et de rebus Sardois edente Cibrario, roy. 4to. *portrait, hf. bd. only* 300 *copies printed*, 20s *Aug. Taurin*, 1835

5148 FARIA y SOUSA, Africa Portuguesa, folio, *old calf, rare*, 32s Lisboa, 1681
The Quatremère copy fetched 80 francs.

5149 ———— Imperio de la China, sacado de las noticias de Semmedo, 1731—Galvadō, Descobrimentos antigos e modernos, até a 1550, 1731—Moreno Porcel, Retrato de Faria y Sousa, sua Vida y sus Escritos, 1733—3 vols. in 1, folio, *a few leaves slightly wormed, calf, rare*, 30s Lisboa, 1731-33
This collection of minor works is generally wanting to sets of Faria y Sousa's works.

5150 FELLOWS (Chas.) Discoveries in Lycia, stout roy. 8vo. *plates and woodcuts of Antiquities, Coins, Greek Inscriptions, etc.* (pub. at £2. 2s) *cloth*, 24s 1841

5151 FIGUEROA, Historia y anal, relacion de las cosas que hizieron los Padres de la Compañia de Jesus en Oriente, (Goa, Etiopia, Madure, Malabar, Japon, Sierra Leone), 1607-8, sm. 4to. *vellum, rare*, 32s Madrid, 1614

5152 FISCHER, Sibirische Geschichte, 2 vols. 8vo. *maps, a valuable geographical and historical work*, 5s St. Peters. 1768

5153 FLANDIN ET COSTE. VOYAGE EN PERSE de MM. Eugène Flandin, Peintre, et Pascal Coste, Architecte, attachés à l'ambassade de France en Perse, pendant les années 1840 et 1841, entrepris par ordre de M. le Ministre des affaires étrangères, d'après les instructions dressées par l'Institut; publié sous la direction d'une commission composée de MM. Burnouf, Lebas et Leclère
  PLATES. Perse ancienne; Planches par Eug. Flandin et P. Coste, 4 vols. *containing* 245 *plates of Views of Ruins, including plans, ancient Architecture, Sculpture, Inscriptions, etc. engraved by the best French artists*
  PERSE MODERNE; Planches par Eug. Flandin, 1 vol. *containing* 100 *beautiful lithographs of Views in Persia, of modern Persian Architecture, and Scenes of Persian Life, exterior and interior*
  TEXT. PERSE ANCIENNE; Text par Eug. Flandin, 8 and 186 pp.
  RELATION DU VOYAGE, par Eug. Flandin, 2 vols. 511 and 536 pp.
  Together 6 vols. roy. atlas folio, *containing* 345 *magnificent plates (the finest work on Persia in existence, published under the auspices of the French Government, in* 72 *numbers, and priced in* 1857, £60.) *neatly half bound French mor.* £24. Paris, 1851

5154 FLINDERS' Voyage to Terra Australis, for the purpose of completing the discovery of that vast country, prosecuted in the years, 1801-3, in the Investigator, the Porpoise, and the Cumberland, 2 vols. roy. 4to. *plates*, with roy. folio atlas of 18 *large plates, hf. calf gilt*, £2. 10s 1814

5155 FORBES' ORIENTAL MEMOIRS, 4 vols. impl. 4to. *many plates of Views and Costumes, and Natural productions of the East, several of the latter brilliantly coloured.* LARGE VELLUM PAPER. *An almost unique copy, having proof impressions of the plates on India paper, with many etchings, and an unpublished sheet, printed only for the large paper copies,* at the close of which is an Autograph of Mr. Forbes; *splendidly bound in olive morocco, broad borders of gold, gilt and marbled edges*, £15. 1813
A superb work, in the finest possible state, previously priced £20.
"This is the original and only complete edition. It was printed at the expense of the author; the composition was the labour and amusement of many years. It abounds with striking pictures of the manners, customs, and the habits of the people of India. In the "Quarterly Review," Vol. XII. is an elaborate account of the work, which occupies 47 pages. The Reviewer observes, "A work more splendid or more complete in its decorations we have seldom seen." At the death of Mr. Forbes some reserved copies were deposited in a warehouse and forgotten, or not a single copy would have remained unsold. It had long been considered scarce, and in consequence his daughter, the late Countess de Montalembert, was induced to re-publish the work in an abridged form, with a portion of the plates, which edition, from the impossibility of securing the present, obtained a rapid sale, and is now out of print. The drawings and collections of Mr. Forbes seem almost to exceed the powers of human industry and perseverance, and this literary monument to his name may fairly be considered the essence of his extraordinary researches. The whole work is very entertaining as well as instructive."—LITERARY GAZETTE.
It is to be regretted that this very splendid and expensive work was not published in a cheaper form, as it abounds in most striking pictures of the manners, customs, &c. of India."—STEVENSON.

5156 FORMALEONI, Fonti degli Errori nella Cosmografia degli Antichi, 8vo. *hf. bd. rare*, 6s Venezia, 1789

5157 FORSTER'S (Rev. C.) Historical Geography of Arabia, with Appendix of Inscriptions, &c. 2 vols. 8vo. *maps and plates, cloth*, 18s; *calf extra*, 28s 1844

5158 FORSTER (G.) Voyage round the World in the Resolution, commanded by Capt. Cook, 1772-75, 2 vols.—Observations made, 1 vol.—together 3 vols. roy. 4to. *map, calf*, 24s 1777-78

5159 FRASER'S Tour through the Himālā Mountains, and to the sources of the Jumna and Ganges, roy. 4to. *map. hf. calf*, 10s 1820

GEOGRAPHY, VOYAGES, TRAVELS. 271

5160 FROBISHER. Forbisseri *Angli, Capitanei,* Historia Navigationis A.C. 1577, jussu Reginae Elisabethae in Septemtrionis et Occidentis tractum susceptae, Latine, a Freigio, smallest 4to. *with the plate of the man in a canoe, darting a harpoon at wild fowl, morocco back, rare,* 25s *Hamb.* 1675

5161 FÜRERI (Christo.) Itinerarium Ægypti, Arabiæ, Palestinæ, Syriæ, aliarumque regionum Orientalium, cum oratione funebri et Auctario, sm. 4to. *fine paper, very beautiful portrait, early impression and plates, remarkably fine copy in rough vellum,* 30s *Norimberyæ,* 1620

"Volume rare et recherché"—BRUNET. Bindley's copy fetched £3. 9s; the White Knight's £2. 4s; Mason's, £3. 13s 6d. Priced, 1840, J. Bohn, mor. £2. 5s; fine copies usually valued £3. 3s.

5162 GARCIA DE CESPEDES (Andres) Regimiento de Navegacion—Segunda parte, Hydrografia, 2 vols. in 1, sm. folio, *engraved title-page, numerous woodcuts of Spheres, &c. and the original engraved* MAP, *slightly stained, good sound copy in limp vellum,* £2. *Madrid, Juan de la Cuesta,* 1606

Rare: not mentioned by Brunet, nor in any of Salva's catalogues.
La seconde partie de cet ouvrage, c'est-à-dire l'hydrographie, contient d'une manière fort détaillée le *Guide de la navigation aux Indes,* et la description de ces pays.

5163 GAZETTEER OF THE WORLD, or Dictionary of Geographical Knowledge, edited by a Member of the Royal Geographical Society, 14 vols. impl. 8vo. *double columns, maps, woodcuts, and* 120 *engravings on steel,* (pub. at £9. 9s) *cloth,* £3. 15s 1836

The best and most complete of all Gazetteers, compiled from the recent authorities, and forming a complete body of modern Geography, physical, political, statistical, historical and ethnographical.

5164 GEOGRAPHIÆ VETERIS SCRIPTORES GRÆCI MINORES, *Gr. et Lat.* (ed. Hudson) 4 vols. 8vo. *maps, old calf gilt, rare,* £5. 15s *Oxonii,* 1698-1712
Priced, 1830, Payne and Foss, morocco, £12. 12s; 1843, £8. 8s.

5165 GEOGRAPHI GRAECI MINORES, recognovit Mullerus, Vol. I: Hanno, Scylax, Dicaearchus, Agatharchis, Scymnus, Dionysius Calliph., Isidorus Charac. Arrianus, etc. *Gr. et Lat.* impl. 8vo. *cxlv. and* 576 *pp. double cols. hf. morocco, gilt edges,* 18s *Paris,* 1855

5166 GEOGRAPHICA ANTIQUA: Scylacis Periplus, etc. *Graece et Lat.* cum animadversione Gronovii, sm. 4to. *fine copy in vellum,* 7s 6d *Lugd. Bat.* 1700

5167 GEOGRAPHICAL SOCIETY. Journal of the Geographical Society of London, from its commencement in 1832 to 1859, Vols. I-XXIX, with Indices to the first twenty volumes, 30 vols. 8vo. *fine set in hf. russia extra, marbled edges,* £12. 12s 1832-59

5168 —— Another set, Vols. I-XVII, 8vo. *hf. calf neat,* £6. 10s 1832-47

5169 GERLACH, Fastes Militaires des Indes Orientales Néerlandaises, stout impl. 8vo. *maps and plates, cloth,* 9s *Zalt-Bommel,* 1859

5170 GOUVEA (F. Antonio de) Jornada do Arcebispo de Goa Dom Frey Aleixo de Menezes Primaz da India Oriental quando foy as Serras do Malavar, y Lugares em que morão os antigos Christaos de S. Thome—Synodo Diocesano da Igreia e Bispado de Angamale, &c. in 1 vol. sm. folio, *very fine copy, red morocco extra,* £4. 10s *Coimbra,* 1606

Not mentioned by Boucher de la Richarderie. This curious and interesting Journey, termed by Brunet "volume rare et recherché," is not in the Grenville collection.

5171 GRELOT, Voyage de Constantinople, 4to. *large view of the Seraglio, and other plates, calf gilt,* 9s *Paris,* 1680

5172 GUERRERO (Fernan) Relacion Anual de las cosas que han hecho los Padres de la Compañia de Jesus en la INDIA ORIENTAL y JAPON en 1600 y 1601, traduzida de Portugues por Colaco, sq. 8vo. *vellum, rare,* 36s *Valladolid,* 1604

5173 HALL (Capt. Basil) Voyage to the West Coast of Corea and Loo-Choo, with Clifford's Loo-Choo Vocabulary, etc. 4to. 7 *coloured plates and* 4 *maps* (pub. at £2. 2s), *calf gilt,* 10s 1818

5174 —— Fragments of Voyages and Travels, *the three series,* 3 vols. each, together 9 vols. 16mo. (pub. at 45s) *bds. scarce,* 30s 1831-33

5175 HAMILTON's Researches in Asia Minor, Pontus and Armenia, with an account of their Antiquities and GEOLOGY, 2 vols. 8vo. *plates* (pub. at 38s) *bright calf gilt,* 18s 1842

5176 HAKLUYT'S COLLECTION OF EARLY VOYAGES, TRAVELS, and Discoveries of of the English Nation, made by Sea, or Overland, within the compass of these 1600 years, (edited by G. Woodfall,) 5 vols. royal 4to. reprinted with additions from the rare edition of 1599, (pub. at £15. 15s) *hf. russia,* £10. 1809-12

Rare: only 250 copies were printed.

5177 HAKLUYT SOCIETY'S PUBLICATIONS, from the commencement in 1847 to 1860, 27 vols. 8vo. *many maps and plates, (printed for subscribers only, at the cost of* £14. 14s) *new in cloth,* £12.   1847-60

The following is a list of the Contents; with the prices affixed at which I can supply separate vols.—

a Hawkins' (Sir Richd.) Observations in his Voiage into the South Sea in 1593, 1622; edited by Capt. C. R. Bethune, 12s 6d   1847
b Columbus, Select Letters, with other original documents relating to his Four Voyages, translated and edited by R. H. Major, 12s 6d   1847
c Ralegh's Discoverie of Guiana in 1595, 1596; edited by Sir R. N. Schomburgk, *map,* 12s 6d   1848
d Sir Francis Drake, his Voyage, 1595, by Thomas Maynarde, edited from the original MSS. by W. D. Cooley, 12s 6d   1849
e Rundall (Thos.) Narative of Voyages towards the North-West in search of a Passage to Cathay and India, 1496 to 1631, 3 *maps,* 12s 6d   1849
f Strachey (Wm.) Historie of Travaile into Virginia Britannia, edited from the MS. by R. H. Major, *map, facsimiles and 5 plates,* 12s 6d   1849
g Hakluyt (Rd.) Divers Voyages touching the discovery of America and the Islands adjacent, 1582; edited by J. Winter Jones, *facsimile and 2 maps,* 12s 6d   1850
h Rundall's Collection of early Documents on Japan, 12s 6d   1850
i Coat's Geography of Hudson's Bay, edited by Jno. Barrow, 12s 6d.   1851
j Hakluyt (Rd.) Discovery and Conquest of Terra Florida by Don Ferdinando de Soto, 1611; edited by W. B. Rye, *map,* 12s 6d   1851
k Herberstein, Rerum Moscovitarum Commentarii: Notes upon Russia, translated and edited by R. H. Major, 2 vols. 2 *facsimile maps and 4 plates,* 12s 6d   1852
l De Veer (Gerrit) Three Voyages by the North-East to China, 1594-6, edited by C. T. Beke, 12s 6d   1852

m Mendoza (Juan Gonzalez de) Historie of China, transl. by Parke, 1588; edited by R. G. Staunton, 2 vols. 25s 1853-4
n D'Orléans (Pierre Joseph) History of the Tartar Conquerors of China, *Paris,* 1688; transl. and edited by the Earl of Ellesmere, 12s 6d   1854
o Fletcher (Francis) The World encompassed by Sir Francis Drake; edited by W. S. W. Vaux, *map,* 12s 6d   1854
p White (Adam) Collection of early Documents on Spitzbergen and Greenland, 12s 6d   1855
q Middleton (Sir Hen.) Voyage to Bantam and the Maluco Islands, 1606; ed. by B. Corney, *map and 5 plates,* 12s 6d 1855
r Bond (Edw. A.) Russia at the close of the 16th Century, 12s 6d   1856
s Benzoni (Girolamo) History of the New World; Travels, 1541-56, *Venice,* 1572; translated and edited by Adml. W. H. Smyth, *facsimiles of old woodcuts,* 12s 6d 1857
t Major (R. H.) India in the 15th Century, 12s 6d   1857
u Champlain, Voyage to the West Indies, 1599-1602; transl. by A. Wilmere, ed. by N. Shaw, 4 *coloured and* 4 *plain facsimiles,* 21s   1859
v Expeditions into the Valley of the Amazons, 1539, 1540, 1639; transl. and edited by C. R. Markham, 12s 6d 1859
w Gonzalez de Clavijo, Embassy to the Court of Timour at Samarcand, 1403-6, by R. Markham, *map,* 12s 6d   1859
x Hudson, (Hen. *the Navigator*) by G. M. Asher, 2 *maps,* 10s 6d   1860
y Early Voyages to Terra Australis, now called Australia, edited by R. H. Major, *maps,* 12s 6d   1859

5178 HANWAY's (Jonas) Historical Account of British Trade over the Caspian Sea; Travels from London through Russia into Persia; and back through Russia, Germany, and Holland, with the History of Nadir-Kouli, 4 vols. 4to. *best edition, portraits, maps and plates, calf gilt,* 12s   1753

5179 HARRIS' Collection of Voyages and Travels, continued with large additions, by Dr. Campbell, 2 vols. large folio, *numerous maps and plates, Mitford's copy in calf gilt,* 30s   1764

Best edition, superseding that of 1705. Priced, 1840, Payne and Foss, £3. 13s 6d.
Vol. I. Introduction. B. 1. c. 1. Circumnavigators from Columbus to Anson.—c. 2. Discov. Settl. and Commerce of East Indies.
Vol. II. c. 3. Discovery, Settl. and Commerce of West Indies. B. 2. c. 1. Discoveries made towards the North, and attempts for N.E. and N.W. Passage. B. 2. c. 2. Northern Parts of Europe; c. 3. Middle Parts of Europe; c. 4. Spain, France, and Navarre; c. 5. Germany, Bohemia, Hungary, &c. B. 3. c. 1. Isles of Archipelago, Turkish Dominions; c. 2. Persia; c. 3. N. E. parts of Asia and China, and parts depending on them.

5180 HAVART, Op- en Ondergangh van Cormandel, 3 vols. in 1, thick sm. 4to. *frontispiece, maps and plates, vellum*, 9s *Amst.* 1693

5181 HELFFRICH (Joh.) Bericht von der Reiss aus Venedig nach Hierusalem von dannen in Aegypten, auff den Berg Sinai, Alcair, Alexandria, und widerumb gen Venedig. sm. 4to. *numerous fine bold woodcuts, one a procession, nearly 40 inches long, the eugravings of Oriental Costume are very attractive, fine tall copy, calf extra, rare,* £2. 10s *Leipzig*, 1581

5182 HELL's Travels in the Caspian Steppes, Crimea, etc. 8 vols. *cl.* 5s 1847

5183 HENTZNER'S Journey into England in 1698, sm. 8vo. *fine copy in Old English calf extra, with the autograph of "Walpole,"* 30s *Strawberry Hill*, 1757
Priced, 1840, Jno. Bohn, mor. £2. 12s 6d.
"Honest Paul Hentzner sets down the peculiarities of an Englishman with the same accuracy that Captain Hall describes the new-found inhabitants of Loo Choo Islands. The travels of a German tutor in England in 1598 must indeed be matter of curiosity to those who wish to know what impression the manners, habits, and amusements, and the general character of their country, made upon a foreigner more than two hundred years ago.—He has certainly noted some particulars which are not to be found elsewhere, and which are equally curious and amusing."—*Retrospective Rev.*

5184 HERTHA : Zeitschrift fur Erd., Völker und Staatenkunde, von Berghaus und Hoffmann, Vols. i-xiii. 8vo. *plates, hf. calf,* 30s *Stuttgart*, 1825-9

5185 HIBBERT's Shetland Islands, a Description, comprising the Geology, Scenery, Antiquities, and Superstitions, 4to. *geological map and plates,* (pub. at £3. 3s) *bds.* £2. 2s *Edinb.* 1822

5186 HOARE (Sir Richard Colt) Recollections Abroad, from 1785 to 1791 inclusive, during his Travels in France, Germany, Istria, Italy, Sicily, Malta, Abruzo, &c.) 4 vols. royal 8vo. *brown* MOROCCO, UNCUT, PRIVATELY PRINTED, EXTREMELY RARE, £12. *Bath*, 1815-18
Priced, 1847, Thorpe, mor. £25.; Lowndes mentions only 3 vols., and says that Coxe's copy fetched £11. 1s.
Only Twenty-five Copies of Vols. I. and II. and Fifty of the Vols. III. and IV. of this interesting work were privately printed, to be given as presents to the friends of the learned baronet, whose writings are much coveted by antiquarians and collectors in general. It contains a description of his four several journeys from London to Paris, Lyons, Turin, Milan, Parma, Modena, Bologna, Florence, Rome, Naples, Geneva, Loreto, Ancona, Rimini, through Switzerland, Holland, Belgium, Sicily, Malta, &c. with description of each place, the paintings, curiosities, &c. forming a most valuable acquisition to the traveller, artist or connoisseur. The above copy is numbered 9, and was presented to T. S. Champneys, Esq., with the author's autograph, and it is believed to be the third complete one which has ever occurred for sale.
Vol. I. contains the Recollections of the Author, the late Sir Richart Colt Hoare, Bart., in France and Italy. Vol. II. Recollections of Germany, Istria and Italy. Vol. III. Sicily and Malta. Vol. IV. Italy, Abruzzo, &c.—*Martin's bibliogr. catalogue of privately printed Books.*

5186*HONTERI (Joannis) Rudimenta Cosmographica (Carmen), 12mo. *woodcut maps (including America), fine copy, with autograph of Desportes the French Poet, old French red morocco, gilt edges, rare,* 21s. *Antverp. J. Richard. s. a.*

5187 HOOKER'S (Sir W. J.) Tour in Iceland, 1809, 2 vols. roy. 8vo. *second edition, with Appendix,* LARGE PAPER, *maps and plates,* (pub. at 36s) *bds.* 18s 1813
"This interesting work has left nothing to be desired on the subject of this extraordinary island."—LOWNDES.

5188 HUGHES, Travels id Greece and Albania, 2 vols. 8vo. *maps and plates, hf. calf,* 10s 1830

5189 HULSIUS TRAVELS, Collations of the First Editions, parts 1-26, 1598-1650, sm. 4to. *to bind with a set,* 8 pp. 21s *Privately printed,* 1860
This careful collation is by a Nobleman, and conducted through the press by the advertiser. The collation is the most correct ever made, giving the contents and date of every part, the number of preliminary, printed, and blank leaves, further the exact description of every map and plate.

5190 HUMBOLDT, Asie Centrale, Recherches sur les Chaines de Montagnes et la Climatologie, Vols. II, III, stout 8vo. *map and 8 tables, sd.* £2. 2s *Paris*, 1843
Sold, 1856, at Sotheby's, 3 vols. £4. 8s.

5191 HUNTER's Journal of Transactions at Port Jackson and Norfolk Island, 1787-92, roy. 4to. *portrait, maps, plates, calf,* 9s 1795

5192 IDES (YSBRANTS) Travels from Moscow to Pekin—Kao's China, in 1 vol. 4to. *map and 29 curious plates, calf,* 12s 1706
Fetched, Sotheby's in 1860, £1. 11s. "Relation curieuse; elle se paye £2. à £4, en Angleterre."—BRUNET.

5192*JOHNSTON (A. Keith) Dictionary of Geography forming a complete Gazetteer of the World, stout 8vo. 1352 pp. *(pub at* 35s) *hf. russia,* £1. 9s 6d 1862

5193 JUSTEL, Recueil de divers Voyages faits en Afrique et en l'Amérique, contenant l'origine, les mœurs, les coûtumes, et le commerce de ces parties du monde, sm. 4to. *several maps and plates, fine copy in vellum,* £2. 2s *Paris*, 1684
Containing Ligon, Histoire des Barbades; Wische, Relation du Nil, Telles, Ethiopie, Extrait, with the two rare maps; L'Empire du Prête-Jean; La-Borde, Relation des Caraibes, des Antilles, et de l'Amerique.

T

5194 JUNGHUHN'S Java, seine Gestallt, Pflanzendecke und innere Bauart; aus dem holländischen übertragen von Hasskarl, 3 vols. in 4, 8vo. *with folio Atlas of Views, Maps, Geological Sections, &c. hf. russia neat*, 36s   *Leip.* 1852-54

The best scientific account of the natural resources of Java, completing the learned work of Raffles.

5195 —— Java, zijne gedaante, zijn Plantentooi en inwendige bouw, 2e. verbeterde Uitg. impl. 8vo. *all published, present. copy to Dr. Horsfield*, 30s *Amst.* 1852, etc.

Afd. I. pp. 1-176; Afd. II. pp. 1-1432; Afd. III. pp. 1-296.

5196 —— Rückreise von Java nach Europa, 8vo. *maps and views, hf. bd.* 3s   1852
5197 KING'S Survey of the Intertropical and Western Coast of Australia, 1818-22, 2 vols. 8vo. *maps and plates* (pub. at 36s) 12s   1827
5198 KLAPROTH, Voyage au Mont Caucase et en Géorgie, 2 vols. 8vo. *map, with vocabularies of various languages, hf. calf*, 7s 6d   *Paris*, 1823
5199 LA CAILLE, Journal du Voyage au Cap de Bonne-Espérance, 16mo. *plate, old red morocco, gilt edges*, 6s   *Paris*, 1763
5200 LAIRD and OLDFIELD'S Expedition into the Interior of Africa, by the Niger, 1832-34, 2 vols. 8vo. *plates, calf*, 12s   1837
5201 LANDER'S Expedition to explore the Niger, 2 vols. 16mo. *maps and plates, calf gilt,* 5s   1838
5202 LANDT'S Description of the Feroe Islands, 8vo. *plates, hf. calf*, 5s   1810
5203 LA PUENTE, Compendio de los Descubrimientos y conquistas de la India Oriental y sus Islas, sq. 8vo. *vellum*, 25s   *Madrid*, 1681
5204 LAVENDER (Theophilus) Travels of Foure English Men and a Preacher into Africa, Asia, Troy, Bythinia, Thracia, and to the Black Sea, begunne in the yeare of Jubile 1600, and by some of them finished in 1611, the others not yet returned, sq. 8vo. 𝔟𝔩𝔞𝔠𝔨 𝔩𝔢𝔱𝔱𝔢𝔯, *hf. bd. from Miss Currer's library, rare*, £2. 2s   *F. Kyngston for W. Aspley*, 1612

Priced, Thorpe, 1845, £2. 12s 6d. The names of the five Englishmen were W. Biddulph (the preacher) Jeffrie Kirbie, E. Abbott, J. Elkin, Jasper Tyon.

5205 LEAKE'S Travels in the MOREA, 3 vols. 8vo. *very large Map of the Morea, and upwards of 30 others, plates of Inscriptions, &c.* (pub. at £2. 5s) *cloth*, 12s 1830
5205* —— Travels in Northern Greece, 4 vols. 8vo. *cloth*, £2. 10s   1835
5206 LE BRUN, Voyages par la Moscovie, en Perse, et aux Indes Orientales, 2 vols. folio, *portrait, and upwards of 320 plates, old French calf neat*, 12s *Amst.* 1718

Priced, 1840, £2. 2s.

5207 —— Travels into Muscovy, Persia and the East Indies, 2 vols. folio, *maps and plates, old calf neat*, 10s   1737
5207*LELEWEL, Geographie du Moyen-age, avec l'Epilogue, 4 vols. 8vo. *with 10 maps and an oblong folio Atlas of 50 plates of Mediaeval Maps, sewed, rare,* £2. 10s   *Bruxelles*, 1852-7
5208 LENGLET DUFRESNOY (Abbé) Methode pour étudier la Geographie, avec un Catalogue de Voyages, Cartes, &c. 7 vols. in 8, 12mo. *maps, fine copy in citron morocco, gilt edges, with the Arms of S. A. R. Madame Sophie de France on sides,* £3. 12s   *Paris*, 1742
5209 LEON (Jean) Historiale description de l'Afrique, thick 12mo. *curious woodcuts, calf,* 10s   *Anvers*, 1556
5210 LETTRES ÉDIFIANTES ET CURIEUSES, écrites des Missions Étrangères, 26 vols. 12mo. *fine copy, old calf gilt, from Miss Currer's library*, £3. 3s 1780-83

Priced, 1824, Rivington, £8 8s; 1844, White, £6. 16s 6d.
This edition is generally preferred to the original, because it has the advantage of being systematically arranged."—"Of which *Fontenelle* said, 'that he had never read a work which answered better to its title.' Of the accuracy of those *Letters*, and the works of *Du Halde* and *Gaubil*, the author has often heard the late *Sir G. Staunton* speak in the highest terms."—*C. Butler*.

5210*LETTRES EDIFIANTES : Choix des lettres édifiantes écrites des Missions Étrangères, précédé d'un tableau de la Chine, 8 vols. 8vo. *calf*, 18s   *Paris*, 1808
5211 LEVCHINE, Description des Hordes et des Steppes des Kirghiz-Kazaks, traduite du Russe par Pigny, roy. 8vo. *map, and plates of Costume, Music, etc.* 7s 6d   *Paris*, 1840
5212 LUCAS Voyage dans la Turquie, l'Asie, Palestine, Egypte, 2 vols. 12mo. *maps and plates, hf. bd.* 5s   *Amst.* 1720
5213 LYALL'S Travels in Russia, the Krimea, the Caucasus, and Georgia, 2 vols. 8vo. *map, hf. calf,* 6s   1825

GEOGRAPHY, VOYAGES, TRAVELS. 275

5214 LINSCHOT, Histoire de sa Navigation aux Indes Orientales, 2me *edition, portrait, folding map of the world including America dated* 1594, *with* 3 *maps and* 36 *plates*, 1619—Grand Routier de Mer, contenent une instruction des routes en la Navigation des Indes Orientales, et a la coste du Bresil, etc. 1619—Description de l'Amerique et des parties d'icelle, *folding map of South America and the West Indies, by A. Florentius à Langren*, 86 pp. 1619—together 3 vols. in 1, folio, *fine copies, vellum*, £2. *Amsterdam*, 1619

5215 —— Histoire de sa Navigation aux Indies Orientales, description des Lieux descouvertes par les Portugais, 2 vols. in 1, folio, *numerous maps and plates, third edition, calf,* 20s *Amst.* 1638
"Linschoten had for fourteen years lived in the Portuguese possessions in the East, and had there collected a vast amount of information."—*R. H. Major's Disc. of Austs.* 1861.

5216 MACKENZIE's Travels in Iceland, 1810, with a dissertation on its Literature by Holland, 4to. (pub. at £3. 3s) *maps, plates, some coloured, hf. calf,* 10s 1811

5217 M'LEOD's Travels in Eastern Africa, and Residence in Mosambique, 2 vols. sm. 8vo. *portrait, map and plate,* 2 vols. 12mo. *cloth,* 7s 6d 1860

5218 MALTE-BRUN, Annales des Voyages, de la Geographie, et de l'Histoire, avec des mémoires historiques sur l'origine, la Langue, les mœurs, etc. des peuples, et une table générale, 25 vols. 1809-14—EYRIÈS et MALTE-BRUN, Nouvelles Annales des Voyages, Vols. I—XXX. 1819-26; together 55 vols. 8vo. *several hundred maps and plates, the first thirty-seven vols, neatly hf. bd, calf, the rest in green cloth,* £4. 16s *Paris*, 1809-26

5219 MANDELSLO et OLEARIUS, Voyages aux Indes Orientales, en Moscovie, Tartarie, et Perse trad. par A. de Wicquefort, 4 vols. in 2, folio, LARGE PAPER, *portraits, maps, and plates, calf,* 32s *Amst.* 1727
Ouvrages assez estiméz.—*Brunet.*

5220 MARCO POLO'S Travels in the XIIIth Century, being a description by that early traveller of remarkable places and things in the Eastern parts of the World, translated from the Italian, with notes by Marsden, stout 4to. *map, calf neat,* £2. 16s 1818

5221 —— the same, LARGE PAPER, royal 4to. *map, bds. uncut,* £3. 16s 1818

5222 —— Recueil de Voyages et de Mémoires, publié par la Société de Geographie: Vol. I. le Voyage de Marc Polo, *in French and Latin,* 4to. *calf,* 30s *Par.* 1818
Marco Polo, once reviled but now the much honoured pioneer of geographical investigation.

5222* —— Historia de las Grandezas y cosas marauillosas de las Prouincias Orientales, traduzida en Romance y añadida in muchas partes por Bolea y Castro, 12mo. *fine copy, Spanish calf neat,* RARE, 30s *Caragoça*, 1601

5223 MARSDEN (W.) Names of Places arranged according to the Arabic and Persian Orthography, obl. roy. 8vo. *neat MS. giving the Oriental names in Arabic and Roman characters, parallel with the common appellations, and the geographical situation,* 107 pp. *hf. bd.* £2. 10s *ca.* 1820
A very interesting Autograph MS., prepared for press.

5224 MARIS CARNEYRO, Hydrografia la mas curiosa asta oy salida, sq. 8vo. *curious Sailing Directions, vellum,* 12s *S. Sebastian*, 1675

5225 MARINI, Historia et Relatione del Tunchino e del Giappone, 4to. *plates, vellum,* 7s; *uncut,* 10s *Romæ*, 1665

5226 MARMOL CARAVAIAL, Primera parte de la Descripcion General de Affrica, con todos los successos de guerras entre los infieles, y el pueblo Christiano, 2 vols. in 1, sm. folio, FIRST EDITION, *the lower margin of 20 leaves wormed, limp vellum,* 25s *Granada*, 1573
Priced, Thorpe, £2. 2s.

5227 —— l'Afrique, traduit par D'Ablancourt, avec l'histoire des Chérifs, 3 vols. 4to. *maps, old calf,* 6s *Paris*, 1667

5228 MARRYAT's Borneo, and the Indian Archipelago, impl. 8vo. *plates of Costume and Scenery,* (pub. at £1. 11s 6d) *calf gilt,* 14s 1848

5229 MARTENS (F.) Spitzbergische oder Groenlandische Reise Beschreibung, gethan 1671, sm. 4to. 15 *plates, calf,* 15s *Hamburgh*, 1675

5230 MAUNDRELL's Journey from Aleppo to Jerusalem, at Easter, 1697, 8vo. LARGE PAPER, *plates, calf, gilt edges,* 20s *Oxford*, 1740

5231 MEYENDORFF, Voyage d'Orenbourg à Boukhara, par Jaubert, 8vo. *map,* 5s *Paris*, 1826

5232 MANDAVILLA (Joanne de) qual tratte de le piu maravegliose cose e piu notabili che se trovino e come presentialmente ha cercato tutte le parti habitabili del mondo, etc. 12mo. *vellum, a very rare edition,* £3. 10s *Venetia*, 1553

T 2

5233 MAUNDEVILE'S (Sir John) Voiage and Travaile, which treateth of the Way to Hierusalem, and of Marvayles of Inde, with other Ilands and Countryes, roy. 8vo. *best English Edition, fine paper, old calf gilt*, £2. 15s   1725
Bindley's copy fetched £3. 15s.
Mandeville set out in 1322, and returned in 1356. He was the first to assert the spherical form of the earth, and the possibility of circumnavigating the same. He was also the compiler of the very earliest original prose volume in the language.
Sir John Mandeville wrote his travels in Latin, whence he translated them into French, and subsequently into English. The literature of the middle ages has scarcely a more entertaining and interesting subject; and to an Englishman it is doubly valuable, as establishing the title of his country to claim as its own the first example of the liberal and independent gentleman travelling over the world in the disinterested pursuit of knowledge; unsullied in his reputation, honoured and respected wherever he went for his talents and personal accomplishments; and in the words of the faithful panegyric inscribed on his tomb, "Moribus, ingenio, candore, et sanguine clarus."

5234 MICHAUD et POUJOULAT, Correspondence d'Orient, 1830-1, 8 vols. in 4, *map, hf. calf gilt*, 9s   *Brux.* 1841

5235 MIÑANO, Diccionario Geográfico-Estadístico de España y Portugal, con el Suplemento, 11 vols. sm. 4to. *maps, cloth, uncut*, £2.; or, *in Spanish calf neat*, £2. 16s   *Madrid*, 1826-29
Priced, 1843, Salva, 150 fr.

5236 MONTEFIORE (Lady) Notes from a private Journal of a Visit to Egypt and Palestine, 8vo. *cloth, privately printed*, 12s   1844

5237 MOORCROFT and TREBECK's Travels in the HIMALAYAN Provinces of Hindustan and the Punjab, Ladakh, Kashmir, Bokhara, &c. by H. H. Wilson, 2 vols. 8vo. *map and plates, cloth*, 10s; or *morocco*, 12s   1841

5238 Moore's (Fr.) Travels into the inland parts of Africa, sm. 8vo. *map of the Gambia and plates, with a Mundingo Vocabulary, calf*, 6s   1738

5239 Moor's Notices of the Indian Archipelago and adjacent countries, 4to. *maps, stained, half bound*, 18s   *Singapore*, 1837

5240 MORISOTI Orbis Maritimi sive rerum in Mari et Littoribus gestarum Historia, continens omnia ad rem maritimam pertinentia, folio, 11 leaves, 726 pp. and Index 9 leaves, *frontispiece, folding plates, curious engravings, and maps, three of which relates to America, vellum*, 25s; or, *in the original dark morocco, original lettering and tooling*, £2.   *Divione*, 1643
A curious and rare work, unknown to Brunet, who mentions three other works of this author, all less important than the above. It is a kind of Encyclopædia on maritime affairs; there is a geographical description of the world, with upwards of 20 maps; of Africa, with 1 map; of America, with 3 maps; interesting for the history of early geographical discovery. At the end of each description in this portion of the book is a list of the names of towns and places differing from the Latin nomenclature. Amongst the illustrations may be noticed a boat with three paddle-wheels, p. 712.

5241 MUNSTERI (S.) Cosmographia Universalis, stout sm. folio, *numerous curious spirited woodcuts, including portrait of the author, many ancient maps (amongst others one of* ENGLAND *and one of the* NEW WORLD), *large folding views of Towns, Costumes, Figures, Monsters, etc. old calf*, 35s   *Basileæ*, 1572

5242 MURRAY'T account of Discoveries and Travels in ASIA, 3 vols. 8vo. *maps, calf*, 9s   *Edin.* 1820

5243 MYRITII Opusculum Geographicum rarum, totius ejus negotii rationem complectens, 2 parts in 1 vol. sm. folio, *portrait and arms of the author, large maps, and several diagrams with moveable pieces, relating to the discoveries in America, etc. vellum, rare*, £2. 2s   *Ingolst.* 1590

MURRAY'S HANDBOOKS:

5244 EGYPT; The Nile, Alexandria, Cairo, Pyramids, Thebes, and Overland Route to India, *map*, (pub at 15s) 12s 6d   1858

5245 GREECE; Ionian Islands, Athens, &c. *maps*, (pub. at 15s) 11s   1854

5246 INDIA; Bombay and Madras, 2 vols. (pub. at 24s) 20s   1854-59

5247 —— Madras, *separately*, (pub. at 12s) 7s 6d   1859

5248 SPAIN, by R. Ford; Andalusia, Grenada, Valencia, Catalonia, Galicia, Madrid, 2 vols. *maps*, (pub. at 30s) 25s   1855

5249 SYRIA and Palestine, 2 vols. *maps and plans*, (pub. at 24s) 20s   1858

5250 NAAUKEURIGE VERSAMELING der gedenkwaardigste REYSEN NAAR OOST EN WEST-INDIEN, mitsgaders andere Gewesten gedaan; beginnende met het Jaar 1246 en eyndigende 1696, 28 vols. in 29, sm. 8vo. *complete with about 500 folding plates and maps in the style of De Bry's, old Dutch calf gilt*, £4.
Leyden, Pieter Van der Aa, 1706-7
I do not find the above curious collection of Travels in Brunet. Boucher de la Richarderie in his Bibliothèque quotes it, "Versammeling den gedenkwaardigsten Beysen, door D. de Bry unter het name Gottfried, Leyde, 1707-10, 30 vols. in 8;" F. Muller in Amsterdam, in his Bibliographie Neerlande-Reyse: "Verzameling der gedenkwardigsten zee-en land-reizen, 1706, 26 tom. en 27 vols. 8vo."—both copies disagree with the present, which is quite perfect, according to the General Table of Contents, bound up with volume XXVIII.

GEOGRAPHY, VOYAGES, TRAVELS. 277

5251 NEWBOLD's British Settlements in the Straits of Malacca, with a history of the Malayan States, 2 vols. 8vo. *maps*, (pub. at 26s) *cloth*, 8s   1839

5252 NIEBUHR (C.) Description de l'Arabie, 1774—Questions proposées aux Savants qui font le Voyage de l'Arabie, par Michaelis, 1774—Voyage en Arabie et en d'autres Pays circonvoisins, par Niebuhr, 2 vols. 1776-80—together 4 vols. 4to. *with 150 maps and plates of Antiquities, Coins, etc. French calf gilt, Lord Orford's copy*, 30s; or, *hf. calf, uncut*, 36s   *Amst.* 1774-80

<small>Niebuhr, a traveller of the greatest merit, and who has collected, upon the state of various countries of the East, more copious and minute information than is to be found perhaps in any other single author. Subsequent travellers have borrowed largely from him.</small>

5253 NIECAMPII Historia Missionis Evangelicae in India Orientali, 4to. *bds.* 6s   1747

5254 NORDEN, Voyage d'Egypte et de Nubie, avec des additions par Langlès, 3 vols. 4to. *upwards of* 150 *maps and plate, vellum paper, hf. bound, uncut*, 25s   *Paris, Didot*, 1795-8

<small>Priced, vellum paper, 1836, £4. 14s 6d. "The merits of Norden's Works are of the most enduring and substantial kind, so far as relates to the Antiquities of Egypt and the Cataracts: it is high and unequivocal commendation of this author, that subsequent travellers have found him a judicious and sure guide."—*Stevenson.*</small>

5255 NOTT and GLIDDON, Types of Mankind, or Ethnological Researches, based on Ancient Monuments, Paintings, Sculptures, and Crania of Races, their geographical and philological History, roy. 8vo. *woodcuts, cloth*, 21s   *Philadelphia*, 1857

5256 ORDONEZ DE ZEVALLOS (Pedro) Historia, y Viage del Mundo: ITINERARIO à las cinco partes de la Europa, Africa, Asia, AMERICA, y Magalanica, sm. 4to. *a good copy in limp vellum, extremely rare*, £4. 4s   *Madrid*, 1691

<small>COLLATION: 6 prel. leaves; pp. 1-432; Tablas, 4 leaves. A valuable description of the author's travels to Goa and Malabar, Cochin-China, the Philippine Islands, New Granada, Quito, Lima, and Peru, the Straits of Magellan, where he met with many English vessels, the West Indies and Mexico, then back to Philippine Islands, India, the Levant, Barbary, Gibraltar and Iceland; returning to Spain after 34 years' absence. This work has been little known to bibliographers. Nic. Antonio could never obtain sight of a copy. I can find no trace of any copy having occurred for sale.
An agreeable and often interesting autobiography of its author, beginning with his birth at Jaen and his education at Seville, and giving his travels for 39 years all over the world, including China, America, many parts of Africa, and the northern kingdoms of Europe. Its spirit is national, and its style simple and Castilian.—*Ticknor.*</small>

5257 OUSELEY (Sir W.) Travels in various countries of the East, particularly Persia, 3 vols. 4to. *numerous plates, calf*, £2. 2s   1819-23

<small>A valuable work, wherein the author has described, as far as his observations extended, the state of those countries in 1810, 1811, and 1812; and has endeavoured to illustrate many subjects of Antiquarian Research, History Geography, Philology, and Miscellaneous Literature, with extracts from rare and valuable MSS.</small>

5258 PACIFIQUE (Père) Voyage de Perse, avec les remarques de la Terre Sainte, 12mo. *vellum*, 10s   *Paris*, 1645

5259 PALLAS, Samlungen historicher Nachrichten über die Mongolischen Völkerschaften, 2 vols. 4to. 29 *plates*, 7s 6d   *St. Petersburgh*, 1776-1801

<small>A very important collection of historical documents illustrative of the Mongolian Races, with Kalmuk Poetry and Specimens of Writing.</small>

5260 PALLAS, Reise durch verschiedene Provinzen des Russischen Reichs, 5 vols. 4to. *numerous plates, sewed*, 7s 6d   *St. Petersburg*, 1801

5261 —— —— Tableau physique et topographique de la Tauride, en 1794, 4to *sd. ib.* 1795

5262 PARRY (Capt. W. E.) Three Voyages for the Discovery of a North West Passage, with the Appendixes, 4 vols. 4to. *plates, calf gilt, fine set*, £4. 10s   1821-6

5263 PASHLEY's (R.) Travels in Crete, 2 vols. 8vo. *map and plates*, (pub. at 24s) *cloth*, 12s 6d   *Cambridge*, 1837

5264 PENA (J.) Nuñez de la) Conquista y Antiguedades de las Islas de la Gran CANARIA, con muchas advertencias de la muy poderosa Isla de Thenerife, 8vo. *hf. calf, rare*, 28s   *Madrid*, 1676

5265 PÉRON ET FREYCINET, Voyage de Découvertes aux Terres Australes, 1800-4, 2 vols. 4to. with 2 royal 4to. *atlases of* 58 *plates, some coloured*—Navigation et Géographie, par Freycinet, 1 vol. 4to. *with* royal folio *atlas of* 32 *maps* —in all 6 vols. *French calf gilt*, £5.   *Paris*, 1807-15

<small>Priced, 1836, Bossange, hf. mor. £7. 7s.</small>

5266 PETRUS MARTYR. Extraict ou Recueil des Isles nouvellement trouvées en la grande Mer Oceane, faict en Latin par Pierre Martyr, et depuis translate, item trois Narrations de Cuba, etc. 8vo. *facsimile title page, otherwise a very good copy, old calf, rare*, £2. 16s   *Paris*, 1532

5267 PEYSSONEL et DESFONTAINES, Voyages en Tunis et Alger, 1724-25, 2 vols. 8vo. *map and plates, hf. calf*, 6s   *Paris*, 1838

5268 PIGAFETTA, Premier Voyage autour du Monde sur l'Escadre de Magellan, 1519-22, 8vo. *maps and plates, come coloured, calf*, 18s *Paris*, 1801
5269 PINTO (Fernão-Mendez) Peregrinaçam, em que da conta de muytas estranhas cousas que viò no reyno da China, em Tartaria, Sornau, Calaminhan, Pegù, Martauão, e outros reynos Orientais, folio, FIRST EDITION, *margins of title and a few leaves at the beginning repaired, otherwise a good copy, vellum, very scarce*, 24s *Lisboa*, 1614

Copies have fetched, 1855, Lord Stuart de Rothesay's, £3. 15s; Sotheby's, £3.; 1858, Sotheby's, £1. 11s.

5270 —— Historia Oriental de las Peregrinaciones, en Castellano por Maldonado, sm. folio, *hf. russia*, 15s *Madrid*, 1627
5271 —— Historia Oriental, folio, *fine copy, brown calf gilt*, 18s *Valencia*, 1645

The extraordinary and amusing adventures related by this traveller have procured for him the reputation of being the Prince of Long-bow-men, and sometimes the name of the "*Prince of Liars.*" Modern research has established Pinto's character for veracity.

5272 POLACK's Manners of the New Zealanders, 2 vols. 8vo. *maps and cuts, cl.* 5s 1840
5273 PORTER'S (Sir R. Ker) Travels in Georgia, Persia, Armenia, Ancient Babylonia, &c. during the years 1817 to 1820, 2 stout vols. 4to. *maps, and 75 plates of* ANTIQUITIES, *those of* COSTUME *coloured*, (pub. at £9. 9s) *hf. calf*, 36s 1821

Copies fetched, 1857, Berry's, hf. bd. £3. 6s; 1859, D. Turner's, bds £2. 10s.

"Few persons combine so many qualifications for a traveller as Sir Robert Kerr Porter, who is an elegant scholar, an accomplished gentleman, a skilful artist, an intelligent observer, and an agreeable writer. To such an individual, the countries he has travelled over presented a field of incomparable richness and abundance: and as he gleaned copiously—yet with great discrimination—he has produced one of the most valuable and interesting works of the day. No one is more competent than he to the task of ascertaining and making us acquainted with the antiquities, manners, and customs of the nations among whom he journeys, and great reliance may be placed both on his judgment and integrity."—*Lit. Chron.*

5274 POTTINGER's Travels in Beloochistan and Sinde, *map, bd.* 15s 1816
5275 PREVOST D'EXILES, Histoire Générale des Voyages, ou nouvelle collection de toutes les relations de Voyages par Mer et par Terre, publiées jusqu'à présent dans les différentes langues de toutes les Nations, 25 vols. 4to. *portrait and a profusion of plates, maps, &c. fine copy, hf. calf, uncut,* £4. 10s *La Haye*, 1747-1780

"Cette édition contient des augmentations considérables, et entre autres l'histoire des possessions Hollandaises dans l'Asie qui forme le 17e. vol.—BRUNET.

5276 PTOLEMY. Geographia Universalis complectens Ptolemaei Enarrationem, *Latine*, etc. sm. folio, 46 *large maps, vellum*, 15s *Basil.* 1540

See ante, under Classics.

5277 PURCHAS, his PILGRIMES, containing PEREGRINATIONS and DISCOVERIES in the remotest North and East parts of Asia, called Tartaria and Asia, by Englishmen and others, and Voyages and Discoveries of the North parts of the World, by land and sea, Polar Regions and North-West of America, also English Northern Navigation, and Discoveries of Greenland, the North-West Passage, and other Arctic Regions; Voyages and Travels to and in the New World, called America, and of the Seas and Islands adjacent, 5 vols. folio, FRONTISPIECE, with ALL THE MAPS *and curious old woodcuts, a* SPLENDID COMPLETE COPY *of this great and desirable work, old russia, gilt edges,* £66. 1625-26

Purchas says in his preface, that he has incorporated the substance of more than twelve hundred writers of voyages and travels. "His work is not only valuable for the various instruction and amusement contained in it, but is also very estimable on a national, and I may add, a religious account'—*Granger.*

"We owe to the zeal and vast erudition of this laborious man, one of the most celebrated collections of voyages which have ever appeared,—valuable alike for the abundance of its materials and its importance in the history of early discoveries, especially those of the English." *Biog. Univers.*

5278 RAFFLES'S (Sir Stamford) History of Java, 2 vols. roy. 4to. *large map and 65 plates, some* COLOURED (pub. at £6. 6s) *bds.* 32s 1817
5279 —— the same, LARGE PAPER, 2 vols. roy. 4to. *map and plates*, (pub. at £8. 8s in bds.) *calf extra*, £4. 4s 1817

Priced, John Bohn, Large Paper, bds. £9. 9s; 1837, Payne and Foss, mor. £12. 12s; 1837, Arch, bds. £7. 17s 6d; 1840, Payne and Foss, L. P. mor. £12. 12s.

A literary master-piece, giving an account of the Natural History, Ethnology, Costume, Manners, Customs, Implements of Arts and Warfare, Mythology, Literature, Poetry, Astronomy, Antiquities and History of Java and the Javanese. This original and best edition has got the Comparative Vocabulary, wanting in the other editions, of the following Languages, viz. English, Maylayu, Javan, (Jawa, Basa Krama, Sunda,) Madurese, (Madura Sumenap,) Bali, Lampung. "An important work, being, on the whole, the best account of this fine Island that has yet appeared. It was principally compiled from materials supplied by the officers subordinate to the author, during the five years of his intelligent and successful government of the island."—MACCULLOCH.

5280 RAFFLES's (Lady) Life and services of Sir T. S. Raffles, in Java, Bencoolen, etc. Commerce and Resources of the Eastern Archipelago, 4to. *maps and plates, bds. or hf. russia*, 12s 1830

GEOGRAPHY, VOYAGES, TRAVELS. 279

5281 RAMUSIO, Primo volume, e seconda edizione delle Navigationi et Viaggi, 3 *woodcut maps, and several woodcuts*, 1554; Secondo volume, 1574; Terzo volume, 1556; 3 vols. folio, *vellum*, £6. *Venetia, Giunti*, 1554-74-76

Best edition of Vol. I. being equally good as that of 1563, and best edition of Vol. II. according to collation, the edition of 1574 (the above) containing 97 pages more than that cited by Brunet as the best.

Collation:—Vol. I. 1554, Title, 1 leaf; Dedication, etc. 3 leaves; Indice, 34 leaves, 3 large woodcut maps, on the back of the first of which is printed note "a gli studiosi di Geographia," not in any other edition; and the leaves to 436.

Vol. II. 1574, Title, with Nomi de gli autori on the back, 1 leaf; Di M. G. B. Ramusio prefatione, 4 leaves; Espositione, 9 leaves; Ramusio alli lettori, 1 leaf; Indice, 12 leaves; Prohemio, 1 leaf; Viaggi, leaves 2 to 248— containing "Commentarii della Moscovia et della Russia per Sigismondo libero Barone in Herberstain," 57 pages, and Commentarii del Viaggio in Persia di M. C. Teno, 40 pages, which pieces are not contained in the edition of 1559. This is a better edition of Vol. 2 than that of 1559.

Vol. III. 1556, Title, 1 leaf; discorso, 4 leaves; Nomi degli autori, 1 leaf; Indice, 34 leaves; and leaves 1 to 456 with 7 large woodcut maps, the last of which is a curious map of North and South America.

5282 RAMUSIO, Primo volume, e terza editione delle Navigationi et Viaggi, 3 *engraved maps, and numerous woodcuts*, 1563; Secondo volume, 1574; Terzo volume, *several very curious woodcut maps included in the paging*, 1565; 3 vols. in 2, stout folio, *old stamped calf*, £6. *Venetia, Giunti*, 1563-74-65

The best edition of Vols. 1 and 3, according to Brunet. The enthusiastic collector should make one copy of these two, and he would then obtain the best edition of every volume.

"Ramusio was the most learned compiler of the age."—*Santarem*.

For the contents of this valuable collection see Gamba, Testi di Lingua, Ven. 1839, 8vo. No. 2751.

"C'est une Collection précieuse, peu vantée par les libraires, peu récherchée par les amateurs des beaux livres, parce qu'elle n'est pas ornée d'estampes, mais seulement de gravures en bois qui n'ont rien d'agréable: elle est estimée par les savans, et regardée encore aujourd'hui par les géographes comme un des recueils les plus importans. Ramusio avoit, soit à raison des voyages qu'il avoit faits lui même, soit a raison de ses grandes connoissances dans l'histoire, la geographie, les langues, soit enfin à raison des correspondances multipliées avec ces personnes qui pouvoient être de quelque utilité à son entreprise, toutes les facilités nécessaires pour former une excellente collection."—*Camus*.

"Ramusio recueillit dès le 5me. siècle les relations qui pouvaient faire connaître les côtes de l'Afrique, une partie de l'Asie et les découvertes faites jusqu'alors dans le *Nouveau Monde*; il enrichit ces voyages de savantes prefaces, et composa des dissertations importantes."—Daru.

"Ramusio's collection of Voyages and Travels, the most perfect work of that nature extant in any language whatsoever; containing all the discoveries to the East, West, North and South; with full descriptions of all the countries discovered; judiciously compiled, and free from that great mass of useless matter, which swells our English Hackluyt and Purchas; much more complete and full than the Latin De Bry, and, in fine, the noblest work of this nature."—Locke.

5283 RAYNAL, Histoire philosophique et politique des établissemens des Européens dans les deux Indes, 5 vols. 4to. 49 *maps, calf*, 15s *Génève*, 1783

Priced, 1829, £2. 10s; 1831, £4. 4s; Fetched, M. Townshend's, £7. 17s. 6d; Fonthill, £1. 13s.

5284 RECUEIL des Voyages de la Compagnie des Indes Orientales, 12 vols. 18mo. *many maps, plates, and charts, old Dutch calf, fine copy*, 18s *Rouen*, 1725

Voyages to all parts of the world. Previously marked £3. 13s 6d.

5285 RENAUDOT, Ancient Accounts of India and China, by two Mohammedan Travellers, 9th Century, translated from the Arabic, 8vo. *fine copy, in russia extra*, 18s 1733

5285*RENNEFORT (Souchu de) Memoires pour servir à l'Histoire des Indes Orientales, sm. 4to. *fine copy, in calf extra, gilt edges, Langles' copy, with his Autograph*, rare, £2. 2s *Paris*, 1688

5286 REPETTI Dizionario Geographico, Fisico, Storico, della Toscana, contenente la descrizione di tutti i luoghi del granducato, ducato di Lucca, Garfagnana e Lunigiana, 5 vols.—Supplemento, Appendice, Introduzione, 1 vol.—together 6 vols. 8vo. *maps, sd.* £2. *Firenze*, 1833-46

Ouvrage très intéressant, et très estimé.

5287 REUSNERUS de Italiâ, 2 pts. 12mo. *red morocco, gilt edges*, 7s 6d *Argent*. 1585

5288 RICCIOLII Geographia et Hydrographia reformata, folio, *with two copious Indexes (both ways) of Latin Ancient Names of Towns, and their Modern renderings, old calf*, 20s *Bonon*. 1661

One of the first works on Physical Geography, based upon profound observations and the reports of early Navigators.

5289 RITTER'S Erdkunde im Verhältniss zur Natur und zur Geschichte des Menschen, oder allgemeine vergleichende Geographie, Vols. I.-XIX.—Ideler's Namen und Sach-Verzeichniss zu Band. II.-XI, 2 vols.; together 21 vols. in 22, 8vo. (*pub. at about Twenty Guineas*) 18 *vols. calf extra, and 4 sewed, with royal folio atlas of Palestine and Sinai, in* 15 *maps. sd.* £12. *Berlin*, 1822-59

Vols. I.-XVIII. with the Index, 2 vols. priced, 1856, £12. 10s; Vols. I.-XVII. 1857, £13.

Ritter's Erdkunde is unrivalled in Geographical literature; indispensable to every public library;—both the Geography and History of the East are related in this learned work with the utmost care.

5290 ——— the same, Vols. I-XII, with Ideler's Index to Vols. II-VI (Ost. Asien), thus divided: Erdkunde von Afrika, 1 vol.; Asien, Vols. I.-VIII, pt. 1, in 11 vols.: Ideler's Index to Ost-Asien, 1 vol.; together 13 vols. sm. 8vo. *twelve hf. bound, one sd.* £3. 10s *Berlin*, 1822-46

5291 ROBIQUET, Recherches historiques et statistiques sur la Corse, impl. 8vo. *plates no atlas, hf. morocco*, 7s 6d *Paris*, (1835

5292 RUSSELL's Natural History of Aleppo, 2 vols. 4to. *hf. bd.* 10s 1794
5293 SACK's Reise nach Surinam, 2 vols. in 1, 4to. *plates, hf. morocco,* 5s 1818
5294 SAGARRA, Historia de la España Transfretana (Fez, Morocco), 2 vols. sm. 8vo. *maps, calf,* 7s *Barcelona,* (1820)
5295 SALT's Voyage to Abyssinia, and Travels into the Interior of that country, 1809-10, with Vocabularies of the Languages, roy. 4to. *map and engravings, bds.* 8s; or *hf. calf,* 10s 1814
5296 ———— the same, Large Paper, impl. 4to. *bds.* 12s 1814
5297 SAMARANG VOYAGE. BELCHER's Narrative of the Voyage of the SAMARANG, 1843-46, with vocabulary of the languages of the Eastern Archipelago, 2 vols. 8vo. *tinted lithographs, hf. russia, gilt,* 15s 1848
5298 SALMON's Present state of Africa, sm. 8vo. *plates, calf,* 7s 1739
5299 SANTAREM, Essai sur l'Histoire de la Cosmographie et de la Cartographie au Moyen-Age, 3 vols. 8vo. *woodcuts, hf. calf, uncut, rare,* £2. 5s *Paris,* 1849-50
5299*SAN ROMAN, Historia General de la India Oriental de Portugal, sm. folio, *title and last page of text injured, no table at end,* EXTREMELY SCARCE *when complete,* 36s *Valladolid,* 1603
   I sold a complete copy in 1861 for £10. "Cet auteur était natif de Valencia et religieux de l'ordre de Saint Benoit."—*Ternaux.*
5300 SCHMIDT (Ulrich von Straubingen) Warhafftige Beschreibunge aller Schiffarten, auch viler unbekanten erfundnen Landtschafften, folio, *some leaves foxed a few of the last slightly wormed, bds.* 28s *Frankf. Feirabend,* 1567
   A rare work, containing five early Portuguese voyages to India, etc. described for the first time by Schmidt; not mentioned by Brunet, Ebert, Camus, nor Boucher de la Richarderie.
5301 SCHOUTEN (Wouter) Oost Indische Voyagie, Zee- en Landt-Gevechten tegen de Portugeesen en Makasseren, etc. 4to. LARGE PAPER, *superb impressions of the numerous fine plates,* PROOFS BEFORE LETTERS, *fine copy in old calf,* 18s *Amst.* 1676
5302 SCHWEIGGER, Reiss Beschreibung nach Constantinopel und Jerusalem, sq. 8vo. *portrait and numerous woodcuts, bds.* 7s *Nürnberg,* 1639
5303 SCORESBY'S (W.) Account of the ARCTIC REGIONS, with a history and description of the Northern Whale Fishery, 2 vols. 8vo. *map and plates, hf. bd. scarce,* 25s.; or *russia, gilt edges,* £2. 2s 1820
5304 SHAW's Barbary and the Levant, 4to. *maps and plates, calf,* 7s 1757
5305 SMITH'S Dictionary of Greek and Roman Geography, 2 stout vols. 8vo. (pub. at £4.), *cloth,* £3. 1856-57
5306 STEPHENS' History of South Australia, 8vo. *maps, cloth,* 6s 1839
5307 STRABON, GÉOGRAPHIE, traduite du Grec en Français par M. M. de la Porte du Theil, Coray et Letronne, avec des Notes et une Introduction par Gosselin, 5 vols. atlas 4to. LARGE VELLUM PAPER, *half red morocco, uncut, by Koehler, very rare,* £12. 10s *Paris,* 1805-19
5308 STRAHLENBERG, das Nord und Oestliche Theil von Europa und Asia, das Russische Reich, Sibirien und die grosse Tartarey, sm. 4to. *with the scarce Polyglott Table, numerous maps and plates, vellum, fine copy,* 10s *Stockholm,* 1730
5309 TAVERNIER (J. B.) Ses Six Voyages, en Turquie, en Perse et aux Indes, 2 vols. sm. 4to. *numerous plates, including many engravings of the* COINS *current in Turkey, Persia, India, Siam, Japan,* etc. *title injured, calf,* 10s *Paris,* 1676
5309*———— the same, nouvelle edition augmentée, 3 vols. small 4to. *plates, old calf gilt,* 28s *Paris,* 1682-79
   Copies fetched, 3 vols. 4to. Amst. 1678-9, 1855, Bernal's, mor. £2. 9s; 1857, Berry's copy, with the "Relation du Serail, 1 vol. 1679, mor. £2. 1s.
5310 TCHIHATCHEFF, Voyage scientifique dans l'Altaï Oriental et les parties adjacentes de la frontière de Chine, fait par ordre de l'empereur de Russie, *with Atlas of* 29 *plates of Views, Fossils,* etc. forming 4 vols. impl. 4to. *hf. bd.* £3. 15s *Paris,* 1845
   "Magnifique ouvrage, qui révele l'immense étendue du terrain paléozoique dans cette partie de l'Asie, en même temps que sa pauvreté sous le rapport des restes organiques."—*Murchison's Russia, Vol. II. pr. X.*
5311 TCHIHATCHEFF, Asie Mineure, description physique statistique, et archéologique de cette contrée, 2 parts in 2 vols. impl. 8vo. of text, *numerous plates, one vol. calf gilt, the other sd. with impl. 4to. Atlas of* 28 *fine plates, including a photographic portrait of the author, and large Map, in two cases,* £2. 5s *Paris,* 1853-56
5312 TEIXEIRA (Pedro) Relaciones d'el origen, descendencia, y succession de los Reyes de Persia, y de Harmuz, y de un Viage hecho donde la India Oriental hasta Italia por tierra, *old calf,* 5s; *fine copy in vellum,* 12s; *red morocco,* 20s *Amberes,* 1610
   At page 129 commences a dissertation on hawking, and on the hunting of the wild animals in the East.

GEOGRAPHY, VOYAGES, TRAVELS. 281

5313 TEMMINCK, Coup d'Oeil général sur les possessions Néerlandaises dans l'Inde Archipélagique, 3 vols. 8vo. *hf. russia*, 18s *Leide*, 1846-49

5314 THEVENOT (Melch.) RELATIONS DE DIVERS VOYAGES curieux, qui n'ont point esté publiées, traduites ou tirées des originaux Français, Espagnols, Allemands, Portuguais, Anglois, Hollandois, Persans, Arabes, etc. nouvelle edition augmentée, 2 vols. folio, *numerous maps, plates, and cuts, very fine copy in old calf gilt*, £5. *Paris*, 1696
This copy has the Spanish fragments in the second volume completed by modern impression like that of the Grenville library in the British Museum.

5315 THUNBERG's Travels in Europe, Africa, and Asia, 1770-79, 4 vols. sm. 8vo. *plates, largely treating of Japan, calf*, 7s 6d 1795-96

5316 TOURNEFORT, Relation d'un Voyage du Levant, contenant l'histoire ancienne et moderne des iles de l'Archipel, de Constantinople, de la mer Noire, de l'Arménie, de la Géorgie des frontières de Perse et de l'Asie-Mineure, 2 vols. 4to. *many plates, calf,* 20s ; *a fine copy, in old French calf gilt, rare*, 30s *Paris*, 1717
Priced, 1830, £2. 2s; 1840-8, £1. 16s; fetched, Stanley's, mor. £6. 6s; White Knight's, £2. 15s.

5317 —— the same, 3 vols. 8vo. *plates, bds. uncut*, 7s 6d *Lyon*, 1717

5318 TOURNEFORT's Voyage into the Levant, 3 vols. 8vo. *maps and plates, original calf gilt, marbled edges, fine copy*, 16s 1741
Stevenson pronounces Tournefort's voyage "rich and valuable in the rare junction of antiquarian and botanical knowledge."

5319 TURNERELLI's Russia on the Borders of Asia : Kazan, 2 vols. sm. 8vo. (pub. at 21s) *cloth*, 7s 6d 1854

5320 UNIENVILLE, Statistique de l'Ile Maurice et ses dépendances, avec une notice sur Madagascar, 3 vols. 8vo. *cloth*, 15s *Paris*, 1838

5320*URRETA, Historia Ecclesiastica, politica, natural, y moral de la ETIOPIA, monarchia de Preste Juan, sq. 8vo. *bds. cut close, rare*, 7s 6d *Valencia*, 1610

5321 VALENTYN, Oud en Nieuw Oost-Indien, &c. A Collection of Voyages to the East Indies, Japan, Moluccas, many Islands in the Eastern Seas, the Cape, etc. *in Dutch*, 5 vols. folio, *numerous engravings of Natural History, Views, Portraits, beautiful impressions, calf neat*, £3. 10s *Dordrecht en Amst.* 1724-26
The author was above twenty years in India, and has given a very complete history, both natural and civil, of that country. Copies are extremely scarce in this country, and noticed by the editor of the REPERTORIUM BIBLIOGRAPHICUM as among the remarkable books in the possession of the Right Hon. T. Grenville and Roger Wilbraham, Esq.; Hope's copy fetched £13. 2s, and Pinkerton's £15. 15s.

5322 VALENTIA'S (Lord) Voyages and Travels to India, the Red Sea, Abyssinia and Egypt, from 1802 to 1806, 3 vols. impl. 4to. LARGE PAPER, PROOF IMPRESSIONS *of the* 69 *fine plates by Angus, Landseer, Warren, &c. from drawings by H. Salt, superbly bound in citron morocco super extra, joints, silk linings, gilt edges*, £4 4s 1809
Only a few copies were printed on Large Paper. The present copy cost its former proprietor £16. 16s.

5323 VERA (Ger. di) Tre Navigationi fatte dagli Olandesi e Zelandesi nella Norvegia, Muscovia, e Tartaria verso il Catai, e Regno de' Sini ; la Nuova Zembla et la Groenlandia, tradotte da Giunio, sq. 8vo. *maps and curious engravings, one of which is worked in red ink, some leaves stained at the end, bds.* 15s *Venet.* 1599

5324 VERDUN DE LA CRENNE, BORDA et PINGRÉ, Voyage fait par ordre du Roi en 1771 et 1772 en divers partie de l'Europe, de l'Afrique et de l'AMERIQUE, pour verifier l'utilité de plusieurs Instrumens servant à determiner la Latitude et la Longitude, 2 vols. sm. 4to. *maps and plates, a beautiful copy in old red* MOROCCO, *gilt edges, arms on sides*, £3. *Paris*, 1778

5325 VIERA y CLAVIJO (Jos de) Noticias de la Historia General de las Islas de CANARIA, 4 vols. sm. 4to. *map and portrait of Bethencourt, Spanish binding, the fourth, which is rarely met with not uniform*, £3. 10s *Madrid*, 1772-83

5326 —— the same, LARGE PAPER, 3 vols. 4to. *map and portait, calf,* 27s 1772-76
"Ce livre est recommandable tant par son mérite historique, que parce qu'il fut écrit par un des hommes qui surent le mieux manier la langue castillane à la fin du siècle dernier. L'histoire des Canaries fut imprimée, a un petit nombre d'exemplaires, tous destinés à des presents; ce qui explique la grande difficulté qu'il y a aujourd'hui à en rencontrer des exemplaires."—SALVA.

5327 WALCKENAER, Recherches sur l'interieur de l'Afrique Sept. 8vo. *map, half calf* 5s 1821

5328 WENTWORTH's New South Wales, 8vo. *hf. bd.* 5s 1820

5329 WERKEN van het KONINKLIJK INSTITUUT voor Taal-, Land- en Volkenkunde van Nederlandsch-Indië : Müller (S.) Reizen in den Indischen Archipel. 2 vols. *maps*, 1857—Vries (Mat. Gerr.) Reize naar Japan in 1643, 1858—Adji-Säkä door Winter, *in Javanese*, with a Javanese Dictionary, by Roorda, 1557— together 4 vols. 8vo. *maps, bds.* 18s *Amst.* 1857-58

5330 WILLIAMS' Missionary Enterprises in the South Sea Islands, 8vo. *plate and cuts*, cloth, 5s 1837

5331 WILSON's Pelew Islands, by Keate, with Vocabulary, roy. 4to. *portrait, map, and* 15 *plates, calf neat,* 7s 1788

5332 —— the same, with Hockin's Supplement, 2 vols. roy. 4to. *map and plates*, bd. 10s 1788-1803

5333 ZIMMERMANN, Analyse der Ritter's Karte von Vorder- Inner- Asien; Kriegstheater Russlands; Lauf des Oxus, in 1 vol. 4to. *cloth*, 7s 6d Berl. 1840-5

5334 ZURLA (Cardinal) di Marco Polo e degli altri Viaggiatori, 2 vols. impl. 4to. *folding plates, vellum gilt,* 12s Venezia, 1818-9

ATLASES AND MAPS.

5335 APIANI CHOROGRAPHIA BAVARIAE: Beschreibung Obern und Nidern Bayern, oblong folio, 25 *maps engraved on copper by P. Weiner, surrounded by Arabesques and Coats of Arms,* PRINTED UPON VELLUM, *interleaved with a* MS. *Contents of each map, very rare if not* UNIQUE *in this state, hf. vel.* £8. 8s ?1550

5336 ARROWSMITH (John) London Atlas of Universal Geography, impl. folio, 95 *large folding maps, the outlines coloured (pub. at* £17. 17s) *hf. bd.* £7. 10s 1842
   There exists no set of Maps more carefully executed than those in Arrowsmith's Atlas.

5337 BLAEU. LE GRAND ATLAS, ou Cosmographie Blauiane, en la quelle est exactemente descrite la Terre, la Mer et le Ciel, 12 vols. impl. folio, *with upwards of a thousand large Maps carefully coloured, many of the maps embellished with illuminated Coats of Arms; the Text forming the most complete body of Geography, political and natural, of the period, very fine copy in gilt vellum, gilt edges.* £10. 10s Amsterdam, 1667

Best edition, that with French text. "On y donne les généalogies des familles les plus illustres et leurs faits historiques, décrits plus amplement que dans l'edition latine."—BRUNET.

CONTENTS.
Vol. I. Europe: The Arctic Regions, Norway, Denmark, Sleswic.
„ II. Sweden, Russia, Poland, Eastern Europe, Greece.
„ III. Germany.
„ IV. Belgium.
„ V. England, contains maps of all the English counties, by Speed and others, surrounded by Portraits of old English Kings, and numerous Coats of Arms.
„ VI. Scotland and Ireland, engraved by Punt.—This is the oldest set of Maps on Scotland.
„ VII. VIII. France, divided into Provinces, and a complete history of every Province, with an account of all the great families settled there.
   The coats of arms of every family are either represented on the maps or described in the text. To the 8th volume is added Savoy and Switzerland.
„ IX. Italy.
„ X. Spain, Africa, and the adjoining Islands.
„ XI. Asia, including China.
„ XII. America, North and South, with a complete digest of the early travels of the Spaniards and English. The map of Bermuda is very curious, giving the names of the English shareholders, amongst whom the native tribes were divided.

This grand Atlas, though very common formerly, is now disappearing from the market. A public library should secure this handsome copy. The maps being all on a very large and comprensive scale, and taken from early and authentic surveys, have in several instances been found important in proving sites of old monuments and landmarks in the courts of law.

5338 MAGINI Geographia tum Vetus tum Nova, cum Ptolomaei ennarationibus, etc. 2 vols. in 1, stout sq. 8vo. 64 *maps, including America, old calf,* 6s Arnhemii 1617

5339 SANSON, l'Europe, l'Asie, l'Afrique, et l'Amérique, en plusieurs Cartes et en divers Traittés, 4 parts in 1 vol. sq. 8vo. *about* 60 *maps, hf. vellum,* 20s Paris, 1683

5340 SANTAREM'S GREAT ATLAS of EARLY PORTOLANI and NAVIGATION CHARTS.—Mr. Q. has some approximately perfect copies nearly ready for sale.

5341 SOCIETY ATLAS. MAPS OF THE SOCIETY FOR THE DIFFUSION OF USEFUL KNOWLEDGE, 2 vols. atlas folio, 218 *large coloured maps, including those of the Stars, with Indexes, the* BEST *General Atlas, hf. russia,* £3. 3s 1844

5342 SPRUNER'S Atlas Antiquus, folio, 27 *large coloured maps, with* 64 *minor maps in the margins, cloth,* 20s Gothae, 1855

5343 STIELER'S PHYSICAL AND POLITICAL ATLAS: Hand-Atlas, über alle Theile der Erde und über das Weltgebäude, SIXTH EDITION, *with* 83 *excellent coloured maps, including Title and Star Maps,* folio (pub. at £2. 2s) *hf. russia,* 24s 1554
   Stieler's Atlas enjoys great reputation for correctness in Germany.

5344 VAN DER MAELEN, ETABLISSEMENT GEOGRAPHIQUE DE BRUXELLES. ATLAS DE L'EUROPE, dessiné par Perkin, gravé sous la direction de Doms, par Charles et Bulen, 3 vols. atlas folio, 165 *sheets on a scale of* $\frac{1}{600,000}$ *with Tableaux of Political Divisions, hf. russia,* £4. 4s Bruxelles, 1833

ATLASES AND MAPS. 283

5345 WELLS (E.) New Set of Maps of ancient and present Geography, impl. folio,
61 *maps, engraved by Burghers and others, rough calf,* 15s   Oxford, 1702
The last plate is entitled "the considerable Plantations of the English in America."

5346 **Africa.** Wyld's Map of Africa, in 6 parts, folded into an imp. 8vo. case, 7s 6d   1851

5347 **America.** POPPLE'S Map of the British Empire in America, with the adjacent French and Spanish Settlements, roy. folio, 21 *large maps, views of New York, Quebec, Mexico, the Niagara, etc. hf. bd. rare,* 36s   1733
"The above maps seem to have been laid down with great accuracy, and to show the position of the provinces more truly than any yet extant."—EDMUND HALLEY.

5348 **Austria.** Das Oesterreichische Kaiserthum, von Fallon gezeichnet, *in* 9 *divisions, each a single sheet, folio on canvas, in a case,* 5s   1822

5349 **Brasil** and Coasts of South America. ROUSSIN, le Pilote du Brésil, ou Description des Côtes de l'Amerique Méridionale, atlas folio, 15 *charts on a large scale, bds. presentation copy to Admiral Otway,* 12s   Paris, 1826

5350 **ENGLAND.** SPEEDE'S England fully described in a compleat sett of Mapps of the County's of England and Wales, with their Islands, roy. folio, *engraved title page and* 58 *large maps, Coats of Arms of the Nobility and Gentry, Plans of the towns, and views, upon the margins,* £2. 5s   1610

5351 SAXTON'S (C.) Shires of England and Wales, being the best and original maps, with additions and corrections by P. Lea, roy. folio, 50 *large coloured maps, hf. calf neat,* £2. 10s   London, Lea, ca. 1690
Very curious on account of the fixing of Old Localities, which have since become unknown. The maps are embellished with numerous Coats of Arms of the County Gentry, and with Plans of the County Towns.

5352 OGILBY's Britannia Depicta, improved by John Owen and Eman. Bower, sq. 8vo. 272 pp. *entirely engraved, containing Maps and plans of the various Roads and Towns through England and Wales, with the Coats of Arms of all the Towns, calf,* 7s 6d   1724

5353 **London.** HORWOOD'S Plan of London and Westminster, Southwark and Parts adjoining, shewing every House, 32 *sheets,* 27¾ in. by 22¼, £3.   1792-99
This beautiful map is engraved by Ash and Spear, and is dedicated by Horwood to the Trustees and Directors of the Phœnix Life Office.

5354 **Shropshire,** a carefully made *coloured* map of Shropshire, on 9 sheets, exhibiting all towns, villages, and hamlets, folio, *hf. bd.* 15s   Llanymynech, 1808

5355 TELFORD's Charts and Plans referred to in the Report relative to the communication between England and Ireland by the N. W. of Scotland, atlas folio, 16 *plates,* 10s   1809

5356 **Yorkshire.** GREENWOOD'S Map, on the Basis of Triangles by Mudge and Colby, 9 sheets, each 32 in. by 26, *an excellent map shewing the Woods, Plantations, Mines, etc.* (pub. at £5. 5s), *with the autograph of Sir M. M. Sykes,* 36s
Leeds and Wakefield, 1817

5357 **Hanover,** Manuscript Map of part of: Carte von Amt-Meppen aufgenommen von Colson, gezeichnet von Russell, 58 in. by 47, *mounted on canvas, with the stamp of the Duke of Cumberland,* 12s   Hasel. 1809

5358 **Holland,** Topographical Atlas of. 'T Hooge Heem Raed-Schap van Rhynland, atlas folio, 14 *Maps on a large scale, beautifully executed in gold and colours, also* 8 *additional maps, calf gilt,* 12s   1740

5359 **Ireland.** HISTORICAL ATLAS. ATLAS OF ULSTER, executed about the year 1609, in 31 Maps, each on a sheet measuring 28 in. by 22, *plain, an extremely important series of Maps,* 31s   1862

5360 ———— the same, *very carefully coloured,* £7. 8s   1862
1. A Generalle Description of Ulster; 2. Tyrone; 3. Tyrconnelle; 4. and 5. Baronie of Knockninnie; 6. Clancally; 7. Clinawley; 8. Maghery Steffanah; 9. Mahhery Roy; 10. Lurgh and Cole Mackernan; 11 and 12. Donganon; 13 and 14. Loghinisholin; 15 and 16. Strabane; 17. Omey; 18. Clogher; 19. Loghtie; 20. Tollagh Garvie; 21. Clanchy; 22. Castle Rahin; 23. Clonmahowne; 24. Tollachconco; 25. Tollaghaghe; 26. Orier; 27. Fues; 28 and 29. Oneilan; 30. Ardmagh; 31. Toghrany. These maps possess much interest, as exhibiting the titles from the Crown of the landed proprietary of the present day in Ulster.

5361 VIEW of the SIEGE OF ENNISKILLEN, 1592, facsimile from the original "made and dun by John Thomas, Solder," *a very curious plan on a large sheet, plain,* 2s 6d; *or coloured,* 11s   1862

5362 NOWELL (Dean) Two Ancient Maps of Ireland (ca. 1566) facsimiled from the original in the British Museum, *on a single sheet,* 1s 6d   1862

5363 ———— Copy of portion of an Ancient MS. in the B. M., *being the text to the above* 2 *Maps,* folio, 20 *pp. lithographed, sd.* 1s   1862

☞ The above **Maps and text, bound together in 1 vol. large folio,** *hf. calf, the maps plain,* £2. 16s; or, *the maps coloured,* £9.   1862

5364 BEAUFORT's Map of Ireland, 1792, 2 *sheets*—Rocque's Plan of Dublin; Survey of the City and Suburbs, 1756, 4 *sheets*—Gibson's Bay and Harbour of Dublin, 1756—D'Anville Orbis Vet., Orbis Romanus, 2 *sheets*—Gallia Ant.; Italia Ant.; Græcia Ant.; Asia; India; and several others, *in all 32 curious and old maps, several on many sheets mounted, in an atlas folio volume, hf. bd.* 16s 1788-1792
5365 **Dublin.** ROCQUE's Atlas of the City, Bay, and Environs of Dublin, with improvements by Scale, 4 large sheets, 30 inches by 22, 10s 1773
5366 IRISH RAILWAY Commission, 6 *maps*, showing the Railway Lines, Density of the Population, etc. impl. folio, *hf. russia*, 7s 1838
5367 **Kildare.** TAYLOR's Map of Kildare, in the County of Kildare, in 6 sheets, 34 inches by 22, 7s 6d 1783
5368 **Japan.** MAP of Japan, Kurile, part of China, Lake Baikal, etc. 4 sheets, in an 8vo. case, 7s 1840
5369 **Malta and Goza.** PALMEUS, Plan de la Ville de Malte, 40 inches by 25, *Paris*, 1757; Palmeus' Map of the Sovereign Principality of Malta and Goza, 42 in. by 23, *Lond.* 1799—2 large sheets, 7s 6d 1757-99
5370 **Silesia.** HOMANN, Atlas Silesiae, id est Ducatus Silesiae, atlas folio, 20 *large folding maps, with picturesque scenes on the margins, title and index mended, hf. bd.* 24s *Norimb.* 1750
5371 **Sweden, Norway,** and **Denmark.** FORSELL, Karta of Sverige och Norrige (och Danmark) eller det fordna sao kallade Skandinavien, 8 parts, each 35 inches by 24, *mounted on canvas, and folded into a stout wooden case, book-shape*, sm. folio, *morocco gilt,* £2. *Stockholm*, 1815-26
5372 **Turkey.** HELLERT, Nouvel Atlas physique, politique, et historique de l'Empire Ottoman, et des Etats limitrophes, avec commentaire par Heck et Plée, roy. folio, 39 *Maps and plans of Towns, Battles, Sieges, etc.* 12s *Par.* 1844

MAPS PUBLISHED by the Topographical and Statistical DEPARTMENT of the War Office.

Ordnance Survey of England and Wales:
5373 GENERAL MAP on the One-Inch Scale, in 110 sheets, £10. 17s 6d
The Counties sold separately at the rate of 6d per quarter sheet.
5374 COUNTY MAPS, on the Six-Inch Scale, published at per sheet from 2s 6d to 5s
5375 PARISH MAPS on the scale of $\frac{1}{2500}$, published at about 2s 6d per sheet
5376 SKELETON MAPS of LONDON and its environs, on the scale of one inch to a mile, 2s per sheet; six inches, at 1s; twelve inches, 1s; and five feet to a mile, at 1s
5377 MAPS OF TOWNS on the scales of 5 feet, 10 feet, $\frac{1}{500}$, and others, at 2s per sheet; also sold coloured

Ordnance Survey of Scotland:
5378 ONE INCH MAPS, published at 1s per sheet; the County and Parish Maps and Town Maps at the same rate as the English.

Ordnance Survey of Ireland:
5379 GENERAL Map, one inch to a mile, in 205 sheets, £5. 2s 6d
Each County separately published in outline at 6d per sheet.
5380 COUNTY Six Inch Maps, and Town Maps, at the same rate as the English and Scotch

EASTERN EUROPE.

Comprising books on the GEOGRAPHY, HISTORY, LANGUAGE *and* LITERATURE *of the Slavonic, and Hungarian, (including the Finnish, Esthonian, and Lettish) Races.*

5381 GUAGNINI (Al.) Sarmatiae Europeae descriptio, quae regnum Poloniae, Lituaniam, Russiam, Moscoviam, etc. complectitur, folio, *in the text a series of woodcut-portraits, also folding woodcut of an assembled council, size of two pages; separate table,* 'Gencalogia Regum Poloniae;' *calf,* £2. 10s *Spirae,* 1581
Not mentioned by Brunet or Ebert, nor have I traced copies sold by auction.
5382 JORDAN (J. C. de) De Originibus Slavicis, opus Chronologico-Geographico-Historicum, 4 parts or 2 vols. in 1, stout folio, *fine copy in the original stamped hogskin,* 32s *Vindob.* 1745
Priced, 1855, Tross, in Paris, 45 fr The fourth part being the "historical apparatus," comprises a valuable chapter "De Lingua Slavorum," wit comparative grammatical tables for all the Slavonic dialects.

5383 MICHEOVO (M. di, *Cracoviense*) Historia delle due Sarmatie, tradotta par Maggi, 16mo. *bds. rare*, 12s *Vinegia*, 1561

5384 ORBINI Rauseo (Mauro) Il Regno de gli Slavi detti Schiavoni, nella quale si vede l'Origine quasi di tutti i Popoli che furono della lingua Slava, con molte guerre che fecero; e i successi de' Rè in Dalmatia, Croatia, Bosnia, Servia, Rassia e Bulgaria, folio, *Coat-of-Arms and 2 etchings, fine copy in old calf*, 36s; or, *a very tall copy, the title not clean*, MOROCCO *extra, gt. edges*, £2. 2s *Paris*, 1601

5385 PEYSSONEL, Observations Historiques et Géographiques sur les peuples barbares qui ont habité les bords du Danube et du Pont-Euxin, 4to. *maps and plates, calf*, 10s *Paris*, 1765

5386 POTOCKI, Fragments Historiques et Géographiques sur la Scythie, la Samatie et les Slaves, Vols. I. (wanting pp. 1-48, of Book 17), II. and IV. with the Supplement, in 3 vols. sm. 4to. *no map, bds. extremely rare*, 12s *Brunsvic*, 1796

Klaproth's copy of the 4 vols. fetched 240 francs. Only a few copies were printed for private distribution.

5387 STRITTERI, Memoria Populorum, olim ad Danubium, Pontum Euxinum, Paludem Mœotidem, Caucasum, Mare Caspium, et inde magis ad Septemtriones incolentium (Gothorum, Vandalorum, Longobard. Hunn. etc.) e Scriptoribus Historiæ Byzantinæ erutæ et digestæ, accedit Index duplex, 4 vols. in 5, 4to. *sewed*, 25s *Petropoli*, 1771-79

Priced, 1857, Asher, Berlin, 4 vols. in 6, *sewed*, 65 francs; fetched by auction, 1857, Sotheby's, £4. 8s.
"Cet ouvrage, important pour l'histoire de la formation de tous les états du nord, a été imprimé aux frais de l'empereur de Russie. Il y a peu d'exemplaires en France."—*Techener.*
"All the passages of the Byzantine history which relate to the Barbarians, are compiled, methodised and transcribed, in a Latin version by the laborious Stritter, in his 'Memoriae, etc.'"—*Gibbon.*

5388 **Bosnia.** PERTUSIER, la Bosnie dans ses rapports avec l'Empire Ottoman, 8vo. *calf gilt*, 5s *Paris*, 1822

5389 **Bohemia.** PUBITSCHKA, Series Chronologica rerum Slavo-Bohemicarum, ab A.C. 490 ad 874, sm. 4to. *old calf gilt*, 6s *Viennae*, 1770

5390 SPROSTNOST KATOLICKA, to gest Pohadky Krestianske, (*the Roman Catholic Missal*), 18mo. black letter, *vellum, scarce*, 10s *Praze*, 1636

5391 **Carniola.** Glossarium Slavicum in supplementum ad primam partem Dictionarii Carniolici, sq. 8vo. *with the cognate words in various languages, bds.* 7s 6d *Viennae*, 1792

5392 **Dalmatia and Illyria.** APPENDINI, Notizie Istorico-Critiche sulle Antichita, Storia e Letteratura de' Ragusei, I. 4to. *plates, hf. cf.* 9s *Ragusa*, 1802

5393 FORTIS, Viaggio in Dalmazia, 2 vols. 4to. *plates, vellum*, 6s *Venezia*; 1774

5394 —— Travels into Dalmatia, with Observations on Cherso and Osero, 20 *plates, russia*, 8s 1778

5395 LUCIO, Historia di Dalmatia, et in particolare delle Città di Trav, Spalatro, e Sebenico, sm. 4to. *vellum*, 12s *Venet.* 1674

5396 MICALIA, Blago Jezika Slovinskoga: Thesaurus Linguae Illyricae, Illyrico-Italo-Latinum, stout 12mo. 863 *pp. double cols. calf neat*, 25s *Ancona*, 1649-51
With the "Grammatika Talianski, *Loretu*, 1649," prefixed.

5397 **Esthonia and Livonia.** HIÄRN's Ehst-, Lyf-, und Lett- laendische Geschichte, 4to. *bds.* 8s *Riga*, 1835

5398 HUPEL's (A. W.) Topographische Nachrichten von Lief und Ehstland, 3 vols. 8vo. *maps and plates, vellum*, 16s *Riga*, 1774-82

"The third volume is often wanting. The second volume contains a chapter on the Livonian Nobility, Vocabularies, etc.; the third contains a valuable Index of Lettish and Esthonian names.

5399 **Finland and Lapland.** GANANDER, Mythologia Fennica, eller Förklaring öfver de Nomina propria Deastrorum, Idolorum, Locorum, Virorum, etc. sm. 4to. *with extracts and translations from old Finnish Poems*, sm. 4to. *hf. bound, scarce*, 10s *Abo*, 1789

5400 KALEWALA, taikka Wanhoja Karjalan Runoja, suomen Kansan muinosista ajoista, 2 vols. 8vo. *sd.* 10s *Helsingissä*, 1835

5401 LEEMIUS, de Lapponibus Finmarchiæ, eorumque linguâ, vitâ et Religione pristinâ, cum notis Gunneri et Jessens, *Danice et Lat.* 2 vols. in 1, 4to. 99 *very curious plates, calf*, 30s *Kiöbenhavn*, 1767

5402 —— LEXICON LAPPONICUM bipartitum; Lapponico- danico-latinum et Danico-Latino-Lapponicum, cum Indice latino, thick sm. 4to. *hf. calf*, £5. *Nidrosiae*, 1768

Very rare; of the second volume nearly all the copies were consumed by fire. Collation of the above copy: Deel I. title, pp. 1-1610; Errata, 3 leaves; Deel II. pp. 1-512, Index latinus, a-vinea, therefore wanting a leaf or two, viz. vo-z.

5403 Rühs' Finland und seine Bewohner, 8vo. *map, cloth,* 5s *Leipzig,* 1809
   Bound up with Bartholdy, Krieg der Tyroler Landleute.
5404 SCHEFFER, Histoire de la Laponie, sa description, l'origine, les mœurs de ses habitans, leur Magie, etc. sm. 4to. *map and many plates, with a chapter of the Language, fine copy in old calf gilt,* 12s *Paris,* 1678
   The Fonthill copy fetched £2. 17s; Hibbert's, £1. 16s.
5405 **Hungary.** GYÖNGYÖSI Istvánnak Költemenyes Maradvanyi egybe-szedett Dugonics Andras, 2 vols. sm. 8vo. *portraits, fine copy in old green morocco, gilt edges,* 10s *Poson. es Pest.* 1796
5406 PALMA, Notitia Rerum Hungaricarum, 3 vols. sm. 8vo. *portrait and genealogical tables, calf,* 8s *Pestini,* 1785
5407 SESTINI, Viaggio per la Valachia, Transilvania, e Ungheria, sm. 8vo. *plates, sd.* 5s *Firenze,* 1815
5408 **Poland, Lithuania, Ruthenia.** BEAURAINS, Methode Pratique de lire le François, 12mo. *with reading lessons, Polish and French, coloured plates, bds.* 3s 6d *Breslau,* 1806
5409 CHODZKO, Tableau de la Pologne, par Malte-Brun, 2 vols. 8vo. *maps, calf neat,* 7s 6d *Paris,* 1830
5410 HERBURTI DE FULSTIN Chronica sive Historiae Polonicae descriptio, sm. 4to. *portrait of Sigismund, clean copy in the original oak bds. rare,* 21s *Basil.* (1571)
5411 KOJALOWICZ, Historia Lituana, de rebus ante susceptam Christianam religionem, et à conjunctione cum Poloniâ ad unionem dominiorum, Vol. I. *wanting title, Dantisc.* 1550; Vol. II. *Antv.* 1669; together 2 vols. sm. 4to. *vellum, very rare,* £3. 10s 1650-69
5412 ——— Historiae Lituanæ a conjunctione Magni Ducatus cum Poloniâ ad unionem eorum dominiorum libri VIII, sm. 4to. *old calf,* 36s *Antverpiae,* 1669
   This latter is the second and scarcer part of Kojalowicz' work on LITHUANIA, the first part having been printed at Dantzic in 1650. Vogt styles it "Liber egregius, et infrequens, quia nec uno loco nec eodem tempore prodiit; hinc Pars Posterior rarissime conspicitur."
5413 LELEWEL, Antiquités de Pologne, de Lituanie, et de Slavonie, No 1, impl. 8vo. 16 *pp. and* 7 *plates containing about* 120 *coins, scarce,* 10s *Paris,* 1842
5414 LENGNICH, Jus publicum regni Poloni, 2 vols. in 1, 12mo. *portrait of Frederick Augustus, calf,* 7s *Gedani,* 1742-46
5415 MIECHOW, CHRONICA POLONORUM, à prima propagatione Polonorum usque ad annum 1504, cum Jod. L. Decii SUPPLEMENTO, sm. folio, *numerous woodcuts, including some very fine portraits, the margins rather soiled, not a fine copy, very rare,* £4. 4s *Cracoviae, Hier. Victor,* 1521
5416 ——— Another copy, sm. folio, *wanting title and first leaf of text,* 30s 1521
   "Edition originale et fort rare de cette chronique. Il s'y trouve ordinairement réuni un ouvrage anonyme de Jod. L. Decius, contenant 'De vetustatibus Polonorum I, de Jagellonum familia II. de Sigismundi regis temporibus III.'"—BRUNET. I can trace the sale of no copy in England.
5417 NEUGEBAUER à Cadano, Historia Rerum Polonicarum concinnata et ad Sigismundum III. deducta, stout sm. 4to. *vellum, rare,* 20s *Hanoviae,* 1618
5418 NOWY TESTAMENT z Greckiego Jezyka na Polski wiernic przetlumaczony, 18mo. *engraved frontispieces, in the original broken morocco, gilt edges, rare,* 30s *Gdansku (Dantzic),* 1633
5419 OGERII (Caroli) Ephemerides, sive Iter Danicum, Suecicum, Polonicum; accedunt Borbonii Epistolæ ad Comitem Avauxium et Ogerii Poemata, sm. 8vo. *vellum, very rare,* 32s *Lut. Paris,* 1656
   "On y trouve, dit l'Abbé Goujet, des particularités curieuses.—Ogier accepta la place de Sécrétaire du Comte D'Avaux nommé ambassadeur près des cours du Nord."—BIOGRAPHIE UNIVERSELLE. "Relation bien faite et d'une grande exactitude; fort estimée dans le nord de l'Europe."—BRUNET.
5420 PIETROWSKI's Story of a Siberian Exile, sm. 8vo. (pub. at 7s 6d) *cloth,* 6s 1863
5421 PISTORII Polonicæ Historiæ Corpus: Polonicarum rerum Latini Scriptores quotquot extant, cum Genealogiis Regum Poloniæ, principumque Silesiæ, Ducum Massoviæ et Lithuaniæ, 3 vols. in 1, stout folio, *Genealogical Tables, a fine copy in the original stamped binding,* 36s *Basil.* 1582
5422 RANOTHOWICZ, Iasna Pochodnia Zycia Apostolskiego, Zywot Stanislawa Kazimierczyka *(Life of St. Stanislaus Casimir, Sec XIV.),* sq. 8vo. *portrait, vellum, gilt edges,* 20s *Krakowie,* 1660
5423 TRETER de Episcopatu et Episcopis Ecclesiæ Varmiensis, folio, *Arms of Polish Bishops, hf. bd.* 15s *Cracov.* 1685

5424 ZALUSKI Specimen Historiae Polonæ Criticae, sq. 8vo. *vellum*, 10s *Warsav*. 1735
5425 **Russia** (*including the Baltic Provinces*). BACMEISTER, Russische Bibliothek zur Kenntniss des gegenwärtigen Zustandes der Literatur in Russland, 11 vols. 12mo. (*complete, with the general Index*), *calf, rare*, 30s *Leipzig*, 1772-87
    A valuable Bibliography of Works published either in Russia, or relating to all parts of the Russian Empire.
5426 BEAUPLAN (Sieur de) Description d'Ukranie, qui sont plusieurs provinces de Pologne contenües depuis les Confins de la Moscovie, jusques à la Transilvanie, sm. 4to. *large folding map*, 2 *plates and engravings, vellum*, 18s *Rouen*, 1661
    Rare; I cannot trace any other copy as having occurred for sale.
5427 BIBLII, siretch Knig' Sphennago Pisania : the Old Testament, *in the Church Slavonic*, 4 vols. 8vo. *old red morocco, gilt edges*, 24s *Moskva*, 1778
5428 CARLISLE, Relation de trois Ambassades du Comte de Carlisle vers le Czar, les Rois de Suède, et de Dannemarc, 12mo. *vellum*, 7s 6d *Amst*. 1669
5429 ERDMANN, Beiträge zur Kenntniss der Innern von Russland, 3 vols. 8vo. *with maps and plates in* 2 8vo. *cases, hf. calf,* 12s *Riga, etc.* 1822-26
    This learned work contains many valuable Statistical Tables and Vocabularies.
5430 ESNEAUX (J.) Histoire philosophique et politique de Russie, 5 vols. 8vo. *calf gilt*, 12s *Paris*, 1828-30
5431 FALK (J. P.) Beyträge zur topographischen Kenntniss des Russischen Reichs, 3 vols. 4to. *with* 39 *plates, mostly of Natural History, sewed,* 7s ; or, *hf. calf,* 10s *St. Petersb*. 1785-86
    Vol. III. pp. 575-582 contains a Vocabulary in 4 Tartar Languages.
5432 GMELIN, Reise durch Russland, zur Untersuchung der drey Natur-Reiche, 4 vols. 4to. *about* 100 *plates, sd.* 7s *St. Petersb*. 1774-84
5433 HAMMER sur les Origines Russes, extraits de MSS. Orientaux, *Arabe* (*et Pers.*) *et Français*, 4to. *sd.* 10s *St. Petersb*. 1827
5434 HAXTHAUSEN (A. F. von) Etudes sur la Russie : la situation intérieure, la vie nationale, et les institutions rurales, Vols. I—III pt. 2, in 4 vols. 8vo. *woodcuts*, (pub. at 10½ *thalers*) *sd.* 16s *Hanovre*, 1847-53
5435 HERBERSTAIN. Comentari della Moscovia et parimente della Russia, composti per Sigismundo libero bar. in Herberstain, tradotti in lingua italiana ; religione delli Moscoviti, discrittione di tutto l'Imperio Moscovitico, e alcuni luoghi vicini. sm. 4to. *large woodcut map and* 6 *woodcuts, occupying each a page*, PALE MOROCCO, *gilt edges*, RARE, £2. 10s *Ven. Pedrezzano*, 1550
    This translation is extremely rare."—*Adelung's Herberstain.* 1818.
5436 —— Rerum Moscoviticarum Commentarii Sigismundi liberi Baronis in Herberstain, Neyperg, et Guettenhag, fol. *folding map, old calf gilt*, £2. *Basil.* 1551
    Contents:—Russiae et Moscoviae descriptio; De Religione; Chorographia; Itineraria in Moscoviam, etc. Bound up is, Machumetis et Successorum Vitae, 1550—Confutationes Legis Mahumeticae—Historiae de Saracenorum sive Turcarum origine. All circa, 1550.
5437 ADELUNG, Siegmund von Herberstein, seine Reisen in Russland, 8vo. *map*, 2 *portrs. hf. vellum,* 6s *St. Pet.* 1818
5438 HERBINII Religiosae Kijovienses Cryptae sive Kijovia subterranea in quibus Labyrinthus sub terra, 12mo. *folding plates, calf gilt, rare,* 15s *Jenac,* 1675
    A description of catacombs at KIEV, containing the remains of Russian primitive Christians.
5439 KARAMSIN (M.) Histoire de l'Empire de Russie, traduite par St. Thomas, Jauffret et Divoff, 11 vols. 8vo. *hf. calf,* 36s *Paris*, 1819-26
    Dr. Hawtrey's copy, 11 vols. fetched, 1853, £2. 12s.
    "Karamzin, a Russian historian of eminence, whose works were expressly excepted from the censorship by the late Emperor Alexander."—*Sir W. Singer.*
5440 LEDOVITCH, Kupetcheskii Sistema i Torgovyi Nauka : a History of Commerce, 2 vols. in 1, stout 4to. *hf. calf,* 10s *Moskva*, 1789
5441 MAYERBERG. Iter in Moschoviam, Augustini Baronis de Mayerberg et Caluuccii ab Imperatore Leopoldo ad Tzarem Alexium Mihalowicz, 1661, ablegatorum, cum Statutis Moschoviticis, sm. folio, *fine copy*, 30s *s. l. & a.* (? 1664)
    Priced, 1857, W. Adolf, Berlin, 18 thalers; fetched, 1855, Lord Stuart de Rothesay's, £1. 18s. "This narration of Baron von Mayerberg's embassy to Russia in 1661, was privately printed, and is of the greatest rarity. It is very interesting and after Herberstein's, the best account of Russia we have at an early period."—*Sir W. Singer.*
5442 MUELLER, Sammlung Russischer Geschichte, 9 vols. sm. 8vo. *Pedigrees, etc. hf. morocco,* 36s *St. Petersb*. 1732-64
5443 NATCHALNOE OUTCHENIE : Introduction to the Holy Scriptures, *in the Church Slavonic*, 12mo. *in the original calf, fine copy,* 24s *Moscow,* 1739
5444 NOVAGO ZAVÉTA : the New Testament *in the Church Slavonic*, stout sm. 4to. 46 *plates, original binding,* 24s *Moskva,* 1755

5445 PALLAS, Voyages en différentes Provinces de l'Empire de Russie et dans l'Asie Septentrionale, traduits de l'Allemand par Gauthier de la Peyronie, 5 vols. 4to. *calf*, and folio atlas, *hf. bd. containing the map and plates*, 16s   *Par.* 1788-93

"Tout est précieux dans son Voyage."—*Boucher de la Richarderie.*

5446 PALLAS, Sravnitelnye Slovar, Otdyelenie Pervoe : Evropeiskie i Aziatskie Yazyki : Linguarum totius orbis Vocabularia comparativa, Augustissimæ curâ collecta, Pars I : Europaeae et Asiaticae Linguae, 2 vols. 4to. *all published, hf. calf*, £2. 10s   *Sankpeterb.* 1787-89

Containing the Preface by Pallas, which is frequently wanting.

5447 —— Sravnitelnyi Slovar : Vocabulaire comparatif de toutes les langues et dialectes de tous les peuples soumis à la Russie, et des différentes langues du monde, y compris celles de l'AFRIQUE ; par les soins de *Theodor* JAN KIEWITCH, *en Russe*, 4 vols. 4to. *hf. calf*, £5. 5s   1790-91

Ouvrages *tres curieux et rares*. Le premier contient un choix de 286 mots Russes, avec leurs traductions dans les diverses langues d'Europe et d'Asie, au nombre de 200. Le second présente les mots similaires des différentes langues du monde, rangés un seul ordre alphabétique et accompagnés de leur traduction russe.
Klaproth says of these works, that they comprise most valuable materials for the study of Comparative Philology, though collected without critical judgment. The work of Jan Kiewitch is a new much enlarged edition of Pallas's work, and includes the African dialects, entirely omitted by Pallas.

5448 PERRY's State of Russia under the present Czar, 8vo. *map, calf, curious*, 10s   1716
5448*POSSENINI Moscovia ; de rebus Moscoviticis, etc. 18mo. *map, calf neat, fine copy*, 10s   *Antv. Plantin*, 1587
5449 PSALTER, KATHISMA, i PESNI, *in the Church Slavonic*, 18mo. *original vellum-covered binding, rare*, 20s   *Kiev.* 1725
5450 RERUM MOSCOVITICARUM AUCTORES varii, unum in corpus nunc primum congesti, quibus et Gentis Historia continetur et Regionum Descriptio, cum Indice, folio, *woodcut maps, large woodcuts, light brown calf extra, gilt edges*, £2. 5s   *Francof.* 1600

Contents : Herberstein commentarii ; P. Jovius de legatione Basilii principis Moscoviae ad Clementem VII. ; Fabri Moscovitarum Religio ; Adamus, Anglorum Navigatio ad Moscovitas ; Gwanini, Regionum Moschoviae descriptio ; Hist. belli Livonici ; Basilidis vita ; Heidenstein, de bello Moschov. ; etc.

5451 RUSSKAGO GEOGRAPHITCHESKAGO OBSHTCHESTVA Zapiski : TRANSACTIONS of the IMPERIAL RUSSIAN GEOGRAPHICAL SOCIETY, from the beginning in 1849 to 1853, Nos. 1-9—MEMOIRS, Nos. 1-5 ; together 14 parts in 13 vols. roy. 8vo. *maps, sd.* 36s   *St. Petersb.* 1849-53
5452 SCHOETTGENIUS de Originibus Russicis, sm. 4to. *hf. bd.* 7s   *Dresd.*, 1731
5453 STRAHL (Philipp) Geschichte der Russischen Kirche, Vol. I. (988-1588) *Halle*, 1830—Strahl und Herrmann, Geschichte des Russischen Staates, 5 vols. (bis 1775) *Hamburg*, 1832-53—6 vols. 8vo. *hf. bd.* 15s   1830-53
5454 SLOVAR TSERKOVNO-SLAVYENSKAGO i RUSSKAGO Yazyka, Imperator. Akadem. Nauk. 4 vols. roy. 4to. *a Dictionary of the Church Slavonic explained in Russian, by the Imperial Academy of Sciences, sd.* £2. 10s ; or 4 vols. in 2, *hf. bd.* £2. 16s   *Sanktpeter.* 1847
5455 TOOKE's View of the RUSSIAN EMPIRE to the close of the present century, 3 vols. 8vo. *calf gilt*, 7s   1799
5456 VERÄNDERTE (das) RUSSLAND, Erster Theil, sm. 4to. *portraits, map and plates, sd.* 9s   *Francfurth*, 1744

This curious work, which contains the whole account of the Trial and Execution of the Czarewitz by order of his father, Peter the Great, was rigidly suppressed by order of the Russian Government.

SCANDINAVIA.

5457 BIORNER, NORDISKA KÄMPA DATER : continens Regum, etc. in Orbe Hyperboreo antiquo res gestas, folio, *comprising all the most important Northern Sagas, in Icelandic, Swedish, and Latin, hf. calf gilt*, 36s   *Stockholm.* 1737

" Livre rare. Vendu 55 flor. Meerman ; 60 fr. Raetzel."—BRUNET.
CONTENTS : Praefatio ; Conspectus Genealogicus ; Origines Norrigiae ; Rhythmi de Carolo et Grimo : Rolf Krakes Saga ; Fridthiof's Saga ; Alf's Saga ; Romund's Saga ; Halfdan Bran. Saga ; Sorles Saga ; Halfdan Ostenson's Saga ; Samson's Saga ; Wolsunga Saga ; Ragnar Lodbrok's Saga ; An's Saga ; Norna Saga ; Thorsten's Saga.

5458 IHRE, GLOSSARIUM SUIO-GOTHICUM, in quo tam hodierno usu frequentata Vocabula, quam in ævi medii scriptis obvia, explicantur, et ex Dialectis Mœso-Gothica, Anglo-Saxonica, Anglica, Alemannica, Islandica, ceterisque illustrantur, 2 vols. folio, *calf, scarce*, £4. 4s   *Upsaliæ*, 1769
5459 KRAKAS MAAL, eller kvad om kong Ragnar Lodbroks Krigsbedrifter og Heltedöd, udgeved af Rafn, 8vo. *facsismile, bds.* 7s 6d   *Kjöben.* 1826

5460 MESSENII (Joh.) SCONDIA ILLUSTRATA, seu Chronologia Sueciæ, Daniæ, Norvegiæ, Islandiæ et Gronlandiæ, edita et aucta à Peringskiöld, 15 vols. and Index, bound in 2 vols. folio, *old calf gilt*, £2. *Stokholm.* 1700-5
A very important and rare work on Northern History and Chronology. Stephen's copy, mor. fetched £3. Priced, Rivington, £2. 12s 6d.
"Cette seconde edition est celle qu'on préfère; les exemplaires en sont rarement complets."—BRUNET.

5461 —— Historia Suecorum Gothorumque per Ericum Olai concinnata, nunc erroribus vindicata, cum indice, sq. 8vo. *vellum, arms on sides, 7s 6d*
Stocholm. 1615 (MDCVXX)

5462 PERINGSKIOLD, Monumenta Sueo-Gothica; Lib. I. Uplandiae pars primaria Thiundia; II, Monumenta Ullerakerensia, cum Upsalia Nova illustrata; omnia *Suecice et Latine*, in 1 vol. *maps, with about 200 curious plates and cuts of Tombs, Monuments, Coins, Runic Inscriptions, Arms*, etc. *fine copy in hf. calf, scarce*, £2. 16s *Stockholm.* 1710-19
Priced, 1824, Rivington, £7. I sold a copy in 1856 for £3. 16s

5463 SWENSKE RIJM KRONIKE. Then gamble Rijm Krönikes första Deel i-hwilken Swenske Konungars, 1222-1439, öffuersced aff Messenio, 12mo, *olive morocco extra, gilt edges, rare*, 30s *Stocholm.* 1616

5464 THORSTENS VIIKINGS-SONS SAGA pao gammal Göthska, medh Anteckningar förbettrad af Reenhielm, 12mo. *old Norse and Swedish, vellum*, 9s *Upsalae*, 1680

5465 SNORRONIS STURLESON Edda Islandorum, *Islandice, Danice, et Latine*, ed. Resenius, sq. 8vo. *old calf gilt*, 18s *Havniae,* 1665

AFRICA.

5466 ALVAREZ (Francisco) Historia de las cosas de Ethiopia. Copia de diversas Cartas de algunos Padres y Hermanos de la Compañia de Jesus de las grandes Marauillas en las Indias, y en el Reyno d'JAPON y en la Tierra de BRASIL, &c. folio, **black letter**, *fine copy in vellum*, VERY RARE, £5. *Caragoça, Millan,*1561

5467 CANNECATTIM, Collecção de Observações Grammaticães sobre a lingua Bunda ou Angolense, com Supplemento e DICCIONARIO CONGUEZA, sq. 8vo. *hf. russia, neat,* 21s *Lisboa,* 1805

5468 **Egypt.** ABD-ALLATIF, Relation de l'Egypte, *en Francais*, suivi de divers extraits d'Ecrivains Orientaux, *Arabe, etc.* enrichi de notes historiques et critiques, par Sylvestre de Sacy, 4to. PAPIER VELIN, *sd.* 24s *Paris,* 1810

5469 BELZONI'S Narrative of recent Discoveries in Egypt and Nubia,—4to. *port. hf. bd.* 10s. 1820

5470 —— The Plates, illustrative of the Researches and Operations in Egypt and Nubia, 44 *plates*—Supplement, 6 *new plates*, 1822—in 1 vol. atlas folio, 50 *finely coloured plates*, £2. 10s 1820-22
The Supplement is scarce, and generally wanting.

5471 BURTON'S Excerpta Hieroglyphica, or Exact Copies of various Hieroglyphical Inscriptions and Sculptured Monuments still existing in Egypt, and Nubia, and at Mount Sinai, &c. &c. 4 parts, complete in 1 vol. oblong folio, *containing 62 curious plates*, PRIVATELY PRINTED, *hf. bd. very rare*, £3. 10s *Cairo,* 1823-7

5471*CADET, Copie figurée d'un Rouleau de Papyrus, trouvé à Thèbes dans un tombeau des Rois, 18 *plates, without title or text, joined into one piece*, 30 feet long and 13 inches broad, *printed on yellow paper, the figures coloured, mounted upon canvas, and fixed on a wooden roller*, 30s (*Paris*, 1805)
Meerman's copy fetched 36 florins.

5472 GAU, Antiquités de la Nubie, ou monuments inédits des bords du Nil, situés entre la première et la seconde cataracte, atlas folio, *with* 78 *plates and vignettes*, 8 *of them coloured* (pub. at 150 fr.), *bds*. £2. *Stuttgart,* 1822
The Vellum Paper copies are published at 240 fr. Cet ouvrage peut être considéré comme le complément à la Description d'Egypte, publiée par ordre de l'Empereur; son exécution le rend digne d'y etre joint.

5473 MINUTOLI, Reise zum Tempel des Jupiter Ammon in der Libyschen Wüste und nach Ober-Aegypten, 1820-21, herausg. von Toelken, impl. 4to. with roy. folio *Atlas of maps and* 38 *plates, bds.* £2. 10s *Berlin,* 1824

5474 GROUT (Rev. L.) The Isizulu; A Grammar of the Zulu Language, with a historical introduction and Appendix, 8vo. 432 pp. *cloth*, 21s *Natal*, 1859

5475 HAHN, Grundzüge einer Grammatik des Herrero (West. Afrika) roy. 8vo. *including a Dictionary of* 94 *pp. double columns, and a comparative table of* 12 *languages, sd.* 8s 6d *Berlin*, 1857

5476 ISENBERG and Krapf's Journals of proceedings in Shoa, and other parts of Abyssinia, 1839-42, 8vo. *maps, cloth,* 6s 1843

5477 **Madagascar.** ELLIS' History of Madagascar, 2 vols. 8vo. *plates* (pub. at 25s), *cloth*, 10s   1838
5478 FLACOURT, Dictionnaire de la Langue de Madagascar, avec quelques mots du langage des Sauvages de la Baye de Saldagne, un petit Catechisme, etc. in 1 vol. 8vo. xvi. 176, iv. 61, viii. and 112 pp. *vellum*, RARE, £4.   Paris, 1658
5479 —— Petit Catéchisme avec des prières, *Malgache et Français*, sm. 8vo. *vellum*, 21s   1658
5480 —— Relation de la grande Isle Madagascar, 4to. *calf*, 6s   Paris, 1661
5481 MÜLLER (W. J.) die Africanische auf der Guineischen Gold- Cust gelegene Landschafft Fetu, mit einem Fetuischen *Wörterbuche*, 12mo. *plates, hf. calf*, 12s   Nürnb. 1675
5482 NEDERDUITSCH ZUID-AFRIKAANSCH TYDSCHRIFT, Deel I.-III, 3 vols. 8vo. *a bi-monthly periodical of general information, half calf, rare*, 24s
Kaapstad, 1824-26
5483 Vossius de Nili et aliorum fluminum origine, cum Appendice ad scriptum de naturâ Lucis, sm. 4to. *calf*, 10s   Hagae, 1666

AMERICA.

Comprising Works relating to the History, Geography, Aboriginal Languages and Antiquities of North and South America.

5484 ACCIOLI de Cerqueira, Memorias historicas e politicas da Provincia da Bahia, 4 vols. sq. 8vo. *sd*. 27s   Bahia, 1835-37
5485 ACOSTA, Historia natvral y moral de las Indias, en qve se tratan las cosas notables del cielo, y elementos, metales, plantas, y animales dellas; y los ritos, y ceremonias, leyes, y gouierno, y guerras de los Indios, sq. 8vo. *clean copy in old calf*, 25s; or, *a fine tall copy, title slightly stained*, 36s   Sevilla, 1590
5486 —— another edition stout sq. 8vo. *limp vellum*, 12s   Madrid, 1608
5487 —— sexta edicion, 2 vols. sq. 8vo. *calf*, 12s   1792
JOSEPH DE ACOSTA, né à Medina del Campo, vers l'an 1539, passa, après avoir professé la théologie, à Ocana, en 1571 aux Indes occidentales, et fut le second Provincial de l'ordre des Jésuites au Pérou ou il séjourna pendant 17 ans. Il mourut recteur à Salamanque, le 11 février 1600. Son ouvrage, estimé à juste titre, a été ré-imprimé assez souvent et traduit dans presque toutes les langues. Nous avons la première édition. (V. de Backer. I, 1.)

5488 ACUGNA, Acarete, Grillet and Bechamel, Voyages and Discoveries in South America, 8vo. 2 *maps, calf*, 18s   1698
5489 ADAIR'S History of the American Indians, containing an account of their Origin, Language, Customs, &c. *map, bds.* 28s; or, *calf neat*, 32s   1775
A very curious work, tracing the Indians to a Hebrew origin. "One of the best and most instructive books of its kind."—DIBDIN.

5490 ALBERDI, Memoria sobre Tucuman, sq. 8vo. *hf. bd.* 6s   Buenos Aires, 1834
5491 ALSEDO Y HERRERA (D. Dionysio de) Compendio Historico de la Provincia, Partidos, Ciudades, Astilleros, Rios y Puerto de Guayaquil en las Costas de la Mar del Sur, 4to. *map, vellum*, EXCESSIVELY RARE, £3. 10s   Madrid, 1741
5492 —— Aviso Historico, Politico, Geographico, con las noticias del Peru, Tierra-Firme, Chile, y Nuevo Reyno del Granada, etc. sq. 8vo. *calf*, 18s Madrid, 1740
5493 AMERICA, or an exact description of the West Indies, especially of those under the dominion of Spain, by N. N. 2 parts in 1 vol. 12mo. *old calf, rare*, 20s 1655
Fetched, 1858, Sotheby's, 20s.
5494 AMERICAN Annual Register, for 1825-31, Vols. I—VI, stout royal 8vo. *bds.* 36s
New York, 1827-32
Contains interesting information respecting the United States.
5495 AMERICAN PHILOSOPHICAL SOCIETY, Transactions of the Historical and Literary Committee, Vol. I, 8vo. i. and 464 pp. *bds.* 12s   Philadelphia, 1819
In three parts: No. I. Heckewelder's History, Manners and Customs of the Indian Nations, pp. 1—347; II. Correspondence between Heckewelder and Duponceau on the Languages of the American Indians, 351—448; III. Lenni-Lenape Words, Phrases, and Dialogues.
5496 AMERICAN PREACHER, Select Discourses from; by some of the Evangelical Ministers in the United States, 2 vols. 8vo. *bds.* 16s   Edinb. 1796-1801
Vol. II. pp. 442-463, contains "A serious address to those who unnecessarily frequent the Tavern, and often spend the evening in Public Houses, by Thomas Foxcoft, Boston, 1726."
5497 AMUNÁTEGUI, la Reconquista Española, apuntes para la historia de Chile, 1814-17, 8vo. *hf. bd.* 7s 6d   Santiago, 1851
5498 ANTIQUITATES AMERICANAE, sive Scriptores Septentrionales Rerum Ante-Columbianarum in America, edidit Soc. Antiq. Septemtr. impl. 4to. *maps and plates, russia*, 36s   Hafniae, 1837

5499 APOLLONII (Levini, *Gandobrugani*) de Peruviae regionis, Novi Orbis celeberrimae, inventione, 12mo. *folding woodcut, map, good sound copy, in limp vellum*, 18s *Antverpiae*, 1566
Priced, 1827, Thorpe, mor. £1. 11s 6d.

5500 ARENAS (Pedro de) Vocabulario Manual de las Lenguas Castellana y Mexicana, en que se contienen las palabras mas comunes en communication entre Españoles e Indios, 16mo. cut close, *bds.* VERY RARE, £2. 10s *Mexico*, 1683
Sold in 1852 for £3. 15s.

5501 AVILA (Francesco de) Arte de la lengua Mexicana, y breves platicas de los mystérios de la n. santa fee catolica, y otros, 16mo. 13 preliminary leaves (including title and leaf of errata) and leaves 1—37, *russia, gilt edges*, VERY RARE. £4. *Mexico*, 1717

5502 BANCROFT, History of the United States, Vols. I—IV. 8vo. *to the year* 1763. *portrait, maps and plates*, (pub. at £2. 8s) *cloth*, 12s *Boston*, 1848-52

5503 BARCIA, HISTORIADORES PRIMITIVOS de las Indias Occidentales, que junto, traduxò en parte, y sacò à luz, illustrados con eruditas Notas, y copiosas Indices, D. Andres Gonzalez Barcia, 3 vols. sm. folio, *a good copy in hf. calf*, £8. ; or, 3 vols. in 2, *Spanish calf*, £10. *Madrid*, 1749
VERY RARE. The price of copies has gradually risen. In 1853 Dr. Hawtrey's copy fetched £7. 10s; 1859, Lady Webster's copy fetched £16.
This invaluable collection consists of reprints of the early historians of the New World, including Columbus, Cortes, Alvarado, Godoy, Oviedo, Gomara, Zarate, Torres, Alvar Nunez, Cabeça de Baca, &c. The original editions of these authors are scarcely ever to be met with. It is said, that positive proof exists of more than 100 copies of some of the parts having been destroyed, so that only about 200 sets could have been completed; the work has, in consequence, become very scarce in Spain.

5504 BARLAEI (Casp.) Historia rerum per octennium in Brasilia et alibi nuper gestarum sub præfectura Mauritii Nassoviæ, etc. roy. folio, LARGE PAPER, *each leaf mounted on guards, 58 large folding maps and fine plates, old calf gilt, fine copy*. £2. *Amst. Blaeu*, 1647

5505 BARTON (B. C.) New Views of the Origin of the Tribes and Nations of America, with Appendix, 8vo. *including* 133 *pp. of comparative vocabularies, hf. calf*, 27s *Philadelphia*, 1798

5506 BARTRAM's Travels through Carolina, Georgia, Florida, the Cherokee, and Chactaw countries, etc. 8vo. *plates, hf. bd.* 6s ; *uncut*, 9s 1792
"A most interesting work."—LOWNDES.

5507 BELKNAP (Jeremy) History of New Hampshire, 3 vols. 8vo. *clean copy, original bds.* £2. 16s *Philadel. and Boston, for the Author*, 1784-92

5508 BELTRAMI, Découverte des Sources du Mississippi et de la Riviere Sanglante, avec des Observations sur plusieurs Nations Indiennes, 8vo. 327 pp. *bds. rare*, 10s *Nouvelle Orleans*, 1824

5509 BENADUCI (Lorenzo) Idea de una nueva Historia General de la America Septentrional, fundada sobra Figuras, Symbolos, Geroglificos, y Manuscritos de Autores Indios, ultimamente descubiertos, sm. 4to. *fine copy in vellum or russia*, RARE, £2. 8s *Madrid, Zuniga*, 1746
Twenty-two prel. leaves, including the engraved frontispiece and portrait: Text 167 pp. followed by 4 leaves and 96 pp. Written during an eight years' residence in Mexico, and as the result of a considerable acquaintance with the manners and customs of the Indians; ancient manuscripts and pictures preserved in the Monasteries, etc. "It contains much important information not before published."—CLAVIGERO.

5510 BENZONIS (H.) Novæ Novi Orbis Historiæ, id est, res ab Hispanis in India Occidentali hactenus gestae, *Lat.* à Calvetone, sm. 8vo. *vellum, fine copy*, 14s *Genevæ*, 1578

5511 BIBLIOTHECA AMERICANA, a chronological Catalogue of the most curious books, pamphlets, papers, etc. upon America, from the earliest period, in print and MS. 4to. *hf. bd. uncut*, 21s 1789

5512 BISSELII (*Soc. Jesu.*) Argonauticon Americanorum, sive historiae Petri de Victoria ac sociorum lib. 15, 16mo. *engraved title and map, fine copy in old red morocco, from Lord Stuart de Rothesay's library*, 18s *Monachii*, 1647

5513 BOCANEGRA (Jean Perez) Ritual, Formulario, e Institucion de Curas, para administrar a los naturales los Sacramentos, *Quechua y Espanol*, sq. 8vo. 16 *preliminary leaves, including title and errata, and pp.* 1-720; *Table*, 4 *leaves, vellum*, VERY RARE, £7. 10s *Lima*, 1631

5514 BOLLAERT's Antiquarian and Ethnological Researches in New Granada, Equador, Peru and Chile, 8vo. *plates, cloth*, 7s 1860

5515 BONNYCASTLE's Spanish America, historical, geographical, and descriptive, stout 8vo. *map*, 582 pp. *bds.* 7s 6d *Philadelph.* 1819

5516 BRASSEUR DE BOURBOURG, Histoire des Nations Civilisées du Mexique et de l'Amérique Centrale, durant les siècles antérieurs à Colomb. écrite sur des documents originaux et entièrement inédits, puisés aux anciennes archives des indigènes, 4 stout vols. large 8vo. *map and woodcuts of the picture writing, sd.* 36s *Paris,* 1857-59

5517 BRIDGES' Annals of Jamaica, 2 vols. 8vo. *bds. suppressed edition,* 12s 1827

5518 BRISSOT, Nouveau Voyage dans les Etats-Unis, 1788, 3 vols. 8vo. *calf gilt,* 10s *Paris,* 1791

5519 BRULII Historia Peruana Ordinis Eremit. S. Augustini, Veteris novaeque Peruviae notitia, de origine, moribus, etc. Peruanorum, 2 vols. in 1, sm. folio, *fine copy in vellum, rare,* £2. 10s *(Antverpiae),* 1652

5520 BUSTAMANTE, Cuadro Historico de la Revolucion de la America Mexicana, 1810-23, 2 vols. in 1, stout sm. 4to. *a weekly periodical in* 65 *Cartas, calf,* 18s *Mexico,* 1823-24

5521 CABECA DE VACA (Alvar Nuñez) Narrative of, translated from the Spanish edition, Valladolid, 1555, by Buckingham Smith, atlas 4to. LARGE PAPER, *printed for private circulation only, cloth, uncut,* £2. 12s *Washington,* 1851
An account of one of the earliest explorations of territory within the limits of the United States.

5522 CAROCHI, Compendio del Arte de la lengua Mexicana, dispuesto por PARADES, in tres partes, sq. 8vo. *frontispiece, and* 12 *preliminary leaves including title and index,* text pp. 1-202, *vellum,* VERY RARE, £5. *Mexico,* 1759

5523 CARROLL's Historical Collections of South Carolina, rare pamphlets, etc. from the discovery to 1776, 2 vols. 8vo. *map, cloth,* 15s *New York,* 1836

5524 CASAS (BART. DE LAS) TRATADOS VARIOS: I. Treynta Proposiciones muy juridicas, en las quales se tocan muchas cosas pertenecientes al derecho sobre los infieles, *Sevilla, Trugillo,* 1552—II. Disputa, o Controuersia entre Bartholeme de las Casas y Gines de Supelveda sobre las conquistas de las Indias, *ib. id.* 1552 —III. Tratado sobre la materia de los Yndios, *ib. id.* 1552—IV. Remedios para reformacion de las Indias, *ib.* Croberger, 1552—in 1 vol. sq. 8vo. 𝔟𝔩𝔞𝔠𝔨 𝔩𝔢𝔱𝔱𝔢𝔯, *fine tall copies, original vellum wrapper,* EXTREMELY RARE, £8. 1552

5525 —— another set: I. Tratado comprobatorio del Imperio soberano de los Reyes de Castilla sobre las Indias, *Sevilla, Trugillo,* 1553—II. Disputa, o Controversia entre Las Casas y G. de Sepulveda sobre las conquistas de las Indias, *ib. ib.* 1552 —III. Brevissima Relacion de la destruycion de las Indias; Pedaço de una carta y relacion, &c. *ib. ib.* 1552—IV. Remedios para reformacion de las Indias, *ib.* Crōberger, 1552—in 1 vol. sm. 4to. 𝔅𝔩𝔞𝔠𝔨 𝔩𝔢𝔱𝔱𝔢𝔯, *fine copies, old binding, gilt edges,* £5. *Sevilla,* 1552-53
Priced, complete, 1858, Asher, Berlin, 275 thalers. Fetched, 1861, £14.
Each of the above volumes contains four of the eight pieces which form a complete set of the Tratados. They should be united, as both together contain six, including the rarest, of these celebrated treatises. The " Relacion de las Indias," in the above copy has the four leaves, " Un Pedaço de una Carte," almost always wanting, unknown to De Bure, and almost all Bibliographers.
De Bure, in whose time only five parts were known, speaks of their excessive rarity. Richarderie has no other particularisation of parts than those noticed by De Bure; nor was Llorente, in his notice of the works of Las Casas, better informed, as he only mentions the first five.

5526 CASAS, Brevissima Relacion—Treynta Proposiciones—Disputa o Controversia—Tratado sobre la materia de los Indios—Remedios—Pedaço de una Carta—in 1 vol. sq. 8vo. 214 *pp. sd. rare,* 30s *Sevilla,* 1552 (*Barcelona,* 1646)
Priced, 1818, Thorpe, £3. 3s; by me, 1855, £2. 2s.

5527 —— Conquista dell' Indie Occidentali, *Spagnuol e Ital.* da Ginammi, sq. 8vo. *being the " Disputa ò Controversia" mentioned above, vellum,* 12s *Ven.* 1645

5528 —— Narratio Regionum Indicarum per Hispanos devastatarum, sm. 4to. *original edition, with fine impressions of the plates by* DE BRY, *fine copy in russia extra, gilt edges,* RARE, £3. 10s *Francofurti,* 1598
Priced, 1826, Payne and Foss, £4. 4s; Roscoe's copy fetched £11. 10s.

5529 —— Regionum Indicarum per Hispanos olim devastatarum descriptio, sq. 8vo. *fine impressions of De Bry's engravings, sd.* UNCUT, *rare,* 36s *Heidelberg,* 1664

5530 —— Umbständige warhafftige Beschreibung der Indianischen Ländern, in Teutsch übersetzt, sq. 8vo. *with the same engravings as the Latin editions, morocco, rare,* 28s 1665

5531 —— Colleccion de las Obras, con su vida, por Llorente, 2 vols. 8vo. *calf,* 15s *Paris,* 1822

5532 —— Œuvres, en Français, avec sa vie, &c. par Llorente, 2 vols. 8vo. *portrait, sd.* 14s *Paris,* 1822

AMERICA. 293

5533 CASAS (Bart. de las) Relation des Voyages et des Découvertes que les Espagnols ont fait dans les Indes Occidentales, 1698—Voyage de Montauban, Capitaine des Filibustiers en Guinée, en 1695, 1698—L'Art de voyager utilement, 1698—in 1 vol. 12mo. *calf extra, gilt edges,* 21s   *Amst.* 1698

"In parting from Las Casas, it must be felt that all ordinary eulogies would be feeble and inadequate   His was one of those few lives that are beyond biography, and require a history to be written in order to illustrate them. His career affords, perhaps, a solitary instance of a man who, being neither a conqueror, a discoverer, nor an inventor, has, by the pure force of benevolence, become so notable a figure that large portions of history cannot be written, or at least cannot be understood, without the narrative of his deeds and efforts being made one of the principal threads upon which the history is strung.   Other men have undertaken great projects of benevolence, and have partially succeeded in them; but there is not any man whose success or failure in such endeavours has led to the great civil or military events which ensued upon the successes and failures of Las Casas.   Take away all he said and did, and preached, and wrote, and preserved (for the early historians of the New World owe the records of many of their most valuable facts to him); and the history of the conquest would lose a considerable portion of its most precious material.—*Helps.*

5534 CATECISMO y Doctrina Cristiana, *Qquechua y Espanol,* impreso in Lima, 1583, lo da nuevamente a luz Gallegos, sq. 8vo. 34 pp. *hf. mor.* 32s *Cuzco,* 1828
5535 CATHECISMO (Tercero) y Exposicion de la doctrina Christiana por sermones, para que los curos prediquen, etc. sq. 8vo. 8 *preliminary leaves including title and table; Approbation and Proem,* 1-8; *text in Spanish, Quichua, and Aymara,* 9-215, *vellum,* very rare, £5. 10s   *Ciudad de los Reyes,* 1585
5536 CAULIN (F. Antonio) Historia Coro-Graphica, natural y evangelica dela Nueva Andalucia, Cumana, Guayana y Vertientes del Rio Orinoco, folio, *map and plates, calf,* 32s   *Madrid,* 1779
  Lord Stuart de Rothesay's copy fetched, 1855, £3. 3s.
5537 Chalmers' Introduction to the History of the Revolt of the American Colonies, from the State Papers of Great Britain, 2 vols. 8vo. *cloth,* 15s *Boston, U. S.* 1845
5538 CHARLEVOIX, Histoire de l'Isle Espagnole, ou de S. Domingue, écrite sur des Manuscrits de J. B. Le Pers, 2 vols. 4to. *maps, calf,* £2. 10s   *Paris,* 1730
5539 ——— Histoire et description générale de la Nouvelle-France, et Journal d'un Voyage dans l'Amérique Septentrionale, 3 vols. 4to. *maps and plates, calf,* £2. 10s   *Paris,* 1744

" De toutes les relations de Canada, c'est dans celle-ci, qu'on peut s'instruire le mieux sur les nombreuses peuplades qui y étaient répandues, et dont quelques-unes subsistent encore."—*Boucher.*

5540 ——— Histoire du Paraguay, avec plusieurs piéces pour servir de preuves et d'éclaircissemens, 3 vols. 4to. best edition, *maps and plans, old calf gilt,* £1. 11s 6d   *Paris,* 1756
  "Relation la plus complète et la plus satisfaisante sur Paraguay."—*Boucher.*
5541 Chaumonot, (*Missionaire dans la Nouv. France,* 1688), Vie, par lui-même, sq. sm. 8vo. large paper, *bds. privately printed,* 15s   *Nouvelle York,* 1858
  With appendix of the "Voeu à la Vierge" in the Huron language.
5542 Chiquitos. Geschichten derer Chiquitos und anderer von denen Patribus der Gesell. Jesu in Paraquaria neu-bekehrten Völker, etc. stout 8vo. *stamped hogskin, rare,* 18s   *Wienn,* 1729
5543 CIECA DE LEON (Pedro de) Parte Primera de la Chronica del Peru, que tracta la demarcacion de sus prouincias, descripcion dellas, fundaciones de las ciudades, costumbres de los Indios, y otras cosas estrañas, folio, Black letter, *numerous curious woodcuts,* fine large and clean copy *in vellum, wanting folio* 21, extremely rare, £6. 6s   *Seuilla, Montesdoca,* 1553

Priced, 1832 and 1837, Payne and Foss, £12. 12s; fetched, Hibbert's, £9. 9s; 1855, Lord Stuart de Rothesay's, £10.—With the Autograph signature of the author at the end of the volume.

5544 CIECA, Parte primera de la Chronica del Peru, 12mo. *second edition, woodcuts, title slightly mended, a fine copy in morocco extra, gilt edges,* 36s *Anvers,* 1554
5545 ——— Cronica del Peru, tradotta per Cravaliz, 16mo. *vellum,* 12s *Venetia,* 1576

"The first part only was printed: the 2nd and 3rd parts were seen in MS. in Madrid some time ago, but it is not known what became of them."—*Rich.*
⁎ Auctor tredecim fere annorum post ad occidentales Indos Peruanamque plagam transfretavit, militiamque ibi secutus, plus quam septemdecim annos in his oris commoratus est. Fructum tam longæ peregrinationis eximium quidem is edidit in libro isto cujus vero *prima tantum pars prodiit : reliquæ tres valde ab omnibus desiderantur.* Meuselius from Nic. Antonius.

5546 CLAVIGERO, Storia Antica del Messico, 4 vols. 4to. *maps and plates, bds.* 35s   *Cesena,* 1780-81
5547 ——— History of Mexico, collected from Spanish and Mexican Historians, MSS. and Ancient Indian Paintings, translated by Cullen, 2 vols. 4to. *maps and numerous plates, hf. russia,* 25s   1787

"A valuable work; besides Natural History there is in this work much learned research on the Ancient History of Mexico."—*Lowndes.*
  Marq. of Townshend's copy fetched 30s; Fonthill copy, £2. 10s.

5548 CLADERA, Investigaciones Historicas sobre los Descubrimientos de los Españoles en el Mar Oceano, sq. 8vo. 5 *portraits and map, calf,* 15s *Madrid,* 1794

5549 COLDEN (Cadwallader) History of the Five Indian Nations of Canada, 2 vols. in 1, 12mo. *no map, fine copy in brown morocco extra, gilt edges, from Miss Currer's library*, 32s 1755
5550 COLUMBUS, BOSSI, Vita di Colombo, 8vo. *portrait and plates, calf gilt*, 6s 1818
5551 CONTEST in America between Gt. Britain and France, 8vo. 6s 1757
5552 CORDEYRO (Ant.) Historia Insulana das Ilhas a Portugal sugeytas no Oceano Occidental, sm. folio, *Title, Prologue, License, Index, etc.* 8 *leaves; text, pp.* 1-528, *upper margin slightly wormed near the end, Lord Strangford's copy, in the original calf, rare*, 24s Lisboa, 1717
5553 CORTÉS (Hern.) Historia de Nueva España, aumentada por Lorenzana, Arzobispo de Mexico, sm. folio, *with map and 32 curious plates of Mexican Antiquities, calf*, £2. 5s Mexico, 1770
COLLATION: Title; Frontispiece; Dedication, 12 pp.; Prologo, 4 pp.; folding map; Viage de Cortes, pp. I-XVI.; Errata, 1 leaf; plate, "Templo de Mexico"; Advertencias, and text, pp. 1-400, with plates 1-32 (the first 14 not numbered); Indice, 16 pp.
5554 CORTESII von dem NEWEN HISPANIEN, so im Meer gegem Nidergang, zwo gantz lustige vnnd fruchtreiche Historien, an den grossmächtigsten vnüberwindtlichisten Herren Carolum V. Römischen Kaiser etc. Künig in Hispanien, etc. small folio, *fine copy, oak boards, rebacked*, £2. 10s Augspurg, Vlhart, 1550
COLLATION: Title, 1 leaf; Dedication, 1 leaf; P. Ulhart zu dem Lesser, etc. 3 leaves; Argument, 1 leaf; the work itself, folios 1 to 60.—RARE; not mentioned by Brunet.
This edition in German contains at the end several letters concerning the settlements of the Germans in Spanish America not found in the Latin or Spanish editions.
5555 —— Despatches of Cortes, addressed to Charles V. during the conquest, by Folsom, large 8vo. *bds.* 6s New York, 1843
5556 COXE'S Description of Carolina, called Florida and Louisiane, and of the Meschacebe River, 8vo. *map, bds.* 7s 6d St. Louis, 1840
5557 DALRYMPLE'S Catalogue of Authors who have written on the Rio de la Plata, Paraguay, and Chaco, 4to. LARGE PAPER, *hf. calf*, 20s 1807
5558 DAVILA (D. Francisco) Tratado de los Evangelios que la Iglesia propone en todo al año con sermones, etc. *Espanol y Quichua*, 2 vols. in 1, sm. folio, *limp vellum*, VERY RARE, £6. 10s Lima, 1648
COLLATION: Vol. I. Title, and Dedicatoria, 4 leaves; Auto, 4 leaves; Oratio, 6 leaves; Petition for Approbation, Approbations, etc. 12 leaves; prefacion, 18 leaves; text, pp. 1-564; Vol. II. Title, Dedication, and Approbations, 6 leaves; text, pp. 1-134; Tabla, 3 leaves.
5559 DAVILA (Gil Gonzalez) Teatro de la Iglesia de las Indias Occidentales, Vol. II. sm. folio, *vellum*, 18s Madrid, 1655
5559*DUFLOT DE MOFRAS, Exploration du Territoire de l'Orégon, des Californies et de la Mer Vermeille, 1840-42, 2 vols. in 4, roy. 8vo. *plates, bds. with folio atlas of 26 maps and plates, hf. bd.* £2. Paris, 1844
5560 EDER, Descriptio Provinciae Moxitarum in regno PERUANO, 8vo. *map and 3 plates, sd.* 10s Budae, 1791
5561 EDWARDS (Jonathan) Observations on the Language of the Muhhekaneew Indians, with notes by Pickering, (and a Vocabulary of Indian languages), 8vo. *hf. bd.* 15s Boston, 1823
5562 ELIOT (John) Grammar of the Massachusetts Indian Language, with notes by Du Ponceau and Pickering, 8vo. *hf. bd.* 36s Boston, 1822
5563 —— COTTON MATHER'S Life of John Eliot, the first preacher to the Indians in America, 16mo. *hf. calf, rare*, 20s 1691
5564 ESCALONA, Gazophylacium Regium PERUBICUM, in quo omnes materiae ad jura regalia Peruana spectantes tractantur, fol. *fine copy, vellum*, 15s Matr. 1775
5565 EYMA, la Republique Americaine, 2 vols.—Les 34 Etoiles de l'Union Américaine, 2 vols.—together 4 vols. 8vo. *sd.* 6s Paris, 1861
5566 FALKNER'S Description of Patagonia, with a short Grammar and VOCABULARY of the language, 4to. *large map in the fold, hf. russia*, 25s Hertford, 1774
5567 FERNANDEZ, Relazione della Nuova Christianità degli' Indiani detti CICHITI (Paraguay), sm. 4to. *vellum, rare*, 9s Roma, 1729
5568 FIGUEIRA, Arte da Grammatica da lengua de Brasil, sq. 8vo. *hf. calf, rare*, 30s Lisboa, 1795
5569 FORBES' California, Upper and Lower, from the first discovery, 8vo. *map and plates, hf. calf*, 7s 1839
5570 FREZIER, Relation du Voyage de la Mer du Sud à Chily et Perou, 1712-14; avec une Chronologie des Viceroys, 4to. *plates and plans, calf*, 9s Paris, 1732
5571 FUNES, Ensayo de la Historia Civil del PARAGUAY, BUENOS-AYRES Y TUCUMAN, 3 vols. sq. 8vo. *hf. calf*, £2. 5s Buenos-Ayres, 1816-17

AMERICA.

5572 GARCIA (Gregorio) Origen de los Indios de el Nuevo Mundo y Indias Occidentales, averiguado con discurso de opiniones, 16mo. FIRST EDITION, *a little stained and wormed, vellum*, 15s; or, *a fine copy, vellum*, 30s   *Valencia*, 1607
The first License to print, 2 pp., is in the Valencian dialect.

5573 ——— Origen de los Indios, *segunda impresion*, enmendada y añadida de opiniones, (por And. Gonz. de Garcia) sm. folio, *sd. uncut*, 15s   *Madrid*, 1729

5574 GARCILASO DE LA VEGA, Commentarios reales de el Origen de los Incas del Peru, de su idolatria, leies, y govierno, de sus vidas y conquistas, 1723—Historia general del Peru, de el descubrimiento, las guerras entre Pizarros y Almagros, 1722—La Florida del Inca, 1723—Ensayo Chronologico para la historia general de la Florida, por Gabriel de Cardenas (Ant. Gonzales de Barcia), 1723—together 4 vols. folio, *vellum or calf*, £4.   *Madrid*, 1722-23

5575 ——— Historia general del PERU, ó comentarios reales de los Incas, 13 vols.—Historia de la Florida, 4 vols.—together 17 vols. 18mo. *Spanish calf, very nice uniform set*, £2. 2s   *Madrid*, 1800-3
"Jolie édition."—BRUNET.
Very authentic and highly esteemed histories. "The author (says Pinkerton), as a descendant of the princes of Peru, has been peculiarly minute relative to the religion, government, laws, customs and manners of the ancient inhabitants of Peru, as well as the productions of that country."
"His knowledge of the Peruvian language has enabled him to correct some errors of the Spanish writers, and he has inserted some curious facts taken from authors whose works are now lost."—*Robertson*.
"A gentle and trusting spirit rather than a wise one, proud of being a son of one of the unscrupulous conquerors of Peru, but always betraying the weaker nature of his mother, who was of the blood royal of the Incas, and never entirely forgetting the glories of his Indian race, or the cruel injuries they had suffered at the hands of Spain. The Commentaries are a striking and interesting book, showing much of the spirit of the old Chronicles."
Ticknor, III. 146.

5576 GILIJ (Abbate F. P.) Saggio di Storia Americana, o sia storia naturale, civile e sacra de' regni e delle provincie Spagnuole nell' America meridionale, 4 vols. 8vo. *map and plates, hf. bd. rare*, 32s   *Roma*, 1782-84
"Le troisième volume contient des détails curieux sur les langues de l'Amérique meridionale."—BRUNET.

5576*GIOSEPPE, *di S. Teresa, Carmelitano Scalzo*, Istoria delle Guerre del Brasile accadute tra Portogallo e Olanda, 2 vols. in 1, sm. folio, *engraved title and numerous large maps, plans, views, etc. vellum*, £2. 2s   *Roma*, 1700

5577 **Greenland.** EGEDE, Dictionarium Grönlandico-Danico-Latinum complectens primitiva cum derivatis, sm. 8vo. *with two Indexes, Danish, and Latin, hf. bd.* 21s   *Hafniae*, 1750

5578 ——— Grammatica Grönlandica Danico-Latina, 8vo. *hf. bd. uncut*, 21s   1760

5579 FABRICIUS, Forsög til en forbedret Grönlandsk Grammatica, 12mo. *hf. bd.* 16s   *Kiöb.* 1801

5580 TESTAMENTE NUTAK: the New Testament *in Greenlandish*, by Fabricius, stout 12mo. *hf. bd.* 5s   *Kiöb.* 1799

5581 TESTAMENTITOKAMIT Salomonib Ajokaersutej, pellisimit Wolfimit, 1828—Profetit Mingnerit, pellisimit Kraghmit, 1829—2 vols. in 1, sm. 8vo. *the Proverbs of Solomon, and the Prophets, calf extra*, 7s   *Kjöb.* 1828-29

5582 GRYNÆI (Simonis) Novus Orbis Regionum ac Insularum Veteribus incognitarum, folio, *original edition, no map, fine copy in vellum*, 32s   *Paris*, 1532
The above volume contains the voyages of Columbus, Cadamosto, Amerigo Vespucci, Marco Polo, etc.

5583 GUADALUPE RAMIREZ, Breve Compendio de todo lo que debe saber el Christiano, en lengua *Othomi (y Castellano)* sq. 8vo. *formerly belonging to Fouché, hf. bd.* £3. 3s   *Mexico*, 1785
Title and Preface, 3 leaves; Censure, 1 leaf; Approbations and cancelled Errata, 4 leaves; New Errata, 1 leaf; pp. 1-80; Epitome, large folding sheet in 5 columns. The first 17 pp. are in explanation of the letters, etc.

5584 **Guatemala.** GACETA del Gobierno de Guatemala, Nos. 1-30, Nov. 1821 to March 13, 1829, with Supplements, folio, *bds.* 14s   *Guatemala*, 1821-9

5585 GACETA del Gobierno supremo de Guatemala, Nos. 1-48, March 1824 to Nov. 1825, 4to. *bds.* 15s   *ib.* 1824-5

5586 INDICADOR (El) Nos. 5-156, Nov. 1824 to Nov. 1827, sm. folio, *bds.* 6s 1824-7

5587 GUMILLA, el Orinoco ilustrado, y defendido, Historia Natural, Civil, y Geographica de este Gran Rio, y de usos, y costumbres de los Indios sus habitadores, 2 vols. sm. 4to. *large map and plates, fine copy in old Spanish* MOROCCO, *gilt edges, rare*, £2. 5s   *Madrid*, 1745

5588 GUMILLA (Jos.) Historia de las Naciones en las Riveras del Orinoco, 2 vols. sm 4to. *portrait, map*, 5 *plates of Indian Antiquities, calf*, 28s   *Barcelona*, 1791
Lord Rothesay's copy fetched, 1855, 33s.

5589 GUZMAN (Jos. Javier) el Chileno instruido en la Historia de su pais, 1 vol. of xvi. 927 and 8 pages, in 2 vols. 8vo. *hf. calf*, 21s   *Santiago de Chile*, 1834

5590 HALIBURTON'S Historical and Statistical Account of Nova Scotia, 2 vols. 8vo. *maps and plates, calf extra, uncut, top edges gilt*, £2. 2s *Halifax*, 1829

5591 HALL'S (Basil) Forty Etchings, from Sketches made with the Camera Lucida, in North America, 1827-28, roy. 4to. *map, 40 etchings, hf. russia*, 18s 1829

5592 —— Travels in North America, 1827-28, 3 vols. sm. 8vo. *hf. rus.* 7s 6d *Ed.* 1829

5593 HAMILTON's History of the United States National Flag, 12mo. *coloured plates, cloth*, 5s *Philad.* 1853

5594 HAWKINS's Picture of Quebec, with historical recollections, sm. 8vo. *plates, cloth*, 7s *Quebec*, 1834

5595 HAYWARD's Gazetteer of New Hampshire, sm. 8vo. *plates, hf. bd.* 6s *Boston*, 1849

5596 —— Gazetteer of the United States, roy. 8vo. *portrait and map, calf*, 7s 6d *Hartford (U. S.)* 1853

5597 HELPS' Spanish Conquest in America and its relation to the history of Slavery and the government of colonies, 4 vols. 8vo. *several woodcut maps*, (pub. at £3.) *new in cloth*, £2. 10s 1855-61

5598 HENNEPIN'S New Discovery of a vast country in America, extending above 4000 miles between New France and New Mexico, with Continuation, 2 vols. in 1, sm. 8vo. *maps and plates, calf*, 20s 1698

5599 HERRERA, Novus Orbis, sive descriptio Indiae Occidentalis : acc. Navigatio Australis Jacobi Le Maire atque Descriptio Indiae Occidentalis, authore Ordonnez de Cevallos, unâ cum descriptione Americae, ex tabulis Bertii, folio, *with* 16 *folding maps and charts, and numerous views, tall copy in the old vellum binding*, £2. *Amstel.* 1622

5600 HERRERA (Antonio de) Historia General de los hechos de los Castellanos en las Islas i Tierra firme del Mar Oceano, *eight Decades, bound in* 4 vols. sm. folio, *fine copy in Spanish calf*, £5. 5s *Madrid*, 1730-36

COLLATION: Title; Historia general de los Hechos de los Castellanos, 1730; 16 prelim. leaves, 78 pp., 14 maps. Decada I. 2 preliminy. leaves, 292 pp.; II. 2 prel. leaves, 288 pp.; III. Dedication 1 leaf, 296 pp.; IV. 2 prel. leaves, 232 pp.; V. 3 prel. leaves, 252 pp.; VI. 2 prel. leaves, 236 pp.; VII. 2 prel. leaves, 245 pp.; VIII. 2 prel. leaves, 251 pp. Each decade with an engraved title; Tabla, ¶ 1—¶ 113, or 225 leaves.

5601 HOADLY'S Records of the Colony of New Haven, 1638-49, and 1653 to the Union, with the Code of 1656, 2 vols. 8vo. *cloth*, 18s *Hartford (Connec.)* 1857-58

5602 HOLGUIN, GRAMMATICA y ARTE nueva de la lengua Qquichua ó lengua del Inca, 1607—VOCABULARIO de la lengua general de todo el Peru, llamada lengua Qquichua ó del Inca, 2 parts in 1 vol. *a little stained, the title and last page slightly injured*, 1608—together 3 parts in 2 vols. sq. 8vo. *red morocco, gilt edges*, EXTREMELY RARE, £36. *Ciudad de los Reyes*, 1607-8

COLLATION of the Grammatica: Title, Dedication, etc. 4 leaves: Arte, ff. 1—144, 143-44 being 4 pages of Tabla. COLLATION of the Vocabulario: Title, Suma de las cosas, Approbacion, 2 leaves; Epistola dedicatoria, Al Christ. Lector, 2 leaves; Al Lector, 1 leaf; pp. 1—375. Libro Segundo, pp. 1—332; Summario, 2 leaves.

5603 HUBBARD (W. *Minister of Ipswich*) Present State of New England, being a narrative of the troubles with the Indians in New England from the first planting in 1607 to 1677: to which is added a Discourse about the War with the Pequods in 1637, small 4to. LARGE WOOD-CUT MAP OF NEW ENGLAND, VERY RARE, £4. 4s *London, Parkhurst*, 1677

This work was reprinted from the first edition, *Boston*, 1677, and must have been issued almost simultaneously. The Boston edition omits the first portion of the title "Present state of New England, being;" the woodcut map is the same in both issues, and is considered the first map printed in the United States. Of the Boston edition two copies were recently picked up at the prices of 1 and 2 shillings, but sold 1856, Sotheby's £5.; 1859, Puttick's £6., and were bought by a bookseller.

Collation: Licence, dated Boston, March 29, 1677—London, June 27, 1677, 1 *leaf*; MAP; *title*, 1 *leaf*; dedication, 2 *leaves*; advertisement, 1 *leaf*; Poems, 2 *leaves*; A Narrative, 131 pp.; a table of Towns inhabited by the English in New England, 7 pp.; Postscript, 3 *leaves*; A Narrative, etc. from Pascataqua to Pemmaquid, 88 pp.

5604 HUMBOLDT, Essai politique sur le Royaume de la NOUVELLE ESPAGNE, 2 vols. impl. 4to. *calf neat*—ATLAS PHYSIQUE et GEOGRAPHIQUE, 20 *large maps*, atlas folio, *hf. bd.*—together 3 vols. (pub. at 250 fr.) £2. 10s *Paris*, 1811

5605 —— le même, 6 vols. 8vo. *map, sd.* 10s 1811

5606 HUMBOLDT (Al. de) Vues des CORDILLÈRES, et Monumens des peuples indigenès de l'Amerique, impl. folio, 69 *large plates of Mexican Picture-writing, Hieroglyphics, Bas-reliefs, Costumes, Views, &c. some* FINELY COLOURED, (pub. at 504 fr.) *hf. red morocco, neat*, £6. 6s *Paris*, 1810

5607 —— the same, impl. folio, VELLUM PAPER, *a few leaves stained, hf. green morocco, full gilt back*, £6. 1810

The greater part of the copies now in the market want from page 272 to page 350, and plates 50-69. The most beautiful and generally interesting part of Humboldt's works, at a fourth of the original price. "Humboldt traced with the hand of a master the outline of a vast picture, future travellers can only assist in filling up."—*Ward's Mexico*.

In this work the Picture-writing of the Mexicans first received the attention and the ample treatment which are due to a literature as strange and important in the records of the New World, as that of Egypt in the Old.

At a great public meeting, held June 21, 1824, it was declared by the executive power of the Mexican Government, that "Mr. Humboldt's 'Political Essay on New Spain,' contained the most complete and most accurate picture of the natural riches of the country, and that the reading of this great work had not a little contributed to reanimate the active industry of the nation, and to inspire it with confidence in its own powers."

"No name stands higher than that of Humboldt, among the lovers of geographical and physical science. In exploring the tropical regions of the New World, this accomplished traveller has displayed a resolution and perseverance. that have never been surpassed by any former adventurer. Very few individuals indeed were better qualified than M. de Humboldt for executing that arduous undertaking. Zealous, active, vigorous; imbued with liberal knowledge, skilful in general physics, and particularly attached to chemistry and its kindred branches, possessing ample means of indulging its taste, while thirsting after discoveries, and fired with emulation and the generous passion of fame, he has directed his inquiries into every department of nature and society. The mass of curious information which he procured in those distant travels, and the superb collection which he was enabled to make, relative to different objects of science, far exceed anything that has heretofore been achieved by the exertions of an individual. Much interesting light is thus cast on the history of our species; the limits of accurate geography are extended; and the stores of botany, zoology, and mineralogy, are enriched with immense additions."
Edinburgh Review, vol. 16, p. 223-4

5608 JAMAICA. Interesting Tracts relating to the Island of Jamaica, curious State papers, Councils of War, Letters, Narratives, etc. from the conquest down to 1702, 4to. 300 pp. *calf gilt*, £2. 2s *St. Jago de la Vega*, 1800
Very rare and important. I never saw a copy before.

5608*JAMAICA. Ordinances of the Common Council of Kingston for the regulation of Internal Affairs, etc. in 1 vol. 4to. *bds. uncut*, 10s *Jamaica*, 1803-9

5609 JEFFERSON (Thomas) Notes on the State of Virginia, 8vo. *map and tables, calf*, 7s 6d *Philadelphia*, 1794

5610 JESUITS. RELATIONS DES JESUITES, contenant ce qui s'est passé de plus remarquable dans les Missions des Pères de la Compagnie de Jésus dans la Nouvelle France, 1611-72, ouvrage publié sous les auspices du Gouvernment Canadien, 3 vols. stout royal 8vo. *double columns, containing reprints of the Journals and letters of the Missionaries in* CANADA, *during a most interesting period, hf. calf, uncut*, £3. 10s ; or *calf gilt*, £4. *Quebec*, 1858
Nothing can be more valuable as a record of the manners and customs of the North American Indians, than the detailed and exact information contained in the collected narratives of men like the Jesuits, admittedly earnest, learned, and intelligent, full of practical wisdom, and possessing opportunities and talents which no single traveller could ever combine.

5611 JEFFERY's Description of the Spanish Islands and Settlements on the Coast of the West Indies, sm. 4to. 32 *maps and plates, calf*, 16s 1762

5612 JUAN Y ULLOA, Relacion historica del Viage a la America Meridional, hecho por orden de S. Mag. para medir algunos grados de Meridiano Terrestre, y venir por ellos en conocimiento de la verdadera figura y magnitud de la Tierra, con otras varias Observaciones Astronomicas y Phisicas—Origen y Succession de los Incas del Peru. Observ. astron. y phisicas en los Reynos del Peru, 5 vols. in 4, high 4to. *large paper, many maps and plates, vellum*, £2. 16s
"Ouvrage fort estimé."—BRUNET. *Madrid*, 1747-48

5613 KEATING's Expedition to the source of St. Peter's River, Lake Winnepeck, etc. 2 vols. in 1, 8vo. *map and plates, those of shells coloured, hf. calf*, 7s 1825

5614 KENNETT (Bp. *of Peterborough*) Bibliothecæ Americanæ Primordia, an Attempt towards laying the foundation of an American Library, sm. 4to. *title cut, calf, scarce*, 32s 1713

5615 KINGSBOROUGH'S (Lord) ANTIQUITIES OF MEXICO : comprising facsimiles of Ancient Mexican Paintings and Hieroglyphics, preserved in the Royal Libraries of Paris, Berlin, and Dresden ; in the Imperial Library of Vienna ; in the Vatican Library ; in the Borgian Museum at Rome ; in the Library of the Institute of Bologna ; and in the Bodleian Library at Oxford ; together with the Monuments of New Spain, by M. Dupaix ; with their respective scales of measurement, and accompanying descriptions ; the whole illustrated by many valuable inedited MSS. 9 vols. impl. folio, *containing upwards of* 1000 *large plates, embracing all the Remains of Mexican Architecture, Art, Religion, etc. hf. morocco, uncut, gilt tops*, £25. 1830-48

5616 ——— the same, *with the plates* COLOURED (pub. at £175.) *hf. morocco, gilt tops*, £50. 1830-48

Cet ouvrage de la plus grande magnificence, a été exécuté aux frais de Lord Kingsborough, qui en a fait hommage à plusieurs bibliothèques publiques du continent, particulièrement à la Bibliothèque royale, a Paris, et à celle de l'Institut de France. Le prix de chaque exemplaire était de 175 livres (2000 fr. Klaproth). Les quatre premiers volumes renferment les planches lithographiées, au nombre de plus de 1000 ; les trois autres contiennent l'explication des planches et plusieurs mémoires inédits, écrits en différentes langues, ainsi que des appendices en anglais. Le septième volume est entièrement rempli par un ouvrage important qui a pour titre : *Historia universa de las cosas de Nueva Espana, por el M. R. P. Fr. Bernardino de Sahagun*."—*Brunet*.

After an interval of seventeen years two more volumes of this extraordinary work have been published, in every respect uniform with the preceding, consisting, 1. of Supplementary Notes in English and Spanish; 2. of Extracts from the works of Torquemada, Acosta and Garcia, illustrating the last portion of the Mexican paintings, contained in the collection of Mendoza, and shewing the correspondence which exists between many of the Mexican and Hebrew laws; 3. Adair's History of the North American Indians, their customs and descent from the Jews; 4. Cartas ineditas de Hernando Cortez; 5. Cronica Mexicana de Tezozomoc; 6. Historia Chichimeca y Relaciones por Fernando de Alva Ixtlilxochitl.

"When, some four centuries ago, the enterprise of Spanish navigators opened the vast continent of America to the admiration of Europe, the civilization of the New World was found to be concentrated in two spots, and two only, of that enormous territory. One of these favoured regions was Peru: the other was Mexico. IT WAS IN MEXICO ESPECIALLY THAT ART, POLITICS, AND SCIENCE HAD RECEIVED THEIR GREATEST DEVELOPMENT. All the rest of North America, from the shores of Hudson's Bay to the mouths of the Mississippi, was desolate and barbarous, diversified only by swamp, forest, or prairie, and populated by savages without knowledge or laws. Mexico alone redeemed the character of the new continent, and presented to the eyes of the invaders a spectacle so marvellous as to satisfy even the expectations which the great discovery had raised. There the Spaniards found an organized State, an ancient polity, and opulent capital, an exalted dynasty, a formidable priesthood, and a people well skilled in mechanical and decorative arts. So great, in fact, was the proficiency of the Mexican workmen, so elaborate the system of government, and so impressive the whole evidence of wealth and grandeur, that for some time the civilization of Mexico was regarded as superior to that of Europe. Although, indeed, the researches of modern inquirers have enabled us to apply some corrective to these ideas, it is really probable that in certain respects the Spaniards found Mexico more advanced than Spain, and we have been recently assured on the authority of a comprehensive history that this civilization was the necessary incident of geographical and natural advantages. Such was the situation and configuration of Mexico that it could hardly fail to make progress, and all that was discovered there in the shape of national wealth or political order represented the extraordinary opportunities which nature had provided."—*Times, Dec.* 8, 1858.

5617 KUNSTMANN (Fr.) The Discovery of America: die Entdeckung Amerikas, nach den ältesten Quellen geschichtlich dargestellt; mit einem ATLAS alter bisher ungedruckter Karten, 4to. Text and very large folio ATLAS of 13 *maps, being facsimiles of Early* PORTULANI, *represented with scrupulous accuracy by J. Schleicher and S. Minsinger,* £4. 5s   München, 1859

The most valuable modern contribution to our knowledge of geographical discovery.

The Royal Academy of Sciences at Munich has done an important service to the cause of Geographical Science, by the publication of this work. It forms a part of the series called "Monumenta Sæcularia," issued by the Academy, and contains a most able account of the several discoveries made in America from the time of the Northmen downwards. Its principal attraction, however, lies in the atlas of the thirteen maps by which it is illustrated. These are in folio, while the letter-press is in quarto, and contains accurate representations of some of the earliest maps of America existing in the Court and State Library at Munich, the Library of the University and the "Haupt-Conservatorium" of the Bavarian Army. They comprise the maps of Pedro Reinel, of the Viscount De Majolo, of Vaz Dourado and others, besides an English map drawn by one Thomas Hood, in 1592, and showing the whole east coast of America down to the Isthmus of Panama. All these are lithographed in the first style of the art, and handsomely coloured to resemble the originals.

5618 LABAT, Nouveau Voyage aux Isles de l'Amerique, contenant l'Histoire Naturelle de ces Pays, l'Origine, les Mœurs, &c. 2 vols. 4to. *maps and plates, old calf gilt,* 18s   La Haye, 1724

Priced, 1836, £2. 8s. Fetched, 1855, Bernal's sale, 30s.

5619 LAET (Jo. de) Novus Orbis seu Descriptio Indiæ Occidentalis, folio, *numerous cuts, maps, &c. neat in calf,* 25s   Lugd. Bat. Elzevir, 1633

"Opus egregium, maximeque rarum et infrequens."—MEUSELIUS.

5620 LAFITEAU, Mœurs des Sauvages Ameriquains, comparées aux Mœurs des premiers temps, 2 vols. 4to. *many plates, illustrating the Religion and Customs of the Indians, calf,* RARE, 32s   Paris, 1724

"Whoever considers the Americans of this day, not only studies the manners of a remote present nation, but he studies in some measure the antiquities of all nations, from which no mean lights may be thrown upon many parts of the ancient authors, both sacred and profane. The learned Lafiteau has laboured this point with great success, in a work which deserves to be read amongst us much more than I find it is."—BURKE.

"This is a very curious work relating chiefly to Canadian manners and customs; the author lived five years in Canada. It is now rare."—DIBDIN.

5621 LAON D'AIGREMONT, Relation du Voyage des Français au Cap de Nord en Amerique, 12mo. *map and plates, calf,* RARE, £2.   Paris, 1654

5622 LE FEBVRE DE LA BARRE, Description de la France Equinoctiale, cydevant appelée Guyanne et par les Espagnols, El Dorado, sm. 4to. *large folding map, old calf gilt,* RARE, £3. 3s   Paris, 1666

5623 LEWIS and Clarke, Travels from St. Louis to the Pacific, 1804-6, with an Indian Vocabulary, 8vo. *maps, bds.* 5s   1806

5623*LLORENTE (Sebastian) Historia del Peru: I, Historia antigua del Peru; II, Historia de la Conquista; III, Historia, bajo la dinastia Austriaca, 1542-98; 3 vols. 8vo. *the first vol. bound, the two others sd.* 32s   Lima, 1860-63

5624 LOZANO, Descripcion Chorographica de las provincias del Gran Chaco, Gualamba, los Ritos y costumbres de las naciones que le habitan, etc. por Machoni, sm. stout 4to. *fine copy, with large map, vellum, or calf,* 30s   Cordoba, 1733

5625 ——— Historia de la Compañia de Jesus en la Provincia del Paraguay, 2 vols. sm. stout folio, *calf, very scarce,* £4. 4s   Madrid, 1754-55

Lady Webster's copy fetched £6. 5s.—"A judicious author."—ROBERTSON.

5626 LUCAS, Charters of the Old English Colonies, 8vo. *bds.* 3s 6d   1850

AMERICA. 299

5627 LUCCOCK, Notes on Rio Janeiro and the Southern Parts of Brazil, 4to. *plans and maps* (pub. at £2. 12s 6d) *bds. 9s* 1820

5628 LUGO, Gramatica en la lengua general del Nuevo Reyno, llamada Mosca, 16mo. *title injured, and folio* 2 *and the last* 3 *pp. in MS. hf. bd.* EXTREMELY RARE, £5. *Madrid, Guzman,* 1619

5629 MACKENZIE's Voyages from Montreal, on the St. Lawrence, and to the Frozen and Pacific Oceans, 1789-93, with account of the Fur trade, 4to. *maps, hf. bd. uncut,* 12s 1801

5630 M'GREGOR's British America, 2 vols. 8vo. *map* (pub. at 30s), *cloth,* 6s 1833

5631 MAGALLANES: Relacion del ultimo Viage al Estrecho de Magallanes, de la Fragata S. Maria de la Cabeza, 1785-86, y Noticia de los Habitantes, etc. sm. 4to. *portraits, tables, and* 5 *large maps, old red morocco, royal arms of Spain on sides,* 32s *Madrid,* 1788

5632 —— Apendice, que contiene el Viage para completar el reconocimiento del Estrecho, 1788-89, sm. 4to. *map, calf,* 10s 1793

5633 MALDONADO, Afectos a Dios . . . Oraciones que predicó en Antequera, Valle de Oaxaca, 8vo. *half russia,* 7s 6d *Valladolid,* 1713

5634 MARQUES, Brasilia Pontificia, sive speciales facultates Brasiliae Episcopis concessae, cum appendice, sm. folio, *calf,* VERY RARE, £3. 16s *Ulyssipone,* 1749

COLLATION: Half title and title, 2 leaves; Dedication, 6 leaves; Ad Lectorem, 2 leaves; Facultates, etc. 2 leaves; Series librorum, 6 leaves; pp. 1-486; Index, pp. 1-69; Errata, p. 70.

5635 MARSHALL's History of Kentucky, 2 vols. 8vo. *calf,* 18s *Frankf. (Kentuck.)* 1824

5636 MASSACHUSETTS Historical Society, Collections of, Third Series, Vol. 1, with Index, 1849; Fourth Series, Vols. 1, 2, 3, 1852-56—the 4 vols. 8vo. *bds.* 30s
Boston, N.E. 1849-56

5637 MATHER (Cotton) Magnalia Christi Americana; or the Ecclesiastical History of New England, from 1620 to 1698, folio, *the map in facsimile, tall copy in the original calf,* £5. 1702

Contents: I. Antiquities; II. The Lives of the Governors of New England; III. The Lives of 60 Divines of New England; IV. An account of the University of Cambridge, New England; V. Acts and Monuments of the Church of New England; VI. Wonderful Providences on divers persons in New England; VII. The Wars of the Lord, or disturbances of the Churches of New England.

5638 MATHER. JENNINGS' Abridgment of the Life of Cotton Mather, by his son Samuel, 12mo. *calf,* 7s 6d 1744

5639 MATRAYA Y RICCI, EL Moralista Filalethico Americano, Tom. I, stout sm. folio, *limp vellum, rare,* 30s *Lima,* 1819

Including a "Catalogo cronologico de las Pragmaticas, Cedulas, Decretos, etc. despues de la publicacion de la recopilacion de las Leyes de Indias en 1680."

5640 MAUDE's Visit to the Falls of Niagara in 1800, roy. 8vo. *several plates, cloth,* 7s 6d 1826

5641 MAXIMILIAN Prinz zu Wied, Reise in das innere Nordamerica, 1832-34, 2 vols. impl. 4to. LARGE PAPER, *map,* 33 *fine plates of Scenery, Costume, Portraits, etc. after drawings by Bodmer, and many woodcuts, fine impressions, presentation copy from Prince Maximilian,* NO ATLAS, *bds.* 27s *Coblenz,* 1839-41

Priced, 1843, Williams and Norgate, £12. 12s, pp. 455-645 are on American Languages.

5642 MEDRANO, Breve Descripcion del Mundo, 12mo. *vellum,* 7s 6d *Brusselas,* 1688

The first fifteen pages are a Geographical description in verse.

5643 **MEXICO.** Celleccion de Ordenes y Decretos de la soberana Junta provisional gubernativa y soberanos congresos generales de la Nacion Mexicana, 5 vols. in 3, sm. 4to. *Spanish calf,* 36s *Mexico,* 1829-31

5644 TRAGE DE INDIO DE MEXICO: Costumbres, Fiestas, Entretenimientos, y diversas formas de proceder de los Indios de Nueva España, sm. 4to. *MS. of* 144 *leaves, beautifully bound in black morocco extra, gilt edges, arms on sides,* £2. 16s
ca. 1780

An interesting and important MS. stated to be copied from the original MS. in the Escurial Library. It was written about the year 1560, and intended to be illustrated by a series of drawings; but, as stated on the first page, "faltan las pinturas." It contains most elaborate and detailed information upon the Religious Worship and various Deities of the Ancient Mexicans; their manners, habits, superstitions, etc. The last 126 pp. contain a "Tratado di los Chichimecas," who are stated to be a wandering race, held in abhorrence by the Mexicans, and whom the author says "se podrian bien comparar a los Alarabes." The information contained in this work has probably never been published.

5645 RIVERA (M. G.) Nueva Colleccion de Leyes y Decretos Mexicanos, en forma de Diccionario, Tom. I, letra A, stout impl. 8vo. 1109 *pp. calf,* 14s *Mexico,* 1853

5646 MISSA GOTHICA, SEU MOZARABICA, et Officium itidem Gothicum, diligenter explanata (à Lorenzanà) in obsequium Decani et Capituli Eccles. Toletanæ Hisp. et Indiarum Primatis, sm. folio, *rubrics and engravings by Nava,*

very fine copy in the original smooth morocco binding, back, sides and leaves gilt,
£3. 3s   *Angelopoli typ. Palafox.* 1770
 Angelopolis or Puebla de los Angelos, where this volume was printed, is a city of Mexico, and formerly the capital of the province of Tlascala. This edition of the Mozarabic Missal is unnoticed by Zaccaria, as well as in any other liturgical or bibliographical work.

5647 MOLINA (Fray Alonso de) VOCABULARIO EN LENGUA MEXICANA y Castellana, 2 vols. in 1, sm. fol. *last leaf neatly mended, russia, gilt edges,* £20. *Mexico,* 1571
 A copy was priced by Thorpe in 1832, £28. which had cost Lord Kingsborough £52. 10s; another priced by Stargardt, in Berlin, 1858, 150 Thalers; fetched at Sotheby's, 1857, *cut close and mended,* £15. 15s; in 1860 at Puttick's, £16. The present copy cost Mr. Heber £31. 10s in the original parchment cover.
 The first and most complete of any of the dictionaries of the American languages. It is cited by Thomas in his History of Printing in America, as a great literary curiosity, it being one of the earliest books printed in the New World. See also Dr. Cotton, Horne, Tenante, and other bibliographical productions.

5648 MOLINA, Historia del reyno de CHILI, traducido del Italiano por Mendoza, y la Cruz, 2 vols. in 1, sm. 8vo. *containing a philological sketch of the Chilene language, Comparative Vocacularies, and a list of writers on Chili, with portrait and map, calf,* or *sd. uncut,* 10s   *Madrid,* 1788-95

5649 MOLLIEN, Voyage dans la République de Colombie, 1823, 2 vols. 8vo *map and plates, calf gilt,* 6s   *Paris,* 1825

5650 MONARDES (Nicolo) Primera y Segunda y Tercera partes de la Historia Medicinal de las Cosas que se traen de nuestras Indias Occidentales que siruen en Medicina, tratado de la Piedra Bezaar, y de la yerua Escuerconera sq. 8vo. *woodcuts, margins stained, vellum,* 20s ; or *a fine copy, slightly stained, and very little cut, in hf. russia,* 30s   *Sevilla,* 1574
 Priced, 1860, £4. 4s; 1858, 31 florins.

5651 —— the same, a later edition, sm. 4to. *vellum,* 20s   *Sevilla,* 1580

5652 —— delle Cose che vengono portate dall' Indie Occidentali pertinenti all' Uso della Medicina, nouamente recata dalla Spagnola; de' Veneni et della lor cura; con libro della Neve, 2 vols. in 1, 12mo. *a few woodcuts,* De Thou's copy in old "*veau fauve," with his large Arms containing Monogram stamped in gold on sides and back,* £2.   *Venetia,* 1575
 This rare work, orignally written in Spanish, has also been translated into English under the title of "Joyfull Newes from the New-found World by Dr. Monardus."

5653 MONTALVO, Informe del nuevo beneficio que se ha dado a los Metales ordinarios de Plata, folio, *vellum,* 18s   *Mexico,* 1643

5654 MOSQUERA, Examen del libelo publicado en el Comercio en Lima por el reo profugo OBANDO, 2 vols. 8vo. *hf. calf,* 9s   *Valpariso,* 1843
 Containing the life of Obando, and an account of the battles between the Spaniards and the Republicans, 1819-30.

5655 MURR'S Nachrichten von verschiedenen Ländern des Spanischen Amerika, 2 vols. in 1, 8vo. *bds.* 12s   *Halle,* 1809-11
 Containing very valuable specimens of various American languages, including a "Tarahumarisches Woerterbuch," "Californische Sprachproben," etc.

5656 NAVARRETE, Colleccion de los VIAGES y Descubrimientos que hicieron los Españoles desde el Siglo XV. con documentos sobre la historia de su Marina y de sus establecimientos en Indias, 5 vols. sm. 4to. *maps and portraits, sd. uncut,* £3. or *calf,* £3. 10s   1825-37
 I sold a copy in 1860, for £4. 10s. "Le *premier* volume de cette importante collection contient le journal original des voyages de Colomb, redigé par las Casas; le *second* est rempli de curieux documents relatifs a l'histoire des mœurs à cette époque; le troisième renferme les expeditions d'Americo Vespucci, et dans les *tomes* 4 *et* 5 sont compris les expeditions de Magellan, Elcano, Loaisa et Saavedra, le tout ou d'après des manuscrits inédits, ou réimprimé sur les editions devenues très rares."—*Brunet.*
 From this collection Washington Irving drew his information regarding Columbus.

5657 NEAL'S (Dan.) History of New England, containing an Account of its Civil and Ecclesiastical Affairs to the Year 1700, with the Present State of New England, and an Appendix, containing their present Charter, etc. 2 vols. 8vo. *large map, fine copy in calf,* 20s   1720

5658 NEW ENGLAND HISTORICAL and GENEALOGICAL REGISTER, published under the direction of the New England Historic-Genealogical Society, FIRST SERIES, COMPLETE, 10 vols. 8vo. *numerous fine portraits, plates, facsimiles, etc. half calf,* RARE, £8. 10s   *Boston,* 1847-56

5659 —— The same, Vols. I.—IX. 8vo. *new in cloth,* £6.   *Boston,* 1847-55
 Including papers on the early Records of the State, facsimile signatures of the first settlers; tracing the families of New England to their European progenitors: a very interesting periodical.

5660 **NEW YORK.** DOCUMENTS relative to the COLONIAL HISTORY of the State of New York, 1663-1778, procured in Holland, England, and France, by J. R. Brodhead, Agent, edited by E. B. O'Callaghan, 10 vols. roy. 4to. *numerous maps, including facsimiles of early charts,* etc. *cloth,* £5. 15s   *Albany,* 1856-58

AMERICA. 301

5661 NEW YORK, Documentary History of the State of New York, arranged under direction of the Hon. C. Morgan, Secretary of State, by E. B. O'Callaghan, 4 vols. stout 8vo. *large coloured* GEOLOGICAL *and numerous other* MAPS, *views, portraits, facsimiles,* etc. *cloth,* £2. 16s *Albany,* 1849-51
A very valuable collection of papers relative to the Indian tribes and settlers in New York.

5662 NEWSMAN'S Interpreter: a Description of several Spanish Territories in America, particularly those against which the English have a Design, 18mo. *2nd edition, 3 folding plans, poor copy, hf. bd. very rare,* 15s *Manchester,* 1741

5663 NODAL (BARTOLOME GARCIA, and GONÇALO DE.) RELACION DEL VIAGE qve hizieron al descubrimiento del Estrecho Nuebo de S. Vicente y reconosimjo. del de Magallanes, sm. 4to. *fine copy in old Spanish red morocco, Arms on sides, with the map from the second edition,* £4. 10s *Madrid, Correa de Montenegro,* 1621

Twelve prel leaves: viz. Engraved title with Portraits of the two brothers Nodal. the reverse blank; 'Fee de apronacion,' 3 pp.; 'Suma del priuilegio,' 1 p.; 'Tassa,' 1 p.; 'Erratas,' 1 p.; 'A Don Fernando Carillo,' 3 pp.; 'Al Lector,' 5 pp.; 'Advertencias,' 3 pp.; 'Variacion de la aguja,'' 3 pp.; 'Reglas,' 2 pp.; Text, 65 folioed leaves; 'Tabla para saler las Horas,' etc. 1 leaf; 'Relacion svmaria de los Servicios de los Capitanes Bartolome Garcia de Nodal, y Gonçalo de Nodal hermanos,' folioed leaves 2-15. At fol. 35 there should be a copperplate Map entitled 'Reconocimiento de los Estrechos de Magellanes,' etc. 'I. de Courbes sculpsit,' 13½ by 15¼ inches. It is supplied, in the copy above described, by the reprint in a smaller form, from the second edition.
Fetched, 1860, Puttick's, £12. "More than one copy has been sold for 30 guineas."—*Rich.* The map is almost always wanting, and from the well-know jealousy, or policy rather, of the Spanish Government, was probably inserted in very few copies. The Rev. Mr. Crofts, believed his own copy to be the only perfect one in England—that in the British Museum being deficient of the chart.

5664 NOVUS ORBIS, id est, Navigationes Primæ in Americam, cum Varrerii discvrsu super Ophyra Regione, 12mo. *a very fine copy in the original calf, gilt back,* 20s
Fetched, 1860, Puttick's, £2. 4s. *Roterodami,* 1616

5664*NYWE TESTAMENT set over in die Creols Tael, tot Dienst van die Deen Mission, stout sm. 8vo. 1166 pp. *calf,* 12s *Copenhagen,* 1781
In the Negro-Dutch dialect, spoken in the West Indian possessions of Denmark.

5665 OBANDO (General) Apuntamientos para manifestacion de la persecucion que ha sufrido, 1837, 8vo. *hf. bd.* 10s *Lima,* 1842

5666 OEXMELIN, Histoire des Avanturiers qui se sont signalez dans les Indes, des Boucaniers, etc. 2 vols. in 1, stout 12mo. *maps and plates, calf,* 18s *Paris,* 1688

5667 OLDENDORPS Geschichte der Mission der Evangelischen Brüder, auf den Caraïb. Inseln, herausg. durch Bossart, 2 vols. in 1, stout sm. 8vo. *with an article "von der verschiedenen Sprachen der Neger," and comparative table, maps and plates,* 18s *Barby,* 1777

5668 ORTIZ, Discursos Exemplares (de un Indiano, etc.) 16mo. *calf,* 7s 6d *Xeres,* 1634

5669 OVALLE, Historica relacion del reyno de CHILE, smallest folio, *large Map,* 36 *plates and* 18 *woodcuts, perfect, red morocco, gilt edges,* £6. 6s *Roma,* 1646

Extremely rare when perfect, copies being generally found defective. COLLATION: Title, Prologo, Advertencia, and Protesta, 4 leaves; text, pp. 1-456, including Index.
The plates in the above volume are curious. One at p. 58 represents a miraculous tree like the Saviour crucified, growing in the valley of Limache, in Chili; another the sudden appearance of the Virgin, at a battle between the Indians and Spaniards; others, the various games, customs, &c. of the Indians, with the manner of transfering their houses from one place to another.
"Ouvrage recherché mais difficile à trouver."—BRUNET.

5670 OVAGLIE (Alonso d') historica relatione del Regno di CILE, e delle Missioni che esercita in quelle la Compagnia di Giesu, very small folio, *plates, vellum or hf. bd.* £2. 10s *Roma,* 1646
In the same year appeared a Spanish edition, slightly differing. COLLATION of the ITALIAN edition: title, 1 leaf; Prolog. 2 leaves; tabula geographica regni Chile; Advertimenti, 1 leaf; the body of the work, pp. 1-378, with 12 unnumbered plates, opposite pp. 50, 90, 92, 94, 106, 168, 180, 182; Seconda protesta, 1 leaf; a Series of Churches and Buildings, etc. 12 pp. engraved on wood; alcune Isole, 6 pp. engraved on wood.

5671 OVIEDO, Historia general y natural de las Indias, Islas y Tierra-firme del Mar Océano, por el Capitan Gonzalo F. De Oviedo y Valdés, Vols. I-IV, folio, *maps and plates, hf. morocco,* £6. 6s *Madrid,* 1851-5
A new and very fine edition of 50 books of Oviedo's History of Spanish America, edited for the Royal Academy of History, by D. José Amador de los Rios.

5672 PALFREY'S History of New England, 2 vols. roy. 8vo. *maps and facsimiles, cloth,* 20s *Boston (U.S.),* 1858-60

5673 **Paraguay.** Coleccion general de Documentos, tocantes a la Persecucion, que los regulares de la Compañia suscitaron, 1644-60, contra B. de Cardenas, 2 vols.—Tomo Tercero: Sucesos tocantes á la segunda Epoca de las conmociones enel Paraguay—Tomo Quarto: Tercera Epoca, el Reyno Jesuitico del Paraguay, por Ibañez de Echavarri—4 vols. sm. 4to. *clean copy, vellum,* RARE, £3. 10s *Madrid,* 1768-70
A valuable work, with a great amount of information on the condition of Paraguay under the Jesuits.

5674 CAUSA Jesuitica de Portugal, guerra de los Jesuitas en el Uruguay y Paraná, sq. 8vo. *hf. calf,* 10s *Madrid,* 1768

5675 PENNSYLVANIA HISTORICAL SOCIETY, 1845-46; containing reprints of Dent's New York, 1670; Senter's Journal, 1775; Townsend's Battle of Brandywine, 1777, 8vo. *cloth,* 6s *Philadelphia,* 1845-46

5676 CONTRIBUTIONS to American History, roy. 8vo. *cloth,* 7s 6d *ib.* 1858

5677 PENNSYLVANIA. REGISTER OF PENNSYLVANIA, devoted to the Preservation of Documents, etc. respecting the State, edited by HAZARD, Vols. I.-XVI., roy. 8vo. *hf. calf, very rare,* £4. 10s *Philadelphia,* 1828-36

5678 PERALTA BARNUEVO, Lima Fundada, o Conquesta del Peru, poema heroico, en que se decanta la historia del Descubrimiento y Sugecion por Pizarro, 2 vols. sq. 8vo. *calf neat, rare,* 36s *Lima,* 1732

Priced, Thorpe, £2. 12s 6d; fetched, 1859, Puttick's, £1. 19s; Sotheby's, £2. 2s.
"This book, having been printed in South America, has escaped the notice of Bayer in his edition of Nic. Antonio. Pinelo speaks of another work of the author, but does not seem to know this work, of which, perhaps, not many copies have reached Europe."—See *Bibliotheca Grenvilliana.*

5679 PHILADELPHIA: Rush's Account of the Bilious remitting Yellow Fever, 1793, 8vo. *cloth,* 6s *Philad.* 1794

5680 PHILOPONI (Honorii) Nova typis transacta Navigatio Novi Orbis Indiæ Occidentalis, Rev. Buellii Catalonii sociorumque Monachorum, ad barbaras gentes Evangelium prædicandi gratiâ delegatorum etc. folio, *engraved frontispiece and* 18 *very curious plates by* Kilian, *in the manner of De Bry, vellum,* £2. *s. l.* 1621

Priced, 1828, £3. 3s; 1853, £6. 16s; 1856, £3. 3s; 1857, £3. 18s; sold in Pitt's sale for £3. 4s, and in Lord Valentia's for the same sum. It contains a very detailed account of Columbus and his discoveries. The plates are very curious, one of which contains a whole-length portrait of Columbus.

5681 PIEDRAHITA, Historia general de las Conquistas del Nuevo Reyno de Granada, folio, *a little stained at the beginning, but otherwise a fine tall copy, hf. calf,* VERY RARE, £4. 4s *Amberes, s. a. (Madrid,* 1688)

Lord Stuart de Rothesay's copy, 1855, fetched £4. 10s.
"Le premier vólume de cet ouvrage important est le seul qui ait paru; il va jusqu'en 1563. Cette perte est d'autant plus regrettable que la Nouvelle-Grenade est une partie de l'Amerique sur laquelle, nous possédons le moins de documens."—*Ternaux.*
COLLATION: Printed Title; Engraved title, with 7 portraits of Indian Chiefs and coat-of-arms of D. Vincente Gonçaga; Dedication "Senor," signed "Lucas Obispo de Santa Marta," 1 leaf; Aprobacion, etc. 7 leaves, with catchwords; engraved title, 'Primera Parte,' with 12 portraits of native chiefs; pp. 1-599; Indice, 7 pp.; and a blank leaf, forming Gggg. 4. In the text, between pp. 62 and 63, there is an engraved title, "Libro Tercero," containing 13 portraits of Spanish Commanders, before the third book.

5682 PIZARRO Y ORELLANA (Fernando) Varones Illustres del Nuevo Mundo, Descubridores, Conquistadores, y Pacificadores del Imperio de las Indias Occidentales; sus vidas, virtud, valor, hazañas, y claros BLASONES sm. folio, *the paper discoloured, vellum,* RARE, £2. 16s *Madrid, Carrera,* 1639

COLLATION: Half title, 1 leaf; Title, 1 leaf; Senor, 1 leaf; Dedication, 2 leaves; Censura, etc. 7 leaves; Prefacion, 6 leaves; Varones, the work itself, pp. 1 to 427; Discurso, pp. 1-72; Indice, Sumario, and Index, 16 leaves.—This work contains an account of the Discoveries and Adventures of Columbus, Cortes, the Pizarros, Almagro, etc.

5683 POEPPIG's Reise in Chile, Peru, und auf dem Amazonenstrome, 1827-32, 2 vols. 4to. *map and music, with folio* ATLAS *of* 16 *plates, bds.* 14s *Leipz.* 1835-6

5684 PRINCE'S (Thos.) Chronological History of New England, from 1602, Vol. I. *reaching to* 1630, 12mo. *calf, rare,* 28s *Boston, N. E.* 1736
All published. There is only this volume in the British Museum.

5685 Quito. BREVE INSTRUCCION, o Arte para entender la lengua comune dos Indios de Quito, 12mo. *title injured, the end wanting, hf. bd.* 12s *Lima,* 1753
Fort rare. Un exemplaire incomplet, 17 fr. Raetzel—*Brunet.*

RAMON DE LA SAGRA,—*see Natural History Catalogue.*

5686 RAVENEAU de Lussan, Voyage à la Mer de Sud, avec les Flibustiers de l'Amerique, 18mo. *calf,* 10s *Paris,* 1690

5687 REGLAMENTO y Aranceles Reales para el Comercio libre de España a Indias, de 12 de Octubre, 1778, 4to. *with the book-plate of* "*El Conde de Tepa*," *calf,* 7s 6d *Madrid,* 1778

5688 REMESAL (F. Antonio de) Historia de la Provincia de S. Vicente de Chyapa y Guatemala de la Orden de S. Domingo, folio, *vellum, or in the original stamped calf,* £5. 5s *Madrid,* 1619
Fetched, 1855 Lord Rothesay's sale, £5.

5689 RIBAS (A. Perez de) Historia de los Triumphos de nuestra Santa Fee entre gentes las mas barbaras del Nuevo Orbe; costumbres, ritos, y supersticiones de

estas gentes, etc. sm. folio, *title mended, otherwise a fine copy in hf. calf,* VERY
RARE, £6. 10s *Madrid,* 1645
COLLATION: Title, and Dedication, 4 leaves; Approbations, and Protesta, 4 leaves; Prologo and Carta, 4 leaves; Tabla, Licencia, and Errata, 8 leaves; pp. 1-756; Indice, pp. 757-64. This copy therefore contains twenty preliminary leaves (erroneously misplaced at the end) while Mr. Stephens mentions but 16; and has also an Index of 4 leaves at the end, of which he was ignorant, and which was not in his copy.

5690 RICH, Bibliotheca Americana Nova: Catalogue of Books relating to America, Vol. II. *books printed from* 1801 *to* 1844, 1846—Supplement to Part I; 1701-1800, 1841—2 vols. in 1, 8vo. *cloth,* 25s 1841-5
The same price will be given by B. Q. for the first volume.

5691 RICHSHOFFER (Ambrosius) Braszilianisch und West Indianische Reisze Beschreibung, 12mo. *fine portrait, engraved title, plates with Coats of Arms of Pernambuco, Rio Grande, etc. bds. fine copy,* 25s *Strasburg, Joszias Städel,* 1677

5692 ROBINSON's (W. D.) Memoirs of the Mexican Revolution, and narrative of the expedition of General Mina, 2 vols. 8vo. *bds.* 6s; or *hf. calf neat,* 9s 1821

5693 [ROCHEFORT] Histoire naturelle et morale des Iles Antilles de l'Amerique, avec un VOCABULAIRE CARAÏBE, 4to. *engravings, calf,* 10s *Roterdam,* 1658

5694 ——— 2e édition, revue et augmentée, sm. 4to. *nearly* 50 *plates, bd.* 18s 1665

5695 ROCHEFOUCAULD-LIANCOURT, Voyage dans les Etats-Unis de l'Amérique, 1795-97, 8 vols. 8vo. *maps, calf gilt,* 20s *Paris,* 1799

5696 RUIZ DE LEON, Hernand. Triumphos de la Fe y Gloria de las Armas Espanoles. Poema heroyco. Conquista de Mexico, Cabeza del imperio septentrional de la Nueva-España, Proezas de Cortes y Grandezas del Nuevo Mundo, small 4to. *olive morocco, gilt edges,* £2. *Madrid,* 1755

5697 RUIZ (Ant.) Tesoro de la lengua Guarani, dedicado a la soberana Virgen Maria, very sm. 4to. *vellum, fine copy,* EXTREMELY RARE, £8. 8s *Madrid, Sanches,* 1639
Dictionnaire des plus rares d'une Langue Américaine presque éteinte. Il se compose de 8 ff. prél. et de 408 ff. à 2 col. "Livre devenu fort rare."—*Brunet.*

5698 RUZ, Yucatecan Grammar translated from the Spanish into Maya; and from the Maya into English by Kingdon, 8vo. *calf,* 15s *Belize,* 1847

5699 SANCHEZ VALVERDE, Idea del Valor de la Isla Española (St. Domingo), y sus utildades, sm. 4to. LARGE PAPER, 2 *maps, calf neat,* 18s *Madrid,* 1785

5700 SANTAREM, Researches respecting Americus Vespucius, by Childe, 12mo. *cloth,* 5s *Boston,* 1850

5701 SCHOOLCRAFT'S Historical and Statistical information respecting the history, condition and prospects of the INDIAN TRIBES of the UNITED STATES, Pts. I. and II. in 2 stout vols. impl. 4to. LARGE PAPER, *about* 150 *plates most of them coloured, of Views, and of Ancient Pottery, Cooking Utensils,* PICTURE WRITING, WRITTEN MUSIC, *Alphabets, etc. of the Indians,* (pub. at £8. 8s) *cloth, uncut,* £3. 10s *Philadelphia,* 1851-52
A work which contains a vast amount of interesting and valuable information on the Manners and Customs, Antiquities, Intellectual capacity, Physical type, Language, *with comparative Vocabularies,* Art, etc. of the American Indians, the whole most profusely illustrated with beautiful coloured plates.

5702 SCHOOLCRAFT's Notes on the Iroquois, contributions to American History, Antiquities and General Ethnology, 8vo. *plates, cloth,* 7s 6d *Albany,* 1847

5703 SCHMIDEL (H.). Vera Historia admirandæ cujusdam Nauigationis, quam Huldericus Schmidel in Americam, juxta Brasiliam et Rio della Plata confecit, 1534-54, quid sustinuerit, quam mirandas regiones ac homines viderit, ab ipso descripta, *charts and several plates,* and bound up with it is, Guil. Ces. de Solis Discorso di Cosmografia, e l'Origine di molte Citta del Mondo, *Padova,* 1602—in 1 vol. sq. 8vo. *vellum,* £3. 3s *Norimbergæ, Hulsius,* 1599
"Collation: Full-length portrait (mounted), title with engraving of Schmidel on horseback, a Coat of Arms on the first page, and 20 plates—102 pp of text (the last blank); added are pp. 3—12 et tabula locorum, 1 leaf of 'Descriptio Regni Guianae in America."

5704 SELKIRK's (Earl) Settlement upon the Red River, its destruction in 1815, 8vo. *maps, bds.* 5s 1817

5705 SHEA (J. G.) French-Onondaga Dictionary from a MS. of the Seventeenth Century, roy. 8vo. 103 *pp. double columns, calf,* 18s *New York,* 1860

5706 SIMON (Pedro) Primera Parte de las Noticias historiales de las Conquistas de tierra firme en las Indias Occidentales, folio, *engraved title, tall copy, vellum,* £5. *Cuenca, Domingo de la Yglesia,* 1627
This copy contains 9 preliminary leaves, being two more than stated by Mr. Steevens, in his collation of a complete copy. VERY RARE; an important relation prepared under the direction of the Council of the Indies. The first part only was published.

5707 SMITH'S (Capt. John) Generall Historie of Virginia, New England, and the Summer Isles; with the Names of the Adventurers, Planters, and Governours from their first beginning Anno 1584 to this present 1624, with the Proceedings of those Severall Colonies and the Accidents that befell them in all their Journeyes and Discoveries, sm. folio, *the portraits of the Duchess of Richmond and Matoaka reprints, fine royal copy in the original calf, with the royal arms of England stamped in gold on the sides*, EXTREMELY RARE, £18. 18s   1624

    A copy fetched at Puttick's in 1861, £23. wanting the two portraits.

5708 SMITHSONIAN INSTITUTION. Squier's Aboriginal Monuments of New York State, *plates and cuts*, 1849—Whittlesey's Ancient Works in Ohio, *plates*, 1852—Mayer on Mexican History and Archaeology, *plates*, 1856—Haven's Archaeology of the United States, 1856—together 4 parts, roy. 4to. *numerous plates, sewed*, 25s   *Washington*, 1849-56

5709 SOLIS (Ant. de) Historia de la Conquista de Mexico, poblacion y progressos de la America septentrional, folio, FIRST EDITION, *frontispiece, calf*, 18s; or, *a fine copy in calf extra*, 24s   *Madrid*, 1684

    Priced, 1824, Thorpe, £1. 11s 6d; 1826, with Salazar, Conq. de Mexico, 1743, 2 vols. vellum, £3. 3s.

5710 —— Historia de la Conquista de Mexico, Segunda parte, por SALAZAR y Olarte, sm. folio, *calf, scarce*, £2. 2s   *Cordoba*, 1743

5711 —— segunda parte, segunda edicion, sm. folio, *calf*, 21s   *Madrid*, 1786

5712 —— the same, both parts, 2 vols. 4to. BEST EDITION, *2 maps, portrait of Cortes by Titian engraved by Selma, portrait of De Solis, and many beautiful plates designed and engraved by Spanish artists, calf gilt*, £2. 16s   *Madrid*, 1783-4

5713 SPIX und Martius, Reise in Brasilien, 2 vols. 4to. *morocco*, 7s   *München*, 1828

5714 SQUIER'S Collection of Rare and Original documents, concerning the Discovery and Conquest of America, chiefly from the Spanish Archives, No. 1. Carta dirijida al Rey por Garcia de Palacio, 1576, Spanish and English, with notes and Index, sm. 4to. *map hf. morocco, uncut*, 18s   *New York*, 1860

    The above "Carta" gives a description of the Ancient Provinces of Guazacapan, Izalco, Cuscatlan, in the Audiencia of Guatemala; with an account of the Languages, Customs, and Religion of their aboriginal inhabitants.

5715 STADE (Hans) Warhafftige Historia unnd Beschreibung einer Landtschafft der wilden menschfresser Leuthen, in der Newen Welt gelegen, sq. 8vo. *several woodcuts, bds. rare*, £3. 13s 6d   *Franckfurdt, s. a.*

    Dated both at the end of the dedication and preface, 1556. According to Grenville, this is the second edition. Collation: Title; A 2-Z 4, ending with a colophon without date; no map. The engravings are entirely different from the Marpurg Vedition of 1557, mentioned by Brunet, a copy of which fetched £6. 12s, at Puttick's in 1861, there stated to be the original edition, although one year later in date than the above.

5716 STEPHENS (J. L.) Incidents of Travel in Central America, Chiapas, and Yucatan, 2 vols. 8vo. *plates of Aboriginal Monuments, cloth*, 18s   *New York*, 1841

5717 TAUSTE (Francisco de) Arte, y Bocabulario de la Lengua de los Indios CHAYMAS, CUMANAGOTOS, Cores, Parias, y otros diversos de la provincia de Cumana, o Nueva Andalucia, sq. 8vo. *title, dedication, approbations, and errata*, 8 *leaves; pp.* 1-187, *vellum*, £10   *Madrid*, 1680

    Extremely rare, unknown to most Bibliographers. The present copy, and one other are the only two that I can trace in bookseller's Catalogues, or public sales.

5718 TOMAS de Cordoba, la Administracion de Puerto-Rico. sm. *calf*, 10s *Madrid*, 1838

5719 TORQUEMADA (Juan de) Monarquia Indiana, con el origen y guerras de los Indios Occidentales, sus poblaciones, descubrimiento, conquista, conversion y otras cosas maravillosas, 3 vols. folio, *engraved titles, map, best edition, nice clean copy in Spanish vellum*, £3. 3s   *Madrid*, 1723

    "Ouvrage fort curieux, et le plus complet que nous ayons sur l'ancien Mexique."—*Brunet*.
    The author was for a long time resident in New Spain, and has inserted in this work some very interesting observations. Gonsalves de Barcia edited this new edition, which Brunet says is "la plus recherchée." "Ouvrages important sur l'histoire d'Amerique reimprimé par les soins de l'infatigable Barcia."—*Salva*.
    Priced, 1824, Thorpe, £3. 13s 6d; Quaritch, hf. cf. £4. 8s; fetched at Lord Rothesay's sale, £4.; 1858, Puttick's £3. 10s. LARGE PAPER, priced, 1824, Thorpe, bds. £8. 8s; 1830 Payne and Foss, bds. £4. 4s and 1833-7, £3. 3s fetched, Condé's, £3. 15s; 1859, Lady Webster's mor. with 2 leaves of Vol. 3 supplied from a small paper, £12.

5720 TORRES RUBIO (Diego de) Arte y Vocabulario de la Lengua QUICHUA general de los Indios de el PERU; añadio el P. Juan de FIGUEREDO; ahora nuevamente corregida y aumentada en muchos vocables y varias notas, etc. 16mo. *vellum, very rare*, £6. 6s   *Lima*, 1754

    I sold a copy in 1858, for £7. 7s. COLLATION: Title and dedication, 6 leaves; Arte de la Quichua, leaf 1-51; Doctrina Christiana, 52-72; Vocabulario Indico Castellano y Vocabulario Castellano Indico, 72-212; Vocabulario de la Lengua CHINCHAISUYO, y algunos modos mas usados de ella, por el P. Juan de Figueredo, 213-231; Confessionario en Quichua, 231-254; Indice, 5 pp.

AMERICA. 305

5721 ULLOA, Noticias Americanas, sobre la America Meridional, y la Septentrional Oriental, sm. 4to. *with remarks on the languages, old calf,* 10s   *Madrid,* 1772
5722 —— the same, sm. 4to. *calf,* 7s   1792
5723 UMFREVILLE's Present State of Hudson's Bay and the Fur Trade, *with a specimen of* 5 *Indian languages,* 8vo. *bds.* 8s   1790
5724 VARGAS MACHUCA (Bernardo de) Milicia y Descripcion de las Indias, 4to. *fine portrait, title wanting, vellum,* EXTREMELY RARE, £3. 10s   *Madrid,* 1599
    I have met with only one other copy, sold for £5.
    Collation: title (wanting) and 7 preliminary leaves; fine portrait, with Coat of Arms and map of America; leaves 1—186; tabla, 17 leaves; declaracion, 3 leaves; colophon, 1 leaf; tail-piece, 1 leaf.
    One of the most interesting and valuable books respecting the Conquest of South America.—SOUTHEY.
5725 VEITIA LINAGE, Norte de la Contratacion de las Indias Occidentales, sm. folio, *fine tall copy with the engraved frontispiece, vellum,* £2. 10s   *Sevilla,* 1672
    Fetched, 1855, Lord Stuart de Rothesay's copy, £4. 15s; 1859, Lady Webster's, cf. £2. 2s.
    "Ce livre est rare, et Salva l'estime, £2. 2s."—BRUNET.
    COLLATION: Engraved title, and printed title, 2 leaves; Censuras, Licence, and Errata, 6 leaves; Dedication, 1 leaf; Al Lector, and Advertencia, 5 leaves; Soneto, 1 leaf; Indice, 2 leaves; pp. 1-299; libro segundo, 1-264; Indice, 35 leaves; Colophon, 1 leaf.
5726 VENEGAS (P. Miguel) Noticia de la CALIFORNIA, y de su Conquista, hasta el tiempo presente, 3 vols. sq. 8vo. *maps, calf,* 36s; *fine copy in limp vellum,* £2. 10s   *Madrid,* 1757
    An important History of North-Western America, based upon materials collected in Mexico in 1739.
5727 VILLAGUTIERRE SOTO-MAYOR, Historia de la Conquista de la provincia de el Itza, de el Lacandon y otras naciones de Indios barbaros, de la mediacion de el regno de Guatimala a las provincias de Yucatan en la America Septentrional, Iª. Parte, *(all published)* stout folio, *frontispiece, limp.* £3. 3s   *Madrid,* 1701
    Very rare; Robertson seems to have been unacquainted with it, although he treats of Guatemala and Yucatan. Priced, 1855, Quaritch, Lord Rothesay's copy, cf ext. £7. 10s; fetched, 1859, Lady Webster's, cf. £4. 12s.
5728 VETANCURT, Theatro Mexicano, descripcion breve de los successos exemplares, historicos, politicos, militares y religiosos del Nuevo Mundo Occidental de las Indias, Parts, I—III, with the Tratado della Ciudad de Mexico, etc. in 1 vol. sm. folio, *hf. bd. rare,* £4.   *Mexico,* 1698
    A copy with the fourth part sold at Puttick's, in 1861, for £13. Complete copies are extremely scarce.
5729 VILLA-SENOR Y SANCHEZ (D. Jos. Ant. de) Theatro Americano, descripcion general de los Reynos y provincias de la Nueva España, y sus Jurisdicciones, 2 vols. sm. folio, *fine copy, bound,* £4. 14s 6d   *Mexico,* 1746-48
    RARE: "As Villa-Senor was Accountant-general in New Spain, and by that means had access to proper information, his testimony with respect to the royal revenue merits great credit. He is the only author who has given its population, and although imperfect, having given only 5 of the 9 dioceses, very useful, having published them from the reports of the magistrates in the several districts, and from his own observations and long acquaintance with most of the provinces."—SEE ROBERTSON'S AMERICA.
    Priced, 1824, Thorpe, £4. 14s 6d; 1825, morocco extra, £8. 18s 6d; 1830, Payne and Foss, £7. 7s; Lord Stuart de Rothesay's copy fetched, 1855, £6. 10s.
5730 VIRGINIA. HISTORY of VIRGINIA, in four parts, viz.—I, History of Virginia to the year 1706; II, The Natural Productions; III, The Native Indians, their Religions, Laws and Customs; IV, The present state of the Country, 1720; in 1 vol. sm. 8vo. 284 pp. 14 *plates, calf, rare,* 27s   1722
5731 WALSH's Notices of Brazil in 1828-29, 2 vols. 8vo. *maps and plates,* (pub. at 34s) *cloth,* 10s   1830
5732 WARD's Mexico in 1827, 2 vols. stout 8vo. *map and plates,* (pub. at £2. 2s) *bds.* 6s   1828
5733 —— the second edition enlarged, 2 vols. 8vo. *map and plates,* 10s   1829
5734 WELD's (J.) Travels through North America, Upper and Lower Canada, 1795-97, 4to. *map and plates, russia neat,* 7s 6d   1799
5735 **West Indies.** WEST- UNND OST- INDISCHER LUSTGART: das ist, Eygentliche Erzehlung wann die Newe Welt erfunden, vnd eingenommen worden, sq. 8vo. *vellum,* 12s   *Cöllen,* 1618
5736 GEOGRAPHICAL and Historical DESCRIPTION of the principal objects of the present war in the West Indies, 8vo. *coloured map, morocco, rare,* 12s   1741
5737 WINTERBOTHAM's Historical, Geographical, Commercial, and Philosophical View of the United States, and the Settlements, 4 vols. 8vo. (pub. at £3. 3s) *plates, maps, and plans, bds.* 12s   1795
5738 WINTHROP (*first Governor of Massachusetts*) History of New England, 1630-49, from his original MSS. with Notes by Savage, 2 vols. 8vo. *portrait by Chorley, hf. morocco,* 18s   *Boston, U.S.* 1825
5738* —— — New edition, with additions and corrections, 2 vols. 8vo. *portrait by Sharpe, cloth,* 36s   *Boston,* 1853

5739 **XERES** (Fr.) Admirable ampla et vera Narratio della Conquista del Peru, et Provincia del Cuzco, conquistata per Francesco Picciarro, tradotta in lingua Italiana per Dominico del Gaztelu, sq. 8vo. *bds.* VERY SCARCE, £4. 10*s*
Vinegia, Steph. da Sabio, 1535

5740 XIMENEZ, las Historias del Origen de los Indios de esta provincia de GUATEMALA, publicadas por Scherzer, 8vo. *sd.* 4*s* *Viena,* 1857

5741 AMERICA, a collection of *Foreign* Tracts relating to, including amongst others: Historia de Santo Domingo, 1806—Voyage de Chastellux, 1785—Indrenii Specimen de Esquimaux, gente Americana, *with vocabulary, Aboœ, Finland,* 1756—Voyage au XVe siècle, par Martyr, 1827; and others, many printed in America, the lot, 20*s* 1756-1850

5742 AMERICA, an extensive and valuable collection of *English* Tracts relating to America, many of them *scarce,* the lot, £3. 10*s* 1740-1836

INCLUDING

Taking of Carthagena by the Buccaniers	1740	Case of Capt. Frye	1754
Conduct of Gen. Shirley	1758	Selkirk (Earl) on the Red River Settlement	1819
Letters of Hutchinson and Oliver at Boston	1774	Researches on America, the Aborigines *Baltimore,*	1816
Transactions respecting Falkland's Islands	1771	Mutiny on the Lady Shore	1798
Answer to the Address of the Congress	1775	Conflagration of the Theatre in Richmond *Philad.*	1812
Price on the American War	1776	Bunker's Hill, a tragedy, by Burk	1797
Tucker on the Arguments of the Mother Country	1775	Considerations upon the American Inquiry	1779
Letters on the Trade of America	1774	Debate on Independence, *with Fox's Speeches*	1782
Rights of Gt. Britain asserted	1776	Addresses by Jamaica to Metcalfe	1842
Bal'nesque's Travels in North America *Philad.*	1836	Voyage of Discovery to Baffin's Bay	1819
Letter on a British War *Providence,*	1812	Otis, Rights of the British Colonies	*s. a.*
Martyrdom at Boston, 1659	1841	West India Diseases	1764

5743 AMERICAN TRACTS: a volume of, containing Account of the Proceedings of the States of Holland and West Friezeland, on the complaint of Sir J. Yorke, 1762 —Defence of the Merchants of England trading to the East Indies against the Dutch East-India Company, 1762—Muller's Voyages from Asia to America, 1761—Dobb's Account of the countries adjoining to Hudson's Bay, *map,* 1744; in 1 vol. 4to. *hf. bd.* 20*s* 1744-62

ASIA; including Works on the History, Literature and Languages of all the Asiatic nations.

5744 BOCK, Oeuvres diverses: Histoire du Sabéisme, avec un Catéchisme Druse; Memoire sur le peuple nomade, appellé Bohémien et Zigeuner; 2 vols. 12mo. *with comparisons of the Gipsey and Indian languages, sd.* 6*s* *Metz,* 1788

5745 D'HERBELOT, BIBLIOTHÈQUE ORIENTALE, avec les corrections et additions de Schultens, continuée par Visdelou et Galand, 4 vols. 4to. BEST EDITION, *fine copy in old calf gilt,* £4. *La Haye,* 1777-79

5746 DEGUIGNES, HISTOIRE DES HUNS, des Turcs, des Moguls, et des autres, Tartares Occidentaux, precedée d'une introduction contenant des Tables Chronologiques, 5 vols. 4to. *old French calf gilt,* £5. 5*s* *Paris,* 1756-58

5747 DE GUIGNES. SENKOWSKI, SUPPLÉMENT à l'Histoire Générale des Huns, des Turks, et des Mogols, 4to. *sd. very rare,* 30*s* *St. Petersb.* 1824

5748 IBN KHALLIKAN, Vies des Hommes Illustres: a curious old French translation of this celebrated work, containing the Monarchs and Conquerors; the Generals, Heroes, and Governors; the Vizirs and Illustrious Women; each classed separately and chronologically (not following the alphabetical arrangement of the original), sm. 4to. 332 *leaves,* 20*s* *Sec.* XVII

5749 JOURNAL ASIATIQUE, ou Recueil de Memoires relatifs à l'Histoire, à la Philosophie, aux Langues, et à la Littérature des peuples Orientaux, PREMIÈRE SÉRIE, 11 vols. 1822-27—SECONDE SÉRIE, 16 vols. 1828-35—TROISIÈME SÉRIE, 14 vols. 1836-42—QUATRIÈME SÉRIE, 20 vols. 1841-52—CINQUIÈME SÉRIE, Vols. I-XX pt. 1, 1853-62—*a complete set, from the beginning in 1822 to July* 1862, *the first 36 vols. hf. bd. the rest in Nos. Jomard's copy,* £25. *Paris,* 1822-62

5750 KLAPROTH, Archiv für Asiatische Litteratur, Geschichte, und Sprachkunde, Band I (*all published*) 4to. *plates, sd.* 10*s; or vellum paper, morocco extra, gilt edges,* 20*s* *St. Petersb.* 1810

Fetched 48 fr. Klaproth's sale.

5751 KLAPROTH, Mémoires relatifs à l'Asie, contenant des Recherches historiques, géographiques, et philologiques sur les peuples de l'Orient, 3 vols. 8vo. *maps and plates, sd.* 35*s* *Paris,* 1826-28

ASIA.

5752 NOTICES et Extraits des Manuscrits de la Bibliothèque du Roi, Vols. I-XII, stout 4to. *numerous plates and facsimiles, sd. uncut,* £6. 10s   *Paris,* 1787-1831
Very rich in Oriental Literature; and containing the contributions of the most distinguished scholars of the age, De Sacy, Quatrèmere, Boissonade, Guérard, etc.

5753 **Arabian Literature.** ALCALA (Pedro de) Arte para ligeramēte saber la lengua Arauiga—Vocabulista Arauigo en letra Castellana—2 vols. in 1, sm. 4to. gothic letter, *very fine large copy in calf extra, gilt edges,* £18. 18s
Granada, 1505
Excessively rare when complete. A copy sold in 1824 for 500 francs.
Collation: Arte. Title, with woodcut on the back, 1 leaf; Prologo, 3 pp.; Arte, a iii reverse, to f viii; together 48 leaves. Vocabulista: Title, with woodcut on the back, 1 leaf; Prologo, 3 pp.; Regla, etc. a iii reverse, to L iv obverse; Al letor, 2 pp.; Numero, 2 pp.; woodcut on last page, being the reverse of L vi; together 270 leaves.

5754 Dictionarium Arabico-Latinum: a MS. in an old Spanish hand, 4to. *267 leaves, double columns, vellum,* 12s   *Saec.* XVII

5755 EBN AL-DINARY Ibn Al-Dawidary, Akhbar ul-Malouk b-Ard Misr: History of the Sultans of Egypt, sm. 4to. *Arabic MS. of* 251 *leaves, written on European paper, green morocco gilt,* 20s   *Sec.* XVIII

5756 KITAB UL-MAANI... Tarfa min Ilm ul- Add wa Khuwassa, etc.: Encyclopaedia of the Sciences, 3 vols. sq. 8vo. *an Arabic MS. of nearly* 2000 *pages, hf. calf, from De Sacy's library,* £3.   *Sec.* XVIII
Treating on Geometry, Astronomy, Geography, Arithmetic, Music, Mines, Precious Stones, Medicine, Anatomy, Metaphysics, etc.

5757 Milad Moolla-na el-Hakim Jalla ... Nativity of our Lord the glorious Hakim, sm. 4to. *Arabic MS. a* Druse *work on the founder of their religion,* 100 *leaves,* 10s   *Sec.* XVIII

5758 PENTATEUCH. Terjemah ul-Turat Mukaddasat. Arabic Translation of the Five Books of Moses, for the use of the Samaritans, folio, *well written MS. of* 246 *pp. hf. bd. from De Sacy's library,* £2. 10s   *ca.* 1810
In the handwriting of Michaal Sabbâgh of Acre, an Arabic author, and well-known copyist, who died at Paris, 1816.

5759 **Armenia.** SAINT-MARTIN, Mémoires historiques et géographiques sur l'Armenie, avec l'histoire des princes Orpélians par Orpélian, *Armenien et Français,* etc. 2 vols. large 8vo. *sd.* 28s   *Paris,* 1819

5760 Dictionary, Armenian, Turkish, and English, 3 vols. 16mo. *the three alphabets complete, the Turkish in Armenian characters, calf neat,* 12s   *Venice,* 1843

5761 **Assyria.** Menant, les Ecritures Cunéiformes, exposé des travaux qui ont prépare l'interprétation des inscriptions, roy. 8vo. *sd.* 10s   *Paris,* 1860

5762 **Burmah.** LATTER'S Grammar of the Language of Burmah, 4to. *bds. rare,* 30s   *Calcutta,* 1845

5763 **Ceylon.** Forbes (Major) Eleven Years in Ceylon, its history and antiquities, 2 vols. 8vo. *plates and cuts,* (pub. at 21s) *cloth,* 8s 6d   1840

5764 Percival's Ceylon, its History, Geography, Natural History, Manners, etc. 4to. *maps, russia,* 7s 6d   1803

5765 —— second edition, imp. 4to. *Large Paper, maps and plates,* (pub. at £2. 12s 6d) *bds.* 9s   1805

5766 Philalethes' History of Ceylon, with its Maxims and Proverbs—Knox's Ceylon, and his Captivity there, 1660-80—2 vols. in 1, 4to. *maps and plates, bds.* 10s   1817

5767 Pridham, Ceylon and its Dependencies, 2 vols. 8vo. (pub. at 28s) *map,* 9s   1849
5768 Ribeyro, Histoire de Ceylon, 12mo. *map, plates, hf. cf.* 5s   *Amst.* 1701
5769 Singaleesch Belydenis Boek, 8vo. *all in Singalese, vellum,* 7s 6d   *Colombo,* 1738
An early printed work,

5770 **China.** Abdallæ Beidavaei Historia Sinensis, *Pers. et Lat.* ed. A. Muller Greiffenhagius; Comment. alphabetica; Basilicon Sinense; Nomenclator Geographicus; Hebdomas observationum; monumentum Sinicum; etc., omnia à Mullero, sq. 8vo. *vellum,* 18s   *Berol.* 1672-89

5771 Callery, Systema phoneticum scripturæ Sinicæ; Dictionnaire Chinois-Latin-Français, 2 vols roy. 8vo. *sd. uncut, rare,* £2. 10s   *Macao,* 1841

5772 CHINESE MISCELLANY designed to illustrate the government, philosophy, religion, arts, manufactures, trade, manners, customs, history and statistics of China, Nos. I-IV. sm. 8vo. *several large curious woodcut engravings, sd. rare,* 28s   *Shanghae,* 1849-50
No. II. contains a translation of a very curious Chinese work, "The Chinaman abroad, an account of the Malayan Archipelago," displaying the traveller's shrewd views of men and manners in the European settlements.

5773 CHOU KING, un des livres sacrés des Chinois, qui renferme leur Gouvernement, etc. recueilli par Confucius, traduit par Gaubil, avec des notes par De Guignes, 4to. *plates, calf,* 14*s* 1770

5774 CONFUCIUS'S Works; containing the original *Chinese* text, with an *English* translation, Vol. I. (all published) very stout 4to. *xxxix,* 725, *and* 17 *pp. bds. uncut, rare,* 42*s* Serampore, 1809

5775 DICTIONARIUM Sinico-Latinum: a neat MS. containing about 2000 monosyllabic Chinese characters, with the sounds expressed in Roman letters, and the explanation in Latin, sm. 4to. 200 *pp. bds.* 36*s* China, Sec. XVIII

5776 EDKINS' Grammar of the Chinese Colloquial Language, called the Mandarin Dialect, sm. 8vo. *sd.* 28*s* Shanghai, 1857

5777 Escayrac de Lauture (Le Comte) Telegraphic transmission of Chinese characters; Sur la rebellion; Fleuves de la Chine; Grammaire du Telegraphe; etc. 5 *valuable tracts on Chinese subjects by a resident there,* 10*s* 1855-62

5778 GONCALVES, Diccionario China-Portuguez e Portuguez-China, 3 vols. in 2, sm. 4to. 2048 *pp. double columns, hf. calf neat,* £3. 3*s* Macao, 1831-33

5778* —— the same, 3 vols. in 4, 1831-33—Arte China, constante de Alphabeto e Grammatica, com modelos das composiçoens, 1829—together 4 vols. in 5, sm. 4to. *sd. uncut,* £7. 10*s* Macao, 1829-33

5779 Gonzalez de Mendosa, Rerum Morumque in Regno Chinensi maxime notabilium historia, ex libris Chinensibus concinnata, *Latine* à Brulio, sq. 8vo. *calf,* 7*s* 6*d* Antv. 1655

5780 HAOU KING, a treatise on Filial Piety, *in Chinese,* roy. 8vo. *consisting of leaves folded so as to form one large sheet if rolled out, part printed in white letters on a black ground, the rest in red letters on a white ground,* 35*s* Sec. XIX

5780*Hernisz, Guide to conversation in English and Chinese, for Americans and Chinese in California and elsewhere, oblong 8vo. 39 and 179 *pp. treble columns, containing the English first, with the Chinese both in native and Roman characters, sd.* 14*s* 6*d* Boston, 1855

5781 INNOCENTIA VICTRIX, sive sententia Comitiorum Imperii Sinici pro innocentia Christianae Religionis, 1669, jussu R. P. A. de Gouvea *Sinico-Latine* exposita, Quam-cheu, metropoli prov. Quam-tum, (*Canton*) 1671—LIFE OF CHRIST, *in Chinese, with* 51 *large woodcuts, almost the size of the page, containing a series of illustrations, executed in the European manner by native artists, a remarkable specimen of Art, ca.* 1670—2 vols. in 1, imp. 8vo. *portrait of the Missionary Schall as a Mandarin inserted, original calf, with the Crucifixion stamped on the sides in gold,* £12. 12*s* Canton, 1671

The first work in this volume, containing the sentence of the Chinese tribunals in favour of the Christian religion, Chinese (native and Roman character) and Latin, is extremely rare. See Rémusat's Catalogue, for a full description of it. The second work is not only rare, but is also extremely curious as a Chinese Block Book, executed in the European Mediaeval style.

5782 KLAPROTH, Dictionarium Sinico-Latino-Germanicum, 4to. *MS. of* 272 *leaves, containing the Chinese in native and Roman character, followed by the explanation in Latin, and in German, hf. bd.* 25*s* ca. 1810

This MS. contains the explanation of about 1600 characters, with the Key in red ink; and was the commencement of an immense undertaking on the part of Klaproth.

5783 Klaproth's Verzeichniss der Chinesischen und Mandshuischen Bücher und Handschriften der K. Bibliothek zu Berlin—Ueber die Sprache und Schrift der Uiguren—2 vols. in 1, folio, *hf. bd. uncut,* 18*s* Paris, 1822

5784 —— Notice d'une Mappemonde et d'une Cosmographie Chinoises, sm. 8vo. *map, sd.* 2*s* 6*d* 1833

5785 Klaproth, Mentzel, Bayer, Lexicon Sinico-Latinum, stout folio, *MS. of upwards of* 500 *leaves, bds.* 25*s* 1750-1820

This MS. written upon paper of the last century, contains all the characters of the Chinese Dictionary "Tser Wei," with the Romanized form and the explanation in Latin, many of them, by the above great scholars. The Chinese characters are in the handwriting of Mentzel. The explanations were inserted afterwards by Bayer and Klaproth.

5786 MAILLAC (Moyria de) Histoire générale de la Chine, ou Annales de cet empire traduites du Tong-Kien Kang-Mou, publiées par Grosier, 12 vols.—Supplement: Grosier, Description de la Chine, 1 vol.—together 13 vols. 4to. *numerous maps and plates, fine copy, old calf gilt,* £4. 10*s* Paris, 1777-85

ASIA.

5787 MEDHURST (W. H.) Chinese-English and English-Chinese DICTIONARY, containing all the words of the Chinese Imperial Dictionary, arranged according to Radicals, 4 vols. 8vo. *bds. very rare*, £10. 10s
Batavia, 1842, *and Shanghae*, 1847

5788 MEMOIRES concernant l'Histoire, les Sciences, les Arts, les Mœurs, les Usages, etc. des Chinois, par les Missionaires de Pékin (Amyot, Bourgeois, Ko et Poirot) 15 vols. 4to. *numerous plates and portraits, old calf*, £5.
Paris, 1776-91

5789 MONUMENT OF YU. A series of 12 roy. folio sheets of *Chinese facsimiles, in white letters on a black ground, reproducing the most ancient Inscription in China, from Klaproth's library*, 6s
ca. 1780

5790 NOEL (Patris F.) Observationes Mathematicæ et Physicæ in India et China factae, 1684-1708, sq. 8vo. *curious star-map, and woodcuts, calf*, 32s *Pragae*, 1710

5791 PREMARE'S Chinese Grammar. NOTITIA Linguæ Sinicæ, large 4to. *sd. rare*, £2. 2s
Malacca, 1831

"Premare is the only Philologist whose mode of treating the subject will be found peculiarly advantageous to those who have acquired even a slight knowledge of the language, as they are thus enabled to imbibe notions of its general literature which they could otherwise procure only by laborious study of the best Chinese authors for many years."—RÉMUSAT.

5792 RÉMUSAT (Abel) Dictionnaire Chinois-Français contenant les caractères les plus usités, leur prononciation, leur ton, et leur signification, avec deux tables de renvois au dictionnaire, sm. 4to. *neat MS. of 270 pp.* £2. *fini, Decbre.* 1808

5793 RÉMUSAT, Histoire de la ville de Khotan, traduite du Chinois, 8vo. *sd.* 3s 6d 1820

5794 SOUCIET, Gaubil, etc. Observations Mathématiques, Astronomiques, Géographiques, Chronologiques, etc. tirées des anciens livres Chinois ou faites aux Indes et à la Chine, 3 vols. in 1, stout 4to. *plates, vellum*, 25s   *Paris*, 1729-32

5795 SZE SHOO. THE CHINESE CLASSICAL WORK commonly called the FOUR BOOKS, translated, with notes, by *Collie*, large 8vo. *cloth, very rare*, 20s *Malacca*, 1828

5796 THSING WEN TIEN YAO: Selection of Precepts for the Mantchou Language, 4 parts in 1 vol. 8vo. *a Dictionary of Chinese phrases explained in Mantchou, hf. bd. from Klaproth's library*, 36s
1739

5797 THSING WEN KHI MENG: Principles of the Mantchou Language, *Chinese and Mantchou*, 4 parts in 1 vol. impl. 8vo. *hf. bd. from Klaproth's library*, £2. 10s
1732

This Grammar was composed for the use of schools by Cheou Ping; all the rules are in Chinese, with the examples given in Mantchou. See Rémusat's analysis of the work, in his "Recherches sur les langues Tartares."

5798 TRIGAULT, SI JOU EUL MOU TSEU: Vocabulary arranged according to the Tones, following the order of the European words, 3 vols. in 1, stout imp. 8vo. *the characters in many instances being expressed in Roman letters, with curious diagram, hf. bd. from Klaproth's library*, VERY RARE, £12. 12s   *China*, 1626

5799 **INDIA.** AYEEN AKBERY. The Institutes of the Emperor Akber, translated by F. Gladwin, 3 vols. 4to. BEST EDITION, *calf gilt*, £2. 10s
Calcutta, 1783-86

5800 CALDWELL'S Comparative Grammar of the Dravidian or South-Indian Family of Languages, 8vo. 528 *pp. a work of profound Philological and Ethnological research, cloth, new*, 21s
1856

5801 COLEBROOKE'S (H. T.) Miscellaneous Essays, 2 vols. 8vo. BEST EDITION, *numerous facsimiles from early Indian MSS. and Inscriptions, bds. rare*, £2. 2s
1837

5802 LASSEN (Chr.) INDISCHE ALTERTHUMSKUNDE, Vols. I-IV, in 11 parts, 8vo. *maps, (pub. at 40 Thalers) half calf, uncut*, £5. 10s *Bonn and Leipzig*, 1847-61

A most learned work on the ancient History and Geography of India, from the earliest period to the Mohammedan Invasion. Some parts are out of print.

5803 MALCOLM (Sir John) Report on the Province of Malwa and adjoining districts, 4to. *calf neat*, 10s
Calcutta, 1822

5804 MANRIQUE (Sebastian) Itinerario de las Missiones del India Oriental que hizo en varias Missiones, con una Relacion del Imperio de Xa-Ziahan Corrombo Gran Mogol, etc. 4to. *a little stained, vellum*, £3. 3s
Roma, 1653

EXTREMELY RARE. Brunet states that the book has no frontispiece, and puts the date (Roma, 1649) in parenthesis; from which it would appear that the book is generally seen without a title page. The privileges, etc. are all dated Rome, 1649. Thorpe priced a copy £4. 4s. COLLATION: Title, 1 leaf; Dedication, 1 leaf; Approbations, etc. 1 leaf; Indice, 2 leaves; Errata and Protesta, 1 leaf; pp. 1-470; Table, pp. 471-76.

5805 POGSON'S History of the BOONDELAS, 4to. *map and plates, calf gilt, rare*, 20s
Calcutta, 1828

5806 **WARREN** (Lieut-Col.) KALA SANKALITA: A collection of Memoirs on the various modes according to which the nations of the Southern parts of India divide TIME, 4to. *cloth*, 20s *Madras*, 1825

5807 **Bengali.** SRI DURGA, Annade Mangala et Bidagasundara, History of the Goddess Durga, *in Bengali*, 2 vols. in 1, 8vo. *several curious plates,* "engraber by Bissonant Mookerjea," *hf. bd.* 7s 6d *Calcutta*, 1814

5808 **Canarese.** BASHAVA PURANA, in the *Kannadi* or Karnataka language, folio, 670 *pp. lithographed, hf. bd.* £2. 16s *Mangalore*, 1850
This is the Sacred Book of the Jangams or Lingavants, and was written about the year 1300 of our era.

5809 **JAIMINI BHARATA**, a poem in the *Kannadi* language, sm. folio, 353 *pp. lithographed, hf. bd.* £2. 2s *Mangalore*, 1848

5810 **Hindostani.** SOUDA (*the greatest of Indian poets*) Intikhab-i-Diwan—Diwan-i-Mir Soz—2 vols. in 1, 4to. *hf. bd.* 12s *Calcutta* (ca. 1810)

5811 LULLOO LAL KUVI, Principles of Inflection and Conjugation in the Brij B,hak,ha, roy. 4to. *calf*, 15s *Calcutta*, 1811

5812 **Karen.** (*Tennasserim*) WADE's Karen-English Dictionary, 4to. *in the Burmese character*, pp. 9-324 (*all published*) *double cols. hf. bd.* 32s (*Tavoy*, 1842)

5813 **Punjabi.** DICTIONARY of the Punjabi language, prepared by a Committee of the Lodiana Mission, 4to. 438 pp. *treble cols.* £2. 16s *Lodiana*, 1854

5814 **Sanscrit.** Bhatti Kavya, a poem on the actions of Rama, *in Sanscrit*, with the commentaries of Jayamangala and Bharatamallika, 2 vols. in 1, roy. 8vo. 847 *and* 512 *pp. hf. russia*, 36s *Calcutta*, 1828
Priced, Dondey-Dupré, 70 fr.

5815 **BHAGAVATA PURANA**, with the commentary of Cridharasvâminis, *Sanscrit*, in Bengali characters, edited by Bhavanicarana, 530 leaves oblong folio, *printed on thick yellow tinted paper, unbound, between two wooden boards, and wrapped in a cover of coarse red cloth*, £6 *Calcutta, Anno Sakae*, 1752 (1830)
The finest and best edition of this great Purana, which celebrates one of Vishnu's Avatars,—his incarnation as Krishna.

5816 **BRAHMA-VAIVARTA-PURANA**: History of the Wanderings of Brahma, stout sm. folio, *remarkably fine old Sankrit MS. green morocco*, £6. Sec. XVII

5817 **CAREY'S** (W.) Grammar of the Sungskrit Language, with examples for Exercise, and a complete List of the Dhatoos, or Roots, stout roy. 4to. *calf gilt, scarce*, £2. 12s *Serampore*, 1806
Priced by Allen, 1829, £8. 8s; 1840, £4. 4s; the above copy cost previously £3. 13s 6d. Fetched, Klaproth's sale, 1839, 81¼fr.

5818 **HARIVANSA**, an account of the family and the deeds of Krishna, *in Sanscrit*, Vol. I.   MS. of 668 *oblong folio leaves, written in bold characters and ruled with red lines, unbound*, 21s Sec. XVIII
A remarkable MS. of this famous work which is regarded as so sacred that the greatest rewards, on earth and in heaven, are offered to those who read it.

5819 **KALIDASA**, the Raghu Vansa, or Race of Raghu, an historical poem, with prose interpretation, *all Sanscrit*, roy. 8vo. 2 *titles, and pp.* 1-638, *sd.* 15s
Calcutta, 1832

5820 **KASHI KHAND**, being a section of the SKANDA PURANA, giving an account of Holy Places at Benares, *in Sanscrit*, stout narrow folio, *a fine MS. of* 386 *pp. hf. bd.* £2. 16s Sec. XVIII

5821 ——— Kasi Khanda, the same work—VAMANA PURANA—*both in Sanscrit, boldly written MSS.* 2 vols. oblong folio, 325 *and* 225 *leaves, not uniform in size, unbound*, £2. 10s Sec. XVIII

5822 **KEDAR KHANDA**, *in Sanscrit*, high 4to. 386 *leaves, well written, ruled in with red lines, green morocco gilt*, 35s Sec. XVIII

5823 **KIRAT-ARJUNIYA.** Kâvyanâma Kirâtârjuniya, Kavinama Bharavi: the famous poem of the Kiratarjuniya, *in Sanscrit*, edited at the desire of Mallatas, by Bâburâma and Vidyâkârâmiçram, roy. 4to. *calf gilt, Chezy's copy with his notes on separate pieces of paper*, £2. 2s *Khidirapur*, 1814

5824 **MANAVA-KALPA-SUTRA**, being a portion of this ancient work on Vaidik Rites, together with the commentary of Kumárila-Swámin, *Sanscrit and English*, with preface by Goldstücker, narrow sm. folio, *printed in the oblong fashion to resemble the original, the Sanscrit text being in facsimile, on thick paper*, (pub. at £4. 4s) *cloth*, £2. 2s 1861

5825 MAHABHARATA: the Great Epic Poem of the Wars between the Pandous and the Kourous: the Kerna Parva; the Anushusan Parva; the Gada Parva; and the Shanti Parva; being various portions of this famous Poem, *in Sanscrit,* 4 vols. oblong folio, *finely written MSS. unbound,* £3. 10s   Sec. XVI-XVIII

5826 NALUS, Maha-Bharati Episodium, *Sanscritè et Latinè,* cum annotationibus criticis, ed. BOPP, sq. 8vo. *nice copy in bright calf gilt,* 24s   *Berolini,* 1832

5827 —— the same, sq. 8vo. THICK VELLUM PAPER, *hf. morocco,* 30s   1832

5828 PANINI-SUTRA-VITRI, or the Grammatical Aphorisms of Panini, in Sanscrit, stout 8vo. *title, and pp.* 1203 *and* 42, *hf. morocco gilt, Langlès' copy, with his autograph,* £2. 16s   *Calcutta,* 1810

"This is the legitimate edition of the grammar of Panini."—GOLDSTÜCKER.

"Panini, the father of Sanscrit Grammar, lived in so remote an age that he ranks among the ancient Sages whose fabulous history occupies a conspicuous place in the Puranas or Indian Theogonies."—*Colebrooke.*

5829 PADMA PURANA: the History of Lakshemi, the Lotus-Goddess, *in Sanscrit,* oblong folio, *well written MS. ruled in with red lines,* £2. 12s   Sec. XVIII

5830 RIG-VEDA-SANHITA: the Sacred Hymns of the Brahmans, together with the Commentary of Sayanacharya, *in Sanskrit,* edited by MAX MÜLLER, 4 vols. very stout royal 4to (pub. at £10. 13s) *cloth,* £7. 10s   1849-62

5831 SISUPALA BADHA, or death of Sisupála, also entitled the MAGHA CAVYA, or Epick Poem of Magha, with Malli Nátha's commentary, edited by Vidya Cara Misra, and Syama Lala, stout roy. 8vo. *title, advertisement, Sanskrit title, etc.* 4 *leaves; pp.* 1-760, *bds.* 25s.   *Calcutta,* 1815

5832 SAMA VEDA, in 8 Ashtakas of about 70 leaves each; with the Mantra Sanhita, 145 leaves; 9 parts, oblong folio, *fine old Sanscrit MSS. unbd.* 32s   Sec. XVII.

5833 VALMIKI'S RAMAYANA, being the great Epic by the Poet Valmiki on the deeds of the Hero Rama, and the downfall of Ravana, the Giant King of Ceylon, stout narrow folio, *a beautiful old Sanskrit MS. finely written,* green morocco, £4. 4s   Sec. XVII

5834 VALMEEKI, THE RAMAYUNA, in the original Sungskrit, with a Prose Translation, and explanatory notes by W. CAREY and J. MARSHMAN, 3 vols. 4to. *hf. russia,* VERY RARE, £8. 10s   *Serampore,* 1806-10

Vols. II, III, were not published; their existence has often been doubted.

5835 WILSON'S DICTIONARY, Sanscrit and English, translated, amended, and enlarged from an original compilation prepared by learned Natives, roy. 4to. 1061 pp. double cols. *hf. russia,* £5.   *Calcutta,* 1819

5836 —— the same, SECOND EDITION, *greatly enlarged,* roy. 4to. *bds.* £12.   1862

5837 **Tamul.** BESCHII Grammatica Latino-Tamulica, de vulgari Tamulicae linguae idiomate Keddun-Tamul dicto, 12mo. *calf,* 7s 6d   *Trangambar,* 1738

5838 —— the same, 1738—WALTHERI Observaciones Grammaticae, 1739—2 vols. in 1, 12mo. *hf. calf,* 10s   *Trangamb.* 1738-39

5839 BIBLIOTHECA TAMULICA, sive Opera praecipua Tamuliensium, ed. GRAUL, I, II, 8vo. *sd.* 12s   *Lipsiae,* 1854-55

Vol. I contains: the Kaivaljanavanita, the Pankadasaprakarana, and the Atmabodaprakasika, all in German; Vol. II contains: the Kaivaljanavanita, in Tamul and English, with glossary, and a Tamil Grammar of 100 pp.

5840 KNIGHT and SPAULDING's English-Tamil Dictionary, or manual Lexicon, revised by Hutchings, 8vo. 22 *and* 831 *pp. double cols. hf. calf,* 32s   *Madras,* 1844

5841 MANUAL DICTIONARY of the Tamil Language, published by the Jaffna Book Society, *all in Tamil,* stout 8vo. *calf,* 15s   *Jaffna,* 1842

5842 PHRASE BOOK, or idiomatic exercises in English and Tamil, 16mo. 372 *pp. double cols. of Dialogues, calf,* 9s   *Jaffna,* 1841

5843 PSALMEN (Eenige) en anderen Lofzangen *in Tamulsche* Digte overgeset door Melho, sm. 8vo. *with the Music, sd.* 12s   *Colombo,* 1755

5844 ROTTLER'S Tamil-English Dictionary, partly revised by Rev. W. Taylor, and Vencatachala Moodelly, 4 parts in 1 very stout vol. 4to. 300, 420, 456, *and* 248 *pp. double columns, bds.* £2. 5s   *Madras,* 1834-41

5845 VOCABULARIO PORTUGUEZ-MALABAR, 16mo. an interesting MS. of 481 pp. *the Tamul in Roman characters, with several curious initial letters in red and black ink, bd. very curious,* 36s   Sec. XVII

The Dictionary is followed by a list of words in Latin, Malabar (Syriac character) and Syriac; and afterwards by Syriac litanies. There are Syriac words also interspersed through the Vocabulary.

5846 **Telugu.** CAMPBELL'S Grammar of the Teloogoo Language, commonly termed the Gentoo, second edition, roy. 4to. *bds. rare*, 30s *Madras,* 1820
5847 ——— Dictionary of the Teloogoo Language, roy. 4to. 601 pp. *double columns, hf. russia, rare,* £2. 10s *Madras,* 1821
5848 **INDIAN ARCHIPELAGO.** BATAVIAASCH GENOOTSCHAP van Kunsten en Wetenschappen, Verhandelingen, derde Druk, Vols. I-XV, *calf gilt,* and Vols. XX, XXI, in 3 vols. *sd.* together 17 vols. in 18, 8vo. *maps and plates, a complete Cyclopaedia of information on the East, especially on the Languages, Ethnology, Antiquities, History, Geography, and Statistics of the Indian Archipelago,* £15. *Batavia,* 1825-48
5849 BOCHARY Djohor, Taj ul-Salatin: de Kroon aller Koningen, *Maleisch en Duitsch,* door Roorda, sm. 4to. *bds.* 20s *Batavia,* 1827
5850 BOWREY'S Dictionary, English and Malayo, Malayo and English, with some Grammar Rules, Miscellanies, Dialogues, etc. 2 vols. in 1, sm. 4to. *map, old calf gilt,* £3. 3s 1701
Excessively rare: Rousseau, the Oriental bookseller, stated in his preface to Howieson's Dictionsry, that he had only seen 3 copies during fifty years. It is a work of great industry and merit. COLLATION: Title, Dedication, Preface, and Errata, 6 leaves; Map; Dictionaries, Signature B to Oo 2, and O3 to Qqq 2; Grammar Rules, 8 leaves; Miscellanies, Dialogues, and Letters, 29 leaves; Computations of Time, 9 leaves; Specimen of the Characters, etc. 5 leaves. Except in this specimen, the Malay is always in Roman characters.

5851 DIALOGUES, *Malayan and Dutch,* with a comparison of the names of the Numerals in three dialects, sm. 4to. *Dutch MS. of* 20 *pp.* 3s 6d Sec. XVIII
5852 LOGAN's Ethnology of the Indian Archipelago, and continental relations of the Indo-Pacific Islanders, 8vo, *sd.* 3s 6d *Singapore, ca.* 1840
5853 MARSDEN'S Grammar of the Malayan Language, with Introduction and Praxis, 4to. *bds.* 18s 1812
5854 ROORDA van Eysinga, Nederduitsch en Maleisch Woordenboek, met Aanhangsel, stout 8vo. 20, 497, and 39 pp. *bds.* 12s *Batavia,* 1824
5855 RUYLL, Spieghel van de Maleysche Tale, in de welcke sich die Indiaensche Jeucht Christlijck ende vermaeckelick kunnen oeffenen, met VOCABULARIUM van de Duytsche ende Maleysche Tale, sq. 8vo. *title and* 3 *preliminary leaves,* and 139 pp. *vellum, very rare,* £3. 16s *Amst.* 1612
5856 **Borneo.** HARDELAND's Versuch einer Grammatik der Dajakischen Sprache, mit Anhang, "Das Augh olo Balian" *Dajakisch und Deutsch,* 8vo. 374 pp. *sd.* 7s 6d *Amst.* 1858
5857 **Formosa.** HAPPART'S Dictionary of the Favorlang Dialect of the Formosan language, written in 1650, translated by MEDHURST, 12mo. *paper discoloured, hf. morocco, rare,* 25s *Batavia,* 1840
5858 FORMOSAANSCHE Woorden- Lijst, volgens een Utrechtsch Handschrift, met Aanmerkingen, door Vlis, 8vo. *sd.* 12s *Socracarta, (Java)* 1842
5859 **Java.** CATECHISMOE (Ichtitsaar) etc. met Uytlegging van eenige Woorden, 16mo. with a Malay Vocabulary, VERY RARE, 28s *Batavia,* 1685
5860 **Macassar** (*Celebes*). MATTHES, Makassaarsche Chrestomathie; oorspronkelijke Makassaarsche Geschriften in Prosa en Poëzy, roy. 8vo. *Makassar in the Bugis character, and Dutch, with notes, bds.* 18s *Amst.* 1860
5861 **Philippine Islands.** BERGANO (Diego) Bocabulario de PAMPANGO en Romance, y Diccionario de Romance en Pampango, folio, *fine copy, in red morocco, gilt edges,* EXTREMELY RARE, £15. *Manila,* 1732
Thorpe priced a copy, 1834, £15. 15s.

5862 BUZETA (Manuel) y Felipe BRAVO, *Misioneros,* Diccionario Geográfico Estadistico, Historico, de las Islas Filipinas, 2 vols. imp. 8vo. *plates and tables, hf. bd.* 24s *Madrid,* 1851
5863 COMBES, Historia de les Islas de Mindanao, Iolo, y sus adyacentes, small folio, *hf. calf,* £3. 10s *Madrid,* 1667
VERY SCARCE, like most of the works on the Philippine Islands.

5864 EXTRACTO Historial del Expediente en el Consejo Real a instancia de Manila y demás de las Islas Philippinas, folio, *vellum, rare,* 10s *Madrid,* 1736
5865 FRANCISCO DE S. JOSEPH, Arte y Reglas de la Lengua Tagala, stout 12mo. *the first four pages slightly stained, limp vellum,* VERY RARE, £5. *Reimpresso en Manila,* 1752
COLLATION: Title, and 15 preliminary leaves, forming four signatures of ¶'s; Arte, folios 1-785; Para el que aprende etc. in verse, 10 leaves; Librong Paguaralan, por Pinpin, Bataan, 1610, Ggggg 2 to Zzzzzz 1; Indice, Zzzzzz 1, verso, to ***** 4, being 47 pp.

ASIA.

5866 JUAN DE LA CONCEPCION, HISTORIA GENERAL de PHILIPINAS, Conquistas de estos Españoles Dominios, establecimientos, progresos, y decadencias, 14 thick vols. smallest 4to. *with 8 maps, in excellent preservation, vellum,* £7. 7s   *Manilla,* 1788-92

This book has been artfully introduced into the London market from Paris. As recently as October 24, 1861, I paid 320 francs for a copy to a Paris bookseller, who now sells it for 200 francs, coolly quoting in his Catalogue my *former* price, based upon the 320 francs paid to him.

Undoubtedly the best work on the Philippine Islands. "Cet ouvrage, le plus volumineux, peut-être, qui ait paru aux Philippines, se trouvent rarement complet."—*Brunet.*

"Comprehende los Imperios y Provincias de Islas y Continentes con quienes ha havido communicacion y comercio por imediatas coincidencias; con noticias geographicas, hidrographicas, de Historia natural, de Politica, de Costumbres y de Religiones, en lo que deba intersarse tan universal titulo."

LIST OF MAPS.

Vol. 1, p 118. Parte de la Isla de Celebes.
" 1, " 291. Mapa de las Yslas Philipinas por Murillo Velarde.
" 2, " 34. Plano de las Islas descubiertas (de Pasion).
" —— Plano del Bajo descubierto.
" 2, " 232. Japonia.
" 3, " 316. Formosa.
" 6, " 319. Isla de Borneo, &c.
" 7, " 145. Ysla de Guaxan.
" —— Saipan.
" 9, " 150. Isla Jap. o Gran Carolina.

5867 MALDONADO DE PUGA, Religiosa Hospitalidad por los hijos de S. Juan de Dios, en su provincia de S. Raphael de las Islas Philipinas, su Fundacion, Progresos, y estado presente, sqr. 8vo. *vellum,* 10s   *Granada,* 1742

5868 MARTINEZ DE ZUNIGA (Fr. Joaquin) Historia de las Islas Philipinas, sq. 8vo. title, 4 prelim. leaves, and pp. 1-687, *fine copy,vellum,* VERY RARE, £3. 3s
Sampaloc, 1803

Printed on paper manufactured from silk at Sampaloc in the Philippine Islands; a specimen of it, especially in this country, is of unfrequent occurrence. Priced, Thorpe, £4. 4s. Livre rare, vendu, 1836, 62 fr.—BRUNET.

5869 MOZO Noticia Historico Natural de los gloriosos triumphos y felices adelantamientos de los Religiosos del Orden de S. Augustin en las Islas Philipinas, y la China, 8vo. *vellum, rare,* 18s   *Madrid,* 1763

Full of very interesting information respecting the manners and customs of the inhabitants of the Philippine Islands.

5870 MURILLO VELARDE (Pedro) Historia de la Provinciale de Philipinas de la Compania de Jesus; progresos de esta Provincia desde 1616, hasta 1716, folio, *printed on silk paper, map, vellum, very rare,* £3. 15s   *Manila,* 1749

This work was intended as a continuation to "Colin, Labor Evangelica, Madrid, 1663." "Ce volume est intitulé seconde partie parce qu'il forme la continuation du pere Chirino."—SALVA.

5871 NOCEDA (El P. Juan de) y el P. Pedro de SAN LUCAR, Vocabvlario de la Lenga Tagala, trabaxado por varios svgetos doctos y graves, sm. folio, *fine copy in limp vellum,* £6. 6s
Manila, Imprenta de la Comp. de Jesus, por N. de la Cruz Bagay, 1754

COLLATION: Title; Epistles, 'Aprobacion,' etc. 6 leaves; Errata, 2 leaves; Prologo, 6 leaves; Vocab. *Tagala, Hispano, pp.* 1-619; 'Apendix,' 34 pp. : Vocab. *Hispano Tagalog,* 190 pp.

I sold a copy in 1861 for £12. 12s.
"Volume fort rare; vendu 243 fr., Salle Silvestre, 1826; £5. 15s 6d, Heber; 150 fr. Raetzel."—BRUNET.

5872 ORTIZ (Thomas) Arte, y Reglas de la lengua Tagala, very small 4to. *fine copy, russia extra, joints, gilt edges,* VERY RARE, £10. 10s   *Sampaloc,* 1740

COLLATION: Title, Licencia, Aprobacion, Censura, Licencia Al Lector, 6 leaves; pp. 1-125; Tabla, 3 pp.; Erratas, 3 pp.

This very curious and interesting volume was executed at Samplai or Sampaloc, situate in the south-western extremity of Lugon, one of the largest of the Philippine Islands. It is printed upon a fine silk paper, manufactured on the spot. Like all the other works which have been since produced there, it is of very great rarity.

5873 JAPAN. ALCALA Vida de San Martin, Proto-Martyr del Japon, sm. 4to. *vellum,* 6s   *Madrid,* 1739

5874 ALCOCK (Sir R.) The Capital of the Tycoon, Narrative of a Three Years' Residence in Japan, 2 vols. 8vo. *maps, coloured plates, and above* 100 *illustrations,* (pub. at £2. 2s) *cloth,* 35s   1863

"We have not previously had a book like this on Japan. As a narrative it is excellent; and as containing the results of large observation and close study among a strangely interesting people, it possesses an importance for all thinking readers."—*Athenæum, Feb.* 21, 1863.

5875 CARTAS que los padres de la compañia de Jesus en los Reynos de Japon escrivieron a los de la misma Compañia, 1549-1571, sm. 4to. *gilt vellum, rare,* 25s   *Alcala,* 1575

Valuable for the early history of Japan, containing information relative to the Manners and Customs, Superstitions, and Religious Worship of its inhabitants.

5876 CHARLEVOIX, Histoire et Description générale du Japon, 9 vols. 12mo. *map and plates, calf,* 21s   *Paris,* 1736

5877 FISSCHER (J. F. Van Overmeer) Bijdrage tot de Kennis van het Japansche Rijk, roy. 4to. *plates of the Costume of the Japanese, &c. in brilliant colouring heightened with gold and silver, calf gilt*, £2. 2s   Amsterdam, 1833

5878 HISTORIEN van Odssi Juky of Dunne Ineeun, imp. 8vo. *a native Japanese work, with the above Dutch title written in pencil on the fly-leaf, curious colored illustrations, apparently of a romantic character, in the style of European Mediaeval Blockbooks, sd.* 36s   Sec. XVIII

5879 HWA SAN . . . Jin, etc. A work in Japanese, with a Chinese and a Japanese title, 2 parts, imp. 8vo. *several large colored illustrations representing the Domestic Life and Occupations of the Japanese, including some curious sketches, such as one native lighting his pipe from that of another, etc. in case,* 32s   Sec. XIX

5880 ICHTHYOLOGY: a native work in Japanese, 2 vols. imp. 8vo. *with about 70 large coloured illustrations, representing all kinds of Fish, including Shell-Fish, sd.* 28s   Sec. XIX

5881 KÆMPFER'S (Dr. E.) History of Japan, state of the Government of that Empire, of its Temples, Palaces, Castles, and other Buildings, of its Natural History, Customs of the Natives, their Manufactures and Trade, translated by Scheuchzer, *with both Appendices,* 2 vols. folio, 45 *plates, calf,* £2. 2s   1727-28

5882 —— the same, 2 vols. roy. folio, LARGE PAPER, *old calf neat,* £4. 4s   1727-28

Drury's copy fetched £5. 18s; Heath's, £8. 15s; the Fonthill copy, £10. 10s; and Stanley's, £14. 14s Still the best book on Japan. "Kæmpfer's Japan is highly valued for its accuracy and fidelity."—LOWNDES.

5883 MAP OF JAPAN, a native publication, on one large sheet, 65 inches by 28, folded into 8vo. size, *with a marginal text in Japanese and Chinese,* 12s   ca. 1800

5884 NATURAL HISTORY, a native work in Japanese, 8vo. *with* 118 *engravings of Birds and Beasts of all species, two of them representing a wild man and wild woman whose features appear to be of the Malay type, sd.* 10s   ca. 1800

5885 NUMISMATA. Naamen der Munten in het Boek Wa Kan Ko Fo Soe Je; Kopere Munten in het Werk Fin Sen Sen Poe; Munten in Fin Qua Ko Fo Dsu Kan; Ro Sen Ki; folio, Lists of Japanese Coins, *in Dutch MS.,* sm. folio, *bd.* 10s.   Sec. XVIII

5886 PINEYRO, Relacion del Sucesso que tuvò nuestra Santa Fe en Japon desde 1612 hasta 1615, 4to. *slightly stained, calf, rare,* 15s   Madrid, 1617

5887 TCHING TE VOU KIEN, a Japanese work, in 7 vols. 12mo. *with numerous small Ornamental and Symbolical illustrations scattered through the text, sd.* 28s   Saec. XVIII

5888 TITSINGH'S (M.) Illustrations of Japan, translated by Shoberl, impl. 4to. *with* 11 *colored plates after Japanese originals, morocco extra, gilt edges,* 28s   1822

5889 —— Japanese and Chinese Chronology. Bedenkingen over de Teidreekening der Chineesen na het Gevoele der Japanners, beneevens eenige Aanmerkingen nopens de Oorspronk der Japanners in eene geregelde Jaartelling van de Opvolging der Chineese en Japanse Vorsten tot het Jaer 1784, large folio, *autograph MS. of Titsingh, sent to his brother in* 1789, *with some lines of continuation to* 1795, 128 *pp. with preface and Index, completely ready for the press, hf. bd. from Klaproth's sale,* 32s   1795

5890 TRIGAUTIUS de Christianis apud Japonios triumphis, 1612-20, sm. 4to. *plates, bd.* 24s   Monachii, 1623

5891 VOCABULARIES, etc. in Dutch and Japanese, an European MS. prepared in the East, in 1 vol. sm. folio, *bds.* 25s   Sec. XVIII

Containing: Vocabulary Dutch and Japanese, 18 pp. double columns; Origine du Syllabaire Siro-Kanoi; Prononciation Japonaise; "Uyt het Boek Sin day no maki," 8 pp. *double columns in Japanese and Roman characters;* Vocabulary Japanese and Dutch, 32 pp. double columns; etc.

5892 Y RO FA NI, a native Japanese Dictionary entirely in Japanese, 12mo. 277 pp. *hf. morocco,* 24s   Sec. XVII

5893 JAPANESE ENGRAVINGS, 5 very large Sheets of native Woodcuts, three of them colored, 28s   Sec. XIX

Worked from woodblocks of extraordinary size, nearly 4 feet long by 2 feet broad. There are two colored portraits of ladies; an immense colored Landscape, representing various scenes and figures; and two large bird's-eye views, one colored, each representing a city of bridges and canals, with public sports, Rope Dancing, and the open-air life of the Japanese, their shops, promenades, etc.

PALESTINE, with the Literature of the Sacred Languages, including Hebrew, Chaldee, Syriac, and Ethiopic.

5894 ABULPHARAGII sive Bar-Hebræi Chronicon Syriacum, *Syriace et Latine*, cum notis Brunsii, edidit Kirsch, 2 vols. sm. 4to. *Fine Paper, old calf, gilt edges, rare*, £2. 18s *Lips*. 1789

"An elegant writer of the Syriac tongue, a poet, physician, and historian. The account of his life and writings is perhaps the most curious article in the Bibliotheca of Assemannus."—*Gibbon.*
" Of all the works of Abulpharagius the most important is his chronicle, which will be an eternal monument to his memory."—*De Rossi.*

5895 ADRICHOMII Theatrum Terrae Sanctæ et Biblicarum Historiarum, folio, 11 *large Maps, in the original stamped calf, gilt back*, 12s 6d *Colon*. 1628

5896 BIBLIA HEBRAICA, sine punctis, cum notis Masoretarum Kri et Ktif, ed. Lederlin, 16mo. *calf*, 9s *Amst*. 1701

"Edition estimée."—BRUNET. A very pretty edition.

5897 BUXTORFII Lexicon Chaldaicum, Talmudicum, et Rabbinicum, cum Indice, stout folio, *portrait and engraved frontispiece*, pp. 10, 2679, and 63, *vellum*, £2. 10s *Basil*. 1639-40

5898 —— de Abbreviaturis Hebraicis, Recensio Talmudi, et Bibliotheca Rabbinica, 16mo. *vellum*, 2s 6d 1613

5899 —— the same, editio locupletior, 2 vols. in 1, 16mo. *vel*. 5s *Franequerae*, 1696

5900 COTOVICI Itinerarium Hierosolymitanum et Syriacum, 4to. *fine plates of the principal Sacred Places in the Holy Land, with all the slips and tables, very fine copy in vellum*, 18s *Antv*. 1619

Presented by the Author to John Van Rhede.

5901 DE ROSSI, Specimen variarum Lectionum Sacri Textus et Chaldaica Estheris additamenta, cum Latinâ versione, 8vo. *hf. morocco*, 12s *Romae*, 1782

5902 GESENIUS' Hebrew and Chaldee Lexicon, translated with additions and corrections by Tregelles, stout sm. 4to. *cloth*, 22s 1857

5903 ISAAC ABOHAB, Sepher Menorath Hammaor: Book of the Candlestick, *in Hebrew*, with Rabbi Moses' commentary entitled Nephesh Yudah or "Soul of Juda," 12mo. *original binding*, 7s 6d *Amst*. 1701

5904 KOEGLERI Notitia Bibliorum Judaeorum in Imperio Sinensi, diatriben addidit Murr, 8vo. *calf*, 3s *Halae*, 1805

5905 LUZZATO, Eloh Beni Haneurim: Hebrew Poems, some in Hebrew and Italian, sq. 8vo. *cloth*, 9s *privately printed*, 1768

5906 MEDINA, Viaggio di Terra Santa, con sue stationi e misterii, tradotto da Buonfanti, sm. 4to. *woodcuts, old calf, rare*, 16s *Fiorenza*, 1590

5907 NOE, Viaggio da Venetia al santo Sepolcro et a Sinai, 12mo. *very rude woodcuts, the first book printed at Roncilio, hf. bd.* 7s *Ronciglione*, 1615

5908 NORBERG, CODEX NASARÆUS, Liber ADAMI appellatus, *Syriacè et Latine*, cum LEXIDIO et Onomastico, 5 vols. sm. 4to. *plates of facsimiles, calf neat*, £5.
Hafniæ, (et Lond. Goth.) 1815-17

Priced, 1836, Black, £6. 6s.
The sect of which the above are the Sacred Books has been known in the East under the various names of Nazareans, Mandaites, Christians of St. John, or Sabæans. Some assert that they are Christians; others the remains of the Hemerobaptists; and Norberg states that their religion is a medley of Chaldæism, Judæism, and Christianity. Others are of opinion that they are those so often alluded to in the Koran, as "the people of the book."—They are principally settled in the neighbourhood of Bussorah; in 1811 their number was about 5000, but in a state of rapid decrease. Their language is a dialect of the Chaldáic or Syriac. In the first part of the *Liber Adami* mention is made of Noah, Abraham, Moses, Solomon, John the Baptist, and Jesus Christ; of the destruction of Jerusalem; of the Christians;" of the Manichæans, Mahomet, the Sassanian dynasty of Persian kings, the conquest of Persia by the Arabs, &c. In the second, *Mana*, or the soul, sent by the Supreme Life to vivify and animate the body of Adam, speaks.

5909 RELANDI Palæstina, 2 vols. in 1, sm. 4to. *vel*. 8s 6d *; or calf*, 10s *Traj*.1714
5909* —— the same, LARGE PAPER, 2 vols. 4to. *vellum, fine copy*, 25s 1714

5910 RADZIVILI (Principis) Ierosolymitana Peregrinatio, ex Polonico sermone in Latinum translata à Tretero, sm. folio, *curious plates, fine copy in the original calf, gilt edges, rare*, 32s *Antv*. 1614

Priced, 1847, £2. 2s; Lord Rothesay's copy fetched £1. 17s; the Fonthill, £2. 11s.
"The second edition, 1614, is in every way preferable to the first."—*Grenville Catalogue.*
The author of the present volume was Duke of Olica and Nieswitz. Being afflicted by a grievous malady, which for a long time defied the powers of medicine, he made a vow, that if he recovered he would visit the Holy Sepulchre. After many fruitless attempts he accomplished his purpose The *Biographie Universelle* says of his work, "La relation de Radziwil est intéressante par les détails qu' elle donne sur la Terre Sainte, l'Egypte et les autres pays que Radziwil a vus, et par la manière dont elle est écrite."

5911 RIVERA, Viage que hize a JERUSALEM, todas las cosas que en el pasaron desde Noviembre de (1)518 hasta Otubre de (1)520, very small 4to. *the engraved title injured, otherwise a fine copy in old calf*, 36s *Seuilla*, 1606
Not in any of Salva's Catalogues. "On trouve dans ce volume la description du même voyage, en vers heroïques, par Juan de la Enzine, qui fut le compagnon du Marquis de Tarifa."—*Brunet.*

5912 ROGER (E.) La TERRE SAINTE, ou description topographique tres-particuliere des Saints Lieux, et de la Terre de Promission, 4to. *plates of Oriental Costume, fine copy, vellum*, 36s *Paris*, 1664
RARE; the Roxburghe copy fetched 34s.

5913 ROXBURGHE CLUB. ITINERARIES of WILLIAM WAY, to Jerusalem, 1462; and to St. James of Compostella, 1456; from the original Manuscript in the Bodleian Library, 4to. *hf. morocco*, £2. 10s 1857

5914 TOBIN'S (Lady) Land of Inheritance: or, Bible Scenes Revisited, a handsome large impl. 8vo. volume, viii *and* 438 *pages, beautifully printed, with the* PORTRAITS *of Lady Tobin and Sir Thomas Tobin, and* 8 *original* VIEWS *in Palestine and Egypt, extra cloth gilt, gilt edges*, 30s 1863

5915 ZIEGLERI Terræ Sanctæ, quam Palæstinam nominant, Syriæ, Arabiæ, Ægypti, et Schondiæ descriptio, folio, 8 *large woodcut maps, margins wormed, otherwise fine copy, stamped binding*, 25s *Argent.* 1536
"Ce livre est rare, et comme on peut en juger par le titre, d'un certain intérét."—*Brunet.*

5916 ZUALLARDO, Viaggio di Gerusalemme, sq. 8vo. *numerous maps and plates, fine copy in vellum*, 16s *Roma*, 1587

5917 **Amharic.** LUDOLFI Lexicon Amharico-Latinum, et Grammatica linguæ Amharicæ, 2 vols. folio, *sd.* 24s *Francof.* 1698

5918 **Ethiopic.** BIBLIA VETERIS TESTAMENTI Aethiopica, ad librorum MSS. fidem edidit Dillmann, cum apparatu critico et notis, Vols. I, II pt. 1, in 4 parts, sm. 4to. *sd.* 20s *Lipsiae*, 1853-61

5919 LUDOLFI (J.) GRAMMATICA AETHIOPICA, accedit prosodia, cum appendicibus, folio, *bds. uncut*, VERY RARE, £2. 2s *Francofurti*, 1702

5920 —— LEXICON AETHIOPICO-LATINUM, editio secunda, folio, VERY RARE, £2. 2s *Francof.* 1699

5921 **PERSIA.** AKBAR NAMEH, the History of the great Emperor Akbar, by his Vizier, the Sheikh ABUL FAZL, 3 vols. folio, a *fine well written MS. of an important work, not quite uniform in size, bound*, £8. 8s A. H. 1044 (1643)
The literary productions of Abul Fazl have raised him to the highest position in Oriental literature, and he was equally distinguished as a statesman. His history of Akbar the Great has never been published.

5922 BERÉSINE, Recherches sur les Dialectes Persans, 3 parts in 1 vol. 8vo. *sd.* 25s *Casan*, 1853
Part I is Grammatical; Part II contains "Textes Guileks, Mazanderans, Guebres, Kurde-Oriental et Kurde-Oriental," with dialogues, etc.; Part III contains "Vocabulaire Francais-Persan, Guilek, Mazanderan, Guebre, Kurde Oriental et Kurde Occidental."

5923 TAWAFIQ-UL-MULK, the Prosperity of Kingdoms, an *Arabic* MS. of Persian execution, elegantly written, on the lives of the Prophets, sm. folio, 530 *leaves, bound in old calf gilt*, £5. 5s *Sec.* XV-XVI
An extremely valuable and important MS. recently bought at the sale of Baron Van Alstein in Ghent.

5924 MATSYA PURANA: a Persian translation of this great Sanscrit Purana, which celebrates the Incarnation of the God Vishnu as a Fish, in 9 vols. large 8vo. *finely written, Vols.* III *and* VI *being adorned with a coloured Drawing on the first page of each, representing the appearance of Vishnu rising from the mouth of a Fish in the sea, before a vessel filled with worshippers, oriental cloth bds.* £2. 10s A. H. 1207
The Matsya Purana was considered by Langlès to be the greatest and most important of all the Puranas. A note in English on the fly-leaf of a couple of the vols. says "Muschee Pooran translated by Gosain Aun und Ghun and it being delevered to Jonathan Duncan Esquire Precedent at Benaras 9th September, Sunday morning, 1792."

5925 MIRKHOND, AL-RAUZAT AL-SAFA FI SIRAT AL AMBIYA WA AL-MULUK WA AL-KHULAFA: The Garden of Purity, of the Merits of the Prophets, the Kings, and the Khalifs; being a General History from the earliest Times to the Death of the Sultan Husain Mirza Abu al-Ghazi Bahadur in A.H. 911 (A.D. 1511), written by Mohammed Ben Khwand Shah Ben Mahmud, better known as Mirkhond, and continued by his Son Khondamir, to whom the last two volumes are attributed, *in Persian*, 8 vols. in 6, sm. folio, *oriental binding*, £12. 12s *Saec.* XVII.
A complete set of this most important work, and of great rarity. This copy cost its former proprietor, Dr. Bird, £20. THE RAUZAT AS-SAFA IS OF THE VERY HIGHEST AUTHORITY BOTH IN ASIA AND EUROPE. A description

of it, by M. Jourdain, will be found in the ninth volume of the Notices et Extraits; the learned Baron Hammer-Purgstall has also given a detailed account of its contents in the Catalogue of his Oriental MSS.

CONTENTS :

Vol. I. A Preface and Introduction on the utility of history. An account of the creation, and of the deluge. Account of the Patriarchs, Prophets, and Kings of Israel, the Virgin Mary, St. John, Jesus Christ, the Seven Sleepers, and St. George. History of the Péshdádian and Kaianian Kings of Persia. Account of Alexander the Great and the ancient philosophers. The Ashkanian and Sasanian dynasties, to Yazdajird, the last of the Kings of the race of Sasan.
,, II. The genealogy and history of Muhammad, and of the first four Khalifs, to A.H. 44 (A.D. 664.)
,, III. The history of the twelve Imams, and of the Khalifs of the Bani Umayyah and Bani 'Abbas dynasties, to A.H. 656 (A.D. 1258).
,, IV. The history of the dynasties contemporary with the 'Abbasides.
,, V. An account of the origin of the Turks traced from Japhet, and of the ancestors of Ginghis Khan. History of Ginghis Khan and his successors to the time of Nushirwan, the last of the race. The Ilkanians, from the death of Hasan Buzurg, in A.H. 757 (A.D. 1356) to the time of Sultan Ahmad Ben Uwais. Domination of Amir Wali, in Astarabad, and of Sayyid Kawam ad-Din, in Mazandaran. The Sarbadarians, from their origin to the time of Khojah 'Ali Muayyad, who submitted to Timur.
,, VI. The history of Timur, his descendants and successors, to the death of the Sultan Abu Sa'id Ghurkan, in A.H. 873 (A.D. 1468).
,, VII. The history of Abu al-Ghazi Sultan Husain Mirza, the fourth in descent from Timur; and VIII. Geographical description of the earth.

Mirkhond was born towards the close of A.H. 836 or the beginning of 837 (A D. 1433). He devoted himself, early in life, to literary pursuits, but he never composed anything previously to his introduction to Mir 'Ali Shir, who immediately took him under his protection, and soon afterwards assigned him apartments in the Khankah Akhlasiyah, a building which the minister had erected to serve as a retreat and asylum to men distinguished by their attainments. A great portion of Mirkhond's work was written whilst he was on a bed of sickness, and he has himself given a painful account of his sufferings whilst engaged in completing his history. For a whole year before his death, which occurred in A.H. 903 (A.D. 1493) he gave himself up entirely to religious duties.

5926 TABAKAT-I-AKBARY: the Tables of Akbar, a general History of India to the reign of Akbar, by Khojah Nizámu-l-dín Ahmad Bakhshi, *in Persian*, sq. 8vo. *neatly written MS.* 110 *pp. bd.* 25s   Saec. XVII

5927 TABARI, Abu Jaffer Mohammed, TARIKH PISR JORAIR: Universal History, from the Creation to 300 A. H. translated from the Arabic, and continued to A. H. 487, by the Vizer Abdulgani, folio, *a beautifully written Persian MS. of 596 pp. in a minute handwriting, with an illuminated heading, each page enclosed by gold and coloured lines, in the original embossed Oriental binding, from the library of Dr. Adam Clarke to whom it had been presented by Lord Teignmouth*, £3.   Saec. XVI

Tabari was born A. H. 224, died A. H, 310. This Persian translation is considered more valuable than the Arabic original, from its numerous and curious additions. Tabari's work is the most accurate and judicious of all Oriental histories; the least disfigured with metaphorical exaggeration.

5928 VEDAS. The Rig Veda; the Yajur Veda; the Sama Veda: and the Atarban Veda; being a Persian translation of the Four Sacred Books of the Sanscrit Theology, in 1 vol. roy. 8vo. *beautifully written MS. with illuminated heading, on various coloured papers, white, yellow, flesh-coloured, blue, green, and orange*, 812 *pp. enclosed within red and blue lines, original bdg. from Adam Clarke's library*, £2. 16s   Sec. XVI

Probably one of the books prepared by order of the great Akbar, when his free-thinking spirit, so much dreaded by devout Mussulmans, led him to have the Indian Scriptures translated and examined.

5929 Ancient Persia. AVESTA, die Heiligen Schriften der Parsen, zum ersten Male *im Grundtexte*, sammt der *Huzváresch*-Uebersetzung, von Spiegel, Vols. I, II pt. 1: Vendidad, Vispered, Yaçna, 2 vols. 8vo. *sd.* 27s   Wien, 1853-58

5930 ZOROASTER'S WORKS in Persian: a Persian MS. labelled on the back "Zoroaster Persien MS." 2 vols. in 1, stout sq. 8vo. *hf. bd.* £2. 16s   Sec. XVII

There is a curious description of the acquisition of the work by an English traveller in Persia on the blank page preceding each volume. The first is written in affectedly old English, stating the procurement of the book from a Dervise, and that it contained the works of Zoroaster. This is signed "Jons. Henricus Somerts, Knite." The second notice is written in simple English about 150 years old, and signed apparently "J. L. Masters."

5931 LORD (Henry) the Religion of the Persees, compiled from a book called their Zundavastaw, sm. sq. 8vo. *bd. rare*, 15s   1630

5932 Phœnicia. BOURGADE, Toison d'Or de la Langue Phéniciene, folio, *with 36 large plates, several of them double, of Ancient Inscriptions and Monuments in Tunis, etc. sd.* 12s   Paris, 1852

5933 FALBE, Recherches sur l'Emplacement de Carthage, Inscriptions Puniques, etc. 8vo. *no plates, sd.* 4s   1833

5934 HAMAKER Miscellanae Phoenicia, sive commentarii de Rebus Phoenicum, quibus inscriptiones multae explicantur, etc., 1828—Diatribe philologico-critica Monumentorum Punicorum, 1829—2 vols. 4to. *large folding plates of Inscriptions, sd.* 10s   Lugd. Bat. 1828-29

5935 MULLER (L.) Numismatique de l'Ancienne Afrique, ouvrage commencé et préparé par Falbe et Lindberg, 2 vols. 4to. *numerous illustrations of the Coins of Cyrenaica, Syrtica, Byzacena, and Zeugitana, sd.* 25s *Copenhague,* 1860-61

5936 **Siam.** ALEXANDRI DE RHODES Catechismus in octo dies divisus, ab illo Latine et Annamitice compositus, in linguam Siamicam translatus operâ Laurentii, sq. 8vo. *MS. of 300 pp. entirely in the Siamese character, very neatly written, with a MS. note by the Abbé Vuillemin and another by Rémusat, hf. morocco,* £2. *ca.* 1690

The note of the Abbé Vuillemin says, "Ce M. Laurent etoit fils de Barkalom, premier ministre du Roy de Siam sur la fin du regne de Louis XIV. Il est ecrit de sa main en langue sçavante. Je l'ai acquis à Bankok."

5937 LA LOUBÈRE, Description du Royaume de Siam, 2 vols. 12mo. *plates, bd.* 5s 1714
5938 PALLEGOIX, Grammatica Linguae Thai, 4to. *hf. bd. rare,* 36s *Bangkok,* 1850
5939 —— Description du Royaume Thai ou Siam, 2 vols. 12mo. *maps and cuts, hf. calf gilt,* 7s 6d 1854
5940 **Tartary.** BERGMANN's Nomadische Streifereien unter den Kalmüken, 1802-3, 4 vols. in 2, 12mo. *plates, cloth,* 7s 6d *Riga,* 1804
5941 GIGANOFF, Slovar Rossiisko-Tatarski, 4to. *the Tatar being expressed both in Arabic and Russian characters,* 682 pp. *hf. bd.* 25s *St. Petersb.* 1804
5942 KLAPROTH, DICTIONNAIRE MONGOL-MANDCHOU, 4 vols. folio, about 2000 pp. *each page containing eight words of Mongolian in black ink with the Mandchou explanation in red ink beside it, and a numeral reference to each, very neatly written MS. by Klaproth's own hand, hf. bd.* £4. 4s *ca.* 1820
5943 LANGLÈS, Rituel des Tartares-Mantchoux, redigé par l'ordre de l'Empereur Kien-Long, *Mantchou et Française,* 4to. *with* 10 *plates of the appurtenances to the Chamanic worship, bds.* 12s *Paris,* 1804
5944 MERGAN ZAMZA : The Lost Cattle, a Mongolian Episode, 17 *pages on narrow strips of paper, printed, with* 7 *pages in MS. the former being an excellent specimen of Mongolian typography,* 7s 6d *ca.* 1800
5945 RÉMUSAT (Abel) Recherches sur les langues Tartares ou Mémoires sur la Grammaire et la Littérature des Mandchous, des Mongols, des Oingours, et des Tibetains, Vol. I. 4to. *all published, sd.* 20s *Paris,* 1820
5946 (ZWICK) Kleines Kalmykisch- Deutsch und Deutsch- Kalmykisches Wörterbuch, 2 vols. sm. 4to. *about* 720 pp. *very neatly written MS. bds.* 36s *ca.* 1820
5947 **Thibet.** BTSCHOM- LDAN- ADAS: Herz der zum jenseit Ufer des Wissens gelangten Allerherrlichst- Vollendenten, obl. 8vo. *all Tibetan, sd.* 3s 1835
5948 HYACINTHE BITCHOURIN, Description de Tubet, *en Français,* revue sur le Chinois par Klaproth, 8vo. *maps, sd.* 5s *Paris,* 1831
5949 NGYEH KRIS : a native work, in Tibetan, 69 pp. on long narrow folio strips of thick paper, *unbound, a very curious specimen, with the figures of three divinities on one page,* £2. *Sec.* XIX
5950 SHAKYA-MUNI. Prayers to Dshak Shimmuni, a Tibetan MS. on 47 leaves, narrow sm. 8vo. size, *unbound,* 16s *Sec.* XVIII
5951 SMON- LAM- BTSCHU, Tübetisches Gebetbuch, obl. 8vo. *all Tibetan,* 2s 1835
5952 **Turkey.** MENINSKI. Complementum Thesauri Linguarum Orientalium, seu Onomasticum Latino-Turcico-Arabico-Persicum, folio, *very fine copy in hf. calf neat, rare,* £2. 5s *Viennae,* 1687

5953 **AUSTRALASIA.** AUSTRALIAN AND NEW ZEALAND GAZETTE from the commencement of the new series in October 1850 to December 1853, an interesting weekly newspaper, bound in 3 vols. sm. folio, *hf. calf,* £2. 2s 1850-53

5954 GREY (now Sir George) Journals of Two Expeditions of Discovery in North West and Western Australia, 1837-39, 2 vols. 8vo. *large map enclosed in the cover, and numerous plates, some coloured, representing Aboriginal Monuments, etc. (pub. at* 36s*) cloth,* 20s 1841

5955 **New Zealand.** KAWENATA HOU: the New Testament in the *Maori* language, 12mo. *calf,* 5s *Ranana,* 1841

5956 **Sandwich Islands** EMERSON'S English-Hawaiian Dictionary : Hoakaolelo no na Huaolelo Beritania i mea Kokua i na Kanaka Hawaii, 8vo. *with a Grammatical preface, x pp. ; the Dictionary, pp.* 184, *double columns, bds.* 36s *Lahainaluna,* 1845

HERALDRY, ANTIQUITIES, MEDIÆVAL HISTORY, CHRONICLES, GENEALOGY AND TOPOGRAPHY.

5957 ABELA, Malta Illustrata, ovvero descrizione di Malta, con le sue Antichità accresciuta e continovata da Ciantar, 2 parts in 1 vol. stout folio, *frontispiece, large map, and 21 plates of Punic Inscriptions, etc. bds. rare*, 20s *Malta*, 1772

5958 ACTA TOMICIANA. Epistolae, Legationes, Responsa, Actiones et Res Gestae Principis Sigismundi I, Regis Poloniæ, (1506-43) edente Comite T. Dzialynski, 7 vols. in 6, folio. (pub. at 36 Thalers), *bds.* £4. 4s *Posnaniae*, 1845-58

5959 AKERMAN'S (J. Y.) Remains of Pagan Saxondom, 4to. *numerous woodcuts, and 40 coloured plates of Fibulæ, Bronzes, Drinking Vessels, Urns, Weapons, Domestic Utensils, etc.* (pub. at £3. 3s) *hf. calf,* 36s 1855

5960 ANDERSON'S Royal Genealogies, or the Genealogical Tables of Emperors, Kings, and Princes, folio, second edition (or issue), with new Addenda and Corrigenda after the preface, folio, *calf,* 36s 1736

5961 ANGLIA CHRISTIANA (Society): Chronicon Monasterii de Bello, nunc primum typis mandatum, 8vo. *hf. morocco, not printed for sale,* 10s 1846

5962 ANTIQUARIES OF SCOTLAND Society, Synopsis of the Museum, sm. 8vo. *plate and woodcuts, thick paper, cloth,* 5s *Ed.* 1849

5963 ARCHAEOLOGIA CANTIANA, being the Transactions of the Kent Archaeological Society, Vols. I—III, 8vo. 50 *plates, some coloured, of Antiquities, Ancient Arms, Ornaments, Facsimiles of Early Charters, etc. cloth, only printed for subscribers, but now out of print and very rare,* £2. 12s 6d 1858-60

5964 ARGELATI Bibliotheca Scriptorum Mediolanensium, seu Acta et Elogia Virorum illustrium, cum SAXII Historiâ Literario-Typographicâ Mediolanensi à 1465 ad 1500 et cum Indicibus, etc. 2 vols. in 4, large folio, *fine clean copy, old calf neat,* £2. *Mediolani*, 1745

Priced, 1818, Longman, £2. 12s 6d; 1826, Thorpe, £4. 14s 6d; 1832, £2. 12s 6d.

5965 ARGOTE DE MOLINA (Gonçalo) Nobleza del Andalusia, folio, *numerous large woodcuts of Arms, calf gilt,* £2. 10s *Seuilla, Fernando Dias*, 1588

A rare work. Priced by Thorpe, 1822, vell. £3 3s; 1824, vell. £2. 12s 6d; by Salva, 1826, £2. 2s; 1829, £3; by myself, 1855, £3.
"Cet ouvrage contient les armoiries de toute la noblesse Andalouse. Il est d'une grande importance, non seulement pour le généalogiste, mais encore pour l'historien et le littérateur. Argote de Molina, en parlant des nobles enfants de sa patrie, rapporte aussi l'histoire du temps où ils vécurent, et en racontant certains faits d'armes ou batailles, il n'oublie pas de citer les romances et les compositions poétiques populaires qui les rappellent. Plusieurs de ces poésies, qui remontent au XIVe. siècle, auraient été perdues pour nous, si le savant annaliste n'eût pris le soin de les transmettre ainsi à la postérité. Soit qu'on recherche beaucoup ce livre en Espagne, soit qu'il n'ait été tiré qu'à un petit nombre d'exemplaires, le fait est qu'aujourd'hui on en rencontre fort peu, et encore manquent-ils le plus souvent du titre."—SALVA.

5966 ASHMOLE'S (Elias) Institutions, Laws, and Ceremonies of the most noble ORDER OF THE GARTER; a work furnished with a variety of matter relating to Honour and Noblesse, with the Appendix, and leaf of Errata, folio, *numerous plates by* HOLLAR *representing the Knights in their Robes, Orders, etc. Grand Processions, Views of Windsor Castle, St. George's Chapel, the Hall, Seals, Arms, etc. remarkably fine copy, calf extra, gilt leaves, by Lewis,* £6. 6s 1672

Priced, 1829, John Bohn, £7. 7s; 1835, Thorpe, £7. 17s 6d; 1843, John Bohn, £7. 7s; 1848, Payne and Foss, £7. 7s
Large Paper copies; 1834 and 36, Thorpe, £16. 16s and £14. 14s; 1837, 1845, 1848, Payne and Foss, £21. £26. 5s. Lane's copy, morocco, fetched, 1856, at Sotheby's £9. 15s.

5967 ASSEMANI Italicæ Historiæ Scriptores ex Bibliothecæ Vaticanæ aliarumque codd. MSS. collecti, 4 vols. 4to. *portrait of the Infante of Spain, vellum, rare,* £5. *Romæ*, 1751-53

"Collection recherchée. Les morceaux qui y sont réunis se rapportent particulièrement aux royaumes de Naples et de Sicile."—BRUNET.

5968 AVILES (Joseph de) CIENCIA HEROYCA reducida a las Leyes Heraldicas del Blason, 2 vols. 12mo. 62 *plates, containing numerous Coats of Arms and Heraldic Insignia, last leaf of Index to Vol. I. injured, calf,* 36s *Barcelona*, 1725

5969 BAGMIHL'S Pommersches Wappenbuch, mit historischen Nachweisen, complete in 5 vols. 4to. 341 *plates of Coats of Arms, uncut,* £2. *Stettin*, 1843-55

5970 BARLANDE, Chroniques des Ducs de Brabant, sm. folio, *Coats of Arms, and* 36 *beautiful engravings by Collaert, of the Dukes and Duchesses of Brabant in the rich costume of their time, calf,* 12s *Anvers*, 1612

5971 BASTARD, Maison de, *Originaire du Comté Nantais, existant encore en Guienne, au Maine, en Bretagne et en Devonshire:* Inventaire de Sources Historiques Manuscrites et imprimées, pour servir de preuves a sa Généalogie, *with Alphabetical Index*—Armoiries des Maisons alliées à la Maison de Bastard, *Arms of* 600 *families*, 54 *being English*—Armoiries de la Maison de Bastard, *several cuts* —together 3 vols. high 4to. bds. £3. Paris, 1847

5972 —— Armoiries de la maison de Bastard—Armoiries des maisons alliées—together 2 vols. high 4to. *numerous coats of arms, bds.* 18s 1847

5973 BATTHYAN (Ign. Comit. de, Episcopi Transyl.) Leges Ecclesiasticæ regni Hungariæ et provinciarum adjacentium, 3 vols. large folio, *engravings of Seals, &c. Large Paper, hf. cf. uncut*, £3. 10s Albæ Carolinæ et Claudiopoli, 1785-1827

5974 BEAU Traicté de la diversité des Fiefs en Flandres, roy. 8vo. *printed on pink coloured paper, russia, gilt edges, silk linings,* 15s Gand, 1839
Printed from an old MS. and containing some words found in no Glossary.

5975 BECKMANN, Histoire des Fürstenthums Anhalt, mit Accessionibus und Continuation, 8 vols. in 3, folio, *nearly* 100 *plates, including about* 40 *fine Portraits, of Views, Monumental and Architectural Antiquities, Seals, Coins, etc. Genealogical Tables, a little stained, fine copy, old calf extra,* £2. 2s Zerbst, 1710-16

5976 BERTRAND, Histoire de Boulogne, 2 vols. 8vo. *map and plates, calf,* 6s 1828-29

5977 BERRY'S County Genealogies, Pedigrees of the Families in the County of HANTS, collected from Heraldic Visitations and other MSS. sm. folio, *numerous Coats of Arms,* cloth, 32s 1833

5978 BIANCOLINI, Notizie storiche delle Chiese di VERONA, 8 vols. in 9, sm. 4to. *Coats of Arms, etc. good copy, hf. bd.* 32s Verona, 1749-71
An important work, containing Lists and descriptions of all the Art Treasures in the Churches of Verona, including the Paintings. In G. Molini's Oper. Bibl. only 4 vols. are quoted; the later volumes are scarce.

5979 BLONDELLI, Genealogiæ Francicæ plenior Assertio, Vindiciarum Hispanicarum, etc. Chiffletii omnimoda Eversio, 2 vols in 1, stout sm. folio, *several pages not printed upon, tables of Genealogy, old calf gilt,* 21s Amstelædami, 1654

5980 BOREL D'HAUTERIVE, Annuaire de la Noblesse de France, et des Maisons Souveraines de l'Europe, 1854-58, 5 vols. sm. 8vo. *plates, sd.* 20s Paris, 1854-58

5981 BOUCHE, Chorographie ou Description de PROVENCE, et l'Histoire chronologique du même Pays, 2 vols. folio, *with the additional leaves, plates, portraits, and Coats of Arms, fine copy in new calf gilt,* £4. Aix, 1664
Ouvrage recherché et rare. Il faut voir si l'on y trouve les additions et corrections qui ont paru à part, et qui occupent 30 pp. pour le tome Ier et 36 pp. pour le tome II.—*Brunet.*

5981*(BOULLEMIER) Recueil des Sceaux du Moyen Age, dits Sceaux Gothiques, sm. 4to. *frontispiece, and* 30 *plates of Seals, hf. calf, rare,* 21s Paris, 1779

5982 BOUTELL'S Monumental Brasses of England, roy. 8vo. 150 *engravings, with descriptive Notices and Indexes of Heraldry, Names and Places,* (pub. at 28s) cloth, 14s 1849

5983 —— Manual of Heraldry, Historical and popular, 8vo. *second edition revised and enlarged,* xiii and 488 pp. *with* 850 *illustrations, cloth gilt,* 8s 6d 1863
A very cheap, useful and carefully compiled book.

5984 BOYER's Great Theater of Honour and Nobility, *French and English,* 4to. *frontispiece and plates of Arms, hf. calf, a useful book,* 10s 1729

5985 BRYDGES (Sir Egerton) Ataviæ Regiæ, a Collection of Genealogical Tables, with Illustrations, impl. 4to. *plate of arms, bds.* 19s Florence, 1820
Privately printed, the impression limited to 60 copies. Priced, 1836, £2. 12s 6d; 1840, Thorpe, £3. 3s; Hanrott's copy fetched £7. 7s.

5986 BRYDGES' Stemmata Illustria, præcipue Regia, roy. folio, *numerous plates of Arms, and additional leaves, hf. bd. uncut,* £2. 5s Paris, 1825
This interesting volume of which but 100 copies were printed, *and only for private distribution,* contains the descents of the noble houses of Lancaster, Leisester, Vere, Sudely, Westmoreland, Warwick, Surrey, Arundel, Clare, Fitzmaurice, Northumberland, Cumberland, Chester, Bridgewater, Pembroke, Winchester, De-la-Zouch, Stafford, Ewe, Montacute, Montford, Gurnay, Cobham, Berkeley, Essex, Lincoln, Salisbury, Norfolk, Courtenay, De Roos, Fitzwalter, Arundel, Derby, Harcourt, &c. &c. The above copy contains the LARGE PLATE of the Arms of Sir Egerton Brydges, with 360 quarterings.

5987 BURGERMEISTER, Bibliotheca Equestris, continens ultra 50 scriptores de Nobilitate et Ordine equestri: item "Das alte Thurnierbuch," 2 vols.—Codex Diplomaticus equestris, 2 vols.—together 4 vols. thick sm. 4to. *calf,* 12s Ulm, 1720-21
To all engaged in Heraldic studies, the above volumes will be of great service.

HERALDRY, ANTIQUITIES, CHRONICLES, GENEALOGY, ETC.

5988 BURGUNDY. (PLANCHER ET MERLE), Histoire générale et particulière de Bourgogne avec des Notes, des Dissertations et les Preuves justificatives, 4 vols. folio, *map, and many large plates of Monumental and Architectural Antiquities, Seals, Coins, etc. and numerous fine Vignettes, old calf gilt*, RARE, £6. *Dijon*, 1739-41-48-81

5989 BURKE, Encyclopædia of Heraldry, or General Armory of England, Scotland, and Ireland, comprising a Registry of all Armorial bearings from the earliest to the present time, third edition, with Supplement, stout roy. 8vo. *illuminated title, about 1150 pp. double cols. cloth, new*, 18s *London, s. a.*

5990 BUTKENS, Annales Genealogiques de la Maison de Lynden; verifiées par chartes, etc. embellies des figures de divers POURTRAICTS, Chasteaux, Sepultures, et anciens Seaux, tirés sur leurs originaux, sm. folio, A HANDSOME VOLUME, *with many Coats of Arms, Portraits, Views, Seats, etc. and the Genealogical Table, old calf*, £10. *Anvers*, 1626
   A very rare and very valuable work, the chef d'œuvre of foreign Genealogical Monographs. No copy appears to have been sold for many years.

5991 CAMDEN'S BRITANNIA, or a Chorographical Description of England, Scotland, and Ireland, new edition, much enlarged, with additions by GOUGH and NICHOLS, 3 vols. large folio, BEST EDITION, *portrait, numerous maps and copperplates of Antiquities*, (pub. at £21.) *russia gilt*, £3. 3s   1789
   "The common sun, whereat our modern writers have all lighted their little torches."—*Nicholson*.

5992 CAMPANILE, Notizie di Nobilità, sq. 8vo. *frontispiece, 2 portraits, and 2 other plates, with numerous large woodcut Coats of Arms, russia extra, gilt edges, very rare*, £2. 10s *Napoli*, 1672

5993 ——— dell' Armi overo Insegne dei Nobili, oue sono i discorsi d'alcune famiglie del regno di NAPOLI, folio, 303 pp. *with frontispiece and numerous Coats of Arms, vellum, fine copy*, 25s *Napoli*, 1681
   "Rare edizione, anteponibile alla antecedente."—*MS. note.*

5994 CANISII Thesaurus Monumentorum Ecclesiasticorum et historicorum, sive Lectiones Antiquæ, cum observationibus et notis, ed. Basnage, 4 vols. folio, *fine copy in old calf gilt*, £2. 2s *Amst.* 1725
   A curious collection of pieces by writers of the early Christian times, and of the middle ages. It contains various early Chronicles; Adamnan's Life of Columna; remnants of St. Gall, and other British Saints; commentaries, some in Greek and Latin; itineraries to the Holy Land, etc. For a list, see Dowling's Notitia, pp. 101—111.

5995 CARPENTIER, Histoire Genealogique des Païs-Bas, ou histoire de Cambray, et du Cambresis, sous les Empereurs et les Rois de France et d'Espagne, 3 vols. in 2, sm. 4to. *large folding map and plate, representing the Noblemen of Cambray at a Convocation, with their respective Arms, nice copy in old calf gilt*, £3. 5s *Leide, chez l'Auteur*, 1664
   A book of importance to many English families, whose ancestors come from Cambray, such as the Lefroys Jolys, etc.

5996 CATEL (G.) Histoire des Comtes de Toulouse, avec quelques Chroniques, 2 vols. in 1, folio, *with the family portraits, fine copy in vellum*, 21s *Tolose*, 1623

5997 CEDERCRONA, SWERIGES Rikes Ridderskaps och Adels Wapen Bok, folio, *Coats of Arms of the Swedish Nobility, hf. bd.* £2. 16s *Stockholm*, 1746
   Rarely met with complete. The work is divided as follows: Ridders och Adelsmaen, 208 leaves, with 1867 Coats of Arms; Grefwar, 14 leaves, with 82 Coats of Arms; Friherrar, 34 leaves, with 204 Coats of Arms.

5998 CIBRARIO e Promis, Documenti, Sigilli e Monete appart. alla Storia di Savoia, 8vo. *Thick Paper, sd.* 7s 6d *Torino*, 1833

5999 CLARK (Hugh) Introduction to Heraldry, 12mo. *43 coloured plates of Insignia, hf. calf*, 10s   1827

6000 COCHET, les Eglises de Dieppe, roy. 8vo. *plates, hf. morocco*, 6s *Dieppe*, 1846

6000*CODICE del sacro MILITARE ORDINE GEROSOLIMITANO riordinato per comandamento del Capitolo celebrato, 1776, sotto il Gran Maestro E. de Rohan, 3 vols. in 1, stout folio, *portrait of the Grand Master*, 27s *Malta*, 1777-82

6001 COLINS, Histoire des choses plus memorables advenues depuis l'an 1130 jusques à notre siècle, sq. 8vo. *old calf gilt, rare*, 20s *Mons*, 1634
   "Ouvrage curieux surtout pour les événements qui se sont passés du temps de l'auteur."—BRUNET.

6002 COLONIA (D. de) Histoire Littéraire de la Ville de LYON, avec une Bibliothèque des Auteurs Lyonnois, 2 vols. roy. 4to. *plates, hf. morocco, uncut*, £2. 2s *Lyon*, 1728-30

6003 COLLECTANEA Topographica et Genealogica, 8 vols. roy. 8vo. *bds.* £5. 1830-43
   Priced, 1854, £7. 7s; 1857, Nichols, £8.; 1857, £7. 7s; fetched, 1859, Sotheby's £6. 6s.
   Containing Additions to Dugdale's Baronage, from the MS. collection of Townsend, *Windsor Herald*, edited by Sir Chas. Geo. Young, *Garter:* Extracts from Cartularies, Registers of Burials in Westminster Abbey, Sales of Bishops' Lands, Sepulchral Inscriptions, Pedigrees of Families, &c. &c.
   The most valuable collection of materials for Family History and Topography ever published. The articles were contributed by the best antiquaries of the day.

6004 CONCILIUM zu CONSTANTZ. Das Concilium so zu Constantz gehalten ist worden, 1413, sm. folio, *with numerous fine woodcuts, including representations of the burning of John Huss, of the German Emperor investing the Nobility in their feudal dignities, of Ecclesiastics, and their Elections, dissensions, etc. giving altogether a very striking picture of the events of that famous Council; with the Coats of Arms of all the Nobles, Citizens, and Ecclesiastics, this being the* FIRST ARMORIAL *ever published, fine tall copy, old binding,* £3. *Augspurg,* 1536

6004*COLLINS' (Arthur) HISTORICAL COLLECTIONS of the NOBLE FAMILIES of CAVENDISHE, HOLLES, VERE, HARLEY, and OGLE; with the Lives of the most remarkable Persons, Lives of the Earls of Oxford, concluding with Aubrey de Vere; of Horace Lord Vere of Tilbury, and Sir Francis his brother, fol. folio, LARGE AND FINE PAPER, WITH FIRST AND BRILLIANT IMPRESSIONS *of the fine portraits by Vertue, splendid copy, orange morocco extra, gilt edges, by Lewis,* £14. 14s 1752

VERY RARE, only a few copies having been printed on this paper. So fine a copy as the present has probably seldom occurred for sale.

6005 COLLINS' Peerage of England, Genealogical, Biographical, and Historical, augmented and continued by Sir E. Brydges, 3 vols. 8vo. BEST EDITION, *Coats of Arms of each family, calf gilt,* £4. 4s 1812

6006 CONTELORII (F.) Mathildis Comitissæ Genealogia, sq. 8vo. *with 3 folding Genealogical Tables, green morocco, by Clarke,* £2. *Interamnæ,* 1557

Mathilda, the great Countess of Tuscany, was one of the most warlike and extraordinary women that ever filled a throne. This volume is excessively rare, and seems to have escaped all her Biographers, as well as all Bibliographers. It is curious, also, from being printed at Terni, 80 years earlier than Mr. Cotton supposed printing to have been introduced there. The type is very rude.

6007 CORMERII Rerum gestarum Henrici II, Regis Galliae, libri V, sm. 4to. *limp vellum,* 12s *Paris,* 1684

6008 CORBINELLI, Histoire Genealogique de la Maison de GONDI, 2 vols. 4to. *many fine plates, and several beautifully engraved portraits by Duflos, with numerous cuts of Arms, neat in calf,* 36s *Paris,* 1705

One of the most elegant and esteemed of the French Family Histories. The celebrated CARDINAL DE RETZ was of the Family of Gondi, and his portrait is inserted; also that of Paule de Gondi, DUCHESSE DE RETZ.

6009 COUSIN (Jean) Histoire de TOURNAY, ou quatre livres des Chroniques, Annales, ou demonstrations, du Christianisme de l'Evesché, 4 vols. in 1, stout sq. 8vo. *plates, calf,* 18s *Douay,* 1620

6010 CRESCENZI, Corona della NOBILTA D'ITALIA, overo compendio dell' istorie delle famiglie illustri, 2 vols. in 1, stout sq. 8vo. *engraved title-page containing two Coats of Arms, calf neat,* 30s *Bologna,* 1639-42

A very rare work on the noble families of Italy. The Roxburghe copy fetched £3. 3s.

6011 CROMERI POLONIA, sive de Origine et rebus gentis Polonorum, stout folio, *portrait and maps, with MS. additions, calf,* 20s *Coloniæ,* 1589

6012 CURICK, der Stadt DANTZIG historische Beschreibung, sm. folio, *portraits, plan of Dantzig, plates of Churches, Buildings, Views, etc. vellum,* 15s *Amst.* 1688

6013 D'ABLAING VAN GIESSENBURG, de Ridderschap van VELUWE, of Geschiedenis der Veluwsche Jonkers, roy. 4to. lxxx and 442 pp. with Alphabetical Index, 7 *plates containing* 94 *Coats of Arms, sd.* 21s *Gravenhaage,* 1859

An important work on the Dutch Nobility, particularly that of the Province of Guelders.

6014 DALLAWAY'S (Rev. J.) Inquiries into the Origin and Progress of the SCIENCE OF HERALDRY in England, with Explanatory Observations on Armorial Ensigns, and an Appendix containing the Lives of Sir W. Dugdale (Garter) and Greg. King (Windsor Herald), an exact copy of the third part of "the Boke of St. Alban's," thick roy. 4to. *many plates, some coloured, russia gilt,* 32s 1793

"This elegant and erudite work is most appropriately dedicated to Charles, Duke of Norfolk, Earl Marshal of England. Mr. Dallaway has here, with the pen of a Tacitus, accurately defined, in a most comprehensive manner, its rise and progress from the earliest through the most interesting periods of British History, accommodating the study to modern system."—*Moule.*

6015 DAMBERGER, Fürstenbuch, 8vo. *morocco*; Fürstentafel der Europäischen Staatengeschichte, folio, *Tables, hf. morocco*—together 2 vols. 9s *Regensburg,* 1831

6015*DANIEL, Histoire de la Milice Françoise, 2 vols. 4to. *best edition, with* 70 *plates of Arms, Armour, Warfare, etc. old calf gilt,* 12s *Paris,* 1721

6016 DENYALDI (Roberti) Rollo-Northmanno-Britannicus, folio, *calf,* FINE COPY, RARE, £2. 16s *Rothomagi,* 1660

This interesting work contains the history of seven dukes of Normandy, in verse and prose, including William the Conqueror. Only two other copies are noticed in the Bibliographer's Manual, the one in the Royal Institution, and a copy which sold for £6. in 1825, J. Bohn, £4. 4s.

HERALDRY, ANTIQUITIES, CHRONICLES, GENEALOGY, ETC. 323

6017 DIECI CIRCOLI delle Germania; Entrate de Principi Spirituali e temporali; Soldati dell' Imperio; Republica di Norimberga; Rinuncia di Carlo V, sm. 4to. *limp vellum, a valuable statistical record, 7s 6d* *Venet.* 1558

6018 DLUGOSSI seu LONGINI Historiae Polonicae libri XII, cum libro XIII° et ultimo; accedit Kadlubkonis historia Polonica, cum commento; Sarnicii annales Polonorum et Lituanorum; Orichovii annales Polonici; Sarnicii descriptio veteris et novae Poloniae itemque Russiae et Livoniae, etc. 2 vols. folio, *a fine copy in old calf, gilt back, from Miss Currer's library*, £3. 3s. *Lips.* 1711-12

6019 DOLFI (P. S.) Cronologia delle Famiglie Nobili di Bologna, con le loro Insegne e nel fine i Cimieri, stout sq. 8vo. *with the Coats of all the great* BOLOGNA FAMILIES, *calf gilt, gilt top, uncut, rare*, £2. 2s *Bologna,* 1670

6020 DORST'S Württembergisches Wappenbuch, 4to. *nearly 250 coloured plates, with Genealogical Notices, bds.* 20s *Halle,* 1846

6021 DUCHESNE (A.) HISTORIÆ NORMANNORUM SCRIPTORES Antiqui, Res ab illis per Galliam, Angliam, Apuliam, Capuæ Principatum, Siciliam et Orientem gestas explicantes, 838—1220, folio, *a fine copy in russia extra, from Miss Currer's library,* £5. 5s *Lutet. Paris,* 1619

6022 MASERES, Historiae Anglicanae circa tempus Conquestûs selecta Monumenta, excerpta ex volumine "Historiae Normannorum Scriptores antiqui," a DUCHESNE edito, 4to. *with English notes, hf. bd.* 9s 1807

6023 DU CHESNE (F.) Historiæ Francorum Scriptores, a Philippo Augusto usque ad Philippi IV tempora cum Epistolis Regum, Pontificum, Ducum, Abbatum, et aliis veteribus Monumentis, 5 vols. folio, *vellum, gilt edges,* £8.; *or a fine copy in old calf gilt, from Miss Currer's library,* £8. 8s *Lutetiæ Paris,* 1636-49

6024 —— Antiquitez des Villes, Chasteaux, etc. de la France, 12mo. *vel.* 6s 1637

6025 DUCANGE, Illyricum vetus et novum, sive historia Dalmatiae, Croatiae, Slavoniae, Bosniae, Serviae, Bulgariae, folio, *plate, hf. vellum,* 16s *Posonii,* 1746

6026 DUELII Excerpta Genealogico-Historica, folio, 60 *fine plates of* SEALS, *Arms, Costumes, and Mediaeval Art, bds.* 15s; *a fine copy in old calf,* 25s *Lips.* 1725

6027 DUGDALE (Sir W.) MONASTICON ANGLICANUM; a History of the Abbies and other Monasteries, Hospitals, Frieries, and Cathedral and Collegiate Churches, with their dependencies in England and Wales, translated and edited with large additions by Caley, Bandinel and Ellis, 8 vols. *numerous plates of Ecclesiastical edifices by John Coney*—HISTORY OF ST. PAUL'S CATHEDRAL, enlarged by Sir H. Ellis, *many fine plates,* 1818, 1 vol.—together 9 vols. folio, *original edition,* (pub. at £141. 15s) *hf. green morocco, gilt top, uncut,* £30. 1817-30

Both works are printed and bound uniformly, and they form the most complete History of the Ecclesiastical establishments in this country.

Copies are rapidly rising in price. Next to Doomsday Book this is the most ancient and ample record of the history and descent of the greatest portion of the landed property of the country; and has been admitted as evidence in a Court of Evidence where the original documents had perished.

6028 DUGDALE'S (Sir William) BARONAGE OF ENGLAND, or an Historical Account of the Lives and most memorable Actions of our English Nobility, 3 vols. in 2, folio, *with the rare leaf of Errata at the end of Vol. I.* FINE LARGE CLEAN COPY, *in old calf,* £6. 10s 1675-6

Sold in the Merly sale for £20., in the Marquis of Townshend's for £16. 5s, and in the Duke of Roxburghe's for £15. 10s.

"A work abounding in the most valuable information."—*Rev. J. Hunter.* "The BARONAGE is distinguished by the most laborious research and extraordinary accuracy, and confers honour on its author."—*Sir H. Nicolas.* It has also been styled by a late author, as "a work which will exist to the latest age a monument of its author's historical knowledge and antiquarian learning."

6029 DU PAZ (F. A.) Histoire genealogique de plusieurs Maisons illustres de Bretagne, stout folio, *many Coats of Arms, good copy in calf, rare,* £4. *Paris,* 1619

6030 DUSBURG, Chronicon Prussiae, res ORDINIS TEUTONICI, 1227-1435: acc. Antiquitates Prussicae, sm. 4to. *map, with a dissertation on the old Prussian language, plates of Arms, Coins, vellum,* 7s *Jenæ,* 1679

6031 ECCARDI Corpus Historicum Medii Aevi sive Scriptores res in orbe præcipue in Germanicâ Gestas a tempore Caroli Magni usque ad finem Saec. XV illustrantes, 2 vols. folio, *vellum,* 36s *Lips.* 1723

"This collection contains many Chronicles and Journals, of which Muratori, in his collection, has omitted many details, particularly those he considered too scandalous for the Popes."—*Sismondi.*

6032 ECCARDI Leges Francorum Salicæ et Ripuariorum Annales Ruinarti, etc. folio, *with lists of old Teutonic words, calf gilt,* 12s *Franc.* 1720

6033 ECKHART (J. G. ab) Commentarii de rebus FRANCIÆ ORIENTALIS et Episcopatus Wirceburgensis, Regum et Imperatorum Franciæ veteris Germaniaeque, &c. Gesta, 2 vols. stout folio, *portrait and numerous plates of Diplomas, Facsimiles, Seals, Coins, etc. fine copy in old calf gilt*, 36s Wirceb. 1729
   Each volume contains specimens and Glossaries of the Ancient Saxon and Theotisc languages, with other interesting philological matter.

6034 EDMONDSON'S (Jos.) Complete Body of HERALDRY, the Origin and Progress of Armories and Heraldry, the proper Method of Blazoning Armorial Bearings, etc. with plates of the Arms of Cities, Towns, etc., Glover's Ordinary of Arms, augmented, an Alphabet of Arms, containing upwards of *Fifty Thousand Coats of Arms with their Crests*, 2 vols. in 1, large folio, *portrait and plates, fine copy, russia*, £3. 10s 1780
   The best book on the subject; it sold in Edwards's sale for £11.; Bindley's, £11. 15s; Brockett's, £14. 3s 6d; Nassau's, £13. 13s; Constable's, £12. 17s.

6035 EICKSTET, Epitome Annalium Pomeraniæ, Genealogia Ducum, etc. ed. Balthasar, sq. 8vo. *calf*, 7s 6d Gryphiswald. 1728

6036 ENGLISH HISTORICAL SOCIETY. The Fine Series of Chronicles, &c. as printed under the auspices of this Club, ON FINE LARGE PAPER, which was restricted to the number of Noblemen and Gentlemen composing the Society, 29 vols. royal 8vo. *very elegantly printed, extra bds. complete sets have now become scarce*, £14. 14s 1838-56

6037 ERNST, Histoire du LIMBOURG, de Daelhem et de Fauquemont, etc. avec notes, et la vie de l'auteur, par Lavalleye, 7 vols. large 8vo. *plates, hf. calf, fine copy,* 27s 1837-47
   The 7th volume contains the "Annales Rodenses," not yet continued.

6038 FAIRBAIRN'S Crests of the Families of Great Britain and Ireland, with the Mottoes, 2 vols. impl. 4to. LARGE PAPER, 144 *plates containing* 2160 *engravings of* CRESTS, CYPHERS, *and* FLAGS, *Proofs on India Paper,* (pub. at £5. 5s) *hf. morocco*, £2. 10s Edinburgh, 1860

6039 FANT (E. M.) Scriptores Rerum Suecicarum Medii Aevi, Vol. I. folio, *facsimiles, bds.* 21s Upsalæ, 1818
   This collection is to be completed in 3 vols. but only two have yet appeared.

6040 FARNESE FAMILY: Reales Exequias de Donna Ysabel Farnesio, Princesa de Parma y Reyna de la Españas, celebradas en la Santa Iglesia Cathedral en la Imperial Corte Mexicana, 27 y 28 Febrero 1767—in 1 vol. sm. 4to. *with the large plate and others, vellum, rare*, 30s Mexico, 1768
   With numerous sonnets, emblems, &c.

6041 FAVINE'S Theater of Honour and Knighthood (*including the Orders of England, Scotland, and Ireland*); a Chronicle of the whole Christian World, the Original of all Monarchies and Estates, the Institution of Armes, Emblazons, etc. 2 vols. in 1, stout folio, *numerous woodcuts of Arms, some of the initials and arms coloured, a fine copy in old calf,* £2. 2s 1623
   "The most valuable Treatise we have in English upon the Foreign Orders of Knighthood, equally worth the attention of the Antiquary and the Historian."—MOULE.

6042 FELIBIEN, Histoire de l'Abbaye Royale de SAINT DENYS en France, fol. *fine plates of Monuments, Interior Views, Gothic Architecture, &c. old calf*, 25s
   Priced, 1832, £2. 2s. Paris, 1706

6043 FLORENCE. NOTIZIA della vera LIBERTA FLORENTINA, con la Disamina, e Confutazione delle Scritture in varj tempi pubblicate per negare i Sovrani Diritti degli Imperadori sovra la Città di FIRENZE e il GRAN DUCATO DI TOSCANA, 3 parts in 2 vols. folio, *fine clean copy in old calf, gilt edges, very rare*, £2. 10s s. l. 1724-26

6044 FRESCHOT, Pregi della Nobiltà Veneta abbozzati in un Giuoco d'Arme di tutte le Famiglie, 12mo. *plate, vellum*, 12s Venezia, 1682

6045 GALLETTI Inscriptiones Romanæ infimi Ævi Romæ exstantes, cum Appendice, 3 stout vols. roy. 4to. *frontisp. fine copy, hf. bd. entirely uncut*, 18s Romae, 1760

6046 GALLIA CHRISTIANA SAMMARTHANI in provincias ecclesiasticas distributa quâ series Archiepiscoporum, Episcoporum, et Abbatum Franciæ vicinarumque dictionum ab origine Ecclesiarum ad nostra tempora deducitur, 13 vols. folio, *fine copy in old French calf gilt*, £25. Paris, 1715-85
   "Ouvrage important. Les 13 volumes publiés ne se trouvent plus que difficilement complets."—BRUNET.
   The above copy has not got the Maps which are to be found in some; but of which I find no mention in Brunet, nor in the catalogues of booksellers, whose descriptions I have examined.

HERALDRY, ANTIQUITIES, CHRONICLES, GENEALOGY, ETC. 325

6047 GARIBAY (E.) Illustraciones Genealogicas de los Reyes de las Españas, de los de Francia, y de los Emperadores de Constantinopla, folio, *fine portrait of Philip III by Perret, cuts of Arms and Genealogical Trees, fine copy in calf extra, gilt edges, scarce,* £4. 4s *Madrid,* 1596

6048 GARIEL, Series Praesulum Magalonensium et Monspeliensium, variis Guillelmorum Monspelii Dominorum historiis locupletata, 451-1665, 2 vols. in 1, folio, *calf,* 18s *Tolosae,* 1665

6049 GASTELIER DE LA TOUR, Genealogie de la Maison de Preissac tirée du Nobiliaire de Languedoc, 4to. *old calf,* 10s *Paris,* 1770

6050 GAUFRIDI, Histoire de PROVENCE, 2 vols. folio, *portrait and Genealogical tables, old calf, rare,* 30s *Aix,* 1694
  An exceedingly important and valuable historical work.

6051 GELENII Historia et Vindiciae B. RICHEZAE, Comitissae Palatinae Rheni, Reginae Poloniarum, cum sua genuina GENEALOGIA, sm. 4to. *MS. notes and corrections, calf, very rare,* 28s *Colon.* 1649
  Not mentioned by Janozki.

6052 GESTEL (C. van) Historia Sacra et Profana Archiepiscopatus Mechliniensis, 2 vols. in 1, folio, *Large Paper, numerous plates, calf gilt,* 10s *Hagæ,* 1725

6053 GETTY's Notices of Chinese Seals found in Ireland, sm. 4to. *frontispiece and* 19 *plates, cloth,* 7s 6d *Dublin,* 1850

6054 GLAFEY, Decas Sigillorum, historiam Italiae, Galliae atque Germaniae illustrans, sm. 4to. *plates of Seals, etc. sd.* 5s *Lips.* 1749

6055 GORE, Catalogus omnium Authorum qui de Re Heraldicâ Latinè, Gallicè, Italicè, Hispanicè, Germanicè, Anglicè scripserunt, sm. 4to. *calf neat, from Miss Currer's library,* 15s *Oxon.* 1674

6056 GORII Symbolæ Litterariæ, Opuscula varia, philologica, scientifica, antiquaria, signa, lapides, numismata, Gemmas, etc. Medii Ævi complectentes, 10 vols in 5, 8vo. *numerous plates of Antiquities, Coins, &c.* 32s *Florentiæ,* 1748-52

6057 GOUBE, Histoire du Duché de Normandie, 3 vols. 8vo. *maps, plates, and tables, hf. calf,* 9s *Rouen,* 1815

6058 GRÄFLICHES TASCHENBUCH, from 1842 to 1859, Hist.-Herald. Handbuch, 1860, *to be supplied separately at* 2s *Gotha,* 1842-60
  FREIHERRLICHES Taschenbuch, for 1848, 55, 57, 59, *to be sold separately at* 2s *Gotha,* 1848-59

6059 GRUPEN, de Uxore Theotisca, von der Teutschen Frau, sm. 4to. *plates, vellum,* 12s *Göttingen,* 1748
  This curious work contains, besides a Treatise on Anglo-Saxon Brides, one on the Marriage of Henry the Lion with Princess Matilda; and much philological matter relating chiefly to Old German and Anglo-Saxon.

6060 GUICHENON, Histoire Généalogique de la Royale Maison de SAVOYE, 2 vols. large folio, *Best Edition, with fine impressions of the numerous portraits, and many engravings of Arms, Coins, Monuments, etc. by Thurneysen, old calf gilt,* £4. 10s *Lyon,* 1660
  " Rare."—MOULE.—" Ouvrage rare et estimé."—DU FRESNOY.
  "Ouvrage peu commun. Il y a une nouvelle édition moins belle et qui ne va aussi que jusqu'en 1660."—BRUNET.

6061 GUIGARD, Bibliothèque Heraldique de la France, 8vo. xxiv. and 527 pp. *double columns* (pub. at 16 fr.) *sd.* 14s *Par.* 1861
  This valuable work, the first that deserves the name, is a Bibliography of the Heraldic Literature of France. It is compiled for the purpose of filling up a vacuum which has hitherto existed in the domain of French erudition; and not only does it supply this grand deficiency for France, but also includes works upon the Heraldry, Nobility, Orders of Chivalry, and Genealogies of the Netherlands, Belgium and French Switzerland. There is an appendix of works in French, similarly relating to the other countries of Europe, with a *table raisonnée* of Authors.

6062 GUILLIM, DISPLAY OF HERALDRY, SIXTH (and best) edition, improved with large additions, stout folio, *with many hundred Coats of Arms in the text, and* 64 *plates, including portraits, a fine copy in calf gilt,* £5. 5s 1724
  Fine copies are now worth from 6 to 10 guineas.

6063 HAER (F. Van der) Les Chastelains de Lille, leur ancien Etat, Famille, etc. les Comtes de Flandres, etc. sq. sm. 8vo. *Genealogical Tables, calf,* 12s *Lille,* 1611

6064 HAECHT, Chroniicke van de Hertoghen van Brabant, small folio, 42 *fine plates of the Dukes of Brabant, all full size in their Costume, calf,* 9s *Antw.* 1612

6065 HAGECII Böhmische Chronica: von Ursprung der Böhmen, von irer Hertzogen und Könige Graffen Adels und Geschlechter Ankunfft, aus Böhmischer Sprache transsferiret durch SANDEL, 2 vols. in 1, thick fol. *woodcut titles and portraits, old stamped calf, sound copy,* RARE, 21s *Prag,* 1596

6066 HAMCONII Frisia, seu de Viris rebusque Frisiæ illustribus, sq. 8vo. *portrait of author, and* 53 *full length portraits with arms, calf,* 10s *Franeck.* 1620
Bound up with "Effigies Regum Francorum a Pharamundo ad Ludov. XIII." *Francof.* 1622, containing 64 portraits. The White Knight's copy fetched £1. 16s

6067 HAMPSON (R. T.) Origines Patriciæ, a deduction of European Titles of Nobility from their sources, with Appendix of an Icelandic poem and Glossarial Index, 8vo. *title cut, cloth, rare,* 21s 1846

6068 HARAEI Annales Ducum seu Principum Brabantiæ Belgiique, usque ad 1609, 3 vols. in 2, sm. folio, 41 *full length portraits, old calf gilt,* 12s *Antv.* 1623
Heath's copy fetched £2. 12s.

6069 HARO (Lopez de) Nobiliario Genealogico de los Reyes y Titulos de España, 2 vols. folio, *many Coats of Arms, calf,* £3. 10s *Madrid,* 1622

6070 ——— the same, Vol. II, only, folio, *many Coats of Arms, vellum,* 36s 1622
The Second Volume is extremely scarce.

6071 HARTARD VON HATTSTEIN, die Hoheit des Teutschen Reichs-Adels, 3 vols. stout folio, *including the Supplements, numerous Coats of Arms of the German Nobility, with the Pedigrees, bds.* 9s ; *hf. calf neat,* 18s *Fulda,* 1729-40
Complete copies are very rare; these have all the Supplements, and the general Index.

6072 HARTKNOCH, Alt- und Neu-Preussen oder Preussische Historien, 2 vols. in 1, folio, *maps, plates, full-length portraits of the Teutonic Knights, and Views, in the style of Hollar, fine copy in vellum,* 15s *Frankfurt,* 1684
The fourth chapter contains a treatise on the Old Prussian Language, with comparisons of various dialects.

6073 HELMOLDI Chronica Slavorum cum supplemento Arnoldi, ed. Reineccius, *Franc.* 1581—Lindenbrogius, Scriptores Rerum Germanicarum, *Franc.* 1609— TORFFAEI Orcades, *Haun.* 1715—3 vols. in 1, folio, *calf,* 24s 1581-1715

6074 HEMRICOURT (Jacques de) Miroir des Nobles de Hasbaye, où il traite des Généalogies de l'ancienne Noblesse de Liége, 1102-1398, par De Salbray, folio, *numerous Coats of Arms, hf. calf, uncut,* 18s ; *old calf gilt,* 25s *Bruxelles,* 1673

6075 HENNINGES. Theatrum Genealogicum ostentans omnes omnium ætatum Familias Monarcharum, Regum, Ducum, Marchionum, Principum, Comitum, atque illustrium Heroum et Heroinarum, item Philosophorum, Oratorum, Historicorum, a condito mundo usque ad hæc nostra tempora cum Supplementis, et Appendice de Saxoniâ, 7 parts bound in 2 vols, very stout folio, *cuts of arms, etc. fine copy in stamped hogskin, rare,* £5. 5s *Hamb. et Magd.* 1590-98

⁎ Distinct portions of this valuable work are allotted to the *genealogies of the principal families of England and Scotland*; it is the first book that was ever published on the subject. " Ce grand ouvrage d'Henninges sur les genealogies est regardé comme un des plus savans et un des plus achevés parmi ceux qui ont été mis au jour sur cette partie. Il est non seulement remarquable par les dissertations interessantes qu'il renferme, mais encore par la vérité qui les charactérise. Il est difficile d'en trouver des exemplaires complets; et quand on est' parvenu à rassembler toutes les parties qui les composent, c'est un ouvrage qui devient alors précieux."—*De Bure*.
The extreme rarity of an entire set like the above results from the historical fact that many copies of the work were destroyed when Magdeburg was sacked by Count Tilly.

6076 HERALDIC ORDINARY, or Arms Book, in 2 vols. folio, *blank, with Shields for the insertion of Arms, the first* 42 *already filled with the Arms of Irish Families, in old handwriting, bound,* 12s ca. 1780

6077 HOFMANNI (J.) LEXICON Universale, Historiam sacram et profanam, Chronologiam, etc. Omnis aevi omniumque gentium explanans, 4 vols. folio, *best edition, vellum,* £2. 2s *Lugd. Bat.* 1698

6078 HOFFMANN (C. G.) Scriptores Rerum LUSATICARUM, 4 vols. in 1, folio, *plates of Slavonic Antiquities, vellum,* 10s *Lips.* 1719

6078*HOFFMANN (T.) Portraits des HOMMES ILLUSTRES DE DANNEMARK, avec leurs TABLES GÉNÉALOGIQUES, 5 parties—Mémoires de Griffenfeld, Adeler, et Torkenskiold, 1 vol.—in 1 vol. sm. 4to. *all the Pedigrees, no Portraits, calf,* 15s *Cop.* 1746

6079 HOLMES (Randle) Accademy of Armory, or a Store House of Armory and Blazon, containeing all thinges borne in Coates of Armes both Foraign and Domestick, with the termes of Art used in each Science, stout sm. folio, *engraved title inlaid, printed title neatly mended, otherwise a fine copy with the Index by Triphook in* 1821, *calf neat, Miss Currer's copy,* £10. *Chester,* 1688
Priced, Thorpe, £12. 12s. A copy was sold at Lord Alvanley's sale for £13.
COLLATION: Engraved title; printed title; Original Prospectus, reprint, inserted; Anagram, etc.; Contents, 4 leaves; pp. 1-108; Table, 8 pp.; Title of Book II.; pp. 1-220; a leaf unpaged; 221-488; Title to Book III; pp. 1-502, with 2 plates of Letters between pp. 414 and 416; Triphook's Index, 1821, title and pp. 1-46.
" The author has contrived to amass in this *storeh' use* a vast fund of curious information upon every branch of human knowledge, such as is not to found in any other work, and of a nature peculiarly adapted to the illustration of the manners and customs of our predecessors, from the highest rank to the lowest menial. It is considered to be one of the *most scarce* of heraldic books, and that not more than *fifty copies* are to be found in the kingdom."— *Moule.* See also Ormerod's *History of Cheshire*.

HERALDRY, ANTIQUITIES, CHRONICLES, GENEALOGY, ETC.

6080 HOPF (Karl) Historisch-Genealogischer Atlas, seit Christi Geburt bis auf unsere Zeit, Abtheilung I: Deutschland, folio, *cloth*, 36s *Gotha*, 1858
A most valuable, indeed, indispensable book of reference for students of history, embodying information as to dynasties and successions, royal and seignorial, secular and ecclesiastical, European and extra-European, pagan and Christian, which at present is only to be found in very large, expensive, and scarce works.

6081 HOZIER (Le Sieur d') Les Noms, Surnoms, Qualitez, Armes et Blasons des Chevaliers de l'Ordre du St. Esprit, sm. folio, *plates, hf. bd.* 36s ; or, *a fine copy in morocco extra, gilt edges*, £2. 16s *Paris*, 1634
Copies are frequently found incomplete ; but the above is perfect, and with the exception of the title which has been strengthened, a beautiful copy.
COLLATION: Engraved title ; printed title ; Dedication and Advertisement, 2 leaves ; 3 large double plates of Ceremonials ; Explication, 2 leaves ; Discours, 6 leaves ; leaves 1-59, with a Coat of Arms engraved on each, except leaf 3 which is a title ; Table and Privileges, 2 leaves.

6082 HUMBRACHT (Jo. Mart.) die höchste Zierde Teutschlandes, und Vortrefflichkeit des Teutschen Adels: Genealogical Tables of German Princes and Families, folio, *beautifully engraved Coats of Arms, calf*, 25s *Franckf.* 1707

6083 IMHOFF (J. W.) Genealogiæ viginti Illustrium in Italiâ Familiarum, exegesi historicâ illustratæ, folio, *portrait, plates of Arms, and Genealogical Tables, fine copy in calf, gilt backs*, 14s *Amst.* 1710

6084 JACOB'S (Al.) ENGLISH PEERAGE, with a History of the Houses of Brunswick, Brandenburgh, Saxe-Gotha, and Mecklenburgh, complete in 3 stout vols. folio, *numerous plates, and Genealogical tables, old calf gilt, fine copy*, £2. 10s 1766-69

6085 JAHRBÜCHER des Vereins von Alterthumsfreunden im RHEINLANDE, Vols. 1-24, and Index, in 8 vols. *plates of Roman Antiquities, bds.* £2. 6s 1842-57

6085*JOANNIS (G. C.) Rerum Moguntiacarum, Vol. I, II. et Tomus novus (III.) 3 vols. folio, *with Genealogical Tables, calf gilt*, RARE, £2. *Francof.* 1722-7
A valuable collection of Early German Chroniclers ; most copies were destroyed by fire.

6086 JOHNSTON (Rob.) Historia Rerum Britannicarum, ut et Gallicarum, Belgicarum, et Germanicarum, 1572-1628, sm. folio, *fine copy in vellum*, 32s *Amst.* 1655
"A work of great merit, whether we consider the judicious structure of the narrative, the sagacity of the reflections, the acute discernment of character, or the classical tincture of the style."—*Lord Woodhouselee.*

6087 JORNANDES de Getarum sive Gothorum origine et rebus gestis cum Isidoro et Procopio, accedit Jornandes de regnorum successione—Vulcanius de Literis et linguâ Getarum—in 1 vol. 12mo. *vellum*, 10s 6d *Lugd. Bat.* 1597

6088 JOSEPHUS Alexander de Vindis Prussiis, et JABLONOWSKI Lech et Czech, sm. 4to. *bds.* 6s *Lips.* 1775

6089 JURISPRUDENTIA HEROICA, sive de Jure Belgarum circa Nobilitatem et Insignia (auctore Christyn), folio, *numerous Coats of Arms, and* 16 *large folding plates of Pedigrees, fine copy in calf, gilt back*, 27s *Brux.* 1668
"Ouvrage excellent, principalement pour connoître la haute Noblesse des Pays Bas."—*Du Fresnoy.* A complete Armorial of Belgium.

6090 KELHAM'S Dictionary of the Norman or Old French Language, 8vo. *calf*, 20s 1779

6091 —— Domesday Book illustrated, containing an Account of that Record, a translation of difficult passages, an explanation of the Terms, Abbreviations, etc. 8vo. 24s 1788

6092 KEYSLER, Antiquitates selectae Septentrionales et Celticæ, 12mo. *hf. vellum*, 7s 6d *Hannov.* 1720

6093 KIRCHMANNUS de Annulis, cum Longo, Gorlæo, Kornmannoque de iisdem, 16mo. *vellum*, 7s 6d *Lugd. Bat.* 1672

6094 KNESCHKE (E. H.) Deutsche Grafen-Häuser der Gegenwart, in herald., histor. und genealog. Beziehung, 3 vols. 8vo. *many Coats of Arms* (pub. at 18 thalers) *cloth*, 32s *Leipzig*, 1852-54

6095 —— die Wappen der Deutschen freiherrl. und adeligen Familien in vollständiger Beschreibung, 4 vols. 8vo. (pub. at 16 Thalers) *sd.* 32s *Leipzig*, 1855-57

6096 KOJALOWICZ, Historia Lituana, Vol. I. *wanting title, Dantisc.* 1550 ; Vol. II. *Antv.* 1669 ; together 2 vols. sm. 4to. *vellum, very rare*, £3. 10s 1650-69

6097 —— Historia Lituana a conjunctione cum Poloniâ ad unionem dominiorum, sm. 4to. *old calf*, 36s *Antverpiae*, 1669

6098 KÖNIGSHOVEN, Elsassische und Strasburgische Chronicke, mit Anmerkungen von Schilter, thick sm. 4to. *fine plates of Mediæval German Art, vellum, rare*, 10s *Strasburg*, 1698

6099 LALAURE, Traité des Servitudes Réelles, sm. 4to. *old calf gilt*, 6s   *Paris*, 1761
6100 LANCASHIRE AND CHESHIRE, Historic History of; Proceedings, Papers, and Transactions, Vol. I—X. 8vo. *numerous plates of Antiquities, hf. green morocco, gilt tops, uncut, a very nice set*, £4. 10s   *Liverpool*, 1829-58
6101 LABBEI ET COSSARTII, SACROSANCTA CONCILIA, ad Regiam editionem exacta, ab initiis Christianismi ad annum 1664, 16 vols.; APPARATUS duo ad Concilia, Jacobatianus, etc. cum Indicibus, 2 vols.; together 17 vols. folio, *old calf*, £8. 15s   *Paris*, 1672

Priced, 1834, Leslie, £13. 13s; 1838, Deighton, £12. 12s; 1841, £10. 10s; 1856, Weigel, 72 Thalers; Heath's copy fetched £19.—"Collection recherchée, 240 à 300 fr."—*Brunet*. This copy has the second apparatus.

6102 LAING'S Descriptive Catalogue of Impressions from ANCIENT SCOTTISH SEALS, Royal, Baronial, Ecclesiastical, and Municipal, from A.D. 1094 to the Commonwealth, 4to. *woodcuts, and* 29 *plates of seals, cloth*, 32s   *Bannatyne Club*, 1850
6103 LANERCOST. Chronicon de Lanercost, MCCI—MCCCXLVI, e codice Cottoniano nunc primum typis mandatum, 2 vols. in 1, stout 4to. *with Notes, illustrative documents and Index by Stevenson*, LARGE PAPER, *superbly bound in morocco extra, edges gauffred and gilt*, £2. 10s   *Bannatyne Club*, 1839
6104 LANGUEDOC. HISTOIRE GENERALE DE LANGUEDOC, avec des Notes et les pièces justificatives, enrichie de divers Monumens, par deux Religieux Benedictins de S. Maur (Claude de Vic et Joseph Vaissete), 5 vols. folio, 39 *plates. and numerous fine vignettes, hf. bd. Sir F. Palgrave's copy*, £6. 6s *Paris*, 1730-45
6105 LANGUEDOC. Memoires, pour l'histoire naturelle de LANGUEDOC, 4to. *maps and plates, calf*, 10s   *Paris*, 1737

The Philological portion extending from page 422-508 is particularly interesting.

6106 LANGEBEK, Suhm, Engelstoft et Werlauff, SCRIPTORES RERUM DANICARUM medii Ævi, partim hactenus inediti partim emendatius editi, 8 vols. folio, *plates and facsimiles, fine copy in new calf gilt*, £12.   *Hafniæ*, 1772-1834

A work of considerable importance both for English and Danish History.

Priced, 1837, Black, £10. 10s; 1847, H. Bohn, £8. 18s 6d and £13. 13s: all the volumes are out of print.
"All preceding collections of *Northern Antiquities* were exceeded equally in splendour, utility, and extent, by the meritorious labours of LANGEBEK, whose collection has now become a work of uncommon occurrence. The editor was doubtless the *Bouquet* of Denmark."—*Dibdin*.

6107 LA ROCHE LA CARELLE, Histoire de Beaujolais et des Sires de Beaujeu, avec l'Armorial de la Province, 2 vols. impl. 8vo. THICK PAPER, *illuminated arms on the title, plates and numerous cuts, bds.* 18s   *Lyons*, 1853

Only a few copies printed.

6108 LAZIUS de aliquot Gentium Migrationibus, folio, *woodcuts, bds.* 10s   *Basil.* 1572

A curious Ethnological work, giving an Account of the Early Migrations of the German, Celtic and Gallo-Greek Tribes, with SPECIMENS OF THEIR LANGUAGES, AND GENEALOGIES of the Great Barons of the Middle Ages.

6109 LE FERON. Histoire des Connestables, Chanceliers, Gardes des Seaux, Maréchaux, Grands-Maîtres de la maison du Roi, Prevosts de Paris, avec leurs blasons, par JEAN LE FERON, 1555; revue et continuée par Denys Godefroy, large folio, *numerous woodcut Coats of Arms, French calf*, £2. 4s   *Paris*, 1658
6110 LE LABOUREUR (J.) Histoire du MARESCHAL DE GUEBRIANT, contenant le recit de la guerre de France et de Suede, et des Estats alliez contre la Maison d'Austriche avec l'Oraison funebre; et HISTOIRE GENEALOGIQUE de la MAISON DES BUDES, 2 vols. impl. folio, *fine frontispiece, plate of Sepulchre, and numerous woodcut Coats of Arms, fine copy, beautifully bound in red* MOROCCO, *gilt edges, by Petit*, £3.   *Paris*, 1676-56
6111 LELLIS (Carlo de) Discorsi delle Famiglie Nobili del Regno di NAPOLI, parti prima, seconda, e terza, 3 vols. sm. folio, *numerous woodcut Coats of Arms, calf gilt, very rare*, £4. 4s   *Napoli*, 1654-63-71

The different parts of this scarce work having been published separately, and at long intervals, it is a circumstance of no ordinary occurrence to find them united.

6112 LELLIS, Discorsi delle Famiglie di Napoli, *parte seconda*, sm. folio, *vellum*, £2.   1663
6113 LE LONG, Bibliotheque Historique de la France, contenant le Catalogue de tous les Ouvrages imprimés et Manuscrits qui traitent de ce Royaume; augmenté par Fontette, 5 vols. folio, *French calf gilt*, £5. 5s; *or a very fine copy, veau fauve gilt*, £8. 8s   *Paris*, 1768-78

"Le Long's historical library if we except some errors, is a very curious and useful work."—*Voltaire*.
This is perhaps the most laborious and most able Bibliographical work which has ever appeared. It is scarcely possible to find a volume or a manuscript in the least connected with French History, but what is fully described here, and it frequently gives curious details respecting our English historians. Brunet says of it—"Cet ouvrage est un des travaux les plus essentiels qu'ait produits la science bibliographique, et il doit se trouver dans toutes les Bibliothèques."

HERALDRY, ANTIQUITIES, CHRONICLES, GENEALOGY, ETC.

6114 LEMPRIERE FAMILY. Payne's Monograph of the House of LEMPRIERE, recording by tabular Pedigrees, Biographical Notices, etc. its history from A.D. 970 to 1862, imp. 4to. 5 *large plates of Arms, several woodcuts, and large folding sheet of Comparative Pedigree, showing the connection with the ducal house of Normandy and several noble families of Great Britain*, cloth, gilt edges, 25s
Only 100 copies printed. *Privately printed*, 1862

6115 Le Roy, Erection de toutes les Terres, Seigneuries, et Familles titrées du Brabant, folio, LARGE PAPER, engraved dedication, *map, and engravings of Castles, with the Arms*, old calf gilt, fine copy, 30s Leide, 1699

6116 Letzeneri Hardessiani, Stammbuch oder Chronick des adelichen Geschlechts von Berlebsch, sq. 8vo. *many large woodcuts, representing Knights in Armour, with their Coats of Arms*, vellum, rare, 15s s. l. 1594

6117 ——— Corbeyische Chronica; Leben und Thaten Ludovici Pii, nebst Beschreibung 30 adelicher Geschlechter und Lehns-Leute des Stiffts Corbey, sq. 8vo. *numerous Coats of Arms*, hf. calf, 10s Leipzig, 1693

6118 Levrier, Chronologie historique des comtes de Genevois, 2 vols. 8vo. *pedigrees*, sd. 7s 6d Orleans, 1787

6119 Licquet, Histoire de Normandie, jusqu' à la Conquête de l'Angleterre, 1066, avec une introduction par Depping sur la Littérature, etc. 2 vols. 8vo. *hf. calf*, 10s Rouen, 1835

6120 LIEGE. Recueil Héraldique des Bourguemestres de la Cité de Liège, ou l'on voit la Genealogie des Evêques et Princes, de la Noblesse et des principales Familles de ce Païs, (par Loyens) sm. fol. *many woodcut Coats of Arms*, calf, 36s Liege, 1720

6121 LINDSAY (Lord) Report of the Speeches of Counsel, the Lord Chancellor and Lord St. Leonards, upon the Claim of James Earl of Crawford to the Dukedom of Montrose, folio, *pp. Genealogical Chart and Facsimile*, cloth, 12s 1855

6122 LOBINEAU (Gui Alexis) Histoire de Bretagne composée sur les Titres et les Auteurs Originaux, avec un Glossaire des mots Bretons, Basques, Gaulois, de Basse-Latinité, etc. 2 vols. large folio, 21 *fine plates, (thirteen of portraits) and 22 plates of 285 Seals*, old French calf gilt, Arms on sides, £2. 10s Paris, 1707

Priced, £4. 10s; the Fonthill copy fetched £6. Priced 1827, £3. 13s 6d; 1832, £3. 3s; the Marquis of Townshend's copy fetched £3. 4s.

"Lobineau (Dom. Gui-Alexis) was born at Rennes, in Brittany, AD. 1666. He entered the Benedictine order in his eighteenth year, and became one of the best historians of his time. His principal work is the History of Brittany, in two folio volumes. It had been begun by Dom Gallois, but was left for Lobineau to finish. His intimate acquaintance with Celtic and Armorican antiquities rendered him eminently qualified for the task; and he in consequence produced a work that has ever since maintained its reputation untarnished."—*H. L. Jones.*

6123 LODGE (J.) Peerage of Ireland, revised by Archdall, 7 vols. 8vo. *plates of arms*, hf. calf, £2. Dublin, 1798

6124 Louvain. Septem Tribus patriciae Lovanienses, 12mo. *genealogical table and coloured plates*, calf, 6s Lov. 1754

6125 Luccari, Ristretto degli Annali di Rausa (Ragusa) le Familie Nobili, etc. sq. 8vo. *MS. additions*, calf, 12s Venetia, 1605

6126 LUCIUS de Regno Dalmatiæ et Croatiæ; Diocleatis Regnum Slavorum; Maruli-Regum Dalmatiæ Gesta; Thomæ Spalatensis Historia Salonitana; Madii Historia Spalatensis; Obsidio Iadrensis; Memoriale Pauli de Paulo (1371-1400); Palladius; Appianus Alexandrinus; etc. cum notis, folio, *Maps and Genealogical Tables*, original calf, 10s; or *a fine copy in calf*, 15s Amstelædami, 1666

"A very rare and valuable work."—*Sir Gardner Wilkinson.* It contains valuable information upon the history and languages of the Slavonic nations.

6127 LUDEWIG (J. P.) Reliquiae Manuscriptorum omnis aevi Diplomatum ac Monumentorum ineditorum, 12 vols. sm. 8vo. *vellum*, 35s Francof. 1720-40

"Depuis quelques années on recherche beaucoup cette collection de pièces inédites et assez curieuses. Les exemplaires n'en sont pas communs, et le prix s'est élevé au-delà de 60 fr.; vendu 88 fr. 70 c. Abrial."—*Brunet.*

6128 LUITPRANDI Opera: Chronicon et adversaria, ed Higuera, cum notis a Ramirez de Prado, folio, *fine copy in vellum*, 16s Antverp. Plantin, 1640

6129 MACKENZIE'S (Sir G.) Observations upon the Laws and Customs of Nations as to Precedency, 1680—The Science of Heraldry, *several plates, the size of the page*—in 1 vol. sm. folio, old calf, 18s Edinburgh, 1680

The first of these fetched, Bindley, £1. 11s 6d. The second has been highly praised by Nicolson, Nesbit, and other writers.

6130 MAGNENEY, Recueil des Armes de plusieurs Nobles Maisons et Familles, tant Ecclesiastiques, Princes, Ducs, Marquis, Comtes, Barons, Chevaliers, Escuyers, et autres de la France, sm. folio, 109 *engraved leaves (of which the first three are title, dedication, and privilege) containing* 636 *fine Coats of Arms, original calf, very rare*, £2. 16s *Paris*, 1633

6131 MAGNI Historia de omnibus Gothorum Sueonumque Regibus, stout sm. folio, *many quaint wood-engravings and initial letters, original edition, with good impressions, fine clean copy in the original limp vellum*, 32s *Romæ*, 1564
Hibbert's copy, mor. fetched £5. 2s 6d. John Magnus, Archbishop of Upsala, was born at Lindkoeping in 1488, and acquired great reputation by the above work. In consequence of the introduction of the Reformation by Gustavus Wasa, Magnus retired to Italy, where he died at Rome in 1544.

6132 MALINGRE, Traicté de la Loy Salique, Armes, Blasons, et Devises des François, 12mo. *cuts of Arms, vellum*, 10s *Paris*, 1614
"Cet ouvrage se trouve difficilement."—BRUNET.

6133 MALTE (H. F. de) Les Nobles dans les Tribunaux, traité de droit, enrichi de plusieurs curiosités du BLAZON, sm. folio, *calf gilt*, 15s *Liége*, 1680

6134 MANNI (D. M.) Osservazioni Istoriche sopra i SIGILLI ANTICHI de' Secoli Bassi, 30 vols. in 15, sq. 8vo. *complete, numerous woodcuts of the* SEALS OF THE MIDDLE AGES, *vellum, scarce*, £5. *Firenze*, 1739-86
A most important work for the History of Italy during the Middle Ages. To the Genealogist and Antiquarian it is almost invaluable, but of the greatest rarity to find complete.

6135 MARCA (P. de) Marca Hispanica sive Limes Hispanicus : accedunt Gesta Comitum Barcinonensium, etc. roy. folio, *map, calf*, 10s *Paris*, 1688
Heath's copy fetched £2. 12s 6d.

6136 MASTER OF THE ROLLS' PUBLICATIONS, 23 vols. roy. 8vo. *hf. bd.* 1858-1860
The set consists of the following articles published at 10s per vol. which can be supplied separately at the affixed prices.

a CAPGRAVE's Chronicle of England, edited by Hingeston, roy. 8vo. *facsimile*, 8s 6d 1858

b CHRONICON Monasterii de ABINGDON, edidit Stevenson, 2 vols. roy. 8vo. *facsimiles*, 17s 1858

c EDWARD THE CONFESSOR. Estoire de Seint Aedward le Rei — Vita Edvardi Regis—Vita Aeduuardi Regis —3 vols. in 1, roy. 8vo. *facsims. hf. bd.* 8s 6d 1858

d MONUMENTA FRANCISCANA : Thomas De Eccleston, Ada de Marisco, Registrum Ff. Minorum, 3 vols. in 1, roy. 8vo. *facsim. hf. bd.* 8s 6d 1858

e FASCICULI Zizaniorum, Wycliffi, cum Tritico, ascribed to Netter, by Shirley, roy. 8vo. *facsim. hf. bd.* 8s 6d 1858

f BUIK of the CRONICLIS of SCOTLAND, a metrical version of Boece, by Stewart, edited by Turnbull, 3 vols. roy. 8vo. *facsim. hf. bd.* 25s 6d 1858

g CAPGRAVE, de Illustribus Henricis, ed. by Hingeston, roy. 8vo. *facs. hf. bd.* 8s 6d 1858

h HISTORIA Monast. S. Augustini Cantuariensis, by Thomas of Elmham, edited by Hardwick, roy. 8vo. *fascs.* 8s 6d 1858

i EULOGIUM (Historiarum sive Temporis), Chronicon ab orbe condito ad an. 1366, edited by Haydon, 2 vols. roy. 8vo. *facsim. hf. bd.* 17s 1858-60

MEMORIALS of HENRY VII. Bernardi Andreae Historia cum aliis quibusdam, edited by Gairdner, roy. 8vo. *fascim. hf. bd.* 8s 6d 1858

k MEMORIALS OF HENRY V. Redmanni Vita ; Versus Rhythmici ; Elmhami liber metricus, edited by Cole, roy. 8vo. *facsim. hf. bd.* 8s 6d 1858

l MUNIMENTA GILDHALLAE LONDONIENSIS, Vol. I : Liber Albus, roy. 8vo. *facs. hf. bd.* 8s 6d 1859
Vols. II and III, containing the (" Liber Custumarum," et " Liber Horn," which complete the work, can be supplied at the same rate.

m JOHANNIS DE OXENEDES Chronica, edited by Sir Henry Ellis, roy. 8vo. *fasc. hf. bd.* 8s 6d 1859

n POLITICAL POEMS and SONGS relating to English history, from Edward III to Richard III, edited by Thomas Wright, Vol. I, roy. *hf. bd.* 8s 6d 1859
Vol. II. which completes the collection can be supplied.

o BACONI (Rogeri) Opera hactenus inedita, ed. by Brewer, Vol. I. roy. 8vo. *facsimiles, hf. bd.* 8s 6d 1859

p COLTON (Bartholomæi de) Historia Anglicana, cum libro de Archiep. et Episcopis, ed. by Luard, roy. 8vo. *facsims. hf. bd.* 8s 6d 1859

q BRUT Y TYWYSOGION, the Chronicle of the Princes, *Welsh and English*, ed. by Williams ab Ithel, roy. 8vo. *facsims. hf. bd.* 8s 6d 1860

r ROYAL and HISTORICAL LETTER during the reign of Henry IV, edited by Hingeston, Vol. I, roy. 8vo. *hf. bd.* 8s 6d 1860

s ANNALES CAMBRIAE, cum Glossario, ed. by Williams Ab Ithel, roy. 8vo. *facsim. hf. bd.* 8s 6d 1860

HERALDRY, ANTIQUITIES, CHRONICLES, GENEALOGY, ETC. 331

6137 MARLOT, Théatre d'Honneur et de magnificence préparé au Sacre des Roys, stout sq. 8vo. 22 pp. and 760 pp. calf, 10s *Reims*, 1643

6138 MARNE, Histoire du Comté de Namur, 4to. *fine copy in calf gilt*, 10s *Liége*, 1754

6139 MARSEILLE. Bousquet, la Major, Cathedrale de Marseille, 8vo. *numerous plates, hf. calf*, 5s *Marseille*, 1857

6140 MATTHAEI Veteris Aevi Analecta seu Vetera Monumenta hactenus nondum visa, quibus continentur Scriptores qui Expeditiones in Terram Sanctam, Res Germaniae, Gelriae, Hollandiae; Gesta Ordinis Teutonici, etc. memoriae prodiderunt : praeterea ITINERARIA, 5 stout vols. sm. 4to. *vell*. 30s *Hagae*, 1738

6141 MATTHÆI PARIS Opera : Historia Major, cum Rogeri Wendoveri, Rishangeri, authorisque Chronicisque MSS. collata, cui accesserunt Vitæ Offarum et XXIII Abbatum S. Albani, &c., cum variis lectionibus, Glossario et Indicibus, editore Wats ; folio, *full length portrait by T. Cecill, calf neat*, 20s ; or *fine clean copy in vellum*, 25s 1640-30

6142 ―――― Historia Major, cum Vitis Regum Offarum, et Abbatum S. Albani, Glossario, etc. editore Wats, folio, *portrait*, BEST EDITION, *large copy, old calf, with rare autograph of Narcissus Luttrell*, 30s 1684
Priced, 1841, £2. 2s; 1813, £2. 5s; 1847, £2. 8s; 1854, £2. 5s.

6143 MATTHÆI WESTMONASTERIENSIS Flores Historiarum, præcipue de Rebus Britannicis, ad annum 1307 : accedit Florentii Wigornensis Chronicon cum continuatione, folio, BEST EDITION, *fine copy in vellum*, 30s *Francof.* 1601

6144 MEGERLE VON MÜHLFELD, Oesterreichisches Adels-Lexikon 1701-1820 nebst Ergänzungs-Band bis 1822, 2 vols. 8vo. *hf. calf*, 9s *Wien*, 1822-24

6145 MÉMOIRES DE L'ACADÉMIE CELTIQUE, ou recherches sur les Antiquités Celtiques, Gauloises et Françoises, 5 vols. 1807-10—MÉMOIRES et dissertations sur les ANTIQUITÉS NATIONALES et étrangères, publiés par la SOCIÉTÉ ROYALE DES ANTIQUAIRES DE FRANCE, 10 vols. 1817-34; Nouvelle série, 10 vols. 1836-50; Troisième série, Vol. I. 1852 ; 21 vols. 1817-52—together 26 vols. 8vo. *plates, calf extra, with imp.* 4to. *atlas of 17 plates to the Mémoires de la Société Royale, hf. calf gilt*, £8. 10s *Paris*, 1807-52

6146 MENESTRIER (C. F.) Eloge Historique de la Ville de Lyon, 4to. LARGE PAPER, 75 *pp. of Coats of Arms*, COLOURED, *fine copy in red morocco extra, with the Arms of Lyons stamped on the sides*, RARE, £2. 10s *Lyon*, 1669

6147 ―――― Traité des TOURNOIS, Joustes, Carrousels et autres Spectacles Publics, sm. 4to. *with Vignettes and Initials, calf*, 18s *Lyon*, 1669

6148 ―――― Nouvelle Méthode raisonnée du Blason, ou de l'Art Heraldique, stout sm. 8vo. *best edition*, 50 *plates, containing several hundred Coats of Arms, old calf gilt*, 15s *Lyon*, 1780

6149 MESSENII Theatrum Nobilitatis Suecanae, folio, *Genealogical tables, poor copy, calf*, 20s *Holmiae*, 1616
MIECHOW, Chronica Polonorum—*See Nos.* 5415 *and* 5416.

6150 MILLES (Thos) Nobilitas Politica vel Civilis, personas scilicet distinguendi, et ab origine inter gentes nobilitandi forma, fol. *plates of the various degrees of Nobility in their Robes, Orders, etc.; and one of* QUEEN ELIZABETH *on the Throne surrounded by her Peers, by Hollar, hf. morocco, fine copy*, 22s 1608
Priced, 1848, Longman's £2. 2s; Brockett's copy fetched £2. 8s.

6151 MIRÆI OPERA DIPLOMATICA et Historica, in quibus continentur Chartæ Fundationum ac Donationum, Testamenta, Privilegia, Fœdera Principum et alia Antiquitatis Monumenta à Pontificibus, Imperatoribus, Regibus, Principibusque BELGII edita, et ad GERMANIAM INFERIOREM spectantia ; EDITIO SECUNDA cum Supplemento, à FOPPENS, 4 vols. folio, *portrait, fine copy in old calf gilt*, 32s *Lovanii et Bruxellis*, 1723-48
An excellent collection of Historical and Genealogical Documents, which comprises the most essential particulars for a history of Holland, Belgium, and Lower Germany.

6152 MODII (Fr.) Pandectae triumphales, sive Pomparum et Festorum ac solennium Apparatuum, Conviviorum, Spectaculorum, et denique omnium nobiliorum tomi duo, fol. *many fine woodcuts by* JOST AMMAN, *of Tournaments, Coats of Arms, etc. tall copy, hf. bd. stamped binding*, RARE, 16s *Francof.* 1586
The author describes a great number of actual Tournaments, with exact particulars of the names and Arms.

6153 MONTFAUCON, Diarium Italicum, sive Monumentorum veterum Bibliothecarum, etc. notitiae, 4to. *plates, calf*, 5s ; or, *a fine copy, calf gilt*, 7s *Paris*, 1702

6154 MORGAN (Sylvanus) Armilogia sive Ars Chromocritica, the Language of Arms by the Colours and Metals, sq. 8vo. *numerous woodcut Coats of Arms, calf*, £2. 10s 1666
A rare book; intended by the author as a Supplement to his great work "The Sphere of Gentry."

6155 MOULE's Heraldry of Fish, notices of the principal Families bearing Fish in their Arms, 8vo. *numerous fine woodcuts, cloth*, 10s 6d   *Van Voorst*, 1842

6156 MOYA, Rasgo Heroyco, Empresas, Armas, y Blasones de los Reynos, Ciudades, etc. de España, 8vo. *hf. bd.* 7s 6d   *Madrid*, 1756

6157 MUNIER (J.) Recherches et Mémoires servans à l'Histoire d'Autun, sm. 4to. *Map and plate of Arms, limp vellum*, 21s   *Dijon*, 1660
The Map and plate are frequently wanting.

6158 MURATORII RERUM ITALICARUM SCRIPTORES, ab anno 500 ad 1500, 24 vols. in 28, *Mediolani*, 1723-51—TARTINII RERUM ITALICARUM SCRIPTORES, 2 vols. *Florent*. 1748-70—together 27 vols. in 30, folio, *numerous frontispieces, vignettes, maps, facsimiles of early Charters, etc. twenty-seven vols. in stamped vellum, gilt backs, the last three in bds.* VERY RARE, £40.   1723-70
The necessary Supplement by Tartinius is rarely found with the original work.

6159 MURATORI, delle Antichità Estensi ed Italiane, 2 vols. folio, *full length portrait of George I. to whom the book is dedicated, fine copy in vellum*, VERY RARE, £3. 10s   *Modena, stamperia ducale*, 1717-40

6160 MUSHARD (Luneberg) Monumenta Nobilitatis Antiquæ Familiarum Illustrium, imprimis Ordinis Equestris in Ducatibus Bremensi et Verdensi, sm. folio, *the text all in German, numerous Coats of Arms, large woodcut initials, vellum*, 36s   *Bremen*, 1708

6161 NABERAT, Histoire des Chevaliers de l'Ordre de S. Jean de Jerusalem, avec les Statuts traduits par Baudoin, les Vies des Grand Maistres, etc. 2 vols. folio, *engraved frontispiece*, 59 *portraits, and other plates, fine copy in the original vellum, calf back*, 30s   *Paris*, 1643

6161* —— the same, folio, *engraved frontispieces*, 59 *portraits, and other plates, old calf rebacked*, 20s   *Paris*, 1659

6162 NESTOR, Hommes Illustres de la Maison de MEDICI; avec abrégé des Comtes de Bolongne et d'Auvergne, sm. 4to. *cuts, devices, hf. bd.* 10s   *Paris*, 1564

6163 NEUGART, Codex Diplomaticus Alemanniæ et Burgundiæ Trans-Juranæ, 2 vols. sm. 4to. *cloth*, 10s   *San-Blas*. 1791-95

6164 NEVILLE's SAXON OBSEQUIES, folio, 40 *coloured plates of Ornaments and Weapons discovered in a cemetery, Cambridgeshire*, 1851, *and plan*, (pub. at £4. 4s) *cloth*, 30s   1852

6165 NICHOLS, Collection of the WILLS now extant of the Kings, Queens, Princes, etc. of England, from the Conqueror to Henry VII, with notes and Glossary, sm. 4to. *hf. russia gilt*, 18s   1780

6166 NISBET'S (A.) System of Heraldry, Speculative and Practical, with the true Art of Blazon; illustrated with Examples of Armorial Figures and Achievements of the most considerable Families in Scotland, &c. Genealogical Memorials, etc. 2 vols. folio, 51 *plates of Arms, etc.* (pub. at £7. 7s) *calf gilt*, £5.
Priced, 1837, £4. 14s 6d; 1840, £5. 5s; 1857, £5. 10s.   *Edinburgh*, 1816

6167 NOBILIARIO del Conde de BARCELOS DON PEDRO, hijo del Rey Dionis de Portugal, traduzido con nuevas ilustraciones por M. Faria i Sousa, sm. folio, *vellum*, 25s   *Madrid*, 1646

6168 NOTICES sur les Familles illustres de la POLOGNE, 8vo. 3 *plates, containing* 32 *coloured coats of Arms, sd.* 10s; or, *hf. calf, gilt top, uncut*, 10s 6d   *Brux*. 1862

6169 OGEE (M.) Dictionnaire Historique et Géographique de la Province de BRETAGNE, 4 vols. 4to. *map of Britanny (? engraved* 1780*) inserted, old calf, bright gilt backs, scarce*, 21s   *Nantes*, 1778-80

6170 **Orders of Knighthood.** CHAPPRONAYE, Reigle et Constitution des Chevaliers de l'Ordre de la Magdaleine; Révélations de l'Hermite Solitaire sur l'estat de la France, 2 vols. in 1, 12mo. *engraved frontispieces and* 10 *curious Allegorical plates, blue mor. gilt edges*, 28s   *Paris, Toussaincts de Bray*, 1617-18
" Cet Ordre prit sa naissance et sa fin en la personne du Sieur de la Chaponeraye, qui, perdant l'esperance de voir l'éxécution de ses bonnes intentions, se retira dans un Hermitage au bout de la Forêt de Fontainebleau et prit le nom d'Hermite Pacifique de la Magdelaine."—*Hist. des Ordres Milit.* vol. 4, p. 296.

6171 ORDERIC VITAL, Histoire de Normandie, 4 vols.—Guillaume de Jumiège, Ducs de Normandie, 1 vol.—par Guizot, 5 vols. 8vo. *sd.* 15s   *Caen*, 1826

6172 PAGLIARINO, Croniche di Vicenza sino al anno 1504, date in luce da Alcaini, sq. 8vo. *with a MS. Index of* NOBLE FAMILIES, *bds. rare*, 12s   *Vicenza*, 1563

6173 PARADIN, Alliances Généalogiques des Rois et Princes de Gaule, folio, *upwards of* 1000 *Coats of Arms, old calf gilt*, 25s   *Paris, Jean de Tournes*, 1636

HERALDRY, ANTIQUITIES, CHRONICLES, GENEALOGY, ETC. 333

6174 PARIS. Gouverneurs, Lieutenans de Roy, Prevôts de Marchands, Echevins, Procureurs, etc. de la Ville de Paris, large folio, *consisting of* 117 *plates, containing upwards of* 2000 *coats of arms, engraved by Beaumont, crimson morocco, gilt edges, arms on sides, dentelle borders, a superb copy,* £6. 15s   ca. 1770

6175 Passarelli Bellum Lusitanum, et separatio a Regno Castellensi, folio, *old calf,* 10s   *Lugduni,* 1684

      Priced, 1830, Payne and Foss, £2. 5s. 1848, £1. 16s.

6176 PECK'S Desiderata Curiosa, or a Collection of divers Scarce and Curious Pieces (relating chiefly to matters of English History), 2 vols. in 1, large paper, *plates, calf,* £1. 10s   1732

9177 PIRRI (Rocci) Sicilia sacra, editio tertia, Continuatione aucta à Mongitore, 2 vols. in 1, stout folio, *sound clean copy, hf. calf, rare,* 36s   *Panormi,* 1733

6178 Peregrinii Historia Principum Langobardorum, sm. 4to. *bds.* 8s   *Napoli,* 1643

  The same volume contains a Tract "Dell Origine della Famiglia di Colimenta."

6179 Perrot, Collection historique des Ordres de Chevalerie civils et militaires, 4to. 39 *coloured plates, sd.* 14s   1820

6180 Persan, Recherches historiques sur la ville de Dole, Jura, 8vo. 7s 6d   *Dole,* 1812

6181 PERTZ, Monumenta Germaniæ Historica, inde ab anno Christi 400 usque ad annum 1500 auspiciis Societatis Aperiendis Fontibus Rerum Germanicarum medii ævi, edidit Geor. Henr. Pertz. ; Vols. I.-XIV. XVI. and XVII.—together 16 vols. and a part, large folio, large paper, *plates of Charters, good sound copy, hf. vellum, uncut, fine set,* £60.   *Hannover,* 1826-61

Vol. 15 is not published yet.

The work consists of two Series: Scriptores, Vol. I.-XII., XVI. XVII. ; and Leges, Vols. I. II., III parts.

An "uncut" large paper copy is not only very scarce but also very desirable, as the early volumes are only met with bound, and usually much cut down.

Of this valuable and stupendous publication very few copies were printed, and occur rarely for sale. Vols. 5, 6, and 7 are out of print ; complete sets sell therefore beyond the publishing price.

6181*Pertz, Monumenta, Vol. IV. folio, *rare,* £2. 5s   1837

6182 Pregitzer Teutscher Regierungs und Ehrenspiegel, besonders des Hauses Hohenzollern, folio, 38 *plates, including Portraits of the Counts of* Hohenzollern, *with their coats of Arms, hf. vellum,* 10s   *Berlin,* 1703

6183 ——— Wirttembergischen Cedern-Baum oder Genealogie des Hauses Wirttemberg, 6 parts in 1 vol. folio, *portrait and pedigrees, calf,* 10s 6d   *Stuttg.* 1734

6184 Pylaie (De la) Etudes Archéologiques et Géographiques, impl. 8vo. *hf. calf,* 6s   *Brux.* 1850

6185 Radulphi, Abbatis de Coggeshal, Opera ed. Dunkin, (Chronicon Terræ Sanctæ, &c.) 8vo. *engraved title and portrait, bds. only* 25 *copies printed,* 6s *Noviom.* 1856

6186 Raoul, Histoire pittoresque du Mont. S. Michel, et de Tombelène, roy. 8vo. 14 *curious etchings by Boisselat, hf. morocco, uncut,* 6s   *Paris,* 1833

6187 Reiffenberg sur les Noms de Familles et de Lieux—Chronologie des Sires de Diest, 4to. *plates, sd.* 5s   *Brux.* 1844

6188 Rena (Cosimo della) Serie degli Antichi Duchi e Marchesi di Toscana, parte I, folio, *all published, with pedigrees, vellum,* 14s   *Firenze,* 1690

  "Uomo nelle Antichità etrusche singolarmente dotto."—*Tiraboschi.*

6189 René (le Duc) Nobiliaire du Duché de Lorraine et de Bar, 12mo. *calf,* 18s 1761

6190 Resenha das Familias Titulares do Reino de Portugal, 8vo. *large folding table* " *Genealogia da Real Casa,*" *hf. calf, gilt top, uncut,* 18s   *Lisboa,* 1838

6191 RIETSTAP, Armorial Général, contenant la description des Armoiries des Familles Nobles et Patriciennes de l'Europe ; précédé d'un Dictionnaire des Termes de Blason, thick 8vo. 1172 pp. *double cols.* 5 *plates of Coats of Arms,* (pub. 45s) *hf. bd. mor.* 32s   *Gouda,* 1861

6192 ——— Handboek der Wapenkunde, 8vo. *with the technical terms in English, French and German as well as Dutch,* 5 *plates, bds.* 9s   1859

6193 Rittershusii Genealogiae Imperatorum, Regum, Ducum, Comitum, aliorumque procerum Orbis Christiani, folio, *vellum,* 10s   *Tubingae,* 1664

6194 Rix, The Fauconberge Memorial, Account of Henry Fauconberge of Beccles, etc. sq. 8vo. 30 *woodcuts of Views, Monuments, Coats of Arms, Facsimiles, Pedigrees, bds. privately printed,* 7s   *Ipswich,* 1849

6195 ROBENS' Ritterbürtige Landständische Adel des Grossherzogthums Niederrhein, 2 vols. 8vo. 86 *plates of Arms, bds.* 15s *Aachen*, 1818
6196 RODERICI Toleti Archiepiscopi rerum in Hispaniâ gestarum Chronicôn libri IX, cum GENEALOGIÂ Regum Hispanorum Alphonsi de Carthagena—Episcopi Gerundinensis Paralipomena Hispaniae—2 vols. in 1, folio, *woodcut titles and initials, fine large copy in the original limp vellum*, 15s *Granatae*, 1545
6197 ROUCK's Nederlandtschen Herauld, folio, *plates of Arms, Costume, etc. old calf*, 9s *Amst* 1645
6198 [ROWLANDS (Rev. W. G.)] The Armorial Bearings of several Families which are or have been connected with SHROPSHIRE, 4to. 24 *leaves containing* 142 *Coats of Arms, with the names and descriptions added, all* COLOURED *and* EMBLAZONED *by the* REV. R. W. EYTON, *hf. bd. privately printed*, £4. 10s *Shrewsbury*, 1834
6199 ROWS' ROL: Thys rol was laburd and finished by Master John Rows of Warwyk, high 4to. *frontispiece with the Arms of Warwick, and* 33 *plates, comprising* 64 *exquisitely drawn* PORTRAITS *of members of the* HOUSE OF WARWICK, *with their* COATS OF ARMS, *all splendidly illuminated and emblazoned in gold and colours, with Introduction, Genealogy of the House of Warwick, Quarterings of Arms, and Historical Index, only a few copies got up, hf. morocco, gilt top, uncut*, £4. 15s *Pickering*, 1845
A very valuable ENGLISH HISTORICAL CHRONICLE, containing much interesting information relative to the History of England during the York and Lancaster Wars.
6200 RUBEI (H.) Historiarum Ravennatum libri X, cum libro XI°, usque ad 1538, locupletati, sm. folio, *woodcuts, vellum*, 20s *Venet.* 1589
6201 RUBEIS (F. B. M. de) Monumenta Ecclesiæ AQUILEJENSIS, cum commentario, etc. roy. folio, LARGE PAPER, *bds.* 10s *Argent.* 1740
6202 RYMER (Tho.) FŒDERA CONVENTIONES, LITERÆ, et cujuscunque generis Acta Publica, inter Reges Angliæ et alios Imperatores, Reges, Pontifices, Principes, vel Communitates, ab anno 1101 ad nostra tempora habita, collata et emendata studio G. Holmes, 10 vols. roy. folio, *plates of Charters, etc. bds. uncut, Mr. Buckle's copy*, £10.; or 10 vols. fol. *a fine copy in hf. vel.* £13. *Hagæ Com.* 1745
Priced, 1840, Leslie, £14. 14s; Payne and Foss, £18. 18s; J. Bohn, £18. 18s; fetched, 1857, Sotheby's, £13.
"By much the best edition, as having a complete and useful Index to the work."—*Dibdin.*
"An invaluable work, and as such it is esteemed both at home and abroad. It is equally interesting to the antiquary and Historian. Whoever wishes to write such a history of Great Britain as will do honour to himself and justice to his country must go to Rymer for his materials."—*Clarke's Bibliog. Dict.*
"Rymer's Fœdera, with the Statutes of the Realm, the Rolls of Parliament, and Wilkins' Concilia, form an outline map of English mediæval history."—*English Review, No.* 2.
The "Index Rerum præcipuarum in novis tomis Fœderum," which was added to this edition, and makes it by far the best, is marked by the most extreme minuteness and accuracy; forming the fourth part of Vol. X., and consisting of 332 close pages, with treble columns.
6203 RUDBECKII (Olai) ATLANTICA, sive Manheim, vera Japheti posterorum sedes ac patria, *Latine et Suecice;* cum INDICE, 2 vols. folio, *curious woodcuts, vellum, sound copy*, £3. *Upsalæ*, 1675-89
"Ouvrage précieux contenant de savantes recherches sur les Antiquités du Nord en général et celles de la Suède en particulier."—*Brunet.*
"I cannot close these observations without making some mention, and enforcing the recommendation, of the celebrated work called RUDBEKII ATLANTICA, which is doubtless among the *greatest guns* of a well chosen collection."—*Dibdin's Lib. Comp.*
6204 RUSHWORTH'S Historical Collections; of Private Passages of State and Law, and of Remarkable Proceedings in Five Parliaments, beginning in the 16th year of James I. 1618, and ending at the Death of Charles I. 1648, with the Trial of the Earl of Strafford, 8 vols. fol. *calf gilt, Arms on the sides*, £3. 16s 1682-1701
"Rushworth's collection is full of vastly curious and valuable matter."—*Bp. Warburton.*
6205 SAINCT JULIEN, de l'Origine des Bourgongnons, et Antiquité des Estats de BOURGONGNE, d'Autun, de Chalon, de Mascon, de l'Abbaye et ville de Tournus, folio, *views of Dijon, Beaûne, Autun, Mascon, and Chalons, and Arms, shield coloured, a very fine copy in overlapping vellum, rare*, £4. *Paris, Chesnau*, 1581
6206 SAINTE MARIE (Honoré de) Dissertations Historiques et Critiques sur la Chevalerie, ancienne et moderne, 4to. 42 *plates, representing the Insignia of Orders, etc. calf gilt*, 36s *Paris*, 1718
6207 SALAZAR Y CASTRO (Luis de) Historia genealogica de la CASA DE LARA, justificada con instrumentos, y escritores, 3 vols.—PRUEBAS de la CASA DE LARA, 1 vol.—together 4 vols. stout folio, *numerous Pedigrees and Coats of Arms, fine copy, vellum*, £6. *Madrid*, 1694-97
Value in Spain, £10.
"Vir, in quo cum summa eruditione integritas humanitasque eximia certant; quippe Antiquitatum patriarum non modo, sed et omnis rei Genealogicæ universæ Europæ peritissimus."—*Franckenau.*
6208 SALIG, de Diptychis veterum, Oblationibus, Martyribus, Missâ, etc. sq. 8vo. *frontispiece, vellum*, 5s *Halae*, 1731

HERALDRY, ANTIQUITIES, CHRONICLES, GENEALOGY, ETC. 335

6209 SALVER, Proben des hohen Teutschen Reichs Adels, folio, *a very handsome book, with many engravings of Tombs, coats of Arms, and Sepulchral Monuments, old calf gilt*, 21s *Wirzburg*, 1775

6210 SANDFORD'S (Fras.) GENEALOGICAL HISTORY of the Kings and Queens of ENGLAND, with Continuation, Additions, and Annotations, the Descents of divers Illustrious Families now flourishing, etc. by Stebbing, folio, BEST EDITION, *numerous fine plates by Hollar of Monumental Effigies, Seals, Arms, Ecclesiastical Architecture, etc. and Tables of Genealogies, calf*, £5. 15s 1707
Priced, 1834, Thorpe, £7. 17s 6d; 1841, Thorpe, £6. 6s; 1844, Rodd, £8. 8s; 1847, mor. £8. 18s 6d; old russia, £7. 10s; 1859, red morocco, £15. 15s. *** Sold in Willett's sale for £10. 10s, Townsend's for £11., and in Nassau's for £13. 13s; 1860, Sotheby's, broken bdg. £6. 10s.
"Sandford has shewn very peculiar genealogical skill in his account of the Royal Family and the correction of its collateral branches. The whole arrangement is well concerted, and the notes and marginal references abound in curious information; to which are added many engravings of seals and funeral monuments."—*Dallaway.*

6211 SANSOVINO, Historia e Huomini Illustri di Casa ORSINA, 2 vols. in 1, sm. fol. *pedigrees and fine large portraits, old vellum*, 14s *Venetia*, 1565

6212 SAUVAGE, CRONIQUE DE FLANDRES (depuis 792 jusqu'en 1383) ancienement composee par auteur incertain, et nouvellement mise en lumière par Sauvage —Continuation (1384-1435)—Memoires de Messire OLIVIER DE LA MARCHE (1435-92) mis en lumière par Sauvage, 2 vols. in 1, stout folio, *clean copy in the original calf binding*, 36s *Lyon*, 1562
The above is the first edition of the very interesting memoirs of Olivier de la Marche.

6213 SCARDEONIUS de Antiquitate Urbis PATAVII, folio, *woodcut view, scarce, fine copy in old calf*, 18s *Basileæ*, 1560
"Opus rarissimum et cujusvis pretii etiam in Italia."—*Zorzi.*

6214 SCHNEIDER'S Hoch-Gräflich-Erbachische Stamm-Tafel, nebst Erklär- und Bewührungen, stout folio, *Genealogical Tables, and 25 plates of Seals, Monumental Antiquities, etc. calf*, 20s *Franckfurt a. M.* 1736

6215 SCHŒPFLINI (J. D.) Historia Zaringo-Badensis, cum Codice Diplomatico, 7 vols. 4to. *portraits, plans, plates of coins, &c. hf. calf*, 25s *Carolsruhae*, 1763-66
A most valuable work. The last three volumes contain the *Codex Diplomaticus* from the year 676 downwards.

6216 SCHOEPFLINI Alsatia Illustrata, Celtica, Romana, Francica, 2 vols. large folio, *numerous plates of Antiquities, Views of Towns, &c. calf*, 18s *Colmariæ*, 1651
"A noble and masterly work."—*Dibdin's Tour in France, &c.* Vol. 3, p. 45.

6217 SCHOETTGENII et KREYSIGII Diplomataria et Scriptores historiae Germanicae Medii Aevi, cum prefatione Buderi de Archivis Germaniae, etc. 3 vols. folio, 20 *plates of Seals and Pedigrees, hogskin, fine copy*, 32s *Alten.* 1753-60

6218 SCHOTTI (A.) HISPANIÆ Illustratæ, seu Rerum Urbiumque Hispaniæ, Lusitaniæ, ETHIOPIÆ, et INDIÆ Scriptores varii, 4 vols. folio, MAPS, WITHOUT the Appendix to Mariana, but WITH *a still rarer Supplement*, "TABULÆ GENEALOGICÆ Regum Aragoniæ et Arag. fam. Lanuzarum; deinde Gentis Nordmannicæ; tertio Gironum familiæ," *calf or vellum*, £2. *Francof.* 1603-8

6219 —— the same, WITH BOTH SUPPLEMENTS (Marianæ libri XXI-XXX, et Tabulæ Lanuzarum), 4 vols. stout folio, *hf. vellum*, £4.; or 4 vols. in 3, *fine copy in stamped vellum*, £5. 5s 1603-8
"Cet ouvrage est tres-estimé, et l'on s'en procure difficilement des exemplaires complets."—*Brunet.*
Priced, 4 vols. Weigel, 36 thalers, 1829; 1832, Payne and Foss, *vellum*, £6. 6s; 1837, Payne and Foss, £9. 9s. In the second volume (pp. 1282-84) will be found the celebrated letter of Columbus "*de Insulis nuper inventis.*"

6220 SCHROT'S (Martin) Wappen Buch des hohen Geistlichen und Weltlichen Stands der Christenheit in Europa, sq. 8vo. *about 500 woodcut coats of Arms, hf. bd. clean copy*, 20s *München*, 1576

6221 —— Wappenbuch des Heiligen Römischen Reichs und allgemainer Christenheit in Europa, insonderheit des Teutschen Keyserthumbs, auch von Franckreich, Hispanien, Engelland, etc. und von den Haiden und Türcken, folio, *nearly a thousand coloured coats of Arms, limp vellum, fine copy*, 30s *München*, 1580

6222 SCHUETZ, Historia Rerum Prussicarum, Beschreibung der Lande Preussen, Ursprung des Deudschen Ordens, und Erbawung der Stadt Dantzig, mit Continuation, folio, *old stamped black morocco, clasps*, 20s *Leipzig*, 1599

6223 SCOHIER (Jean, *Beaumontois*) Généalogie et descente de la maison de CROY, 4to. *numerous coloured coats of Arms, vellum, rare*, 35s *Douay*, 1589
One of the rarer books printed at Douay, unmentioned by Brunet and Ebert.

6224 SCOHIER, Estat et comportement des Armies, livre necessaire a tous Gentilshommes et Officiers d'Armes, sm. folio, *numerous cuts of Arms, Pedigrees, etc. hf. vellum*, 20s *Bruxelles*, 1597
"Schohier naquit en 1560 dans la petite ville de Beaumont en Haynaut, d'une famille noble et ancienne. Il fut chanoine à Bergopsom."—*Duthilloeul, Bibl Douaisienne*, p. 67.

6225 SCOHIER, Estat et Comportement des Armes, *woodcuts, coloured, Brux.* 1629— Walthausen, Art de Chevalerie (*no plates*) *Francf.* 1616—Winzingeroda de Ordine S. Georgii et Periscelidis in Anglia, *plate, Jenæ*, 1701—in 1 vol. sq. 8vo. *calf gilt,* 12s   1616-1701

6226 SCOTTI, Helvetia profana e sacra, 2 parts in 1 vol. sq. 8vo. *cf.* 7s *Macerata*, 1642

6227 SCROPE AND GROSVENOR ROLL. CONTROVERSY between Sir Richard Scrope and Sir Robert Grosvenor in the Court of Chivalry, A.D. 1385-1390, printed from the Original Roll in the Tower of London, with notes and HISTORY OF THE FAMILY OF SCROPE, &c. by Sir NICHOLAS HARRIS NICOLAS, 2 vols. impl. 8vo. *all printed, cloth bds. scarce,* £10.   1832

Priced, 1834, Thorpe, £12. 12s; 1840, Payne and Foss, £14. 14s.

Privately printed at the expense of an association of noblemen and gentlemen. This curious and interesting memorial of early honours contains the evidences of upwards of three hundred earls, barons, knights and esquires; of each an interesting biographical notice is given; and their depositions abound in interesting information, illustrative of the history, manners and customs, of this country in the fourteenth century. Only a small edition was printed, and none of the copies was intended for sale. This celebrated dispute was carried on in the Court of Chivalry, during a period of five years, with great spirit by both parties, who enlisted as witnesses some of the most distinguished knights and warriors who flourished in that age of chivalry. One of the witnesses was "Geffrey Chaucere, Esquier," who mentions his captivity in France. See an interesting account of it in Mr. Martin's Catalogue of privately printed Books.

6228 SEGAR (Sir W.) Honor, Military and Civill, contained in foure Bookes, sm. folio, *with fine impressions of the eight full length portraits, which illustrate the costumes of different Orders, hf. russia,* RARE, £2. 2s   1602

6229 SETON (George) Law and Practice of Heraldry in Scotland, 8vo. 105 *woodcuts and* 14 *plates of Arms, Crests, Seals, etc. new in cloth,* 25s   *Edinb.* 1863

6230 SIBBALDI, Miscellanea quaedam eruditae Antiquitatis, ad Borealem Britanniam pertinentia, sm. folio, 3 *plates, hf. calf,* 12s   *Edin.* 1710

6231 SICOTIÈRE et POULET, Le Departement de L'ORNE Archéologique et Pittoresque, large folio, 326 *pp. with* 108 *fine lithographs of Views, Ancient Buildings, Architectural Ornaments, Facsimiles, etc. hf. morocco,* £2. 6s   *Laigle,* 1845

6232 SIEBMACHER, das erneurte DEUTSCHE WAPPENBUCH, in welchem des h. Römischen Reiches hohe Potentaten, Fürsten, Grafen, Herren, Stände und Städte, Wappen, etc. aussgebildet zu ersehen, 5 vols. with the Appendix to Vol. V. together 6 vols. in 3, oblong smallest 4to. 1145 *plates containing thousands of coats of Arms, original impressions, two volumes in old red morocco, and one volume in old calf,* £2. 10s   *Nurnberg,* 1657

6233 ———— the same, 6 vols. in 3, oblong 4to. *the margins at the end of Vol.* 6 *slightly injured, vellum,* 30s   1657

6234 SIGONIUS de Rebus Bononiensibus, Vita And. Doriæ, folio, *cf. gt.* 8s *Franc.* 1604

6235 SMITH (C. Roach) Antiquities of Richborough, Reculver and Lymne, in Kent, very sm. 4to. *plates and cuts of Antiquities, cloth,* 12s   1850

6235* ———— Catalogue of his Museum of London Antiquities, roy. 8vo. *numerous plates and cuts of Ancient Bronzes, Coins, Ornaments, Potteries, Tiles, etc. hf. calf, gilt top uncut, printed for subscribers only,* 25s   1854

6236 ———— INVENTORIUM SEPULCHRALE, an Account of some Antiquities dug up in Kent, by the Rev. B. Faussett, 1757-73, edited with Notes and Introduction by C. Roach Smith, 4to. *portrait of J. Mayer, map, numerous cuts and twenty plates (several brilliantly coloured), cloth, (printed for subscribers only at the price of* £2. 2s*)* 30s   1856

6236* ———— the same, roy. 4to. LARGE PAPER, (price to subscribers, £4. 4s) *cl.* £2. 10s 1856

6237 SOCIÉTÉ DES ANTIQUAIRES de la MORINIE, Mémoires, Vols. I–IV, 8vo. *facsimiles of Charters and MSS. plates of Ancient Edifices, Coins, etc. hf. calf gilt,* 28s   *St. Omer,* 1834-39

6238 SOHIER, La Veritable Origine de la tres Ancienne et illustre Maison de SOHIER, avec Table Genealogique, large folio, *portrait of Constantine Sohier, and many coats of Arms, col. cf. Arms of the Family on the sides, rare,* 36s *Leyden,* 1681

6239 SOMMERSBERG (F. W. de) Silesiacarum Rerum Scriptores adhuc inediti, acc. Diplomatarium Bohemo-Silesiacum, 3 vols. in 2, folio, *with pedigrees, fine copy, stamped hogskin, rare,* £3. 16s   *Lips.* 1729-32

6240 SOUSA (A. Caetano de) Historia Genealogica da CASA REAL PORTUGUEZA, desde a sua origem até o presente, com as familias illustres, 12 vols. in 14—Provas da Historia Genealogica tiradas dos archivos, 6 vols.—Indice geral, 1 vol.—21 vols. royal 4to. *Vol. IV. containing* 49 *plates of* SEALS, *Coins, and Medals; a few leaves of text wanting, and some volumes stained, the set sold not subject to collation; neat in old calf, rare, Lord Stuart de Rothesay's copy,* £4. 10s   *Lisboa,* 1735-49

"Ouvrage capital dans son genre."—*Brunet.* One of the best Genealogical works published in Europe; it is now getting very rare. Priced, 1847, H. Bohn, £13. 13s; sold by auction, 1853, Purton Cooper's copy, £13. 13s; Lord Stuart de Rothesay's copy dropped cheap.

HERALDRY, ANTIQUITIES, CHRONICLES, GENEALOGY, ETC.

6241 Sousa (A. C. de) Memorias Historicas e Genealogicas dos Grandes de Portugal, sm. 4to. *cuts of arms, a few coloured, with MS. notes on the margins, old calf,* 12s *Lisboa*, 1755

6242 Sovrani del Mondo, Genealogie delle loro Famiglie, etc. 4 vols. 12mo. *including an Article on Japan, numerous Arms, vellum,* 9s *Venezia*, 1720

6243 Spangenberg's Mansfeldische Chronica, Theil I. folio, *all published, best edition, fine copy, in stamped hogskin,* 10s *Eisleben*, 1572
The binding is dated 1574; the crucifixion in the centre is beautifully preserved.

6244 SPANO (G.) Bulletino Archeologico Sardo, ossia Raccolta de Monumenti Antichi in ogni genere di tutta l'Isola di Sardegna, Vols. I—VIII, part 2, 8vo. *numerous plates and cuts of Sardinian Antiquities, six vols. bound in 3, hf. morocco, the rest sewed,* £4. 4s *Cagliari*, 1855-62

6245 Speneri (J. C.) Notitia Germaniae antiquae et mediae, sm. 4to. 6s *Halae*, 1717

6246 Speneri (P. J.) Insignium Theoria, seu Operis Heraldici partes generalis et specialis, folio, 36 *plates of about* 300 *coats of Arms, vellum,* 15s *Franc.* 1717

6247 SPROTT'S (Thomas) Chronicle of Profane and Sacred History, translated from the original Manuscript, 4to. *with an exact anastatic facsimile of the entire original Codex, in a case, very scarce, only a few copies were printed at the private expense of Mr. Joseph Mayer,* 25s *Liverpool*, 1851

6248 SPRUNER'S Historical Atlas : Historisch-Geographischer Hand-Atlas zur Geschichte der Staaten Europa's vom Anfang des Mittel-alters bis auf die neueste Zeit, folio, 73 *fine large coloured maps, with text, hf. russia,* £2. 16s *Gotha*, 1846
The best Historical Atlas published.

6249 STANIHURST (Dan. *Dublin*) de Rebus in Hibernia gestis cum Appendice ex S. Giraldo Cambrensi, sm. 4to. *very fine copy in vellum,* 21s *Antv.* 1584

6250 Stroobant, Notice sur les Seigneurs de Tyberchamps, 1851—Seigneurs de Braine le Chateau et Haut-Ittre, 1849, 2 vols. roy. 8vo. *plates,* 6s *Brux.* 1849-51

6251 STUKELEY (Dr. W.) Itinerarium Curiosum : or an account of the Antiquitys and remarkable Curiositys in Nature or Art, observ'd in travels thro' Great Britain, folio, first edition, *with* 100 *plates of celebrated ancient Sites, Roman and Celtic Remains and Ruins, etc., fine copy in old russia, gilt,* £2. 10s 1724
A facsimile reprint edition appeared about 1810.

6252 ——— the same, 1724—STONEHENGE, a Temple restor'd to the British Druids, *portrait and* 35 *plates,* 1740—ABURY, a Temple of the British Druids, *volume the second,* 40 *plates,* 1743—together 3 vols. fol. 176 *curious plates, not quite uniform, in old calf gilt,* an original copy, £6. 1724-43
The Stonehenge and Abury were reprinted *circa* 1835. Priced, 1825, Thorpe, the original edition, "Stonehenge and Abury" only, £14. 14s; 1828, Payne and Foss, £14. 14s; 1855, Baker's copy fetched, £5. 7s 6d.

6253 ——— Itinerarium Curiosum : or an Account of the Antiquities and remarkable Curiosities, in Nature or Art, observed in Travels through Great Britain, second edition, *with large additions,* 2 vols. in 1, folio, *bds.* £3. 10s 1776
The Centuria I (or Vol. I.) contains the Itinerarium, with the 100 plates of the first edition of 1724, and an additional plate of the "Solar Eclipse, 1724;" Centuria II. (or Vol. II.) the following unpublished works : The Brill, pp. 1-16; Iter Boreale, pp. 17-78; Ricardi Monachi de Situ Britanniæ, pp. 79-108; Richard of Cirencester, pp. 109-150; Carolus Bertram, pp. 151-168; The Weddings, pp. 169-178; Indices, 6 leaves; plates, 1-102, 75 leaves, and Map of Roman Britain.
A long account of this most interesting work will be found in Savage's Librarian, together with a biographical sketch of the author, vol. 2, pp. 145-180. Sold in Mr. Dent's sale for £11. 11s, in the Duke of Roxburghe's for £16. 16s, in Dr. Heath's for £16. 16s, and at King's and Lochee's, in 1806, for £21; 1855, Baker, £5. 2s 6d; 1856, Lane, with the Stonehenge and Abury, £11. 15s.
"Stukely, the most zealous of English Antiquaries."—*Palgrave's Commonwealth,* p. 349.

6254 Suecia : Exegesis commemorans Causas ob quas Ordines Regni Sigismundum III. Poloniæ Succano exuerunt Diademate et Carolum IX. coronarunt, sm. 4to. *vellum,* 10s *Stokhol.* 1610

6255 SWIDHUN (St.) Legends of St. Swidhun and Sancta Maria Aegyptiaca, Gloucester Fragments, *Anglo-Saxon,* copied in photozincographic facsimile, at the Ordnance Office, Southampton, with elucidations, translation, and an essay by Rev. John Earle, roy. 4to. *bds.* 28s 1861

6256 TAILLEFER (Wlgrin de) Antiquités de Vesone, cité Gauloise, remplacée par Périgueux, 2 vols. 4to. 25 *plates of Coins, etc. bds.* 15s *Périgueux,* 1821-26

6257 Teutsche Reichs-Herold (der), Genealogie der Familien, etc. stout folio, *half vellum,* 12s *Franck.* 1727

6258 Thaumassiere, Commentaires sur les Coutumes des Pays et Duché de Berri, folio, *calf gilt,* 6s *Bourges,* 1701

6259 THULEMARII Tractatio de Bulla Aurea, Argentea, Plumbea, et Cerea; de Aurea Bulla Caroli IV. folio, *numerous facsimiles, hf. bd. 9s* *Franc.* 1697

6260 THURINGIA SACRA, sive historia Monasteriorum, quae olim in Thuringia floruerunt, stout folio, *numerous plates of Monuments, Views, etc. vell.* 14s *Franc.* 1737

6260*TIRABOSCHII Vetera Humiliatorum Monumenta, Dissertationibus, etc. 3 vols. 4to. *vellum, rare*, 21s *Mediolani*, 1766-68
An important work, full of interesting biographies and documents from the XIIth Century to the XVth, in which this powerful and formerly illustrious Ecclesiastical Order was suppressed in consequence of the abominations discovered amongst its members.

6261 TORFFAEI Orcades seu Rerum Orcadensium historia, folio, *bds. uncut, rare*, 24s   Priced, 1824, Rivington, £2. 12s 6d.   *Havniae*, 1715
An authentic account of the Early History of the Orkneys.

6262 TURKHEIM, Tablettes Genealogiques des Ducs de Zaeringen, Margraves et Grands-Ducs de Bade, 8vo. VELLUM PAPER, *mor. gilt edges*, 7s 6d *Darmst.* 1810

6263 TWYSDENI (Rogeri) Historiæ Anglicanæ Scriptores X, ex vetustis MSS. nunc primum in lucem editi; adjectis variis Lectionibus, Glossario, Indiceque copioso, 2 vols. in 1, folio, FINE PAPER, *vellum or calf*, £4. 10s   1652

6264 UPTONUS de Studio Militari; J. De Bado Aureo, Tractatus de Armis: Spelmanni Aspilogia, ed. Bissæus, folio, *very fine portrait by Faithorne, excellent impressions of the plates, some by Hollar, and numerous coats of Arms, old calf*, 20s   1654
Priced, 1830, Payne and Foss, £3. 3s.; 1841, £2. 5s; 1856, with the plates coloured, £5. 5s; Fetched, 1856, with the Arms emblazoned, at Sotheby's, £2. 18s.
"Upton served under Thomas de Montacute, Earl of Salisbury, during which time he compiled his treatise, 'De Studio Militari,' which comprises the military code established by Henry V. at Minuce in France. The work is divided in five books, I. Officers of Arms. II. Veterans now styled Heralds. III. Duels. IV. Colours. V. Figures, making the whole a systematic Grammar of Heraldry."—*Dallaway*.

6265 VALVASOR, Topographia Archiducatus Carinthiae antiquae et modernae: Chronik des Erz-Herzogthums Kärndten, folio, 225 *pretty Views, vel.* 15s   1688

6266 ——— die Ehre dess Hertzogthums CRAIN: Belegenheit dieses Römisch-Keyserlichen Erblandes, mit Erzehlung seiner Landschafften, Böden, Felder, Wälder, Berge, Wassern, etc. erweitert durch E. Francisci, 4 stout vols. folio, *frontispiece, with portrait and a profusion of fine plates of Scenery, Arms, Maps, etc. old green boards, gilt backs*, £4.   *Laybach*, 1689
The most complete and comprehensive work upon Carniola. The Scenery of this beautiful but neglected province is amply depicted in the fine engravings with which the book is crowded; its Antiquities, Customs, Costumes, etc. is well represented; and there are several hundred Coats of Arms. Vol. II, Book VI. chapter 1 treats upon the CARNIOLAN and SLAVONIC LANGUAGE, with a plate of Cyrilic and Glagolitic Slavonian Alphabets, and a comparative list of words in Latin and thirteen Slavonic dialects.

6267 VELTRONII (Fr. Ptolemæi) Statuta HOSPITALIS HIERUSALEM cum Indice Materiarum, sm. folio, *numerous curious plates with woodcut borders, including* 52 *portraits of Grand Masters, etc. vellum*, 30s   *Romæ*, 1588
"Vol. rare; vend. 51 fr. La Serna."—BRUNET. Fetched at the Borluut sale 38 fr. "Liber eximiæ raritatis, vix centesimo visus."—VOGT.

6268 VERTOT, Histoire des Chevaliers Hospitaliers de St. Jean de Jerusalem appellez aujourd'hui les Chevaliers de Malte, 4 vols. 4to. LARGE PAPER, *maps and* 72 *fine* PORTRAITS, *beautiful impressions, calf*, £2. 2s   *Paris*, 1726
Mead's copy fetched £3. 3s; the Devonshire copy £2. 16s.

6269 VOET, Origine et Gestes des Seigneurs de Brederode, traduits du Flamand par Pailhot, 4to. *vellum*, 10s   *Amst.* 1663

6270 VREDII (Olivarii) Historia Comitum Flandriæ à Cæsare ad Clodovæum, 3 parts in 1 vol. 1650—Genealogia Comitum Flandriæ a Balduino Ferreo ad Philippum IV, 3 parts in 1 vol. 1642-50—Sigilla Comitum Flandriæ et Inscriptiones Diplomatum, 1639—Historia Flandriæ Christianæ—together 4 vols. sm. folio, *numerous very fine plates of Seals and Arms, Genealogical Tables, old calf, gilt back*, £4. 4s   *Brugis*, 1639-50
A complete set of these valuable works. There is a long essay, with illustrations, on the old Frank language in the second part of the "Historia Comitum."

6271 WAGNERI Descriptiones Genealogicæ praecipuarum Familiarum Magnatum in Europâ—Breviarium Orbis terrarum—2 parts in 1 vol. 12mo. *fine copy in vellum*, 12s   *Ulmæ*, 1663

6272 WALLACE's Origin of Feudal Tenures, and Descent of Ancient Peerages in Scotland, 4to. *hf. morocco*, 10s   *Edinb.* 1783

6273 WATER, Adelyk en Zeelant, 8vo. 2 *large plates of Arms, uncut*, 8s *Middel.* 1761

6274 WAP, Geschiedenis van het Land en de Heeren van CUYK, met Stamlijsten, A.D. 800-1400, 4to. *coloured plates of Arms, etc. cloth*, 20s   *Utrecht*, 1858

HERALDRY, ANTIQUITIES, CHRONICLES, GENEALOGY, ETC. 339

6275 WESTPHALEN (J.) MONUMENTA INEDITA Rerum Germanicarum praecipue Cimbricarum et Megapolensium, quibus varia Antiquitatum, Historiarum, Legum Juriumque Germaniæ, Holsatiae, etc. argumenta illustrantur, 4 vols. thick folio, *illustrated with numerous curious plates of Idols, Inscriptions, Monuments, Costumes, Arms, Portraits, &c. a good copy, hf. bd. uncut,* 30s ; or *vellum,* £3.
Lips. 1739-45

6276 WEEVER'S (John) Ancient Funerall Monuments within the united Monarchie of Great Britaine, Ireland, and the Islands adjacent, with the Dissolved Monasteries therein contained, folio, *brilliant impression of the portrait and frontispiece by Cecill, fine tall copy, elegantly bound in blue morocco, gilt edges,* £6. 1631
This really fine copy has the Index, which was published after the work itself, and is extremely rare.
Collation: Portrait, Engraved title-page, Printed title-page, Dedication to Charles, the "Author to the Reader," 8 pp. Table, 1 leaf; Errata, 1 leaf; "Discourse of Funerall Monuments," pp. 1—871; Index, 12 pp.

6277 WILLEMENT'S Regal Heraldry; The Armorial Insignia of the Kings and Queens of England, from coeval Authorities, roy. 4to. LARGE PAPER, 36 *coloured plates of Arms,* (pub. at £4. 4s) *bds.* 25s   1827

6278 WILLEMS (T. F.) Belgisch Museum voor de Nederduitsche Tael- en Letterkunde en de Geschiedenis des Vaderlands, 10 vols. 8vo. *plates, portraits and facsimile, hf. bd. uncut,* £2. 6s   *Gent,* 1837-1846
Interesting Collection of Treatises about old Flemish Literature and History.

6279 WILTHEMII Vita Yolandæ priorissæ ad Mariæ Vallem, cum append. de Margaritâ Henrici VII. Imp. sorore, et Genealogiâ Comitum Vienn. in Arduennâ, 12mo. *plates, vellum,* 12s   *Antv.* 1674

6280 WILDE (J.) Sueciæ historia pragmatica quæ vulgo Jus publicum dicitur, sq. 8vo. *calf, Chancellor D'Aguesseau's copy, having his devices, the bâton and shells, as tooling,* 16s   *Holmiæ,* 1731

6281 WILDEISEN, Brandenburg-Onolzbach. genealogischer Lust-Wald oder Geschlecht-Register, 2 vols. in 1, royal folio, *pedigrees, bds. rare,* 10s   *Onolzbach,* 1680

6282 WILLEMENT'S (Thomas) Lithographed Fac-simile of a Contemporary Roll, with the Names and Arms of the Sovereigns, and of the Spiritual and Temporal Peers who sat in Parliament in the Sixth Year of Henry VIII, 1515—Index to the Roll of Arms—2 vols. in 1, obl. roy. 4to. 29 *leaves of Coats of Arms, richly coloured in strict imitation of the original vellum, hf. russia, rare,* £4. 15s   *Privately printed,* 1829
Only 50 copies were printed, and none of these for sale.

6284 WINSEMII (P.) Chronique van Vrieslant, folio, *portraits and plates,* black letter, *fine copy in the original old black* MOROCCO, *gilt gaufré edges, the sides and back richly ornamented with gold tooling,* 36s   *Franeker,* 1622
The binding is a good specimen of Dutch skill in the early part of the XVIIth century.

6285 WOGEN's Gottesdienstlichen Alterthümer der Obotriten, sm. 4to. *numerous curious plates of Slavonic Antiquities, old red morocco,* 8s   *Berlin,* 1771

6286 WILTSHIRE. ARCHAEOLOGICAL INSTITUTE, Memoirs illustrative of the History and Antiquities of Wiltshire and the City of Salisbury, 8vo. *numerous plates of Ancient Monuments, Stained Glass Windows, Seals, etc. cloth,* 15s 1851

6287 WOLZOGEN und Neuhaus, Geschichte des Reichsfreiherrlich von Wolzogen'schen Geschlechts, 2 vols. in 1, large 8vo. *portraits, Arms and Pedigrees, hf. cf. uncut,* 10s   *Leipzig,* 1859

6288 WYRLEY'S (Will.) True Use of Armorie, shewed by History and plainely proved by Example, and other matters of Antiquitie, incident to the advancing of Banners, Ensignes, and Marks of Noblenesss and Chevalrie, *cuts of Arms, coloured by a former possessor, 16th Century, and noted by him, tall copy in the original binding,* RARE, £2. 10s   1592
Priced, 1832, Thorpe, £3. 3s; morocco, £4. 14s 6d; fetched, 1858, Sotheby's, morocco, £3. 5s.
Two long poems in seven line stanzas, upon the lives of Sir John LORD CHANDOS, and Sir John de Gralhy, CAPITALL DE BUZ, follow the "Use of Armes."

6289 YORKE (*James of Lincoln, Blacksmith*) The UNION of HONOUR, containing the Armes, Matches, and Issues of the Kings, Dukes, Marquesses, and Earles of England, from the Conquest until 1640, with the Armes of the English Viscountes and Barons now being, and the Gentry of Lincolnshire ; whereunto is annexed, a Briefe of all the Battels fought by the English since the Conquest, folio, *with the* RARE ENGRAVED FRONTISPIECE, *containing portrait, and with many woodcuts, singularly fine tall copy, calf,* £3. 16s   1640-41

6290 ZEDLITZ-NEUKIRCH, neues Preussisches Adels- Lexicon, 5 vols. 8vo. *sd.* 8s
Leipzig, 1836-39

CHRONOLOGY, HISTORY OF THE CALENDAR.

6291 ART DE VERIFIER LES DATES des Faits Historiques, des Inscriptions, des Chroniques, et autres Anciens Monumens, avant l'Ere Chrétienne, 5 vols.—Depuis la Naissance de Notre Seigneur jusqu'à 1770, 18 vols.—Depuis 1770 jusqu'à nos jours, 18 vols.—Tables Générales, 3 vols. in 1—together 42 vols. 8vo. *hf. bd. uniform, large copy, very little cut,* or *another copy, calf gilt,* £9. *Paris,* 1819-44

6292 ART DE VÉRIFIER LES DATES, troisième édition, Vol. III, very stout folio, 864 *and xc pp. containing the Chronologies of all the Minor States of Europe, beginning with the Counts of Flanders, bds. uncut,* 25s *Paris,* 1787

Comprenant les *Annales comparatives de tous les Peuples et de tous les Rois du Monde;* ouvrage qu'on peut, à juste titre appeler la clef de l'Histoire générale; car point de bons livres sans l'Art de Verifier les Dates; point d'homme savant s'il ne connait à fond ce precieux travail "

"A splendid monument of learning, which has left little to be done by subsequent chronologists, besides the humble duties of translation and abridgement."—*Sir Harris Nicolas.*

"The great treasure of historical information."—*Sir Jas. Mackintosh.*

"It may truly be said that no book ever held so important a place in modern historical literature as this. It contains a most exact summary of the history of all nations; so, exact, that to detect any error in it may, commonly speaking, be called an impossibility. The decisions of this book are always looked upon as final; he who possesses a copy of it has indeed a treasure."

6293 BAYERUS de Horis Sinicis et Cyclo Horario, cum Parergo de Calendariis Sinicis, 4to. 8 *plates, hf. morocco, uncut,* 7s 6d *Petrop.* 1735

6294 GRAVII Epochae celebriores Chataiorum, Arab. etc. ex trad. Ulug Beigi, *Pers. et Lat.*—Abulfedae Chorasmia, Arab. et Lat.—in 1 vol. sq. 8vo. *vellum,* 5s 1750

6295 GRESWELL, Fasti Temporis Catholici and Origines Kalendariae, 5 vols. 8vo. *plates,* with 4to. atlas (*pub. at* £3. 5s *in cloth*) *a valuable and important work, newly bound,* £3. *Oxford,* 1852

6296 HALES' (Dr. W.) NEW ANALYSIS of CHRONOLOGY and Geography, History and Prophecy, 4 vols. 8vo. *plates, best edition, calf neat, scarce,* £2. 10s 1830

"The most elaborate system of Chronology in our language, there is scarcely a difficult text in the sacred writings not illustrated."—*Horne.*

6297 HALTAUS, Jahrzeitbuch der Deutschen des Mittelalters, 4to. a singularly learned work, explaining obscure Names, etc. *hf. bd.* 6s *Erlangen,* 1797

6298 IDELER (Dr. L.) Handbuch der Mathematischen und technischen Chronologie, 2 vols. 8vo. *hf. calf,* 15s *Berlin,* 1825

6299 LALAMANTII Exterarum Gentium Anni ratio et cum Romano collatio, 12mo. *limp vellum,* 7s 6d *Haed. Burg. (Autun),* 1571

6300 PERPETUO CALENDARIO e Lunario Sardo, con aggiunte filologiche, 8vo. *hf. vellum,* 7s 6d *Cagliari,* 1818

6301 POTOCKI (Comte Jean) Principes de Chronologie, pour les temps antérieurs aux Olympiades, 4to. *Papier velin,* 84 pp. and leaf of Errata, RED MOROCCO, *gilt edges,* 18s *St. Petersbourg,* 1810

Rare: printed for presents only.

6302 PETAVII Opus de Doctrinâ Temporum, cum Dissertatione de LXX hebdomadibus Harduini, 3 vols. folio, *portrait, old calf neat,* 24s *Antverpiæ,* 1703

DIPLOMATICS, MÆDIEVAL LATIN GLOSSARIES.

6303 ANDERSONI Selectus DIPLOMATUM et NUMISMATUM SCOTIÆ Thesaurus cum Indice Nominum et expositione praecipuarum Familiarum curâ Ruddimanni, roy. folio, *containing* 180 *plates of* COINS, ANCIENT SEALS, CHARTERS, &c. *fine impressions, hf. bd.* £8. 8s ; *or whole russia,* £9. 9s *Edinb.* 1739

The only record of the Genealogies of the Great Families of Scotland. Nearly the entire edition of this extremely scarce and valuable work was destroyed by fire. Hibbert's copy fetched £12.

6304 KNIGHT'S Essay on the Greek Alphabet, roy. 4to. 9 *plates, bds.* 5s 1791

6305 MABILLON DE RE DIPLOMATICA libri VI ; accedunt commentarius de antiquis regum Francorum palatiis, veterum Scripturarum varia specimina, etc. 1709—SUPPLEMENTUM, 1704—2 vols. in 1, stout roy. folio, LARGE PAPER, *upwards of* 60 *large plates of Facsimiles of Old Charters, etc. and woodcuts, calf, gilt back,* 36s *Lut. Paris,* 1704-9

Priced, 1818, Longman, £6. 10s; 1831. £3. 10s; 1854, £3. 13s 6d.

"Ce livre est regardé comme le chef-d'œuvre du savant bénédictin, qui en est l'auteur. Le supplément est beaucoup plus rare que le livre auquel il appartient, parceque, selon toute apparence, les exemplaires en ont été tirés a plus petit nombre."

6306 RUSSELL (J.) Complete Book of Cyphers, obl. 4to. 24 *plates, including the Emperor Charlemagne's Crown, sd.* 12s 1794

6307 TERRY'S New and Complete Book of Cyphers for the use of Artists and others, 4to. *engraved on* 25 *plates, sd.* 15s 1786

6308 WALTHERI Lexicon Diplomaticum, Abbreviationes Syllabarum et Vocum in Diplomatibus et Codicibus a Sec. VIII ad XVI usque occurrentes exponens, junctis Alphabetis et Scripturae Speciminibus, cum prefatione Jungii, 3 parts in 1 vol. folio, *last edition,* 225 *plates of Mediaeval Alphabets and Contractions, and* 28 *plates of Facsimiles, all with explanations, calf, sound copy,* £2. 16s; or *tall copy in calf gilt, uncut, top edges gilt,* £3. 3s *Ulmæ,* 1756
A magnificent volume. In consequence of variations existing between copies, the collation of the above is given. Title and 11 prel. printed leaves; the Alphabet of Contractions in 459 columns; facsimile specimens of Early Manuscripts, Tab. 1-28; printed index, 19 leaves.
For a complete List of this Class of Works, see ante Nos. 55—117.

NUMISMATA AND MEDALLIC HISTORY.

6309 (AINSLIE), Illustrations of the Anglo-French Coinage, from the Cabinet of a Fellow of the Antiquarian Societies of London and Scotland, *with* 7 *plates engraved by Finden,* India Proofs—Supplement, with 2 plates, *India Proofs,* 1847—2 vols. in 1, large 4to. (pub. at about £3. 10s) *cloth,* 25s 1830-47
Bound up with the above is Sotheby's Catalogue of General Ainslie's Numismatic collection, priced and with purchasers' names.

6310 AKERMAN (J. Y.) Descriptive Catalogue of Rare and Unedited Roman Coins, to the extinction of the Empire, under Palæologus, 2 vols. roy. 8vo. *numerous plates,* large paper, (pub. at £4. 4s) *cloth,* 35s 1-34
This work, besides containing every coin described in the work of Mionnet, comprises descriptions and engravings of numerous rare and unique pieces, among which are several hundred coins of Allectus and Carausius.

6311 ———— Tradesmen's Tokens in London and its vicinity, 1648-72, 8vo. 8 *plates,* (pub. at 15s) *cloth,* 7s 6d 1849
6312 ARGELATUS (P.) de Monetis Italiæ, variorum illustrium virorum dissertationes, partes III, cum Appendice ad tertiam, 4 vols. in 3, 4to. *cuts of several hundred coins, some very large, vellum,* 20s *Mediol.* 1750
6313 AUGUSTINI (Ant.) Dialogos de Medallas, Inscriciones, y otras Antiguedades, sq. 8vo. *with* 52 *leaves of engraved coins and a Scale, red morocco, portrait inserted, gilt edges,* £2. 5s *Tarragona,* 1587
"Edition originale et très rare. Vend. 210 fr. Gaignat; 141 fr. De Colle; 199 fr. D'O———; 70 fr. Chartin; 88 fr. MacCarthy; 120 fr. Millin; et 105 fr. Debure."—Brunet.

6314 Augustini, Dialogos de Medallas, sq. 8vo. 51 *engraved pp. of coins, and scale, calf,* 7s *Madrid,* 1744
6315 AVELLINO, Opuscoli diversi (sopra talune Medaglie della Italia, e dalla Sicilia; Osservazioni Numismatiche, Hispania, Italia, etc.; sopra un inedito diploma militare di Severo; Iscrizioni e Antichità) 3 vols. 8vo. *plates of coins, etc. hf. bd.* 32s *Napoli,* 1826-36
6316 ———— Rubastinorum Numi, Alla Memoria di Avellino, &c. 3 Tracts, 4to. *plates, sd.* 5s *Napoli,* 1844-55
6317 BANDURIUS: TANINII Supplementum ad Bandurii Numismata Imperatorum Romanorum, folio, *plates, containing Byzantine coins, old red morocco, broad borders, richly tooled corners, rare,* £2. 10s *Romae,* 1791
6318 BARATAIEFF (Prince Michel) Documents Numismatiques du Royaume de Géorgie, impl. 8vo. 14 *plates of numerous coins, with description in Russian and French, hf. calf,* 18s *St. Petersb.* 1844
6319 Bayeri (T. S.) Historia Osrhoena et Edessena, ex nummis, 4to. *plates of coins, bd.* 5s *Petrop.* 1734
6320 Bayerius (F. Perez) de Numis Hebræo-Samaritanis, roy. 4to. *portrait and plates of coins and Samaritan inscriptions, calf,* 10s *Valent.* 1781
6321 Bettange, Traité des Monoyes, 2 vols. 12mo. *calf,* 7s 6d *Avignon,* 1760
6322 BIRCHEROD, Specimen Antiquæ Rei Monetariæ Danorum, sq. 8vo. *frontispiece and numerous plates of coins, fine copy, vellum,* 25s *Hafniæ,* 1701
6323 BIZOT, Histoire Métallique de la République de Hollande, folio, *numerous finely engraved medals, old French red morocco, with Royal Arms and Crest on the back and sides,* 36s *Paris,* 1687
A remarkable peculiarity of this book is, that the arms of Colbert are introduced in the course of the work, as vignettes, in nearly a dozen places.

6324 BONNEVILLE, Traité des Monnaies d'Or et d'Argent qui circulent chez les différens Peuples, folio, 188 *plates of about* 1000 *coins, bds.* 30s; *green calf gilt,* £2. *Paris,* 1806
A standard book of reference.

6325 BOUDARD, Études sur l'Alphabet Ibérien et sur quelques Monnaies autonomes d'Espagne, 8vo. 10 *plates of alphabets, hf. calf,* 7s *Béziers,* 1852
6326 ———— Essai sur la Numismatique Ibérienne précédé de Recherches sur l'Alphabet et la Langue des Ibères, 4to. 39 *plates, nine of Ancient Alphabets, etc. thirty of several hundred coins, hf. red morocco, gilt top, uncut,* 32s *Paris,* 1859

6327 BUDELIUS de Monetis et Re Numariâ, etc. 3 vols. in 1, sm. 4to. *woodcuts, calf,* 10s *Colon.* 1591

6328 BUONARROTI, Osservazioni sopra alcuni Medaglioni Antichi, 4to. 38 *plates of Coins, Medals, etc. vellum,* 6s *Roma,* 1698

6329 BURN's Catalogue of the London Traders' Tokens, XVII Century, presented by Beaufoy to the Corporation Library, 8vo. *cloth,* 6s 1853

6330 CARELLII Nummorum Veterum Italiæ, quos ipse collegit, et ordine Geographico disposuit, descriptio, cum Avellinii adnot. folio, 200 *fine plates, containing figures of several thousand coins, hf. russia, uncut, only* 100 *copies printed for private circulation,* £4. 4s *Neapoli,* 1812-34

6331 —— NUMI ITALIÆ VETERIS, edidit Cavedonius, accesserunt Carellii Numorum quos ipse collegit descriptio, et Avellinii adnotationes, folio, 202 *plates, hf. morocco,* £4 4s Only 100 copies were printed. Sold, 1855, at Sotheby's, £4. 16s. *Lips.* 1850
The most extensive and rarest collection of the coins of Magna Græcia ever brought together, many of which were unknown to Mionnet and other eminent Numismatists.

6332 CAVEDONI, Biblische Numismatik, von Werlhof, 2 vols. in 1, 8vo. *plates of coins, hf. calf,* 7s 6d *Hannover,* 1855-56

6333 CINAGLI (A.) MONETE DE' PAPI descritte in Tavole sinottiche, folio, *plates of coins, calf gilt,* £2. 10s *Fermo,* 1848
Priced, 1856, *sewed,* £2. 16s. This is the only good work on Papal coins.

6334 COHEN (H.) Description générale des MONNAIES de la RÉPUBLIQUE ROMAINE communément appelées MÉDAILLES CONSULAIRES, stout 4to. 75 *plates containing several hundred coins, sd. or hf. calf,* 30s *Paris,* 1857

6335 —— Description historique des Monnaies frappées sous L'EMPIRE ROMAIN appelées MÉDAILLES IMPERIALES, 6 vols. large 8vo. *above* 100 *plates containing several hundred coins, sewed,* £5. *Paris,* 1859-62

6336 COMBE, Nummorum veterum Populorum et Urbium, qui in MUSEO HUNTER asservantur, descriptio, roy. 4to. 71 *plates containing several hundred coins, calf,* £2. 12s 6d : or *red morocco, gilt edges,* £3. 3s 1782

6337 —— (Taylor) Veterum Populorum et Regum Numi qui in Museo Britannico adservantur, roy. 4to. *calf,* 21s 1814

6338 CORDERO, della Zecca e delle Monete degli Antichi Marchesi della Toscana, 8vo. *hf. calf,* 7s 6d Bound up with Ferlini, Scavi nella Nubia, 1837. *Pisa,* 1828

6339 COVARRUVIAS, Veterum collatio Numismatum, 8vo. *portr. calf,* 7s 6d *Val.* 1775

6340 DANISH COINS : Beskrivelse over DANSKE MYNTER og MEDAILLER i den Kongelige Samling (Description of Medals and Coins in the Royal Cabinet of Denmark, by Nielson, Müller, Kölle and Spengler,) 2 very stout vols. roy. folio, *with* 326 *plates, calf, scarce,* £3. *Kiöbenhavn,* 1791
Priced, 1824, Thorpe, bds. £18. 18s. This magnificent publication, printed at the private expense of the King of Denmark, is of great rarity. The first volume is a letter-press description of the coins in the second.

6341 DOMINICIS (Fr. de) Repertorio Numismatico per conoscere qualunque moneta Greca tanto Urbica che dei Re, 2 vols. in 1, stout 4to. *neatly bd.* 12s *Nap.* 1826
A work of the greatest importance to the Numismatist, being an exact description of every Greek Coin, in a tabular form ; it is, in fact, a digested and comprehensive edition of the more costly works of Mionnet.

6341*DONALDSON (T. L.) ARCHITECTURA NUMISMATICA, or Architectural Medals of Classic Antiquity, royal 8vo. xxxii and 341 pp. 46 *plates and numerous woodcuts,* (pub. at £3. 3s) *cloth,* 24s 1859
Architectural medals have not received that attention to which they are entitled ; they reflect the customs of the ancients in reference to their buildings, and reveal matters of historical interest, otherwise imperfectly known, of which they alone offer evidence.
CLASSIFICATION : 1. *Sacred.* Temples ; Altars ; Tabernacles ; Funeral Edifices ; etc.—2. *Monumental.* Commemorative Columns ; Votive Arches ; Trophies—3. *Public Utility.* Forum ; Basilica ; Thermæ ; Bridges—4. *Public Games.* Theatres ; Stadia ; etc.—5. *City Gates.* Cities ; Camps ; Ports.
"A work worthy of Professor Donaldson's high reputation."—*Gentleman's Mag.* Vol CCVII.

6342 DUANE (M.) COINS OF THE SELEUCIDÆ, Kings of Syria ; from the Establishment by Seleucus Nicanor, to the determination of it under Antiochus Asiaticus, royal 4to. *with* 24 *plates by Bartolozzi, a good copy,* £5. 15s 1803
VERY RARE. Very few copies of this valuable work were printed ; even the Coppers have disappeared.

6343 DUBY (Tobiésen) Traité des Monnoies des BARONS DE FRANCE, des Pairs, Evêques, Abbés, Chapitres, Villes, et autres Seigneurs, 3 vols. impl. 4to. *with* 120 *plates, containing about* 2000 *coins struck by the Nobility of France, hf. calf, rare,* £2. 8s : or *a fine copy in* 2 *vols. French calf gilt,* £2. 10s *Paris,* 1790
Brockett's copy fetched £3. 1s ; the Marquis of Townshend's, £3. 4s.

6344 DUTENS, Oeuvres : Origines des Decouvertes attribuées aux Modernes, 1796 —Recherches sur l'usage des Voûtes chez les Anciens, 1805—Oeuvres mêlées, 2 vols. 1796—Explication de quelques Médailles Grecques et Phénic. et Paléographic Numismat. 7 *plates,* 1776—5 vols. in 2, 4to. *calf extra,* 15s 1776-96

6345 ECKHEL (J. H.) DOCTRINA NUMORUM VETERUM, cum supplemento, 9 vols. 4to. *plates, sd.* £5. 15s *Vindob.* 1792-1826
6346 ——— Addenda ad Doctrinam Numorum, 4to. *portrait*, 5s *Vindob.* 1826
The grand work on the numismatic science of antiquity. Lord Strangford's copy fetched £7. 17s 6d. "Ce bel ouvrage, dans lequel l'auteur a embrassé la numismatique toute entière, en a disposé les différentes parties dans le meilleur ordre, les a soumises à la critique la plus savante et la plus ingénieuse, et a dissipé les ténèbres dont plusieurs étaient encore couvertes, a mis le comble à sa gloire littéraire."—*Biographie Universelle.*
6347 ECKHEL, Traité élémentaire de Numismatique Ancienne, augmenté par Jacob, 2 vols. in 1, 8vo. *plates, hf. calf,* 9s 1825
6348 FELLOWS (Sir Chas.) COINS OF ANCIENT LYCIA, before the reign of Alexander, royal 8vo. *map and* 20 *plates of coins, cloth,* 15s 1855
6349 FILLON, Considérations Historiques et Artistiques sur les Monnaies de France, 8vo. 4 *plates and several cuts of coins, sd.* 6s *Fontenay-Vendée,* 1850
6350 FIORELLI, Annali di Numismatica, 2 vols. impl. 8vo. *plates, sd.* 12s *Nap.* 1851-53
6351 FOLKES' (Martin) Tables of English Silver and Gold Coins, published by the Society of Antiquaries, 4to. *best edition, with the Supplement,* 67 *plates, fine copy in russia extra,* 25s *Soc. of Antiq.* 1763
"Folkes' Silver Coins afford much valuable information subsequent to the reign of Richard III."—*Ruding.*
6352 FLOREZ, Medallas de las Colonias, y Pueblos Antiguos de España; Coleccion de las que se hallan en diversos autores, y de otras hasta hoy nunca publicadas, 3 vols. sm. 4to. *maps and* 67 *plates, also* 8 *plates of the Coins of the Goths, calf,* £2. 5s *Madrid,* 1757-73
6353 ——— the same, Vols. I, II, LARGE PAPER ; III, *small paper,* 3 vols. sm. folio, *calf gilt,* £2. 1757-73
Priced, 1824, Rivington, £3. 13s 6d; 1840, Jas. Bohn, £2. 12s 6d; 1843, Salva, 60 fr. "Cet ouvrage du savant Florez est le plus complet qui existe sur la numismatique espagnole."—*Salva.* "Opera pregiatissima e rara specialmente in Italia."—*Cicognara.* "The ancient coins of Spain will be found to much advantage."—*Pinkerton.*
6354 Fox (Gen. C. R.) Engravings of Unedited or rare Greek Coins, Parts 1, 2, (Europe, Asia and Africa), 4to. 16 *plates, sd.* 12 1856-62
6355 [FRAEHN ?] zur Münzkunde Russlands, 8vo. *hf. bd.* 6s *St. Petersb.* 1805
6356 FRAEHNII Recensio Nummorum Muhammedanorum Acad. Imp. Scient. Petropolitanae, 4to. 744 pp. *cloth,* 20s *Petrop.* 1826
6357 ——— De acad. imp. scientiarum Petrop. Museo Numario Muslemico prolusio prior, *Petr.* 1818—Novae symbolae ad rem numariam Muhammed. 2 *plates, Petr.* 1819—De Numorum Bulgharicorum antiquissimo, *Casani,* 1816—3 pts. 4to. 12s 1816-19
6358 ——— Münzen der Chane vom Ulus Dschutschi's, nebst denen anderen Muhamm. Dynastien, 4to. 18 *plates, sd.* 12s *St. Pet.* 1832
6359 GAILLARD, recherches sur les Monnaies des Comtes de FLANDRE, 4to. 22 *plates of Coins, sd.* 6s *Gand.* 1852
6360 GESSNERI (J. J.) Specimen Rei Numariæ, cum prolegomenis, observationibus doctissimorum virorum de Numismate Græco, etc. 2 vols. folio, *about* 340 *plates of several thousand coins, fine copy in russia, gilt edges,* £5. *Tiguri,* 1735-38
COLLATION : Vol. I. 1, Printed Title Numismata Macedoniæ ; 2, Avertissement, etc. 2 leaves ; 3, Text, pp. 1-226 (126) continuation engraved, 227-354 ; 4, Engraved title "Num. Pop. et Urb." ; 5, Macedonia. 7 plates ; 6, Engraved title, Syria, Egypt, Parthia ; 7, Syria, 9 plates, Egypt, 3 plates, Parthia, 4 ; 8, Engraved title Sicilia, and 5 plates ; 9, Reges Gent. Minor, 3 plates ; 10, Engraved title, Reges et Viri Illustres, and 4 plates ; 11, Engraved title, Populi et Urbes, and plates 1-19, 19-85—Vol. II. 12, Numism. Imperatorum, engraved title and 184 plates ; 13, Familiarum Romanarum, engraved title, and plates 1-34.
6361 GUSSEME (T. A. de) DICCIONARIO NUMISMATICO general, para la perfecta inteligencia de las Medallas Antiguas, sus Signos, Notas, e Inscripciones, y generalmente de todo lo que se contiene en ellas, 6 vols. sm. 4to. *calf neat,* £2. 5s
Valued by Salva at £3. 10s. *Madrid, Ibarra,* 1773
6362 HALLENBERG (J.) Collectio Nummorum Cuficorum, sm. 8vo. 10 *plates of Coins and Alphabets,* 6s *Stockh.* 1800
6363 HAWKINS. The Silver Coins of England arranged and described, with remarks on British Money previous to the Saxon dynasties, 8vo. 47 *plates of coins, half morocco, uncut,* 18s 1841
6364 HENNIN, Histoire Numismatique de la Revolution Française ou description raisonnée des Médailles, Monnaies, et autres Monumens Numismatiques, relatifs aux Affaires de la France, 1789-99, 2 vols. in 1, 4to. 95 *plates containing* 927 *Medals, hf. russia,* £2. 5s *Paris,* 1826
The best work on the Coins struck during the French Revolution. Priced, 1845, Rodwell, bds. £5. 5s.
6365 HICKCOX (John H.) an historical Account of AMERICAN COINAGE, roy. 8vo. LARGE PAPER, *with* 5 *plates, hf. calf, uncut,* £2. *Albany, N. Y.* 1858
Very rare: only 6 copies were printed on Large Paper ; 200 on the small paper.

6366 JUNCKER, Vita LUTHERI, *nummis* illustrata, 12mo. *plates, vellum*, 5s *Franc.* 1699
6367 KIRCHER. L'ÆS GRAVE del Museo Kircheriano, ovvero le Monete Primitive de' Popoli dell' Italia media, 4to. *map and* 39 *plates of early Roman coins,* (pub. at £2. 2s) *hf. calf,* 14s *Roma,* 1839
A highly useful work to the Numismatist and to the Classical Scholar.
6368 KOEHLERS HISTORISCHE MÜNZ-BELUSTIGUNG, mit Supplementen und Register, 24 vols. in 12, stout sq. 8vo. *numerous plates of coins, vellum, a fine copy*, £3. 10s *Nürnberg,* 1729-64
6369 LANGLOIS (Victor) Numismatique des Nomes d'Egypte Romaine, 4to. 4 *plates, sd.* 7s *Paris,* 1852
6370 ——— Num. de la Géorgie au Moyen-Age, 4to. 4 *plates, sd.* 6s 6d 1852
6371 ——— Numismatique de l'Arménie dans l'Antiquité, 4to. 6 *plates, sd.* 10s 1859
6372 ——— Numismatique des Arabes avant l'Islamismé, 4to. 4 *plates of coins, sd.* 10s *Paris,* 1859
6373 LASSEN's Points in the History of the Greek and Indo-Scythian Kings in Bactria, Cabul, and India, by Roeer and Torrens, 8vo. *cloth, scarce,* 10s *Calcutta,* 1840
6374 LASTANOSA (Vincencio Juan de) Museo de las Medallas desconocidas Españolas, smallest 4to. *portrait and* 35 *plates of* 175 *coins, old veau fauve extra, gilt edges, from the libraries of Girardot de Prefond, and of Ford, with his notes,* 30s *Huesca, por Juan Noques,* 1645
6375 ——— the same, *a fine tall copy, the pagination of one leaf torn away, and the margin of one in the index restored, in red morocco, gilt edges, from Miss Currer's library,* £2. 6s 1645
Fetched at Nicol's sale £2. 4s; Towneley's, £4. 9s.
"Liber inter rariores rarissimus," Vogt, edit. 1747, p. 398—"Ouvrage éstimé et fort recherché des Curieux. Les exemplaires en sont rares," De Bure, No. 5853.
6376 ——— Museo de las Medalles, *Huesca,* 1745—Tratado de la Moneda Jaquesa y otras del Reyno de Aragon, 10 *plates of coins, Zaragoza,* 1681—VICO, Imagini degli Imperatori, tratte dalle Medaglie, *numerous fine plates of coins,* (*Venet. Aldo*) 1548—3 vols. in 2, sq. 8vo. *fine copies in Spanish calf extra,* £3. 3s 1548-1645
Brunet mentions the "Moneda Jaquesa" as very rare; the MacCarthy copy of it fetched 60 francs. This edition of Vico is also scarce.
6377 LEAKE (W. M.) NUMISMATA HELLENICA: a Catalogue of Greek Coins, collected by himself, *map, etc.,* with the Appendix containing a Geographical and GENERAL INDEX, 4to. *map,* 1854—A Supplement to Numismata Hellenica: Catalogue of Greek Coins, 1859—together 2 vols. 4to. (pub. at £4. 4s) *cloth,* £2. 8s 1854-59
6378 ——— the Supplement, *separately,* 4to. 16s 1859
6379 LELEWEL, Numismatique du Moyen Age, 2 vols. 8vo. *with the Atlas of* 25 *plates, neatly hf. bd.* 38s; or, *hf. calf, gilt tops, uncut,* £2. 2s *Paris,* 1835
6380 LENORMANT (C.) Lettres à De Saulcy sur les plus anciens Monuments Numismatiques de la série Mérovingienne, roy. 8vo. 16 *plates, sd.* 18s 1848-54
6381 LENORMANT (F.) Medailles et Antiquités du Cabinet du Baron Behr, 8vo. *plates,* 5s 1857
6382 LOCHNER (J. H.) Samlung merkwürdiger Medaillen, 8 vols. sm. stout 4to. *numerous very beautiful engravings of Medals, calf gilt,* 32s *Nürnberg,* 1737-44
6383 LUYNES (H. de) Essai sur la Numismatique des Satrapies et de la Phénice sous les Rois Achæménides, avec Supplement, 2 vols. impl. 4to. 17 *plates, bds. very rare,* £3. 10s *Paris,* 1846
6384 ——— Numismatique et Inscriptions Cipriotes, impl. 4to. 12 *plates, bds.* 36s *Paris,* 1852
6385 MAKRIZI Historia Monetæ Arabicæ, *Arab. et Lat.* ed. Tychsen, sm. 8vo. *calf neat, gilt top, uncut,* 7s 6d *Rostoch.* 1797
6386 MARSDEN (W.) NUMISMATA ORIENTALIA Illustrata. The Oriental Coins, Ancient and Modern, of his Collection, described and historically illustrated, 2 vols. 4to. 57 *plates, comprising upwards of* 1000 *fine engravings of Eastern Coins, bds.* £4. 10s; *calf neat,* £5. 5s 1823-25
6387 ——— the same, Vol. II, LARGE PAPER, 4to. *plates,* 28-57, *bds. uncut,* 20s 1823
6388 MIONNET (T. E.) Description de MEDAILLES ANTIQUES, GRECQUES ET ROMAINES, 7 vols. *one of them containing the plates,* 1806-13—Supplément à la même, 9 vols. 1819-37—De la Rareté et du prix des Médailles Romaines, 2 vols. 1858 –together 18 vols. 8vo. *neat in hf. russia, uncut, a fine perfect set,* £30. 1806

6389 MIONNET, de la Rareté et du Prix des Médailles Romaines, seconde edition augmentée, 2 vols. 8vo. 39 *plates, hf. calf,* 21s *Paris,* 1827

6390 MIRKHOND's History of the Atabeks of Syria and Persia, *Persian* by Morley, roy. 8vo. 7 *plates of Coins, with descriptions, cloth,* 9s 1848

6391 MIERIS, Histori der Nederlandsche Vorsten, uit de Huizen van Beijere, Borgonje en Oostenryk, 3 vols. folio, *portrait by Houbraken, and a profusion of superbly engraved Coins and Medals, fine copy in stamped vellum, rare,* 25s *Graavenhaage,* 1732-35

Priced, 1848, £2. 2s; 1857, Heussner, 50 fr.; Brockett's copy fetched £2. 15s; 1855, Sotheby's, £3.

6393 MILLINGEN, Considérations sur la Numismatique de l'Ancienne Italie, 8vo. *bds.* 9s *Florence,* 1841

6394 MOELLER de Numis Orientalibus numos Chalifarum et Cuficos exhibens, *plate,* 1826—Catalogus Librorum MSS. et impressorum Bibliothecae Gothanae, 2 parts, *with* 4 *coloured plates,* 1826—3 parts in 1 vol. 4to. *bds.* 8s *Gothae,* 1826

6395 MORELLI, THESAURUS MORELLIANUS, sive FAMILIARUM ROMANARUM Numismata omnia, accuratissime delineata et disposita ab Andr. Morellio, cum Nummis miscellaneis nunc primum editis a Havercampo, *Amstellædami,* 1734, 2 vols. 184 *plates*—Thesaurus Morellianus, sive Schlegelii, Havercampi et Gorii commentaria in XII. priorum IMPERATORUM ROM. Numismata, delineata ab Morellio, cum præfatione Wesselingii, *Amst.* 1752, 3 vols. 200 *plates*—together 5 vols. folio, £4. 10s *Amst.* 1734-52

Priced, 1832, 37, 40, Payne and Foss, £8. 8s; 1847, Bohn, £10. 10s; Hearne, £6. 6s. Hibbert's copy fetched £6. 8s 6d; Brockett's, £13.; Townley's £7. 12s 6d.

6396 MORIN, Numismatique du DAUPHINÉ, Archevêques de Vienne, Evêques de Grénoble, Dauphins de Viennois, 4to. *Large Paper,* 23 *plates, hf. morocco neat,* 32s Priced in French Catalogues at £4. *Paris,* 1854

6397 MÜLLER (L.) die Münzen des Thracischen Königs Lysimachus, 4to. 2 *plates of Coins and* 7 *plates of Symbols used on the Coins, sd.* 4s *Kopenhagen,* 1858

6398 —— Numismatique d'Alexandre-le-Grand; avec les Monnaies de Philippe II et III, 8vo. xvi. and 402 pp. *with a* 4to. *Atlas of* 29 *plates, sd.* 10s; *hf. calf,* 12s *Copenhague,* 1855

6399 MÜNTZ BUCH, darinnen zu besehen die besten unnd schönsten so wol alte als newe Gelt Müntze, sm. 4to. *cuts of several hundred coins, vellum,* 7s *Hamb.* 1631

6400 NOEHDEN (Dr.) Specimens of Ancient Coins of Magna Græcia and Sicily, from the Cabinet of Lord Northwick, atlas 4to. 20 *very fine plates by H. Moses, hf. calf,* 18s 1826

6401 NUMISMATIC JOURNAL, CHRONICLE, and Numismatic Society's Proceedings, from the beginning in 1836: Journal, 2 vols. 1837-38; Chronicle, Vols. I-XX, 1838-58; together 22 vols. 8vo. *numerous plates, hf. bd. calf neat,* £18. 18s 1836-58

Complete sets are very scarce. Several numbers in stock for the completion of sets; also parts of the "Proceedings."

6402 OBSERVAZIONE sopra di un libro, Dell' Origine della Monetae delle Zecche d'Italia, 4to. *bds.* 7s *Roma,* 1752

6403 ORSINI (Ign.) Storia delle Monete de Granduchi di Toscana della casa de' MEDICI, 29 *plates of coins,* 1756—ORSINI, Storia delle Monete della republica FIORENTINA, 6 *plates, and about* 1000 *cuts of coins, coats of Arms, Cyphers, etc.* 1760—2 vols. 4to. *half calf, gilt top, uncut, rare,* £3. 3s *Firenze,* 1756-60

6404 PANEL, Remarques sur les Maccabées, ou sur une Medaille d'Alexandre, sq. 8vo. 8 *plates, calf,* 6s *Valence,* 1753

6405 PELLERIN, ŒUVRES SUR LES MÉDAILLES, Recueil de Médailles de Rois, pas encore publiées, 22 *plates, Paris,* 1762—Recueil de Médailles de Peuples et de Villes, 3 vols. 136 *plates, Paris,* 1763 — Mélange de diverses Médailles, pour servir de Supplément aux Recueils, 2 vols. 32 *plates, Paris,* 1765—Quatre Suppléments aux Recueils, 2 vols. 21 *plates, Paris,* 1765-67 — Deux Lettres de l'auteur, 7 *plates, Francfort,* 1770 — Additions aux neuf volumes de Recueils, 4to. *plates, Paris,* 1778—together 10 vols. 4to. *fine copy in old French calf, gilt back,* £5. 5s 1762-78

6406 —— The same, a tall copy, 10 vols. in 9, 4to. *old veau fauve extra, gilt edges,* £5. 5s 1762-78

The title to "Additions aux Neuf Volumes," possesses the engraved head of Ptolemy upon it.
Ouvrage très estimé; vendu 403 fr. en 1889.—*Brunet.* Recommended for perusal by Pinkerton; he says: "These volumes chiefly contain coins never before published, and are justly held in high esteem. The view of his plates almost equals that of the coins themselves."

6407 PELLERIN. LE BLOND, Observations sur quelques Médailles du Cabinet de Pellerin, 4to. *sd.* 10s *Paris,* 1823

6408 PEMBROKE COINS. Numismata Antiqua in tres partes divisa, collegit olim et æri incidi vivens curavit Thomas Pembrochiae et Montis Gomerici Comes, 4 parts in 1 vol. large stout 4to. 308 *plates, calf, privately printed*, 36s   1746
6409 ——— the same, folio, LARGE PAPER, *russia, presented by the Countess of Pembroke to Richard Westmacott, rare*, £2. 16s   1746
    The present copies possess the fourth part, containing the "Nummi Anglici et Scotici." Large Paper copies were priced, 1832 and 1840, Payne and Foss, £7. 7s.
6410 PIETRASZEWSKI, Numi Mohammedani, Fasc. I. continens numos Mamlukorum, Maavidarum, Ortokidarum, Regum Siciliae, etc. etc. 4to. 15 *plates, hf. calf*, 10s 6d   *Berol.* 1843
6411 POEY D'AVANT (F.) Description des Monnaies Seigneuriales Françaises composant sa Collection, Essai de Classification, 4to. 26 *plates, hf. calf, uncut, scarce*, 36s   *Fontenay-Vendée*, 1853
6412 PRAUN von dem Münzwesen älterer und neuerer Zeiten, 8vo. *bds.* 5s *Leipz.* 1784
6413 PRINSEP, Historical results of recent discoveries in Afghanistan, 8vo. 17 *plates of Bactrian coins, Inscriptions, etc. cloth*, 3s 6d   1844
6414 ——— Essays on Indian Antiquities, historic, NUMISMATIC, and palaeographic, with his Useful Tables of Indian Coinages, etc. edited with notes and additions, by THOMAS, 2 vols. 8vo. *with many engravings of Indian and Bactrian coins*, (pub. at £2. 12s 6d) *cloth*, £2. 2s   1858
6415 PROMPTUARIUM Iconum insignium hominum, subjectis eorum vitis, 2 vols. in 1, sm. 4to. *several hundred fine woodcut Portraits after Ancient and Modern Medals*, CHOICE IMPRESSIONS, *fine copy, limp vellum*, 18s   *Lugduni*, 1553
6416 PRONTUARIO DE LE MEDAGLIE de piu illustri huomini, 2 parts in 1 vol. sm. 4to. *several hundred fine woodcuts of medals, including many English portraits, with that of Mary Queen of Scots, vellum*, 10s   *Lione*, 1577
6417 RACZYNSKYI, le MEDAILLER de POLOGNE, 3 vols. 4to. 256 *fine plates, text in French and Polish ; the Supplement in Polish only, sd. a bargain*, 15s   1841-45
6418 RAOUL-ROCHETTE, Lettre au Duc de Luynes sur les Graveurs des Monnaies Grecques, 4to. *plates, sd.* 6s 6d   *Paris*, 1831
6419 RASCHE (J. C.) LEXICON universæ REI NUMARIAE VETERUM et praecipue Graecorum et Romanorum cum observationibus antiquariis, geographicis, chronologicis, historicis, criticis, et passim cum explicatione monogrammatum—Tom. I-VI, Pars I. (A—Z); Supplementorum tomi I, II, III (A—J)—together 9 vols. in 14, 8vo. QUITE COMPLETE, *as far as published, hf. bd. uncut*, £5 ; or in 13 vols. *calf, very neat*, £6.   *Lips.* 1785-1804
    In 1853, Borrell's copy fetched £8.; 1854, Gardner's copy, russia, £7. 18s.
6420 ——— Lexicon universæ Rei Numariæ, (A—Z) 6 vols. in 11, 8vo. FINE PAPER, *calf*, 25s   1785
"Un des livres les plus remarquables de la Science Numismatique, travail prodigieux de patience et d'érudition. C'est sans contredit un des ouvrages de Numismatique les plus utiles qui existent."—*Hennin*.
6421 RAMUS, Catalogus Numorum Veterum Graecorum et Latinorum Musei Regis Daniae, 2 vols. 4to. *Thick Paper*, 13 *plates, bds.* 18s   *Hafn.* 1816
    Priced, 1841, Hearne, £2. 2s; 1854, £2. 12s 6d; 1847, H. Bohn, £2. 8s; a copy sold in 1853 at Sotheby's, £2. 2s.
6422 RENAULDIN, Etudes sur les Médecins Numismatistes, 8vo. *a singularly well executed work, sd.* 5s   *Paris*, 1851
6423 RENESSE-BREIDBACH, Histoire Numismatique de l'Evêqué et Principauté de Liége, 8vo. 78 *plates, hf. cf. uncut*, 10s   *Brux.* 1831
6425 RICCIO, Monete delle Antiche Famiglie di Roma, co' suo Zecchieri dette Consolari, 4to. 55 *plates of many thousand Medals, vellum*, 12s   *Napoli*, 1836
6426 ——— the same, *seconda edizione*, 4to. 72 *plates, hf. calf*, 25s   *Napoli*, 1843
6427 ROBERT, Etudes Numismatiques sur une partie du Nord-Est de la France, roy. 4to. *Thick Paper*, 18 *plates, containing figures of about 200 early Gaulish and Frank coins*, (pub. at 55 fr) *sd.* 25s   *Metz*, 1852
6428 RUDING (R.) Annals of the Coinage of Great Britain and its Dependencies, third edition enlarged, 3 vols. 4to. *illustrated by several beautiful figures of coins on* 159 *plates, cloth*, £3. 10s   1840
6429 SABATIER, Description générale des MONNAIES BYZANTINES frappées sous les Empereurs d'Orient, depuis Arcadius jusqu' à la prise de Constantinople, 2 vols. 8vo. 70 *plates, containing many hundred coins, sd.* 36s   *Paris*, 1862
    Suite et complément de la description des Memoires de l'Empire Romain par Cohen.
6430 SAINTHILL (Richard, *of Cork*) An Olla Podrida: or Scraps, Numismatic, Antiquarian, and Literary, 2 vols. royal 8vo. *portraits and plates of coins, cloth, printed for private circulation only*, £2. 2s   1844-53

NUMISMATA, MEDALLIC HISTORY. 347

6431 SAULCY (F. de) Classification des Suites Monétaires BYZANTINES, 8vo. xvi. and 488 pp. with 4to. *Atlas of* 33 *plates* (pub. at 38s) *sd.* 20s ; *hf. calf,* 25s *Metz,* 1836
6432 —— —— Recherches sur la Numismatique JUDAÏQUE, 4to. 20 *plates of about* 200 *coins, sd.* 24s *Paris,* 1854
6433 SCILLA, Monete Pontificie sino a Clemente XI, sm. 4to. *vellum,* 8s *Romæ,* 1715
6434 SESTINI (D.) LETTERE e DISSERTAZIONI NUMISMATICHE, FIRST SERIES, Vol. I to IV: Collezione Ainslieana, *Livorno,* 1789-90—Vol. V. Collezione Ainslieana e di altri Musei, *Firenze,* 1821—Vol. VI. Museo Knobelsdorffiano, *Berlino,* 1804—Vol. VII. Museo Nazionale di Francia, *ib.* 1805—Vol. VIII. Museo Regio di Berlino e di altri Musei, *ib.* 1805—Vol. IX. Museo Ducale di Gotha e Continuazione del Museo Nationale di Francia, *ib.* 1806—together 9 vols. in 6, 4to. LARGE PAPER, *many plates, hf. bd. vellum* 1789-1806
Lettere e Dissertazioni Numismatiche, SECOND SERIES, 9 vols. 4to. *plates, sd.*
Milano, &c. 1813-20
Descriptio Numismatum e Museo olim de Camps nunc Bibl. Berol. 1808
Medaglie antiche relative alla Confederazione degli Achei, *plates Milano,* 1817
Descrizione degli Stateri Antichi, 9 *plates Firenze,* 1817
Descrizione delle Medaglie Ispane nel MUSEO HEDERVARIANO, Vol. I. II. III. e Continuazione, being 4 vols. *with* 41 *plates Firenze,* 1818-29
—— Medaglie Antiche greche, *Parte Europea,* 2 vols. 6 *plates ib.* 1830
Descrizione di molte Medaglie antiche greche in pie Musei, 14 *plates ib.* 1828
Medaglie greche del Museo di Crestiano Federigo di Danemarca, 2 *plates* 1821
Medaglie greche del MUSEO di C. d'Ottavio FONTANA di Trieste, 3 vols. 43 *plates* —Serie Consolare, 4 *plates ib.* 1822-27
Medaglie greche del MUSEO del Barone St. di CHAUDOIR, 6 *plates ib.* 1831
Together, THE WHOLE SET, 34 vols. *with many thousand engravings of Rare hitherto undescribed coins,* £10. 10s 1789-1831
As the binding of this valuable Numismatic Series would require particular care, Mr. Q. proposes to bind it into ten volumes, each with contents lettered.

6435 SESTINI, Lettere e dissertazioni Numismatiche, sopra alcune Medaglie rare della collezione Ainslieana e di altri Musei, 5 vols. large 4to. LARGE PAPER, *many plates, vellum,* 30s *Livorno,* 1789—*Roma,* 1794
6436 —— the same, *second edition,* Vol. 5, 4to. *plates, sd.* 6s *Firenze,* 1821
6437 —— Classes Generales, sive Moneta Vetus Urbium, Populorum, et Regum, ed. sec. 4to. *plates, hf. calf,* 15s *Florent.* 1821
6438 —— Descrizione d'alcune Medaglie Greche del Sign. Fontana di Trieste, 4to. 12 *plates, sd.* 6s *Firenze,* 1827
6439 —— degli Stateri Antichi illustrati con le Medaglie, 4to. 9 *plates, sd.* 7s *ib.* 1817
6440 SMYTH (Capt. *now Admiral*) Descriptive Catalogue of a Cabinet of Roman Imperial Large Brass Medals, 4to. *cloth,* 15s *Bedford, Privately printed,* 1834
6441 —— descriptive Catalogue of Roman Family Coins, belonging to the DUKE OF NORTHUMBERLAND, roy. 4to. *cloth, privately printed,* £2. 10s 1856
A very well executed and excellent work.

6442 SNELLING'S WORKS : I, View of the Silver Coin and Coinage of England, 7 *plates,* 1762—II, View of the Gold Coin and Coinage of England, 17 *plates,* 1763—III, View of the Copper Coin and Coinage of England, 8 *plates,* 1766— IV, Miscellaneous Views of the Coins struck by English Princes in France, Counterfeit Sterlings, Coins of the East India Company, West India, and Isle of Man, etc. 7 *plates,* 1769—V, View of the Origin of Jettons or Counters, Black Money and Abbey Pieces, 7 *plates,* 1769—VI, View of the Silver Coin and Coinage of Scotland, 6 *plates ;* to which are added 4 *plates* of the Gold, Billon, and Copper Coins of the same Kingdom, 1774—VII, Supplement to Simon's Essay on Irish Coins, 3 *plates*—the 7 parts complete in 1 vol. royal 4to. *all* ORIGINAL EDITIONS, *with a portrait and additional plate inserted, fine copy in russia extra,* £5. 5s 1762-74
Copies have fetched at sales so much as £11, £12, and £13.

6443 SPASSKII, Bosphor Kimmeriiskii : a Russian work on the Crimea, roy. 4to. 7 *plates containing numerous coins, bds.* 10s *Moskva,* 1846
6444 SPERLINGIUS de Nummis non cusis, sq. 8vo. *calf,* 5s *Amst.* 1700
6445 SPIES, Brandenburgische Historische Münzbelustigungen, 5 vols. sm. 4to. *numerous engravings of coins, medals, seals, etc. hf. bd.* 7s *Anspach,* 1768-74
6446 TAFURI (M.) MONETE CUFICHE battute da principi Longobardi Normanni e Suevi nel regno delle due Sicilie interpretate e illustrate dal D. Spinelli, roy. 4to. 30 *plates of Cufic coins, uncut,* 20s *Napoli,* 1844

6447 THOMAS (E.) Coins of the PATAN SULTANS of Hindustan, 8vo. 7 *plates*, 3s 1847
6448 ——— Coins of the PATAN SULTANS of Hindustan, 7 *plates*, 1847—Supplementary Contributions, *woodcuts, extremely rare, Delhi*, 1852—8vo. 16s   1847-52
6449 ——— Supplementary Contributions, *reprinted from the Delhi edition, but without the engravings, very rare*, 4s   London, 1852
6450 ——— Coins of the Kings of Ghazni, A.D. 961-1171, with Supplement, 8vo. 3 *plates, sd.* 3s 6d   1848
6451 ——— the same, 1848—Supplementary Contributions, *plate*, 1859—2 parts, 8vo. 5s   1848-59

Mr. Thomas was for several years "The British Resident" at Delhi, and had there peculiar advantages in collecting and describing the Coins of the Mohammedan Rulers of India. His works are of the greatest historical value. See above PRINSEP. The great merits of his literary labours are pointed out in a Review of that work, attributed to MAX MÜLLER, in "The Guardian," Oct. 20, 1858.

6452 TYCHSEN, OPERA: De Numis Hebraicis, 1791; Res Numaria Muhammed. 1794; De Arabum ponderibus, 1800—the 3 books, 8vo. 5s   1791-94
6453 VAILLANT, Arsacidarum et Achæmenidarum Imperium, 2 vols. 4to. *engravings of Parthian, Bithynian, etc. calf,* 8s   Paris, 1725
6454 ——— Numismata Imperatorum Romanorum, a Julio Caesare ad Postumum, cum appendice, 3 vols. 4to. *plates, a fine copy in vellum,* 15s   Romæ, 1743
6455 VAN LOON, Histoire Metallique des PAYS-BAS, depuis Charles V. (1555) jusqu'à 1716, 5 vols. folio, *several hundred fine engravings of Coins and Medals by Houbraken, including many English and Scotch, calf, the Marquis of Donegal's copy,* £2. 10s   La Haye, 1732-37
6456 VERKADE (P.) Muntboek bevattende de Namen en Afbeeldingen van Munten, geslagen in de zeven voormalig vereenigde NEDERLANDSCHE PROVINCIEN, etc. 2 vols. 4to. 228 *plates, bds.* £2.   Delft, Schiedam, 1831-48
6457 VELASQUEZ, Ensayo sobre los Alphabetos de las Letras desconocidas, que se encuentran en las Antiguas Medallas de España, 4to. 20 *plates,* 6s Madrid, 1752
6458 VERGARA, Monete del Regno di Napoli da Roggiero sino a Carlo VI. Imp. (1100—1700), fol. *numerous engravings of Coins, old calf neat,* 24s Roma, 1716
6459 VERMIGLIOLI della Zecca e delle Monete Perugine, large 4to. *plates, sd.* 9s 1816
6460 (VETTORI) IL FIORINO D'ORO antico, da un Accademico Etrusco, 4to. xviii. and 540 pp. *numerous cuts of Coins, sd.* 20s   Firenze, 1738
6461 VIRTUOSO'S COMPANION and Coin Collector's Guide, complete, 3 vols. in 2, 12mo. 240 *plates, containing several hundred Tradesmen's Tokens, etc. with Index of names, calf gilt,* 36s   M. Denton, 1795-96
The complete set should have 240 plates, 1795-97.

6462 WADDINGTON, Voyage en Asie-Mineure, 8vo. 11 *plates of coins, hf. calf,* 6s 1853
6463 WILSON'S ARIANA ANTIQUA: A Descriptive Account of the Antiquities and Coins of AFGHANISTAN, with a Memoir on the Buildings called Topes, 4to. *map and* 36 *plates of Bactrian Antiquities and Coins, cloth,* 36s; *half vellum,* £2. 1841
The best account of the Ancient Bactria, or Modern Afghanistan, of equal importance to the Scholar and to the Antiquary. This valuable work is out of print, and will not be reprinted, the plates being destroyed.

6464 ZOEGA, Numi Aegyptii Imperatorii prostantes in Museo Borgiano Velitris, 4to. 22 *fine plates, containing about* 200 *Medals, Coins, etc. calf,* 12s Romae, 1787
6465 CATALOGUES OF COIN SALES: a Collection of 102 PRICED English Sale Catalogues, bound in 14 vols. 8vo. *with an* INDEX, *hf. calf,* £6. 10s   1841-55
These Catalogues comprise all the chief collections of Coins recently dispersed in England; and they form a true key to their value and rarity. It is difficult now to obtain such a large suite of priced Catalogues.

6466 ——— another Collection, bound in 3 vols. 8vo. *hf. blue morocco, most of them with prices and purchasers' names,* £2. 10s   1818-44
To give some idea of the extent of this collection a short list of contents is here subjoined.
CONTENTS:—Henderson's English, Scotch, and Irish Coins, *with prices and purchasers' names*, 1818—Earl of Morton's Greek and Roman Coins, *with prices and purchasers' names*, 1830—Broad's Greek and Roman Coins, *priced*, 1838—Steuart's Greek and Roman Coins, *priced*, 1840—Baron Bolland's Coins and Medals, *prices and purchasers' names*, 1841—John Knight's Greek and Roman Coins and Medals, *prices and purchasers' names*, 1842—British Museum Duplicates, 1842—MATTHEW YOUNG's Library and very extensive, highly valuable, and important collection of Coins and Medals, *with prices and purchasers' names*, 1838-42.

6467 GOETZSCHE Sammlung von Münzen verkauft November, 1792, sm. 8vo. 5s 1792
6468 MILLER (Joseph) Catalogue of his Coins and Medals, etc. sold at Sotheby's, February 1829, 8vo. *with the prices and purchasers' names neatly written in, hf. calf,* 5s   1829
6469 ROGERS (Sam.) Catalogues of his Works of Art, and of Greek and Roman Coins, etc. sold at Christie's, April and May, 1856, in 1 vol. 8vo. *hf. morocco,* 6s 1856
6470 THOMAS (Thos.) Catalogue of his Collection of Coins and Medals, of his Library, Prints, and Bronzes, in 1 vol. 8vo. *with the prices and purchasers' names, hf. morocco, gilt top, uncut,* 18s   1843

6471 TILL (W.) Catalogue of his Collection of Coins and Medals, sold at Sotheby's, 1845-46, 5 parts in 1 vol. 8vo. *with prices and purchasers' names neatly written in, hf. morocco, gilt top, uncut*, 10s   1845-46

6472 TRATTLE, Catalogue of his collection of Coins and Medals, sold at Sotheby's, 1832, 8vo. *prices and purchasers' names in neat MS. sd.* 7s   1832

6473 —— the same, with Catalogues of Paintings, Plate, etc. *a Fine Paper copy, interleaved, and illustrated with 2 portraits of Trattle, one a proof before letters, and many engravings of Coins and Medals,* 3 parts bound in 1 vol. 4to. *hf. morocco, gilt top, uncut,* £2. 2s   1832

6474 TYSSEN (Samuel) Catalogue of his entire Museum, Coins and Medals, Books and MSS., Portraits, Prints, Antiquities, and Curiosities, with Index, sold at Sotheby's, in 2 vols. 8vo. *portrait,* FINE PAPER, *with the prices and purchasers' names neatly written on interleaved pages, green morocco, gilt top, uncut,* VERY RARE, £2. 16s   1800

This copy fetched at Mr. Combe's sale, 1827, £2. 7s; cost a former proprietor £5. 13s; and was sold at Thomas' sale for £4. 12s.

6475 YOUNG (Matthew) Sale Catalogue, in 9 parts, of his exceedingly valuable and extensive Collection of Coins, 8vo. *prices and purchasers' names neatly written in, J. T. Brockett's copy in hf. russia, uncut,* 20s   1839-41

FINE ARTS, BOOKS OF PRINTS, PAINTING.

6476 ABEKEN. Mittel Italien vor den Zeiten römischer Herrschaft, 8vo. 11 *large plates of Early Italian Art, sd.* 6s   Stuttg. 1843

6477 Africa. SMITH's Thirty different Drafts of Guinea, by W. SMITH, Surveyor to yᵉ Royal African Company of England, oblong folio, *large map of Africa and* 30 *Views by Gray, calf,* 20s   London, J. Clark, s.a.

The map is dedicated to Sir Isaac Newton.

6478 AGINCOURT'S (Seroux d') Histoire de l'Art par les Monumens, depuis sa Décadence au quatrième Siècle, jusqu'à son Renouvellement au seizième, 6 vols. in 3, impl. folio, *with* 325 *plates,* (pub. at £45.) bds. £10.; or, *hf. bd. red* MOROCCO *extra, gilt edges,* £14.   Paris, 1823

6479 —— MONUMENTS OF ART; Denkmaeler der Architectur, Sculptur und Malerei vorzugsweise in Ialien, vom IV. bis zum XVI. Jahrhundert, royal folio, 328 *beautiful plates, with* 3835 *engravings, comprising an immense amount of Detail, with text, in* 4to. *hf. morocco,* £2.   Frankfurt, 1846

6480 —— The History of Art by its Monuments, from its Decline in the Fourth Century, to its Restoration in the Sixteenth Century; with 3335 Subjects on 328 plates, Architecture, Sculpture, Painting; translated from the French by OWEN JONES, 3 vols. in 1, folio, (sells for £5. 5s) *half russia,* £2. 10s   1850

6481 —— STORIA dell' ARTE col mezzo dei Monumenti, edizione prima italiana, con aggiunte, 6 vols. in 4, royal folio, *with* 325 *plates re-engraved, and the text improved, hf. calf,* UNCUT, £5. 15s   Milano, 1824-25

The division of this grand work is into three parts: *Architecture.* 73 plates; II. *Sculpture,* 51 plates; III. *Painting,* 204 plates. To Antiquaries and lovers of the Fine Arts, this work is indispensable; it connects the works of Winckelman and Cicognara, and forms with them a most interesting series.

"This fine work was the first in which the idea of exhibiting the Progress of Art, by a series of its noblest monuments, was perfectly carried out. By a series of accurate Engravings from celebrated Monuments, we trace the transitions of Art from the classic period to our own times. Sculpture Painting, the Art of Illumination, and the Art of Engraving on Wood, on Gems, and on Medals, are similarly represented.

"It is a work that has long been sought and prized by all who could afford the high price at which only it was to be procured. This English Edition will now be within the reach of all, and it is anticipated that no Library, Architect, Painter, Sculptor, or any one connected with the Fine Arts, will be longer without such a work."

AMMAN (Jost) see post "Woodcuts."

6482 ANGELICO (Fra.) S. MARCO, Convento dei Padri Predicatori in Firenze, illustrato e inciso principalmente nei dipinti del B. Giovanni Angelico; con la VITA dello stesso pittore, e un sunto storico del convento medesimo, del P. Vinc. MARCHESE, impl. folio, *with* 40 *beautiful plates,* INDIA PROOFS, *hf. bd. red morocco, gilt top, uncut,* £5. 15s   Firenze, 1853

6483 ANNALS of the Fine Arts, for 1816-20, 5 vols. 8vo. *fine portraits and plates, hf. russia,* 15s   1817-20

6484 ARCHAEOLOGISCHE ZEITUNG, herausg. von GERHARD, Jahrgang 1-16, in 3 SERIES: Series I. 4 vols.—Series II. 2 vols.—Series III. with the additional Title: "Denkmaeler, Forschungen und Berichte," Vols. 1-10—together 16 vols. 4to. 192 *plates, (subscription price* 48 *Thalers), new and clean in parts, from W. Hamilton's library,* £5.   Berlin, 1843-58

6485 **ARMOUR, Ancient and Mediaeval.** Meubles et Armures Anciennes et du Moyen Age, large folio, 144 *plates of every kind of Armour, and elegant specimens of Old Furniture*, no text was published with this work, *hf. bd. uncut,* £2. 4s *Paris, Veith and Hauser, s. a.*
The Armour has chiefly been taken from the Cabinets of Prince Soltykoff at St. Petersburg, of M. Baron, of M. Soulage, and other private collections.

6486 CLAESEN, Recueil d'Ornements et de sujets pour être appliqués à l'Ornementation des Armes, impl. 4to. 32 *plates of elaborate designs for Ornamental Arms, Guns, Pistols, many of the Ornaments equally applicable to other embellishments,* hf. morocco, 25s *Liege,* (? 1858)

6487 HEWITT'S Ancient Armour and Weapons in Europe, 3 vols. 8vo. *numerous plates and woodcuts,* (pub. at £2. 10s) *new in cloth,* £2. 2s 1860

6488 LOSTELNEAU, le Mareschal de Bataille, contenant le Maniment des Armes, les Evolutions, etc. folio, 48 *fine plates of Mousquetaires in their full Costume practising their Musket Exercise, calf, gilt edges,* 32s *Paris,* 1647

6489 ARTAUD DE MONTOR, Peintres Primitifs, collection de Tableaux rapportée d'Italie et publiée par lui, reproduite sous la direction de Challamel, roy. 4to. 60 *large plates beautifully executed in Lithography on India paper,* (pub. at 60 fr. sd.) *hf. bd.* 32s *Paris,* 1843

6490 ——— the same, 4to. *calf extra, gilt edges,* £2. 1843

6491 ARTS SOMPTUAIRES (les) Histoire du Costume et de l'Ameublement et des Arts et Industries qui s'y rattachent, 3 vols. 4to. *several hundred beautiful plates, in* RICH COLOURS, (pub. at 400 fr.) *sewed,* £12. 12s 1854-59

6492 ARNETH, Monumente des Münz-und Antiken-Cabenettes in Wien, royal folio, *with* 25 *plates of* ANTIQUE CAMEOS, *hf. morocco,* 18s *Wien,* 1849

6493 ARUNDEL SOCIETY PUBLICATIONS, from the commencement in 1849 to 1855 incl. *quite complete,* VERY RARE, £10. 1849-55
For a detailed list see ante, No. 163.

6494 VASARI'S Life of Giovanni Angelico da Fiesole, translated by Bezzi, impl. 8vo. 1 *plate of Angelico's Monument, and* 20 *fine engravings on India paper, of his works,* £2. 2s 1850

6495 GIOTTO and his Works in Padua, by Ruskin, part I. impl. 8vo. *sd.* 5s 1854

6496 WYATT'S Notices of Sculpture in Ivory, 4to. 9 *photographic plates of print, hf. bound, rare,* 20s 1856

6497 ART TREASURES of the United Kingdom; consisting of Examples from the Manchester Exhibition of 1857, with descriptive Essays by OWEN JONES, DIGBY WYATT, A. W. FRANKS, WARING, J. C. ROBINSON, and G. SCHARF, folio, 100 *extremely beautiful* PLATES, MOSTLY IN GOLD AND COLOURS, *executed in the highest style of chromo-lithography,* by F. Bedford, (pub. at £19. 19s) *gilt cloth,* £7. 7s 1857-8
As originally intended, this work is THE MOST BEAUTIFUL EVER PRODUCED in colours. The series of one hundred plates has been produced in the highest style of chromo lithography, with all the advantages of the present advanced state of the art. As the selection was made from the most choice and prominent subjects of the Art Treasures' Exhibition, it follows that, whilst the collection consisted of the *chef-d'œuvres* of the art of the entire kingdom, this work contains none but the most precious gems that could be gathered therefrom. Only 750 copies were printed, and the stones have been destroyed, so no more can be produced.

6498 BAGLIONE, Vite de' Pittori, Scultori, Architetti ed Intagliatori, e Vita di Salvator Rosa da Passari, 4to. *vellum,* 9s *Napoli,* 1733

6499 BARDON, Histoire universelle traitée relativement aux Arts de peindre et de sculpter, ou Tableaux de l'histoire, 3 vols. 12mo. *old red morocco extra, gilt edges, "exemplaire de Madame Elizabeth de France," with the royal arms of France on the sides,* 25s *Paris,* 1769

6500 BARTHOLI (P. S.) Picturæ Antiquæ Cryptarum Romanarum et Sepulcro Nasonum, illustratæ a J. P. Bellorio et M. A. Causseo, editio nova, cum APPENDICE nunquam antehac edita, 4 parts in 1 vol. impl. folio, 94 plates, *hf. russia,* 15s *Romae,* 1791

6501 BARTSCH, Catalogue Raisonné de toutes les Estampes qui forment l'Oeuvre de REMBRANDT, et de ses imitateurs, 2 vols. sm. 8vo. *portraits and plates, hf. bd.* 20s *Vienne,* 1797

6502 BARTSCH, LE PEINTRE GRAVEUR, 21 vols. 8vo. *with the* 16 *extra etchings, calf neat, an* ORIGINAL *copy,* £10. 10s *Vienne,* 1803-21
Cet ouvrage, dont l'auteur est mort à Vienne, le 21 Aout, 1820, est certainement le plus exact qu'on possède en ce genre. Les quelques exemplaires qu'on avait pu compléter au moyen de la réimpression des premiers volumes étant déjà disparus du Commerce, cet ouvrage est devenu de nouveau très rare.

FINE ARTS, BOOKS OF PRINTS, PAINTING.

6503 BARONIAL HALLS and Ancient Picturesque Edifices of England, with Descriptions by S. C. Hall, 2 vols. in 1, stout impl. 4to. *71 large and finely executed plates, from Drawings by Hurdinge, Cattermole, Prout, Muller, Fairholt, and other eminent Artists,* PROOFS, *also many woodcuts in the text, antique morocco, gilt edges,* £4. 4s 1844, etc.
The Drawings of this attractive work are executed in the highest style of Art, by the most eminent Living Artists, and comprise the most ancient Castles and Mansions now existing in England; it was published at £14. 14s.

6503*BAUDICOUR (Prosper de) Le Peintre-Graveur français continué, ou Catalogue raisonné des estampes gravées par les peintres et les dessinateurs de l'école française nés dans le dix-huitième siècle; *ouvrage faisant suite au Peintre-Graveur français de M. Robert Dumesnil,* 2 vols. 8vo. *sd.* 10s 6d *Paris,* 1859-61

6504 BAUR (Jo. Gul., *pictor*) Iconographia, 4 vols. in 1, oblong folio, *portrait, 4 titles, and 146 fine plates by* MELCHIOR KYSELL, *comprising two series of the Life and Passion of Christ, Views, Ports, Palaces, Gardens, and Miscellaneous Compositions, forming the* COMPLETE WORKS, FINE IMPRESSIONS, *blue* MOROCCO, *gilt edges, rare in this complete state,* £3. 16s *Augspurg, M. Kysel,* 1682
Part I. the Passion and Resurrection of Christ, and emblematic engravings, 37 plates; part II. the Birth, Life and Miracles of Christ, 36 plates; part III. Views in Italy, Historical pieces, 36 plates; part IV. Sea Ports, Gardens, Palaces, principally in Italy, 37 plates.

6505 **BELGIUM**, STROOBANT, MONUMENTS D'ARCHITECTURE ET DE SCULPTURE en Belgique, dessinés d' après nature et lithographiés en plusieurs teintes par F. Stroobant; avec des notices historiques et archéologiques par F. Stappaerts, 2 vols. folio, *containing 63 beautiful tinted plates of Exteriors and Interiors of Buildings in* ANTWERP, LIEGE, NAMUR, BRABANT AND FLANDERS, (pub. at 300 francs in parts) *whole bound impressed foreign morocco, gilt edges,* £6. *Bruxelles,* 1853

6506 BERBRUGGER, Algérie historique, pittoresque et monumentale. Recueil de vues, monuments, combats, cérémonies, costumes et portraits dessinés dans les provinces d'Alger, Oran, Bone et Constantine, avec texte historique et descriptif, 5 parts in 3 vols. atlas folio, *beautiful illuminated title,* 149 *fine plates in tints, comprising Views, Antiquities, Costume, Battle Pieces, etc. the Botany in colours, and* 21 *vignettes, hf. morocco,* £6. 1843

6507 BERJEAU, Varieties of Dogs, as found in old Sculpture, Pictures, Engravings and Books, sq. 8vo. 52 *plates, containing upwards of* 100 *specimens, new in cloth,* 10s 6d 1863

6508 BERNINO, *Scultore*, Vita, da Baldinucci, 4to. *portr. and 9 plates, hf. bd.* 6s 1682

6509 BERTELLI, Vere Imagini et descritioni delle piu nobilli Città del Mondo, 4to. *engraved title and 22 double plates of Cities, old calf, rare,* 18s *Venetiis,* 1572

6510 **BIBLE ILLUSTRATIONS:** BIBLE (La Sainte) en *Latin* et en *François,* avec des notes, 4 vols. folio, *illustrated with a fine series of several hundred large* ENGRAVINGS *by Picart, Hoet, Houbraken, Poole, etc. with explanations under each in* SIX LANGUAGES, *La Haye, Hondt,* 1728, *calf gilt,* £2. 16s *Paris,* 1715
Cost the late J. J. de Hochepied Baron Larpent 200 francs.

6511 FIGURES historiques de la Vie de Jesus-Christ, 18mo. 189 *pretty woodcuts, hf. bd.* 10s *Lyon,* 1672

6512 ICONES BIBLICAE: Figgers of the Bible in who (sic) almost every History of the Holy Scriptures are described, with descriptions in Latin, French, German, English and Dutch Quatrains, 3 vols. in 1, small obl. 4to. *about* 500 *pretty plates, fine impressions, blue morocco,* £2. 10s *Amsterdam, Cornelis Danckertz,* 1648-59

6513 KÜSELL (MELCHIOR) Icones Biblicæ Veteris ac Novi Testamenti, sm. 4to. *consisting of* 242 *beautiful engravings by this very pleasing artist,* BRILLIANT IMPRESSIONS, *red morocco extra, gilt edges,* £6. 10s *Augsburgh,* 1680
Fort belles épreuves. Le volume se compose ainsi: Vieux Testament, 1 frontisp., 1 titre gravé, 51 pl., 1 titre, 51 pl., 1 titre, 50 pl., 1 fleuron.—Nouveau Testament, 1 frontisp., 1 titre, 47 pl., 1 titre, 42 pl., 1 fleuron. Ce charmant volume a été vendu 299 fr. chez la Vallière.

6514 LAVATER, Jesus Messias, 5 vols. 8vo. *with* 72 *fine plates by* CHODOWIECKI, *calf gilt,* 7s 6d *Zürich,* 1783

6515 NATALI, EVANGELICÆ HISTORIÆ IMAGINES, fol. *text and* 153 *beautiful engravings, illustrative of the Life of Christ, and of the New Testament, by the celebrated* WIERXES, *brilliant impressions, blue morocco, fine copy,* £9. *Antv.* 1594
Dawson Turner's copy fetched in 1853, £15. 10s.
The Plates are 153 in number, designed by Martin de Vos, Bern. Passer Romanus, and engraven by Adr. Collaert, Ant. J. and Jer. Wierx, and others. This copy is the FIRST EDITION with the text, and has brilliant impressions of the Plates in their original state.
Three later issues appeared; Antv. 1595, 1596 and 1607; they are as might be expected only the shadow of the genuine book.

6516 SCHEUCHZER, PHYSIQUE SACRÉE, ou Histoire Naturelle de la Bible, traduite du Latin, 8 vols. folio, *fine impressions of the* 750 *plates, old red morocco, gilt leaves,* £10. 10s *Amst.* 1732-37
Priced, 1825, Thorpe, *morocco*, £31. 10s; 1837, Payne and Foss, *morocco*, £24.
A most beautiful picture book of the Bible, containing 750 fine plates of scenes recorded in the Holy Scriptures, of Trees, Plants, Animals, Fossils, etc.

6517 SICHEM (Christ. à) Historien ende Prophecien, mit der H. Schrifturen, thick 12mo. *with upwards of* 500 *woodcuts of Biblical Illustrations, first impressions, fine copy in russia, gilt edges,* 25s Antwerpen, P. J. Faets, 1644

6518 STIMMERI (Tobiæ) Novæ Sacrorum Bibliorum figuræ, versibus Latinis et Germanicis exposita, sm. 8vo. *brilliant impressions of the numerous beautiful woodcuts, very fine copy, old vellum, rare,* £2. Strassburg, 1590
"Recueil des 173 planches gravées en bois. On en fait assez de cas, sous le rapport de la composition."—*Brunet.*

6519 VIE (la) de nostre Seigneur Jesu Christ, par figures, selon le texte des quattre Evangelistes, avec toutes les Evangiles, Epistres et Propheties de toute l'année, "par grace et privilege de la Majesté Imperiale," 12mo. lettres gothiques, *several hundred fine woodcuts by an eminent French artist, olive morocco extra, gilt edges,* 36s
The volume ends "Le jour dedacesse, Apoca. XXI. a;" the colophon being apparently wanting. The prologue is signed "Esprit dempres *Gand, aux Chartreus, les xxv de Decembre l'am MDXXXVII.*"

6520 BIRCH'S (Sam.) History of Ancient Pottery, 2 vols. 8vo. *with coloured plates and numerous woodcuts, cloth,* 27s 1858

6521 BLAKIANA. The Life of William Blake, in MS. extracted from Cunningham's Lives of the Painters, ILLUSTRATED *with numerous specimens of his works of most singular design and execution, including portions of his* "Songs of Innocence and Experience;" "Book of Ahania;" "Europe, a Prophecy;" "Books of Thel and Urizen;" "Gates of Paradise;" "The Elements;" "Canterbury Pilgrimage," *the large and scarce print, etc. in all* 114 *plates, some duplicates in different states and tinted by the artist: also* 14 *portraits of the artist, his friends, and contemporaries, including* A PORTRAIT OF THOMAS HAYLEY, AN ORIGINAL DRAWING, BY W. BLAKE: *a Manuscript Index to the Songs of Innocence, believed to be in the autograph of the artist: list of Original Drawings and Sketches sold by auction in* 1862, *with the prices realised, etc. in* 1 *vol. impl.* 4to. *hf. bound, crimson morocco. A very rare, curious, and exceedingly interesting Collection,* £21. 1790, etc.

6522 BLAKE (William) THE BOOK OF THEL, *Motto, title, and* 6 *designs,* 1789— VISIONS OF THE DAUGHTERS OF ALBION, 11 *designs,* 1793—*the two pieces in one volume,* roy. 4to. *olive morocco, gilt edges, by C. Lewis,* £15. 15s 1789-93
⁂ The cuts in both pieces coloured in the artist's peculiar style.

6523 BLAKE (W.) Illustrations to Dante, 7 *plates, designed and engraved by W. Blake, with quotations from F. Pollock's Version of Dante, very neatly written, portrait of the Artist by Schiavonetti, and two of Dante, inserted, half crimson morocco gilt,* £3. 10s s. a.

6524 BLOEM-HOF (den) van de Nederlantsche Jeught, obl. sm. 4to. Dutch Sonnets, Epigrams, and Songs, *with* 12 *fine plates, calf,* 25s *Amst.* 1608

6525 BOCK (Dr. F.) Geschichte der Liturgischen Gewänder des Mittelalters, Vol. I. thick 8vo. 47 *carefully executed illuminated plates of Woven Stuffs, Silks, etc. hf. calf,* 15s Bonn, 1859

6526 BÖTTIGER's Ideen zur Kunst-Mythologie, 2 vols. 8vo. *Fine Paper, plates of Greek and Roman Art, bds.* 6s Dresden, 1826-36

6527 BOLOGNA'S BAS-RELIEFS IN FLORENCE: a very beautifully engraved Series of 12 large plates by VASCELLINI, *comprising Bas-Reliefs by G. Bologna, Cellini, and Ghiberti existing in Florence.* obl. atlas fol. *hf. vell.* 15s Firenze, 1782

6528 **Book-Binding.** CUNDALL on Ornamental Art, applied to ancient and modern Bookbinding, 4to. 8 *plates, further illustrated by* 44 *additional plates, in gold and colours, chiefly copies of Grolier's bindings, hf. red morocco,* £2. 10s 1848

6529 BORGIA, de Cruce Vaticana, cum Ritu Salutationis Crucis, Syr. et Lat. sm. folio, *curious plates of Crosses, hf. bd.* 7s Romae, 1779

6530 BOSSUIT. CABINET de l'Art de Schulpture, par Francis van Bossuit exécuté en Yvoire, ou ébauché en terre, gravées d'après les desseins de GRAAT par POOL, 4to. 104 *leaves entirely engraved, with about* 150 *engravings of Sculptures in ivory, frontispiece, two portraits, the text to these being in Dutch, French, and English, fine copy in bright calf extra, gilt edges,* £2. 2s *Amst.* 1727

FINE ARTS, BOOKS OF PRINTS, PAINTING. 353

6531 BOTTA'S NINEVEH: Monument de Ninive découvert et décrit par Botta, mesuré et dessiné, par Flandin, 5 vols. atlas folio, *with 871 magnificent plates of Architecture, Sculpture, and Inscriptions*, (pub. at £110. and usually sold for 50 guineas), *hf. bd.* morocco *extra, gilt edges*, £32. 10s *Par.* 1849-50
6531* ——— the same work, with all the plates on India Paper, 5 vols. elephant folio, *hf. bd.* morocco, *gilt edges, the only copy ever offered for sale in England*, £40. 1849-50

This magnificent work was published by order of the French Government, and under the direction of a committee of the Institute. Contents, Vols. I. and II. Architecture and Sculpture, 168 plates; Vols. III. and IV. Inscriptions, 203 plates; Vol. V. Text.

"To Botta is due the honour of having found the first Assyrian Monument."—*Layard.*

The cuneiform system of letters was a species of picture writing, invented, not by the Semitic inhabitants of Babylon, but by those who preceded them. This writing was, however, reduced by the Semitic race to letters, and adapted to the articulation of their language. Their mode of writing consisted of several elements. There was the ideographic, or picture-writing, and the phonetic, which was equivalent to the alphabet of their language. The cuneiform inscriptions were divided into three branches, Persian, Scythic, and Assyrian.

6532 **Brabant:** SANDER'S Brabant: Groot Toneel des Hertogdoms van Brabant, large folio, *with upwards of 110 large engravings of Cathedrals, Views of Towns, Portraits, etc. calf gilt*, 15s *Graavenh.* 1727

See also Le Roy.

6532*BREITKOPF, Ursprung der Spielkarten, Anfang der Holzschneidekunst, etc. 2 vols. 4to. 14 *plates, Vol. II. containing the History of Penmanship, Woodcarving, Painting, Mosaics, Frescoes. Miniatures, etc. hf. bd.* 16s *Leipz.* 1784-1801
6533 ——— the same, 2 vols. 1784-1801—Erfindung der Buchdruckerkunst, 1799— Ueber Bibliographie, 1793—in 1 vol. 4to. *calf*, 25s 1784-1801
6534 Brisbane's Anatomy of Painting, folio, *a double series of 6 plates with keys in outline, with Flaxman's autograph, bds.* 15s 1769
6535 BRITTON'S Works: ARCHITECTURAL ANTIQUITIES of Great Britain, 5 vols. *with 360 engravings by* Le Keux *of the most interesting Ancient Edifices of this country*, 1827-26—Billings' Architectural Antiquities of Durham, 64 *plates, Durham*, 1846—BRITTON'S CATHEDRAL ANTIQUITIES of England, 14 parts (Canterbury, York, Salisbury, Norwich, Oxford, Winchester, Lichfield, Hereford, Wells, Exeter, Worcester, Peterborough, Gloucester, and Bristol) in 5 vols. 311 *plates by Le Keux*, 1836—Wild's Cathedral Church of Lincoln, by Britton, 16 *large plates*, 1837—Billings' Architectural Illustrations of Carlisle Cathedral, etc. 50 *plates*, 1840—Billings' Geometric Tracery from Carlisle Cathedral, 19 *plates*, 1842—Billing's Cathedral Church at Durham, 75 *plates*, 1854—together 15 vols. in 13, 4to. 895 *fine plates, with vignettes,* (*pub. at about* £76.) *a handsome uniform set in hf. morocco, uncut, top edges gilt,* £15. 15s 1826-43
6536 BRONGNIART, Traité des Arts Céramiques ou des poteries considérées dans leur pratique et leur théorie, 2e *édition*, 2 vols. 8vo. 1548 pp. *and* 4to. *atlas of* 60 *plates of Vases, Jars, &c. showing also the Machinery and the Mechanical Process in the Manufacture of Pottery in Ancient and Modern Times, hf. bd.* morocco, 38s 1854

The best book on Pottery. The first edition, on Vellum Paper, 1844, sold, 1854, at Sotheby's, King Louis Philippe's copy, £6. 15s.

6536*BRONGNIART et Riocreux, Description Methodique du Musée Ceramique de la Manufacture Royale de Porcelain de Sevres, avec Table des Monogrammes, 4to. *the plates finished in colours, hf. morocco, gilt tops, uncut*, £5. 15s *Paris,* 1845

In 1857 Utterson's copy fetched £6. 2s 6d; in 1859, Lady Webster's, £7. 10s.

6537 BRULLIOT, Dictionnaire des Monogrammes, Marques figurées, Lettres initiales, Noms abrégés, etc. des Peintres, Graveurs, Sculpteurs, etc. 4to. *best edition, many cuts of Monograms, hf. bd.* morocco, £2. *Munich,* 1832
6538 BRYAN'S Dictionary of Painters and Engravers, containing their Lives, a list of their principal works, with Critical Analyses, their Cyphers, Monograms, Marks, &c. from the earliest period, 2 vols. 4to. *original edition, bds.* 28s 1816
6539 BUCK'S (S. and N.) Antiquities; or, Venerable Remains of above 400 Castles, Monasteries, Palaces, etc. in England and Wales, 2 vols. royal folio—Views of nearly 100 Cities and Towns in England and Wales, royal folio—together 3 vols. *old calf*, £18. 1774
6540 BURGKMAIER'S (Hans) Turnierbuch, herausgegeben von J. von Hefner, folio, *coloured title and* 35 *fine large plates of* Knights in Armour, *richly executed by hand in* gold and colours, *hf. bd.* morocco, £3. 16s *Frankfurt,* 1853

2 A

6541 BURNET (John) PRACTICAL HINTS ON PAINTING, viz.: On Composition, Chiaroscuro and Colouring, *portrait and 38 beautiful etchings*, 1827—On Light and Shade in Painting, *illustrated by examples from the Italian, Flemish, and Dutch Schools*, 39 *fine plates*, 1826—On Colour in Painting, 23 *coloured plates and 8 plain, India Proofs*, 1827--An Essay on the Education of the Eye, with reference to Painting, *illustrated by 7 copper-plates and woodcuts*, 1837—together 4 vols. royal 4to. LARGE PAPER, ORIGINAL INDIA PROOFS, (pub. at £7. 7s unbound) *hf. bd. green morocco, gilt tops, uncut*, £5.   1826-37

"Mr. Burnet has just completed his 'Practical hints on Painting;' and a more interesting Work has not come under our notice. In this last part of it, he has shewn with great ability that, as in composition and in chiaroscuro, so also in the general management of colour in a picture, the great masters proceeded upon principles, varying, yet harmonious; and which, while they occasionally seemed to be in direct hostility to one another, always tended to the same triumphant results. To the professor these remarks must be invaluable; and the library of no lover of the Fine Arts can henceforth be considered complete without Mr. Burnet's Work."—*Literary Gazette.*

6542 BUSCEMI, Notizie della Basilica di San Pietro, detta la Cappella Regia, 4to. *frontispiece and 17 plates, hf. calf*, 10s   *Palermo*, 1840

6543 CAMPO SANTO DI PISA: Pitture a Fresco del Campo Santo, disegnate da Rossi ed incise da Lasinio figlio, roy. folio, 46 *fine plates, with text, bds. entirely a new edition*, £2. 8s   *Firenze*, 1832

The Campo Santo was erected in the fourteenth century, and its pictures, consisting of Scriptural subjects, will always be interesting as shewing the state of the art in Italy at that early period. Raphael and other great painters of Italy are said to have studied them attentively--indeed some of the finest compositions of the succeeding period will be found mainly indebted to them. Lanzi, in his *History of Painting*, says, "The Campo Santo, which does high honour to the magnificence of the Pisans, would be an inestimable museum, if the pictures there, executed by Giotto, by Memmi, by Stefano Florentino, by Buffalmacco, by Antonio Veneziano, by the two Orcagni, by Spinello Aretino, and by Laurati had been carefully preserved; but the greatest number have unfortunately been injured by damp."

6544 CAMPO (A.) CREMONA FIDELISSIMA CITTA, e nobilissima Colonia de i Romani rappresentata in disegno col suo Contado ed illustrata d'una breve Istoria delle cose piu notabili apartenenti ad esso et i RITRATTI Naturali de i Duchi e Duchesse di Milano e Compendio delle loro Vite, folio, *plates and* PORTRAITS *of the Dukes of Milan by Caracci, calf extra, gilt edges*, £2. 4s   *Cremona*, 1585

Priced, 1847, Bohn, £3. 3s to £3. 10s; 1848, Payne and Foss, £5. 5s; 1856, Weigel, 30 th. It fetched: La Valliere, 172 fr.; Edwards' £5. 5s.

The portraits in this volume are engraved by Augustine Caracci, and include those of the Dukes and Duchesess of Milan, Charles V. and Philip II. of Spain, and his four successive wives, among whom is that of Mary, Queen of England.

Editio Cremonensis admodum rara est, et pretiosa. Vid. *Catalogus Historicorum* Fresnolo-Mencken, p. 369. *Biblioth. Historico* Struvio-Buderiana, p. 1395. et Nic. Franc. Haym *Notiz. de Libri rari*, p. 59, cujus hæc sunt verba: "Questa edizione è rarissima, e stimata per gl' intagli in rame d'Agostino Caracci. Fu anche impressa in Milano 1643, in 4. ma e di gran lunga inferiore all' edizione in fol.

6545 CANINA (Cav. L.) Descrizione della Antica città di Veji, royal folio, *with* 44 *plates of Etruscan Art, cloth*, £2.   *Roma*, 1847

Only a few copies were printed for presents.

6546 CANOVA'S WORKS, THE ORIGINAL EXTREMELY RARE ITALIAN EDITION: Recueil de Statues, Groupes, Busts, Mausolées, Colosses, et Monumens de tout genre, executés par CANOVA, dessinés et gravés sous les yeux de l'auteur a Rome, elephant folio, (meas. 26 inches by 32), *portrait, four printed leaves of French text, and* 71 MOST MAGNIFICENT PLATES, BRILLIANT IMPRESSIONS, *perhaps the finest and most beautifully executed work of the graver produced during this century, hf. morocco*, £15.   *Roma*, 1805, etc.

Priced, 1841, H. Bohn, 66 engravings only, mor. £38. This is one of the few complete copies which have escaped the barbarous decree of the Pope, by which it was ordered that all engravings of statues should appear in decent habiliments.

6547 CARPENTER (W. H.) Pictorial Notices; consisting of a Memoir of Sir Ant. VAN DYCK, with Catalogue of his Etchings, 4to. *facsimile and portraits, cloth*, £2.   1844

6548 CAYLUS, Recueil d'Antiquités Egyptiennes, Etrusques, Grecques, et Romaines, 7 vols. 4to. 826 *fine etchings of Ancient Sculpture, Gems, Jewels, Utensils, &c. calf*, 1752-67—Grivaud de la Vincelle, Recueil de Monumens Antiques pour faire suite à Caylus, 2 vols. 43 *plates*, 1817—together 9 vols. in 8, 4to. *calf gilt, a handsome set from Miss Currer's library*, £4.   *Paris*, 1752-1817

Priced, without the Supplement, 1824, Rivington, £12. 12s; 1834, Bohn, £8.; 1843, Rodd, £12. 12s; North's copy fetched £10. 10s; the White Knight's, £18. 5s.

A book still sought after by our Antiquaries as containing representations of Works of Art and Curiosities to be found nowhere else.

6549 CHINESE COSTUME: A singularly beautiful collection of 32 Drawings, representing the great DIGNITARIES OF STATE; appended are a few COURT-LADIES in their rich Costume, *meas. 10 inches by 14, mounted on stout drawing paper, olive morocco, gilt edges*, £12. 12s   *Saec. XVII*

FINE ARTS, BOOKS OF PRINTS, PAINTING.

6550 **CHRISTIAN ART.** ARINGHI (P.) Roma subterranea novissima, in qua post Bosium Antiqua Christianorum et praecipue Martyrum Coemeteria, monimenta, epitaphia, inscriptiones, illustrantur, 2 vols. in 1, large folio, *numerous plates of Inscriptions, Monuments, &c. old calf gilt,* £2. 10s *Lutet. Paris.* 1659

6550*AYALA, Pictor christianus eruditus, sive de erroribus passim admissis circa pingendas atque effingendas sacras Imagines, sm. folio, *vellum,* 12s *Matr.* 1730

6551 DIVERS WORKS OF EARLY MASTERS, IN CHRISTIAN DECORATION, with an Introduction containing biography, journal of travel, contemporaneous associations in art, and a critical account of the works of ALBERT DURER; notices of his master WOHLGEMUTH and his friend Pirckheimer; Adam Krafft and his Sacrament-House at Nuremberg. With examples of Ancient Painted and Stained Glass from York, West Wickham, Kent, and St. George's Chapel, Windsor; the ancient Church and Sacrament-House at Limbourg; the Works of Dirk and Wouter Crabeth, &c,; also a succinct account, with illustrations, of Painted and Stained Glass at Gouda in Holland, and the Church of St. Jacques, at Liège, illustrated by very beautiful vignettes and facsimiles of rare subjects connected with Albert Durer, Adam Krafft, and the Crabeths, 2 vols. royal folio, *many fine plates of early engravings and Ancient Painted and Stained Glass, Architecture, &c. &c.* AN ORIGINAL COPY, (pub. at £10. 10s) *elegant in half green morocco, gilt edges,* £3. 16s *J. Weale,* 1846

Of this beautiful book many inferior copies have for some years been in the market, but the above is an original copy, and is much superior to those, it having been COLOURED in a much more ARTISTIC STYLE. The copy, with the original Drawings, and some additions, bound in 4 vols. russia, was offered by Mr. Weale for £210.

6552 DIDRON (M.) Iconographie Chrétienne. Histoire de Dieu, 4to. *numerous curious woodcuts of early representation of the Deity,* 624 pp. *a learned and valuable work, cloth,* 16s *Paris,* 1843

6553 TWINING's (Louisa) Types and Figures of the Bible, illustrated by the Art of the Early and Middle Ages, sm. 4to. 54 *plates, several illustrations on each plate,* (pub. at 24s) *cloth,* 14s 1855

6554 CICOGNARA (L.) STORIA DELLA SCULTURA dal suo Risorgimento in Italia sino al Secolo XIX, per servire di Continuazione alle opere di Winkelman e di D'Agincourt, complete in 3 vols. large folio, *with* 181 *fine plates, original impressions, half bound, uncut,* £6. *Venezia,* 1813-18

This Work contains nearly seven hundred Engravings of the principal Monuments of the Art of Sculpture in Italy. A considerable part of the third volume is occupied by a Critical Examination, accompanied with Engravings, of the Works of Canova.

6555 CICOGNARA, Catalogo ragionato dei Libri d'Arte e d'Antichità posseduti da lui, 2 vols. 8vo. *calf gilt,* 28s *Pisa,* 1821

A valuable Catalogue, with notes, of the Author's splendid collection of Works of Art.

6556 COLLART et WIERX: Vita Jesu Salvatoris, variis Iconibus ad Adriano Collart expressa, 24mo. 94 *beautiful old engravings, with the original broad margins, blue morocco, gilt edges,* £5. (? 1600)

Collation: Vita, etc. title and plates 1-35—Passio et Resurrectio Jesu Christi, title and plates 2-23, unnumbered plates 9—Admodum Patri Claudio Aquaviva praeposito Generali Societatis Jesu HIERONYMUS WIERX faciebat, title and plate 1-8, and Portrait 1—Triumphus Jesu Christi Redemptoris, engraved by Th. Galle, front. and plates 1-7, and 8 miscellaneous engravings.

6557 CLAUDE LORRAINE, Liber Veritatis, or 200 Prints (in Aquatinta) after his designs in the Devonshire Collection, engraved by R. Earlom, with descriptive catalogue, 2 vols. folio, ORIGINAL IMPRESSIONS, *elegantly bound in old calf gilt,* £7. 7s *Boydell* [*text printed by Bulmer*] 1777

In 1856, West's copy fetched £10. 12s; 1857, mor. £9. 9s.

6558 —— Liber Veritatis, a Collection of 300 Prints after the original designs of Claude de Lorrain, engraved by Earlom in the manner of the Drawings, 3 vols. folio, (pub. at £20. 9s 6d) *hf. bd. uncut,* £10. 10s 1777-1819

A very early copy of the second issue of Vols. I and II; of the Vol. III, the impressions are ORIGINAL and very fine. In 1854, Gardner's copy fetched £16.; priced, 1840, Jas. Bohn, mor. £52. 10s.

6559 CONCA, Descrizione odeporica della SPAGNA in cui si dà notizia delle Belle Arti, 4 vols. 8vo. *Thick Paper, hf. bd.* 20s *Parma,* 1793-97

6560 CONSTABLE's (J.) GRAPHIC WORKS, chiefly Landscapes, many of them now first published, *comprising* 40 *large and highly finished* MEZZOTINTO *engravings by David Lucas,* with Descriptions by C. R. Leslie, R.A. folio, (pub. at £5. 5s) *half morocco,* 27s 1855

An exceedingly beautiful volume of Landscapes by this eminent Master, well deserving a place beside Claude's Liber Veritatis.

6561 CONSTABLE (John, *R.A.*) Memoirs of the Life of, composed chiefly of his Letters, by C. R. LESLIE, sm. 4to. *portrait and* 4 *plates,* (pub. at 21s) *cloth,* 9s 1845

6562 COOKE'S (E. W.) Views of the Old and New London Bridges; the text by Sir J. Rennie, royal folio, 21 *beautiful plates*, ORIGINAL INDIA PROOFS, *half morocco*, 27s 1833

6563 **COSTUME:** BEVY, Histoire des Inaugurations des Rois, Empereurs, etc. 8vo. 14 *plates of the costumes of various ages, calf*, 12s 6d Paris, 1776

6564 MALLIOTT (J.) Recherches sur les Costumes, les Mœurs, les Usages des Anciens Peuples, 3 vols. 4to. *with* 296 *plates containing above* 1000 *outline engravings, calf extra*, 32s Paris, 1809

6565 MARECHAL (S.) Costumes civils actuels de tous les Peuples connus, 4 vols. 8vo. *with about* 300 *coloured plates of the Costume of all Nations, calf gilt, Princess Elizabeth's copy*, £2. 12s 6d Paris, s. d. (? 1788)

6566 SPAIN. Coleccion de Trajes de España, 65 *coloured engravings*—Costume of Minorca, *Drawings of* 26 *subjects in water-colours*—Costume of Naples, &c. 26 *coloured drawings*—Costume of Italy, 18 *drawings in body-colours, by Gatta and C. Castelli*—in one vol. sm. folio, *hf. calf gilt, an interesting volume*, £2. 10s

6567 COLECCION general de los TRAGES que en la Actualidad se usan en España, 12mo. 104 COLOURED *plates, autograph of H.R.H., blue morocco, gilt edges*, £2. 2s Madrid, 1801

6568 VECELLIO (Cesare) Habiti Antichi et Moderni di tutto il Mondo, di nuova accresciuti di molte figure, thick 8vo. 507 *beautiful woodcuts of full length* COSTUME, *after the designs of Titian, elegantly bound in pale morocco, gilt edges, very fine copy*, £10. 10s Venetia, Sessa, 1598

Best edition of this elegant and highly esteemed work, invaluable to artists.

This has Sessa the printer's large woodcut of a cat, respecting which it is observed in Dibdin's Decameron, that "the late Bishop of Ely used to say, 'When ever you see a cat and mouse in the frontispiece, seize upon it, for the chances are as three to four, that it will be found both curious and valuable.' Admonition from such a quarter is not to be lightly rejected."

6569 VECELLIO, COSTUMES ANCIENS et MODERNES, *Italien et Français*, 2 vols. 8vo. 513 *fine woodcuts of the Costume of all ages, text and plates within elaborate woodcut borders*, (pub. at 48 fr.) 36s; or, *hf. morocco, gilt tops, uncut*, £2. 8s; or, *whole* MOROCCO, *extra, gilt tops, uncut*, £3. Paris, Didot, 1860

Ce recueil offre, en effet, aux artistes en tout genre, sculpteurs, peintres, graveurs, dessinateurs, un choix nombreux de modèles aussi exacts que pitoresques, et au public ami des arts un ensemble d'objets agréables et instructifs. Les dames mêmes y trouveront un attrait tout particulier par l'originalité, la grace, la noblesse, la naïveté et quelquefois la bizarrerie des costumes, qui souvent pourront leur suggérer d'heureuses inspirations.

6570 DIDOT, Essai typographique et bibliographique sur l'Histoire de la Gravure sur Bois, pour faire suite aux Costumes de Vecellio, 1 vol. xvi and 315 pp. *double columns, small type, sd.* 4s 6d; or, *hf. morocco, to match Vecellio*, 12s 1863

6571 CRISPIN DE PAS. De la Lumière de la Peinture et de la Designature, dans laquelle ou demonstre avec une facile manière à tirer toutes les parties du corps, par une figure proposée avec la mesure; commençant de la teste jusques aux mains, jambes, pieds, tant des hommes que des femmes et enfans, folio, *with* 205 *plates of Studies, vellum, rare*, £2. Amst. 1643

Cet ouvrage (texte Italien, Français, Hollandais, Allemand) se compose de cinq parties, dont la 2e et la 3e sont datées de 1644 modifié par 1624). Il a en tout un frontispice et deux cent cinq planches, tant sur cuivre que sur bois; la 1re. partie renferme 36 pl.; la 2de partie, une planche double, 25 fig. académiques et 11 pl. de perspective; la 3me partie, 2 pl. de proportions et 18 de femmes nues; la 4e partie, 47 fig. vêtues; la 5e partie 47 pl. de quadrupèdes, 12 d'oiseaux et 6 de poissons et insectes.

6572 CUVILLIÈS (Français de) OEUVRES D'ORNAMENTS et D'ARCHITECTURE: Morceaux de Caprice à divers usages, 2 vols. impl. folio, *consisting of* 281 *fine large plates, comprising above* 318 *engravings of Ornaments, Decorations, Iron and Silver Work, Chandeliers, Altars, Rural and Landscape Architecture, Fountains, Gates, Furniture, Ceilings, etc. hf. calf*, £16. 16s

Paris et à Munich, chez l'Auteur, 1750-68

"Recueil rare et assez bien exécuté."—*Brunet*.

6573 DAHLBERG, Suecia Antiqua et Hodierna, 3 vols. folio, LARGE PAPER, *containing upwards of* 350 *fine engravings of the Palaces, Gardens, Churches, Castles, Public Buildings, etc. of all parts of Sweden, with the Coats of Arms of the Nobility and Gentry, a fine copy in old calf gilt*, £5. 5s Holmiæ, 1693-1714

Fort bel ouvrage publié aux frais du roi de Suède, par le comte de Dalberg. Les figures sont bien executées et représentent les villes, des ports, des palais, des vues, des antiquités, des portraits, etc.

6574 DANCE OF DEATH; exhibited in elegant engravings on wood, with a dissertation on the several representations of that subject, by DOUCE, 8vo. *facsimiles by Bonner and Byfield of the* 50 *designs by* HANS HOLBEIN, *hf. morocco*, 16s 1833

FINE ARTS, BOOKS OF PRINTS, PAINTING. 357

6575 LANGLOIS, Essai historique, philosophique, et pittoresque sur les Danses des Morts, complété par Pottier et Baudry, 2 vols. 8vo. *upwards of 50 plates containing several hundred compartments of Figures in facsimile of the ancient engravings, with many vignettes, hf. calf neat, 24s* Rouen, 1852

6576 DELICES DE DIVERS PAYS: **England.** BEEVERELL, les Delices de la Grande Bretagne et de l'Irlande, 8 vols. 12mo. *several hundred pretty plates, original impressions, old calf*, 35s *Leide*, 1707

6577 ——— the same, 8 vols. 18mo. *with all the plates, old calf gilt*, 30s 1727
This is a beautiful and scarce book; it contains the whole of Kip's Views of the Seats of the Nobility and Gentry of England, and a portion of Loggan's Oxford and Cambridge, reduced, and very neatly engraved.

6578 **Italy.** Les Delices de l'Italie, 4 vols. 18mo. *many pretty Views, old calf gilt*, 15s *Paris*, 1707

6579 DENNIS (G.) Cities and Cemeteries of Etruria, 2 vols. 8vo. *many fine plates and woodcuts, cloth,* 36s 1848

6580 DONATI, Dittici degli Antichi, sm. 4to. *5 plates of Diptychs, hf. bd.* 6s *Lucca*, 1753

6581 DOPPELMAYR'S Nachricht von den NÜRNBERGISCHEN Mathematicis und Künstlern, fol. *with 15 plates of early Nurnberg Art, the splendid* FOUNTAINS, *Monuments, &c. bds.* 9s *Nürnberg*, 1730

6582 DORÉ'S ILLUSTRATED WORKS:
a DANTE, l'Inferno, colle figure di G. Doré, large folio, *the text beautifully printed and 75 beautiful plates on India Paper, cloth,* £3. 16s *Parigi*, 1861
b PERRAULT, Contes, dessins de G. Doré, folio, *with about 60 very spirited plates on India Paper, richly gilt cloth*, £2. 10s *Paris*, 1862

6583 DRAWINGS BY THE OLD MASTERS: A Collection of nearly 200 Sketches, principally by Masters of the Italian School, and of every description of subject, neatly arranged and mounted, royal folio, *half bound in calf,* £6. 10s (? 1550)

6584 DUCHESNE, ainé, Essai sur les Nielles des Orfévres florentins, au XV Siècle, 8vo. *plates, sd.* 10s *Paris*, 1826

6585 DUPLESSIS, Histoire de la Gravure en France, 8vo. *sd.* 6s *Paris*, 1861

6586 DURAND CABINET: Catalogue de la Vente, (Vases, Terres Cuites, Bronzes, Pierres gravées), 8vo. *sd.* 4s; or, *with the prices, hf. bd.* 6s *Par.* 1836

6587 DURERI (A.) de Symmetria partium humanorum Corporum, folio, *woodcuts, calf,* 25s *Par.* 1557

6588 DURER'S (Albert) Passion of Our Lord Jesus Christ, edited by H. Cole, square 12mo. 36 *woodcuts, facsimiles of the originals by Albert Durer, antique calf neat,* 10s 1844

6589 DU SOMMERARD, LES ARTS AU MOYEN AGE, a complete and original copy, both divisions with the Atlas, bound in 5 vols. impl. folio, 510 *most beautiful plates, executed in imitation of the originals, in gold, silver, and colours, comprising* MONUMENTS, FURNITURE, SCULPTURE, PAINTINGS, PAINTED GLASS, FACSIMILES OF MANUSCRIPTS, ARMOUR, GEMS, IVORY, JEWELS, SILVERSMITH'S WORK, *splendid* COSTUME, *with* 5 vols. 8vo. *of text*—together 10 vols. *sumptuously whole bound in* MOROCCO *super extra, gilt edges,* £85. *Paris*, 1838-48
This fine work of Art was published at £80. in parts, the binding has cost £30. making the original cost £110. The copies which are *now* sold in Paris are far inferior, the colouring not having been done, as in the original copies, under the immediate inspection of Monsieur Du Sommerard, *père.*
Lord Rutherford's copy sold for £100. 10s; Bernal's for £110.

6590 **EMBLEMS:** BOISSARDI Emblemata, ab auctore delineata et a DE BRY sculpta, sq. 8vo. *frontispiece, portrait, and* 51 *fine engravings of Emblems, vellum,* £2. 16s *Francof.* 1593

6591 CAMERARII Symbolorum et Emblematum ex Re HERBARIA, ex ANIMALIBUS, Quadrupedibus, ex VOLATILIBUS et Insectis, ex AQUATILIBUS et Reptilibus desumptorum Centuriæ IV; 4 vols. in 1, smallest 4to. *400 very pleasing cuts, illustrative of Flowers, the Habits of Animals, Birds, Fishes, Insects, Sea-Marvels, etc. vellum,* 24s *Francof. John Ammon,* 1654-64
A former edition appeared, Norimb. 1590-95-96-1604.

6592 CAMILLI, Imprese Illustri di diversi, con Discorsi, 3 parts in 1 vol. sq. 8vo. *three engraved title pages, and about* 100 *beautiful Emblematic engravings by Porro, calf gilt*, 36s *Venet.* 1586
Priced by Thorpe, £2. 12s 6d.

6593 (CHESNEAU) Emblemes Sacrez sur le saint Sacrement de l'Eucharistie (traduit par Lubin), sm. 8vo. 101 *engravings of Emblems, with mottoes in French and Latin, calf neat,* 25s *Paris*, 1667

6594 DILHERR, Heilig-Epistolischer Bericht und Licht: Emblematische Fürstellung der Episteln; Augen und Hertzens Lust; 2 vols. in 1, stout sm. folio, *with about 200 remarkably pretty engravings by* M. KÜSELL, *illustrative of Biblical Truths*, FIRST IMPRESSIONS, *calf*, 28s ; *or, stamped hogskin*, 30s *Nürnberg*, 1663

6595 FLAMEN (Albert) Devises et Emblesmes d'Amour, 12mo. *engraved title and 50 curious plates, calf, rare*, 36s *Paris*, 1653

6596 FREITAGHII (Arnoldi) Fabulæ, sq. 8vo. *no title, with* 124 *fine Etchings, hf. bd. fine large copy, rare*, 30s *Antverp.* 1579

6597 PARADIN. Devises Heroiques de Paradin, Symeon, et autres aucteurs, 18mo. *nearly two hundred curious woodcut Emblems, with Latin devises above the French text, calf*, 30s *Anvers, Plantin*, 1567

At the end of this little volume, there are 18 pp. of contemporary MS. additions at the end, containing the description and explanation of forty one special Devices borne by various Kings of France, and others of royal or noble French blood.

6598 PETRASANCTA (S. à) de Symbolis Heroicis, sq. 8vo. *with portrait of* " *Caraffa Episcopus Tricaricensis*," *and* 260 *very pretty emblematic engravings, each with a motto, and in a different Cartouche, original edition, with fine impressions, a slight wormhole in the first and the last few pages, vellum, rare*, 36s *Antv.* 1634

6599 ——— the same, sq. 8vo. *vellum*, 16s *Amst.* 1682

Collation: Frontispiece by Rubens, engraved by Galle; Elogium ac Stemma gentis Carafacae, pp. i-xxx; De Symbolis, pp. 1-480; Index. The Reprint has not got the portrait of Caraffa.

6600 ROLLENHAGII Nucleus Emblematum selectissimorum quæ Itali vulgo Impressas vocant, sq. 8vo. *engraved title; portrait; preface*, 2 *leaves; and* 100 *fine emblematic engravings, by* CRISPIN DE PAS, *brilliant impressions, with mottoes, calf extra, rare*, 36s *Coloniæ, C. Passæus*, (1611)

Fetched, 1860, Sotheby's, £2. 9s.—"Volume recherché à cause des jolies gravures qui le composent."—*Brunet*.

6601 RUNDALL (Mary Ann) Symbolical Illustrations of the History of England, 4to. *with* 40 *plates of emblematic designs*, THE DEDICATION COPY (" to H.R.H. the Princess Elizabeth,") *with an autograph letter from the authoress, splendidly bound in purple* MOROCCO, *broad joints, silk linings, gilt edges, the sides richly ornamented with gold tooling, very rare*, £5. 1815

6602 RUSCELLI, Imprese Illustri, sq. 8vo. *upwards of* 100 *very fine engravings, in ornamental cartouches, each with the* COAT OF ARMS *of the Venetian* FAMILY *to which the Emblem relates, the headline at the top, and the imprint partly cut off, Sir Kenelm Digby's copy with his autograph, old calf*, 25s *Venetia*, 1572

6603 SAMBUCI Emblemata et aliquot Nummi antiqui operis altera editio cum auctario—Hadriani Junii Emblemata—in 1 vol. 12mo. *about* 300 *pretty woodcuts within borders, including* 16 *pp. of coins, green morocco extra, gilt edges,* RARE, £2. 10s *Antverp.* 1566

6604 SCHOONHOVII Emblemata moralia et civilia, acc. Poemata, sq. 8vo. 74 *engravings of Emblems, vellum*, 14s *Goudae*, 1618

6605 VILLAVA, Empresas Espirituales y Morales, sq. 8vo. 99 *rude woodcut Emblems, vellum*, 20s *Bacça*, 1613

6606 WITHERS' (GEORGE) COLLECTION OF EMBLEMS, Ancient and Modern, quickened with metrical Illustrations, moral and divine, and disposed into Lotteries that Instruction and good Counsel may be furthered by recreation, folio, *frontispiece by Marshall, fine portrait of Wither by Payne, and* 200 *engravings of Emblems by* CRISPIN DE PAS, *frontispiece inlaid, preposition, title, and last leaf neatly mended, fine copy in russia extra, gilt edges*, £5. *A. M. for R. Milbourne*, 1635

VERY RARE. COLLATION: Preposition to the frontispiece, 1 leaf; Frontispiece; Printed Title; To the Reader, etc, Portrait, and preliminary verses, 7 leaves; pp. 1-62; Title to Book II, and preliminary verses, 3 leaves; pp. 63-124; Title to Book III, and preliminary verses, 3 leaves; pp. 135-196; Title to Book IV, and prelim. verses, 3 leaves; pp. 209-270; Table, verses, etc. including curious large woodcut of a Lottery Dial, 5 leaves.

Priced, 1818, Longmans, £10. 10s ; 1822, Thorpe, £5. 15s 6d ; 1858, £8. 18s 6d. Fetched, 1850, Sotheby's £7.; 1851, £7.; 1855, £4. 15s; 1856, £4. 12s; 1858, £5. 12s 6d.

"Collectors of engravings, and old woodcuts, are familiar with that class of curious books which aim at the typification of moral truths by symbolical images and devices. In the middle of the 16th century this class of books assumed in Italy the character of a distinct literature; and its tendency to multiply passed to France, Germany, Holland, Spain, and England, until their issue was so large as to form a considerable library, when brought together by collectors. At this day, it is hardly possible to form a notion of the number of these works or of their characteristic quaintness. The symbolism of the Middle Ages was secularized for their production, and art, although then eminently realistic, was inexhaustible in the eccentricity of the conceptions which it sought to turn into pictures for their embellishment.

"Such works have long passed out of fashion, and the specimens which turn up at book sales are now so rare as to command very high prices. There is no class of books more attractive to the true bibliophile who cares for distinctive excellence rather than rarity."—*Times, Nov.* 24, 1859.

FINE ARTS, BOOKS OF PRINTS, PAINTING.

6607 ESPANA ARTISTICA y MONUMENTAL: l'Espagne Artistique et Monumentale; Vues et descriptions des sites et des Monuments Artistiques les plus notables de l'Espagne, avec des Dessins et des notices sur les Usages, les Armes, et les Costumes des époques qui peuvent le plus intéresser l'histoire de l'Art, par une Société d'Artistes, de gens de lettres et de capitalistes Espagnols : Directeur artistique, Don Genaro Perez de Villa-Amil; Redacteur du texte, Don Patricio de la Escosura; Planches lithographiées par V. Adam, Arnout, Asselineau, Bachelier, etc. etc. 3 vols. imperial folio, 144 *large plates in tinted lithography, beautifully executed, (published unbound, at* 576 *francs, in parts) plates, half bd. morocco, gilt edges,* £8. 8s ; or, *half bd. morocco extra, gilt edges,* £10. *Paris,* 1842-50

6608 ——— the same, a picked copy, 3 vols. impl. folio, *whole bound red* MOROCCO *extra, gilt edges,* £18. 18s   1842-50
Fetched, 1855, at Sotheby's, *half morocco,* £16. 16s.
This superb work is the most complete ever published in illustration of the Antiquities and Art Treasures of Spain; a country so frequently spoken of, yet so little known. Many Spanish gentlemen, numbering amongst them the most celebrated names, have bestowed their labour of love, literary and artistic, upon the "Espagne Artistique;" and the land of the Cid, in all its grand and romantic beauty, with all its old historic pride, seems present to the eye that rests upon those beautiful illustrations. In some, the outer life of the people, and scenes beneath the bright sun and pellucid atmosphere of Spain, contrasts with others which shadow forth the dark and solemn majesty of Cathedral aisles. No Art library is complete without this magnificent work.

6609 ETCHING CLUB: GOLDSMITH (O.) DESERTED VILLAGE, a Poem illustrated by the Etching Club, large folio, in portfolio, £4. 4s   1841

6610 ——— the same, atlas folio, FIRST INDIA PROOFS ON THE LARGEST PAPER, *half scarlet morocco extra, uncut edges,* £8.   1841
The chef-d'œuvre of the Etching Club. COLLATION: engraved title, table of contents, and 40 beautiful plates.

6611 ETRURIA PITTRICE, OVVERO STORIA DELLA PITTURA TOSCANA, dedotta dai suoi Monumenti che si esibiscono in Stampa dal Secolo X sino al presente, 2 vols. roy. folio, *containing* 120 *beautiful engravings, exhibiting the chefs-d'œuvre of as many artists of the Florentine school, with vignette portraits of each, and bibliographical sketches, vellum,* RARE, £10.   *Firenze,* 1791-95
Priced, 1829, J. Bohn, mor. £18.; it fetched, 1856, Adamson, hf. bd. £11. 5s.
The text is in Italian and French, and was contributed by M. Pacini. The plates are said in the Preface to be engraved by the first artists of Italy.
The greater part of these paintings are not engraved in any other collection, but many of them are described in Lanzi's History of Painting in Italy. Brunet says of the work, " Ouvrage composé de 120 pl. avec un texte en Italien et en Français par le savant Lastri ; on le trouve rarement en France."

6612 ETRUSCAN ART. GERHARD's Gottheiten der Etrusker, 4to. *plates, hf. cf.* 5s 1847

6613 MUSEUM Etrusque de Lucien BONAPARTE, Fouilles de 1828-29, roy. 4to. 42 *plates, bds.* 7s 6d   *Viterbe,* 1829

6614 EVELYN's Sculptura; or the History and Art of Chalcography and Engraving in Copper, sm. 8vo. *portrait and head, calf,* 12s   1755

6615 **FAYENCE or Henry II. Ware:** DELANGE (C. et H.) Recueil de toutes les pièces connues jusqu'à ce jour de la Faïence Française dite de Henri II, et Diane de Poitiers, impl. folio, *with* 52 *beautifully coloured plates, a perfect copy, with the Supplement, whole bound red morocco, gilt edges,* £10. 10s *Paris,* 1861
Only 150 copies were printed.

6616 FERRARIO (Giulio) Monumenti delle Basilica di Sant' Ambrogio in MILANO, folio, *with* 31 *tinted plates, comprising many fine specimens of* EARLY CHRISTIAN ART, *hf. calf,* 18s   *Milano,* 1824

6617 ——— the same, folio, *the plates* COLOURED, *and some highly finished in* SILVER *and* GOLD, AN ORIGINAL COPY, *blue morocco, gilt edges,* £4. 10s *Milano,* 1824

6618 FICORONI (F.) Dissertatio de Larvis Scenicis et Figuris comicis antiquorum Romanorum, 4to. *with* 84 *plates of Ancient Works of Art, with* MASKS, *fine copy in old calf gilt,* 25s   *Romæ,* 1750

6619 ——— Gemmæ antiquæ litteratæ à Galeotti, 4to. 29 *plates, hf. bd.* 5s *ib.* 1757

6620 FIELDING's Index of Colours and Mixed Tints, roy. 8vo. 18 *plates of* 360 *colours,* (pub. at 21s) *bds.* 5s   1830

6621 ——— Theory of Painting, roy. 8vo. *coloured plates* (pub. at 26s) 6s 1836

6622 FIESOLE (Giov. de) La Vita di Gesu Christo dipinta, incisa da Nocchi, atlas folio, 56 *very large beautiful engravings from the famous Paintings in the Florentine Gallery, hf. morocco,* £2.   *Firenze,* 1843

6623 FINDEN'S Views of Ports and Harbours, Watering-places, Fishing villages, and other picturesque objects on the ENGLISH COAST, 4to. *numerous beautiful plates, hf. morocco,* 20s   1836

6624 FIORILLO'S WERKE: Geschichte der zeichnenden Künste von ihrer Wiederauflebung bis auf die neuesten Zeiten, oder Geschichte der Mahlerey in Rom, Toscana, Venedig, Bologna, und den Hauptstädten der Lombardey; Neapel, Genua, etc.; in Frankreich; in Spanien; in Gross Britannien; in Deutschland und den vereinigten Niederlanden, 9 vols.—Kleine Schriften artistischen Inhalts, 2 vols in 1—together 11 vols. 8vo. *calf gilt*, £2.   *Gött.* 1798-1820

6625 FLAXMAN'S Compositions from the Hell, Purgatory, and Paradise of Dante, oblong folio, *two frontispieces and* 110 *beautiful plates,* FIRST IMPRESSION, *half bound,* 36s   1807

6626 FLORENCE: GHIBERTI, Le Tre Porte del Battistero di San Giovanni di Firenze, incise ed illustrate, atlas folio, LARGE PAPER, 75 *beautiful engravings representing Biblical subjects, on* 46 *large plates, by* LASINIO, *old impressions, the text in Italian and French, hf. calf,* £3. 5s   *Firenze,* 1821

6627 ——— the same, Papier Vélin, impl. fol. *First Proof Impressions, hf. bd.* £4. 1821

Only 24 copies were printed; Dawson Turner's copy, 1853, fetched. £4. 15s.

COLLATION: PRIMA PORTA, opera in bronzo di Andrea Pisana, plan 1 plate, section 1 plate, and 28 engravings on 14 plates; SECONDA PORTA, opera in bronzo di Lorenzo Ghiberti, view and 30 engravings on 15 plates; TERZA PORTA, di Ghiberti, plan and 13 plates.

Cette magnifique porte, faite en concours des Brunellesco, Donatello, Jacopo dalla Quercia, Niccolo d'Arezzo, Francesco da Vandabrina, Simo e da Colle, et qui, un siècle plus tard, faisait dire à Michel-Ange qu'elle était digne de fermer le paradis, est encore de nos jours l'admiration des artistes de talent et des connaisseurs.

Ghiberti's great gate from the Baptistery at Florence is one of the two pronounced by Michael Angelo to be fit for the "gates of Paradise." A pupil of Giotto, Ghiberti is said to have begun them when just of age, carrying off the palm from his rivals Donatello and Brunalleschi, finishing them after twenty years labour, in which he was aided by his father and nine other sculptors.

'The beautiful compositions by Ghiberti, in the Gates of the Baptistery at Florence, are as good examples as could be brought before you, of their kind."—*Athenæum, March* 6, 1858.

6628 FOWLER'S Coloured Engravings of MOSAIC PAVEMENTS, STAINED GLASS WINDOWS, NORMAN TILES, and Specimens of Gothic Architecture in Great Britain, a volume atlas folio, *containing* 28 *beautiful plates, including the dedication, twenty-two plates of Tessellated Pavements, and six of Stained Glass Windows, with eight of the* DESCRIPTIVE ADVERTISEMENTS, *hf. morocco, gilt edges,* £7. 7s   1796-1804

The Advertisements are very seldom found with the engravings to which they form a sort of text, so that the above copy is peculiarly valuable in this respect.

6629 GALERIES.—AGUADO GALLERY: Choix des principaux Tableaux de la Galérie du Marquis de las Marismas del Guadalquivir, par C. GAVARD, atlas folio, 38 *very fine engravings after exquisite specimens, by* MURILLO, VELASQUES, etc. *cloth,* £4. 10s   *Paris,* 1839

Priced, 1845, in 12 livraisons, £7. 10s. A copy, India Proofs, before the inscriptions, date 1843, 32 plates, from Louis Philippe's library fetched, 1853, at Baron Taylor's sale, £17.

'Admirable in Illustration. as far as it goes, of the Spanish School of Art."—*D. Turner.*

6630 VIARDOT, Notices sur les Peintres de l'Espagne, roy. 8vo. *hf. cf.* 7s 6d   1839

6631 BLUNDELL GALLERY OF MARBLES AT INCE. Engravings of the Statues, Busts, Bas-Reliefs, Gems, Cinerary Urns, Bronzes, etc. in the Collection of the late HENRY BLUNDELL, ESQ. at Ince, near Liverpool; with descriptive letter-press, impl. folio, *containing* 158 *fine plates, original red morocco,* VERY RARE, £18.   1809

PRIVATELY PRINTED. ONLY 50 COPIES WERE TAKEN OFF, AS PRESENTS, and more than half of them given to public libraries, chiefly abroad.

Priced, 1834, Thorpe, £21.; 1840, Payne and Foss, £31. 10s.; 1845 and 48, P. & F. £42; 1847, H. Bohn, £42.; in 1847, I sold a copy for £28. 10s.

This princely collection was formed by the late Mr. Blundell, while at Rome with Mr. Townley, and contains the well known Marbles of the Villas Mattei, Lanti, and D'Este. Sir J. E. Smith says (Life, vol. 2, p. 303)—"The most interesting place I have seen, in itself, is Mr. Blundell's, of Ince: rich in a profusion of antique sculptures and marbles."

COLLATION:—Vol. I. Portrait, Frontispiece, View of the Park Pantheon; Title; (Preface) 1 leaf; Plates 1-77, all numbered.—Vol. II. Frontispiece, View of the *Garden* Pantheon; Title; (Preface) 1 leaf; a page of text to plate 78, (one leaf half size); Plate 78, not numbered; Plates 79-126, all numbered; 127, numbered in MS.; 128 and 129 numbered; 130-39 not numbered; 140 and 141 numbered in MS. on one plate; 142 not numbered; 143 numbered in MS.; 144-151 numbered; 152 not numbered, composed of 7 different pieces, containing 13 figures; 153 and 154, (so altered in MS. from the former printed Nos. 145-146,) both on one plate; one plate not numbered; 155 numbered; 156-158, 3 plates, not numbered.

6632 BLUNDELL'S Account of the Statues, Busts, Bass-Relieves, and Paintings at Ince, 4to. *calf, privately printed,* 20s   *Liverpl.* 1803

Fetched, 1857, Sotheby's, £2. 3s.

6633 FLORENCE ACADEMY GALLERY: Galleria dell' I. e R. Accademia delle Belle Arti di Firenze, descritta da Vinc. MARCHESE, impl. folio, 60 superb plates, executed by the first Italian engravers, after the Paintings of Cimabue, Giotto, Angelico da Fiesole, Pietro Perugino, Raphael, Del Sarto, etc. *fine impressions, hf. morocco, uncut,* £5. 15s   *Firenze,* 1845

6633*GALERIE DES PEINTRES FLAMANDS, HOLLANDAIS, ET ALLEMANDS: ouvrage enrichi de 201 planches, gravées d'après les meilleurs tableaux de ces maîtres, par les plus habiles artistes de France, de Hollande, et d'Allemagne, par J. P. B. LEBRUN, 3 vols. large folio, 201 *beautiful engravings after celebrated pictures*, ORIGINAL BRILLIANT IMPRESSIONS, *bright old calf gilt, a remarkably beautiful copy*, £14. *Paris*, 1792-96

6634 GALERIE ROYALE DE DRESDE, 2 vols. atlas folio, *containing* 102 *very large and beautiful engravings after the old Masters, executed by Kilian, Folkema, Houbraken, Ridinger, Tanjé, Basan, Beauvarlet, and all the best artists of the day*; GOOD IMPRESSIONS, *including the two additional and rare* PORTRAITS *of Augustus III. King of Poland, and his Queen, old bds*. £10. *Dresden*. 1753-57

Priced, 1831, H. Bohn, mor. £33.; 1847, £30.; £31. 10s. The M. of Lansdowne's copy fetched £32. 11s.; 1853, D. Turner's, £19.; 1853, Baron Turner's, £15.; 1854, Prince de Paur's, £17. 5s; 1856, a copy in boards like the above, £13.

The rarest and most magnificent of all the old picture galleries. This choice copy came from the Library of the late Queen of Wittemberg, and has since been bound at the expense of £10. 10s. Brunet, who calls the work "*Recueil Précieux*," states that the portrait of *Augustus* alone sold for 164 francs, *Alibert* in 1803, and for 125 francs *Saint-Yves*.

6635 GALLERY OF THE OLD GERMAN MASTERS, formerly at Stuttgard, in the possession of the Brothers BOISSERÉE, now removed to Munich, 84 superb plates, executed under the direction of STRIXNER, engraved in lithography, heightened by tints, and so admirably done as to be scarcely distinguishable from the most perfect line engravings; mounted on drab coloured drawing paper, elephant folio, *hf. russia, a bargain*, £8. 8s *Stuttg. and Mun.* 1821-36

Published at 100 Guineas. Priced, in 1841, H. Bohn, morocco, £63.
In 1857, a copy in 2 vols. morocco, with 118 plates only, fetched at Sotheby's £40.; in 1857, the Earl of Shrewsbury's copy, 120 engravings, hf. russia, fetched £6. 10s.
A copy India Paper Proofs (no number of engravings stated), fetched, 1856, at Sotheby's, £19. 10s.
A similar work exists under the title: Königl. Bayr. Gemäldesaal, zu München und Schleisheim. 2 Bde. 200 Tafeln, lithograp., von Strixner, Piloty, etc. München, 1817-31, price 200 Thalers.
This work is the admiration of the most fastidious connoisseurs. It is impossible to conceive the perfection which lithographic engraving has attained at Munich, without seeing this *chef d'œuvre*. The stones, from their uncommon size, being valuable, were cleaned off and used as the work proceeded; and as a very limited number were struck off, sets are already scarce.

6636 PARMESE GALLERY: Le piu insigni Pitture Parmensi, 4to. *text in French and Italian*, 59 *fine plates, bds*. 12s *Parma*, 1809

6637 TURIN GALLERY: GALLERIA REALE di Torino, illustrata da Roberto d'Azeglio, 39 fascicoli, making nearly 4 vols. royal folio, 156 *superb plates*, PROOFS BEFORE LETTERS, BRILLIANT IMPRESSIONS, *a Subscriber's copy, in parts*, £17. 17s *Torino*, 1836-59

The Continuation will be supplied on its appearance.

6638 VIENNA GALERIE IMPÉRIALE AU BELVÉDÈRE à VIENNE; d'après les dessins de M. S. de Perger, peintre de la cour, gravées par différents Artistes, avec un texte par C. Haas, 4 vols. 4to. *containing* 240 *highly finished line engravings, superb impressions, equal to* PROOFS, (subscription price 120 Thalers), *red* MOROCCO *extra, gilt edges*, £14. *Vienne*, 1821-28

Of all the celebrated Continental Picture Galleries, this is perhaps the most popular and pleasing, the subjects being selected with the most consummate taste and judgment; it was published in 60 parts, 4to. Priced, 1847, Bohn, £20.; 1855, Artaria, Manheim, 200fl. A few copies were issued of the Large Paper Proofs before Letters, sold by me, 1859, for £24. The coppers of this work have recently passed into other hands, and are worked again.

6639 GALERIE DE VIENNE: Galerie impériale et royale du Belvédère à Vienne, 4 vols. in 2, 4to. 240 *plates, the text in French only, hf. mor.* £2. 16s *Franc*. (1858)

6640 GEMS. EBERMAYER, Capita Deorum et illustrium hominum, Abraxea, et Amuleta in Gemmis incisa, ed. Reusch, folio, 30 *fine plates of Gems, hf. vellum*, 9s *Francof*. 1721

6641 GORIUS, Dactyliotheca Smithiana, cum Historia Glyptographica, 2 vols. folio, 100 *very fine engravings of* ANTIQUE GEMS, *formerly in possession of Consul Smith, calf*, 16s *Venet*. 1767

6642 GORLÉE (A.) Cabinet de Pierres Antiques gravées, Egyptiennes, Etrusques, Grecques, &c. 2 vols. sm. folio, *portrait, and* 282 *plates, containing* 216 RINGS, *and* 682 GEMS, *calf neat*, 24s *Paris*, 1776

6643 MARIETTE, Traité des Pierres Gravées, 2 vols. folio, *with upwards of* 250 *plates of Gems, calf neat*, £2. 2s *Paris*, 1750

Mariette's own copy fetched at Paris's sale, £10. 10s.

6644 MÜLLER (L.) Description des Intailles, Camées et Monnaies Antiques du Musée Thorwaldsen, 8vo. *plates, hf. calf*, 25s *Copen*. 1847

6645 PONIATOWSKI GEMS. PHOTOGRAPHIC FACSIMILES of the Antique Gems, formerly possessed by Prince Poniatowski, (collected by the Kings of Poland), *both series*, 2 thick vols. 4to. *nearly* 500 *plates, executed in the first style of Photographic Art, with descriptions by* Prendeville *and Dr*. Maginn, (pub. £21.) *cloth*, £3. 16s 1857-59

Of this beautiful work only 75 copies were executed, and no more can be produced.

6645 *ZOBI, Notizie storiche sul Stabilimento dei Lavori di Commesso in Pietre dure, 8vo. *hf. bd. uncut*, 7s 6d *Firenze*, 1841

6646 STOSCH (P. de) Pierres Antiques gravées, sur lesquelles les Graveurs ont mis leurs noms, expliquées par P. Stosch, Fr. et Lat. folio, 70 *finely engraved plates by B. Picart, veau fauve, gilt edges*, 25s *Amst.* 1724

6647 GÖZ, Leidenschaftliche Entwürfe für empfindsame Kunst- und Schauspiel-Freunde, 4to. 228 *pp. of Text, (interspersed with etchings) and a series of* 160 *plates, entitled* "LENARDO UND BLANDINE, ein Melodram nach Bürger in 160 Leidenschaftlichen Entwürfen." *These* 160 *spirited Etchings, representing all the attitudes and expressions of the Actors, varying from indifference to the greatest degree of passion, rage, affection, distress, agony, hf. red morocco, gilt tops, uncut, rare*, 32s *Augsburg*, 1783

6648 GOZZINI, MONUMENTI SEPOLCRALI della TOSCANA, incisi da LASINIO, folio, 47 *fine plates of Funeral Monuments, bds.* 21s *Firenze*, 1819
" Ouvrage exécuté avec soin."—*Brunet*. Sykes' copy fetched, £2. 12s 6d. The edition of 1821, though with 29 additional plates, is an inferior book.

6649 GRUNER'S ORNAMENTAL ART, selected from the best Models of the Classical Epochs, 1 vol. atlas folio, *containing the* SUPPRESSED PLATES *and the* 80 *most exquisitely beautiful plates comprising the most perfect specimens of Paintings, Carvings, Friezes, Ceilings, Ornaments and Decorations of the Thirteenth, Fourteenth, Fifteenth and Sixteenth Centuries, executed in the Palaces and Churches of Rome, Verona, Mantua, Milan, &c. by* JACOBO DELLA TURRITA, BRAMANTE, LUINI, GIULIO ROMANO, RAPHAEL D'URBINO, *etc. many of the plates sumptuously* COLOURED *and* HEIGHTENED *with* GOLD ; *with the* 4to. *volume of explanatory text, and the additional plates*, (pub. at £12. 12s in bds.) *rare*, £12.   1850
This book is now entirely out of print.
Published by authority of the British Government, which placed copies in every Government School of Design, and paid for them at the rate of £25. each. "Gruner's Ornamental Art" is a foundation from which every Artist may get a correct notion of true Art, its principles and adaptation. Almost all the Designs are now published for the first time, and are all drawn from the Originals expressly for this work. The branches of Ornamental Art and Industry illustrated in this work are principally, besides the different styles of Architecture and their simple and ornamental mouldings—Decorative Painting, of the different styles from the first to the sixteenth century; Glass Painting and Glass Mosaics, symbolic of Pagan and Christian Worship; Etruscan and Modern Pottery; classic Terra Cottas, and of the fifteenth century; Bronzes; Ornamental Wood-work, inlaid and carved; Flowers from Nature, as materials for Embroidery, Silks, Printed Goods, and Decorative Painting; ornamental Gold, Silver, and Iron Work, comprising Chased Arms, Enamels, of Limoges, &c. &c.

6650 GRUNER'S Ornamental Art, the explanatory text and additional plates by Emil Braun, 4to. 7 *plates sd. often wanting to Gruner's "Ornamental Art,"* 7s 6d 1850

6651 GRUNER'S ITALIAN FRESCO PAINTINGS : Fresco Decorations and Stuccoes of Churches and Palaces in Italy during the Fifteenth and Sixteenth Centuries, a splendid volume, imp. folio, 56 *very large, elaborate and most interesting engravings, after the original Paintings of Raphael, Giulio Romano, Giovanni da Udine, Baldassare Peruzzi, Sebastian del Piombo, Correggio, Moretto, Ambrogio da Fossano, Bramantino, Bernardino, Luini, Pinturicchio, &c. several* ELABORATELY FINISHED IN COLOURS, *and coloured key-plates are given to shew the colouring of the rest* (only 150 copies printed at £7. 7s) *half morocco uncut*, £4. 15s   1854
Accompanying this fine work is an Essay by J. J. Hittorff, on the Arabesques of the Ancients as compared with those of Raphael and his School. This magnificent work is no less valuable to the *Architect* than to the *Painter*. It does not profess (says the *Quarterly Review* in an elaborate article) to exhibit fresh decorative painting in that highest walk chosen by Michael Angelo and Raffaelle (except as a handmaid), but as *a purely decorative Art and subservient to Architecture*. Owing its very existence to the exigencies of the sovereign art, and deriving its appropriate locality, scale and effect, from the edifice, it no less assists the *Architecture*, in return, by its arabesques and other tasteful accessories.

6652 GRUNER'S Decorations of the Garden-pavilion in the Grounds of Buckingham Palace. With an introd. by JAMESON, fol. 15 *coloured plates*, (pub. at £5. 5s) *cloth*, £2. 2s *London*, 1846

6653 GRUNER. Die Basreliefs an der Vorderseite des Domes zu ORVIETO. Marmorbildwerke der Schule der Pisaner, mit erläut. Text von E. BRAUN, obl. fol. 80 *plates on India paper*, (pub. at £6. 6s) £4. 4s *Leipzig*, 1858

6654 GUERCINO. HERCOLANI, Notizie della Vita e delle Opere del Guercino, 4to. *portrait, bds.* 7s 6d *Bologna*, 1808

6655 HEINECKEN (Baron) Idée Generale d'une Collection complette d'Estampes, avec une Dissertation sur l'Origine de la Gravure, et sur les premiers Livres d'Images, stout 8vo. *facsimile plates of the early Block Books, and other engravings in the infancy of the art, calf extra, gilt edges*, £2. 16s *Leipsic*, 1771
The Roxburghe copy fetched £2. 16s; Roscoe's, £3

FINE ARTS, BOOKS OF PRINTS, PAINTING 363

6656 HAMILTON'S (Sir Wm.) CAMPI PHLEGRÆI, or the Volcanoes of the two Sicilies, with SUPPLEMENT, *the text in English and French, an autograph letter of Sir W. Hamilton inserted*, 3 vols. in 1, large folio, THE ORIGINAL NEAPOLITAN EDITION, *with* 60 *plates of Volcanic Eruptions, etc. finely* COLOURED IN IMITATION OF DRAWINGS, *crimson morocco extra, with joints, broad borders of gold on the sides, and gilt edges, Dawson Turner's copy*, £7. Naples, 1776-9
The above copy has the scarce Supplement: To Joseph Banks, Esq. London, Naples, Oct. 1, 1779; 30 pp. and dedication, 1 leaf.
Copies fetched: Stanley's, £31. 10s; Dent's, £29.; White-Knight's, £11. 11s; Nassau's, £16. 5s 6d; Hibbert's £16. 5s 6d; Talleyrand's, £19. 8s 6d; Roxburghe's, £21.; 1855, Bernal's, £7. 15s; 1855, Baker's (originally Dent's copy) £11.

6657 HELLER's Handbuch für Kupferstichsammler, oder Lexicon der vorzüglichsten Kupferstecher, Formschneider, etc. 8vo. *second much improved edition*, 946 pp. *half bound morocco, uncut*, 16s Leipzig, 1850

6658 HERTZ (B.) A Catalogue of the Collection of Pearls and Precious Stones, formed by H. P. HOPE, ESQ. atlas 4to. *with* 42 *plates on India paper, cloth, rare*, £2. 1839
Privately printed.

6659 HEYNS (Zacharias) Const-Thoonende Juweel (the Jewel of Dramatic Art) published by the Honourable City of Haerlem in XII Emblematic PLAYS or MORALITIES, with Prologues and Songs arranged according to the regulations of the City Authorities, sm. 4to. *numerous plates of* THEATRICAL FIGURES *and* COSTUMES, *a remarkably fine copy, vellum*, £2. Zwol. 1607
This copy has also the additional play of Haerlems Juweel, with plates, separately published in the following year, 1608. The above, recently in the library of an eminent Dramatic critic, will be found of great interest to all who study Mediæval manners and customs. I know of no similar work, having all the costumes so fully represented. This rare collection of early moralities is rendered particularly interesting by the plates representing the characters in each play in stage costume preceded by their standard-bearers. The plays were performed on a stage in the Town-hall at Harleem, by members of the twelve principal towns of Holland, and Leyden obtained the highest prize for the best morality. The book is so rare in a perfect state that the late Mr. Douce could not succeed in obtaining a complete copy.

6660 HOGARTH RESTORED; The whole Works of William Hogarth, now re-engraved by Th. Cook, atlas folio, *portrait and* 94 *large plates;* with an impl. 8vo. volume, "Anecdotes and Descriptions of the plates," *hf. bd. russia*, 32s 1801-3

6661 HOPE'S (Thomas) Costume of the Ancients, 2 vols. 4to. LARGE PAPER, 300 *fine outline engravings by Moses* (pub. at £5. 5s in bds.) *fine copy in blue morocco, gilt edges*, £4. 4s 1812

6662 HORSEMANSHIP: NEWCASTLE (William Cavendish, Duke of) General System of Horsemanship in all its Branches, 2 vols. in 1, large folio, 43 *splendid large folding plates, containing Portraits of the Cavendish Family after Diepenbeke, engraved by Vosterman and Clouet, with* 21 *additional plates of Horses, also head-pieces and vignettes in the text, calf*, £5. 1743
Original English edition, to which a second volume, with 21 plates of engravings of Horses, their Anatomy, Farriery, etc. are added, not contained in the French edition.

6663 HUBER, et ROST, Manuel des Curieux et des Amateurs de l'Art, notice des principaux graveurs, leurs ouvrages, etc. 8 vols. 12mo. *calf*, 20s Zurich, 1797-1804

6664 HUMPHREYS' (H. N.) ILLUMINATED BOOKS of the Middle Ages, with an Account of the development and progress of the Art of Illumination from the IVth to the XVIIth centuries, impl. folio, LARGE PAPER, *illustrated by a series of* 31 *examples of the size of the originals, selected from the most beautiful of the MSS. of the various periods, executed on stone, and most beautifully printed in gold, silver and colours by* OWEN JONES, (pub. at £16. 16s) *hf. bd. red morocco*, £7. 7s. 1849
An extremely low price for such a beautiful work. In 1855, Bernal's copy, mor. fetched £12.
The illustrations, all of the exact size of the originals, are from the most celebrated and splendid MSS. in the Imperial and Royal Libraries of Vienna, Moscow, Paris, Naples, Copenhagen, and Madrid; from the Vatican, Escurial, Ambrosian, and other great Libraries of the Continent; and from the rich Public, Collegiate, and Private Libraries of Great Britain.

6665 INGHIRAMI (F.) Galleria Omerica o raccolta di Monumenti Antichi per servire allo Studio dell' Iliade e dell' Odissea, 3 vols. 8vo. *containing* 388 *plates, chiefly in tints, with letter-press descriptions, cloth, uncut*, £4. Fiesole, 1831-36

6666 INSTITUTO di CORRISPONDENZA ARCHEOLOGICA di ROMA: Text, Bulletino, 1829-44, 5 vols. *hf. calf*, 4 pts.—Annali, 1829-43, 6 vols. *hf. calf*, 6 pts. *Plates, Monumenti inediti*, Vol. I. 60 *plates*—Vol. II. 60 *plates*, Vol. III. 24 *plates; no list of plates to Vol.* 3—*together* 11 vols. 10 pts. *and the plates in a folio parcel*, £10. Roma, 1829-44

6667 ITALY. Collection de Vues Pittoresques de l'Italie, dessinées d'après nature, et gravées à l'eau forte à Rome, par trois peintres allemands: DIES, REINHART et MECHAU, royal folio, 72 *fine large plates of Picturesque Views*, ORIGINAL IMPRESSIONS, *calf, Baron Larpent's copy*, £2. Nuremberg, 1799
The coppers have recently been worked again.

6668 BROCKEDON (W.) ITALY, Classical, Historical, and Picturesque, impl. 4to. 60 *beautiful steel engravings by Willmore, Cousens, etc. after drawings by Turner, Stanfield, Roberts, Harding, and others,* (pub. at £5. 10s unbound) *and a coloured French plate of Lake Maggiore inserted, a fine copy strongly bound in green morocco extra, gilt edges,* £4. 4s   1842-44

6669 JACQUEMART et LE BLANT, Histoire de la PORCELAINE, accompagnée de recherches sur les sujets et emblèmes qui la décorent, les marques et inscriptions, les variations des prix et les collections où ils sont conservés, stout folio, *with* 28 *plates, a very elegantly got-up book, red* MOROCCO *extra, gilt edges,* A SUPERB COPY, £6. 6s   *Paris,* 1862

6670 JAMESON'S (Mrs.) Sacred and Legendary Art, 2 vols. 1857—Legends of the Monastic Orders, as represented in the Fine Arts, *second edition enlarged,* 1852 —Legends of the Madonna, as represented in the Fine Arts, *second edition,* 1857 —together 4 vols. 8vo. *many hundred plates and woodcuts, a beautiful series, cloth,* £3. 10s   1852-57

6671 ——— Legends of the Madonna, as represented in the Fine Arts, 8vo. *original impressions of the numerous plates and woodcuts, cloth,* 18s   1852

"Mrs. Jameson has done much to familiarize her countrymen, not only with the noble works of Early Italian Art, but with the origin and progress of the great revival at present going on in Germany."—*Lord Lindsay's Christian Art.*

6672 JANSEN, Essai sur l'Origine de la Gravure en Bois et en Taille-Douce, des Cartes à jouer et géographiques, 2 vols. 8vo. 20 *curious plates after Early Engravings, well bound,* 14s   *Paris,* 1801-8

Brockett's copy, £1. 13s.

6673 JONES'S (Owen) GRAMMAR OF ORNAMENT, a Series of 101 *large and exquisitely coloured plates, executed in* CHROMO-LITHOGRAPHY, *comprising* 3000 *examples of the* DECORATIONS *of all ages and nations,* with descriptive letterpress, *illustrated with woodcuts,* impl. folio, (pub. at £19. 19s) *elegantly half bound morocco, gilt leaves,* £9. 9s   1856

A splendid work of designs, selected from the best works of all styles. The aim of the author is to present the student with a TEXT-BOOK of design, selected from the best works and styles, and to show that, by returning to the works of nature for fresh inspiration we may yet go forward, and, whilst availing ourselves of the experience of all time, may be enabled to produce works in harmony with our own times, instead of blindly following the past.

6674 JONES' (Owen) ALHAMBRA; Plans, Elevations, and Sections of the Alhambra, with the elaborate details of this beautiful specimen of Moorish Architecture minutely displayed in 100 *beautifully engraved plates,* 67 *of which are* HIGHLY FINISHED IN GOLD AND COLOURS, from Drawings taken on the spot, by Jules Goury and Owen Jones, with a complete translation of the Arabic Inscription, and an historical notice of the Kings of Granada, by P. de Gayangos, 2 vols. impl. folio, (pub. at £24.) *half bound, morocco, gilt edges,* £10.   1842

6675 ——— the same, LARGE PAPER, atlas folio, 100 *plates,* 67 *of them in* GOLD AND COLOURS, *the others on* INDIA PAPER, (pub. at £36.) *hf. bd. morocco,* £14.   1842

A most gorgeous and magnificent work—it cost the artist—Owen Jones, years of labour, and Jules Goury lost his life whilst engaged upon the work—the plates in the large paper copies are more highly finished than those on small paper. The Alhambra Court at the Sydenham Crystal Palace was decorated under the superintendence of Owen Jones.

6676 JONES's (Owen) Designs for MOSAIC and Tesselated Pavements, with Essay on their Materials and Structure, roy. 4to. 10 *coloured plates,* (pub. at £1. 11s 6d) *hf. bd.* 14s   1842

6677 JORIO, Opere; Real Museo Borbonico; Officina de' Papiri, *plates,* 1825—Viaggio di Enea all' Inferno, 1831—Musée Bourbon, Guide pour la Galerie, 16 *plates,* 1830—Plan de Pompéi, 4 *plates,* 1828—Mimica degli Antichi, 21 *plates,* 1832— in 2 vols. 8vo. *hf. morocco, uncut,* 14s   *Napoli,* 1825-32

6678 JOUBERT, les Dessinateur pour les Fabriques d'Etoffes d'Or, d'Argent, et de Soie, 8vo. *woodcut patterns, hf. bd.* 7s 6d   *Paris,* 1774

6678*JOUBERT, Manuel de l'Amateur d'Estampes, 3 vols. 8vo. *calf extra,* 30s *Par.* 1821

6679 JUBINAL (A.) les Anciennes Tapisseries du 11me Siècle jusqu'au 16me savoir D'Aix et Aulhac, 12 *plates;* de Bayeux, 24 *plates;* de Beauvais, de Louvre; Alexandre roi d'Escosse, 15 *plates;* de Berne, 12 *plates;* de Dijon et du Chevalier Bayard, 6 *plates;* de Nancy, 6 *plates;* de Rheimes, 10 *plates;* de Valenciennes, 6 *plates;* La Chaise Dieu, 32 *plates*—in 1 vol. oblong folio, *together* 123 *plates,* PROOFS ON INDIA PAPER, *with descriptions and dissertations,* (pub. at 880 fr.) *hf. bd. red morocco,* £7. 10s   *Paris,* 1838

6680 ——— Recherches sur les Tapisseries Historiées, jusqu'au XVI Siècle, 8vo. *plates, sd.* 5s   1841

6681 KEMPIS, IMITATION DE JÉSUS-CHRIST, Traduction du chancelier de Marillac, avec la reproduction des anciens manuscrits depuis le VIe jusqu'au XVIIe siecle, 2 vols. impl. 8vo. A MOST SUMPTUOUS EDITION, *the text printed within borders, extending to upwards of 400 pages, each of which is decorated with elegant designs, copied from exquisite specimens in* EARLY BYZANTINE, GREEK, ORIENTAL, FLEMISH, ITALIAN, *or* FRENCH ART; *and coloured according to existing originals in Missals, Books of Devotion, Poems, &c. &c. many pages finished in gold and silver, each leaf mounted on a guard so as not to obtain a proper symmetry,* (pub. at £12. in parts, cost of binding £4.) *richly bound in purple morocco, gilt edges,* £12. 12s   Paris, Curmer, 1856

Accompanied with another or Appendix Volume, in which is given an account of the presumed writers of this well-known work, a history of the designs executed in the most superbly decorated Manuscripts known to exist; a Bibliographical Catalogue of Books and Manuscripts from which the ornaments in the other volume have been copied ; Holbein's Dance of Death, and La Danse Macabre, with facsimiles, &c. of which the exact titles follow:
Delaunay, l'abbé.—Des auteurs présumés de l'Imitation de Jésus-Christ; in 8 avec 4 portraits photographiés.
Denis, Ferd.—Histoire de l'ornementation des manuscrits; gr. in-8, avec lettres ornées et fleurons, d'après les manuscrits du VIe au XVIIe siècle.
Catalogue bibliographique des manuscrits reproduits dans l'Imitation de Jésus-Christ et des imprimés cités dans l'Histoire de l'ornementation des manuscrits, accompagné d'ornements.
Index des manuscrits et imprimés reproduits ou cités dans l'Imitation, avec l'indication des dessinateurs, etc., accompagné des figures de H. Holbein, Hans Beham et Jollat.

6682 KING (Thos.) Orfévrerie et Ouvrages en Metal du Moyen Age, 2 vols. roy. folio, 200 *plates of Mediaeval Art-Workmanship,* (pub. at £8.) *bds.* £3. 8s   Par. 1852-57
A very useful work for all practical Artists.

6683 KRAMER, über den Styl und die Herkunft der bemahlten griechischen Thongefässe, 8vo. *morocco,* 6s   Berlin, 1837

6684 KUGLER's Handbuch der Kunstgeschichte, 8vo. THICK PAPER, *cf. extra,* 10s   1842

6685 KUNST-BLATT, redigirt von SCHORN, FÖRSTER, und KUGLER, *vom Anfang,* 1820-49 (wanting 1848), 29 vols. *Stuttgart*—Deutsches Kunstblatt, von Kugler, Passavant, Waagen, etc. herausg. von EGGERS, Vols. I-VIII, *Leipzig und Berlin,* 1850-57—together 37 vols. twenty-six sm. 4to. eleven roy. 4to. *numerous plates to illustrate Early Engraving, Modern Art, Architecture, etc.* (pub. at 150 thalers) *bds.* £12. 12s   1820-57
I sold a copy, 1820-56, of this valuable Art Journal for £18.

6686 LABORDE, MONUMENS DE LA FRANCE, classés chronologiquement, et considérés sous le rapport des faits historiques et de L'ETUDE DES ARTS, 2 vols. atlas folio, PAPIER VÉLIN, *with about 270 engravings of the Antiquities of France, many with architectural details, hf. bd. uncut,* £7. 10s   Paris, 1816-36

Issued in 54 livraisons, in 3 states: the ordinary edition was published at 810 fr.; Vellum Paper, at 1350 fr.; Vellum Paper, Proofs before Letters, at 2250 fr.
This grand and important work of equal interest to the lovers of Works of Art to the Architect, contains Views of many highly interesting Monuments which were destroyed during the French Revolution.
Parmi les belles planches dont se compose cet ouvrage, on remarque surtout la representation des antiquités romaines d'Arles, Autun, Nismes, Orange, Frejus, Cavaillon, Saint-Camas, Vienne, Vaison, Reims, Saintes, Metz, Trèves, etc.
Les belles cathédrales d'Amiens, Auxerre, Auch, Arles, Angoulême, Bourges, Bayeux, Coutances, Caen, Chartres, Clermont, Dijon, Lyon, Mende, Metz, Narbonne, Orleans, Paris, Poitiers, Reims, Bodez, Rouen et Saint-Ouen, Sens, Strasbourg, Saint-Denis, Saint Gilles, Toul, Tours, Toulouse, etc.
Et parmi les châteaux, le Louvre, Ecouen, Blois, Chambord, Chaumont sur-Loire, Chenonceaux, Châteaudun, Chinon, Clisson, Jostelin, Meillant, Ussé, Joinville, Gaillon, Saint-Germain, La Rochefoucauld, etc. etc.

6687 LACROIX et SERÉ, LE MOYEN AGE et LA RENAISSANCE, 5 vols. 4to. *containing a series of fine engravings* (MANY SPLENDIDLY COLOURED) *from curious, exquisitely beautiful, and singular objects of Middle-Age Art, illustrative of Ancient Costume, Manners, Designs in Fresco, Paintings, Stained Glass, Missal and other illuminations, Furniture, Jewellery, Armour, etc.* £14. 10s   Par. 1848-51

A superb and very interesting work. Utterson's copy, in morocco, fetched, 1857, £24. 10s; Bernal's copy fetched £19, and was resold for £23.
A very beautiful work, the engravings exhibiting specimens of curious objects in Mediæval Art from all parts of Europe; there is indeed no other publication giving such a faithful picture of everything connected with the Middle Ages: as a drawing room book no other work could surpass it in beauty and interest.

6688 LAVATER'S ESSAYS ON PHYSIOGNOMY, translated by Hunter, 5 vols. roy. 4to. BEST AND ONLY COMPLETE EDITION, *with about 800 beautiful engravings, by* THOS. HOLLOWAY, BARTOLOZZI, *and others,* BRILLIANT IMPRESSIONS, *A* SUBSCRIBER'S COPY, *hf. cf. neat, with many rough leaves, almost uncut, a bargain,* £5.   1789-98

A fine original copy of this beautiful work, with early impressions of the plates, and quite free from the usual stains, similar to the above, seldom occurs. It has the rare list of subscribers at the end of Vol. V.

6689 **LAWRENCE'S** (Sir T.) CHOICEST WORKS, royal folio, 53 *most beautiful plates, engraved in the first style, by Cousins, Ward, &c.* FIRST PROOFS, LARGE PAPER, (pub. at £28. 7s) *hf. bd. red morocco, gilt edges, from Dr. Hawtrey's library,* £7. 7s 1835
One of the most charming works ever published. Independent of presenting no less than 50 and 3 additional of the choicest pictures of this great master, the volume forms likewise a most desirable companion to Sir Joshua Reynolds's Works, of which Dr. Hawtrey's splendid proof copy is also in my stock.

6690 **LENOIR**, MUSÉE DES MONUMENS FRANCAIS, Description historique et chronologique des Statues, Bas-Reliefs, et Tombeaux, pour servir à l'Histoire de France et de l'Art, avec l'Histoire de la Peinture sur Verre, Description des Vitraux anciennes et modernes, et une dissertation sur les COSTUMES de chaque siècle, 8 vols. 8vo. *upwards of 294 plates, calf gilt,* £3. Paris, 1800-21

6691 **LAZZARINI** (Giov. Andr. *Canonico*) Opere, 2 vols. 8vo. *port. sd. 5s* Pesaro, 1806
Contains a dissertation on Painting, and critical notices of Pictures at PESARO.

6692 **LEAR'S** (Edw.) Views in ROME and its ENVIRONS, impl. folio, *consisting of 25 fine lithographs, tinted,* (pub. at £4. 4s) *hf. bd. morocco,* 25s 1841
In 1855, Bernal's copy fetched £2. 12s 6d.

6693 ——— Illustrated Excursions in ITALY, 2 vols. atlas 4to. 65 *plates in double tints, and numerous very pretty woodcuts,* (pub. at £7. 7s) *cloth,* £2. 16s 1846

6694 **LITTA, FAMIGLIE CELEBRI ITALIANE**, a complete set, as far as published, 147 parts or dispense, arranged in 8 vols. roy. folio, A SERIES OF PEDIGREES, *with several thousand fine plates of Antiquities, Medals, Sculpture, and Paintings, the* PORTRAITS BEAUTIFULLY ILLUMINATED, *so as to resemble the Original Paintings by Early Italian Masters, all the* COATS OF ARMS *elaborately emblazoned* (pub. at 1796 francs in Italy, London selling price £80.) *clean and uncut, with* TITLES, TABLE *of* CONTENTS, *and* GENERAL INDEX *expressly printed for this copy,* £52. 10s Milano, 1819-63

6695 ——— the same, parts 1—136, bound in 8 vols. royal folio, quite perfect, the last eleven parts (137—147) in a uniform portfolio, *strongly hf. bd. red morocco, gilt tops, uncut,* £63. 1819-63
THE GRANDEST WORK OF THIS KIND PUBLISHED IN EUROPE. The earlier parts are out of print. The late noble author devoted his whole life and a large fortune to its publication. ☞ S e t s c o m p l e t e d and bound for possessors of copies.
To show the extent of this immense work, a List of the Families published is given.

Acciaioli di Firenze sp. 1834	Eccelini della Marco di Trevigi	Ordelaffi di Forli
Accolti di Arezzo spenta 1699	Erizzo di Venezia	Orseolo di Venezia spenta
Acquaviva di Napoli	Este (marchesi d')	Orsini di Roma
Adorno di Genova	Euffreducci di Fermo	Ottobono di Venezia sp. 1740
Aldobrandini di Firenze	Facchinetti di Bologna sp. 1685	Pallavicino
Alidosio d'Imola spenta	Faggiuola (Della) nel Montefeltro	Paleologo marchesi di Monferrato
Alighieri di Firenze sp. 1558	Farnesi duchi di Parma	Pazzi di Firenze
Altempo di Roma	Ferrero di Biella	Peretti di Montalto sp. 1655
Alviano (D') d'Orvieto sp. 1837	Fogliani di Reggio sp. 1785	Pico della Mirandola sp. 1787
Appiani di Pisa	Foscari di Venezia	Piccolomini Todeschini di Siena
Archinto di Milano	Fregoso di Genova	Pio di Carpi
Arcimboldi di Milano sp. 1727	Gaddi di Firenze spenta 1607	Pusteria (della) di Milano
Ariosto di Bologna sp. 1786	Gallio di Como spenta 1800	Rangoni di Modena
Barbo di Venezia	Gambacorta di Pisa sp. 1725	Rossi di Parma spenta 1825
Bentivoglio di Bologna	Gambara di Brescia	Rovere di Savona, Duchi d'Urbino
Bevilacqua di Verona	Gherardesca di Pisa	Roverella di Ferrara
Birago di Milano	Ghilini d'Alessandria	Sanvitale di Parma
Bojardo di Reggio sp. 1560	Giovio di Como	Savoja (duchi di)
Bonacolsi di Mantova sp. 1328	Giustiniani di Venezia	Scaligeri di Verona sp. 1598
Boncompagni di Bologna	Gonzaga di Mantova	Sforza Attendolo di Romagna
Bonelli di Roma	Gozzadini di Bologna	Simonetta di Calabria
Borromeo di S. Miniato	Grassi di Bologna spenta 1848	Sinibuldi di Pistoja sp. 1497
Buonarrato di Firenze	Guicciardini di Firenze	Soderini di Firenze
Buondelmonte di Firenze	Lando di Venezia sp. 1734	Stampa di Milano
Calcagnini di Ferrara	Lannoy di Napoli sp. 1604	Steno di Venezia
Camino (da) di Trevigi sp. 1422	Lodovisi di Bologna sp. 1699	Strozzi di Firenze
Candiano di Venezia sp. 1018	Macchiavelli di Firenze sp. 1727	Suevi re di Napoli sp. 1268
Cantelmi di Napoli sp 1749	Madruzzo di Trento sp 1658	Tiepolo di Venezia
Carraresi e Pappafava di Padova	Malaspina	Torelli di Ferrara
Carpegna, conti di, sp. 1749	Manfredi di Faenza	Torriani di Valsassina
Casali di Cortona	Marescotti di Bologna	Tornabuoni di Firenze spenta
Castiglioni di Milano	Martelli di Firenze	Trimci di Foligno sq. 1452
Cavalcabó di Cremona	Massimo di Roma	Trivulzio di Milano
Cavaniglia di Napoli sp. 1792	Mauruzi di Tolentino	Urbino, Duchi di
Cesarini di Roma spenta 1685	Medici di Firenze	Valori di Firenze spenta 1687
Cesi di Roma	Monferrato (marchesi di)	Varano di Camerino
Colonna di Roma	Monte (del) di Montesansovino	Verme (dal) di Verona
Concini di Arezzo sp. 1631	Monte Sa. Maria dell' Umbria (Marchesi del)	Vettori di Firenze
Contrari di Ferrara sp. 1575		Villani di Firenze sp. 1617
Corraro di Venezia	Montefeltro (conti del) sp. 1508	Visconti di Milano
Correggio da Correggio sp. 1711	Navagero di Venezia sp. 1713	Visconti già Aicardi di Milano
Da Polenta di Ravenna	Normanni Re di Sicilia sp. 1195	Vitelli di Citta di Castello

FINE ARTS, BOOKS OF PRINTS, PAINTINGS. 367

6696 LE ROY (Jac.) Notitia Marchionatus S. R. J., hoc est Urbis, et Agri Antverpiensis, folio, *numerous plates of Castles, Views, Seats, Coats of Arms, Monuments, etc. many by Hollar, fine impressions, drawing of arms from a stained glass window at Antwerp inserted, vellum*, 36s *Amst.* 1678

This copy has the FRENCH INDEX, *La Haye*, 1781, mentioned by Brunet; it has also the two Plates said to be frequently wanting. Nicol's copy fetched £3. 6s; at Evans's 1818, £3. 10s; Sotheby's 1856, £3.

6697 LE ROY, Castella et Prætoria Nobilium BRABANTIÆ, Cænobiaque celebriora, folio, FIRST EDITION, *several hundred beautiful engravings of Public Edifices, Castles, Chateaux, Churches, etc. by Van Croes, including the Antwerp Cathedral, by W. Hollar*, BRILLIANT IMPRESSIONS, *old calf gilt*, £4. 4s
Antverpiae, sumptibus autoris, 1697

Fetched 1818, Evans, £5. 10s. A second issue appeared, *Lugd. Bat.* 1699; another, *Amst.* 1705. Ouvrage recherché à cause des nombreuses vues des châteaux et dont plusieurs ont été gravées par Perelle, Hollar, Horrewyn et d'autres.

6698 LONDESBOROUGH. Catalogue of a collection of Ancient and Mediæval Rings and Personal Ornaments formed for Lady Londesborough, 4to. *x and 88 pp. woodcuts and 2 plates, hf. morocco, uncut*, £2. *Printed for private reference*, 1853

6699 LONDONIO. The Works of Francis Londonio, comprising Etchings of Cattle Pieces, Goats, Sheep, and large Pastoral Subjects, atlas fol. 154 *beautiful plates, most of them in rare states, printed on coloured paper and tinted, mounted in a large Scrap Book, half bound, dark blue morocco*, £3. 16s

The larger subjects are etched by the Artist after his own Paintings. In all these works the combination of the groups of Shepherds and Cattle are singularly life-like.

6700 LUINI. Lo SCAFFALE, or presses in the Sacristy of the Church of Sta. Maria delle Grazie at MILAN; illustrations of the painted decoration by Bernardino Luini, chromo-lithographed under the direction of L. GRUNER, roy. folio, 30 *plates of Festoons, Borders, Panels, Shields, etc, finely executed in colours*, (pub. at £3. 3s) *cloth*, 32s 1859-60

6701 LUYNES (le Duc de) et F. J. DEBACQ, MÉTAPONTE (in Magna Grecia) atlas folio, *with 10 plates of Early Grecian Art, bds. privately printed*, 28s *Par.* 1833

6702 LYSONS (SAMUEL) COLLECTION OF GLOUCESTERSHIRE ANTIQUITIES, Engraved on One Hundred and Ten Plates, *etched by the talented author, depicting Churches, Castles, Ancient Houses, Tombs, Sculpture, Stained Glass, Seals, &c. &c.* A VERY EARLY AND ORIGINAL COPY OF THIS VALUABLE PICTORIAL VOLUME *on Colombier paper, with the plates of stained glass, effigies, &c. coloured by hand under the direction of the editor.* ONLY TWELVE COPIES SO EXECUTED, *russia, gilt edges, broad gold borders*, £12. 1804

This noble volume is further illustrated by Engravings peculiar to the County from other sources, neatly laid down; also by a copy of the Rev. Cooper Willyams's History of Sudeley Castle, in Gloucestershire, with a View; THREE DRAWINGS, BY ROBINS, of the Thatched House, near Cheltenham, taken in 1745, the Views being those of A south-east prospect of Sudeley Castle and Town of Whinchcombe; south-east prospect of Hales Abbey, County Gloucester—*both in colours*; a west prospect of the Spa and Town of Cheltenham *in indian ink*—this latter is on VELLUM, and being taken when only 35 years had elapsed after the Mineral Spa had been discovered, and long before much of a place of fashionable resort had been built up around it, deserves the especial attention of the Gloucestershire collector.

6703 MAMACHI, de' COSTUMI de' primitivi Cristiani, 3 vols. 8vo. *numerous plates representing Martyrdoms, vellum*, 25s *Roma*, 1753

6704 MARRYAT. Collections towards a History of Pottery and Porcelain in the Fifteenth, Sixteenth, Seventeenth, and Eighteenth Centuries; with a Description of the Manufacture, a Glossary, and a List of Monograms, by Joseph Marryat, 8vo. *illustrated with coloured plates and woodcuts, cloth*, 36s 1850

6705 ——— the same, LARGE PAPER, 4to. *with* 12 LARGE COLOURED PLATES, *and upwards of* 100 WOODCUTS, *these on* INDIA PAPER, *hf. morocco*, £10. 1851

BEST EDITION, very rare, only a few copies were executed in this style.

6706 ——— the same, second edition, revised and augmented (as regards the text), 8vo. *with 2 coloured plates, each containing 2 vases, and many woodcuts*, 25s 1857

" As a handbook the value of this work is very great, and we know of no other in which so large an amount of interesting matter connected with pottery and porcelain is to be found. The book is anecdotical throughout. Any one taking it up will be astonished with it. Its numerous coloured plates and woodcuts and its fine type gratify the eye, and on every page will be found information of the most curious and varied kind."—*Athenæum*.

6707 MEYRICK: SKELTON'S (Jos.) Antient Arms and Armour, from the Collection of Llewelyn Meyrick, and with the Descriptions of Dr. Meyrick, 2 vols. impl. 4to. *with 150 plates of Arms and Armour, hf. bd. morocco, gilt tops*, (pub. at £11. 11s) £4. 5s *Lond.* 1830

6708 MEYRICK'S PAINTED ILLUSTRATIONS OF ANCIENT ARMS AND ARMOUR, a Critical Inquiry into Ancient Armour as it existed in Europe, but particularly in England, from the Norman Conquest to the Reign of Charles II., with a Glossary, &c., by SIR SAMUEL RUSH MEYRICK, LL.D., F.S.A., &c. new and greatly improved edition, corrected and enlarged by the Author himself, with the assistance of Literary and Antiquarian Friends (Albert Way, &c.) 3 vols. impl. 4to. *illustrated by more than* 100 *plates, splendidly* ILLUMINATED, *mostly in gold and silver, exhibiting some of the finest specimens existing in England, also a new plate of the Tournament of Locks and Keys,* (pub. at £21.) *neatly hf. bd. morocco, gilt extra, full gilt backs and edges,* 8s 8s   1842

   Sir Walter Scott justly describes this collection as "the incomparable Armoury."
"This most superb Archæological work is animated with numerous novelties, curious and historical disquisitions, and brilliant and recondite learning—Learning going to Court in the full, rich costume of the Order of the Garter.—Plates as fine as the monuments of Westminster Abbey. Really and truly the work is admirably executed, and deserves every eulogy."—*Edinburgh Review.*

6709 MICHAEL ANGELO'S SISTINE CHAPEL, oblong folio, general View and 41 beautiful plates in brown aquatint, INDIA PROOFS, *hf. bd. calf,* VERY RARE, £5. 5s   *Engraved and published by J. Linnell,* 1833

6710 MICHIELS (A.) Histoire de la Peinture FLAMANDE et HOLLANDAISE, avec le Supplément, 4 vols. 8vo. *hf. morocco,* 18s   Bruxelles, 1845-48

6711 —— the same, 4 vols. 8vo. *Papier Vélin, hf. calf,* 25s   1845-48

6712 MILLIN, Antiquités Nationales, ou Recueil de Monumens pour servir à l'Histoire générale et particulière de l'Empire François, tels que Tombeaux, Inscriptions, Statues, Vitraux, Fresques, etc. 5 vols. 4to. *with several hundred fine engravings of early Paintings, Inscriptions, Tombs, Monuments, etc. calf gilt,* £2. 5s   Paris, 1790-98

6713 —— Monumens Antiques Inedits, ou nouvellement expliqués, 2 vols. 4to. 99 *plates of Statues, Bas-Reliefs, Paintings, Mosaics, Inscriptions, Medals, etc. bds.* 20s   Paris, 1802-6

6714 —— Dictionnaire des Beaux-Arts, 3 vols. 8vo. *vellum,* 7s   Paris, 1806

6715 —— Voyage dans les Départemens du Midi de la France, 4 vols. in 5, 8vo. *calf, with* 4to. *atlas of* 51 *plates of Antiquities, hf. russia,* 25s   Par. 1807-11

  North's copy fetched £2. 12s. "Un des ouvrages de Millin les plus intéressants."—*Brunet.*

6716 MOLANUS de usu vero Imaginum Picturarumque, ed. Paquot, 4to. 8s   Lov. 1771

6716*MONTANI (Arii) Humanæ Salutis Monumenta, 8vo. *containing portrait and* 71 *beautiful engravings to the Old and New Testament, by the* WIERXES, *David, Bolswert, and others; fine impressions, blue morocco, gilt edges,* £2. 12s 6d   Antv. Plantin, 1571

   The Towneley copy fetched £5. 7s 6d.

6717 MONTFAUCON, l'Antiquité expliquée et representée en Figures, avec le Supplément, 15 vols. in 10, folio, *upwards of* 1300 *fine plates, representing every kind of Greek, Roman, and Etruscan Art Monuments, classified according to subjects, old calf gilt, Mr. Buckle's copy,* £10.   Paris, 1722-4

"Of the importance of this great book to the antiquarian and the historical world it is hardly possible to speak too highly. Its object was to lay before the public a vast series of objects of ancient art, of architecture, of sculpture, etc., and to illustrate the whole by plates, executed in the highest style which the age admitted of. This the learned author effected most completely; and it is to this very book that the foundation of all our most important branches of archæological knowledge at the present day may be ascribed. The obligations of the continental antiquary to Montfaucon are immense; and his work will stand the test of future ages, as one of the most astonishing and certainly one of the most extensive monuments of antiquarian research ever made by one man. The price is still from fifteen to twenty guineas, and it is likely to increase rather than to sink in value."
                H. L. Jones. Gent.'s Mag. Dec. 1855.

6717*MONTFAUCON'S (Bernard de) Regal and Ecclesiastical Antiquities of FRANCE, translated from the French, 2 vols. in 1, folio, *illustrated with* 304 *plates, calf neat,* £4.   1750

  This is an English issue of the "Monarchie Françoise, 5 vols. folio," a book which is now very rare, and has greatly risen in price.

6718 MONUMENTA illustrium Virorum et Elogiæ, sm. folio, *with about* 100 *engravings of Funeral Monuments, Tombs, Inscriptions, Urns, etc. vellum,* 30s   Traj. ad Rhenum, 1671

6719 MOYEN-AGE MONUMENTAL ET ARCHEOLOGIQUE, Vues, Details, et Plans des Monumens les plus remarquables de l'Europe, depuis le VIe. jusqu'au XVIe Siècle, lithographiés par les Artistes les plus distingués de la Capitale, d'après les Dessins de M. Chapuy, avec l'Histoire de l'Architecture au Moyen-Age, par Daniel Ramée, 2 vols. royal folio, *containing* 444 *finely executed lithographic engravings of Views, Details, and Plans of Architectural Monuments and Sculptures of the Middle Ages,* (pub. at £20. in parts) *hf. bd. red morocco, uncut,* £12.   Paris, 1843-45

  This is a work of similar character to the following article, the Moyen Age Pittoresque, published in 1837, with 180 Plates, and should be united with it.

FINE ARTS, BOOKS OF PRINTS, PAINTINGS.

6720 MOYEN AGE PITTORESQUE, Monumens et Fragmens d'Architecture, Meubles et Armes, du X au XVI Siècle, dessinés d'après Nature par CHAPUY, 2 vols. large folio, *containing* 180 *fine lithographic engravings of the Architecture, Ornaments, and Furniture of the Middle Ages*, with descriptive Letter-press, (pub. at £15. 15s bds.) *half bound morocco, top edges gilt*, £4. 10s
Paris. Veith and Hauser, 1837-40

Priced, 1847, £9. 9s: in 1855, Bernal's copy fetched, russia, £7. 15s; priced, 1847, INDIA PAPER, £11. 11s; the PLATES COLOURED, mor. £21.

6721 MÜLLER (K. O.) Ancient Art and its remains; by Leitch, 8vo. (pub. at 18s) *cloth*, 10s   1847

A most valuable manual of the Archaeology of Art.

6722 MUELLER (C. O.) DENKMAELER der ALTEN KUNST, gezeichnet und radirt von C. Oesterley, 2 vols. in 1, oblong sm. folio, 149 *plates of ancient Art, hf. morocco extra, gilt edges*, £2.   *Göttingen*, 1835-56

6723 MÜLLER (F. H.) Beiträge zur Teutschen Kunst- und Geschichtskunde durch Kunstdenkmale, 2 vols. in 1, impl. 4to. 41 *plates of Monuments and Stained Glass (in colours), Ivory Carvings, &c. hf. mor.* 10s   *Darmstadt*, 1832-33

The title-page to the first volume is bound at the end of the second.

6724 MURPHY'S ARABIAN ANTIQUITIES OF SPAIN, atlas folio, AN ORIGINAL COPY, *with* 100 *fine plates of Architecture, Ornaments, etc. by Le Keux and others*, (pub. at £42.) *whole bd.* MOROCCO *super extra, gold borders, gilt edges*, £7. 15s 1813

6725 MURR, Bibliothèque de Peinture, de Sculpture, et de Gravure, 2 vols. 12mo. *with Alphabetical Index of Authors, hf. bd. uncut*, 6s   *Francfort*, 1770

6726 —— Journal zur Kunst-Geschichte und zur allgemeinen Litteratur, 17 vols. in 9, 12mo. *plates, hf. bd.* £2. 2s   *Nürnberg*, 1775-89

A very valuable and learned repository of Antiquarian, Artistic, Philological and Literary Treatises, positively indispensable to a public library.

6727 MUSÉE FRANCAIS, ou, COLLECTION COMPLETTE DES TABLEAUX, STATUES ET BAS-RELIEFS, qui composent la Collection Nationale, avec l'Explication des Sujets et des Discours sur la Peinture, la Sculpture, et la Gravure par S. C. Croze, Magnan, Robillard, Peronville, Laurent, Visconti et David, 4 vols. atlas folio, 343 *superb plates*, ORIGINAL EDITION, *with very brilliant impressions of The Laocoon, The Transfiguration by Raphael, St. Cecilia, Infant Hercules, &c. hf. bound russia, uncut*, £45.   *Paris*, 1803-11

The present copy was carefully selected by Mr. Dawson Turner, while in Paris in 1808.
Published in 80 livraisons of 48 francs each, being 3840 fr.; priced, 1824. Rivington's, £190.; 1820, J. Bohn, £105., mor. £130.; 1831, H. Bohn, £120.; 1840, Payne and Foss, £105.; 1817, £52. 10s.—By auction, copies fetched at Sotheby's, 1832, £56.: 1855, Southgate's, mor. £51.; 1856, Sotheby's, russia, £53.
Proofs before letters were published, 96 francs the livraison, being 7680 fr.; priced, 1829, Longman, £180.; 1831, H. Bohn, £150.—By auction, copies fetched, 1855, J. Wilks's, £81.; 1855, Baker's, £86. 2s.

6728 MUSÉE ROYAL, Recueil de Gravures d'après les plus beaux Tableaux, Statues et Bas-reliefs de la Collection Royale, par LAURENT, 2 vols. atlas folio, *brilliant impressions of the* 161 *beautiful plates, half morocco, fine* ORIGINAL COPY, £16. 16s   *Paris*, 1816-18

6729 MUSÉE FRANCAIS ET MUSÉE ROYAL; ou Recueil des Tableaux et Bas-Reliefs qui composent les Galéries Napoleon et Royale par Robillard-Peronville, et Laurent, 7 vols. atlas folio, **both series**, *original and brilliant* **Proofs before the Letters**, *richly bound in green morocco, broad leather joints inside, gold borders round the outsides, which also are decorated with the Imperial insignia worked in gold in the centres*, £170.   *Paris*, 1803-16

Selected by express command for the late Mr. Beckford, at the dispersion of whose effects at Fonthill this fine copy was purchased by its late proprietor. The volumes are each enclosed in separate cases lined with leather. A matchless copy of the grandest series of Engravings by the most distinguished artists from such a collection of Paintings by Masters of the several Schools as can never again be united.
These two works, the MUSÉE FRANÇAIS and MUSÉE ROYAL, form ONE SET; they were priced, 1840, 6 vols. £100.; the RE-ISSUE of both Works, 6 vols. can be supplied for about £30. PROOFS BEFORE LETTERS, the 2 Series were priced, 1847, H. Bohn, £168, and morocco, £200.

L'un des plus beaux monumens élevés aux arts est,sans contredit,cette vaste collection d'estampes, commencée en 1802, sous le nom de Musée Français, continuée et terminée sous le titre de Musée Royal, per MM. Laurent père et fils. A l'exposition de 1819, la medaille d'or fut decernée à Mr. Henri Laurent, le jury considerant cet ouvrage comme le plus parfait qui ait eu lieu depuis l'existence de la gravure.

This very interesting publication is undoubtedly the most magnificent work that has issued from the Parisian Press; and will perpetuate the matchless collection which formerly graced the Louvre, combining, as it did, nearly all the excellence of which the various countries on the Continent could boast in painting and sculpture. And although a chain of wonderful events has restored many of the brightest gems of art to their rightful owners, so much of excellence still remains, that the gallery of the Louvre is yet, to the man of taste, the greatest attraction in Paris, and the very circumstance of the dispersion of so many wonderful productions gives additional value to the work which describes them in a collected state.

It is necessary to observe, that this work is not a mere collection of Prints, as it contains many luminous and masterly dissertations upon the state of the arts in different ages, observations upon the style, excellence, and defects of the various schools in painting; a minute description of every painting, &c. drawn with extreme care and correctness.

6730 MUSEO BORBONICO (Real) 15 vols. 4to. *with upwards of* 800 *beautiful engravings of Statues, Bas-Reliefs, ancient Paintings, Vases, Candelabra, &c. very fine subscription copy, whole bound vellum, fine copy*, £20.   *Napoli*, 1828-59
One volume more will complete the work.
6731 MUSEO BORBONICO (REAL) fasc. 8-40 inclusive, 4to. *many beautiful plates*, £2. 10s   *Napoli*, 1827-34
6732 MUSEUM WORSLEYANUM: a Collection of Antique Basso-Relievos, Busts, Statues, and Gems, with Views in the Levant, taken on the spot in 1785-6 and 7, formerly in the possession of Sir R. Worsley, 2 vols. impl. 4to. *with above* 150 *exquisitely beautiful engravings, fine impressions*, (pub. at £12. 12s) *whole russia, gilt tops, uncut*, 36s   1824
Subscription copy, No. 40.
6733 MUSEUM of PAINTING and SCULPTURE, or, Collection of the principal Pictures, Statues, and Bas-Reliefs in the Public and Private Galleries of Europe, drawn and etched by REVEIL, with descriptive critical and historical notices by Duchesne, senior, *Text in English and French*, 17 vols. 12mo. *with near* 1200 *outline engravings*, EARLY IMPRESSIONS, *cloth, gilt tops*, £4. 4s   1828-33
6734 NAGLER'S (G. K.) DICTIONARY OF ARTISTS: Neues allgemeines Künstler-Lexicon, oder Nachrichten von dem Leben und den Werken der Maler, Bildhauer, Baumeister, Kufperstecher, Formschneider, &c. 22 vols. 8vo. *bds. scarce*, £8. 10s   *München*, 1825-52
The best book of its kind, now very scarce.
6735 NASH'S (Jos.) MANSIONS OF ENGLAND in the Olden Time. The FOUR SERIES COMPLETE, *consisting of upwards of* 100 *large and tinted lithographic drawings of existing Views, depicting the most characteristic Features of the Domestic Architecture of the Tudor Age, and also illustrating the Customs, Habits, and Recreations of our Ancestors, with Descriptions,* 4 vols. imp. folio, *hf. morocco,* AN ORIGINAL COPY (pub. at £16. 16s) *hf. morocco*, £10. 10s   1839-49
6736 NASH'S Old Mansions of England and Wales, as now existing, a COMPLETE COLOURED SET of this beautiful and interesting work, atlas folio, *consisting of nearly* 100 FINE LARGE PLATES, BEAUTIFULLY COLOURED LIKE DRAWINGS, *mounted on tinted cardboards (published at £42) and enclosed in* 2 *portfolios, in this state very scarce*, £21.   1839-49
"Nash's Mansions" has always been considered one of the most beautiful and attractive works ever published, and has met with a proportionate success.
6737 NASH'S ARCHITECTURE OF THE MIDDLE AGES, exhibiting Sketches of Ecclesiastical and other Edifices, drawn from Nature on stone, and tinted, imp. folio, 25 *plates* (pub. at £4. 4s) *hf. morocco, a genuine copy*, 36s   *London*, 1838
6738 —— Views of the Interior and Exterior of WINDSOR CASTLE, impl. folio, 26 *lithographic views* (pub. at £4. 4s) *hf. morocco*, 25s   1852
6739 NEALE'S (J. P.) VIEWS of the SEATS of Noblemen and Gentlemen in ENGLAND, WALES, SCOTLAND, and IRELAND, 11 vols. large 8vo. 720 *fine plates*, (pub. at £27. 10s) £8. 10s   *Lond.* 1822-29
6740 NEALE'S VIEWS of the Seats of Noblemen and Gentlemen in England, Wales, Scotland, and Ireland, SECOND SERIES, 5 vols. 4to. *complete, with* 300 *pretty plates*, INDIA PROOFS, *bds.* £4. 10s   1824-29
6741 NOVELLI. Gallo, Elogio di Pietro Novelli, Pittore, Architetto, ed Incisore, sm. folio, *portrait and* 8 *plates, half calf, gilt top, uncut*, 9s   *Palermo*, 1830
6742 **ORNAMENTS.** ANTONELLI, Collezione de' migliori Ornamenti Antichi nella Città di VENEZIA, oblong royal 4to. 120 *plates of Ornaments, Fresco Paintings, Borders, etc.* cloth, 32s   *Venezia*, 1831
6743 BORSATO (Gius.) OPERE ORNAMENTALI, pubblicate per cura dell' I. R. Accademia di Belle Arti di Venezia; con cenni storici dell' Ornato Decorativo Italiano di VALLARDI, royal folio, *with* 60 *highly finished Etchings of Monuments, Altars, Chimney Pieces, Candelabra, Lamps, Tables, Seats, Pilasters, Beds, &c.* (pub. at £4. 4s) *hf. bd.* 30s   *Milano*, 1831
6744 HOFFMAN et KELLERHOFEN, Recueil de Dessins relatifs à l'Art de la DECORATION, 2 vols. royal folio, 80 *plates, of which* 41 *are richly executed in colours* (pub. at 150f.) *hf. morocco*, £5. 10s   *Paris*, 1858
6745 KOLB (J. C.) neu inventirtes Laub Bandl und Groteschgen Werck, vor Mahler, Bildhauer und Stucator, oblong folio, 10 *elegant plates of Arabesque Ornaments in the style of Raphael*, 7s 6d   *s. l. e. a.* (? *Augsburg*, 1600)
6746 PRANGEY (Girault de) Choix d'Ornements Moresques de l'Alhambra, large folio, 30 *plates on India paper by Peyre, hf. morocco*, 16s   *Paris, Hauser*
See also, Cuvilliès, Jones, Pergolesi.

FINE ARTS, BOOKS OF PRINTS, PAINTINGS. 371

6747 OTTLEY'S Inquiry into the Origin and EARLY HISTORY OF ENGRAVING upon Copper and in Wood; with an Account of the Engravers and their Works, from the invention of Chalcography by Maso Finiguerra to the time of Marc Antonio Raimondi, 2 vols. 4to. *illustrated with numerous facsimiles of ancient, rare, and curious engravings,* (pub. at £8. 8s in bds.) red morocco, £6.   1816

In 1860, Scarisbrook's copy, calf, fetched £6. 12s 6d.

6748 —— the same, 2 vols. impl. 4to. LARGE PAPER, PROOF IMPRESSIONS ON INDIA PAPER, *only 50 copies printed (pub. at £16. 16s bds.) hf. bd. russia, joints, gilt tops,* £18. 18s   1816

This magnificent book is printed uniformly with Dibdin's Ames, and with that work forms a grand series of the History of Printing and Engraving.

"Mr. Ottley is the first among us who has treated of the early art of Engraving in a manner which it deserves to be treated; and the embellishments which he has introduced are equally distinguished for their felicity and fidelity.—*Dibdin.*— " See Ottley's excellent History of Engraving.—*Lord Lindsay's Christian Art,* v. iii. p. 354.

6749 OTTLEY'S Italian School of Design, being a series of Facsimiles of Original Drawings of the most Eminent Painters and Sculptors of Italy, with Notices of their Lives and Works, impl. folio, LARGE VELLUM PAPER, *with 84 beautiful plates,* FIRST PROOF IMPRESSIONS, (pub. at £25. 4s) *hf. bd. russia, joints, scarce,* £8. 8s   1823

A *hf. bd.* copy fetched, 1853, Sotheby's, £8. 8s. The ordinary edition is common, published at £12. 12s.

6750 **PAGEANTS.** ENTRÉE solennelle et pompeuse de Robert Dudley, COMTE DE LEYCESTER, à la Haye en Hollande, lors qu'il y vint en qualité de Gouverneur pour Elizabeth Reine d'Angleterre, en 1535, 20 *plates of the magnificent reception, Triumphal Arches, Allegorical representations,* etc. by F. T. DE BRY; fine PORTRAITS of Queen Elizabeth in her Youth, and of the Earl of Leicester, both engraved by Crispin de Pass,

Marriage of the English Princess Matilde with the Elector of the Palatinate, in 1594, 6 *fine plates by Keller,* 1613

Ponte fatto dalla Citta di Messina a Don Gioan d'Austria, 1571, 4 *plates*

Magnificences faites à la Cour de Florence pour le Mariage de Cosme de Medicis, avec Marie d'Autriche, 1603—Battaglia Navale rap. in Arno per le Nozze del Principe di Toscana, 1608—61 *fine plates, chiefly by Giulio Parigi*

Carousel fait à Boulogne par l'Academie des Terbidi pour le Gr. Duc de Toscane, 1628, 14 *large plates by* CORIOLANO

Opera repr. à Munich pour la Naissance du Prince Maximilien, 1662, 17 *remarkably spirited plates by* M. KÜSELL

Vosmeri Principes Hollandiae, *Antv.* 1578, 31 *fine full length portraits,* in full COSTUME, engraved by P. Galle

Further 37 miscellaneous engravings of Entries, etc. making in all 172, the whole carefully collected and mounted in 1 vol. atlas folio, by FOSSARD "ordinaire de la Musique du Roi" in 1691, and bound in spotted vellum, £10.

6751 VITALE (Pietro) Relazione delle massime Pompe festive de' Palermitani per la Vittoria ottenuta contro i Collegati con le forze di Filippo V. folio, *with* 14 *plates of Public Festivities, vellum,* 25s   *Palermo,* 1711

6752 WRIT (G. M.) Ragguaglio della solenne Comparsa fatta in Roma, 8 Gennaio, 1687, dall' Conte di Castlemaine Ambasciatore straordinario di Giacomo II, sm. folio, 16 *fine engravings by A. van Westerhout, of the Procession and Ceremonials, one a large six-folded plate of a Banquet, vellum,* 15s   *Roma,* 1687

6753 PALEY'S Illustrations of Baptismal Fonts, 8vo. *a series of* 125 *fine wood engravings, with descriptions, hf. morocco,* 12s 6d   1844

6754 PANOFKA, Tod des Skiron und des Patroclus—Verlegene Mythen—Griechinnen und Griechen—Aegialea, Vendetta di Venere—Die Heilgötter der Griechen; and others, in all 9 Tracts, in 1 vol. imp. 4to. *numerous fine plates of Vases, Coins, Figures, etc. from Bunsen's library,* 21s   1836-48

6755 PASCOLI (L.) Vite de PITTORI, SCULTORI, ed ARCHITETTI moderni, 2 vols. 4to. *calf neat,* 18s   *Roma,* 1730-36

6756 —— the same, 2 vols.—Vite de' Pittori Perugini, *Roma,* 1732—together 3 vols. sm. 4to. *calf,* 25s   1730-36

6757 —— Vita de' Pittori, Scultori, ed Architetti Perugini, 4to. *vellum,* 10s   1732

6758 PERGOLESI, Collection of 370 Designs on 55 Plates, impl. folio, *the Ornamental portion extremely beautiful, the centres designed by Cipriani, and engraved by Bartolozzi, hf. bd. uncut, rare,* £2. 16s   1777-85

6759 PIPPI. Istoria della Vita e delle Opere di G. Pippi Romano, scritta da Carlo d'Arco, large folio, 90 *plates, half calf, gilt top*, £2. 16s *Mantova*, 1838

6760 PIRANESI, OPERE D' ARCHITETTURA, etc. A GRAND WORK on the ANTIQUITIES, ARCHITECTURE, and CLASSICAL ORNAMENT of ANCIENT ROME: AN UNRIVALLED SERIES OF ENGRAVINGS, ORIGINAL ROMAN COPY, comprising:

I.-IV. ANTICHITÀ ROMANE, 4 vols. atlas folio, *with the letterpress and* 218 *plates, fine old impressions* *Roma*, 1756

V. RACCOLTA de' TEMPJ Antichi, *Sciographia, a folding plate; dedication, a printed leaf; text, pp.* 1-24; *plates*, 1-13—TEMPIO DELL' ONORE e della Virtu, *title and text, pp.* 1-10; 8 *plates* 1780

VI. ANTICHITÀ ROMANE de' Tempi della Repubblica e de' primi Imperatori, parte I, *plates* 1-15, *title included;* Antichità Romane, parte II, *engraved title and plates* 16-29 *Roma, s. a.*

VII. DE ROMANORUM MAGNIFICENTIA ET ARCHITECTURA, *engraved title, portrait of Clement XIII.; dedication, a leaf; text, pp.* 1-212; *engraved Italian title, and* 38 *plates, several folded* *Roma*, 1761

VIII. TROFEI di Ottaviano Augusto, con altri ORNAMENTI ANTICHI, *engraved title and a small engraving on one plate, and* 28 *plates, mostly folding, of Ornaments and Vases* *s. a.*

IX. DEL CASTELLO DELL' ACQUA GIULIA, *engraved title,* 26 *pp. text and* 19 *plates on* 18 *s. a.*

LAPIDES CAPITOLINI sive Fasti Consulares triumphalesque Romanorum, *a printed and an engraved title, engraved dedication, preface,* 2 *leaves of text, and very large folding plate; printed text,* 61 *pp.* 1761

DELLE ANTICHITA DI CORA, *a printed and an engraved title, pp.* 1-15, *printed on page* 16 *an engraving, and* 10 *folding plates* *s. a.*

X. CAMPUS MARTIUS antiquae urbis, *engraved title,* 1 *plate; ground plan,* 1 *plate; dedication,* 4 *printed leaves; text, pp.* 1-70; *Index, pp.* 1-12; *Catalogus*, 1-18; *plates* 1-48; *the large sheet* 5-10 *mounted on canvas* *Roma*, 1762

XI. ANTICHITÀ D'ALBANO e di Castel Gandolfo, *printed title, engraved title, dedication, a folding plate; dedication, a printed leaf; text, pp.* 1-26; *plates,* 1-26—Descrizione e Disegno del Emissario del LAGO ALBANO, *engraved title, text, pp.* 1-20: *Roma,* 1762; *plates* 1-9; *text,* 1-10, *Roma,* 1762; *plates,* 1-12—together 50 *plates, fine Roman impressions* *s. a.*

XII.-XIII. VASI, CANDELABRI, Cippi, Sarcofagi, Tripodi, Lucerne ed Ornamenti antichi, 2 vols. elephant folio, *containing* 112 *beautiful engravings, bound in the full size,* NOT FOLDED, *the title to Vol. I. in* 2 *plates, Vases, etc. plate* 2—112, *plate* 22 *a double one; title to Vol. II. forms plate* 56 *Roma*, 1778

XIV. TROFEI de Daci, de Sarmati, ed altri popoli alleati, scolpiti nella fascia e nel piedestallo della COLONNA TRAJANA, 24 *plates, viz. title a double plate; inscription* 2 *plates; portrait of Clement XIV., tav. III. the Trajan Column,* 10 *feet long, pasted together, IV. a double plate, V.-XX. plates* 13 *and* 14 *pasted together* *s. a.*

COLONNA eretta in memoria dell' Apoteosi di ANTONINO PIO, 6 *plates, and the folding plate of the Column* *s. a.*

XV. PAESTUM. Differentes Vues de quelques Restes de trois grands Edifices qui subsistent encore dans le milieu de l'ancienne Ville de Pesto, autrement Possidonia, *frontispiece, and* 20 *superb folding plates, brilliant impressions* *s. a.*

XVI.-XVII. VEDUTE DI ROMA, 2 vols. elephant folio, *consisting of* 136 *grand and* SPLENDID VIEWS, *viz., title, plan in* 2 *plates pasted together, and* 133 *large plates bound in full size,* NOT FOLDED, *original and choice Roman impressions* *s. a.*

XVIII. STATUE ANTICHE, 41 *fine plates, four of them folding* *s. a.*

XIX. TEATRO d' ERCOLANO, *printed title, engraved title, a folding plate, text,* 4 *leaves,* 9 *folding plates* *Roma*, 1782

XX. DIVERSE Maniere d'adornare i Camini, *printed title, engraved title, folding plate, dedication, a printed leaf, printed text, pp.* 1-36, *and* 67 *plates* *Roma*, 1769

XXI. OPUSCULA VARIA ET INEDITA, Catalogo, 1 *plate;* Villa d'Horazio, 4 *small plates, inlaid*—LETTERE (due) di Giustificazione a Milord Charlemont, 4to. *engraved title, and* 8 *plates, inlaid, Roma,* 1757—Osservazioni di G. B. Piranesi sopra la lettere de M. Mariette, 1754, *Roma,* 1765, *engraved title,* 24 *printed pages, with vignettes*—Lettere, 32 pp. 4to. *inlaid*

Together 21 vols. bound in 19, five of them bound full size, elephant folio, the remainder in atlas folio, *comprising upwards of* 1000 MOST MAGNIFICENT PLATES, GENUINE EARLY ROMAN IMPRESSIONS, WHOLE BOUND RED MOROCCO, *gilt edges, a splendid set of books,* £95. *Roma,* 1756-82

The Marquis of Townshend's copy, 14 vols. fetched £157. 10s; North's, £252.; the Fonthill, £168. Piranesi's Works are a most imposing and at the same time most attractive set of books; nowhere is the grandeur of Ancient Rome better expressed than by Piranesi's bold designs.

6761 PIRANESI, le Magnificenze di Roma: stampe rappresentanti le più cospicue Fabbriche di ROMA MODERNA, oblong atlas folio, 70 *plates,* EARLIEST IMPRESSIONS, *old calf gilt,* £4. *Roma,* 1751

Collation: Portrait, printed title; VEDUTE DI ROMA, engraved title, 33 plates; INVENZIONI DI CARCERI, engraved title, and 13 plates, THE ORIGINAL ETCHINGS, *differing from the regular issue;* ARCHITETTURE e Prospettive, engraved title, and 16 plates, with 7 other plates and a plan.

6762 PIRANESI, Carceri d'Invenzione, impl. folio, 14 *very fine bold plates, Proof Impressions, bds.* £2. 2s *Roma, s. a.*

6763 PLOOS VAN AMSTEL'S IMITATIONS OF DRAWINGS BY THE PRINCIPAL DUTCH and FLEMISH MASTERS. Collection d'Imitations de Dessins d'après les principaux Maîtres Hollandais et Flamands; avec des Renseignemens historiques et detaillés sur ces Maîtres et sur leurs Ouvrages; et un Discours sur l'Etat ancien et moderne des Arts dans les Pays Bas, 3 vols. atlas folio, *containing* 103 *beautiful Engravings after Ostade, Teniers, Rembrandt, Van Dyck, Terburg, Gerard Douw, Rubens, Brouwer, Netscher, Jan Steen, Wouvermans, Paul Potter, Van de Velde, Berghem, Cuyp, Bakhuizen, Ruysdael, Both, and many others,* EXECUTED IN EXACT IMITATION OF THE ORIGINAL DRAWINGS, MANY BEAUTIFULLY COLOURED, edited by C. Josi of the British Museum, (pub. at £63.) *hf. bound, an original copy, rare,* £20. 1821

Of this beautiful work only 100 copies were executed; the above is a genuine subscriber's copy, for which the price of sixty guineas was paid. Even inferior copies now rarely occur for sale.

6764 PLOOS VAN AMSTEL. Opera aeri incisorum Extyporum, quasi manu exarata et delineata excellentissimorum inter Belgas Pictorum imitantium, folio, THE ORIGINAL EDITION, COMPLETE, *Dedication, and* 61 *inimitable Engravings, mounted on* 59 *leaves, executed in an unique manner, reproducing the designs of the Flemish Masters so as to resemble the originals,* (15 *of them are variations, Artists' Proofs*) *half bd. calf, with* 8vo. *text,* £10. 1765

A perfect copy of the original edition. "Mr. Corneille Ploos van Amstel a inventé une manière tout à fait particulière pour graver des desseins, tellement qu'il n'st pas aisé d'en comprendre le procédé, c'est à dire le méchanisme."—*Heineken Idée,* p. 109.

6765 POMPEI. GELL AND GANDY'S Pompeiana: the Topography, Edifices, and Ornaments of Pompeii, the result of Excavations before 1819, forming the *first series,* 2 vols. in 1, royal 8vo. *containing* 77 *fine plates, by Cooke, Heath, and Pye, original edition, morocco extra, gilt edges, scarce,* £3. 3s 1817-19

6766 —— the same, 4to. LARGE PAPER, *Proofs, bd. gilt edges,* £4. 4s 1817-19

Better impressions than the issue of 1821 and 1824.

6767 —— Pompeiana, *second series,* being the result of Excavations since 1819, 2 vols. royal 8vo. *upwards of* 100 *fine plates* (pub. at £6. 6s) *hf. morocco, uncut,* £2. 12s 1832

Large Paper, pub. at £20. 4s. Priced, 1836, Bryant, £11. 11s; 1853, calf, £8. 8s; 1856, mor. £7. 15s; fetched, 1860, mor. £9. Proofs and Etchings on India Paper, priced, 1834, Arch, £26. 5s.

6768 **PORTRAITS:** BULLART, Academie des Sciences et des Arts, contenant les Vies et les Eloges historiques des Hommes illustres, 2 vols. in 1, folio, *with* 274 *Portraits,* 86 *of them those of Artists, engraved by Boulonnois, Larmessin, Hollar, etc. calf,* 28s 1695

6769 CURTII (C.) Virorum illustrium ex Ordine Eremitarum D. Augustini Elogia, sm. 4to. *brilliant impressions of the beautiful portraits by C. Galle, fine copy in vellum,* 27s *Antverpiæ,* 1636

6770 DESCAMPS, la Vie des Peintres Flamands, Allemands et Hollandais, 4 vols. *numerous portraits, calf neat,* 1753-63—Voyage pittoresque de la Flandre, 1792, *hf. calf*—together 5 vols. sm. 8vo. *neat,* 30s 1753-92

6771 DOMINICI (Bernardo de) Vite de Pittori, Scultori ed Architetti NAPOLETANI, 3 vols. sm. 4to. *portrait, vellum,* £2. *Napoli,* 1742-45

6772 —— another copy, 3 vols. sm. 4to. *no portrait, and no title to Vol. III. hf. bd.* 12s 1742-45

"It is extremely scarce, and but for the kindness of friends both in Italy and England, I should have been unable to refer to it. The first volume of a reprint (quite void of notes) appeared in 1840. The work is a storehouse of information respecting the Neapolitan artists of the sixteenth and seventeenth centuries, and many citations are also given verbatim from the MS. collections of the painters Giovanni Angelo Criscuolo, Massimo Stanzioni, and others, respecting the history of art at Naples."—*Lord Lindsay's Christian Art,* Vol. II. p. 148.

6773 DANISH KINGS: Holst, Regum Daniae Icones, accurate expressae, 4to. 102 *portraits, calf, rare*, £2. 2s *Hafniae, A. Haelwegh fecit et excudit,* (s. a. ? 1642)

6774 FOPPENS, BIBLIOTHECA BELGICA, sive Virorum in Belgio Vitâ Scriptisque illustrium Catalogus Librorumque Nomenclatura, 2 vols. 4to. *with* 156 *fine Portraits, including* 14 *which are* ADDITIONAL, *very fine copy, old calf gilt,* £4. 4s *Bruxellis*, 1739

6775 GOOL, Nieuwe Schouberg der Nederlantsche Kunstschilders, 2 vols. 8vo. *many very fine portraits of Dutch Painters, calf*, 18s *Gravenhage*, 1750

6776 GRAMMONT (Comte de) Memoires de, par Hamilton, 2 vols. in 1, 8vo. *numerous fine portraits of English Ladies and Gentlemen, calf, gilt edges*, 20s 1811

6777 HOLLANDI (Henr.) HERWOLOGIA ANGLICA, hoc est, clarissimorum et doctissimorum aliquot ANGLORUM, qui floruerunt ab A.D. 1500 usque ad 1620, vivæ effigies, vitæ et elogia, duobus tomis, authore H. H. Anglo Britanno, small fol. 67 *splendid portraits, and the one of the two monuments,* BRILLIANT IMPRESSIONS, *a genuine tall copy, issued before those with the "post prefatio," old calf,* £7.
Impensis CRISPINI PASSÆI *chalcogr. et Jansonii bibliop. Arnhem. s.a.* [1620]
A most desirable copy of this beautiful series of English Portraits, the first ever issued. As few copies are as perfect as the present, I add the COLLATION:—
Engraved title; Text: Augustissimo, 1 leaf; Praefatio, 2 leaves; (*no Post-Prefatio*, 2 leaves); Ejusdem, a leaf; (*no* Quidquid, a leaf); Encomium, a leaf; iret, a leaf; non jam, 1 leaf, *with portrait*; pp. 1-240, with a PORTRAIT on nearly every leaf; List of plates, 1 leaf. SEPARATE PLATES: (*no* Monument of Queen Elizabeth after p. 44); Frobisher's portrait, after p. 96; J. Harrington, after p. 138; J. Balaeus, after p. 164. Without the ADDITIONAL PORTRAITS: E. Ledenberg, Rumoldus Hogerbeerts, usually wanting.
Williams's copy fetched £27. 16s 6d; Willett's £18. 18s.

6778 HOWELL'S (James) Familiar Letters, illustrated in a fine series of 90 Old Portraits, preceded by a beautiful Indian Ink DRAWING *of a full-length* PORTRAIT *of the* AUTHOR, 1 thick vol. 8vo. *russia, gilt edges*, £5. 5s 1754
From the library of the late Joseph Tasker, Esq., of Middleton Hall, Essex, who paid £8. 8s for it.

6778*HOUBRAKEN, Schouburgh der Nederlantsche Konstschilders en Schilderessen, 3 vols. 8vo. *numerous fine portraits, uncut*, 12s *Gravenhage*, 1753

6779 KNIGHT'S GALLERY OF ENGLISH AND FOREIGN PORTRAITS, 2 vols. folio, 168 *fine Portraits, very beautifully engraved for the Society for the Diffusion of Useful Knowledge,* PROOFS ON INDIA PAPER, *the Biographies accompanying the Colombier* 8vo. *edition were not printed for the proofs, hf. bd. mor.* £6. 1833-37
This is a singularly fine Series of Portraits, by such excellent engravers as Woolnoth, Holl, Wagstaff, J. W. Cook, Scriven, R. Hart, and others. To produce a similar series in our days would not be possible.

6780 LIONI, Ritratti di alcuni Celebri Pittori del Sec. XVII. sm. 4to. 12 *fine portraits, vellum*, 12s *Roma*, 1731

6781 MALVASIA, FELSINA PITTRICE, Vite de Pittori Bolognesi, 2 vols. 4to. *numerous portraits and woodcuts, good clean copy in vellum, calf backs*, 18s *Bologna*, 1678

6782 —— Felsina Pittrice con aggiunte e note inedite di Zanotti, 2 vols. large 8vo. *text in double columns, portraits, hf. calf, uncut,* 28s *Bologna*, 1841

6783 CRESPI, Vite de' Pittori Bolognesi, *non descritte* nella Felsina Pittrice, 4to. *nearly 50 portraits, hf. bd.* 18s *Roma*, 1769

6784 —— FELSINA PITTRICE, 2 vols.—CRESPI, Vite non descritte nella Felsina Pittrice, 1 vol.—together 3 vols. sm. 4to. *numerous portraits, hf. vellum,* 30s; *vellum*, 36s 1678-1769

6785 VITTORIA, Osservazioni sopra la Felsina Pittrice, per difesa di Raffaello, dei Caracci, etc. 8vo. *vellum*, 5s *Roma*, (ca. 1680)

6786 MANDER, Leven der Nederlandsche en Hoogduitsche Schilders, door De Jongh, 2 vols. 8vo. 51 *plates, containing* 150 *Portraits, hf. bd. uncut,* 14s *Amst.* 1764

6787 MEMORIE de' PITTORI MESSINESI e degli esteri che in Messina fiorirono, 8vo. 28 *portraits, hf. calf, uncut,* 18s *Messina*, 1821

6788 MEYSSENS (Jean) Image de divers Hommes d'Esprit, small folio, *a fine series of* 121 *Portraits, some by* Hollar, *old impressions, hf. bd.* £2.2s *Anvers*, 1649
Collation of this copy, which is more complete than those quoted by Brunet: engraved title, engr. frontispiece, Portraits of N. Bruyant, and of A. Brouwer; the regular Series, 1-120, and 121 not numbered, but no Nos. 65 and 117.

6789 NEUGEBAVERI Icones et vitae Principum ac Regum Poloniae, sq. 8vo. *numerous fine woodcut portraits, old calf,* 7s 6d *Francof.* 1620

6790 REUSNERI Icones sive Imagines vivae, literis cl. virorum Italiae, Graeciae, Germaniae, Galliae, Angliae, Ungariae; c. elogiis variis, 12mo. 90 *spirited woodcut portraits, vellum*, 32s *Basil.* 1589

FINE ARTS, BOOKS OF PRINTS, PAINTINGS. 375

6791 RIDOLFI, Maraviglie dell' arte, ovvero Vite de gl'illustri PITTORI VENETI, 2 vols. in 1, stout sq. 8vo. *frontispieces, and* 38 *plates of Portraits, fine impressions, the plates somewhat discoloured, hf. calf,* 20s *Venetia,* 1648
Ouvrage rare très estimé. Priced, 1847, Payne and Foss, £2. 2s.

6792 SERIE degli Uomini i piu illustri nella PITTURA, SCULTURA, et ARCHITETTURA, e Ritratti in Rame, 12 vols. 4to. *containing* 300 *Lives and* 300 *fine Portraits of Painters, Sculptors, and Architects, by Cecchi, hf. vellum,* 36s *Firenze,* 1769-75
Priced, 1829, £8. 8s; 1841, £7. 7s.

6793 TOMASINI (J. P.) Illustrium Virorum Elogia, iconibus exornata, 2 vols. sm. 4to. *upwards of* 100 *Portraits of eminent Italians, calf,* 12s *Patavii,* 1630-446

6794 TRAGICUM Theatrum Actorum et Casuum Tragicorum Londini publice celebratorum, 18mo. *contains fine portraits (brilliant impressions) of Strafford, Laud, Fairfax, Cromwell, Charles I., Earl of Holland, and View of the Execution at Whitehall, vellum,* VERY SCARCE, £1. 10s *Amst.* 1649
The Townley copy sold for £4. 4s.

6795 VISCONTI FAMILY. Le Vite dei XII Visconti che signoreggiarono Milano, descritte da P. Giovio, 4to. *fine ports. early impressions,* 20s *Milano,* 1645

6796 VICI (Aeneæ) Augustarum Imagines æneis formis expressæ, cum vitis et signorum explicatione, sm. 4to. *frontispiece and* 62 *plates of Portraits of the Roman Empresses from* COINS, *with cuts, vellum,* 25s *Venetiis,* 1558
Fine copy, apparently Large Paper.

6797 VITE E RITRATTI DI ILLUSTRI ITALIANI, complete, 2 vols. royal 4to. 60 *beautiful portraits, engraved by* RAPHAEL MORGHEN, LONGHI, *and others, also* 24 *engravings of Napoleon Medals,* (pub. at £20.) *elegantly bound in crimson morocco, full gilt, joints, gilt edges,* £7. 7s *Padova,* 1812; *Mil.* 1820
"This copy was selected for me by Longhi himself, who wished me to buy it, as containing some of the finest works of his graver."—*D. Turner.* A few copies exist, folio, VELLUM PAPER, proof impressions of the portraits before the letters, published at £25.

6798 ZANOTTI (Giamp.) Storia dell' Accademia Clementina di BOLOGNA, 2 vols. 4to. *portraits, calf,* 14s *Bologna,* 1739

6798*——— the same, 2 vols. roy. 4to. *portraits, hf. bd. red morocco, uncut,* 22s 1739

6799 POTTERY: PICCOLPASSI (Cyp.) Les trois Libvres de l'Art du Potier esquels se traicte non seulement de la practique mais de tous les secretz ; translatés de l'italien par Claudius Popelyn, atlas 4to. *with* 38 *plates of* MAJOLICA *Ware, sd.* 21s *Paris,* 1861

6799*PUGIN'S GLOSSARY OF ECCLESIASTICAL ORNAMENT AND COSTUME, setting forth the Origin, History, and Signification of the various Emblems, Devices, and Symbolical Colours, peculiar to Christian Design of the Middle Ages, with especial reference to the Decorations of the Sacred Vestments and Altar Furniture, formerly used in the English Church, impl. 4to. *illustrated by nearly* 80 *plates, splendidly printed in gold and colours by the new lithochromatographic process, containing examples of the Ecclesiastical Costume of the Roman, English, French, and German Bishops, Priests and Deacons ; Altar Furniture, Embroidery, Diaperings, Bordures, Powderings, Floreated Crosses, Holy Emblems, Holy Monograms, Examples of the Nimbus, Conventional Forms of Animals and Flowers for Heraldic and Church Decoration, Funeral Palls, &c. &c. &c.* (pub. at £7. 7s) *half morocco extra, top edges gilt, the back and sides ornamented with appropriate devices in gold,* £3. 10s 1846

6800 RACZYNSKI (*Comte Athanase*) Histoire de L'ART Moderne en ALLEMAGNE, 3 vols. impl. 4to. *with* 240 *fine woodcuts, calf neat ;* and the large folio ATLAS *of* 38 *superb Engravings, in half calf, uniform, rare,* £8. *Paris,* 1836-9-41
Priced, 1846, £15. 8s; 1847, bds. £14. 14s. Only a small number of the copies were printed.

6801 RAFFAELLE. LOGGIE NEL VATICANO, 4 vols, atlas folio, comprehending the Arabesques, Stuccoes, and Ceilings of the Vatican, finely engraved by Volpato and others, from the drawings of Camporesi, after the original works, in three series of 14, 13, and 12 each, with the General View, Plan of the Gallery on three sheets, the two plates of the Doors, marked A. and B., and the scarce FOURTH part, "Raphael's Bible," *in all* 92 *superb prints,* VERY BRILLIANT IMPRESSIONS, *the pilasters are folded, a* SUPERB COPY, *whole red* MOROCCO *extra, gilt edges,* £20. *Roma,* 1772-89
Complete copies like the above are of rare occurrence. Raphael's Loggie are the most elaborate "Encyclopædia of Ornament" ever published. The Fonthill copy fetched, £19. 18s 6d; Dent's, with coloured plates, £32. 12s; priced, 1847, £31 10s.
Collation: General title, being a fine VIEW of the Interior ; one leaf of Text, dated: Rome, 1772; the DOORS, 2 plates ; LARGE VIEW, shewing the 12 Windows and the outlines of the Frescoes, 3 sheets, making 1 large plate FRESCO DECORATIONS of the Arabesques and Stuccoes in 2 SERIES, each with an engraved title; the first 14, to second Series, 12 double plates; the CEILINGS, with Bible Illustrations, 13 plates—Fatti piu celebri della SAhe; BIBLIA, 52 plates, 2 on each leaf, 1789—in all 92 plates.

6802 RAFFAELLE, Loggie nel Vaticano, atlas folio, 36 *plates by Volpato, fine impressions, calf,* £3. *Roma,* 1772
  Collation: Frontispiece, being the View of the Interior, 1 plate; the Gates, A. B. 4 plates; the Elevation, 3 plates; the Arabasques, I.—XV. 28 plates.
6803 ——— Frescoes in the Loggie nel Vaticano, oblong atlas folio, 14 *double plates, half bound,* 32s *Roma, s. a.*
6804 ——— TESTE SCELTE di Personaggi Illustri in Lettere e in Armi, dipinte nel Vaticano da Raffaelo d'Urbino, disegnate ed incise secondo la loro grandezza da P. Fidanza, 5 vols. in 2, impl. folio, *consisting of* 180 *extraordinary fine and boldly engraved Portraits, selected from the Pictures of Raphael and Michael Angelo in the Vatican, hf. bd.* £4. 10s *Roma,* 1769
6805 ——— Recueil de Tetes choisies, arranged in 2 vols. bound into 1, atlas folio, *the* 180 *superb Portraits executed in bistre, whole bound red morocco extra, gilt edges, a sumptuous and magnificent book,* £7. 7s *Rome,* 1785
  This grand Series of Portraits forms the best set of Artist's Studies in existence. An extraordinary book, whether viewed as a Portrait Gallery by the Divine Raphael, or as Studies for Artists.
6806 RAPHAEL and RUBENS : Raphael (Sanctius Urbinus) Pinacotheca Hamptoniana a Nicolao Dorigny aere incisa : *the Seven Cartoons of Raphael, engraved in the line manner on a scale of* 2 *ft.* 5 *in. by* 1 *ft.* 2 *in. very fine impressions,* (1715)—Achilles's Life, painted by P. P. RUBENS, and engraved by B. Baron, *Lond.* 1724, *frontispiece and* 8 *magnificent plates*—Two plates, one after Titian, by Baron—in 1 vol. atlas folio, *calf,* £7. 1715-32
  A set of Raphael's Hampton Court Cartoons fetched, 1803, £14. 10s ; Edwards's, £13. 2s 6d.
6807 Quatremere de Quincy, Istoria della Vita e delle Opere di Raffaello Sanzio da Urbino, ampleata per Longhera, 4to. *fine portraits and numerous plates, calf gilt,* 24s *Milano,* 1829
6808 Rembrandt. Descriptive Catalogue of the Prints of Rembrandt, 8vo. 7s 1836
6809 ——— the same, *Large paper,* roy. 8vo. *cloth,* 10s 1836
6810 RETZSCH'S Outlines to Shakspeare : Hamlet, Macbeth, Romeo and Juliet, King Lear, 4 parts, impl. 4to. *with* 56 *beautiful plates, original impressions,* (pub. at £3. 12s) *bds.* £2. 2s *Leipzig,* 1828-38
  These fascinating plates are now offered to the public at the above much reduced price. For gracefulness of design, truth of expression and variety, the outlines of Retzsch are unsurpassed,—they nobly represent the thoughts of the immortal Shakspere.
6811 REVOLUTION. Tableaux Historiques de la Revolution Française, contenant les gravures de différentes scenes de la révolution, depuis l'assemblée des notables jusqu'au 18 brumaire, avec un texte historique et les portraits des personnages les plus remarquables, (par Fauchet, Champfort, Ginguené et Pagès), 3 vols. royal folio, papier vélin, *containing* 160 *fine engravings of Revolutionary Scenes, giving at the same time the only correct* Architectural Record *of Paris during that period, and* 65 *Ports.* Early Impressions, *a good copy, in French calf, gilt edges, or russia, marbled edges,* £7. 7s 1791-1804
  Priced, 1845, Bossange, 300 fr. ; 1855, Tross, 300 fr. ; Lord Stuart de Rothesay's copy fetched, 1855, hf. bd. £9. 15s. The re-issue of 1817 is of little value.
6812 REYNOLDS (Sir Joshua) Graphic Works, consisting of engraved Titles and 356 beautiful Engravings, (comprising 429 subjects) after this delightful painter, engraved on Steel, by S. W. Reynolds, 3 vols. royal folio, *original edition,* proof impressions on india paper, *an early and very choice subscriber's copy,* (pub. in 60 parts, at £2. 12s 6d each, making £157. 10s) *from the library of the late Dr. Hawtrey, Provost of Eton, hf. bd. red morocco, gilt edges,* £60. 1820
  It is very difficult to obtain a perfect copy, the latter part being usually wanting.
  Collation: Vol. I. Portraits of Gentlemen ; engraved title to Vol. 1, engraved general title and engr. dedication, 138 plates with 191 Portraits.
  Vol. II. gen. title and Portraits of Ladies, engraved title to Vol. 2, gen. title and dedication, 116 plates with 136 Portraits.
  Vol. III. Historical and Fancy Subjects ; engraved title to Vol. 3, gen. title and dedication, 102 plates.
6813 REYNOLDS' (Sir Joshua) Graphic Works, 3 vols. folio, *consisting of* 300 *beautiful copper-plate engravings of* Portraits *and fancy subjects, engraved by S. W. Reynolds* (pub. at £36.) *elegantly hf. bd. morocco, full gilt backs and gilt edges,* £10. 10s 1834, etc.
  In taste, in grace, in facility, in happy invention, and in the richness and harmony of colouring, he was equal to the greatest masters of the renowned ages. In portrait he went beyond them; for he communicated to them that description of the art, in which English artists are most engaged, a fancy, and a dignity, derived from the higher branches, which even those who professed them in a superior manner did not always preserve when they delineated individual nature. His portraits remind us of the invention and the amenity of landscape."—*Burke.*
6814 REYNOLDS' (Sir Joshua) Discourses, *illustrated by explanatory notes and* 12 *Plates by John Burnet,* 4to. *cloth,* 24s 1842

FINE ARTS, BOOKS OF PRINTS, PAINTING. 377

6815 RICHARDSON'S (C. J.) Studies of Ornamental Design, atlas folio, the ARTIST'S OWN COMPLETE COPY, *consisting of 55 engravings and the preparatory Drawings, hf. red morocco, uncut*, £6. 6s 1847, etc.

6816 RIO, Poésie Chrétienne, Forme de l'Art: Peinture, 8vo. *sd. 6s* Paris, 1836

6817 ROBERTS'S Sketches in the HOLY LAND, SYRIA, IDUMEA and ARABIA, EGYPT and NUBIA, etc. complete, 6 vols. in 3, atlas folio, *portrait and* 248 *beautiful and most attractive plates of all the Remains and sites famous in* BIBLE HISTORY, *the chief Monuments of Art and Nature in* EGYPT, *etc. executed in tints, original subscriber's copy,* (sold at £36. in parts) *hf. bd.* MOROCCO, *gilt edges,* £18.
Lond., F. G. Moon, 1842-44

6818 ——— HOLY Land, Syria, Idumea and Arabia, complete in 3 vols. atlas folio, *portrait and* 124 *plates,* (pub. at £18. in parts) *hf. bd. mor. gilt edges,* £10. 1842

6819 ROBERTS'S HOLY LAND, Syria, Idumaea and Arabia, with historical descriptions by Croly, 3 vols. atlas folio, 125 *magnificent plates,* **coloured** LIKE THE ORIGINAL DRAWINGS, *each plate mounted on cardboard, and fastened on guards,* 1842—EGYPT and NUBIA, from Drawings made on the spot, by David Roberts, R.A., with historical descriptions by Brockedon, complete, 21 parts in 13, forming 3 vols. atlas folio, 123 PLATES MOST BEAUTIFULLY coloured TO IMITATE THE ORIGINAL DRAWINGS, *and mounted on cardboard,* (pub. at £44. 2s) 1846-9—together 6 vols. atlas folio, *hf. bd. blue* MOROCCO, *full gilt backs, a magnificent set,* £70. 1842-49

GENUINE COLOURED COPIES; some speculator had a few ordinary copies coloured, but these are easily detected by the fact, that the ordinary copies have the Vignettes on the text, whilst in the PROOFS, and in the ORIGINAL COLOURED copies the vignettes are on separate plates.

Roberts' "Holy Land and Egypt" is a really noble and grand publication. The great artist has represented, in his masterly style, all the famous sites and stupendous Architectural Remains of the Land of the Bible, of Ancient Egypt, Nubia, etc. such as they appear now. Every one of the Engravings is a perfect work of Art; to every Bible Reader, every Oriental Scholar, and to gentlemen who resided or travelled in the East, Roberts's works will afford the most pleasant reminiscences.

6820 **ROME:** THOMAS (M.) Un An à Rome et dans ses Environs, folio, 72 *lithographed plates* COLOURED, *with text, hf. blue mor.* 36s Paris, Didot, 1823
Roman domestic, Public and Religious Life is well drawn here; coloured copies are scarce.

6821 NUOVA PIANTA di Roma data in luce da G. NOLLI, l'anno 1748, royal folio, *with* 18 *large folding plates, calf,* 12s 1748

6822 ROSELLINI (Ippolito) I MONUMENTI DELL' EGITTO E DELLA NUBIA, disegnati dalla Spedizione Scientifico Letterario Toscano in Egitto, 389 *fine plates in outline, many beautifully* COLOURED, 3 vols. elephant folio, and 9 vols. of descriptive text, in 8vo. *hf. bd. morocco gilt,* £30. *Pisa,* 1832-44

6823 RUBENS'S WORKS, a magnificent series of 88 large Engravings, comprising the Works of Rubens, and a few Engravings after Paintings by Van Dyck, *engraved by Bolswert, Pontius, Gillis, Hendericx, Vorsterman, Galle, and others, old binding, from the library of Baron Hochepied de Larpent,* £10.
Antwerpiae, 1620, etc.
An important and very rare set of Engravings, desirable to the admirer or collector of Rubens' and Van Dyck's Paintings.

6824 RUMOHR's Italienische Forschungen, 3 vols. in 1, 12mo. *hf. calf,* 9s *Berlin,* 1827

6825 RUSKIN'S Works on Art, 9 vols. roy. 8vo. *a very fine* COMPLETE SET, *many plates and woodcuts,* (pub. at £15. 3s) *cloth,* £11. 15s 1851-60

6826 RUSKIN'S (J.) MODERN PAINTERS, 5 vols. impl. 8vo. *plates and woodcuts,* (pub. at £8. 6s 6d) *cloth,* £5. 1851-60
CONTENTS:
Vol. 1, containing Parts I. and II.—"Of General Principles, and of Truth."
Vol. 2, containing Part III.—"Of the Imaginative and Reflective Faculties."
Vol. 3, containing Part IV.—"Of Many Things," with eighteen illustrations, drawn by the Author, and engraved on steel.
Vol. 4. containing Part V.—"Of Mountain Beauty, with thirty-five illustrations engraved on steel, and 116 woodcuts.
Vol. 5, containing Part VI.—"Of Leaf Beauty. Part VII.—"Of Cloud Beauty." Part VIII.—"Of Ideas of Relation: 1. Of Invention Formal." Part IX.—"Of Ideas of Relation: 2. Of Invention Spiritual." With an Index to the whole Five Vols. with thirty-four Engravings on steel, and 100 Woodcuts.

6827 RUSKIN's THE STONES OF VENICE, 3 vols. impl. 8vo. *plates,* (pub. at £5. 15s 6d) *new in cloth,* £4. 10s 1851-53
Contents: Vol. 1. "The Foundations," second edition, imperial 8vo. with twenty-one plates.
Vol 2. "The Sea Stories," imperial 8vo. with twenty plates.
Vol. 3. "The Fall," imperial 8vo. with twelve plates.

6828 ——— THE SEVEN LAMPS OF ARCHITECTURE, impl. 8vo. *second edition, with fourteen plates drawn by the Author.* (pub. at 21s) *new in cloth,* 17s 6d

6829 SALVATOR ROSA'S Works: 60 *beautiful plates of Human Figures, mostly Men in Arms, neatly inlaid*, sm. 4to. *russia, gilt edges*, £2. *Paris, Bonnart, s. a.*

6830 SCHREINER (J. G.) Fresco- Gemälde in der K. Allerheiligenkapelle zu München, elephant folio, 43 *fine extremely large lithographs of the Frescoes in the* ALL SAINTS' CHAPEL AT MUNICH, *with descriptive text, hf. bd. red morocco, gilt edges*, £5. *München. s. a.* (? 1850)

6831 SCRIVERII (P.) Principes Hollandiæ, Zelandiæ et Frisiæ, ab anno Christi DCCCLXXIII et primo Comite Theodorico usque ad ultimum Philippum Hispaniarum Regem, aeri omnes incisi ac fideliter descripti, impl. folio, 38 *fine* PORTRAITS *of the largest size, with each individual's shield of arms, engraved after pictures by Titian, Rubens, and others, brilliant impressions, dutch vellum, gilt edges*, £3. 3s *Harlemi*, 1651

6832 SCOTLAND: BILLINGS' (R. W) Baronial and Ecclesiastical Antiquities of Scotland, 4 vols. 4to. *with* 240 *plates from the designs of Le Keux, &c. fine impressions,* (pub. at £8. 8s) *cloth,* £4. 1852

6833 ——— the same, 4 vols. 4to. *hf. green morocco extra, gilt edges,* £6. 10s 1852
The only extensive Pictorial work on the Architectural Monuments of Scotland.

6834 SCULPTURE. DESCRIZIONE del Giardino Reale di BOBOLI, 4to. *large plan and* 46 *plates of Sculptures, bds.* 7s 6d *Firenze*, 1789

6835 PEMBROKE'S (Earl of) Marble Antiquities at Wilton, consisting of Statues, Bustos, Bas-Reliefs, etc. 4to. 74 *plates etched by Cary Creed, hf. mor.* 21s 1731

6836 SELVATICO, sulla Capellina degli Scrovegni nell' Arena di PADOVA, e sui freschi di GIOTTO in essa, roy. 8vo. 20 *plates, bds.* 6s; *hf. morocco,* 8s *Pad.* 1836

6837 SERRADIFALCO (Duca di) Antichità della Sicilia, Vols. I.—IV. folio, containing 131 *fine plates, chiefly of Architectural Subjects, with elevations and details,* (pub. at £12, 12s in bds.) *hf. bd. red morocco,* £6. *Palermo*, 1834-40
The work complete, 5 vols. 1834-42, 180 plates, can be supplied for £12.

6838 SHAW'S Illuminated ORNAMENTS, from the Sixth to the Seventeenth Century, selected from Manuscripts and early printed Books, 4to. *engraved on* 59 *copper-plates, with descriptions by Sir Frederick Madden, the whole of the plates highly finished with opaque colours,* (pub. at £5. 5s) *cf. ext. gt. edges,* £21. 6s 1833

6839 ——— the same, LARGE PAPER, *the Illuminations carefully executed in colours and gold, maroon morocco, gilt edges,* £5. 15s 1833
In 1858, Bliss's copy fetched £9.
"The design of this work is unique, and its execution beautiful. The elaborate richness of decoration, and the splendour of the combinations of colour and blazonry, which render illuminated missals so curious and valuable, afford many useful hints for embellishment in colour and design."—*Spectator.*
"This work is got up with great care. It is, we believe, the first work of the sort that has been attempted, and cannot fail of success."—*Athenæum.*

6840 SHAW'S DRESSES and DECORATIONS of the MIDDLE AGES, from the Seventh to the Seventeenth Centuries, with Historical Descriptions, ORIGINAL EDITION, 2 vols. impl. 8vo. 85 *beautifully* COLOURED *copper-plate engravings, woodcuts, a profusion of beautiful initial letters, and examples of curious and singular ornaments* (pub. at £7. 7s in parts) *hf. bd. morocco, gilt edges,* £4. 4s 1843

6841 ——— Another copy, 2 vols. impl. 8vo. FINELY COLOURED PLATES, *morocco extra, gilt edges,* £5. Fetched, 1861, Southgate's, £8. 8s. 1843

6842 SHAW'S DRESSES AND DECORATIONS OF THE MIDDLE AGES, 2 vols. impl. 4to. LARGE PAPER, *the plates accurately* COLOURED *and* HEIGHTENED WITH GOLD *from the best existing authorities,* (pub. at £18. 18s) *hf. bd. uncut, rare,* £15. 1843
In 1855, Bernal's copy fetched £16. 5s; Utterson's fetched £18. 10s.
The "ORIGINAL Large Paper" copies of this splendid work on Mediaeval Costume are so incomparably superior to those on "small paper," that in point of fact they are two different works; the execution of the beautiful illuminations in these Large Paper copies quite equal to the choicest miniatures. No more copies equalling the above can ever be produced.
"This work, which has occupied for several years a great portion of the time and talents of Mr. H. Shaw, is at length completed. It forms a splendid addition to antiquarian literature, and rescues from oblivion a multitude of rare gems, which in a short time, without such a record, must have been obliterated and lost. To say anything in praise of the compiler of the book is superfluous; the services he has before the appearance of it rendered to antiquaries, artists, and to all persons of genuine taste and proper appreciation, have secured his reputation, excited respect for his research, and gratitude for the results. This book is beautifully printed; the initial letters of the various chapters are themselves amongst the most rare and beautiful specimens of the art of printing; they are facsimiles of ancient letters, copied from manuscripts and documents contained in the museums, libraries, and collections of this country and the continent. Some of them are of the most exquisite workmanship, executed with an elaborate delicacy which is hardly conceivable to those not conversant with such things. The illuminations consist of coloured plates, copied with fidelity from pictures, coloured glass, jewelled ornaments, pieces of ancient armour, weapons, domestic ornaments, costumes, reliquaries, mitres, sceptres, crowns, &c., and form a perfect museum of the curious vestiges of 500 years. The letter-press, by the eminent antiquary Mr. Thomas Wright, explains the history, the use, and the application of all these things, and whether, as a book of reference for artists, of instruction for antiquaries, or of illustration for those who read history, is important and almost indispensable for a right understanding of the subject on which it treats."—*Times, Jan.* 29, 1844.
"All lovers of art, and all who delight in the matchless gorgeousness of the Middle Ages, should secure to themselves copies of one of the most correctly beautiful works which has hitherto appeared in England."
Athenæum, Aug. 13, 1842.

FINE ARTS, BOOKS OF PRINTS, PAINTINGS. 379

6843 SHAW'S Dresses and Decorations of the Middle Ages, 2 vols. impl. 8vo. *new edition, with all the plates and woodcuts richly* COLOURED, (pub. at £7. 7s) *whole morocco extra, gilt edges,* £6. 6s 1858

6844 SILVESTRE'S UNIVERSAL PALEOGRAPHY, or a Collection of Facsimiles of the Writings of every Age, taken from the most authentic Manuscripts existing in the Libraries of France, Italy, Germany, and England; by M. Silvestre, *containing upwards of* 300 *large and most beautifully executed* FACSIMILES, *taken from Missals and other MSS. most richly illuminated in the finest style of art,* new and improved edition, 2 vols. atlas folio, the text in 2 vols. royal 8vo.— together 4 vols. *elegantly half bound morocco extra, gilt edges,* £27. 10s 1850 etc.

The best work on the manuscript Literature of Ancient and Mediaeval times. The finest possible specimens are given of MSS. in every European and Oriental Language; of such Languages as GREEK and LATIN many Specimens of every century and every style are represented. The number of reproductions of ITALIAN, FRENCH, and GERMAN MINIATURES is very considerable.

6844*SILVESTRE, Alphabet Album, ou Collection de 60 feuilles d'Alphabets, historiés et fleuronnés, tirés des plus beaux MSS. de l'Europe ou composés par J. B. Silvestre, large folio, 60 *plates of Alphabets, hf. bd.* 30s *Paris,* 1830

La grande variété, la beauté des alphabets, la pureté du dessin, la réunion de tous les styles, forment en quelque sorte l'histoire de la lettre artistique de tous les pays, de tous les siècles.

6845 SINGER'S (S. W.) Researches into the History of Playing Cards, with illustrations of the origin of Printing and Engraving on Wood, 4to. *plates, calf gilt,* £3. 10s 1816

6846 SMITH (John) CATALOGUE RAISONNÉ of the Works of the most eminent DUTCH, FLEMISH, and FRENCH PAINTERS, with Biographical Notices of the Artists, and a copious Description of their principal Pictures, also the prices at which they have been sold, *complete,* with the Supplement, 9 vols. royal 8vo. £9. 1829-42

This elaborate work, by Mr. Smith, the eminent picture dealer, is indispensable to the collector of pictures.

6847 SMITH'S (J. T.) ANTIQUITIES of WESTMINSTER, the Old Palace, St. Stephen's Chapel (now destroyed), imp. 4to. 39 *plates containing* 246 *engravings, very fine impressions, many executed in* GOLD *and* COLOURS, *a subscriber's copy,* (pub. at £6. 6s) *bds. uncut,* 28s 1807

6848 SOLIS (V.) Drinking Cups, Vases, Ewers, and Ornaments, 4to. 21 *facsimiles of extremely rare etchings, hf. bd.* 9s 1862

6849 **SPAIN.** LOCKER'S Views in Spain (illustrative of a tour with Lord John Russell in 1813), roy. 4to. LARGE PAPER, 60 *plates, proofs on India paper,* (pub. at £7. 4s) *russia, gilt edges,* 25s 1824

6850 PONZ (Antonio) Viage de España, en que se da noticia de las cosas mas apreciables, y dignas do saberse, que hay en ella, 18 vols. *Madrid,* 1787-94—Viage fuera de España, 2 vols. *ibid.* 1785—in all 20 vols. 16mo. *many fine plates of Views, Antiquities, Architecture, Portraits, etc. complete, Spanish calf,* £2. 5s
Madrid, 1787-94

Priced, 1821, Thorpe, £7. 7s; 1829, John Bohn, £8. 18s 6d; 1840, Jas. Bohn, £6. 6s; Drury's copy fetched £4. 16s.

6851 VIVIAN'S Scenery of Portugal and Spain, impl. folio, 31 *very attractive Lithographs,* (pub. at £4. 4s) *hf. morocco,* £2. 2s 1839

6852 **SPANISH ART.** AYALA (Jo., Interian de) Pictor Christianus Eruditus; sive de erroribus, qui passim admittunter circa pingendas, atque effingendas SACRAS IMAGINES, folio, *vellum,* 12s *Mad.* 1730

A very interesting and critical Analysis of modern Christian Art. A Spanish translation appeared by L. de Duran y Bartero, 2 vols. 4to. *Mad.* 1782.

6853 BUTRON (J. de) Discursos apologeticos en que se defiende el Arte de la PINTURA, sm. 4to. *engraved title, limp vellum, fine copy,* 18s *Madrid,* 1626

6854 CARDUCHO (V.) Dialogos de la PINTURA, sq. 8vo. *engraved title and six allegorical plates, bottom margin of some leaves slightly stained,* £2. *Madrid,* 1633
"Volume recherché et peu commun."—*Brunet.*

6855 CEAN-BERMUDEZ, Diccionario historico de los mas ilustres Professores de las BELLAS ARTES en ESPAÑA, 6 vols. 12mo. *sd. ;* or *calf neat,* 36s *Madrid,* 1800
The best Spanish account of Spanish artists. With this book as his guide, Soult plundered the Spanish galleries.

6856 LA FORGE, Arts et Artistes en Espagne, jusqu'à la fin du 18e Siècle, 8vo. 372 pp. *elegantly printed, uncut,* 16s *Lyon,* 1859

6857 LLAGUNO Y AMIROLA, Noticias de los ARQUITECTOS y Arquitectura de ESPAÑA desde su Restauracion, ilustradas con notas por Cean-Bermudez, 4 vols. 8vo. 24s *Madrid,* 1829

6858 PALOMINO (A.) DE CASTRO Y VELASCO. El Museo Pictorico y escala optica; Teorica de la pintura.—El Parnaso español pintoresco laureado, con las VIDAS de los PINTORES, etc. 3 vols. in 2, sm. folio, *vellum*, £2. 16s Madrid, 1715-24
A second edition without additions appeared Madrid, 1795. Ouvrage peu commun et très-recherché.
6859 ——— the same, second edition, 3 vols. in 2, folio, *Spanish bdg.* £2. 2s 1795-97
6860 QUILLIET, les Arts Italiens en Espagne, ou Histoire des Artistes Italiens qui contribuèrent à embellir les Castilles, folio, *hf. vellum, presentation copy from Wm. Stirling to R. Ford, rare*, 21s *Rome*, 1824
6861 STIRLING (W.) Annals of the Artists in Spain, 3 vols. 8vo. *numerous fine plates and woodcuts, cloth, very rare*, £5. 5s 1848
6862 STEEN. WESTRHEENE (T. van) Jan Steen: Etude sur l'Art en Hollande, roy. 8vo. *vi and* 191 *pp. portrait, sd.* 5s La Haye, 1856
6863 ——— the same, THICK PAPER, royal 8vo. *hf. bd. morocco*, 10s 6d 1856
A singularly well written Biography of this eminent Dutch master. Contents: the historical portion, 96 pp.; the List of Jan Steen's Paintings, 482 in all, with careful critical and commercial notices, pp. 97-173; the engravings, pp. 171-182.
6864 SPENCE'S (Josh.) Polymetis, or an Enquiry concerning the Agreement between the Roman Poets and the Remains of the Ancient Artists; being an Attempt to illustrate them mutually from one another, folio, FIRST EDITION, *portrait by Vertue, and* 41 *fine plates of the Heathen Mythology, engraved by Boitard, all free from stains, very fine copy, in russia, joints, gt. edges*, £2. 10s 1547
With the bookplate of "Sir John Anstruther of that ilk, Baronet." Priced, 1828, Payne and Foss, vell. £6. 6s.
6865 SPRUGGINS' GALLERY.—Portraits of the Spruggins' Family, by Richard Sucklethumkin Spruggins, Esq. 4to. *a series of* 44 *ludicrous Caricatures, with descriptive letter-press, hf. morocco, uncut,* £2. 10s 1829
Privately printed for presents. A *jeu d'esprit* by the Countess of Morley, being a very severe satire on the mania for publishing memoirs of obscure families. Utterson's copy fetched £3. 3s.
6866 STOTHARD'S MONUMENTAL EFFIGIES OF GREAT BRITAIN, selected from our Cathedrals and Churches, for the purpose of bringing together and preserving correct representations of the best Historical Illustrations extant, from the Norman Conquest to the Reign of Henry VIII., with Historical Descriptions and Introduction, by Alfred John Kempe, Esq. F.S.A., royal folio, LARGE PAPER, *containing* 147 *beautifully finished Etchings, all of which are more or less tinted, and some of them highly illuminated in* GOLD *and* COLOURS, *including the extra plates of the Effigies at Fontevraud, and Geoffrey Plantagenet,* (pub. £28.) *elegantly hf. bound morocco, uncut,* £7. 15s 1817
A fine ORIGINAL copy.
6867 STRUTT'S (Joseph) Biographical Dictionary of Engravers, from the earliest period of the Art to the present time, and a list of their most esteemed Works, 2 vols. in 1, 4to. *with the Cyphers, Monograms, and Marks used by each Master, and specimens of the performances of the ancient Artists, hf. bd. morocco, uncut,* £2. 1785
Priced, 1824, Arch. £4. 4s; 1828, Thorpe, £4. 14s 6d; 1837, Macpherson, bds. £4. 4s; 1837, Payne and Foss, bds. £5. 5s; by auction, 1855, Baker's, £7. 10s.
6868 STRUTT'S Complete View of the DRESS and HABITS of the PEOPLE OF ENGLAND, from the Establishment of the Saxons in Britain to the Present Time, Illustrated with Engravings taken from the most Authentic Remains of Antiquity, with General Description of the Ancient Habits in Use among Mankind, 2 vols. impl. 4to. LARGE PAPER, 153 COLOURED PLATES, *very fine copy in bright calf, gilt edges,* £12. 10s 1796-99
Priced by Thorpe, £14. 14s; in 1824, Sir Mark Sykes's copy, in bds. fetched, £16. 5s.
6869 ——— the same copy, with "The Sports and Pastimes of the People of England, with 40 COLOURED PLATES, 1801"—together 3 vols. impl. 4to. LARGE PAPER, *a very handsome uniform copy, bright calf extra, gilt edges,* £14. 1796-1801
6870 ——— SPORTS and PASTIMES of the People of England, including Rural and Domestic Recreations, May-Games, Mummeries, etc. royal 4to. *with* 40 CO-LOURED PLATES, *representing upwards of* 200 *ancient Popular Diversions, calf neat,* £3. 3s 1801
All First and best editions, with the original colouring of the plates.
6871 STRUTT (J. G.) SYLVA BRITANNICA, or Portraits of Forest Trees, distinguished for their Antiquity, Magnitude, and Beauty, impl. folio, 50 *beautiful Etchings, with descriptive text,* (pub. at £9. 9s) *hf. red morocco extra, gilt edges,* £4. 4s 1826
6872 ——— the same, ORIGINAL INDIA PROOFS, imp. 8vo. *hf. mor. gt. edges,* £5. 5s 1826
"This is one of those works of art which do not merely charm the eye, but appeal forcibly to the imagination, and delight the mind. Of all the productions of nature, there are none with which so many agreeable and even

FINE ARTS, BOOKS OF PRINTS, PAINTINGS. 381

affecting feelings are associated as with the trees of the forest, and especially with those remarkable specimens which historical or romantic circumstances have caused to be distinguished from their venerable compeers. Forty of such trees in England, and eight in Scotland, are figured in this publication, from very clever drawings, which are admirably etched, in a style well calculated to preserve their characteristics and perpetuate their remembrance, when old Time shall have mowed them down, like the Hainault Oak, or that of Epping Forest, under which generations of gipsies spread their canvas, and generations of citizens enjoyed their annual festival. The local details and anecdotes attached to so many of these subjects are extremely curious and interesting. SOME OF THE ETCHINGS RESEMBLE THE PAINTINGS BY WATERLOO VERY STRIKINGLY ; BUT THE WHOLE ARE VARIOUS, BEAUTIFUL, AND INTERESTING; GIVING PERFECTLY THE CHARACTER OF EVERY SPECIES."—*Literary Gazette*.

6873 **SWITZERLAND.** BEATTIE'S Switzerland illustrated, in a series of views taken on the spot and expressly for this work by Bartlett, 2 vols. sm. 4to. *numerous plates, hf. calf gilt*, 16s 1834

6874 GESSNER'S Schweizerische Prospecten, obl. 8vo. *a series of 51 pretty views, designed and engraved by Gessner, calf, 7s 6d* ca. 1780

6875 TARBÉ, Trésors des Eglises de Reims, sm. folio, 31 *plates by Maquart, of Reliquaries, Ecclesiastical Ornaments, etc. of elaborate workmanship, mostly presented by the French Kings, bds.* 15s *Reims*, 1843

6876 THORWALDSEN'S WORKS: Leben und Werke des Dänischen Bildhauers Bertel Thorwaldsen, dargestellt von Thiele, 2 vols. folio, 158 *fine outline engravings, with text*, (pub. at 40 thalers in boards) *beautiful copy, calf super extra, gilt edges*, £4. 10s *Leipzig*, 1832-34

6877 TROOST. SCENES tirées de la VIE DOMESTIQUE DES HOLLANDAIS au XVIII. Siècle, peintes par Corneille Troost, oblong atlas folio, *a series of 32 magnificent plates in the style of Hogarth, engraved by Houbraken, Tanjé, Fokke, etc. hf. bound*, £4. 4s *Amsterdam*, 1811
   Nagler speaks in the highest terms of praise of Troost's works.

6878 TUDOT (E.) Collection de Figurines en Argile; oeuvres premières de l'Art Gaulois, avec les noms des Ceramistes, impl. 4to. *numerous woodcuts in the text and 75 plates of Gaulish Pottery, hf. red morocco, uncut*, £2. 1860

6879 TURNER'S (J. M. W.) Picturesque Views on the SOUTHERN COAST OF ENGLAND, an original copy, 2 vols. impl. 4to. 80 *most beautiful plates, engraved by W. and G. Cooke*, EARLY IMPRESSIONS, *hf. bd. morocco, uncut*, £5. 5s 1826

6880 —— Picturesque Views on the SOUTHERN COAST OF ENGLAND, 2 vols. folio, LARGE PAPER, 80 *most beautiful plates, engraved by W. and G. Cooke*, PROOF IMPRESSIONS *with the open letters*, (subscription price, £14. 8s) *russia extra, gilt edges*, £10. 10s 1814-21
   An original and very fine subscriber's copy of this beautiful work.
   Turner's Southern Coast has always ranked as his greatest performance, as well as one of the most perfect works of English Scenery ever produced. Original copies like the preceding, were immediately bought up at the full publication price, and the INDIA PROOFS, of which only 25 sets are said to have been taken off, soon rose to the value of £40. and upwards.

6881 TURNER'S VIEWS IN ENGLAND AND WALES, with descriptive and historic Illustrations by H. E. Lloyd, complete, 2 vols. in 1, large 4to. *containing 88 beautiful engravings*, (pub. at £16. 16s) £8. 8s 1832

6882 TURNER and his Works, illustrated with Examples from his Pictures by John BURNET, and a Memoir by Peter Cunningham, 4to. *with 10 plates, cloth*, 12s 6d 1852

6883 VAN DYCK. CARPENTER (W. H.) Pictorial Notices, consisting of a Memoir of Van Dyck, descriptive Catalogue of his Etchings, and particulars relative to other Artists patronized by Charles I., 4to. *portraits, and facsimile of a letter of Van Dyck, cloth*, £2. 2s 1844

6884 VASARI, VITE de' piu eccellenti PITTORI, SCULTORI, e ARCHITETTORI, di nuovo dal medesimo riviste et ampliate, con i ritratto loro, et con l'aggiunta delle Vite de' vivi et de' morti dall' 1550 insino al 1567, 3 vols. 4to. *numerous spirited woodcut portraits, a leaf of the Index to Vol. III. supplied in MS. the beginning of this volume stained, bright old veau fauve gilt, from Lord Calthorpe's library*, £3. 10s *Florenza, Giunti*, 1568
   This edition is rare and much sought after; of late it has very much increased in price. Priced, 1830, Payne and Foss, mor. £7. 7s; and 1840, mor. £10. 10s; 1858, calf, £6. 16s 6d. Fetched: Towneley's £5. 18s; 1855, Sotheby's, russia, by R. Payne, £9.

6885 VASARI, Vite de' Pittori, nuova ediz. per Manolessi, 3 vols. sm. 4to. *portrait of the Giunti edition, and some additional, calf*, 18s *Bologna*, 1648-63

6886 —— Vite de' Pittori, etc. per cura d' una Societa di Amatori delle belle Arti, 13 vols. 12mo. *plates, sd. best modern edition*, £2. 2s *Firenze*, 1846-57

6887 VATICANO (Il) descritto ed illustrato da Erasmo PISTOLESI, con disegni a contorni diretti dal Pittore Camillo Guerra: The Vatican described and illustrated

by Erasmus Pistolesi, with fine Plates, in Outline, of all the Ornaments, Frescoes, Paintings, Statues, Marbles, etc. contained in that celebrated Edifice, including all its Architecture and Details, 86 parts forming 8 vols. royal folio, *containing upwards of 850 large and beautiful engravings,* FINE ORIGINAL IMPRESSIONS, (pub. in parts at £60.) *hf. bd. russia, uncut,* £25. *Roma,* 1829-38
"Description la plus étendue, et la plus exacte, de ce magnifique edifice."—*Brunet.*
This magnificent book has now become scarce; the above copy is a remarkably beautiful one, its impressions have all the vividness of Proofs.

6888 RIGHETTI, DESCRIZIONE DEL CAMPIDOGLIO, complete in 50 parts, forming 2 vols. roy. folio, *containing 390 fine plates of Statues, Bas-reliefs, Busts, etc. brilliant original impressions,* (pub. at £20.) *sewed, uncut,* £7.; or, *half russia, to match the Vaticano,* £8. 10s *Roma,* 1833-39
These two superb works, the Vaticano and Campidoglio ought to be purchased together; they are both a desideratum, and an ornament to any Library.

6889 VENICE. BOSCHINI Descrizione di tutti le pubbliche Pitture di Venezia, 16mo. *calf,* 7s 6d 1732

6890 URBIS VENETIARUM Prospectus celebriores ex ANTONII CANAL. tabulis 38 ære expressi, in tres partes distributi 1742-51, *the paintings by Canaletti, engraved by Visentini*—Another Series of 19, *engraved by Brustolini, after subjects from scenes in Venice by Canaletti,* in 1 vol. impl. folio, *plan and 57 fine large Views, half calf,* £2. 10s

6891 CANALETTI'S Views in Venice: Prospectus Aedium Viarumque insigniorum Urbis Venetiarum, quas Ant. Canale coloribus expressit et J. B. BRUSTOLONI aere incidit, large folio, *engraved title and 21 large folding plates, good impressions, with 4 Views in* VIENNA *added, hf. bd. from the library of Baron Hochepied de Larpent,* £2. 5s *Venice, L. Furlanetto,* 1763
CICOGNARA, Fabbriche di Venezia—*see post,* ARCHITECTURE.

6892 VERSAILLES. Les Plans, profils et elevations des Ville et Château de Versailles avec les Bosquets et Fontaines, 40 *large plates by Blondel*—La Chapelle Royale de Versailles, 10 *plates*—together 50 *very richly coloured plates, red morocco,* £2. 10s 1716

6893 VICI (Aeneæ) Augustarum Imagines æreis formis expressæ, cum vitis et signorum explicatione, sm. 4to. *frontispiece and 62 plates of Portraits of the Roman Empresses from* COINS, *with cuts, vellum,* 28s *Venetiis,* 1558
Fine copy, apparently Large Paper.

6894 VIOLLET-LE-DUC, Dictionnaire raisonné du MOBILIER FRANÇAIS, de l'epoque Carlovingienne à la Renaissance, large 8vo. *with several hundred woodcuts and plates, some in colours,* (pub. at £3. 3s) *hf. vellum, a pretty book,* 38s *Paris,* 1858

6895 VISCONTI (Ennio Quirino) OPERE DELLA HISTORIA DELLE BELLE ARTI:
IL MUSEO PIO CLEMENTINO, 7 vols. *portrait and 426 plates* 1818-22
IL MUSEO CHIARAMONTI, 1 vol. 50 *plates* 1820
ICONOGRAFIA ROMANA, 2 vols. in 1, 40 *plates* 1818-19
ICONOGRAFIA GRECA, 3 vols. 169 *plates* 1823-25
MUSEO WORSLEJANO, 1 vol. *portrait and* 78 *plates* 1835
MONUMENTI GABINI della Villa Pinciana, 1 vol. 22 *plates* 1835
MONUMENTI SCELTI BORGHESIANI, 1 vol. 46 *plates* 1837
OPERE VARIE Italiane e Francesi, 4 vols. 80 *plates* 1827-31
—together 20 vols. 8vo. in 19, *upwards of* 900 *plates,* (pub. at about £18. 18s in parts; value of binding, £7. 7s), *uniformly and elegantly bound in Roman vellum, contents lettered, very cheap,* £8. 8s *Milano,* 1818-37
Visconti's works, complete, comprising an immense amount of Ancient and Early Italian Art.

6896 VISCONTI, MUSEO PIO CLEMENTINO, e Museo Chiaramonti, 8 vols. atlas folio, 431 *large fine plates,* ORIGINAL IMPRESSIONS, *hf. bd. red morocco, gilt edges,* "*a great and magnificent work,*" £15. *Roma,* 1782-1808

"Excellent ouvrage tant pour le texte que pour les planches. En voici la description: tome 1, 1782, 52 pl. de statues, avec 2 pl. marquées A. B. Au commencement doivent se trouver le portrait de Pie VI. et le plan général du Museo (le texte de ce volume est de J. B. Visconti, père d'Ennio Quirino).—II. 1784, 32 pl. de statues, 2 pl. *di monumenti illustrativi,* et le portrait au commencement.—III. 1788, 50 pl. de statutes. un nouveau portrait du pape, et *tre travole illustrative.*—IV. 1790, 45 pl. de bas reliefs, *due tavole di monumenti illustrativi,* et les statues d'Apollons de Venus et de Meléagre, gravées par Louis Cunego, pour servir d'appendice au 1er vol.—V. 1796, 45 pl. de bas reliefs, 2 *tav. illustrativa,* et un sarcophage.—VI. 1797, 61 pl. de bustes, 2 *tav. illustrativa.*—VII. 1807, *Miscellanea del Museo Pio Clementino,* dédié au pape Pie VII. et avec son portrait, 50 pl. et 2 *monumenti illustrativi.*—VIII. 1808, *il Museo Chiaramonti,* aggiunto al Pio Clementino da Pio VII. (con *l'esplicazione di Fil.-Aurel. Visconti e Guis.-Ant. Guattani, pubbl. da Ant. d'Este e Gasp. Capparona),* 44 pl. de monuments de différents genres, avec 1 *tav. illustrativa* et un second portrait du pape Pie VII.,"—*Brunet.*

FINE ARTS, BOOKS OF PRINTS, PAINTINGS. 383

6897 VISCONTI, Villa Borghese: Sculture del Palazzo della Villa Borghese detta Pinciana, 2 vols. 258 *plates*—Monumenti Gabini della Villa Pinciana, descritti da E. Q. Visconti, 1 vol. 59 *plates*—together 3 vols. 8vo. *fine impressions of the plates, blue morocco, gilt edges,* £2. 2s   Roma, 1796-97
Priced, 1857, Weigel, 30 thalers; in 1854, sold by me, Large Paper, mor. £3. 3s.
These works were executed by Lamberti and Visconti, and were privately printed for presents only, at the expense of Prince Borghese. The marbles were removed to the Louvre, being purchased by Napoleon.

6898 VOLPATO e RAFFAELLE MORGHEN, Principj del Disegno, tratti dalle più eccellenti Statue Antichi, atlas folio, 36 *fine plates of famous specimens of* Antique Sculpture, *with artistic details, hf. bound,* 32s   Roma, 1786
Original and best edition, preferred to that of Vallardi, Milano, 1831.

6899 Voyage d'un Amateur des Arts en Flandre, dans les Pays-Bas en Italie, etc. par De la R***, 3 vols. 12mo. *half bound,* 7s 6d   Amst. 1783

6900 VOGTHERR (*Heinrich, der elter und junger*) Ein frembdes und wunderbarliches KUNSTBUECHLIN, allen Molern, Bildtschnitzern, Goltschmiden, Steynmetzen, Waffen-und Messerschmiden hoch nützlich zu gebrauchen; dergleichen vor nie keines gesehen, oder in dem Truck kommen ist, square 8vo. (smallest 4to.) *two woodcut portraits on the title, with several hundred bold and very original designs to serve as copies for Artists, all engraved on wood, beautiful copy, morocco, gilt edges,* £4.   Strassburg, 1572
Collation: Sign A.—G. in fours, H 2 leaves; both sides of the leaves filled with woodcuts.

6901 WAAGEN'S Kunstwerke und Künstler in England und in Paris, 3 vols. 12mo. *cloth,* 4s; or, 3 vols. in 2, *calf,* 7s   Berlin, 1837-9

6902 —— Treasures of Art in Great Britain, account of the chief collections of Paintings, Drawings, Sculptures, Illuminated MSS. 3 vols. 8vo. (pub. at £1. 11s 6d) *cloth,* 18s   1854

6903 **WALES.** COLOURED VIEWS in, viz.—North view of the Ancient City of Saint David, 2 *views;* South view of the Ancient City of St. David; View of the North side of the Cathedral of St. David's; View of the South side of the Cathedral; Architectural views of the East and West sides of the Cathedral, 2; Ground plans, view of the Interior, etc. 4 *views*—in all 11 *drawings, about 3 ft. by 2 ft. beautifully executed in the middle of the last century, in water colours, exhibiting considerable artistic skill and mathematical precision,* £3. 3s

6904 WALKER'S Beauty, illustrated chiefly by an Analysis and Classification of Beauty in Woman, roy. 8vo. *with* 22 *elegant lithographs, bds.* 21s   1836

6905 WARING (J. B.) The Arts connected with Architecture, illustrated by Examples in Central Italy, of Stained Glass, Fresco Ornament, Marble and Enamel Inlay, Wood Inlay, etc. from the Thirteenth to the Fifteenth Century, impl. folio, 41 *beautiful plates in* colours, with descriptive text (pub. at £10. 10s, reduced to £6. 6s) *hf. bd. morocco,* £5. 10s   1858
"So elaborate, costly, and suggestive a work as that which has been produced by Mr. J. B. Waring, with the aid of Mr. Vincent Brooks, deserves to be set as prominently before those who are interested in the subject of it, or are likely to be acted on by it, as our means will admit of. To produce a work by means of chromolithography, containing forty-one large folio plates, blazing with colour, accompanied with historical and descriptive letter-press, on paper *de luxe*, solidly bound, involves no small risk financially; and the effort, when worthily made, as this is, should be supported by those who concern themselves with the arts of the country. It is not every individual, however well-disposed, who can afford six guineas for a book; but the more wealthy buyers, public bodies, municipal libraries, and schools of design should consider it their duty to assist in such cases by the purchase of copies. For years our architecture has been bald and lifeless;—restricted to ill-understood imitations, and permitted no aid from her children arts.
"The forty-one plates in the work before us are appropriated to stained glass, eight; fresco ornament and figures, eight; wood inlay, five; and marble and enamel inlay, twenty."—*Builder.*

6906 WARRINGTON'S (W.) History of Stained Glass, from the earliest period of the Art to the present time, illustrated by coloured Examples of Entire Windows in the various styles, with Biographical Notices of some of the most eminent Artists in Glass Painting and Staining, from the Twelfth Century to the present time, 26 *fine beautifully* coloured *plates*, impl. folio (pub. at £8. 8s) *hf. bd. morocco extra, gilt edges,* £3.   1845

6907 WATTEAU'S Ornamental Designs, collected from his works, and lithographed by Nichol, royal folio, *portrait and* 88 *elegant plates, hf. bd.* £2. 16s   1841
Fifty Pounds would be given for a set of the original edition of Watteau's works in 4 vols.

6908 WELCKER'S alte Denkmäler: Vol. I. die Giebelgruppen und griechische Statuen; Vol. II. Basreliefe und geschnittene Steine: Vol. III. Griechische Vasengemälde, 3 vols. 8vo. 36 *folding plates of Greek Art,* 16s   Gött. 1849-51

6909 WESTWOOD (J. O.) Palæographia Sacra Pictoria : a Series of Illustrations of the Ancient Versions of the Bible, copied from Illuminated MSS. executed between the Fourth and the Sixteenth Centuries, impl. 4to. 40 *plates, heightened in gold and colours, hf. red morocco*, £2. 10s　　　　　　　　　　1845

6910 [WILSON (T.)] Catalogue Raisonné of the Select Collection of Engravings of an Amateur, with some copies after rare prints; and several etchings after designs by G. CRUIKSHANK, impl. folio, LARGE PAPER, *with 43 facsimiles and plates, First India Proofs before the letters, cloth, uncut*, £3. 10s　　1828

Priced, Small Paper, 1834, Thorpe, £4. 4s; of Large Paper, only about 10 copies were got up.

PRIVATELY PRINTED, as presentations to the collector's friends. The present was Dr. Dibdin's copy, and has an autograph letter of Mr. Wilson's. The Catalogue is drawn up with admirable judgment, with brief biographical notices of the masters, and particular anecdotes of the prints, the marks of Engravers, &c.

The decorative initial letters are etchings by Mr. Wilson, from designs by Mr. Howard. These are five fine facsimiles from several of the unique and costly engravings in the collection, and the tail-pieces, etched by George Cruikshank, are unequalled in any work for richness of humour and effect.

6911 WINCKELMANN'S Werke, herausgegeben von Fernow, 8 vols. 8vo. *calf neat*, and 4to. Atlas *hf. calf, with portrait, and* 64 *plates of Ancient Art*, (pub. at £6. 10s) 28s　　　　　　　　　　　　　　　　　　Dresden, 1808-20

6912 ―― Sämtliche Werke, von Eisclein, 12 vols. 12mo. *sd. with large folio Atlas*, 2 *parts in* 1 *vol. hf. russia, containing portrait and* 67 *plates of upwards of* 300 *figures*, 20s　　　　　　　　　　　　　　　　Donauöschingen, 1825-35

6913 ―― MONUMENTI ANTICHI inediti, spiegati ed illustrati, Seconda Edizione, aggiuntovi alcune erudite Addizioni nel Fine dell' Opera, 2 vols.—RAFFEI Dissertazioni VIII, 1 vol.—together 3 vols. folio, 226 *plates, hf. calf, uncut*, £2. 2s ; or *neat in vellum*, £2. 10s　　　　　　　　　　　　　　　　　1821

The first edition, 3 vols. folio, Roma, 1767-79, is less complete.

6914 WINKELMAN, Histoire de l'Art chez les Anciens, 3 parts in 2 vols. 4to. *numerous plates, calf extra, gilt edges*, 30s　　　　　　　　Paris, 1802-3

6915 WINKLES'S BRITISH CATHEDRALS, containing Architectural and Picturesque Illustrations of the Cathedrals of Salisbury, Canterbury, St. Paul's, York, Wells, Ely, Norwich, &c. *making* 181 *engravings*, with Descriptions by T. Moule, 3 vols. impl. 8vo. 1838-42—Illustrations of the principal Cathedrals of FRANCE, from Drawings by R. Garland, engraved by B. Winkles, with Historical and Descriptive Accounts, 4to. 50 *plates*, 1837—together 4 vols. 4to. *beautiful* EARLY IMPRESSIONS *of the plates* (pub. at £4. 4s) *hf. calf gilt*, £2. 8s 1837-42

A very beautiful copy of this deservedly popular work, with splendid impressions. Copies with recent impressions of the plates can be had cheaper.

6916 WYATT'S (D.) Industrial Arts of the Nineteenth Century : a Series of Illustrations of the choicest specimens produced by every Nation at the Great Exhibition of Works of Industry, 1851, 2 vols. royal folio, *with* 158 *elaborate plates executed in the exact* COLOURS *of the originals*, SCULPTURES, METAL-WORK, TEXTILE FABRICS, LACE AND EMBROIDERY, PORCELAIN, WOOD AND IVORY CARVING, etc. (pub. at £17. 17s in bds.) *whole bound morocco, gilt edges*, £10.　　1851

This beautiful work forms in itself a perfect cyclopædia of Design in all branches of Art. The plates have the appearance of original paintings, and have never been equalled in gorgeousness of colouring.

6917 WYATT'S (D.) METAL WORK and its Artistic Design, impl. folio, 50 *splendid plates, executed in colour, and resembling Drawings* (pub. £6. 6s) *cloth*, 36s 1852

6918 ―― Art of Illuminating, as practised in Europe from the earliest times, illustrated by Borders, Initial Letters, Alphabets, &c. selected from the British Museum, South Kensington Museum, and other important Collections, by W. TYMMS, with an Essay on the Art, and Instructions as to its Practice in the Present Day, by M. DIGBY WYATT, 4to. (pub. at £3. 10s) *richly bound in full gilt cloth*, 32s　　　　　　　　　　　　　　　　　　　1860

This magnificent and serviceable work contains 102 plates, ALL FULLY ILLUMINATED, and printed in colours and gold on vellum paper, and 104 pages of Text, surrounded by borders in colours. Counting the various specimens of letters and borders given on the 102 pages, there will be found 1008 Illuminated Figures.

6219 ZUCCARI (Fratelli, T. F. e O. *Pittori celeberrimi e Scolari di Michel Agnolo Buonarotti*) ILLUSTRI FATTI FARNESIANI, coloriti nel Real Palazzo di Caprarola, incisi in Roma da G. G. de PRENNER, impl. folio, 42 *fine plates, brilliant impressions, fine copy in vellum*, £3. 3s　　　　　　　　　　Roma, 1748

Priced, 1837, Payne and Foss. Collation : Title, portrait, dedication, and index, 5 large plates of the Building, with the ground-plans : Sala de Fatti Farnesi, 21 plates, *including some fine portraits*; Anticamera del Concilio, 15 Symbolical engravings.

6220 **XYLOGRAPHY**. AN EXTREMELY IMPORTANT VOLUME, CURIOUSLY ILLUSTRATING THE SUBJECT OF WOOD ENGRAVING. A MANUSCRIPT VOLUME OF PRAYERS, IN THE GERMAN LANGUAGE, *on paper, in which is* INSERTED A LEAF POSSESSING

FINE ARTS, BOOKS OF PRINTS, PAINTINGS. 385

TWO IMPRESSIONS (THE CRUCIFIXON, AND CHRIST IN THE LAP OF MARY) FROM WOOD BLOCKS EXECUTED IN THE VERY INFANCY OF THE ART. *Enclosed in a well-made case in green morocco for its more careful preservation*, £9.   *ante* 1445

*** THIS VERY INTERESTING MANUSCRIPT, WRITTEN ANTERIOR TO THE DISCOVERY OF METAL PRINTING, was for many years the property of W. Y. Ottley, Esq. and by him highly prized, but reverted back on his decease to the family by whom it had originally been presented. Mr. Ottley obtained a translation of a prayer in the volume, which is as follows:—" In the name of God. Amen.—Prologue—I, a poor cell Monk of the Carthusian Order, am so idle in my peaceful tranquility in consequence of the corrupted nature of my soul, that I must always devise and exercise some new Act of Devotion, and as a new year is now begun, (Anno Domini 1445), I feel disposed from that to send all hearts a New years Gift that they may pray to God for my Soul. Life is gone—Time flies away—Death comes. The Lord grant that we may die in a proper manner. In the first place I shall compose Three Short Prayers for the Feast of Christmas, likewise for all the Festivals of our Lady Mary," &c. &c.

The cuts are placed opposite a prayer for Good Friday. The MS. has in the beginning and at the end—" This book belongs to the Monastery at St. Kather. prdis. orden. in nur'rga."

6921 AMMON (Jost) Kunstbüchlin, Fürbildung vieler geistlicher unnd weltlicher Hohes und Niderstands Personen, etc. sq. 8vo. *consisting of 275 fine spirited woodcuts of Equestrian Figures, Knights in Armour, Costumes of Kings, Nobles, Ladies, and persons of every degree, original vellum, sold with all faults*, £3. 3s   *Franckfurt, Feyrabend*, 1599

" In the cuts of the Horse, the action of the animal is frequently represented with great spirit: his men generally have a good seat, and his ladies manage their heavy long-tailed steeds with great ease and grace."—*Jackson*.

6922 AMMAN. LONICERI (P.) CHRONICA TURCICA, 3 vols. in 1, folio, *many hundred spirited woodcuts by Jost Amman, calf*, 14s   *Francof. F. Feyrabent*, 1578

The third volume is almost exclusively devoted to the Life and Adventures of Scanderbeg. Goldsmith's copy fetched £2. 4s; 1855, Lord Rothesay's copy, hf. mor. fetched £2. 12s, and was sold afterwards for £3. 3s.

6923 AMMAN. CLERI TOTIUS ROMANÆ ECCLESIÆ subjecti, seu Pontificiorum Ordinum omnium omnino utriusque sexus Habitus artificiosissimis figuris, a JUDICO AMMANNO expressi; 4to. *with* 103 *fine woodcuts, calf gilt*, 36s   *Francof.* 1585
Fetched, 1855, at Sotheby's, £3. 1s.

6924 AMMAN. BOCKSPER'S Neuw Thierbuch, sm. 4to. *first edition, with about* 200 *very pretty engravings of Quadrupeds, with German verses under each, beautiful impressions, a remarkably sound and fresh copy in the original, stamped calf*, £4. 4s   *Franckfurt, Feyerabend*, 1569

6925 BEWICK (T.) Fables of Æsop, and others, 8vo. *many very spirited woodcuts, hf. green morocco*, £2. 2s   *Newcastle*, 1818

6926 BEWICK (T. and J.) Select Fables, with Memoir and Catalogue of their Works, 8vo. *portraits and many woodcuts, hf. green morocco*, 28s *Newcastle*, 1820

6927 —— the same, LARGE PAPER, royal 8vo. *bds. uncut*, £2. 2s   1820

6928 BLARRORIVO (Petri de) Liber Nanceidos, Opus de Bello Nanceiano (Carmen historicum), hac primum exaratura elimatissime nuperrime in lucem emissum, sm. folio, *numerous very beautiful and spirited woodcuts, beautiful copy (with both Mandements) in blue* MOROCCO *extra, gilt edges by* DE ROME, £7.
Impressum in celebri Lothoringie pago divi Nicolai de portu per petrum jacobi presbyterum, loci paganum, 1518

This volume, printed in a village near Nancy, is extremely rare, and very curious. It is ornamented with many woodcuts by Jacobus, executed in a spirited style, which represent the various events of the war of Lorraine. "The celebrated *Liber Nanceidos*." "It is a poem written in Latin hexameter verse by P. Blaru, descriptive of the memorable siege of Nancy in 1476, by Charles the Rash, Duke of Burgundy, who perished before the walls. His death is described in the sixth book, the passage relating to it beginning—
' Est in Nanceijs aratro locus utilis aruis.'
A woodcut portrait of the commanding French general, Renet, is in the frontispiece. A good copy of this handsomely printed, and rather interesting work should always grace the shelves of an historical or classical collector."
Dibdin's Tour, vol. ii. p. 543.

6929 CAOURSIN. Historia von Rhodis, wie ritterlich sie sich gehaltē mit dem tyrannischen Keiser Machomet uss Türckyē, lustig ūn lieplich zu lesen, sm folio, *large woodcut on title, and numerous large and curious woodcuts throughout the text, hf. russia*, £2. 2s   *Strassburg*, 1513

Priced, 1858, Butsch in Augsburg, 41 flor.; Fetched, Libri Sale, 1859, red mor. by Niedrée, £4. 10s.
This is a most interesting description of the famous siege of Rhodes by the Turks, written by the Chancellor of the Order himself. It contains the most minute particulars of every transaction during the protracted defence.

6930 DYALOGUS CREATURARUM optime moralizatus omni materie morali jocundo et edificativo modo applicabilis : ad laudem dei et edificationem hominum, folio, *first edition, with* 132 *very rude and very quaint* WOODCUTS, BEAUTIFUL CLEAR IMPRESSIONS, *very fine copy in purple morocco, gilt edges*, £18. 18s
Presens liber " Dyalogus Creaturarum appellatus jocundis fabulis plenus," per Gerardum Leeu in opido Goudensi inceptus munere dei finitus est A. D. MCCCCLXXX

THE EXTREMELY RARE FIRST EDITION of this popular work. Collation: blank leaf; preface 10 leaves, one of them blank; Dyalogus, etc. 93 leaves, the first leaf with a rich border, curious cut and capital letter.
Fine specimen of this printer, who has a double claim to the attention of an English Collector, as he printed

2 C

an Edition of Caxton's Chronicle, and translated the Game of Chess into Dutch. *See* the Spencer Catalogue, Vol. IV. p 120, Col. Stanley's copy of this book sold for £42.

Première édition dont les exemplaires sont tres-rares. Elle est imprimée en lettres gothiques à longues lignes, sans chiffres et réclames, avec signatures; il y a des gravures en bois à chaque fable. On trouve à la tête du volume 9 feuillets qui renferment une préface, la table des fables, au nombre de 122, et une table alphabétique des matières. Le texte suit, et au recto du dernier feuillet, se trouve la souscription précédée d'un grand écusson d'armoiries gravé en bois.

6931 FIGURE DE LA BIBLIA, illustrate di stanze toscane, per Gabriel Symeoni, 12mo. *with about* 100 *very neatly executed woodcuts,* (? *by Le Petit Bernard*) *veau fauve,* 21s   Lyone, 1565

6932 HANS SACHS im Gewande seiner Zeit oder Gedichte dieses Meistersängers, von Becker, impl folio, *frontispiece and* 22 *very large bold woodcuts, with text in Old German verse underneath, bds.* 12s   Gotha, 1821

6933 HOLBEIN (Hans) Icones Veteris Testamenti: Illustrations of the Old Testament on Wood, from Designs by Hans Holbein, with Verses from Scripture, in English, Latin, French, Italian, and Spanish, and an Introduction by Dr. Dibdin, 8vo. 91 *most beautiful woodcuts by John and Mary Byfield, hf. bound,* 10s 6d   1830

6934 JACKSON AND CHATTO'S Treatise on WOOD ENGRAVING, historical and practical, impl. 8vo. BEST EDITION, *xvi. and* 749 *pp. with upwards of* 300 *beauful woodcut illustrations, including facsimiles from the works of Albert Dürer, with the rare slip, hf. bound morocco,* £2. 16s   1839

MAXIMILIAN (Emperor of Germany) his Series of Illustrated Works.

6935 THEURDANCK. Der allerdurchleuchtigste Ritter, oder Grosz-Thaten, Abentheuer, Glücks-Wechslungen und Siges-Zeichen des Heldens Maximilian I. durch M. Pfinzing in Reimen verfaszt, folio, 117 *woodcuts by Hans Schaeuffelein, vellum, fine copy,* 32s   Augspurg, 1679

6936 DER WEISS KUNIG, eine Erzehlung von den Thaten Kaiser Maximilian des Ersten; von M. Treitzsaurwein: THE WISE KING, ILLUSTRATIVE OF THE LEARNING, WISDOM, AND ADVENTURES OF THE EMPEROR MAXIMILIAN, folio, 237 *large woodcuts by Hans* BURGHMAIR, *from the original old blocks* (1510) *bds. uncut,* £4.   Wien, 1775

To this copy is added a French Text, dated "Vienne, 1799."

Copies on ordinary paper usually sell for £5. 1855, Bernal's, £6. 16s 6d; on Thick Paper, 1853, Dr. Hawtrey's copy fetched £9. 9s.

There are 237 large cuts in this fine work, 92 contain Burghmair's mark, H. B., and one that of Schaeuffelein; they are executed in a very bold manner, all those which contain the mark of Hans Burghmair show a decided superiority in point of engraving.

"Le livre étrange auquel nous avons emprunté la gravure et les lignes qui précèdent a été commencé en 1512 par l'empereur Maximilien lui-meme, et terminé d'après son ordre, en 1514, par Marx Treitzsaurwein, l'un de ses secrétaires. L'ouvrage entier est resté inédit pendant près de trois siècles. Georges-Christophe van Schallenberg avait découvert, le premier, pendant son sejour à Vienne (1631) quelques-unes des gravures sur bois du *Weiss Kunig*, avec une note autographe de Maximilien; il entreprit de les publier en les complétant, mais il mourut laissant son travail inachevé. Plus tard on découvrit d'autres planches a Graez en Styrie, en on les porta à la bibliotheque impériale de Vienne, où était déjà le manuscrit de Treitzsaurwein. Enfin on publia en 1775 le texte avec les gravures sur bois, dont les planches avaient été rassamblées à grand'peine au nombre de 237. La bibliotheque imperiale de Vienne possede de plus 13 gravures dont les planches n'ont pas été retrouvées. L'object du livre est l'histoire de la naissance, de l'éducation et des actions de Maximilien; on le suit pas à pas depuis son enfance jusqu'a son âge mûr."

Magasin pittoresque, 1835.

6937 KAISER MAXIMILIANS I. TRIUMPH: Le triomphe de l'Empereur Maximilien I. et une suite de 135 *planches gravées en bois,* d'après les dessins de HANS BURGHMAIR, accompagnées de l'ancienne description dictée par l'Empereur à son secrétaire Marc Treitzsaurwein, oblong impl. folio, *good impressions of this wonderful series of woodcuts, hf. bd.* £7. 10s   Vienne, 1796

6938 —— the same, FINE PAPER, impl. folio, *brilliant impressions, calf neat,* £10.   1796

6939 IMAGES de SAINTS et Saintes de la Famille de l'Empereur Maximilien I. folio, 119 *fine large woodcuts by various old engravers after designs by* H. BURGMAIER, *antique calf,* £3. 5s   Vienne, 1799

6940 OVID. La Vita et Metamorphoseo d'Ovidio, figurato in forma d'Epigrammi da M. G. Symeoni, 12mo. *with nearly* 200 *very pretty woodcuts, surrounded by a great variety of singularly chaste and beautiful* ORNAMENTS, *some in the style of the Ancient Missals, others in that of Finiguerra, and adapted for Silversmith Work, by "Le Petit Bernard," brown morocco extra,* £2. 8s   Lione, 1559

6941 PAPILLON, Traité historique et pratique de la Gravure en Bois, 2 vols. 8vo. *portrait and numerous facsimile-woodcuts and engravings representing the processes of woodcut printing, some coloured, calf,* 20s   Paris, 1766

FINE ARTS, BOOKS OF PRINTS, PAINTINGS.

6942 PASSIO Domino nostri Jesu Christi, ex Evangelistarum textu, &c. smallest fol. 30 *leaves, with 25 large bold woodcuts, the size of the page, calf, scarce,* £2.
The Latin edition has got the woodcut on the last page. *Argent. Knobloch*, 1507

6943 PLUTARCHI Vitae (*Latine*) post Jodocum Badium repositae, cum Probi vitis, folio, *numerous woodcuts, vellum,* 15s *Venetiis, Sessa*, 1516
With the Cat and Mouse vignette.

6944 POLICARII (J.) der heiligen XII Aposteln Ankunfft, Beruff, Glauben, Lere, Leben und seliges Absterben, folio, *woodcut title and* 15 *beautiful engravings by* LUCAS CRANACH, *morocco,* £2. *Wittemburg*, 1549

6945 POLIPHILI Hypnerotomachia, ubi Humana Omnia, non nisi Somnium esse docet, atque obiter Plurima scitu sane quam digna commemorat, folio, *fine copy, with the numerous beautiful woodcuts from designs by Andrea Mantegna, Italian calf gilt, gilt leaves,* £13. 13s *Venet. Aldus*, 1467 (1499)
Quite perfect, with all the woodcuts, and the list of Errata.
For a detailed account of this interesting vol. vide Renouard Annales de l'Imp. des Alde, vol. 1, p. 50, where there are upwards of three pages devoted to its description.

6946 POLIPHILE. (COLONNA) Hypnerotomachie, ou Discours du Songe de Poliphile, déduisant comme Amour le combat, à l'occasion de Polia, traduit de langage Italien (par Beroalde de Verville), folio, 197 *fine woodcuts, old calf gilt,* £4. 4s *Paris, Kerver*, 1561
Priced, 1860, Duquesne, Gand, 140 fr.; fetched, 1858, Sotheby's, £5.
Des trois éditions de cette traduction, celle ci est la plus recherchée. Elle est augmentée d'un avertissement de J. Gohory.
"It is not generally known that Goujon re-drew the embellishments of Beroalde de Verville's translation of the Politilo, and that these, beautiful as they are in the Aldine edition, acquired new grace from the French artist." *Sir F. Palgrave, in Turner's Letters from Normandy*, I. p. 201.

6947 RUEXNER (G.) THURNIER BUCH: Anfang, Ursprung und Herkommen des Thurnirs in Teutscher Nation, folio, FIRST EDITION, *facsimile title, with numerous very fine woodcuts of* TOURNAMENTS, *Festivities, etc. beautiful impressions, also about* 1000 COATS OF ARMS *carefully illuminated, very good copy, vellum,* £3. 10s
"Edition rare, la première de cet ouvrage tres curieux." *Siemern*, 1530

6948 SCHATZBEHALTER (der) oder Schrein der waren Reichthümer des Heils, stout folio, *with* 95 *remarkably beautiful large woodcuts, the full size of the page, by* MICH. WOHLGEMUTH, *in the original stamped oak covers,* £6. 6s
Nurmberg, Koberger, 1491
A tall clean copy of an extremely rare and curious work. The woodcuts in this most extraordinary volume, which occupy the whole length of the page, represent subjects of the Old and New Testament, but chiefly the life and passion of our Saviour. Many of the designs are highly singular, and are evidently the work of WOLGEMUTH, the tutor of ALBERT DURER, and the engraver of the cuts for the NUREMBERG CHRONICLE. Strutt characterises the productions of this artist as "bold in execution and original in design."

CATALOGUES of Pictures and Works of Art.

6949 BERNAL COLLECTION. Catalogue of Works of Art, from the Byzantine Period to Louis Seize, 8vo. *with prices and purchasers' names, plates, hf. calf,* 7s 6d 1855

6950 BRITISH INSTITUTION (The) from 1808 to 1850, (wanting 1809-12, 1831, 1833, 1840, 1848) with the Second Exhibitions for 1819, 1821-23, 1825-28, 1830, 1836-38, 1847; together 48 parts, 4to. 20s 1808-50

6951 CORSHAM HOUSE, Historical Account, with Catalogue of the Pictures, by Britton, 8vo. *bds.* 3s 6d 1806

6952 MARIETTE. BASAN, Catalogue Raisonné du Cabinet de feu M. Mariette, stout 8vo. *several plates of Etchings of the Old Masters, interleaved, with prices and purchasers' names, French calf extra,* 32s *Paris*, 1775
At the end are several pages in manuscript, in elucidation of the Cyphers and Monograms of early Engravers.

6953 MISCELLANEOUS AUCTION and other CATALOGUES of Italian, French, Flemish, Dutch, and English PICTURES, Drawings, Prints, Antiquities, Bronzes, Portraits, Painted Glass, Old China, Coins, Books, &c. &c. *a very extensive collection, consisting of several hundred Catalogues, many of them with the prices and purchasers' names, arranged in* 12 *4to. cases, hf. bd. vellum, from Dawson Turner's library,* £2. 10s 1798-1850

6954 ———— another collection of Art and Sale Catalogues, comprising Royal Academy, British Institution, and numerous Auction Catalogues, including Robins' Strawberry Hill with portrait of Horace Walpole, Beckford's, Willett's, Lord Kinnaird's, etc. Society of Water Colours, and others, *many with prices,* about 80 in number, 20s 1780-1850

6955 NOTICES de Tableaux recueillis à Venise, Florence, Turin, etc. Dessins originaux, Emaux, Miniatures, etc. 4 vols. 16mo. *calf,* 7s 6d *ca.* 1802

6956 POLAND (the King of) DESENFANS, Catalogue, with remarks and anecdotes, of Pictures bought for his late Majesty, to be exhibited, 8vo. *hf. bd.* 10s   1802

6957 PORTLAND MUSEUM, Catalogue of the, to be sold April 1786, *with the purchasers' names, and the prices,* 1786—Catalogue of the Prints, Drawings, etc. of J. Blackburne, to be sold March 1786—with other pieces in 1 vol. 4to. *calf,* 21s 1786-89
   There is an original drawing by Repton inserted to illustrate Miss Seward's Louisa, which is one of the pieces in the volume.

6958 PRAUN CABINET. MURR, Description du Cabinet de P. de Praun à Nuremberg, 8vo. *portrait and 6 other plates, bds.* 16s   *Nuremb.* 1797

6959 ROBINSON'S Catalogue of the Works of ART, forming the collection of Matthew UZIELLI, large 8vo. *plates of Gems, etc. cloth,* 7s 6d   1860

6960 ROYAL ACADEMY, Exhibition Catalogue of, from 1810-1862, a few wanting, 48 Catalogues, 4to. *sd.* 30s   1810-62

6961 WINDSOR CASTLE. Catalogue of the Pictures, Busts, Bronzes, etc. in the corridor of Windsor Castle, 4to. *cloth,* 7s   *Privately printed,* 1843

6962 WOBURN ABBEY. CATALOGUE of Miniature Portraits in Enamel, by Henry Bone, in the collection of the Duke of Bedford, roy. 8vo. *portrait, bds. privately printed,* 12s   1825

ARCHITECTURE, ENGINEERING, MACHINERY.

6964 ALBERTOLLI, Ornamenti diversi, 23 *very beautiful plates of Architectural Ornaments for Roofs, Pillars, etc.* 1782—Alcune Decorazioni di nobili Sale ed altri Ornamenti, 23 *fine plates,* 1787—Miscellanea, 23 *beautiful designs for Ornaments,* in 1 vol. atlas folio, *hf. bd. uncut,* £3. 6s   1782-96

6965 ANDROUET DU CERCEAU, Edifices antiques Romains, fol. 98 *carefully designed plates of Roman Buildings, as they were, calf gilt, rare,* 36s   *Paris,* 1584

6966 ARCHITECTURAL SOCIETY'S PUBLICATIONS, from the beginning in 1848 to 1859, divided as follows : ESSAYS AND ILLUSTRATIONS published during the first five years, 12 parts, *with* 99 *plates and* 66 *woodcuts,* VERY RARE, 1848-53 —DICTIONARY OF ARCHITECTURE, including the Biographical as well as Techcal and other portions of the Art and Science, with the Series of Illustrative Plates, 15 parts, *with* 84 *plates and upwards of* 200 *woodcuts,* 1852-59—together 27 parts or nos. roy. 4to. 183 *plates and* 270 *cuts, sd.* £10. 10s   1848-59
   A few odd parts for sale.
   This important and comprehensive work (the only one of the class in any language), honoured by the support and countenance of the leading scientific and artistic bodies, is an invaluable authority for reference on all matters relating to the art or science of Architecture, and will be found to merit a foremost place in the libraries of all amateurs and artists, and of public bodies and educational establishments of all countries. The Annual Subscription is One Guinea.

6967 ARTARIA, Il Duomo di Milano, descrizione di questo Tempio e degli oggetti d'Arte che lo adornano, 4to. 63 *plates of Architecture, Sculpture, and Ornaments, bds.* 10s   1831

6968 BELIDOR, ARCHITECTURE HYDRAULIQUE, ou l'Art de conduire, d'élever, et de ménager les Eaux, 4 vols. 4to. *numerous plates, cf. gt.* £3.   *Paris,* 1782-88-70

6969 BLONDEL, ARCHITECTURE FRANÇOISE ou Recueil des Plans, etc. des Maisons Royalles et de quelques Eglises de Paris, et de Chateaux et Maisons de Plaisance de France, royal folio, 69 *large folding plates, old french calf,* £4. 4s
   Paris, Mariette, s. a.

6970 BÖCKLER, Nova Architectura Curiosa ; das ist, Neue ergötzliche Sinn- und Kunst-Reiche, auch nützliche Bau- und Wasser-Kunst, folio, 320 *plates of Ornamental Fountains, Gardens, etc. vellum, fine copy,* 30s   *Nürnberg,* 1664

6970* ———— the same, folio, *calf,* 24s   *ib.* 1704

6971 BOISSEREE'S Denkmale der Bau-kunst, vom 7ten bis zum 13ten Jahrhundert am Nieder Rhein : Memorials of the Architecture of the Lower Rhine, from the Seventh to the Thirteenth Century (in German), impl. folio, 72 *fine tinted lithographs,* (pub. £7. 10s) *hf. morocco extra, gilt edges,* 36s   1833

6972 BRANDON'S Analysis of Gothic Architecture, with upwards of 200 Examples of Doorways, Windows, etc. and Remarks on the Details of an Ecclesiastical Edifice, 2 vols. royal 4to. (pub. at £5. 5s) *cloth,* 32s   1858

6973 ———— Open Timber Roofs of the Middle Ages, impl. 4to. *with* 43 *plates of Church Roofs,* (pub. at £3. 3s) *cloth* 20s   1849

ARCHITECTURE, ENGINEERING, ETC.

6974 CAMPBELL'S Vitruvius Britannicus; or, the British Architect, containing the Plans, Elevations, and Sections of the regular Buildings in Great Britain, with New Designs and the Continuation by Woolfe and Gandon, *about three hundred plates, with Descriptions in French and English,* 5 vols. atlas folio, *half russia,* £6. 15s 1715-71

6975 ——— NEW VITRUVIUS BRITANNICUS, consisting of Plans and Elevations of Modern Buildings, public and private, by Celebrated Architects, 2 vols. impl. fol. 72 *plates from original drawings by* GEORGE RICHARDSON, *russia, gilt edges,* £2. 1802

6976 CATANEO (Pietro, Senese) L'Architettura, alla quale sono aggiunti il V, VI, VII, e VIII, libro del ornato per le fabbriche, dell acque, dei bagni, di Geometria e di Prospettiva, folio, *best edition, very numerous woodcuts, some the full size of the page, calf neat, gilt edges,* 25s *Venetia,* 1567
Priced, 1833, Thorpe, £1. 8s; 1840, Payne and Foss, £2. 2s; the Fonthill copy fetched £2. 4s. Ouvrage bien exécuté.

6976*CHEVOTET, BLONDEL, etc. Architecture Françoise, oblong folio, 140 *plates of Buildings in Paris and its Environs, comprising Plans, Elevations, Sections and Details, no title, old calf,* £2. 10s *Paris, Mariette, s. a.*

6977 CICOGNARA, LE FABRICHE piu cospicue di VENEZIA, 2 vols. atlas folio, FIRST and BEST EDITION, 250 *fine engravings of Buildings, with Architectural details, including all the best specimens of Venetian Architecture,* (pub. at £24.) *hf. bd.* £9. 9s *Venezia,* 1815-23

6978 ——— Le Fabbriche e Monumenti cospicui di Venezia; edizione con copiose note ed aggiunte di F. Zanotto, 2 vols. atlas folio, *with* 259 *plates, the text in Italian and French, hf. bd. calf,* £8. 1858

6979 CLAYTON'S (J. Arch.) Collection of the Ancient Timber Edifices of England, impl. folio, *with* 26 *fine large tinted plates of Timber Buildings, including Details,* (pub. at £4. 4s) *hf. morocco, an interesting work,* £2. 16s 1846

6980 CONTANT ET FILIPPI, Parallèle des principaux Théatres Modernes de l'Europe, et des Machines Théatrales Françaises, Allemandes et Anglaises; dessins par Clément Contant, Architecte, ancien Machiniste en Chef du Théatre Impérial de l'Opéra; texte par Joseph de Filippi: 1re Partie. Théatres (Plans, Coupes et Élévations), à l'échelle de 5 millim. 2me Partie. Machines Théatrales, à l'échelle de 1 centim. par mètre; 2 vols. royal folio, *with* 134 *plates and* 172 *pp. of text,* (pub. at 160 francs unbound) *hf. morocco,* £5. 15s 1860

6981 CRESY'S ENCYCLOPÆDIA OF ENGINEERING, Historical, Theoretical, and Practical, in 1 thick vol. 8vo. *illustrated by upwards of three thousand engravings on wood by R. Branston,* (pub. at £3. 13s 6d) *cloth,* 36s 1861

6982 DIETTERLIN (Wendel) LE LIVRE DE L'ARCHITECTURE, recueil de planches donnant la division, symétrie et proportion des Cinq Ordres, appliqués à tous les travaux d'Arts qui en dependent tels que FENÊTRES, CHEMINÉES, CHAMBRANLES, PORTAILS, FONTAINES et TOMBEAUX, royal folio, a new edition, 210 *plates, printed on a tinted ground, an exact reproduction of the original prints, hf. morocco,* £5. 5s *Liege, Claesen,* 1862

6983 GLOSSARY OF ARCHITECTURE, or of Terms used in Grecian, Roman, Italian, and Gothic Architecture, with the Companion, *fourth edition,* 3 vols. 8vo. *cloth,* 21s *Oxford,* 1845-46

6984 GOETGHEBUER (J. P.) Choix des Monuments Edifices et Maisons les plus remarquables des PAYS-BAS, roy. fol. PAPIER VÉLIN, 150 *plates, hf. green morocco,* £2. *Gand,* 1827
The only work giving designs of the best Modern Buildings in Holland and Belgium.

6985 GWILTS Encyclopædia of Architecture, historical, theoretical, and practical, thick 8vo. *with more than* 1000 *wood engravings, cloth,* 36s 1859

6986 HART'S (Capt. P. D.) Architectural Illustrations of the principal Mahometan Buildings of BEEJAPORE, executed under the direction of Bartle Frere, B. C. S. edited by James FERGUSON, impl. folio, 73 *large Photographs of Plans, Sections, etc. hf. red morocco, uncut,* £3. 1859

6987 HITTORF et ZANTH, Architecture moderne de la Sicile, ou Recueil des plus beaux monuments religieux, et des édifices publics et particuliers les plus remarquables de ce pays, imp. folio, PAPIER VELIN, 75 *plates, with text, hf. bd. red morocco, uncut,* £4. *Paris,* 1835

6988 HONDIUS, l'Architecture; avec quelques belles Ordonnances mises en Perspective, par Vredman, sm. folio, *numerous fine plates, vel.* 18s *Amst.* 1628

6989 INSTITUTION of Naval Architects, Transactions from the beginning in 1860 to 1862, edited by E. J. Reed, Vols. I-III, 4to. 42 *folding plates of Ship Building, etc.* (pub. at £6. 6s) *new in cloth*, £4. 4s   1860-62

6990 JOMBERT, Architecture Moderne, 2 stout vols. 4to. *numerous plates, old calf*, 10s
Paris, 1764

6991 KNIGHT'S (Henry Gally) Ecclesiastical Architecture of Italy, from the time of Constantine to the Fifteenth Century, with an Introduction and Text, impl. folio, *First and Second Series, containing* 81 *beautiful and highly interesting Views of Ecclesiastical Buildings in Italy, several of which are expensively illuminated in gold and colours*, (pub. at £10. 10s) *hf. bd. morocco*, £7.   1843-44
Bernal's copy fetched, 1855, £7. 15s.

6992 LA FAYE [M. de] Recherches sur la Préparation que les Romains donnoient à la Chaux ou sur la manière de Bâtir des Anciens, 2 vols. in 1, 8vo. *old French red* morocco, *arms of Madame Elizab. de Bourbon on sides*, 18s Paris, 1777-78

693 **LANDSCAPE GARDENING.** BLONDEL, de la Distribution des Maisons de Plaisance, et de la decoration des edifices en général, 2 vols. large 4to. 160 *fine plates of Gardens and Mansions, with Architectural details, fine copy, in the original calf gilt*, £4. 15s   Paris, 1737-8
The best book on the subject; eagerly sought after in France.

6994 CAUSE, de Koninglycke Hovenier, folio, 16 *plates of Flowers, aad* 32 *well planned designs of* Flower-Beds, *hf. bd.* 10s   Amsterdam, s. a. ca. 1676

6995 DIESEL, Erlustierende Augenweide in Vorstellung herrlicher Garten und Lustgebäude, 50 *plates of Gardens, Cascades, Palaces, etc.*—40 Miscellaneous Etchings of German Views—in 1 vol. fol. 90 *plates, hf. calf*, 25s   Aug. Vin. ca. 1700

6996 HIRSCHFELD'S Theorie der Gartenkunst, 5 vols. 4to. *Fine Paper, numerous engravings of Gardens, Summer-Houses, etc. bds.* 16s   Leipzig, 1779-85

6997 KLEINER, Plans et Veües des Maisons et Jardins de Plaisance, &c. Impériales, Schwartzenberg, Lichtenstein et Althan, Part I, folio, *engraved title and dedication, and* 33 *plates of Palaces, Gardens, etc. hf. calf*, 18s   (Augsburg, 1724)

6998 NÜRNBERGISCHE HESPERIDES, oder Beschreibung der Citronat, Citronen und Pomerantzen-Früchte, 4 vols. in 1, folio, 111 *beautiful plates by* Dekker, *of Gardens, Views, Country-Houses, etc. filled up with engravings of* Fruit, *calf*, 18s   Nürnberg, 1708

6999 PERCIER et FONTAINE, Choix des plus célèbres Maisons de Plaisance de Rome, et de ses Environs, atlas folio, 75 *plates of Palaces, Country-Houses, Landscape Gardening, &c. fine early impressions of the plates, with descriptive text, bds.* Flaxman's copy, £2. 10s   Paris, 1802

7000 —— the same, *hf. bd. uncut*, £3. 3s   1802
"Ouvrage estimé pour la correction des dessins et l'exactitude de la gravure."—*Brunet.* All the beautiful Villas and Country Palaces of the Roman Nobility, faithfully represented.

7001 ROBINSON'S Designs for Ornamental Villas, (including Residences in the Swiss, Grecian, Palladian, modern Italian, Tuscan, Old English, Castellated, Anglo-Norman, Elizabethan, Ancient Manor House, and other Styles), etc. roy. 4to. 96 *plates by Harding*, (pub. at £4. 4s) *hf. morocco, uncut*, 28s   1836

7002 —— Village Architecture, a series of Picturesque Designs for the Inn, the Schoolhouse, Parsonage, Church, etc. roy. 4to. 41 *plates by Davis and Allom*, (pub. at 36s) *hf. morocco*, 16s   1838

7003 SCHENCKII Paradisus Oculorum sive conspectus elegantissimi ex delineatione Jacobi Romani, oblong 4to. 100 *plates of Views of Gardens, Palaces, etc. vellum, rare*, 30s   (ca. 1700)

7004 LEUPOLD'S Works on Machinery: Theatrum Machinarum Hydrotechnicarum, 51 *plates of Waterworks*, 1724—Theatrum Machinarum Hydraulicarum, 2 vols. 107 *plates*, 1724-25- Theat. Mach. 56 *plates of Pulleys, Presses, etc.* 1725—Theatrum Pontificale, 56 *plates of Bridges*, 1726—Theatrum Staticum, 4 parts in 1, 57 *plates of Scales, Weights, Measures, etc.* 1726—Theatrum Arithmeticogeometricum, 43 *plates of Mathematical Instruments, etc.* 1724 — Theatrum Machinarum Molarium, 43 *plates of Mill Wheels, etc.* 1734—Supplementum, 40 *plates*, 1774—together 9 vols. fol. 453 *plates, with German text, old binding*, 30s   Leipzig, 1772-74
Priced, 1847, vellum, £5. 5s. Cet ouvrage, le plus considérable que nous ayons sur la Mécanique, n'est pas commun en France."—*Brunet.*

7005 MAROT (J.) Petit Œuvre d'Architecture, impl. 4to. *consisting of* 215 *designs for Palaces, Castles, Churches, &c. calf*, £2. 16s *Paris*, 1764
This work contains : Ouevres d'Architecture ou Recueil des plans de Palais, Chasteaux, Eglises, etc. batis dans Paris et aux Environs, 122 *plates*—Tombeaux ou Mosolées, 19 *plates*—Livre d'Autels et Tabernacles, 18 *plates*—Portes des Hostels de Paris, 20 *plates*—Petits Temples, 36 *plates*.

7006 MAROT (J.) Recueil des Plans, profils, et elevations des plusieurs Palais, Chasteaux, Eglises, Sepultures, Grotes et Hostels, 62 *plates*—Desseins par Lepeintre, 12 *plates*—obl. sm. 4to. *plates, old calf*, 15s *Paris, s. a.*

7007 MOLLER'S MEMORIALS OF GERMAN ARCHITECTURE : Denkmäler der Deutschen Baukunst, *second edition*, 2 vols. in 1, roy. folio, 128 *fine plates of Gothic Architecture, Plans, Sections, Elevations, Ornaments, Monuments, and Details*, (pub. at £4. 4s) *bds.* 22s *Darmstadt, s. a.* (? 1840)
Vol. I. contains on 72 plates the History of Architecture from the VIII. to the XVth century. Vol. II. contains Marburg Cathedral, 18 plates; Limburg and Worms Cathedrals, 18 plates; Freiburg Cathedral, 19 plates. The first edition appeared in 1821.

7008 NICHOLSON's Principles of Architecture, 3 vols. 8vo. *upwards of* 200 *plates, calf*, 15s 1795

7009 NORMAND *aîné*, PARIS MODERNE, ou Choix de Maisons, construites dans la Capitale et dans les Environs, 3 vols. impl. 4to. 480 *carefully engraved plates, with all the Architectural details*, (pub. at £9.) *hf. calf neat*, £4. *Paris*. 1843-49

7010 PALLADIO, Architettura, e della case private, sm. folio, ORIGINAL EDITION, *numerous beautiful plates, remarkably fine copy in overlapping vellum*, UNCUT, 28s *Venetia*, 1570

7011 PUTTRICH (Dr. L.) Architecture of the Middle Ages in the Kingdom and Duchy of Saxony and the Prussian Province of Saxony ; Denkmale der Baukunst des Mittelalters in Sachsen, 5 vols. folio, *with* 387 *plates, representing all the Old Buildings of interest, with numerous plates of Antiquarian and Architectural details, with German text*, (pub. at £18. 18s) *bds.* £7. *Leipzig*, 1835-52
Among the principal buildings are those at Wechselburg, Freiburgh, Anhalt, Schwarzburgh, Meissen, Altenberg, Weimar-Eisenach, Coburg-Gotha, Meiningen-Hildburghausen, Reuss, Dresden, Leipzig. Altenzelle, Zwickau, Bautzen, Oybin, Merseburg, Membleben, Schulpforte, Freiburg, Naumburg, Eisleben, Seeburg, Sangerhausen, Querfurt, Conradsburg, Halle, Petersberg, Landsberg, Jüterbog, Zinna, Treuen-Brietzen, Erfurt, Stolberg, Lausitz, Mühlhausen, Nordhausen, Heligenstadt, Wittenberg, Mühlberg, Zeitz.

7012 QUATREMERE DE QUINCY, Histoire de la Vie et des Ouvrages des plus célèbres Architectes, du XIe Siècle jusqu'à la fin du XVIIIe, 2 vols. roy. 8vo. *with plans of the most celebrated Buildings, bds.* 15s ; *calf gilt*, 22s *Paris*, 1830

7013 RAM RAZ, Essay on the Architecture of the Hindus, impl. 4to. *with* 48 *plates, comprising specimens of the celebrated Buildings in India, with Architectural measurements and details*, 10s 1834

7014 RENNIE (Sir John) On the Theory, Formation and Construction of BRITISH and FOREIGN HARBOURS, copious explanatory text, illustrated by numerous examples, 2 vols atlas fol. *portrait and* 121 *fine large plates, hf. morocco*, £13. 10s 1854
The history of the most ancient maritime nations affords conclusive evidence of the importance which they attached to the construction of secure and extensive Harbours, as indispensably necessary to the extension of commerce and navigation, and to the successful establishment of colonies in distant parts of the globe.
To this important subject, and more especially with reference to the vast extension of our commerce with foreign nations, the attention of the British Government has of late years been worthily directed; and as this may be reasonably expected to enhance the value of any information which may add to our existing stock of knowledge, in a department of Civil Engineering as yet but imperfectly understood, the contribution at the present time may become generally useful to the Engineering Profession.
The Plates are executed by the best mechanical Engravers; the views finely engraved under the direction of Pye: all the Engineering Plates have dimensions, with every explanatory detail for professional use.

7015 RUGGIERI Studio d'Architettura Civile [di Firenze], 3 vols. folio, *plates of Gates, Windows, etc. with plans and elevations of remarkable buildings in* FLORENCE, *a very nice copy in old calf gilt, from Lord Calthorpe's library*, £2. 5s *Firenze*, 1722-28

7016 SCAMOZZI, Architettura Universale, 2 vols. in 1, stout sm. folio, *portrait on frontispiece, with a profusion of plates and woodcuts, vellum*, 18s *Venezia*, 1694

7017 SCHINKEL'S SAMMLUNG ARCHITECTONISCHER ENTWÜRFE, enthaltend theils Werke, welche ausgeführt sind, theils Gegenstände, deren Ausführung beabsichtigt wurde, (Collection of Architectural Designs, containing both Works which are finished, and those whose erections are contemplated) atlas fol. *with* 162 *fine plates, comprising Plans, Elevations, and Sections*, (pub. at £21.) *with an* ADDITIONAL MS. TEXT, *descriptive of all the plates in* ENGLISH, *whole green morocco, gilt edges*, £12. *Berlin*, 1820-26

7018 SERLIO, Extraordinario Libro di Architettura, folio, 77 *plates of Porticoes, Gates, Arches, etc. bds.* 7s 6d *Venetia*, 1557

7019 —— ARCHITETTURA, fol. *many hundred cuts and plates, hf. vel.* 10s *Sessa*, 1559

7020 SERRADIFALCO (Duca di) del Duomo di Monreale et di altre Chiese Siculo Normane, impl. folio, *with 28 plates, descriptive of the Ecclesiastical Architecture of Sicily, bds. scarce,* £2. 16s *Palermo,* 1838

7021 SHARPE'S (E.) ARCHITECTURAL PARALLELS, or the Progress of Ecclesiastical Architecture in England through the XIIth and XIIIth Centuries, 121 *large and elaborate plates,* (pub. at £12. 12s) *The Priory Church at Tynemouth,* 4 *plates—The Full sized* MOULDINGS *of the Abbey Churches,* 60 *plates,* (pub. at 30s)—together 185 *tinted plates,* (pub. at £14. 2s) *in parts,* £10. 1848
A splendid and valuable work; the examples are selected from the following Abbey Churches: Fountain, Kirkstall, Furness, Roche, Byland, Hexham, Jervaulx, Whitby, Rievaulx, Netley, Bridlington, Tintern, St. Mary's York, Guisborough, Selby and Howden.

7021*SHIP-BUILDING. WITSEN's Scheeps-Bouw en Bestier, sm. folio, *frontispiece and* 114 *plates, hf. bd. uncut,* 20s *Amst.* 1671

7022 SIMM'S (J.) PUBLIC WORKS of GREAT BRITAIN, consisting of Railways, Rails, Chairs, Blocks, Cuttings, Embankments, Tunnels, Arches, Viaducts, Bridges, Stations, Locomotive Engines, &c.; Cast-Iron Bridges, Iron and Gas Works, Canals, Lock-gates, Centering Masonry and Brickwork for Canal Tunnels; Canal Boats: Dock-gates, Walls, Quays, and their Masonry; Mooring-chains, and other important Engineering Works, with Descriptions; the whole rendered of the utmost utility to the Civil Engineer and to the Student 131 *plates*—Elmes's Survey of the Harbour and Port of London, 22 *plates* —in 1 vol. impl. folio, 153 *plates of Railways, Arches, Docks, Bridges, etc. etc.* (pub. at £4. 4s in bds.) *hf. bd. morocco, uncut,* £2. 10s 1838

7022*SOANE (Sir John) Description of his House and Museum, roy. 4to. 16 *plates, not published, calf gilt,* 10s 1832

7023 STIEGLITZ (C. L.) Plans et Dessins, tirés de la BELLE ARCHITECTURE, ou Représentations d'Edifices exécutés ou projettés, folio, 115 *plates, bds* 30s 1801

7024 STUART'S and Revett's Antiquities of Athens, 4 vols. impl. folio, 384 *finely engraved impressions, russia extra, gt. edges, by Staggemeier,* £10. 10s 1762-1816
Very superior to the copies usually met with. The first and third volumes, the plates of which are seldom fine, have all the appearance of proof impressions.
Priced, 1829, John Bohn, mor. £52. 10s; 1837, Payne and Foss, £37. 16s; 1840, Jas. Bohn, mor. £42.; 1841, Rodwell, hf. bd. £21.
"Stuart's Athens is a work of surprising exactness, presenting to the eye, in one group, a collection of the noblest specimens of Grecian art and of Attic taste now existing."—*Eustace.*

7025 ANTIQUITIES OF ATHENS and other places in Greece, Sicily, &c. delineated and illustrated by Cockerell, Kinnaird, Donaldson, Jenkins, and Railton, impl. folio, 60 *fine plates,* (pub. at £6. 12s) *cloth,* £2. 10s 1830
Supplementary to the esteemed work of Stuart and Revett, and being printed on a large paper of an equal size, becomes a very important and necessary addition.

7026 TATHAM'S Etchings, representing the best Examples of Ancient Ornamental Architecture, drawn from the Originals in Rome and other parts of Italy, during the years 1794-1796, folio, *best edition,* 102 *plates of Friezes, Vases, Altars, Marble Chairs, Pilasters, &c. original impressions, hf. cf. uncut,* 25s 1799

7027 TAYLOR and CRESY'S Architectural Antiquities of Rome, 2 vols. impl. folio, 129 *most accurate plates of all the Old Buildings in Rome, carefully measured,* (pub. at £12. 12s) *hf. bd.* UNCUT, £4. 1821-22

7028 **TURNING.** BERGERON, Manuel du Tourneur, ouvrage dans lequel on enseigne tout ce que l'Art a produit de plus ingéniex, 3 vols. 4to. *original edition, the third vol. consisting entirely of* 72 *large plates, many of them double, including* 8 *coloured plates of* 72 *different species of wood, hf. cf.* £2. 8s *Paris,* 1792-96

7029 CAMPIN's Practice of Hand Turning in Wood, Ivory, Shell, etc. sm. 8vo. *cuts, cloth, new,* 5s 1861

7030 HANDBOOK of Turning, with Patterns, 12mo. *coloured plates, cloth,* 5s 1842

7031 IBBETSON's Specimens in Eccentric Circular Turning, with practical instructions, 8vo. *plates and cuts, bds.* 10s 1818

7032 PLUMIER, l'Art de Tourner, ou de faire en perfection toutes sortes d'Ouvrages au Tour, folio, *with* 71 *plates, slightly stained, calf,* 16s *Lyon,* 1701

7033 —— nouvelle edition augmentée, folio, 79 *plates, old calf gilt,* 36s *Paris,* 1749

7034 SUPPLÉMENT à tous les Ouvrages sur l'Art du Tourneur, 4to. 22 *folding plates, sd.* 7s 6d *Paris,* 1848

7035 VERDIER ET CATTOIS, Architecture civile et domestique au Moyen Age et à la Renaissance, 2 vols. impl. 4to. *woodcuts in the text, and* 113 *very accurate and carefully engraved plates of* ORNAMENTAL ARCHITECTURE, *hf. bound, calf gilt,* £4. *Paris,* 1855-57

I. CURIOSA MANUSCRIPTS. 393

7036 VITRUVIUS de Architecturâ, 12mo, *cuts, calf gilt, 7s 6d*   *s. l.* 1523
7037 ―――― Les X Livres d'Architecture de Vitruve, corrigez et traduits, avec des notes, par Perrault; seconde edition augmentée, large folio, *with 65 plates and numerous cuts, calf,* 24*s*   *Paris,* 1684
7038 ―――― Civil Architecture, translated by W. Wilkins, and illustrated by numerous Engravings, with an Inroduction, containing an Historical View of the Rise and Progress of Architecture among the Greeks, atlas 4to. *fine impressions of the plates,* (pub. at £6. 6s unbound) *green morocco extra, gold borders and gilt edges,* £2.   1812
7039 ―――― Architecture, translated by Gwilt, 4to. *Large Paper,* 10 *plates, vignettes on India paper,* (pub. at 36*s*) *bds.* 9*s*   1826
7040 WEALE'S Designs of Ornamental Gates, Lodges, Palisading and Iron Work of the Royal Parks, atlas 4to. 50 *fine engravings,* (pub. at £2. 2*s*) *cloth, morocco back,* 18*s*   1841
7041 WILARS. Facsimile of the Sketch-Book of Wilars de Honecort, an Architect of the XIIIth century, with commentaries and descriptions by Lassus and Quicherat; translated and edited, with many additional notes by Professor R. Willis, roy. 4to. *portrait, plans,* 63 *plates, and* 43 *woodcuts, cloth,* £2. 2*s*   1859
    Valuable to the Scholar of Mediæval Antiquities and Architecture.

CURIOSA:

MANUSCRIPTS, EARLY PRAYER BOOKS, EARLY SCIENCE, SPECIMENS OF EARLY PRINTING.

I. MANUSCRIPTS.

7042 BASILIUS MAGNUS de Utilitate Studii in libros Gentilium, ad Nepotes, *Latine,* à Leonardo Aretino—Sibillarum Oracula de Christo—Nomina Offitiorum et Dignitatum Urbis Romæ—in one volume, 12mo. *neat MS. upon vellum, with two drawings, one large initial elaborately interlaced and ornamented, and minor illuminated initials, executed in the Italian style of the XVth century, in the original stamped binding,* £5. 5*s*   *Sec.* XV.
    The book is dedicated by Leonardo Aretino to "Colucium Florentinum," and begins thus with a fine large initial "Ego tibi hunc librum ex media, Coluti, ut aiunt, Grecia delegi." There are several curious proverbial phrases scattered here and there through the pages in a contemporary handwriting; and on the fly-leaf an interlinear translation of the Lord's Prayer and the Hail Mary into Greek, with a peculiar spelling of the Greek.

7043 CAYÉ de LARS du CANONAGE (Cahier de l'Art) sm. 4to. *a* **French** *MS. of the last century, containing numerous Tables of Calculations,* 14 *coloured Drawings of Cannons of various shapes and sizes, and the mode of moving and using them, and colored diagrams to illustrate the size of the Balls, the power of impulsion, and the range, with explanations, etc. a very curious MS. to which the experiments of the present day give double interest,* 20*s*   *ca.* 1720

7044 FIRDOUSI, SHAH NAMAH, *in* **Persian***, large folio,* A MAGNIFICENT PERSIAN MS. *beautifully written, on* 886 *pp. in quadruple columns, each page ruled in with lines of gold, black, green, and orange,* WITH SIXTY-SEVEN LARGE ILLUMINATED DRAWINGS, *chiefly representing scenes of Warfare, illuminated heading to the prefatory life of the poet, and* TWO SPLENDID ANWANS *or opening pages,* RICHLY ILLUMINATED, *strong oriental morocco binding, rebacked, from the library of Dr. Clarke,* £20.   A. H. 1030 (A. D. 1620)
    An extremely fine Manuscript, in the most perfect preservation; such a specimen of Persian artistic workmanship as is seldom seen in Europe.

7045 LIFE OF KRISHNA, *in* **SANSCRIT***, stout sm.* 4to. *a fine Brahminical MS. of* 960 *pp. written in a bold plain hand, in the Devanagari character,* WITH 147 LARGE DRAWINGS, *each the full size of the page, all brightly colored and many of them silvered, representing every incident of the Incarnation or Avatar, oriental stamped binding, from the library of Dr. Clarke,* £30.   *Sec.* XVIII
    The style of the illustration is rude, the character of the incidents depicted is singular and grotesque; but altogether this MS. forms a remarkable specimen of Indian Art from the great number, freedom, and variety of the drawings.

7046 PSALTERIUM DAVIDIS, Græco-Latine, sm. 4to. A FINE MANUSCRIPT *of Italian workmanship, on* 130 *leaves, the Greek and Latin in parallel columns, with rubricated initials, bound in old green vellum,* £4. 15*s*   *Sec.* XV.
    There are some prayers in Italian at the end of the Psalms, the orthography of which can determine the age of the MS. The Greek is written in a small upright character, very clear; and the Latin in a somewhat larger hand, with the peculiar long f occurring in every position of a word.

7047 RECEUL des ANTIQUITEZ de FLANDRES, sm. folio, *a curious old Flemish MS. in French, written in the latter part of the Fifteenth Century, 7 leaves of Index and 216 leaves of Text, in the original stamped binding*, £20.   ca. 1460

A most interesting Manuscript, which formerly belonged to Sander, the great writer upon Flanders, and has his autograph "Antoni Sanderi Gandavensis" written on the fly-leaf. Beneath this signature, is a curious notice stating its purchase at Sander's sale: —" Ce livre et histoire Je Phlp. de L'Espinay. Prr. de la Chapelle Elp. ay achete a Ypre de la Vendue tenue publiqumnt des livres de Mesr. Anthoine Sanderus Chainoisne de Ypre. The MS. begins with a table of chapters in 13 pp.; and the text begins on leaf 1 with the chapter "Des Forrestiers Contes et Contesses de Flandres," and ends with the 143rd Chapter on page 431, which carries the history down to about the year 1440. The wars between England and France for the throne of the latter country are of course treated upon; the great Duke of Bedford's name being converted to Bechfort, and that of Duke Humphrey to Clocestre. The troubles of the celebrated Duchess Jacqueline of Hainault are specially recorded, and a bitter phrase states the union of the Duke of Gloucester, on his divorce from her, with a woman of low degree. There is some disorder in the style of the narration; the chronicler frequently recurring to the "Baudewyns" and the times of the Crusades, on the mention of a name whose history he desires to tell. There are also some memorandums at the end concerning the chateau of Courtrai, and the name of "Jehan Des Martin" appears signed in a couple of places, with the date 1584. For its genealogical, as well as historical value, this MS. demands special attention at the hands of the Antiquary and the Collector. The writing is clear and tolerably regular, the style very quaint, and the orthography rather primitive.

7048 ROIZ SILVERA (Francisco) Reformação da Milicia e Governo do Estado da India Oriental—Discursos sobre a Reformaçam de Justiça da Comarca da Beira e Antre Douro e Minho, e outras Cosas, 2 vols. in 1, sm. 4to. the ORIGINAL MANUSCRIPT, *beautifully written and apparently quite prepared for the Press, with complimentary Sonnets by Vargas and Pacheco, and Stanzas by Botelho, in the original ornamented binding, with gilt gauffré edges*, £4. 10s   ca. 1590

The first work is dedicated to the Infanta Margarita, and the second to the King.

A most important MS. for the history of Portuguese domination in India. The author seems to have been most intimately acquainted with the state of affairs there; and he points out most particularly the abuses of the government, with recommendations how to reform them. The historical details are extremely interesting.

7049 VILADAMOR (Antoni) Primera Part de la Historia General de Cathaluña en la qual se contenen las Vidas dels Reys y Emperadors que la governaren des del Diluvi fins aques perde abtot lo restant de España en temps del Rey Don Rodrigo; ahont tantbe stan continuadas las vidas dels Papas, folio, MS. *of 219 leaves, vellum*, £5.   1585

AUTOGRAPH MS. OF A LOST CHRONICLE. Pedro Antono Viladamor was "His Majesty's Secretary and Archivist under the Crown of Arragon," and flourished at Barcelona in the latter half of the sixteenth century. The only work which he is known to have written, is the above Chronicle of Catalonia, composed in his native dialect, and concerning which there has been no information save a scanty allusion in the Bibliotheca Hispana of Antonio, who seems merely to have known that such a chronicle had been left in MS, and been largely used by Pujades in his work published 1609. The handwriting of the MS. is bold and clear; it is dedicated to the "Illustrious Congregation of the three states of Catalonia convoked by his Majesty in the Cortes of Monço, 1585." It has evidently received the author's final arrangement for publication; being in every way complete. In our limited knowledge of Viladamor, we cannot say what was the cause that it never went through the printer's hands; but it may be conjectured that his death took place soon after the conclusion of the MS. There are two notes, which follow the table of chapters, in one of which he excuses the absence of a list of authors in consequence of his want of books; and in the other, mentions that he had been unable, through illness, to prepare an index. The MS. no doubt fell into the hands of Pujades, then a young man, who had probably very little scruple in appropriating the labors of Viladamor, although indeed he frequently quotes his name as an authority.

7050 ZALDIVIA, Suma de las cosas CANTABRICAS y GUIPUZCOANAS compuestas por Zaldivia natural de la villa de Tolosa, año de 1564, sm. folio, 161 pp. *half bound*, £2. 16s   *copied circa* 1700

A very valuable MS. apparently copied about one hundred and fifty years ago from the original, doubtless to preserve the record. The name of the author, and the existence of his work, seem to be unknown to all the biographers and bibliographers; yet the dedication is addressed to a patron of high rank, one of the Manriquez de Lara, a family which gave Governors and Viceroys to Naples, Valencia, and Catalonia. The name of Zaldivia moreover occurs during the progress of the narration as that of a family of distinction and influence. The first and second chapters of the work treat on the Geography and Physical peculiarities of the country, the third on its original inhabitants, the fourth is a curious essay on the LANGUAGE; and the historical portion begins in the seventh chapter with the wars of the CANTABRIANS and Augustus Caesar. There can be no doubt that the matter of this interesting volume has never been published.

II. EARLY PRAYER BOOKS.

7051 HEURES A L'USAIGE DE ROME, sm. 4to. PRINTED UPON VELLUM, *ornamented with twenty large, and numerous smaller most exquisite finished engravings, representing the Life and Passion of our Saviour, with other subjects of scripture history; each page surrounded by an engraved border composed of Scriptural and other subjects, the borders to the "Vigiliæ Mortuorum" representing the "Dance of Death," pale calf gilt, richly tooled on sides, with clasps*, £6. 6s

Paris, Simon Vostre, 1498.

Sir Mark Sykes' copy fetched £8. 8s; Dr. Hawtrey's, 1853, £16. COLLATION of this copy: Title, preliminary matter, and Almanack, 5 leaves, being ã i. to ã v; text, ã vi. to ii., being 60 leaves; making altogether 65 leaves.

A CHARMING VOLUME, in which the delicacy of finish in the engraved illustrations is peculiarly remarkable; so much so, as to make it almost doubtful whether they have been worked from *wood-blocks*, as has generally been supposed. The text is also beautifully worked, and is enriched with numerous capitals in gold and colours, which, with the brilliancy of the ink used by the printer, renders the whole a "*chef-d' œuvre*" of typographic skill. For artistic beauty of design, this is considered the finest of all the Books of Hours. Some of the marginal decorations are so singularly fine, that they have been introduced into the Bibliographical Decameron.

7052 HORTULUS ANIME, (seu Officium B. Mariæ Virginis), stout 12mo. gothic letter, *printed in red and black, with 86 curious woodcuts, every page surrounded by an elaborate woodcut border, fine copy, in dark stamped morocco, gilt edges, by Clarke and Bedford, rare*, £4. *Nurenberg, Koberger*, 1521
This work has always been esteemed and sought for, on account of its finely designed woodcut illustrations. The present edition seems unknown to the bibliographers.

7053 OFFICIUM GLORIOSÆ VIRGINIS MARIÆ secundum Sanctam Ecclesiam Romanam nuper ex concilio Tridentino reformatum—Devota Preparatione innanzi al divino Uffizio, per la *Riforma* della Chiesa; in 1 vol. 12mo. *printed in red and black,* Gothic letter, *woodcut initials, etc. in black morocco, gilt edges, fine large copy*, £5. 5s *Venetiis, Leuncinus*, 1571
VERY RARE and curious. The volume begins with a Calendar in Italian, and finishes with 72 pages of Prayers in that language, as used by the "Fratelli di S. Maria dell' Humiltà" in Venice.

7054 HEURES A L'USAIGE DE ROUEN, toutes au long sans rien requerir, 12mo. gothic letter, *printed in large well cut type, red and black, with 60 large and very curious woodcuts, and numerous woodcut initials, calf extra, bound by Simier*, £6. 6s *Paris, J. Kerver*, 1577
Many of the woodcuts are of a singularly grotesque character. There are numerous very curious couplets and quatrains interspersed through the beginning of the book, and many odd phrases quite in keeping with the style of the illustrations.

7055 SAILLY (P. Thomæ) Thesaurus Litaniarum ac Orationum, cum Apologiâ adversus Sectarios, *printed in red and black, with nearly 30 engravings, Bruxellæ*, 1598—Litaniæ Septem Virgini musice decantandæ, 56 *leaves of* MUSIC, *with all the parts, Tenor, Bass, etc. Antv.* 1598, 2 vols. in 1, stout sm. 8vo. *vellum, rare*, 36s 1598
The first work in this volume was stigmatized in the Roman Index Expurgatorius.

7056 SENAULT (Elizabeth) Heures Nouvelles dediees a Monseigneur Dauphin, 16mo. *title, dedication, and pp.* 1—212 *entirely engraved in a most tasteful and delicate manner by the authoress herself, with ornamental initials, etc. old French red morocco extra, gilt edges*, £3. 3s *Paris, s. d. (ca.* 1660)

7057 VEREPÆI (Simonis) Catholicum Precationum selectissimarum enchiridion, ex Patrum Scriptis, etc. concinnatum, 16mo. 90 *beautiful small engravings, executed with marvellous delicacy, and most exquisitely finished, brilliant impressions, bound in old olive morocco, gilt edges, arms on sides*, £5. *Antverp.* 1603
The name of the artist nowhere appears; but the fine style of these small engravings—each being 2 inches by 1½—and their minute, yet perfect workmanship, prove an extraordinary skill in the use of the graver, and a complete mastery over the art.

7058 BOSSU (le R. P.) Heures Royales contenant les Offices, Vespres, etc. le tout en François, 1677—Vie de N. Seigneur, de la Vierge, et des Apostres, 1678—in 1 vol. 18mo. *portraits of Louis XIV. and his Queen, original morocco*, 12s
Paris, 1677-78

7059 LIVRE D'HEURES d'après les Manuscrits de la Bibliothèque Royale, 12mo. *containing* 184 *pp. entirely executed in chromo-lithography by Engelmann, richly finished in* COLOURS *and* GOLD, *comprising* 16 FINE MINIATURES, *full page size, with beautiful borders, and other illuminations of smaller figures, birds, flowers, capitals, initials, etc. in facsimile of the finest MSS. of the Royal Library, XIII.-XVI. Century, bound in black stamped morocco, clasps, gilt edges, a charming book*, £2. *Paris*, 1846
Fetched, 1855, Sotheby's, £4. 8s; 1857, £3. 4s.

7060 HEURES ILLUSTRÉES, Prières Quotidiennes, La Sainte Messe, Les Vêpres, etc. sq. 8vo. *magnificently printed in* GOLD *and* COLOURS *on* 78 *leaves of enamel cardboard, with elegant borders surrounding every page, enclosing Figures, Flowers, and Ornaments of every description, illuminated initials, etc. in imitation of Ancient illuminated Missals, solidly bound by Hayday, in antique brown morocco, edges gilt and gauffré*, £3. 3s *Paris, ca.* 1854

III. CURIOSA VARIA:
Miscellanies, Magic, Witchcraft, Early Science.

7061 BRANDT (Sebastiaen) Affghebeelde Narren Speel-schuyt, overgheset door A. B., sq. 12mo. *fine engraving on title, portrait of Brand, and* 103 *curious woodcuts, calf, rare*, 32s *Amstelredam*, 1635

7062 EULENSPIEGEL. Periandri (Ægidii) Noctuæ Speculum, 12mo. *a rare poem on the adventures of Eulenspiegel or Howleglass, with* 103 *woodcuts by Jost Amman, calf gilt, fine copy*, 25s *Francof.* 1567

7063 EULENSPIEGEL. Les Aventures de Tiel Ulenspiegel illustrées par Lauters, 12mo. *numerous pretty woodcuts, calf gilt,* 7s 6d *Brux.* 1840

7064 **Freemasonry**. Manual de los Masones Libres del Rio de la Plata; Constitucion de la Masoneria Escoc. para la Confed. Arg.; Regl. de la Log. de S. Juan; in 1 vol. 8vo. *morocco,* 7s 6d *Buenos Aires,* 1856-58

7065 DESAGULIERS (Dep. Grand-Master) Constitutions of the Freemasons, for the use of the Lodges, with Songs and Choruses, 4to. *frontispiece and Music, old calf,* 10s 1723

7066 FRANCKENBERG, Raphael oder Artzt-Engel, 4to. *plate and symbolical cuts, bds. a very singular and learned work, bds.* 7s 6d *Amst.* 1676

7067 LARCHER, Mémoire sur la Déesse Vénus, auquel l'Acad. des Inscript. a adjugé le prix, 1775, 12mo. *calf, a learned and curious work,* 12s 6d *Paris,* 1776

7068 MERCURY, or the Secret and Swift Messenger, how a man may with privacy and speed communicate to any distance, by J. W. 12mo. *calf,* 10s 1641

7069 **MAGIC**. AGRIPPAE (H. Cornelius) Opera, 2 stout vols. 12mo. *portrait, hf. calf,* 18s *Lugduni, s. a. Bering.*
This copy agrees in every point with Brunet's description of the best issue and best edition.
The La Valliere copy fetched 52 fr.; Maucune's, 40 fr. Priced, 1832, 1837, and 1840, Payne and Foss, mor, £3. 3s.

7070 BELLIERE, Physionomie raisonnée ou Secret curieux pour connoître les inclinations de chacun, 16mo. *vellum,* 6s *Paris,* 1664

7071 BODINO, Demonomania degli Stregoni, cioè Furori et Malic de' Demoni col mezo de gl' Huomini, sm. 4to. *vellum,* 14s *Ventia, Aldo,* 1592
A prohibited book. Priced, Thorpe, £2. 2s; Renouard's copy, fetched, £1. 12s.
Very interesting, as containing, at the end of the table a catalogue of books printed by the Manutii, with the sizes and prices.

7072 CHAMBRE, L'Art de connoistre les Hommes, 16mo. *vel. curious,* 7s 6d *Amst.* 1660

7073 **Chiromancy**. LA SCIENCE CURIEUSE, ou Traité de la Chyromance, sm. 4to. 88 *curious plates, containing several hundred compartments of figures, vellum, rare,* 28s *Paris,* 1665

7074 RAMPALLE, la Chyromantie naturelle de Ronphile, 12mo. *engravings, vellum,* 10s *Paris,* 1655

7075 DEFOE's History of the Life and Adventures of Duncan Campbell, who writes down future contingencies of Fortune, 8vo. *portraits and 3 plates, calf,* 7s 1720

7076 ECKARTSHAUSEN, Aufschlüsse zur Magie, 4 vols. 8vo. *bds.* 6s 1791

7077 HILDEBRANDI Magia Naturalis, das ist Kunst und Wunderbuch, 4 vols.— Kunstbüchlein vor die Kürschner, etc.—Planeten-Buch, *curious cuts and tables*—6 vols. in 4, sq. 8vo. *bd.* 10s *Erffurdt,* 1611-13

7078 HORST (G. C.) Zauber-Bibliothek, oder von Zauberei, Theurgie und Mantik, Hexen, Dämonen, Gespenstern, etc. 6 vols. 8vo. *curious cuts, hf. calf,* 32s *Mainz,* 1821-26

7079 MONCÆJUS de Magia Divinatrice, sq. 8vo. 2 *curious cuts, vellum,* 6s *Franc.* 1683

7080 PLANCY, Dictionnaire Infernal, ou Recherches sur les Démons, etc. 2 vols. in 1, 8vo. *cloth,* 12s *Paris,* 1818

7081 RAGON Cours philosophique des Initiations, 8vo. *cloth,* 5s *Paris,* 1841

7082 SALVERTE, des Sciences Occultes; ou essai sur la Magie, les Prodiges et les Miracles, 2 vols. 8vo. *hf. calf,* 12s *Paris,* 1829

7083 SANDERS' Physiognomie and Chiromancie, Metoposcopie, the proportions and moles of the body, Dreams, the Art of Memory, etc. sm. folio, *fine portrait, and numerous curious woodcuts, in the original binding,* 25s 1653

7084 SHARP (Jérome) Les Petites Aventures de, contenant autant de Tours ingénieux que de Leçons utiles, avec le supplément (par DECREMPS) 4 vols. in 2, 8vo. *cuts of Legerdemain tricks, hf calf neat,* 12s *Paris,* 1792-93

7085 SOLDAN's Geschichte der Hexenprocesse, 8vo. *hf. calf,* 5s *Stuttg.* 1843

7086 TASGRESTI, vera e falsa Astrologia e Chiromanzia, 12mo. *vellum,* 6s *Roma,* 1683

7087 WIEGLEB (Johann Christian) die NATÜRLICHE MAGIE, aus allerhand belustigenden und nützlichen Kunststücken bestehend, mit Martius' Unterricht, 20 vols. in 19, 8vo. *numerous plates, hf. calf,* 32s *Berlin und Stettin,* 1789-1805

7088 WIER, Histoires, disputes et discours des Illusions et Impostures des Diables, des Magiciens, etc. avec deux dialogues d'Erastus, stout 12mo. *limp vel.* 16s 1579

7089 **SCIENCE (Early)**. AGRICOLÆ (Georgii) De Re Metallica Libri XII. quibus Officia, Instrumenta, Machinæ ac omnia ad Metallicam spectantia describuntur et per effigies, adjunctis Latinis Germanicisque appellationibus, ob oculos ponuntur; cum Libro de Animantibus Subterraneis, folio, LARGE PAPER, *with several hundred large and fine woodcuts of Mining Operations, Tools, Instruments, Machinery, etc. old calf, from the Old Electoral Library of Bavaria, very fine copy*, £2. 12*s* *Basiliæ*, 1556

7090 BEAUSARDI Arithmeticae Praxis, ad quam veterum exempla explicantur, 12mo. *title and 15 other preliminary leaves, folios 1—120, vellum*, 24*s* *Lovanii*, 1573

7091 DANFRIE (P.) Declaration du l'usage du Graphometre et Traicté de l'Usage du Trigometre, sans reigle d'Arithmetique, 12mo. 91 *and* 34 *pp. and Extraict 1 leaf, printed in " Lettres de Civilité," engravings, neat in vellum*, VERY SCARCE, 20*s* *Paris*, 1597

7092 GOMPARST (Godefroyd) Ung Liuret du Copte, contenant plusieurs simples exemples questions et demandes a la Rigle de Troix et Practique duysantes conuenables et prouffitables a la marchandise, oblong 24mo. black letter, *bd.* £2. 16*s* *Anvers, Symon Cocq*, n. d. (*ca.* 1520)

VERY RARE AND CURIOUS. COLLATION: A to S, in eights, including the title, and the preface, "Au benivolent Lecteur." This preface is curious and quaintly-phrased, and has an odd conclusion in rhyme of a dozen lines sonnet-fashion. Gomparst seems to have been a teacher " de ceste subtile industrie dAlgorisme."

7093 MENNHERR, Arithmeticque contenant plusieurs belles Regles et questions utiles aux Marchands, 12mo. *bd. rare*, 36*s* *Anvers*, 1570

A curious old work of questions in Exchange, Practice, and other arithmetical rules. COLLATION: a to x, in eights, including title, dedication, etc. at the beginning, and the address, "Au Lecteur," and subscription at the end.

7094 STEINMETZ (M.) Arithmeticæ Praecepta in quaestiones redacta cum exemplis, 12mo. *vellum*, 21*s* *Lips.* 1568

EARLY PRINTED BOOKS, ROMANCE LITERATURE.
I. FRANCE.

7095 **Lyon.** MANTUAN (Baptiste) LA PARTHENICE MARIANE, trāslatée de Latin en Francoys (par Jacques de Mortières), smallest folio, *fine copy in green morocco extra, gilt edges*, £5. *Lyon, Claude Nourry et Jehan Besson*, 1523

VERY RARE. COLLATION: Title, Privilege, and Table, 3 leaves; dedication to the Duchess d'Alençon, etc. 1 leaf; Feuillets 1-86; Sept petis couplets, 1 leaf. This last leaf of couplets, addressed to the Duchess d'Alençon, is the rarest part of the volume, and generally wanting. The only copy in the British Museum (formerly Mr. Grenville's) does not possess it.

7096 **Paris.** BOUCHET (Jehan), Sensuyt le LABYRINTH DE FORTUNE & seiour des troys nobles Dames, compose par lacteur des Regnars Trauersans et Loups Rauisans, surnomme le trauerseur des voyes perilleuses, sm. 4to. lettres gothiques, *curious woodcuts on title and last page, fine copy in old French red morocco, gilt edges*, £5. *Paris, Alain Lotrian, s. d.*

A poetical volume of considerable rarity; dedicated to Marguerite, duchesse de Berry et d'Alençon, sister to Francis the First.

7397 KEMPIS. DE IMITATIONE CHRISTI: Incipit liber primus Johannis Gerson, 16mo. gothic letter, *a scarce edition, with woodcut device of Jehan Petit on title page, and that of Gaspard Philippe on reverse of last page, fine large copy in French red morocco, gilt edges, by Wright, the bottom margins almost all uncut*, 24*s* *Parisiis, pro J. Parvo*, 1505

7098 MONSTRELET. LEPREMIER (SECOND ET TIERS) VOLUME DE ENGUERRAN DE MONSTRELLET, ensuyvant Froissart, des Croniques de France, Dangleterre, Descosse, Despagne, de Bretaigne, de Gascongne, de Flandres, et lieux circonvoisins, etc. 3 vols. in 2, smallest folio, gothic letter, *very fine copy in red morocco extra, gilt edges, from Dr. Hawtrey's library, very rare*, £10. *Paris, Jean Petit et M. Lenoir*, 1512

Priced, Tross, 1856, 300 fr.; Flaxman's copy fetched £12; the Solar copy 480 fr.

7099 MONSTRELLET, Croniques de France, d'Angleterre, d'Escoce, d'Espaigne, de Bretaigne, de Gascongne, de Flandres, &c. 3 vols. in 1, fol. black letter, *very tall copy, with a few uncut leaves*, £6. 15*s* *Paris, Fr. Regnault*, 1518

This edition is augmented with a continuation from 1498 to 1516.

7100 BIBLE FRANCAISE. Les Paraboles de Salomon, les Prophetes, et les Machabees, (par Le Febvre d'Estaples), folio, *triple woodcuts of the chapter headings, and woodcut initials, bd.* £2. 10*s* ? *Anvers*, 1528, or 1534

The edition of 1534, of Le Fevre's Bible, which was originally brought out irregularly and in different portions in consequence of the persecution he endured, is extremely rare, having been rigorously suppressed.

7101 MOLINET (Maistre Jehan) Les Faictz et dictz de feu de bône memoire Maistre Jehan Molinet, contenans plusieurs beaulx Traictez, Oraisons, et Champs royaulx folio, lettres gothiques, 3 *leaves, 1 blank leaf and cxxxiii leaves, device of Jehan Longis on the title, superb copy in red* MOROCCO *super extra, gilt edges, broad borders of gold, by Petit,* £7. 10s *Paris, J. Longis et Veufue Sainct Denys,* 1531

7102 VINCENT [de Beauvais] MIROIR HISTORIAL, translaté de Latin en Francois (par J. de Vignay), 5 vols. in 3, folio, lettres gothiques, *large and spirited woodcuts*, £10. *Paris, N. Couteau,* 1531

Brunet states that this second French edition is as scarce as the first; he quotes no copy.

7103 VIRGILLE, les Oeuvres de, translatees de Latin en Francoys, et nouvellement corrigees oultre la premiere impression, sm. folio, *title in black and red within curious engraved border, numerous woodcuts, corners of the last two leaves torn off, original calf, arms on sides,* £3. 16s *Paris, Yvernel, Le Messier,* 1532

7104 ROMMANT DE LA ROSE, nouvellement reveu et corrige oultre les precedentes impressions, stout 12mo. gothic letter, *woodcuts, old calf,* £4.
Paris, Pierre Vidove, 1538

Priced, 1829, £4. 4s; recently, £6. 6s; fetched, 1860, £4. 4s; Dr. Hawtrey's copy, £4. 14s 6d. A very rare and highly esteemed edition of this celebrated poetical romance.

7105 CAVICEO, Dialogue tres elegant intitule le PEREGRIN, traictant de l'honneste et pudicq amour, traduict de vulgaire Italien par Françoys Dassy, Secretaire du Roy de Navarre ; avec les Annotations, par Jehan Martin, Secretaire de Maximilian Sforce Visconte, 12mo. *a very fine clean copy in French calf gilt,* £2. *Paris, Vincent Serthenas,* 1540

Caviceo (Jaques) prêtre Italien, eut de grand diferens avec l'évêque de Parme sa patrie. Il en fut exilé, et commit un homicide, a son corps defendant, dont il fut absous. Il mourut en 1511, a 68 ans. Il s'est fait connoitre par son roman de Peregrino, traduit en François par Francois Dassy."—*Dict. Universel, Paris,* 1810

Under the assumed name of Peregrino, Caviceo in this work relates his own adventures. "Ce livre faisait en France au commencement du règne de François I. les délices de la jeunes', et donnait lieu aux prédicateurs d'en blâmer fortement la lecture comme dangereuse."—*Niceron.*

7106 MARGUERITE DE VALOIS, Royne de Navarre, L'HEPTAMERON des Nouvelles, 4to. SECOND EDITION, but the *first containing 72 Novels, and equally scarce with the earlier impression, very* FINE COPY, *old red* MOROCCO, *in the style of De Rome, Sen. from the Collection of Girardot de Prefond, with his book-plate,* £9. 10s *Paris, Benoist Prevost,* 1559

7107 Troyes. THOISON D'OR. GUILLAUME [FILLASTRE] jadis Evesque de Tournay, Le premier [et second] volume de la Thoison d'Or, auquel sont contenus les haulx faictz, tant des maisons de France, Bourgogne et Flandres que d'autres roys et princes, 2 vols. in 1, sm. folio, black letter, *with curious woodcuts, and woodcut capital letters, fine copy, with the title-page of J. Petit, hf. calf,* £3. 6s *Troyes, par N. le Rouge,* 1530

Into this account of the Order of the Golden Fleece, the Author has introduced a Romance of Jason and Medea.   Lord Rothesay's copy fetched, 1855, £6. 10s.

II. GERMANY.

7108 MENSA PHILOSOPHICA. Incipit tabula in librum qui dicitur Mensa philosophica. *In fine,* Presens liber que mensam philosophicā vocāt unicuique p'utilis compēdiose p̄ractās in primis qd in cōviviis p CIBIS et POTIBUS sumendū est . . deinde qui sermones illis s'm exigētiam psonarum habendi sunt, et que q'stiones discutiēde ; q' insuper FACETIE sive JOCI interserendi . Feliciter explicit, (auctore Theobaldo Anguilberto, HIBERNO), smallest 4to. 96 *leaves, the first of which is a blank, 27 lines to a full page, printed on stout paper, with all the initial letters painted in, a very large copy in remarkably sound condition, bound in the year* 1788 *in calf,* £8. *sine loco aut anno aut nomine typog.* ca. 1473

AN EXTREMELY RARE EDITION, and probably THE FIRST. Ebert, Panzer, Hain, and Brunet are all ignorant of it. The latter three mention an edition, being the first without a date, but supposed to be printed by Johannes Guldenschaaf, at Cologne before 1480. This edition is exactly described by Hain, and seems to approach very closely in all particulars to that set forth above ; the only differences being in the division of the words at the end of the lines, and the circumstance that there are 26 lines per page in Hain's edition, while there are 27 in this.

The volume consists of 96 leaves, the first blank, having signatures a to r (a in six leaves, b to f, each in 8, g in 6, h to l each in 8, and m, n in 6), with 27 lines to a full page. The book contains some curious tales and facetious jokes. This work has often been falsely attributed to Conrad of Halberstadt, he also having written a Treatise entitled Mensa Philosophica.

7109 WECZDORFF DE TRIPTIS (Jodocus) Ars Memorandi nova secretissima continens precepta paucissimis bonarum artium militibus visa, sm. 4to. *a curious work of 8 pages, with large woodcut title, several peculiar woodcut characters, and woodcuts of symbols, beautifully bound in red morocco extra, gilt edges, uncut,* £5. 5s *s. l. et a.* (ca. 1480)
Unknown to all the bibliographers. This is the only copy I can trace.

7110 FREYDANCK. PROUERBIA ELOQUENTIS FREYDANGKS innumeras in se vtilitates coplectentia. Ich bynss genant bescheidenheit Die aller tugende krone treit Mich hat gemacht frydanck, etc. *old German and Latin,* sq. 8vo. 36 ff. *fine copy, last leaf mended, hf. calf,* £3. 10s *Absque ullâ notâ (circa* 1490)
Cette édition, en vers allemands et latins est la première que l'on ait de ce poëme originairement écrit dans le XIIIe. Siècle. Déjà en 1508 elle était si rare que le célèbre Seb. Brant en entreprit une édition refondue, comme il fait remarquer sur titre, pour sauver l'ouvrage de l'oubli.

7111 **Augsburg.** GREGORII (S.) LIBER DIALOGORUM TEUTSCH. Hye hatt ain end das puch genant dyalogus sancti Gregorii pape, gedruckt da mā zelt nach Cristi gepurd, M,CCCC,LXXIII, jar—Visio Tundali, zu teutsch, die gesicht Tundali.—Von einem Bischoff Forsee genant.—Wunderzaichen in Sicilia.—Ars moriendi, Teutsch—Tractatus quatuor novissimorum, Teutsch, M,CCC,LXXIII,— in 1 vol. folio, *printed with a very quaint gothic type on* 194 *leaves including the frontispiece, calf neat, fine copy, with xylographic frontispiece representing Saint Gregory in conversation with his Deacon Peter, extremely rare,* £3. 10s 1473
Priced, 1841, 1842, Thorpe, £4. 14s 6d. These six tracts, "in den Kloster St. Ulrich gedrukt, 1473," bear the same degree of rarity as our books printed at St. Albans. It is one of the very rare productions of the press established by the Prior Melchior de Stamham, in the Monastery of St. Ulrich and Afra at Augsburg, and is minutely described by Panzer in his Annalen, 1788, p. 71.

7112 **Cologne.** VOCABULARIUS Fructuosus omni aetati perutilis ex Papia, Britone, Catholico, Alano, Ysidoro, aliisque quamplurimis Magistris collectus, qui alio nomine Brevilogus nuncupatur, folio, *remarkably fine copy, russia extra, very rare,* £4. 10s *(Coloniæ, per Conradum de Hoemborch,* 1470)
A noble specimen of typography in the infancy of the art; printed without signatures, paginatior, catchwords, and colophon. The capitals filled in by hand with red ink. Not mentioned by Brunet nor Hain.

7113 BIBLIA SACRA LATINA, continens Vetus Testamentum et Libros Apocryphicos, in 1 stout volume, sm. folio, all the CAPITALS filled in by hand and illuminated, *a superb copy of this fine early Monument of Typography,* UNCUT *throughout, with very ample contemporary MS. notes partly in the margins, partly interleaved, original hogskin binding.* This copy belonged in 1553, to Brother Hermann de Affelin, £8. 8s *Sine anno, loco aut typographo,* (sed COLONIÆ, *typis* UDALRICI ZELL, 1470)

7114 **Frankfort.** HELDENBUCH, darinn viel seltzamer Geschichten und kurzweilige Historien von den grossen Helden und Rysen, sm. 4to. *numerous woodcuts engraved within ornamental borders, by Feyerabend, most excellently designed, and representing scenes of Chivalry, romantic incidents, and illustrating the Costume of the Middle Ages, a rare poetical Romance, in the original oak binding, leather covered and stamped, with clasps,* £3. 10s *Franckfort,* 1590
Fetched, at Sotheby's in 1860, £5. 10s

7115 **Hamburg.** MEIGER, de Panurgia Lamiarum, Sagarum, Strigum ac Veneficarum totiusque cohortis Magicae Cacodaemonia, entirely *in Low German,* sm. 4to. *antique calf,* 32s *Hamborch,* 1587

7016 **Lubeck.** SUMMA JOHANNIS, FIRST EDITION, in *Low German,* sm. folio, *very fine copy, in old calf, not mentioned by Scheller,* £4. 10s *Lubek, S. Arndes,* 1487
COLLATION: Table of contents, 8 *leaves*; the book commencing: Hir hevet sik an de vorrede disses bokes genomet Suma Johannis, welker de eerwerdige vader lezemester Johannes van Vryborgh prediker ordens to latine ghemaket unde uth deme hylligen decret boke getoge hefft. Unde van latine in dat dudesche gemaket dorch einen hochgelerden doctore geheten brod. Bartold, *sheets* A—S (in eights) T *in* 10 *leares.* "This version in the language of Lower Saxony is very rare and highly interesting in a philological point of view. The colophon is curious: Here ends the Summa Joannis which is taken out of the holy book of Decretals, which is most useful to the instruction of the people to their soul's happiness."—*Singer's MS. note.*

7117 **Mentz.** HERP (Henrici) SPECULUM AUREUM decem Præceptorum Dei, stout folio, *fine copy bound in the original leather covered oak boards, uncut leaves,* £2. *Maguneiæ, P. Schoyffer de Gernsheym,* 1474
With the Printer's Shield in red, and the very curious Imprint respecting Typography having been discovered at Mentz.

7118 **Nuremberg.** LUTHER'S Deutsch Catechismus, mit newen Vorrhede unnd Vermanunge zu der Beycht, 12mo *title in red and black, with woodcut border, and numerous woodcuts through the text, vellum,* A RARE AND PRECIOUS EDITION, £5. *Nürenberg, Formschneyder,* 1531
Heber's copy fetched £5. 5s. The woodcuts render this edition peculiarly valuable.

7119 **Strassburg.** [LICHTENBERGER]. Hec practica narrat de presenti āno et sequētibus annis, DE NOVIS RARIS ET INAUDITIS REBUS, et gestis que futura sunt, sq. 8vo. *numerous allegorical woodcuts, singularly fine copy, calf extra, by Simier,* £2. 10s *Urbs Argent.* 1499
Collation: A, C, E, in eights; D, F, G, H, in fours; the last leaf being a woodcut.

7120 CAOURSIN, Historia van RHODIS, wie ritterlich sie sich gehalten mit dem tyrannischen Keyser Machomet uss Türckyē, lustig un lieplich zu lesen, sm. folio, *large woodcut on title, and numerous woodcuts representing the Siege of Rhodes, the heroism of its Defenders, etc. hf. bd.* RARE, £2. 2s *Straszburg*, 1513

III. HOLLAND AND BELGIUM

7121 **Antwerp.** CHRONICLE OF FLANDERS. Dits die excellente Cronike vā Vlaenderē, beghinnende vā Liederick Buc den eersten Forestier tot desen onsen doorluchtichsten Keyser Karolo, stout sm. folio, *large woodcuts on the front and reverse of title, representing Charles V. on horseback, with numerous large woodcuts throughout the text, containing Portraits, Historical Scenes, etc. vellum,* £3. 3s *Antwerpen, Vorsterman,* 1531

7122 SPELEN VAN SINNE vol scoone Moralisacien Wtlegginghen end Bebiedenissēn op alle loeflijcke Consten ; ghespeelt binnen der stadt van Andtwerpen op d'landtjuweel by die veerthien cameren van Rhetorycken, 3en Augusti M,D,LXI. stout small 4to. *many curious woodcuts, very fine copy, Dutch calf gilt,* £4. 4s *Antverpen, Silvius,* 1562
Tres-bel exemplaire de cette édition rare et recherchée.

7123 **Delft.** PASSIONAEL (dat) WINTER STUCK : eñ is gehietē in Latijn : Aurea Legeda, d'beduut in Duytsce, die gulde legende, 4to. *numerous large, rude, and curious woodcuts of the Crucifixion, the Adoration of the Magi, the Murder of the Innocents, Saints, Bishops, etc.* Black letter, *double columns, with printer's device, Dutch calf gilt,* £2. *Delff in Holland,* 1487

7124 **Haerlem.** (GLANVIL) BARTOLOMEUS ENGELSMAN, Boeck welck ghehieten is bartholomeus vanden Proprieteyten der Dinghen, stout folio, 445 leaves, Black letter, 12 *large woodcuts, on separate leaves, including the printer's device at the end ; the initial letters of each of the* 19 *books are painted, those of each chapter rubricated ; fine large copy in vellum, in excellent preservation,* £4. 4s *Haerlem, Bellaert,* 1485
Priced, 1826, Baynes, cf. extra, £6. 6s.
A magnificent specimen of early printing. The paper and type are equally admirable. After all the pretensions of a fabulous Coster, it must be ranked among the first productions of the Haarlem press, and is the ONLY book known to have been printed by Bellaert. It is a volume of great rarity. The present is a particularly choice, clean, large copy, with all the woodcuts complete. This is a circumstance of very rare occurrence, since in most copies, some one or other of these cuts are always wanting. The printer's device, surrounded with a curious border, occupies a separate leaf at the end. All the woodcuts are faintly coloured, apparently by the rubricator or by a contemporary hand.

IV. ITALY.

7125 **Florence.** APOLLONIOU RODIOU Argonautika, *Graece,* sm. 4to. EDITIO PRINCEPS, *fine large copy in the original green vellum, gilt back,* £4. 10s *Phlorentia,* 1496
VERY RARE. Collation: A to X iv. in eights, making 171 leaves of text, and one blank at the end. The text is entirely printed in capitals in the middle of the pages, the side and foot margins being occupied with the commentary in small characters. The La Valliere copy fetched 254 fr. ; Ditot's, 504 fr. ; Larcher's, 192 fr. ; £9. 9s., Hibbert; 150 fr. Coulon; £7. 7s, citron mor. Libri.

7126 **Genoa.** PSALTERIUM Hebreum, Grecū, Arabicū et Chaldeū, cum tribus latinis interpretationibus et glossis, cura Justiniani, folio, LARGE PAPER, *old calf gilt, binding injured,* £4. 4s *Genuæ, Porrus,* 1516
This is the first Polyglott ever printed with the characters peculiar to each language. It is remarkable for Giustiniani's commentary upon the 19th Psalm, "coela enarrant," where his pride as a Genoese in the recent glories of his compatriot Columbus, induced him to insert an account of America and a life of its discoverer.

7127 **Milan.** MOMBRITIUS (Boninus) de Dominica Passione, sm. 4to. *very fine large and clean copy, in the original vellum,* EXTREMELY RARE, £3. 15s *Mediolani, Ant. Zarotum, absque anno, sed circa* 1475
Priced, 1840, Payne and Foss, £4. 4s
⁎ Bonini Mombrizio, the author of this very rare Poem, was one of the most learned men of his time, to whom posterity is indebted for the revival of letters. The works written by him are in great estimation for their intrinsic merit, as well as on account of their rarity, and they are likewise distinguished for the elegance and correctness with which he caused them to be printed.

7128 CECCO D'ASCOLI. Lo Illustra Poeta Cecho Dascholi con cometo novamente trovato, et nobilmente historiato, revisto et emendato, sq. 8vo. *title surrounded by a woodcut border in several compartments, with a profusion of curious woodcuts through the text, morocco extra, gilt edges,* RARE, £3. 3s
Milano, Scinzenzeler, 1511

7129 **Manual.** JOSIPPON BEN GORION, Historiæ Judaicæ libri sex, usque ad tempus Flavii Josephi, *Hebraice*, 4to. editio princeps et rarissima, *beautifully printed with broad margins, the title on the first printed leaf in MS.* 266 pp. *sd.* £4. 10s *Constantinopoli*, 1490 *sed Mantovæ, Ab. Conat, ca.* 1476
Vendu 55 fl. Crevenna.—*Brunet.*
Very rare. The first edition of this rare work, which has been proved by De Rossi, notwithstanding the apparent internal evidence that it was printed at Constantinople in 1490, to have been produced at Mantua, sometime between 1476 and 1480, under the editorship of Abraham Conat, a Jewish physician. There was an edition at Constantinople in 1510, in small 4to. size, less elegantly printed, but with some additions to the text. The author, known as Josephus Gorionides, is stated to have lived sometime between the sixth and ninth centuries, opinions not agreeing as to the exact period. The work is a garbled Hebrew version of Flavius Josephus, interwoven with numerous Rabbinical fictions; and it is supposed, the author intended that his co-religionists should look upon it as the genuine original of Josephus, which it was long believed to be.

7130 **Rome.** RODERICI SANTII (de Arevalo) Historia Hispanica, sm. folio, *calf gilt, rare,* 20s *(Romæ), Udalricus Gallus, s. a.* (ca. 1470)
Without the preliminary table : with a few marginal notes in an old handwriting.

7131 **Trevigi.** MAII PARTHENOPEI (Juniani) de priscorum Proprietate Verborum Opus, stout folio, *a beautifully printed* LATIN ENCYCLOPAEDIA, *with references throughout to the Classics, very fine copy, in the original oak binding, with brass studs and clasps,* £2. *Tarvisiæ, per Bernardum de Colonia,* 1477
This copy has on the inside of cover the autograph signature of "Joannes Protzer, M CCCC XC," and at the end a friendly epistle. The paper of this volume is perhaps the best ever used for printing.

7132 **Venice.** PSALTERION : Psalterium Græcum, edente Justino Decadyo, sq. 8vo. 150 *leaves printed in red and black, fine clean copy in the original stamped calf,* VERY RARE, £6. 6s *En Enetiais, Ald. Manoutios, circa* 1498
Fetched 198 fr. D'Ourches; £8. 8s Sykes; £6. 6s Renouard. The above is one of the rarer copies in which he omission on the first page of signature i 1 has been supplied in smaller type.

7133 POETAE CHRISTIANI MINORES, Vol. II.: Sedulii Mirabilia, Juvencus, Arator, Proba Falconia, Vitae Martini et Nicolai, Homerocentra, Annuntia. Virginis, etc. stout sm. 4to. *very large and fine copy in vellum,* 20s *Ald.* 1501-2

V. SWEDEN.

7134 THET NYIA TESTAMENTIT paa Swensko, sm. folio, *title supplied in MS., some leaves mended and mounted, and the last leaf of Index partly supplied in MS., therefore sold not subject to collation, old calf, very rare, from the Duke of Sussex's library,* £3. 3s *Stockholm,* 1526
COLLATION: Fürsprack, 10 pp.; St. Matthew to the Acts, leaves 1-97; Fürsprack, 12 pp.; Paulus till the Romerska, to the Apocalypse, leaves 1-79; Register, 10 pp. On the fly-leaf of the present copy is a MS. note :—
' Presented to H.R.H. the Duke of Sussex by Count Björnstjerna, Envoy Extraordinary of the King of Sweden and Norway, 18th December, 1832."
"Cette traduction de L. Andrea est le premier livre biblique qu'on ait imprimé en Suédois."—BRUNET.

SHORT-HAND, STEGANOGRAPHY.

7135 MORLAND (Sir Samuel) New Method of Cryptography, folio, *fine portrait engraved by Lombart after Sir Peter Lely inserted, and several coloured diagrams, hf. cf. a rare and curious work,* 24s 1666
7136 TRITHEMII (Jo.) Polygraphiae libri vi., cum Clave, sm. folio, EDITIO PRINCEPS, **Black letter,** *fine woodcut title and ornamental capitals, fine copy, solid russia binding, from Philip Lord Hardwicke's library,* £2. 16s *Haselberg de Aia,* 1518
EXTREMELY RARE, The *first publication on* SECRET WRITING.
7137 SELENI (Gustavi) Cryptomenytice et Cryptographia, cum planissimâ Steganographiæ Trithemii enodatione, folio, *four engravings on the borders of title, numerous cuts and tables, old calf,* 21s *Lunæburgi,* 1624
7138 VIGENERE (B. de) Traicté des Chiffres ou Secretes manières d'Escrire, 4to. *with numerous curious Alphabets, and alphabetical complications, old calf, stained,* 18s *Paris,* 1586
7139 ——— the same, sm. 4to. *Fine Paper ;* a fine copy from the late Earl of Aberdeen's Library, *in calf, gilt edges,* 24s 1587
7140 ANGELL (J.) Stenography, or Short-hand improved, sm. 8vo. 21 *plates, calf,* 10s
Preface signed in MS. by J. Angel, No. 142. *s.a.* (? 1765)
7141 BYROM (J.) Universal English Short-Hand, 8vo. *plates, portrait, inserted, calf,* 6s *Manchester,* 1767
7142 GIBB's Historical account and essay towards improvement of Short-hand, 8vo. 60 *printed and* 56 *engraved pages, calf,* 5s 1736
7143 MASON (W.) Art's Advancement, the most exact and easy method of Short-hand writing, 16mo. *portrait and* 23 *engraved leaves, old calf,* 10s 1682

2 D

7144 MACAULAY, Polygraphy, or Short-hand made easy, 16mo. 119 *engraved pages, calf*, 5s   1747
7145 MITCHELL's Most rational and easy Method of writing Short-hand, 8vo. *calf*, 6s   1784
7146 RAMSAY (Ch. Al.) TACHÉOGRAPHIE ou l'art d'escrire aussi viste qu'on parle, 16mo. *fine copy in old red morocco, gilt edges, rare*, 36s   Paris, 1681
7147 WESTON (James) Stenography compleated, or the art of Short-hand brought to perfection, 8vo. *portrait, and 200 engraved pages, calf*, 10s   1730

PROVERBS OF ALL NATIONS.

7148 DUPLESSIS, Bibliographie Parémiologique, études sur les ouvrages consacrés aux Proverbes dans toutes les langues, avec un choix de curiosités parémiologiques, 8vo. *sd.* 9s   Paris, 1847
7149 MERY, Histoire générale des Proverbes, Adages, Apophthegmes, 3 vols. 8vo. *sd.* 9s   Paris, 1828-29
7150 MOORE's Dictionary of Quotations from ancient and modern Languages, with *English* translations, 8vo. *cloth*, 7s   1831
7151 **Arabic.** FREYTAG, AMTHAL AL ARAB: ARABUM PROVERBIA, vocalibus instruxit, Latiné vertit, commentario illustravit et edidit G. W. Freytag; insunt à Meidanio collecta Proverbia, commentatio, indices tres et Addenda, 4 parts in 3 vols. 8vo. 2900 pp. (pub. at £4. 14s 6d) *uncut*, 35s   Bonnae, 1838-43
7152 —— the same, 4 vols. 8vo. *hf. cf. uncut*, £2. 5s   1838-43
7153 BURCKHARDT'S Arabic Proverbs of the Modern Egyptians, 4to. *bd. very rare*, £3. 3s   1830
7154 —— Arabische Sprüchworter, oder die Sitten und Gebräuche der neueren Aegyptier, 8vo. 5s   Weimar, 1834
7155 **Basque.** OIHÉNART, Proverbes et Poésies Basques, sm. 8vo. *hf. cf.* 21s   1847
7156 **Dutch.** TUINMAN, Oorsprong en Uitlegging van Nederduitsche Spreekwoorden, 2 vols. in 1, stout sq. 8vo. *vellum, fine copy*, 7s   Middelburg, 1726-27
7157 **English and Scottish.** BLAND's Proverbs, with examples from other Languages, 2 vols. in 1, sm. 8vo. *calf*, 6s   1814
7158 DYKES, English Proverbs, accommodated to the humour of the present age, 8vo. *calf*, 6s   1713
With a curious tract called "The Union Proverb," relating to the union between England and Scotland.
7159 JANUA LINGUARUM, (turned from the Spanish into English by Wm. Welde,) sm. 4to. *containing* 1200 *proverbs in English and Latin, calf*, 12s   1621
7160 KELLY's Collection of Scotish Proverbs, sm. 8vo. *calf, gilt edges*, 10s   1721
7161 PALMER's Moral Essays on curious English, Scotch and Foreign Proverbs, 8vo. *calf, rare*, 12s   1710
7162 RAY's English Proverbs, also Scotch, Italian, French, Spanish, etc. with a collection of English words not generally used, 8vo. *third edition, calf*, 6s   1742
7163 —— The same, *fourth ed.* 8vo. *calf*, 9s; or a *fine copy, calf gilt*, 12s 6d 1768
7164 **English and Italian.** Garland full of delightfull Flowers, gathered out of Italian Authors, by P. P. 18mo. *calf*, 7s   1660
7165 **French.** BACKER, Dictionnaire des Proverbes François, 12mo. *cf.* 5s 1710
7166 CRAPELET, Proverbes et Dictons Populaires, avec les dits du Mercier et des Marchands, et les Crieries de Paris, aux XIIIe et XIVe Siècles, impl. 8vo. PAPIER D'HOLLANDE, *facsimiles, bds.* 16s   Paris, 1831
Only 7 copies were printed on Large Dutch Paper.
7167 LE ROUX DE LINCY, Livre des Proverbes Français, avec Essai par Denis sur la philosophie de Sancho Pança, 2 vols 12mo. *hf. calf*, 10s   Paris, 1842
7168 MATINEES SENONOISES, ou Proverbes Français, 8vo. 548 pp. *calf*, 5s Sens, 1789
7169 WODROEPHE (John) The Marrowe of the French Tongue, with two Bookes of Dialogues (French and English) the Springwell of Honour and Vertue, Sentences Proverbiales, &c. 4to. *wanting title, a rare and most curious volume, filled with quaint Proverbs and Sayings, hf. russia, from Miss Currer's library*, 36s   (1625)
7170 **Gaelic.** MACKINTOSH's Gaelic Proverbs, *Gaelic and English*, 12mo. 5s 1819
7171 **German.** FRANCK's Sprichworter, schöne, weise, herzliche Clugreden unnd Hoffsprüch, 2 vols. in 1, sm. 4to. 6, 163 and 211 leaves, *original stamped vellum, rare*, 12s   Franckenfurt, 1541
FREYDANCK. See *Early Printed Books*.

7172 **Low German.** Schambach's Niederdeutsche Sprichwörter, 8vo. containing 717 *proverbs, with explanations, etc.* 4s — *Gött.* 1863

7173 **Italian.** Buoni (T.) Nuovo Thesoro de'Proverbij Italiani, 2 vols. in 1, 16mo. 714 pp. *russia gilt,* 16s — *Venetia,* 1610

7174 Fiacchi, dei Proverbi Toscani, con dichiarazione de' Proverbi di Cecchi, 8vo. *sd.* 5s — *Firenze,* 1820

7175 FLORIO his Firste Fruites which yeelde familiar Speech, merie Proverbes, wittie Sentences, and golden Sayings, also a perfect introduction to the Italian and English Tongues, sq. sm. 8vo. *bd. rare,* £2.2s *Dawson for Woodcocke,* 1578

7776 —— Second Fruites to be gathered of Twelve Trees of divers but delightsome Tastes to the Tongues of Italians and Englishmen, to which is annexed his Gardine of Recreation yeelding six thousand Italian Proverbs, 2 vols. in 1, *fine copy in vellum;* or, *in red morocco extra, joints, gilt edges, from Miss Currer's library,* £3. 16s — *T. Woodcocke,* 1591

Collation of Vol. I.: title and 11 prel. unnumbered leaves; leaves 1-159. Mr. W. Stirling's copy has leaves 160-163, these consisting of a separate treatise beginning "*Regole necessarie per indurre gli' taliani a posferir la lingua Inglese.*" It ends at bottom of first side fol. 163, "Imprinted at London, by Thomas Dawson for Thomas Woodcocke." The back of leaf is blank. The missing leaves appear to have been added after the book had been printed, and perhaps do not occur in all copies.

Collation of Vol. II.: title and 5 prel. leaves; pages 1-205; 3 unnumbered pages, 1 blank;—Giardino di Ricreatione nel quale crescono fronde fiori e frutti, vaghe, leggiadri, e soavi sotto nome di Sei mila Proverbij, etc. Londra, 1591, title, 3 unnumbered leaves; pp. 1-216; the last page (218) contains the Colophon.

7177 PENSA, Epigrammi Toscani, 8vo. *bds.* 7s ; or, *old red morocco, gilt edges,* 12s — *Monte Regale (Sicily),* 1570

7178 PESCETTI (Orlando) Proverbi Italiani, 1603—Proverbi Italiani e Latini per uso de' fanciulli, 1602—in 1 vol. 18mo. *vellum, fine copy,* 15s — *Verona,* 1602-3

7179 —— the same, another edition, 2 vols. in 1, 18mo. *vellum,* 12s *Venetiæ,* 1629

7180 Bonifacio, Proverbi Lombardi, 12mo. 464 pp. *sd.* 5s — *Milano,* 1860

7180*Cassani, Saggio di Proverbi Triestini, 12mo. *sd.* 3s — *Trieste,* 1860

7181 Pasqualigo, Raccolta di Proverbi Veneti, 3 vols. 12mo. *sd.* 7s 6d *Ven.* 1857-58

7182 **Jewish.** Ben Siræ Proverbia, *Hebr. et Lat.* à Drusio, cum scholiis, etc. sq. 8vo. *calf neat,* 5s — *Franeker.* 1597

7183 Tendlau (Abraham) Sprichwörter und Redensarten Deutsch-Jüdischer Vorzeit, als Beitrag zur Volks-, Sprach-, und Sprichwörter-Kunde, 8vo. 12 and 425 pp. *half calf,* 7s — *Frankfurt,* 1860

7184 **Maltese.** Vassalli, Motti, Aforismi, e Proverbii Maltesi raccolti ed interpretati con note filologiche, 8vo. *bds.* 4s — *Malta,* 1828

7185 **Persian and Hindoostanee.** Roebuck's Proverbs, and Proverbial Phrases in the Persian and Hindostanee Languages, compiled and translated chiefly by the late Capt. T. Roebuck, edited by Professor H. H. Wilson, stout 8vo. 36s — *Calcutta,* 1824

In addition to the translation of the Proverbs, many of them are further illustrated by a comparison with the analogous proverbial phrases of the West, and by an explanation of their tendency, or the circumstances on which they were founded.

7186 **Portuguese.** ADAGIOS Proverbios, Rifãos e Anexins da lingua portugueza, por F. R. I. L. E. L., 8vo. *half calf, almost uncut,* 12s ; or, *a fine copy, in old calf, gilt back,* 16s — *Lisbon,* 1780

7187 **Sanscrit.** MORTON'S Collection of Proverbs, Bengali and Sanscrit, with their English Translation, 8vo. *cloth,* 20s — *Calcutta,* 1832

7188 **Spanish.** Barros (Alonso de) La Perla: Proverbios morales, 16mo. *bd.* 12s — *Zaragoça,* 1656

Very rare. Collation: title and prel. leaves, 8; Proverbios, fol. 1-66, leaf 9 slightly injured.

7189 CARO y Cejudo (G. M.) Refranes y modos de hablar Castellanos, con los Latinos que les corresponden, y la Glosa, sq. 8vo. *bd.* 16s — *Madrid,* 1792

The first edition of this excellent work was printed in 1675. Though little known and unnoticed by the Bibliographers, this volume contains the most complete and best explained collection of the Proverbs of Spain;—it is the production of a philologist of no ordinary skill.

7190 Collins' Dictionary of Spanish Proverbs, compiled from the best authorities in the Spanish Language, translated into English, with explanatory illustrations from the Latin, Spanish, and English Authors, sm. 8vo. 392 pp. *cloth,* 10s 1828

"I am of opinion, Sancho, that there is no Proverb which is not true, because they are all sentences drawn from experience itself, the Mother of all the Sciences."—*Don Quixote,* part I. cap. 21.

7191 Leiva (Diez de) *Medicio de Santo Domingo,* Antiaxiomas morales medicos, etc. sm. 8vo. *the last leaf injured, vellum, rare, not in Mr. Stirling's catalogue,* 10s — *Madrid,* 1682

7192 NUNEZ, Refranes o Proverbios en Romance que coligio y glossa el Comendador Hernan Nuñez; la FILOSOFIA VULGAR de Juan de MAL LARA, en mil refranes glossados, todos hasta aora impressos; las quatro Cartas de Blasco de Garay, hechas en refranes, stout sq. 8vo. *fine copy in limp vellum, from Miss Currer's library*, VERY RARE, £2. 16s *Madrid*, 1619
This is the first edition containing the Proverbs of Mal Lara. The Colophon is dated 1618. Nunez' work is indispensable to the readers of Don Quixote. In the last edition the editors have left out many proverbs which they thought objectionable.

7193 NUNEZ, Refranes o Proverbios; la Filosofia Vulgar de Juan de Mal Lara; Las quatro cartas de Blasco de Garay, sm. 4to. *calf*, RARE, 36s *Lerida*, 1621

7194 NUNEZ, Refranes o Proverbios en Castellano, por el orden Alfabetico, revistos y emendados por Luis de Leon, 4 vols. 16mo. 30s *Madrid*, 1804
"Cette dernière edition renferme de nombreuses augmentations."—*Brunet*.

7195 PROVERBIOS. Primera parte de las sentencias hasta nuestros tiempos para edificacion de buenos costumbres escritas, sq. 8vo. *old calf, 7s 6d* *Coimbra*, 1554

7196 SORAPAN DE RIEROS (Dr. Juan) Medicina Española, contenida en Proverbios vulgares de nostra Lengua, stout sq. 8vo. *vellum or calf*, 20s *Madrid*, 1616
"Ce livre, très rare et fort curieux est, ainsi que son titre l'annonce, un véritable Traité de Médicine fondé sur les Proverbes vulgaires de l'Espagne. . . . . Ce livre, dont la conception est assez originale, m'a semblé fort curieux, et l'auteur y fait preuve d'une érudition singulière et très étendue."—DUPLESSIS, *Bibl. Paremiolog.*

7197 XIMENEZ PATON. Proverbios morales, Heraclito de Al. de Varros, concordados, por Bart. Ximenez Paton, sm. 4to. *bd*. 30s *Baeça*, 1615

7198 —— the same, new edition, sq. sm. 8vo. *calf, Ford's copy,* 12s *Lisboa*, 1617

7199 **Swedish.** PRINTZ, GRUNDEN, BOETHIUS, Dissertationes de Adagiis suio-Gothicis, in Reg. Acad. Upsal. praesîde IHRE propositae, 1769-71, 3 parts in 1 vol. sm. 4to. *hf. calf, uncut, very rare,* 36s *Upsaliae*, 1769-71

FRENCH LITERATURE.

7200 **FRENCH LANGUAGE:** COTGRAVE's (Randle) French and English Dictionary, with another in English and French, a large Grammar, and a dialogue of all Gallicismes, with additions of Proverbs, by James Howell, folio, *old calf gilt*, 24s *Printed by W. H. for Rd. Whitaker*, 1650

7201 —— another edition, folio, *calf*, 25s *William Hunt in Pye-Corner*, 1660

7202 DICTIONNAIRE de L'ACADÉMIE Française, sixième édition, 2 vols. LAST EDITION, *calf gilt*, 30s *Paris, Didot*, 1835

7203 —— the same, 2 vols. 1835—COMPLÉMENT du Dictionnaire de l'Académie, 1856 —together 3 vols. stout 4to. *hf. red morocco, gilt edges*, £2. 2s 1835-56

7204 DU GRES, Grammatica Gallica, 18mo. *with autograph,* "*Lib. Roberti Heywood, ex dono ipsius Authoris,*" *vellum*, 10s *Cantabr. Author*, 1636

7205 DUVIVIER, Grammaire des Grammaires, 5e *edition*, 2 vols. 8vo. *calf gilt*, 5s 1822

7206 FAUCHET, Recueil de l'Origine de la Langue et Poesie Françoises, 1610—BOREL, Tresor des Antiquitez Gauloises et Françoises, 1655- in 1 vol. sm. 4to. *fine copies in veau fauve gilt*, 15s *Paris*, 1610-55

7207 FLEMING et TIBBINS, Grand Dictionnaire Français-Anglais et Anglais-Français, avec la prononciation figurée, 2 vols. royal 4to. £2. 2s *Paris*, 1841-44

7208 —— Grand Dictionnaire Français-Anglais, roy. 4to. *hf. calf*, 16s 1845

7209 LEROUX (P. J.) DICTIONNAIRE COMIQUE, Satyrique, Critique, Burlesque, Libre et Proverbial, avec une explication de toutes les manières de parler burlesques, etc. dans les meilleurs Auteurs, tant anciens que modernes, 2 vols. sm. 8vo. *best edition, old French calf gilt*, 20s *Pampelune*, 1786

7210 —— the same, 2 vols. sm. 8vo. *fine large copy in calf extra, gilt edges* 28s 1786
A work of great utility in reading the old French authors.

7211 MENAGE, Dictionnaire Etymologique de la Langue Françoise, augmenté par Jault, 2 vols. folio, BEST EDITION, *old calf gilt*, £2. 2s *Paris*, 1750
La meilleure édition de cet ouvrage le plus complet que nous ayons en ce genre. Elle est enrichie des étymologies de Huet, de Le Duchat, de Vergy, etc. et contient aussi *le Trésor des recherches gauloises de Borel*.

7212 MICHEL (Francisque) DICTIONNAIRE D'ARGOT, ou Etudes de philologie comparée sur l'argot et sur les idiomes analogues parlés en Europe et en Asie, 8vo. lvi. and 516 pp. *sd*. 9s *Paris*, 1856
Besides a complete French Slang Dictionary, the above contains also a Supplement on the Argot or Slang of ITALY, SPAIN, PORTUGAL, GERMANY, ENGLAND, HOLLAND, JUTLAND, RUSSIA and ALBANIA.

7213 POUGENS Archéologie Française, Vocabulaire de mots tombés en désuétude, propres à être restitués, **2 vols. in 1,** 8vo. *hf. bound,* 7s 6d *Paris*, 1821-25

FRENCH LITERATURE. 405

7214 SPIERS' FRENCH DICTIONARY. Dictionnaire général Français-Anglais et Anglais-Français, nouvellement redigé d'après les Dictionnaires Français de l'Académie, de Laveaux, de Boiste, de Bescherelle, etc. et les Dictionnaires Anglais de Johnson, Webster, Richardson, 2 vols. 8vo. 14*th edition, sewed*, 13*s*; or *neatly bound*, 18*s* 1861
 "A work of very great research, admirable in its arrangement, of great perspicuity, and a production of a very high character. The Dictionary of Dr. Spiers was by far the best (French and English) Dictionary he had ever seen."—*Vice-Chancellor Sir W. P. Wood, Times, Feb.* 26, 1858.
7215 TARVER'S Royal Phraseological English-French, French-English Dictionary, 2 vols. stout royal 8vo. (pub. at £2. 10*s*) *hf. calf neat*, 30*s* 1845-50

7216 **ABRÉGÉS HISTORIQUES** : ABRÉGÉ CHRONOLOGIQUE de l'Histoire Universelle, traduit du Latin de PETAU, 4 vols. 12mo. *calf gilt*, 9*s*   *Paris*, 1715
7217 **Church History.** Abrégé chronologique de l'Histoire Ecclesiastique, des Schismes, des Hérésies, etc. 3 vols. 12mo. *calf gilt*, 15*s*   *Paris*, 1768
7218 **France.** HENAULT, NOUVEL ABRÉGÉ chronologique de l'Histoire de FRANCE, 2 vols. 4to. *numerous fine portraits, old French calf gilt*, 9*s*   *Paris*, 1768
7219 HENAULT, NOUVEL ABRÉGÉ chronologique de l'Histoire de FRANCE, 3 vols. 12mo. *calf*, 9*s*   *Paris*, 1768
7220 —— the same, 5 vols. 12mo. *calf*, 10*s*   *Paris*, 1788
7221 —— the same, 5 vols. 12mo. *calf gilt*, 8*s* 6*d*   *Rouen*, 1789
7222 **Germany.** ABRÉGÉ chronologique de l'Histoire d'ALLEMAGNE, 2 vols. 12mo. *calf*, 5*s*   1766
7223 **Italy.** ABRÉGÉ chronologique de l'Histoire générale d'ITALIE, par Saint-Marc, 6 vols. 12mo. *hf morocco, uncut*, 16*s*   *Paris*, 1761
7224 **Nord.** ABRÉGÉ chronologique de l'Histoire du NORD : Dannemarc, Russie, Suède, Pologne, Prusse, Courlande, la Laponie, les Tartares, etc. par Lacombe, 2 vols. 12mo. *calf gilt*, 7*s* 6*d*   *Paris*, 1762
7225 **Spain.** ABRÉGÉ de l'Histoire d'ESPAGNE, par Desormeaux, 5 vols. 12mo. *calf gilt*, 7*s* 6*d*   1759

7226 ALETHEIUS DEMETRIUS (J. O. de la Mettrie) Ouvrage de Penelope, ou Machiavel en Medecine, avec Supplément, 3 vols. 12mo. *beautiful copy in old French* MOROCCO, *richly gilt back*, 18*s*   *Geneve*, 1748
 A very violent Satire against the Medical Profession.
7227 AMADIS DE GAULE, L'onziesme livre de, sm. 8vo. or 12mo. *fine woodcuts, good copy, old calf*, 10*s*   *Paris, Longis*, 1560
7228 —— le quatriesme et le cinquiesme livre d'Amadis de Gaule, 2 vols. in 1, stout 18mo. *bds.* 7*s* 6*d*   *Lyon*, 1574-75
7229 AMI des Filles, 12mo, *frontispiece, hf. calf*, 5*s*   1761
7230 AMOURS des DAMES ILLUSTRES de notre siècle, stout 16mo. *calf*, 24*s*   *Col.* 1703
 Containing the Histoire amoureuse des Gaules, by Bussy-Rabutin, Amours de Madame, de Mademoiselle, and several other pieces.
7231 ANACRÉON, SAPHO, Bion, et Moschus, traduction en prose, avec la Veillée des Fêtes de Vénus, par M. C(lairfont) 8vo. *numerous pretty engravings by Eisen, fine copy in old French red morocco, gilt edges*, 20*s*   *Paphos et Paris*, 1773
7232 ANCIENS POETES FRANCAIS, Recueil de leurs ouvrages : La Farce de Pierre Pathelin ; Poesies de Guillaume Coquillart ; Œuvres de François Villon ; Poesies de Guillaume Cretin ; Œuvres de Racan, 2 vols. ; Poesies de Martial d'Auvergne, 2 vols. ; Œuvres de Jean Marot ; Bordigné, Legende de Pierre Faifeu ; 10 vols. 12mo. *old calf gilt*, £2 10*s*   *Paris, Coustelier*, 1723-24
 Collection recherchée ; vendue 119 fr. m. r. BRUNET.
7233 ANCIEN THEATRE FRANCOIS ; ou Ouvrages Dramatiques, les plus remarquables depuis les Mystères jusqu'à Corneille, publiés par Viollet le Duc, avec Glossaire, 10 vols. 12mo. *whole blue morocco, edges uncut, top edges gilt*, £5. 10*s*   *Paris, typ. Elzev. chez P. Jannet*, 1854
7234 APOPTHEGMES (Les) cest a dire promptz, subtilz, et sententieulx Ditz de plusieurs Royz, chefz darmee, Philosophes, et autres grans personnaiges, translatez de Latin par Lesleu Macault, 12mo. *fine copy in dark morocco, gilt edges*, 36*s*   *Paris, Soleil d' Or*, 1539
7235 ARRETIN [L'] (par l'Abbé du Laurens), 2 vols. in 1, 12mo. *calf, rare*, 30*s*   *Rome, Congreg. de l'Index* (? *Amst.*) 1763
 First Edition of a very curious work of sarcastic and free character.
7236 BALZAC, Romans et Contes philosophiques, 3 vols. 8vo. *hf. calf*, 6*s*   *Paris*, 1831

7237 BARANTE, Histoire des Ducs de Bourgogne de la maison de Valois, 1364-1477, 8 vols. sm. 8vo. *with portraits, sd.* 36s *Paris*, 1860

A noble work—a masterpiece of historical narration. The author relies entirely upon contemporary information, and introduces, as far as possible, the same language; he gives, in the style of Froissart, a most faithful picture of that eventful period of English and French History, the possession of France by the English. The peculiar position of the Dukes of Burgundy, first as masters of France, and afterwards as almost independent Sovereigns of Burgundy, Picardy, Flanders. Holland, and Luxembourg, their struggles for power in France, their combats with the proud cities of Flanders, their magnificence in public entries and tournaments, their great influence in the affairs of Europe, and their extinction in the Battle of Nancy, by the victorious Swiss, are all of the most stirring interest, and serve indeed as the best guide for the understanding of Mediæval History, its glory and its misery.

7238 BAZANCOURT, L'Expédition de CRIMÉE, jusqu'à la prise de Sebastopol, 2 vols. 8vo. *hf. calf gilt*, 12s *Paris*, 1856

7239 BECKET. VIE de St. Thomas Archevesque de Cantorbery et Martyr, par De Beaulieu (*i. e.* Du Combout de Pontchasteau), 4to. *very fine copy in old French red morocco, gilt edges*, 27s *Paris*, 1674

7240 BEKKER, le Monde enchanté, ou examens des communs sentimens touchant les ESPRITS, leur nature, leur pouvoir, et les éfets que les hommes produisent par leur communication, 4 vols. 18mo. *calf gilt*, 18s *Amst.* 1694

An interesting work now that the question of "Spirit Communication" is agitating the whole of England.

7241 BERANGER, ŒUVRES complètes, 2 vols. 53 *beautiful plates*, 1851—MUSIQUE des Chansons de Béranger, *fine plates*, 1851—together 3 vols. 8vo. *uniform in hf. morocco*, 27s *Paris*, 1851

7242 BIBLIOTHEQUE BLEUE. Romans de Chevalerie des XII.-XVI. Siècles, publiés sur les meilleurs textes par une Société sous la direction de Delvau, 3 vols. 4to. *about* 1400 *pp. double cols. with numerous woodcuts, hf. calf*, 24s 1860

7243 BIBLIOTHÈQUE ELZEVIRIENNE. A Collection of Reprints of Early French Poetry, Voyages, Romances, Historical and Literary Curiosities, &c., 60 vols. 12mo. *cloth*, £6.6s *Paris, Jannet*, 1853-8

Laudonnière, la Floride; St. Aubin, Mémoires; Théophile, Œuvres 2 vols.; St. Amant, Œuvres, 2 vols.; Anciennes Poesies Françaises, 7 vols.; Anciens Poetes; Sénèce, 2 vols.; Somaize, Dictionnaire des Précieuses, 2 vols.; Fournier, Variétés historiques et littéraires, 8 vols.; Courcelles, Mémoires; Jehan de Paris; Caquets de l'Accouchée; D'Aubigné, Adventures de Faeneste, et les Tragiques, 2 vols.; Morlini Novellæ; Hitopadesa; L'Escurel, Chansons; Evangiles des Quenouilles; Tachereau, Hist. de Corneille; Roger de Collerye, Œuvres; Coquillart, Œuvres, 2 vols.; La Guette, Mémoires; Dolopathos par Brunet et Montaiglon; Floire et Blanceflor par Duméril; Gérard de Rossillon par Michel; Nouvelles du 13e et 14e Siècle. 2 vols.; Courriers de la Fronde, 2 vols.; Nuits de Straparole, 2 vols.; Oliva, Hist. du Pérou; Campion, Mémoires; Tabarin, Œuvres, 2 vols.; Hervé, Temple des Oracles; Tavannes, et Balthazar, Mémoires; Violier des Hist. Romaines; Carlisle, Ambassades; Gaultier Garguille; Chartier, Chronique, Vol. I.; Gringore, Vol. I.

7244 BIGNON, Histoire de France, depuis le 18 Brumaire (Novembre 1799) jusqu'à la Paix de Tilsitt (Juillet 1807), 6 vols. 8vo. *calf gilt*, 18s *Paris*, 1829-30

7245 BIOGRAPHIE UNIVERSELLE, ANCIENNE ET MODERNE, 52 vols.—Mythologie, 3 vols.—Supplément, 29 vols.—in all 84 vols. 8vo. A COMPLETE SET, *blue calf gilt, lettered*, £25. 10s *Paris*, 1811-62

Complete sets like the above are of the rarest occurrence, even in France. The last volume of the set brings the Supplement down "Van."

None of the modern imitations of this valuable work have been completed yet, and none comes up to it in correctness; the Biographies, including those of Englishmen, were written with great care by the most eminent writers.

7246 BLANC (Louis) Histoire de Dix Ans, 1830-1840, 5 vols. in 2, 12mo. *hf. calf*, 6s *Bruxelles*, 1846

7247 BOILEAU, ŒUVRES, avec des esclaircissemens historiques par lui même, augmentées de remarques et de dissertations critiques, 5 vols. sm. 8vo. *fine copy in old veau fauve extra, tooled back, gilt edges*, 32s *Paris*, 1772

7248 ——— the same, 5 vols. A SUPERB COPY *in old French red* MOROCCO, *gilt edges*, £6. 5s 1772

"If I am not deceived there is something in all the compositions of Boileau, so finished, so removed from conceit, and from forced thought; there is such an ardent zeal for propriety in sentiment and in expression, such a sense of the dignity of the human character. when undebased; such a hatred of hypocrisy; such a love of purity; such an abhorrence of all profaneness, and of indecency, and even of indelicacy; that I am not able to name a man whose works, as a poet and a critic, may be read and studied with equal advantage."—*Pursuits of Literature, &c.* p. 49.

7249 (BORDELON), Voyage forcé de Becafort Hypocondriaque, qui s'imagine être obligé de dire ou d'écrire, 12mo. *calf gilt, gilt edges, curious*, 10s *Paris*, 1709

7250 ——— Les Tours de Maître Gonin, 2 vols. 12mo. *numerous curious plates, calf gilt, rare*, 14s *Paris*, 1713

7251 ——— Histoire des Imaginations extravagantes de M. Oufle, 5 parts in 2 vols. 12mo. *plates, fine copy in veau fauve, gilt back*, 18s *Paris*, 1754

7252 BOUCHET (G.) les SERÉES de, 3 vols. 12mo. *old calf gilt*, RARE, £2. 12s 6d *Rouen*, 1635

Fetched at Col. Stanley's sale, £8. 18s 6d; 1857, Sotheby's, £2. 14s.

"Sterne has generally concealed the sources of his curious trains of investigation and uncommon opinions, but in one instance he breaks through his restraint, by mentioning Bouchet's Evening Conferences among the treasures of Mr Shandy's library. This book is now become so extremely scarce, that for a long period it had escaped all my inquiries and exertions."—*Ferriar's Illustrations of Sterne.*

7253 BOUHOURS, Manière de bien penser dans les ouvrages d'esprit, 12mo. *very fine copy in old citron morocco, richly gilt, gilt edges*, 6s   *Paris*, 1715
7254 BOUILLET, DICTIONNAIRE Universel D'HISTOIRE et de GEOGRAPHIE, 17e edition, avec un Nouveau Supplément, 2 vols. stout roy. 8vo. *hf. russia extra*, 22s   *Paris*, 1861
7255 BOURRIENNE, Memoires, 10 vols. sm. 8vo. *hf. calf*, 10s   *Paris*, 1829
7256 BRANTOME (P. de Bourdeilles, Seigneur de) ŒUVRES, avec des Remarques historiques et critiques, par Le Duchat, Lancelot et Prosper Marchand, 15 vols. 12mo. *calf gilt*, £2. 2s   *Londres (Maestricht)*, 1779
"Brantôme is frequently an amusing and instructive writer, but his naiveté often borders on what must be considered not a little licentious. He has preserved many important facts, as well as entertaining anecdotes, which must have otherwise perished. It is pleasant to find the unaccountable omission of his name by La Harpe, supplied by a short, but smart notice of him, by Barbier."—*Dibdin's Library Companion*, p. 538.
The reader will find the notice mentioned by Mr. Dibdin in Barbier's *Bibliothèque d'un Homme de Gout*, vol. 4, p. 17.
Mr. Dibdin adds in a note, "We owe to Brantôme, I believe, the preservation of the affecting song which Mary sung in the vessel, while quitting the shores of France, to return to her kingdom. Yet there may be reasonable doubts of its authenticity. Was the sensitive mind of a woman in her situation in a state to warble ditties?"

7257 BUCHON (J. A. G.) PANTHÉON LITTERAIRE, 17 vols. impl. 8vo. *sd.* £2. 12s   *Paris*, 1838-40
Contents of the Series: Chroniques étrangeres relatives aux expéditions Francaises pendant le XIIIe. siecle, 1 vol.—Œuvres de Brantome, 2 vols.—Chroniques de Froissart, 3 vols.—Chroniques et Memoires sur l'histoire de France, 11 vols.—together 17 volumes.
7258 BUHLE, Histoire de la Philosophie Moderne depuis la Renaissance jusqu'à Kant, précédée d'un abrégé sur la Philosophie ancienne, traduite par Jourdan, 6 vols. 8vo. *calf neat*, £2. 2s   1816-17
Ouvrage tres estimé, et dont l'édition est devenue rare.—BRUNET.
7259 BUTLER, HUDIBRAS, traduit en vers François (par TOWNELEY) avec des remarques, etc. 3 vols. 12mo. *English and French on opposite pages, portrait and plates after Hogarth*, ORIGINAL EDITION, *fine copy in old French calf gilt*, 25s 1757
Priced, 1845, Thorpe, £2. 2s; North's copy fetched £3. 13s 6d; the Fonthill, £7.; Inglis's, £8. 10s 6d.
7260 BUTLER, Hudibras, poëme, traduit en vers français par TOWNELEY, 3 vols. 12mo. *portrait and plates after Hogarth, hf. calf*, 15s   *Paris*, 1819
The best French translation of an English Classic. possessing all the wit, force, and compactness of the original.
7261 BYRON (Lord) ŒUVRES de, précédées d'une notice par Nodier, 8 vols. 8vo. *numerous fine plates on India paper, calf gilt, gilt edges*, 24s   *Paris*, 1823
7262 CABINET DES FÉES, ou Collection choisie des Contes des Fées et autres Contes merveilleux, 41 vols. 8vo. *numerous fine plates from designs by Marillier, in old calf neat*, £4.   *Genève*, 1785-89
Priced 41 vols. (*Amsterdam*) 1840, Jas. Bohn calf, £12. 12s; 1840, Payne and Foss, calf, £10. 10s; 1844, Jas. Bohn, calf gilt, £9. 9s; Bossange, £7. 7s; 1853, hf. calf, £6. 6s. The Fonthill copy fetched £7.; North's, £6. 6s.; Goldsmid's, £7. 7s.
This extensive work embodies all the Fairy Tales and Popular Stories of Europe.
7263 CABINET DU ROY de France, dans lequel il y a trois Perles precieuses d'inestimable valeur, 12mo. *red morocco extra, tooled on the sides, watered silk linings, gilt edges by Riviere, Buckle's copy*, 28s   1581
"Une satire très-vive et tres-méprisable; une des plus violentes qui aient paru. Les trois perles sont le Clergé, la Noblesse, et le Tiers-Etat; et l'on propose au roi de s'emparer des Revenus Ecclesiastiques, etc. L'auteur qui etoit Huguenot outre les choses au point qu'il n'est plus croyable."—*LeLong*.
The prejudices of LeLong, and his antipathy to the opinions of the anonymous author, are evident from his critique; the counsels of the satirist, and his charges against the clergy, are full of truth and good sense.
7264 CABINET SATYRIQUE, ou Recueil des Vers piquans et gaillards, 2 vols. in 1, 12mo. *frontispieces, calf*, RARE, £3. 16s   *Mont-Parnasse*, 1697
7265 CALLIÈRES, des Bons Mots et des Bons Contes, de leur usage, raillerie des anciens, etc. 12mo. *frontispiece, hf. bound*, 5s   *Paris*, 1692
7266 CAMUS (A. G.) Profession d'Avocat : Recueil de pièces concernant l'exercice de cette profession contenant les Lettres de Camus, etc. par Dupin aîné, 2 vols. 8vo. *best edition, hf. calf gilt*, 25s   *Paris*, 1832
7267 [CAMUS, Evêque de Bellay] Le Rabat-Joye du Triomphe Monacal, 12mo. *vellum*, 7s 6d   *A l'Isle*, 1634
7268 CARIOX (Jehan) Livre des Chroniques, traduit par Le Blond, stout 16mo. *calf*, 8s   *Paris*, 1547
The first edition of the French translation.
7269 CASANOVA. MEMOIRES de J. Casanova de Seingalt, écrits par lui-même, *édition originale*, 12 vols. 12mo. *russia*, RARE, £3. 10s   *Leipsic*, 1826-38
These curious Memoirs show a most extraordinary insight into human nature.
7270 CASE, Le Galatee, *Italien, Latin, Espagnol et Francois*, 24mo. *vellum, scarce*, 5s
The French is printed in Lettres de Civilité.   *Lyon*, 1598
7271 CASTIGLIONE. Le parfait Courtisan, *Italien et François*, par Chapuis, 12mo. *calf*, 6s   *Lyon*, 1585

7272 CAUSES CÉLÈBRES et intéressantes, avec les Jugemens qui les ont décidées, 20 vols. 12mo. *fine copy in old French calf gilt*, £2. 16s *Paris*, 1734-50

Priced, 1837, £3. 3s; 1840, £2. 12s 6d; 1855, £2. 10s; fetched at Steevens', £2. 14s.

7273 CAYET, Chronologie novenaire, histoire de la guerre sous Henry IIII, 3 vols. 12mo. *portrait, bound, 5s* *Paris*, 1608

7274 (CAYLUS, Montesquieu, et autres) Etrennes de la Saint-Jean, 16mo. *facetious, curious portrait, calf gilt*, RARE, 6s *Troyes*, 1751

7275 CAZOTTE, Œuvres badines et morales, historiques et philosophiques, 4 vols. 8vo. *best edition, curious plates, calf gilt*, 21s *Paris*, 1816

7276 —— Œuvres choisies et badines, 6 vols. in 3, 16mo. *calf*, 7s 6d *Paris, an VI.*

7277 CERVANTES, le valeureux Don Quixote de la Manche, on l'histoire de ses grands exploicts d'armes, fidèles amours, et aventures estranges, (traduit par Oudin et Rosset), 2 vols. 16mo. *vellum, rare*, 12s *Par.* 1632, *Rouen*, 1636

7278 —— Histoire de l'admirable Don Quichotte de la Manche, traduite par Filleau de Saint Martin, avec un essai par Auger, 6 vols. 8vo. *portrait and plates, calf*, 12s *Paris*, 1825

7279 —— l'ingenieux Hidalgo Don Quichotte de la Manche, traduit et annoté par Viardot, 2 vols. roy. 8vo. *numerous vignettes by Tony Johannot, half calf, gilt edges*, 15s *Paris*, 1836

7280 CHAPELAIN, la PUCELLE, ou la France delivrée, poëme heroïque, 16mo. *plates, vellum, rare*, 12s 1656

7281 CHARLES I. Histoire du Procez de Charles Stuart, Roy d'Angleterre, 16mo. *vellum*, 7s 1650

7282 CHATEAUBRIAND, ŒUVRES COMPLÈTES, 32 vols. 8vo. *portrait and numerous plates,* (pub. at 220 francs) *neat in half red morocco gilt, contents lettered,* £7. 7s *Paris*, 1834-38

CONTENTS.

Vol. I. Essai sur la Vie.
II. III. Essais sur les Révolutions.
IV—VII. Etudes Historiques.
VIII. Melanges Litteraires.
IX—XI. Itinéraire de Paris à Jerusalem.
XII. Voyage en Amerique.
XIII. —— en Suisse, en Italie.
XIV—XVII. Génie du Christianisme.
XVIII. Atala.

Vol. XIX—XXI. Les Martyrs.
XXII—XXIII. Les Natchez.
XXIV. Poésies.
XXV. Mélanges Historiques.
XXVI—XXVII. —— Politiques.
XXVIII—XXIX. Polémique.
XXIX—XXXI. Opinions et discours.
XXXI. Oeuvres diverses.
XXXII. Table des Matieres.

7283 CHATEAUBRIAND, Memoires d'Outre-Tombe, 6 vols. in 12, 12mo. *calf gilt*, 25s *Brux.* 1849

7284 CHOIX DE POESIES MORALES et Chretiennes depuis Malherbe jusqu'à nos jours, 4 parts in 3 vols. 12mo. VERY FINE COPY *in old French citron morocco extra, gilt and marbled edges, with the arms of Madame Elizabeth on the sides,* £2. 10s *Paris*, 1740

7285 CHRONIQUE du bon Chevalier Messire GILLES de CHIN, publiée d'après un MS. de la Bibl. de Bourgogne à Bruxelles, 8vo. *headings and initials in red and blue, Thick Paper, red morocco extra, gilt edges*, 36s *Mons*, 1837

Forming No. IV. of the publications of the "Société des Bibliophiles de Mons."

7286 CHRONIQUE SCANDALEUSE, memoires pour l'histoire de la géneration presente, avec des anecdotes piquantes, 5 vols. 12mo. *calf*, 20s *Paris*, 1785-91

7287 CICERON, ŒUVRES COMPLÈTES, traduites en Francais avec le texte en regard, édition, publiée par Leclerc, 30 vols. 8vo. *portrait* (pub. at 150 francs, unbound) *fine copy in veau fauve gilt,* £3. 16s *Paris*, 1825

"Cette édition, fort remarquable sous tous les rapports, mérite bien le succes qu'elle a obtenu."—BRUNET.

7288 COMMINES, MÉMOIRES, nouvelle édition, enrichie de notes par Messieurs Godefroy, augmentée par Lenglet du Fresnoy, 4 vols. 4to. *portraits, with the suppressed dedication to Marshal Saxe, choice set in veau fauve gilt, very fine copy,* £3. 3s *Paris*, 1747

"You will find in Philip de Comines (says Montaigne) united to an excellent disposition, the language of true simplicity and pure narrative, in which the good faith of the author is everywhere apparent, without vanity or affectation."—"No English historical collection can be complete without the Memoirs of P. de Comines. The best edition is that of 1747."—*Dibdin*.

7289 COMMINES, Memoires, augmentez, avec Supplement de la Chronique Scandaleuse, par Godefroy, 4 vols. 12mo. *portraits, old calf gilt*, 10s *Brusselle*, 1706-13

FRENCH LITERATURE.

7290 CONDÉ (Le Prince de) Mémoires, contenant ce qui s'est passé de plus memorable en Europe, sous les règnes de François II. et Charles IX., avec le Supplément, (édition augmentée par Lenglet Du Fresnoy), 6 vols. 4to. LARGE PAPER, *fine copy in old French calf gilt*, 30s *Paris*, 1743
Priced, 1831, Bohn, £4. 14s 6d; 1837, Payne and Foss, £4. 4s.
"Ouvrage curieux et instructif, et qui est dans les bibliothèques où l'on rassemble les morceaux recherchés."
These Memoirs contain much matter relating to Mary Queen of Scots and Queen Elizabeth.

7291 [CONTI (la Princess de)] Amours du Grand Alcandre, (Henry IV.) sq. 8vo. *old calf, Arms on sides*, 9s *Paris*, 1652
7292 CORNEILLE (P.) ŒUVRES, avec le Commentaire de Voltaire, et des observations critiques par Palissot, 12 vols. 8vo. *French calf gilt*, £2. 5s *Paris*, 1801
7293 COTTIN (Madame) Oeuvres complètes, avec notice sur sa vie et ses écrits, 12 vols. 12mo. *plates, pretty set in calf gilt*, 10s *Paris*, 1818
7294 CRÉTINEAU-JOLY, Histoire religieuse, politique, et littéraire de la COMPAGNIE DE JÉSUS, 6 vols. 8vo. *portraits and numerous facsimiles, half calf gilt*, 32s *Paris*, 1844-46
The best work on the history of this famous Order.
7295 CULTE des Dieux Fétiches, 12mo. *calf*, 6s 1760
7295*D'ALEMBERT, ŒUVRES, Philosophiques, Historiques, et Littéraires, 18 vols. sm. 8vo. *old French calf gilt*, £2. 10s *Paris*, 1805
7296 DARU, Histoire de la République de VENISE, 7 vols. 8vo. *good type, plates, hf. morocco, uncut*, 24s *Paris*, 1819
7297 —— the same, 8 vols. 8vo. BEST EDITION, *hf. calf neat*, £2. *Paris*, 1821
7298 —— the same, 8 vols. 8vo. *calf gilt*, £2. 7s 1821
7299 —— Histoire de Venise, 2 vols. roy. 8vo. *calf*, 12s *Brux.* 1838
"The author, Count Daru, has enjoyed opportunities for consulting a far greater number of authentic documents than any preceding writer on Venetian History. He had not only free access to the secret archives after their removal to Paris, but his efforts seem to have been indefatigable in collecting such further materials as the great libraries of the continent could afford.

7300 D'AUBIGNÉ (J. H. Merle) Histoire de la RÉFORMATION du XVI Siècle, 5 vols. 8vo. *half calf gilt*, 38s *Paris*, 1853
7301 [DE CHALLES] Les Illustres Françoises, Histoires Veritables, 4 vols. in 2, 12mo. *plates, calf, gilt edges*, 8s *Amst.* 1748
7302 DÉMEUNIER, l'Esprit des Usages et des Coutumes des différens peuples, 3 vols. 8vo. *a very choice copy in old French calf gilt*, 12s *Londres*, 1776
7303 DESCARTES, Œuvres, publiées par V. Cousin, 11 vols. 8vo. *plates*, £4. 4s *Paris*, 1824-26
"It is indeed a very observable fact, that while Richelieu, with such extraordinary boldness, was secularizing the whole system of French politics, and by his disregard of ancient interests, was setting at naught the most ancient traditions, a course precisely similar was being pursued, in a still higher department, by a man greater than he; by one, who, if I may express my own opinion, is the most profound among the many eminent thinkers France has produced. I speak of René Descartes, of whom the least that can be said is, that he effected a revolution more decisive than has ever been brought about by any other single mind."—*Buckle's Civilization*, Vol. I, 1858, p 529.
7304 DES PERIERS, Nouvelles Récreations et joyeux devis, 24mo. 2 *leaves in MS. calf neat*, 5s *Paris*, 1568
7305 D'ESPINELLE Les Muses R'alliées, thick 18mo. *engraved title by Gaultier, calf extra, gilt edges*, 18s *Paris*, 1603
A curious volume of old French poetry, printed in Italics.
7306 DES-PORTES, Prèmieres Œuvres, contenant Diane, Amours, Elégies, Epitaphes, Bergeries, Masquarades, &c. thick 12mo. *corner of leaf 237 torn, olive morocco extra, gilt edges*, 16s *Rouen*, 1600
Edition belle et peu commune,—BRUNET.
7307 D'HERBELOT, BIBLIOTHEQUE ORIENTALE, avec les corrections et additions de Schultens, continuée par Visdelou et Galand, 4 vols. 4to. BEST EDITION, *portraits, half bound, fine copy*, £5. *La Haye*, 1777-79
7308 DIDEROT, ŒUVRES, publiées par Naigeon, 15 vols. 12mo. *portrait, calf, gilt back*, 32s *Paris*, 1800
7309 —— Œuvres philosophiques, 6 vols. 8vo. *including the Bijoux Indiscrets, plates, old calf gilt*, 16s *Amst.* 1772
7310 —— le Pere de Famille, comédie, 2 vols. in 1, 8vo. *old blue morocco, gilt edges*, 6s *Amst.* 1758
7311 —— les BIJOUX INDISCRETS, 2 vols. 12mo. *curious plates, hf. calf*, 30s *Monomotapa*, ? 1730
7311*—— the same, 12mo. *fine copy in old calf gilt*, 36s ? 1730
7312 DU BARRI (la Comtesse) Memoires, 4 vols. 8vo. *cloth*, 10s *Paris*, 1829
7313 DU DEFFAND (Marquise) Letters to Horace Walpole, and to Voltaire, 1759-75, (*in French*), 4 vols. 12mo. *portrait, hf. calf*, 7s 1810

7314 DU FAIL, Contes et Discours d'Eutrapel avec Discours d'aucuns Propos Rustiques et Facecieux, 3 vols. in 2, 12mo. *calf, scarce*, 21s   1732
" The pictures of ancient rural manners in France, before the vices of the Court began to affect the Provinces are extremely curious and interesting."—*Ferrier*.

7315 Du LORENS, Les Satyres de, sq. 8vo. *title cut and mounted, calf*, 9s Paris, 1646
Les Satyres de Du Lorens ont fourni a Boileau plusieurs traits des siennes.—*Brunet*.

7316 Du TILLIOT, Memoires pour l'histoire de la fête des Foux, qui se faisoit autrefois dans plusieurs Eglises, 12mo. *curious plates, calf gilt*, 6s   Lausanne, 1751
Most of the rhymes in old Southern patois.

7317 EFFEN (Van) Le Misantrope, édition augmentée, 2 vols. 12mo. *old red morocco, gilt edges*, 8s   La Haye, 1726

7318 ERASME, les Colloques traduits par Gueudeville, 6 vols. in 3, 12mo. *vignettes, calf*, 7s 6d   1720

7319 ESTIENE (Henri) Introduction au Traité de la conformité des Merveilles anciennes avec les modernes, stout 12mo. *old calf gilt*, 7s 6d   1572
Entirely consisting of obscene accusations against the priests.

7320 FAUCHET, Œuvres reveues et corrigees avec additions, in 1 vol. stout sq. 8vo. *old calf gilt*, 12s   Paris, 1610
Contents: Antiquitez Gauloises; Dignitez et Magistrats de France; Origine des Chevaliers, Armoiries, etc.; Ordonnances, armes, et instruments; Libertez de l'Eglise Gallicane; LANGUE et Poesie Françoise.—Col. Stanley's copy fetched £5. 10s.

7321 FELIX [de Nisart] (J.) Satyres sur les Femmes Bourgeoises, qui se font appeler Madame, 8vo. *very curious plates, old calf extra, gilt edges*, EXTREMELY RARE, 32s   La Haye, 1713

7322 FENELON, ŒUVRES complètes, avec un essai sur la personne et les écrits de Fénélon, suivi de son éloge historique, 10 vols. 8vo. *portrait and fine plates by Moreau, calf neat*, £2.   Paris, 1810

7323 ———— Les AVANTURES de TELÉMAQUE, Fils d'Ulysse, 5 parts in 2 vols. 16mo. RARE, *beautiful copy in French red morocco super extra, doublé with purple leather linings, gilt edges*, £2.   La Haye, Moetjens, 1699-1700
This copy contains the second edition of Tome I. 1699; the fifth of Tome II. 1700; the fourth of the Suite du IIe Tome, 1699; the fifth of 2e Suite du IIe Tome, 1699; and the fifth of Tome III.; thus forming a complete set, the difficulty of effecting which is but too well known to collectors.

7324 FONTENELLE, Œuvres de, 11 vols. 12mo. *portrait and plates, fine copy, calf neat*, 15s   Paris, 1766

7325 ———— the same, 11 vols. 12mo. *portrait and plates, French calf gilt*, 15s   1767

7326 ———— Œuvres, 3 vols. 8vo. *facsimile, calf gilt*, 12s   Paris, 1818

7327 FROISSART, Histoire et Cronique, reveue et corrigée sus divers exemplaires, et suyvant les bons auteurs, par Denis Sauvage, 4 vols. in 2, folio, *fine copy in the original calf, back full gilt and stamped with arms*, £4. 4s
Lyon, Jan de Tournes, 1559-61
On the title of Vol. I, is written; " Ce livre est a moy Phles. Sire de Croy, Duc Darschot, Prince de Chimay, Conte de Beanmot et Senghem, 1565, J'y parviendray, Croy."—Cette édition, devenue peu commune, est très belle, et mérite d'etre recherchée; Elle est infiniment supérieure aux précédentes."—BRUNET.—The entire set of the four volumes is rarely met with, the third and fourth being generally added from other editions.

7328 FROISSART (Sire Jean) Les Chroniques, avec notes, tables, et Glossaire par BUCHON, 3 vols. roy. 8vo. *cloth*, 21s   Paris, 1837

7329 FROMMENT, Actes et Gestes merveilleux de la Cité de Geneve, en fourme de Chroniques, 8vo. *a History of the Reformation in Geneva, printed on tinted paper, with plates, vellum, uncut*, 25s   Géneve, 1854

7330 FUNESTES Effets de l'Amour et les desordres de cette passion, 2 vols. in 1, 16mo. *calf neat, curious*, 6s   Luxembourg, 1707

7331 GABRIELLE D'ESTRÉES, Memoires, 4 vols. 8vo. *hf. calf*, 12s 6d Paris, 1829

7332 GARASSUS, la Doctrine Curieuse des Beaux-Esprits, pernicieuse à l'Éstat, à la Religion et aux bonnes Mœurs, combattue et renversée, 4to. *old calf, a very curious book*, 15s   Paris, 1623

7333 GAUTIER (Théophile) Fortunio; Une Larme du Diable, etc.; Les Roués Innocents; Jean et Jeannette; 4 vols. 16mo. *hf. calf gilt*, 10s   Brux. 1839-50

7334 ———— Caprices et Zigzags; Un Trio de Romans; Italia; Les Grotesques; Constantinople; 5 vols. 12mo. *hf. calf gilt*, 15s   Paris, 1852-53

7335 GILLES, Croniques et Annales de France, nouvellement imprimées sur la correction de Denis Sauvage, 2 vols. in 1, folio, *woodcut titles, portraits, and genealogical tables, first title neatly repaired, calf*, 15s Paris, N. du Chemin, 1566

7337 GILLET, Triomphe de l'Amour honneste, sm. 4to. *vellum, 7s* *Paris*, 1642
7338 GOSSELIN (P. F. J.) Recherches sur la Géographie des Anciens, 4 vols. 1798-1813—Géographie des Grecs analysée, ou Systèmes d'Eratosthenes, de Strabon, et de Ptolomée comparés, 1790—together 4 vols. roy. 4to. 80 *maps, calf, gilt backs,* 36s *Paris,* 1790-1813
Priced, 1844, £4. 4s; 1855, Techener, 72 fr.—Toutes les grandes bibliothcques doivent faire une place à ce savant ouvrage, qu'aucun au!re ne peut remplacer.
7339 GRECOURT, Œuvres completes, 4 vols. 8vo. *portrait and fine plates, calf gilt,* 36s *Paris,* 1796
A handsome library edition.
7340 GRECOURT, Œuvres diverses, 4 vols. 16mo. *portr. and frontisps. by Eisen, calf,* 6s *Luxemb.* 1761
Rather poor as a poet, the reputation of Grécourt was obtained by the licentiousness of his imagination and a facility for rhyme, which he abused. In conjunction with the Duke D'Aguillon, Vinot and the Princess de Conti, he added much to the loose and erotic literature of France under the Regency; and his productions are still read with gusto.
7341 GREGOIRE, Explication des Cérémonies de la Fête-Dieu d'Aix en Provence, 12mo. *portrait of René d'Anjou, plates of processions, bds.* 6s *Aix,* 1777
7342 GRÉGOIRE DE TOURS, Livres des Miracles et autres opuscules, Latin et Français, par Border, 2 vols. large 8vo. *hf. red morocco, uncut,* 12s *Paris,* 1857
7343 GRESSET, Œuvres, 2 vols. 8vo. *portrait and plates, calf gilt,* 7s 6d *Paris,* 1811
7344 GRILLET, Dictionnaire Historique, Littéraire et Statistique, du Mont-Blanc et du Leman, contenant l'Histoire de Savoie, des personnes distinguées, etc. 3 vols. 8vo. *calf neat,* 12s *Chambery,* 1807
7345 GRIMM et DIDEROT, Correspondance Littéraire, Philosophique et Critique, depuis 1753 jusqu'en 1790, 16 vols.—Supplément, 1 vol.—together 17 vols. 8vo. *calf gilt,* £2. 2s *Paris,* 1813-14
"A magazine of good sense, lively anecdote, spirited criticism, and laughable whim, such as no collection of *Ana* or table talk that we are acquainted with exceeds or even rivals."—*Quar. Rev.*
7346 GUIZOT, Histoire de la Civilisation en EUROPE depuis la chute de l'Empire Romaine, 1 vol. 1840—Histoire de la Civilisation en FRANCE, 4 vols. 1840—together 5 vols. 8vo. *hf. calf,* 20s *Paris,* 1840
7347 ——— Histoire de la Révolution d'Angleterre, 2 vols. 8vo. *portraits of Charles I. and Cromwell, vellum gilt,* 8s *ib.* 1845
7348 HEEREN, Essai sur l'influence des Croisades, par Villers, 8vo. *calf,* 5s 1808
7349 HIPPOCRATE, Traité des Airs, des Eaux, et des Lieux, *Grec et Franç.* par Coray, 2 vols. 8vo. *frontisp. bds.* 5s 6d *Paris,* 1800
7350 HISTOIRE Générale des LARRONS, 3 vols. in 1, stout 12mo. *calf neat, a curious and amusing work,* 10s *Rouen,* 1657
7351 HISTOIRE de la RESTAURATION et des causes de la chute de la branche ainée des Bourbons, par un homme d'état, 10 vols. 8vo. *hf. calf,* 10s *Paris,* 1831-33
7352 HISTORIETTES Galantes, 12mo. *frontisp. calf,* 5s *La Haye,* 1730
7353 INTRIGUES GALANTES de la Cour de France, 2 vols. 12mo. *frontispiece, old red morocco extra, gilt edges,* 25s *Cologne,* 1695
7354 JEANDET (J. P. Abel) PONTUS de TYARD, Seigneur de Bissy, Evêque de Chalon (*See XVI.*) 8vo. *printed in antique style, with portrait and facsimile, hf. green morocco, gilt top, uncut,* 10s *Paris,* 1860
7355 JEHAN DE SAINTRÉ. Histoire et plaisante Cronicque du petit Jehan de Saintré de la jeune Dame des Belles Cousines sans autre nom nommer, avec de notes critiques, etc. 3 vols. 16mo. *a pretty set in old veau fauve gilt,* 25s *ib.* 1724
7356 JOVIO (Paolo, *Evesque de Nocera*) HISTOIRE sur les Choises faictes et advenues de son Temps, traduictes en François par Denis Sauvage, 2 vols. in 1, folio, *fine copy in russia extra, gilt edges, from Miss Currer's library,* 36s *ib.* 1581
7357 JOYEUSETEZ Facecies, et Folastres Imaginacions de Caresme Prenant, Gauthier Garguille, Tabarin, etc. 16mo. *only 76 copies printed, hf. crimson morocco gilt, gilt top, uncut,* 21s *ib.* 1834
7357*KARAMSIN, Histoire de Russie, traduite par St. Thomas et Jauffret, 11 vols. 8vo. *complete, calf neat,* 36s *Paris,* 1819-26
7358 LA FONTAINE, Fables, 2 vols. 8vo. *portrait, hf. calf,* 5s *Paris,* 1825
7359 ——— CONTES et Nouvelles en vers, 2 vols. 12mo. *numerous plates, old calf gilt,* 21s *Amst.* 1732
7360 LAMARTINE, Histoire des GIRONDINS, 8 vols. 8vo. *finely printed, calf gilt,* £2. 5s *Paris,* 1847
7361 LAZARE, Histoires tragiques de nostre temps, 12mo. *engraved title, vellum,* 7s *Rouen,* 1641

7362 LAZARILLE DE TORMES, Vie et Aventures, 2 parts in 1 vol. 16mo. *portraits and plates, calf gilt*, 10s *Brusselles*, 1699

7363 LA SUZE (la Comtesse de) et M. Polisson, Recueil de Pieces Galantes, 3 vols. in 1, 12mo. *old calf*, 5s *Paris*, 1674-75

7364 LE GRAND D'AUSSY, Histoire de la Vie privée des François, avec des Notes par Roquefort, 3 vols. sm. 8vo. *cloth*, 7s *Paris*, 1815

7365 LESAGE, Œuvres, précédées d'une Notice sur sa Vie et ses Ouvrages, 12 vols. 8vo. *plates, hf. calf*, £2. 12s 6d *Paris*, 1828

7366 —— Œuvres, avec une Notice sur Lesage, et une liste de ses ouvrages, 14 vols. 12mo. *numerous plates, calf gilt*, 24s *Paris*, 1820-21
"Le Sage knew more of the world than the Abbé Prevost, and his works are consequently more imbued with this knowledge. His Gil Blas is a faithful picture of every situation in life, and it is instructive as well as amusing."—*Barbier's Bibl.* vol. 5, p. 30.

7367 LETTENHOVE (Kervyn de) Histoire de FLANDRE (792-1792), 6 vols. large 8vo. *hf. red morocco*, 32s *Bruxelles*, 1847-50

7368 LIAISONS DANGEREUSES, 4 vols. in 2, 12mo. *hf. calf neat*, 9s *Amst.* 1788

7369 LIVRE de la FEMME FORTE et vertueuse, declaratif du cātique de Salomon, etc. 16mo. *edition unknown to Brunet,* lettres gothiques, *device of Romaine Loriot on front, and woodcut of the Annunciation on back of title, stamped binding*, 32s *Paris, Le Dru, pour Frellon et Loriot, sans date* (? 1500)

7370 LONGUS, Les Amours Pastorales de DAPHNIS et de CHLOE, traduits par Amyot, 12mo. 28 *plates, including " les Petits Pieds," after the designs of the Regent of Orleans, by Audran, old French red morocco extra, gilt edges,* £3. 10s *Paris*, 1718
"Vendu 125 fr. De Bure; 147 fr. Parison; 99 fr. Solar;" and even much higher prices have been fetched for this publication of the celebrated Regent.

7371 LOUVET de Couvray, Vie du Chevalier de FAUBLAS, 7 vols. 16mo. *hf. calf*, 10s 1795

7372 —— Vie de FAUBLAS, avec une notice sur l'auteur, etc. 4 vols. 12mo. *portrait, hf. morocco*, 10s *Paris*, 1807

7373 MABLY, Collection complète des ŒUVRES, 15 vols. sm. 8vo. *calf*, 16s *Paris*, 1795

7374 MAINTENON, Mémoires pour servir a l'histoire de Madame de Maintenon, et à celle du Siecle passé (par M. de la Beaumelle), 16 vols. 12mo. *best edition, calf gilt*, 32s *Maestricht*, 1789

7375 MAINVILLE, Bonheur et Malheur du Mariage, 16mo. *vellum*, 6s *La Haye*, 1684

7376 MAISON-NEUFVE, Plaisante et delectable Histoire de GERILEON D'ANGLETERRE, contenant ses hauts faicts d'armes, et chevaleureuse proüesses, etc. 183 *leaves*, 1602—Second Livre de Gerileō d'Angleterre, 160 *leaves, and, at the end, 6 of Sommaires et Extraicts*, 2 *of woodcuts*, 1589—2 vols. in 1, 18mo. *good clean copy, calf, gilt back*, 36s *Lyon*, 1602-1589
The above copy has the third edition of the first part, and the first edition of the second part. All editions of this romance are rare. A copy of the edition, Paris, 1586, 'Le premier et second livre' fetched, 1856, at Sotheby's, £5. 12s 6d.

7377 MALEBRANCHE, Œuvres, 2 vols. 12mo. *hf. calf*, 5s *Paris*, 1846

7378 MANLEY (Madame) L'Atlantis, contenant les Intrigues politiques et amoureuses de la Noblesse d'Angleterre, 2 vols. 12mo. *old calf gilt, curious*, 10s *Selon la copie impr. a Londres*, 1714

7379 MARGUERITE DE VALOIS, Reine de Navarre, HEPTAMERON FRANCOIS Nouvelles, etc. 3 vols. sm. 8vo. *numerous fine plates and vignettes by* FREUDENBERG, *superb impressions, with printed and engraved titles, hf. red morocco, gilt edges*, £4. 10s *Berne*, 1780-81

7380 —— the same, 3 vols. 8vo. *hf. green morocco gilt*, ENTIRELY UNCUT, *the late Earl of Aberdeen's copy*, £6. 6s *Berne*, 1792
There is no difference between these two copies, 1792 being merely the date of a new title, as the entire impression of the plates was printed off in 1780.

7381 MARGUERITE, Contes et Nouvelles, 8 vols. in 4, 12mo. *numerous plates, hf. calf*. 16s. *Paris*, 1807

7382 —— MEMOIRES, 16mo. *vellum, fine copy*, 20s (ca. 1628)
Unknown to Brunet, and evidently the second issue of the first edition, with corrections. It has the appearance of a privately printed or an unfinished book, being without date, place, or name of printer.

7383 MARIVAUX, Œuvres complettes, 12 vols. sm. 8vo. *port, calf gilt*, 25s *Paris*, 1781
Contents: Vols. 1-5, Théâtre; Vols. 6, 7, Discours à l'Académic, Effets de la Sympathie, Vie de Marianne; Vol. 8, Le Paysan Parvenu; Vol. 9, Le Spectateur Français, L'Indigent Philosophe, Cabinet du Philosophe; Vol. 10, L'Iliade travestie; Vol. 11, Le Don Quichotte Moderne; Vol. 12, Œuvres melées, Priced, 1848, Payne and Foss, £12.; Dent's copy, large paper, fetched £11.

7384 MARMONTEL, ŒUVRES complètes, 18 vols. 8vo. BEST EDITION, *portrait and plates, calf gilt*, £2. 10s *Paris*, 1818-19
" Belle edition sortie des presses de Firmin Didot."—BRUNET.

7385 MARMONTEL, Œuvres complètes, 18 vols. 12mo. *nice copy in calf gilt*, 32s
Paris, 1819

7386 MAROT (Clement) Œuvres, 2 vols. 16mo, *fine copy, red morocco, gilt edges, by Simier*, 35s
La Haye, Elzevir, 1700
Priced, 1840, J. Bonn, £6. 6s. Fetched, 1813, Col. Stanley's, £10. 10s; 1859, at Sotheby's, £4.
"Ce Poète avait un esprit enjoué et plein de saillies, sous un extérieur grave et philosophique. Marot a surtout réussi dans le genre epigrammatique. Du Verdier dit en parlant de lui qu'il a été le Poëte des Princes, et le Prince des Poetes.—BIBL. D'UN HOMME DE GOUT.

7387 MARTENS, Recueil de Traités d'Alliance, de Paix, de Commerce, de limites, et plusieurs autres actes servant a la connoissance des relations étrangères, 1761 à 1808, 8 vols. 1817-35—Nouveau Recueil, continué par Saalfeld et Murhard, 16 vols. in 19, 1817-42—Nouveaux Supplémens, 3 vols. 1839-42—Table Générale, 2 vols. 1837-43—Nouveau Recueil Général, continué par Murhard, Pinhas, Samwer, etc. vols. I.-XV, 1843-57—together 47 vols. 8vo. (*pub. at* 165 *Thalers, sd.*) *hf. calf neat, a complete set up to* 1857 *of this extremely valuable collection*, £12. 12s
Goettingue, 1817-57

7388 MATTHIEU, Histoire de France, du regne de Henri IV, 2 vols. 12mo. *bd.* 7s 1620

7389 MATTHIEU PARIS, Grande Chronique, traduite par Huillard-Bréholles, avec des Notes et une introduction par le Duc de Luynes, 9 vols. 8vo. *hf. calf gilt*, 27s
Paris, 1840-41

7390 MAURY, Essai sur les Legendes Pieuses du Moyen-Age, 8vo. *hf. calf, gilt top, uncut*, 12s
Paris, 1843

7391 MAZARINADES. A Collection of 128 French Tracts, Poems, Satires, Burlesque Pieces, etc. upon Cardinal Mazarin, all contemporary with him, and all of the utmost interest, in 2 vols. sq. 8vo. *hf. bd.* VERY RARE *and* CURIOUS, 25s
1649-50
"This singular collection contains many of the celebrated, but extremely coarse and vulgar pieces entitled 'Mazarinades.'" A collection of only 54 of these tracts relating to Mazarin fetched at Hibbert's sale £3. 5s.

7392 MAZURE, Histoire de la Révolution de 1688, en Angleterre, 3 vols. 8vo. *calf neat*, 9s
1825

7393 MELANGES tirés d'une Grande Bibliothèque, par Messieurs Paulmy et Coulant D'Orville, 64 vols. 8vo. *hf. bd.* £2. 10s
Paris, 1779-1787
Les premiers volumes de ces Melanges renferment les extraits d'un grand nombre d'ouvrages Français antérieurs au 17e siècle ; et sous ce rapport ils ne sont pas sans intérêt pour les personnes qui veulent connaître notre ancienne littérature ; malheureusement les derniers volumes de l'ouvrage n'ont pas a beaucoup près le meme mérite que le commencement ; et c'est ce qui fait que cette volumineuse collection est peu recherchée.—*Brunet.*

7394 **MEMOIRS.** COLLECTION UNIVERSELLE des Mémoires Particuliers relatifs à l'Histoire de France (recueillis par Roucher, A. Perrin, Dussieux et autres) avec TABLE générale, 67 vols. sm. 8vo. *calf neat*, £5.   *Paris*, 1785-91
Priced, 1827, Thorpe, £15. 15s.

7395 PETITOT, Collection Complete des Mémoires sur la France, PREMIÈRE SÉRIE, depuis le règne de Philippe Auguste jusqu'au commencement du XVIIe Siècle, avec des notices sur chaque ouvrage, 52 vols. *Paris*, 1819-26—PETITOT et MONMERQUÉ, Collection complete des Memoires sur l'Histoire de France, SECONDE SÉRIE, depuis l'avènement de Henri IV. jusqu'à la Paix de Paris en 1763, avec des notices sur chaque ouvrage, 79 vols. *Paris*, 1820-29—together 131 vols. (pub. at £40. unbound) *hf. calf, clean set*, £27.   *Paris*, 1819-29

7396 —— the same, 131 vols. in 132, 8vo. *fine set, entirely uniform in hf. purple morocco, gilt top, uncut*, £28. 10s   *Paris*, 1819-29

7397 COLLECTION (NOUVELLE) DES MEMOIRES, pour servir à l'HISTOIRE DE FRANCE, depuis le XIIIme siècle jusqu'à la fin du XVIIme, précédés de Notices pour caractériser chaque auteur des Mémoires et son epoque; suivis de l'analyse des Documents historiques qui s'y rapportent, par MM. MICHAUD et POUJOULAT. Collection terminée, 33 vols. royal 8vo. *double columns, neatly half bound, calf gilt, contents lettered*, £16. 16s   *Paris*, 1850

7398 MÉMOIRES pour l'Histoire de France et de Bourgogne, contenant un JOURNAL de PARIS sous Charles VI et Charles VII, 4to. *calf*, 7s   *Paris*, 1729

7399 MÉMOIRES (Bibliothèque des) relatifs à l'histoire pendant le XVIII Siècle, avec notices, par BARRIÈRE, 12 vols. sm. 8vo. *calf neat*, 32s   *Paris*, 1846-48

7400 MÉMOIRES de la Comtesse de B., 2 vols. in 1, 12mo. *old calf*, 5s   *La Haye*, 1744

7401 MERCIER, Tableau de Paris, 12 vols. in 6, 1783—Nouveau tableau de Paris, 6 vols. in 2—together 18 vols. in 8, 8vo. *calf neat*, 10s   1783-93

7402 MICHAUD, Histoire des Croisades, avec la Bibliographie des Croisades, analysant toutes les Chroniques, 7 vols. 8vo. *maps, calf neat*, 15s *Paris*, 1819-22
7403 —— septième édition, augmentée d'un Appendice par Huillard-Bréholles, 4 vols. large 8vo. *frontispieces, fine copy from Dr. Hawtrey's library, in calf extra*, £2. 8s *Paris*, 1849
7404 MICHEL (Francisque) Lais Inédits des 12e et 13e Siècles, sm. 8vo. *calf extra, gilt edges*, 7s 6d *Paris, Techener*, 1836
7405 MICHELET, Histoire de France, 14 vols. 8vo. *complete as far as published, rare*, £3. 10s *Paris*, 1833-62
Vols. I-V bring the history down to 1461; Vol. VI, Louis XI et Charles le Téméraire; VII, Renaissance; VIII, Réforme; IX, Guerres de Religion; X, La Ligue et Henri IV; XI, Henri IV et Richelieu; XII, Richelieu et la Fronde; XIII, Louis XIV; XIV, Louis XIV et le Duc de Bourgogne.

7406 —— Histoire de France (jusqu'à 1483) 9 vols. in 7, 16mo. *cloth*, 9s *Brux.* 1834-44
7407 —— Histoire de France, (jusqu'à 1483) 9 vols. 16mo. *sd.* 6s *ib.* 1840-43
7408 —— Histoire de la Révolution Française, 7 vols. 8vo. *hf. calf*, 36s *Par.* 1847-49
7409 MIRABEAU, Oeuvres, avec une notice sur sa vie et ses ouvrages par Mérilhou, 8 vols. 8vo. *hf. bd.* 15s *Paris*, 1834-35
7409*MOLIÈRE, OEUVRES, nouvelle édition augmentée, 6 vols. in 3, stout 12mo. *portrait and plates, vellum*, 21s *Paris*, 1716
7410 —— ŒUVRES, avec un discours, la Vie de l'auteur et des reflexions par M. Petitot, 6 vols. 8vo. *portrait and plates, from designs by Moreau le jeune, French calf gilt*, 32s *Paris*, 1812
7411 —— ŒUVRES, nouvelle edition, avec des remarques par BRET, 6 vols. 8vo. *plates, calf gilt*, 38s *Paris*, 1804
7412 —— Œuvres, avec un commentaire historique et littéraire, et la vie de Moliere par Petitot, 6 vols. 8vo. *calf, very neat, contents lettered*, 27s *Paris*, 1821
7413 —— Œuvres, précédées d'une notice sur sa vie et ses ouvrages par Sainte Beuve, 2 vols. roy. 8vo. *portraits and numerous woodcuts by Tony Johannot, cloth*, 12s *Paris*, 1835-36
7414 —— the same, 2 vols. roy. 8vo. *calf extra, gilt edges*, 32s 1835-36
7415 MOLL et GAYOT, ENCYCLOPÉDIE pratique de l'AGRICULTEUR, Vols. I-VIII, large 8vo. *containing letters A-Indr, complete as far as yet published, with numerous woodcuts of Horses, Dogs, Cattle, Implements, etc. about* 6000 *pp. double cols.* (pub. at 84 francs) *sd.* 36s *Paris, Didot*, 1859-63
The engravings of the Animals are by the best Artists of France, and are very beautiful.

7416 MONSTRELET, Chroniques, avec notice biographique par Buchon, roy. 8vo. *hf. bd.* 10s *Paris*, 1836
7417 MONTAIGNE, ESSAIS, 5 vols. 8vo. *portrait, cloth*, 15s *Paris*, 1818
7418 —— ESSAIS, avec les notes de tous les commentateurs, édition publiée par Le Clerc, 5 vols. 8vo. FINE PAPER, *portrait and maps, hf. blue morocco, uncut*, £2. 12s 1826
7419 MONTESQUIEU. ŒUVRES, 5 vols. 8vo. *portrait, calf gilt*, 25s *Paris*, 1788
7420 —— Oeuvres, 5 vols. 8vo. *portrait and maps*, PAPIER D'HOLLANDE, *fine copy in old French red morocco extra, gilt edges*, £5. *Paris*, 1796
7421 —— Œuvres complètes, 6 vols. 8vo. *port. calf extra, gilt edges*, 36s *Par.* 1816
7422 MONTRESOR, Memoires: diverses Pieces durant le Ministere de Richelieu, 2 vols. 12mo. *original edition, fine copy in old morocco, gilt edges*, 10s *Cologne*, 1663-65
7423 MORALISTES ANCIENS, collection des: Epictète; Confuce; Auteurs Chinois, 5 vols.; Isocrate; Senèque, 3 vols.; Ciceron; Theophraste; Sages Grecs; Socrate, 2 vols.; Jésus Christ, 2 vols.: together 18 vols. 16mo. *French red morocco, gilt edges*, £2. 10s *Paris*, 1782-95
7424 MOREAU, HISTOIRE DE FRANCE, 18 vols. 8vo. *fine copy in old French* RED MOROCCO EXTRA, *gilt edges, arms on sides*, £5. 5s *Paris*, 1778-86
7425 MORELLET, Mélanges de Littérature et de Philosophie du XVIIIe Siecle, 4 vols. 8vo. *hf. calf neat*, 7s 6d *Paris*, 1818
7426 MOTTEVILLE (Madme. de) Memoires pour l'histoire d'ANNE d'AUTRICHE, épouse de Louis XIII, 6 vols. 12mo. *calf gilt*, 32s *Amst.* 1783
7427 MOUHY (le Chevalier de) LA PAYSANNE PARVENUE, ou les Mémoires de la Marquis de L. V., 12 parts in 3 vols. 12mo. *calf*, 7s 6d *Paris (et la Haye)* 1726-27
7428 —— Les Mille et une Faveurs, tirées du Gaulois par la Reine de Navarre, 8 vols. 18mo. *portrait, calf*, 10s 1740
7429 MOULINET, la vraye histoire comique de Francion, stout 16mo. *cf.* 7s *Rouen*, 1673

7430 MOUSIN, Discours de l'Yvresse et Yvrongnerie, ensemble la maniere de Carousser des anciens, 12mo. *fine copy in veau fauve extra, edges gilt, rare,* 30s
"Ouvrage rare et singulier."—*Brunet.* *Toul,* 1630

7431 MOYEN DE PARVENIR, (par Beroalde de Verville), 2 vols. 18mo. *a nice copy in old French blue morocco extra, gilt edges,* 30s *Nullepart,* 1739
7432 —— the same, 2 vols. 18mo. *hf. bd.* 12s *Nullepart,* 1754
"Un répertoire de petits contes joyeux et de quolibets . . . quelquefois très plaisants et toujours fort libres."

7433 NAPOLEON. LAURENT de l'Ardèche, Histoire de l'Empereur Napoléon, roy. 8vo. *many hundred wood engravings after Horace Vernet, calf,* 10s *Paris,* 1839

7434 NISARD, Histoire des Livres Populaires depuis le XVe siècle, 2 vols. roy. 8vo. *numerous woodcuts, dark antique calf, Buckle's copy,* £2. 10s *Paris,* 1854
This interesting History of French Chap Books and popular Literature was undertaken under a Commission issued by the French Government. The numerous singular woodcuts (taken on India paper) are from the original blocks discovered in various parts of France. The few copies which were issued are now all dispersed.

7435 NOSTRADAMUS, les vrayes Centuries et Propheties, 16mo. *vellum,* 7s *Leyde,* 1650
7436 NOUGARET, la Folle de Paris, ou les Extravagances de l'Amour, 2 vols. in 1, 12mo. *calf,* 7s 6d 1787
7437 OUDEGHERST, Chroniques et Annales de Flandres, sm. 4to. *fine copy, limp vellum,* 12s *Anvers, C. Plantin,* 1571
7438 PAGANEL, Histoire de SCANDERBEG ou Turks et Chretiens ou 15e Siecle, 8vo. *cloth,* 7s *Paris,* 1855
7439 (PANCOUCKE) Art de désopiler la Rate, sive de modo c— prudenter, en prenant chaque feuillet pour se t— le d—, 2 vols. 12mo. *calf,* 5s *Venise (Paris)* 1788-73

7440 PASCAL (Bl.) ŒUVRES: Pensées, Lettres Provinciales, Œuvres Mathematiques, etc. 5 vols. 8vo. *portrait, hf. calf,* 24s; *or hf. calf neat, uncut,* £2. *La Haye,* 1779
7441 —— Œuvres, nouvelle édition, avec un Essai sur l'origine de la langue Française, et une liste des livres Français imprimés avant 1500, 5 vols. 8vo. *portrait and plates, hf. vellum,* £2. 2s *Paris,* 1819
7442 —— les Provinciales, avec les variantes, et leur réfutation en introduction et notes par l'Abbé Maynard, 2 vols. 8vo. *sd.* 4s *Paris,* 1851
7443 PASTORET, Histoire de la Législation, 11 vols. 8vo. *calf,* £2. 10s *Paris,* 1817-35
7444 PATIN (Gui) Lettres, nouvelle édition, avec des lettres inédites, remarques historiques, etc. par Reveillé-Parise, 2 vols. 8vo. *portrait and facsimile, calf extra, uncut, top edges gilt, by Rivière, Mr. Buckle's copy,* 28s *Paris,* 1846
Dernière édition d'une correspondance non moins curieuse pour l'histoire littéraire et pour celle de la médicine, que pour la connaissance des moeurs et usages du XVIIe siècle.—*Brunet.*

7445 PETRARQUE. LES TRIUMPHES Petrarque, 18mo. 289 *numbered leaves (including title), and leaf with printer's device, numerous woodcuts, red morocco extra, joints, gilt edges,* £2. *Paris, Estienne Croulleau,* 1554
A peculiarity in the translation by Marot of Petrarch's Visions, at the end of this volume, is that there is a special character with a line across it to represent the silent *e.*

7446 PHILADELPHE, le Reveille-Matin des Francois et leurs voisins, 2 parts in 1 vol. 12mo. *a curious Huguenot work attributed to Beza, fine copy, vellum,* 12s *Edimbourg, (Génève)* 1574
7447 PHILOSOPHIE DIVINE, appliquée aux Lumières naturelle magique, astrale, etc. 3 vols. 8vo. *calf,* 10s 1793
7448 PIGAULT-LEBRUN, ŒUVRES COMPLÈTES, 22 vols. 8vo. VELLUM PAPER, *three portraits and a double set of three plates by Chasselet,* PROOFS AND ETCHINGS, *superb copy in calf extra, marbled and gilt edges, from the Collection of the Comte de Labedoyere,* £21. *Paris,* 1822-41
This copy will be found to contain beyond the ordinary works of this great French Novelist—Le Voyage dans le Midi de la France, Le Joyeux Testament ou Mémoires de Pigault-Lebrun, ou les Souvenirs de Barba.
"A writer possessing all the energy and graphic force, with more than the grossness, of him whom Gregory XVI used to call 'Questo amabile signore Paolo di Kokko.'"

7449 PITZIPIOS, L'Eglise Orientale, sa séparation et sa réunion avec Rome; accord des deux Eglises dans les dogmes, apostasie du Clergé de Constantinople, etc. 4 parts in 1 vol. roy. 8vo. *cloth,* 9s *Rome,* 1855
7450 PLATON, Œuvres complètes, traduites en Français, accompagnées d'arguments philosophiques, notes historiques et philologiques par Victor COUSIN, 13 vols. in 12, 8vo. (pub. at 130 fr.) *with numerous pencil marks, hf. cf.* £2. 8s *Paris,* 1822-40
Le nom si connu du traducteur est une suffisante garantie du mérite de cette traduction, préférable d'ailleurs à toutes les autres à cause des notes dont elle est enrichie.
Priced, 1853, £5. 13s; 1855, £3. 3s; fetched 1855, Sotheby's, £3. 6s.

7451 POETES FRANCAIS, Recueil des Chefs-d'œuvre de la Poésie Française depuis les origines jusqu'à nos jours, avec une notice sur chaque poëte, et introduction par Ste. Beuve, Vols. I-III, stout 8vo. (pub. at 22½ francs) *sd.* 15*s* *Paris*, 1861
   The collection is completed in 4 volumes.

7452 POTHIER, Oeuvres, nouvelle édition publié par Siffrein, 17 vols. 8vo. *portrait*, 36*s* *Paris*, 1820-22
   The reputation of this learned writer has been established as one of the greatest Jurisconsults of Europe.

7453 POGONOLOGIE, ou histoire philosophique de la Barbe, *Constantinople*, 1786— Eloge des PERRUQUES, par Akerlio—in 1 vol. 12mo. *calf gilt, curious,* 7*s* 6*d* 1786

7454 POLITIQUE (le) du Temps, ou conseil sur les mouvemens de la France, 24mo. *calf extra, rare,* 5*s* *Charle-Ville,* 1678

7455 PUISIEUX, Conseils a une Amie, 1749—Les Caracteres, 1750—in 1 vol. 12mo. *calf, gilt back,* 6*s* *Privately printed,* 1749-50

7456 QUINZE JOIES de MARIAGE, sq. 16mo. *printed in Gothic type, with facsimile of an early MS. of the work, and pretty small woodcuts, red morocco gilt, uncut, by Capé,* 20*s* *Paris, Techener,* 1837
   " Edition faite sur celle de Treperel (circa 1499) ornée de jolies gravures."

7457 RABELAIS, ŒUVRES, avec des remarques et critiques, 6 vols. 12mo. *portrait and plates, calf,* 21*s* (*Paris*), 1732

7458 —— ŒUVRES, avec précis de sa vie, etc. 2 vols. 8vo. *calf gilt,* 12*s* 1738

7459 —— ŒUVRES, avec les Remarques de Le Motteux par Cesar de Missy, 3 vols. 8vo. *portrait and* 76 *characteristic plates, fine impressions, calf gilt,* £2. 10*s*
   Il n'en a été tiré que 250 exemplaires. *Paris,* 1798

7460 —— ŒUVRES, ÉDITION VARIORUM, augmentée de piéces inédites, des Songes Drolatiques de Pantagruel, ouvrage posthume, des remarques de Le Duchat, de Voltaire, &c. ; et d'un commentaire historique et philologique par Esmangart et Eloi Johanneau, 9 vols. 8vo. BEST EDITION, *map,* 10 *vignettes,* 2 *portraits of Rabelais, and* 120 *very curious woodcuts, bds. uncut,* £3. 10*s*; or *hf. calf,* £3. 15*s* *Paris,* 1823

7461 —— the same, PAPIER VELIN, 9 vols. 8vo. *sewed, uncut,* £5. 5*s* 1823
   Fetched, 1855, at Sotheby's, morocco, £7. 7s.

7462 —— Œuvres de, 3 vols. 8vo. *hf. morocco,* 18*s* 1823
   Vol. 3 contains a Glossary, and a Catalogue of "Erotica Verba."

7463 RACINE (J.) ŒUVRES, avec des Commentaires par Luneau de Boisjermain, 7 vols. 8vo. *portrait and plates after Gravelot,* BEST EDITION, *with the suppressed leaves and cancels, French calf extra, gilt edges,* £2. 10*s* *Paris,* 1768

7464 —— the same, 7 vols. 8vo. *fine copy on* THICK DUTCH PAPER, *French calf gilt,* £3. 3*s* 1768
   Priced, 1837, Payne and Foss, *Dutch paper, fine copy,* £12. 12*s* ; 1840, J. Bohn, £3. 3*s* ; 1848, Payne and Foss, £3. 13*s* 6*d* ; Heath's copy fetched £6. 12*s* 6*d* ; Bailley's, Dutch paper, 172 fr. ; 1860, Sotheby's, £4. 2*s*.
   Bibliographers do not seem to have been aware of copies with cancelled leaves, a fact not even alluded to by Brunet.
   Les deux derniers volumes de cette édition, n'obtinrent pas de privilège (ils contiennent l'histoire de Port-Royal), et furent imprimés sous la rubrique de Londres, sans nom d'éditeur ; mais par une singulière anomalie, la liste des souscripteurs se trouve dans le 7e volume, imprimée en cachette, et le Roi s'y trouve porté pour 200 exemplaires.

7465 —— ŒUVRES, avec des commentaires par Géoffroy, 7 vols. 8vo. *portraits, fac-simile, and plates, calf gilt,* 20*s* *Paris,* 1808
   On placera toujours au nombre des principales éditions, celle de Géoffroy,

7466 —— ŒUVRES complètes, avec les notes de tous les commentateurs, publiées par Aimé-Martin, 6 vols. 8vo. *fine plates, calf gilt,* 32*s* *Paris,* 1820

7467 —— ŒUVRES, avec les Notes de tous les Commentateurs, par Aimé-Martin, 7 vols. 8vo. *portrait, hf. calf neat,* 25*s* *Paris,* 1825

7468 RÉCREATIONS historiques, etc. histoire des Fous en titre d'office, 2 vols. 12mo. *calf,* 5*s* *La Haye,* 1768

7469 RECUEIL des Dépêches, Rapports, et Mémoires des Ambassadeurs de France en Angleterre et en Ecosse pendant le 16e Siècle, publiés par Chas. Purton COOPER, 7 vols. 8vo. *hf. calf,* 15*s* *Paris,* 1838-40

7470 RECUEIL des plus belles Pieces de Poëtes François (depuis Villon) avec l'histoire de leur vie (*par Fontenelle*), 5 vols. 18mo. *calf gilt,* 12*s* *Amst.* 1692

7471 RETZ. MÉMOIRES du Cardinal de Retz, de Guy Joli, et de la Duchesse de Nemours, 6 vols. 8vo *portrait and facsimile, library edition, large type, hf. calf gilt,* 18*s*; or, *calf gilt,* 25*s* *Paris,* 1820

7472 —— Memoires du Cardinal de Retz, 4 vols. 12mo. *calf gilt,* 7*s* *Geneve,* 1777

7473 RÉVOLUTION FRANCAISE ou Analyse complette et impartiale du Moniteur, 3 vols. ; suivie d'une Table Alphabétique des Personnes et des choses, 4 vols. in 3—together 6 vols. stout 4to. *numerous ports. hf. russia*, 20s *Paris*, 1801-2
7474 BUCHEZ et Roux-Lavergne, Histoire Parlementaire de la Revolution Francaise, ou Journal des Assemblées Nationales depuis 1789 jusqu'en 1815, 40 vols. 8vo. *hf. calf neat*, £5. *Paris*, 1834-38
This important collection was priced in 1845, *sewed*, 160 francs.
7475 Courrier de Provence : Mirabeau, Lettres à ses Commettans—Courier de Provence pour faire suite aux Lettres, Nos. 20-97 and 118-162—together 7 vols. 8vo. *hf. bd*. 12s 1789-90
7476 Delandine, Tableau des Prisons de Lyon, pendant la tyrannie de 1792-93, sm. 8vo. *hf. calf*, 7s 6d *Lyon*, 1797
7477 Mallet du Pan, Mercure Britannique, ou notices sur les affaires du tems, 5 vols. sm. 8vo. *hf. bd*. 15s 1798-1800
7478 ROLAND (Madame) Appel a l'impartiale Posterité, ou Recueil de ses Ecrits pendant sa détention à l'Abbaye et à Sainte-Pelagie, 4 parts in 1 vol. 8vo. *bds*. 21s *Paris, ca*. 1795
Full of the most curious and interesting information about the French Revolution.
7479 Tracts and Pamphlets, Robespierre, Rapport du Comité de Salut Public ; Montesquieu, Réponse à Claviere, 1793 ; Gasc, Discours au Club des Revolutionnaires, 1793 ; Rapport du Comité des Quinze, 1793 ; Réflections sur le procès de la Reine, 1793 ; Mallet, sur la Revolution, 1793 ; Interet de la France à une Constitution Monarchique, *Berlin*, 1791 ; 5 Manuscript pages on the outbreaks at Perpignan and Aix, 1790 ; 5 tracts on the troubles in Sicily, 1796-9 ; and others—together 48 *rare and interesting tracts*, 8vo. 12s 1790-99
7480 Reybaud, Jérome Paturot à la recherche d'une position sociale, roy. 8vo. *many fine humourous engravings by Grandville, hf. red mor. gilt edges*, 10s *Paris*, 1846
7481 ROCHEFOUCAULD (Le Duc de la) Maximes, et Reflexions Morales, 8vo. *fine portrait, Large Fine Paper, ruled with red lines, blue morocco extra, silk insides, by Bradel, uncut*, 38s *Paris, l'Impr. Royale*, 1770
7482 **Romances.** ROMANS des CROISADES. Li Romans de Bauduin de Sebourc IIIe Roy de Jhérusalem, poëme du XIV Siècle, publié pour la première fois d'après les Manuscrits de la Bibliothèque Royale, 2 vols. impl. 8vo. *facsimile*, large vellum paper, *whole bound in light blue Turkey morocco, gilt tops, edges uncut*, £5. 5s *Valenciennes*, 1841
Only thirteen copies were printed on this paper.
7483 ROMANS des DOUZE PAIRS de France publiés par Paulin Paris, Francisque Michel, et autres : Berthe aus grans piés ; Garin de Loherain, 2 vols. ; Raoul de Cambrai ; Chansons des Saxons, 2 vols. ; Parise la Duchesse ; Romancero Français ; 8 vols. sm. 8vo. papier d'Hollande, *only 200 copies printed, elegantly bound in calf extra, gilt edges*, £5. *Paris*, 1833-40
7484 ROMAN du RENART, d'après les MSS. des XIIIe, XIVe, et XVe Siècles, par Méon, etc. 4 vols. 1826—Supplément, variantes, et corrections, par Chabaille, 1835—together 5 vols. roy. 8vo. *plates, hf. calf extra, gilt tops, uncut*, £2. 10s *Paris*, 1826-35
7485 ROMAN de la VIOLETTE, ou de Gerard de Nevers, en Vers du XIII Siècle, par Gibert de Montreuil, publié pour la première fois par F. Michel, large 8vo. *six facsimile plates and coloured initials, bds., or hf. morocco*, 32s *Paris*, 1834
7486 —— the same, 8vo. papier d'Hollande, one of the twenty-five copies, with duplicates of the six curious illuminations, *in exact imitation of the ancient Miniatures, citron morocco super extra, broad dentelle borders, gilt edges, by Mackenzie*, £4. 10s 1834
7487 Histoire de Huon de Bordeaux, 2 vols. in 1, sq. sm. 8vo. *hf. bd*. 12s *Lille*, 1726

7488 ROSSET (François de) Romant des Chevaliers de la Gloire, contenant plusieurs hautes et fameuses adventures aux Courses faites à la Place Royale pour la feste des Alliances de France et d'Espagne, avec les Blasons, etc. sq. 8vo. *title soiled, otherwise a fine copy in limp vellum*, 25s *Paris*, 1613
Priced, 1855, Techener, Paris, 68 fr.
7489 —— Histoires Tragiques de nostre Temps, Morts funestes de plusieurs Personnes, arrivées par leurs Ambitions, Amours déréglés, &c. thick 12mo. *vellum*, 12s *Rouen*, 1688

7491 ROUSSEAU, Œuvres, 26 vols. 18mo. *portrait and numerous pretty plates,* *calf,* 18s 1791

7492 —— Œuvres complètes, avec des éclaircissements et des notes historiques par Auguis, 27 vols. 8vo. VELLUM PAPER, *portrait and plates,* PROOF IMPRESSIONS, *hf. calf,* £4. *Paris,* 1825

7493 SACY, Traité de la Gloire, 12mo. *fine copy, old red* MOROCCO, *gilt edges,* 5s 1745

7494 (SAINT-AMANT) la Rome ridicule, caprice, 12mo. *vellum,* 15s (*Paris*), 1643
A curious Satire against the vices of the Court of Rome.

7495 (SAINT-HYACINTHE) Recueil de divers Écrits sur l'Amour, etc. 12mo. *calf extra, gilt edges,* 5s *Paris,* 1736

7496 SAINT-RÉAL (l'Abbé) Œuvres, 8 vols. 16mo. *a pretty set in* OLD RED MOROCCO *extra, gilt edges,* 32s *ib.* 1757

7497 SAINT-SIMON, ses Mémoires complets et authentiques sur le Siècle de Louis XIV. et la Régence, publiés pour la première fois, 21 vols. 8vo. BEST EDITION, *hf. calf, scarce,* £3. 3s *ib.* 1829-31
Priced, 1837, £8. 15s; 1844, £13. 13s; 1853, £8. 8s; fetched, 1843, Mainnemarre's sale, 185 fr.; 1853, Dr. Hawtrey's, £10. 10s; 1855, Puttick's, £6. 12s 6d; 1859, Christie's, £5. 7s 6d; 1860, Sotheby's, £6.
"It becomes my business, as usual, to mention such works, not as may, but must be, read. The great magazine from which subsequent writers of history and compilers of anecdote have drawn their materials, is the 'Mémoires du Duc de St. Simon.'"—*Smyth's Lect. on Mod. Hist.*
"Nous ne croyons pas qu'aucuns mémoires du temps puissent etre lus avec autant de plaisir que ceux du Duc de Saint-Simon. Le style est toujours vif, piquant, énergique; ses tournures sont neuves et hardies. Son talent marqué, c'est celui des portraits, et il les fait de main de maître."—*Barbier, Bibl. d'un Homme de Goût.*

7498 SAINT-SURIN, L'Hôtel de Cluny au Moyen-Age, sm. 8vo. *old French poems, calf extra, gilt edges, by Bedford,* 7s 6d *Paris,* 1835

7499 SAINTE-CROIX, Recherches sur les Mystères du Paganisme, seconde édition, par De Sacy, 2 vols.—VILLOISON de Veterum Mysteriis—together 3 vols. in 2, 8vo. *plates, hf. calf,* 15s *ib.* 1817

7500 SALGUES, des Erreurs et des Préjugés répandus dans la Société, 3 vols. 8vo. *calf neat, gilt top, uncut, a profound and interesting work,* 21s 1811-13

7501 SAVARY. MÉMOIRES du Duc de ROVIGO, pour l'histoire de l'Empereur Napoléon, 8 vols. 8vo. *sd.* 18s *Paris,* 1828

7502 SCARRON, Œuvres de, 7 vols. 8vo. *portrait, calf, gilt edges,* 30s *ib.* 1786

7503 SCHMID (Chanoine) Contes, roy. 8vo. *many illustrations by* GAVARNI, *hf. morocco,* 12s *ib.* 1843

7504 SÉVIGNÉ (Mad. de) LETTRES, nouvelle edition enrichie de notes, augmentée de lettres, etc. par Grouvelle, 8 vols. 8vo. *portraits of all the celebrated characters at Louis XIV's court, and facsimiles, bds.* 36s *ib.* 1806

7505 —— LETTRES, 8 vols. 8vo. *portraits and plates, calf gilt,* 32s *ib.* 1806

7506 —— LETTRES, par Grouvelle, 13 vols. 12mo. *pretty copy, calf gilt,* 36s *ib.* 1818-19

7507 —— LETTRES, avec notice bibliographique par Monmerqué, notice sur Madame de Sévigné par Saint Surin, etc. 10 vols. 8vo. FINE PAPER, *numerous portraits, Arms, facsimiles, and other plates, calf gilt,* £2. 5s *ib.* 1818
"Edition la meilleure que l'on ait ju-qu'ici de cette immortelle correspondence."—*Brunet.*

7508 —— LETTRES, avec un essai biographique et littéraire (par Campenon), 12 vols. 8vo. *portraits, cloth,* 28s *ib.* 1822-23

7509 —— LETTRES, avec les notes de tous les commentateurs, 7 vols. 12mo. *portrait, half calf gilt,* 20s *ib.* 1856-7

7510 —— Lettres Inédites, Opuscules de la Fontaine, 8vo. *portrait and facsimiles, cloth,* 5s *ib.* 1827

7511 SISMONDI, HISTOIRE DES FRANÇAIS, avec Table générale alphabétique, 31 vols. sm. 8vo. BEST EDITION, *calf neat,* £8. 15s *ib.* 1821-44

7512 —— Histoire des Français; Vols. I—XXIX, 8vo. *first ₁ velve vols. hf. bd. edges cut, the remainder uncut,* 29 vols. 8vo. £2. *ib.* 1821-31
Vols. 30 and 31 complete the work.
The best History of France is undoubtedly that of the learned Sismondi, who diligently studied all the original Sources, and guided by a sound critical judgment, and by liberal political views, produced a work which supersedes all rivals. Sismondi's style is noble and vivid; he gives life to every character he describes. Many pages of Sismondi illustrate English History; and of the French Historians he is the most honest and candid with regard to this country. Guizot recommends Sismondi's History of France as the best book of its kind. Since Mezeray's time a vast amount of additional matter has been gathered in illustration of persons and events, all of which Sismondi has used in his work. "The author of the historical work now before us is already well known to our readers. * * * On the field which he has now chosen, Sismondi must be considered not as having rivals to surpass, but as having an entire deficiency to supply, Daniel, and even Mezerai are no longer read."—*Edinburgh Review,* vol. 35.

7513 SISMONDI, Histoire des RÉPUBLIQUES ITALIENNES du Moyen Age, 16 vols. 8vo. *hf. bd.* £2. *ib.* 1818
A work that will yet always be read for the beauty of its style, and the richness and wisdom of its reflections. "The analogy between the republics of ancient Greece and those of Italy during the Middle Ages is also well deserving of attention. Between the population of Athens and that of Florence there is no greater apparent difference than might be ascribed to mere local causes. In both there is the same fervour for democratic rule, the same

fickleness, the same thirst for pleasure, similar innate love of the fine arts, the same passionate vehemence of admiration or of hatred, and it would be difficult to establish any important moral difference between a Florentine of the age of Lorenzo the Magnificent, and a Greek of the age of Pericles. Whoever would wish to trace the commerce, the philosophy, art, literature, and policy of modern Europe, must make the period of the Italian republics a particular study."—*Gent.'s Mag.* Oct. 1844.

7514 SOLDAT (Le) FRANÇOIS — Le Pacifique, ou l'Anti-Soldat François — Apologie Royalle — Le Capitaine au Soldat — Le Soldat au Capitaine — Le Roy au Soldat — in 1 vol. 16mo. *woodcut on title, vellum, curious*, 10s Paris, 1604

7515 SOLDAT NAVARROIS, 16mo. *woodcut on title, vellum*, 5s ca. 1604

7516 SPINOZA, Œuvres, traduites par Saisset, 2 vols. 12mo. *cloth*, 6s 1842

7517 STAEL (Mme. de) OEUVRES complètes, 17 vols. 8vo. *portrait, calf gilt, contents lettered*, £2. 16s Paris, 1820-21

7518 STRAPAROLE, Les Facecieuses Nuicts, traduictes par Jean Louveau, 18mo. *old blue morocco, gilt edges*, 32s Lyon, 1596

7519 SULLY, Memoires ou Oeconomies Royales d'Etat, domestiques, politiques et militaires de HENRI LE GRAND, 12 vols. 18mo. *a pretty set in calf gilt, gilt edges*, 30s Amst. (avec la Sphère), 1725

7520 ——— Mémoires, avec Remarques par l'Ecluse des Loges, 8 vols. 12mo. *calf neat*, 10s 1778

7521 ——— the same, 8 vols. 12mo. *portraits, a very fine copy in veau fauve gilt, gilt edges*, 24s 1778

7522 (TABOUROT) BIGARRURES DU SEIGNEUR DES ACCORDS avec les Apophthegmes de Gaulard, 2 vols. in 1, 18mo. *one leaf defective supplied in MS. vellum*, 10s Lyon, 1600-1599

7523 ——— BIGARRURES et TOUCHES du Seigneur DES ACCORDS, avec les Apophtegmes de Gaulard, et les Escraignes Dijonnoises, édition augmentée, 5 parts in 1 vol. stout 16mo. *woodcuts, vellum*, RARE, £3. 3s Rouen, 1621-16

7524 ——— the same, in 2 vols. 12mo. *red morocco, gilt edges*, RARE, £3. 3s Rouen, 1640
This is the curious work to which Swift is said to owe so much of the drollery displayed in the Art of Punning. It contains humour, wit, wisdom, learning, and coarseness enough for a score of books.

7525 TAILLANDIER, Études sur la Revolution en Allemagne, 2 vols. 8vo. *hf. morocco, gilt edges*, 7s Paris, 1853

7526 TALLEMANT DES RÉAUX, les Historiettes, revues par Monmerqué et P. Paris, 6 vols. 12mo. *leather backs*, 25s ib. 1862

7527 THIÉBAULT, Souvenirs de Vingt Ans à Berlin, ou Frédéric le Grand, sa cour, etc. 5 vols. 8vo. *calf gilt*, 9s ib. 1805

7528 ——— Frédéric Le Grand, souvenirs de 20 ans à Berlin, 4me édition, 5 vols. 12mo. *half calf*, 12s ib. 1826

7529 THIERRY, Histoire de la Conquête de l'Angleterre par les Normands, 4me. édition, 4 vols. 8vo. *hf. calf*, 12s ib. 1836

7530 ——— 5me edition, 4 vols. 8vo. *numerous plates, hf. morocco, neat*, 36s ib. 1838

7531 ——— 7me edition, 4 vols. in 2, stout 12mo. *calf gilt*, 15s ib. 1846
One of the best written French works on English History. Nowhere is the long struggle of the Saxons against their Norman Conquerors, and their final amalgamation, better recited than in Thierry's stirring pages.

7532 THIERS, Histoire de la RÉVOLUTION FRANÇAISE, quatrième édition, 10 vols. 8vo. *map, and about 200 fine plates after the designs of Ary Scheffer and Tony Johannot, hf. calf neat*, 32s ib. 1834

7533 ——— RÉVOLUTION FRANÇAISE, 10 vols. in 5, 8vo. *hf. calf*, 30s ib. 1838-39

7534 ——— Révolution Française, 2 vols. impl. 8vo. *map, numerous woodcuts and vignettes, sd.* 6s Brux. 1844

7535 ——— Révolution Française, avec table analytique, 10 vols. 8vo. *54 portraits and plates, calf gilt*, £3. 12s Paris, 1854
"The History of the French Revolution by Thiers is a celebrated and popular book in France — and I believe in Europe. He was, in the highest degree, one of that quality of minds which take a marvellous grasp of all things - rapid in the acquirement of knowledge — one of those fine and unsullied pages on which so much may be written. He set himself to examine into the facts and the men of the Revolution. He inquired into its laws, its orations, its battles, its victories, its defeats. He occupied himself with researches of a thousand kinds;—war he discussed with he generals—finance with the financiers—diplomacy with the diplomatists. Nothing escaped his enthusiastic, persevering, and enlightened mind. The History of the French Revolution unites in itself all the kinds of merits which characterise those various brief historic relations, which are not history itself, though nearly related to it. Its pages contain admirable passages. There are in many parts of this great book, whole chapters, which read as if they had been written with the sword."—*Jules Janin.*

7536 TOCQUEVILLE (A. de) La Démocratie en Amérique, douzième édition augmentée, 4 vols. 8vo. *hf. calf gilt*, 36s Paris, 1848
Best edition of this excellent standard work, which will be read with double interest in consequence of the present revolution in America.

7537 TÖPFFER, Nouvelles Genevoises, large 8vo. *most amusing tales, a profusion of numerous woodcuts, hf. morocco, gilt edges*, 9s ib. 1845

7538 TÖPFFER VOYAGES en ZIGZAG ou excursions dans les Cantons Suisses, impl. 8vo. *numerous beautiful woodcuts, hf. green morocco, gilt edges*, 14s   Paris, 1850
7539 TRESSAN, Corps d'Extraits de Romans de Chevalerie, 4 vols. 16mo. *calf gilt*, 7s   *ib.* 1782
7540 VALLEMONT, Physique Occulte, ou Traité de la Baguette Divinatoire, 16mo. *frontispiece and curious plates, calf extra, gilt edges*, 12s   Amst. 1693
7541 VAUBLANC, la France au temps des Croisades ou recherches sur les mœurs et coutumes des Français aux XIIe et XIIIe siècles, 4 vols. 8vo. *woodcuts, calf gilt*, 27s   Paris, 1844-47
7542 VÉRON (Dr. L.) Mémoires d'un Bourgeois de Paris, 6 vols. 8vo. *sd.* 12s   1853-55
7543 VERTOT, Histoire de l'Ordre des Chevaliers de Malte, 7 vols. 8vo. *calf*, 9s *ib.* 1819
7544 VILLETTE (Marquis de) Œuvres, *a beautiful copy in old French red* MOROCCO *extra, gilt edges*, 15s   Londres, 1784
7545 VOLNEY (C. F. de) ŒUVRES complètes, avec une Notice sur sa Vie et ses Écrits par Bossange, 8 vols. 8vo. *portrait and plates, sd.* 12s   Paris, Didot, 1826
7546 —— the same, 8 vols. 8vo. *calf gilt*, £2.   1821-26
7547 VOLTAIRE, ŒUVRES COMPLÈTES, avec les notes de Beaumarchais, 92 vols. 8vo. LARGE FINE PAPER, *beautiful plates*, PROOFS, *the volume of the "*PUCELLE,*" containing double impressions, proofs and proofs before the letters, calf extra, gilt edges*, £10.   Paris, 1785-89

Priced, 1829, Longmans, £25.; Kemble's copy fetched £17. 17s; and Lady Webster's, £12.
The paper of this beautiful edition is of the fourth quality; and the addition of the "proofs before letters" to the fine plates of "La Pucelle" make this copy singularly desirable.

7548 VOLTAIRE, ŒUVRES COMPLÈTES, 4 vols. stout 8vo. *portrait, double columns, a very compact and beautifully printed edition, calf gilt*, 30s   *ib.* Didot, 1827
7549 —— La Henriade et autres pièces, 2 vols. sm. 8vo. *plates after Eisen, very fine copy in old red morocco extra, gilt edges by De Rome*, 24s   1770
7550 VRAYE et entiere HISTOIRE des Troubles et choses mémorables, avenues tant en France qu'en Flandres, depuis l'an 1562; et Considerations sur les GUERRES CIVILES des François, thick 12mo. *vellum, rare*, 20s   La Rochelle, 1573
7551 HISTORICAL TRACTS, A curious collection of, relating to France, some of them of the utmost rarity, bound in 1 vol. sm. 4to. *hf. calf*, 20s   1650-1717

CONTENTS:
Apologie des Frondeurs   no place or printer, 1650
Lettre au Cardinal de Rets, par un de ses confidents   1655
Relation de l'estat des Eglises reformées de France   1660
Remonstrance du Clergé de France au Roy   1680
Memoires présentés au Roy par Tellier   1695
Harangue au Roy par l'Eveque de Troyes   1710
Conclusions de la Faculté de Theologie, touchant la Souveraineté des Rois, *last leaf torn* Paris, 1717

7552 BIBLIOGRAPHY. DELANDINE, Bibliotheque de Lyon: Manuscrits de la Bibliothèque, leur ancienneté, leurs auteurs, leur écriture, etc. 3 vols.; Livres de Belles Lettres, 2 vols.; Théâtre, 1 vol.; together 6 vols. 8vo. *French calf gilt*, 20s   Paris, 1812
7553 DELEPIERRE, Analyse des travaux de la Société des Philobiblon de Londres, 8vo. *hf. morocco, gilt top, uncut*, 7s 6d   1862
7554 LACROIX DU MAINE et DU VERDIER, Bibliotheques Françoises, nouvelle édition augmentée par La Monnoye, Bouhier, Falconnet, et Rigolet de Juvigny, 6 vols. 4to. LARGE PAPER, *old French calf, gilt edges*, £2. 10s   Paris, 1772-73

Priced, Thorpe, £3. 13s 6d; fetched at Treuttel's sale £5. 12s 6d.
"Ouvrage tres précieux pour l'histoire littéraire de la France antérieurement à la fin du 16e siecle."—BRUNET.

7555 PUY DE MONTBRUN, Recherches Bibliographiques sur quelques Impressions Neêrlandaises du 15e et du 16e Siecle, 8vo. *fucsimiles, hf. calf*, 7s 6d Leide, 1836
7556 PARIS (Paulin) Les Manuscrits François de la Bibliothèque du Roi, leur Histoire et celle des textes Allemands, Anglois, Hollandois, Italiens, Espagnols de la même collection, 7 vols. 8vo. *hf. calf*, 32s   Paris, 1836-48

Fetched, 1857, Sotheby's, £3. "Cette histoire de nos MSS. a pour but de faire connaitre quel est le nom des principaux scribes – ou l'on exécutait les plus beaux MSS.—quels sont les ornemens les plus anciens, les plus curieux, les plus bizarres; – dans quels volumes l'on trouve des dessins d'églises, de vaisseaux, de costumes, &c.—, la date des MSS. et des reliures; les bibliotheques ou ils ont passé;—les plus vieux MSS. &c.

7557 VRIES (A. de) Eclaircissement sur l'Histoire de l'Invention de l'Imprimerie, et Arguments des Allemands en faveur de leur prétention à l'Invention, trad. par Noordziek, 2 vols. royal 8vo. *hf. calf gilt, uncut, gilt tops by Riviere*, 18s   La Haye, 1843-5

FRENCH LITERATURE. 421

7558 **GEOGRAPHY.** Perez-Rosales, Essai sur le Chili, 8vo. *map, sd.* 5*s* 1857
7559 **POLITICAL ECONOMY.** TURGOT, Œuvres, avec les Notes de Dupont de Nemours, des lettres inédites, etc. 2 vols. *portrait*, 1844—Economistes Financiers du 18e Siècle: Vauban, Boisguillebert, Law, Melon, Dutot, 1843—Physiocrates, Quesnay, Dupont de Nemours, Mercier de la Rivière, Baudeau, Le Trosne, 1846—Les tous publiés par Eugène DAIRE; together 4 vols. large 8vo. *uniform in hf. russia gilt*, 36*s* *Paris*, 1843-46
7560 **PHILOLOGICAL WORKS.** Du Ponceau, Mémoire sur le Système Grammatical des langues de quelques nations Indiennes de l'Amerique du Nord, 8vo. *calf gilt*, 12*s* *Paris*, 1838
7561 EICHHOFF, Parallele des Langues de l'Europe et de l'Inde, ou études des langues Romanes, Germaniques, Slavonnes, et Celtiques, comparées entre elles et à la langue Sanscrite, 4to. *half calf neat, gilt top, uncut*, 27*s* *Paris*, 1836
7562 Le Pileur, Tableaux Synoptiques de Mots Similaires dans les langues Persane, Samskrite, Grecque, Latine, Moeso-Gothique, Island., Suco-Goth., Anglo-Sax., Bretone, Francique, etc. 8vo. *comparative tables, hf. calf*, 7*s* (*ca.* 1812)
7563 **Arabic.** KAZIMIRSKI Dictionnaire Arabe Français contenant toutes les racines de la langue Arabe, leurs dérivés, tant dans l'idiome vulgaire que dans l'idiome littéral, 2 stout vols. roy. 8vo. 1638 *pp. double columns, hf. calf, uncut*, £4. 10*s* *Paris*, 1846-60

" M. Kazimirski de Biberstein a terminé son Dictionnaire arabe-français, que est fondé sur le Kamus, avec additions de termes tirés de lectures de l'auteur, et d'un certain nombre de significations plus modernes, empruntées aux Mille et Une Nuits. C'est un travail fait avec beaucoup de soin, qui a occupé M. Kazimirski pendant bien des années."—Mohl. R. A. Journ. Asiat. 1863.

7564 **DE SACY.** Grammaire Arabe, seconde édition, augmentée, avec un traité de la prosodie et de la métrique, 2 vols. stout 8vo. 1345 pp. 8 *plates and numerous tables, cloth*, £5. 10*s* *Paris*, 1831
7565 **Basque.** Bidassouet, Histoire des Cantabres, les premiers colons de l'Europe, et des Basques, avec leur Langue reduite aux principes de la Française, 8vo. 416 *pp. of which 200 are upon the Language, Grammar, etc. hf. calf gilt, uncut, gilt top*, 12*s* *Paris*, 1825
7566 **Breton.** LEGONIDEC, Dictionnaire Breton-Français et Français-Breton, avec la Grammaire Celto-Bretonne; enrichi des mots Gallois et Gaëls correspondants par Villemarqué, 2 vols. 4to. *sd. uncut*, 32*s* *Saint Brieuc*, 1847-50
7567 **Chinese.** LI KI, ou Mémorial des Rites, *Chinois et Français*, avec des notes, etc. par Callery, large 4to. *sd.* 15*s* *Turin*, 1853
7568 **Romance.** ROQUEFORT, Glossaire de la langue Romane, avec le Supplément, et des dissertations, 3 vols. 8vo. *frontispiece und facsimile, hf. calf neat*, £2. 2*s* *Paris*, 1808-20
7569 WACE, Oeuvres: Roman de Rou, avec observations philologiques par Raynouard, 3 vols. *Rouen*, 1827; Roman de Brut, avec description des MSS. par Le Roux de Lincy, 3 vols. *Rouen*, 1836; Fête de la Conception Notre-Dame, *Caen*, 1842; together 7 vols. 8vo. *facsimiles, Glossaries, and notes, hf. calf extra, gilt tops, uncut*, £4. 4*s* 1827-42
See also " Romances" *ante*, Nos. 7482-87
7570 **Romansch.** La Sacra Bibla stampada in lingua Rumanscha d'Ingadinna Bassa, 4 vols. in 1, stout folio, *with the Apocrypha, in poor condition, original binding, very rare*, £5. *Scuol, (Schuls) Jacob Dorta*, 1679
7570*   **Sanscrit.** RIG VEDA, ou livre des Hymnes, traduit du Sanscrit, par Langlois, 4 vols. large 8vo. *uncut*, 30*s* *Paris*, 1848-51
7571 **Sanscrit and Tibetan.** BURNOUF, Introduction à l'Histoire du Bouddhisme Indien, Vol. I, roy. 4to. (*all published.*) *sd.* £2. *Paris*, 1844
7572 **Scandinavian.** Wolff, Runakefli, le Runic Rim-Stok, ou Calendrier Runique, avec le Thryms-Quida ou le Rapt du Marteau de Thor, *Islandais*, 8vo. *plates of Runic inscriptions, hf. calf, gilt top, uncut*, 7*s* 6*d* *Paris*, 1820
7573 **SCIENCE AND NATURAL HISTORY.** LACROIX (S. F.) Traité du Calcul Différentiel et du Calcul Intégral, 3 vols. 4to. *seconde* (*la dernière*) *édition, plates, hf. calf*, £2. 12*s* *Paris*, 1810-19
7573*——— the same, 3 vols. 4to. *calf neat*, £3. 5*s* 1810-19

7574 LAPLACE, Œuvres, édition publiée par le Gouvernement, 7 vols. 4to. *cloth, uncut,* RARE, £6. 6s *Paris, Impr. Royale,* 1843-47
Priced, 1858, Asher in Berlin, 160 francs.
Contents: Vols. I—V, Traité de Mecanique Celeste; Vol. VI, Exposition du Systeme du Monde; Vol. VII, Théorie des Probabilités.

7575 MONTUCLA (J. F.) Histoire des Mathématiques, depuis leur origine jusqu'à nos jours; tableau et développement des découvertes, vies et contestations des Mathématiciens, etc. 4 vols. 4to. *portrait and plates, calf neat,* £4. 4s
The best and only complete History of the Mathematical Sciences. *Paris,* 1799-1802

7576 OLIVIER, Entomologie, ou Histoire Naturelle des Insectes, (COLÉ-OPTÈRES), 6 *vols.* roy. 4to. 363 *plates,* FINELY COLOURED, *fine tall copy, bds. uncut, with the plates bound separately in 4 vols. green* MOROCCO *extra, gilt edges,* £9. *Paris,* 1789-1800
7577 ——— the same, 6 vols. stout 4to. *hf. bd.* £10. 1789-1800
7578 ——— the same, 6 vols. in 8, large 4to. *or fine tall copy in half morocco neat,* £10. 10s 1789-1800
The best and most complete work upon Beetles which has yet appeared.

7579 TREMBLEY, Mémoires pour servir a l'Histoire des Polypes d'Eau douce, avec l'Essai de Baker sur les Polypes, 3 vols. 12mo. *plates, old cf. gilt,* 10s *Par.* 1744

GERMAN LITERATURE.

7580 **German Language.** ADELUNG'S Great German Dictionary: Grammatisch-kritisches Wörterbuch der Hoch-deutschen Mundart, mit Vergleichung der übrigen Mundarten, 4 stout vols. 4to. *hf. bd.* 18s *Leipzig,* 1793-1801

7581 CAMPE'S Wörterbuch der deutschen Sprache, 5 vols. 1807-11—Wörterbuch der aufgedrungenen fremden Ausdrücke, 1813—together 6 vols. large 4to. *hf. bd.* 12s *Braunschweig,* 1807-13

7582 EBERHARD'S deutsche Synonymik in einem Wörterbuche, von Maas, 4 vols. 8vo. *calf gilt,* 9s *Halle,* 1819-20

7583 EBERHARD und MAASS, teutsche Synonymik, *dritte Ausgabe* von Gruber, 6 vols. 8vo. *hf. bd.* 7s 6d *Halle,* 1826-30

7584 FLÜGEL'S German-English and English-German Dictionary, 2 stout vols. 8vo. *about* 3000 *pp. double cols. hf. russia,* 24s *Leipzig,* 1847

7585 FRISCH'S Teutsch-Lateinisches Wörterbuch, 2 vols. 4to. *portrait, calf, Mr. Singer's copy,* 16s *Berlin,* 1741
A most excellent Dictionary often quoted by Grimm.

7586 GRIMM (Jacob) Deutsche Grammatik, zweite Ausgabe, 4 vols. stout 8vo. *half calf,* £2. 10s *Göttingen,* 1822-37
7587 ——— Geschichte der Deutschen Sprache, 2 vols. 8vo. *cloth,* 20s *Leipzig,* 1848

7588 HEINSIUS, Wörterbuch der Deutschen Sprache, 4 vols. in 5, very stout 8vo. *calf gilt,* 14s *Hannover,* 1818-22

7589 HEYSE, Handwörterbuch der Deutschen Sprache, 6 vols. 8vo. *calf gilt,* 24s *Magdeburg,* 1833-49
A valuable German Etymological Dictionary, with all the High and Low German Synonyms, Provincialisms, Derivations from the Dutch, Old German, Scandinavian, Latin, and Greek Languages, etc.

7590 HILPERT'S German-English and English-German Dictionary, with preface by Kaercher, 4 vols. in 2, 4to. *half morocco,* 36s 1846
7591 ——— the same, the German-English part only, 2 vols. in 1, stout 4to. 1688 *pp. treble columns, calf,* 20s *Karlsruhe,* 1846

7592 ——— German Dictionary, in two parts, English-German and German-English, 2 parts in 1, very stout volume, 8vo. (pub. *sd.* at 18s) 1097 *pp. double cols., half calf,* 12s 1851

7593 KALTSCHMIDT'S Sprachvergleichendes Wörterbuch der deutschen Sprache, stout 8vo. *a very valuable work, calf gilt,* 9s *Leipzig,* 1839

7594 KLAUER KLATTOWSKY'S German Manual for Self-tuition, 2 vols. 12mo. *thick paper, cloth,* 7s 1845

7595 MOZIN, Dictionnaire Allemand-Français et Français-Allemand, 4 vols. in 3, large 4to. *vellum,* 12s *Stuttgart,* 1823-28

7596 SELECTION from the German Prose Writers, with double translation, on the *Hamiltonian* system, 8vo. *cloth,* 5s 1828

7597 ALEMAN, Der Landstörtzer Gusman von Alfarache, Teutsch durch Albertum, 12mo. *vellum, first German translation*, 5s   *München*, 1615
7598 AMALIE (Prinzessin von Sachsen) Original Beiträge zur Deutschen Schaubühne, 6 Bände ; Neue Folge, Band I ; 7 vols. 12mo. *calf extra*, 24s   1836-44
7599 ARNIM (Ludwig Achim von) SÄMMTLICHE WERKE, herausgegeben von W. Grimm, 19 vols. in 17, 8vo. *portrait, hf. calf, full gilt backs*, £2.   *Berlin*, 1839-46
7600 ARNIM und BRENTANO, des Knaben Wunderhorn, alte deutsche Lieder, 3 vols. 8vo. *sd.* 15s   *Heidelberg*, 1806
7601 ——— zweite Auflage, 3 vols. 8vo. *calf gilt*, 22s   *ib.* 1808-19
7602 ——— neue Ausgabe, 3 vols. 8vo. *hf. bd.* 16s   *Berlin*, 1846
7603 BAEHR'S Geschichte der Römischen Literatur, (bis zum Karolingischen Zeitalter), 3 vols. 8vo. *calf extra, Dr. Hawtrey's copy*, 18s   *Carlsruhe*, 1832-40
7604 BARTHOLDY's Krieg der Tyroler Landleute, 1809, sm. 8vo. *fine paper, music, red morocco, gilt edges*, 6s   *Berlin*, 1814
7605 BALLADENBUCH (Deutsches) mit Holzschnitten von Ehrhardt, Oer, Plüddemann, Richter, und Schurig, roy. 8vo. *a profusion of fine woodcuts, cloth extra*, 6s 1861
7606 BECKER'S (K. F.) Weltgeschichte, herausg. von Loebell, mit Fortsetzungen von Woltmann und Menzel, 14 vols. in 5, stout 8vo. *seventh edition*, (pub. at £2. 16s sd.) *hf. calf*, 32s   *Berlin*, 1844
   An Universal History of great popularity in Germany.
7607 BECKER (W. A.) Gallus, 2 vols.—Charikles, 2 vols.—4 vols. in 2, 8vo. *plates, hf. bd.* 7s   *Leipz.* 1838-40
7608 BÖRNE'S Gesammelte Schriften ; Dramaturgische Blätter, Erzählungen, Reisen, Schilderungen und Briefe aus Paris, Gebiete der Länder und Völkerkunde, etc. 11 vols. ; Nachgelassene Schriften, 4 vols. ; Börne's Leben von Gutzkow ; together 16 vols. 12mo. *original editions, portrait and facsimile, hf. calf*, 32s   *Hamburg, Mannheim*, 1829-47
7609 ——— Gesammelte Schriften, 4 vols. 12mo. *sd.* 10s   *Hamburg*, 1862
7610 BÖTTIGER's Amalthea oder Museum der Kunstmythologie und bildlichen Alterthumskunde, 3 vols. 8vo. 18 *plates of Ancient Art, hf. morocco. Dr. Hawtrey's copy*, 14s   *Leipzig*, 1820-25
7611 BOUTERWEK (F.) Geschichte der Poesie und Beredsamkeit, seit dem Ende des XIII Jahrhunderts (History of Italian, Spanish, Portuguese, German, English, and Dutch Literature), 12 vols. 8vo. *hf. calf gilt*, 24s *Götting.* 1801-19
   Priced, 1847, £3. 10s and £4. ; Asher in Berlin, 45 fr. ; Brockett's copy fetched £2. 9s.
7612 BRENTANO, Der Goldfaden, 12mo. *curious woodcuts, calf*, 5s   *Heid.* 1809
7613 BUCH der LIEBE, von Büsching und Hagen, Vol. I. 8vo. containing "Tristan und Isalde, Fierabras," etc. *hf. bd.* 5s   *Berlin*, 1809
7614 BÜRGER's sämmtliche Werke, herausg. von Reinhard, mit Leben von Döring, 8 vols. 12mo. *calf gilt*, 12s   *Berlin*, 1823-26
7615 BYRON'S sämmtliche Werke, von Böttger, 12 vols. in 6, 12mo. *portrait and plates, cloth*, 10s   1841
7616 CHAMISSO'S Werke, mit Leben durch Hitzig, 6 vols. 16mo. *portrait, calf gilt*, 12s   *Leipzig*, 1842
7617 ——— Gedichte, 18mo. *morocco*, 5s   *Leipzig*, 1852
7618 CONVERSATIONS-LEXICON : Allgemeine Deutsche Real-Encyclopaedie für die gebildeten Stände, 15 vols. 8vo. NINTH EDITION, *hf. bd.* 30s *Leip.* 1843-48
7619 DRUMANN'S GESCHICHTE ROMS in seinem Uebergange von der republikanischen zur monarchischen Verfassung, 6 vols. 8vo. *hf. russia, or hf. calf gilt*, 30s 1834-44
7620 FICHTE'S Werke : Kritik aller Offenbarung, 1793—Bestimmung des Gelehrten, 1794—System der Sittenlehre, 1793—Der geschlossne Handelstaat, 1800—Grundlage der Wissenschaftslehre, 1802—Reden an die deutsche Nation, 1808—Bestimmung des Menschen, 1825—Leben und Briefwechsel, 1830—8 vols. 8vo. and 12mo. *bds.* 15s   1798-1830
7621 FLEMMING's (Paul) Geist- und Weltliche Poemata, 18mo. *front. bds.* 5s *Jena*, 1660
7622 FREILIGRATH'S sämmtliche Werke, 6 vols. in 3, stout 12mo. *bright calf gilt*, 14s   *New York*, 1858
7623 ——— Gedichte, 18mo. *morocco, gilt edges*, 5s   *Stuttg.* 1852
7624 GERVINUS, GESCHICHTE DER POETISCHEN NATIONAL LITERATUR der Deutschen von der ersten Spuren der deutschen Dichtung bis zur Zeit der Befreiungskriege, 5 vols. in 3, 8vo. (pub. at £2. 16s) *hf. calf*, 16s   *Leipz.* 1840-2
7625 ——— the same, 5 vols. 8vo. *cloth*, 24s   1840-44

7626 GESCHICHTE der Künste und Wissenschaften seit der Wiederherstellung derselben bis an das Ende des XVIIIen Jahrh. A COMPLETE SET, *bound in 44 vols. 8vo. (pub. at £26. 8s 6d) hf. calf, contents lettered*, £3. 10s 1796-1808

Contents: Cultur und Literatur des neueren Europa von Eichorn, 2 vols.; Zeichnende Künste von Fiorillo, 5 vols.; Poesie und Beredsamkeit von Bouterwek, 9 vols.; Studium der classischen Literatur von Heeren, 2 vols.; Historische Forschung und Kunst, von Wachler, 2 vols.; Neuere Philosophie von Buhle, 6 vols.; Mathematik, von Kastner, 4 vols.; Kriegskunst, von Hoyer, 2 vols.: Physik von Fischer, 8 vols. *plates;* Chemie von Gmelin, 3 vols.; Technologie, von Poppe, 3 vols.; Christliche Moral von Stäudlin, 1 vol.; Praktische Theologie, von Ammon, Vol. I.; Schrifterklärung, von Meyer, 5 vols.

7627 GOETHE'S sämmtliche Werke, vollständige, neugeordnete Ausgabe, 40 vols. in 20, sq. 16mo. *hf. calf, full gilt back*, £3. 15s *Stuttgart*, 1840

7628 ——— sämmtliche Werke, vollständige neugeordnete Ausgabe, 30 vols. in 19, stout 8vo. *plates*, BEST LIBRARY EDITION, *hf. calf*, £4. 10s *Stuttg.* 1850-51

7629 ——— the same, 30 vols. in 18, stout 8vo. *a handsome copy in hf. morocco, contents lettered*, £6. 15s 1850-51

7630 ——— Gedichte, erläutert von Viehoff, 3 vols. 12mo. *hf. calf*, 8s *Düsseld.* 1846-53

7631 ——— Gedichte, 2 vols. in 1, 18mo. *morocco extra*, 6s *Stuttg.* 1851

7632 ——— Briefwechsel mit einem Kinde, 2 vols. 12mo. *2 plates, hf. cf.* 7s *Berl.* 1835

"Goethe is held, by the unanimous voice of Europe, to have been one of the greatest poets of our own, or of any other time."—*Whewell.*

"Goethe, simple yet profound, united the depth of philosophical thought to the simplicity of childish affection, and striking with almost inspired felicity the chord of native affliction, produced that mingled flood of poetic meditation and individual observation, which has rendered his name unbounded in the Fatherland."—*Alison.*

7633 GRIMM (Jacob) Deutsche Rechts-Alterthümer, 2 vols. 8vo. *sd.* 10s *Göttin.* 1828

7634 ——— Deutsche Mythologie, zweite Ausgabe, 2 vols. 8vo. *bds.* 14s *Göttin.* 1844

7635 GRIMM (die Brüder) Deutsche Sagen, 2 vols. 8vo. *bds.* 16s *Berlin*, 1816-18

7636 ——— Irische Elfenmärchen, 12mo. *calf gilt*, 7s *Leipzig*, 1826

7637 Gundling, Gundlingiana über Jurisprudentz, Philosophie, Historie, Critic, Litteratur, etc. in 5 vols. 12mo. *portrait, cloth*, 5s *Halle*, 1715-32

7638 Hans Sachs Trauerspiele, Schauspiele, Fabeln, etc. von Büsching, 2 vols. 8vo. *hf. bd.* 7s *Nürnb.* 1816-19

7639 HEINE, Buch der Lieder, 1839—Neue Gedichte, 1844—Romanzero, 1851— 3 vols. 12mo. 8s *Hamb.* 1839-51

7639*HELDENBUCH (Das) welchs auffs new corrigiert und gebessert ist, mit schönen Figuren geziert, sm. folio, *title printed in black and red, with large woodcut, and numerous woodcuts through the text*, BEAUTIFUL LARGE COPY *in dark olive morocco extra, antique style, gilt edges, by Bedford*, £10. 10s
Frankfurdt, Han und Feierabendt, 1560

Collation: Title, 1 leaf; An den Leser, 3 pp.; Erster Theil, leaves 1-73, with 73 woodcuts; blank leaf; Ander Theil, leaves, 75-141, with 70 woodcuts; blank leaf; Dritt Theil, leaves 143-167, with 28 woodcuts; blank leaf; Vierdter Theil, leaves 169-184, 13 woodcuts; Geschlecht der Helden, leaves 184-187, one woodcut; blank leaf. The woodcuts in all number 185, and the text is printed in double columns.

7640 HERDER (J. G. von) Sämmtliche Werke: zur Religion und Theologie, 18 vols. in 9—zur Philosophie und Geschichte, 22 vols. in 11—zur schönen Literatur und Kunst, 20 vols. in 10—together 60 in 30, 16mo. *uniformly hf. bd. contents lettered*, £2. 10s *Stuttgart*, 1827

7641 ——— Ideen zur Philosophie der Geschichte der Menschheit, 4 vols. sq. 8vo. *calf*, 6s *Riga*, 1784-91

7642 Hippel's (J. G. von) Sammtliche Werke, 12 vols.—Hippel's Leben und Briefe, 2 vols.—14 vols. in 6, 12mo. *portrait and plates, hf. calf*, 14s *Berlin*, 1827-35

7643 HISTORISCHES TASCHENBUCH, mit Beiträgen von Passow, Raumer, Voigt, Wachler, Wilken, herausgegeben von Raumer: Series I, 10 vols.; Series II, 10 vols.; Series III, 9 vols; Series IV, 2 vols.—together 31 vols. 12mo. *portraits, the last two sewed, the rest in hf. calf*, £2. 4s *Leipzig*, 1830-60

7644 HOFFMANN'S sämmtliche Werke, stout impl. 8vo. *portrait*, 1157 *pp. double columns, hf. blue morocco extra, gilt top, uncut*, 18s *Paris, Baudry*, 1841

7645 ——— gesammelte Schriften, 12 vols. 12mo. *numerous pretty woodcuts, hf. calf gilt*, 25s *Berlin*, 1844-45

7646 Houwald's gesammelte Schriften, 10 vols. in 5, 16mo. *hf. cf. gt.* 8s *Wien*, 1826-27

7647 Jacobi's Werke, von Roth, 6 vols. in 8, 8vo. *cloth*, 12s *Leipzig*, 1812-25

7648 JEAN PAUL'S sämmtliche Werke, Vols. 1-55, 8vo. *bds.* 28s *Berlin*, 1826-28

7648* ——— the same, 60 vols. sm. 8vo. *uncut*, £2. 2s 1826-28

7649 ——— sämmtliche Werke, 33 vols. in 16, 12mo. *portrait, hf. calf gilt*, £4.
Berlin, 1810-42

A very nice and desirable library copy.

7650 JEAN PAUL's sämmtliche Werke, 4 vols. roy. 8vo. *fine portrait, hf. calf gilt*, £2.
Paris, 1843
7651 ────── ausgewählte Werke, 16 vols. sm. 8vo. *sd. uncut*, 25*s*   *Berlin*, 1847-49
"One of the chosen men of Germany, colossal spirit, lofty original thinker, genuine poet, keen, impetuous, far-grasping, extorter of hidden and refractory truth."—*Carlyle.*
7652 JÖRDEN'S Lexikon Deutscher Dichter und Prosaisten, mit Supplement bande, 6 vols. 8vo. *cloth*, 15*s*   *Leipz.* 1806
7653 KINKEL's Gedichte, 18mo. *morocco, gilt edges*, 5*s*   *Stuttg.* 1852
7654 KNEBEL's Literarischer Nachlass und Briefwechsel, herausg. von Varnhagen von Ense und Mundt, 3 vols. in 1, 8vo. *portraits, hf. calf gilt*, 5*s*   *Leipz.* 1840
7655 KOTZEBUE'S (A. von) THEATER, 40 vols. 12mo. (pub. at £3. *sd.*) *hf. calf gilt, a pretty set*, £2. 12*s*   *Wien*, 1840-41
7656 KUGLER's Geschichte Friedrichs des Grossen gezeichnet von Menzel, impl. 8vo. *several hundred spirited woodcuts, hf. morocco*, 7*s* 6*d*   *Leip.* 1850
7657 LEO, Geschichte der Europäischen Staaten, herausgegeben von Heeren und Ukert, 5 vols. 8vo. *fine copy in calf gilt*, 30*s*   *Hamburg*, 1829-32
7658 LE SAGE, Geschichte des Gil Blas, 4 vols. in 2, 12mo. *etchings, calf*, 5*s*   1768
7659 LESSING'S SÄMMTLICHE WERKE, 30 vols. 12mo. (pub. at about £2. 10*s*) *hf. bd.* 21*s*   *Carlsruhe*, 1823-25
7660 ────── sämmtliche Schriften, 32 vols. in 16, 12mo. *hf. calf*, 32*s*   *Berlin*, 1825-28
7661 ────── sämmtliche Schriften, von Lachmann, mit dem Supplement-Bande, 13 vols. 8vo. *best library edition, portrait, hf. calf gilt*, £2. 2*s*   *Berlin*, 1838-40
7662 LICHTENBERG's vermischte Schriften, 9 vols. in 3, stout 12mo. *portrait and woodcuts, hf. calf gilt*, 10*s*   *Wien*, 1844
7663 LIEDER-LEXIKON, alphabet. Sammlung aller Deutschen Lieder, 4 vols. in 2, 12mo. *hf. calf*, 6*s*   *Leipz.* 1847
7664 MANNERT (K.) Geographie der Griechen und Römer, aus ihren Schriften dargestellt, 10 vols. in 14, 8vo. *an excellent standard work, maps*, (pub. at £5. 16*s*) *hf. calf*, 30*s*   *Nürnberg*, 1788-1825
7665 MARBACH, Volksbücher: Popular German Stories, illustrative of Mediaeval Legends and Romances, 5 vols. 12mo. *numerous woodcuts, some of these vols. out of print, hf. calf*, 15*s*   *Leipz.* 1838
7666 MATTHISSON, Schriften, 9 vols. 12mo. *vellum paper, calf gilt*, 18*s*   *Zürich*, 1825-33
7667 MENZEL's Geschichte der Deutschen, 3 vols. roy. 8vo. *portrait, hf. calf*, 9*s*   1843
7668 MÜLLER'S (Johann von) sämmtliche WERKE, herausg. von J. G. Müller, 40 vols. in 20, 16mo. *cloth*, 30*s*   *Stuttgart*, 1831-35
7669 ────── Allgemeine Geschichte der Europäischen Menschheit, 3 vols. 12mo. *hf. calf*, 7*s*   *Tübing.* 1817
7670 ────── Geschichten Schweizerischer Eidgenossenschaft, fortgesetzt von Hottinger, 7 vols. in 8, 8vo. *hf. calf*, 14*s*   *Leipzig und Zürich*, 1825-29
7671 NIBELUNGEN Noth, die Bearbeitung des Textes von Pfizer, 4to. *with fine woodcuts after Schnorr and Neureuther, hf. morocco*, 21*s*   *Stuttgart*, 1843
7672 OPITII Deutsche Poemata, 2 vols. in 1, stout 12mo. *frontispiece, early German Poems, vellum*, 7*s*   *Bresslaw*, 1629
7673 PIERER'S Universal Lexikon oder encyclopädisches Wörterbuch der Wissenschaften, Künste und Gewerbe, 34 vols. in 17, large 8vo. with oblong sm. folio ATLAS, *hf. bd.* £3. 16*s*   *Altenb.* 1840-46
7674 RANKE'S (Leopold) die römischen Päpste, ihre Kirche und ihre Staat im 16ten und 17ten Jahrhundert, 3 vols. 8vo. *hf. calf*, 16*s*   *Berlin*, 1838-36
7675 ────── Deutsche Geschichte im Zeitalter der Reformation, 3 vols. 8vo. *hf. calf*, 10*s*   1839-40
7676 ────── Preussische Geschichte, 3 vols. sm. 8vo. *hf. morocco*, 14*s*   1848
7677 RAUMER'S Geschichte der Hohenstaufen und ihrer Zeit, 6 vols. 8vo. *map, plans, and plate, neatly bound*, 18*s*   *Leip.* 1823-25
7678 ────── the same, 6 vols. 8vo. *hf. bd.* 22*s*   *Leip.* 1840-42
7679 RAUPACH's dramatische Werke, ernster Gattung, 8 vols. in 4, 12mo. *calf gilt*, 16*s*   *Hamburg*, 1835-37
7680 RITTER'S Erdkunde im Verhältniss zur Natur und zur Geschichte des Menschen, oder allgemeine vergleichende Geographie Vols. I.-XIX.—Ideler's Namen- und Sach-Verzeichniss zu Band II.-XI, 2 vols.; together 21 vols. in 22, 8vo. (pub. at about *Twenty Guineas*) 18 *vols. calf extra, and* 4 *sewed, with royal folio atlas of Palestine and Sinai only, in* 15 *maps, sd.* £12.   *Berlin*, 1822-59

7681 Röder von Diersburg, des Markgrafen Ludwig Wilhelm von Baden Feldzüge wider die Türken, (1683-92) 2 vols. 8vo. *portrait and plans, morocco, gilt edges,* 10s *Carlsruhe,* 1839-42

7682 ROTTECK'S allgemeine Geschichte, 9 vols. 8vo. *plates, bds. 7s 6d Frei.* 1824-26

7683 ROTTECK und WELCKER, Staats-Lexicon oder Encyclopädie der Staatswissenschaften, neue durchaus verbesserte und vermehrte Auflage, 12 vols. large 8vo. *a handsome copy, in bright calf gilt,* £4. 10s *Altona,* 1845-48

A learned Encyclopaedia of Political Economy, Diplomacy, Public Law, History, Government Administration, etc.

7684 Rückert, Gedichte, 12mo. *portrait, calf extra,* 5s *Frankf.* 1846

7685 SAVIGNY'S Geschichte des Römischen Rechts im Mittelalter, 7 vols. 8vo. 28s *Heidelburg,* 1834-51

"His researches have thrown a new light upon the origin of the laws and government, prevailing in modern Europe."—*Palgrave's Commonwealth, pref.* 6.

7686 SCHELLING'S Werke, Abtheil. I, 1, 2; 4 vols. 8vo. *bds.* 10s 1856-57

7687 —— Opera Varia Philosophica: 12 vols. 8vo. *various bindings, rare,* 20s 1799-1832

Contents of this Collection:

Einleitung zu seinem Systems der Naturphilosophie, *hf. calf* 1799	Kritisches Journal der Philosophie, 2 vols. in 1, *hf. calf* 1802
Erster Entwurf eines Systems der Naturphilosophie, *bds.* 1799	Philosophie der Natur, 2 vols. in 1, *bds.* 1808
	Von der Weltseele, *bds.* 1809
Zeitschrift für spekulative Physik, 2 vols. in 1, *hf. calf* 1800	Philosophische Schriften, Vol. I. *hf. calf* 1809
	Zeitschrift von Deutschen, 2 parts, *bds.* 1813
Transscendental Idealismus, *bds.* 1800	Ueber Faraday's neueste Entdeckung, *bds.* 1832

7688 SCHILLER'S sämmtliche Werke, 12 vols. sm. 8vo. *portrait and fine plates, a nice edition, hf. calf gilt,* £2. *Stuttgart,* 1835-36

7689 —— Werke, 12 vols. in 6, 12mo. *portrait, sd.* 12s; or 12 vols. *cloth bds.* 18s *Stuttgart,* 1838

7690 —— Gedichte, 2 vols. in 1, 18mo. *portrait and frontispiece, mor.* 7s *Stuttg.* 1838

"Schiller, uniting the ardour of a soldier to the soul of a statesman and the hand of an historian, has pourtrayed the shades of former times with dramatic power, and in a noble spirit."—*Alison.*

7691 Schildtberger, ein wunderbarliche und kurzweilige History, sq. 12mo. *a popular Chap-book, with many quaint woodcuts of Eastern adventures, title mended, bds.* 10s *Franckfurdt, Weygandt Han,* ? 1560

7692 SCHLEGEL'S (Fr.) sämmtliche Werke, 10 vols. in 5, sm. 8vo. *calf neat,* 21s *Wien,* 1822-3

7693 —— the same, *Fine Paper,* 10 vols. in 5, 8vo. *hf. calf,* 25s 1822-3

7694 SCHMIDT (M. J.) Geschichte der Deutschen, (bis 1584) 5 vols. *portrait,* 1785-87—Neuere Geschichte der Deutschen bis 1806 und algemeines Register, 17 vols. in 9, 1785-1808—together 22 vols. in 14, *hf. cf. neat,* 22s *Ulm,* 1785-1808

7695 Schubert's Geschichte des Lebens, 3 vols. 8vo. *calf,* 5s *Leip.* 1806-21

7696 Seume's sämmtliche Werke, von Wagner, impl. 8vo. *portrait, calf,* 5s 1835

7697 SHAKSPEARE'S Dramatische Werke, übersetzt von Schlegel, ergänzt von Tieck, 9 vols. sm. 8vo. *in calf gilt,* 35s *Berlin,* 1825-33

7698 —— the same, third edition, 12 vols. in 6, *hf. calf gilt,* 21s *Berlin,* 1843-44

The names of Schlegel and Tieck are sufficient warrant for the excellence and spirit of this translation, by which that of Eschenburg, and others are completely superseded.

7699 Shakspeare's dramatische Werke, übersetzt von Ortlepp, 16 vols. in 8, 16mo. *portrait and plates, bds.* 9s *Stuttgart,* 1842

7700 Simrock's Handbuch der Deutschen Mythologie, 8vo. *hf. calf,* 6s *Bonn,* 1855

7701 Tausend und Eine Nacht, Arabische Erzählungen, deutsch von Habicht, Von der Hagen und Schall, 15 vols. in 7, 12mo. *frontispieces, bds.* 10s *Breslau,* 1840

7702 TIECK'S sämmtliche Werke, 2 vols. roy. 8vo. *compact double column edition, portrait, hf. calf,* 16s *Par.* 1837

7703 —— Phantasus, eine Sammlung von Mährchen, Erzählungen und Schauspielen, 3 vols. 12mo. *half calf,* 7s *Berlin,* 1812-16

7704 Ulrici's Geschichte der Hellenischen Dichtkunst, 2 vols. 8vo. *hf. bd.* 6s 1835

7705 Van der Velde's sämmtliche Schriften, 8 vols. in 4, 12mo. *hf. cf.* 6s *Stuttg.* 1828

7706 WACKERNAGEL'S Deutches Lesebuch, Prosa und Poesie, 3 vols. stout 8vo. *hf. blue morocco,* 35s *Basel,* 1847

Vol. I. contains Old German Poems and a Glossary; II. and III., Poetry and Prose since 1500.

7707 Weber's Sagen der Vorzeit, 7 vols. 12mo. *vignettes, hf. bd.* 5s 1790-8

GERMAN LITERATURE.

7708 WELCKER'S Geschichte des Tempelherrenordens, 2 vols. in 1, stout sm. 8vo. *morocco extra, gilt edges, 7s 6d* *Leipz.* 1826-27

7709 WIELAND'S SÄMMTLICHE WERKE, 45 vols. 12mo. *fine paper, hf. calf, £2.*
Leipzig, 1794

" Wieland charmed every imagination by the brightness of his fancy, the richness of his language, and the sparkling freshness which he has thrown over all the subjects which his pencil touched."—*Alison.*
" Wieland, the prince of the German poets,"—*Hufeland.*

7710 WOLFF'S Poetischer Hausschatz des deutschen Volkes, mit Einleitung, etc. 8vo. 1170 *pp. double cols. calf extra,* 8s   1832

7711 ZEDLITZ, Gedichte, 18mo. *morocco, gilt edges,* 5s   *Stuttg.* 1844

7712 ZSCHOKKE'S ausgewählte Dichtungen, Erzählungen und Novellen, zweite verbesserte Ausgabe, 10 vols. 12mo. *hf. calf,* 12s   *Aarau,* 1830

7713 —— dritte vollständige Original-Ausgabe, 8 vols. *hf. calf gilt,* 21s   1836

7714 —— ausgewählte Novellen und Dichtungen, siebente Original-Auflage, 10 vols. 12mo. *a very pretty set, calf extra, gilt edges,* £2.   *Aarau,* 1845

7715 **PHILOLOGICAL AND HISTORICAL WORKS.** CURTIUS, Grundzüge der Griechischen Etymologie, 2 vols. large 8vo. *a valuable work of Comparative Philology, hf. calf, gilt tops, uncut,* 14s   *Leipzig,* 1858-62

7716 GRAFF, ALTHOCHDEUTSCHER SPRACHSCHATZ, oder Wörterbuch der althochdeutschen Sprache (Dictionary of the Old German Language, with references to the Greek and Latin, Oriental, Northern, and other Languages), 6 vols.— Massman's Vollständiger Index, 1 vol.—together 7 vols. 4to. *sd.* 36s; or *hf. bd.* £2. 2s   *Berl.* 1834-46

7717 KLAPROTH, ASIA POLYGLOTTA, 4to. 14 and 400 pp. *with the folio Atlas of Languages, comprising* 59 *Tables of Vocabularies, map, hf. calf, uncut,* 30s   *Paris,* 1823

7718 LASSEN (Chr.) INDISCHE ALTERTHUMSKUNDE, Vols. I-IV, 8vo. *maps* (pub. at 40 Thalers) *hf. russia neat, gilt tops, uncut,* £5. 10s   *Bonn and Leipzig,* 1847-61

"L'Archéologie de l'Inde par M. Lassen donne l'exemple le plus brillant de la maniere dont on peut reconstruire, avec ces matériaux épars, l'histoire d'un pays. La fin du quatrième volume de cet ouvrage, qui a paru l'an passé, contient surtout le tableau de la civilisation hindoue du IVe. au XIe. siecle; elle traite de l'histoire de la religion et des sectes brahminiques pendant cette époque, du bouddhisme, de son extinction dans la péninsule, et de ses conquêtes en dehors de l'Inde, de la secte des Djainas, de l'histoire de la langue et de l'écriture, de la poésie épique et du théâtre, de l'astronomie, de l'architecture et du commerce de l'Inde. Il serait superflu de vouloir caractériser un ouvrage dont l'excellence est aussi généralement reconnue."—MOHL, *Rap. Ann. du Journ. Asiat.* 1863.

7719 PARROT'S Sprache, Abstammung, Geschichte, und Mythologie der Liwen, Lätten, Eesten, 8vo. with folio Atlas of POLYGLOTT TABLES, *hf. calf gilt,* 14s   *Berlin,* 1839

7720 POTT'S Doppelung als ein wichtiges Bildungsmittel der Sprache, 8vo. *sd.* 5s   *Lemgo,* 1862

7721 ZEITSCHRIFT der DEUTSCHEN MORGENLÄNDISCHEN GESELLSCHAFT, Vols. I-VI. 8vo. *hf. calf gilt, uncut, gilt tops,* £2. 10s   *Leipzig,* 1847-52

7722 **Chinese.** ENDLICHER'S Anfangsgründe der Chinesischen Grammatik, 8vo. 24 and 376 pp. *the Chinese words in Chinese and Roman characters, cloth,* 9s   *Wien,* 1845

7723 **Ethiopic.** DILLMANN'S Grammatik der Aethiopischen Sprache, 8vo. *sd.* 10s   *Leipzig,* 1857

7724 **Gothic.** ULFILAS. Veteris et Novi Testamenti versionis Gothicæ Fragmenta quæ supersunt, *Goth. et Lat.* cum Glossario, et Grammatica, ed. Gabelentz et Loebe, 2 vols. in 3, 4to. *facsimiles, hf. russia,* 32s   *Lipsiæ,* 1843-46

7725 **Old Teutonic.** OTFRIDI EVANGELIORUM liber, veterum Germanorum Grammaticæ Poeseos, Theologiæ, praeclarum monumentum : Evangelien Buch, mit Gunst des Herrn Hermann Riedesel in truck verfertiget, 12mo. *fine copy in old red morocco extra,* £4. 10s   *Basil,* 1571

"Liber inter rariores rarissimus nuncupatus."—*Vogt.* The third and fourth leaves of the " Prefatio," being signatures *a* 4 and *a* 5, are wanting. COLLATION: Title, Praefatio, Vorred, Dictionary, etc. being signatures a to ζ 4 in eights; prologus, text, etc. pp. 1-574.

7726 **Phenician.** MOVERS, DIE PHÖNIZIER : Band I, Untersuchungen über die Religion und die Gottheiten ; Band II, Theil I,II, III, pt. 1, das Phönizische Alterthum ; together, 4 vols. 8vo. *sd.* 21s   *Bonn u. Berlin,* 1841-56

7727 —— the same, 4 parts in 3 vols. 8vo. *hf. calf, and a part,* 25s   1841-56

7728 **Romance.** KELLER'S Romvart, Beiträge zur Kunde mittelalterlicher Dichtung, 8vo. 718 pp. *of extracts from early Romance MSS. in Italian libraries, hf. calf extra, gilt top, uncut,* 8s 6d   *Mannheim,* 1844

7729 **Sanscrit.** BOPP'S Ausführliches Lehrgebände der Sanskrita-Sprache, 4to. *bds.* 24*s* *Berlin*, 1827

7730 **SCIENCE AND NATURAL HISTORY.** ANNALEN DER CHEMIE und Pharmacie, herausgegeben von Wöhler und LIEBIG, Vols. LIII-LXXIV (wanting LIX-LX) in 10 vols. 8vo. *hf. calf gilt*, £2. *Heidelberg*, 1845-50

7731 ANNALEN DER PHYSIK und Chemie, herausgegeben von POGGENDORF, Band LXIV-LXXIX (der ganzen Folge CXL-CLV) mit Ergänzungsbande, 17 vols. 8vo. *plates, hf. calf gilt*, £3. *Leipzig*, 1845-50

7732 ENDLICHER (S.) Genera Plantarum, secundum ordines naturales disposita, cum tribus Supplementis et Indice, stout imp. 8vo. (pub. at £3. 16s 6d, sd.) *half calf*, £3. 3*s* *Vindobonæ*, 1836-43

7733 LINNAEA, ein Journal für Botanik in ihrem ganzen Umfange, herausgegeben von Schlechtendal, Vols. I-XXIX, from the beginning in 1826 to 1858, 29 vols. 8vo. *numerous plates (pub. at 174 Thalers) hf. calf*, £4. 10*s*
Vols. I-XXIII, priced, 1856, £8. 10*s*. *Berlin und Halle*, 1826-58

7734 FLORA, oder BOTANISCHE ZEITUNG der Regensburgischen Königl. Botanischen Gesellschaft, herausg. von Hoppe und Fürnrohr, *from the beginning in 1818 to June* 1841, with the Literaturberichte, 1831-39, 9 vols. in 3; together 41 vols. 12mo. *plates (pub. at 80 Thalers) hf. bd.* 25*s* *Regensburg*, 1818-41
In the series of the Flora, 38 vols., there are wanting 1823 pt. 1, 1834 pt. 2, 1837 pt. 1, 1838 pt. 1.

7735 STURM'S Deutschland's Fauna in Abbildungen nach der Natur mit Beschreibungen; KÄFER (*Coleoptera*), Vols. I-X, bound in 4 vols. 12mo. 227 *coloured plates (pub. at about 30 Thalers) hf. green morocco, gilt tops, uncut*, £2. 18*s* *Nürnberg*, 1805-36

7736 SCHNIZLEIN, Iconographia Familiarum naturalium Regni Vegetabilis, parts 1-15 (wanting No. 6) 4to. *text in Latin and German, with* 280 *plates partly* COLOURED *(pub. at* 28 *Thalers) unbd.* 36*s* *Bonn*, 1843-59

7737 SAINT-ANGE, Praktische Eisenhüttenkunde, oder systematische Beschreibung des Verfahrens bei der Roheisenerzeugung und der Stabeisenerfabrication, bearbeitet von Hartmann, zweite vermehrte Auflage, 3 vols. 4to. with atlas folio Atlas *containing* 78 *large plates of Machinery by Le Blanc, hf. calf*, £2. 16*s* *Weimar*, 1842-43

ITALIAN LITERATURE.

7738 **Italian Language.** ALBERTI, GRAND DICTIONNAIRE Français-Italien et Italien-Français, 2 vols. stout roy. 4to. *hf. calf*, 30*s* *Milan*, 1834-35

7739 —— the same, 2 vols. stout roy. 4to. *fine copy in calf gilt*, £3. *Milan*, 1840

7740 —— le même, nouvelle édition, augmentée par Ambrosoli et Sergent, 2 vols. 4to. *last and best edition, hf. morocco gilt*, £2. 16*s* *Milan*, 1842

7741 ALUNNO, Richezze della Lingua Volgare, folio, *fine copy in vellum, edges gilt and gauffré*, 6*s* *Vinegia, Aldus*, 1543

7742 BARETTI (G.) Dizionario Italiano ed Inglese, corretto ed ampliato, *Bologna*, 1830—Barretti, English-Italian Dictionary, augmented, *Florence*, 1832—2 vols. in 1, stout large 4to. 1347 *pp. treble columns, strongly bound in russia extra, gilt edges*, 36*s* 1830-32

7743 CARENA (G.) Prontuario di Vocaboli attenenti a parecchie Arti, ad alcuni Mestieri, a cose Domestiche, ecc. per Saggio di un Vocabolario Metodico Italiano, 3 vols. 8vo. *sd.* 15*s* *Torino*, 1851-60

7744 FERRARII (O.) Origines Linguæ Italicæ, folio, *a Dictionary, with the Etymologies, calf, very beautiful copy*, 18*s* *Patavii*, 1676

7745 FILIPPI, Dizionario Italiano-Tedesco e Tedesco-Italiano, 2 parts in 4 vols. stout 8vo. *nearly* 3000 *pp. double cols. hf. bd.* 12*s* *Vienna*, 1817

7746 FLORIO'S Worlde of Worldes; or a Dictionarie in Italian and English, sm. fol. *engraved title*, 25*s* *A. Hatfield*, 1598
Second edition, now scarce. Collation: Title; Dedication to the Reader, etc. 8 leaves; and pp. 1-462.

7747 —— Queen Anna's New World of Words, or Dictionarie of the Italian and English Tongues—Necessary Rules for the speedie learning of the Italian Tongue, 1611; 2 vols. in 1, folio, *fine portrait of the author, by Wm. Hole, original old calf*, 25*s* 1611
This Dictionary, 'for the variety of words, was far more copious than any extant in the world at that time.'
Ant. à Wood.

7748 GRAN DIZIONARIO della LINGUA ITALIANA, 7 vols. 4to. *sd.* 18*s*; or *hf. calf*, 27*s* *Bologna*, 1819-1828

7749 MILLHOUSE'S Italian-English and English-Italian Pronouncing and Explanatory Dictionary, 2 vols. post 8vo. 1254 *pp. double cols. sd.* 10s *Milan*, 1855-57
7750 ———— the same, 2 vols. 8vo. *hf. calf neat*, 15s   1855-57
7751 NAPIONE, dell' Uso e dei Pregi della Lingua Italiana, coi suoi Opuscoli, 2 vols. sm. 8vo. *vellum paper, cloth, gilt tops, uncut*, 9s   *Firenze*, 1813
"Opera degna di quell' ingegnoso Scrittore, il piu giusto conoscitore ed il più valoroso Apologista della nostra lingua."—*Tiraboschi.*
7752 TOSELLI, Dizionario Gallo-Italico, 2 vols. 8vo. *hf. bd.* 15s   1833
A valuable dictionary of Comparative Philology, by which the vocabulary of the Italian language is traced to Celtic roots, with illustrations from other tongues.
7753 UGOLINI, Vocabolario di Parole errate comunemente in uso, 12mo. *sd.* 4s 1861
7754 VOCABOLARIO DEGLI ACCADEMICI DELLA CRUSCA; cresciuto d'assai migliaja di voci, le più trovate da Veronesi; Sopraggiunta; Indice; Autori e Libri (citati); Vocabolario dell' Arte del Disegno: Voci e Maniere di Dire e Osservazioni (di Medicina e di Cirurgia), 7 vols. 4to. *hf. bd.* 32s   *Verona*, 1806-4
7755 ———— the same, 7 vols. 4to. *a fine copy in Italian vellum, gt. back,* £2. 5s 1806-4
An enlarged edition of the celebrated Vocabolario della Crusca; and, although not so handsome as the original in six folio volumes, is much superior to it for practical purposes.
7756 **Thieves' Slang.** TRATTATO dei Bianti over Pitocchi e Vagabondi, col modo d'imparare la Lingua Furbesca, 16mo. *hf morocco, gilt top, uncut,* 21s *Italia*, 1828
Only a limited number printed. Pp. 73-120 contain the *Modo da parlar Furbesco*, with Vocabularies, etc.

7757 ALAMANNI, OPERE TOSCANE, 16mo. *in morocco, gilt edges, the old richly ornamented sides, gilt in the Grolier style, having been preserved and carefully let in by C. Lewis,* 15s   *Lugd. Gryphius*, 1532
Gamba states this edition to be rare, and that both editions of 1532 were ordered to be burnt by Pope Clement VII.
7758 ALBERI. RELAZIONI degli AMBASCIATORI VENETI al Senato, raccolte, annotate, ed edite da E. Alberi, *the three series complete with Appendix,* in 15 vols. 8vo. *(pub. at about* 135 *francs sewed)* ten vols. *hf. calf gilt, the other five sewed,* £4.   *Firenze*, 1839-62
Series I: Relazioni degli Stati Europei tranne l'Italia, 6 vols.—Series II: Relazioni degli Stati Italiani, 5 vols. —Series III: Relazioni dell' Impero Ottomano, 3 vols.—Appendice, 1 vol. A very important collection for the political history of Europe in the sixteenth century.
7759 ALBERTI (L.) Descrittione di tutta L'ITALIA; Dito di essa, Costumi de Popoli, Condicioni de Paesi; huomini famosi che l'hanno illustrata, con tutte l'Opre maraiugliose della Natura, stout sm. folio, *fine portrait, autograph signature "Di Odoardo Biseto,"* BRUNCK'S COPY *in veau fauve, full gilt back,* 25s
Bologna, 1550
7760 ANDREA DA BERGAMO, SATIRE alla Carlona, primo e secondo libro, *Vinegia,* 1648-65—Quattro Dialogi di Garnero con alcune curiosità, *Geneva,* 1627—Sette dialogi e piacevoli ragionamenti utili a i desiderosi di questa lingua, 1645 — 4 vols. in 1 vol. stout 12mo. *fine copies in old red morocco extra, gilt edges,* £2.
1548-1645
Pages 179-227 of this second work contain Proverbs arranged alphabetically. The Satirist's true name was Pietro Nelli. "*Queste satire sono graziossime e molto rare.*"—*Haym*, ii. 122.
7761 ANDREA DA BERGAMO, Satire alla Carlona, 2 vols. in 1, 16mo. *calf extra, gilt edges by C. Lewis,* 12s   *Venegia,* 1566
7762 ANDRES (G.) dell' Origine, Progressi e Stato attuale di ogni Letteratura, 8 vols. in 9, 4to. *hf. vellum,* 20s   *Roma,* 1808-17
7763 ANGELONI (F.) Historia di TERNI, 4to. *frontispiece, portrait of the author, plan of Terni and portrait of Cardinal Mazarin, etched by J. A. Canini, fine copy in Italian vellum,* 12s   *Roma,* 1646
7764 ANTONINI, Archiepiscopi Florentiæ, CONFESSIONALE in vulgari sermone . . . Omnis mortalium cura, etc. . . . *In fine,* Finisse lo confessionale stampato a Venesia per Christophoro Arnoldo a laude et gloria de Iesu Christo omnipotente, MCCCCLXIII, sm. 4to. FINE TALL COPY *in vellum, almost* UNCUT, *with numerous untouched leaves,* £2. 16s   *Venesia,* 1473
VERY RARE. This edition is mentioned by no bibliographer; Brunet only speaks of one which might be taken for the above, but that is supposed to consist of 96 leaves, while the present edition contains 116.
7765 ARETINO (Pietro) La prima (e seconda) parte de RAGIONAMENTI—Commento di Ser Agresto da Ficarvolo sopra la Ficata del padre Siceo, con la Diceria de Nasi—3 vols. in 1, stout 16mo. *old red morocco extra, gilt edges,* RARE, £2. 16s
Bengodi ne la gia felice Italia, 1589
Fetched in 1857 at Sotheby's, *blue morocco,* £3. 3s.
COLLATION: Title, and prefatory matter, 5 leaves, pp. 1-198; title to part 2, and dedication. 3 leaves; pp. 1-330; Commento di Ser Agresto, pp. 1-118 including title and preface.

7766 ARETINO, Capricciosi e Piacevoli Ragionamenti, col Commento delle Fiche, 12mo. *old calf, rare*, 24s *Cosmopoli*, (*Amst. Elzevir*), 1660
" Edition la plus belle et la plus correcte."—*Brunet.*

7767 —— I Quattro Libri de Humanita di Christo, 16mo. *woodcut portrait on title, some pages a little water stained, original stamped calf, rare and curious*, 18s (*Venetia*), 1539

7768 —— Humanita di Christo, 1539—I Sette Salmi della Penitentia, 2 vols. in 1, 16mo. *woodcut portrait, calf gilt,* Arms *on sides*, 20s (*Venetia*), 1539

7770 —— Quattro Comedie, cioè il Marescalco, la CORTEGIANA, la Talanta, l'Hipocrito, 18mo. *woodcut portrait, calf gilt*, 6s 1588

7771 —— the same, 18mo. *old Italian calf, broad borders of gold, gilt edges, fine copy*, 25s 1588
Fetched at Nodier's sale, 58 francs.

7772 ARIOSTO, ORLANDO FURIOSO alla sua integrita ridotto, con alcune stanze del S. Aluigi Gonzaga in lode del medesimo, aggiuntevi per ciascun canto alcune allegorie, e col Espositione dei Vocaboli di Dolce, sm. 8vo. (12mo.) *numerous beautiful woodcuts, including two portraits, very choice copy in old red* MOROCCO *extra*, £5. 15s *Vinegia, Giolito*, 1546
A remarkably pretty and very rare edition. Priced, 1833, Payne and Foss, mor. £6. 6s.

7773 —— ORLANDO FURIOSO, tutto ricorretto et di nuove Figure adornato, con le Annotationi di Ruscelli, la Vita dell' Autore da Pigna, Vocabolario, etc. 4to. *printed in italic type, engraved title, 46 large woodcuts the size of the paper, and numerous woodcut initial letters, clean copy, old calf neat, full gilt back*, 20s *Venetia, Valgrisi*, 1556
Priced, 1840, Jas. Bohn, £1. 11s 6d. "Première edition de ce poëme donnee par les Valgrise, et la plus belle, qui soit sortie de leurs presses. Les gravures en bois dont elle est ornée ont été faites sur les dessins de Dosso Dossi peintre ferrarais."—*Brunet.*

7774 —— Orlando Furioso, con Annotationi da Ruscelli, Vita da Pigna, e li cinque Canti aggiuntovi, sm. 8vo. *numerous large woodcuts, calf*, 10s *Valgrisi*, 1566

7775 —— ORLANDO FURIOSO, novamente adornato di figure da Porro, colle Osservatione di Lavezuola, etc. 4to. *engraved title and plates, Italian calf binding, gilt edges*, 20s *Ven.* 1584
The plate to Canto 34 is a duplicate of the plate to Canto 33 as is always the case.

7776 —— ORLANDO FURIOSO, 4 vols. roy. 8vo. BASKERVILLE'S SPLENDID EDITION, edited by P. Molini, *portrait and numerous fine plates after Eisen, Cipriani and others, engraved by Bartolozzi, etc. a fine copy in red morocco, double bands, gilt edges, by Walther*, £4. 10s *Birm.* 1773
Priced, 1824, Thorpe, £6. 6s; 1830-2, Payne and Foss, £5. 5s; 1840, Jas. Bohn, £6. 16s 6d. Fetched in the Merly sale, £6.; Hibbert's, £5. 12s 6d; North's, £5. 7s 6d; 1856, Sotheby's, £7. 7s.

7777 —— Orlando Furioso, 4 vols. large 8vo. *portr. calf gilt*, 20s *Baskerville*, 1773

7778 —— l'Orlando Furioso, con annotazioni, 4 vols. large 8vo. THICK PAPER, *sd.* £2. *Firenze*, 1821

7779 —— Orlando Furioso, 12mo, *portrait, bd.* 5s *Lione*, 1842

7780 GUIDI, Annali delle Edizioni e delle Versioni dell' Orlando Furioso, 8vo. *port. sd.* 6s *Bologna*, 1861
"Ariosto has been, after Homer, the favourite poet of Europe. His grace and facility, his clear and rapid stream of language, his variety and beauty of invention, his very translations of subjects, so frequently censured by critics, but artfully devised to spare the tediousness that hangs on a protracted story, left him no rival in general popularity. Above sixty editions of the Orlando Furioso were published in the sixteenth century. There was not one, says Bernardo Tasso, of any age, or sex, or rank, who was satisfied with a single perusal."—*Hallam.*

7781 ARLOTTO (il Piovano, Prete Fiorentino) FACETIE, Piacevolece, Fabule, e Motti, 16mo. *small rude woodcuts, unmutilated edition, the foot margins of numerous leaves uncut, very fine copy in red morocco, super extra, gilt edges*, £4. 4s *Venetia, Bindoni*, 1549
VERY RARE. COLLATION: Title, with woodcut half the size of the page, Dedication to Pietro Salviati, Life of Arlotto, together 3 leaves; Motti, etc. to the end, 89 leaves, being A iv. to M iv. in eights.

7782 ASCETTI, la Cellidora overro il Governo Malmantile, sq. 8vo. *rus.* 5s *Firenze* 1734

7783 ATHENAGORA, *philosopho christiano*, Risurrettione de Morti, Natività di Christo, da Faleto, sm. 4to. iv. and 56 leaves, *vellum*, 8s *Venetia, Aldus*, 1556
Chardin's copy fetched 36 fr.

7784 AUTORI ITALIANI, cioè: ARIOSTO, 4 vols.—BOCCACCIO, 3 vols.—PULCI, 3 vols.—Carteromaco, 3 vols.—Tassoni, 1 vol.—Corsini, 2 vols.—Guarini, 1 vol.—Lippi, 1 vol.—MACCHIAVELLI, 8 vols.—Vocabulario, 1 vol.—in all 27 vols. 18mo. *portrait and frontispieces, uniform in calf gilt, a pretty set*, £2.
Parigi, M. Prault, 1768

7785 BALDASSINI (G.) Memorie Istoriche dell' antichissima Citta di Jesi, 4to. *hf. calf*, 7s 6d *Jesi*, 1765

ITALIAN LITERATURE. 431.

7786 BALDI (B.) Vita e fatti di Federigo, Duca d' URBINO, da Zuccardi, 3 vols. 8vo. *sd.*
10*s* *Roma*, 1824

7787 BANCO, Bizzarrie Politiche, over raccolta delle più notabili Prattiche di Stato, 16mo. *red morocco, gilt edges,* 10*s* *Franechera*, 1658
The most curious piece in this volume is the Squitinio della Libertà Veneta by the Marquis of Bedemar, whose plot against Venice is so famous.

7788 BANDELLO, Novelle, 4 vols in 3, 4to. LARGE PAPER, *fine copy in old calf, gilt backs,* SCARCE, £2. 2*s* *Lond. Harding*, 1740
Harding's reprint of the Lucca edition of 3 parts, 1554, and of the Lyons edition of the 4th part of 1573. Only a few copies were printed on Large Paper. Priced, 1830, Payne and Foss, russia, £5. 5*s*.

7789 BANDELLO, Novelle, la quarta parte, sm. 4to. *containing* 28 *Novels, portrait, calf,* 10*s* *Lione, Marsilii,* 1573, repr. *Londra*, 1740

7790 —— Novelle, con la sua vita da Mazzuchelli, 9 vols. sm. 8vo. *portrait, calf,* 25*s* *Londra*, 1791-3
" Edition entière et qui est plus correcte que la premiere el e-meme."—*Brunet*.
" In point of composition these Novels, although inferior to those of Boccaccio, are written with a degree of vivacity and nature which seldom fails to interest the reader; and which, combined with the singularity of the incidents, will probably secure a durable, although not a very honourable, reputation to the author."—*T. Roscoe*.

7791 BARGAGLI (Scip.) I Trattenimenti (Narrate, Novelle e Cantate amorose, Canzonette), 4to. *original and most correct edition, vel.* 20*s Venetia, Giunti,* 1587

7792 BARLAAM E GIOSAFATTE, Storia di, 8vo. *calf, gilt edges,* 5*s* *Roma*, 1816

7793 BAROTTI (G.) Memorie istoriche di LETTERATI FERRARESI, Vol. I. stout folio, LARGE AND THICK PAPER, *engraved title, fine portraits, vignettes, etc. vellum,* 25*s* Nicol's copy fetched £2. 12*s* 6*d*. *Ferrara*, 1777

7794 —— Letterati Ferraresi, 2da edizione, 2 vols. 4to. *plate, calf,* 20*s Fer.* 1792-93
7795 —— Continuazione, 4to. *sd.* 10*s* *ib.* 1811

7796 BASILE, il Conto de' Conti, trattenimento a' Giovani, 12mo. *rude woodcuts, hf. calf, scarce,* 15*s* *Napoli*, 1747

7797 —— il Conto de' Conti, trattenimento a' Fanciulli, trasportato dallo Napoletano, 12mo. *rude woodcuts, vellum,* 12*s* *Napoli*, 1769

7798 BELIANIS. HISTORIA del Magnanimo et invincibil Principe don BELIANIS, figliuolo dell' Imperator di Grecia, tradotta da Rinaldi, 2 vols. 16mo. *fine copy, hf. calf,* RARE, 18*s* *Ferrara,* 1586—*Verona,* (1587)

7799 BENTIVOGLIO (Cardinal) Opere Storiche: Relazioni; Guerra di Fiandra; Memorie, 5 vols. 8vo. *portrait, russia,* 6*s* *Milano,* 1806-7

7800 BENVENGA (Ab. M.) L'Arpa overo Poesie Liriche, sm. 8vo. *portrait of Pope Clement XI., old red morocco extra, gilt edges, richly ornamented, with the Papal Arms on sides,* 30*s* *Roma,* 1718
The Dedication copy of Pope Clement XI., and a fine specimen of his library.

7801 BERNI, CASA, Mauro, Varchi, Dolce et d'altri Auttori, RIME piacevoli, 3 vols. 18mo. *red morocco, gilt edges,* 10*s* *Venetia,* 1627
" Vendu, 31 fr. 50 c. Mac Carthy."—*Brunet*.

7802 BERNI, CASA, Varchi, Mauro, Bino, Molza, Dolce, Firenzuola, OPERE BURLESCHE, 3 vols. 12mo. *portrait, vellum,* 7*s* *Usecht,* 1760

7803 BERTOLDO, con Bertoldino e Cacasenno, roy. 4to. *fine spirited plates, vellum, Lord Rothesay's copy,* 8*s* *Bologna,* 1736
The best and handsomest edition of this famous Comic Poem, composed by various Wits of the day, such as the two Ranotti, Bruffaldi, Zampieri, Barotti, and others.

7804 BERTOLDO, Bertoldino e Cacasenno, 12mo. *curious plates, vellum,* 6*s* *Venez.* 1737

7805 BIANCOLINI, dei Vescovi e Governatori di VERONA, sm. 4to. 3 *large plates and plans, one coloured, vellum,* 6*s* *Verona,* 1757

7806 BIBBIA, cioè i Libri del Vecchio e del Nuovo Testamento, nuovamente traslatati da DIODATI, 3 vols. in 1, stout 4to. *vellum, gilt edges,* 21*s* 1607
FIRST and rare edition of Diodati's Bible; some one has inserted the letter L before the VII on the title, so that at first sight the date appears to be 1657.

7807 BLASI (G. E. di) Storia Civile del Regno di SICILIA (sino all' anno 1768) col Indice generale, 17 vols. sq. 8vo. *vols. XI and XIII want titles, sold not subject to collation, scarce,* 20*s* *Palermo,* 1811-21
This is the best and most complete history of Sicily.

7808 BOCCACCIO, il DECAMERONE nuovamente corretto et con diligentia stampato, sm. 4to. *dark olive mor. extra, gilt edges,* £2. 2*s Firenze,* 1527, (*Venezia,* 1729)
This is a copy, in beautiful condition, of the famous forgery, executed at Venice, for Consul Smith, under the care of Stefano Orlandini and Salvatore Ferrari; of which 300 copies were printed.

7809 BOCCACCIO, il Decamerone, nuovamente stampato e ricorretto per Brucioli, 4to. 10 *and* 274 *leaves, portrait of Boccacio on title, large margins, but of which the lower corners are stained nearly all through the book, with the autograph of* " *Borthwell,*" *third husband of Mary Queen of Scots, limp vellum,* £3. 3*s*
Vinetia, G. G. da Trino, 1538

7810 BOCCACCIO, il DECAMERONE, nuovamente stampato et ricorretto per Messer Antonio Brucioli, con dichiaratione di piu regole dela lingua Toscana, sq. 8vo. *woodcut title with portrait, and woodcut initials and vignettes, russia extra*, 36*s*
Venetia, Iolito di Ferrarii, 1542

" Edition rare et estimée ; vendue £6., White Knights."—BRUNET.

7811 ——— il Decamerone, nuovamente corretto, historiato, et con diligenza stampato, stout 16mo. *woodcuts, bound in old red* MOROCCO EXTRA, *the sides covered with beautiful ornamentation, gilt edges*, 32*s* *Venetia*, 1545

An interesting specimen of binding.

7812 ——— il Decamerone, di nuovo emendato, con vita, note, &c. sq. 8vo. *portrait, hf. morocco,* 9*s* *Vinegia, Giolito de Ferrari*, 1550

7813 ——— il Decamerone, alla sua vera lezione ridotto da SALVIATI, sm. 4to. *with the rare facsimile of the seal and autograph of Salviati, vellum,* 12*s Venezia*, 1582

First and rare edition of Salviati's text. Copies having the facsimile of the seal and autograph are seldom met with.

7814 ——— il Decameron, riscontrato con testi antichi da Salviati, sq. 8vo. *hf. bd.* 20*s*
Venezia, Giunti di Firenze, 1585

Not mentioned by Gamba.

7815 ——— il Decameron, sq. 8vo. *vellum,* 5*s* *Firenze, Giunti*, 1587
7816 ——— il Decameron, riscontrato con testi antichi da Salviati, sm. 4to. *numerous woodcuts, French calf neat, gilt backs,* 16*s* *Venetia, A. Vecchi*, 1597
7817 ——— il Decameron, da Salviati, sq. 8vo. *numerous woodcuts, fine sound copy, in the original vellum,* 16*s* *Venetia*, 1614

"Teneva il supremo scanno fra i letterati il Salviati, il quale di per se stesso nelle cose di lingua era si procacciata con tanto autorita, ch'era venerato come l'oracolo di Firenze, della Toscana e dell' Italia."—*Baldelli.*

7818 ——— il Decameron, 2 vols. 12mo. *fine copy, vellum,* UNCUT, RARE, 18*s Amst.* 1679
7819 ——— il Decamerone, 2 vols. sm. 8vo. *old red morocco, gilt edges,* 7*s Amst.* 1718

An excellent edition of which there was also an inferior issue ; this copy being the genuine book.

7820 ——— il Decameron, stout 16mo. *morocco, flexible backs,* 5*s* *Firenze*, 1820
7821 ——— il Decamerone, da Ugo Foscolo, 3 vols. sm. 8vo. *hf. red morocco, gilt tops, uncut,* 14*s* *Pickering*, 1825
7822 ——— the same, 3 vols. 8vo. LARGE PAPER, *with an original set of Stothard's plates,* PROOF IMPRESSIONS, (pub. £4. 14*s* 6*d*) *cloth,* 36*s* 1825
7822*——— il Decameron, stout 18mo. *morocco, gilt edges,* 6*s* *Firenze*, 1827
7823 MANNI, Istoria del Decamerone, sm. 4to. *vellum paper, tall copy, calf extra, by Smith,* 6*s* *Firenze*, 1742
7824 BOCCACCIO, l' amorosa Fiammetta, 16mo. *vellum,* 6*s* *Vinegia*, 1575
7825 ——— il CORBACCIO, altrimenti, LABERINTO D'AMORE, da Dolce, 1551—Apuleio, Asino d'oro, per Firenzuola, 1550—in 1 vol. 16mo. *vellum, edges gilt and gauffréd,* 12*s* *Vinegia*, 1550-51
7826 Boccaccio, Testamento ; VITA di DANTE, 8vo. *hf. calf,* 5*s* (? 1836)
7827 BALDELLI, Vita di G. Boccacci, large 8vo. *thick paper, portrait, sd.* 4*s* 1806
7828 BOETIO, Consolatione de la Filosofia, tradotto da Bartoli, 12mo. *large copy in limp vellum,* 6*s* *Fiorenza*, 1551
7829 BOCCALINI, PIETRA DEL PARAGONE POLITICO, con una nuoua aggiunta, 16mo. *engraved title and plates, old red morocco, a curious satire,* 20*s* *Cosmopoli,* 1675
7830 BOIARDO. Gli Quarto, Quinto e Sesto Libri dello INNAMORAMENTO DI ORLANDO, compositi per Nicolo delli Agostini, sq. 8vo. 167 *leaves, woodcut on the first, and a map of central Europe on the reverse of leaf* 46, *the margins of a few leaves slightly stained, old calf gilt,* 28*s* *Vinegia, Nicolini da Sabbio*, 1539

"This is the first edition of the Quarto libro by Agostini, and two edd. of the Orlando Inam. by Boiardo preceded it: Venice 1500 ; 4to. Milan, 1518."— *Rev. J. Mitford's MS. note.* This statement of Mitford is incorrect, as according to Gamba three books of Agostini were published with an edition of Boiardo, Venezia, Zoppino ; and according to Brunet, the fourth book was adjoined to the editions of Venice and Milan, 1506 ; and the three books (4th, 5th and 6th) were printed by Zoppino, 1525-6-4.

7831 BOIARDO, ORLANDO INNAMORATO, insieme co i tre libri di Nicolo de gli Agostini, riformato per Domenichi, 2 vols. sq. 8vo. *woodcuts, vellum, nice copy,* 36*s*
Vinegia, Girolamo Scotto, 1553

7832 BOIARDO, Orlando Inammorate, co i tre libri di Agostini, riformato per Domenichi, sq. 8vo. *portraits and woodcuts, calf,* 10s *Venecia, Comin da Trino,* 1560
This edition contains only three books, and not the three books of Agostini, as mentioned on the title.

7833 —— Orlando Innamorato, co i tre libri di Agostini, riformati per Domenichi, sq. 8vo. *many woodcuts in ornamental borders, the title, margins of the first three and last two leaves very slightly wormed, otherwise a nice copy, in old russia extra,* 21s *Venetia, Imberti,* 1602

7834 —— Orlando Innamorato, insieme con i tre libri di Nicolo de gli Agostini, già riformati per L. Domenichi, stout sm. 8vo. *a profusion of woodcuts, old French veau fauve gilt,* 18s *Venetia,* 1655
"A Rifacimento of the Orlando appeared by one Domenichi, who spoiled many of the beauties, without improving the style of his original."—*Prescott s Miscell. p.* 382. Dr. Illll, of Dublin, however, was of quite a contrary opinion; he states in his catalogue, that Dominichi has performed his task "with the strictest fidelity and true poetic excellence; whilst on the contrary, Berni, indulging his natural propensity and luxuriant imagination, has departed so widely from his original, in giving a comic cast to its grave chivalrous style, in altering the texture of the poem, and in making so many interpolations and additions, as to render his rather an entirely new work, than a Rifacimento of his valuable prototype."

7835 BOIARDO ed ARIOSTO, Orlando Innamorato ed Orlando Furioso, with an Essay on the Romantic Narrative Poetry of the Italians, memoirs and notes by Panizzi, 9 vols. sm. 8vo. *cloth,* 36s *Pickering,* 1830-4
This edition is highly praised by Hallam. The poem as written by Boiardo had never been reprinted since 1544.

7836 BONINI, Echo della Fama, Panegirico nella Coronatione della Regina di Polonia, 12mo. *vellum, Imperial Austrian Arms on sides,* 7s *Vienna,* 1670

7837 BORGHI, l'Oplomachia Pisana, la Battaglia del Ponte di Pisa, sq. 8vo. *woodcuts, calf, uncut,* 10s *Lucca,* 1713

7838 BORGHINI (Raffaelo) il Riposo, in cui della PITTURA e della SCULTURA si favella, de' Pittori e Scultori, e delle loro famose opere, stout 12mo. *fine copy in old red morocco, gilt edges, rare,* 32s *Firenze,* 1584
Contains notices on the lives and works of about 300 Italian Painters and Sculptors "Ouvrage estimé et rare de cette édition."—*Brunet.*

7839 BOTERO (Ab. Giov.) la Primavera e le Rime spirituali, 12mo. *vell.* 7s *Torino,* 1609
Rare. The only edition of the work that I have been able to trace is one printed at Milan, 1611, priced, 1824, by Thorpe, vellum, £3. 3s.

7840 BOTTA (C.) Storia d'Italia dal 1789 al 1814, 8 vols. in 4, 8vo. *portrait, calf neat,* 22s *Italia,* 1824

7841 —— the same, 4 vols. 8vo. *hf. calf neat,* 11s *Italia,* 1826

7842 —— Storia d'Italia, continuata da quella del Guicciardini sino al 1789, 15 vols. 16mo. *portrait, calf gilt,* 12s *Parigi,* 1832

7843 —— Storia della Guerra Americana, 7 vols. 8vo. *hf. vellum,* 35s *Liv.* 1825-26

7844 BOUGUAINVILLE, *Franzese,* la Nuova Citerea, sq. 8vo. *a curious Italian Poem, vellum,* 9s *Forli,* 1770

7845 BREVIO, e CADEMOSTO, NOVELLE, 2 vols. in 1, sm. 8vo. *calf, only 80 copies printed,* 10s *Privately printed,* 1819

7846 BROFFERIO, Storia del Piemonte dal 1814 ai nostri giorni, 5 vols. in 1, stout 8vo. *hf. russia,* 12s *Torino,* 1849-52

7847 BRUNO (Giordano) Opere, per la prima volta raccolte e pubblicate da Wagner, 2 vols. in 1, 8vo. *portrait, sd.* 7s ; or, *hf. calf,* 10s *Lipsia,* 1830

7848 —— the same, 2 vols. 8vo. *calf gilt,* 15s 1830
"Giordano Bruno was burnt as a heretic in 1600, in consequence of the opinions in a work which he published in England, and dedicated to Sir Philip Sidney, 'Spaccio della Bestia Trionfante,' which contains a bitter satire on the Catholic religion, and the papal government."—*Whewell.*

7849 BURCHIELLO e altri, Sonetti, 8vo. *portrait, bds.* 6s *Londra (Lucca),* 1757

7850 CALVI, Scena Letteraria degli Scrittori Bergamaschi, 2 parts in 1 vol. stout sq. 8vo. *frontisp. and many portraits, vellum,* 20s *Bergamo,* 1664

7851 CARAZOLI DE LITIO, SPECHIO DELLA FEDE, sm. folio, *fine copy in old citron morocco, gilt edges,* £5. 15s *Venetia, Zoanne di Lorenzo de Bergamo,* 1495
VERY RARE. COLLATION: Title, Epistle, etc., 1 leaf; text, leaves 1—164, being a i to a u iii; Table, colophon, and Register, 5 pp., ending on the reverse of leaf 166, being a a v. The work consists of 45 Sermons on various subjects.

7852 CARLO V. Vita da DOLCE, sq. 8vo. *fine portrait, bds.* 5s *Vinegia,* 1567

7853 CARAFFA. PROSE e Versi sulla Memoria della Princ. Livia Doria Caraffa, 4to. *fine plates, calf extra,* 7s *Parma, Bodoni,* 1784

7854 CARITONE AFRODISIEO, Racconti Amorosi, tradotti dal Greco (da Giacomeli), sm. 4to. *old crimson morocco, arms on sides,* 7s *(Roma),* 1752

7855 CASIMIRO, Memorie della Chiesa di S. Maria in Araceli di Roma, sm. 4to. *plates of Early Art, vellum*, 6s *Roma,* 1736

7856 CASTI, Opere varie, 6 vols. 16mo. *printed on bluish paper, portrait, calf gilt,* 10s *Parigi,* 1821
Contents: Gli Animali parlanti; Poesie Liriche; Poesie dramatiche.

7857 —— Gli Animali parlanti, poema epico, 3 vols. large 8vo. *calf gilt*, 7s 1802

7858 CASTIGLIONE, Il libro del Cortegiano, 16mo. *calf*, 5s *Vinegia, Aldi,* 1547
"Edizione molto elegante e accurata."—*Gamba.*

7859 —— Il Corteggiano, revisto da Dolce, 16mo. *fine copy in vell.* 5s *Vinegia,* 1564

7860 —— Libro del Cortegiano restituito alla sua prima integrita, 2 vols. in 1, sq. 8vo. *portrait, vellum, uncut,* 9s *Vinegia,* 1771

7861 CASTONE (Conte de la Torre Rezzonico) Opere, pubblicate da Mochetti, Vols. I.—VIII. 4to. *portrait,* LARGE VELLUM PAPER, *hf. bd. uncut,* 25s *Como,* 1815-20
Vols. IX. and X. published to 1830, complete the collection, of which the general price in the above state is 120 fr.

7862 CELLINI (B.) Vita di, con illustrazioni e documenti inediti da Tassi, 3 vols. large 8vo. *thick paper, fine portrait, sd.* 6s *Firenze,* 1829

7863 —— Vita, curata da Molini, 2 vols. 8vo. *hf. calf*, 5s 1832

7864 CIBRARIO, Storia della Monarchia di SAVOIA, 2 vols. 8vo. *calf*, 11s *Torino,* 1840-41

7865 CISANO (Giov.) Tesoro di CONCETTI Poetici, scelti da' piu illustri Poeti Toscani, con annotationi, 2 vols. stout 16mo. *very fine copy, vellum, uncut,* 15s *Ven.* 1610

7866 COLLENUCCI (Pandolfo) COMPENDIO dell' Istoria di Napoli, di Collenuccio di Roseo, et di Costo, 3 vols. in 2, sm. 4to. *old calf*, 12s *Venetia, Giunti,* 1613
VERY RARE. This is the original edition of the text which was afterwards reprinted in the Collection of Neapolitan Historians.

7867 COLLETTA, Storia di NAPOLI, 1734-1825, 2 vols. 8vo. *calf*, 7s 6d *Parigi,* 1837

7868 CONCLAVI de' PONTEFICI ROMANI, stout 16mo. 880 pp. *calf*, 5s *s. l.* 1668

7869 CONTALGENI, Endecasyllabi Fidentiani, Difesa de Pedanti, etc. 18mo. *vellum, curious,* 5s *Fior.* 1641

7870 CONTARINO, Vago e dilettevole Giardino, infelici fini di huomini illustri, opere delle Sibille, etc. 2 vols. in 1, stout sq. 8vo. *vellum,* 6s *Vicenza,* 1602

7871 COSTANZO (A. di) Historia del Regno di NAPOLI, accresciuta con Indice, e colla Vita dell' autore, 4to. LARGE PAPER, *mor. extra, gilt edges,* 21s *Napoli,* 1735

7872 COSTO (Tomaso) il FUGGILOZIO, diviso in otto giornate, 18mo. *calf gilt,* £2.
"Cette édition est rare."—*Brunet.* *Venetia,* 1600

7873 —— Fuggilozio, 12mo. *calf neat*, 20s *Venetia,* 1610

7874 —— Fuggilozio, 12mo. *fine large copy, with rough lower margins, vellum,* £2. 5s *Venetia,* 1620
A curious collection of Novelle, &c. on the Malice of Women and Arrogance of Men, Witty Sayings, Remarkable Deeds, &c. Colonel Stanley's copy sold for £3.

7875 CRISPOLTI, PERUGIA augusta, sq. 8vo. *vellum,* 6s *Perugia,* 1648
Pp. 281 to the end (384), contain the lives of the most illustrious men of Perugia.

7876 DANDOLO, (C. T.) FIRENZE sino alla caduta della Repubblica, 8vo. *bds.* 6s 1843

7877 DANDOLO (G.) Caduta della Repubblica di VENEZIA, con Appendice, 2 vols. in 1, stout 8vo. *hf. calf,* 18s *Venezia,* 1855-57

7878 DANTE, OPERE, col comento di LOMBARDI, ora nuovamente arricchito di molte illustrazioni edite ed inedite, 6 vols. 8vo. *calf gilt,* £3. 3s *Padova,* 1822-27

7879 —— the same, 6 vols. 8vo. *portrait, being an exact reprint of the text of the Padova issue, vellum, gilt backs,* £5. *Firenze, Ciardetti,* 1830-41
Contents of this splendid edition, acknowledged to be the best:—I, Inferno; II, Purgatorio; III, Paradiso; IV, Rimario, Convita, Vita Nuova, etc.; V, Rime e Biografia; VI, Opere minori; Egloghe latine, i tratatti del volgar eloquio, etc.

7880 —— DIVINA COMMEDIA; corretta, spiegata, e difesa da LOMBARDI, 4 vols. 4to. *portrait and plates, fine copy, calf gilt,* by C. Lewis, £3. *Roma,* 1815-17
Priced, 1830, Payne and Foss, £5. 5s; Harward's copy at Sotheby's, 1858, fetched £3. 18s.
Considered by many to be the best edition of the "Divina Commedia," with a Rimario, Dante's Life, La Visione, and Index.

7881 —— DIVINA COMMEDIA, col Comento di Biagioli, 3 vols. *hf. calf neat,* 15s
Parigi, 1818-19

7882 —— the same, 3 vols. 8vo. *calf gilt,* 20s 1818-19
With an excellent Commentary explaining the beauties of the poet. "Bella e nitida e correttissima edizione."—*Colomb. de Batines.*

ITALIAN LITERATURE. 435

7882*DANTE. L'OTTIMO COMMENTO della Divina Commedia, testo inedito d'un contemporaneo di Dante citato dagli Accademici della Crusca, 3 vols. 8vo. *portrait, hf. red morocco extra, gilt tops, uncut*, £2. 2s *Pisa*, 1827
7883 —— la Commedia, illustrata da Ugo Foscolo, 4 vols. 8vo. *a good edition, sd.* 18s *Londra*, 1842-3
7884 —— le Prime Quattro Edizioni della DIVINA COMMEDIA letteralmente ristampate per cura di LORD VERNON, (con un discorso sulle medesime da PANIZZI), stout folio, 20 *and* 748 *pp.* (pub. at £4. 4s) *five plates of facsimiles, hf. morocco, uncut*, £3. 3s *Londra*, 1858
  A beautiful and careful reprint of the four first and most important editions. Each page exhibits at one view the differences of the four.
7885 —— la Divina Commedia, con comento analitico di Gabrielle ROSETTI : L'INFERNO, 2 vols. 8vo. *all published* (pub. at £2.) *bds.* 25s *Londra*, 1826-7
  The best edition of Dante's Inferno.
7886 COLOMB DE BATINES, BIBLIOGRAFIA DANTESCA, ossia Catalogo delle edizioni, traduzioni, Codici Manoscritti e Comenti della Divina Commedia, delle Opere Minori, etc. 2 vols. in 3, 8vo. *half French morocco*, 38s *Prato*, 1845-46
7887 DAVILA, Istoria delle Guerre Civili di Francia, 6 vols. 8vo. *portrait, fine copy, calf gilt*, 14s *Milano*, 1807
7888 DENINA, Rivoluzioni d'Italia, 10 vols. 18mo. *port. calf gilt*, 8s *Firenze*, 1826
7889 —— Rivoluzioni della Germania, 8 vols. 8vo. *calf gilt*, 16s *Firenze*, 1804
7890 —— Istoria della Italia Occidentale, 6 vols. in 3, 8vo. *calf neat*, 9s *Torino*, 1809
7891 DOLCE (Lod.) Le Trasformationi (di Ovidio), sq. 8vo. *woodcut title and numerous woodcuts in text, calf*, 9s *Vinegia, Giolito*, 1561
7892 DOMENICHI (Lodovico) Detti et Fatti de diversi Signori, i quali si chiamano Facetie. Motti et Burle, 16mo. *calf extra, gilt edges*, 12s *Venetia*, 1562
7893 DONI, Novelle, (raccolte da Gamba), 8vo. *with a Life of Doni and Bibliography of his works, fine paper, vellum, uncut*, 16s MDCCCXV.
  These 40 Novels, diffused amongst Doni's letters and various works, were extracted and put together by Gamba. Only 80 copies of the edition were printed.
7894 DONI, LA ZUCCA: Cicalamenti, Baie, Chiachiere, Post Scritta, 12mo. FIRST EDITION, *numerous cuts, amongst others, the woodcut head forming the original of the received likeness of Caxton, hf. bd. rare, good copy*, 18s *Vinegia*, 1551
  All later editions suffered retrenchments.
7895 —— la Zucca, espurgata de Capugnano, thick 12mo. *vellum*, 6s *Venetia*, 1591
  The first edition with the humourous introduction "Anatomia sopra la Zucca." Fetched, 1856, Gancia, £1. 8s.
7896 —— Mondi celesti, terrestri, e infernali, de gli Academici Pellegrini, 16mo. *woodcut on title, hf. bound*, 5s *Vicenza*, 1597
7897 DOPPIA (la) IMPICATA, 16mo. *vellum, rare and curious*, 5s *Orbitello*, 1667
7898 EQUICOLA, libro di Natura d'amore, corretto da Dolce, 16mo. *calf*, 5s *Vin.* 1554
7899 FACETIE, Motti, Burle e Buffonerie del Piovano Arlotto, Gonella, Barlacchia, &c. 16mo. *calf, gilt edges*, 10s *Venetia*, 1617
7900 —— another edition, 16mo. *hf. bound*, 5s *ib.* 1693
7901 FELLECCHIA, Viaggio della Regina di Bohemia da Madrid a Napoli, sq. 8vo. *vellum*, 5s *Napoli*, 1630
7902 FERRARIO (Giulio) Storia ed Analisi degli Antichi Romanzi di CAVALLERIA e dei Poemi Romanzeschi d'Italia con Dissertazioni sull' origini de' Cavalieri, sulle Corti d'Amore, Tornei, &c. 4 vols. 8vo. 34 *plates of Armour, military processions, &c. hf. calf neat, gilt tops, uncut*, £2. 16s *Milano*, 1828-29
  Few copies have the tinted plates. The first two volumes of this curious and valuable work contain the historical part, the third the Analysis of the contents, and the fourth a complete Bibliography of all the Italian romances.
7903 FERRARIO, Storia ed Analisi degli antichi ROMANZI di CAVALLERIA, 1828—MELZI, Bibliografia dei Romanzi d'Italia, 1829—2 vols. in 1, roy. 8vo. LARGE VELLUM PAPER, *hf. morocco gilt*, 16s *Milano*, 1828-29
  Only 25 copies printed on this paper for presents.
7904 FIORAVANTI, Compendio de Secreti rationali, (*Alchimia, etc.*) 1660—FALOPIA, Secreti diversi et miracolosi (Secreti di Alchemia), 1650 — 2 vols. in 1, stout 16mo. *vellum*, 5s *Venetia*, 1660-50
7905 FORTEGUERRI, il Ricciardetto, 4 vols. 12mo. *portrait, calf gilt*, 5s *Pisa*, 1813-14
7906 FRIANORO (R.) il Vagabondo, overo Sferza de Bianti e Vagabondi, 16mo. *calf gilt*, 20s *Trevigi*, 1654
  This curious and very rare book formerly belonged to the Right Hon. Thomas Grenville, and has his arms on the inside of cover.

7907 FRIZZI, Memorie per la storia di FERRARA, con giunte e note di Laderchi, 5 vols.—Diario di Frizzi in continuazione della storia di Ferrara, Fasc. 1, 222 pp.—6 vols. roy. 8vo. *sd.* 18*s* *Ferrara*, 1847-57
7908 ——— Storia di FERRARA, 5 vols. roy. 8vo. *hf. calf neat*, 10*s* *ib.* 1847-48
7909 GALLUZZI (Riguccio) Istoria del Granducato di TOSCANA, sotto il Governo della Casa Medici, 5 vols. 4to. LARGE PAPER, *plates, hf. calf,* 18*s* *Firenze,* 1781
Priced, 1848, Thorpe, £5. 5s.
7910 ——— Nuova edizione, 11 vols. in 5, 8vo. *portraits, hf. calf,* 20*s* *ib.* 1822
7911 GAMBA, Serie dei Testi di Lingua Italiana, sm. 4to. *hf. calf,* 6*s* *Venezia*, 1828
7912 ——— Serie dei Testi di Lingua e di altre opere importanti nelle Italiana letteratura, Sec. XIV—XIX, quarta edizione, roy. 8vo. *portrait, vellum,* 15*s* 1839
Best edition of this valuable work of Italian Bibliography.
7913 GAZANO, Storia della SARDEGNA, 2 vols. in 1, stout 4to. *a few margins stained, hf. bd. neat,* 18*s* *Cagliari,* 1777
" Cet ouvrage a été payé 140 fr. a la vente Millin."—*Brunet.*
7914 GIANNONE, Istoria Civile del Regno di NAPOLI, 4 vols.—Opere Postume, 2 vols.; together 6 vols. 4to. *portrait, vellum,* 15*s* *Venezia,* 1766-68
7915 ——— Istoria di Napoli, 8 vols.—Opere Postume, 2 vols.; together 10 vols. in 5, *portrait, vellum, neat,* 24*s* *Italia,* 1821
7916 GIOBERTI, Primato Morale e Civile degli Ital'ani. 3 vols. 8vo. *sd.* 5*s* 1846
7917 GIRALDI CINTHIO, Hecatomithi, overo Cento Novelle, 2 vols. in 1, sm. 4to. *old russia extra, gilt edges, rare,* 30*s* *Venetia,* 1608
"Of all the Italian Novelists *Cinthio* appears to have been the greatest favourite with our old English dramatists. Two of the most popular of Shakspeare's plays were taken from his Novels, *Othello* and *Measure for Measure*; also the plots of two other plays by Beaumont and Fletcher, *The Laws of Candy* and the *Custom of the Country*—and Dryden's tragedy of *Amboyna*, and the incidents of many scattered scenes in the works of these dramatists may be traced to the same source."—*Dunl p's History of Fiction.*
7918 GOZZI (Gasparo, *Conte*) Opere, colla sua Vita, da Dalmistro, 8vo. *hf. calf, uncut, contents lettered,* 18*s* *Padova,* 1818
"Edition la plus complete que l'on ait de ce célèbre ecrivain."—BRUNET.
7919 GUALTERIO (F. A.) gli Ultimi Rivolgimenti Italiani, 4 vols. 12mo. *hf. morocco, gilt tops, uncut,* 10*s* *Firenze,* 1852
7920 GUALDI, Vita di Donna Olimpia Maldachini che governò la Chiesa, 1644-55, 16mo. *vellum, curious,* 10*s* *Ragusa,* 1676
7921 GUAZZI (Marco) Historie di tutte le cose degne di memoria quai del anno 1524 sino al presente, sono occorse, etc. sq. 8vo. *woodcut on title and woodcut portrait, hf. bound, fine clean copy,* £2. 12*s* 6*d* *Venet. Zoppino,* 1540
VERY RARE: a copy was priced by Thorpe, £6. 16s 6d. The work is an interesting chronicle of contemporary events in all parts of the world, and may take its position amongst the earliest productions of NEWSPAPER Literature. It includes, besides European affairs, news from "Turkey, Persia, India, and other places, by sea and land, with the names of many learned men," as stated on the title. Brunet appears ignorant of this book, although his accurate list of Guazzi's works contains one of similar character published in 1547, but referring to an earlier period.
7922 GUERINO detto il Meschino, 16mo. *calf neat,* 8*s* *Bassano,* (? 1750)
7923 GUICCIARDINI, Historia d'Italia, 4 vols. 4to. *portrait, tall copy in calf, several rough leaves,* 20*s* *Friburgo,* 1775-76
Guicciardini may be considered the first of Italian historians, but such was the jealousy or the fear of the higher classes of his countrymen that the text of his history continued in a very mutilated state, till, from an uncastrated MS. in the Magliabechi library, a new and perfect edition appeared in 1775, 4to. 4 vols.; and those who do not possess this edition, have not the *legitimate* text of Guicciardini."—*Dibdin.*
7924 GUICCIARDINI, Istoria d'Italia, 10 vols. 8vo. *calf,* 10*s* *Milano,* 1803
7925 ——— the same, 10 vols. in 5, 8vo. *hf. calf gilt,* 16*s* 1803
7926 HERVAS (Don Lorenzo) Idea dell' Universo: la Storia della Vita dell' Uomo ; Elementi Cosmografici ; Viaggio al Mondo Planetario; Storia della Terra ; 16 vols. sm. 4to. *hf. vellum,* 30*s* *Cesena, (Lorenzo).* 1778-84
The philological works of Hervas form a continuation in 5 vols. to the above.
7927 LALLI, Franceide overo del Mal Francese, poema giocoso, 16mo. *vellum,* 5*s* 1629
7928 LIPPI (Lorenzo) Il MALMANTILE RACQUISTATO, di Perlone Zipoli, colle note di Puccio Lamoni (Paolo Minucci) e d'altri, 2 vols. 4to. *two fine portraits, fine copy in old French red morocco extra, gilt edges,* 32*s* *Firenze,* 1731
7929 LAZARIGLIO DI TORMES, il Picariglio Castigliano, trasportata dal Spagnuolo, 2 vols. sq. 16mo. *vellum,* 5*s* *Venetia,* 1635
7930 LEGGENDA divotissima di piu Vergini & martyri, intitulato Libro delle Vergini, sq. 8vo. clxvi leaves and Index, *vellum, rare,* 10*s* *s. l. e. a.* (? 1520)
The printer's mark at the end seems to be that of Hieronymo Benedetto of Bologna.
7931 LEPOLEMO. Historia del valorosissimo Cavallier della Croce, tradotta dal Spagnuolo, 2 vols. 16mo. *good copy of this celebrated Romance, in old calf gilt,* 20*s* *Venetia,* 1629
7932 LEPOREO (Ludov.) Compositioni, sm. 4to. *vellum,* 10*s* *Roma,* 1688
Curious Poems which shew the richness of the Italian language, by the peculiarity of the metres.

ITALIAN LITERATURE. 437

7933 LETTERE VOLGARI di diversi Ingegni, 3 vols. 16mo. *ruled, veau fauve, gilt edges,*
10s *Vinegia,* 1564
Amongst the writers are Bocaccio, Bembo, Petrarch, Sannazaro, Lorenzo de'Medici, Aretino, Michael Angelo, Guicciardini, Ariosto, etc.
7934 LOREDANO, Bizarrie Academiche, 2 vols. 1654—Sei Dubbi Amorosi—NOVELLE, 1656—in 1 vol. 16mo. *calf,* 5s *Venetia,* 1654-56
7935 LOREDANO e Michiele, Il Cimitero, EPITAFIJ Giocosi, 3 parts in 1 vol. 12mo. *a curious and rather gross collection, blue mor. extra, gilt edges,* 15s (*Ven.*) 1545
7936 MACHIAVELLI, Tutte le Opere, sq. 8vo. *portrait on title, calf,* 6s 1650
7937 ———— Istorie ed altre OPERE, 10 vols. large 8vo. *best edition, portrait and facsimile, sd.* 28s *Firenzi, Conti,* 1818-21
7938 ———— the same, 10 vols. 8vo. *Roman vellum, gilt backs, a fine set,* £3. 3s 1818-21
7939 ———— OPERE, 9 vols. 12mo. *portrait, calf gilt,* 25s *Milano,* 1820-22
7940 ———— OPERE, 10 vols. 8vo. *portrait, large type, sd.* 32s *Italia,* 1826
" Machiavel was the first writer who discovered the secret of what may be called *comparative history.* He it was who first sought in ancient history for materials to illustrate the events of his own times."—*D'Israeli.*

7941 MAFFEI (G.) Storia della Literatura Italiana sino a' nostri giorni, 2 vols. 8vo. *hf. calf,* 9s *Italia,* 1834
7942 MANFREDI (Eustachio), Poesie, con vita, sq. 8vo. *portrait, Large Paper, calf neat,* 7s *Parma,* 1793
7943 MANNO (G.) Storia di SARDEGNA, 3 vols. 8vo. *sd. a classical work,* 10s *Torino,* 1826
7944 MANUZIO (P.) LETTERE, large 8vo. *thick paper, sd.* 5s *Parigi,* 1834
7945 MANZONI, Opere Scelte, sm. 8vo. *portrait on frontispiece, and plates,* 500 *pp. double columns, bds.* 5s *Firenze,* 1832
7946 ———— I PROMESSI SPOSI, stout 12mo. *calf gilt,* 7s 6d *Firenze,* 1829
7947 ———— I Promessi Sposi, 2 vols. 12mo. *sd.* 4s *Londra,* 1848
7948 ———— Storia della Colonna Infame, 12mo. *calf gilt,* 5s *Parigi.* 1843
7949 MELZI, Bibliografia dei Romanzi e Poemi Cavallereschi Italiani, 8vo. viii and 380 pp. *portrait of Ariosto, hf. calf, gilt top, uncut,* 10s *Milano,* 1838
7950 ———— Dizionario di Opere Anonime e Pseudonime di Scrittori Italiani, ò come che sia, aventi relazione all'Italia, 3 vols. impl. 8vo. *upwards of* 1600 *pp. double columns, half calf, gilt tops, uncut,* £2. *Milano,* 1848-59
This important work of Count Melzi is considered one of the best ever published; it has been highly praised.

7951 METASTASIO Opere, 17 vols. 8vo. *portrait, bds.* 10s *Padova,* 1810-12
7952 ———— Opere, 16 vols. 8vo. *portrait, half calf neat,* 34s *Firenze,* 1819
7953 ———— the same, LARGE PAPER, 16 vols. in 8, large 8vo. *portrait, hf. vellum, gilt backs, uncut, tops gilt,* £3. 1819
7954 ———— Opere scelte, 2 vols. 12mo. *calf gilt,* 5s 1821
7955 MOLIERE, Opere, tradotte da Castelli, 4 vols. 16mo. *portrait and plates, gilt vellum,* 9s 1698
7956 MONALDI, Irene overo della Bellezza con altri due Dialoghi, dell' Havere, & della Metafisica, 4to. *beautiful copy in red* MOROCCO *extra, gilt edge, with the Arms of* PRINCE EUGENE *on sides,* 25s *Venetia,* 1599
7957 MONTI (Vincenzo) Opere, 8 vols. 12mo. *port. vellum gilt,* 18s *Bologna,* 1827-28
7958 MORSO, descrizione di PALERMO Antico, 8vo. *plates of inscriptions, half morocco,* 10s *Palermo,* 1827
7959 MURATORI (L. A.) ANNALI D'ITALIA, sino all' anno 1750, 13 vols. 4to. *portraits, calf,* 32s *Napoli,* 1773
7960 NARBONE (Alessio) BIBLIOGRAFIA SICOLA sistematica, o Apparato Methodico alla Storia letteraria della SICILIA, 4 vols. in 2, stout 8vo. *hf. calf gilt, gilt tops, uncut,* £2. 16s *Palermo,* 1850-55
A work indispensable to the student of Sicilian History and Literature.
A classified catalogue of 2000 pp. with Index of authors' names.

7961 NOVELLE AMOROSE de' Signori Accademici incogniti, 2 parti in 1 vol. sm. 4to. *vellum,* 5s *Venetia,* 1650
7962 NOVELLE SCELTE RARISSIME, stampate à spese di XL Amatori, sm. 8vo. *a collection of scarce Italian Novelle, edited by S. W. Singer, only* 50 *copies privately printed, bds. uncut, very scarce,* £2. *Londra,* 1814
1857, Utterson's copy fetched £4. 1s.
7963 ODONI (Rinaldo) Discorso per Via Peripatetica, ove si dimostra, se l'Anima è mortale o immortale, sm. 4to. *fine copy in hf. vellum,* 12s *Venetia, Aldus,* 1557
7963* ———— the same, sq. 8vo. *citron morocco, gilt edges,* 27s 1557
7964 PALERMO (Fr.) Classazione dei Libri a stampa dell' I. e R. Palatina in corrispondenza di un nuovo ordinamento dello Scibile Umano, imp. 8vo. *a valuable work on the Science and Practice of Bibliography, blue Turkey morocco extra, gilt edges,* 21s *Firenze,* 1854

7965 PALLAVICINO, La Susanna; La Bersabee; Il Principe Hermafrodito; Il
 Giuseppe; La Taliclea; in 3 vols. 16mo. *vellum*, 15s *Venetia*, 1654
7966 —— Il Divortio Celeste, 16mo. *vellum*, 5s *Villafranca*, 1643
7967 —— Continuazione del Corriero Sualigiato, 1660—la Rete di Vulcano, 1660—
 Anima di Pallavicino, 2 *parts*, 1643-65—in 1 vol. 18mo. *vellum*, 5s 1643-65
7968 PALMERINO D'INGHILTERRA, et Floriano dal Deserto suo fratello, con
 alcuni gloriosi fatti del Principe Florendo, tradotto dal Spagnuolo, 3 vols. 12mo.
 fine copy in green morocco extra, gilt edges, from Miss Currer's library, £2. 2s
 RARE. Priced, Thorpe, £3. 13s 6d. *Venetia*, 1609
7969 PARMA. DUE ORAZIONI in lingua Toscana: Accusa contra Leon, Secretario;
 e Difesa, 8vo. *bds. rare*, 10s *Parma, Setto Viotto*, 1547
 A rare tract relating to a case of treason in connection with the papal government of Parma, after the French expulsion.
7970 PANTHERA (G. G.) Monarchia del nostro Signor Giesu Christo, 16mo. *a very
 fine copy, in vellum, rare*, 15s *Vinegia*, 1552
7971 PARNASO ITALIANO, overro Raccolta de' Poeti Classici Italiani, 56 vols.
 12mo. *many pretty vignettes*, £2. 10s *Venezia*, 1784-91
 A complete set of all the important Italian Classics.
7972 PETRARCA (Sonetti e Canzoni, e Triomfi) con l'espositione di Vellutello, sm.
 4to. *woodcut title, vellum*, 20s *Vinegia, Giolito de Ferrari*, 1552
7973 PETRARCA (Il) 18mo. *old red morocco*, 9s *Lione*, 1547
7974 —— Rime bravemente sposto per Lodovico Castelvetro, 3 parts in 1 vol. 4to.
 old calf gilt, 25s *Basilea, Pietro de Sedabonis*, 1582
7975 —— the same, *a fine copy in green morocco extra, gilt edges, tooled on sides,
 from Miss Currer's library*, 36s 1582
 Priced, 1829, Longman's, old mor. £3. 10s; 1837, Payne and Foss. mor. £2. 12s; 1840, Payne and Foss, mcr.
 £2. 2s, russ. £1. 11s 6d; Heath's copy, mor. fetched £3. 3s
 "Edition rare, la première de ce commentaire fort estimé. Le texte est celui de l'édition d'Alde, 1514, mais
 imprimé très incorrectement: 8ff prelimin. y compris le titre, au verso duquel est un privilège du roi de France.
 Prem. part. 447 pp. 2e et 3e part 398 pp. y compris 2 pp. et denie d'errata.
7976 —— Rime, 2 vols. 12mo. *vellum paper, blue* MOROCCO, *joints, gilt edges, by
 Walther*, 14s *Parma, Bodoni*, 1799
 According to Brunet, this pretty edition is more correct than the folio published by Bodoni.
7977 PETRARCA, RIME, edizione publicata per opera e studio di MARSAND, 2 vols.
 imp. 4to. VELLUM PAPER, *containing beautiful portraits of Petrarch and Laura,
 by Gandolfi and Raphael Morghen, facsimile of his handwriting, and other engravings in bistre*, FINE COPY, *in green morocco extra, gilt edges, with numerous rough leaves*, RARE, £3. 3s *Padova*, 1819-20
 Priced, 1848, Payne and Foss, £7. 7s; 1856, priced £4. 14s 6d; fetched, 1853, Sotheby's £3. 12s.
 "Belle édition donnée avec des soins infinis par M. Antoine Marsand. C'est la meilleure que l'on ait de Pétrarque et celles que suivent les imprimeurs jaloux de reproduire un bon texte."— BRUNET.
7978 PETRARCHA, Rime (da Marsand), 2 vols. 8vo. *portraits, an elegant edition in large
 type, smooth morocco, gilt edges*, 15s *Livorno, Masi, 'cariteri di Didot,'* 1820
7979 —— RIME, corrette sovra i testi migliori, colle note di Tassoni, Muzio, e Muratori, 2 vols. stout 8vo. *facsimile, sd.* 10s *Roma*, 1821
7980 —— Rime, con illustrazioni, 2 vols. large 8vo. *plates, sd.* 9s *Firenze*, 1821
7981 —— Rime, 16mo. *printed on tinted paper, calf gilt*, 9s *Firenze*, 1822
7982 —— Rime, 2 vols. 8vo. *calf gilt*, 9s *Milano*, 1824
7983 —— Rime, con annotazioni, 16mo. *a pretty book, hf. morocco, gilt top, uncut*,
 8s *Firenze*, 1822
7984 PETRARCA SPIRITUALE (Il) novamente ristampato, et dall' auttore con nuova
 additione reconosciuto, 16mo. *beautiful woodcut portrait on title, and engraving the size of the page on the reverse, fine copy, old red morocco extra, gilt
 edges*, £2. 5s *Ven.* 1545
 The verses of Petrarch are here adapted to spiritual subjects by Hieronimo Maripetro.
7985 PIGNOTTI, Storia della Toscana, 5 vols. 16mo. *calf gilt*, 6s *Pisa*, 1815
7986 —— Storia della Toscana, 6 vols. 8vo. *portrait, sd.* 7s *Firenze*, 1824
7987 —— the same, 6 vols. in 3, 8vo. *calf neat*, 14s 1824
7988 PORTA (Luigi da) Rime e Prosa, con vita da Zorzi, sm. 4to. LARGE PAPER, *red
 morocco, gilt edges*, 7s 6d *Vicenza*, 1731
 Containing the novel upon which "Romeo and Juliet" was founded.
7989 PULCI, MORGANTE MAGGIORE, nuovamente corretto per Domenichi, sm. 4to.
 woodcuts, rough calf, 14s *Vinegia, Girolamo Scotto*, 1545
 "Edition recherchée et rare, sans être cependant la meilleure de ce poëme, ainsi que plusieurs bibliographes
 l'ont prétendu: 40 fr. Guignat; 28 fr. mar. r., La Vallière; £1. 6s, and £6. 10s, mar. bl. Heber."—*Brunet*.
7990 PULCI, MORGANTE MAGGIORE, nouamente stapato e corretto, sq. 8vo. *rude wood-*

ITALIAN LITERATURE. 439

    cuts, title, 194 *leaves and* 1 *leaf with the printer's device, fine copy, calf neat,*
RARE, £2. 16*s*   *Venetia, G. Padoano,* 1552
This edition is mentioned neither by Haym nor by Brunet.

7991 RENUCCI, Storia di CORSICA, 2 vols. 8vo. *portraits, sd.* 7*s*   *Bastia,* 1833-34
7992 RINGHIERI, Cento Giuochi liberali et d'Ingegno, sm. 4to. *original edition, vellum,* 9*s ; fine copy in calf,* 21*s*   *Bologna,* 1551
7993 ROSINI, Luisa Strozzi, Storia del Sec. XVI, 2 vols. 12mo. *hf. calf gilt,* 5*s*   1833
7994 ———— la Monaca di Monza, storia del sec. XVII, 2 vols. 12mo. *calf gilt,* 5*s* 1830
7995 ROSMINI, Historia di G. J. TRIVULZIO, 2 vols. 4to. *hf. bd.* 6*s*   *Milano,* 1815
7996 RUSCELLI, Fiori delle Rime de' Poeti illustri, 12mo. *calf,* 7*s* 6*d*   *Lucca,* 1729
7997 SABELLICO (Marco Ant.) CRONICHE che tractano de la origine de Veneti, de la Guere in Italia, Dalmacia, Grecia, contra li infideli, etc. volgarizate per M. Vesconte, sm. folio, 9 *prelim. leaves, including title, and blank leaf; text, leaves* 2-183, *and the rare last leaf, blank on the obverse, on the reverse* " *Deche de lorigine de Veneti,*" *in red Gothic letters, vellum, rare,* 30*s*
    Venet. Lompugnano, s. a. (ca. 1480)
Priced, 1855, Asher, Berlin, 50 fr.
The first edition of this work in Italian. It is unknown to Brunet, Molini, and Ebert, who mention that of 1554 as the first; ignorant, not only of the above, but also of an edition dated, Venice, 1504.

7998 SANSOVINO (F.) CENTO NOVELLE scelte da piu nobili Scrittori della lingua volgari, sq. 8vo. *fine woodcuts, Italian red morocco, from Lord Rothesay's library,* 36*s*   *Venetia,* 1566
Priced, 1848, Payne and Foss, £3. 3s. Fetched, Borromeo sale, £2. 15s; Fonthill, £4. 3s.

7999 ———— Cento novelle, sq. 8vo. *woodcuts, sd.* 9*s*   *Venetia,* 1571
8000 SANSOVINO, Origine et Fatti delle Famiglie illustri d'Italia, sq. 8vo. *limp vellum* 12*s*   *Vinegia,* 1582
8001 .SANUTO (Marin, *Cronista de Secoli* XV-XVI) Ragguagli sulla sua Vita e sulle sue Opere, 3 parts or vols. 8vo. *sd.* 10*s ;* or, in 1 vol. stout 8vo. *hf. vellum,* 12*s*
    Vinezia, 1837-38
8002 SARDI (G.) Libro delle Historie Ferraresi, di più quattro libri di Faustini, sm. 4to. *portraits, best edition, fine copy in old calf gilt,* 18*s*   *Ferrara,* 1646
8003 SARPI, Vita del Padre Paolo, 16mo. *vel.* 5*s ; old red* MOROCCO, 7*s*   *Leida,* 1646
8004 SCALIGGER, Trastulli della villa distinti in sette giornate, 16mo. *blue* MOROCCO, 7*s*
    Venetia, 1627
8005 SCINA (D.) Prospetto della Storia Letteraria di SICILIA nel Secolo XVIII, 3 vols. 8vo. *sd.* 18*s*   *Palermo,* 1824-27
8006 ———— the same, 3 vols. 8vo. *hf. bd.* 22*s*   1824-27
A learned and valuable work, with general Index.

8007 SPAGNA (La), li gran fatti, e le mirabili Battaglie del Re Carlo, 16mo. *woodcuts, vellum,* 10*s*   *Ven.,* 1783
8008 SOCIO, Miserie de li Amanti, sq. sm. 8vo. *hf. morocco, uncut,* 12*s*   *Vinegia,* 1533
8009 SPELTA, la SAGGIA PAZZIA, fonte d'allegrezza; colla Dilettevole Pazzia e la Pazziazza furiosa, 2 vols. in 1, sq. 8vo. *some curious cuts, old calf, arms on sides, rare,* 21*s*   *Pavia,* 1607
" Un livre singulier."—*Brunet.*

8010 TASSO (Bernardo) LETTERE, stout 12mo. FIRST EDITION, LARGE AND THICK PAPER, *original vellum neat,* VERY RARE, *probably unique,* 36*s*   *Vinegia,* 1549
Unknown even to the editors of the edition of 1733.

8011 ———— Lettere, con vita dell' Autore da Seghezzi, 3 vols. in 2, stout 12mo. *best edition, portrait, vellum, rare,* 15*s*   *Padova,* 1733-5
The third volume is frequently wanting.

8012 TASSO (Bern.) l'Amadigi, 4to. *title slightly soiled, a small piece in last leaf mended, otherwise a fine copy, citron morocco, gilt edges,* 20*s*   *Venetia, Zoppini,* 1583
8013 TASSO (Torquato) OPERE, colle Controversie sopra la Gerusalemme Liberata, 6 vols. sm. folio, *port. fine copy in Italian calf gilt, rare,* £2. 10*s*   *Firenze,* 1724
Priced, 1829, Longman, £7. 7s ; Duke of Grafton's copy fetched £4. 9s
" Edition donnée par Bottari, avec une bonne preface."—*Brunet.*

8014 ———— OPERE, con le Controversie sopra la Gerusalemme Liberata e con le Annotazioni intere di varj Autori, 12 vols. 4to. *hf. morocco, uncut,* £2. *Ven.* 1735-42
Complete sets of the works of Tasso are of unusual occurrence ; Volume XII. has a good Index of the work. Gardner's copy, in red morocco, fetched, 1854, £12. 5s.

8015 TASSO, il Goffredo, overo GERUSALEMME LIBERATA, sm. 4to. *hf. bd.* 9*s* *Vin.* 1585
Rare, neither mentioned by Gamba, Haym, nor Brunet.

8016 TASSO, GERUSALEMME LIBERATA, con le Figure di Bernardo Castello (AGOSTINO CARACCI) e le Annotazioni di Scipio Gentili e di Giulio Guastivini, 4to. *apparently upon Large Paper, fine impressions of the* 20 *plates by A. Caracci and J. Franco,*

the engraved title mounted, a portrait of Tasso engraved by Sadeler, 1617, inserted, richly bound in the original citron morocco, fine copy, rare, £2. 10s
Genova, 1590

This edition is much esteemed on account of the plates of Ago. Caracci, which it contains. In many copies the plate to Canto IV. is the same as that to Canto V., which imperfection greatly diminishes the value of the book. The present copies have the proper plate. "In questa rara edizione vi sono nove figure intagliate dal celebre AGOSTINO CARACCI, oltre il frontispizio, che sono stimatissime. Nicola Francesco HAYM, illustre antiquario e Bibliografo Romano, nella lettera al Lettore premessa alla sua bella edizione del Tasso loda grandemente questa stampa, dicendo: L'edizione in quarto di Genova di questo celebratissi. Poema è fin ora stata preferita ad ogn' altra e presentemente è divenuta sì rara, ch'è difficile il rinvenirla. Ella fu fatta con il consentimento del Tasso, come apparisce per la lettera dedicatoria del Castelli, e stimasi che vi facesse diversi miglioramenti: e per gli adornamenti disegnati dal predetto B. Castelli, è certo, che non ha invidia ad alcun altro libro, che fin ad ora sit sortita dalle stampe."—*Serassi, Vita di Tasso, p. 547.*

Priced, 1828, Payne and Foss, calf neat, £3. 3s; 1830, Payne and Foss, morocco, £4. 4s. and £5. 5s; 1840, James Bohn, morocco, £6. 6s. Fetched, the Stanley copy, 238, with an additional set of plates from a German translation published in 1626, morocco, £10. 10s, resold at Mr. Heber's sale for £10. 15s; Roscoe's 1183, morocco, £5. 17s 6d; Askew's 639, mor. £2. 12s 6d; 1853, Dr. Hawtrey's, £1. 12s; 1855, Sotheby's, morocco extra, £4.

8017 TASSO, IL GOFFREDO, overo Gierusalemme Liberata, stout 16mo. *vellum*, 10s 1590

8018 ——— Gerusalemme conquistata, sm. 4to. *vellum*, 10s   *Pavia,* 1594
A scarce edition containing a table of the first lines of each stanza.

8019 ——— Goffredo, overo Gerusalemme Liberata, congli Argomenti di Ariosti, 24mo. *title within woodcut border, and several small pretty woodcuts in the text, 18 leaves and 502 pp. neatly printed in minute type, in the original vellum,* 36s
Venetia, Giunti, 1609

8020 ——— GERUSALEMME LIBERATA, con le annotationi di Scipion Gentili, figurata da Benardo Castello, sm. folio, *plates after the designs of A. Caracci and J. Franco, with the suppressed one to Canto IV, and both the frontispieces, calf, fine copy,* 32s
Genova, 1617

Fetched at Paris' sale, £6. 6s. The plates are different from the preceding editions of Genova, 1590 and 1604. The first frontispiece contains the portrait of Carlo Emmanuel Duke of Savoy, the second one that of Tasso, Many copies have the plate of Canto 5 repeated to Canto 4.

8021 TASSO, Gerusalemme Liberata, 2 vols. 8vo. *portraits and numerous beautiful plates and vignettes by Gravelot, French calf, gilt edges,* 11s   *Parigi,* 1771

8022 ——— GERUSALEMME LIBERATA, 2 vols. roy. 4to. DIDOT'S BEAUTIFUL EDITION *on large vellum paper, with the* 41 *fine plates after Cochin, russia extra, gilt edges,* 28s
Parigi, n. d. (ca. 1790)

8023 ——— Gerusalemme liberata, 2 vols. 8vo. *sd.* 6s   *Firenze,* 1818

8024 ——— la Gerusalemme, edizione sopra quella di Mantova, 1584, 2 vols. 8vo. *portrait, hf. calf, uncut,* 14s   *Milano, Tosi,* 1820

8025 ——— la Gerusalemme e l'Aminta, con note da Buttura, 2 vols. 8vo. *portrait, sd.* 7s
Par. 1823

8026 ——— the same, 2 vols. sm. 8vo. *calf extra,* 12s   1823

8027 ——— Gerusalemme Liberata, &c. colle varianti e con note critiche, 2 vols. 8vo. *portrait,* BEST EDITION, *calf extra, gilt edges,* 28s   *Firenze, Molini,* 1824

8028 ——— La GERUSALEMME LIBERATA con illustrazioni, 3 vols.—RIMARIO della Gerusalemme liberata, 1 vol.—together 4 vols. roy. 8vo. *bds.* 18s   *Pisa,* 1830-31

8029 MANOSCRITTI INEDITI, ed altri pregevoli documenti per sua biografia, illustrati da Alberti, folio, *portraits, and* 33 *plates of facsimiles, hf. vellum, uncut,* 32s
Lucca, 1837

8030 SERASSI, Vita del Tasso, 4to. *portrait on title, calf gilt,* 12s   *Roma,* 1785

8031 TASSONI (Aless.) la SECCHIA RAPITA, Poema Eroicomico, 16mo. *portrait and plates, red morocco extra,* 5s
Venezia, 1711

8032 ——— la Secchia Rapita, colle Dichiarazioni di Salvini e le annotazioni di Rossi, sm. 8vo. *portrait and humourous plates, fine copy, French veau fauve gilt, Arms on sides,* 27s
Venezia, 1747

" A graceful facility and light humour make this a very amusing poem. It is exempt from the bad taste of the age; and where the burlesque tone disappears, is versified with much elegance. The Count di Culagna, one of his most ludicrous characters, bears a certain resemblance to Hudibras."—*Hallam.*
A valuable notice of Tassoni's various works will be found in T. C. Walker's Memoirs of the Poet.

8033 TEATRO ITALIANO ANTICO, con note da Ferrario, 10 vols. 8vo. *portraits, blue morocco, gilt edges,* £2. 2s   *Milano,* 1808-12

8034 TIRABOSCHI (G.) Biblioteca Modenese, o Notizie degli Scrittori di Modena, 6 vols. 4to. *calf gilt,* £2.   *Modena,* 1781-6

8035 ——— STORIA della LETTERATURA ITALIANA, col Indice, 9 vols. in 11, 8vo. *hf. calf,* 30s
Firenze, 1805-13

8036 ——— the same, 9 vols. in 14, 8vo. *calf,* 34s   1805-13

8037 ——— the same, 9 vols. in 16, 8vo. *hf. calf gilt,* £2. 2s   1805-13

8038 ——— another edition, 9 vols. in 11, 8vo. *hf. calf,* 24s   *Venezia,* 1822-13

"This work has long held a distinguished rank among the histories of literature."—*Horne.*
" A strict adherence to veracity, a thorough acquaintance with the subject in all its details; a spirit of

candour, raised far above the influence of party; a discernment in criticism, deep and correct; and, above all, a clear and unbiassed *principium et fons recte scribendi*, pervade every part of this astonishing work, and give it a perfection very unusual in literary productions so comprehensive and so complicated."—*Eustace*.

The Storia della Litteratura Italiana of the immortal Tiraboschi cannot fail to be admitted into every judicious library. Italy boasts of few literary characters of higher class.

8039 TOMMASEO, Canti Popolari Toscani, Corsi, Illirici, Greci, con opuscolo originale, 4 vols. 8vo. *plates, hf. calf neat*, 36s *Venezia*, 1841-42

8040 TORELLI. Rime amorose del Conte Pomponio Torelli detto il Perduto nell' Accademia degli illustri innominati di Parma, sq. 8vo. *very fine copy, rough leaves, in the original vellum binding*, 18s *Parma, Viotti*, 1575

8041 TROIANO (Massimo) Dialoghi delle cose notabili delle Nozze di Guglielmo VI, Conte Palatino e Duca di Baviera, e di Mad. Renata di Loreno, sm. 4to. *Italian and Spanish, port. of Troianus, woodcuts of emblems, calf gilt*, 14s *Venetia*, 1569
" Della rarita di questro libro (di cui parla Bianconi nelle Lettere sopra la Baviera, Lucca, 1763) vedi l'opera di Napione della lingua Italiana, Milano, 1819."—*Tomitano*.

8042 TROYA, condizione de Romani vinti da' Longobardi, 8vo. *calf extra*, 5s *Mil.* 1844

8043 TRUCCHI. Poesie Italiane inedite di Dugento Autori, raccolte da Trucchi, dall' origine della lingua, infino al Sec. XVII, 4 vols. large 8vo. *hf. morocco, gilt tops, uncut,* 25s *Prato,* 1846-47
Commencing with the "Trovatori," and ending with the "Poeti Secentisti," with biographical notices.

8044 TUTTI I TRIONFI, Carri, Mascherate, o CANTI CARNASCIALESCHI andati per Firenze dal Tempo del Magnifico Lorenzo De Medici, fino all' anno 1559, in questa seconda edizione corretti con diversi MSS. collazionati, 2 parts, sq. 8vo. *engraved title,* 40 *portraits, first issue of this edition, bds.* UNCUT, *from the libraries of the Duke of Roxburghe and Isaac Disraeli,* 32s *Cosmopoli (Lucca)*, 1750

8045 ——— the same, 2 vols. 8vo. *old French calf, gilt edges,* 36s 1750

8046 ——— the same, 2 parts in 1 vol. stout 8vo. *second issue, old calf gilt,* 20s 1750
The Stanley copy fetched £2. 2s. Besides the 'Canti' of Lorenzo de Medici, this volume contains those of 47 other poets. A few of the poems are in Italian dialects. "The merits of these Carnival Songs are principally to be estimated by the purity of the Florentine diction, which is allowed to be there preserved in its most unadulterated state. They are frequently cited by the Academicians della Crusca, in their celebrated dictionary, as authorities for the Italian tongue, and consequently composed a part of those works, selected for the purity of their style, and known by the name of Testi di lingua."—*Roscoe*.

"A strange existence, truly, was that of Lorenzo! After working with all the power of his intellect and his will at the making of new laws, which should crush out some last remnant of liberty—after using his influence to obtain some new decree of confiscation or sentence of death, he would enter the Platonic Academy, and dispute with vehemence on virtue and the immortality of the soul—issuing thence, and mingling with a company of utterly depraved young men, he would sing his '*Canti Carnascialeschi*,' or Carnival Songs (of infamous celebrity), and give himself up to wine and women, then return home again, and at table, in the society of Pulci and Politian, recite verses and discourse on poetry, and to each of these pursuits he gave himself up so wholly that each seemed to be the sole aim of his life."—*Prof. Villari, Life of Savonarola, quoted in the Athenæum,* Aug. 18, 1860.

8048 VARCHI (B.) STORIA FIORENTINA, con aggiunte, correzioni e note per cura di Lelio Arbib, 3 vols. 8vo. *calf gilt,* 24s *Firenze,* 1843-44

8049 VENICE. CONTARINO La Republica e i Magistrati di Vinegia, 1545—ROSELLO, Ritratto del vero Governo del Principe dal essempio vivo del Gran Cosimo, 1552 —PATRITIO, La Citta Felice, etc. 1553—3 vols. in 1, 16mo. *olive morocco, gilt back, gold borders on the sides,* 12s *Vineg.* 1545-53

8050 QUIRINO (Ant.) Advis donné à l'Estat et Republique de Venise, sur les difficultez avec Paul V, 1606—SQUITINIO DELLA LIBERTA VENETA, le raggioni dell' Impero Romano sopra la signoria di Venetia, *Mirandola,* 1619—2 vols. in 1, 12mo. *vellum, from Lord Orford's and Lord Roxburghe's libraries,* 21s 1606-19
The author of the curious second piece in this volume was the famous Marquis of Bedemar, Spanish Ambassador at Venice, 1607-10, who formed the plot to seize that city for Spain.

8051 VENICE. RACCOLTA degli Scritti, nella Causa del P. PAOLO V. co' signori VENETIANI, sm. 4to. *containing* 19 *rare works on the quarrel between Pope Paul V. and the Republic of Venice, calf,* 25s *Coira,* 1507 (1607)

8052 VASARI, OPERE: Vite de piu celebri Pittori, Scultori e Architetti, dal 1200 al 1568; Lettere pittoriche; Vite degli Artefici; etc. 6 vols. in 12, 18mo. *about* 150 *portraits, a pretty set in calf gilt,* 25s *Firenze,* 1822-23
This is the first complete edition of the works of Vasari.

8053 VILLANI [Giovanni] Cronica, a miglior lezione ridotta coll ajuto de' Testi a Penna, 8 vols. impl. 8vo. *portrait engraved by Lasinio the younger,* 1823—VILLANI [Matteo e Filippo] Cronica, 6 vols. 8vo. 1825-6—together 14 vols. LARGE VELLUM PAPER, *sd.* £3. 6s *Firenze,* 1823-6

8054 ITALIAN DIALECTS. Bergamesc. TASSO, il GOFFREDO, trauestito alla Rustica *Bergamasca* da Carlo Assonica, 4to. *with philological footnotes, hf. bd.* £2. *Venetia, Pezzana,* 1670
Traduction rare, avec le texte original en regard.
An edition exactly similar to the above, published at Cosenza, 1737, was priced, 1856, myself, with a few leaves stained, £2. 2s. The difference between the two is merely in the title.

8055 TASSO, il Goffredo, con il Travestimento *Bergamesco* di Assonica, 2 vols. 12mo. *portrait, half calf, uncut*, 18s *Bergamo*, 1778

8056 ZAPPETTINI, Vocabolario Bergamasco-Italiano, 8vo. 540 *pp. hf. calf, uncut*, 12s *Bergamo*, 1859

8057 **Bolognese.** AURELI, Nuovo Dizionario del dialetto Bolognese, 12mo. *hf. calf, uncut*, 8s 6d *Bologna*, 1851

8058 FERRARI, Vocabolario Bolognese-Italiano, con squarci di componenti Bolognesi, prefazione sulla Ortografia, ed Appendice, stout 4to. *Italian vellum, gilt back*, 25s *Bologna*, 1835

8059 DEGRAZI d'Bertuldin dalla Zena, miss' in rima Bulognesa, da G. M. B. sm. 4to. *etchings, bds.* 8s ; *calf neat*, 12s *Bologna*, 1736

8060 LOTTI (Lotto) Ch' n' ha cervel hapa gamb, poemetto giocoso, *Parma*, 1685—Rimedi per la Sonn, *Milano*, 1704 ; 2 vols. in 1, 12mo. *plates, vellum*, 6s 1685-1704

8061 —— Rimedi per la Sonn da liezr alla Banzola, sq. 8vo. *bds.* 3s 1703

8062 **Brescian.** MELCHIORI, Vocabolario Bresciano-Italiano, 2 vols. 8vo. *sd.* 10s *Brescia*, 1817

8063 —— the same, 2 vols. Appendice, 1 vol.; together 3 vols. in 1, 8vo. *hf. calf, uncut*, 25s 1817-20

8064 **Calabrese.** TASSO GERUSALEMME Liberata, in Lingua Calabrese da Cusentino, sm. 4to, *Italian and Calabrian, vellum*, 12s *Cosenza*, 1737

8065 **Ferrarese.** NANNINI, Vocabolario Ferrarese-Italiano, 12mo, 280 pp. *double columns, vellum*, 10s *Ferrara*, 1805

8066 **Genoese.** CAVALLI, Cittara Zeneize, con Rime antiche Genovesi, 12mo. *vellum*, 9s *Genova*, 1745

8067 FRANCHI, Ro Chittarrin, Strofoggi dra Muza, 12mo. *vellum*, 8s *Zena*, 1772
  Prefaced with "Regole dell' Ortografia Zeneize."

8068 —— the same, NEW EDITION, 16mo. *sd.* 6s *Genova*, 1823

8069 OLIVIERI, Dizionario Genovese-Italiano, 12mo. 559 *pp. sd.* 4s 6d *Gen.* 1851

8070 **Milanese.** CAPPELLETTI, Vocabolario Milanese-Italiano-Francese, 16mo. 553 *pp. sd.* 5s 1848

8071 CHERUBINI, Vocabolario Milanese-Italiano, 2 vols. 8vo. *hf. calf*, 10s 1814

8072 —— the same, 2 vols. 8vo, *calf neat*, 16s 1814

8073 COLLEZIONE delle migliore Opere scritte in Dialetto Milanese, 12 vols. 16mo. *sd.* 18s 1816-7

8074 TASSO, Gerusalemme Liberata, travestita in lingua Milanese da Balestrieri, folio, *Italian and Milanese, bd.* 10s *Milano*, 1773

8075 **Neapolitan.** POETI NAPOLETANI. COLLEZIONE di tutti i Poemi in Lingua Napoletana, con Vocabulario, 28 vols. in 14, 12mo. *neat in hf. calf, scarce*, £2. 12s *Napoli*, 1783-89

8076 POETI NAPOLETANI. Another copy, 27 vols. (Vol. 5 wanting), 12mo. *hf. morocco*, 25s *Napoli*, 1783-89

8077 CAPASSI, Varie Poesie, 4to. *portrait, vellum*, 5s *Napoli*, 1761
  Several are in the Neapolitan dialect.

8078 TASSO, Gierosalemme Libberata, da Fasano, folio, *Italian and Neopolitan, plates after Caracci, vellum*, 7s *Napoli*, 1689

8079 —— another edition, 2 vols. 12mo. *bd.* 5s *Nap.* 1786

8080 VOCABOLARIO del dialetto Napoletano con Ricerche Etimologiche, 2 vols.—Del Dialetto Napoletano—3 vols. 16mo. *vellum*, 15s *Nap.* 1789

8081 **Parmese.** MALASPINA, Vocabolario Parmigiano-Italiano, accresciuto di più che 50,000 voci, con Giunte e Correzioni, 4 vols. 8vo. about 1900 *pp. double columns, sd.* 30s *Parma*, 1856-59

8082 PESCHERI, Dizionario Parmigiano-Italiano, col Appendice, 3 vols. in 1, stout sm. 8vo. *calf gilt, gilt top, uncut*, 15s *Parma*, 1828-31

8083 —— Dizionario Parmigiano-Italiano, rifuso, corretto, accresciuto, 2 vols. 8vo. 47 *and* 1194 *pp. double columns, bds.* 28s *Borgo San Donnino*, 1836

8084 **Piedmontese.** CALVI, Poesie Piemontesi, 8vo. *sd.* 5s *Torino*, 1816

8085 PIPINO, Poesie Piemontese, *Torino*, 1783—Rancher, La Nemaida, et Aperçu sur le patois Niçard, *Nissa*, 1823—Coye, Œuvres complètes Provençales ; Lou Novy Para, coumediou, *Arles*, 1829—Cholera in Pavia, *Pavia*, 1836 ; 5 vols. in 1, 8vo. *hf. russia*, 10s 1783-1836

8086 SANT' ALBINO, Gran Dizionario Piemontese-Italiano, roy. 4to. 16 *and* 1237 *pp. double columns, hf. calf, uncut*, £2. 8s *Torino*, 1859

8087 ZALLI DI CHIERI, Dizionario Piemontese, Italiano, Latino e Francese, edizione seconda riordinata e arrichita, colle Appendici, 2 vols. in 1, stout 4to. *calf gilt, gilt tops, uncut*, 30*s*   *Carmagnola*, 1830

8088 **Romanesc.** BERNERI, Il Meo Patacco overo Roma in Feste, poema giocoso nel Linguaggio Romanesco, stout 12mo. *vellum*, 4*s*   *Roma*, 1695

8089 MORRI, Vocabolario Romagnola-Italiano, large 4to. 886 *pp. double columns, hf. calf, uncut,* £2. 5*s*   *Faenza*, 1840

8090 PERESIO, il Maggio Romanesco, ouero il Palio conquistato, con indice dei Proverbij, etc. stout 12mo. *vellum*, 9*s*   *Ferrara*, 1688
Bel exemplaire de ce poeme fort rare.

8091 **Sardinian.** PORRU, Saggio di Gramatica sul dialetto SARDO Meridionale, 8vo. *calf, scarce*, 20*s*   *Cagliari*, 1811

8092 PURQUEDDU, Tesoro della Sardegna ne Bachi e Gelsi, poema *Sardo e Italiano*, 12mo. *front. and plates, stiff covers, uncut, fine copy*, 15*s*   *Cagliari*, 1779

8093 SPANO, Oitografia Sarda nazionale, ossia Gramatica della lingua Logudorese, 2 vols. in 1, 8vo. *map*, 434 *pp. hf. calf, uncut*, 20*s*   *Cagliari*, 1840

8094 ——— Vocabulario Sardo-Italiano, e Italiano-Sardo, coll' Aggiunta dei Proverbj Sardi, 2 vols. in 1, high 4to. *hf. calf, uncut*, £2. 2*s*   *Cagliari*, 1851

8095 BIUNDI, Dizionario Siciliano-Italiano, 12mo. 578 *pp. sd.* 5*s*   *Palermo*, 1857

8096 **Sicilian.** CARINI, Lu Vivu Mortu, effectu di bruttu amuri, 16mo. *hf. vel.* 6*s*   *Palermu*, 1783

8097 LEONARDI, Poema supra di lu Vinu, si sia utili o dannusu, cantatu intra l'Accademia di li Etnei, 1789, 8vo. THICK PAPER, *portrait, vellum*, 32*s*   *Gatania*, 1798
Copies on thick or vellum paper are VERY RARE. Each page of this curious work has learned philological foot-notes, explaining all the etymologies of the difficult Sicilian words.

8098 MORTILLARO, Nuovo Dizionario Siciliano-Italiano, 4to. 976 *pp. double columns, hf. calf, uncut*, 36*s*   *Palermo*, 1853

8099 PASQUALINO (Mich.) Vocabulario Siciliano etimologico, Italiano, e Latino, 5 vols. sm. 4to. *russia extra, by Clarke,* £3. 3*s*   *Palermo*, 1785-95
Very rare. "Selon Eber, l'Auteur de cet ouvrage peu connu en France a fait de profondes et heureuses recherches sur les etymologies."—*Brunet.*

8100 RAU E REQUESENS (D. S.) Rime, 16mo. *vellum*, 18*s*   *Venetia, Giunti*, 1672
This very scarce volume contains the Author's CANZUNI SICILIANI, written in the Sicilian dialect. On the fly-leaf at the end is a Manuscript sonnet, " Risposta data dal Gran Visir al Re di Prussia," also in the Sicilian dialect.

8101 SCIMONELLI (Ign.) Poesie, 2 vols. 8vo. *portrait, hf. citron morocco, rare,* £2.   *Palermo*, 1826

8102 TEMPIU (*Duminicu*) Operi, Vols. I, II, in 1 vol. 8vo. *hf. rus.* 15*s* *Catania*, 1814
These poems were completed in the third volume, published 1815.

8103 **Siennese.** GIGLI (Girolamo) Vocabulario Cateriniano, ove si spiega alcune Voci e Frasi di S. Caterina da Siena, usate nelle sue opere, secondo IL DIALETTO SANESE, 4to. FIRST EDITION, 320 pp. (A—R), *all published, very rare,* £2.   (*Roma*, 1717)
La premiere édition de cet ouvrage parut, Rome, 1717, mais elle fut arrêtée et saisie lorsquil n'y avait encore que 320 pages d'imprimées, parce que l'ouvrage contenait une satire continuelle des académiciens de la Crusca. Comme l'édition est fort rare, on en a fait une réimpression in 4to, " con aggiunte di Martelli, A—Z," avec un supplément, sans date, mais sous l'indication de *Manila nell'isole Filippine.*
This work was never perfected, but burnt by the hangman, by order of the Grand Duke of Tuscany, who conceived himself injuriously mentioned therein. The inhabitants of Siena believe the dialect of the Italian Language as spoken by them the purest, and have therefore at various times roughly handled the Academy della Crusca.

8104 GIGLI, Vocabulario Cateriniano, con aggiunta, seconda impressione, 4to. *portrait, hf. bd. uncut*, 18*s*   *Manilla, nell' Isole Filippine, s. a.*
To this edition has been added some fragments left by the author, and some letters of Academicians concerning the work; but it has been purged of the obnoxious passages.

8105 **Venetian.** BAFFO (Georgio) Opere, 4 vols. sm. 4to. *portrait, hf. bd.* £2. 8*s*   *Cosmopoli*, 1789
"Poesies obscènes en patois Vénitien, imprimées aux frais du Comte de Pembroke."—BRUNET.

8106 BOERIO, Dizionario del Dialetto Veneziano, roy. 4to. 802 pp. *treble cols. hf. bd.* 28*s*   *Venezia*, 1829

8107 BOSCHINI (Marco) Carta del Navegar Pitoresco, dialogo tra un Senator Venetian deletante e un Professor de Pitura (*in quartine in Dialetto Veneziano*), sq. 8vo. *frontispiece, portrait and plates etched by the Author himself, vellum,* 25*s*   *Venetia, per li Baba*, 1660

8108 ——— the same, sm. 4to. *with all the Etchings, hf. bd. entirely uncut*, 32*s* 1660
"This is an enthusiastic patriotic attempt to place the Venetian School above all others, and is bitter against Vasari. Lanzi says, that with all its defects this work is valuable for historic notices and pictorial precepts. " Sotto quaderni in lingua Veneziana descrivonsi le migliori pitture di Venezia, opera rara e delle più interessanti per l'arte."—" Operetta interessantissima fatta da un insigne conoscitore delle arti, e piena di accorgimento, scritta in dialetto Veneto, col ritratto dell' autore, e una galleria di pitture al fine in 26 tavole illustrate, e inventate dall' autore medesimo."—*Cicogna. Bibliogr. Ven z.*

8109 COLLEZIONE delle migliori Opere scritte in dialetto Veneziano, 12 vols.—
Poeti antichi, 2 vols.—14 vols. 16mo. *sd.* 18*s*; or, 14 vols. in 5, 16mo. *calf extra*,
30*s*   *Venezia*, 1817
8110 PATRIARCHI (Gasparo) Vocabolario Veneziano e Padovano, 4to. *hf. bd.* 6*s*   1821
8111 TASSO, El Goffredo, canta alla Barcariola, 2 vols. 12mo. *Italian and Venetian,
woodcuts, bds.* 12*s*   *Venezia*, 1771
8112 **ITALY**: GINGUÉNÉ (P. L.) Histoire Littéraire d'Italie; augmentée
par Danou, et continuée par SALFI, 12 vols. 8vo. *sd.* 35*s*   *Paris*, 1812-34
8113 ———— the same, COMPLETE, 14 vols. 8vo. *hf. morocco, very rare,* £4. 4*s*   1811-35
The latter volumes are extremely rare, many having been destroyed by fire.
8114 DENNISTOUN'S Memoirs of the Dukes of Urbino, illustrating the Arms,
Arts, and Literature of Italy, from 1440 to 1630, 3 vols. 8vo. *with numerous
engravings, comprising portraits, views, medallions, facsimiles of handwriting,
&c.* (pub. at £1. 8*s*) *extra cloth gilt*, 17*s* 6*d*   1851
This valuable work has already taken a high place in historical literature. Though professing only to record
the history of Urbino, the birth-place of Raphael, it largely illustrates the history and condition of Italy during the
Middle Ages, especially her literature, arts, and artists. The work has been the labour of a life; and the materials
employed, manuscript and printed, exceed 500 volumes, as will be seen by the printed list of them, extending to
eight closely printed pages. The illustrations were engraved in Italy from authentic sources, and have been highly
praised for their truth and delicacy.
8115 FERRARI, Histoire des Révolutions d'Italie, ou Guelfes et Gibelins, 4 vols. 8vo.
cloth, 12*s*   *Paris*, 1858
8116 ROSSETTI (G.) The Antipapal Spirit which produced the Reformation, its secret
influence on the Literature of Italy, 2 vols. post 8vo. *cloth*, 6*s* 1834
8117 **MUSIC**. PICITONO (Frate Angelo da) FIOR ANGELICO DI MUSICA, nel
qual si contengono bellissime dispute contra quelli che dicono la Musica non
esser Scienza, sq. 8vo. *woodcut title, and printer's device at end, with numerous
specimens of Music, and diagrams, title very slightly injured and neatly mended,
otherwise a fine copy in antique calf gilt, by Bedford,* £4. 4*s*   *Vinegia*, 1547
VERY RARE. COLLATION: Title, Dedication, etc. 2 leaves; Table, 2 leaves; Libro primo, 60 leaves, unnumbered,
A to P; Libro secondo, 35 leaves, Q to & 3; Colophon, 1 leaf.

ENGLISH LITERATURE.

8118 **Language and Dialects.** ASH (J.) Dictionary of the English Language,
2 vols. 8vo. *calf*, 9*s*   1775
"An excellent old dictionary."
8119 BAKER'S (A. E.) Glossary of Northamptonshire Words and Phrases, with the
Customs of the County, 2 vols. 8vo. (pub. at 24*s*) *cloth*, 15*s*   1854
8120 BARNES' Poems in the Dorset Dialect, first collection, 12mo. *cloth*, 5*s*   1862
8121 BEE, Sportsman's Slang, a dictionary of terms used on the TURF, the RING, and
BON TON, 12mo. *coloured front. bd.* 7*s*   1825
8122 BOBBIN'S (Tim) MISCELLANEOUS WORKS (by JOHN COLLIER), containing his
view of the LANCASHIRE DIALECT, and his Poems with Glossary, *portrait and
curious plates, half morocco, very rare*, 36*s*   *Manchester*, 1775
8123 ———— the same, 1775—BRICE'S EXMOOR Scolding, and Courtship, with Vocabulary of the Language, 1771—2 vols. in 1, 12mo. *plates, calf,* £2. 2*s*   1771-75
8124 BOBBIN'S Miscellaneous Works, with his Life, *portraits and plates,* 1812—
Plebeian Politics, dialogue between two Lancashire Clowns, etc. by Tim Bobbin
the Second, with Glossary, *portrait*, 1801—2 vols. in 1, 8vo. *calf neat*, 20*s*
                                                                       Salford, 1801-12
8125 BOBBIN'S Works in prose and verse, with Memoir of the Author by Corry,
and Glossary of Lancashire Words and Phrases, large 8vo. *portrait and plates*,
BEST EDITION, *fine paper, calf extra, gilt edges,* £2. 2*s*   *Rochdale*, 1819
8126 BOBBIN'S Lancashire Dialect and Poems, 12mo. *plates by Cruikshank, half
morocco,* 7*s* 6*d*   1828
8127 BONAPARTE (Prince L. L.) SONG OF SOLOMON, *in twenty-five English
dialects*: Lowland Scotch, three versions; of Northumberland; Newcastle,
two versions; Cumberland, two varieties, North and Central; Durham, Westmoreland, North Yorkshire, Craven, North Lancashire, West Yorkshire,
Sheffield, Lancashire (Bolton), Devonshire, East Devonshire, Somersetshire,
Wiltshire, Dorset, Cornwall (living dialect,) Sussex and Norfolk, and Saxon-
English; 25 parts, 16mo. £3. 5*s*   1858-63
8128 BOUCHER (J.) Glossary of Archaic and Provincial Words, Introduction, and
A-BLA, (*all published*), 4to. *an unfinished work, cloth,* 5*s*; or *calf gilt,* 7*s* 6*d* 1832

8128 *BOPP'S Comparative Grammar of the Sanscrit, Zend, Greek, Latin, Lithuanian, Gothic, German, and Sclavonic Languages, translated from the German by Lieut. Eastwick, conducted through the press by H. H. Wilson, 3 vols. 8vo. *second edition, complete,* (pub. at £3. 7s 6d), *cloth,* 36s 1856
Professor Bopp gives numerous and undeniable proofs of the close connexion which subsists between the sacred language of the Hindus and the languages of ancient Greece and Rome, as well as those of the Celtic, Teutonic, and Sclavonic nations.

8129 COLE's English Dictionary, 12mo. *calf,* 5s 1692
8130 COTGRAVE'S French-English and English-French Dictionary, with Grammar and Proverbs, by Howell, folio, *calf,* 24s 1650
8131 —— another edition, folio, *calf,* 25s 1660
8132 CRAVEN DIALECT in the West Riding of the County of York, with a copious GLOSSARY and Dialogues, 2 vols. sm. 8vo. (pub. at 20s) *cloth,* 14s 1828
8133 DIALOGUES, Songs, and Ballads, in the Westmoreland and Cumberland dialects, with Glossary, 12mo. *cloth,* 7s 1839
8134 DICTIONARY (A new) of the Terms Ancient and Modern of the CANTING CREW, Gypsies, Beggars, Thieves, Cheats, with proverbs and phrases, by B. E., 12mo. 6 *and* 176 *pp. double columns, calf, rare,* 30s (ca. 1700)
8135 FORBY (R.) Vocabulary of East Anglia (Norfolk and Suffolk), with Life by Dawson Turner, 2 vols. 8vo. *portrait, cloth,* 14s 1830
8136 —— the same, 2 vols. in 1, sm. 8vo. *calf gilt,* 15s 1830
8137 FULLER's Collection of *English, French, Scotch, Spanish, and Italian* Proverbs, 18mo. *calf extra,* 6s (? 1800)
8138 GIL (Alexandri) Logonomia Anglica quâ gentis sermo facilius addiscitur, secundò edita, correctior, ad usum communem accomodatior, sq. 8vo. *a little wormed towards the end, otherwise fine copy, calf gilt, old style,* £3. 3s 1621
A very rare and curious work, being an English Grammar in Latin, on a singular Phonetic system, with examples from Anglo-Saxon, German, and other languages. The author (whose son and namesake was the teacher of Milton) was evidently a man of extensive learning and acquirements. His phonetic spelling sometimes looks rather uncouth; as, for instance, when such a combination as *Dzyudzyh* represents the word *Judge*.

8139 GRADUS AD CANTABRIGIAM, Dictionary of Cant Terms, 12mo. 2s Lond. 1803
8140 GROSE'S (Captain) Classical Dictionary of the Vulgar Tongue, 8vo. FIRST EDITION, *containing many indecorous words and explanations not given in after editions, clean copy, rare, bds.* 15s 1785
Of this edition an illustrated issue exists, with the title changed to "Blackguardiana," or a Dictionary of Rogues, Bawds, Pimps, etc. *illustrated with* 18 *portraits (of bad characters) by Caulfield, interspersed with Anecdotes and Flash Songs* (reprinted from "A new Canting Dictionary, 12mo., 1725,") 8vo. s. a.

8141 GROSE, the second edition, corrected and enlarged, 8vo. *bds.* 9s 1788
8142 —— Lexicon Balatronicum, originally by Grose, now enlarged by a member of the Whip Club, Hell-Fire Dick, etc. 8vo. *bds.* 5s 1811
8143 —— the same, *with a large plate, "Bang-up Dinner" by Cruikshank inserted, bds.* 7s 6d 1811
8144 —— Lexicon Balatronicum: Dictionary of Buckish Slang, University Wit, and Pickpocket Eloquence, altered and enlarged by J. Disney, H. Clarke, Dick Owen (Hell-Fire Dick), and others, 8vo. *prepared for a new edition,* WITH COPIOUS MANUSCRIPT ADDITIONS, *hf. russia, uncut,* £2. 2s 1811
8145 GROSE's Provincial Glossary, with a collection of Local Proverbs and Popular Superstitions, 8vo. 5s 1785
8146 —— the same, 2nd edition, *calf,* 7s 1790
8147 HALLIWELL'S Dictionary of Archaic and Provincial words, obsolete phrases, and Ancient Customs, from the fourteenth Century, 2 vols. 8vo. *cloth,* 15s 1852
8148 HARTSHORNE (C. H.) SALOPIA ANTIQUA, or an enquiry from personal survey into the Druidical, Military, and other early remains in Shropshire, and the North Welsh borders, with observations upon the names of places and a Glossary of words used in the County of Salop, 8vo. *illuminated title and plates, cloth,* 10s 1841
The Glossary is very complete, extending over 324 pages.

8149 HULOET'S (R.) Dictionarie (English, Latin, and French) enlarged by John Higgins, (Editor of Mirror for Magistrates), sm. folio, black letter, *engraved title, with the coat of arms of Sir Geo. Peckham on the reverse, large copy, calf,* 2 *leaves of sheet* K *and* 1 *leaf of sheet* T t *wanting, calf, scarce,* 32s
T. Marsh, 1572
Amongst the commendatory verses is an English Poem of 38 lines by Thomas Churchyarde. Collation: Engraved title; Dedication, 1 leaf; To the reader and verses, 2 leaves; Dictionary, sig. A—A a a, 251 leaves; Table, 1 leaf.
"In fact this is almost a new book from the various additions and improvements it contains."—*Ant. à Wood.*

8150 HUNTER'S (Jos.) Hallamshire Glossary, sm. 8vo. *cloth*, 5s 1829
8151 (HUTCHINSON) Advantages of a good Language to a Nation, 8vo. *bds*. 5s   *s. a.*
8152 JAMIESON (DR. JOHN) ETYMOLOGICAL DICTIONARY OF THE SCOTTISH LANGUAGE, illustrating their significations from ancient and modern Writers, shewing their Affinity to other Languages, and elucidating National Rites, Customs, and Institutions, in their Analogy to those of other Nations, with the Supplement, 4 vols. 4to. (pub. £8. 8s *in cloth*), *calf gilt, rare*, £7. 10s   *Edinb.* 1808-25
This valuable work is rapidly getting scarce; the second edition, 2 vols. 4to. 1841, advertised as including "The Supplement," contains only a selection of the words from the Supplement, with short Explanations, but *without* the many quotations in the original Supplement.

8153 JAMIESON'S ETYMOLOGICAL DICTIONARY OF THE SCOTTISH LANGUAGE, SECOND EDITION, with the additional Words in the Supplement incorporated, 4 vols. 4to. (pub. at £8. 8s) *cloth.* £6.   *Edinb.* 1840-41
This is universally admitted to be one of the most important lexicographical works published in any country and has long maintained a high price in the book market.
"An admirable Dictionary, which has been of great use to me."—*R. Nares.*

8154 —— the same, abridged from the Dictionary and Supplement, stout 8vo. *portrait*, 715 pp. *double columns*, (pub. at 21s), *new in cloth*, 12s   *Edinb.* 1846

8155 JENNINGS on some of the Dialects in the West of England, particularly SOMERSETSHIRE; with a glossary of words now in use there, and poems and other pieces exemplifying the dialect, 18mo. *scarce*, 12s 1825

8156 JOHNSON'S (Samuel) Dictionary of the ENGLISH LANGUAGE, in which the Words are deduced from their Originals, and illustrated in their Different Significations by Examples from the best Writers, FIRST EDITION, 2 vols. large thick folio, *old calf extra, backs mended, arms on sides,* £2. 1755
Priced, 1840, Jas. Bohn, £4. 4s.

8157 —— Dictionary of the English Language, second edition, (exactly the same as the first) 2 vols. large thick folio, *calf neat*, 36s   1755-56
"It is well known that in the later editions of this immortal production numerous errors and abridgments are to be found, especially with regard to the examples; hence the desirableness of securing the first edition."—*Lowndes.*
This edition contains some curious explanations suppressed by subsequent editors; as, "Excise, a hateful tax levied upon the commodities, and adjudged, not by the common judges of property, but wretches hired by those to whom excise is paid." "LEXICOGRAPHER, a harmless drudge." "PENSION, an allowance made to any one without an equivalent. In England it is generally understood to mean pay given to a state hireling for treason to his country." "PENSIONER, a slave of state hired by a stipend to obey his master," &c. &c.

8158 JOHNSON'S Dictionary of the English Language; with numerous corrections, and the addition of several thousand words, by TODD, 4 vols. 4to. *calf gilt*, 30s   1818-19

8159 JUNII Etymologicum Anglicanum, edidit accessionibus multis E. Lye, cum vita Auctoris et Grammatica Anglo-Saxonica, folio, *portrait from Vandyke by Vertue, in old calf, rare*, 21s   *Oxon.* 1743

8160 LANE'S Key to the Art of Letters, or English a learned Language, full of Art, Elegancy and Variety, 16mo. *old morocco*, 7s 1700

8161 LATHAM'S English Language, third enlarged edition, stout 8vo. (pub. at 15s), *cloth*, 9s 1850

8162 MARRIOTT'S Collection of English Miracle Plays or Mysteries, containing 10 Dramas, with Glossary, 8vo. *bds.* 7s   *Basel*, 1838

8163 MOOR'S (E.) Suffolk Words and Phrases; or an attempt to collect the Localisms of that County, 12mo. 18s   *Woodbridge*, 1823

8164 MULLER'S (Max) Lectures on the SCIENCE OF LANGUAGE, delivered at the Royal Institution, 1861, 4th edition, 8vo. (pub. at 12s) *cloth*, 10s   1864
The most profound philological work of modern days; written at the same time in such a simple manner as to be understood by the general reader.

8165 MURRAY'S English Grammar, 2 vols. 8vo. 3*rd edition. hf. calf*, 6s   *York*, 1816

8166 NARES (Archdeacon) GLOSSARY, or Collection of Words, Phrases, Names, and allusions to Customs, Proverbs, &c. which require Illustration, in the Works of English Authors, particularly SHAKESPEARE, and his contemporaries, 4to. (pub. at £2. 15s) 20s 1822

8167 —— the same, 4to. FINE PAPER, (pub. at £4. 4s) *bds.* 27s 1822

8168 OWAIN MILES, and other inedited fragments of Ancient English Poetry, (edited by Turnbull), sm. 8vo. *uncut, only 32 copies printed*, 24s   *Edin.* 1837

8169 PARKER (Geo.) Life's Painter of variegated Characters in public Life, 8vo. *portrait, bd.* 7s 1789
A work which must have enjoyed an immense popularity to judge by the extensive list of subscribers. Chapter XIV. contains: Original Cant Songs; the Slang Language; a Glossary and a Key. Chapter XV. Glossary.

ENGLISH LITERATURE.

8170 PIERS PLOUGHMAN, his Vision and Creed (by Robert or William Longlande), with Introduction, notes and Glossary (by Wright), 2 vols. 12mo. *woodcut title and illustration, ruled with red lines, calf gilt*, 16s   *Pickering*, 1832

8171 PICKERING's (John) Vocabulary of Words and Phrases peculiar to the United States, 8vo. 15s   *Boston, U. S.* 1816

8172 POTTER's Dictionary of all the Cant and Flash Languages, ancient and modern, 8vo. 62 pp. 6s   *ca.* 1795

8173 RICHARDSON'S Dictionary of the English Language, comprising explanations with Etymology, and illustrated by quotations from the best authorities, 2 vols. with the SUPPLEMENT, 4to. (pub. at £4. 16s) *cloth bds.* £3. 16s   1858

8174 —— the same, 2 vols. 4to. *hf. russia*, £4. 14s 6d   1858

8175 —— the Supplement separately, for possessors of the earlier issues, 4to. 126 pp. *cloth*, 10s   1858

Richardson's Dictionary appeared in 1833-7; since then there have been numerous issues with fresh titles and later dates. The book being stereotyped, there is no difference in the copies. The above Supplement *should go with every copy*, it is printed in such a manner as to correspond with each volume of the Dictionary, and to bind up with them.

8176 RIVE (Edmund) Ten Grammaticall chapters, with Latine, construed to introduct unto the understanding of Lillie's Grammar, sm. 4to. 62 pages, Black letter, *hf. morocco*, 32s   *London, printed by Authority*, 1620

In the same volume are bound up, Certaine rules for this time of pestilential contagion, with a caveat to those that wear *impoisoned Amulets as a preservative from the Plague*, 1603; a relation of the departure of Frederick, King elect of Bohemia, with his royall Ladie Elizabeth, 1619; Fenton's Treatise of Usurie, 1611; and other curious tracts.

8177 ROGET'S Thesaurus of English Words and Phrases, arranged to facilitate literary composition, 8vo. (pub. at 14s) *cloth*, 10s   1853

8178 SANFORD (J.) Entrance to the SPANISH TONGUE, sq. 12mo. *with folded table, rare*, 24s   *Th. Haveland, for Nath. Butter*, 1611

8179 SCOUNDREL'S DICTIONARY, or an Explanation of the Cant Words, used by Thieves, Housebreakers, Street Robbers, and Pickpockets about Town, with Flash Songs, and a Glossary, sm. 8vo. *hf. bd.* 18s   1704

A copy fetched, 1857, at Sotheby's, £3. 7s.

8180 SKINNER (S.) Etymologicon Linguæ ANGLICANÆ, seu explicatio vocum Anglicarum etymologica ex 12 Linguis, folio, *good copy in old calf*, 25s   *Londini*, 1671

An early and valuable Etymological Dictionary of the English Language, not superseded by any subsequent work.

8181 SMITH's (Capt. Alex.) History of the Lives and Robberies of the most notorious Highwaymen, Foot-Pads, Shop-Lifts, and Cheats, Vols. II, III, 12mo. *bd.* 14s
Vol. II. contains "The Thieves' new Canting Dictionary," 1719.   1719-14

8182 STAGG's Poems, some in Cumberland dialect, 12mo. *bds.* 3s   1805

8182* —— another edition, sm. 8vo. *bds.* 4s   1808

8183 THOMAS (W.) Principal Rules of the ITALIAN GRAMMAR, with a Dictionarie for the better understandynge of Boccace, Pethrarcha, and Dante, newly corrected and imprinted, sq. 12mo. Black letter, *woodcut border round the title, fine copy in maroon morocco*, RARE, £2. 16s   *H. Wykes*, 1567

Priced, 1820, Thorpe, £3. 3s. The author was executed at Tyburn, for a conspiracy against Queen Mary.

8184 TOOKE'S (J. Horne) ΕΠΕΑ ΠΤΕΡΟΕΝΤΑ, or the Diversions of Purley, new edition by Taylor, 2 vols. 8vo. *bds.* 9s; or *hf. calf*, 12s   1829

8185 VAUX (James Hardy) Memoirs, by himself, 2 vols. sm. 8vo. *cloth*, 10s   1819
Pages 147-227 contain a VOCABULARY OF THE FLASH LANGUAGE.

8186 VERSTEGAN'S Restitution of Decayed Intelligence, in Antiquities concerning the English Nation, BEST EDITION, *plates of Anglo-Saxon Antiquities, no title*, 1605—(CAMDEN) Remaines concerning Brittaine, its Languages, Names, Moneys, Apparell, Proverbs, Epitaphs, etc. 1629—2 vols. in 1, sq. 8vo. *original old calf, from the collection of Thomas Havers*, 12s   1605-29

Verstegan is particularly valuable for the philological portion; Camden's works is rich in proverbs.

8187 WILBRAHAM's CHESHIRE Glossary, 12mo. *bds.* 3s 6d   1820

8188 WITHALS' DICTIONARIE, in English and Latine, for Children and yong beginners; with Phrases and Rythmicale and Proverbial Verses, added by Evans, Fleming, and Clerk, thick 12mo. *pp.* 10 *and* 623, *double columns, calf*, 28s   *London, Purfoot*, 1616

8189 —— the same, *title mounted, otherwise a good copy, old calf*, 18s   1616

8190 ABBOTSFORD CLUB. PAPERS relative to the Regalia of Scotland, 4to. *plates and facsimiles, bds.* 35s   *Edinb.* 1829

8191 ROMANCES of Sir GUY OF WARWICK and Rembrun his son, now first edited from the Auchinleck MSS. 4to. *plate, cloth*, 32s   *Edinb.* 1840

8192 A PENNI WORTH of Witte : Florice and Blaunchefleur ; and other Pieces of ancient English Poetry, from the Auchinleck MS. 4to. *cloth*, 28s *Edinb*. 1857

8193 MEMOIRS of the INSURRECTION in Scotland in 1715, by John, Master of Sinclair, from the original MS. with notes by SIR WALTER SCOTT, stout 4to. *cloth*, £4. 4s *Edinb*. 1858

8194 OPPRESSIONS of the Sixteenth Century in the Islands of ORKNEY and ZETLAND, from original documents, with introduction, appendix, and a Glossary, 4to. *cloth*, 30s *ib*. 1859

8195 ADAMS' Index Villaris ; or an Alphabetical Table of all the Cities, Market Towns, Parishes, Villages, and Private Seats, in ENGLAND and WALES, folio, LARGE PAPER, *very fine copy in rich old red* MOROCCO, *gilt leaves, with a MS. note " The gift of the ingenious author Mr. Adams, March 31st, 1683," and the crest of Sir William Boothby, Ashburne Hall*, 36s 1680
With copies of a later issue, an Appendix and a map have occasionally been found ; such a copy was priced, 1834, Thorpe, £5. 5s.

8196 ADDISON'S (Joseph) Works, BASKERVILLE's beautiful edition, 4 vols. roy. 4to. *portrait by Guignon, and plates, quite free from stains, fine copy, in calf gilt, scarce*, £4. 4s Birmingham, 1761
Priced, 1856, £4. 14s 6d ; Maddison's copy fetched, £8. 10s ; Willett's, £6. 12s 6d ; Williams, *morocco by De Rome*, £14. 14s ; 1853, Sotheby's, morocco, £10. 10s ; 1858, £5. 10s ; 1858, £5. It is very uncommon to meet with an unstained copy. "He who hath the Baskerville edition hath a good and even a glorious performance."—*Dibdin*.

8197 ALISON'S (Sir A.) HISTORY OF EUROPE, from the commencement of the French Revolution in 1789, to the Restoration of the Bourbons in 1815, 10 vols. 8vo. (pub. at £7. 15s in bds.) *calf*, £6. 6s 1835-42

8198 ——— the same, a New Library Edition (being the Tenth), in 14 vols. demy 8vo. *with portraits*, and a copious Index, (pub. at £10. 10s) *cloth*, £8. 15s 1863

8199 ——— another edition, in crown 8vo. (pub. at £6.) *cloth*, £5. 1863

8200 ——— a People's Edition, 12 vols. *closely printed in double columns*, and Index volume, (pub. at £2. 11s) *cloth*, £2. 5s 1863
" An extraordinary work, which has earned for itself a lasting place in the literature of the country, and within a few years found innumerable readers in every part of the globe. There is no book extant that treats so well of the period to the illustration of which Mr. Alison's labours have been devoted. It exhibits great knowledge, patient research, indefatigable industry, and vast power."—*Times, Sept*. 7, 1850.

8201 ——— HISTORY OF EUROPE from the fall of Napoleon in 1815, to the accession of Louis Napoleon in 1852, 9 vols. 8vo. (pub. at £6. 7s 6d) *cloth, clean copy*, £4. 10s 1854-60

8202 ——— ATLAS TO ALISON'S HISTORY OF EUROPE, containing 109 Maps and Plans of Countries, Battles, Sieges, and Sea-Fights, constructed by A. Keith Johnston, F.R.S.E., with Vocabulary of Military and Marine Terms, demy 4to. Library Edition, £3. 3s ; People's Edition, crown 4to. £1. 11s 6d 1863

8203 ALPHABETS, Ornamental and Early English, Initials, etc. for Engravers and Decorators, roy. 8vo. *cloth*, 5s *ca*. 1845

8204 ANDERSON'S ROYAL GENEALOGIES, or the Genealogical Tables of Emperors, Kings, and Princes, folio, second edition (or issue), with new Addenda and Corrigenda after the preface, roy. folio, LARGE PAPER, *calf gilt*, £6. 6s 1736
" The most useful and valuable work of the kind, and probably the most difficult and laborious ever undertaken by author or printer."—*Lowndes*.

8205 ANTAR, a Bedoueen Romance, translated from the Arabic, by T. Hamilton, 4 vols. 8vo. 20s 1820
The best picture of Bedoueen Life.

8206 ANTIQUARIAN and TOPOGRAPHICAL CABINET, containing a series of elegant Views in Gt. Britain, with letterpress, 10 vols. 12mo. *numerous pretty plates, calf gilt*, 27s 1807-11

8207 ARABIAN NIGHTS' ENTERTAINMENTS, a new translation, with copious Notes on the Language, Manners, and Customs of the Egyptian Arabs, by Edward William LANE, 3 vols. roy. 8vo. ORIGINAL AND BEST EDITION, *with upwards of one thousand woodcuts, by the most eminent artists, after designs by* W. HARVEY, *cloth gilt*, £2. 12s 6d 1839-41
" Much of the nightmare which has oppressed our judgment as to the supposed extravagance and impossibility of this collection has vanished with the darkness of past hours ; the fidelity of the descriptions has been recognised as giving the best picture possible of Eastern manners ; and this adherence to the truth on one, and so material a point, gives earnest of accuracy on others upon which we cannot be so well informed. Much of this information, however, Mr. Lane has supplied, and no one who is acquainted with his unrivalled and delightful volumes on Egypt, can doubt that he was ABSOLUTELY THE FITTEST OF WRITERS for the task he has undertaken. The doubtful and obscure becomes truth and elucidation in his hands ; we are improved in spite of ourselves, and even by the very means we seek to avoid it ; the customs, and manners, and habits of thought, become familiarised with us, even as amongst the chosen playthings of indolent recreation. The parent need no longer fear, the maiden no longer blush.

to take up the work, and place it in the hands of a child. Were this the only praise, it would be no ordinary recommendation ; but the beauty of the type, correct pictorial embellishments, and faithful expression, render this one of the most delightful of works:—a walking dream, to soothe and wile the listless and vacant hours that creep along during 'the long siesta of a summer's day!'"—*Foreign Quarterly Review, July,* 1838.

8208 ARCHAEOLOGIA CANTIANA, being the Transactions of the Kent Archaeological Society, Vols. I, II, 8vo. *many plates, some coloured, of Antiquities, Ancient Arms, Ornaments, Facsimiles of Early Charters, etc.* cloth, only printed for subscribers, now out of print and very rare, £2. 12s 6d   1858-59

8209 ARTHUR OF LITTLE BRITAIN. The History of that Valiant Knight Arthur of Little Britain, a Romance of Chivalry, originally translated by Lord Berners, new edition, (by Utterson), sm. 4to. FINE PAPER, *with* 25 PLATES, *coloured after ancient illuminated manuscripts, blue morocco extra, with joints and gilt leaves,* £4. 4s   1814

Copies with illuminated plates have been priced, 1837, Baldwin, mor. £7.; 1843, morocco, £5. 5s; 1822, Baldwin, mor. £6.; Hibbert's copy fetched £5. 10s; 1857, Utterson's copy, mor. £6. 15s. "The editor of this elegant volume uses extraordinary diligence in tracing out the name of the original writer of the above Romance, the time of its composition, and other much wished for particulars."—*Holme's Catalogue.*

8210 ARTHUR (King) The Byrth, Lyf and Actes of KYNG ARTHUR; of his noble Knyghtes of the Rounde Table, theyr merveyllous Enquestes and Adventures, thacheyeuyng of the Sanc Greal ; and in the end Le Morte Darthur, reprinted from Caxton's Edition of 1485, with Introduction and Notes by SOUTHEY, 2 vols. 4to. *bds. uncut,* £4. 4s   1817

8211 —— the same, 2 vols. sm. 4to. *a fine copy in olive* MOROCCO *extra, by* BEDFORD, £6. 10s   1817

With the following note in Sir F. Palgrave's autograph: "This publication, produced when the Bibliomania was an epidemic, proved an utter failure to the booksellers. Southey received £100. for the work."

8212 ASCHAM (Roger) Toxophilus, the Schole or Partitions of Shooting, *portrait, calf,* 10s   London, 1571; *Wrexham, reprinted* 1788

8213 ASTLE'S Origin and Progress of Writing, illustrated by Engravings from Marbles, MSS. and Charters, roy. 4to. BEST EDITION, *with additions, portrait, and* 31 *plates of facsimiles of MSS., Alphabets, &c. bds. uncut,* 28s   1803

8214 —— the same, roy. folio, LARGE PAPER, *portrait, and* 31 *plates of facsimiles of MSS. Alphabets, &c. several illuminated,* (pub. at £10. 10s *in bds.*) *hf. morocco, uncut,* £4.   1803

Very few copies were printed on this paper.

8215 **Atlas.** SAXTON'S Maps of England and Wales, folio, *the* ORIGINAL EDITION, COLOURED, *wanting Index and* 13 *Maps, original old binding,* £4. 4s   1579

Containing:—Frontispiece, with portrait of Elizabeth, injured; England; Southampton; Essex; Hertfordshire; Berkshire, Buckinghamshire, and Oxfordshire; Norfolk, Northampton, Cambridge, Bedford, Huntingdon, and Rutlandshire; Warwick and Leicestershire; Staffordshire; Shropshire; Hereford; Derby; Cheshire; Yorkshire; Lancashire; Northumberland; Glamorgan; Pembroke; Montgomery and Merioneth; Denbigh and Flint; Anglesey and Caernarvon; in all 22 maps, coloured, with the Arms engraved in the corner of each.

8216 SAXTON'S ATLAS ; another set, the 35 maps, complete, without Index, folio, *in the original old calf,* £5.   1573-1642

Containing:—England and Wales; Cornwall; Devon; Somerset; Dorset; Southampton; Kent; Essex; Suffolk; Norfolk; Northampton; Hartford; Oxford, Buckingham and Berks; Wiltshire; Gloucester; Hereford; Salop; Worcester; Warwick and Leicester; Lincoln and Nottingham; Darbieshire; Stafford; Cheshire; Lancaster; Yorkshire, Durisme; Cumberland and Westmoreland; Northumberland; Monumeth; Penbrok; Glamorgan; Radnor, Breknok, Cardigan, and Caermarden; Montgomeri and Merionidh; Anglesey; Denbigh and Flint. This is the complete Atlas, and has been engraved from the original coppers, with the alteration only of the date. The alteration is visible on each plate.

8217 AUBREY'S Letters, written by eminent Persons in the XVIIth and XVIIIth Centuries, now first published, 3 vols. 8vo. *bds.* 12s   1813

Priced, 1840, J. Bohn, 24s; Dr. Bliss's copy, 1858, fetched £2. 5s. Including Hearne's Journey to Reading and to Whaddon Hall, with lives of eminent men who lived about this date.

8218 ASSIZE OF BREADE. Here beginneth the Booke, named the Assise of Breade, and also the Assyse of Ale, Weyght of Butter and Cheese, etc. very small 4to. 𝕭𝖑𝖆𝖈𝖐 𝖑𝖊𝖙𝖙𝖊𝖗, 4 *curious woodcuts on the title, and* 4 *small woodcuts of loaves of bread on nearly every page, fine copy in* RED MOROCCO EXTRA *by Bedford,* VERY RARE, £4. 15s   London, Hugh Jackson, s. a. (? 1600)

8219 BACON (Francis) *Lord Chancellor of England,* WORKS, a new edition, by BASIL MONTAGU, 16 vols. in 17, 8vo. *portraits, views, facsimiles, etc. fine copy in calf gilt,* £8. 10s   Pickering, 1825-34

The most complete edition extant: it contains translations as well as the original of the Latin Works, and is illustrated by Portraits, Views, and Facsimiles, with a New Life.

8220 BACON'S WORKS ; new edition, collected and edited by R. L. Ellis, J. Spedding, and D. D. Heath, Vols. I. to V. comprising the Division of Philosophical Works, 5 vols. 8vo. £4. 6s. Vols. VI. and VII., comprising the Division of Literary and Professional Works, 2 vols. 8vo. £1. 16s—together, 7 vols. 8vo. *cloth,* £5.   1858, &c.

2 G

8221 BAINE'S LANCASHIRE. HISTORY of the County Palatine and Duchy of
LANCASTER, the Biographical Department by Whatton, 70 Nos. forming 4 vols.
stout royal 4to. LARGE PAPER, *with proof impressions on India paper of the numerous fine plates of Portraits, Views, Antiquities, Machinery, etc. with maps,
and numerous woodcuts of Arms, etc. as well as an immense number of Pedigrees,*
in numbers, £12. 1831-36
<small>In Vol. I. of the above set, pp. 377-84 are wanting. In Vol. II. a plate of Power Loom Weaving is wanted.
In Vol. III. pp. 25-64 (being No. 35) are wanting; the lower margins of No. 41 injured by oil; and four plates
(Moreton Hall, Gillibrand Hall, Warrington Market Place, and portrait of J. P. Kemble) wanting. In Vol. IV.
pp. 121-160 (No. 56), three plates (Liverpool from Toxteth Park, Interior of St. John's Market, Liverpool, Lancaster
Sands), and the Stanley Pedigree, are wanting. A complete copy should also be accompanied by the series of 46 plates
of Views, etc., which were subsequently engraved as suitable for insertion in the work.</small>

8222 BANKERS' MAGAZINE, Journal of the Money Market, and Railway Digest,
from January 1848 to December 1862, published monthly, being Nos. 46 *bis*,
to 225 (wanting No. 47, for February 1848), together, 180 Nos. 8vo. (pub. at
£13. 10s), *sd.* £3. 10s 1848-62

8223 BANKRUPTS' REGISTER, continued monthly, from December 1827 to
December 1846, in 5 stout vols. 8vo. *hf. calf,* 25s 1827-47

8224 PERRY'S Bankrupt and Insolvent Weekly Gazette, a complete Register of
English, Scotch, and Irish Bankrupts, etc. from 1825 to 1858 inclusive,
7 vols. 4to. *hf. bd.* £2. 16s 1852-58

8225 BANKS (T. C.) History of the Ancient Noble Family of MARMYUN, their singular office of King's Champion by the Tenure of Scrivelsby Manor, etc. 4to.
LARGE PAPER, *portraits (including one of Henry VIII. inserted), facsimiles,
pedigrees, etc., hf. russia, uncut,* 28s 1817

8226 BANNATYNE CLUB. REGISTRUM Episcopatus Glasguensis: Munimenta
Ecclesie Metrop. Glasg. a Sec. XII. ad reformatam Religionem (ed. Innes),
2 vols. 4to. *plates of seals, etc. cloth,* £2. 16s Edinb. 1843

8227 BLACK BOOK of TAYMOUTH, with other Papers from the Breadalbane
Charter Room, stout 4to. *printed in black letter facsimile, with numerous
ILLUMINATED plates of Knights in Armour, cloth,* £7. 15s Edinb. 1855

8228 ADAMNANI Vita Sancti COLUMBÆ: Life of St. Columba, in Latin, with
Irish and Latin extracts, and copious notes and dissertations by Reeves,
stout 4to. *facsimiles, cloth,* £4. 10s Dublin, 1857

8229 COLVILLE (J.) Letters (1582-1603) to which is added his Palinode, 1600,
with a Memoir of the Author, stout 4to. *facsimile, presented by the Earl of
Selkirk, cloth,* £2. Edinb. 1858

8230 BARONIAL HALLS and Ancient Picturesque Edifices of England, with
Descriptions by S. C. Hall, 2 vols. folio, LARGE PAPER, ORIGINAL ISSUE, 71 *large
and finely executed plates, from Drawings by Harding, Cattermole, Prout, Müller, Holland, and other eminent Artists,* PROOFS ON INDIA PAPER, *also many
woodcuts in the text, green morocco super extra, gilt edges,* £10. 10s 1848
<small>The Drawings of this attractive work are executed in the highest style of Art, by the most eminent Living
Artists, and comprise the most ancient Castles and Mansions now existing in England; the small paper issue was
published at £14. 14s.</small>

8231 BARRIFFE (Capt. W.) Militarie Discipline; or, the Young Artillery-man,
sq. 8vo. *with the scarce portrait and cuts, calf, curious,* 10s 1643
<small>COLLATION: Portrait; Title; Dedication, etc. 3 leaves; pp. 1-261; Contents, 3 pp. At pp. 174 and 259
there are 3 slips of woodcuts.</small>

8232 BECKFORD'S Biographical Memoirs of extraordinary Painters, 12mo. *plate, bds.*
6s 1834
<small>Sharp satires on the Dutch and Flemish schools.</small>

8233 BEHN (Mrs.) All the Histories and Novels of, published by Charles Gildon, with
Life of the Author, 2 vols. 12mo. *portrait and plates, hf. bd. rare,* £2. 10s 1735
<small>The character that Mrs. Behn has acquired for gross and licentious writing, is a blot on her reputation for
judgment and ability, which was so great that Charles II. thought fit to entrust her with the conduct of some
political affairs in Holland.</small>

8234 BENTHAM'S (Jeremy) WORKS, now first collected; under the superintendence
of his executor, John Bowring, 22 parts, forming 11 vols. large 8vo. *portrait,*
(pub. at £9. 18s) *cloth,* £5. 5s 1838-43

8235 ———— Collection of his minor, but important Judicial, Legal, and Political
Pamphlets, formed into 3 vols. 8vo. *hf. calf,* £2. 2s 1793-1832

8236 ———— Panopticon, or the Inspection House, with a plan of Management, 2 vols.
12mo. *bds.* 5s 1791

8237 ———— Scotch Reform considered, with illustrations from English Non-reform,
8vo. *cloth,* 5s 1808

8238 ———— on Codification and Public Instruction, 8vo. *bds.* 5s 1817

ENGLISH LITERATURE. 451

8239 BENTHAM (J.) Chrestomathia for the extension of instruction to the higher branches of learning, 8vo. *tables, bds.* 5s 1816
8240 ——— Defence of Usury, with a Letter to Adam Smith, and a Protest against Law taxes, 12mo. *bds.* 5s 1818
8241 ——— Plan of Parliamentary Reform, in the form of a Catechism, 8vo. *bds.* 5s 1813
8242 ——— Church-of-Englandism and its Catechism examined, 8vo. (pub. at 20s) 10s 1818
8243 ——— Fragment on Government, 8vo. *second enlarged edition, bds.* 5s 1823
8244 ——— Book of Fallacies, 8vo. *two leaves of preface and contents wanting, bds.* 6s 1824
8245 ——— Rationale of Judicial Evidence, specially applied to English practice, 5 vols. 8vo. (pub. at £3.) *bds.* 20s 1827
8246 ——— Justice and Codification Petitions, 8vo. *bds.* 6s 1829
8247 ——— Constitutional Code for all Liberal Nations and Governments, Vol. I. (all pub.) 8vo. *cloth,* 6s 1830
8248 ——— Deontology; or the Science of Morality, edited by Bowring, 2 vols. 8vo. *bds.* 6s 1834

"Dr. Parr considered Jeremy Bentham as the wisest man of his time, whose powerful and penetrating mind had anticipated the improvements of coming ages; and who, on the all-important subject of jurisprudence, has discovered and collected knowledge, which will scarcely find its way to the great mass of human intellect, perhaps through the course of another century."—*Field's Life of Parr.*

8249 [BENTLEY (S.)] Excerpta Historica; or Illustrations of English History, royal 8vo. (pub. at 21s) *facsimiles of autographs, etc. cloth,* 16s 1833

BERRY'S COUNTY GENEALOGIES:

8250 PEDIGREES and Arms of the Families in the County of KENT, with a List of the Sheriffs from 1066 to 1830, collected from Heraldic Visitations, and other MSS. folio, *woodcuts of Arms,* (pub. at £6. 6s) *bds.* £4. 4s 1830
The Genealogies of this County contain the whole of the Pedigrees entered at the Visitation in 1619 of John Phillipot, Rouge Dragon, Deputy for William Camden, Clarenceux.

8251 PEDIGREES and Arms of the Families in the County of SUSSEX, with a List of the Sheriffs from 1154 to 1830, folio, *numerous woodcuts of Arms,* (pub. at £6. 6s) *rare,* £4. 4s 1830
The Genealogies of this County contain the whole of the Pedigrees entered at the Visitation in 1663 of Sir R. St. George, Clarenceux, and Sir J. Burrough, Norroy, by the Deputies, John Philipot and George Owen.

8252 PEDIGREES and Arms of the Families in the County of HERTFORD, folio, *engravings of Arms, entirely lithographed,* (pub. at £3. 10s) *only 150 copies printed, bds.* £2. 2s (1844)

"These Collections of Pedigrees will be found of great utility, though not of sufficient proof in themselves to establish the claims of kindred set forth in them; but affording a ready clue to such necessary proof whenever it should be required, by pointing out the places of nativity, baptism, marriages, and burials, and such other legal documents, as localities will otherwise afford; and the modern entries in the Herald's College are of no better authority, requiring the very same kind of proof for legal purposes."—*Preface.*

8253 BERNI, Orlando Innamorato, by Rose, 12mo. *bds.* 5s; or, *calf gilt,* 7s 1823
8254 BERTIE'S (Lady G.) Five Generations of a Loyal House, part I. containing the Lives of Richard Bertie and his son Peregrine Lord Willoughby, stout sq. 8vo. *cuts of Coats of Arms, Views, etc. finely printed, bds.* 22s 1845
8255 BEWICK (T. and J.) Select Fables, with Memoir and Catalogue of their Works, 8vo. LARGE PAPER, 5 *portraits and* 300 *woodcuts,* £2. Newcastle, 1820
8255*BIBLE, that is, the HOLY SCRIPTURES, translated by MYLES COVERDALE, 1535, stout sm. 4to. *portrait and facsimiles,* (pub. at 35s) *calf gilt,* 1535; repr. 1845
8256 BLAIR's Chronological and Historical Tables, impl. 8vo. (pub. at 31s 6d) *half morocco,* 9s 1851
8257 BLAKE (William). GILCHRIST'S Life of WILLIAM BLAKE, "Pictor Ignotus," with selections from his Poems and other writings, 2 vols. large 8vo. *portrait, facsimile plates, and numerous woodcut engravings from Blake's works,* (pub. at 32s) *cloth gilt extra,* 27s 1863

"One of the strangest and most noticeable works of the year."—*Athenæum* (No. 1880).
"There is is something in the madness of this man (Blake) which interests me more than the sanity of Lord Byron or Walter Scott."—*Wordsworth.*

8258 BLOMEFIELD'S Essay towards a TOPOGRAPHICAL HISTORY of the County of NORFOLK, continued by the Rev. Charles Parkin, 5 vols. stout folio, *numerous plates of Antiquities. Monuments, Arms, Seals, Portraits, etc. and many Pedigrees, bound,* VERY RARE, £15. *Fersfield (and Lynn),* 1739-75

In the above set: Vol. I. the Blomefield Pedigree, p. 74, is wanting; the rare List of Subscribers is bound up with Vol. II. In Vol. II. the Dedication, the plan of Norwich and folded sheet, and three plates (Bishop Hall's Monument, Manby's Monument, and facsimile Grant) are wanting. In Vol. III. are wanting Title, preface and errata; also pp. 679-870 and Index; the end is slightly wormed; plate of Marsham Monument, portrait of Calthorpe, and views of Houghton Hall, are wanting; a MS. index added. In Vol. V. a plate of Arms and Seals is wanting.

2 G 2

8259 BLOUNT (T.) Fragmenta Antiquitatis, or Ancient Tenures of Land, and Jocu-
lar Customs of Manors, corrected and enlarged by J. and H. M. Beckwith,
with Index of obsolete words, roy. 4to. *best edition*, LARGE FINE PAPER, (pub. at
£3. 3s) *bds.* £2. 2s 1815

8260 BLUNDEVILLE's Exercises, containing eight Treatises necessarie to be learned of
all that desire to learn Cosmographie, Astronomy, Navigation, etc. stout sq.
8vo. black letter, *a curious book with many diagrams, some with moveable pieces,
calf,* 10s 1613

8261 BOMBAY LITERARY SOCIETY Transactions; translations from the Chinese, the Persian, etc. dissertations on Hindoo Mythology, Ethics, Antiquities,
Mohammedan Mysticism, comparison of the Gipsy and Hindostanee languages,
plan of a comparative Vocabulary of Indian Languages by Sir J. Mackintosh,
on Cuneiform Inscriptions, etc. 3 vols. 4to. *numerous plates of Antiquities, facsimiles, etc. hf. calf.* £2. 2s 1819-23

8262 BONDE (Cimelgus) SCUTUM REGALE, the Royal Buckler, or Vox Legis, a lecture to Traytors, who most wickedly murthered Charles I. and banished Charles
II. stout 18mo. *frontispiece, portrait of Charles II. and of a blind Shepherd,
calf neat,* 16s *London,* 1660
A RARE WORK on English History, it was probably privately printed, as there is no name of printer.

8263 BOOK (The) OF DATES, comprising the principal events of all ages, with Index,
stout sm. 8vo. pp. 738, and 64, *double columns, cloth,* 7s 6d 1862

8264 BORROW (George) Lavengro, the Scholar, the Gipsy, the Priest, 3 vols. *portrait,* 1851—The Romany Rye, 2 vols. 1857—together 5 vols. sm. 8vo. (pub.
at £2. 10s), *cloth,* 25s 1851-57

8265 BRADFORD's History of Plymouth Plantation, reprinted from the Massachusetts
Historical Collections, edited with notes, by Deane, royal 8vo. *cloth,* £2. 2s
privately printed, Boston, 1856
Bradford was second Governor of the Colony, and wrote his history more than two hundred years ago.

8266 BRATHWAITE's (R.) ENGLISH GENTLEMAN, sq. 8vo. *fine copy, with the elegant
frontispiece by Vaughan, and the explanatory broadside, calf gilt,* 10s 1633

8267 ———— BARNABÆ ITINERARIUM, or Barnabee's Journal, with Life of the Author,
and Bibliography of former editions, 12mo. *English and Latin, humourous
engravings, calf neat,* 11s 1818

8268 BREE (J.) Cursory Sketch of the Naval, Military and Civil Establishment, &c.
of this Kingdom during the XIVth Century, 4to. *autograph notes of* CRAVEN
ORD, *who has also inserted engravings of Seals, hf. bd.* 12s 1791

8269 BRIGGS (Col. T.) History of the Rise of Mahommedan Power in India till the
year 1612, translated from the Persian of Ferishta, 4 vols. 8vo. *title and a few
pages in Vol. IV. slightly injured, hf. calf gilt,* £2. 4s 1829

8270 BRITISH ESSAYISTS; containing the Tatler, Spectator, Guardian, Rambler,
Adventurer, World, Connoisseur, Idler, Mirror, Lounger, Observer, and
Looker-on, with prefaces, historical and bibliographical, by Alexander Chalmers,
45 vols. 12mo. *portraits, a very pretty set in calf gilt, gilt borders, contents
lettered,* £3. 1803
Priced, 1840, Jas. Bohn, £11. 11s.
"But the most memorable consequence of Swift's frolic was the establishment of the Tatler, the first of that
long series of periodical works which, from the days of Addison to the days of Mackenzie, have enriched our literature with so many effusions of genius, humour, wit, and learning."—*Sir W. Scott.*

8271 BRITISH PROSE WRITERS; a Selection of the best pieces in Prose, from
the Works of Bacon, Clarendon, Temple, Locke, Boyle, Goldsmith, Gray,
Delolme, Dr. Johnson, Bp. Horne, Franklin, Burke, Sir W. Jones, Horace
Walpole, Sir J. Reynolds, Beattie, etc. 25 vols. 16mo. *fine portraits and vignettes, a very pretty set. bound in whole green morocco, gilt edges,* (formerly
priced £11. 11s) £4. 10s 1819-20

8272 BRITISH POETS, from Chaucer to Cowper, including Translations, with
Johnson's Prefaces, Biographical and Critical, and additional Lives by A.
Chalmers, 100 vols. 12mo. *beautifully printed by Whittingham,* (pub. at £25.
unbound), *a pretty set in calf extra,* £18. 18s *Chiswick,* 1822

8273 BROADSIDES, BALLADS, and PAPERS. Among others, The History of Titus
Andronicus—Life and Death of Richard III.—Deposing of Richard II.—Jane
Shore; and various Garlands and many other Songs, *laid upon blotting paper,
and bound in imp. folio, lettered on the back "English Bishops,"* 32s
Several of these are political and satirical, some relate to the pretended plot of Oates, and the cabals that
marked the close of Charles II.'s reign; some to the Union with Scotland; others to the Amours of the Aristocracy,
with well known Actresses, such as Mrs. Bracegirdle, etc.; and others to Swift as the Drapier and Wood's Copper
Coinage, etc. It is altogether an interesting collection.

8274 BROMLEY (H.) Catalogue of Engraved British Portraits, with Appendix, *with the names of the designers and engravers, and specification of all the various portraits of each person, hf. russia*, 10s   1793

8275 BROOKE (Raphe) Catalogue of the Kings, Princes, Dukes, Marquesses, Earls and Viscounts of England since the Norman Conquest to 1619, very sm. folio, *first edition, cuts of Shields of Arms, with woodcut border round title, fine copy in old calf*, 25s   1619

8276 BROUGHAM (H. *now Lord*) Inquiry into the Colonial Policy of the European Powers, 2 vols. 8vo. *calf, scarce,* 20s   *Edinb.* 1803

8277 BROUGHAM (Lord) Lives of Men of Letters and Science of the time of George III. 2 vols. roy. 8vo. *very fine portraits, calf neat*, 38s   1845-46

8278 BROWNE (Thomas) Lectures on the Philosophy of the Mind, with Memoirs by Welsh, 4 vols. 8vo. *portraits, calf gilt*, 32s   *Edinb.* 1851

8279 BROWNE'S History of Roman Classical Literature, 8vo. *new in cloth*, 6s   1853

8280 BRUCE (J. C.) THE ROMAN WALL, a description of the Barrier of the Lower Isthmus from the Tyne to the Solway, st. 8vo. *numerous plates and cuts of Antiquities, Coins, etc. hf. morocco*, 16s   1853

8281 BRYDGES (Sir Egerton) Restituta, or Titles, Extracts, and Characters of Old Books in English Literature revived, 4 vols. 8vo. (published at £5. 12s) *bds.* £2. 16s   1814-16

8282 ——— The Topographer, a Series of Original Articles illustrative of the Local History and Antiquities of England (edited by Stebbing Shaw, and Sir Egerton Brydges), 4 vols. 8vo. 48 *plates, hf. russia, uncut*, £2. 5s   1789-1791
Bindley's copy fetched £2. 5s; the Fonthill, £3. 10s; the Stowe copy, £2. 2s.

8283 **Buckinghamshire.** LIPSCOMBE'S History and Antiquities of the County of Buckingham, 8 parts in 4 vols. roy. 4to. *numerous maps, plates and woody cuts,* (pub. at £16. 16s) £12. 18s   1831-4_7_

8283*——— the same, Parts 1, 2, 8, roy. 4to. *plates,* (pub. at £6. 6s) *sd.* £3. 3s 1831-4_7_

8284 BUCKLE'S HISTORY OF CIVILIZATION in England, 2 vols. 8vo. *third edition*, (pub. at 37s), *new in cloth*, 31s   1861-64

8285 BUNYAN'S PILGRIM'S PROGRESS, with notes by Scott, sq. 8vo. *portrait, and Stothard's beautiful plates and vignettes, blue morocco, gilt edges*, 32s   1840

8286 BURKE (J. and J. B.) Genealogical and Heraldic History of EXTINCT and dormant BARONETCIES, stout 8vo. *portrait of James I. and illuminated title, woodcuts of shields, cloth*, 12s   1838

8287 ——— Genealogical and Heraldic Dictionary of the LANDED GENTRY of Great Britain and Ireland, with Supplementary Alphabet, Addenda, General Index of 10,000 names, etc. 3 vols. roy. 8vo. (pub. at £3. 15s) *with numerous very interesting MS. notes by Mr. Turnbull, cloth,* £2. 18s   1846-49

8287*——— another copy, *in bright calf gilt*, £2. 18s   1846-49

8288 BURKE (Sir Bernard) Landed Gentry of Great Britain and Ireland, fourth edition, roy. 8vo. (pub. at £2. 16s), *cloth*, £2. 6s   1864

8289 ——— Peerage and Baronetage for 1864, roy. 8vo. (pub. at 38s), *cloth*, 32s   1864

8289*BURKE (E.) Works and Correspondence, 8 vols. 8vo. *portrait,* (pub. at £4. 16s. *unbound*) *new calf gilt*, £4. 15s   1852
Best library edition of the works of this great statesman.

8290 BURNEY, General History of Music from the earliest Ages, 4 vols. 4to. *plates by Bartolozzi after Cipriani, fine copy in calf neat*, £4.   1776
"Dr. Burney gave dignity to the character of the musician by joining with it that of the scholar and philosopher."—SIR W. JONES.

8291 BURNS'S (Rob.) WORKS, with his life, a criticism on his writings, and observations on the Scottish Peasantry, 4 vols. *portrait*, 1800—Cromek's Reliques of Robert Burns, 1817—together 5 vols. 8vo. *calf gilt*, £2. 2s   1800-17

8292 ——— Works, with Life, a Criticism on his Writings, and Observations on the Scottish Peasantry, 4 vols. 8vo. *portrait, fine copy, calf gilt*, 38s   1803
At the end of Vol. III. is a Glossary.
"Robert Burns, the greatest of all, the brightest glory of English song-writers, the bard of nature, the self-taught, glowing, ardent child of genius and of song, the poet of every passion and of every feeling that heaven has placed in the breast of man, whose lays are the outpourings of his own great, deep heart"—*Irish Quarterly.*

8293 BURTON'S Anatomy of Melancholy, with Life of the author, 2 vols. 8vo. *best edition, calf gilt*, 14s   1813

8294 BUTLER (Chas.) Philological, Biographical, and other Works, together 14 vols., 8vo. *several presentation copies to the late Sharon Turner, hf. calf,* VERY SCARCE, £4.   1817-26
There has never been a collected edition of the works of this able writer, and the occurrence of so complete a set as the above is very rare. The great learning and industry of Butler have received due acknowledgment; only by means of so much assiduous labour, and such a system as he adopted, could any one attain a similar extent of multifarious knowledge.

8295 BUTLER'S (Sam.) HUDIBRAS, in three parts, written in the time of the late wars, corrected and amended, with additions, 12mo. *portrait and plates* BY HOGARTH, *calf neat, rare*, 32s   1726
8296 ——— Hudibras, with annotations and preface by Zachary Grey, 2 vols. 8vo. *portrait and plates after Hogarth, hf. calf,* 10s   1799
8297 ——— Hudibras, with Grey's Annotations, 3 vols. 8vo. *portraits and plates, cloth,* 20s   1819
8297*——— the same, 3 vols. 8vo. *Large Paper, portrait and plates,* PROOFS ON INDIA PAPER, *hf. calf neat*, £2. 2s   1819
    Dr. Hawtrey's copy sold for £4. 18s ; Duke of York's, impl. paper, £7. 7s.
    Concerning Hudibras there is but one sentiment—it is universally allowed to be the first and last poem of its kind. The learning, wit and humour certainly stand unrivalled. Various have been the attempts to describe the two last; the greatest English writers have tried in vain—Cowley, Barrow, Dryden, Locke, Addison, Pope, and Congreve, all failed in their attempts; perhaps they are more to be felt than explained, and to be understood rather from example than precept; if any one wishes to know what wit and humour are, let him read Hudibras with attention, he will there see them displayed in their brightest colours."

8298 BYRON (Lord) COMPLETE WORKS, with a biographical and critical notice by Lake, 7 vols. 8vo. *fine portrait, perfectly complete edition, good large type, hf. bd.* £2. 10s   *Paris*, 1825
8299 CALENDAR OF STATE PAPERS, DOMESTIC SERIES, preserved in the State Paper departments of the Record Office, 1547-1628, 7 vols. impl. 8vo. *cloth,* £3. 10s   1856-59
    Including:—Reigns of Edward VI. Mary, Elizabeth, 1547-1580, by Lemon; and Green's Reign of James I, 1603-25, 4 vols.; and Bruce's Charles I. 1625-28, 2 vols.
8300 CALENDARIUM CAROLINUM, a new Almanack after the old fashion, 1662, with the Gesta Britannorum for 1600-62, 16mo. *calf*, 7s 6d   1662
3301 **Camberwell.** ALLPORT'S Collections, illustrative of the Geology, History, and Antiquities of CAMBERWELL, roy. 8vo. *plates and cuts, cloth*, 6s   1841
8302 CAMPBELL'S Poetical Works, 12mo. *portrait and woodcuts, morocco,* 7s   1840
8302*CAPPER'S Port and Trade of London, historical, statistical, local, and general, 8vo. (pub. at 15s) *cloth, new,* 12s 6d   1862
8303 CARDS. BLOME'S 52 *Armoriall Cards, n. d.*—Geographical, 52 *maps, with four titles, and including small portraits of Charles II. and Queen Mary, scarce, n.d.* in 1 vol. 16mo. 12s   *ca.* 1660
8303*CAREW'S (R.) Survey of Cornwall, sq. 8vo. FIRST AND ONLY UNCASTRATED EDITION, *fine copy in calf, gilt edges,* £2. 12s 6d   1602
    COLLATION: Title, Dedication, etc. 3 leaves; leaves 1—159; corrections, and Tables, 5 leaves.
8304 CARLISLE (N.) Collections for a History of the Ancient Family of BLAND, roy. 4to. *woodcut Coats of arms, bds.* PRIVATELY PRINTED, £2. 12s 6d   1826
8305 CARLISLE FAMILY. COLLECTIONS for a history of the ancient Family of Carlisle, roy. 4to. *several woodcuts of Arms, privately printed for presents only, bds.* £2.   Priced, 1829, J. Bohn, £5. 5 ; 1843, £2. 12s 6d   1822
8306 CARLYLE (Thomas) Cromwell's Letters and Speeches, with elucidations and with Supplement, 2 vols. 8vo. *portrait* (pub. at 41s) *cloth,* 18s   1845-46
8307 ——— History of Friedrich II. of Prussia, called Frederick the Great, Vols. I—III, 8vo. *portraits and plans* (pub. at £3.) *cloth,* £2. 2s   1860-62
8308 CASTIGLIONE. THE COVRTYER of COVNT Baldessar CASTILIO, divided into foure bookes, very necessary, and profitable for yonge Gentilmen and Gentilwomen, abiding in Court, Palaice, or Place, done into Englyshe by Thomas Hoby, sq. 8vo. *woodcut title, with autograph notes of G. Harvey on the title and margins, large copy, calf extra, by Bedford,* £3.   *London, Wyllyam Seres,* 1561
    Collation : Title, 1 leaf; The Printer to the reader, 1 leaf; Hoby's dedication to Lord Hastings, 4 leaves; on the reverse of the last leaf commences, " Unto Lord Mychaell," 5 leaves; blank leaf; The book itself, A to Z in fours, and Aa to ZZ 4; A Letter of Syr J. Cheekes, 1 leaf.
    On the last leaf is " A Letter of Syr J. Cheekes."—" This letter being omitted in the subsequent editions, for the singularity of its orthography and the learned writer's opinion concerning our language, I have given entire."—*Amos.*
8309 CAXTON. BLADES (W.) Life and Typography of William Caxton, with evidence of his typographical connection with Colard Mansion, the printer at Bruges, 2 vols. 4to. *portrait and more than 60 facsimile plates by Tupper, hf. morocco, uncut, only a limited number of copies printed,* £5. 5s   1861-63
    This work, besides copious quotations from Original Documents, and sources hitherto unexplored, illustrative of the Life and Times of Caxton, includes the whole of his Prologues and Epilogues to books printed by him; also his own historical work, entitled ' Policronicon Liber Ultimus.' The second volume is devoted to a Bibliographical and Literary account of all the Works printed by or ascribed to the Press of Caxton, including many undescribed by Dibdin and others; with careful collations of them, and a list of Copies of Caxton's Books, in number more than four hundred and fifty, now in Public and Private Libraries, noticing their sales, the purchasers' names, etc.
8310 CERVANTES, Life and Exploits of DON QUIXOTE, translated by Jarvis, 2 vols. sm. 8vo. *numerous plates after Vanderbank, calf gilt*, 18s   1749
8311 ——— the same, by Jarvis, 4 vols. 16mo. *portrait, calf gilt,* 10s   1821

8312 CHAMBERS' MISCELLANY of useful and entertaining Tracts, Vols. I—XX, in 10 vols. 12mo. *numerous woodcuts, hf. red morocco gilt*, 35s *Edinb.* 1844-48

8313 CHAP BOOKS. BOOK OF HISTORIES, containing the Battle on Chevy Chase; Life of Long Meg of Westminster; Ducks and Green Peas, or the Newcastle Rider; Nine Pennyworth of Wit for a Penny; and many others, *being reprints of early Romances*, etc. in 1 vol. 12mo. *with very quaint cuts, calf gilt,* 38s
Reprinted by Angus, Newcastle, 1810

8314 The UNFORTUNATE HAPPY LADY—HISTORY of Tom True Blue—The Unfortunate Twin Sisters, Lucy and Fanny Bently—Sabine's Annual Valentine Writer for 1800—Cheapside Apprentice—Madge Blarney—Miss Sally Johnson, the unfortunate Magdalen—Life of Miss C(a)tl(e)y, Singer and Courtezan—Barker's Unfortunate Shipwright, 1795—History of Harriott Fairfax —Shepherdess of the Alps—in 1 vol. sm. 8vo. *numerous very curious cuts, hf. russia*, 30s *Sec.* XVIII.

8315 HISTORY of Guy of Warwick, *thick paper*—Burn's Farewell, etc. Waterford— Jack and the Giants, *Nottingham*—Tom Thumb, 3 parts, *thick paper;* and others, *mostly printed in the provinces*, in 1 vol. 16mo. *curious cuts, hf. morocco,* 9s *ca.* 1780

8316 CHARLES I. Declaration to his Subjects concerning LAWFUL SPORTS to be used on Sundays: "The Kings Maiesties Declaration to his Subjects, concerning lawfull Sports to bee used," sm. 4to. 24 *pp. the second time reprinted on tinted paper in exact imitation of the original by Whittingham, hf. morocco, uncut*, 5s " ¶ *Imprinted at London by Robert Barker, Printer to the Kings most Excellent Maiestie : And by the Assignes of John Bill,* 1633."
Reprinted, 1862, *by Bernard Quaritch*, 15 *Piccadilly.*

8317 LARGE DECLARATION concerning the late Tumults in Scotland, by the King (Dr. Balcanquhal, Dean of Durham), sm. folio, *fine portrait of Charles I. original calf, arms on sides,* 18s 1639

8318 ΕΙΚΩΝ ΑΚΛΑΣΤΟΣ, the Image Unbroaken, a perspective of the Libell entitled Eikonoklastês, against Eikôn Basilikê, sq. 8vo. *vellum, rare,* 15s *s. l.* 1651

8319 BATII Elenchus Motuum nuperorum in Angliâ, 12mo. *portrait of Charles I. calf,* 7s 1661

8320 **Cheshire.** KING'S (D.) VALE-ROYALL of England, or the County Palatine of CHESTER illustrated, a Geographical and Historical Description of that famous County, its hundred Seats of the Nobility, Gentry, &c. Rivers, Towns, Castles, Buildings, with a discourse of the Island of Man, sm. folio, *engraved and printed titles, maps and plates, by Hollar and King, including the rare one of Hugh Lupus sitting in Parliament, fine copy in old russia,* £6. 6s 1656

In reality the Vale Royal was written by W. Smith, Rouge-Dragon, and W. Webb, Clerk to the Mayor's Court at Chester. King was merely the publisher, and, as he himself tells us, his claim consists in adding "several Prospects and other Pieces of Sculpture for the ornament of the whole work; as also, through the help of some that are well-wishers thereto, a translation of divers Monastery Foundation-Charters, with other things of good note."

8321 LEYCESTER'S (Sir Peter) Historical Antiquities, in two Books; the first treating in general of Great Brettain and Ireland, the second containing particular Remarks concerning CHESHIRE, faithfully collected out of authentick Histories Old Deeds, Records, etc. folio, *map and coats of arms, fine copy in old russia extra, gilt edges,* £2. 2s 1673
Priced, Thorpe, £2. 12s 6d; Heath's copy fetched £5. 7s 6d.

8322 ORMEROD'S (George) History of the County Palatine and City of CHESTER; compiled from original evidences in Public Offices, the Harleian and Cottonian MSS., Parochial Registers, Private Muniments, Unpublished MS. Collections of Cheshire Antiquaries, and a personal Survey of every Township in the County: incorporated with a Republication of King's Vale Royal and Leycester's Cheshire Antiquities, 3 vols. folio, *nearly* 200 *fine engravings, plates and woodcuts, including portraits, cloth,* UNCUT, VERY SCARCE, £36. 1819
Priced, 1854, £42.; 1859, £36. 15s; fetched, 1854, Sotheby's, £37.

8324 CLARENDON GALLERY. LEWIS (Lady Theresa) Lives of the Friends and Contemporaries of Lord Chancellor Clarendon, illustrative of Portraits in his Gallery, 3 vols. 8vo. *portraits*, (pub. at £2. 8s) *cloth*, 18s 1852

8325 COLENSO, the Pentateuch and Book of Joshua critically examined, by the Right Rev. J. W. Colenso, D.D., Bishop of Natal, Part IV., the First 11 Chapters of Genesis examined and separated, with Remarks on the Creation, the Fall, and the Deluge, 8vo. (pub. at 10s 6d) *cloth, new,* 8s 9d 1864

8326 **CHETHAM SOCIETY'S PUBLICATIONS**, consisting of Remains Historical and Literary connected with the Counties of Lancaster and Chester, complete from the beginning in 1843 to the conclusion in 1863, 60 vols. with General Index, 1 vol., together 61 vols. sm. 4to. *cloth, gilt back, contents lettered,* £22. 10s   1844-63

CONTENTS.

I, Brereton's Travels, 1634-35, by Hawkins.
II, Ormerod's Military Proceedings in Lancashire, Civil War.
III, Chester's Triumph, 1610.
IV, Martindale's Life, by Parkinson.
V, Hibbert-Ware, Lancashire Memorials of 1715.
VI, Pott's Discovery of Witches, by Crossley.
VII, James, Ites Lancastrense by Corser.
VIII, Raines' Notitia Cestriensis.
IX, Heywood's Norris Papers.
X, XI, Hulton's Chartulary of Walley Abbey.
XII, Heywood's Moore Rental.
XIII, Worthington's Diary by Crossley, I.
XIV, Assheton's Journal, by Raines,
XV, S. Werburge's Life, by Hawkins.
XVI, Whalley Chartulary, III.
XVII, Beamont's Warrington, 1465.
XVIII, Newcome's Diary, by Heywood.
XIX, Notitia Cestriensis, II, 1.
XX, Whalley Chartulary, IV.
XXI, XXII, Notitia Cestriensis, II, 2, 3.
XXIII, Robinson's Golden Mirror.
XXIV, Chetham Miscellanies, I.
XXV, Allen's Defence of Stanley.
XXVI, XXVII, Autobiography of Newcome.
XXVIII, Jacobite Trials at Manchester, 1694.
XXIX, Heywood's Stanley Papers, I.
XXX, Hulton's Penwortham Documents.
XXXI, Stanley Papers, II.

XXXII, Byrom's Journal and Remains, I, 1.
XXXIII, Lancashire and Cheshire Wills.
XXXIV, Byrom's Journal, 1, 2.
XXXV, Harland's Shuttleworth Accounts.
XXXVI, Diary of Worthington, II, 1.
XXXVII, Chetham Miscellanies, II.
XXXVIII, French's Church Libraries of Turton.
XXXIX, Ffarington's Farington Papers.
XL, Byrom's Journal, II, 1.
XLI, Shuttleworth Accounts, II.
XLII, Booker's Didsbury and Chorlton Chapels.
XLIII, Shuttleworth Accounts, III.
XLIV, Byrom's Journal, II, 2.
XLV, Wilson's Miscellanies, by Raines.
XLVI, Shuttleworth Accounts, IV.
XLVII, Booker's Birch Chapel, Manchester.
XLVIII, Jones' Tracts on Popery.
XLIX, L, Lancashire Lieutenancy under Tudor and Stuarts, 2 vols.
LI, Lancashire and Cheshire Wills, II.
LII, Corser's Collectanea Anglo-Poetica, I.
LIII, Harland's Mamecestre, I.
LIV, Lancashire and Cheshire Wills, III.
LV, Collectanea Anglo-Poetica, II.
LVI, Mamecestre, II.
LVII, Chetham Miscellanies, III.
LVIII, Mamecestre, III.
LIX, LX, Chantries of Lancaster, by Raines.
LXI, General Index.

The following Nos. can be supplied separately.

8327 28. JACOBITE TRIALS at Manchester in 1694, from an unpublished MS. edited by Beamont, sm. 4to. *cloth*, 12s   *Manchester*, 1853

8328 32, 34, 40, 44. BYROM (John) Private Journal and Literary Remains, edited by Richard PARKINSON, 2 vols. in 4, sm. 4to. *port. cloth*, £2. 2s   *ib.* 1854-57

8328* 48. JONES (Thomas) Catalogue of the Collection of Tracts for and against Popery, in the Chetham Manchester Library, Part 1, (*all published*) 4to. *cloth*, 12s   *ib.* 1859

8329 CLIFFORD'S (Sir Thomas and Arthur) Topographical and Historical Description of the Parish of Tixall, Stafford, 4to. *portraits, plates, and Genealogical tables, hf. calf gilt*, 36s   *Privately printed, Paris*, 1817

8330 CLINTON'S (Henry Fynes) Fasti Hellenici. The Civil and Literary Chronology of Greece, from the earliest Accounts to the Death of Augustus, 3 vols. 4to. *last and best edition of each volume*, £6. 6s   *Oxford, Clarendon Press*, 1834-41-51

8331 CLINTON, Fasti Romani. The civil and literary Chronology of Rome and Constantinople from the death of Augustus to the death of Justin II., 2 vols. 4to. *new, calf extra, gilt edges,* £4. 4s   *Oxf.* 1845-50
The set, 5 vols. bound uniform, a very elegant library copy, £10.

8332 COBBETT's Political Works, Selections from, by J. M. and J. P. Cobbett, 6 vols. 8vo. *bds.* 12s   (1837)
"The most racy and idiomatic of all our writers."—*Buckle's Civilization,* I. pa. 744, 1858.

8333 COLEBROOKE'S (H. T.) Miscellaneous Essays, 2 vols. 8vo. BEST EDITION, *numerous facsimiles from early Indian MSS. and Inscriptions, bds.* 36s   1837

8334 COLEMAN'S (C.) MYTHOLOGY of the Hindus, 4to. *with 39 plates illustrative of the principal Hindu Deities, cloth, rare,* £2. 10s   1832

8335 COLTON'S Works: Lacon, or many things in few words; Poems, etc. 2 vols. 8vo. *bds.* 5s   1822

8336 COLLINS'S Peerage of England, Genealogical, Biographical and Historical, greatly augmented and continued to the present time, by Sir Egerton Brydges, Bart., 9 vols. 8vo. BEST EDITION, *many coats of arms,*(pub. at £9. 9s in bds.) *calf gilt,* £4. 10s

A standard library book of noted excellence. A supplementary volume by a conscientious Genealogist would be a boon.
A valuable work. "Sir George Naylor, York Herald (the late Garter) furnished copies of all, or most of the Pedigrees of the New Peers which have been entered at the Heralds' Office."—*Moule.*

ENGLISH LITERATURE. 457

8337 CONGREVE'S Works, consisting of his Plays and Poems, 3 vols. in 2, 12mo. *old calf gilt*, 14s 1730
8338 ——— Works, consisting of his Plays and Poems, with Life, 3 vols. roy. 8vo. BASKERVILLE'S FINE EDITION, *portrait and plates by Grignon, quite free from spots or stains, old calf gilt*, £2. 16s *Birmingham*, 1761
    The Fonthill copy, £3. 17s; Dent's, in morocco, £7. 15s. Copies are very seldom found without stains.
8339 C[ORBET] (R[ichard]) Poetica Stromata, a collection of Sundry Pieces of Poetry, 12mo. *privately printed, good clean copy, calf*, 7s 6d 1648
    Containing 24 Poems addressed to the Duke of Buckingham, Lord Mordant, Prince Charles, etc.
8340 [COTTON (Sir Robt.)] Short View of the Life and Raigne of Henry III. of England, presented to King James, sq. sm. 8vo. *fine portrait of Henry III., hf. bd. rare*, 9s 1627
    This is the rare original edition which was anonymously printed.
8341 **Cornwall.** BORLASE'S (W.) Observations on the Antiquities, Historical and Monumental, of the County of Cornwall, with VOCABULARY of the CORNU-BRITISH Language, &c. 1754—The Natural History of Cornwall, 1758—together 2 vols. folio, *numerous plates, fine copies, in old calf gilt, newly rebacked,* £3. 3s 1754-58
    Priced, 1831, Egerton, £4. 14s 6d; 1840, Thorpe, £3. 13s 6d; Dent's copy fetched £8. 8s; Dawson Turner's, 1853, £3. 12s.
8342 CORNUCOPIAE. Pasquil's Night-Cap, or Antidot for the Headache, 8vo. *old humorous poetry, bds.* 6s *London*, 1612, reprinted 1819
8343 CORNWALLIS (*Charles, First Marquis*) Correspondence, edited with Notes by C. Ross, 3 vols. 8vo. *portrait and pedigree, calf gilt, by Riviere*, £2. 10s 1859
    A valuable collection of papers which illustrate the character of Lord Cornwallis, and also much light upon the history of those times. Mr. C. Ross has performed his arduous task most carefully, having examined all the printed books and MSS. which were at all likely to be of service to him.
8344 COWPER'S LIFE and Works, including his Correspondence, by Southey, 15 vols. 12mo. *fine portraits and plates, hf. morocco neat, gilt tops, uncut,* £2. 2s 1835-57
8345 ——— Poems, with biographical and critical Introduction, by Dale, 2 vols. 8vo. *with 75 pretty woodcuts, engraved by Smith after Gilbert, cloth gilt*, 10s 1841
8346 CORTES (Hernando) Pleasant Historie of the Conquest of the Weast India, now called New Spaine, translated by T(homas) N(icholas), sq. 8vo. 𝔅lack letter, *title slightly mended, otherwise a fine copy in green morocco, gilt tops, from Miss Currer's library,* RARE, £3. 3s *by Henry Bynneman* (1578)
    COLLATION: Title; Dedication to Sir F. Walsingham, 2 leaves; To the Reader, 1 leaf; Stephen Gosson in prayse of the translator, and In Thomai Nicolai occident. Indiam St. Gosson, 1 leaf; Text, pp. 1-405; Table, 3 pp.
8347 CROMWELL AND THE COMMONWEALTH. An Extensive Collection of the Acts of Parliament passed during the period of the Commonwealth and Protectorship of Oliver Cromwell, 1648-1659, arranged in Chronological order, in 3 stout vols. folio, 𝔅lack letter, *old calf*, £8. 10s 1648-59
    A very curious and important collection, comprising amongst other Acts, those for "Authorizing Col. Blake to be Admiral and General of the Fleet;" "Declaring and constituting the People of England to be a commonwealth and Free State;" "Against unlicensed and scandalous Books and pamphlets;" "For the sale of Fee-farm Rents;" "For securing Moneys for the Navy and Army;" "For repealing an ordinance whereby Sir Thomas Fairfax was constituted Commander-in-chief;" "The Militia of the Commonwealth of England;" and many Acts on Trade, Rents, Lands, Corn, Meal, the Army, Navy, Internal Administration, Challenges, Duels, Creditors, the Postal Service, Popery, Customs, Excise, Debts, Tythes, etc. etc.
8348 CROMWELL'S ACTS. Another Collection of Statutes and Proclamations, in 3 vols. folio, *containing many Acts printed as Broadsides, russia, edges uncut,* £9. 1649-1659
    "This equally curious collection contains most precious historical Documents, such as the Act "prohibiting the Proclaiming any person to be King of England," "For abolishing the House of Peers;" "What Offences shall be adjudged Treason;" "Letters of Mart;" further, many Acts about the Militia, Mortgages, Trade, Rents, General Pardon, Army, Navy, Cock-Matches, Highwaymen, Hackney Coaches, General Monck, many Proclamations, etc.
    Each of the above collections contains some pieces in common with the other; but united they constitute a body of information invaluable for the history of the time.
8349 CRUIKSHANK (R.) Northcote's Fifty-one Original Fables, with Plutarch's Seven Sages, 8vo. 85 *humourous woodcuts, cloth*, 10s 1833
8350 DANIEL (Sam.) Certaine small workes heretofore divulged, now corrected and augmented, 16mo. *title and last leaf mended, calf neat, rare*, 15s *London*, 1607
    "The Atticus of his day."—*Headley.* "For sweetness and rhyming, second to none."—*Drummond.*
8351 DANCE OF DEATH, painted by HOLBEIN, and engraved by HOLLAR, with the Daunce of Machabree in Verse by Lydgate, Monke of Bury, (the preface and description by Douce), sm. 8vo. 2 *portraits and* 30 *plates, impressions from the* ORIGINAL COPPERS, *calf gilt*, 27s (1792)

8352 DARRELL (John) Detection of that sinnful and ridiculous discours of Samuel HARSNET, "Discoverie of the frawdulent practices of John Darrell," wherein is showed the impossibility of the counterfayting of Somers, Darling, Wright and the others, in Lancashire, sm. 4to. *some of the marginal notes, etc. cut into, hf. bd. very rare*, 30s *Imprinted* 1600

Collation: Title, 4 prel. leaves, and pp. 3-211. "In this treatise, 'full of sound and fury,' Darrell has contrived to render it somewhat doubtful whether he was a dupe or an impostor."—*Gifford*.

8353 DAVISON'S (Francis) Poetical Rhapsody, with several other pieces, Memoirs and Notes, by Sir Harris Nicolas, 2 vols. 8vo. *facsimile plate of signatures of the various contributors*, (Sir Ph. Sidney, Sir W. Raleigh, Fulke Greville, Wotton, etc.) bds. 21s 1826

"In addition to the notes, the editor has given us Memoirs of the contributors, so that the Rhapsody is no longer a book of songs only, but a lively picture of the time, including particulars of interesting subjects, which have never before seen the light. We may allude to the curious letter, hitherto unpublished, from Sir Edward Dyer to Sir C. Hatton, respecting Queen Elizabeth, which, in our opinion, sets at rest the question as to the chastity of the *Virgin* Queen."—*New Monthly Magazine.*

8354 DEBRETT's Baronetage of England, revised, corrected, and continued by Collen, stout 8vo. *several hundred woodcut coats of arms*, (pub. 28s) *hf. morocco*, 6s 1840

8355 DE FOE's Robinson Crusoe, his Life and Adventures, 2 vols. sm. 8vo. *numerous engravings by Cruikshank, calf gilt*, 12s 1831

8356 DENNISTOUN'S Memoirs of the DUKES OF URBINO, illustrating the Arms, Arts, and Literature of Italy, from 1440 to 1630; 3 vols. 8vo. *with numerous engravings, comprising portraits, views, medallions, facsimiles of handwriting, &c.* (pub. at £2. 8s) extra cloth gilt, 17s 6d 1851

8357 —— the same, 3 vols. 8vo. *newly bound in whole calf gilt*, 35s 1851

8358 **Devonshire.** POLWHELE'S (Rich.) History of Devonshire, 3 vols. in 1, stout roy. folio, *map and fine plates of Castles, Churches, Gentleman's Seats, etc.* £4. 18s *Exeter*, 1797-1806

8359 DIALOGUES of CREATURES MORALIZED, applicable and edifying to every Merry and Jocund Matter, and right profitable to the Governance of Man, edited by Haslewood, sm. 4to. *beautifully reprinted in* Black letter, *with 125 curious woodcuts, from the Latin edition of* 1481, (pub. at £5. 5s) *antique calf, gilt top, uncut*, £4. 4s 1816

Only 98 copies of this handsome volume were printed, and but 42 were preserved from Bensley's fire. The work will be found curious to the Philologist, interesting to the lover of Natural History, and amusing to the Moralist.

8360 DIBDIN'S BIBLIOTHECA SPENCERIANA, or Descriptive Catalogue of the Books printed in the 15th Century, and of many valuable First Editions, in the possession of the Earl Spencer, 4 vols.; Ædes Althorpianæ, or an Account of the Mansions, Books and Pictures at Althorp, with a Supplement to the Bibliotheca Spenceriana, 2 vols.; Descriptive Catalogue of the Books printed in the 15th Century, lately forming part of the Cassano Library; with General Index to the 7 vols. of the Spencer Collection—7 vols. impl. 8vo. *numerous fine facsimiles of early woodcuts, and a Series of Portraits contained in the Picture Gallery* (pub. at £22.) bds. uncut, £12. 12s 1814-23

8361 —— the same, 7 vols. in 6, impl. 8vo. *magnificent copy in red turkey morocco extra, joints, gilt and marb. edges, from Miss Currer's library*, £18. 18s 1814-23

Published as follows: Bibl. Spenc. 4 vols. 1814, £14. 14s; Aedes Althorpianae, portraits and plates, 2 vols. 1822, £6. 6s; Cassano Catalogue, 21s—Priced, 1825, Wheatley, mor. £29. 8s; 1829, Longman's, mor. £18. 18s; 1837, Payne and Foss, mor. £18. 18s; 1840, Jas. Bohn, £18. 18s.

8362 DIBDIN'S BIBLIOGRAPHICAL DECAMERON, or Ten Days pleasant Discourse upon Illuminated Manuscripts and subjects connected with Early Engraving, Typography and Bibliography, 3 vols. roy. 8vo. *with a beautifully engraved series of* WOODCUTS *and* COPPER-PLATES *of* PORTRAITS, *Illuminations, etc. beautiful copy in red turkey morocco extra, joints, gilt leaves*, £12. 1817

8363 DIBDIN'S BIBLIOMANIA, or Book Madness, new edition, with Supplement, and a Key to the Names, *wood engravings*, stout roy. 8vo. *uniform in size with the author's other Bibliographical Works, woodcuts of facsimiles, etc.* bds. £3. 6s 1842

8364 DIETRICHSEN's Almanack and Book of General Information, 1838 to 1863, 26 years in 5 vols. *hf. calf*, and 3 Nos. sm. 8vo. *rare*, 15s 1838-63

8365 DOMESDAY BOOK for Kent, Sussex, and Surrey, *translated*, with Introduction and Notes by Henshall and Wilkinson, *London*, 1799—BAWDEN's Translation of Domesday for Yorkshire, Derbyshire, Nottingham, Rutland, Lincoln, Middlesex, Hertford, Buckingham, Oxford, and Gloucester, with Glossary and Indexes, 2 vols. *Doncaster*, 1809-12—together 3 vols. in 2, 4to. *hf. calf gilt*, £3. 4s 1799-1812

8366 DOMESDAY BOOK. BAWDWEN's Translation of the record called Domesday, so far as relates to the Counties of Middlesex, Hertford, Buckingham, Oxford, and Gloucester, 4to. *bds.* 15*s* *Doncaster*, 1812

8367 ELLIS (Sir Henry) General Introduction to Domesday Book, official copy for the use of the Record Commissioners, 4to. *hf. bd.* £2. 2*s* *Not pub.* 1817
Extremely rare; I have never seen another copy. It is possible that only three or four may have been printed in this form.
See also *ante*, Nos. 691-711.

8368 DIODORUS SICULUS, Historical Library, translated by G. Booth, with the fragments, 2 vols. roy. 8vo. *russia gilt*, 24*s* 1814

8369 DONNE (Dr.) Poems by J. D., with Elegies on the Author's Death, 16mo. *old calf*, 15*s* 1639
Priced, 1841, 27*s*. "Donne was the greatest wit of this nation."—*Dryden*.

8370 **Dorsetshire.** HUTCHINS (John) History and Antiquities of the County of Dorset, with a copy of Domesday Book, and the Inquisitio Gheldi, for the County, etc. 2 vols. folio, *map and 56 fine plates (not including some worked in the letter-press) of Views, Gentlemen's Seats, and other Buildings, Antiquities, etc. with numerous Pedigrees, fine copy in the original calf, neat,* £5. 5*s* 1774
Fetched at the Townley sale, £8. 10*s* 6*d*; at Heath's, £11.; Townshends, £7. 17*s* 6*d*; Edwards', £6. 10*s*; Bindley's, £6. 8*s* 6*d*.

8371 LYSONS, Mosaic Pavements, discovered near Frampton in Dorsetshire, atlas folio, 7 *coloured plates*, with descriptions, *half morocco*, 20*s* 1808

8372 DOUGLAS (Rev. Jas.) NENIA BRITANNICA; a Sepulchral History of Great Britain (in which are engraved the Antiquities discovered by Dr. Faussett), roy. folio, 36 *plates of Celtic and Anglo-Saxon Antiquities, fine copy in hf. russia, uncut,* £5. 5*s* 1793
This valuable work includes a complete series of the British, Roman and Saxon Sepulchral Rites and Ceremonies, with the contents of several hundred Burial Places, opened under the careful inspection of the author. The Barrows contain Urns, Swords, Spear-heads, Daggers, Knives, Battle-Axes, Shields, and Armillae; Decorations of Women, consisting of Gems, Pensile Ornaments, Bracelets. Beads, Gold and Silver Buckles; Magical Instruments, and other Relics.

8373 DRAKE (Sir Francis) Revived, being a summary and true Relation of foure severall Voyages made by him to the West Indies, sq. 8vo. *port. hf. bd.* £2. 1653
The Nassau copy fetched £4. 1*s*; Jadis', £2. 15*s*; Sotheby's, 1859, £2. 11*s*.
COLLATION. Portrait, title, etc. 3 leaves; pp. 1—87; The World encompassed, title (1652), 1 leaf, and pp. 1 —108; Summarie Discourse, title (1652) 1 leaf, and pp. 3—41; Relation of another Voyage, title, (1652) 1 leaf, and pp. 45—60.

8374 DRAMATIC TABLE TALK, 3 vols. 18mo. *plates, hf. calf,* 5*s* 1825

8375 DRUMMOND'S (Rt. Hon. W.) Academic Questions, Vol. I. 4to. *all published, bds.* £2. 2*s* 1805

8376 DRYDEN'S (John) WORKS, with notes historical, critical, and explanatory, and a life of the author, by Sir Walter Scott, 18 vols. 8vo. SECOND AND BEST EDITION, *portrait, calf gilt,* £10. 1821
Fetched, 1856, at Sotheby's, £10. 10*s*.
"Purchase *either* of the *two* editions, in eighteen goodly octavo volumes, of which *Sir Walter Scott* is the editor —and then you may brandish your mother-of-pearl paper-cutter, and open the instructive pages of Dryden, to your heart's content!"—*Dibdin*.

8377 DUFF'S History of the MAHRATTAS, 3 vols. 8vo. *two maps mounted on canvas, and frontispieces, hf. calf gilt,* £4. 1826
A most elaborate work, entirely based upon original documents, unpublished MSS., official Papers, &c. hidden in the palaces, temples, and private repositories of the natives. The History begins with the Conquest of the Deccan by the Mahommedans, A.D. 1000, and extends to the British possession in 1819.

8378 DUGDALE (Sir William) ORIGINES JURIDICIALES, or Historical Memorials of the English Laws, Courts of Justice, etc.; also a Chronologia of the Lord Chancellors, Keepers, etc. FIRST AND MOST CORRECT EDITION, *with beautiful impressions of the fine portraits by Hollar, numerous plates of Arms, fine copy, in red morocco extra, gilt and marbled edges by Bedford,* £6. 16*s* 6*d*
F. and T. Warren for the Author, 1666
Pepys in his amusing Diary says, "1667, April, Bought Dugdale's History of the Inns of Court, of which there was but a few saved out of the fire."

8379 DUGDALE'S BARONAGE OF ENGLAND, or an Historical Account of the Lives and most memorable Actions of our English Nobility, 3 vols. in 1, stout folio, FINE CLEAN COPY *in russia gilt, edges marbled and gilt, sides tooled in the Harleian style,* £7. 10*s* 1675-76

8380 ―― Ancient Usage in bearing Arms, with Catalogues of the Nobility of England, Scotland, and Ireland, 16mo. *Shields of Arms, calf neat,* 7*s* 6*d* *Oxf.* 1682

8381 DU HALDE'S General History of China, a Geographical, Historical, Political, and Physical description of China, Chinese Tartary, Corea and Thibet, 4 vols. sm. 8vo. *several maps and plates, fine copy in old English red morocco, gilt edges,* 32*s* 1736

8382 DUNLOP'S HISTORY OF FICTION, 3 vols. 12mo. *half calf,* 14s 1814
　An interesting literary account of the Romances of France, England, Italy, renowned during the middle ages. "A mind which has feasted on the luxurious wonders of Fiction has no taste for the insipidity of truth."—*Johnson.*

8383 DUNTON'S (John, *London Mariner*) True Journall of the Sally Fleet, proceedings of the Voyage, list of Sally Captives, and places where they dwell, sq. sm. 8vo, *map of the three Towns, calf gilt,* 36s 1637
　Priced, 1825, by Thorpe, morocco, £4. 14s 6d.
　The author was commander of the ship Leopard, in this expedition against the Turkish and Sallee pirates, under Admiral Carteret.

8384 **Durham.** HUTCHINSON'S History and Antiquities of the County Palatine of DURHAM, 3 vols. 4to. *no plates,* (pub. at £6.) *bds.* 27s Durham, 1823

8385 EARL MARSHALL OF ENGLAND. The Office of Earl Marshall, taken from a Manuscript dated 1572, in the possession of John Edmondson, Esq. Mowbray Herald Extraordinary, 8vo. *very neatly copied in Italic characters, with headings, etc. in black and red, containing 27 Shields of Arms, elegantly executed in colours (? by Capt. Montagu) orange morocco, broad border of gold, gilt edges,* £2. 16s (1825)
　This valuable MS. contains numerous interesting and curious particulars.

8386 EDEN (Sir F. M.) STATE OF THE POOR, or an History of the Labouring Classes in England from the Conquest to the present, with appendix containing a comparative and chronological table of prices, etc. 3 vols. 4to. *presentation copy, calf, rare,* £3. 3s 1797
　A book of singular importance, and the only one published upon the Social Annals of the English people. No work, professing to be a history of England, can pretend to any real value, unless based upon the statistics which shew forth the inner life of the masses, and their gradual progress through the phases of civilization. These statistics are collected here; and it may be remarked as a rather curious fact that the late Mr. Buckle, for whose work, these details of domestic history would have been amongst its most valuable ingredients, seems to have been wholly ignorant of Eden's State of the Poor.

8387 EDWARDS' (President Jonathan) Works, with Memoirs and Index, 8 vols. 8vo. *portrait, tall copy, hf. calf,* £2. Leeds, 1806-11
　"That great master-mind, Jonathan Edwards, whose close-sighted observations, clear judgment, and unbending faithfulness, were of the highest order."—*Dr. Pye Smith.*

8388 ENCYCLOPÆDIA BRITANNICA, or Dictionary of Arts, Sciences and General Literature, EIGHTH AND LAST EDITION, 21 vols. 4to. *numerous plates, half russia,* £25. 1860

8389 ENCYCLOPÆDIA METROPOLITANA, or Universal Dictionary of Knowledge, comprising the two-fold Advantages of a Philosophical and an Alphabetical Arrangement, edited by Smedley, Rose, and others, with a General Index, 30 vols. 4to. *several hundred plates and maps,* (pub. at £61. 19s *in parts*) *hf. russia gilt,* £10. 1844-45
　Priced, 1847, £25. 10s; £25.; 1853, £15. 15s; £21.; 1854, £20.; 1857, £15.; £15. 10s; fetched, Sotheby's, 1851, £11.; 1855, £13. 10s; 1857, Puttick's, £13.

8390 EDMONDSON (Joseph) BARONAGIUM GENEALOGICUM, or the Pedigrees of the English Peers deduced from the earliest times, originally compiled by Sir W. SEGAR, continued by Edmondson, complete with Supplement, 6 vols. imp. folio, *wholly engraved, above* 500 *sheets of Pedigrees, with Coats of Arms, including those of the Earls of Radnor and Anglesey, frequently wanting, fine copy in hf. russia, uncut,* £8. 8s 1764-84
　This copy cost a former proprietor £21. Priced, 1840, J. Bohn, £12. 12s; Hibbert's copy, fetched £15. 4s; Edwards' £19. 10s; Dawson Turner's copy fetched, 1853, £12.

8391 **Epitaphs.** COLLECTION of Epitaphs and Monumental Inscriptions, with Johnson's Essay, 2 vols. 12mo. *bds.* 10s 1806

8392 DEROZARIO'S Monumental Register, containing all the Epitaphs in and about Calcutta, etc. 8vo. *morocco, gilt edges, rare,* 18s Calcutta, 1815

8393 DUNCAN, Elogia Sepulchr.; Monumental Inscriptions from Burial Grounds, Edinburgh, 8vo. *bds.* 5s Edinb. 1815

8394 KELKE's Churchyard Manual, 12mo. *cuts, cloth,* 3s 6d 1851

8395 ORCHARD's Epitaphs and Remarkable Inscriptions, 8vo. *port. bds.* 3s 6d 1827

8396 KILKHAMPTON ABBEY, or Monumental Records for the year 1780, compiled to ascertain the manners of Great Britain in the 18th Century, 2 parts in 1 vol. 4to. *hf. morocco, uncut,* 7s 6d 1780

8397 WRECK OF WESTMINSTER ABBEY, a Selection from the Monumental Records of the conspicuous personages who flourished in the latter half of the eighteenth Century, 4to. *curious plate of George III. and Queen Charlotte, half morocco, uncut,* 10s MMI. (ca. 1780)
　Both of these two books contain only mock and sarcastic Epitaphs upon the remarkable characters of the time, and reveal the details of their private lives, with all their foibles and criminal actions. The names are disguised by omission of letters, but so slightly that they are easily discovered.

8398 ERSKINE (W.) History of India, under the two first sovereigns of the House of Taimur, Báber and Humáyun, 2 vols. 8vo. (pub. at 32*s*) *cloth*, 10*s*   1854
8399 EXMOUTH (Admiral Viscount) Life by Ostler, 8vo. *portrait, bds. 7s 6d*   1835
8400 FABER'S ORIGIN OF PAGAN IDOLATRY, ascertained from historical testimony and circumstantial evidence, 3 vols. 4to. 3 *plates and maps, hf. calf*, RARE, £5. 12*s* 6*d*   1816

"Mr. Faber, in his admirable work on the Pagan Idolatry, has collected and separately examined all the different systems of the Heathen Mythology ; and has shewn that there is such a singular, minute, and regular accordance among them not only in what is *obvious* and *natural*, but also in what is *arbitrary* and *circumstantial*, both in *fanciful speculations* and in *artificial* observances as to render untenable every other hypothesis than this—'that they must all have originated from some common source.'"—*Cory's Ancient Fragments.*

8401 FABYAN. THE CHRONICLE OF FABIAN, which he nameth the Concordaunce of Histories, newly perused and continued from the beginning of Kyng Henry the Seventh to the ende of Queene Mary, 2 vols. in 1, sm. folio, 𝔅lack letter, *fine copy of the* BEST FOLIO EDITION, *massively bound in smooth dark green morocco, ancient style, being covered over bevilled oak boards, joints inside, gilt edges, from Miss Currer's library*, £12. 12*s Jhon Kyngston, mense Aprilis,* 1559

The Roxburghe copy fetched £15. 15*s*; the Marquis of Lansdowne's £16. 16*s*.

Fabian was an eminent Merchant and some time Sheriff of London: he is very particular in this Chronicle in the affairs of London, many things being noted by him, which concern the Government of that City, hardly to be met with elsewhere; he gives the names of all the Bailiffs, Mayors, and Sheriffs, with the chief transactions in their several years. Cardinal Wolsey is said to have procured all the copies of this Chronicle that he could meet with to be burned, because he thought the Church's Patrimony was thereby too plainly discovered.

8402 FELLOWS (Charles) Journal during an Excursion in ASIA MINOR, roy. 8vo. (pub. at 28*s*) *cloth*, 15*s*   1839
8402*—— Discoveries in Lycia, stout roy. 8vo. *plates and woodcuts of Antiquities, Coins, Greek Inscriptions, etc.* (pub. £2. 2*s*) *cloth*, 24*s*   1841
8403 FENN'S ORIGINAL LETTERS, written during the Reigns of Henry VI, Edward IV, and V, Richard III, and Henry VII, by various persons of Rank, or consequence, (members of the PASTON FAMILY,) containing many curious Anecdotes relative to that turbulent, but hitherto dark period of our history, 5 vols. 4to. SECOND AND BEST EDITION, *with portraits shewing the costumes, coloured, and numerous facsimiles of autographs and seals, fine copy in marbled calf gilt, the fifth vol. bound to match*, £9.   1787-1823
8404 —— the same, *a very tall fine copy, in bright calf extra, rough gilt edges, with numerous leaves entirely uncut*, £12.   1787-1823

"The Paston letters are an important testimony to the progressive condition of society, and come in as a precious link in the chain of the moral history of England, which they alone in this period supply. They stand indeed singly in Europe; for though it is highly probable that in the archives of Italian families, if not in France or Germany, a series of merely private letters equally ancient may be concealed, I do not recollect any that have been published. They were all written in the reigns of Henry VI and Edward IV, except a few as late as Henry VII, by different members of a wealthy and respectable, but not noble family: and are, therefore, pictures of the life of the English gentry in that age."—*Hallam.*

*** This interesting publication consists of the original correspondence of the family of Paston, of Norfolk; they are valuable reliques of the old times, and were written during the troublesome times of the wars between the houses of York and Lancaster, in the Reigns of Henry VI, Edward IV, Edward V, Richard III, and Henry VII. They treat of the political history and of the military transactions of the day, and they also descant on the amours, the marriages, &c. of private life; relieved again by observations on domestic occurrences, and the details of rural occupations. "They altogether form a delightful picture of the times, of the manners and customs of the middle ages, and may be read with pleasure and advantage, even by those who profess abhorrence of whatever is ancient."

See an elaborate article respecting the original Ms. of these Letters by Sir Frederick Madden in *Notes and Queries*, Feb. 5, 1859.

FINLAY'S (G.) History of Greece under Foreign Domination, 7 vols. 8vo. viz. :
8405 GREECE UNDER THE ROMANS, B.C. 146 to A.D. 717, a Historical View of the Condition of the Greek Nation from its Conquest by the Romans until the Extinction of the Roman Power in the East, second edition, (pub. at 16*s*) 13*s* 6*d*
8406 HISTORY OF THE BYZANTINE EMPIRE, A.D. 716 to 1204, and of the Greek Empire of Nicæa and Constantinople, A.D. 1204 to 1453, 2 vols. (pub. at £1. 7*s* 6*d*) 23*s*
8407 MEDIÆVAL GREECE AND TREBIZOND. The History of Greece, from the Conquest by the Crusaders to its Conquest by the Turks, A.D. 1204 to 1566; and the History of the Empire of Trebizond, A.D. 1204 to 1461, (pub. at 12*s*) 10*s*
8408 GREECE UNDER OTHOMAN AND VENETIAN DOMINATION, A.D. 1453 to 1821 (pub. at 10*s* 6*d*) 8*s* 9*d*   1856
8409 HISTORY OF THE GREEK REVOLUTION, 2 vols. 8vo. (pub. at £1. 4*s*) 20*s*   1860

"His book is worthy to take its place among the remarkable works on Greek history which forms one of the chief glories of English scholarship. The history of Greece is but half told without it."—*London Guardian.*

"His work is therefore learned and profound. It throws a flood of light upon an important though obscure portion of Grecian history. . . . In the essential requisites of fidelity, accuracy, and learning, Mr. Finlay bears a favourable comparison with any historical writer of our day."—*North American Review.*

8410 FIELDING'S (H.) WORKS, with his Life, 8 vols. 8vo. *calf*, £2. 10*s*   1771
8411 —— the same, 8 vols. 8vo. *fine copy in bright old calf gilt.* £4. 10*s*   1771

Priced, 1824, Rivington, £5. 5*s*; fetched, 1855, Bohn's, £5. 5*s*.

8412 FIELDING'S Works, with Life, *new edition*, to which is now added, The Fathers, or the Good-natured Man, 10 vols. 8vo. *portrait and frontispiece, calf,* £2. 10s 1784

8413 ——— the same, 10 vols. 8vo. *fine copy in calf gilt*, £3. 3s 1784
"Of all the works of the imagination to which English genius has given origin, the writings of Henry Fielding are perhaps most decidedly and exclusively her own. The persons of his story live in England, travel in England, quarrel and fight in England: and scarce an incident occurs, without it being marked by something which could not well have happened in any other country. In strong and national humour, and forcible yet natural exhibition of character, the *Father of the English Novel* remains unapproached, even by his successful followers."—*Sir Walter Scott.*
"What a master of composition Fielding was! upon my word I think the Œdipus Tyrannus, the Alchemist and Tom Jones, the three most perfect plots ever planned, and how charming, how wholesome Fielding always is! to take him up after Richardson is like emerging from a sick room heated by stoves, into an open lawn on a breezy day in May."—*S. T. Coleridge.* "The prose Homer of human nature."—*Lord Byron.*

8414 FORTESCUE (Thomas) The FOREST, or collection of Histories no less profitable than pleasant and necessarie, dooen out of French into English, sq. sm. 8vo. Black letter, *cut rather close but otherwise a* FINE COPY, *morocco elegant, gilt leaves*, £2. 2s 1571
Priced, Thorpe, £2. 12s 6d; fetched at the Gordonstown sale, £4. 7s; Bindley's, £4.; Hibbert's, £4. 15s; Towneley's, £4. 17s 6d; Lloyd's, £5. 15s 6d; 1842, Sotheby's, £3.; 1858, £3. 8s.
A rare and interesting volume. COLLATION; Title, dedication, To the Reader, and Advertisement, 6 leaves; text, leaves 1-187; table, 4 leaves.

8415 FISHER (Byshop Johan) Mornynge Remembrance at the Moneth Minde of Margarete Countesse of Richmonde and Darbye, Moder unto Henry VII., 12mo. *reprint in* Black letter, *from Wynkyn de Worde's edition, plates of Arms and Monument, old calf*, 12s 6d 1708

8416 FLETCHER of Salton, Tracts: Discorso delle cose di Spagna, *Napoli,* 1698—Speeches in Parliament, Edinburgh, 1703—Right Regulation of Government, Ed. 1704 ; in 1 vol. 16mo. *calf gilt,* 5s 1698-1704

8417 FOOTE'S (Sam.) Works, with Remarks on each play, and an essay on his life and writings, by BEE, 3 vols. 12mo. *portrait, hf. morocco,* 15s 1830

8418 FORD (John) Dramatic Works, with introduction and explanatory notes by Weber, 2 vols. 8vo. *calf gilt*, 20s *Edinb.* 1811

8419 FOSBROKE (T. D.) Abstracts and Extracts of Smyth's Lives of the Berkeleys, with History of Berkeley, and Life of Jenner, 4to. *frontisp. bds.* 7s 6d 1821

8420 FOSS (Edward) The Judges of England; with Sketches of their Lives, and notices connected with the Courts at Westminster, from the time of the Conquest to 1485, Vols. I.-IV. 8vo. (pub. at £2. 16s *in cloth*) *calf extra*, £2. 1845-51

8421 ——— the same, Vols. 5, 6,—2 vols. 8vo. (pub. at 28s) *cloth*, 21s 1857
"A work which cannot be too highly estimated, whether for the importance of its object, or the great learning, extraordinary research, judgment, and impartiality bestowed on all parts of its composition."—*Legal Observer.*
"Mr. Foss has written a book which has added more to our knowledge of legal history than any single book published since 'Madox's History of the Exchequer.'"—*Gentleman's Magazine.*

8422 FOWLER (J.) History of the Troubles of Suethland and Poland, with the Life and Death of Sir George Douglas, 8 *portraits*—PARIVAL's History of this Iron Age, 1500-1656, 13 *portraits, including Charles I., Cromwell, Strafford, Mazarin, etc.* 2 vols. in 1, sm. folio, *fine impressions of the* 21 *portraits, fine copy, in the original old English calf,* 36s 1656
The second edition of Parival, which was published in 1659, contains only 12 portraits; and in these are but eight of the 13 mentioned.

8423 FOX (The Right Hon. Charles James) SPEECHES in the House of Commons, edited by Wright, 6 vols. 8vo. *hf. russia neat,* RARE, £5. 5s 1815

8424 FRENCH (G. R.) Royal Descent of Nelson and Wellington from Edward I. sm. 8vo. *hf. morocco, uncut,* 8s *Pickering,* 1853

8425 FROISSART'S (Sir John) Chronicles of England, France, Spain, Portugal, Scotland, etc. translated from the French by Lord Berners, reprinted from Pynson's Edition of 1523 and 1525, with Memoir of the Translator, and a copious Index, edited by Utterson, 2 vols. roy. 4to. *facsimiles,* (pub. at £7. 7s) *hf. bd. entirely uncut, scarce,* £2. 16s 1812
Priced, 1840, J. Bohn, £6 6s; 1841, £3. 10s; 1844, Payne and Foss, £5. 5s; 1850, White, £4. 4s: fetched, 1855, Sotheby's, £3. 12s; 1856, £3. 6s; 1858, Hodgson's, £3. 7s.
"Froissart is an historian consulted by every writer whose subject leads him to the period in which he wrote; he is the chief source of information we are possessed of with regard to one of the proudest portions of our national annals. Even the readers of romances must be gratified and charmed with Froissart, for there is as much gallantry, love, and adventure in the chronicles of Froissart as in any romance, Don Quixote scarcely excepted."—*Quart. Rev.*

8425*FROUDE'S History of England from the fall of Wolsey to the death of Elizabeth, Vols. I—VIII. 8vo. (pub. at £5. 12s) *cloth, new,* £4. 13s 6d 1858-64

8426 ——— the same, Vols. VII, VIII, 8vo. *cloth,* (pub. at 28s) 24s 1864

8426*FUSELI'S Life and Writings, by Knowles, 3 vols. 8vo. *portrait,* (pub. at 21s in bds.) *calf extra, gilt edges,* 20s 1831

8427 GARCILASSO DE LA VEGA, Works, in English, with his Life, etc. by Wiffen, sm. 8vo. *portrait, calf gilt,* 6s 1823

ENGLISH LITERATURE. 463

8428 GARLANDS collected by John Bell, Garland of Northumberland Heroes; Contented Cuckold; Garland of Bells; Whittell's Poetical Works, part 1, 1815; Poor Jack's Garland; Greenwich Pensioner's Garland; Jem of Aberdeen's Garland; and many others, Reprints of rare old Songs, Ballads, etc.; in 1 vol. 12mo. *fine paper, with curious cuts, calf gilt*, £2. 2s *Newcastle*, 1814

8429 GAY'S Fables, with Life, 2 parts in 1 vol. 16mo. *Heptinstall's very pretty edition, with frontispiece, portrait and 70 elegant vignette engravings by John Scott and others, blue morocco, gilt edges, scarce*, 20s 1796

8430 GEDDES (James) Essay on the Composition and manner of writing of the Antients, particularly Plato, sm. 8vo. FINE PAPER, *a learned and interesting work, old veau fauve, gilt edges*, 12s *Glasgow, Foulis*, 1748

8431 GIBBON'S ROMAN EMPIRE, with Notes, by Dean Milman and M. Guizot, edited with additional Notes by W. Smith, 8 vols. 8vo. *portrait and maps*, (pub. at £3. 3s) cloth, £2. 5s 1854

8432 —— MISCELLANEOUS WORKS, with memoirs of his Life and Writings, by himself, and notes, etc. by Lord Sheffield, 5 vols. 8vo. *portrait and plates*, (pub. at £3. 13s 6d) *calf gilt*, £2. 1814

8433 GIPSIES. GRELLMANN'S Dissertation on the Gipsies, translated by Raper, 4to. *calf gilt*, 10s 1787

8434 GLADSTONE'S (W. E. *Chancellor of the Exchequer*) Financial Statements of 1853, 1860, 1862, 1863, 8vo. 462 pp. (pub. at 10s 6d) *cloth*, 9s 1863
These famous Budget Speeches are here united into one volume; they give the clearest account of the Financial policy of Great Britain for the last ten years.

8435 GLADSTONE'S (W. E.) Studies on HOMER and the Homeric Age, 3 vols. 8vo. *cloth, out of print*, £2. 2s *Oxford*, 1858

8436 GLEIG'S Family History of England, 3 vols. 12mo. *plates of Costume, etc.* (pub. at 19s 6d) *cloth*, 10s 1836

8437 GOLDSMITH'S (Oliver) Works, edited by Peter Cunningham, 4 vols. 8vo. *portrait and frontispieces, calf gilt*, 38s 1854

8438 —— Poems, edited by Willmott, sm. 4to. *elegantly printed, with Illustrations by Birket Foster and Humphreys printed in colours, red morocco extra, blind tooled, gilt edges*, 21s 1859

8439 GOUGH (R.) BRITISH TOPOGRAPHY, an account of what has been done for illustrating the Topographical Antiquities of Great Britain and Ireland, 2 vols. stout sm. 4to. BEST EDITION, *many plates, calf neat*, 21s 1780

8440 GRAFTON'S Chronicle or History of England, with his Table of the Bailiffs, Sheriffs, and Mayors of London, from 1189 to 1558, 2 vols. roy. 4to. *bds.* 30s 1809

8441 GRATTAN'S Speeches in the Irish, and in the Imperial Parliament, edited by his Son, 4 vols. 8vo. *portrait, calf gilt*, 32s 1822

8442 GRAY'S (Thos.) Works, containing his Poems and Correspondence, with Memoirs of his life and writings, 2 vols. 8vo. *portrait, bds.* 9s 1825

8443 GREENE'S (Robert) Dramatic Works, with his Poems, some account of the Author, and notes by Dyce, 2 vols. sm. 8vo. *cloth*, 27s *Pickering*, 1831
The Plays of Greene are of extreme rarity and with one exception have never before been reprinted. Greene was one of the most popular poets of the Elizabethan period. His dramas contain much real poetry, and are especially valuable as pictures of the wild roystering life of the age.

8444 GRESHAM'S (Sir Thos. *Founder of the Royal Exchange*) Life and Times, with notices of his contemporaries, 2 vols. 8vo. *portrait and plates*, (pub. at 30s) *hf. calf*, 9s 1839

8445 GROTE'S History of Greece, 12 vols. 8vo. *with portrait and maps*, (pub. at £9. 12s) *cloth*, £7. 7s 1851-56

8446 —— History of Greece, new edition, complete in 8 vols. 8vo. *portrait and maps, calf gilt*, £7. 1863
"A great literary undertaking, equally notable whether we regard it as an accession to what is of standard value in our language, or as an honourable monument of what English scholarship can do."—*Athenæum*.

8447 GREY (Sir George) POLYNESIAN MYTHOLOGY and Traditional History of the New Zealand Race, sm. 8vo. *cuts*, (pub. at 10s 6d) *cloth*, 7s 1855

8448 GROSE'S MILITARY ANTIQUITIES respecting a History of the English Army, from the Conquest to the present time, 2 vols. 4to. *numerous plates, calf gilt*, £2. 2s 1786-88

8449 GUTCH'S Collectanea Curiosa; Tracts relating to the History and Antiquities of England and Ireland, chiefly published from the MSS. of Archb. Sancroft, 2 vols. 8vo. *bds.* 9s *Oxf.* 1781

8450 GYLL'S (G. W. J.) History of the parish of WRAYSBURY, Ankerwycke Priory, and Magna Charta Island; Horton, and Colnbrook, Bucks, 4to. *map and* PEDIGREES, *etc. new in cloth*, 15s 1862

8451 HAKLUYT SOCIETY'S PUBLICATIONS, from the commencement in 1847 to 1860, 27 vols. 8vo. *many maps and plates, (printed for subscribers only, at the cost of* £14. 14s) *in cloth,* £10. 1847-60
Separate volumes supplied.

8452 HALES' (John) GOLDEN REMAINS, sm. 4to. FIRST EDITION, *beautiful frontispiece and title by* HOLLAR, *dated* 1659, *original cf. excellent copy,* 20s Lond. 1659
"He had read more, and carried more about him, in his memory, than any man I ever knew; he was one of the least men in the kingdom, and one of the greatest scholars in Europe."—*Clarendon.*

8453 HALES' (Dr. W.) NEW ANALYSIS of CHRONOLOGY and Geography, History and Prophecy, in which their Elements are attempted to be exclaimed, harmonized and vindicated, upon Scriptural and Scientific Principles, 4 vols. 8vo. *second and best edition, scarce,* £2. 1830
Dr. Hawtrey's copy fetched £2. 18s.
"This work ought to have a place in the library of every biblical student who can procure it. It is not only the most elaborate system of Chronology extant in our language, but there is scarcely a difficult text in the sacred writings which is not illustrated."—*Horne.*

8454 HALLAM'S WORKS : The State of Europe during the Middle Ages, 3 vols.— The Constitutional History of England, from Henry VII. to George II. 3 vols. —The Literature of Europe in the XVth, XVIth, and XVIIth Centuries, 4 vols.—together 10 vols. 12mo, *new calf gilt,* £4. 4s 1860

8455 HAMPSON (R. T.) Origines Patriciæ, a deduction of European Titles of Nobility from their sources, with Appendix of an Icelandic poem and Glossarial Index, 8vo. *cloth, rare,* 18s 1846

8456 ——— Medii Aevi Kalendarium, or Dates, Charters and Customs of the Middle Ages with Kalendars of the X-XVth Centuries, and GLOSSARY, etc. 2 vols. 8vo. *facsimile,* (pub. at 42s) *bds.* 32s 1841

8457 **Hampshire.** WARNER'S (R.) Collections for the History of HAMPSHIRE and the Bishopric of Winchester, the Isles of Wight, Jersey, Guernsey and Sarke, 6 vols. in 3, 4to. *many fine portraits and plates of Antiquities, &c. fine copy in calf gilt,* £10. 10s 1789-96

8657* ——— the same, Vol. VI. only, LARGE PAPER, containing Hampshire extracted from Domesday Book, in Latin and English, with Introduction upon the Anglo-Saxon form of Government, and Glossary, roy. 4to. *hf. calf, uncut,* £5. 1789
No doubt wanting to a set.
Only 250 copies of this valuable work were printed. It includes the original Domesday Book of the County, with a translation, a view of the Anglo-Saxon times, the Ancient Form of Government, Glossary, etc.

8458 HARRIS' Life of Lord Chancellor HARDWICKE, with selections from his Correspondence, Diaries, Speeches, and Judgments, 3 vols. 8vo. *portrait, facsimile and 2 plates, calf gilt,* 32s 1847

8459 HARDY's (T. Duffus) Description of the Close Rolls in the Tower of London, 8vo. *cloth,* 6s *Privately printed,* 1833

8460 HARLEIAN MISCELLANY, a Collection of scarce and curious Pamphlets and Tracts, in Manuscript and Print, found in the late Earl of Oxford's library, with historical Notes by Malham, 12 vols. 8vo. *green morocco extra, gilt edges,* £5. 10s 1808-11
Priced, 1831, Longman, £6. 6s; 1836, Bryant, £6. 6s; 1843, £5. 15s 6d; 1847, £5. 10s.

8461 HARTE'S History of GUSTAVUS ADOLPHUS, King of Sweden, 2 vols. in 1, roy. 8vo. *portraits and plans, red morocco, gilt edges,* 18s 1807

8462 HAZLITT'S (W.) View of the English Stage, or a Series of Dramatic criticisms, 8vo. *title spotted, half bound,* 6s 1818

8463 ——— Life of NAPOLEON BUONAPARTE, 4 vols. 8vo. *calf gilt,* 27s 1830

8464 ——— Lectures on the Dramatic Literature of the age of Elizabeth, *portrait,* 1821—Lectures on the English Poets, 1819—2 vols. 8vo. *calf gilt,* 14s 1819-21

8465 ——— The Plain Speaker: opinions on Books, Men and Things, 2 vols. 8vo. *calf gilt,* 12s 1826

8466 HEAD'S and KIRKMAN'S ENGLISH ROGUE, described in the life of Meriton Latroon, a Witty Extravagant, comprehending the most eminent Cheats of both Sexes, 4 vols. in 2, *complete, portrait and many curious plates, a few pages injured, bd.* VERY RARE, £2. 16s 1680-71
Priced, 1827, Thorpe, £5. 5s; 1837, £3. 3s; fetched at Stanley's sale, £7. 2s 6d; Fonthill, £8. 8s; 1859, Gardiner's, fine copy, £7. 10s.
R. Head, the dissolute author of this very rare and amusing work, was the Bampfylde Moore Carew of his day, having the peculiar talent of transforming himself to any shape suitable to his roguish purposes. According to Mr. Aubrey, he was at one period of his life a bookseller in Little Britain. See Letters from the Bodleian Library, Vol. iii. p. 439. Copies almost invariably want some of the plates.

8467 (HEAD'S) Canting Academy, or the Devil's Cabinet Opened, with a complete CANTING DICTIONARY, several Catches and Songs, etc. 16mo. *bds. rare and curious,* 20s 1673

8468 HEEREN'S HISTORICAL WORKS, translated from the German by Bancroft, etc.: African Nations, Carthaginians, Ethiopians, Egyptians, 2 vols.; Asiatic Nations, Persians, Phenicians, Babylonians, Scythians, Indians, Appendices, 2 vols.; Europe and its Colonies; Ancient Greece, Historical Treatises; Manual of Ancient History; together 7 vols. 8vo. (pub. at £6. 6s) *cloth*, 36s 1838-47

8469 HELP'S Spanish Conquest in America, its relation to the history of Slavery and the Government of Colonies, 4 vols. 8vo. (pub. at £3.) *an excellent standard work, new in cloth*, £2. 10s 1855-61

8470 HENRY (Dr. Rob.) History of Great Britain written on a new plan, 12 vols. 1814—ANDREWS' Continuation, 2 vols. 1806—together 14 vols. 8vo. *portrait, calf neat*, 27s 1806-14

Fetched, 1855, Sotheby's, £3.; Bernal's sale, £3.

8471 HERBERT (Hon. and Rev. W.) Works, with additions and corrections, 3 vols. 8vo. (pub. at 31s 6d in bds.) *coloured calf gilt by Hayday*, 18s 1842

8472 Hertfordshire. CLUTTERBUCK'S (Robert) History and Antiquities of the County of HERTFORD, compiled from the best Authorities and Original Records, 3 vols. roy. folio, *numerous fine plates*, (pub. in bds. at £25. 4s) *half morocco neat, gilt tops, uncut*, £21. 1815-27

8473 HEWITT (J.) Ancient Armour and Weapons in Europe, from the Iron Period of the Northern Nations to the end of the XVIIth Century, 3 vols. 8vo. *very numerous plates and woodcuts*, (pub. at £2. 10s) *cloth extra, gilt tops, uncut*, £2. 2s 1860

8474 HERTSLET'S Complete Collection of Treaties and Conventions between Great Britain and Foreign Powers, compiled from authentic documents, with General Index, 8 vols. 8vo. (pub. at £8. 5s) bds. £4. 4s 1820-51

A valuable collection; containing the treaties in the foreign languages and English, side by side.

8475 HIGGINS (Godfrey) CELTIC DRUIDS: or an attempt to shew that the Druids were the Priests of Oriental Colonies, who emigrated from India, and were the Introducers of the first or Cadmean System of Letters, and the Builders of Stonehenge, of Carnac, and other Cyclopean works in Asia and Europe, 4to. LARGE PAPER, *map and numerous lithographic plates of Druidical Monuments, bds.* RARE, £2. 2s 1829

8476 —— ANACALYPSIS, an attempt to draw aside the veil of the Saitic Isis, or an Inquiry into the Origin of Languages, Nations and Religions, 3 vols. in 1, stout 4to. xxxii. and 867 *pages, five plates containing 34 compartments of figures, etc. bds.* £6. 10s 1833-36

8477 HOBBES' (Thomas *of Malmesbury*) COMPLETE WORKS, English and Latin, collected and edited by Sir W. MOLESWORTH, with Indexes, 16 vols. 8vo. *portrait and plates,* (pub. at £9. 12s) *new in cloth,* £2. 10s 1839-45

An elegantly printed ed¹tion, and the only complete one, of this fine old English philosopher.
"Hobbes may be numbered among those eminent persons born in the latter half of the XVIth Century who gave a new character to European philosophy in the succeeding age. A permanent foundation of his fame consists in *his admirable style, which seems to be the very perfection of didactic language.*"

8478 HOGG'S (*the Ettrick Shepherd*) Poetical Works, 4 vols. 12mo. (pub. at £2. 12s 6d) *half calf gilt*, 18s Edinb. 1822

8479 HOLINSHED'S CHRONICLES OF ENGLAND, SCOTLAND, AND IRELAND, (corrected and enlarged by Abraham Fleming), 3 vols. in 4, folio, *with the Indexes and greater part of the reprinted Castrations,* BEST EDITION, *old russia, broken binding, gilt edges,* VERY RARE, £7. 7s 1586-7

Sold in Steeven's sale for £23.; Roxburghe, £31. 10s; and Willett's for £36. 4s 6d.

8480 [HOLLAND (Philemon)] REGIMEN SANITATIS Salerni; or the Schoole of Salernes Regiment of Health, enlarged by P. H. sq. 8vo. 𝔅𝔩𝔞𝔠𝔨 𝔩𝔢𝔱𝔱𝔢𝔯, *old calf,* 16s 1649

8481 HOLLIS (Thomas) Memoirs of, 2 vols. in 1, impl. 4to. *with fine impressions of the 37 beautiful plates engraved by Bartolozzi from Cipriani's designs, including portraits of Milton, A. Marvell, Algernon Sydney, Locke, Newton, and others, strongly bound in stamped russia, neat,* £2. 2s Privately printed, 1780

Quite complete with the starred additional pages, the Index, and the portrait of Newton, which are often wanting. Priced, 1860, £3. 3s; Heath's copy fetched £4. 7s; copies with the starred pages used to sell formerly for £7. 7s. These splendidly illustrated Memoirs contain a great deal of curious and interesting literary matter, especially respecting Milton, not to be found elsewhere.

8482 HOOK (Theodore) Life of Sir DAVID BAIRD, 2 vols. 8vo. *portrait* (pub. at 24s) *bds.* 10s 1838

8483 HOUSEHOLD BOOKS. Privy Purse Expenses of Elizabeth of York, Wardrobe Accounts of Edward IV. and Memoir of Elizabeth, by Sir Harris Nicolas, 1830—Regulations of the Household of Henry Percy, fifth Earl of Northumberland, by Bishop Percy, 1827—Privy Purse Expenses of Henry VIII. 1529-1532, by Nicolas, 1827—Privy Purse Expenses of Princess, afterwards Queen Mary, with a Memoir and Notes, by Sir Frederic Madden, 1830—4 vols. 8vo. (pub. at £4. 4s) *cloth*, £2. 10s 1827-30

8484 NORTHUMBERLAND (Earl of) Regulations and Establishment of the Household of Henry Algernon Percy, fifth Earl of Northumberland, at his Castles of Wresill and Lekinfield in Yorkshire, 1512, edited by BISHOP PERCY, 8VO. WITH THE PREFACE, *old red morocco, gilt edges*, £2. 2s 1770

<small>Sold in Mr. Dent's sale for £8. 12s 6d, in Joshua Smith's for £6. 16s 6d, in Sir M. M. Sykes's for £8. 15s, Mr. Brockett's £10. 10s, and in the Fonthill for £20. 1s 6d.</small>

8485 HOPTON (Arthur) Concordancy of Yeeres, containing an exact computation of Time, with the use of the English and Roman Kalender, 12mo. *a curious Diary or Chronology, vellum*, 7s 6d 1615

8486 HOWELL'S (James) Dendrologia, Dodona's Grove; or, the Vocall Forest, sq. sm. 8vo. *engraved title, good copy, vellum*, 8s 1644
<small>A curious allegory of the principal incidents in the history of Europe, 1603-40.</small>

8487 HUGHES' (T. S.) HISTORY OF ENGLAND, from the accession of George III, to the accession of Queen Victoria, third edition, corrected and enlarged, with preliminary essay, 7 vols. 8vo. *calf elegant, portrait*, £2. 2s 1846
<small>Indispensable as being the best continuation to Hume and Smollett.</small>

8488 HUME (David) PHILOSOPHICAL WORKS, including all the essays, with the important alterations, 4 vols. 8vo. *port. calf gilt, scarce*, £2. 2s Edinburgh, 1826

8489 HUME AND SMOLLETT'S History of England, from the Invasion of Julius Cæsar to the death of George II, 10 vols. 8vo. *two portraits, calf gilt, fine copy*, £3. 10s 1830

8490 HUNTER (Rev. J.) South Yorkshire: History and Topography of the Deanery of DONCASTER, 2 vols. folio, *portrait, plans and plates of Ecclesiastical Antiquities, Monuments, etc. with woodcuts of Arms, bds.* RARE, £7. 10s 1828-31
<small>A copy with the arms emblazoned by Dowse fetched, 1856, Sotheby's, £12.</small>

8491 ——— Three Catalogues describing the contents of the Red Book of the Exchequer, the Dodsworth MSS. in the Bodleian, and the MSS. in Lincoln's Inn Society Library, 8vo. *hf. calf*, 16s Pickering, 1838

8492 HYETT'S (W. H.) Sepulchral Memorials, Engravings from the Altar, Tombs, Effigies, and Monuments, in the County of Northampton, 3 parts in 1 vol. roy. folio, LARGE PAPER, 15 *fine plates*, (pub. at £3.) *hf. calf, uncut*, 25s 1817
<small>A very desirable addition to Baker's Northamptonshire.</small>

8493 (ILLINGWORTH) Topographical Account of the Parish of Scampton in the County of Lincoln, Roman Antiquities discovered there, and anecdotes of the Bolles Family, 4to. 13 *plates, including 2 maps and large tabular Pedigree, calf extra, gilt edges, scarce*, 36s Privately printed, 1808
<small>There was a second edition of this work *published* two years later, which, although containing 2 more plates than the privately printed edition, does not contain the large Genealogical sheet.</small>

8494 INNES AND BRABAZON FAMILIES. HISTORICALL Account of the Origine and Succession of the family of Innes, from an original MS. in possession of the Duke of Roxburghe, *illuminated initial*, Edinb. 1820—GENEALOGICAL History of the Family of BRABAZON, *plates, coats of Arms, and Genealogical tables*, privately printed, Paris, 1825—2 vols. in 1, 4to. *calf extra, gilt edges*, RARE, £3. 16s Edinburgh, 1820

8495 ISLA, History of Friar Gerund de Campazas, by Salazar, 2 vols. 8vo. *fine copy, calf gilt*, 8s 1772

8496 JACOBITE TRACTS. The Present State of England—The Price of Abdication—Now or Never; or, the Last Cast for England—Great Britain's Just Complaint, 1692—Account of the late Depredations of the Dutch upon the English, 1695—Reply to Dr. Welwood's Answer to King James's Declaration, 1693—A Dialogue between K. W. and Benting—Detection of the Corruptions, of some Persons of Great Trust, 1695—and several others, *an important Collection*; in 1 vol. sq. 8vo. *bds.* 20s 1692, &c.
<small>The Dialogue between King William and Benting is an extremely curious fictitious colloquy, in which the King accuses himself of every crime, and is visited by the ghost of Queen Mary, who cries to him—" Repent; for me it's too late, not yet for you."</small>

ENGLISH LITERATURE.

3497 JACOBITE TRACTS — another collection. Executions ot Ashton, of Anderton, and others; Letters on the late Tryals, the pretended Plot; Gallienus Redivivus (the Massacre of Glencoe), etc. in 1 vol. sq. 8vo. *bds.* 15*s* 1690-95
A very curious collection of pieces, written by partizans of James II, concerning the legitimacy of the Prince f Wales, the executions for Jacobite conspiracies, the Massacre of Glencoe, etc.; comparing " W. R." (William III.) o the tyrants of antiquity.

3498 JOHN BULL (The) Weekly Newspaper, from the beginning in Dec. 17, 1820, to March 31, 1860, with the titles and Indexes, 39 vols. folio, and 13 Nos. (pub. at £51. 11*s unbound*) *hf. calf, a clean set*, £9. 1820-60

3499 JONSON'S (Ben) WORKS, with notes, critical and explanatory, and Memoir by W. GIFFORD, 9 vols. 8vo. *portrait*, LIBRARY COPY, *in calf gilt, contents lettered*, SCARCE, £6. 6*s* 1816
Cost the former proprietor £8. 2*s*. Fetched, Sotheby's, 1859, *morocco*, £9. 15*s*; 1860, Sotheby's, £6. 15*s*.

3500 JONES (Gen. Sir H. D.) Reports relating to the Re-Establishment of the Fortresses in the Netherlands, 1814-30, 8vo. *map, cloth, printed for private circulation*, £2. 1861

3501 JONES (Sir W.) Works, with Life, by Lord Teignmouth, 13 vols. 8vo. *hf. calf,* 30*s* 1807
Bernal's copy fetched, 1855, £5. 15*s*.
" His writings everywhere breathe pure taste in morals as well as in literature; and it may be said with ruth, that not a single sentiment has escaped him which does not indicate the real elegance and dignity which ervaded the most secret recesses of his mind. No author is better calculated to inspire those generous sentiments f liberty, without which the most just principles are useless and lifeless."—*Sir James Mackintosh.*

3502 KELHAM'S Dictionary of the Norman or Old French Language, with the Laws of William the Conqueror, in Latin, Old French, and English, 2 vols. in 1, 8vo. *calf gilt, rare,* 30*s* 1779

3503 —— Domesday Book illustrated, containing an Account of that Record, a translation of difficult passages, an explanation of the Terms, Abbreviations, etc. 8vo. *calf gilt,* 30*s* 1788

3504 KEMBLE (J. M.) Horæ Ferales, or, Studies in the Archæology of the Northern Nations, edited by R. G. Latham, and A. W. Franks, roy. 4to. 34 *plates*, 11 *coloured, price* £3. 3*s* 1864

3505 KEMPIS, Imitation of Christ, translated with notes by Dibdin, 8vo. *plates, cloth*, 10*s* 6*d* 1828

3506 KENNETT'S (Bishop White) Complete History of England, with the Lives of all the Kings and Queens to the Death of William III, 3 vols. folio, BEST EDITION, *old calf,* £2. 1719
Priced, Longman, £4. 4*s*; J. Bohn, £4. 14*s* 6*d*; Pickering, £3. 3*s*; fetched, 1859, Sotheby's, £3. 7*s*.
" Much abuse was drawn upon him by the Jacobite party, who thought it not sufficiently favourable to their rinciples of passive obedience.—*Roose's Ecclesiastica.*

3507 KEIGHTLEY's History of England, 3 vols. 8vo. (pub. at 36*s*) *cloth,* 14*s* 1839

3508 —— the same, 3 vols. 8vo. *hf. russia gilt,* 20*s* 1839

3509 KENNEDY and GRANGER's Present State of the Tenancy of Land in Great Britain, 2 vols. 8vo. *frontispieces*, (pub. at 30*s*) *cloth,* 10*s* 1828-29

3510 KENNETT'S (W.) Parochial Antiquities attempted in the History of Ambrosden, Burcester, and other adjacent parts in the Counties of OXFORD and BUCKS, 2 vols. 4to. *portrait and plates, calf gilt,* £2. Oxford, 1818

3511 **Kent.** PHILIPOTT's Villare Cantianum, or Kent Surveyed and Illustrated, sm. folio, *with the original map and* 4 *plates on the letterpress engraved by* HOLLAR, *old calf,* 12*s* 1659
Priced, 1840, £2. 2*s*; 1858, a copy fetched 33*s*. " A valuabl performance."—*Lowndes.*

3512 KIMBER and JOHNSON, Baronetage of England, with account of Nova Scotia Baronets of English Families, and a Dictionary of Heraldry, 3 vols. 8vo. 36 *engraved pp. containing* 427 *Shields of Arms, calf,* 12*s* 1771
Priced, 1834, Thorpe, £1. 11*s* 6*d*.

3513 KING's Italian Valleys of the Pennine Alps, a tour through the less frequented " vals" of North Piedmont, 8vo, *map, plates, and cuts,* (pub. at 18*s in bds.*) *calf extra,* 12*s* 1858

3514 KINGLAKE'S Invasion of the Crimea, 2 vols. 8vo. *fourth edition,* (pub. at 32*s*) *cloth, new,* 27*s* 1863
With an interesting advertisement of 22 pages, reviewing the criticisms and corrections.

3515 KORAN (Al) of Mahomet, translated out of Arabique into French, and now newly Englished, sq. 8vo. *bd.* 10*s* 1649
The first English translation.

3516 —— translated from Arabic into English with explanatory notes, by G. SALE, 2 vols. 8vo. *very neatly bound,* 16*s* 1825

2 H 2

8517 LAMBETH PALACE. TODD'S (Archdeacon) Catalogue of the Archiepiscopal Manuscripts in the Library at Lambeth Palace, with account of the Archiepiscopal Registers and other Records there preserved, folio, *plates of facsimiles from early MSS., bds. uncut,* PRIVATELY PRINTED, *very rare*, £4. 14s 6d   1812
Priced, 1842, Thorpe, £5. 15s 6d; fetched at Dawson Turner's sale, 1853, £4. 16s.

8518 LANCASHIRE and CHESHIRE HISTORIC SOCIETY'S Proceedings, Papers, and Transactions, First Series, 12 vols.—New Series, Vols. I, II.—together 14 vols. 8vo. complete from the beginning, *numerous plates of Antiquities,* (pub. at £7. 10s) *sd.* £4. 16s   Liverpool, 1849-60

8519 ——— the same, Vols. I—X. 8vo. *hf. green morocco, gilt tops, a very nice set,* £4. 15s   1849-58

8521 LANDOR'S (Walter Savage) Works, 2 vols. stout roy. 8vo. (pub. at 32s) *cloth,* 21s   1846

8522 LAPPENBERG'S History of England under the Anglo-Saxon Kings, translated from the German by Thorpe, with additions and corrections, 2 vols. 8vo. (pub. at 21s) *cloth,* 10s   1844

8523 LATHAM, The Nationalities of Europe, 2 vols. 8vo. (pub. at 32s) *cloth,* 22s   1863

8524 LEAKE'S Travels in NORTHERN GREECE, 4 vols. 8vo. *maps, plates, and cuts, cloth,* £2. 10s   1835

8525 LE GRAND, Fabliaux or Fables abridged from French MSS. of the XII and XIII Centuries, translated into English verse, with preface, notes, and appendix, by Way and Ellis, 2 vols. roy. 8vo. *woodcuts by* BEWICK, *fine copy in red morocco super extra, ornamented sides, joints, gilt and marbled edges, by Kalthoeber,* £3. 3s   1796-1800

8526 LE MARCHANT, Report of the House of Lords Proceedings on the claim to the Barony of Gardner, with Appendix of Legitimacy Cases, 8vo. *bds.* 12s   1828

8527 LEMPRIERE'S Notes in Mexico in 1861 and 1862, politically and socially considered, sm. 8vo. *map and plates,* (pub. at 12s 6d) *cloth,* 7s   1862

8528 LE NEVE'S Lives, Characters, Deaths, Burials, and Epitaphs of all the Protestant Bishops since the Reformation, 2 vols. large 8vo. LARGE PAPER, *fine clean copy in old calf gilt,* 21s   1720
Fetched £2. 1s at the Rev. T. Williams' sale. No more was published than these two parts.

8529 LETTER WRITER. A President for yong Penmen, or the Letter Writer, full of variety, delight, and pleasure, sm. 8vo. 𝕭lack 𝕷etter, *containing very curious epistolary specimens, margin of title mended, calf gilt,* 18s   1638

8530 LHUYD (Humfrey) BREVIARY of BRITAYNE, as this Iland was of ancient time divided into England, Scotland, and Wales, Englished by Thomas Twyne, 16mo. 𝕭lack 𝕷etter, *green morocco, tooled on sides, gilt edges,* VERY RARE, £4.
Imprinted by Richard Johnes, 1573
"This Edition of the Breviary of Britain is so scarce that Mr. Tho. Hearne of Oxford never could meet with a compleat copy but that in the Earl of Oxford's Library; Bishop More offered to Mr. Ralph Thoresby for this copy its weight in gold."—MS. note.

8531 LIBERAL (The), Verse and Prose from the South, 2 vols. 8vo. *hf. calf,* 8s 1822-23
All original contributions by Lord Byron, Shelley, Leigh Hunt, etc.

8532 LILLY (W. *the Astrologer*) Monarchy or No Monarchy in England, Grebner his Prophecy concerning Charles son of Charles, English, Latin, Saxon, Scottish, and Welsh prophecies, etc. sq. 8vo. 19 *curious woodcuts of Predictions fulfilled, allegorical prophecies, etc. calf, from Miss Currer's library, rare,* 28s   1651

8533 LINCOLNSHIRE. Rennie (F.) Report concerning the Drainage of Wildmore Fen, and of the East and West Fens, folio, *map, sd.* 7s 6d   1800

8534 LINDSAY'S (Lord) HISTORY OF CHRISTIAN ART, 3 vols. 8vo. *cloth,* £2. 12s 1847
RARE; the best English work on Christian art, based on profound historical studies and close inspection of the existing Christian Art Treasures. Contents:—Vol. I. The Ideal and the Character and Dignity of Christian Art—The Symbolism of Christianity—The Mythology of Christianity—General Classification of Schools and Artists—Roman Art—Byzantine Art. Vol. II. Lombard and Gothic Architecture—Sculpture of the Lombards, &c.—Niccolo Pisano and his School—Giotto and his School. Vol. III. School of Siena—Semi-Byzantine School of Florence—Primitive School of Bologna—Sculpture and Painting North of the Alps—Postscriptum.

8535 LINDSAY (Lord) Lives of the Lindsays, a Memoir of the Houses of Crawford and Balcarres, 3 vols. 8vo. *facsimiles,* (pub. at 42s) *cloth,* 25s   1849
"A work calculated to illustrate both the public and domestic history of Great Britain, in the most important as well as pleasing manner, by a succession of lively chronological biographies, each of which presents a faithful picture of the statistics, customs and leading events of the era, from the thirteenth century to our own times."
Strickland's Queens of England, Vol. VI, p 260.

ENGLISH LITERATURE. 469

536 LINGARD'S (Dr.) History of England, from the first invasion by the Romans to the close of the reign of James the Second, 14 vols. 8vo. *third and library edition*, (*pub. at £8. 8s*) *bds. £2. 10s*   1825-31

537 —— the same, 14 vols. 8vo. *a handsome set in calf gilt*, £4. 10s   1825-31

538 —— the same, 4*th edition*, 14 vols. 8vo. *sd.* 28*s*   Paris, 1826-31

"Dr. Lingard's History is the fruit of great industry, learning, and acuteness, directed by no ordinary talents, d written in a clear and agreeable manner. He possesses what he claims, the rare merit of having collected his iterials from original historians and records. To one desirous of making a study, and not a mere amusement of a history of his country, we know no general history of England that we should sooner recommend than this."
Edinburgh Review.

539 LOCKE'S (John) Works, with Life, 10 vols. 8vo. *port. hf. cf. neat*, 36*s*   1812
Priced, 1844, £3. 16*s*; 1851, £3. 3*s*

540 LODGE (Edmund) Life of Sir Julius Cæsar, Chancellor of the Exchequer, and Privy Councillor to James I and Charles I, with memoirs of his family and descendants, impl. 4to. *pedigree and* 17 *portraits, that of Mrs. Aberdeen as usual wanting, blue morocco, tooled joints, gilt edges*, 15*s*   1827

541 LONDON GAZETTE from the beginning, November 9, 1665, to March 22, 1668, being Nos. 1-349; in 1 vol. sm. folio, *hf. bd.* £5. 5*s*   1665-68

542 —— another set, from the beginning to March 28, 1670, in 1 vol. stout sm. folio, *not quite perfect, there being about* 20 *Nos. missing from the series, hf. bd.* £6. 6*s*   1665-70

The first 23 Nos. were printed at Oxford with the heading "Oxford Gazette" in consequence of the plague London. Both of the above sets will be sold not subject to collation, as some of the edges are frayed, and the argins occasionally cut into. This, however, is but a trifling drawback to the interest which must attach to such a llection: these numbers give the earliest official accounts of the Great Plague in 1665, the Fire of 1666, and of her occurrences during a most eventful period.

543 **London.** COWPER's Millwall, the Isle of Dogs, 8vo. *cloth*, 3*s* 6*d*   1853

544 FISHER'S (P.) Catalogue of the memorable TOMBS, Grave-stones, Plates, etc. in the demolisht or extant churches of LONDON, sq. 8vo. *imperfect at the end, hf. calf*, 25*s*   1668

545 LONGFELLOW'S Poetical Works, large 8vo. *portrait, and upwards of one hundred designs by J. Gilbert, engraved by Dalziel, cloth, sides covered with gilt tooling, gilt edges*, 17*s* 6*d*   1856

546 LORD (Henry) The Religion of the PERSEES, as compiled from a book of theirs, written in the Persian character, and called the Zundavastaw, sq. sm. 8vo. *bd.* 21*s*   1630

COLLATION: Title, Epistle Dedicatory, etc. 6 leaves; text, pp. 1-53.
An extremely curious and interesting volume: it is the first European Work which makes known the istence of the Parsee race and religion in India. The first chapter describes the origin of this people, and hence they had come. Then follows an exposition, from the Zendavesta, as "interpreted by a learned Parsee," the Parsee religion, with a life of Zertust (Zoroaster); which it would be a curious study to compare with nquetil Duperron's work. Lord was in the service of the East India Company.

548 LYSONS'S (Samuel) Collection of GLOUCESTERSHIRE ANTIQUITIES (a series of one hundred and ten Plates of the Remains of former times existing in the County of Gloucester, including Churches, Castles, Old Houses, Ruins, Tombs, Effigies, Sculpture, Stained Glass, Seals, etc. with Descriptions, royal folio, LARGEST PAPER, 110 *large etchings of Ancient Crosses, Tombs, Doors, Gateways, Churches, Painted Glass, Seals, Brasses,* COLOURED THROUGHOUT, *uncut,* £5. 5*s*
1804

The ordinary issue on Small Paper was published at £6. 6*s*; the Large Paper at £10. 10*s*; but of the Largest aper, with the entire set of plates coloured, only a very few copies were printed, to match the author's *Reliquiæ ritannico-Romanæ.*

549 LYTTELTON'S (Lord) and Mr. GLADSTONE'S Translations, new edition, sm. 4to. contains in ADDITION to the matter of the first Edition, 1861, which is entirely exhausted:
TENNYSON'S Ulysses, translated into Latin, by Lord Lyttelton.
HOMER's first book, translated into English, by the Right Honourable W. E. GLADSTONE, M.P.

⁎ As this Second Edition is again issued in a small number, early application for copies is required. Price half morocco, 9*s*   1863

TWENTY-FIVE COPIES are on LARGE PAPER, 1 vol. 4to. *hf. morocco, uncut,* £1. 8*s*; *whole morocco, gilt edges,* £2. 2*s*   1863

8550 MACAULAY'S (Lord) HISTORY OF ENGLAND, from the accession of James the Second (to the death of William the Third, 1702), 5 vols. 8vo. *best edition*, (pub. at £4. 2s in cloth), *elegantly bound in calf gilt*, £4. 4s   1860-61

8551 —— the same, with Memoir, 8 vols. 12mo. *new edition, revised and corrected, portrait*, (pub. at 48s), *cloth*, £2.   1863-62

8552 M'CULLOCH (J. R.) on the Succession to Property vacant by Death, 8vo. *Author's autograph inscription, hf. morocco extra*, 5s 6d   1848

8553 —— Treatise on the Principles and Practical Influence of TAXATION and the Funding System, 8vo. *third edition, revised, corrected, and improved*, xviii. and 524 pp. *cloth*, 10s   *Edin.* 1863

8554 MACKAY (Charles) Memoirs of Extraordinary Popular Delusions, 3 vols. 8vo. (pub. at £2. 12s 6d) *portraits, hf. calf neat*, 27s   1841

8555 MACHIAVEL (Nicholas) The Arte of Warre; set forth in English by Peter Withorne, sq. 12mo. *elaborate woodcut title and two woodcuts*, 𝔟𝔩𝔞𝔠𝔨 𝔩𝔢𝔱𝔱𝔢𝔯, *with MS. notes, neatly written in the autograph of G. Harvey, a very fine large copy in calf extra, by Bedford*, £2. 10s   1573

8556 MACKINNON'S History of Civilisation, 2 vols. 8vo. (pub. at 24s) *cloth*, 10s   1846

8557 MACKINTOSH (Sir James) History of England, continued by Bell, 10 vols. 12mo. *hf. red morocco, gilt tops, uncut*, £2.   1830-40

8558 McLEAN's Notice of a Twenty-five Years' Service in the Hudson's Bay Territory, 2 vols. sm. 8vo. *with Vocabularies of Languages*, (pub. at 21s) *cloth*, 10s   1849

8559 MACRAY's Manual of British Historians to A.D. 1600, chronological account of Early Chroniclers and Monkish Writers, 8vo. *hf. morocco*, 8s 6d   *Pickering*, 1845

8560 MAGAZINE of the FINE ARTS, and Journal of Literature and Science, 4 vols. 8vo. *portraits, cloth*, 20s   1833-34

8561 MAITLAND'S The Dark Ages, Essays intended to illustrate the State of Religion and Literature in the 9th, 10th, 11th, and 12th centuries, 8vo. *cloth*, 15s 1844

8562 **Man (Isle of)**. FELTHAM'S Tour through the Island of Man, 1797-98, 8vo. *map and plates, bds.* 7s 6d; *or hf. morocco, uncut*, 10s   *Bath*, 1798

8563 SACHEVERELL's Account of the Isle of Man, its Inhabitants, Language, etc. with an account of the Antient Druids, by Thos. Brown, 12mo. *hf. bd.* 4s 6d   1702

8564 MANNING's Lives of the Speakers of the House of Commons, roy. 8vo. (pub. at 24s), *cloth*, 7s 6d   1850

8565 MANSHIP (Henry, *Town Clerk, temp. Elizabeth*) History of Great Yarmouth, edited, with CONTINUATION, by PALMER, 2 vols. *plan, and plates of Antiquities, coins, seals, etc. including Photographic facsimile of King John's Charter, hf. bd.* 36s   *Yarmouth*, 1854-56

8566 MARLOWE'S (Christopher) Works, with notes, and some Account of his Life and Writings by Dyce, 3 vols. sm. 8vo. *cloth, uncut*, 32s   *Pickering*, 1850

Best edition, based upon the collation of early copies of the various pieces.
"Marlowe, renown'd for his rare art and wit,
Could ne'er attain beyond the name of Kit."—*Thomas Heywood.*

8567 MARSDEN's (Wm.) Memoirs, (edited by his Widow, the present Mrs. Col. Leake), 4to. *hf. morocco*, 6s   *Privately printed*, 1838

8568 MARSHALL'S Rural Economy of Norfolk, Gloucester, Yorkshire, Midland, Southern and Western Counties of England, 12 vols. 8vo. *hf. bd.* 25s   1789-89

These are Glossaries of Provincialisms for the various counties; that for Yorkshire, containing 65 pp., is nowhere else to be found.

8569 MARTEN'S (Coll. Henry) Familiar Letters to his Lady of Delight, also her kinde returns, and Pellingall's Heroicall Epistles, 8vo. *calf gilt, rare and curious*, 16s   1662

8570 MAY (Erskine) Constitutional History of England, since the accession of George III, 1760-1860, 2 vols. 8vo. *second edition*, (pub. at 33s) *new in cloth*, 27s 6d   1863

This excellent and remarkable history has already obtained the position of a standard work.

8571 MAY's (Thomas) History of the (Long) Parliament of England, which began May 1640, (edited by Maseres), 4to. *portrait and plate, hf. calf*, 7s 6d   1812

8572 MAYHEW'S (H.) LONDON LABOUR and the LONDON POOR; a Cyclopædia of the condition and earnings of those that *will* work, those that *cannot* work, and those that *will not* work, *with the extra volume*, COMPLETE, 4 vols. 8vo. *numerous woodcuts, from photographs, cloth*, 28s   1861-62

An extraordinary work. Its contents are entirely original, either supplied by the Police authorities, or gathered from the unfortunate parties themselves, and in addition to numerous deeply-interesting autobiographies, the work contains reliable statistical and social information, showing, not only the actual state of the dangerous and vicious classes of the metropolis, but what is doing for their reformation and elevation.

8573 MERIVALE (Charles) History of the Romans under the Empire, 7 vols. 8vo. *fourth edition*, (pub. at £5. 6s), *new in cloth*, £4. 8s 6d   1862

This great work places Mr. Merivale in the foremost rank of historians; his title to stand beside Gibbon is now universally conceded.

8574 MILL'S (J.) History of BRITISH INDIA, fifth edition, with notes and continuation by H. H. WILSON, 10 vols. 12mo. (pub. at £2. 16s), *new in cloth*, 36s   1858

8575 MILL (John Stuart) Principles of Political Economy, with their applications to Social Philosophy, 2 vols. 8vo. fifth edition, (pub. at 30s) *cloth, new*, 25s   1862

8576 ——— System of Logic, Ratiocinative and Inductive, 2 vols. 8vo. *fifth edition*, (pub. at 25s) *cloth, new*, 21s   1862

8577 MILMAN'S History of Christianity from the birth of Christ, to the abolition of Paganism in the British Empire, 3 vols. 8vo. *revised edition*, (nearly ready)   1864

8578 ——— History of Latin Christianity, including that of the Popes to the Pontificate of Nicholas V. 6 vols. 8vo. (pub. at £3. 12s) *new in cloth*, £2. 18s   1857

"He is a Christian scholar, of wide and generous sympathies, sagacious, shrewd, far-seeing, tolerant, who has won for himself a great and deserved reputation by his History of Latin Christianity, a work of which England has reason to be proud."—*Athenæum, May 16, 1863*.

8579 MILLER (Hugh) Testimony of the Rocks, 8vo. *cuts, cloth*, 5s   *Edin.* 1857
8580 MILLS (Ch.) History of the Crusades, 2 vols. 8vo. *calf*, 9s   1822
8581 MILTON'S WORKS, in Verse and Prose, *printed from the Original Editions, with a Life of the Author by the Rev. John Mitford*, 8 vols. 8vo. *an exact reprint of Pickering's edition*, (pub. £4. 4s cloth), *calf extra*, £5. *Chiswick Press,* 1863

At Pickering's Great Sale the entire stock was disposed of, and the book rapidly became SCARCE; up to the present time copies have realised at sales from four guineas to five guineas each. This edition is nearly exhausted, and must speedily rise in value.

8582 MILTON'S (John) POETICAL WORKS, with notes of various authors, illustrations, account of his Life and Writings, Glossary and Verbal Index, by Todd, 7 vols. 8vo. *portraits and 2 plates, calf gilt*, £2. 5s   1809
Previously priced, £5. 15s 6d.

8583 ——— third edition, 6 vols. 8vo. *portrait and plates, calf gilt*, £2. 12s   1826
8584 ——— Poetical Works, with Memoir and Remarks, by Montgomery, 2 vols. sm. 8vo. *with 120 fine engravings from Harvey's designs*, (pub. at 24s) *cloth gilt, new*, 10s   1859

8585 MIRROR FOR MAGISTRATES, collated and edited from the several early editions, with preface and historical notes by JOSEPH HASLEWOOD, Esq. 3 vols. sm. 4to. *cloth*, £3. 5s   1815

Only 150 copies were printed. "The popularity of this work, and its influence on our national poetry, throughout the reigns of Elizabeth and James the First, were very considerable. Even in its earliest and most unfinished state it had attracted the admiration of Sir Philip Sydney, who says, 'I account the Mirrour of Magistrates meetely furnished of beautiful partes;' and in its last and most perfect form it seems to have been considered as a book necessary to the accomplished gentleman; for in Chapman's Comedy, entitled Mayday, and printed in 1611, a character, versed in the elegant literature of the time, is described as 'One that has read Marcus Aurelius, Gesta Romanorum, and the Mirrour of Magistrates'; its pages present us with innumerable specimens of dramatic speeches, incidents, characters, and it has thrown into a metrical form the most interesting passages of the Ancient Chronicles."—*Drake's Shakspeare and his Times.*

8586 MITCHELL (Sir Andrew) Envoy from Great Britain to Prussia, 1756-71, Memoirs and Papers by Andrew Bissett, 2 vols. 8vo. *portrait*, (pub. at 30s), *cloth*, 10s   1850

8587 MITFORD'S History of Greece, 8 vols. 8vo. *hf. calf gilt*, 24s   1820

8588 MOMMSEN'S HISTORY OF ROME, translated with the author's sanction and additions, by the Rev. William P. Dickson, 3 vols. 8vo. (pub. at £1. 8s 6d) *new in cloth*, 24s   1862-63

Dr. Mommsen displays great qualities which have won for him justly a high place among the restorers of classical history. To deep and clear appreciation of his subject, and insight into the political relations and social state of the ancient world, he adds considerable artistic skill; and he has the faculty of lucid arrangement and of plain, manly, and vigorous expression. This picture of a notable episode in the mighty epic of the Res Romana accordingly bears the stamp of truth; it is full, rational, and pregnant with thought; and if it is somewhat wanting in animation, it is very attractive to a philosophic reader. As Niebuhr and Arnold have only touched this period in a cursory manner, and it does not fall within the scope of Mr. Merivale's excellent work, Dr. Mommsen is certainly the greatest historian who has hitherto tried to reproduce it and place it in an intelligible aspect. Accordingly, we leave him, with thanks for the philosophic depth and great ability displayed in this volume; and, in conclusion, especially grateful that in his account of the decay of the Republic he has carefully abstained from misleading the reader by false analogies in modern history. The more we study the peculiar institutions and character of the Imperial City that gradually won universal empire, the more we dwell on the circumstances which led to this extraordinary phenomenon, the more we shall feel that the one differs essentially from every political organization, and the other from every series of events of which we have an authentic record."—*Review of the 3rd volume,* TIMES, *Dec.* 29, 1863.

8589 MOORE'S IRISH MELODIES, illustrated by MACLISE, magnificent edition, imp. 8vo. *the text entirely engraved with* 161 *beautiful designs*, PROOF IMPRESSIONS, *every page enclosed within an elegant border,* (pub. at £6. 6s *without the binding*) *green morocco extra, gilt edges,* £4. 10s   1846

8590 MOORE'S IRISH MELODIES, parts I-III, sm. folio, ORIGINAL EDITION, *containing* 37 *Melodies, with the music for the voice and the pianoforte, and* 22 *harmonised airs, hf. bd.* 32s   *Dublin,* 1807-13

8591 MORAVIANS. Commenius' Exhortations of the Churches of Bohemia to the Church of England, sq. 8vo. *hf. purple morocco, rare,* 10s   1661

8592 MORGAN'S Phœnix Britannicus, being a miscellaneous Collection of scarce and curious Tracts, with choice Pieces from original MSS. sm. 4to. 8 and 584 pp. *calf,* £1. 1s   1731
This volume contains some very rare and curious tracts relating to London, particularly, Decker's Wonderful Year, a Picture of London lying sicke of the Plague, 1605.

8593 MORLEY (H.) Memoirs of Bartholomew Fair, 8vo. *with* 81 *curious facsimile woodcuts by Dalziel, new in cloth, stamped with grotesque figures, cloth,* 9s   1859

8594 MOTHERWELL (W.) Minstrelsy, Ancient and Modern, with historical introduction and notes, sq. 8vo. *frontispiece and vignette title-page, and* 9 *pp. of engraved Music, hf. green morocco, uncut, top edge gilt,* 36s   *Glasgow,* 1827

8595 MOTTLEY's History of the Life and Reign of the Empress Catherine, 2 vols. 8vo. *portraits and plates, calf gilt,* 15s   1744

8596 MÜLLER (C. O.) Scientific System of Mythology, by Leitch, 8vo. *cloth,* 5s 1844

8597 MURE'S Critical History of the Language and Literature of Antient Greece, 2nd edition, 5 vols. 8vo. (pub. at £3. 9s) *new in cloth,* £2. 10s   1854-5

8598 NARES' (Rev. Dr.) Memoirs of the Life and Administration of William Cecil, LORD BURGHLEY, Secretary of State under Edward VI. and Lord High Treasurer under Queen Elizabeth, Historical View of his Time, and the illustrious Persons with whom he was connected, now first published, 3 vols. 4to. *fine portraits and facsimile plates of Burghley's MS. Journal,* (pub. at £9. 9s) *fine copy in calf gilt,* £2. 4s   1828-31
Priced, 1856, £4. 4s. "A publication of the highest national interest, and a great and valuable accession to our knowledge of English History, at a period when that history is most important. It corrects many errors in Rapin, Strype, Neale, Lingard, and others."—*Athenæum.*

8599 NAVAL HISTORY. DERRICK'S Memoirs on the Rise and Progress of the Royal Navy, 4to, *plate, thick paper, calf,* 12s   1806

8600 NEALE's Views of the Seats of Noblemen and Gentlemen, Vol. I. 4to. LARGE PAPER, 36 *fine plates.* PROOFS ON INDIA PAPER, *hf. calf,* 12s   1818

8601 NETHERCLIFT'S Hand-Book to Autographs, a ready guide to the handwriting of distinguished men and women of every Nation, with biographical Index, sq. 12mo. *about* 600 *Autographs, cloth,* 18s   1862

8602 NEWCASTLE (Duchess of) CCXI SOCIABLE LETTERS, small folio, *whole-length figure of the Duchess standing in a recess, after Diepenbeke, engraved by Van Schuppen, mounted, good sound copy in old calf,* £2. 16s   1664

8603 ——— Natures Picture drawn by Fancies Pencil to the Life, being feigned Stories in Verse and Prose, sm. folio, second edition, *with the scarce plate of the Duchess seated in a chair, but the last line of verse cut off, fine copy in calf,* £3. 16s   1671
Amidst many extravagances and much want of taste it must be allowed that she had great powers of imagination and invention. All the works of the Duchess are rare.

8604 NICOLAS (Sir Harris) History of the Battle of AGINCOURT, and the Expedition of Henry V. into France, with the Roll of Men at Arms, sm. 8vo. *emblazoned frontispiece and map* (pub. at 21s) *bds.* 12s 6d   1827
Only 250 copies printed.

8605 NICOLSON'S (Archbp. Wm.) English, Scotch, and Irish Historical Libraries, giving a short View and Character of most of our Historians, either in print or manuscript; account of Records, Law-Books, Coins, &c. roy. 4to. BEST EDITION, *russia gilt,* 27s   1776
"The best preparatory book for the study of Irish history."—*Bibliotheca Hibernica.*
In this work Bp. Nicholson has pointed out the sources whence all information relating to the history of this country is to be derived.—*Roose's Ecclesiastica.*

8606 NICOLSON and BURN, History and Antiquities of the Counties of WEST-
MORELAND and CUMBERLAND, 2 vols. 4to. *maps, calf gilt, by Clarke, scarce*,
£3. 18s 1777
Priced, 1841, Rodd, £4. 10s; fetched, Willett's sale, £4.
8607 NISBET (Alexander) Essay on the ancient and modern use of Armories, with
Index of Names, sm. 4to. *several plates of Arms, fine clean copy, in old calf,*
21s *Edinburgh*, 1718
8608 NORFOLK ARCHÆOLOGY, or Miscellaneous Tracts, relating to the Antiquities of the County of Norfolk, published by the Norfolk and Norwich
Archæological Society, Vols. I.-V. part 1, 8vo. *numerous plates of Architectural
and Ecclesiastical Antiquities, Coins, Seals, etc. scarce*, £5. 5s *Norwich*, 1847-56
8609 **Nottinghamshire.** THOROTON (Robert) ANTIQUITIES of NOTTING-
HAMSHIRE, extracted out of Records, Original Evidences, Leiger Books, other
Manuscripts, and authentick authorities beautified with Maps, Prospects,
and Portraictures, sm. folio, A VERY FINE LARGE COPY, (13¼ by 9 *in.*) *many
plates by Hollar and others, pedigrees, numerous engraved Coats of Arms, but
wanting the " slip and the privilege," old calf gilt*, £8. 8s 1677
Copies with the slip of Arms, priced, 1834, Thorpe, £10. 10s; 1835, £12. 12s; 1843, Payne and Foss, £12. 12s;
1848, £18. 18s; Jeffery's copy fetched £17. 17s; Heath's £14. 5s; the Roxburghe, £16. 16s; Willett's £15. 10s; 1856,
at Sotheby's, £10. 10s.
8610 NOVELS. SELECT COLLECTION of Novels, 6 vols. 12mo. *plates, old calf gilt*,
15s 1720-21
8611 NUMISMATIC JOURNAL, CHRONICLE, and Numismatic Society's Proceedings, from the beginning in 1836: Journal, 2 vols. 1837-38; Chronicle, Vols.
I.-XX, 1838-58; together 22 vols. 8vo. *plates, hf. calf*, £18. 18s 1836-58
8612 OLDFIELD's Representative History of Great Britain and Ireland, being a history
of the House of Commons, 6 vols. 8vo. *bds.* 7s 6d 1816
8613 ORD (J. W.) History and Antiquities of CLEVELAND, comprising the Wapentake
of Langbargh, Yorkshire, 4to. *maps, plans, views, vignettes, and pedigrees*, (pub.
at £2. 2s) *cloth*, 30s 1846
8614 **Orkneys.** BARRY'S History of the Orkney Islands, by H. Eadrick, 4to.
map and plates, hf. calf, 10s 1808
8615 WALLACE (J.) Description of the Isles of Orkney, and Essay on the Thule of the
Ancients, 16mo. *map and plates, russia, gilt edges*, 12s *Edinb.* 1693
8616 ———— another edition, 12mo. *map and plates, hf. bd.* 7s 1700
8617 OTTLEY'S Inquiry concerning the Invention of PRINTING, reviewing the Systems of Meerman, Heinecken, Santander, and Koning, with notices on Block
Books, and Introduction by BERJEAU, 4to. 37 plates of Facsimiles and numerous woodcuts, (pub. at £3. 3s) *new in hf. morocco uncut*, £2. 12s 6d 1863
8618 OVID's Art of Love, translated by Dryden, Congreve, etc. with the Remedy, the
Court, and the History of Love, sm. 8vo. *plates, green mor. gilt edges*, 10s 1712
8619 **Oxford.** PLOT'S Natural History of Oxfordshire, *second and best edition*,
with additions and corrections, account of the Author, etc. sm. folio, *map surrounded with Coats of Arms, and* 16 *plates, neat in old calf*, 32s 1705
In this interesting work is related a long and ludicrous account of some 'unaccountable things,' and 'strange
passages,' which are stated to have taken place at the Palace of Woodstock, in 1649, when Cromwell's commissioners
for surveying the Manor House, park, deer, &c., sat and lodged there; and upon which Scott's romance " Woodstock " is written.
8620 CATALOGUE of all Graduates, Masters of Arts, and Drs. of Music, 1659-1735,
etc. 2 parts in 1 vol. 8vo. *old blue morocco, gilt edges*, 7s 6d *Oxford*, 1727-35
8621 GRIFFITH's Index of Wills, etc. proved at Oxford, roy. 8vo. *cloth*, 3s 6d *Oxf.* 1862
INGRAM'S Memorials of Oxford, 3 vols. 8vo. *numerous beautiful engravings
by Le Keux, and many woodcuts, cloth*, 24s 1837
8622 OXFORD GUIDE, or Companion through the University, sq. 8vo. *interleaved with
numerous neatly written MS. additions in a hand of the last century relating to
Antiquities, Paintings, etc. probably by Ives the antiquary, hf. bd.* 15s (ca. 1750)
8623 OXFORD UNIVERSITY. A collection of about 72 modern Tracts and Opuscula
relating to Oxford, including several Nos. of the Oxford Magazine, University
Squibs, etc. 10s *Sæc.* XIX.
8624 POINTER's Oxoniensis Academia, or Antiquities and Curiosities of the University,
12mo. *bd.* 7s 6d 1749

8625 PALGRAVE'S (Sir F.) Rise and Progress of the ENGLISH COMMONWEALTH,
with Proofs and Illustrations, 2 vols. 4to. *cloth, very scarce*, £4. 10s 1832
" This is, beyond all competition, the most luminous work that has ever been produced on the early institutions of England. It is to Mr. Palgrave that recourse will be had by the curious antiquary, the inquirer into the
origin of English jurisprudence, and by him who loves to trace, in the calm mirror of history, the restless waves of
human action."—*Edinburgh Review.*

8626 PASHLEY (R.) Travels in Crete, 2 vols. 8vo. *map and plates, tree marbled calf extra, by Clarke*, 32s *Camb.* 1837

8627 ——— the same, 2 vols. imp. 8vo. LARGE PAPER, 10 *plates and* 56 *woodcuts of Antiquities and Art*, PROOF IMPRESSIONS, *cloth*, £2. 2s 1837
Only 25 copies were printed on Large Paper. The small paper was published at £2.

8628 PARKES (Fanny) Wanderings of a Pilgrim in search of the Picturesque during 24 years in the East, with revelations of life in the Zenana, 2 vols. imp. 8vo. *a profusion of plates of Costume, Views, Architecture, Mythology, etc. several coloured*, (pub. at £2. 12s 6d) *cloth gilt*, £2. 2s 1850

8629 PATENTS. Indexes of Patent Inventions, etc. from 1818 to December 1851, 3 vols. 8vo. *cloth*, 10s 1846-52

8630 PEELE'S (George) Works, collected and edited with some account of his Life and Writings by the Rev. Alexander Dyce, 3 vols. sm. 8vo. £2. 18s 1829-39

8631 PERCY'S (Thos.) RELIQUES of ANCIENT ENGLISH POETRY, consisting of Old Ballads, Songs, and other pieces of our earlier Poets, 3 vols. 12mo. THE ONLY UNCASTRATED EDITION, *calf*, 36s 1765

8632 PETTIGREW (T. J.) History of Egyptian Mummies, 4to. 13 *plates, three of them coloured*, (pub. at £2. 2s) *calf gilt*, 21s 1834

8633 PHILIPOT'S (J.) Catalogue of the Chancellors, the Keepers of the Seale, and the Lord Treasurers of England, sq. 8vo. *bds.* 5s 1636

8634 PHILOBIBLON SOCIETY. HERBERT LORD CHERBURY'S Expedition to the Isle of Rhe, edited by Lord Powis, sq. 8vo. *genealogical tables, cloth*, £3. 3s 1860

8635 PHILOXENUS Secundus, Persian Recreations, with account of two Ambassadors from Iran to James I and George III, 8vo. *portrait, bds.* 5s 1812

8636 PLINY'S Historie of the World, commonly called the Naturall Historie, translated by Philemon Holland, 2 vols. in 1, stout folio, *calf gilt, scarce*, 35s 1634
Priced, J. Bohn, 1829, £3. 10s; 1841, £2. 18s; 1844, White, £2. 18s.
"A work of immense labour, and what few men of his time could have executed in a superior manner."

8637 PLOT (Robert) HISTORY OF STAFFORDSHIRE, folio, *with the rare large folding Map mounted on canvas, having the Arms of the Nobility and Gentry, and their names in alphabetical order, engraved round the borders, and with* 37 *plates of Views of Seats, Antiquities, Natural Curiosities, etc. without the slip of " Armes omitted," but with the " Directions for a right understanding of the Map," very fine and* VERY LARGE *copy in russia extra, gilt edges*, £7. 7s *Oxford*, 1686
Lowndes states the size of Small Paper copies in the original binding to be 12¼ by 7¼ inches in one case, and 13 by 7¼ inches in another: the size of the pages in this copy is 13 7/16 by 8¼ inches.

8638 POLITICAL TRACTS, concerning King Charles I and the Parliament, the Royal Prerogative and the people's rights, 36 works bound in 2 vols. square sm. 8vo. *calf*, VERY RARE, £5. 1643
A most curious and important collection of works all published in the year 1643. The contents are as follow:—

I, Ferne's Conscience satisfied, that there is no warrant for arms taken up by subjects.
II, Answer to Dr. Ferne.
III, Stephen Marshall's Letter against the aspersions of the Mercurius Aulicus.
IV, Maximes Unfolded, Elections of English Kings, etc.
V, Secrets discovered.
VI, Subject of Supremacy, Right of Caesar.
VII, Contra-Replicant's Complaint to his Majestie.
VIII, Plaine English.
IX, Touching the fundamentall Laws.
X, Declaration to the Commons.
XI, Reasons to adhere t the Parliament.
XII, The Kingdom's Case.
XIII, England's Petition to the King.
XIV, The Moderator.
XV, Review of Observatins n His Majesty's Answers
XVI, The Observator defended.
XVII, Records of things done in Parliament.
XVIII, The Subjects Liberty set forth.
XIX, No post from Heaven nor yet from Hell.
XX, The Pope's Nuntioes.
XXI, The English Pope.
XXII, Political Catechisme.
XXIII, Lawfullnesse of Defence.
XXIV, Pym's Discovery of the Great Plot.
XXV, Fine Designe discovered, and Irish Rebels landed.
XXVI, Narrative of the late horrid Designe.
XXVII, Ward's Analysis of the vow enjoyned by Parliament.
XXVIII, Vow appointed by Parliament to be taken by every man.
XXIX, Remonstrance of the Commons.
XXX, Disclaimer of the Commons to the Remonstrance.
XXXI, Of resisting the lawful Magistrate.
XXXII, Spirituall Snapsacke for the Parliament Souldiers.
XXXIII, Treatise of Monarchie.
XXXIV, Proceedings in the Treaty of Peace.
XXXV, Herle's Independency on Scriptures of Church independency.
XXXVI, Satisfaction concerning mixed communions.
XXXVII, Foulke Grevill's Five Years of King James.

8639 POLITICAL MERRIMENT; or, Truths told to some Tune, by a Lover of his Country, 12mo. *calf, gilt edges, scarce*, 30s 1714-15
Most amusing Ballads, etc. against the Church and the Parliament; dedicated "to the Jacobitical Torie and Traiterous Rioters of Great Britain" by "Your Merry Physician Philopat."

ENGLISH LITERATURE. 475

8640 POPE'S WHOLE WORKS: Juvenile Poems, Translations and Imitations, Moral Essays, Satires; Dunciad; Miscellaneous Pieces; Letters; Homer's Iliad and Odyssey, with Notes by Warburton, together 20 vols. 8vo. *plates*, FINE COPY *in the original calf neat*, £2. 16*s* 1760-66
Priced, Thorpe, morocco, £18. 18*s*; calf, £6. 6*s*; Leslie, £6. 6*s*.

8641 POPE'S HOMER: the Iliad and the Odyssey, with Essay, notes, etc. 5 vols. impl. 8vo. LARGE PAPER, *many plates, a beautiful edition printed by Bensley, fine copy in* RED MOROCCO *extra, gilt edges, silk linings, by Bozerian*, £5. 1802

8642 PRESCOTT'S History of the Conquest of Peru, with preliminary view of the civilisation of the Incas, 2 vols. 8vo. *portraits*, (pub. at 32*s*) *cloth*, 21*s* 1847

8643 —— History of the Reign of Philip II, 2 vols. 8vo. *portraits and facsimile*, (pub. at 28*s*) *cloth*, 18*s* *Boston*, (*N.A.*) 1855
Prescott, the historian of both hemispheres, whose name will not be forgotten in either, but whose honours will always be dearest to those who have best known the discouragement under which they have been won, and the modesty and gentleness with which they are worn."—*Ticknor*.

8644 PRINCE (John) Danmonii Orientales Illustres, or the WORTHIES OF DEVON, with the Lives of the most famous Divines, Statesmen, Swordsmen, Writers, and other Persons, natives of that Province, from before the Conquest to the present Age, with description of their Seats and Habitations, etc. folio, ORIGINAL AND BEST EDITION, 143 *Coats of Arms, good copy in the original old calf*, £3. 10*s*
Exeter, 1701
Priced, 1814, Longmans, £10.; 1848, Payne and Foss, £6. 6*s*; Dr. Heath's sold for £12. 1*s* 6*d*, and Willcott's for £10. 12*s* 6*d*.

8645 PROUT'S (Father) Reliques (by F. Mahony), 2 vols. 12mo. *many humourous engravings, hf. calf*, 12*s* 1836

8646 PRYNNE, God no Impostor nor Deluder, an answer to a Popish and Armenian cavill in defence of Free Will, 8vo. *morocco back, uncut*, 5*s* 1629

8647 RACING CALENDAR, containing an account of Plates, Matches, and Sweepstakes run for in Great Britain and Ireland, with an abstract of engagements for future years, by the WEATHERBYS, from 1804 to 1862, 59 vols.; RACING CALENDAR, of Races to come, 1847-62, 16 vols.; together 75 vols. 12mo. *calf*, £6. 6*s* 1805-62

8648 RAINE'S Memoir of the Rev. John Hodgson (*Historian of Northumberland*), 2 vols. 8vo. *portrait and plates*, (pub. at 28*s*) *cloth*, 24*s* 1857-58

8649 RAPIN'S History of England, with CONTINUATION by N. TINDAL, 5 vols. folio, *fine impressions of the* PORTRAITS, *plates of Medals, maps, and plans of battles, and cities, by Vertue and Houbraken, a handsome copy, old* CALF GILT, *gilt borders*, £3. 10*s* 1732-47
Fetched, 1854, calf gilt, £6.; 1855, old gilt russia, Baker's sale, £14. 14*s*; Hollis's sale, £17. 10*s*, and in the Duke of York's, £16. 10*s*. "No historical library can be complete without this best edition of Rapin, adorned by the heads of Vertue and Houbraken. A copy in fine condition is worth £31. 10*s*."—*Library Companion*.

8650 RAY'S Works: Philosophical Letters, 1718—The Wisdom of God in the Works of Creation, 1727—Discourses on Chaos, the Deluge, and the Dissolution of the World, 1732—Life and Remains, 1760—ENGLISH PROVERBS, also Scotch, Italian, French, Spanish, etc. 1768; together 5 vols. sm. 8vo. *two portraits of Ray, calf*, 15*s* 1718-68

8651 RAY's (Jas.) Compleat History of the REBELLION, 1745, to its Suppression at Culloden, 1746, 12mo. *port. fine copy, calf neat*, 10*s* *Printed for the Author*, 1757

8652 [REDDIE (John)] Scope and Uses of Military Literature and History, pt. 1, 8vo. *cloth*, 7*s* 6*d* *Calcutta*, 1846

8653 REVOLUTION SOCIETY: Abstract of its History and Proceedings, 8vo. 6*s* 1789

8654 REES'S CYCLOPÆDIA: or UNIVERSAL DICTIONARY of the Arts, Science, History, Biography, and Literature, 45 vols. 4to. *including the six vols. of plates, a complete set, hf. calf*, £5. 10*s* 1819
A stupendous and still valuable work, the most complete English Encyclopædia; cost the former proprietor nearly 100 guineas.

8655 RELPH's Miscellany of Poems, 8vo. *calf*, 5*s* *Glasgow*, 1747
Some of the Poems are in the Cumberland dialect, with a Glossary.

8656 RERESBY (Sir J.) Travels and Memoirs, (by himself, 1654-89) large 8vo. 30 *plates, several being coloured, containing* 30 *portraits of the most noted characters of the time and others, and* 10 *Views of places*, (pub. at £3. 3*s* in bds.) *blue morocco extra, gilt edges*, 28*s* 1813

8657 RHIND'S Thebes, its Tombs and their Tenants, excavations in the Necropolis, etc. roy. 8vo. *cold. plates and cuts*, (pub. at 18*s*) *cloth*, 10*s* 6*d* 1862

8658 —— Facsimiles of Two Papyri found in a Tomb at Thebes, with translation by Birch, obl. roy. folio, 16 *plates*, (pub. at £2. 2*s*) *cloth*, 36*s* 1863

8659 RICHARDSON (M. A.) THE BORDERER'S TABLE BOOK; or Gatherings of the Local History and Romance of the English and Scottish Border, 8 vols. in 4, roy. 8vo. *about* 900 *woodcuts, hf. green morocco, gilt edges,* £4. 12s Newcastle, 1841
Fetched, 1855, Sotheby's, £5. 10s.
"This chronology of local occurrences, from the earliest times when a date is ascertainable, possesses an especial interest for the residents of the Northern Counties; but, inasmuch as it records Historical events as well as trivial incidents, and includes Biographical notices of men whose fame extended beyond their birth-places, it is not without a value to the general reader. The work is divided into two portions, the larger consisting of the chronicle, and the lesser of the traditions and ballads of the country. Some of these are very characteristic and curious; they invest with poetic associations almost every ruin or plot of ground; and the earlier legends of moss-troopers and border-strifes afford an insight into the customs and state of society in remote periods. The handsome pages are illustrated with woodcuts of old buildings and other antiquities."—*Spectator.*

8660 RICHTER (Jean Paul F.) Flower, Fruit and Thorn Pieces, Life, Death and Wedding of Firmian Stanislaus Siebenkäs, translated by Noel, 2 vols. 12mo. *cloth, scarce,* 16s 1845

8661 RIDDELL (J.) Inquiry into the Law and Practice in Scottish Peerages, 2 vols. 8vo. (pub. at 31s 6d) *cloth,* 24s *Edinb.* 1842

8662 RITSON'S (J.) Select Collection of English Songs, with the MUSIC, 3 vols. sm. 8vo. *fine vignettes by Stothard,* FIRST EDITION ON FINE PAPER, *old marbled calf gilt, very scarce,* £2. 2s 1783
Priced, 1834, Pickering, £3. 3s.

8663 RITTER'S History of Ancient Philosophy, translated by Morrison, 4 vols. 8vo. (pub. at £3. 4s) *cloth, rare,* £2. 2s 1838-46

8664 ——— the same, 4 vols. 8vo. *calf gilt,* £2. 18s 1838-46
The most comprehensive and best digested work upon the Greek and Roman systems of philosophy. Its great value is amply recognized by the fact that it has been translated and adopted as a text-book both in England and France; for it has superseded all the books previously written upon the subject. It is now becoming scarce.

8665 RIX (S. W.) FAUCONBERGE Memorial; an Account of Henry Fauconberge of Beccles, and the Endowment provided by his Will to encourage Learning, 4to. LARGE PAPER, *plates, bds. privately printed,* 15s *Ipswich,* 1849

8666 ——— DIARY and Autobiography of EDMUND BOHUN, Licenser of the Press under William and Mary, with memoir, notes, etc. by Rix, sm. 4to. *Genealogical Table, and numerous illustrations of Arms, Antiquities, Autographs, etc. bds. uncut, privately printed,* 25s *Beccles,* 1853

8667 ROBERTSON'S Tour through the Isle of Man, impl. 8vo. *plates tinted, calf,* 5s 1794

8668 ROBIN HODE, A lytell Geste of, with other ancient and modern Ballads relating to this celebrated Yeoman, his History and Character, etc. by J. M. Gutch, 2 vols. 8vo. *numerous illustrations by Fairholt, and portrait of Ritson, cloth,* 20s 1847

8669 ROBSON (Thomas) History of Heraldry, inquiries into its origin, account of its progress, and a complete GLOSSARY of the Science, roy. 4to. LARGE PAPER, 31 *plates containing upwards of* 300 *figures, bds.* 24s Sunderland, 1830

8670 ROBY'S (J.) TRADITIONS OF LANCASHIRE, BOTH SERIES, 4 vols. 8vo. *with* 22 *exquisite engravings by* FINDEN, *and* 20 *woodcuts, clean copy, cloth, uncut, a beautiful book, scarce,* £3. 10s 1829-31
"A work which must be seen to be estimated as it ought."—*Literary Gazette.*
Sir Walter Scott speaks highly of this work, which he calls "very elegant," and frequently quotes in his "Letters on Demonology and Witchcraft," and "Tales of the Crusaders."

8671 ROGERS'S (Samuel) Italy, a Poem, *with* 56 *engravings after* TURNER *and* STOTHARD, 1830—POEMS (Pleasures of Memory, Human Life, Jacqueline, &c.) *with* 72 *plates after* STOTHARD *and* TURNER, 1834—together 2 vols. 8vo. *original editions, with early impressions, fine clean copies, bds. scarce,* £3. 3s 1830-34

8672 ——— the same, 2 vols. sm. 8vo. *original copies, in green morocco extra, gilt edges, presentation copy to Lord St. Helens, with Rogers' autograph inscription,* £5. 1834
"The illustration of this poem was the last task for the public undertaken by the author:—a task, it may be added, beyond the compass of any one less easy in fortune, since the production of that volume is said to have cost £10,000, and the days had not then set in when cheap literature on the one hand had been balanced by a luxury in typography and engraving undreamed of by our fathers. There can be no question that the taste, no less than the cost, brought to bear on this volume, in which some of the most exquisite designs of Turner alternate with those of Stothard, mark a period in the history of English book illustration. To this day Rogers's 'Italy' remains without a peer."—*Athenæum,* Dec. 22, 1855.

8673 ROSE'S BIOGRAPHICAL DICTIONARY, 12 vols. 8vo. *second edition,* (pub. at £5. 8s in bds.) *calf gilt, very neat,* £4. 15s 1857

8674 ROY'S (Major-General Wm.) Military Antiquities of the Romans in North Britain, published by order and at the expense of the Society of Antiquaries, impl. folio, 51 *fine large plates, hf. morocco, gilt top, uncut,* 30s 1793
This excellent work gives an account of the Roman Military Antiquities in North Britain, particularly their system of Castrametation, illustrated from vestiges of the camps of Agricola; and comprehends also a treatise, rectifying the ancient geography, from Richard of Cirencester, and a description of the wall of Antoninus Pius, commonly called GRIME'S DYKE, with remarks on various other antiquities.

ENGLISH LITERATURE. 477

8675 ROXBURGHE CLUB. HOUSEHOLD BOOKS of John Duke of Norfolk and Thomas Earl of Surrey, from the original MSS. in the Library of the Society of Antiquaries, edited by J. PAYNE COLLIER, sm. 4to. *hf. mor.* £4. 1844

8676 RUDING (R.) Annals of the Coinage of Great Britain and its Dependencies, third edition, enlarged, 3 vols. 4to. 159 *plates, cloth, new*, £2. 10s 1840
"A valuable national work, and one which says, upon as good security as the Bank of England, 'I promise to pay all the information which you can desire upon the subject of our national money;' and which no man can take without 'value received.'"—*Gent.'s Mag.*

8677 RUMP, or a Collection of the Choycest Poems and Songs relating to the late Times, by the most Eminent Wits from 1639 to 1661, both parts complete in 1 vol. 12mo. *curious frontispiece and engraved title, fine copy, good impressions of both plates, hf. bd.* VERY RARE, £2. 10s 1662
"These excellent Songs overflow with wit and humour. It was the period," says Ellis, "in which they had wit enough, and more than enough."
Copies with both the frontispiece and engraved title are very scarce. Priced, 1840, Thorpe, £4 14s 6d; Stanley's copy fetched £12. 1s 6d; Sir M. Sykes', £5. 5s; Gardner's, 1854, £4. 14s 6d; at Sotheby's, 1857, Utterson's, £4. 4s; 1854, Puttick's, £5. 10s; 1860, Sotheby's, £4. 18s.

8678 RUSHWORTH'S HISTORICAL COLLECTIONS of Private Passages of State and Law, and of Remarkable Proceedings in Five Parliaments, 1618-48, with the Trial of the Earl of Strafford, 8 vols. folio, *portrait, calf gilt*, Arms on the sides, £3. 16s 1682-1701

8679 RUSSELL (Lord John) History of the principal States of Europe, from the peace of Utrecht, 2 vols. sm. 8vo. *(all published of this edition) bds. 7s 6d* 1826

8680 [RUSSELL (J.)] Letters from a young Painter abroad to his Friends in England, 2 vols. 8vo. LARGE PAPER, *plates of Arms, Monuments, etc. red morocco extra, gilt edges*, 21s 1750

8681 RYVES (Bruno) Angliae Ruina, or England's Ruine in the Outrages of the Sectaries committed upon his Maj : Loyal Subjects : MERCURIUS RUSTICUS, or the Countries Complaint, 2 parts, 1646-47—Querela Cantabrigiensis, apologie for the banished members of the University of Cambridge, Cambridge, 1647—Micro-Chronicon, or Chronology of the Battels, Sieges, etc. between the king and parliament, with a catalogue of the Lords, Knights, and Commanders slain therein, 1647—in 1 vol. 12mo. *calf gilt*, 18s 1646-47
A rare and curious collection of tracts, the first alone of the edition of 1646, fetched, Sykes' sale, russia, £2.

8682 SANDFORD'S (Fras.) GENEALOGICAL HISTORY of the Kings and Queens of ENGLAND, with Continuation, additions, and annotations, the descents of divers Illustrious Families now flourishing, etc. by Stebbing, folio, BEST EDITION, *numerous fine plates by* HOLLAR *of Monumental Effigies, Seals, Arms, Ecclesiastical Architecture, etc. and Tables of Genealogies,* BEAUTIFUL COPY *in red Turkey morocco extra, gilt edges, by Clarke and Bedford*, £10. 1707
Priced, 1859, red morocco, £15. 15s. *∗* Sold at Willett's sale for £10. 10s, Townsend's for £11., and in Nassau's for £13. 13s.

8683 SANDYS and Forster, History of the Violin, and other instruments played with the bow, with an account of the principal makers, 8vo. *engravings, cloth, price* 14s 1864

8684 SAVILE (Sir Henry) A Book of Offices, as well of his Mãties Courtes of Recorde, as well as of his Mãts most honorable Houshould, the Connsells of the North, of Wales and the Marches, the Admiraltye, the Minte, the Armorye, Islandes, Townes of Warre, Howses, Parkes, etc. with the fees to everie particuler officer, collected, 1610, sm. folio, OFFICIAL MANUSCRIPT *of 78 pp. wih the autograph of Sir H. Savile on the first leaf, in the original vellum binding, stamped in gold with four crowns*, £5. 5s 1610
A most valuable statistical Record, giving the names of every office of State in connection with the Royal Household, Exchequer, etc. and the salaries of the officials, from the highest to the lowest.

8685 SCHLAGINTWEIT (E.) Buddhism in Tibet illustrated by literary documents and objects of religious worship. With an account of the Buddhist systems preceding it in India, 8vo. text and large folio *Atlas of 20 plates of facsimiles of Tibetan Prayers,* (pub. at £2. 2s) *cloth*, 36s 1863
"M. Émile Schlagintweit, frère, cadet des trois voyageurs bien connus, a publié un ouvrage sur le Bouddhisme au Tibet. Ce travail consiste en deux parties essentiellement distinctes : l'une est un exposé du dogme et de l'histoire du Bouddisme, d'après les travaux récents ; l'autre est un tableau du Bouddisme vivant, tel que M. Robert Schlagintweit, un des frères de l'auteur, l' a trouvé au Tibet. C'est naturellement dans cette partie de l'ouvrage que la science peut puiser avec avantage : nous y trouvons bien des détails curieux et nouveaux sur l'état actuel du culte, les monastères, les représentations figurées des dieux, les cérémonies, les superstitions et les pratiques magiques et astrologiques, accompagnés de textes et d'images."—MOHL, *Rap. Ann. du Journ. Asiat.* 1863

8686 SCHLAGINTWEIT (H., A. and R. de) Results of a scientific mission to India and High Asia. Undertaken between the years 1854 and 1858, by order of the Court of Directors of the Honourable East India Company, Vol. III. Route-Book, Glossary, 4to. text and folio, *Atlas of 5 plates and 2 maps*, £4. 1863

8687 SCLOPPETARIA, or Considerations on the nature and use of RIFLED BARREL GUNS, by a Corporal of Riflemen, roy. 8vo. *frontispiece, and* 12 *plates of experimental improvements, etc.* calf extra, VERY RARE, £6. 6s 1808

This work, which is of extraordinary scarcity, embodies ideas and opinions which were half a century in advance of their time. It was published at £3. 3s, as mentioned in Lowndes; and no copy can be traced in booksellers' or sale catalogues, which proves that only a very limited number can have been printed.

8688 SCOTLAND AND IRELAND. An important collection of 69 Tracts and Minor Works relating to the Civil Wars, 1641-51, bound in 3 vols. sq. 8vo. *with a MS. Index of the contents,* hf. bd. VERY RARE, £10. 10s 1640-1703

The pieces in this collection are of the greatest rarity and interest. They relate chiefly to the proceedings of the Scottish Parliament, Army, and People, and their dealings with the English Parliament during the bloody and tumultuous period of the Civil Wars. They will be found invaluable material for the history of the period.

8689 SCOTT'S (Sir Walter) COMPLETE WORKS, viz. WAVERLEY NOVELS, 48 vols. 1829-36—PROSE WORKS, (containing his Biographies, Pieces of Criticism, etc.) 28 vols. 1834-36—POETICAL WORKS, 12 vols. 1833-34—together 88 vols. 12mo. *frontispieces and vignettes after Turner, and others, to each volume, original impressions,* (pub. at £38.) hf. calf gilt, contents lettered, £12. 12s *Edinburgh,* 1829-36

8690 ——— WAVERLEY NOVELS; the SPLENDID ABBOTSFORD EDITION, 12 vols. stout roy. 8vo. *embellished with* 120 *beautiful steel engravings and* 2000 *fine woodcuts,* (pub. at £16. 16s) a clean copy, £8. 8s 1842-47

8691 ——— Waverley Novels, 48 vols. 12mo. 96 *engravings* (pub. at £12.) cloth, contents lettered, £4. 15s *Edinb.* 1855-56

"The works of Scott produce their effect rather by the combination of many qualities than the predominance of any. In depth of feeling we think he yields to the author of *Anastasius;* in invention of incident, and disposition of plot, he is equalled by many; his humour will hardly bear comparison with that of Sterne, or the best parts of Fielding: and in the direct and forcible expressions of the stronger passions, we should be inclined to give the preference both to Godwin and the author of *Valerius.* But his strength lies in the possession and harmonious adjustment of most of the qualities requisite to the novelist, none engrossing the whole mind, none excluding another, but all working together in kindly unison; learning arrayed in the most picturesque combinations; observations of life embodied, not in abstractions, but in living forms; humour springing out of tenderness, like smiles struggling through tears; the spirit of ancient knighthood leavening the worldly wisdom of modern times; and the imagination of the poet adorning, without impairing, the common sympathies and good-humoured sagacity of the man."

8692 SCOTT'S (Sir Walter) BORDER ANTIQUITIES of ENGLAND and Scotland, comprising specimens of Architecture and Sculpture, and other vestiges of former Ages, with descriptions, illustrations of remarkable Incidents in Border History and Tradition, and original Poetry, 2 vols. impl. 4to. LARGE PAPER, *genuine* PROOF IMPRESSIONS *on* INDIA PAPER *of the* 94 *beautiful plates,* (pub. at £18. 18s) hf. morocco, gilt edges, an original copy, £5. 1814

8693 SEGAR (Sir W.) Honor, Military and Civill, contained in four Bookes, sm. folio, *with fine impressions of the eight full length portraits, which illustrate the costumes of different Orders,* fine copy in red morocco, gilt edges, £3. 3s 1602

8694 SEVEN CHAMPIONS: JOHNSON'S famous History of the Seven Champions of Christendom, their Honourable battles by Sea and Land, their Tournaments for Ladies, their Combats with Monsters, etc. 2 parts in 1 vol. sm. 4to. calf, rare, 25s 1705

The Gordonstoun copy fetched 38s.

8695 SHADWELL'S Dramatick Works, edited with his life by his son, 4 vols. 12mo. *portrait, beautiful copy in* calf extra, gilt edges, RARE, £2. 16s 1720

The abuse which Dryden heaped upon Shadwell has unjustly deprived him of the attention that is due to his merit and high talents.

8696 SHAKESPEARE'S PLAYS, with the Corrections and Illustrations of various Commentators; to which are added Notes by JOHNSON and STEEVENS, FOURTH OR "STEEVENS' OWN" EDITION, 15 vols. 8vo. *plates and facsimile,* calf gilt, £3. 3s 1793

8697 SHAKESPEARE'S PLAYS, with the Corrections and Illustrations of various Commentators, the Notes of JOHNSON and STEEVENS, revised and augmented by Reed, with a Glossarial Index, 21 vols. 8vo. *portrait and facsimiles, fine copy,* calf gilt, £4. 1803

This is an improved and enlarged edition of the one in 15 vols. 1793, and Dr. Dibdin says must be considered as the *Editio Optima* of Shakspeare.—Priced, 1832, Thorpe, £6. 6s; 1856, Willis, £9. 18s; Fetched, 1856, Russell's, £10.; 1856, at Sotheby's, morocco, £13.

8698 SHAKESPEARE'S Comedies, Histories and Tragedies, the celebrated facsimile reprint of the FIRST EDITION of 1623, folio, *portrait after* DROESHOUT, (pub. at £5. 5s *in bds.) fine copy in* russia extra, gilt edges, SCARCE, £4. 4s 1808

Priced, 1860, £5. 15s 6d; 1860, £7. 7s; fetched, 1856, Sotheby's, £5; 1857, £5. 2s 6d; 1860, £6. 12s 6d.

ENGLISH LITERATURE. 479

8699 SHAKESPEARE'S Plays, from the Text of Steevens and Malone, with explanatory and historical notes, and life of the poet by Alexander Chalmers, 8 vols. 8vo. *portrait and plates*, (pub. at £4. 16s in bds.) *calf gilt*, £3. 1823

8700 —— Works, the text formed from an entirely new collation of the old editions, with various readings, notes, life, and a history of the early English stage, by Collier, 8 vols. 8vo. *portrait*, (pub. at £4. 16s) *with an autograph letter of the editor inserted, cloth*, £2. 16s 1844

8701 —— Works, the text revised by the Rev. Alexander Dyce, 6 vols. 8vo. *printed on very thick paper, portrait*, (pub. at £4. 4s) *cloth*, £2. 18s *Moxon*, 1857

8702 —— the Stratford Shakspere, with life, notes, and Glossary by C. Knight, 6 vols. 12mo. *cloth*, 21s 1860

8703 —— Dramatic Works, with Glossary, new edition, stout sm. 8vo. *printed in black and red, double columns, ruled in with red lines, with portrait and numerous beautiful plates, after Stothard and others* (pub. at 30s) *antique morocco, stamped, edges gilt, and gauffred*, 25s 1863

8704 —— the Cambridge edition, edited by William G. Clark and John Glover, Vol. I.-III, demy 8vo. *beautifully printed in antique type, new in cloth, each* 10s 6d *Cambridge*, 1863

To be completed in 8 vols. published at intervals of four months. The text is based on a thorough collation of the 4 folios, and all the 4to. and subsequent editions, with notes and conjectural emendations at the foot of each page. The lines of each Scene are separately numbered, and where a quarto edition varies much from the other, the variation is printed *literatim* in smaller type.

8705 SHAKESPEARE'S Comedies, Histories, and Tragedies, a reprint of the first edition, the folio of 1623, Parts I and II, sm. 4to. *with a photograph of the House at Stratford on the title page* (pub. at 21s 6d) *new, in cloth gilt*, 17s 6d 1863

The third part will complete this reprint, and will contain a photograph from the best impression of Droeshout's portrait, as well as a general title page in exact facsimile of the original.

8705*SHAKESPEARE'S Comedies, Histories and Tragedies, Part I. sm. folio, *a reprint in* facsimile, *by the photozincographic process of the* 1623 *edition*, (pub. at 10s 6d) *new*, 9s 1864

To be completed in 16 parts, published at 10s 6d each.

8706 Ayscough's (S.) Index to the remarkable passages and words made use of by Shakespeare, stout roy. 8vo. *calf*, 10s 1790

8707 **Shropshire.** OWEN'S (H.) and Blakeway's History of Shrewsbury, 2 vols. 4to. *numerous beautiful plates and etchings of Views, Antiquities, Coins, etc. a very fine copy in russia, marbled edges, scarce*, £7. 12s 1825

One of the most valuable topographical works published.

8708 PEARSON'S Selection of Antiquities in the County of Salop, Churches, Castles, and other ancient buildings, with topographical and historical accounts, impl. 4to. large paper, *very fine impressions of the* 43 *beautiful etchings by Pearson, cloth*, 25s 1824

8709 SIDNEY (Sir P.) Miscellaneous Works, with notes and life by Gray, roy. 8vo. large paper, bds. rare, 24s *Oxford*, 1829

8710 SIMS (R.) Index to the Pedigrees and Arms contained in the Heralds' Visitations, and other Genealogical MSS. in the British Museum, 8vo. *cloth, scarce*, 30s 1849

8711 —— Manual for the Genealogist, Topographer, Antiquary, and Legal Professor, 8vo. *second edition* (pub. at 15s) *new in cloth*, 12s 1861

8712 SMEATON (John) Narrative of the building, and a Description of the Construction of the Edystone Lighthouse, with an Appendix upon the Lighthouse at Spurn Point, roy. fol. 23 *large plates, hf. bd. uncut*, 25s 1791

The original cost of this valuable work was £6. 6s.

8713 SMEETON'S Reprints of Scarce and Curious, Historical and Biographical Tracts, (collected and bound in 2 vols.) sq. 8vo. *numerous fine portraits and plates, calf*, 32s *Westminster*, 1820

8714 SMITH (Dr. W.) DICTIONARY of the BIBLE, comprising its Antiquities, Biography, Geography, and Natural History, 3 vols. stout large 8vo. *numerous woodcuts*, 3154 pp. *double columns*, (pub. at £5. 5s) *cloth*, £4. 4s 1860-63

"We consider the Dictionary of the Bible as a very satisfactory book: liberal in the true sense, learned in the best sense: a work which is a credit to English scholarship and English enterprise."—*Athenæum*, No. 1888, Jan. 1864.

8715 SMITH (Dr. W.) Dictionary of Greek and Roman Biography and Mythology, 3 stout vols. 8vo. *illustrated by numerous engravings on wood*, (pub. at £5. 15s 6d) *cloth*, £3. 18s 1844-49

8717 —— Dictionary of Greek and Roman Geography, 2 stout vols. 8vo. (pub. at £4.) *new in cloth*, £3. 3s 1856-57

8718 —— Dictionary of Greek and Roman Antiquities, stout 8vo. 1100 pp. 500 *woodcuts, second edition* (pub. at £2. 2s), *cloth*, 33s 1859

8719 SMITH'S CLASSICAL DICTIONARY of Biography, Mythology, and Geography, stout 8vo. *numerous plates of Coins, etc.* (pub. at 18s) *new in cloth,* 15s 1859

8720 SMOLLETT'S (Tobias) WORKS, with his life, a view of the commencement and progress of Romance, etc. by Dr. John Moore, 8 vols. 8vo. BEST EDITION, *portrait, fine copy in red morocco extra, gilt edges,* £4. 4s 1797
Priced, 1840, J. Bohn, £5. 5s.

8721 —— MISCELLANEOUS WORKS, with Memoir of his life and writings by Anderson, 6 vols. 8vo. *portrait, calf gilt,* 38s Edinb, 1806

8722 SMYTH'S (Capt. W. H.) ÆDES HARTWELLIANÆ, or Notices of the Manor and Mansion of Hartwell, Co. Bucks (Dr. Lee's Residence), large 4to. *plates, and upwards of 50 illustrations on wood and stone, with autograph letter from Dr. Lee to Mr. Duffield,* PRIVATELY PRINTED, cloth, £2. 2s 1851

8723 SMYTH (Vice-Admiral W. H.) CYCLE OF CELESTIAL OBJECTS continued at the Hartwell Observatory to 1859, with a notice of recent discoveries and details from the Aedes Hartwellianæ, roy. 4to. *plates (one coloured) and woodcuts, cloth, rare,* £3. 15s *privately printed,* 1860

8724 SNORRO STURLESON, the HEIMSKRINGLA, or Chronicle of the Kings of Norway, translated from the Icelandic, with a preliminary dissertation by Samuel Laing, 3 vols. 8vo. (pub. at 36s) *cloth,* 14s 1844

8725 SOMNER (Wm.) Treatise of Gavelkind, both name and thing, with his Life by Kennett, sm. 4to. *best edition,* LARGE PAPER, *calf,* 18s 1726

8726 **Songs.** BELLAMY'S Lyric Poetry of Glees, Madrigals, Catches, Rounds, Canons, and Duets, 8vo. 624 *pp. cloth,* 7s 6d 1840

8727 CALLIOPE, or the Musical Miscellany; a collection of English, Scotch and Irish Songs, *set to Music,* 8vo. *calf,* 10s 1788

8728 MERRY COMPANION, or Universal Songster, consisting of a new collection of Scots Songs, English Love-Songs, Battle-Songs, etc. 16mo. *old calf neat,* 7s 6d 1750

8729 MUSICAL MISCELLANY, being a Collection of Choice Songs set to the Violin and Flute by the most eminent Masters, 6 vols. 12mo. *frontispieces with Music and Words of about 400 Songs,* £2. 12s 6d 1729-31
Goldsmid's copy fetched £3. 3s.

8730 POPERY. COLLECTION of the newest and most ingenious Poems, Songs, Catches, etc. against Popery, sm. 4to. *hf. bd. rare,* 10s 1689

8731 SONGS and BALLADS, a collection, printed uniform, in 1 vol. folio, *containing about 280 engraved pages of Music, with the words, including some of the most admired compositions of the last century, hf. bd.* 10s ca. 1770

8732 THOMSON'S collection of the Songs of BURNS, SIR W. SCOTT, and other eminent lyric poets, arranged with Symphonies and Accompaniments for the Pianoforte by Pleyel, Haydn, Beethoven, etc. 6 vols. impl. 8vo. *portraits and plates,* (pub. at £2. 8s) *bds.* 25s s. a. (? 1840)

8733 VOCAL MUSIC, or the Songster's Companion, a choice collection of Songs, Cantatas, *with the Music prefixed to each,* 2 vols. 16mo. *calf,* 6s ca. 1760

8734 SOUTHEY'S HISTORY OF BRAZIL, 3 vols. 4to. (pub. at £8. 8s) *calf gilt, scarce,* Buckle's copy, £4. 4s 1822-17-19
" Dr. Southey is doubtless the '*facile princeps*' of the historians of the Brazils; but this title is hardly commensurate with the bearing and extent of his work, as it comprises the rise and progress of all the European Colonies, from the Andes to the Atlantic, and from the Plata to the River of the Amazons. Numerous will be the impressions which the next half century will cause to be circulated of so ample and instructive a work."—*Dibdin.*

8735 SOUTHEY'S Sir Thomas More, or Colloquies on the Progress and Prospects of Society, 2 vols. 8vo. *portrait and plates of Lake Scenery,* (pub. at 30s *in bds.*) *calf gilt,* 25s 1829

8736 SOUTHGATE (Henry) Many Thoughts on Many Things, being a Treasury of reference, consisting of selections from the known great and the great unknown, sm. 4to. *second edition, frontispiece* (pub. at 21s) *new in cloth extra, gilt edges,* 17s 6d 1861
A useful book of reference, consisting of the choicest selections arranged in the alphabetical order of their subjects, with analytical contents.

8737 SOUTHGATE'S Many Thoughts of Many Minds, 8vo. (pub. at 12s 6d) *new in cloth extra, gilt edges,* 10s 6d 1863

8738 —— the same. sq. 8vo. *whole bound morocco, very neat, gilt edges,* 17s 6d 1863
Another collection of elegant extracts, similarly arranged to the above, with Index of subjects.

8739 SPEKE (Captain J. H.) Journal of the Discovery of the Source of the NILE, 8vo. *map, portraits, and woodcuts, cloth, price* 21s 1864

ENGLISH LITERATURE. 481

8740 SPENSER'S (Edmund) Works, with Glossary, explaining the old and obscure words, published by J. Hughes, 6 vols. sm. 8vo. LARGE PAPER, *plates, clean copy in old calf neat*, 21s *London, Tonson*, 1715
Priced, 1842, Thorpe, £3. 3s. LARGE PAPER copies are scarce.
8741 ——— Works, with the principal illustrations of various Commentators; notes, Life of Spenser, and Glossarial and other Indexes, by Todd, 8 vols. 8vo. *portrait, hf. russia*, £2. 2s *Lond.* 1805
8742 ——— the same, 8 vols. 8vo. *nice set in calf gilt*, £3. 10s 1805
"This edition is assuredly a very valuable one, and the public are greatly indebted to Mr. Todd for his fidelity and labour."—*American Review.*
8743 ——— Works, edited by J. Payne Collier, with Life of the Author, 5 vols. 8vo. *beautifully printed*, (pub. at £3. 15s sewed) *hf. cf. extra, gt. tops, uncut*, £4. 4s 1862
A really handsome edition of Spenser was long wanted, and is at length supplied. It is founded upon a collation of all the early impressions; and with regard to the purity of the text, the paper and type, this is undoubtedly the handsomest modern impression of any of our early poets.
" No author ever possessed and combined, in so brilliant a degree, the requisite qualities of a poet."—*Scott.*
8744 SPIRA (F.) Relation of the fearful estate of, after he turn'd Apostate from the Protestant Church to Popery, also the woful deaths of John Child who hang'd himself and Mr. G. Edwards who shot himself, 16mo. *extremely rude cuts, old calf*, RARE, 10s *London*, 1718
A very curious old English Chap-book.
8745 STANHOPE (Lady Hester) Travels, forming the completion of her Memoirs, by her physician, 3 vols. post 8vo. *plates and cuts*, (pub. at 18s) *cloth*, 9s 1846
8746 STARK'S (James) Scenery of the Rivers of Norfolk, comprising the Yare, Waverney, and Bure, with historical and geological descriptions by Robberds, impl. 4to. INDIA PROOFS, consisting of 36 splendid Engravings by George Cooke, W. J. Cooke, E. Goodall, John Burnet, and other eminent Engravers, (pub. at £6. 6s in bds.) *green morocco super extra, broad borders of gold, gilt edges, by Clarke*, £3. 3s *Norwich*, 1834
" An exceedingly beautiful and interesting volume. The paintings combine in subject, composition, and detail, the united excellencies of Hobbima, Ruysdael, and Vander Velde, and exhibit the known talents of Mr. Stark, and of the able engravers employed, to the greatest possible advantage. Their execution may vie with that of the best performances in the same class of art, which this or any other country has yet produced."—*Literary Gazette.*
8747 STATE PAPERS (Miscellaneous) from 1501 to 1726, 2 vols. 4to. *hf. russia, neat*, 21s 1778
A selection of such interesting documents and letters as, with the addition of notes and anecdotes, best illustrate the characters of the successive sovereigns.
8748 STATISTICAL SOCIETY'S Journal, from the beginning in May 1838 to December 1853, Vols. I-XVI, 8vo. (pub. at £8. 5s) *hf. calf*, £3. 16s 1839-53
8749 STATISTICAL SOCIETY's Journal: Index to Vols. I-XXV. 2 vols. 8vo. 7s 1853-63
8750 STATUTES: An. Reg. CAROLI Regis Angliae, Scotiae, Franciae, et Hiberniae, 16-18o. at the Parliament at Westminster, 1640-42, sm. folio, *titles within elegant borders*, 𝔅lack letter, *calf*, 16s 1640-42
8751 STUD BOOK (General) containing Pedigrees of Race Horses, etc. from the earliest accounts, Vols. II, III, IV, 8vo. *first editions*, (pub. at £3. 5s) *bds.* 20s 1822-27-36
8752 ——— the same, Vols. III-VIII, 8vo. *second editions*, (pub. at £7. 5s) *one vol. hf. bd. the rest in bds.* £3. 16s 1832-57
8753 STERNE'S (Lawrence) Works, with a life of the Author by himself, 4 vols. 8vo. BEST EDITION, *portrait and vignettes, by Stothard and others, calf gilt*, 24s 1808
8753*——— the same, 4 vols. 8vo. *fine copy in red morocco extra, gilt edges*, £2. 2s 1808
"The style of Sterne, though fancifully ornamented, is vigorous and masculine, and full of that animation and force which can only be derived by an intimate acquaintance with the early English prose-writers. In the power of approaching and touching the finer feelings of the heart, he has never been excelled, if indeed he has ever been equalled; and may at once be recorded as one of the most affected and one of the most simple of writers:—as one of the grandest plagiarists, and one of the most original geniuses, that England has produced."—*Sir Walter Scott.*
8754 STEWART'S (Dugald) Collected Works, edited by Sir WM. HAMILTON, with the Supplementary volume, 11 vols. 8vo. *portrait, complete*, (pub. at £6.) *cloth, clean copy*, £4. 4s *Edinb.* 1854-60
" Concise, unaffected, intelligible."—*Smyth.*
"Stewart cast a luminous glare over the philosophy of mind, and warmed the inmost recesses of metaphysical enquiry by the delicacy of taste, and the glow of eloquence."—*Alison.*
8755 STOW (John) ANNALES, or a General CHRONICLE OF ENGLAND, continued and augmented unto the ende of this present year, 1631, by Edmond Howes, folio, 𝔅lack letter, *woodcut title, containing portraits of James I., Q. Mary and Prince Charles*, BEST EDITION, *a very fine tall copy, with rough leaves, calf extra, rough gilt edges*, VERY RARE, £10. *Londini, R. Meighen*, 1631-2
" We now come to Stow, a laborious and honest man; content to state simple facts, without any enlarged views, and in a style the most unpretending imaginable, But there are those who rank him even above Holinshed and the contemporaneous Chroniclers. That he was a diligent and careful collector of facts, and far better acquainted with manuscript authorities (even with some of which all traces are now lost) than any writer in his day, may be unequivocally allowed."—*Dibdin.*

2 I

8756 STRICKLAND'S Lives of the Queens of England, from the Norman Conquest, 8 vols. 8vo. *fourth edition, with all the late improvements, portraits of every Queen,* (pub. at £4. 4s) *cloth*, £3. 3s 1852-54

8757 ——— Lives of the QUEENS OF SCOTLAND and English Princesses connected with the regal succession of Great Britain, 8 vols. 8vo. *fine portraits* (pub. at £4. 4s) *clean as new, cloth,* 38s 1852-59

8758 STRUTT'S HORDA ANGEL-CYNNAN, or a Complete View of the Manners, Customs, Arms, Habits, &c. of the Inhabitants of England, from the arrival of the Saxons to the present time, 3 vols. 4to. 157 *fine tinted plates of Costumes, Arms, Armour, Domestic Life, etc. fine copy in old calf gilt,* £9. 9s 1775-76

The rarest and most valuable of all Strutt's works. Priced, 1839, Longmans, £13. 13s; Macpherson, £12. 12s; 1854, £10. 10s; Hibbert's copy fetched £15.; Bindley's, £16. 5s; the Roxburghe, £16. 16s; Willett's £22.; Beckford's, £22. 5s; Hanrott's £17.

8759 SURTEES SOCIETY'S PUBLICATIONS, a complete set, from the beginning to 1860, 38 vols. 8vo. (pub. at £29. 14s 6d) *cloth,* £16. 16s 1835-60

For a list of the separate Articles, see No. 684.

The following three Nos. which form the continuation can be supplied at the usual reduction of 2d in the 1s from the prices marked.

39. The Lindisfarne and Rushworth Gospels, part 2, 10s 1861
40. Depositions from the Castle of York, relating to Offences committed in the Northern Counties in the XVIIth Century, 15s 1861
41. Tonge's (Thomas, *Norrey King of Arms*) Heraldic Visitation of the Northern Counties in 1530; with an appendix of other Heraldic Documents relating to the North of England, edited by Longstaffe, *Coats of Arms,* 18s 1863
42. Walbran's Memorials of Fountains Abbey, Vol. I. *woodcuts of seals, etc. out of print,* 32s 1863

8760 SWIFT'S (Dean) WORKS, arranged by Thomas Sheridan, with notes, historical and critical, new edition, corrected and revised by JOHN NICHOLS, 19 vols. 8vo. *portrait, calf neat,* £2. 18s 1801

Fetched, Strettell's sale, £6.; Drury's sale, £4. 14s 6d.

8761 SWIFT'S (Dean) WORKS, containing additional Letters, Tracts, and Poems, not hitherto published, with Notes and his Life by SIR WALTER SCOTT, 19 vols. 8vo. *portrait,* BEST EDITION, *calf gilt, fine copy, scarce,* £9. 9s *Edinb.* 1824

"This edition contains upwards of a hundred letters, and other original pieces of Swift's, never before published; and, among the rest, all that has been preserved of his correspondence with the celebrated Vanessa. Explanatory notes and remarks are supplied with great diligence to all the passages over which time may have thrown any obscurity; and the critical observations that are prefixed to the more considerable productions, are, with a reasonable allowance for an editor's partiality to his author, very candid and ingenious."—*Edinb. Review.*

8762 TAAFFE'S History of the Order of St. John of Jerusalem, Knights Hospitallers, Templars, of Rhodes, and of Malta, 4 vols. in 2, 8vo. *cloth,* 9s 6d 1852
8763 TASSO'S Jerusalem Delivered, done into English by Fairfax, 8vo. *calf,* 6s 1749
8764 TASSONI, la Secchia Rapita, the Rape of the Bucket, an heroicomical poem, translated by Atkinson, 2 vols. 12mo. *calf neat,* 8s 1827
8765 TAYLOR (Jeremy) WHOLE WORKS, with Life by Heber, revised and corrected by Eden, in 10 vols. 8vo. *portrait,* (pub. at £5. 5s) *cloth,* £3. 16s 1852-54

"We will venture to assert that there is in any one of the prose folios of Jeremy Taylor more fancy and original imagery, more brilliant conceptions and glowing expressions, than in all the odes and epics that have since been produced in Europe."—*Edinburgh Review.*

8766 TAYLOR'S Lays of the Minnesingers, or German Troubadours, sm. 8vo. *plates, bds.* 4s; *hf. calf,* 6s 1825
8767 TENISON (Lady Louisa) Castile and Andalucia, impl. 8vo. 44 *fine plates and vignettes, the plates executed in tinted lithography of Scenery, Antiquities, Ecclesiastical Architecture, Figures, etc.* (pub. at £2. 12s 6d *in bds.*) *olive morocco, super extra, gilt edges,* £2. 2s 1853
8768 TENNENT (Sir James Emerson) History of Modern Greece, from B.C. 146 to the present time, 2 vols. 8vo. (pub. at 32s) *bds.* 9s 1845
8769 THIRLWALL'S History of Greece, Lardner's Cabinet Edition, 8 vols. 12mo. *frontispieces, calf gilt, a pretty set,* 36s 1839-44
8770 THOMAS, View of Heathen Worship, and Observations on Homer's attachment to Eastern Idolatry, 8vo. *calf,* 7s 6d 1809
8771 THOMSON'S (James) Works, with his last corrections and improvements, 4 vols. 12mo. *plates, pretty copy in old English calf gilt,* 18s 1773
8772 ——— Seasons, and Castle of Indolence, with Life by Gilfillan, sq. 8vo. *fine illustrations,* (pub. at 18s) *cloth extra,* 10s 1857

8773 TOBIN'S (Lady) Land of Inheritance, or Bible Scenes Revisited, a handsome large impl. 8vo. volume, viii *and* 438 *pages beautifully printed, with the portraits of Lady Tobin and Sir Thomas Tobin, and* 8 *original Views in Palestine and Egypt, extra cloth gilt, gilt edges,* 30s 1863

8774 TRADESCANT, Musæum Tradescantianum, or a Collection of Rarities preserved at South Lambeth, neer London, by John Tradescant, 16mo. *with Hollar's portrait, and* ADDITIONAL PLATES, *russia extra, gilt edges,* 36s 1656

COLLATION: Plate of Arms; title; *three sets* of the two portraits of Tradescant, senior and junior, *the first set* being remarkably fine and brilliant impressions, the second a modern re-engraving with the Monument; Dedication, and Latin and English anagrams, 4 leaves; To the Reader, 4 leaves; text, pp. 1—183; and the same plate of arms as at the beginning, 1 leaf; with portrait of Hester Tradescant inserted at page 179. Thus there are 5 additional plates

8775 TROLLOPE (Rev. W.) History of the Royal Foundation of CHRIST'S HOSPITAL, with a narrative of the rise and suppression of the Grey Friars, 4to. *fine portraits and plates,* (pub. at £3. 3s) bds. 15s 1834

8776 TUCKER'S (Abraham) Light of Nature pursued, second edition, revised and corrected, with Life of the Author, by Sir H. Mildmay, 7 vols. 8vo. BEST EDITION, *calf gilt, scarce,* 25s 1805

Priced, 1854, Rivington, £4. 14s 6d; 1844, McPherson, £4. 4s.
"There is more original thinking on the several subjects that he has taken in hand than in any other, not to say than in all others put together; his talent for illustrations is unrivalled."—*Paley.*
"A work the most original and profound that has ever appeared on moral philosophy."—*Mackintosh.*

8777 TUFTON FAMILY, Memorials of the Family of Tufton, Earls of Thanet, 8vo. *plates, bds.* 7s 6d Gravesend, 1800

8778 TURNER'S (Sharon) HISTORY OF ENGLAND; the Anglo-Saxons, 3 vols.; Middle Ages, 5 vols.; Henry the Eighth, 2 vols.; and the Reigns of Edward, Mary, and Elizabeth, 2 vols.; together 12 vols. 8vo. *all published* (pub. at £11. 10s, bds.) *fine set in calf gilt, contents lettered, from Mr. Buckle's library,* £8. 8s 1823

Priced, Walther, £10. 10s; 1834, Arch, £9. 9s; 1841, £8. 10s; 1847, £8. 18s 6d; 1855, £8. 18s; 1856, £9. 9s.

8779 TURNER'S HISTORY of the ANGLO-SAXONS, 3 vols. 8vo. *hf. calf, neat,* 24s 1828

8780 ——— Sacred History of the World, 3 vols. 8vo. *bds.* 15s 1833-37

Priced, 1843, J. Hearne, calf gilt, £2. 15s.
"We regard Mr. Turner's work as a very valuable addition to our national histories; from numerous and recondite sources he has collected much that is interesting and curious, respecting both the manners and the events of the periods which he describes. There certainly was occasion for such a work, and the execution of it leaves no room to regret that it devolved on Mr. Turner."—Eclectic Review.

8781 TURBERVILLE'S (George) The Noble Art of Venerie or Hunting, collected for the pleasure of all Noblemen or Gentlemen, out of the best Authors, reduced into such termes as are used in this Realme, sq. sm. 8vo. Black letter, *fine large woodcuts of animals and hunting groups, the latter curious for the costume, good copy, hf. bd.* 32s London, Purfoot, (1611)

8782 TUSSER (T.) Five Hundred Points of Good Husbandry, together with a Book of Huswifery, a new edition, with notes and Glossary by Mavor, sm. 4to. BEST EDITION, LARGE PAPER, *calf gilt,* 24s 1812

8783 TYRRELL (James) History of England, both Ecclesiastical and Civil, from the earliest time to the Reign of Richard II. taken from the most Ancient Records, MSS. and printed Historians, with memorials of eminent Persons in Church and State, the Foundations of Monasteries and Universities, 3 vols. in 4, folio, *old calf,* £2. 10s 1696-1704

"The work abounds with equally curious and important matter. The author was professedly a Whig."—
"Perfect sets are becoming rarer and rarer every day."—*Dibdin.*

8784 UNIVERSAL HISTORY, Ancient and Modern: Ancient, 18 vols., Modern, 42; together 60 vols. 8vo. SECOND AND BEST EDITION, *maps and plates, fine copy in the original full calf gilt,* £8. 8s 1772-84

Priced, 1834, J. Bohn, £20.; 1836, Arch, £14. 14s; 1845, Rodwell, £10. 10s; 1846. £9. 9s; 1847 and 1849, £10. 10s.
In addition to the separate Index of each vol. Vol. 56 contains a General Index to the entire modern part; and Vols. 57-60 are supplementary, containing the history of the British Isles.

Universities of Oxford and Cambridge.

8785 HUBER on the ENGLISH UNIVERSITIES, translated from the German, edited by Newman, 3 vols. 8vo. 3 *coloured frontispieces,* 15 *portraits, and* 19 *other plates,* (pub. at 30s) *cloth,* 10s 1843

8786 OXFORD UNIVERSITY Statutes, translated by Ward and Heywood, 2 vols. 8vo. (pub. at 16s) *cloth,* 7s 6d 1845-51

These are the Statutes still in force, existing only in Latin at Oxford.

8787 FOUNDATION STATUTES and Documents of MERTON COLLEGE, collected by Heywood, edited by Halliwell and Percival, 2 vols. 8vo. *cloth,* 3s 6d 1843-47

8788 CORPUS CHRISTI COLLEGE, Foundation Statutes of Bishop Fox, 1517, translated, with Life of the Founder by Ward, 8vo. *plates, cloth,* 10s   1843

8789 CAMBRIDGE STATUTES, first and second Series: Collection of the Statutes of Cambridge, including various early Documents, with Appendix and Elizabeth's Statutes, in English, by Heywood, 1840—Early Cambridge Statutes, from the 13th to the 16th Century, with the Statutes of Peterhouse, Clare Hall, and Pembroke College, in English, by Heywood, 1855—together 2 vols. 8vo. *cloth, scarce,* 10s   1840-55

8790 CAMBRIDGE UNIVERSITY TRANSACTIONS during the Puritan Controversies of the 16th and 17th Centuries, some in Latin and English, edited by Heywood and Wright, 2 vols. 8vo. *cloth,* 7s 6d   1854

The above valuable works on the English Universities were published at the expense of that indefatigable University Reformer, J. Heywood, Esq., formerly M.P. for Manchester.

8791 UPCOTT (W.) Original Letters, Manuscripts, and State Papers, impl. 4to. *facsimiles of interesting letters, including one of the Duke of Monmouth, hf. bd. privately printed,* 10s   1836

8792 UPHAM'S (E.) History and Doctrine of Budhism, with notices of the Kappooism, or Demon Worship, and of the Bali, or planetary incantations of Ceylon, impl. 4to. *with 43 coloured plates of Mythological figures from Singalese designs, hf. morocco, uncut,* £4. 4s   1829

8793 UTTERSON'S Select Pieces of Early Popular Poetry, republished from the early black letter copies, with Glossary, 2 vols. sm. 8vo. *facsimile vignettes,* (pub. at 35s) *hf. morocco, gilt tops, uncut,* 30s   1817

Fetched, 1858, Sotheby's, £1. 19s. There were only 250 copies printed.

8794 VAUGHAN (Rob.) The Protectorate of OLIVER CROMWELL, and the state of Europe in the early part of the reign of Louis XIV, 2 vols. 8vo. *2 portraits,* (pub. at 32s) *russia gilt,* 16s   1838

8795 VIRTUOSO'S COMPANION, and Coin Collector's Guide, 4 vols. 12mo. *frontispiece and* 240 *plates containing engravings of several thousand Tradesmen's Tokens, etc. neat in calf, fine copy,* £2. 10s   1795-97

8796 WACE (Master) Chronicle of the Norman Conquest from the Roman de Rou, translated with notes by Taylor, 8vo. *many curious woodcuts, being facsimiles from ancient MSS. Tapestry, etc. russia extra, tooled back and sides, gilt edges,* 18s   1837

"Wace is superior to them all in the fluency and metre of his verse."—*Turner.*

8797 WALCOTT'S William of Wykeham, and his Colleges, roy. 8vo. LARGE PAPER, *plates of Music, and woodcuts, cloth,* 12s 6d   1852

8798 WALFORD (Edward) County Families of the United Kingdom, royal manual of the titled and untitled Aristocracy of Great Britain and Ireland, with the descent, birth, marriage, residence, and other particulars relative to each person, roy. 8vo. *cloth,* price 36s   1864

8799 WALFORD'S Men of the Time, a Biographical Dictionary of living characters, stout sm. 8vo. *hf. bd.* 9s   1862

8800 WALKER'S (Clem.) History of INDEPENDENCY, 1640-60, 4 parts complete, sq. 8vo. *with Faithorne's curious plate of Cromwell and his adherents cutting down "the Royall Oake of Brittayne," calf, good copy,* 25s   1661

A curious historical volume of the transactions during the Civil Wars until the death of King Charles, and continued to the Restoration, Argyle's proceedings, and parallel betwixt him and Cromwell, &c.

"A rich legacy bequeathed to posterity, of all their (the Rump Parliament) great misdoings and their petty villanies, and above all their secret history."—*Disraeli's Cur. of Lit.*

The Author was imprisoned in the Tower by Cromwell, 1649, for writing the History of Independency, where he died 1651.

8801 WALPOLE'S (Horace, Earl of Orford) WORKS, containing his Fugitive Pieces, Account of Royal and Noble Authors, Castle of Otranto, Miscellanies, Account of Strawberry Hill, Anecdotes of Painting, Account of Engravers, etc. 5 vols. roy. 4to. *numerous fine portraits and plates, fine copy in russia extra,* £3. 10s   1798

Priced, 1839, Thorpe, £6. 6s; 1846, Longmans, £5. 5s; 1847, priced £5. 10s; fetched at Dowell's sale £8. 15s; Splidt's, £10. 10s.

"There is an irresistible charm in all the writings of Horace Walpole; we expect to see fresh Humes and fresh Burkes before we again fall in with that peculiar combination of moral and intellectual qualities to which his productions owe their extraordinary popularity."—*Edinb. Review.*

"It is the fashion to underrate Horace Walpole; firstly, because he was a nobleman; and secondly, because he was a gentleman; but to say nothing of the composition of his incomparable letters, and of the Castle of Otranto, he is the 'Ultimus Romanorum,' the author of the Mysterious Mother, a tragedy of the highest order, and not a puling love play. He is the father of the first romance, and of the last tragedy in our language, and surely worthy of a higher place than any living writer, be he who he may."—*Byron.*

ENGLISH LITERATURE. 485

8802 WALPOLE's Anecdotes of Painting in England, with some account of the Artists, and Catalogue of Engravers, 5 vols. 12mo. *calf gilt, 16s* 1786

8803 WALTON AND COTTON'S COMPLETE ANGLER, with original Memoirs and Notes by Sir HARRIS NICOLAS, 2 vols. impl. 8vo. PICKERING'S SPLENDID EDITION, *with* 61 *plates, portraits and vignettes, by Stothard, Inskipp, etc.* (pub. at £10. 10s) *very fine copy, calf extra, gilt edges*, £5. 1836

8804 WEEVER'S (John) Ancient Funerall Monuments within the united Monarchie of Great Britaine, Ireland, and the Islands adjacent, with the Dissolved Monasteries therein contained, folio, *brilliant impression of the portrait, and frontispiece by Cecill, fine tall copy, elegantly bound in blue morocco, gilt edges*, £6. 1631

This really fine copy has the Index, which was published after the work itself, and is extremely rare. Collation: Portrait, Engraved title-page, Printed title-page, Dedication to Charles, the "Author to the Reader," 8 pp. Table, 1 leaf; Errata, 1 leaf; "Discourse of Funerall Monuments," pp. 1—871; Index, 12 pp.

8805 WELLESLEY'S (Marquess) Despatches, Minutes and Correspondence during his Administration in India, edited by Montgomery Martin, 5 vols. 8vo. *portrait, maps, plans, etc.* (pub. at £6. 10s) *rare,* £4. 1840

"Lord Wellesley's letters are admirable compositions; they are evidence of a highly gifted mind, and this collection of historical facts cannot but be highly appreciated."—*Naval and Military Gazette.*
"As a body of authentic facts, and of sound views on Indian policy, this will be an indispensable literary work."—*Asiatic Journal.*
"The despatches may truly be called national records, of which England may justly be proud."—*Metrop. Mag.*
"A publication of peculiar and extraordinary interest."—*Edinb. Rev.*

8806 WEST'S History of Tasmania, 2 vols. 8vo. *cloth, rare*, 36s *Tasmania*, 1853
Vol. I contains the Discovery, the History down to 1852, and the Zoology; Vol. II, the Aborigines, Transportation, and Conclusion.

8807 WEST's Antiquities of Furness, 4to. *map, plan, etc. bds.* 7s 6d 1774

8808 WELLINGTON'S DESPATCHES during his Campaigns in India, Denmark, Portugal, Spain, the Low Countries, and France, 1799-1818, by Gurwood, 12 vols. 8vo. BEST EDITION, (pub. at £12. 10s) *fine copy in calf gilt*, £6. 6s 1837-38

8809 WHEATON'S Elements of Internal Law, sixth edition, with the last corrections of the author, additional notes, etc. by Lawrence, stout roy. 8vo. *cxcvi. and* 728 *pp.* (pub. at 31s 6d) *cloth*, 18s *Boston, U. S.*, 1857

8810 WHITAKER's (John) Life of SAINT NEOT, the oldest of Alfred's brothers, 8vo. *hf. calf*, 7s 1809

8811 WHITAKER'S (Thos. Dunham) LEEDS, Vol. I: THORESBY'S Ducatus Leodiensis, or the Topography of the Town and Parish of Leeds and parts adjacent, with Catalogue of his Museum, second edition, with notes and additions by Whitaker; Vol. II: WHITAKER's Loidis and Elmete, an attempt to illustrate the districts described in those words by Bede, with the APPENDIX and plates published in 1820, 2 vols. roy. folio, *with* 67 *beautiful plates and portraits,* 20 *vignettes,* 34 *separate tables of Pedigrees, and fine woodcut initials, calf gilt,* UNCUT, £8. 8s   RARE in this uncut state; priced, 1857, £9. 9s. 1816

8812 WHITWORTH's (Ch.) Succession of PARLIAMENTS, lists of the Members, 1660-1761, stout 12mo. *calf,* 6s 1764

8813 WILKINSON (Sir G.) MANNERS AND CUSTOMS OF THE ANCIENT EGYPTIANS, including their Private Life, Government, Laws, Arts, Manufactures, Religion, Early History, and Agriculture, etc. derived from a comparison of the paintings, sculptures, and monuments still existing, with the accounts of ancient authors, BOTH SERIES, and Supplement, 6 vols. 8vo. BEST EDITION, with Index, *and* 600 *plates and cuts illustrative of their Paintings, Monuments, Sculptures, etc. some in* COLOURS, *cloth gilt,* £4. 10s 1837-41

8814 WILLIAMS (Sir C. H.) Works, from the originals in the possession of his grandson and others, with notes by Horace Walpole, Earl of Orford, 3 vols. sm. 8vo. *portraits, fine copy in blue morocco extra, joints, silk linings, gilt edges,* £2. 2s 1822

8815 WILLIS'S (Browne) Notitia Parliamentaria; History of the Counties, Cities, and Boroughs in England and Wales, &c. their Antiquities, Charters, Privileges, Lands, &c. List of Knights, Citizens, and Burgesses, Account of Roman Towns, Titles of Nobility, etc. 3 vols. sm. 8vo. *divided into counties, hf. bd.* 25s 1715-16

Copies fetched, Dent's £7.; Brockett's £7.; Sir M. Sykes's £6. 10s; Dr. Heath's £6. 6s; and Stace's £5. 7s 6d. 1854, Gardner's £2. 2s. The first volume was reprinted 1730.

8816 WILLIS'S History and Antiquities of the Town, Hundred, and Deanery of Buckingham, 4to. *hf. bd. uncut*, 36*s* 1755
Heath's copy sold for £17.; Willett's, £12.; Towneley's, £9. 5*s*.
8817 —— Survey of the Cathedral-Church of St. Asaph, 8vo. *plates, old calf*, 10*s* 1720
8818 —— Survey of St. Asaph considerably enlarged and brought down to the present, with additions, Memoirs, a second Appendix containing an account of the Archbishoprics, etc., and the author's life, by Edwards, 2 vols. 8vo. *portrait, bds. uncut*, 12*s* *Wrexham*, 1801

" His weatherbeaten wig was of a colour for which language affords no name; his slouched hat, having passed the stage between black and brown, was in the same predicament as the wig, and the lower part of his equipments had obtained for him in his own neighbourhood the appellation of Old Wrinkle Boots, for during the wear and tear of forty years they had contracted as many wrinkles as their quantum of calf skin could obtain. Having lived long enough to hold a distinguished place among antiquities himself, he left behind him the character of a diligent and faithful antiquary, in which he will long continue to be remembered."—*Quarterly Journal.*

8820 WILSON (H. H.) Select Specimens of the Theatre of the Hindus, 3 vols. 8vo. *original edition, bds. uncut*, 20*s* *Calcutta*, 1827
8821 —— Ariana Antiqua: Descriptive Account of the Antiquities and Coins of Afghanistan, with a Memoir on the Buildings called Topes, 4to. *map and 36 plates of Bactrian Antiquities and Coins, cloth*, 36*s* 1841
8822 —— —— Essays Analytical, Critical and Philological on Subjects connected with Sanskrit Literature, edited by Dr. Reinhold Rost, Vols. I—II, 8vo. (pub. 24*s*) *cloth*, 20*s* 1864
8823 [WILSON (John)] The English Martyrologie containing a summary of the lives of the glorious and renowned Saints of the three Kingdoms, with a catalogue of those who have suffered death for the Catholick cause, since Henry VIII, by a Catholicke priest, 12mo. *vellum*, RARE, £2. 10*s* *Permissu Superiorum*, 1608
   Collation: Title, Dedication, Calendar, and Advertisement, 8 leaves; text, pp. 1-356; table, 5 leaves; authors alledged, 1 leaf; catalogue of those who have suffered, 8 leaves. There is no place or name of printer mentioned in the book.

8824 **Wiltshire.** HOARE (Sir R. C.) History of Modern Wiltshire: Benson and Hatcher, Old and New Sarum or Salisbury, very stout roy. folio, *with numerous plates of Antiquities, Coins, Monuments, etc. some illuminated, bds.* £2. 16*s* 1843
   Added is Hatcher's preface, claiming for himself the entire authorship; and also plate of his Monument.

8825 WIT'S RECREATIONS. Facetiæ; Musarum Deliciæ or the Muses' Recreation, 1656, and Wit Restored, 1658, also Wit's Recreations with a thousand outlandish Proverbs, printed from edition 1640, and preface (by Park and Dubois) 2 vols. sm. 8vo. *with all the curious woodcuts from the original edition, only 150 copies printed, fine copy in red morocco extra, gilt edges*, £3. 3*s* 1817
8826 WORSLEY (Sir Richard) History of the Isle of Wight, roy. 4to. *map and numerous fine plates of Scenery, Antiquities, etc. calf neat*, 20*s* 1781
   Heath's copy fetched £2. 19*s*; Willett's, £3. 4*s*; Edwards', £3. 5*s*.
8827 Wright's Essays on Archæological subjects, and questions connected with Art, Science, and Literature in the Middle Ages, 2 vols. sm. 8vo. *map, plates, and cuts*, (pub. at 16*s*) *cloth, new*, 13*s* 6*d* 1861
8828 —— Essays on subjects connected with the Literature, Superstitions, and History of England in the Middle Ages, 2 vols. sm. 8vo. (pub. at 16*s*) *cloth, new*, 12*s* 6*d* 1846
   The 2 works for 25*s*.
8829 WRIGHT'S Volume of Vocabularies X—XV Century, *Latin and Anglo-Saxon, Old English*, roy. 8vo. *cloth*, £2. *privately printed for J. Meyer*, 1857
8830 Wycliffe's Life and Opinions, illustrated from his unpublished MSS. by Vaughan, 2 vols. 8vo. (pub. at £1. 1*s*) *bds.* 9*s* 1831
8831 Wylie's Fairford Graves, a record of Researches in an Anglo-Saxon Burial place in Gloucestershire, 4to. 13 *plates, bds. new*, 9*s* *Oxford*, 1852
8832 YULE'S (Capt. Henry) Narrative of the Mission sent by the Governor General of India to the Court of Ava in 1855, with notices of the country, government, and people, 4to. *large map enclosed within cover, 29 tinted plates of Scenery, Figures, Temples, etc. and numerous woodcuts* (pub. at £2. 12*s* 6*d*) *calf gilt, gilt edges*, 30*s* 1858
   The Appendix treats, amongst other things, on the Literature and Languages of Burmah, and contains a polyglot Vocabulary of English words rendered into 15 Burmese and Siamese languages or dialects.

8833 YOUNG'S (Arthur) Agriculture of Great Britain; viz.: Six Weeks' Tour through the Southern Counties of England and Wales, 1769—Six Months' Tour through the North of England, 4 vols. 1771—Farmer's Tour through the East of England, 4 vols. 1771—Farmer's Guide in Stocking Farms, 2 vols. 1770—Rural Economy, Essays on the practical part of Husbandry, 1770—Farmer's Kalendar, 1771—Farmer's Letters to the people of England, 2 vols. 1771—together 15 vols. 8vo. *many plates, fine copies in old gilt calf,* SCARCE, £5. 1769-71
8834 —— Farmer's Guide in hiring and stocking Farms, 2 vols. *plate,* 1770—Farmer's Letters, containing the sentiments of a practical Husbandman, 2 vols. 1771—together, 4 vols. 8vo. *old calf gilt,* 20s 1770-71
8835 YOUNG'S (Thomas) Miscellaneous WORKS, 3 vols. 8vo. *portrait,* (pub. at £2. 5s) *cloth,* 28s 1855
CONTENTS: Vols. I. and II. Scientific Memoirs, edited by G. Peacock; Vol. III. HIEROGLYPHICAL ESSAYS and Correspondence, edited by J. Leitch.
8836 YOUNG (M.) Life and Times of Aonio Paleario, or a history of the Italian Reformers in the Sixteenth Century, 2 vols. stout 8vo. (pub. at 28s) *cloth, new,* 16s 1860

8837 **Language.** BARTLETT'S Dictionary of Americanisms: a Glossary of Words and Phrases colloquially used in the United States, 8vo. *calf gilt,* 10s 6d
New York, 1849
8838 ROGET'S Thesaurus of English Words and Phrases, arranged to facilitate literary composition, 8vo. (pub. at 14s *in cloth,) calf extra,* 12s 1853

8840 ALLEN's Principles of Modern Riding for Ladies, roy. 8vo. *numerous plates* (pub. at 21s) *calf gilt,* 15s 1825
8841 ANSTED and LATHAM, the Channel Islands, stout 8vo. *plates and numerous elegant woodcuts* (pub. at 26s) *cloth,* 16s 1862
8842 BARROW (Sir John) Autobiographical Memoir of, (1764-1847), 8vo. *portrait* (pub. at 16s) *cloth,* 7s 6d 1847
8843 BELL (H. N.) the Huntingdon Peerage, a detailed account of the evidence, etc. connected with the restoration of the Earldom, History of the House of Hastings, etc. 4to. *Genealogical Table, and portraits, calf gilt,* 18s 1821
8844 BLUNDEVILL (T.) The Four Chiefest Offices belonging to Horsemanship, Breeder, Rider, Keeper and Ferrer, 4 vols. in 1, sq. sm. 8vo. black letter, *titles within woodcut borders, and several woodcuts of Bits, Snaffles, Hooves, etc. calf,* 28s 1609
The second, third, and fourth tracts in this curious little volume, have each a different title, and a separate pagination.
8845 BRADBURY (H.) Nature-Printing, its origin and objects, 1856—Security and Manufacture of Bank Notes, *specimen plates,* 1856—Printing, its Dawn, Day, and Destiny, 1858—3 vols. in 1, 4to. *morocco, gilt edges,* 10s 6d 1856-58
8846 BRITISH ARCHÆOLOGICAL ASSOCIATION, Journal of the, Vol. XIX, 8vo. (pub. at 31s 6d) *new,* 26s 6d 1864
8847 BURTON's Anatomy of Melancholy, with account of the author, 2 vols. 8vo. (pub. at 24s) *calf gilt,* 18s 1827
8848 CAMDEN SOCIETY'S PUBLICATIONS, being reprints of exceedingly rare and curious Books, and Publications of inedited MS., etc. with copious Introductions and Notes, from the beginning in 1838 to 1860, 78 vols. sm. 4to. *cloth,* £10. 10s 1838-61
8849 MORTON (J.) The ANCREN RIWLE; a Treatise on the Rules and Duties of Monastic life, edited and translated from a Semi-Saxon MS. of the 13th Century, sm. 4to. 480 pp. *cloth,* 16s *Camden Soc.* 1853
8850 CAREW (Bampfylde Moore, King of the Beggars) Apology for, being his Life, (by Goadby), 12mo. *hf. calf neat,* 7s 6d n. d. (1749)
CHETHAM SOCIETY'S PUBLICATIONS, 61 vols. sm. 4to.—The following Nos. can be supplied separately Manchester, 1844-63
8851 III. CHESTER's Triumph in honor of her Prince, 1610, with introduction and notes, by Corser, 10s 1844
8852 VI. JAMES' Iter Lancastrense, 1636, with notes and memoir by Corser, *plate and pedigree,* 12s 1845
8853 IX. HEYWOOD's Norris Papers, 10s 1846
8854 X, XI. HULTON's Coucher Book or Chartulary of Whalley Abbey, 2 vols. 30s 1847
8855 XII. HEYWOOD's Moore Rental, *plan of Liverpool,* 1650, 12s 1847
8856 XIII. WORTHINGTON's Diary and Correspondence, by Crossley, Vol. I, 10s 1847

8857 XXVIII. JACOBITE TRIALS at Manchester, 1694, by Beaumont, 12s   1853
8858 XXXII, XXXIV, XL, XLIV. BYROM (John) Private Journal and Literary Remains, by PARKINSON, 2 vols. in 4, *portrait*, £2. 2s   1854-57
8859 XLI. SHUTTLEWORTH House and Farm Accounts, by Harland, Part II, *portrait*, 10s   1856
8860 XLVII. BOOKER's Ancient Chapel of Birch, Manchester Parish, *plates*, 10s 1859
8861 XLVIII. JONES (Thomas) Catalogue of the Collection of Tracts for and against Popery, in the Chetham Manchester Library, Part 1, *(all published)* 4to. *cloth*, 12s   *ib.* 1859
8862 LII, LV. CORSER's Collectanea Anglo-Poetica, a bibliographical and descriptive catalogue of early English Poetry, with extracts, 2 vols. 20s   1860-61
8863 LVII. CHETHAM Miscellanies, Vol. III, *including 84 pp. on the Lancashire dialect*, 15s   1862
8864 LIX, LX. RAINES' History of the Lancashire Chantries, Reports of the Royal Commissioners of Henry VIII, Edward VI, and Mary, 2 vols. 30s   1862
8865 LXI. General Index to Vols. I—XXX, 25s   1863

8866 CLARKE (W. N.) Parochial Topography of the Hundred of Wanting, with other Records relating to the County of Berks, 4to. *many Genealogical Tables, calf gilt*, RARE, £2. 10s   Oxford, 1824
8867 COKER'S Survey of DORSETSHIRE, containing the Antiquities and Natural History of that County, with a Genealogical account of 300 Families, etc. sm. folio, *map and plates of Arms, calf*, 36s   1732
8868 DUGDALE'S ANTIQUITIES OF WARWICKSHIRE, second edition, printed from a copy corrected by the author, the whole revised, augmented, and continued to the present time, by THOMAS, 2 vols. folio, *fine portrait by Hollar, and numerous plates, fine tall copy in the original old calf*, VERY RARE, £32.   1730
8869 DUTHY'S Sketches of HAMPSHIRE, embracing the Architectural Antiquities, Topography, etc. of country adjacent to the River Itchen, roy. 8vo. *map, plates, and several woodcuts, cloth*, 16s   Winchester, 1839
8870 ELEGANT EXTRACTS, Prose, Verse, and Epistles, 2 vols. each, together 6 vols. large 8vo. *frontispieces, calf gilt*, 28s   1791-1804
8871 FANSHAW (Lady) Memoirs, by herself (1610-70) with extracts from Sir R. Fanshawe's correspondence (edited by Sir Harris Nicolas), 8vo. *portrait, tree-marbled calf extra, by Riviere*, 12s   1829
8872 GAGE [John Gage-Rokewode] History and Antiquities of Hengrave, Co. Suffolk, roy. 4to. 30 *plates of portraits, views, etc.* (pub. at £3. 13s 6d in bds.) *hf. morocco, uncut*, £2.   1822

"A work valuable no less for the ornamentation and useful illustrations, than for the very curious details of private history and biography, and of ancient customs and characters which it exhibits."

8873 GELL (Sir W.) Geography and Antiquities of Ithaca, roy. 4to. *map and many plates of Greek Archæology* (pub. at £3. 3s), *hf. green morocco, uncut, top edge gilt*, 12s   1807
8874 —— Itinerary of Greece, with a commentary on Pausanias and Strabo, and an account of the antiquities existing in Greece, 1801-6, roy. 4to. 28 *fine plates*, (pub. at £2. 12s 6d), *hf. green morocco, gilt top, uncut*, 10s   1810
8875 —— Itinerary of the Morea, 1817—Narrative of a Journey in the Morea, 1823—2 vols. 8vo. *map and many plates, hf. green morocco, gilt tops, uncut*, 12s   1817-23

"That laudable curiosity concerning the remains of classical antiquity which has of late years increased among our countrymen, is in no traveller nor author more conspicuous than in Mr. Gell."—*Lord Byron.*

8876 GORHAM (G. C.) History and Antiquities of Eynesbury and St. Neot's in Huntingdonshire, and of St. Neot's in Cornwall, 2 vols. 8vo. *numerous plates and cuts*, on INDIA PAPER, *calf gilt*, 25s   1824
8877 HANSARD'S Book of Archery, stout 8vo. 15 *fine plates, impressions on India paper, with 24 plates of outline illustrations*, (pub. at £3. 3s) *green morocco extra, gilt edges*, 21s   1840
8878 HARLEIAN MISCELLANY, a Collection of scarce, curious, and entertaining Pamphlets and Tracts, selected from the Library of the Earl of Oxford, with historical, political, and critical notes, by Oldys and PARKES, with the Supplement, 10 vols. royal 4to. BEST EDITION, (pub. at £33. 12s in bds.) *fine set, whole bound in russia gilt*, £16. 16s   1808-13

Priced, 1831. Longmans, £18.; 1837, Arch, £18. 18s; 1840, J. Bohn, £21.; 1845, Rodwell, £16. 16s; fetched at Sotheby's, 1855, *c df extra*, £22. 10s.

8879 ENGLISH TRACTS: a Collection of 7 extremely curious and SCARCE ENGLISH TRACTS relating to VULGAR PROPHECIES, etc. in 1 vol. sm. 4to. *hf. bd.* £2. 1610-44
PROPHECIE (A.) of a White King of Britain, from the library of Sir R. Cotton 1643
PROPHESIE (A.) that hath lyen hid above these 2000 years, wherein is declared all about the Church of Rome, BLACK LETTER, *wants a leaf* 1610
SALTER (Robert) Wonderful Prophecies hidden under Parables W. Jones, 1627
MERCURIUS COELICUS: or, a Caveat to all that have read the pamphlet called "A New Almanack and Prognostication" 1644
LILLY (W.) Prophecy of the White King; and Dreadfull Deadman explained 1644
VOX POPULI, or Newes from Spayne, which may serve to forewarn both England and the United Provinces how farre to trust to Spanish pretences 1620
TOM-TELL-TROTH, or a free discourse touching the murmurs of the times
"This pamphlet written in James ye first his raign is very witty."—*Contemporary MS. note on title.*

8880 **ENGLAND.** TEN TRACTS relating to English History, in 1 vol. sm. 4to. *hf. bd. an important collection,* £2. 16s 1612-84
Comprising the following:—
Declaration du Roy de la Grand Bretaigne touchant le faict de Conradus Vorstius *Londres,* 1612
Reddition de Dunkerque entre les mains des Anglais *Paris,* 1658
Memoire présenté au Protecteur par l' Ambass. du Roy Cathol. en Angleterre 1658
Articles de deux Traités entre la France et l'Angleterre 1658
Arrest contre un livre intitulé, Relation d'un Voyage, au desavantage de la Nation Angloise 1664
Lettre des Etats des Pais Bas au Roy de la G. Bretagne touchant quelques differends 1664
Responce du Roy de la G. Bretagne 1665
Replique du Chev. Downing, Envoyé de la G. Bretagne aux Etats des Prov. Unies 1665
Diverses Piece en réponse aux discours des Hollandais 1565
Lettre des Etats des Pais Bas au Roy de la G. Bretagne, sur le rappel de leur Ambassadeur 1666
Requeste et Pieces pour Milord Comte d'Aran, touchant la restitution du Duché de Chastellerault 1685

8881 CARTE (Tho.) Catalogue des Rolles Gascons, Normans et Francois, conservés dans les Archives de la Tour de Londres, 2 vols. folio, *fine copy in old calf gilt,* £5. 5s *Londres, et Paris,* 1743
Edwards' copy fetched £7.
Carte's Preface was cancelled by order of the French Government, and another, by Bougainville, was inserted in almost all the copies in its place. This copy has the SUPPRESSED PREFACE, of eight pages.

8882 DESCRIPTION de tout ce qui s'est passé dans les Guerres entre Angleterre, la France, les Pays Bas, et l'Evesque de Munster, 1664-67, avec une introduction sur l'Exile et la Restitution du Roy d'Angleterre, sq. 8vo. *some pages discoloured, several fine engravings of Naval Battles, vellum,* 36s *Amst.* 1668

8883 DEFENCE de la RELIGION REFORMÉE et de la Monarchie et Eglise Anglicane contre l'impiété et la tyrannie de la Ligue rebelle d'Angleterre, 12mo. *with the rare portrait of Charles II. by Hollar, vellum, scarce,* 28s 1650

8884 HEARNE (Thomas) Liber Niger Scaccarii, cum Wilhelmi Worcest. Annalibus, etc. ed. Hearne, 2 vols. 8vo. *calf,* 12s 1771

8885 HERMANNIDÆ (Rutgeri) Britannia Magna, sive Angliae, Scotiæ, Hiberniæ et adjacentium Insularum geographico-historica descriptio, stout 16mo. *maps and plans, vellum, fine copy,* £2. 2s *Amst.* 1661

8886 JOVII (Pauli) Descriptio Britanniæ, Scotiæ, Hyberniæ et Orchadum, sq. 8vo. *portrait of "Alvarus Nonius Ludor" inserted, excellent copy in the original old stamped calf,* 21s *Venet.* (1548)

8887 MISSON (M.) Mémoires et Observations en Angleterre, avec une Description particulière de Londres, 12mo. *frontisp. map and* 19 *curious plates of the Public Buildings in London, etc. calf gilt, gilt edges,* 10s *La Haye,* 1698

8888 PARSONS (Robert) Elizabethæ Angliæ Reginæ hæresim Calvinianam propugnantis sævissimum in Catholicos sui regni Edictum, promulgatum Londini, 20 Nov. 1591, cum Responsione ad singula capita, qua non tantum sævitia deteguntur et confutantur, par A. Philopatrum, smallest 4to. *fine copy, morocco elegant, gilt edges,* £2. 10s *Romæ,* 1593

8889 TANNERI BIBLIOTHECA BRITANNICO-HIBERNICA, sive de scriptoribus qui in Anglia, Scotia et Hibernia, ad sæculi XVII initium floruerunt, commentariis edidit D. WILKINSON, folio, *fine portrait by Vertue, clean copy in old calf, binding injured,* VERY RARE, £8. 8s 1748
In the margins are notes in pencil by the late Mr. Petrie of the Tower.

8890 TWYSDENI (Rogeri) Historiæ Anglicanæ Scriptores X, ex vetustis MSS. nunc primum in lucem editi; adjectis variis Lectionibus, Glossario, Indiceque copioso, 2 vols. folio, FINE PAPER, *vellum or calf,* £4. 5s 1652

8891 VERIDICUS (Th.) Elenchus motuum nuperorum in ANGLIA, sq. 8vo. *vellum,* 7s *Francof.* 1650

8892 **IRELAND.** ANTHOLOGIA HIBERNICA, of Science, Belles Lettres and History, from its beginning in January 1793 to December 1794, Vols. I-IV, 8vo. *a monthly Magazine, literary and political, with many plates and portraits, hf. bound,* 18s *Dublin,* 1792-94

8893 ARCHDALL'S (*Mervyn*) MONASTICON HIBERNICUM; or an History of the Abbeys, Priories, and other religious houses in Ireland, Memoirs of their Founders, Benefactors, Abbots, &c. 4to. *map, and* 18 *plates of Monastic and Knightly Costume, &c. calf, rare*, £2. 8s   Dublin, 1786
"A valuable and esteemed work."—LOWNDES.

8894 BELING (Sir Richard) Vindiciarum Catholicorum Hiberniæ, rerum in Hibernia gestarum, 1641-49, synopsis; libelli famosi in Hiberniæ Proceres, qui cum regiis pacem inierunt, confutatio, 2 vols. in 1, 12mo. *vellum*, 32s   Paris, 1650
Priced, Thorpe, £3. 3s; 1840, J. Bohn, £5. 5s; fetched, 1855, Sotheby's £2. 10s
This very scarce little book, published under the name of Philopater Irenæus, was unknown to Nicolson and other writers. It was written in defence of the Confederate Catholics of Ireland. Beling's account is esteemed more worthy of credit than any written by the Romish party.
"Countrymen! have you read this book? If not, you are ignorant of your history."—*Columbanus ad Hibernos.*

8895 CARVE'S ITINERARY: Itinerarium Thomæ Carve, Tipperariensis, Sacellani Majoris Anglorum, Scotorum et Hybernorum sub exercitu Cæsareæ Majestatis militantium, cum historia facti Butleri, Gordon, Lesly et aliorum; nova editio, tres partes in uno volumine complectens, cum imagine auctoris, acc. quædam de vita Itinerantis, necnon Index generalis, 3 vols. in 1, sm. 4to. xxiv. and 432 pp. *portrait, hf. morocco, uncut*, 30s   Quaritch, 1859
Only 100 copies are printed, and very few remain for sale.

8896 —— the same, roy. 8vo. PRINTED ON VELLUM, *hf. red morocco gilt, uncut,* £5. 5s   1859
Only two copies were printed on vellum.

8897 —— LYRA, sive Anacephalæosis Hibernica, in qua de exordio, seu Origine-Nomine, Moribus Ritibusque gentis Hibernicæ succinte tractatur, cum Annalibus Hiberniæ, et rerum gestarum per Europam 1148-1650, editio secunda, sq. 8vo. *with the 5 plates so often wanting (including portraits of Carve, Charles I. and Donagh O'Brien) fine large copy in the original stamped hogskin, with clasps*, £5. 10s   Sulzbaci, 1666
Priced, 1832, Thorpe, £8. 18s 6d; 1833, £8. 8s; 1835, £9. 9s; Nicol's copy fetched £10. 10s; Bindley's £12. 12s.

8898 CASTLEHAVEN (Earl of) Memoirs of his engagement and carriage in the Wars of Ireland, 1642-51, 12mo. *edition suppressed by the author, calf*, 15s 1680
8899 —— Review, or his Memoirs, enlarged and corrected, with Appendix, 12mo. *calf*, 10s   1684
8900 —— Review, or his Memoirs of his carriage in the Irish Wars, with Lord Anglesey's letter thereon, 8vo. *best edition, hf. russia*, 12s   Dublin, 1815
8901 CLANRICARDE'S (The Marquis of) Memoirs, and Letters, 1650-51, with historical Introduction, 1744 — CASTLEHAVEN'S Memoirs, with introduction by Lynch, 1815, 2 vols. in 1, 8vo. *hf. morocco*, 7s 6d   Dublin, 1744-1815
8902 COTTON (Archdeacon H.) Fasti Ecclesiæ Hibernicæ: the Succession of the Prelates and Members of the Cathedral Bodies in Ireland, 5 vols. 8vo. *four vols. in hf. morocco, uncut, the fifth in cloth*, £3. 3s   Dublin, 1847-60
An extremely valuable work on Irish History and Antiquities, with Index.
8903 CURRY's (J.) Reviews of the Civil Wars in Ireland, from Elizabeth to William III. 2 vols. 8vo. *calf*, 6s   1786
8904 D'ALTON (J.) Illustrations, Historical and Genealogical of King James's Irish Army List (1689) second enlarged edition, 2 vols. 8vo. *new in cloth, only printed for subscribers*, 18s   Dublin, 1860
8905 DOLLY'S BRAE RIOTS. BATTLE of Magheramayo, Report of the Evidence at the court, Castlewellan, July to September 1849, 12mo. *map, bd.* 12s Newry, 1849
8906 EACHARD (Lawrence) Exact Description of Ireland, chorographically surveying all its provinces and counties, with an Index that may serve for a Geographical Dictionary of Ireland, 18mo. *five maps, hf. morocco, from Heber's library, rare and curious*, 36s   1691
8907 GEOGRAPHICAL DESCRIPTION of the Kingdom of Ireland, according to the 5 Provinces and 32 Counties, declaring the right of England unto that Kingdom, relation of the former Rebellions, etc. sq. sm. 8vo. *blue morocco, gilt edges*, VERY RARE, 36s   1642
The only copy I can find anywhere mentioned is Hibbert's, which fetched £2. 2s.
8908 GRACE (Sheffield) Grasagh Aboe, the War-Cry of the Grace Family, the original *Irish*, with English, French, Italian, German, Spanish, Greek, and Latin translations, roy. 8vo. *music, portraits, plates, and Coates of Arms, cloth, only* 50 *copies privately printed*, 10s   1839

8909 HISTORICAL ATLAS OF IRELAND: Atlas of Ulster, executed about the year 1609, in 31 Maps, each on a sheet measuring 28 in. by 22, *plain, an extremely important series of Maps* 1862
—— the same, *very carefully coloured* 1862

1. A Generalle description of Ulster; 2. Tyrone; 3. Tyrconnelle; 4 and 5. Baronie of Knockninnie; 6. Clancally: 7. Clinawley; 8. Maghery Steffanah; 9. Mahhery Roy; 10. Lurgh and Cole Mackernan; 11 and 12. Donganon; 13 and 14. Loghinisholin; 15 and 16. Strabane; 17. Omey; 18. Clogher; 19. Loghtie; 20. Tollagh Garvie; 21. Clanchy; 22. Castle Rahin; 23. Clonmahowne; 24. Tollachconco; 23. Orier; 27. Fues; 28 and 29. Oneilan; 30. Ardmagh; 31. Toghrany.

NOWELL (Dean) Two Ancient Maps of Ireland (ca. 1566) $\frac{1}{152,000}$ and $\frac{1}{3,648,000}$ facsimiled from the original MS. in the British Museum, coloured round the margins, *on a single sheet* 1862
—— Copy of portion of an Ancient Manuscript in the British Museum, by Lawrence Nowell, Dean of Lichfield, who died in 1576; *being the text to illustrate the above Maps*, folio, *of 20 pp. lithographed, sewed* 1862
Containing an authentic description of Ireland, from the time of Henry II., and giving the princes and chiefs, with details of their troops, resources, etc.

VIEW of the Siege of Enniskillen 1592, taken from McGuire by Capt. Dowdall, facsimile of the original plan "made and dun by John Thomas, Solder," *a very curious plan on a large sheet, representing an episode of Elizabeth's Wars in Ireland, plain; or coloured* 1862
These Maps possess much interest, as exhibiting the titles from the Crown of the landed proprietary of the present day in Ulster.

☞ The above **Maps and text, bound together in 1 vol. large folio,** *hf. calf, the maps plain*, £2. 16s 1862
8910 —— the same, complete, the Maps coloured, *calf*, £9. 9s 1862
8911 IRISH HISTORICAL TRACTS: Papist and Protestant Properties in Ireland, 1689—Letter from Tyrconnel from Limerick, 1690—Walker's Invisible Champion foyl'd, an Appendix to the Siege of Derry, 1690—Diary of the Siege of Limerick, with the Articles, 1692—Proposal for raising Money out of the forfeited estates, 1694—Discourse concerning the different Interests of Ireland, (1697?)—Essay on an Union of Ireland with England, 1704—together 7 tracts, *all of them extremely rare*, 30s 1689-1704
8912 HAMILTON's Letters on the Northern Coast of Antrim, its Antiquities, Manners, and Customs, 12mo. *portrait, maps and plates, bds.* 7s 6d *Belfast*, 1822
8913 HARDIMAN's Ancient Irish Deeds and Writings relating to landed property, Sec. XII—XVII, 4to. *Irish and English, hf. bd.* 9s *Dublin*, 1826
8914 HARRIS (W.) Fiction Unmasked, or an Answer to a Dialogue of the Irish Rebellion in 1641, 8vo. *calf*, 6s *Dublin*, 1752
8915 JONES (H.) Remonstrance of divers remarkable Passages concerning the Church and Kingdome of Ireland, sq. sm. 8vo. *olive morocco extra, gilt edges by Mackenzie*, 21s 1642
A rare and curious little work on the Rebellion of 1641.
8916 KEATING'S General History of Ireland, containing an account of the first Inhabitants of that Kingdom, the original of the Gadelians, Wars of the Irish against the Danes, &c. THIRD EDITION, with Appendix, collected from the Remarks of Dr. Anthony Raymond, folio, LARGE PAPER, *a fine portrait of Brian Boroimhe, maps, 23 plates of pedigrees of the noble Families of Ireland, and 12 plates of Coats of Arms, an extraordinarily fine, large and tall copy, old calf, neat*, £5. 5s 1738
8917 KEATING's General History of Ireland, 2 vols. 8vo. *calf neat*, 9s *Dublin*, 1809
8918 LELAND'S (Dr. Thomas) History of Ireland from the Invasion of Henry II, with a preliminary Discourse on the Ancient State of the Kingdom, 3 vols. 4to. *calf gilt*, 21s 1773
Priced, 1836, £3. 3s; 1840, £4. 4s; 1848, £4. 4s.
This book was highly prized on its first appearance for its style and manner.
8919 MASON (W. S.) Bibliotheca Hibernica, a descriptive Catalogue of a select Irish Library, collected for the Right Hon. R. Peel, 8vo. *facsimile, privately printed, bds.* 18s *Dublin*, 1823
8920 MORYSON'S (Fynes) Ten Yeeres Travell through the Twelve Dominions of Germany, Bohmerland, Sweitzerland, Netherland, Denmarke, Poland, Italy, Turky, France, England, Scotland, and Ireland, folio, FINE COPY *in calf gilt*, £6. 6s 1617
A very interesting, valuable, and much esteemed work. Among other matters it contains a long account of the Rebellion of Hugh O'Neill, in Ireland, and his subjugation.
"Moryson," says Dr. Drake, "is a sober-minded and veracious traveller, and that part of his book which

relates to the manners and customs of England and Scotland is particularly useful and interesting." "He began his travels," relates Fuller, "May 1st, 1591, over a great part of Christendome, and no small share of Turky, even to Jerusalem, and afterwards printed his observations in a *large book*, which, for the truth thereof, is in good reputation, for of so great a traveller, he had nothing of a traveller in him, as to stretch in his reports. At last he was secretary to *Charles Blunt*, Deputy of Ireland. saw and wrote the conflicts with, and conquest of Tyrone; a discourse which deserveth credit, because the writer's *eye* guides his *pen*, and the privacy of his place acquainted him with many secret passages of importance."

8921 O'CONOR FAMILY. MEMOIRS of the Life and Writings of the late Charles O'Conor, of Belanagare, by the Rev. Charles O'Conor, Vol. I *(all published)* 8vo. *calf neat*, £3. 3s *Dublin, printed by J. Mehain, no date* (1796)
Excessively rare, only a few copies having been printed for the author's friends; with autograph of Lady Morgan when Miss Owenson, dated Dublin, 1811, pages 117-118 torn across, but nothing wanting; no portrait and no arms on title-page.
Sir Mark Sykes' copy fetched £14.; and afterwards sold at Hibbert's sale for £6. The work is said to have been suppressed.

8922 O'CONOR's Chronicles of Eri, translated from the original in the Phœnician Dialect of the Scythian Language, 2 vols. 8vo. *bds*. 5s 1822

8923 O'CONOR's (Rev. C., *D.D.*) Columbanus ad Hibernos, No. 2, with Historical Address on the Calamities of foreign influence in the nomination of Irish Bishops, pts. 1 and 2, 2 vols. 8vo. *bds*. 8s *Buckingham*, 1810-12

8924 O'CURRY's Lectures on the Manuscript Materials of Ancient Irish History, stout 8vo. 26 *plates of facsimiles of Ancient Irish MS. cloth*, 12s *Dublin*, 1861

8925 O'FLAHERTY (Roderici) OGYGIA, seu Rerum Hibernicarum Chronologia, ex pervetustis Monumentis eruta, sq. 8vo. *vellum*, 21s 1685
Priced, Rivington, £3. 3s; Payne and Foss, £2. 12s 6d; 1844, Longman's, £2. 2s; fetched 39s.
A great fund of knowledge and information relating to Ancient Ireland.

8926 O'PHELAN, Epitaphs on the Tombs in the Church of St. Canice, Kilkenny, with preface and notes by Shee, sm. folio, *frontispiece and several plates of Monuments, with interesting biographical, historical, and antiquarian matter, bds*. 10s 6d *Dublin*, 1813

8927 O'REILLY'S Irish-English Dictionary, with a Grammar, 4to. 30s *Dublin*, 1817

8928 PAMPHLETS and Tracts by Sheridan and others on the Legislative Independence of Ireland, List of Absentee Landlords, etc. in 1 vol. 8vo. *hf. calf*, 7s 6d 1779-83

8929 PLOWDEN'S Historical Review of the State of Ireland, from the Invasion under Henry II. to its Union with Britain, 2 vols. in 3, 4to. *port. calf*, 12s 1803
Sold Sotheby's, 1856, calf, £2. 2s.

8930 PLOWDEN's Historical Letters to Charles O'Connor, Columbanus, with Appendix, 8vo. *portrait of O'Connor of Belanagare, bds*. 10s *Dublin* (1812)

8931 ROYAL SOCIETY. Collection of papers communicated to the Royal Society, referring to curiosities in Ireland, sm. 4to. *numerous plates, bds*. 6s 1726

8932 SCALE's Hibernian Atlas, a general description of the Kingdom of Ireland, sm. 4to. 37 *maps, coloured, with engraved text, hf. bd*. 15s 1798

8933 SHIRLEY'S (E. P.) Account of the Territory or dominion of FARNEY, in the province or earldom of ULSTER, 4to. *woodcuts, cloth, scarce, only a limited number of copies printed, presentation copy*, 36s 1845
Containing a large variety of genealogical and historical information concerning the old Irish families. The sixteenth and seventeenth centuries are most extensively treated on, and are peculiarly interesting.

8934 SMITH'S Antient and Present State of the County and City of WATERFORD, 8vo. *maps and views of Waterford, Lismore and Dungarvan, cf*. 10s 6d *Dub.* 1746

8935 STANIHURST (R.) de rebus in Hibernia gestis, sq. 8vo. *fine copy in vellum*, 21s *Antverpiae*, 1584

8936 (STOCK), Narrative of what passed at Killalla, in the County of Mayo, during the French Invasion in 1798, 1800—Impartial Relation of the Military Operations in Ireland on the landing of French Troops in 1798, 1799—2 vols. in 1, 8vo. *hf. bd*. 18s *Dublin*, 1799-1800
On the title-page of the first piece is the autograph of Lady Morgan when Miss Owenson, and on the fly-leaf the following note by her: "This admirable Narrative was written by Dr. Stock, Bishop of Killala, whose preferment was stopt for ever by its publication. He was eminently learned, pious, benevolent and courteous, but all these qualities were neutralized in the eyes of the Irish Government by the patriotism of his politics. This book was given me by his son, J. Stock, Esq. Barrister-at-Law."

8937 STAFFORD'S PACATA Hibernia, or a History of the Wars in Ireland during the Reign of Queen Elizabeth, 2 vols. impl. 8vo. *portraits, maps and plates, facsimiled after the originals, fine copy in russia*, 21s *Dublin*, 1820

8938 STORY'S (G.) Impartial History of the Wars of Ireland, with the Continuation, 2 vols. in 1, sm. 4to. *complete with the* 14 *maps and plans of Towns, Battles, etc. old calf*, £2. 10s 1693
Priced, Rivington, £3. 3s; 1829, £3. 13s 6d; 1843, J. Bohn, £2. 12s 6d.
"Story was an eye-witness, and has intermixed curious accounts of the customs and traditions of the several provinces and countries through which the army passed."—*Lowndes*.

8939 Todd (Dr. J. H.) St. Patrick, Apostle of Ireland, memoir of his life and mission, with introductory dissertation; 8vo. (pub. at 14s), *cloth, new*, 12s   *Dublin*, 1844
8940 WALSH (Peter) The more ample Accompt, the Answers to the Exceptions, etc. in the Advertisement annexed to the late Remonstrance of the Roman Catholick Clergy of Ireland, etc. 12mo. *hf. bd.* VERY RARE, 36s   1662
<small>I cannot trace the sale of any copy. All the works of Walsh are rare, and doubtlessly found many enemies. With the above there are two other small Roman Catholic works bound up.</small>
8941 WARNER's (F.) History of the Rebellion and Civil-War in Ireland, stout 4to. *map, calf*, 9s   1767
8942 WILDE's (W. R.) Descriptive Catalogue of the Antiquities in the Museum of the Royal Irish Academy, 8vo. *numerous woodcuts, bds.* 4s 6d   *Dublin*, 1857
8943 WELD's (Isaac) Illustrations of the Scenery of Killarney, 4to. 19 *plates, maps, vignettes, hf. calf*, 6s   1807

8944 **SCOTLAND**. Anderson (J.) Historical Essay shewing that the Crown and Kingdom of Scotland is imperial and independent, sm. 8vo. *plates of seals, calf*, 5s   *Edinb*. 1705
8945 ARROWSMITH's Map of Scotland, Memoirs relative to the Orkneys and Shetlands, 2 *folding maps*, roy. 4to. (pub. at 16s) *bds.* 9s   1809
8946 BOECE (Hector) HISTORY and CHRONICLES of Scotland, translated from the Latin by John Bellenden, 2 vols. sm. 4to. *two facsimile woodcuts, calf gilt, very scarce*, £4.   *Edinb*. 1821
<small>Of this handsome reprint only 200 copies were executed.</small>
8947 [BOTFIELD (B.)] Journal of a Tour through the Highlands, 1825, sm. 8vo. *map and views, bds. privately printed*, 15s   *Norton Hall*, 1830
8948 BRISTED (J.) Pedestrian Tour through part of the Highlands of Scotland, 2 vols. 8vo. *coloured frontispiece, calf neat*, 12s   1803
8949 BUCHANAN'S (G.) History of SCOTLAND, with notes, and a continuation to the Union, by Aitkin, 4 vols. 8vo. *portraits and map, calf*, 30s   *Glasgow*, 1827
8950 BUCHANAN (W. of Auchmar) Historical and Genealogical Essay upon the Family and Surname of Buchanan, with an enquiry into the Genealogy of ancient Scottish Surnames, particularly the Highland Clans, 2 vols. in 1, sq. 8vo. *plate of arms, calf*, RARE, £3.   *Glasgow*, 1723
<small>A work fraught with curious information not elsewhere to be met with.</small>
8951 ——— Inquiry into the Genealogy and Present State of Ancient Scottish Surnames, the Highland Clans and Buchanan Family, 8vo. *calf*, 16s   *Edin*. 1775
8952 CAMERARII (*David Chambre*) de Scotorum fortitudine, doctrinâ et pietate libri 4, sm. 4to. *vellum*, 27s   *Parisiis*, 1631
<small>COLLATION: Title and Indexes, 6 leaves; pp. 1—288; Index Capitum, Privilége, and Dedication to Charles I, 5 leaves.</small>
8953 CAMPBELL's Highlands of Scotland, 8vo. *half mor.* 5s   1752
8954 CHAMBERS' (R.) Biographical Dictionary of eminent SCOTSMEN, 4 vols. 8vo. 1835—Supplement, 1 vol. roy. 8vo. 1855—together 4 vols. *numerous fine portraits, calf extra*, £2. 5s   1835-55
8955 CARDONNEL, Picturesque Antiquities of Scotland, 2 pts. in 1 vol. 54 *fine etchings of Ruins, etc. calf gilt*, 10s   1788
8956 CHALMERS' (G.) CALEDONIA: or, an account, historical and topographical of NORTH BRITAIN, from the most ancient to the present times, with a Dictionary of places, chorographical and philological, 3 vols. 4to. *all published*, LARGE PAPER, *maps, plates, and genealogical tables*, (pub. at £14. 14s) *very fine copy in calf gilt*, £8. 8s   1807-24
8957 ——— the same, Vol. III, impl. 4to. LARGE PAPER, *hf. calf*, 30s   1824
<small>The third volume is wanting to many copies; complete copies are scarce now.
"It is impossible to speak too highly of the excellencies of this elaborate work—more elaborate, indeed, and copious, more abounding with original information, than any work on British history or antiquities which ever came from one author."—*Quarterly Review*.
" We cannot fail to offer the meed of praise to the truly gigantic labours of Mr. George Chalmers; who, in his *Caledonia*, seems disposed to leave no department untouched, and no event, historical as well as local, unrelated or unnoticed. This gentleman is THE ATLAS OF SCOTCH ANTIQUARIES AND HISTORIANS; bearing on his own shoulders whatever has been collected, and with pain *separately* endured by his predecessors; whom neither difficulties tire nor dangers daunt."—*Dibdin's Library Comp*.</small>
8958 CLAVERHOUSE. MEMOIRS of Viscount Dundee, the Massacre of Glencoe, etc. 12mo. *hf. calf*, 7s 6d   1711
8959 COUPER's Poetry in the Scottish Language, 2 vols. 12mo. *bds.* 7s   *Invern*. 1804
8960 CROMEK's Remains of Nithsdale and Galloway Song, 12mo. *cf. neat*, 7s 6d   1810

8961 DOUGLAS (R. *of Glenbervie*) BARONAGE OF SCOTLAND, containing an Historical and Genealogical Account of the Gentry of that Kingdom, with Continuation and Introduction by Morison, Vol. I, (*all published,*) folio, *coats of arms. hf. bd.* 42s   1798

"This work is intended to delineate the Genealogies of the Baronets, and the lesser Barons or landed Gentry of Scotland."

8962 FAG (F.) The Recess; or Autumnal Relaxation in the Highlands and Lowlands, a Serio-comic Tour to the Hebrides, 8vo. *calf extra,* 7s 6d   1834
8963 GALLOWAY'S Poem, in the *Scottish Dialect,* 16mo. *calf,* 9s   *Glasgow,* 1788
8964 GORDON'S (Sir Rob.) Genealogical History of the Earldom of SUTHERLAND, from its origin to 1651, folio, *fine portrait, plate of Arms, and facsimile Charter,* (pub. at £5. 5s) *hf. morocco, gilt top, uncut,* £2. 2s   *Edin.* 1813

"Contains an interesting authentic account of the transactions which took place during a distant period in a remote part of Scotland, with many particulars not mentioned by contemporary writers, relative to private families, as well as to more general history."

8965 HEADRICK'S View of the Island of Arran, 8vo. *calf,* 5s   *Edin.* 1807
8966 HOGG'S Jacobite Relics of Scotland, being the Songs, Airs, and Legends of the Adherents of the House of Stuart, *with the Music,* both series, complete, 2 vols. 8vo. *calf extra, gilt edges, very scarce,* £2. 16s   *Edinb.* 1819
8967 —— the same, first series, 1 vol. 8vo. *calf gilt,* 25s   1819
8968 IRVING'S (David) History of Scottish Poetry, with Memoir and Glossary, by J. Carlyle, stout 8vo. *cloth,* 14s   *Edinb.* 1861

Valuable and interesting, because there is no other work of the kind, and because it contains a great deal of accurate and solid information. The Glossary is copious.

8969 JAMES I. Nostòdia. In Jacobi Regis felicem in Scotiam reditum, Acad. Edinb. congratulatio, sq. 8vo. *Latin poems by Adamson and others, vellum,* 7s 6d   1617
8970 LESLAEI (J.) de Titulo et Jure serenissimæ Principis Mariæ Scotorum Reginæ, quo Regnum Angliæ sibi vendicat, cum Paraenesi ad Anglos Scotosque—Ejusdem de Illustrium Foeminarum in rep. admin. authoritate libellus—2 vols. in 1, sq. 8vo. *with the very rare folding woodcut of Mary's Genealogical Tree, which is generally wanting, calf, scarce,* 28s   *Rhemis,* 1580

Priced, Thorpe, £4. 4s; *morocco,* £7. 17s 6d; 1841, Bohn, £2. 5s; in a contemporary catalogue, £3. 3s ; Hibbert's copy fetched £3. 6s.
Bp. Lesley was one of the staunchest adherents of Mary, and several times suffered imprisonment for his endeavours in her interest. The *Biographie Universelle* says, "Indépendamment des écrits qu'il publia pour sa défense, ouvrages savants, éloquents et dictés par les plus courageux dévouement, c'est à lui que les Ecossais doivent le premier recueil de leurs lois, &c."

8971 LESSELIE, Droïct et Tiltre de Marie Royne d'Escosse, et de Jacques VI, 12mo. *woodcut border round title, no genealogical table, vellum,* 10s *Rouen* (1587)
8972 LEYDEN, The COMPLAYNT of SCOTLAND, written in 1548, with a preliminary Dissertation and Glossary, 2 vols. in 1, 8vo. *bds. uncut, scarce,* £2. 5s *Edin.* 1801

The preliminary dissertation is a learned and laborious work of 292 pages; the text, a curious protest against the state of affairs in Scotland, and English encroachment, occupies pp. 1—302 ; and the Glossary is comprised in pp. 305—384.

8973 LYNDSAY (SIR DAVID), Facsimile of an ancient Manuscript emblazoned by Sir David Lyndsay, of the Mount, Lyon King of Armes, 1542, (edited by David Laing) folio, *emblazoned title, and* 133 *plates containing several hundred Shields of Arms, in their proper colours, with alphabetical Index, hf. bd. morocco, uncut,* £9. 9s   1822

Only 100 copies printed by subscription, now very scarce.
A copy in morocco fetched £9. 15s at Sotheby's in 1853 ; the work has gradually risen above its original value which was about £5.

8974 MACLEAN. HISTORICAL and Genealogical Account of the Clan MACLEAN from its first settlement at Castle Duart, 8vo. *bds.* 7s 6d   1838
8975 MACKENZIE'S (Sir George) Memoirs of the Affairs of Scotland from the restoration of Charles II. 4to. LARGE PAPER, *russia extra, gilt edges,* 18s *Ed.* 1821
8976 MARTIN'S Description of the Western Islands of Scotland, and of Orkney and Schetland, sm. 8vo. *map and plate, old calf neat,* 10s   1703
8977 **Mary Queen of Scots.** JEBB, Scriptores 16 de Vita et Rebus gestis Mariæ Scotorum Reginæ, 2 vols. folio, *portrait by Vertue, and genealogical table, calf,* 24s   1725
8978 UDALL (W.) Historic of the Life and Death of Mary Stuart, Queene of Scotland, 16mo. *portrait and frontispiece by W. Marshall, old calf neat,* RARE, *fine copy,* 20s   1636

Priced, 1840, Payne and Foss, £1. 11s 6d; fetched, 1858, at Sotheby's £2. ; 1859, £1. 12s 6d

ENGLISH LITERATURE. 495

8979 MICHEL (Francisque) Les Ecossais en France, les Français en Ecosse, 2 vols. 8vo. *woodcuts of Arms*, (pub. at 32s) *cloth*, 25s 1862

8980 MONTROSE (Marquis of) Memoirs, from the Latin of Wishart, with Appendix, 12mo. *calf, 7s 6d* *Edinb.* 1756

8981 NICOLAS (Sir Harris) History of the Earldoms of Strathern, Monteith and Airth, with Report on the claims, of R. B. Allardice, to the Earldom of Airth, 8vo. *cloth, a present from Sir C. G. Young, Garter, to Mr. Turnbull, with inscription*, 18s 1842

8982 PINKERTON, Ancient Scotish Poetry, 1420-1586, never before in Print, now published from the MS. collections of Sir Richard Maitland of Lethington, with Essay on Scotch Poetry, Notes, Appendix, and GLOSSARY by PINKERTON, 2 vols. sm. 8vo. *calf*, 18s 1786

8983 —— the same, 2 vols. sm. 8vo. *facsimile, a very fine copy in old red morocco*, 32s 1786

8984 RAMSAY'S (Allan) Poems on several occasions, 2 vols. 12mo. *hf. calf neat, uncut*, 9s *Edinburgh*, 1780

8985 —— the GENTLE SHEPHERD, a Pastoral Comedy, 4to. *with a Glossary of Scots words, and* 18 *pages of* MUSIC, *portrait and* 12 *plates, calf, rare*, 25s *Foulis*, 1788

8986 ROBERTSON'S Topographical Description of CUNNINGHAME, (Ayrshire); with a genealogical account of the FAMILIES, impl. 4to. *plates, bds.* 20s *Irvine*, 1820

8987 ROBERTSON (J. A.) Comitatus de Atholia: the Earldom of Atholl, its boundaries stated, the extent therein of the possessions of the Family of De Atholia, and their descendants the Robertsons, with proofs, 8vo. *large folded map, cloth, presentation copy*, PRIVATELY PRINTED, 36s *Edinb.* 1860

8988 SCOTTISH ELEGIAC VERSES, 1629 to 1729, with notes and appendix, 8vo. *cloth*, 12s
Only 115 copies printed. *Edinb.* 1842

8989 SCOTTISH TRACTS, a bundle of 19, 4to. and 8vo. mostly written about the time of the Union, 10s *Edinb.* 1775

8990 SHAW's History of the Province of MORAY, 4to. *plates, bds.* 18s 1661-1787

8991 SINCLAIR (Sir John) Statistical Account of SCOTLAND, from the Communications of the Ministers of Parishes, 21 vols. 8vo. *bds.* 10s 1791-99
"A most valuable publication, in which are united the labours of about nine hundred individuals."
Priced, 1834, Jas. Bohn, £4. 4s.

8992 STEWART's (Col. D.) Sketches of the Character, Manners, and present state of the Highlanders of Scotland, and military services of Highland Regiments, 2 vols. 8vo. *map*, (pub. at 28s) *calf gilt*, 18s *Edinb.* 1822

8993 STUART's (R.) Caledonia Romana; a Descriptive Account of Roman Antiquities of Scotland; with a view of the Country and its inhabitants in the First Century, etc. 4to. 5 *maps and* 15 *plates, cloth*, 18s 1845

8994 TYTLER (P. F.) HISTORY OF SCOTLAND, with Index, *third edition*, 8 vols. 8vo. (pub. at £4. 9s) *cloth*, £3. 3s *Edinb.* 1845-50
Fetched, 1860, Sotheby's, £3. 5s; 1862, £3. 10s, without Index.

8995 —— the Index separately, 8vo. *cloth*, 5s 1850

8996 VIRGIL'S ÆNEIS translated into Scottish Verse by Gawin Douglass, with large Glossary and account of the author's Life, sm. folio, *calf*, 28s *Edinb.* 1710
"The completion of such a poem in eighteen months, at a time when no metrical version of a classic (excepting Boethius) had yet appeared in English, is really astonishing; for the work is executed with fidelity and spirit and is recommended by many beautiful specimens of original poetry, under the name of Prologues."—*Ellis*.

8997 WALLACE. METRICAL HISTORY of Sir WILLIAM WALLACE, Knight of Ellerslie, by Henry, commonly called Blind Harry, *in Old Scotch*, with Notes and Glossary, 3 vols. 16mo. *portrait and two frontispieces inserted, old red morocco*, 25s *Perth*, 1790

8998 WILSON's (Dan.) Archaeology and Prehistoric Annals of Scotland, royal 8vo. 6 *plates and* 195 *woodcuts in the text*, (pub. at 28s) *cloth, new*, 16s 1851

8998* —— the same, 2nd edition, 2 vols. 8vo. (pub. at 36s), *cloth gilt, new*, 30s 1863
"A comprehensive, learned, and well-written work."—*Athenæum*.
A most valuable work devoted to the elucidation of Scottish Antiquities, and to the recovery of the earliest traces of arts and civilisation. It is divided into four parts: I. The Primeval or stone period; II. The Archaic or bronze period; III. The Teutonic or iron period; IV. The Christian period.

8999 **WALES.** CAMBRIAN REGISTER, the complete series, 1795-1818, 3 vols. 8vo. *frontispieces and maps, a rare and valuable periodical, illustrating the Language, Literature, History, and Antiquities of Wales, hf. calf*, £2. 2s 1795-1818

9000 CAERNARVON. Registrum vulgariter nuncupatum, "The Record of Caernarvon;" roy. folio, LARGE PAPER, bds. 30s *Record Commission*, 1838
9001 CARADOC of Llancarvan, History of Wales, translated by Powell, augmented by Wynne, with Price's Description of Wales, *a new edition enlarged with Pedigrees of Families*, 8vo. maps, bds. 12s 6d *Merthyr Tydvil*, 1812
9002 CATHRALL'S History of NORTH WALES, comprising topographical descriptions of Anglesey, Caernarvon, Denbigh, Flint, Merioneth, and Montgomery, 2 vols. 4to. 16 *plates of Views, etc. hf. calf gilt*, 30s *Manchester*, 1828
9003 COXE'S (W.) Tour in Monmouthshire, 2 vols. in 1, 4to. *with fine Views by Sir R. C. Hoare, map, etc. hf. calf neat*, 22s 1801
9004 CYMMRODORION, or Metropolitan Cambrian Institution, Transactions, Vol. I, 8vo. *various essays on Welsh Language, Literature, and Antiquities*, 5s 1822
9005 DILLWYN's Contributions towards a History of Swansea, 8vo. *woodcuts, cloth*, 5s *Swansea*, 1840
9006 DODRIDGE (Sir John) History of the Principality of Wales, Dutchy of Cornewall and Earldome of Chester, sq. 8vo. *first edition, painting on vellum of the arms of the Duchy of Cornwall inserted, calf, gilt edges*, RARE, 36s 1630
9007 FENTON'S (Richard) Historical Tour through PEMBROKESHIRE, imp. 4to. *fine impressions of the portrait and* 30 *plates,* (pub. at £3. 13s 6d) *fine copy in hf. russia neat, uncut*, 32s 1810
Sold in Sir M. M. Sykes's sale for £3. 15s.
A book full of interesting matter relating to the history and antiquities of Wales; published under the patronage and with the literary assistance of the late Sir Richard Colt Hoare.
9008 GIRALDUS CAMBRENSIS' Itinerary of Abp. Baldwin through Wales, A.D. 1188, with historical and topographical Illustrations, by Sir R. C. Hoare, 2 vols. 4to. *map and* 59 *beautiful engravings*, £2. 1806
"Giraldus is the oldest topographer of Wales; everywhere quoted at large by Camden as an author of undoubted credit and reputation."—*Nicolson*.
9009 HANES CYMRU, A Chenedl y Cymry, o'r Cynoesoedd hyd at Farwolaeth Llewelyn ap Gruffydd; gan y Parch. Thomas Price, thick 8vo. *cloth*, 10s 1842
This work is a History of England from a Welsh point of view; it extends from the earliest history to the time of Cromwell, 1653; it also includes notices of the Welsh in America.
9010 HUGHES, Horae Britannicae, studies in Ancient British History, 8vo. *bds.* 6s 1819
9011 JONES (John) History and Antiquities of Wales, 8vo. *portrait, bds.* 7s 6d 1824
9012 LHOYD'S (H.) History of Cambria, now called Wales, written in the Brytish Language, above two hundreth Years past, and now Englished by Lhoyd, augmented and continued by D. Powell, sq. 8vo. 𝕭𝖑𝖆𝖈𝖐 𝖑𝖊𝖙𝖙𝖊𝖗, *woodcut portraits of the Kings, title neatly mended, otherwise a good copy in green morocco, joints, gilt edges, from Miss Currer's library*, RARE, £4. 4s 1584
Priced, 1818, Longman's, £8. 8s; the Grafton copy fetched £8.; Hibbert's, £5. 2s 6d; and a copy at King's auction, 1810, £9. 9s.
9013 MEYRICK (S. R.) History and Antiquities of the County of Cardigan, stout 4to. *many plates of Views, Antiquities, etc. calf neat, fine copy*, £2. 5s 1810
9014 NASH's TALIESIN, or the Bards and Druids of Britain, a translation of the Remains of the earliest Bards, and examination of the Mysteries, 8vo. *cloth*, 10s 6d 1858
9015 PARRY's Cambrian Plutarch, Memoirs of eminent Welshmen, 8vo. *hf. calf*, 5s 1824
9016 PHILLIPS's (Sir T.) Wales, its language, social condition, with treatise upon Scotland, Ireland, Brittany, Man, etc. 8vo. (pub. at 14s) *cloth*, 6s 1849
9017 PRICE (Thomas Carnhuanawc, *Vicar of Ciomdû, Breconshire*) Literary Remains, 2 vols. 8vo. *portrait and plates, cloth*, 18s *Llandovery*, 1854
Full of facts relating to the History, Literature, and Language of Wales.
9018 PUGH'S (Edward) CAMBRIA DEPICTA, a Tour through North Wales, 4to 70 *plates of views, etc.* (pub. at £5. 5s) *bds.* 12s 1816
9019 ———— the same, 4to. *calf extra*, 24s 1816
9020 ———— the same, roy. 4to. LARGE PAPER, *with the plates coloured, russia extra, gilt edges, tooled on sides*, £2. 1816
9021 ROWLAND's History of Anglesey, and Memoirs of Glendower, 4to. *sd.* 5s 1775
9022 STEPHENS' Literature of the Kymry; Essay on the History of the Language and Literature of Wales, 1080-1322, with specimens of Poetry, etc. 8vo. (pub. at 12s 6d) *cloth*, 10s 6d *Llandovery*, 1849
9023 SWANSEA Philosophical and Literary (*afterwards* Royal) Institution's Proceedings, 1835-50, 2 vols. 8vo. *hf. morocco*, 7s *Swansea*, 1838-50
9024 THOMAS (J.) Cambrian Minstrel, a Collection of the Melodies of Cambria, with original words in English and Welsh, by J. Thomas, sq. 8vo. *two leaves stained, hf. calf*, 6s *Merthyr Tydvil*, 1845

9025 WILLIAMS (Owen) Royal Songs of Sion, or the new Welsh Harmony, consisting of Ancient and Modern British Melodies: Brenhinol Caniadan Sion neu Cynghanedd Newydd Cymraeg, Vol. I (? *all published*) 4 parts in 1 vol. oblong 8vo. *calf neat*, 20s *London*, W. Mitchell, ? 1800
Arranged for one, two, three, four, six and eight voices. The words are the metrical translation and composition of the two chief sacred Welsh Poets.

9026 WILLIAMS (Rev. Rob.) Enwogion Cymru, a Biographical Dictionary of Eminent Welshmen, 8vo. *cloth*, 13s 6d *Llandovery*, 1852

9027 Williams' (W.) Observations on the Snowdon Mountains, Genealogical account of Penrhyn families, etc. 8vo. *bds.* 10s 1802

9028 YORKE'S (Ph.) Royal Tribes of Wales, 4to. *an interesting Genealogical and Historical work, with 12 fine portraits, bds.* 18s *Wrexham*, 1799

9029 —— the same, 4to. *with first impressions of the plates, bds.* 25s 1799

ART AND ARCHITECTURE.

9030 BALDWIN'S Collection of Gems, royal 4to. *44 plates, with letter-press descriptions, the whole finely lithographed by T. Bouvier, hf. morocco extra, gilt top, uncut,* PRIVATELY PRINTED, £2. 2s *ca.* 1830
The possessor of this collection was, at the time of printing this volume, Egyptian Consul; his death prevented the completion of the work, which remains in an unfinished state, without title, etc.

9031 BEAUMONT (Vicomte A. de) Sketches in Denmark, Sweden, Lapland, and Norway, roy. folio, 25 *large and beautiful plates,* FINELY COLOURED (pub. at £4. 4s), *hf. morocco, uncut,* £2. 2s 1840
Fetched, 1854, Sotheby's, £3. 10s; 1856, £3. There exist few works on Northern Art, Costume, and Scenery.

9032 BLAKE (William) The Gates of Paradise, impl. 4to. LARGE PAPER, *hf. morocco, gilt top, uncut,* £6. 15s 1793
Consisting of twenty engraved leaves, the first being the title with an etching headed "for the Sexes," and ten lines of verse. The second is the frontispiece, which represents man as a humanfaced Chrysalis developing into the Butterfly; then follow the Engravings, Nos. 1-16; concluding with 2 leaves containing an epilogue or Dedication, in 39 lines, "To the Accuser who is the God of this World," with etchings. Every engraving is followed by a line or two of verse. The wild sublimity and vast conceptions of the illustrations can only be equalled by the vague grandeur of the poetry.

9033 BRITISH MUSEUM. (Combe's) Description of the collection of Ancient Terracottas in the B. M., 4to. *40 plates by Alexander,* (pub. at 31s 6d) *bds.* 20s 1810

9034 (COMBE, Cockerell, and Hawkins) Description of the collection of Ancient Marbles in the B. M., parts I, II, III, 4to. *77 fine plates by Alexander and others,* (pub. at £5. 17s 6d), *bds.* 25s 1812-18

9035 CARTER'S Ancient Architecture of England, including the Orders during the British, Roman, Saxon, and Norman Eras; also under the Reigns of Henry III and Edward III, chronologically arranged; new edition, with Indexes, alphabetical, chronological and systematic, and illustrative notes by Britton, 2 vols. in 1, roy. folio, 109 *plates,* (pub. at £12. 12s, reduced price, £4. 4s) *hf. morocco, gilt top, uncut,* £2. 16s 1837

9036 —— Specimens of Gothic Architecture and Ancient Buildings in England, 4 vols. 16mo. 120 *etchings of views, bds. uncut,* 16s 1824
Priced, 1837, Payne and Foss, £2. 2s.

9037 Cooke (G.) Animals after the first Masters for examples in Drawing, oblong sm. folio, 30 *plates, finely etched, from designs by the most celebrated Artists* (pub. at £2. 12s 6d) *bds.* 15s 1829

9038 DANCE of Death, with a dissertation on the several representations, by Douce, 8vo. *woodcut facsimiles of the 50 designs by* Holbein, *cloth,* 14s 1833

9039 DOLLMAN and Jobbins, Analysis of Ancient Domestic Architecture, 2 vols. roy. 4to. *160 plates of the best existing specimens in Great Britain, hf. bd. uncut, top edges gilt,* price £5. 5s 1863

9040 —— the same, 2 vols. impl. 4to. LARGE PAPER, price £10. 10s 1863

9041 FALKENER (E.) Daedalus, or the causes and principles of the excellence of Greek Sculpture, roy. 8vo. 15 *fine Photographs and Chromo-Lithographs of Greek Art, with woodcuts, cloth extra, gilt edges,* 21s 1860

9042 Fine Arts Quarterly Review, Nos. I, II, May and October 1863, 2 stout Nos. roy. 8vo. *plates,* (pub. at 12s) *sd.* 7s 6d 1863

9043 GELL and GANDY'S Pompeiana: the Topography, Edifices, and Ornaments of Pompeii, the result of Excavations before 1819, forming the *first series,* 2 vols. in 1, royal 8vo. *containing 77 fine plates, by Cooke, Heath and Pye, original edition, morocco extra, gilt edges, scarce,* £3. 3s 1817-19

2 K

9044 GELL AND GANDY, POMPEIANA, the Topography, Edifices, and Ornaments of Pompeii, the result of Excavations since 1819, 2 vols. royal 8vo. SECOND SERIES, *upwards of* 100 *fine plates* (pub. at £6. 6s) *hf. morocco. uncut*, £2. 2s   1832

9045 GWILT'S Encyclopædia of Architecture, historical and practical, thick 8vo. *with more than* 1000 *wood engravings*, (pub. at £2. 2s) *cloth*, 36s   1859

9046 HARDING'S Elementary Art, or the use of the Lead Pencil advocated and explained, imp. 4to. 28 *plates*, (pub. at £2. 2s) *cloth*, 21s   1834

9047 HAVELL'S Picturesque Views of Noblemen's and Gentlemen's Seats, roy. folio, *a Series of* 20 *large engravings, beautifully* COLOURED *in exact imitation of the original Drawings by Turner, Fielding, De Wint, and other eminent Artists, with Descriptions*, (pub. at £8. 8s) *hf. morocco, gilt top, uncut*, £3. 16s   1823

9048 JERDAN (W.) NATIONAL PORTRAIT GALLERY of illustrious and eminent Personages of the XIXth Century, with Memoirs, 5 vols. impl. 8vo. *about* 180 *fine portraits, green morocco, gilt edges*, £4. 4s   1830-34

9049 LOUDON'S Encyclopædia of COTTAGE, FARM, and VILLA ARCHITECTURE and Furniture, new edition by Mrs. Loudon, very stout 8vo. 2342 *woodcuts of Designs for Buildings, Garden Scenery*, (pub. at £2. 2s) *cloth, new*, £1. 15s 1863

9050 MAJOR (J.) Theory and Practice of Landscape Gardening, 4to. *portrait, plates and woodcuts* (pub. at £2.) *cloth*, 15s   1852

9051 NASH'S MANSIONS OF ENGLAND in the Olden Time, the FOUR SERIES COMPLETE, *consisting of above* 100 *large tinted lithographic Drawings of existing Views*, depicting the most characteristic features of the Domestic Architecture of the Tudor Age, and illustrating the manners of our ancestors, with descriptions, 4 vols. impl. folio, (pub. at £16. 16s) *hf. morocco*, £9. 9s   1839-49

9052 —— the same, 4 vols. in 2, impl. folio, *whole bound red morocco, gilt edges, tooled back and sides*, £12. 12s   1839-49

9053 NEALE'S VIEWS of the Seats of Noblemen and Gentlemen in England, Wales, Scotland, and Ireland, 6 vols. roy. 8vo. *first series, with* 432 *plates, fine impressions*, (pub. at £10. 8s) *hf. calf*, £2.   1822-23

9054 OTTLEY'S Collection of 129 Facsimiles of Scarce and Curious PRINTS by the early Italian, German, and Flemish Masters, illustrative of the History of Engraving from the Invention of the Art, impl. 4to. *with the* 12 *duplicate Niellos finished in silver*, (pub. £15. 15s) *hf. mor. gilt top, uncut*, £5. 10s   1828

9055 PIEROTTI (Erneste) Jerusalem Explored, being a description of the Ancient and Modern City, translated by Bonney, 2 vols. impl. 4to. *upwards of* 100 *illustrations, consisting of Views, Ground-plans, and Sections*, £4. 4s   1864

The various remains of Jewish and Christian architecture are fully illustrated by engravings, and in particular the subterranean conduits, aqueducts, and cisterns.
The appointment of Dr. Pierotti as architect-engineer to the Pasha of Jerusalem, involving his professional employment in the Haram-es-Sheriff—The Temple Close, has allowed him free access to all the buildings and substructures within the sacred enclosure, to which the European traveller has been permitted, at the most, only a hurried visit; while his operations, in all parts of Jerusalem, as Surveyor for the various Christian communities, and agent for the purchase of land, have put him in possession of a fund of information bearing on the ancient topography of the city.

9056 PUGIN'S CONTRASTS, or a parallel between the Noble Edifices of the Middle Ages and buildings of the present day; shewing the decay of taste, 4to. 20 *plates containing generally two engravings on each, cloth, gilt edges*, 30s   1841
This very remarkable production is the rarest of all Pugin's works.

9057 —— True Principles of Pointed or Christian Architecture, 4to. *original edition*, 9 *plates, and numerous woodcuts, cloth, gilt edges*, 12s   1841

9058 —— Apology for the Revival of Christian Architecture in England, 4to. 10 *plates, cloth*, 9s   1843

9059 —— Treatise on Chancel Screens and Rood Lofts, 4to 14 *plates, cloth, morocco back, gilt edges*, 10s 6d   1851

9060 —— GLOSSARY OF ECCLESIASTICAL ORNAMENT AND COSTUME, setting forth the Origin, History, and signification of the Emblems, Devices, and Symbolical Colours, peculiar to Christian Design of the Middle Ages, with reference to the Decorations of the Sacred Vestments and Altar Furniture, formerly used in the English Church, impl. 4to. *nearly* 80 *plates, splendidly printed in gold and colours by the new lithochromatographic process, of the Ecclesiastical Costume of the Roman, English, French, and German Bishops, Priests, and Deacons; Altar Furniture, Embroidery, Bordures, Crosses, Emblems, Monograms, Palls, &c. &c. &c.* (pub. at £7. 7s) *hf. morocco extra, top edges gilt, back and sides ornamented*, £3. 10s   1846

9061 RICHARDSON (C. J.) Studies from OLD ENGLISH MANSIONS, their Furniture, Gold and Silver Plate, etc. the FOUR SERIES complete, 4 vols. roy. folio, LARGE PAPER, 139 *large and elegant plates, coloured and tinted*, (pub. at £14. 14s) *hf. mor.* £5. 1841-48
9062 ROBINSON'S RURAL ARCHITECTURE, a series of designs for Ornamental Cottages, 4to. 96 *plates, original edition*, (pub. at £4. 4s) *hf. bd. uncut*, 30s 1823
9063 ——— New Series of Designs for Ornamental Cottages and Villas, being a sequel to the Rural Architecture and designs for Ornamental Villas, roy. 4to. 56 *plates*, (pub. at £2. 5s) *hf. morocco, uncut*, 20s 1838
9064 ——— Designs for Farm Buildings, roy. 4to. 56 *plates, original edition*, (pub. at £2. 2s) *bds.* 16s 1830
9065 TURNER'S (T. Hudson) Account of Domestic Architecture in England from the Conquest to the end of the 13th century, 3 vols. in 4, 8vo. *about* 400 *plates and woodcuts*, (pub. at £3. 12s) *new in cloth*, £3. *Oxford*, 1851-59
9066 WARING (J. B.) The Arts connected with Architecture, illustrated by Examples in Central Italy, of Stained Glass, Fresco Ornament, Marble and Enamel Inlay, Wood Inlay, etc. from the Thirteenth to the Fifteenth Century, impl. folio, 41 *beautiful plates in* COLOURS, with descriptive text, (pub. at £6. 6s) *hf. morocco*, £5. 15s 1858
9067 ——— the same, impl. folio, LARGE PAPER, (pub. at £10. 10s) *hf. mor.* £9. 10s 1858
This grand work, which has already appeared in my catalogue of Fine Arts, No. 6905, was there by mistake stated to be published at £10. 10s and reduced to £6. 6s. This error arose from ignorance that there existed a Large Paper issue, and that it was only this issue which had been published at £10. 10s. The book has *not* been reduced in price, and the publisher has entered into a bond that there shall be no reduction.
9068 YOUNG'S (John) PORTRAITS of the EMPERORS of TURKEY, from the foundation of the Monarchy to the year 1815, atlas folio, *consisting of* 30 EXQUISITELY COLOURED *proof plates, in imitation of the original paintings, with an historical vignette beneath each portrait, and biographical accounts in English and French*, (pub. at £26. 5s) *red morocco super extra, broad borders of gold, gilt edges*, £8. 8s
Bulmer, (1815)
"This work was undertaken at the command of the late SULTAN SELIM, and completed under the orders of the present Emperor of the Turks. The whole of the impression was, I believe, sent to the Ottoman Court. It is a very magnificent work."—*Dibdin's Bibliographical Decameron, tome II. p.* 39. It is said that only six copies were so coloured in imitation of the paintings.

ENGLISH BIBLIOGRAPHY.

9069 BRITISH MUSEUM. Librorum Impressorum qui in Museo Britannico adservantur Catalogus, 8 vols. 8vo. *russia gilt*, 30s 1813
9070 SOTHEBY (S. Leigh) PRINCIPIA TYPOGRAPHICA: the BLOCK-BOOKS, or Xylographic Delineations of Scripture History, issued in Holland, Flanders and Germany, during THE FIFTEENTH CENTURY, exemplified in connexion with the Origin of Printing, with Notices on the Paper-Marks of the period, 3 vols. impl. 4to. *illustrated with* 120 *large engravings, some in colours, in exact similitude of the very rare Original Block Books, hf. morocco, uncut*, £8. 1858
Only 215 copies of this work, out of the 250 printed, were sold. The remainder have been presented to Public Libraries and otherwise specially reserved, but not for sale.
9071 RICH'S Catalogue of Books relating principally to America, Parts I and II, (1500-1700) in 1 vol. 8vo. *calf gilt*, 32s 1832
Quoted by Lowndes with a valuation of £2. 12s 6d.
9072 RICH, Bibliotheca Americana Nova: Catalogue of Books relating to America, Vol. II. *books printed from* 1801 *to* 1844, 1846— Supplement to Part I; 1701-1800, 1841—2 vols. in 1, 8vo. *cloth*, 25s 1841-5
These two articles compose the entire series of Rich's valuable Bibliography, and contain the books upon America from 1500 to 1844.

GEOGRAPHY AND TRAVELS.

9073 ARROWSMITH (John) London Atlas of Universal Geography, impl. folio, 95 *large folding maps, the outlines coloured* (*pub. at* £17. 17s) *hf. bd.* £7. 10s 1842
There exists no set of Maps more carefully executed than those in Arrowsmith's Atlas. It is by far the most scientific and complete work of the kind, published in this country.
9074 ATLAS. THE GREAT and newly enlarged SEA ATLAS or Water-World, containing exact descriptions of all the Sea Coasts of the whole World, impl. folio, *frontispiece or title, and* 153 *large* COLOURED MAPS, *double size, with a text in the beginning, an interesting and excellent Atlas in the original old calf gilt, stamped on the sides*, £2. 10s *Amsterdam, Van Keulen*, 1682

9075 **Atlases.** ROGERS (Professor, *of Boston)* and KEITH JOHNSTON, Atlas of the United States, Canada, New Brunswick, Nova Scotia, Newfoundland, Mexico, Central America, Cuba and Jamaica, with Introduction, folio, 29 *coloured Maps,* (pub. at £3. 3*s*) *hf. morocco, gilt edges,* 32*s* (1857)

9076 SPRUNER's Historico-Geographical Hand Atlas, from the year 476, obl. 4to. 26 *coloured maps,* (pub. at 15*s*) *cloth,* 10*s* 6*d* 1861

9077 BELCHER (Sir E.) The Last of the Arctic Voyages in Search of Sir John Franklin, being a narrative of the expedition in H.M.S. Assistance, 1852-54, with Notes on the Natural History by Richardson, Owen, Ball, Salter, and Reeve, 2 vols. roy. 8vo. *maps, coloured plates and woodcuts,* (pub. at 36*s*) *new in cloth,* 16*s* 1855

9078 BRUCE'S Travels to discover the Source of the Nile, 5 vols. roy. 4to. *first and best edition, original impressions of the plates,* FINE TALL COPY, *cf. gilt,* 25*s* 1790

9079 BURCKHARDT'S Travels in Syria and the Holy Land, *portrait and maps, hf. calf,* 30*s* 1822

9080 ——— Notes on the Bedouins and Wahabys, collected during his Travels in the East, 4to. *hf. calf gilt,* 36*s* 1830

9081 CHINA. Notices concerning China, and the Port of Canton, with remarks on the Fire, etc. roy. 8vo. *with list of Imports and Exports, and English and Chinese Index, hf. bd.* 7*s* 6*d* Malacca, 1823

9082 CORYAT (Tom) CRUDITIES, reprinted from the edition of 1611, with his Letters from India, etc. 3 vols. 8vo. *reduced copy of the scarce original frontispiece, portrait and other plates, calf,* £2. 16*s* 1776

9083 ERSKINE (J. E.) Journal of a Cruise among the Islands of the Western Pacific, 8vo. *maps and plates,* (pub. at 16*s in bds.) calf extra,* 10*s* 1853

9084 EYRE (E. J.) Journals of Expeditions of Discovery into Central Australia, 1840-44, 2 vols. 8vo. *map on cloth, and several plates, including many of Natural History,* (pub. at 36*s in bds.) calf extra,* 25*s* 1845

9085 GEOGRAPHICAL SOCIETY: JOURNAL of the Geographical Society of London, from its commencement in 1830 to 1859, Vols. I. to XXIX. with Indices to the first twenty volumes, 31 vols. 8vo. *numerous maps, sd.* £9. 1832-59

9086 ——— another set, Vols. I. to XVII. 8vo. *many maps, half calf neat, uncut,* £5. 15*s* 1832-47

9087 ——— another set, Vols. I. to XIV. 8vo. *half calf neat,* £4. 4*s* 1832-44

9088 ——— Proceedings from 1855-56 to 1860-61, 5 vols. 8vo. Vols. I, II, *hf. calf, the rest in* 16 *parts,* 25*s* 1855-61

9089 GRAAH's Expedition to the East Coast of Greenland, translated from the Danish by Macdougall, 8vo. *chart, cloth,* 5*s* 1837

9090 JUKES (J. B.) Narrative of the Surveying Voyage of H.M.S. Fly (under Blackwood) in 1842-46, to Torres Strait, New Guinea, Eastern Archipelago, and an excursion into East Java, 2 vols. *plates,* 8vo. *maps, cuts, and many plates, including some on Natural History,* (pub. at 36*s*) *calf extra,* 20*s* 1847

9091 LYNCH's Official Report of the United Expedition to the Dead Sea and the Jordan, 4to. *large folding map, and* 16 *plates of Natural History, containing about* 150 *figures, sewed,* 10*s* Baltimore, (U. S.) 1852

9092 MARTIN's Hudson's Bay Territories and Vancouver's Island, 8vo. *map,* 5*s* 1849

9093 MOORCROFT and TREBECK's Travels in the Himalayan Provinces of Hindustan and the Punjab, Ladakh, Kashmir, Bokhara, &c. by H. H. Wilson, 2 vols. 8vo. *maps and plates,* (pub. at 30*s in bds.) calf gilt,* 15*s* 1841

9094 NEW SOUTH WALES. CARY (Henry, District Judge) Collection of Statutes affecting New South Wales, containing all the Statutes of practical utility to the present time, 2 vols. imp. 8vo. (pub. at £4. 4*s*) *cloth,* £2. 2*s* Sydney, 1861

9095 PERRY (Commodore) Narrative of the Expedition of an American Squadron to the China Seas and Japan, 1852 to 1854, under the command of Commodore Perry, U. S. N. 3 vols. stout 4to. *with numerous large folding maps, upwards of* 100 *tinted plates, representing Life, Manners, Portraits, Views, and Natural History in Japan, those of Natural History* BEAUTIFULLY COLOURED, *and several hundred Astronomical and other woodcuts, cloth,* £2. 10*s* Washington, 1856

Published by Order of the Congress of the United States. The first volume is edited by F. Hawkes, the second is by Commodore Perry, and contains in an appendix much matter relative to the Japanese language, with a facsimile of the Japanese-American treaty; and the third, which consists of "Observations on the Zodiacal Light from April 1853 to April 1855" is by the Rev. George Jones.

GEOGRAPHY AND TRAVELS.

9096 POCOCKE (R.) Description of the East, and other countries, 2 vols. large folio, with 112 *fine plates of Antiquities, Architecture, Inscriptions, Utensils, Natural History, Phenomena, calf,* 20s 1743-45

9097 —— Description of the East, 2 vols. in 3, 1743-45—Inscriptiones Latinæ, Græcæ et Latinæ, cum Catalogo Numismatum, à Pocockio typis mandatæ, 1752 —together 4 vols. large folio, *very fine copy in old calf gilt,* £2. 10s 1743-52
" A book of superior learning and dignity."—*Gibbon.*
The two vols. pric ed, 1840, Jas. Bohn, £5. 5s; 1840, Payne and Foss, £7. 7s; 1848, £8. 8s. Dr. Hawtrey's copy fetched, 1854, *russia,* £3. 17s.

9098 STEPHENS (J. L.) Incidents of Travel in CENTRAL AMERICA, CHIAPAS and YUCATAN, 2 vols. 80 *engravings,* 1841—Incidents of Travel in YUCATAN, 2 vols. 124 *engravings,* 1843—together 4 vols. 8vo. 204 *engravings,* (pub. at £3. 14s in bds.) *uniform in calf gilt, by Clarke,* £2. 10s 1841-43

9099 STOKES (J. L.) Discoveries in Australia during the Voyage of H.M.S. Beagle, 1837-43, 2 vols. *several maps on cloth, numerous plates, including Natural History, and cuts* (pub. at £2. 10s *in bds.) calf gilt,* 30s 1846

9100 STURT (Capt. C.) Narrative of an Expedition into Central Australia, 1844-46, with a Notice of South Australia, 1847, 2 vols. 8vo. *plates and cuts, those of Natural History coloured,* (pub. at 36s *in bds.) cloth extra,* 25s 1849

9101 TOURNEFORT (M.) Voyage into the Levant, 2 vols. sm. 4to. *numerous plates of maps, cities, figures, Natural History, &c. calf gilt,* 15s 1718

9102 TUCKEY's Narrative of an Expedition to explore the River Zaire, usually called the Congo, South Africa, 1816, with the Journal of Professor Smith, appendix of Natural History, etc. 4to. 14 *plates,* (pub. at £2. 2s) *bds.* 7s 6d 1818

9103 WELLS' Geographical Dictionary or Gazetteer of the AUSTRALIAN COLONIES, 8vo. 438 *pp. with several coloured maps, bds.* 25s *Sydney,* 1848

9104 **India, and Indian Publications.** ACTS of the Governor General in Council, for the years 1851, 1852, 1854, 1855, 1858, 1859, by Theobald, with abstracts and index, 6 vols. roy. 8vo. *sd.* 10s *Calcutta,* 1852-60

9105 ARNOLD (Edwin) The Marquis of Dalhousie's Administration of British India, Vol. I, 8vo. (pub. at 15s) *cloth,* 7s 6d 1862

9106 BAPTIST MISSIONARY SOCIETY, Periodical Accounts relative to, 6 vols. 8vo. *portraits, hf. bd.* 20s; or, *calf extra,* 36s *Clipstone,* 1800-17
A very valuable and rare publication, with contributions by Carey, Ward, Marshman, and other learned missionaries on the Religious Systems, the Antiquities, Natural History, &c. of India.

9107 BOMBAY BRANCH of the ROYAL ASIATIC SOCIETY, Journal from the beginning in 1841 to 1857, being Vols. I-V, or Nos. 1-20, 8vo. *numerous maps and plates of Ancient Inscriptions, Coins, Scientific Observations, etc.* £7. 10s *Bombay,* 1844-57
Containing translations and articles by the most learned writers upon the Languages and Literatures of India, its Ancient Temples and Worships, Historical Antiquities and Numismata; as well as its Natural History, etc.

9108 BOMBAY GEOGRAPHICAL SOCIETY'S Transactions and Proceedings, from the beginning, in 1836, to 1862, Vols. I—XVI, (XIII and XV wanting) 8vo. *numerous plates, some coloured,* £10. *Bombay, etc.* 1836 (44)-63
A scarce and valuable periodical, containing much historical and ethnological matter, Vocabularies and grammatical sketches of several languages and dialects, etc. Now completed.
This publication became so rare that it was reprinted at Bombay in 1844, and sets are chiefly made up of the reprint; but the above set consists in great measure of the original edition, and has moreover the titles and indexes which were only issued with the reimpression.

9109 BOMBAY MEDICAL AND PHYSICAL SOCIETY's Transactions, from the beginning in 1838 to 1857: FIRST SERIES, Vols. I—VIII, and X, 1838-50; NEW SERIES, Vols. I and III, 1851-56; together 11 vols. 8vo. four vols. in one, *the rest unbound, rare,* £5. 10s *Bombay,* 1838-57

9110 BOMBAY QUARTERLY REVIEW. QUARTERLY MAGAZINE and Review, Nos. 1, 4-6, 8-10, 12, 8 Nos. *Bombay,* 1850-53—BOMBAY QUARTERLY REVIEW, from the commencement, January 1855 to September 1858, Vols. I—VII, being Nos. 1 to 14, 1855-58—together 22 Nos. 8vo. £6. 10s *Bombay,* 1850-58
Containing many valuable articles on the Ethnology, Philology, and Natural History of India. Sets completed.

9111 BUIST (Dr. George, *late of Bombay, Member of several learned Societies*) Personal Memoranda, Miscellaneous Letters, *MS.;* Memoir with Testimonials, printed *Cupar,* 1846; and 2 Books of pencil Drawings, containing some curious sketches; with a lot of more than 100 volumes or Nos. of Tracts, Pamphlets, Opuscula, etc. printed at various towns and cities in India, etc., and collected by him, *including books printed at Agra, Bangalore, Poona, Lahore, Delhi,*

Colombo, Trevandrum, Madras, Roorkee, Allahabad, Bombay, Calcutta, Secunderabad, Aden, Cape Town, the Mauritius, £2. 16s   1830-60

Including several of the Bengal, Bombay, and North Western Government Reports, including valuable Historical and Geographical papers; Briggs' Gujarashtra, 2 parts; portion of the Delhi Sketch Book, 1855, with amusing illustrations in the style of Punch, *very rare;* Bulst's Manual of Physical Research; several numbers of the Cases and Reports of the Sudder Adawlut; Carter's Geography of South Arabia; Carter's Geology of India; Singhalese Vocabulary; Mauritius Meteorological Society's Transactions; Punjab Agra Horticultural Society; Bailey's Letters on Budhist Idolatry; McCosh's Topography of Assam; Ancient Reservoirs at Aden, etc.

9112 BUTTER's Topography and Statistics of Southern Oud'h, roy. 8vo. *maps, bds.* 3s 6d   *Calcutta*, 1839

9113 CALCUTTA Journal of Natural History, exhibiting the progressive discoveries in Indian Geology, Zoology, Botany, etc. conducted by JOHN McCLELLAND, W. GRIFFITH, and others, from the beginning in April 1840 to July 1847, being Nos. 1-30, or Vols. I.-VIII. pt. 2, (in Vol. IV. No. 15 is wanting), 8vo. *numerous plates, six volumes bd. in hf. calf neat, the rest in 5 Nos. sd. very rare,* £5. 15s
        Calcutta, 1841-47

This valuable periodical was completed in eight volumes.

9114 CALCUTTA REVIEW, from the beginning in 1844 to Dec. 1859, being Nos. 1—66 (without No. 39-40, intended for the Index). COMPLETE; together 33 vols. 8vo. 24 vols. *in hf. russia neat, the remainder in* 18 *quarterly parts, uncut,* £10.
        Calcutta and Serampore, 1844-59

9115 DIXON'S Sketch of MAIRWARA, origin and habits of the Mairs, their subjugation, civilization, etc. 4to. 32 *plates and large Maps, including a very large coloured Map on canvas, calf gilt, privately printed,* 21s   1851

9116 ELLIOT's Supplement to the Glossary of Indian Terms, (A—J, *all printed*) 2 Maps, 447 pp. *in Persian, Nagari, and Roman characters, bds.* 5s   *Agra*, 1845

9117 —————— another copy, *wormed at beginning and end,* 2s 6d   1845

9118 GLOSSARIES of Indian Terms. A collection partly MS. and partly consisting of printed Glossaries to Law Cases, containing an immense number of words and phrases from all the languages of India, in a stout folio parcel, 20s   1820-50

9119 HAMILTON's Account of the Kingdom of Nepal, and the territories annexed by the House of Gorkha, 4to. *map and plates, calf,* 5s   *Edinb.* 1819

9120 HEDAYA (The) or Guide; a Commentary on the Mussulman Laws; translated by order of the Governor-General and Council of Bengal, by Charles Hamilton, 4 vols. 4to. *bds.* £4.   1791

9121 —————— another copy, 4 vols. 4to. *wanting the last two leaves in Vol. I, bound,* £2.   1791

9122 HEYNE's Tracts, Historical and Statistical, on India, with account of Sumatra, etc. 4to. *maps and plates,* (pub. at £2. 2s) *bds.* 5s   1814

9123 HISTORICAL SKETCH of the Princes of India, 8vo. *bds.* 3s 6d   *Edinb.* 1833

9124 HUTTMANN's Abstract of State Trials at Jyepoor of Sunghee Jotha Ram and others, for a plot, roy. 8vo. *plan, bds.* 5s   *Calcutta,* 1837

9125 INDIA REVIEW and Journal of Foreign Science and the Arts, edited by Corbyn, Vol. III. 8vo. 700 and xiv pp. *numerous views, scientific plates, maps, and Authentic Portraits no where else to be found, boards,* EXCESSIVELY RARE, 25s   *Calcutta,* 1837

9126 INDIAN ANNALS of MEDICAL SCIENCE, from October 1854 to October 1857, being Nos. II.-VII, stout 8vo. *plates, sd. rare,* £2. 10s   *Calcutta,* 1854-56

9127 McCUDDEN's Oriental Eras, with chronol. notices of events connected with India and the East, 4to. *bd.* 7s 6d   *Bombay,* 1846

9128 MADRAS JOURNAL of LITERATURE and SCIENCE, edited by Messrs. Cole and Brown, Vols. I.-XVI, forming the FIRST SERIES, or Nos. 1-37 (wanting 32, 34 and 36) — NEW SERIES, Nos. 1-6, being Vols. I-III, in 6 parts, (forming Vols. XVII-XIX, or Nos. 40-45, of the entire series) — together 19 vols. 8vo. *with numerous plates of Hindoo Mythology, Antiquities, Geography, Natural History, Vols. I—IV bound in* 3, *hf. russia; the rest in bds. and sd.* £16. *Madras,* 1833-50

9129 —————— the same, Vols. I—XII only, 8vo. *half russia neat,* £8. 8s   1833-40

9130 MORLEY'S INDIAN LAW-REPORTS: ANALYTICAL DIGEST of all the Reported Cases decided in the Supreme Courts of Judicature in India, in the Courts of the Hon. East-India Company, and on Appeal from India, by Her Majesty in Council, together with an Introduction, Notes, illustrative and explanatory, and an Appendix, by William H. Morley, of the Middle Temple, Esquire, Barrister-at-Law, Member of the Royal Asiatic Society, and of the Asiatic Society of Paris, 3 vols. royal 8vo. (pub. at £10. 10s) *cloth,* £4. 4s   1850-52

PHILOLOGICAL WORKS. 503

9131 MORLEY'S Indian Law Reports. The same, 3 vols. roy. 8vo. *hf. calf,* £4. 14s 6d; *calf gilt,* £5. 1850-52
This valuable work throws a great light upon the various RACES OF INDIA, their Manners, Customs, and Prejudices, and it is the best " Picture of India as it really is " ever printed. An extensive Glossary of Indian Technical and other Legal Terms is added.
"If it be asked how the Law shall be ascertained when particular cases are not comprised under any of the general rules, the answer is this: that which well-instructed Brahmans propound shall be held incontestable law."
Menu, B. xii. v. 108.

9132 MONTGOMERY (R.) Statistical Report of the District of CAWNPOOR, roy. 4to. *many maps, showing the smallest Hamlets in that famous District, cloth, privately printed,* RARE, 27s *Calcutta,* 1849
A pattern volume of a good topographical work; the list of villages contains their names in Urdu and English, classification of the Population, etc.

9133 O'BRIEN's Glossary of Revenue Technicalities, in the vernacular language, 4to. *Persian and Roman character, sd.* 10s *Agra,* 1840

9134 ORME'S (Robt.) History of the Military Transactions of the British Nation in Indostan from 1745, with Dissertation on the Establishment made by Mahomedan Conquerors, 3 vols. 4to. *folding maps and plates, old cf. neat,* 20s 1763-78
This valuable historical work "occupies so vast a field, that every future historian of modern India must unavoidably trench, in a greater or less degree, upon his premises."—*Quarterly Review.*

9135 PHAYRE's Report on the administration of Pegu, 1855-58, 2 parts, roy. 4to. 7s 6d *Calcutta,* 1858, *Rangoon,* 1858

9136 (PRINSEP) Memoirs of Mohummud Ameer Khan, from the Persian of Busawun Lal, 8vo. *map and plan, bds.* 7s 6d *Calc.* 1832

9137 PUNJAB and NORTH-WESTERN PROVINCES, a Collection of Official Reports on Administration, Popular Education, Selections from Government Records, Public Correspondence, etc. 51 parts and vols. 8vo. and sm. 4to. 25s
Agra, Lahore, etc. 1850-58

9138 REPORTS on Projected Canals in the Delhi Territory, sm. folio, *about 50 leaves of engraved plans, surveys, etc.* 5s *Allahabad, ca.* 1845

9139 SELECTIONS from the RECORDS of the Government of India, published by authority, Nos. 1-3, 5, 7, 8 and Supplement, 9-12, 14-17, 19-21, 23; Geological Survey, Vol. I, part 1, and II, part 1, (Cuttack, Talcheer, and Bhundelcund); together 21 vols. or Nos. roy. 8vo. *numerous large maps, many of them coloured, cloth,* £2. 16s *Calcutta,* 1853-59
Each No. contains a special subject, so that there is no interruption of sense in the absence of any one of the series. The information is varied and valuable.

9140 SHAKESPEAR's Statistics of the North Western Provinces of Bengal, 1848— Comparative Tables of the District Establishments of the North West Provinces, 1853, 2 vols. roy. 8vo. 7s 6d *Calcutta,* 1848-53

9141 SLEEMAN's Report on the depredations of the Thug Gangs, stout 8vo. *map, bds.* 12s 1840

9142 TIPPOO SULTAN. DIROM's Campaign in India, 1792, *maps and plans of Seringapatam,* 1793—RENNELL's Memoirs of a Map of the Peninsula of India, *maps,* 1793—BEATSON's View of the War with Tippoo, *portrait, maps and plates,* 1800—3 vols. in 1, 4to. *hf. bd.* 7s 6d 1793-1800

9143 WILSON and NEWMARCK, Complete Index to the Laws and Regulations passed 1834-57, 4to. *cloth,* 7s 6d *Calc.* 1858

9144 INDIAN LAW and ADMINISTRATION. A collection of 15 volumes, 4to. and 8vo. *bound and unbound, upon the Legislation, the Government, the Revenue, etc. of India, a bargain,* 7s 6d *Madras and Calcutta,* 1826-51

PHILOLOGICAL WORKS.

9145 AMERICAN ETHNOLOGICAL SOCIETY'S Transactions, Vol. I-III, part 1, 8vo. *plates and cuts, sd. rare,* 38s *New York,* 1845-53
Comprises valuable Papers, including VOCABULARIES of the MEXICAN NATIONS.

9146 BIBLIA SACRA POLYGLOTTA, complectentia Textus Originales, Hebraicum, (cum Pentateucho Samaritano), Chaldaicum, Græcum, versionesque antiquas, Samaritanam, Græcam, Chaldaicam, Syriacam, Arabicam, Æthiopicam, Persicam, et Vulgatam Latinam, cum omnium translationibus Latinis, et apparatu, appendicibus, tabulis, &c. edidit BRIANUS WALTONUS, 6 vols. *fine portrait by Lombart, engraved title and other plates by* HOLLAR, *with the very* RARE ROYAL DEDICATION, 1657—CASTELLI, Lexicon Heptaglotton, Heb. Chald. Syr. Sam. Æthiop. Arab. et Pers. cum omnium Grammaticis, 2 vols. *portrait by Faithorne,* 1699—together 8 vols. roy. folio, *fine copy in the original old calf, rebacked,* £28. 1657-69
Priced, 1831, Thorpe, with both prefaces, £45.; 1831, Payne and Foss, vellum, £36.; 1837, Payne and Foss, with the Royal dedication, mor. £52. 10s, russia, £42. By auction a copy sold in 1855, with the dedication to Charles II., and the reprint, morocco, £35.

9147 BIBLE OF EVERY LAND, a History of the Scriptures in every Language in which translations have been made, with specimens of Characters, Alphabets, Ethnographical Maps, etc. 4to. *numerous maps and plates of specimens*, (pub. at £2. 2s) *hf. morocco*, 30s 1848

9148 LATHAM's Elements of Comparative Philology, stout 8vo. (pub. at 21s) *cloth*, 16s 1862

9149 OUSELEY'S ORIENTAL COLLECTIONS, consisting of dissertations, translations, etc. illustrating the History and Antiquities, the Arts, Sciences, and Literature of Asia, Vols. I, II, 4to. *several plates, calf gilt*, 21s 1797-98

9150 WELLESLEY (Dr. H.) Anthologia Polyglotta, a selection of versions in various languages, chiefly from the Greek Anthology, 8vo. 464 pp. *cloth*, 10s 1849

9151 WESTON's Conformity of the European Languages with the Oriental, especially Persian, sm. 8vo. *bd.* 5s 1803

9152 **Amharic.** ISENBERG'S Amharic-English and English-Amharic Dictionary, 2 vols. in 1, 4to. 216 and 218 pp. (pub. at £2.) *cloth*, 28s 1841

9153 ——— Amharic Grammar, roy. 8vo. *cloth*, 18s 1842

9154 **Anglo-Saxon.** ÆLFRIC SOCIETYS PUBLICATIONS, *the Complete Series;* the Homilies of Ælfric, parts 1-10—Poetry of the Codex Vercellensis, 2 parts—The Dialogues of Salomon and Saturn, 3 parts, edited by J. M. Kemble—together 15 parts, 8vo. £2. 2s 1843-48

9155 ANCIENT LAWS and Institutes of England, comprising Laws enacted under the Anglo-Saxon Kings, *Anglo-Saxon and English*, with the Laws of Edward the Confessor, William the Conqueror, and Henry I; Monumenta Ecclesiastica Anglicana, ancient Latin version of the Anglo-Saxon Laws, and a compendious GLOSSARY, etc. 2 vols. roy. 8vo. *cloth bds.* 30s 1840

9156 BASIL (St.) Hexameron, etc. Anglo-Saxon Version, *Anglo-Saxon and English*, by Norman, 8vo. *sd.* 3s 1849

9157 BEOWULF. Poems of Beowulf, the Travellers' Song, and the Battle of Finnes-Burh, *Anglo-Saxon and English*, with historical Preface, Glossary, and Philological Notes, by John Mitchell Kemble, 2 vols. 12mo. *fine copy in citron morocco, extra gilt edges*, £2. 16s 1833-37

9158 BOSWORTH'S Anglo-Saxon Dictionary, with a Preface on the Origin and Connection of the Germanic Tongues, a Map of Languages, and the Essentials of Anglo-Saxon Grammar, roy. 8vo. BEST EDITION, *calf*, £2. 12s 6d 1838

9159 ——— Compendious Anglo-Saxon and English Dictionary, 8vo. 278 pp. *treble columns, cloth*, 9s; *calf gilt*, 12s 1848

9160 CAEDMON's Metrical paraphrase of Scripture History, an illuminated Manuscript of the X century, in the Bodleian Library, by Ellis, 4to. 53 *quaint engravings of Saxon Art, hf. calf*, 10s 1833

9161 GOSPEL according to St. Matthew, *in Anglo-Saxon and Northumbrian versions*, 4to. *cloth*, 12s Cambridge, *University Press*, 1858

9162 HICKESII LINGUARUM VETT. SEPTENTRIONALIUM *(Anglo-Saxon. Moeso-Goth. Franco-Theotisc. Island.)* Thesaurus Grammatico-Criticus et Archæologicus, 3 vols. in 2, folio, *facsimiles and plates of Anglo-Saxon coins, old calf*, £4. 10s Oxon. 1703-5

9163 ——— the same, 3 vols. folio, *new calf gilt*, £5. 15s 1703-5

Sold in Horne Tooke's sale for £14. 10s, and in Willett's for £12. 12s; priced, 1836, Thorpe, £8. 8s; 1840 and 1848, Payne and Foss, £12. 12s.

9164 ——— the same, LARGE PAPER, *size of the pages* 17¼ *inches by* 11, *portrait, facsimiles and plates of Coins, very fine copy in the original calf*, £6. 6s Oxon. 1703-5

Copies on really Large Paper are very rare. Priced by Payne and Foss, £14. 14s; a very fine copy in morocco, £30.; priced, 1837, £12. 12s; Heath's copy fetched £15. 4s 6d; Brockett's, £26. 15s.

"This work has had so many just praises given to it at home and abroad, that few English readers can be strangers to its contents."—NICOLSON. Many valuable portions of this grand work are taken from original Saxon MSS. now lost. An indispensable work for consultation to the student of Anglo-Saxon Literature, containing Icelandic, Anglo-Saxon and Gothic Grammars and Dictionaries; also valuable Anglo-Saxon fragments. "Hickes displays throughout great erudition, unwearied industry, and sometimes successful investigation; it is enriched with numerous engravings of Ancient Monuments, Runic Inscriptions, various documents, and specimens of Poetry that are not elsewhere to be found."

9165 HOARE (Sir R. C.) REGISTRUM WILTUNENSE, *Saxonicum et Latinum*, ab anno 892 ad 1045, cum notis J. I. Ingram, S. Turner, T. D. Fosbroke, T. Phillipps, R. C. Hoare, *plate*, 1827—CHRONICON VILODUNENSE, sive de vita et miraculis S. Edithæ Regis Edgari filiæ Carmen vetus Anglicum, ed. Black, 1830, 2 vols. in 1, large folio, *neat in russia*, £2. 2s 1827-30

Only 100 copies printed, all for private distribution. Priced, Thorpe, £3. 13s 6d; Macpherson, £4. 4s; Rodd, £3. 3s; 1841, £4. 4s.

9166 KLIPSTEIN's Analecta Anglo-Saxonica, with Ethnological Essay and notes, 2 vols. 12mo. 876 pp. *cloth*, 10s *New York*, 1849
9167 ORMULUM (The) now first edited, *in Anglo-Saxon*, from the original MS. with notes and Glossary, by White, 2 vols. 8vo. 3 *facsimiles*, (pub. at 36s) *bds.* 18s *Oxford*, 1852
9168 RASK's Anglo-Saxon Grammar, enlarged edition, by Thorpe, 8vo. *facsimile, fine paper, bds. rare*, 15s *Copenhagen*, 1830
9169 **Arabic.** LANE'S Arabic-English Lexicon: an Arabic-English Lexicon, derived from the best and most copious Eastern Sources; comprising a very large Collection of Words and Significations omitted in the Kamoos, with ample Grammatical and Critical Comments, and Examples in Prose and Verse, by Edward William Lane, Vol. I part 1, impl. 4to. 367 *pp. treble columns, cloth*, 25s 1863

To be completed in eight parts.

"Son livre est un *Thesaurus* au il traite chaque mot selon son sens primitif et ses nuances et applications, en citant pour chaque cas ses autorités et des exemples."—MOHL, *Rapp. Ann. Journ. As.* 1863.

9170 **Armenian.** AUCHER'S Armenian-English and English-Armenian Dictionary, 2 vols. in 1, very stout impl. 8vo. 983 *and* 640 *pp. double columns, calf*, £2. *Venice*, 1821-25
9171 **Celtic.** LHUYD'S Archæologia Britannica, the Languages, Histories, and Customs of the Original Inhabitants of Great Britain from collections in Wales, Cornwall, Bas-Bretagne, Ireland and Scotland, folio, *fine tall copy, calf*, £2. 10s *Oxf.* 1707
9172 **Chinese.** ESOP'S Fables, *in Chinese*, by Mun Mooy Seen-Shang, in the Chinese character, with the Nankin Mandarin and the Canton pronunciation both expressed in Roman characters, a double translation, and rules for pronunciation, (by THOM), roy. 4to. 104 *pp. sd.* RARE, 25s *Canton*, 1840
9173 MARSHMAN'S Chinese Grammar, with a dissertation on the Characters and Colloquial Medium, and Appendix of the Ta-Hyoh, *Chinese and English*, 4to. £2. *Serampore*, 1814
9174 MEDHURST (W. H.) Chinese English and English-Chinese DICTIONARY, containing all the words of the Chinese Imperial Dictionary, according to Radicals, 4 vols. 8vo. *bds. very rare*, £10. 10s *Batavia*, 1842, *and Shanghae*, 1847
9175 ——— the same: Chinese-English Dictionary, 2 vols. 8vo. 1486, 30, *and* 28 *pp. rare*, £5. 5s *Batavia*, 1842-43
9176 MORRISON (Dr. R.) Dictionary of the Chinese Language, 3 parts in 5 vols. roy. 4to. *bds.* £9. *Maçao*, 1815-23
9177 ——— Chinese Grammar, 4to. *in Chinese and Roman characters, bds.* 30s *Serampore*, 1815
9178 ——— View of China for Philological purposes, Chinese Chronology, Geography, Customs, etc. 4to. *bds.* 10s 6d *Macao*, 1817
9179 SHUCK's Portfolio Chinensis, a collection of State Papers, *Chinese and English*, with notes, etc. 8vo. *Chinese bds.* 7s 6d *Macao*, 1840
9180 **Danish.** WOLFF'S Danish-English Dictionary, 1779—BERTHELSON English-Danish Dictionary, 1754—2 vols. in 1, very stout sm. 4to. *treble columns, calf gilt, fine copy*, 36s 1754-79

The most copious English-Danish Dictionary.

9181 **Gaelic.** ARMSTRONG'S Gaelic-English and English-Gaelic Dictionary, with Gaelic Grammar, 4to. (pub. at £3. 13s 6d) *calf neat*, 30s 1825
9182 **Greek.** LIDDELL and SCOTT's Greek-English Lexicon, fourth edition, augmented, stout 4to. 1654 *pp. double columns*, (pub. at 31s 6d) *new in cloth*, 26s 6d *Oxford*, 1861
9183 YONGE's English-Greek Lexicon, 4to. 558 pp. sq. 8vo. *cloth*, 18s 1861
9184 **Hebrew.** NORDHEIMER'S Hebrew Grammar, with Grammatical Analysis of selections from the Scriptures and Exercises in Composition, 3 vols. large 8vo. *cloth, very rare*, £2. 16s 1845-38
9185 **Hindustani.** SHAKESPEARE'S Dictionary, Hindustani and English, and English and Hindustani, *fourth (the last edition), greatly enlarged*, very stout 4to. (pub. at £5. 5s) *bound*, 30s 1849
9186 ——— the same, with new title, 4to. *cloth*, £2. 1861
9187 **Italian.** BARETTI'S Italian-English and English-Italian Dictionary, with Grammar of each language, new edition, enlarged by Thomson, 2 vols. 8vo. *treble columns, cloth*, 20s 1839

9188 **Pali.** CLOUGH'S Pali Grammar, with Vocabulary, 8vo. *cloth,* 25s
Colombo, 1824
9189 **Persian.** JOHNSON'S Dictionary of Persian, Arabic and English, stout impl. 4to. 1240 *pp. treble columns,* (pub. at £4.) *cloth,* £3. 6s ; *bound in russia extra, and enclosed in morocco case,* £4. *London,* 1852
9190 RICHARDSON'S English-Persian-Arabic Dictionary, edited with additions by Wilkins, roy. 4to. *hf. bd. neat,* £2. 10s 1810
9192 **Romaic.** LOWNDES'S Modern-Greek-English and English-Modern-Greek Dictionary, 2 vols. 8vo. *the title to Vol. II mended and inlaid, calf neat,* £3. 8s *Corfu,* 1827-37
9193 **Sanscrit.** HAUGHTON (Sir Graves C.) Bengali and Sanskrit Dictionary explained in English, with an Index serving for a reversed Dictionary, bound in 2 vols. 4to. (pub. at £7. 7s) *calf gilt,* 36s 1833
9194 MANAVA-DHERMA-SASTRA, or the Ordinances of Menu, according to the Gloss of Calluca, comprising the Indian System of Duties, religious and civil, translated by Sir W. Jones, new edition, with notes by HAUGHTON, *in Sanscrit and English,* 2 vols. 4to. (published at £4. 4s) *hf. russia, not uniform in size,* £2. 16s 1825
9195 MENU SANHITA, the Institutes of Menu, with the Commentary of Killuka Bhatta, *all in Sanscrit,* 2 vols. 8vo. *calf gilt,* 36s *Calcutta,* 1830
9196 PANINI: his place in Sanskrit Literature, by GOLDSTÜCKER, impl. 8vo. xvi. and 268 pp. *cloth,* 12s 1861
9197 PRINSEP's English-Sanscrit Vocabulary, roy. 8vo. 104 *pp. doub. cols. cl.* 5s 1847
9198 WILLIAMS (Monier) Sanskrit Manual, 16mo. *morocco,* 2s 6d 1862
9199 **Sindhi.** WATHEN'S Grammar of the Sindhi Language, with Vocabulary *of nearly* 3000 *words,* 4to. *maps, and plates of characters and facsimiles, calf gilt, rare,* 32s 1836
9200 **Sunda.** RIGG'S Dictionary of the Sunda Language of Java, 4to. 16 and 542 pp. *bds.* 18s *Batavia,* 1862
9201 **Swedish.** WIDEGREN'S Swedish-English Dictionary, *Stockholm,* 1788 —SERENIUS, English-Swedish Dictionary, *Nykoping,* 1757—together 2 vols. sm. 4to. *forming the best Swedish and English Dictionary, about* 1800 *pp. double columns, hf. calf,* 36s 1757-88
9202 **Virginian.** ELIOT (John, *the Apostle of the Indians*) Indian Grammar begun, sm. 4to. *the title only, reprinted in exact facsimile,* 10s
Cambridge (New England), 1666 [*London,* 1863]
9203 **Welsh.** EVANS (Rev. D. S.) English-Welsh Dictionary adapted to the present State of Science and Literature, 2 vols. stout 8vo. 1962 *pp. double cols. cloth,* 30s *Denbigh,* 1852-58
9204 EVANS (W.) New English-Welsh Dictionary, thick 8vo. interleaved with many important notes by Canon Newling, *calf,* £2. 2s *Carmarthen,* 1771
The above was Canon Newling's copy. It is interleaved throughout, and full of his MS. notes containing much philological information, the result of many years study. At the end will be found some curious derivations of the names of towns.
9205 GAMBOLD's Welsh Grammar, a short and easie introduction to the Welsh tongue, 16mo. *old calf, rare,* 15s *Carmarthen,* 1727
9206 PUGHE (W. OWEN) Welsh-English Dictionary, with Welsh Grammar prefixed, second edition, 2 vols. *portrait,* 1832—WALTERS, English-Welsh Dictionary, with dissertation on the Welsh Language, third edition, 2 vols. 1828—together 4 vols. roy. 8vo. *forming the best Welsh and English Dictionary, calf neat, not quite uniform,* £4. 4s *Denbigh,* 1828-32
9207 WELSH COMPARATIVE DICTIONARY: a MS. Collection of Words in the Welch Language which are similar to Words, in other Languages, of the same Signification, 8vo. *nearly* 400 *pp. calf,* £3. 3s *circa* 1783
The author of this work, the Rev. Canon NEWLING, was indefatigable in his researches among all authors from whom any information on this subject could be gained. At the beginning of the MS. he gives a list of the rare works he has consulted, such as the "Dictionarium Anglo. Brit. Gwilym, Salisburi 1547, Dictionnaire Celtique de Bullet, &c. &c. Below I give a few comparisons from this unpublished and valuable Manuscript, which would have proved extremely useful to Bopp and Zeuss:

Abl, abal, able, habilis.
Cantwr, singer, chanter, canter
Cwpl, cwplus, copula, couple.
Dwbl, double, duplex.
Egr, eager, acer, acid, aigre
Gwic, "Wich," vicus, village.

Gwiber, viber, viper, vipera.
Gwyth, vectis, Isle of Wight.
Hagr, ugly, hag, haggard.
Mold, model, mold.
Pantri, pantry, panarium.
Sicer, secure, securus, sure.

9208 WELSH MANUSCRIPT SOCIETY:
  a. LIBER LANDAVENSIS, Llyfr Teilo, or Ancient Register of the Cathedral Church of Llandaff, in Latin, with English Translation and Notes, by Rev. W. J. Rees, roy. 8vo. *facsimiles, cloth, scarce,* 28*s* Llandovery, 1840
  b. IOLO MANUSCRIPTS. A Selection of Ancient Manuscripts in Prose and Verse, from the Collection made by E. Williams, Iolo Morganwg, with English Translations and Notes by his Son Taliesin Williams ab Iolo, roy. 8vo. *plate, cloth,* 28*s* Llandovery, 1848
  c. REES (W J.) Lives of the Cambro-British Saints of the Fifth and immediate succeeding Centuries, royal 8vo. *frontispiece and facsimiles, cloth,* 28*s* 1853
  d. DOSPARTH EDEYRN Davod Aur: Ancient Welsh Grammar, compiled in the 13th Century by Edeyrn the Golden-tongued; with y Pum Llyfr Kerddwriaeth or Rules of Welsh Poetry, and translation and notes by the Rev. J. Williams Ab Ithel, 8vo. *(price to non-members,* £2. 2*s) cloth,* 16*s* 6*d* Llandovery, 1856
  e. MEDDYGON MYDDFAI, MEDICAL PRACTICE OF RHIWALLON and his Sons; with the Llyn-y-Fan, or Legend of the Lady of the Lake: edited by Williams Ab Ithel, with notes and translations by John Pughe, *cloth,* 16*s* 6*d* 1862
9209 WELSH MS. Sermons: a MS. of 350 pages containing 37 Sermons in the Welsh Language, preached by the Rev. D. S. Davies, circa 1818, 12mo. *calf,* 7*s* 6*d* 1818

9210 FROUDE'S History of England from the fall of Wolsey to the death of Elizabeth, Vols. I—VIII, 8vo. (pub. at £5. 12*s*) *cloth, new,* £4. 13*s* 6*d* 1858-64
9211 ——— the same, Vols. VII, VIII, 8vo. *cloth, just published,* 24*s* 1864

SCIENCE AND NATURAL HISTORY.

9212 AMERICAN JOURNAL of Science and Arts, conducted by Professor SILLIMAN, B. Silliman, Jr., and James D. Dana, SECOND SERIES, November 1849 to September 1861, being Vols. VIII pt. 4 to XXXII, or Nos. 24 to 96 inclusive, (wanting Vols. XV-XVI) *numerous plates,* bound in 11 vols. stout 8vo. *hf. calf, and a part,* £5. 5*s* New Haven, 1849-61
9213 AINSLIE's Materia Medica of Hindoostan, and Artisan's and Agriculturist's Nomenclature, sq. 8vo. *the names given in various Indian languages, with numerous MS. Memoranda of Col. Graham, hf. bd.* 7*s* 6*d* Madras, 1813
9214 ——— the same, second edition, 2 vols. 8vo. *the names of the Ingredients in Tamul, Cingalese, Arabic, Persian, Malay, Cochin-Chinese, French, German, Italian, Spanish, Chinese, etc. poor copy, hf. calf,* 16*s* 1826
9215 ANDERSON's Dura Den (*Fifeshire*), a Monograph of the Yellow Sandstone and its remarkable Fossil remains, roy. 8vo. *coloured plates and woodcuts, cloth,* 7*s* 6*d* 1859
9216 AUDUBON and BACHMAN's VIVIPAROUS QUADRUPEDS of North America, TEXT, 3 vols. impl. 8vo. 155 BEAUTIFULLY COLOURED *plates, these completing the large folio series, elegantly bound in blue morocco extra, sides tooled, gilt edges,* £10. 10*s* New York, J. J. Audubon, 1851-54
9217 BARTON (W. C. P.) Flora of North America, 3 vols. 4to. 106 COLOURED PLATES, *hf. green morocco, gilt tops, uncut,* £3. 3*s* Philadel. 1821-3
9218 BELL'S History of British Quadrupeds, including the Cetacea, 8vo. *nearly* 200 *fine woodcuts, hf. calf, out of print,* 27*s* 1837
9219 BENTHAM (G.) Handbook of the British Flora, a description of flowering plants and ferns, sm. 8vo. *calf extra,* 10*s* 1858
9220 BEWICK'S History of BRITISH BIRDS, Vol. I, roy. 8vo. FIRST EDITION, LARGE PAPER, *about* 200 *fine woodcuts, bds.* £2. 10*s* Newcastle, 1797
9221 BOOTT'S (Francis) Illustrations of the GENUS CAREX, stout folio, 200 *large plates, hf. morocco extra,* £5. 5*s* 1858
9222 BOSTON Journal of Natural History, papers by the Boston Society of Natural History, Vols. VII Nos. 1-3, 3 parts, 8vo. 6 *plates, sd.* 10*s* Boston, 1859-62
9223 BRITISH MUSEUM PUBLICATIONS. GÜNTHER's Catalogue of Acanthopterygian Fishes in the B. M. Collection, 4 vols. 8vo. *cloth, price* 37*s* 6*d* 1859-62
9224 WALKER'S List of the Specimens of Lepidopterous Insects in the B. M. Parts 1—27, 12mo. *sd. price* £5. 0*s* 6*d* 1854-63
9225 WESTWOOD'S Catalogue of Orthopterous Insects in the B. M. Collection, Part I.: Phasmidæ, roy. 4to. 48 *plates, cloth, price* £3. 1859

9226 BROWN (R.) Prodromus Floræ Novæ Hollandiæ et Insulæ Van Diemen, Vol. I. (*all published*) sm. 8vo. *hf. calf, rare,* 25s   1810

9227 CAMBRIDGE PHILOSOPHICAL SOCIETY's Transactions, from the beginning, Vols. I.—III. 4to. *numerous Scientific and Geological plates, some coloured, hf. calf, scarce,* £3. 16s   *Cambridge,* 1822-30

9228 CAUTLEY (Sir T. Proby) Report on the GANGES CANAL WORKS, from their commencement until the opening of the Canal in 1854, 4 vols. being 2 vols. 8vo. of text, *with numerous plates and cuts, cloth;* 1 vol. 4to. of Appendices, *plates, etc. cloth;* and 1 vol. atlas folio *of* 66 *immense folding Plans of Bridges, Canals, Elevations and other public works in India, hf. morocco, uncut,* £12.   1860

This great work, which was undertaken upon a vast and liberal scale, cost £50. in the production of each single copy; but was by direction of Government sold at the rate of £21. The impression is almost exhausted, nearly the entire number of copies having been sent to India and dispersed there.

9229 CURTIS'S BOTANICAL MAGAZINE, from the commencement in 1786 to 1859, as follows: 1786-1859

    SERIES I, COMPLETE, Vols. 1—53; *plates,* 1—2704, with text; Index 1 vol. [1786]   1793-1826.

    The last volume (53) ends also Dr. John Sims' Series, called the NEW SERIES, which begins with Vol. 43.

    SERIES II, COMPLETE, conducted by S. Curtis and Sir W. J. Hooker, Vols. 54 —70; or New Series, Vols. I—XVII: *plates,* 2705—4131, with text and INDEX to the SECOND SERIES—17 vols.   1827-44

    SERIES III, by Sir W. J. Hooker, Vols. 71—85, or Third Series, I—XV. *plates,* 4132—5158, with text   1845-1859

    This, the scarcest portion, was published at 2 guineas per volume, making 30 guineas.

    Together, First and Second Series, 71 vols. *uniform in hf. green morocco, gilt edges;* Third Series, in Numbers, £50.   1786-1859

9230 DILLENII HISTORIA MUSCORUM; in qua circiter 600 species distribuuntur, stout 4to. *original and best edition,* 85 *plates with upwards of* 1000 *figures, green morocco extra, gilt edges, by Hering,* 18s   *Oxon.* 1741

9231 —— the same, large 4to. LARGE FINE PAPER, *hf. calf,* 20s   1741

Scarce, only 250 copies were printed, and of these very few on Large Paper. Priced, 1854, £3. 10s; fetched at Edwards' sale, morocco, £13. 2s 6d; Treuttel's, morocco, £9.

9232 DUPPA's Illustrations of the Lotus of the Ancients, impl. 4to. *frontispiece and* 11 *coloured plates, cloth, privately printed,* 12s   1816

9233 FITZROY'S (Admiral) Weather Book, a manual of practical Meteorology, second edition, augmented, 8vo. 16 *plates,* (pub. at 15s) *cloth,* 12s   1863

9234 FOLKARD'S Wild Fowler, a Treatise on Ancient and Modern Wild Fowling, historical and practical, stout 8vo. *numerous fine plates,* (pub. at 21s) *cloth,* 16s 6d   1859

9235 FORSTER (J. R. et G.) Characteres Generum Plantarum, in itinere ad Insulas Australes collectarum, roy. folio, LARGE PAPER, 78 *plates, old calf,* 12s   1776

9236 GOULD'S Mammals of Australia, Parts I-XII. impl. folio, 180 *beautiful coloured plates* (pub. at £37. 16s) *Mr. Bell's original subscription copy in parts,* £25.   1845-60

9237 —— the same, Part XIII. (*completing the work*) impl. folio, 15 *coloured plates, bds. price* £3. 3s   1863

9238 —— Introduction to the Trochilidæ, or Humming Birds, 8vo. *cloth,* not published, 12s   1861

9239 GREVILLE'S (R. K.) SCOTTISH CRYPTOGAMIC FLORA, or coloured figures and descriptions of Cryptogamic plants belonging chiefly to the order Fungi: and intended to serve as a continuation of English Botany, 6 vols. large 8vo. 360 *coloured plates of Fungi, hf. green morocco, gilt edges,* £6.   *Edinburgh,* 1823-28

9240 HARRISON'S FLORICULTURAL CABINET and Florist's Magazine, from the beginning in March 1853 to December 1856, 24 vols. 8vo. *with nearly* 300 COLOURED *plates, containing about* 1000 *figures* (pub. at about £9.) *hf. morocco,* £3. 3s   1833-56

9241 HASKOLL (W. D. *late Resident Engineer on the Smyrna and Aidin Railway*) RAILWAY CONSTRUCTION, Second Series, also Railways in the East and all high thermometric Regions, 2 vols. imp. 8vo. 91 *folding plates of Elevations, Plans, Sections, Implements, etc. with French and English scales* (pub. at £3. 3s) *new in cloth,* £2. 16s   1864

9242 HERSCHEL (Sir J. F. W.) Results of Astronomical Observations made, 1834-38, at the Cape of Good Hope, impl. 4to. 18 *plates,* (pub. at £4. 4s) *presentation copy, cloth, scarce,* £2. 12s 6d   1847

Printed at the expense of the Duke of Northumberland.

SCIENCE AND NATURAL HISTORY.

9243 HILL (Sir J.) Horti Malabarici pars prima adornata per Van Rheede, etc. nunc secundum species Linnæanas, ed. Hill, 4to. 57 *plates, morocco, 7s 6d* 1774
9244 HOOKER (J. D.) Rhododendrons of Sikkim-Himalaya; being an Account of the Rhododendrons recently discovered in the Mountains of Eastern Himalaya, edited by Sir W. Hooker, 3 parts, impl. folio, *with* 39 *large* COLOURED *plates by W. Fitch*, (pub. at £3. 16s) *unbound*, £2. 2s 1849-51
9245 HOOKER (Sir W.) Second Century of Ferns, being figures with descriptions of 100 rare and imperfectly known Ferns, stout impl. 8vo. 100 FINELY COLOURED PLATES (pub. at 48s) *hf. morocco, gilt top, uncut*, £2. 1864
9246 ———— Genera Filicum, or Illustrations of the Genera of Ferns, from the original drawings of Bauer, Parts 1, 5-7, 10-12, impl. 8vo. *with* 70 *coloured plates, sd.* 10s 1838-42
<small>The work was complete in 12 parts with 120 plates, each part pub. at 12s.</small>
9247 ———— Species Filicum, being descriptions of the known Ferns, 3 vols. roy. 8vo. *with* 210 *plates* (pub. at £5. 14s) *hf. green morocco, gilt tops, uncut*, £3. 10s 1846-60
9248 HULL'S (Jonathan) Description and Draught of a new invented Machine for carrying Vessels or Ships out of or into Harbour, against wind or tide, 12mo. *plate of a steamship, hf. morocco*, 28s 1737 (1855)
<small>A privately printed re-impression (only 39 copies taken) of the rare original work, which fetched £7. 12s 6d at Gardner's sale. It contains the first printed description of a steamboat.</small>
9249 HUTTON'S Philosophical and Mathematical Dictionary, 2 vols. 4to. *best edition*, 41 *plates, and many diagrams*, (pub. at £6. 6s) *hf. russia*, 28s 1815
9250 JAMESON (R.) Mineralogy of the Scottish Isles, with observations made in a tour through the mainland, 2 vols. in 1, 4to. *maps and plates, hf. morocco, uncut, top edge gilt*, 10s Edinb. 1800
9251 JOHNSTON (G.) Introduction to Conchology, or Elements of the Natural History of Molluscous Animals, stout 8vo. *numerous woodcuts* (pub. at 21s in bds.) *hf. calf*, 20s Van Voorst, 1850
9252 JOHNSONI (Th.) Mercurius Botanicus, sive itinerum descriptio, ed. Ralph, 2 parts in 1 vol. sq. 8vo. *hf. vellum*, 9s 1849
9253 KIRBY and SPENCE, Introduction to Entomology, 4 vols. 8vo. *portraits and* 58 *plates, many coloured, calf gilt*, 28s 1818-26
9254 LEACH'S (Wm. E.) ZOOLOGICAL MISCELLANY, being descriptions of new, or interesting Animals, illustrated by NODDER, 4 vols. in 2, roy. 8vo. 150 *finely coloured plates, hf. morocco, uncut,* VERY RARE, £3. 16s 1814-17
9255 LEWIN'S Natural History of Lepidopterous Insects of New South Wales, 4to. 18 *beautifully coloured plates, on grounds, and interleaved,* LARGE PAPER, *medium size, fine copy in russia extra, from Miss Currer's library*, £2. 16s 1805
9256 LINDLEY'S Genera and Species of ORCHIDEOUS PLANTS, from the Sketches of Bauer, 4 parts complete, impl. 4to. 40 *large and finely coloured plates* (pub. at £6.) *sd.* £5. 1830-34
<small>The fourth part completed this work.</small>
9257 LINDLEY'S Swan River Botany: Appendix to Edwards's Botanical Register, Vols. 1-23, consisting of a complete Index, 64 pp. together with a Sketch of the Vegetation of the Swan River Colony, 60 pp. impl. 8vo. *with* 9 *coloured plates containing* 18 *coloured figures of plants, and* 8 *woodcuts*, (pub. at 10s 6d) reduced to 5s 1839
9258 LINDLEY'S SERTUM ORCHIDACEUM, royal folio, *frontispiece and* 49 *plates*, £3. 10s 1840
9259 ———— the same, the 50 PLATES COLOURED, *Mr. Gauci's, the artist's own copy, coloured with extra care*, £7. 10s 1840
<small>Both copies without text.</small>
9260 LINDLEY and HUTTON, Fossil Flora of Great Britain, or figures and descriptions of Vegetable Remains found in a fossil state, 3 vols. 8vo. 240 *plates, new in cloth, out of print*, £6. 6s 1831-37
9261 LINNEAN SOCIETY'S Proceedings from the commencement in November 1838 to October 1863: Proceedings, 1838-55, 2 vols.—Journal of the Proceedings, Vols. I.-VII. being Nos. 1-27, with the Supplements—together 9 vols. 8vo. (pub. at about £5. 15s) *eight vols. bd. in cloth, uncut, the rest in* 7 *Nos.* £3. 5s 1838-63
9262 LONG'S Astronomy, 2 vols. roy. 4to. LARGE PAPER, *plates, calf*, 15s 1742-84
<small>The second volume of this work is a bibliographical curiosity; the publication was begun in 1764, and brought to a close in 1784; the first date appears on the title, the latter on the last leaf.</small>
9263 MADRAS OBSERVATORY. TAYLOR'S Result of Astronomical Observations for the years 1831-39, Vols. I.—V. (*wanting* IV. 1836-37) 4 vols. impl. 4to. *sd.* 10s Madras, 1832-39

9264 MAGNETIC and METEOROLOGICAL OBSERVATIONS: Toronto Observatory, Vol. I. 1840-42, by Sabine, 1845; St. Helena Observatory, Vol. II. 1844-49, by Sabine, 1860; 2 vols. stout roy. 4to. *plates*, (pub. at £4. 4s) *cloth*, 20s   1845-60

9265 MAURITIUS ROYAL SOCIETY of Arts and Sciences, Transactions from September 1847 to August 1849, 2 parts (being Vol. I. pt. 2, and Vol. II. pt. 1) 8vo. *plates, sd.* 5s   *Mauritius*, 1849-50
Each part contains the transactions and proceedings for a year; and two parts form a volume. These parts contain a variety of information upon general and local scientific subjects, and include also Ethnological disquisitions on the Malagasy, Malay, and Polynesian Races: some of the papers are in English, some in French.

9266 MINING REVIEW and Journal of Geology, Mineralogy, and Metallurgy, edited by English, from April 1831 to July 1835, Nos. V, VI, VII, 8vo. *plates, sd.* 10s   1831-35

9267 MOORE (Thomas) Illustrations of ORCHIDACEOUS PLANTS, a series of figures representing the principal groups, with descriptions and directions for cultivation, stout roy. 8vo. 100 COLOURED PLATES, (pub. at £3. 10s) *hf. morocco, gilt tops, uncut*, 36s   1857

9268 MURCHISON'S SILURIAN SYSTEM, founded on Geological Researches, in various Counties of England and Wales, with Descriptions of the Coal Fields, and Overlaying Formations, 2 vols. roy. 4to. *geological maps, engravings, and plates of Fossils, with the very rare large Map in 4to. case* (pub. at £8. 8s) *sd.* £7. 7s   1839

9269 —— GEOLOGY OF RUSSIA in Europe and the Ural Mountains, by Murchison, Verneuil, and Keyserling; Vol. I. Geology: Vol. II. Paléontologie (*in French*), 2 vols. roy. 4to. 7 *Maps and Sections*, 12 *Views, and* 53 *plates of Fossil Remains, and numerous woodcuts*, (pub. at £8. 8s) *cloth,* £5. 15s   1845
Contents: Vol. I. Geology, with Views, plates of Corals and 7 large Maps. Vol. II. Palæontology, 50 plates.

9270 NORTH (Roger) Treatise on Fish and Fish Ponds, roy. 4to. 18 *beautifully coloured plates of Fish, by* ALBIN, *hf. morocco, gilt edges*, 21s   (1794)

9271 OVERMAN (F.) The Manufacture of Iron in all its various branches, and an Essay on the Manufacture of Steel, 8vo. 150 *cuts, cloth*, 10s   *Philadelphia*, 1850

9272 OWEN (Professor) on the Archetype and Homologies of the Vertebrate Skeleton, 8vo. *plates, cuts and tables, cloth, rare*, 25s   *Van Voorst*, 1848

9273 —— On Parthenogenesis, 8vo. *plate, cloth*, 7s 6d   1849

9274 —— On the Nature of Limbs, 8vo. *plates, cloth, rare*, 14s   1849

9275 —— Lectures on the COMPARATIVE ANATOMY and Physiology of the INVERTEBRATE ANIMALS; delivered at the Royal College of Surgeons, 2nd edition, 8vo. *numerous woodcuts*, (pub. at 21s) *cloth*, 17s   1855

9276 PETIVERI (Jacobi) Opera Historiam Naturalem spectantia, or Gazophylacium, containing several thousand figures of Birds, Beasts, Reptiles, Insects, Fishes, Plants, Fossils, Minerals, &c. &c. with Latin and English names, 2 vols. folio, *to which are added a number of scarce tracts, printed on broad sheets, between the years* 1693 *and* 1727, *and folded in at the end of Vol. II, completing all he ever wrote on Natural History, nearly* 300 *plates, containing* 10,000 *articles, plain morocco, rare,* £3. 3s   1764
Priced, 1836, J. Bohn, £7. 7s. "The Publications of Petiver have been of essential service to Zoology and Botany, and are, even now, as works of reference, in high repute; but they have become scarce. His Museum was purchased by Sir Hans Sloane for £4000, a great sum in those days, and is now deposited in the British Museum."
Haworth.

9277 PHARMACEUTICAL SOCIETY'S JOURNAL and TRANSACTIONS, from the beginning in 1841 down to the end of 1863; FIRST SERIES, edited by Jacob BELL, 18 vols. *hf. calf*, with Index to Vols. I—XV, 1 vol. *cloth*; NEW SERIES, Vols. I—V No. 6, two vols. *hf. calf, the rest in Nos.*—together 24 vols. 8vo. *portraits and cuts,* (pub. at £14. in Nos.) twenty vols. *uniformly bound in hf. calf neat, one vol. in cloth, and thirty Nos.* £5.   1842-63

9278 PHILLIPS (John) Illustrations of the Zoology of Yorkshire, a description of the Strata and Organic remains, 2 parts: the Yorkshire Coast, and the Mountain Limestone District, 2 vols. 4to. *coloured Geological Map, and* 49 *plates of Sections and Fossils, some coloured*, (pub. at £4. 4s) *bds.* £2. 4s   1835-36

9279 RASHLEIGH'S (Philip) Specimens of British Minerals, with descriptions of each article, 2 vols. in 1, large 4to. 54 *finely coloured plates, hf. russia, uncut, scarce,* 25s   1787-1802
Priced, 1834, Pickering, £3. 13s 6d; 1843, J. Bohn, £3.—Part I only priced, 1836, £3. 3s. The second part is often wanting.

9280 ROXBURGH'S PLANTS OF THE COASTS OF COROMANDEL, Vols. I—II, in 1 vol. atlas folio, *with* 200 FINELY COLOURED PLATES, *fine copy in whole bound russia gilt,* VERY RARE, £7. 10s   1795

9281 ——— the same, Vol. III, part 3, 4, atlas folio, *coloured plates* 251-300, *bds.* RARE, £2. 10s   1819
9282 ROXBURGH'S Flora Indica, or Descriptions of Indian Plants, edited by Carey, with additions by Wallich, Vol. I, 8vo. *MS. memoranda, hf. bd.* 15s
Serampore, 1820
This edition which was completed in 2 vols. contains Wallich's "invaluable notes and additions," which were necessarily omitted in the second.
9283 ——— the same, second edition, by Carey, 3 vols. 8vo. *bds.* £4. 4s   *ib.* 1832
9284 **ROYAL SOCIETY.** PHILOSOPHICAL TRANSACTIONS of the Royal Society of London, from 1824 to 1861 inclusive, 4to. *sewed*, £21. 1824-61
9285 PROCEEDINGS of the Royal Society from the beginning. ABSTRACTS of the Papers printed in the Philosophical Transactions, and communicated to the Royal Society, 1800-54, 6 vols. 1832-54—PROCEEDINGS, in continuation of the Abstracts, from February 1854 to June 1863, (being Nos. 1—56, or Vols. VII—XII, pt. 8), 6 vols. 1856-63—together, 12 vols. 8vo. *plates*, (pub. at £5. 10s in *Nos.*) eleven vols. *hf. russia, and eight Nos.* £3. 10s   1832-63
9286 ROYLE'S Illustrations of the Botany of the Himalayas and the Flora of Cashmere, *Supplementary Number*, (Part XI) impl. 4to. 2 *plates, sd.* 12s   1840
9287 RUSSELL (Dr. P.) Account of Indian Serpents, 46 *plates*, 1796—CONTINUATION, 42 *plates*, 1801·9—together 2 vols. in 1, roy. folio, *with* 88 *coloured plates, hf. bd.* VERY RARE, £14.   1796-1809
9288 SAMOUELLE's Entomological Cabinet, being a Natural History of British Insects, 2 vols. 16mo. 144 *coloured plates* (pub. at £2. *in Nos.) hf. calf*, 24s   1833-34
9289 SOWERBY (James) Coloured Figures of English Fungi or Mushrooms, with descriptions, 3 vols. sm. folio, *complete with the scarce* SUPPLEMENT, 440 *coloured plates, hf. calf*, £14.   1797-1809
COLLATION: Vols. I-III, 400 plates and Index; Supplement, plates 401-440. There is no plate 427, the figures being represented on plate 425; and plate 438 is on plate 420.
9290 SOWERBY (J. and G. B.) Genera of Recent and Fossil Shells, Nos. II-XXI, and XXXVIII-XLII, together 25 monthly Nos. 8vo. *with* 155 BEAUTIFULLY COLOURED PLATES, (pub. at £7. 10s) £2. 10s   *ca.* 1820-22
9291 SPRY's Suggestions received by the Agricultural Society of India for the cultivation of useful and ornamental Plants, 8vo. *cloth*, 5s   Calcutta, 1841
9292 VAN DER HOEVEN's Handbook of Zoology, translated from the second Dutch edition by Clark, 2 vols. 8vo. 24 *plates*, (pub. at £3.) *cloth, new*, £2. 2s 1856-68
9293 VICTORIA PHILOSOPHICAL INSTITUTE's Transactions, edited by Macadam, Vol. IV pt. 2, (September-December, 1859) 8vo. *maps, plates (some coloured) and facsimile, bds.* 10s   *Melbourne*, 1860
This volume completes the proceedings of the Institute.
9294 VOIGT, Hortus Suburbanus Calcuttensis: a Catalogue of Plants cultivated at the E. I. Co.'s Botanical Gardens, Calcutta, by Griffith, roy. 8vo. *cl.* 27s *Cal.* 1845

Wight's Publications on Indian Botany :
PUBLISHED BY THE AUTHOR HIMSELF AT GREAT EXPENSE IN MADRAS.

9295 WIGHT.—ICONES PLANTARUM INDIÆ ORIENTALIS; or Figures of Indian Plants. By Dr. Robert Wight, F.L.S. Surgeon to the Madras Establishment, 6 vols. with the scarce GENERAL INDEX, royal 4to. 2101 *plates, including all those given in the author's* "ILLUSTRATIONS" *and* "NEILGHERRY PLANTS," *but plain instead of coloured,* (pub. at £27. 10s), *cloth*, £12. 12s   Madras, 1838-56
"A most important work, with 2101 invaluable representations of Indian Plants."
H. CLEGHORN, *compiler of the General Index to Wight's Icones*.
"This is not the place to dwell on the extraordinary exertions in the cause of Science of the author of this great work, which is the best proof of his wonderful energy, and shows what can be accomplished by perseverance under apparently insurmountable obstacles. At the period of the publication of the earlier numbers, the art of Lithography was in a very rude state in India, and the Plates are consequently very imperfect; but in the latter volumes the improvement is great, and the outline Drawings are admirably reproduced. The Volumes form the most important contributions, not only to Botany, but to Natural Science, which have ever been published in India, and *they have been of the greatest service to us throughout our labours.*"

"It is admitted that Dr. Wight has accomplished a great work, which is as essential to the student of the Indian Flora, as Sowerby's English Botany is in Britain."
HOOKER AND THOMSON, *in the Introductory Essay to the Flora Indica.*
SOLD SEPARATELY:

Vol. II. with 418 *plates*, 4to. 1840-42, £5.
Vol. III. with 326 *plates*, 4to. 1843-47, £6.
Vol. IV. with 459 *plates*, 4to. 1848-50, £6.
Vol. V. with 299 *plates*, 4to. 1852, £4.
Vol. VI. with 181 *plates*, 4to. 1853, £2. 10s
* Sets completed at a reduced rate.

9296 WIGHT.— ILLUSTRATIONS OF INDIAN BOTANY; or Figures Illustrative of each of the Natural Orders of Indian Plants, described in the Author's "Prodromus Floræ Peninsulæ Indiæ Orientalis," but not confined to them. By Dr. R. Wight, F.L.S. Surgeon to the Madras Establishment, 2 vols. 4to. *containing* 205 COLOURED PLATES, *cloth, only a few copies left,* (pub. at £9. 9s) £6. 6s   Madras, 1838-50

SOLD SEPARATELY:

Vol. II. containing 104 *coloured plates*, £4. 12s   Madras, 1841-50
Odd Parts may also be obtained to complete Sets.

9297 WIGHT.—SPICILEGIUM NEILGHERRENSE; or a Selection of Neilgherry Plants, drawn and coloured from Nature, with brief descriptions of each ; some General Remarks on the Geography and Affinities, and occasional Notices of their Economical Properties and Uses. By Dr. Robert Wight, F.L.S. 2 vols. 4to. *with* 202 COLOURED PLATES, (pub. at £6.) *cloth, only a few copies left,* £5. 5s   Madras, 1846-50

Vol. II. containing 100 *coloured plates*, separately, £3.

9298 WIGHT.—PRODROMUS FLORÆ PENINSULÆ INDIÆ ORIENTALIS; containing abridged Descriptions of the Plants found in the Peninsula of British India, arranged according to the Natural System. By Drs. R. Wight, F.L.S. and Walker Arnott, Vol. 1, 8vo. (pub. at 16s), *cloth*, 7s 6d   Lond. 1834

9299 WIGHT.—CONTRIBUTIONS TO THE BOTANY OF INDIA. By Dr. Robert Wight, F.L.S. 8vo. (pub. at 7s 6d), *cloth*, 5s   London, 1834

The whole set, of which only a few can still be made up, viz.

	Published at
The Icones Plantarum Indiæ, 6 vols. 4to. 2101 *plates*	£27 10 0
The Illustrations of Indian Botany, 2 vols. 4to. 205 *coloured plates*	9 9 0
The Neilgherry Plants, 2 vols. 4to. 202 *coloured plates*	6 0 0
The Prodromus, 1 vol.	0 16 0
The Contributions, 1 vol. 8vo.	0 7 6

Instead of £44 2 6, for £21.

* Imperfect sets completed.

9300 WOOD'S INDEX ENTOMOLOGICUS, a complete illustrated Catalogue of the Lepidopterous Insects of Great Britain, new and revised edition, with SUPPLEMENT, by Westwood, roy. 8vo. 59 *beautifully coloured plates, containing* 1944 *figures*, (pub. at £4. 4s) *hf. morocco, gilt top, uncut*, £2. 16s   1854

9301 YARRELL'S History of British Fishes, with the Supplement, 2 vols. 8vo. ORIGINAL EDITION, *nearly* 400 *beautiful woodcuts*, (pub. at £3. 8s) *cloth*, £2. 8s   Van Voorst, 1836-39

THE KNOWSLEY MENAGERIE.

9302 GLEANINGS FROM THE MENAGERIE AND AVIARY at KNOWSLEY HALL, edited by J. E. GRAY, impl. folio, 17 *beautifully* COLOURED *plates from the series of drawings made by* MR. E. LEAR   Knowsley, 1846

CONTENTS OF THIS VOLUME.

Plate.
1 Vitoe. Nyctipithecus felinus.
2 Whiskered Yarke. Pitheciar ufiventer.
3 Red Macauco. Lemur rufus.
4 Yagouarondi. Leopardus Yagouarondi.
5 Banded Mungous. Mungos fasciatus.
6 Javan Squirrel. Sciurus Javensis.
7 Quebec Marmot. Arctomys Empetra.
8 Eyebrowed Guan. Penelope superciliaris.
9 Plicated Guan. Penelope pilcata.

Plate.
10 Piping Guan. Penelope pipilis.
11 Purplish Guan. Penelope purpurescens.
12 American Emu. Rhea Americana.
13 Wattled Crown Crane. Balearica regulorum.
14 Stanley Crane. Scops Paradisea.
15 Maned Goose. Chenalopex jubata.
16 Eyebrowed Rollulus. Rollulus superciliosus.
17 Eyed Tyrse. Tyrse Argus.

GLEANINGS from the MENAGERIE and AVIARY at KNOWSLEY HALL: **HOOFED QUADRUPEDS**, edited by J. E. GRAY, of the British Museum, impl. folio, 62 *fine plates, many very superbly* COLOURED, *from drawings by W. Hawkins* *Knowsley*, 1850

The Plates of this volume are selected from the series of Drawings of Ungulated Quadrupeds made by Mr. Waterhouse Hawkins for the Right Honourable the Earl of Derby, chiefly from the animals living in his Lordship's Menagerie at Knowsley Hall. They have been lithographed by Mr. W. Hawkins, and coloured under his superintendence.

The Plates are accompanied by Lord Derby's notes on their habits, and by a brief description of the specimens of the various Genera, chiefly derived from the study of the animals at Knowsley, or in the British Museum.
J. E. GRAY.

Together 2 vols. impl. folio, 79 *large plates, many of them finely* COLOURED, *cloth, very rare,* £10. 10s   1846-50

PRINTED FOR PRIVATE DISTRIBUTION amongst the friends of the late Earl of Derby, to whose zeal for Natural History these volumes will remain a lasting monument. The editorship of Dr. Gray of the British Museum is a further guarantee for the excellence of this work, which is indeed the most correct and the most beautiful, especially as far as the MAMMALS are concerned, printed in Europe. The few single volumes which have at rare intervals turned up at sales, have fetched high prices. The above is the first complete copy ever offered for sale.

A most valuable book, printed for PRIVATE CIRCULATION amongst the friends of the late Earl of Derby, and not hitherto offered for sale. To all Public Libraries this work is necessary, as the plates present most accurate delineations of rare Birds and Mammals, made by first-rate Artists from living specimens. The plates and the text in the great work of Cuvier et Geoffroy St. Hilaire, "Histoire naturelle des Mammifères, 3 vols. folio, 1824-35," are inferior in beauty and accuracy to the above;—the Knowsley Menagerie forms a necessary complement to Cuvier and Geoffroy St. Hilaire.

Immediate application will be necessary to secure a copy at the price of ten guineas cash.

9303 GRAY'S FIGURES OF MOLLUSCOUS ANIMALS, selected from various authors; etched for the use of students, by Maria E. Gray, 5 vols. 8vo. *portrait and* 381 *most delicately executed plates* (pub. at £3.) *cloth*, 36s   1859

Now entirely out of print; the tracings from which these Etchings of Molluscous Animals have been taken, were originally made by Mrs. Gray, for my use, with the view of their being added to my collection of figures of Shells, and to aid me in their arrangement. Hoping that others may find such a collection of figures—*many of them copied from expensive works, and brought together from sources not easily accessible to Conchologists*—as useful as they have been to myself.—J. E. GRAY, *British Museum.*

THEOLOGICAL WORKS

From the library of the late **THOMAS HAVERS**, *Esq., of Thelton Hall, Norfolk.*

9304 ADVOCATE of CONSCIENCE. LIBERTY, or an Apology for Toleration, 12mo, *old English blue morocco, gilt edges,* 15s   *no place or name of printer,* 1673

9305 BYBLE (The) IN ENGLYSHE, that is to say the contēt of al the holy scripture both of yᵉ Olde and Newe Testamēt, with a prologe thereinto made by the Reverende father in God, Thomas Archbysshop of Cantorbury, stout folio, 𝔅lack letter, *with woodcuts, sold as per collation below,* £18. 18s   MDXL.

A COPY OF CRANMER'S CELEBRATED FIRST EDITION OF THE HOLY SCRIPTURES; the two leaves of Prologue being from the edition of *July*, 1540; having a large ornamented letter at the commencement of Romans. with the initials E. W. (Edward Whitechurch) within the same wood block, and title to the New Testament designed by Holbein, with the Arms of Thomas Lord Cromwell not defaced, though defective in the under portion of that leaf, and also fol. LXVI marked XLVI.

No title; Prologue, 2 leaves (the third wanting); Names of the Bookes, 11 af; Genesis, etc., leaves i—iii, vi—lxxxiv, the last deficient; title to second parte, 1 leaf; Job, etc. leaves ii—cxviii, cxx—cxxv (marked cxxiii); Psalmes, etc. ii—cxxxi (marked cxxxii); Esdras, etc. ii—lxxx; New Testament, title, 1 leaf, deficient; Matthew, etc., leaves ii—cl. Thus there are about twelve leaves, including titles, altogether wanting. I am enabled to state, on the high authority of F. Fry, Esq., that the entire of this interesting volume is of the FIRST edition, April 1540, with the exception only of the two Prologue leaves which are from the edition of July.

The whole of the titles are wanting in the Old Testament except that to the "second parte of the Bible;" and some other leaves are wanting, but the volume HAS VERY LARGE MARGINS, AND IS FINE AND SOUND with very few exceptions.

9306 BYBLE (The Whole) faythfully translated into Englyshe by Myles COVERDALE, sm. 4to. 𝔅lack letter, *imperfect,* containing folios LXXXIX to CCCXCIX, or from Deut. xxiii to end of Malachy, *cut close, sold with all faults, old calf gilt,* £3. 16s   *Printed for Andrewe Hester (at Zürich by C. Froschover)* 1550

This second edition of Coverdale's Bible is quite as rare as the first in folio; Lea Wilson's copy fetched £38. a copy, supplied in facsimile, fetched at Sotheby's in 1857, £28. 10s.

9307 BIBLE (The Holie) faithfully translated into English out of the avthentical Latin, with Annotations, etc. by the English College at Doway, 2 vols. in 1, very stout sq. 8vo. *in the original old calf,* £3. 3s   *Doway*, 1609-10

Priced, 1840, J. Bohn, morocco, £7. 7s. This is the first edition of the English Roman Catholic version; the translators were Cardinal Allen, Gregory Martin, and Richard Bristow.

9308 NEWE TESTAMENT of our Sauiour Jesus Christe faithfully translated out of the Greeke, with the notes and expositions of the darke places therein, sm. 4to. *title in red and black with portrait of Edward VI,* 𝔅lack letter, *numerous woodcuts, wanting the last leaf, russia,* VERY RARE, £10.   *Richard Jugge* (1566)

A copy of this edition fetched at Pickering's sale, £15. 15s. COLLATION: Title, Almanack, Epistle to Edward VI. and Calendar, 8 leaves; Table, Reckoning of the Yeares, Exhortation, 9 leaves; Description of Palestine, with map, and Life of Matthew, 1 leaf; text, 𝔄 i to 𝔔 q 3. 𝔔 q 4 is wanting, which should contain the conclusion of the table of Epistles, and the colophon of the book.

9309 NEW TESTAMENT, translated by the English College at Rhemes; set forth the second time by the same College returned to Doway, with New Tables of Heretical Corruptions, and annotations augmented, sq. 8vo. *old calf, scarce,* £2. 2s *Antwerp, Vervliet,* 1600
The second edition is as scarce as the first.

9310 [CARWOLD (Thomas)] Labyrinthus Cantuarensis, or Dr. Lawd's Labyrinth, being an answer to his relation of a Conference between himselfe and Mr. Fisher, by T. C. sm. folio, *old calf,* 10s *Paris,* 1658
This is a Roman Catholic work written by a Jesuit named Thomas Carwold.

9311 MANUALE ad usum Ecclesiæ SARISBURIENSIS, 4to. *printed in* 𝔤𝔬𝔱𝔥𝔦𝔠 𝔩𝔢𝔱𝔱𝔢𝔯 *black and red type, with the* MUSIC *noted upon red lines, wanting title, first leaf, and leaves* 115-118, *and* 120-127, *somewhat wormed, in the original boards, binding gone,* VERY RARE, £3. 3s *Paris, Fr. Byrckman,* 1515

9312 MANUALE SECUNDUM USUM insignis ac preclare ECCLESIÆ SARŪ optimis typis impressum, sm. folio, 𝔤𝔬𝔱𝔥𝔦𝔠 𝔩𝔢𝔱𝔱𝔢𝔯, *printed in red and black, with the* MUSIC *noted upon four red lines, two large woodcuts and several woodcut initials, the first few pages and the last page a little wormed, otherwise a good, large, and perfect copy in the original oak boards, covered with leather,* £21.
Antwerp, Endow ; venūdantur Londini apud P. Kaetz, 1523

RARE; such specimens of the old Roman Catholic Divine Service in England are daily becoming scarcer. The entire book is in Latin, with the significant exception of the " Majoris Excommunicationis Articuli generales." These are given in plain English, and extend over twelve pages, full of mortal denunciations against those who should invade the rights and privileges of " al holi moder chyrche." Independently of the curious fact illustrated here, that the Church, always incapable of concession, never clung to her power with more tenacity than when it was declining, the language itself is a curious study, being fully a hundred years in arrear of the time.

SPANISH LITERATURE.

9313 **Language:** ALDRETE, Origen y principio de la lengua Castellana o Romāce, sq. 8vo. *first edition, engraved title, and facsimiles of ancient writing, vellum,* 6s *Roma,* 1606
9313* ——— the same, sm. folio, *best edition, calf,* 16s *Madrid,* 1674
9314 CABRERA (Rámon) Diccionario de Etimologias de la lengua Castellana, 2 vols. in 1, stout sq. 8vo. 1154 *pp. Spanish* MOROCCO, *uncut,* 18s *ib.* 1837
9315 CAMPUZANO, Diccionario de la lengua Castellana, stout 16mo. 1157 *pp. double cols. hf. russia,* 10s *ib.* 1852
9316 CONNELLY (T.) y T. HIGGINS, Diccionario de las dos Lenguas Española ó Inglesa; Spanish-English and English-Spanish Dictionary, 4 vols. 4to. *calf,* 36s *ib.* 1797-98
9316* ——— another copy, 4 vols. 4to. *slightly wormed, bound,* 20s 1797-98
The Dean of Peterborough's copy fetched £3. 8s. The best and most complete Spanish and English Dictionary, comprising all the Idioms, Proverbs, Marine Terms, Metaphorical Expressions, &c. in both languages.

9317 COBARRUVIAS OROZCO, TESORO de la LENGUA CASTELLANA o Española, stout sm. folio, *title inlaid, calf neat,* 20s *Madrid,* 1611
9317* ——— the same, *fine copy in old calf gilt, or limp vellum,* 28s 1611
9318 DICCIONARIO DE LA LENGUA CASTELLANA, en que se explica el verdadero sentido de las Voces, con las phrases, los Proverbios ó refranes, etc. compuesto por la REAL ACADEMIA Española, 6 vols. folio, BEST EDITION, *very fine copy, calf,* £5. 5s *Madrid,* 1726-39
The above is the first and best edition of the Spanish Academy Dictionary, as the *subsequent* editions have been reduced to *one volume,* and omit the quotations and authorities. All the celebrated Ancient Spanish *Proverbs* are contained in this fine work.
" Ce Dictionnaire est très recherché et les exemplaires en sont devenus rares. Ou trouve au commencement du premier vol. une préface relative à la composition de ce grand ouvrage, trois discours sur l'origine de la Langue Castillane, sur les etymologies et sur l'orthographe, avec une liste des auteurs choisis par l'academie pour servir d'autorité à ses decisions."—*Brunet, Nouvelles Recherches.*
" Cet ouvrage est devenu tres-rare, même en Espagne, ou il se vend actuellement fort cher."—SANTANDER.

9319 DICCIONARIO de la lengua Castellana, compuesto por la Real Academia Espanola, *sexta edicion,* folio, THICK PAPER, 869 *pp. treble columns, calf,* 24s 1822
9320 ——— the same, *8va edicion,* sm. folio, *calf,* 18s *ib.* 1837
9320* ——— the same, *novena edicion,* sm. fol. *hf. morocco,* 36s ; or *calf,* £2. *ib.* 1843
9321 FRANCESON, Grammatik der Spanischen Sprache, 8vo. *sd.* 3s *Leipzig,* 1850
9322 LEBRIXA (Antonio de) Grammatica sobre la Lengua Castellana, roy. 8vo. *fine copy in calf,* 18s *Salamanca,* 1492 (1770)
Priced, 1826, Salva, 36s. "This edition though a counterfeit is scarce."—*Salva.*

9322*McHENRY's Spanish Grammar, Exercises, Key to the Exercises, and Synonyms, 4 vols. 12mo. *bd.* 8s 1826-36

9323 NEUMAN and BARETTI'S Spanish-English and English-Spanish Dictionary, *fourth edition*, 2 vols. 8vo. *calf*, 12s   1823
9323*———— the same, *fifth edition*, enlarged and revised by Seoane, 2 vols. 8vo. 1650 pp. *double columns*, (pub. at 32s) *bds.* 20s   1837
9324 NUÑEZ DE TABOADA, Diccionario Frances-Español y Español-Frances, 2 vols. 8vo. *hf. calf*, 7s 6d   *Paris*, 1826
9325 OLLENDORFF'S NEW METHOD of Learning to Read, Write, and Speak the Spanish Language, with Appendix, Practical Rules for Spanish Pronunciation, and Models of Correspondence; designed for self-instruction, by Velasquez and Simonné, with the KEY TO THE EXERCISES, 2 vols. 12mo. *bd.* 10s 6d   1854
9325*———— THE KEY, separately, 12mo. *cloth*, 4s   1859
9326 PERCYVALL (R.) Bibliotheca Hispanica, containing a Grammar with a Dictionarie in Spanish, English and Latine, sq. 8vo. *one wormhole extending through great part of the Dictionary, otherwise a good clean copy in the original calf*, 10s   1591

9326*SALVÁ, Grammatica de la lengua Castellana, stout 12mo. *sd.* 4s   *Paris*, 1835
9327 SANFORD (John) Propylaion, or an Entrance to the Spanish Tongue, sm. 8vo. *with folding table of Verbs, cut close, smooth red morocco gilt, from Mr. Ford's library, with his autograph*, 24s   1611
9328 **Mexican.** ALDAMA Y GUEVARA, Arte de la Lengua Mexicana, 12mo. *fine clean copy, old calf gilt*, £4. 10s   *Imprenta de la Bibliotheca Mexicana*, 1754
RARE. COLLATION: Title, Approbations, Licences, and Prologue, Table of Contractions, and Vocabulary, 9 leaves; De el Alphabeto, etc., 73 leaves, or Signatures A to T 2, in fours, (except A which has only three leaves).
9329 MOLINA (Fray Alonso de) VOCABULARIO EN LENGUA MEXICANA y Castellana, 2 vols. in 1, sm. fol. *last leaf neatly mended, russia, gilt edges*, £20.   *Mexico*, 1571
9329*———— the same, sm. folio, *a very tall copy, slightly wormed, eight or nine words in the imprint defective, red morocco, by Bedford*, £18.   1571
A copy was priced by Thorpe in 1832, £28. which had cost Lord Kingsborough £52. 10s; another priced by Stargardt, in Berlin, 1858, 150 Thalers; fetched at Sotheby's, 1857, *cut close and mended*, £15. 15s; in 1860 at Puttick's, £16. The first of the above copies cost Mr. Heber £31. 10s in the original parchment cover.
The first and most complete of any of the dictionaries of the American languages. It is cited by Thomas in his History of Printing in America, as a great literary curiosity, it being one of the earliest books printed in the New World. See also Dr. Cotton, Horne, Tenante, and other bibliographical writers.
9330 **Tagala.** NOCEDA (El P. Juan de) y el P. Pedro de SAN LUCAR, Vocabvlario de la Lenga Tagala, trabaxado por varios svgetos doctos y graves, sm. folio, *fine copy in limp vellum*, £5.
          Manila, Imprenta de la Comp. de Jesus, por N. de la Cruz Bagay, 1754
COLLATION: Title; Epistles, 'Aprobacion,' etc. 6 leaves; Errata, 2 leaves; Prologo, 6 leaves; *Vocab. Tagala-Hispano*, pp. 1-619; 'Apendix,' 34 pp.: *Vocab. Hispano Tagalog*, 190 pp.
I sold a copy in 1861 for £12. 12s.
"Volume fort rare: vendu 243 fr., Salle Silvestre, 1826; £5. 15s 6d, Heber; 150 fr. Raetzel."—BRUNET.

9330*ABULCACIM TARIF, Historia del Rey Don Rodrigo traducida de Arabigo per Mig. de Luna, 2 vols. in 1, sq. 8vo. *vellum*, 5s   *Madrid*, 1676-5
9331 ACOSTA (Christoval, Affricano) Tratado en Loor de las Mugeres, con varias Historias, 8vo. *engraved title, hf. russia, good copy, rare*, 20s   *Venesia*, 1592
9331*ACOSTA (J.) Historia natvral y moral de las Indias, elementos, metales, plantas, y animales dellas; ritos y guerras de los Indios, sq. 8vo. *fine copy, vellum*, 20s   *Madrid*, 1608
9332 ACUNA (H. de) el Cavallero determinado, 12mo. *the rarest Spanish translation of Olivier de la Marche's romance*, 12 WOODCUTS *the full size of the page, title and five leaves in MS. calf*, 16s   *Barcelona*, 1565
9333 ———— another edition, sm. 8vo. *with the full series of* 20 *well-designed woodcuts, good large copy in vellum*, £2. 12s 6d   *Salamanca*, 1573
This edition like the other two printed in Spain is very rare.
9334 ———— another edition, sm. 8vo. *with the* 20 *illustrations engraved on steel, fine copy in old calf gilt, rare*, £2. 2s   *Anvers, Plantin*, 1591
"One of the best editions of the Cavallero Determinado."—*Ticknor*, 1849, I, 458.
9335 ALCAZAR (Bartholeme, de la Comp. de Jesus) Vida Virtude y Milagros de San Julian, segundo Obispo de Cuença, folio, 2 *plates after* PALOMINO, *vellum*, 24s   *Madrid*, 1692
Rare; not mentioned by Brunet nor in Salva's catalogues. The history extends from 1030 to 1690.
9336 ALDRETE (B.) Varias Antiguedades de España, Africa, y otas provincias, sm. 4to. *calf or vellum*, 12s   *Amberes*, 1614
A learned work on Phœnician, Syriac, and Arabic Philology, the origin of the Spanish Language, etc.
9337 ALEMAN (Matteo) Primera Parte de Guzman de Alfarache, sm. 4to. 392 pp. *wormed in the margin, calf*, 5s   *Lisboa*, 1600

9338 ALEMAN, Primera Parte de Guzman de Alfarache, sm. 4to. *a rare edition, not mentioned by Brunet nor in Salva's catalogues, vellum,* 12s *Sevilla,* 1602
9339 ———— Vida de Guzman de Alfarache, 1ra. parte, 16mo. *vel.* 6s *Tarrag.* 1603
9340 ———— Primera Parte de la Vida del Picaro Guzman de Alfarache, 1604—Segunda Parte por M. Luxan de Sayavedra (Juan Marti), 1604—2 vols. in 1, 16mo. *vellum, very scarce,* 18s *Brucellas,* 1604

The first is a rare edition of the primera parte. The segunda parte is not by Aleman, but by Juan Marti under the assumed name of Matheo Luxan de Sayavedra. Aleman himself complained of having been, through a prodigal communication of his papers, robbed of his original materials; and in the title-page of his own 'segunda parte' says; "Let the reader take notice, that the second part published before this is none of mine, and that this is the only one I recognize."

9341 ALEMAN, Primera y segunda Parte de Guzman de Alfarache, 2 vols. in 1, stout sq. 8vo. *vellum, rare,* 25s *Burgos,* 1619

Fetched, 1824, Dr. Hawtrey's sale, calf, £2.

9342 ———— Guzman de Alfarache, sq. 8vo. *antique calf,* 7s *Madrid,* 1661
9343 ———— Vida y Hechos de Guzman de Alfarache, sq. 8vo. *vellum,* 9s *ib.* 1750

"The Spanish Proteus, which, though writ
But in one tongue was formed with the world's wit;
And hath the noblest mark of a good booke,
That an ill man doth not securely looke
Upon it; but will loathe or let it passe
As a deformed face doth a true glasse."—*Ben Jonson.*

"The first edition of the first part appeared, Madrid, 1599, and two editions besides in the same year. The most ample portraiture of the *Cantariberas,* or the gayer one of Picaros, that is to be found in Spanish Literature. It was very successful, falling in with the vices and humours of the times of the loose Court of Philip III. after the hypocrisy and constraint of the last dark years of Philip II. The genuine second part appeared, Valencia, 1605. The Second part, published 1603, under the name of Mateo Luxan de Saavedra, though not without literary merit, is a forgery."—*Ticknor,* 1849, *III. p.* 26.

9344 ALFONSO (Mosen, Aragones) Historia de la Donzella Teodor, sm. 4to. *rude woodcut title and illustrations, a scarce Romance, bds.* 25s *Sevilla, Pastrana,* 1641
9345 ALFONSO EL SABIO, LAS SIETE PARTIDAS, cotejadas con varios Codices antiguos por la Real Academia, 3 vols 4to. *hf. russia neat,* 25s *Madrid,* 1807
9345*———— the same, 3 vols. 4to. *sd. uncut, new,* 28s 6d 1807

Best edition of this famous and remarkable code, with the variants at foot of each page. It is a monument of Language as well as of Legislation. See a long description in Purton Cooper's Catalogue of the Spanish Law books in Lincoln's Inn Library.

9346 ALFONSO el Sabio, Opúsculos Legales, cotejados con códices antiguos, por la Real Academia: Espejo de los Derechos, Fuero Real, etc. 2 vols. 4to. *sd.* 15s 1836
9347 ALVAREZ Y BAENA, Hijos de Madrid, ilustres en Santidad, Armas, Ciencias, y Artes, Diccionario Historico alfabetico, 4 vols. sq. 8vo. *calf gilt,* 25s *ib.* 1789-91

"A book whose materials are abundant and important, especially in what relates to the literary history of the Spanish capital."—*Ticknor.*

9348 ANTONIO (Nic.) Bibliotheca Hispana, vetus et nova, sive Hispani Scriptores qui ab Octaviani Augusti ævo ad 1684 floruerunt, curante Franc. Perezio Bayerio, 4 vols. folio, *fine copy in Spanish calf gilt,* £4. *Matriti,* 1778

An invaluable body of information concerning Spanish books and authors. It must be considered as the keystone of every Spanish library. Dr. Dibdin in his "Library Companion," regrets its rarity, and values the small paper at £12. 12s.

9349 APIANO (Alexandrino Sophista) los Triumphos de (traducion del bachiller Juan de Molina), very sm. folio, Black letter, *woodcut of Arms on title, first and last pages surrounded by woodcut border, margins cut very close, Spanish coloured calf, rare,* 18s *Valencia, Juan Joffre,* 1522
9350 ———— the same, sm. folio, *the woodcut of Arms on title coloured, a very fine tall copy in Spanish calf gilt,* £2. 12s 6d 1522

Priced, 1826-9, Salva, £3. "In the preface to this work we find a very long and interesting account of the disturbances of Valentia at the time that it was printed."—*Salva.*

9351 ARETINO (Pietro) Coloquio de las Damas, traduzido de lengua Toscana por Fernan Xuarez, 16mo. *fine copy in calf,* VERY RARE. £2. 10s 1548

COLLATION: Title within woodcut border, and preliminary matter, 12 leaves; text leaves 13-94; Sonnet, 3 pages. Of the three preliminary pieces addressed to the Reader, one of six pages contains the "Determinacion de la Duda si es pecado de leer libros prophanos come este Coloquio."

9352 ARGOTE DE MOLINA (Gonçalo) Nobleza del Andaluzia, folio, *numerous large woodcuts of Arms, calf gilt,* £2. 10s *Sevilla, Fernando Dias,* 1588
9352*———— another copy, *some leaves mended, some supplied in MS., many of the Arms emblazoned, vellum,* 20s 1588
9353 ARIOSTO, Orlando Furioso, traduzido en Romance Castellano por Don Jeronimo Urrea, primera y SEGUNDA parte, con el verdadero Sucesso de la famosa batalla de Roncesvalles por Espinosa, 2 vols. sq. 8vo. *numerous woodcuts, fine copy in Spanish calf gilt,* £2. 12s 6d *Anvers,* 1558-56

It is very uncommon to meet the second part by Espinosa in conjunction with the first as above. The second alone sold in Stanley's sale for £10. 10s; it is not a translation, but an original Spanish supplement to Ariosto.

9354 ARIZ (Luys) Historia de las Grandezas de la Ciudad de Avila, sm. folio, *cuts of Arms, borders a little wormed, calf,* 9s *Alcala de Henares,* 1607

9355 ARIZ (Luys) Historia de las Grandezas de la Ciudad de Avila, sm. folio, *with frontispiece*, FINE COPY *in Spanish morocco*, 25*s*   *Alcala de Henares*, 1607
Priced by Salva, £2. 2s. The fourth part of this work treats exclusively upon the Nobility of Avila.

9356 ARIZA (D. Juan de) El Dos de Mayo, novela historica (de la Guerra de la Independencia), 12mo. *portraits, hf. russia*, 5*s* 6*d*   *Madrid*, 1846

9357 ARRIAZA (J. B. de) Poesias Patrioticas, sm. 8vo. *with* 17 *engraved pages of Music, bds.* 2*s* 6*d*   *Londres, Bentley*, 1810

9358 AUGUSTIN (Arzobispo de Tarragona) Dialogos de las Armas, i linages de la Nobleza de España, con la vida del autor par Mayans i Siscar, 2 vols. in 1, sq. 8vo. *portrait, hf. bd.* 18*s*   *Madrid*, 1734

9359 AVILA Y CUNIGA, Comentario de la Guerra de Alemaña hecho de Carlo V., 1546-47, 12mo. *map,* 2 *large plans of Battles, and cuts, original broken calf binding*, 36*s*   *Anvers*, 1550
The first edition was printed in 1548, but that of 1550 is the best. "This is an account of the campaigns of Charles V. in Germany, in 1546-47, prepared probably from information furnished by the Emperor himself, and bearing external evidence of having been composed at the very time of the events they record, and the whole is evidently the work of one of the few personal friends Charles V. ever had."—*Ticknor*, 1863, III. p. 174.

9360 AYGUALS DE IZCO, (W.) Maria la Hija de un Jornalero, novela original, 2 vols. in 1, impl. 8vo. 8,14 *pp.* 200 *woodcuts, hf. morocco*, 12*s* 6*d Madrid*, 1845-46

9361 —— La Marquesa de Bellaflor, ó el Niño de la Inclusa, historia-novela original, 2 vols. in 1, impl. 8vo. 1000 pp. *numerous illustrations, hf. red morocco*, 14*s*   *ib.* 1846-47
Sensational novels, full of incident, and in the style of Eugène Sue.

9362 AYORA (Gonzalo) Cartas, 1503, con su vida, 12mo. *sd.* 2*s*   *ib.* 1794

9363 BACALLAR Y SANNA, Commentarios de la Guerra de España e historia del Rey Phelipe V, el animoso, desde el principio de su Reynado hasta la Paz de 1725, 2 vols. in 1, folio, *original edition, vellum*, 9*s Genova, Garvizza, n. d.* (1729)

9364 —— Comentarios de la Guerra de España, e Historia de Phelipe V, 1700-1725, 2 vols. *Genova, s. a.*—Memorias politicas, y militares para servir de continuacion, por Campo-Raso, 1726-42, 2 vols. *Madrid*—together 4 vols. sm. 4to. *best edition, Spanish calf*, 20*s*   *Genova y Madrid*, 1729-93
Priced by Salva £2. 2s. "Ouvrage fort estimé, surtout sous le rapport militaire."—*Brunet*. This edition is preferred to the folio, and contains the best text of these interesting Memoirs. One volume was originally printed at Madrid, but suppressed in consequence of its revelations adverse to the honour of several noble families. The earliest complete edition was that of Genoa, (1729).

9365 BALBUENA, El Bernardo, poema heroyco, 3 vols. 12mo. *hf. calf,* 7*s Madrid*, 1808
One of the most successful poems of its kind. See Ticknor.

9366 BALLESTER (M. F. F.) Sacro Plantel de varias, si divinas Flores, 16mo. *vellum, rare*, 12*s*   *Valencia*, 1652

9367 BARRIOS (Miguel de) Flor de Apolo, 4to. *Spanish Poetry, engravings by Diepenbeke, hf. bd.* 18*s*   *Bruselas*, 1665

9368 —— Coro de las Musas, st. 18mo. *port. of Fr. de Mello, calf,* 20*s Amst.* 1672

9369 **Basque Provinces.**—COLECCION DE CEDULAS, Cartas-patentes, Provisiones, Reales Ordenes y otros documentos concernientes á las PROVINCIAS VASCONGADAS, 6 vols, sq. 8vo. *Spanish calf,* £4.   *Madrid*, 1829-33
Vol. VI. is usually wanting. A curious collection of documents. They contain valuable materials for tracing the decay of the Latin by documents dated from the year 804 downwards.—*Ticknor*.

9370 BEDOYA, Historia del Toreo y de las principales Ganaderias de España, impl. 8vo. *many portraits of Toreros and plates of Bull Fights, with several woodcuts, bds.* 14*s*   *Madrid*, 1850

9371 BEÑA, Lyra de la Libertad, Poesias Patrioticas—Fabulas Politicas—2 vols. 8vo. *calf gilt, privately printed,* 7*s* 6*d*   *Londres*, 1813

9372 BERGANZA (Fr. de) Antiguedades de España propugnadas en las Noticias de sus Reyes, y Condes de Castilla la Vieja, en la Historia del CID Campeador, y en la Coronica del Monasterio de S. Pedro de Cardeña, con Apendice de Instrumentos hasta aora no publicados, 2 vols. sm. folio, *rare, limp vellum*, £4. 4*s*   *Madrid*, 1719-21

9373 —— the same, 2 vols. in 1, *fine copy in old stamped calf, clasps,* £4. 15*s* 1719-21

9374 BERNI, Creacion, Antiguedad, y privilegios de los Titulos de Castilla, *Valencia*, 1769 -RAMOS, Aparato para la correccion, y addicion de la obra de Berni, *Madrid*, 1777—together 2 vols. folio, *with numerous and valuable MS. notes, cloth,* 22*s*   1769-77

9375 —— Creacion, Antiguedad, y Privilegios de los Titulos de Castilla, folio, *engraved title and portrait, fine copy, calf or vellum,* 35*s*   *Valencia*, 1769

9376 BERTOLDO, Bertoldino, y Cacaseno, traducida del idioma Toscano por Bartholome, 12mo. *humorous woodcuts, vellum*, 3s 6d *Barcelona*, 1769

9377 BEUTER (P. A.) Coronica general de toda Espana, y especialmente del Reyno de Valencia, 2 vols. in 1, folio, *woodcuts and Coats of Arms, very fine copy, old calf gilt*, 25s *Valencia*, 1604
Lord Stuart de Rothesay's copy fetched, 1855, £2. 4s.

9378 —— the same, 2 vols. 1604—DIAGO, Anales de Valencia, hasta Don Jayme el Conquistador, 1613—3 vols. in 1, folio, *old calf, rare*, 36s *Valencia*, 1604-13

9379 BIBLIOTECA CASTELLANA, publicada por Keller y Possart: Tom. I, Juan Manuel, el CONDE LUCANOR, 1839; Tom. II, ROMANCERO DEL CID, 1840— —together 2 vols. 12mo. sd. 5s; *hf. bd*. 7s 6d *Stuttg*. 1839-40
The beauty of the Cid Romances is too well known to require further praise. The prose Romance " Et Conde Lucanor" is one of the oldest literary monuments of Spain; it is the oldest collection of Novels of the Spaniards, composed during the XIVth Century; the first edition appeared at Seville, 1575. The tales are famous for the fascination of their style, and as connecting the Prose Literature of the East and West, many of the tales being derived from Moorish sources. The work was exceedingly rare, no new edition having appeared for the last 200 years. For an elaborate account see *Ticknor's Spanish Literature*.

9380 BIBLIA del Vicio y Nuevo Testamento, conferida con los Textos Hebreos y Griegos, por Cypriano de Valera, sm. folio, *old calf gilt*, 28s *Amst*. 1602

9381 BIBLIA VULGATA Latina, traducida en *Espanol* y anotada por el P. Phelipe de S. Miguel: Viejo Testamento, 15 vols.—Nuevo Testamento, 4 vols.—Lamy, Aparato Biblico, 2 vols.—together 19 vols. sm. 8vo. *numerous maps and plates, Spanish calf*, £3. 5s *Amst*. 1794-97

9382 BLEDA (Jayme) Coronica de los Moros de España, stout sm. folio, a cropt copy, *first three leaves mended, vellum*, 12s *Valencia, Felipe Mey*, 1618
9383 —— the same, sm. folio, *a good copy in limp vellum, or calf*, 30s 1618
9384 —— the same, *a fine copy strongly bound in vellum*, £2. 10s 1618
The most important Spanish Chronicle relating to Moorish dominion in Spain. Priced, 1824, Thorpe, vellum, £3. 13s 6d; 1830, Payne and Foss, russia, £3. 13s 6d; fetched, Colonel Stanley's, £7. 10s; White Knights, £7. 7s; 1818, Evans, mor. £4. 11s; 1853, Dr. Hawtrey's £2. 10s.
"The subject of this Chronicle is full of frightful interest, and the author is called, by Musellus, 'the torch and trumpet' by which the expulsion of the Moors was effected. Bleda was one of their most inveterate enemies. His book, nevertheless, contains some very curious particulars, and is of rarity."—See *Dibdin's Library Companion*, "Ouvrage estimé et dont les exemplaires sont rares."—*Brunet*,

9385 BOCACIO (Juan) Libro llamado Cayda de Principes (trasladado por Zamora), sm. fol. 𝔅lack letter, *curious woodcut on title, calf*, £2. 2s *Alcala de Henares*, 1552

9386 BOSCÁN, Obras, y algunas de GARCILASSO DE LA VEGA, 12mo. *a few MS. notes, otherwise a good copy in bds*. £2. 2s *por M. Antonio de Salamanca*, 1547
All the early editions are rare; the first appeared in 1543.

9387 BOSCAN Y GARCILASO, another edition, stout 16mo. *wanting title, preliminary leaf and last leaf, vellum*, 7s *Barcelona*, 1554
A rare edition, the first containing the "Conversion."

9388 BOSCAN Y GARCILASO, las mismas Obras, de nuevo enmendadas y en mejor orden delo que hasta agora han sido impressas, 18mo. *good copy, calf, gilt edges*, 25s *Enveres, Martin Nucio*, (1556)

9389 —— las mismas Obras, restituidas à su integridad, 16mo. *leaves 15 and 27 a little damaged, in calf extra, gilt edges*, 21s *Anvers, Bellero*, 1597

9390 —— the same, 16mo. *fine copy, red morocco extra, gilt edges*, 36s *Nucio*, 1597
These two are of the same edition—probably the best—although one title bears Bellero's name, the other that of Nucio.

9391 BOTELLO DE MORAES y Vasconcelos, el Nuevo Mundo, Poemma Heroyco, sq. 8vo. *vellum*, 6s *Barcelona*, 1701

9392 —— el Alphonso (poema heroico), 16mo. *three pages wormed, calf*, 5s 1712

9393 BRIZ MARTINEZ, Historia de la Fundacion y Antiguedades de S. Juan de la Peña, y de los Reyes de Sobrarve, Aragon, y Navarra, stout sm. folio, *good copy in calf*, 24s *Caragoça*, 1620
Priced, 1826, Salva, parch. £1.16s.

9394 BULAS APOSTOLICAS. A Collection of Legal Documents relating to Spanish Monasteries and Benefices, in 1 vol. folio, *engravings, vellum*, 6s (? 1710)
BULL-FIGHTING. See Bedoya, Delgado, Noveli.

9395 BUSCAYOLO (Marques de) Opusculos, 16mo. *calf*, 7s *Valencia*, 1669
A curious and rare book, with a Memorial of Services, Treatises on Fortification, etc.

9396 CABRERA (Luis, Cronista del Rey Felipe II.) Relaciones de las Cosas sucedidas en la Corte de España, 1599-1614, impl. 8vo. 664 pp. *sd*. 15s *Madrid*, 1857

9397 CALDERON DE LA BARCA, AUTOS Sacramentales Alegoricos, y Historiales, por Apontes, 6 vols. sq. 8vo. BEST EDITION, *portrait, vellum*, 25s   Madrid, 1759

9398 —— COMEDIAS, 11 vols. in 10, sm. 4to. *best edition, hf. calf, gilt backs, or in vellum*, £2. 10s   *ib.* 1760-63

9399 —— Comedias, cotejadas con las mejores ediciones hasta ahora publicadas, por Keil, 4 vols. roy. 8vo. *portrait, sd.* 16s   Leipsique, 1827-30

"Calderon, a celebrated Spanish writer of the 17th century, one of the most copious and esteemed dramatists in Spain, equal to Lope de Vega."

"His boundless and inexhaustible fertility of invention, his quick power of seizing and prosecuting everything with dramatic effect, the unfailing animal spirits of his dramas, if we may venture on the expression, the general loftiness and purity of his sentiments, the rich faculty of his verse, the abundance of his language, and the clearness and precision with which he embodies himself in words and figures, entitle him to a high rank as to the imagination and creative faculty of a poet."—*Quarterly Review.*

9400 CAMPOMANES, Antigüedad Maritima de CARTAGO, sq. sm. 8vo. *map and plan, calf*, 6s   Madrid, 1756

9401 CANCIONERO DE JUAN ALFONSO DE BAENA (Siglo XV.) ahora por primera vez dado a luz, con notas y commentarios, impl. 8vo. lxxxviii. and 732 pp. *with 2 facsimiles, hf. morocco, uncut*, 18s   Madrid, 1851

9402 —— the same, *red morocco extra, gilt leaves*, 36s   *ib.* 1851

Of this valuable collection of 576 Old Romances, only 500 copies were printed, of which few remain for sale. The introduction comprises an Essay on the Castilian Poetry during the 14th and 15th centuries. The notes are historical, critical, and philological; the work concludes with a Glossary of Obsolete Words.

9403 CANCIONERO de Obras de BURLAS provocantes a risa, con Glosario, 12mo. *bds. uncut*, 25s   Madrid, Sanchez, (London, Pickering, ? 1840)

The only collection of Spanish *facetious* poetry.

9404 CANCIONERO DEL PUEBLO: coleccion de Novelas, Comedias, Leyendas, Canciones, Cuentos y Dramas, escritos por Villergas y Ayguals de Izco, 6 vols. in 3, 18mo. *hf. morocco extra*, 12s   Madrid, 1847

9405 CANDAMO (F. A. de Bances) Obras Lyricas: Sonetos, Dezimas, Romances Heroicos, Silvas, Poema Epico, 24mo. *first edition, vellum*, 9s   Madrid, Abad, (1720)

This edition is certainly of the date of 1720, and differs from that which Ticknor considers the first, of 1729.

9406 —— the same, 24mo. *second edition, vellum*, 5s   *N. R. Francos*, (1729)

9407 CAPELLA (Galeacio) Historia de las cosas q hā passado en Italia, 1521-30, sobre la restituciō del duque FRACISCO SFORCIA enl ducado d. MILA, victorias del Empador Carlos hasta su coronaciō: batallas q el rey de Frācia pdio, etc. traduziola d. latin Bernardo Perez canonigo de Cadis, sm. folio, QUITE COMPLETE, *woodcut title, curious initial letter, large woodcut repeated on two pages,* Black letter, *top margins of a few leaves slightly stained, otherwise a remarkably fine tall copy in vellum*, EXTREMELY RARE, £2. 12s   Valencia, 1537

COLLATION: Woodcut title, 1 leaf; Prologo, 2 leaves, the last leaf with a coat of arms, surrounded with a woodcut border; folios 3 to 48.

9408 CAPITULOS Generales de las CORTES celebradas en Madrid, 1607, 11, 15; Prematicas y Cedulas Reales, 1619-20, sm. folio, *vellum*, 5s   Madrid, 1619-20

9409 CAPMANY y MONTPALAU, Memorias historicas sobre la Marina, Comercio y Artes de Barcelona, 4 vols. 4to. *with the* SUPPLEMENTS, *calf gilt*, 20s   1779-92

9410 —— Ordenanzas de las Armadas Navales de la Corona de Aragon, 4to. *in Spanish, with the original Limousin and Latin texts, sd.* 10s   Madrid, 1787

9411 —— Codigo de las Costumbres Maritimas de Barcelona, llamado "LIBRO DEL CONSULADO," con Apendice, 2 vols. 4to. *Catalan and Spanish, best edition of this famous Naval Code, sd.* 18s   1791

9413 CARAMUEL y Lobkowitz (J. de) Η Σπανο-Σθήμα, Declaration mystica de las Armas de España, invictamente belicosas, sm. folio, *frontispiece and 12 plates, the size of the page, of Coats of Arms of the different parts of Spain, clean copy, original vellum wrapper, or in old calf, arms on sides*, 36s   Bruselas, 1636

A VERY RARE work on the origin and progress of Symbolism and Heraldry, particularly as regards Spain. "This edition bears an earlier date than that which Nicholas Antonio mentions, unless by a typographical error 1639 has been put instead of 1636."

9414 CARO, Antiguedades de SEVILLA, y Chorographia de su Convento o Chancilleria, folio, *vellum*, 7s   Sevilla, 1634

Priced, 1826, Salva, £1. 4s; 1843, Salva, Paris, 30 francs. "Rodericus Caro, vir elegantiori literatura praestans, et Historiae patriae gnarissimus."—*Franckenau.*

9415 CARO Y CEJUDO, Refranes y modos de hablar Castellanos, con los Latinos que les corresponden, y la Glosa, sq. 8vo. *fine copy, hf. morocco*, 18s   Madrid, 1792
9416 CARRILLO y Soto Mayor (Luys) Obras, square 8vo. *engraved title, old calf*, 25s   Priced, 1826, Salva, 30s.   Madrid, 1613
9417 **Cartas de Hidalguia.** COPIA de la REAL CARTA Executoria de Hidalguia despachada en la Real Chancelleria en favor de Don JUAN FRANCISCO OSORIO (descendiente de Don Juan Gomez BUTRON), 4to. MANUSCRIPT ON VELLUM, *attested by the autograph of Don M. A. Brochero the King at Arms, with seven Coats of Arms of the Osorio, Butron, Mora, Escovar, Arnalte and Castellanos families emblazoned in colours, vellum wrapper*, £2. 2s   Madrid, 1771
9418 DESPACHO CONFIRMATORIO de los BLASONES de Armas, Noblesa, y Genealogia, Enlaces, Entronques, Meritos, y Servicios, que per sus dos Lineas paterna y materna a Don CLEMENTE FERNANDEZ DE VELASCO, Garcia de Sedano, Rubio de San Pedro, y Solo de Zaldivar, sm. folio, THE ORIGINAL GRANT, *in MS. very neatly written upon* VELLUM, *emblazoned in gold and silver, with Genealogical Tables, Initials, Coats of Arms, &c. represented in* HERALDIC COLOURS, *with official Seal of the King at Arms, and autographs, Spanish binding*, £8. 8s   Madrid, 1798
    A fine specimen of Spanish Calligraphy and Ornamental Art. The Charter itself contains interesting historical information in connection with the Genealogical descent of the VELASCO FAMILY, and its connection with other noble houses, including the most noted and famous names of the old Spanish Aristocracy.
9419 CASCALES, Tablas Poeticas, 16mo. *first edition, calf*, 7s   Murcia, 1617
9420 —— Discursos Historicos de Murcia y su Reyno, sm. folio, *Best Paper, second title engraved with portrait, and 17 plates containing* 163 *Coats of Arms, good copy in old calf gilt*, 32s   Murcia, 1775
9421 CASIRI Bibliotheca Arabico-Hispana Escurialensis, sive Librorum omnium MSS. quos Arabice compositos Bibliotheca Escurialensis complectitur recensio, 2 vols. folio. *fine copy in old calf gilt*, 30s   Matriti, 1760-70
9422 CASTELLANOS (Juan de) Primera Parte de las Elegias de Varones Illvstres de Indias, sq. 8vo. *title mended, fine tall copy in vellum*, 30s   Madrid, Gomez, 1589
    The first part only was printed.—" After employing the greater part of his life in writing the biography of the conquerors of the New World, Castellanos devoted the remainder to putting his writings into verse."—*Rich*.
9423 CASTILLEJO (Christoval de) Obras, 18mo. *wants. pp*. 78, 79, *vellum*, 5s   1577
    A very rare edition, not in Salva's Catalogues. The earliest edition mentioned by Antonio is that of 1598.
9424 —— Obras, stout 16mo. *calf gilt*, 25s   Anvers, Nucio, 1598
9425 —— the same edition, *with different printer's name and mark on title*, 16mo. *fine clean copy in vellum*, 28s   Anvers, Bellero, 1598
9426 —— Obras, stout 16mo. *fine copy, calf extra, gilt edges*, 20s   Madrid, 1600
    Also a scarce edition. Collation: title, 7 leaves, the last blank; folios 1—438.
    "The Canciones of Castillejo," says Bouterwek, "are so exquisite, that it is scarcely possible to resist the temptation of placing their author in the very foremost rank of poets.
    " Ce poete du commencement du XVIe siècle, est un de ceux qui se distinguèrent le plus, tant par la grace et par la pureté du style, que par la verve satirique."—*Salva*.
9427 CASTILLO SOLORZANO (Alonso de) Historia de Marco Antonio y Cleopatra, 16mo. *first edition, vellum*, 15s   Caragoça, 1639
9428 —— las Aventuras del Bachiller Trapaza, segunda impression, 12mo. *fine copy, old russia extra, tooled back and sides, gilt edges*, 12s   Madrid, 2733 (1733)
    Not in Salva's catalogues. All the works of this author are scarce; Lope de Vega speaks very highly of him in his Laurel de Apollo.
    " Castillo Solorzano est un des nouvellistes les plus célèbres du XVII siècle."—*Salva*.
9429 CASTILLO (Hernando de), Historia general de SANCTO DOMINGO, y de su orden de Predicadores, 2 vols. sm. folio, *vellum*, 36s   Madrid, Sanchez, 1584-92
9430 CASTRO Y ANAYA (P. de), Auroras de Diana, 16mo. *last leaf mended, slightly stained, calf*, 12s   Madrid, 1631
    This edition of Castro's tales is unknown to Ticknor.
9431 CATALOGO de los Cuadros del Real Museo de Pintura y Escultura, por Madrazo, sm. 8vo. *sd*. 5s   Madrid, 1850
9432 CATALUNA, Conquista de, por el Marques de Olias y Mortara, sm. folio, *limp vellum*, 20s   (ca. 1653)
    Apparently a privately-printed book, having only a title without date, place, or name of printer. It is an interesting history, evidently by some one connected with state affairs, of the subjugation of the rebellious Catalans.
9433 CAYRASCO DE FIGUEROA (Bart.) Templo Militante, Triumphos de Virtudes, Festividades y Vidas de Santos, 2 parts in 1 vol. sq. 8vo. *first edition, engraved title page, inner margin of a few leaves stained, calf*, £2. 2s   Valladolid, 1603

9434 CEAN-BERMUDEZ, Diccionario historico de los mas ilustres Profesores de las BELLAS ARTES en ESPAÑA, 6 vols. 12mo. *calf,* 36*s* *Madrid,* 1800
9435 —— Sumario de las Antiguedades Romanas que hay en España, en especial las pertenecientes á las Bellas Artes, sm. folio, *sd.* 7*s* *Madrid,* 1832
9436 CERNADAS (Ant.) *Cura de Fruime,* Obras en prosa y verso, 6 vols. sq. 8vo. *vellum,* 7*s* *Madrid,* 1778-80
9437 CERVANTES, DON QUIXOTE de la Mancha, primera, segunda, tercera y quarta parte, 12mo. *being Vol. I., title soiled, vellum,* 9*s* *Bruselas,* 1617
9438 —— Don Quixote, 2 vols. sm. 8vo. 2 *frontispieces and plates, the text ruled throughout, old calf, gilt backs, binding cracked,* 18*s* *Bruselas,* 1662
9439 —— Don Quixote, 2 vols. sm. 4to. *engravings, hf. bound,* 5*s* *Madrid,* 1714
9440 —— EL INGENIOSO HIDALGO DON QUIXOTE DE LA MANCHA, corregido por la REAL ACADEMIA ESPAÑOLA, 4 vols. roy. 4to. BEST EDITION, GOOD IMPRESSIONS *of the numerous fine plates by the best Spanish artists, Spanish calf gilt, gilt edges, a fine copy,* £5. 5*s* *Madrid, Ibarra,* 1780
Très bel exemplaire de cette édition splendide et très estimée. C'est un vrai chef d'oeuvre typographique. Les nombreuses gravures dont l'édition est ornée, ont été gravées par les premiers artistes de l'Espagne. Priced, 1848, Payne and Foss, mor. £12. 12*s*, calf, £6. 6*s*. Bernal's copy, mor. fetched, 1855, £14. 14*s*.

9441 CERVANTES, Don Quixote, nueva edicion por la Real Academia, 4 vols. 12mo. *portrait and many pretty plates, calf,* 32*s* *Madrid, Ibarra,* 1782
9442 —— tercera edicion por la Academia, 6 vols. 12mo. *pretty plates, calf,* 20*s* *ib. id.* 1787

9443 —— Don Quixote de la Mancha, nueva edicion corregida de nuevo, con nuevas notas, con nuevas estampas, con nuevo analisis y con la vida de el autor por D. Juan Antonio Pellicer, 5 vols. sm. 8vo. *many plates, very neat,* £2.; or, *calf extra,* 45*s* *Madrid, Sancha,* 1797-98
9444 —— the same, 5 vols. 8vo. LARGE AND THICK PAPER, *calf, rare.* £3. 3*s* 1797-98
"Un exemplaire en Gr. Pap. vendu 135 fr. Labedoyère."—*Brunet.*
The notes of Pellicer contain a vast body of erudition and research. The text is remarkable for its correctness, and the embellishments are all the work of Spanish artists, and admirably illustrate the spirit of the text. "Pellicer has greatly improved the text, and in his numerous annotations has displayed much erudition in tracing the sources whence the author drew his supplies; in pointing out the passages in the old romances alluded to in Don Quixote; in detailing at large the historical facts which are there mentioned; and in collecting biographical, bibliographical, and critical information concerning the several authors whose writings Cervantes has either directly or indirectly noticed."—*Lockhart's Don Quixote.*

9445 CERVANTES, Don Quixote, nueva edicion, conforme à la de la Academia, 7 vols. 16mo. *calf gilt, gilt edges, pretty copy,* 16*s* *Paris,* 1814
9446 —— Don Quixote, cuarta edicion corregida por la Real Academia Española, 4 vols. *fine plates*—NAVARRETE, Vida de Cervantes, 1 vol.—together, 5 vols. sm. 8vo. *cloth,* 36*s* *Madrid,* 1819
9448 —— DON QUIJOTE DE LA MANCHA, comentado por DON DIEGO CLEMENCIN, 6 vols. sm. 4to. *portrait, cloth, uncut,* £3. 3*s* *Madrid,* 1833-39
9449 —— the same, 6 vols. sm. 4to. *calf gilt, uncut, top edges gilt,* £4. 4*s* 1833-39
"Le commentaire de Clemencin est le plus étendu qu'on ait publié sur l'immortel ouvrage de Cervantes. En conséquence, cette édition doit etre recherchée par tous les étrangers et par tous ceux qui désirent étudier a fond le Don Quichotte."—*Salva.* "One of the most complete commentaries that has been published on any author, ancient or modern. It is written, too, with taste and judgment in nearly all that relates to the merits of the author; it is rare to find an obscure point which it does not elucidate."—*Ticknor,* 1849, *III.* 383.

9450 AVELLANEDA, Quarta Salida de Don Quixote y quinta parte de sus Aventuras, sq. 8vo. *best edition, vellum.* 7*s* *Madrid,* 1732
9451 —— nueva edicion, 2 vols. 16mo. *calf gilt,* 5*s* *Madrid,* 1805
This work is according to Salva an admirable production, only second to Don Quixote in this style of romance.

9452 BENENGELI (Cid Amet) Adiciones à la historia de Don Quixote, por Delgado, 16mo. *calf,* 6*s* *Madrid,* (*ca.* 1770)
9453 HISTORIA del famoso Escudero Sancho Panzo desde la muerte de Don Quixote, con la Moral, 3 vols. 16mo. *calf,* 5*s* *Madrid,* 1793
9454 CERVANTES, Comedias y Entremeses, 2 vols. sq. 8vo. *hf. bd.* 10*s* *Madrid,* 1749
9455 —— El Buscapié, obra inedita con notas por A. de Castro, 12mo. *sd.* 2*s* 6*d* *Cadiz,* 1847
This is the work lately discovered whose genuineness is still disputed.

9456 MAYANS i Siscar, Vida de Cervantes, sq. 8vo. *vellum,* 5*s* *Madrid,* 1751
9457 CESPEDES y Meneses, Historia de Felipe III, Rey de las Españas, folio, *vellum,* 10*s* *Barcelona,* 1634
Priced, 1826, Salva, £1. 4*s*.

9458 CID, Romancero e Historia del, en lenguage antiguo por Escobar, 12mo. *vellum,*
5s *Madrid* (1695)
9459 ——— the same, 16mo. *bds.* 3s *Cadiz,* 1702
9460 ——— another edition, 16mo. *vellum,* 4s *Madrid,* 1747
9461 ——— the same, 16mo. *calf,* 3s 6d *ib.* 1818
9462 ——— Chronica del Cid Ruydiez Campeador, con Introduccion historico-literaria por Huber, roy. 8vo. *half morocco,* 12s *Marburg,* 1844
9463 CIENFUEGOS (N. A.) Poesias, 12mo. *calf,* 4s *Valencia,* 1816
9464 ——— Obras Poeticas, 2 vols. 12mo. *calf gilt,* 6s *Madrid,* 1816
Both the above contain the Tragedies and Comedies of Cienfuegos.
9465 CIRUELO, Reprovacion de las Superstitiones y Hechizerias, sm. 4to. **black letter,** *with a leaf at the end containing two large woodcuts, being printers' curious devices, fine copy, vellum, rare,* 25s *Alcala de Henares,* 1547
9466 ——— Tratado de las Superstitiones, sq. 8vo. *vellum,* 5s *Barcelona,* 1628
9467 CLADERA, Investigaciones Historicas sobre los Descubrimientos de los Españoles en el Mar Oceano, sq. 8vo. 5 *portraits and large map, fine copy, calf gilt,* 24s *Madrid,* 1794
9468 CLAMADES. HISTORIA de Clamades y de la Linda Clarmonda, sq. 8vo. *wanting title and first leaf, half morocco,* 30s (? *Alcala,* 1603)
VERY RARE. This celebrated romance consists of but 20 leaves, both in the first, and in the above (which is the second) edition. A copy of the first edition fetched, 1858, Salle Sylvestre, 230 francs.
9469 COLECCION GENERAL de las PROVIDENCIAS hasta aqui tomadas sobre el estrañamiento y ocupacion de temporalidades de los regulares de la Compañia en España, Indias, e Islas Filipinas, 3 vols. in 1, sm. 4to. *old red morocco, gilt edges,* 20s *Madrid,* 1767
9470 COLLECCION de POESIAS ESPAÑOLAS : (PADILLA) los Doze Triumphos de los Doze Apostoles, por el Cartuxano, sacado à luz por Riego, *facsimile*—Appendice : Poesias de Riego, *portraits*—in 1 vol. 4to. *half bound,* 7s 6d 1841
Vol. I. of a projected collection, containing a reprint of two very rare poetical works: los Doze Triumphos, written in 1818, and printed at "Sevilla, por Juan Varela," 1521 ; and ' Retablo de la Vida de Cristo,' written in 1500, and printed in Sevilla, por Kromberger, 1505, with other modern poems. The writer of the 'Doze Triumphos' has been called the Homer and the Dante of Spain.
9471 COLLECCION de diversos POETAS ESPAÑOLES, publicada por Don Ramon FERNANDEZ, Vols. I-XIX, in 14 vols. sm. 8vo. *calf,* 35s *Madrid,* 1786-1805
The collection is complete in 20 vols.
9472 COLOMA, Guerras de los Estados Baxos, 1588-99, sm. 4to. *engraved title, vellum,* 14s *Amberes,* 1625
Priced, 1826, Salva, £1. Coloma speaks, not only with authority, but with the natural vivacity which comes from being so near the events he records, that their colour is imparted to his language."—*Ticknor.*
9473 [COLUMNA (Guido de)] Chronica Troyana ; en que se contiene la destruycion de la nombrada Troya (en Romance por Delgado), folio, **black letter,** *part of title deficient and last leaf mended, sold not warranted perfect, half morocco,* 14s
Toledo, M. Ferrer, 1562
This edition is not mentioned by Brunet, and does not occur in Salva's catalogues, who prices a bad copy of an edition, Sevilla, 1540, £3. 13s 6d, and a much later edition, Medina, 1587, £4.
9474 CONDE, Historia de la Dominacion de los ARABES en ESPAÑA, sacada de varios manuscritos y memorias Arabigas, 3 vols. sm. 4to. *plates of Arabic Inscriptions,* BEST EDITION, *Spanish calf,* 20s *Madrid,* 1820-21
Priced, 1826, Salva, £3. 13s 6d.
9475 ——— a new edition, in 1 vol. 8vo. *hf. calf,* 6s *Paris,* 1840
9476 CONTRERAS, Dechado de varios Subjectos, 12mo. *essays written in prose and verse, old brown morocco,* 20s *Alcala de Henares,* 1581
This edition is quite as rare, if not rarer, than the first printed at Caragoça, 1572, which was priced, 1826, by Salva, £1. 11s 6d.
9477 **Coronicas.** COLECCION de las CRONICAS y Memorias de los Reyes de Castilla, 7 vols. 4to. *portraits,* £3. 10s *Madrid, Sancha,* 1779-87
9478 ——— the same, LARGE PAPER, 7 vols. imp. 4to. *sd. uncut,* £5. 5s 1779-87
9479 ——— the same, one vol. *half mor. uncut, the rest in Spanish calf,* £6. 1779-87
Priced, 1844, £6. 6s; 1845, £5. 5s; 1848, £5. 5s; 1857, Asher, 150 francs. Priced, Large Paper, 7 vols. 1824, Thorpe, bds. £18. 18s; 1826, Salva, bds. £15. 15s; 1829, Jno. Bohn, £12. 12s; 1830, Payne and Foss, calf extra, £12. 12s; 1837, Payne and Foss, £12. 12s. Fetched, 1853, Dr. Hawtrey's, hf. mor. £11. 10s.
Odd volumes in stock, and can be supplied.
Contents: Cronicas de los Reyes D. Pedro, D. Enrique II, D. Juan I, y D. Enrique III, por Lopez de Ayala, 2 vols.—Cronique de D. Pedro Nino, Historia del Gran Tamorlan, y Somario de los Reyes de Espana, 1 vol.—Memorias de D. Alonso el Noble, VIII del nombre, por Mondexar, Vol. I. (*all published*) 1 vol.--Cronica de D. Alvaro de Luna, Libro del Passo Honroso, y Seguro de Tordesillas, 1 vol.—Cronica del Rey D. Enrique IV, por Enriquez de Castillo, Coplas de Mingo Revulgo, y Carta del Levantamiento de Toledo, 1 vol.—Cronica de D. Alfonso XI, por Cerda y Rico, Vol. I. (*all published*).
" A la tete de l'histoire littéraire des auteurs Espagnols du XVe Siècle qui ont écrit en prose, nous devons placer les Chroniques. Tandis que dans tout le reste de l'Europe, les chroniques étaient l'ouvrage des moines; en Espagne elles étaient écrites par des chevaliers dont plusieurs étaient poetes."—*Bouterwek.*

9480 CORONICA de ESPANA, abreviada por mādado de la muy poderosa Señora Doña Isabel Reyna de Castilla, etc. (por Diego de VALERA) sm. folio, *title in red ink within woodcut border,* black letter, *small woodcut portraits of the Kings (one of these, with the few lines of text on the back, deficient), half vellum, rare,* £2. 2s *Sevilla, Cromberger,* 1543

9480*CRONICA DE ESPANA: Las quatro partes enteras dela Cronica de España, que mando componer el Serenissimo Rey DON ALONSO llamado EL SABIO; Vista y emendada por Florian d'Ocampo, thick folio, black letter, *stained at the beginning, title injured, but otherwise* FINE COPY, *limp vellum, rare,* £2.
Zamora, 1541

Priced, Salva, £8. 8s; Heber's copy, mor. fetched £7. 15s. This book has often been confounded with the "Quatre libros primeros" of Ocampo, printed also at Zamora, in 1543, from which it is entirely distinct. It is among the rarest of the Chronicles printed in the 16th century.

9481 CRONICA del Rey Dō RODRIGO con la Destruycion de España y como los Moros la ganaron, sm. folio, black letter, *without initials, a small portion of the title deficient, and the margins of two or three leaves slightly injured, vellum,* RARE, £2. 16s *Toledo, Juan Ferrer,* 1549
Hibbert's copy fetched £8. 2s.

9482 CORONICA de los Señores Reyes de Castilla, Sancho el Deseado, Alonzo VIII, y Enrique I. (1136-1217) por A. Nuñez de Castro, folio, *vellum,* 18s *Madrid,* 1665
Priced, 1826, Salva, £1. 11s 6d; 1828, Beckley, vellum, £3. 3s; 1837, Payne and Foss, mor. £3. 13s 6d.

9483 CHRONICA del muy esclarecido principe y Rey Don ALONSO el Sabio, y Chronica de Sancho el Bravo, in 1 vol. sm. folio, *imperfect, beginning with folio ix and ending with folio* lxxii, *the four leaves wanting at end supplied in MS. vellum,* 15s *Valladolid, Martinez,* 1554
A copy priced by Thorpe, morocco, £7. 17s 6d; Hibbert's copy fetched £6.

9484 CRONICA del esclarescido Rey Don ALONZO ONZENO deste nombre, Padre que fue del Rey don Pedro, folio, black letter, *woodcut borders to the title and folio* v.; *fine tall copy, vellum,* EXTREMELY RARE, £3. 3s
Colophon: Valladolid, P. de Espinosa y Ant. de Zamora, 1551
[*Medina del Campo,* 1563]

9485 ——— the same, sm. folio, *very fine clean copy in calf gilt, gilt edges,* £4. 4s 1563
The author of this scarce Chronicle was Juan Nunez de Villasan, whose name is not mentioned in this edition. Priced, 1825, Thorpe, vell. £8. 8s; 1833, Thorpe, morocco, £3. 13s 6d. It only differs in the title page from the edition of 1551, which fetched £20. at the White Knight's sale.

9486 CRONICA del Rey Don Alonzo el onzeno, por Juan Nuñez de Villasan, folio, *a few leaves mended, vellum,* 10s *Toledo, P. Rodriguez,* 1595
9486*——— the same, *a good copy in vellum,* 20s 1595
Priced, 1832-5, Thorpe, vell. £2. 2s. This edition is described by Dibdin as very rare.—See *Library Companion,* p. 303.

9487 CRONICA del serenissimo Rey Don Pedro, hijo Alonso de Castilla, folio, *woodcuts, wanting the last leaf of the Index, vellum,* 12s *Pamplona,* 1591
This Chronicle contains the histories of 'Don Enrique I.' and 'Don Juan I.'; no mention of this continuation is made on the title. Priced, 1822, Thorpe, £4. 14s 6d; 1824, Thorpe, vell. £3. 3s; 1826, Salva, £3. and £2. 12s 6d; Fetched, Sams, £1. 11s; White Knight's, £3. 13s 6d.

9488 CRONICA del Rey Don Juan II. folio, *calf extra,* 25s *Pamplona,* 1591
Priced, 1825, Thorpe, oak binding, £5. 15s; 1826, Salva, £2. 12s 6d; 1841, H. G. Bohn, mor. £3. 3s.

9489 CRONICA del Señor Rey Juan II., por Fernan Perez de Guzman, con las Generaciones de Enrique III, Juan II, y otros, adicionada por L. Galindez de Carvajal, folio, *sewed,* 15s *Valencia, Monfort,* 1779

9490 ——— the same, THICK PAPER, *old Spanish calf neat, gilt edges, fine copy,* 34s
"The best of all the editions is the beautiful one printed at Valencia, 1779."—*Ticknor.* 1779

9491 LA PUENTE (J. M.) Epitome de la Cronica del Rey Don Juan II. de Castilla, sm. folio, *limp vellum,* 7s *Madrid,* 1678

9492 CHRONICA de los muy altos y esclarecido reyes Catholicos don Fernando y doña Ysabel por Nebrixa, (*Pulgar*) folio, *first edition of Pulgar's Chronicle, title and first leaf mended, vellum,* 9s *Valladolid,* 1565

9493 PULGAR (Hernando) Critica de los Señores Reyes Catolicos Fernando y Isabel, folio, *calf,* 12s *Valencia,* 1780
9493*——— the same, folio, *hf. morocco neat, fine copy,* 20s 1780
"By far the best edition is the beautiful one, Valencia, 1780."—*Ticknor.*

9494 CRONICA del Gran Capitan Gonçalo Fernandez de Cordova y Aguilar, con la vida de Diego Garcia de Paredes, nuevamente añadida, folio, *fine large woodcut of a mounted Knight on the title; fol.* 126 *and* 155-8 *wanting, the following leaves are damaged, a few letters of the text being destroyed; Title, Elogio,* 2nd *leaf of* ' *Vida de Paredes,' and fol.* 1 *and* 20, *portions of fol.* 71 *and* 79 *restored in manuscript, old binding,* 36s *Sevilla, Andrea Pescione,* 1580
A very rare edition, Dibdin in his last publication, the Library Companion, says: "What must be said of, or given for, the Chronicle of the great Captain Gonzalo Hernandez de Codova, folio, printed in 1584 at Alcala"—evidently knowing nothing of this edition. Collation: Title, with a large woodcut: Elogio, 1 leaf; Vida de Diego Garcia de Paredes, 3 leaves; blank leaf; Text, fol. 1—160.

9495 SALAZAR Y MENDOÇA, CRONICA de el GRAN CARDENAL de España, Don Pedro Goncalez de Mendoca, Arçobispo de la Yglesia, Primada de las Espanas, Patriarcha de Alexandria; Canciller Mayor de Castilla y Toledo, folio, *with the portrait and genealogical plate,* FINE COPY, *bound,* £2. 16s *Toledo,* 1625
Priced, 1824, Thorpe, £5. 5s; 1827, £3. 3s.

9496 CORTES (G.) Tratado de los Animales Terrestres y Volatiles, 12mo. *many woodcuts, vellum,* 15s *Valencia,* 1672

9496*CORTES (Hern.) Historia de Nueva España, aumentada por Lorenzana, Arzobispo de Mexico, sm. folio, *with map and* 32 *curious plates of Mexican Antiquities, old calf gilt,* £2. 16s *Mexico,* 1770

9497 CORTES, COLECCION DE CORTES de los Reynos de Leon y de Castilla dada a luz por la Real Academia, 38 parts (*all published*) 4to. *sd.* 32s *Madrid,* 1836-45
This, which is the original edition, was never completed, owing to the disturbances which prevailed at the time in Spain. The following article is the new and modified publication.

9498 CORTES de los Antiguos Reinos de Leon y de Castilla, por la Real Academia, Tomo I, stout sm. folio, 640 *pp. well printed on thick paper, sd.* 20s 1861
This edition is carefully arranged in chronological order, and exactly reproduces the ancient texts, with notes. This first volume includes the Cortes of the years 1020-1348.

9499 COBARRUBIAS (Pedro de) Remedio de Jugadores, sq. sm. 8vo. *woodcut on title, a small portion of the lower margin of title, and last two leaves mended, a very curious history and treatise on Chess, and various other games, rare,* 30s *Salamanca,* 1543
"Ouvrage curieux, ou il est traité de toutes sortes de divertissemens, divisés en spirituels, humains et diaboliques."

9500 CRUZ Y CANO (Don R. de la) Teatro ó coleccion de sus Saynetes y demas Obras dramaticas, 10 vols. 12mo. *calf,* 28s *Madrid,* 1786-91
"An attractive and amusing author, especially in reproducing the life of the lower classes with their picturesque dresses, and unchanging manners."—*Ticknor.*

CURITA—see ZURITA

9501 DANTE. Traduciō del dante (en verso Castellano) por don Pero Fernādez de VILLEGAS, dirigido ala señora dona Juana de Arago, stout sm. folio, **Black letter**, *the margins of a few leaves slightly wormed, with a valuable and extensive commentary, sound copy in Spanish calf, extremely rare,* A REAL BIBLIOGRAPHICAL TREASURE, £20. *Burgos, Fadrique Aleman de Basilea,* 1515
I can trace only one perfect copy; it was priced £25.
COLLATION: Title, with large woodcut Coat of Arms full size of the page, reverse blank, 1 leaf; Suma c 2 to c 7, 6 leaves; Prohemio, vida del poeta, etc. A 1 to A 4, 4 leaves, on the reverse of the 4th leaf, A 4, the work commences with Canto primero; Sheets A 5 to z 8, each sheet with 8 leaves; two other sheets, 16 pp.; Sheets A to o 8, each sheet with 8 leaves; Breue tratado, Sheets P and Q in sixes; the last leaf contains a Latin verse and the colophon, and the printer's device, on the reverse of which is a woodcut Coat of Arms, full size of the page.
The *Glosa* is very copious, in some places occupying whole pages together without the intervention of any text; much curious matter relating to Dante, and the times in which he lived, and those also contemporary with the translation, will be found elucidated in it. Another work, written by the translator, was strictly prohibited in Spain, and the author severely condemned; and it is very probable, from its extreme rarity, his Dante shared a similar fate.
"A very rare book, and one of considerable merit."—See *Ticknor*, 1849, *L.* 374.

9502 DAVILA (Sancho, Obispo de Jaen) Veneracion a los Cuerpos de los Sanctos, y la singular con que se a de adorar el cuerpo de Jesu Christo en el Sacramento, sm. folio, *engraved title and plate, vellum,* 14s *Madrid,* 1611
A rare work on Veneration due to Relics and to the Eucharist, not mentioned in Salva's catalogues.

9503 DAVILA (Juan) Passion del Hombre-Dios, sm. folio, *engraved title and fine plate, vellum,* 9s *s. a.* (? 1661)
A poetical work on the Passion of Our Lord.

9504 DELGADO (J. *vulgo, Hillo*) Tauromaquia ó Arte de Torear á Caballo y á Pié, 12mo. 30 *coloured plates of the various modes of Bullfighting, the instruments, etc. hf. russia,* 27s *Madrid,* 1804

9505 DELGADO (A.) Memoria sobre el Gran Disco de Theodosio, sm. 4to. *large plate, sd.* 2s 6d *Madrid,* 1849

SPANISH LITERATURE. 525

9506 DESCLOT, Historia de Cataluña, &c. traduzida de su lengua Catalana por Cervera, sq. 8vo. FIRST EDITION, *very rare, vellum*, 7s *Barcelona*, 1616
Priced, Salva, 36 fr.

9507 DIAZ DE LUCO (Juan Bernal) Contemplaciones del Idiota, nueuamente traduzidas en Castellano, 16mo. *woodcut on title and back of last leaf, Spanish morocco, gilt edges, Ford's copy*, 30s *Anvers, J. Steelsio*, 1620
Very rare: not mentioned by Brunet, nor in Salva's Catalogues.

9508 DIAZ VARA CALDERON, Grandezas y Maravillas de Roma, folio, *portrait and plates, calf*, 7s *Madrid*, 1673

9509 DICCIONARIO GEOGRÁFICO-HISTÓRICO de España por la Real Academia, Seccion II: La Rioja, Logroño, etc. por Govantes, con Supplemento, 4to. *sd.* 7s 1846-51

9510 DICCIONARIO de Voces Españolas Geograficas, 4to. *sd.* 2s *(ca.* 1820)

9511 DORMER, Discursos Varios de Historia, con muchas escrituras reales antiguas, 8vo. *vellum, rare*, 18s *Zaragoça*, 1683
This copy belonged to Mr. Ford, by whom it it designated a curious work.

9512 DUENAS (Juan de) Tercera parte del ESPEJO de CONSOLACION, en la qual se veran muchas historias de la sagrada Escriptura, para cõsolaciõ de los q padescen tribulaciõ, sm. folio, black letter, *large woodcut Coat of Arms on title, a* VERY FINE TALL COPY, *vellum*, £4. 16s *Valladolid*, 1550
VERY RARE: unknown to Antonio, Brunet, and Salva.

9513 ECHEVERRIA, Paseos por GRANADA y sus Contornos, colleccion historica de Antiguedades y noticias curiosas pertenecientes a la ciudad de Granada, 2 vols. sq. 8vo. *the original edition, as issued in* 58 *and* 46 *periodical Nos. no titles printed, vellum, rare*, 25s *Granada*, 1764-67

9514 —— Paseos por Granada, ahora nuevamente reimpresos y illustrados con notas por J. M. Perez, 2 vols. sq. 8vo. *hf. bd.* 9s *Granada*, 1814
Priced, 1843, Salva, 23 francs.
Ouvrage d'un grand intérêt pour l'historien, l'antiquaire et le voyageur. On y trouve non-seulement une description minutieuse et fort détaillée des antiquités arabes de Grenade, la province d'Espagne ou il reste le plus de vestiges de la domination musulmane, notamment le célèbre palais de l'Alhambra, mais encore des examens de plusieurs questions relatives à la partie historique, depuis les temps les plus reculés.

9515 ERCILLA, la Araucana, con la continuacion de Santistevan, OSORIO, 2 vols. in 1, folio, *vellum*, 8s *Madrid*, 1733-35
No later edition contains the fourth and fifth Cantos by Osorio.

9516 —— la Araucana, 2 vols. 12mo. *calf*, 5s *Madrid*, 1803
"An author single and unparalleled in the host of poets. The great and singular work which has justly rendered Ercilla immortal, is his poem. 'Araucana' Cervantes, in speaking of Don Quixote's library, has ranked it amongst the choicest treasures of the Castilian Muse. With all his defects, he appears to me one of the most extraordinary and engaging characters in the world."—*Hayley.*
"Ercilla is to be counted among the many instances in which Spanish poetical genius and heroism were one feeling."—*Ticknor.*

9517 ESCOBAR (Fr. Luis de) Las quatrocientas Respuestas a otras tantas Preguntas, con Proverbios y glosas, sm. folio, black letter, clxxij leaves, *large coat of arms on title page, best edition, poor copy, very rare*, 25s *Valladolid*, 1550
Priced, 1840, Payne and Foss, £2. 12s 6d; a copy wanting the title page was priced by Salva, in 1856, £6. A second part appeared in 1552; a copy of the 2 parts sold for £75. 15s at the White Knight's sale.

9518 ESCOBAR, Las Quatrocientas Respuestas, 16mo. *two or three leaves slightly wormed, calf extra, gilt edges*, 25s *Envers, Martin, Nucio, s. a.*
"Jolie édition imprimée vers 1560. Elle se compose de 34 ff non chiffrés et de 298 ff. chiffrés."—*Brunet.*
The name of the Author of this rare book is to be seen only in an acrostic on some couplets on the reverse of leaf 135. A more curious collection of miscellaneous pieces, religious observations, and of moral doctrines and proverbs, in questions and answers, and in verse and prose, is not to be found in the whole range of Spanish Literature.

9519 ESCOIQUIZ, Mexico Conquestada poema heroyco, 3 vols. 12mo. *calf*, 6s 1798

9520 ESCORIAL. FRANCISCO DE LOS SANTOS, Description del Monasterio de S. Lorenzo del Escorial, sm. folio, *portrait of Philip IV, and plates of Architectural Antiquities, Ornaments, etc. vellum*, 7s 6d *Madrid, Imp. Real*, 1657
"Ouvrage curieux; vendu 23 fr. Hurtault."—*Brunet.*

9521 XIMENEZ, Descripcion del Monasterio de S. Lorenzo del Escorial, folio, *plates of Architecture and Ecclesiastical Ornament, Spanish binding*, 7s 6d 1764

9522 —— the same, two works, Santos and Ximenez, in 1 vol. stout sm. folio, *Spanish morocco, gilt*, 18s 1675-1764
Both valuable works, containing full descriptions of the Library, and of some ancient MS. found there.

9523 Escosura y Hevia, Juicio del Feudalismo en España, roy. 8vo. *sd.* 2s 6d 1856

9524 ESPINEL, Relaciones de la Vida del Escudero Marcos de Obregon, sq. 8vo. FIRST EDITION *of this famous Romance, vellum*, 30s *Madrid*, 1618

9525 ESPINEL, the same, 12mo. *slightly stained, hf. bd.* 8s *Sevilla,* 1641
9526 —— the same, sq. 8vo. *vellum,* 10s *Madrid,* 1744
9527 ESPINOSA, Historia, Antiguedades, y Grandezas de Sevilla, 2 vols. in 1, sm. folio, *hf. bd.* 5s *Sevilla,* 1727-30
9528 ESPINOSA (Pedro) Primera parte de las Flores de Poetas ilustres de España, sq. 8vo. *title and last leaf wanting, otherwise a sound copy, vellum,* VERY RARE, 20s *Madrid,* 1605

Priced, 1826, Salva, £5. 5s. Pedro de Espinosa compiled, with much taste and judgment, this collection of the poets of his time, and published a great number of compositions that were inedited before, and some of which are not to be found in any other work."—*Salva.*

9529 ESPRONCEDA (Don Jose de) Poesias, sm. 8vo. *hf. russia,* 7s 6d *ib.* 1840
9530 ESQUILACHE, Borja el Principe, Obras en Verso, 4to. *green morocco, gilt edges,* 18s *Amberes,* 1654

Pages 397—562 are Romances.

9531 EVIA, Ramillete de Flores Poeticas, sm. 4to. *calf, title damaged,* 5s *Madrid,* 1676
9532 FABER (Don J. N. Böhl de) Floresta de Rimas Antiguas Castallanos, 3 vols. 8vo. *calf gilt,* 24s *Hamburgo,* 1821-25
9533 —— the same, 3 vols. large 8vo. LARGE PAPER, *uncut,* 25s ; or *hf. morocco gilt, gilt tops, uncut,* £2. 2s 1821-5
9534 FARIA Y SOUSA, Imperio de la China, sacado de las noticias de Semmedo, sm. folio, *calf,* 30s *Lisboa,* 1731
9535 FELIZES, el Cavallero de Avila, por la Santa madre Teresa de Jesus, en Fiestas, y Torneos de Caragoça, POEMA HEROICO, stout 12mo. *fine copy in vellum,* 20s

RARE ; not mentioned by Brunet, Antonio, nor Salva. *Caragoça,* 1623

9536 FERNANDEZ DE ROZAS, Noche de Invierno sin Naypes, en varias poesias Castellanas, 2 parts in 1 vol. sq. 8vo. 16 *and* 164 *leaves, vellum,* 16s

Very rare : mentioned neither by Brunet nor Salva. *Madrid,* 1662

9537 FERRER DEL RIO, Galeria de la Literatura Española, 8vo. *ports.* 4s 1846
9538 —— Historia del Reinado de Carlos III, en España, 4 vols. large 8vo. *sd. an important work on the history of an important period,* 25s *ib.* 1856
9539 FEYJOO (B. J.) THEATRO CRITICO Universal, o Discursos varios para desengaño de Errores Comunes, 9 vols. 1746-50—Illustracion Apologetica al Theatro, 1 vol. 1746—Cartas Eruditas y Curiosas, 3 vols. 1748-50—Anti-Theatro Critico y Replica a la Ilustracion, por Mañer, 3 vols. 1729-31—Demonstracion Critico-Apologetica por Sarmiento, 2 vols. 1732—Reflexiones sobre las obras de Feyjoo, por Soto i Marne, 2 vols. *Salamanca,* (1748)—together 20 vols. sq. 8vo. *old Spanish calf,* 25s *ib.* 1732-50
9540 FIGUEROA (Chr. Suarez de) Hechos de Don Garcia Hurtado de Mendoça, Marques de Cañete, sq. 8vo. *title engraved with portrait, etc. Spanish calf,* VERY RARE, £2. 18s *Madrid, Impr. Real,* 1616

This scarce work describes the same events which are celebrated poetically in the Araucana of Ercilla, and narrates some curious events in the life of the soldier-poet.

9541 FLOR DE VIRTUDES (Libro llamado) agora nuevamente impresso, sq. 8vo. 𝔅lack letter, *woodcut title page, fine copy in limp vellum,* 18s *Toledo, Ferrer,* 1558

A VERY RARE EDITION of this Spanish translation from the *Fiore di Virtu.* Collation : 36 leaves, including title and the last leaf which is blank.

9542 FLORESTA ESPAÑOLA de Apotegmas ó Sentencias de algunos Españoles por Santa Cruz, continuada por Asensio, 3 vols. 16mo. *calf,* 9s *Madrid,* 1790
9544 FLOREZ (Henrique) ESPAÑA SAGRADA Theatro Geographico-Historico de la Iglesia de España, continuado por Manuel Risco y otros, Vols. I-XLVII, sq. 8vo. *plates, sd.* £14. 2s *ib.* 1754-1850
9545 —— the same, Vols. I-XX, in 10 vols. stout sq. 8vo. *plates, very neat in old calf gilt,* £5. 1754-65

" Un exemp. 46 vol. 440 fr. en 1840 ; 47 vols. 400 fr. Quatremère."
A most important historical work, embracing a far wider range of research than, from the title, it would seem to do. Florez is styled by Mr. Ford, " the Dugdale, Muratori, and Montfaucon of Spain""
"Une source abondante ou se trouvent un grand nombre de documents exacts sur la géographie et l'histoire du Moyen-Age, beaucoup de diplômes jusqu' alors inédits, ainsi que des textes corrigés sur d'anciens MSS."—*Brunet.*

9546 FLOREZ, Medallas de las Colonias y Pueblos Antiguos de España ; Coleccion de las que se hallan en autores, y de otras nunca publicadas, 3 vols. sm. 4to. *maps, with* 67 *plates, also* 8 *of Gothic Coins, calf,* £2. 5s *Madrid,* 1757-73

9547 FLOREZ, la Cantabria, disertacion sobre su sitio etc. en tiempo de los Romanos, 1786 —Florez vindicado del Vindicador de la Cantabria, Ozaeta, por RISCO, 1779— 2 vols. 8vo. *sd. 6s 6d* 1779-86
9548 —— la Cantabria, sq. 8vo. *vellum, 5s* *Madrid*, 1786
9549 —— Memorias de las Reynas Catholicas, Historia Genealogica de la Casa Real de Castilla y de Leon, 2 vols. sq. 8vo. 15s *ib.* 1790
9550 MENDEZ, Noticias sobre la Vida de Florez, sq. 8vo. *portrait, sd. 4s* 1860
9551 FRANCO (Francisco) Libro de Enfermedades contagiosas, y preservacion dellas, 1569—Tractado de la Nieve y del uso della, **black letter**, 1569—2 vols. in 1, sq. sm. 8vo. *titles within woodcut borders with figures of birds, beasts, and flowers, neatly hf. bd. 15s* *Sevilla, Alonso de la Baviera*, 1569
9552 FRASSO (Ant. de lo) Fortuna de Amor, 2 vols. 8vo. *Prose interspersed with Canciones, Glosas, Sonetos, and Villancios, portrait and plates, calf, 10s; or calf gilt, 16s* 1740

Col. Stanley's copy fetched £3. 13s 6d.
" 'This,' said the Barber, opening another, 'is the Ten Books of the Fortune of Love, composed by Antonio de lo Frasso, a Sardinian Poet.' 'By the holy orders I have received,' said the Priest, ' since Apollo was Apollo, the muses muses, and the poets poets, so humourous and whimsical a book as this was never written ; it is the best and most singular of the kind that has appeared in the world: and he who has not read it may reckon that he never read any thing of taste; give it here, gossip, for I am better pleased at finding it, than if I had been presented with a cassock of Florence satin.' "—*Don Quixote.*

9553 **Fueros.** FUERO viejo de CASTILLA, con notas por Jourdan de Asso, y Manuel y Rodriguez, sm. folio, *calf, 6s* *Madrid*, 1771
9554 FUERO REAL de España, hecho por Alonso IX, glosado por Diaz de Montalvo, con las Siete Partidas, folio, *large woodcut of Arms on title, the title and a few other leaves mended, limp vellum, 30s* *s. l. aut nom typ.* 1544
9555 —— the same, sm. folio, *good copy in vellum, 36s* 1544
Valued by Salva £3. 10s. "At the head of these distinguished jurisconsults, undoubtedly must be placed Alfonso Diaz de Montalvo, who illustrated three successive reigns by his labours."—*Prescott.*
9556 FUEROS, Privilegios, Leyes y Ordenanzas de GUIPUZCOA, Nueva Recopilacion, folio, *engraved title of "Blason y Divissa de Guipuzcoa," old calf, gilt edges, 22s* *Tolosa*, 1696
9557 FUERO-JUZGO ó Recopilacion de las Leyes de los Wisi-Godos Españoles, con Discurso preliminar, por Llorente, sq. 8vo. *calf, 6s* *Madrid*, 1792
Pages 41-84 contain a glossary of ancient Spanish words.
9558 —— en Latin y Castellano, cotejada con los mas antiquos y preciosos Codices por la Real Academia Española, folio, *with a Glossary of ancient Spanish Words, 36s* *ib.* 1815
"The Visigothic Code, Fuero Juzgo, (Forum Judicum) originally compiled in Latin, was translated into Spanish under St. Ferdinand III. in the middle of the XIIIth century. This completion, notwithstanding the apparent rudeness and even ferocity of some of its features, may be said to have formed the basis of all the subsequent legislation of Castile."—*Prescott.*
9559 FUEROS del Reyno de NAVARRA, por Chavier ; Baraibar de Haro, Diccionario para inteligencia de los Fueros, 2 vols. in 1, folio, *fine folding plate of the King of Navarre's Coronation, calf, 12s* *Pamplona*, 1815
9560 FUERO, Privilegios, Franquezas, y Libertades de los Cavalleros Hijos dalgo del Señorio de VIZCAYA, sm. folio, *title engraved with the Arms of Biscay, good copy in vellum, 10s* *Bilbao, Huydrobo*, 1643
9561 FUEROS, privilegios, franquezas y libertades de VIZCAYA, sm. folio, *frontispiece, calf, 6s 6d* *Bilbao*, 1762
9562 COLLECCION de Fueros y Cartas-Pueblas de España por la Real Academia, Catalogo, 4to. *sewed, 5s* 1852

9563 GANDARA, Armas i Triunfos, hechos heroicos de los Hijos de Galicia, elogios de su Nobleza, stout sq. 8vo. *bd. 10s* *Madrid*, 1662
Scarce, like most Spanish genealogical works ; a new edition appeared in 1677.
9564 GARAU, la Fee triunfante en 4 Autos en Mallorca, 16mo. *two leaves damaged, vellum, scarce, 9s* *Mallorca*, 1755
9565 [GARCIA] La Desordenada Codicia de los Bienes Agenos (La Antiguedad y Nobleza de los Ladrones), 16mo. *calf extra, scarce, 12s* *Paris*, 1619
Original edition of this curious work.
9566 GARCI LASSO DE LA VEGA, Obras, con anstaciones del Licenciado Francisco Sanches, 18mo. *green morocco*, RARE, 14s *Salamanca, Lasso*, 1574
9567 —— OBRAS, con anotaciones de Fernando de Herrera, sq. 12mo. *limp vellum, 16s* *Sevilla, Barrera*, 1580
COLLATION: Title, 1 leaf; preliminary leaves, 3 ; pp. 1 to 691; tabla, 2 leaves; pages 61 to 64 are left out.
9568 GARCILASSO, Obras, con anotaciones de Sanchez, 12mo. *vellum, 8s* *Madrid*, 1612

9569 GARCILASSO, Obras, con anotaciones de Tamaio de Vargas, 32mo. *calf,* 7*s*
"Edition estimée."—*Brunet.* Madrid, 1622

9570 GARCILASSO DE LA VEGA (El Ynca) Primera parte de los Commentarios Reales, del Origin de los Yncas, *Lisboa,* 1609—Historia General del Peru, *Cordova,* 1607—2 vols. sm. folio, FIRST EDITION, *not uniform,* £2. 1609-1617
"L'edition originale, peu commune et très recherchée."—*Brunet.* I sold a copy in 1858 for £4.; priced 1824, Thorpe, £4. 4*s*; a copy fetched, 1859, Sotheby's, £4. 10*s*.

9571 GARCILASSO DE LA VEGA, Historia general del Peru, ó comentarios reales de los Incas, 13 vols.—Historia de la Florida, 4 vols.—together 17 vols. 12mo. *Spanish calf, very nice uniform set,* £2. 2*s* Madrid, 1800-3

9572 GARIBAY (E.) ILLUSTRACIONES GENEALOGICAS de los Reyes de las Españas, de los de Francia, y de los Emperadores de Constantinopla, folio, *fine portrait of Philip III by Perret, cuts of Arms and Genealogical Trees, fine copy in calf extra, gilt edges,* £4. 4*s* *ib.* 1596

9573 —— the same, large folio, *a very tall copy in vellum from Southey's library, with his autograph,* £4. 10*s* 1596

9574 —— Compendio Historical de las Chronicas y Universal Historia de todos los Reynos de España, 4 vols. sm. folio, *margin and a few letters in the last leaf of the Index to Vol.* 4 *destroyed, vellum,* 32*s* Barcelona, 1628
Priced, 1824, Thorpe, vell. £2. 12*s* 6*d*; 1826, Salva, £3. 3*s*; 1841, H. G. Bohn, £2. 15*s*.
"Garibay, one of the most distinguished among the Spanish historians."—*W. Irving.*

9575 GAVILAN VELA, Discurso contra los Judios traducido de Portuguese, sq. 8vo. *vellum,* 10*s* Madrid, 1680

9576 GAZETA DE MADRID, del 6 de Agosto, 1771, hasta at 29 de Deciembre 1780, in 10 vols. sq. 8vo. *vellum,* 36*s* Madrid, 1771-80
An official newspaper, published weekly till September, 1778, when it began to appear twice a week. It contains the political, parliamentary, and military intelligence of all the states of Europe during the period embraced.

9577 GIL POLO, La Diana Enamorada, con notas, 12mo. *calf,* 3*s* 6*d* *ib.* 1778
9578 —— la Diana Enamorada, sm. 8vo. *calf, gilt top, uncut,* 6*s* *ib.* 1802
9579 GIRALDO, Vida y Heroycos hechos de Diego de Arze Reynoso, Obispo de Tuy, etc. sm. folio, *portrait, calf extra,* 9*s* *ib.* 1695
RARE: not in Salva's catalogues.

9580 GOMARA (Lopez de) Historia General de las INDIAS Y NUEVO MUNDO, con mas la Conquista del Peru y de Mexico—Cronica de la Nueva España— 2 vols. in 1, sm. folio, 𝕭𝖑𝖆𝖈𝖐 𝖑𝖊𝖙𝖙𝖊𝖗, *wood-cuts on titles, fine copy, elegantly bound in maroon morocco extra, joints, gilt edges by* BEDFORD, EXTREMELY RARE, £12. 12*s* Zaragoça, Augustin Millan, 1554
"Gomara's historical merit is considerable; his mode of narration is clear, flowing, always agreeable, and sometimes elegant. The copies of his Historias de las Indias and of his Chronica were called in by a decree of the Council of the Indies, and were long considered as prohibited books."—*Robertson.*
COLLATION: Title, with dedication on the reverse, 1 leaf; Table, 3 leaves; folios i-xcix; colophon, 1 leaf; Cronica de Nueva Espana, title and dedication, 1 leaf; folios ii-cxiv, the last leaf numbered in error cxiii.

9581 GOMEZ (A. E.) Academias Morales de las Musas, sq. 8vo. *containing various Poems and four Comedies, second edition, old calf gilt, rare,* 20*s* Madrid, 1668
9582 —— Academias Morales de las Musas, sq. 8vo. *vellum,* 7*s* Barcel. 1704
9583 GONGORA Y TORREBLANCA (Garcia de) Historia apologetica y Descripciõ del Reyno de Navarra, su mucha Antiguedad, Nobleza, y calidades, Reyes de su Real casa, sucessos, y hechos heroycos de sus naturales, folio, *fine copy in vellum, rare,* 36*s* Pamplona, 1628
At folio 111 is Catalogo de los Emperadores, y Reynes Gentiles, Christianos, y Moros que ha auido en Espana, y naciones estrangeras, que la senorearon despues del diluvio universal aca, que ha cerca de quatro mil anos.

9584 GONGORA (Luis de) Todas las Obras en varios Poemas, recogidas por Gonzalo de Hozes y Cordova, sq. 8vo. *vellum,* 24*s* Madrid, 1634
9585 —— Obras, comentadas por Garcia de Salcedo, 3 vols. stout sm. 4to. *engraved titles, limp vellum,* 35*s* *ib.* 1636-45-48
"On trouve difficilement ces trois volumes réunis."—*Brunet.*
9586 —— Obras, por Hozes y Cordova, sq. 8vo. *fine copy in vellum,* 20*s* *ib.* 1654
9587 GONGORA Y LOPE DE VEGA, Quatro Comedias, par Sanchez, 12mo *cf.* 6*s* *ib.* 1617
9588 GONZALEZ. Vida y Hechos de Estevanillo Gonzalez, hombre de buen humor, compuesto por el mismo, 16mo. *fine copy, calf gilt,* 25*s* *ib.* 1655
A scarce edition. This work is the original of Le Sage's novel, and is said to be the autobiography of Gonzales who was Fool to the Duque de Amalfi.

9589 GONZALEZ DE ACEVEDO (Lazaro) Memorial i Discursos del Pleito, que las Ciudades, i lugares de los Arzobispados de Burgos i Toledo, etc. tratan con el Arzobispo de Santiago, folio, *vellum,* 12*s* *ib.* 1771

SPANISH LITERATURE.

1590 GONZALEZ DE MENDOÇA (Fr. Joan) Historia de las Cosas mas notables, Ritos y Costumbres, del Gran Reyno dela China, con un Itinerario del NUEVO MUNDO, (por Ignatio), 12mo. *stamped vellum, gilt edges*, RARE, £2. 12s 6d   *Roma*, 1585

"Ouvrage tiré du Chinois, et dans lequel parurent pour la première fois, en Europe, les caractères de cette angue. L'edition de Rome est rare."—*Brunet*.

1591 GONCALEZ DE MENDOÇA (Pedro) Historia del Monte Celia de Nuestra Señora de la Salceda, stout folio, *engraved title and 4 plates including views of the interior of the Chapel, with upwards of 70 engraved portraits of the Archbishops of Granada (including the author, with the Mendoza Arms) in the text, fine copy in calf or vellum*, 21s   *Granada*, 1616

1592 GREGORIO DE SALAS, Coleccion de sus Epigrammas y otras Poesias Criticas, satiricas, y jocosas, 16mo. *calf*, 5s   *Madrid*, 1806

1593 GREGORIO DE CAMPOS MARTINEZ Amorosa Contienda de Francia, Italia y España sobre Carlos III, certamen poetico, sq. sm. 8vo. *hf. calf*, 21s   *Mexico*, 1761

A rare compilation of a vast number of poetical pieces publicly spoken in the University of Mexico, on the oronation of Charles III.

1594 GUDIEL (G.) Compendio de algunas Historias de España, donde se tratan muchas antiguedades dignas de memoria, especialmente de la FAMILIA DE LOS GIRONES, y de otros linages, folio, *genealogical trees, vellum*, £2. 12s   *Alcala*, 1577

1595 GUADALAJARA Y XAVIERR, Memorable Expulsion y justissimo Destierro de los MORISCOS de España, 2 parts—Ripol, Dialogo de Consuelo por la expulsion de España, 2 vols. in 1, sm. 8vo. *vellum, or calf gilt*, 24s   *Pamplona, Assiayn*, 1613

Priced, 1826, Salva, 1 vol. £2. 2s; 1836, Tross, Paris, 2 vols in 1, vellum, 40 fr.

1596 GUEVARA (Ant. de) Despertador de Cortesanos, 16mo. *vellum*, 4s   1605

1597 —— Epistolas Familiares, cosas notables, razonamientos muy altos, exposiciones de figuras, Medallas, etc. 2 vols. in 1, stout 12mo. *sound copy in vellum*, 9s   *Anveres*, 1648

1598 GUMILLA (Jos.) Historia de las Naciones en las Riveras del Orinoco, 2 vols. sm. 4to. *portrait, map, 5 plates of Indian Antiquities, calf*, 28s   *Barcelona*, 1791

1599 —— the same, 2 vols. in 1, sm. 4to. LARGE PAPER, *hf. calf*, £2. 12s 6d   1791

1600 HARO (Fernandez de Velasco, El buen Conde de) SEGURO DE TORDESILLAS, sacole à luz de entre antiguisimos papeles que se conservan en la libreria del Condestable de Castilla, su secretario Pedro Mantuano, con Vida del Conde de Haro por Pulgar y Relacion del linage de Velasco, sm. folio, *fine copy, calf, very rare*, £2. 10s   *Milan*, 1611

C'est la première édition du *Seguro de Tordesillas*, le fait le plus extraordinaire du règne de Jean II. et peut-tre de l'histoire d'Espagne. Salazar de Mendoza et Nic. Antonio ne parvinrent apparemment pas à voir cet ouvrage, uisque le premier, dans ses *Dignidades de Castilla*, et le second dans sa *Bibliotheca hispana*, commettent de graves rreurs en le citant. Ce qui prouve suffisamment (comme l'observe l'edition faite en 1784) que même fort peu de emps après sa publication, ce livre était difficile a trouver.

1601 HARO (Lopez de) NOBILIARIO GENEALOGICO de los Reyes y Titulos de España, 2 vols. folio, *many Coats of Arms, bound*, £3. 10s   *Madrid*, 1622

1602 HEREDIA (J. M.) Poesias, 2 vols. 12mo. *calf gilt*, 5s   *Toluca (Mexico)* 1832

1603 HEREDIA BARNUEVO, Mystico Ramillete, Don P. de Castro y Quiñones, etc. sm. folio, 5 *curious plates of Spanish Saints, vellum*, 6s   *Granada*, 1741

1604 HERNANDEZ (F.) Opera cum edita, tum inedita, ad autographi fidem et integritatem expressa, jussu Regio, 3 vols. 4to. *fine copy in old crimson morocco extra, gilt edges*, 36s   *Matriti, Ibarra*, 1790

Priced, 1841, c. lf, £2. 10s. These 3 vols. contain the Historia Plantarum Novæ Hispaniæ Libri xxiv. much nlarged from the Author's Manuscript.

1606 HURTADO DE MENDOZA (Diego) Historia de las Guerras Civiles de Granada, sm. 8vo. *russia extra, gilt edges*, 12s   *Paris*, 1660

1607 —— Guerra de Granada, publicada por Tribaldos de Toledo, sq. 8vo. *vellum*, 5s   *Madrid*, 1674

1608 —— Guerra de Granada contra los Moriscos, con vida del autor por Portalegre, sm. 4to. *portrait, best edition, hf. calf, uncut*, 9s   *Valencia*, 1776

The first edition appeared in Madrid, 1610. "There is a freshness and a power in Mendoza's sketches that arry us at once into the midst of the scenes and events he describes."—*Ticknor*, 1849, I. 478.

1609 IGLESIAS de la Casa, Poesias, (Amatorias) 3 vols. 24mo. *calf*, 6s   1840

2 M

530   B. QUARITCH, 15 PICCADILLY, LONDON.

9610 ILLESCAS (Gonz. de) Historia Pontifical general y catolica, con Continuacion por Luis de Bavia, Guadalaxara y Xavierr, y Baños de Velasco, COMPLETE in 6 vols. folio, *vellum, a good copy*, £3. *Madrid*, 1622-13-12-30-78
Priced, 1857, vellum, £5. A very interesting General History of the World, with copious particulars about the Spanish Possessions in America, etc. No copy is mentioned in any of Salva's Catalogues. "On trouve difficilement cet ouvrage complet."—*Brunet*.

9611 INDICE Ultimo de los LIBROS PROHIBIDOS, 1790—SUPLEMENTO desde 1789 hasta 1805, 2 vols. in 1, 4to. *hf. calf*, 7s 6d   *Madrid*, 1790-1805

9612 INDICE de los Documentos procedentes de los Monasterios suprimidos, conservados en la Real Academia, Sec. I: Castilla y Leon, roy. 8vo. 7s 6d *Madrid*, 1861

9613 INFORME sobre la Discipline Ecclesiastica, 8vo. *sd.* 1s 6d   1786

9614 ISLA. HISTORIA del famoso Predicador FRAY GERUNDIO de Campazas, por F. L. de Salazar, (*i. e.* J. F. de Isla) con las Cartas Apologeticas de Marquina, y Varias Piezas relativas al Gerundio, 3 vols. sm. 4to. *hf. calf*, 10s *Madrid*, 1787
9615 —— the same, 3 vols. sm. 4to. *calf*, 14s   1804
9616 —— —— Fray Gerundio de Campazas, 4 vols. 12mo. *neatly bound*, 7s   1813
"Written throughout with great spirit; and not only are the national manners and character everywhere present, but in the episodes and in the occasional sketches Isla has given of conventual and religious life in his time, there is an air of reality which leaves no doubt that the author drew freely on the resources of his personal experience. His plan resembles slightly that of 'Don Quixote,' but its execution reminds us oftner of Rabelais and his discursive and redundant reflections, though of Rabelais without his coarseness."—*Ticknor*.

9617 JANER, Condicion social de los Moriscos de España, causas de su expulsion, etc. imp. 8vo. *sd.* 6s; *hf. calf gilt top, uncut*, 9s   *Madrid*, 1857

9618 JAUREGUI (Don Juan de) Rimas: Aminta, Rimas varias i sacras, sm. 4to. FIRST EDITION, *the margins of a few leaves ink-stained, vellum, rare*, 30s *Sevilla*, 1618
Containing the translation of Tasso's Aminta, which Cervantes declared to be so perfectly done, so as to leave in doubt which was the original and which the transfation. Priced by Salva, £2.

9618*JOSEPHO, Antiguedades Judaycas su vida, etc. traduzido de Latin, sm. folio, *calf*, 12s   *Anvers, Nucio*, 1554
Pellicer does not mention this translation, which was prohibited by the Spanish Inquisition.

9619 JUAN DE LA CONCEPTION, HISTORIA GENERAL de PHILIPINAS, Conquistas de estos Españoles Dominios, establecimientos, progresos, y decadencias, 14 thick vols. smallest 4to. *with 8 maps, in excellent preservation, vellum*, £6. 6s   *Manila*, 1788-92

9620 JUAN DE LA CRUZ, Obras Espirituales, con la vida del de Jesus, sq. 8vo. FIRST EDITION, *engraved title, plate of the Saviour's appearance to the author, and a mystical map, a few pages wormed in the inner foot margin, otherwise a fine clean copy, vellum*, RARE, £4. 4s   *Madrid*, 1618

9621 —— Obras misticas y espirituales, añadense unos Romances, etc. stout sm. 4to. *frontispiece, and the same engravings as in first edition, fine copy, with rough leaves, in the original vellum*, £2.   *ib.* 1649
A curious mystical work containing Canciones and Romances. This edition appears to be the first known to Salva. "Saint Jean de la Cruz est considéré comme l'un des meilleurs écrivains, tant en prose qu'en vers."—*Salva*.

9622 JUAN (Jorge) Y ULLOA, Relacion historica del Viage a la America Meridional, hecho de orden de S. Mag. para medir algunos grados de Meridiano Terrestre, y venir en conocimiento de la verdadera figura, magnitud de la Tierra, etc. con el Origen y Sucession de los Incas, y Observaciones astronomicas y physicas en los Reynos del Peru, 5 vols. in 2, roy. 4to. LARGE PAPER, *many maps and plates, two vols. hf. calf, the third sewed*, £2. 10s   *Madrid*, 1748-73
9623 —— the same, 5 vols. in 3, roy. 4to. *fine copy in old calf gilt*, £3. 3s   1748

9624 JUAN (Jorge) Compendio de Navegacion para el uso de los Cavalleros Guardias-Marinas, sq. 8vo. *12 plates, old red morocco, gilt edges*, 7s 6d   *Cadiz*, 1757

9625 LA RIPA (Fray de) Defensa historica por la Antiguedad del Reyno de Sobrarbe, folio, *frontispiece, good clean copy, vellum*, 15s   *Caragoça*, 1675
"Curieux et rare, et pas moins estimé que les Annales du P. Moret."—*Lenglet*.

9626 LA RIPA, Corona Real del Pireneo establecida y disputada, 2 vols. folio, *clean copy, vellum*, 24s   *ib.* 1685-8
Priced, 1826, Salva, vell. £1. 14s. The work is an essential Supplement to Zurita's Anales de Aragon.

9626*LARRA (Dom. M. J. de) Obras completas de Figaro, 4 vols. sm. 8vo. *portrait, hf. morocco*, 36s   *Madrid*, 1843
This celebrated writer and dramatist gained his best laurels under the pseudonym of Figaro, by a series of articles on life and manners, whose vigour of thought, pungent force of observation, and vivacity of style have been largely admired.

9627 LEDESMA (A. de) Conceptos Espirituales, 16mo. *complete, slightly stained, sound copy, hf. calf, £4. 10s* *Madrid,* 1600
Very rare. This book belongs to the class of Spanish Romanceros and Cancioneros, and not only does it contain beautiful poems in various styles, but the author has had the merit of applying to spiritual subjects the *letrillas, romances, villancios, recondillas,* and other kinds of composition employed in the old Romanceros and Cancioneros.
Colmenares in the 17th century stated, that the whole of the editions were out of print, and lamented its scarcity and high price.

9628 Leon (Antonio de) Epitome de la Bibliotheca Oriental i Occidental, Nautica i Geografica, sq. 8vo. *fine copy, calf gilt,* 36s *ib.* 1629
Unmentioned by Brunet and Boucher de la Richarderie. Not in the Grenville collection.

9629 LEON (F. Luis de) Obras, cotejadas con varios MSS. por A. Merino, 6 vols. sm. 8vo. *sd. uncut,* 36s Priced by Salva, 90 *francs.* *ib.* 1804-16
" One of the greatest masters of eloquence in his native Castilian. The characteristics of his prose compositions, even those which from their nature are the most strictly didactic, are the same everywhere; and the rich language and imagery of the passage cited afford a fair specimen of his style. But besides this, he was a poet of no common genius. Nearly all his best poetical compositions are odes in the old Castilian measures, with a classical purity and vigorous finish before unknown and hardly attained since."—*Ticknor,* 1849, II. p. 46-47.

9630 LE SAGE, Aventuras de Gil Blas de Santillana restituidas a su lengua nativa, (por Isla) con Adicion a las Aventuras, 7 vols. sm. 8vo. *best edition, Spanish calf gilt,* 20s *Valencia,* 1791-92
9631 ———— the same, 7 vols. in 3, sm. 8vo. *many plates, hf. calf gilt,* £2. 1791-92
Priced, Salva, £2. 10s.
9632 ———— the same, 7 vols. sm. 8vo. *plates, calf,* 30s *Madrid, (y Valencia),* 1797-91
9633 LIVIO, las Quatorze Decadas, trasladadas in Castellano (por Pedro de la Vega) divided into 3 vols. sm. folio, 𝔅lack letter, *coloured Coat of Arms on title, with large woodcut on reverse, and about* 205 *very fine and bold* woodcuts *of Battles, Sieges, Camp Life, Embassies, etc. showing very minutely the Spanish Costume of the period, remarkably fine copy in Spanish calf,* very rare, £7. 7s *Caragoça,* 1520
This copy cost Mr. Heber £15. 15s. The work is so very rare as to have escaped the researches even of N. Antonio, although he gives an account of the translator, and others of his works.

9634 Llorente, Memoria historica sobre la opinion nacional de España acerca de la Inquisicion, 8vo. *sd.* 2s 6d 1812
9635 Loores de la Virgen nuestra Señora, sq. 8vo. *woodcut of the Virgin's Arms on the title,* 𝔅lack letter, *vellum,* 6s *Alcada de Henares,* 1552
9636 LOPE DE VEGA CARPIO, Colleccion de las Obras sueltas de, assi en prosa como en verso, 21 vols. sm. 4to. *portrait, very neat, in old Spanish calf gilt, fine copy,* £5. 5s *Madrid, Sancha,* 1776-79
Priced by Salva, £10.; 1824, Rivington, £15. 15s; 1827, Thorpe, £8.; J. Bohn, 1840. £8 8s.
9637 Lope de Vega, the same, 21 vols. impl. 8vo. large paper, *calf,* £5. 5s 1776-79
Priced, 1824, Thorpe, £21.; 1830, Payne and Foss, £14. 14s. Large Paper copies are very rare, as there were but a few copies printed, and these were intended exclusively for the public libraries of Spain.

9638 LOPE DE VEGA, Jerusalem conquistada, Epopeya Tragica, stout sq. 8vo. first edition, *woodcut bust of Lope de Vega and full-length portrait of Alphonso VIII., calf or vellum,* £2. *Madrid,* 1609
"This edition has escaped the notice of Antonio." This work is not a 'translation from Tasso, nor does it celebrate even the same history, but is an epic poem upon the Crusade of Richard Cœur-de-Lion.
Priced, 1825, Thorpe, £3. 10s; 1826, Salva, calf, £3. 13s 6d; Hibbert's copy fetched £2. 3s.

9639 ———— La Circe, con otras Rimas y Prosas, sq. 8vo. first edition, *no title, vellum,* 9s *ib.* 1624
9640 ———— Laurel de Apolo, con otras Rimas, sm. 4to. first edition, *good copy, fine impression of the beautiful portrait of Lope, by J. de Courbes, calf, or vellum,* 15s *ib.* 1630
This work mentions the characters and works of nearly 300 Spanish poets.

9641 ———— Rimas humanus y divinas de Tome de Burguillos, sq. 8vo. first edition, *portrait, vellum, fine copy,* 20s *ib.* 1634
Consisting chiefly of humourous, burlesque, and satirical poems of the gayest and lightest character, written under the name of Tomè de Burguillos, a theatrical personage whom Lope had invented and made popular by his sharp sayings The chief piece in the volume is the *Gatomachia,* which is the first in order of merit, of its kind, in the Spanish language. See Ticknor, 1863, II. pp. 181-84.

9642 ———— Rimas Sacras, 1658—Soliloquios Amorosos de un alma a Dios, 1644, 2 vols. 12mo. *fine copies, Spanish calf, gilt backs,* 18s *Lisboa,* 1658-44
9643 ———— Pastores de Belen, prosas y versos divinos de Lope de Vega Carpio, 16mo. *fine copy, calf extra,* 12s *Brusselas,* 1614
9644 ———— Justa Poetica, y alabanzas justas que hizo Madrid en las Fiestas de San Isidro, 8vo. *portrait of the Saint on title, fine copy in vellum,* 15s *Madrid,* 1620
This work contains all the poems sent in on the occasion of the festival, with the names of the writers. Lope was the president who distributed the prizes, and spoke the opening poem, as well also as those humourous pieces under the name of the Maestro de Burguillos, which he first adopted here.

9645 LOPE DE VEGA, Romancero Espiritual, y Estaciones del Via-Cruces, 12mo. *rude minute woodcuts, wanting title and last leaf of table, the top margins stained, vellum*, 21s *Madrid*, 1725

VERY RARE; not in Salva's catalogues. "Antonio n'a point connu ce Romancero."

Great as Calderon was, he cannot, without a large reserve, be named as the greatest genius of the Spanish stage. In wealth of invention, in prodigious fertility, in dramatic fire, he is far surpassed by Lope, who also had the merit of creating the stage on which Calderon rose. The fresh natural grace of Lope's style, and his vivid conciseness in gay or passionate moments, have a living charm beyond the finished ease and rich exuberance of Calderon's manner:—while Lope excelled in some departments,—as in his chivalrous pictures of Old Spain, and in a certain indescribable sweetness, and glow of gracious womanhood in his female characters,—in both of which Calderon is wanting. Both lived long, and wrote to the latest moment.—but Lope's very last pieces are as bright as his earliest, and bear no sign of age; whereas Calderon waned after sixty, and grew verbose and artificial as his years declined."—*Athenæum*, Nov. 20. 1853.

"The prodigy of nature, the great Lope de Vega."—*Cervantes*. "No man ever had a greater genius for comedies than Lope de Vega. He possessed fertility of wit, joined with great beauty of ideas, and wonderful readiness of conception."—*Rapin*.

9646 LOPEZ DE CORELAS (Alonso) TREZIENTAS PREGUNTAS de cosas naturales, cõ sus respuestas y alegaciones d'auctores, agora respondidas y glosadas en este año de 1546, sq. 8vo. black letter, FIRST EDITION, *the printer's device on title and last leaf, blank margin of A 2 torn off, otherwise a fine copy in vellum*, VERY RARE, £3. 3s *Valladolid, Francisco Fernandez de Cordova*, 1546

Priced, 1826. Salva, £4. 4s. COLLATION: 10 preliminary leaves, and 78 pages, unnumbered.

9647 LOPEZ MADERA (Grego. *fiscal de su Magestad*) Discursos de las Reliquias descubiertas en GRANADA, 1588-98, sm. folio. *engraved title, vellum*, 32s *Granada*, 1601

A very rare work on the antiquities of Granada

9648 —— the same, sm. folio, *original edition, carrying the discoveries only down to* 1595, *no title, apparently an unfinished work, unknown to bibliographers, with facsimiles of old gothic inscriptions, which are omitted in the second edition, vellum*, £2. 10s (1595)

9649 LOPEZ DE MENDOCA (Don Iñigo, Marques de Santillana) OBRAS, con vida y notas por Amador de los Rios, roy. 8vo. LARGE PAPER, *portrait and illuminated facsimile*, PRESENTATION COPY *from the Duke de Osuna, with two autograph notes to Mr. Ford, green morocco with joints, silk linings, gilt edges*, £3. 16s *Madrid*, 1852

A handsome reprint, containing the Proverbs and Poetical Works, with a Glossary.

9650 LOPEZ DE MENDOCA (Yñigo) Memorial de Cosas notables, folio, *Spanish calf, rare*, £2. 8s *Guadalajara*, 1564

9651 —— Proverbios, sm. folio, gothic letter, *woodcut title page, wanting folio xvii, fine large copy in bds.* 15s *Toledo, Juan de Ayala*, 1537

A copy fetched, 1858, Sotheby's, £2. 6s.

9652 —— Proverbios; Coplas de Mingo Revulgo; Coplas de Manrique, 3 vols. in 1, 24mo. *calf or vellum*, RARE, 12s *Anvers, Nucio*, 1594

9653 LOPEZ PINCIANO (Alonso) Philosophia Antigua Poetica, sq. 8vo. *Coat of Arms on the back of title, vellum, fine copy*, 30s *Madrid*, 1596

"Pinciano is deserving of honourable remembrance, for he was the first writer of modern times who endeavoured to establish a philosophic art of poetry."—*Bouterwek*.

9654 LOPEZ SOLAR, Los Bandos de Castilla, ó el Caballero del Cisne, 3 vols. 24mo. *a Romance in Scott's style, fronts. calf*, 7s 6d *Valencia*, 1830

9655 LOUBAYSSIN DE LAMARCA, Historia Tragicomica de Don Henrique de Castro, stout 12mo. *engraved title, an historical romance, full of fanciful adventures, fine copy in calf gilt*, 15s *Paris*, 1617

9656 LOZANO (Chr.) Soledades de la Vida, etc. Novelas Exemplares, sm. 4to. *vellum*, 9s *Madrid*, 1713

9657 LUCANO, Poeta antiguo, traduzido por Lasso de Oropesa, 12mo. *fine copy in old veau fauve extra, gilt edges*, 10s 6d *Anvers*, 1585

9658 MAL LARA (Joan de) La Philosophia Vulgar, primera parte que contiene MIL REFRANES glosados, folio, *woodcut title-pages, the corners of some leaves cut off, first edition, vellum*, 35s *Sevilla*, 1568

This work was reprinted at Madrid 1618, and Lerida in 1621, 4to.

"Mal Lara (a Sevillan) selected a thousand of Nunez' collection and added a commentary to each. A volume which, notwithstanding its cumbersome learning, can be read with pleasure, both for the style in which many parts of it are written, and for the unusual historical anecdotes with which it abounds."—*Ticknor*, iii. p. 159.

9659 MANRIQUE (Don Jorge) Coplas, con una Glossa de un religioso de la Cartuxa, etc., Coplas de Mingo Revulgo glossadas por Pulgar; Cartas en Refranes de Blasco de Garay; Dialogo entre el Amor y un Cavallero viejo, por Cota, 16mo. *sound copy in calf*, 30s *Madrid*, 1614

9660 —— Coplas de Manrique, con las Glosas de Guzman, Valdepeñas, Perez, y Cervantes, 12mo. *hf. calf*, 5s *ib.* 1779

"No earlier poem in the Spanish language, if we except perhaps, some of the early ballads, is to be compared with the Coplas of Manrique for depth and truth of feeling. Its versification, too, is excellent; free and flowing with occasionally an antique air and turn, that are true to the character of the age that produced it, and increase its picturesqueness; and effect. But its great charm is to be sought in a beautiful simplicity which, belonging to no age, is the seal of genius in all."—*Ticknor*, 1849, I. 373.

9661 MANUEL (D. Aug.) Vida y Acciones del Rey Don Juan II de Portugal, sm. 4to. *vellum*, 16s *Madrid*, 1639
Pp. 159-60 (a cancel) are torn across and imperfect, but the second nos. 159-60 are complete.
Highly praised by Lorenzo Gracian; the author was beheaded for treason in Lisbon in 1641.

9662 MANUEL RODRIGUEZ (Miguel de) Memorias para la vida de Fernando III, folio, *fine portrait, calf, gilt edges*, 10s *ib. Ibarra*, 1800

9663 MARIANA, HISTORIA GENERAL DE ESPANA, 2 vols. sm. folio, *hf. cf.* 18s *ib.* 1650

9664 —— Historia General de España, con la Continuacion de Miñana, traduzida por Romero, 3 vols. folio, *fine copy, Spanish calf neat*, ' *the Continuacion,*' *not quite uniform*, 36s *ib.* 1780-1804

9665 —— Historia General de España, ilustrada de tablas cronologicas, notas y observaciones criticas, con la vida del autor, 9 vols. folio, *best edition, vignettes and portrait, Spanish calf, gilt backs*, £6. 15s *Valencia, Montfort,* 1783-96
" Edition bien exécutée, que les notes dont elle est enrichie rendent très recommendable."—*Brunet.*
Priced, 1840, Payne and Foss, £18. 18s; 1848, the same, mor. £12. 12s; 1854, £8. 8s; fetched, Stanley's, £22. 1s; General Capel's, £9.

9666 —— Historia general de España, con la CONTINUACION de MINIANA, 10 vols. sm. 8vo. *Spanish calf*, 20s *Madrid*, 1794-95

9667 —— Historia General de Espana, ilustrada con notas historicas y criticas por Sabat y Blanco, 20 vols. large 8vo. *hf. calf gilt*, £4. *ib.* 1817-22
" Cette édition, qui par son format est digne de figurer dans une bibliothèque, est la plus convenable, en raison le ses notes et de ses sommaires, pour ceux qui désirent avoir une connoissance approfondie de l'histoire d'Espagne. Among Spanish prose compositions, the style of Mariana is all but unrivalled. The fourth edition, printed in the very year of his death, is much enlarged and in every way improved. " The proudest monument erected to the history of Spain. His willing belief in the old chronicles, tempered, as it necessarily is, by his great learning, gives an air of truehearthedness and good faith to his accounts, and a picturesqueness to his details, which are singularly attractive."—*Ticknor,* III. 137. " Mariana a obtenu une reputation meritée pour l'élegance de sa narration. La diction est irreprochable, ses descriptions sont pittoresque sans pretention poetique, et pour le temps, ou il a vecu il a conservé assez d'impartialité et d'amour de la liberté."—*Sismondi.*

9668 MARINA (F. M.) Teoria de las Cortes o grandes Juntas Nacionales de los Reinos de Leon y Castilla, 3 vols. in 1, 4to. BEST EDITION, *scarce, having been suppressed in Spain, hf. calf*, 30s *ib.* 1813

9669 —— the same, 3 vols. 4to. *Spanish calf neat*, £2. 2s 1813

9670 —— Ensayo sobre la Legislacion de Leon y Castilla, y el Codigo de las Siete Partidas, 4to. *calf*, 5s *ib.* 1808

9671 —— the same, 2 vols. in 1, 8vo. *calf neat*, 8s *ib.* 1834

9672 MARMOL CARVAJAL (Luys del) Historia del Rebelion y Castigo de los MORISCOS DEL REYNO DE GRANADA, sm. folio, FIRST EDITION, *vellum or calf* £3. 10s *Malaga, Rene, a costa del auctor,* 1600

9673 —— the same, folio, *calf extra, gilt edges*, £5. 1600

9674 —— Historia del Rebelion de los Moriscos de Granada, 2 vols. in 1, sq. 8vo. *hf. russia, large pictorial map of Granada,* 18s *Madrid*, 1797

9675 —— the same, 2 vols. sq. 8vo. *calf gilt*, 24s 1797
"Ouvrage fort curieux."—*Brunet.* "This History of the rebellion of the Moors of Granada, in the author's own times, will be found peculiarly interesting."

9676 MARMOL CARVAJAL, Primera Parte de la DESCRIPTION GENERAL DE AFFRICA, con todos los successos de guerras entre los infieles, y el pueblo Christiano, &c. 2 vols. in 1, stout sm. folio, FIRST EDITION, *title mended, otherwise a fine copy in old calf*, 36s *Granada*, 1573

9677 MARQUEZ (J. Micheli) Deleite y Amargura de las dos Cortes, Celestial y Terrena, con la assistencia de los ingenios, y lagrimas erramadas en la CORTE DEL DIOS MOMO, sq. 8vo. *fine copy, vellum*, 12s *Madrid*, 1642

9678 —— TESORO MILITAR DE CAVALLERIA antiguo y moderno, modo de Armar Cavalleros, sm. folio, *many woodcuts illustrative of Knighthood and Chivalry,* RARE, 24s *ib.* 1642
Quite a complete copy, even a second title page having been added in consequence of a variation, one having an ornamental woodcut, the other an engraved Coat of Arms in the centre. It is extremely rare to find a copy not in some respect deficient.

9679 MARTIN (Manuel Joseph) COLLECCION de VARIAS HISTORIAS, asi sagradas como profanas, de los mas celebres Heroes del mundo, etc. 2 vols. sq. 8vo. *numerous curious woodcuts, vellum,* £4. *ib.* 1780
This collection contains 40 different pieces, in the style of Chap Books, each headed by a rude woodcut, and containing prose narratives of famous lives, mythical histories, tales of apparitions, miracles, and other extraordinary circumstances. The various pieces were issued separately, and all afterwards united by the publisher, Martin, in 2 volumes, of 20 parts each, to which he printed a title page and contents. They form a remarkable specimen of the Spanish " Romancero " Literature in the last century, and will be highly prized by those who know the extreme difficulty of forming collections of the sort.

9680 MARTINEZ DE LA ROSA (Fr.) Obras Literarias, 5 vols. 12mo. *a pretty set in green calf neat*, 21s *Paris, Didot,* 1830-34
9681 —— Doña Isabel de Solis, Reina de Granada, novela historica, 3 vols. 12mo. *plates, calf,* 10s *Madrid,* 1837-46
9682 MASDEU *(Juan Francesco de)* Historia Critica de Espana, y de la Cultura Española, 20 vols. sq. 8vo. *fine copy, Spanish calf, rare,* £4. 10s *ib.* 1783-1805
Priced, 1825, Salva, £12 ; 1829, G. Bohn, £10. 10s; 1843, Salva, 140 fr.
Ce livre est un de ceux qui deviennent indispensables dans une bibliothèque publique.

9683 MEDINA (Pedro de) Grandezas y Cosas Memorables de España, folio, 𝕭lack letter, *with curious woodcuts of towns, etc. and maps including one of America on leaf* 64, *fine copy in vellum,* VERY RARE, £5.
1548—*in fine, Alcala de Henares, Robles y Villanueva,* 1566
Pinello says, "Pedro de Medina, en las Grandeças de Espana, trae algunas cosas de el Decubrimiento de Colon;" this circumstance will partly account for the extreme scarcity of this work, even in Spain.

9684 MEDRANO (Julian de, *Cavallero Navarro*) La Silva Curiosa en que se tratan diversas cosas sotilissimas, y curiosas, mui convenientes para Damas, y Cavalleros, sm. 8vo. *first edition, good copy in old calf, scarce,* 36s *Paris,* 1583
"Ouvrage renfermant nombre de proverbes Espagnols et diverses pieces de poésies du bon temps de cette littérature."—*Brunet.*
"In this collection we find a great quantity of Spanish proverbs, and many pieces of poetry of the best times of our literature, which are not easily met with in any other collection."—*Salva.*

9685 MEMORIAS de DON FERNANDO IV. de Castilla: Tomo I., su Cronica ; Tomo II., la Coleccion Diplomatica que comprueba la Cronica ; arregladas y anotadas por Benavides, de la Academia, 2 vols. 4to. £1. 17s 6d *Madrid,* 1860
9686 MEMORIAS de la REAL ACADEMIA de la Historia, Vols. I.-VIII., 4to. *many plates, sd.* £4. 10s *ib.* 1796-1852
9687 DISCURSOS leidos en las Sesiones Publicas, desde 1852, impl. 8vo. *sd.* 7s 6d 1858
9688 MEMORIAL HISTORICO ESPANOL : Coleccion de Documentos, Opusculos, y Antiguedades que publica la Real Academia, Vols. I.-XV., sq. 8vo. *plates of Coins, etc. sd.* £4. 2s 6d *ib.* 1851-62
9689 MEMORIAS Literarias de la REAL ACADEMIA SEVILLANA de Buenas Letras, Tomo 1. sm. 4to. *plates of inscriptions, medals, etc. calf,* 6s *Sevilla,* 1773
9690 MENA (Juan de) Obras, con la Coronacion y otras coplas, sm. folio, *wanting a leaf containing title and prologue, fol. ij damaged, vellum,* 9s *Sevilla,* 1528
9691 —— Obras, con la Coronacion y otras Cartas y Coplas, sm. folio, 𝖌𝖔𝖙𝖍𝖎𝖈 𝖑𝖊𝖙𝖙𝖊𝖗, *engraved title, wanting fol.* 35-8, *upper corners stained, vel.* 18s *Valladolid,* 1536
Priced, 1858, Lord Rothesay's copy, *mor.* £3. 10s.
9692 —— todas las Obras del famosissimo poeta, con la Glosa de Nunez, thick 12mo. *vellum,* 5s *Anvers, M. Nucio,* 1552
9693 —— Obras, declaradas por Sanchez, 16mo. *Spanish calf,* 5s *Salamanca,* 1582
9694 MENDEZ SILVA (R.) Poblacion General de Espana, sus Trofeos, Blasones, etc. folio, *margin of title cut into, calf,* 5s *Madrid,* 1645
Fetched, 1832-48, Payne and Foss, £2. 2s; 1829, Salva, £1. 1s.
9695 MENDEZ (Fr.) Typographia Española, ò Historia de la introduccion, propagacion, y progresos del Arte de la Imprenta en España, Tomo I (all published), sq. 8vo. *fine portrait, hf. vellum, entirely uncut, scarce,* 20s *ib. Ibarra,* 1796
Ouvrage curieux, quoiqu'il ne comprenne que la XVe Siècle.—*Brunet.*
9696 MERCADO (P. de, *Medico y philosophe*) Dialogos de Philosophia natural y moral, 12mo. FIRST EDITION, 𝖇𝖑𝖆𝖈𝖐 𝖑𝖊𝖙𝖙𝖊𝖗, *woodcut, Coat of Arms of a Cardinal on the title, good copy in vellum,* 20s *Granada, Mena y Rabut,* 1558
VERY RARE: not mentioned by Brunet; Salva prices it 31s 6d.
9697 MEXIA (Pero) SILVA de varia Lecion, stout 16mo. *fine copy in olive morocco extra, gilt edges, by Smith,* RARE, 24s *Anveres, Nucio,* 1544
9698 —— Silva de Varia Lection, nuevamente agora anadido en ella la QUARTA PARTE, sm. folio, 𝕭lack letter, *engraved title, hf. calf,* 30s *Sevilla, Diaz,* 1570
9699 —— COLOQUIOS o dialogos, en los quales se disputan diversas cosas de mucha erudicion, FIRST EDITION, 12mo. 𝕭lack letter, *calf,* 9s *Sevilla,* 1547
9701 MEXIA (Diego) Primera parte del Parnaso Antartico, de obras amatorias, sq. 8vo. *title mended, and part of leaf* 111 *torn off, otherwise a good sound copy in vellum, rare,* 20s *Sevilla,* 1608
Priced, 1826, Salva, £2. 10s. No more was published than this part, which is written, according to Ticknor, "in pure and elegant Castilian verse."

9702 MINADOY, Historia de la Guerra entre Turcos y Persianos, 1576-1585, traducida de Italiano, por Herrera, sq. 8vo. *vellum*, 10s *Madrid*, 1588
Priced, 1826, Salva, £1. 1s. Printed with a peculiar figure 5, somewhat similar to an Arabic 6.

9703 MIRABEL, Jardin de las Damas, y recreo de cavalleros, o desagravio de las mugeres à las nobilissimas Damas, 12mo. *fine clean copy*, 12s *ib*. 1720

9704 MONARDES, *Medico*, (el Licenciado) Sevillana Medicina la quel sirve pā qlquier otro lugar destos reynos, obra ātigua digna dē ser leyda, sq. sm. 8vo. *title in red and black within woodcut borders*, 𝔟𝔩𝔞𝔠𝔨 𝔩𝔢𝔱𝔱𝔢𝔯, *margins a little wormed, vellum*, 25s *Sevilla*, 1545
Monardes in his prologue speaks of the author as having lived in the 14th Century, but does not name him.

9705 MONCON, Espejo del Principe Christiano, sm. folio, *title in red and black within an elegant woodcut border*, 𝔟𝔩𝔞𝔠𝔨 𝔩𝔢𝔱𝔱𝔢𝔯, *vellum*, RARE, 36s *Lisboa*, 1544

9706 MONDRAGON Censura de la Locura humana, 16mo. *vellum*, 6s *Lerida*, 1598

9707 MONDEJAR (Ibañez de Segovia Peralta i Mendoza) Memorias historicas del Rei Alonzo el Sabio, folio, *fine clean copy, calf*, 18s *Madrid, Ibarra*, 1777
Priced, 1826, Salva, bds. £2.

9708 MONFORTE (P. Rodriguez de) Descripcion de las Honras de Phelippe IV (Muerte, Exequias, etc.) sm. 4to. *engraved title, portrait, a series of* 46 *curious emblematical plates, representing the life and death of the King, etc. and several engravings of his arms, calf*, 36s *Madrid*, 1666

9709 MONTEMAYOR, Parte primera y Segunda de la DIANA (la segunda parte por A. Perez), 2 vols. in 1, 16mo. *Spanish calf, gilt back*, 18s *ib*. 1602

9710 ——— los siete Libros de la Diana, *Espagnol et François*, par P(avillon), 12mo. *vellum, calf back*, 10s *Paris*, 1611

9711 ——— La Diana, primera y segunda parte, nuevamente emendada, stout 12mo. *old Spanish brown morocco*, 10s *Lisboa, Craesbeeck*, 1624
This work, in Prose and Verse, formed part of Don Quixote's library. The second part is by Alonzo Perez. Shakespeare is said to have taken the plot of the Two Gentlemen of Verona from Young's translation of it.
"George Montemayor was the inventor of the Spanish Pastoral Romance, and ranks as a poet among the best of his age."

9712 MONTALVAN (Perez de) Sucessos y Prodigios de Amor, en ocho novelas exemplares, añadido en esta impression el Orfeo, 12mo. *fine copy, vellum*, 32s *Barcelona*, 1640

9713 MONTSERRAT. LIBRO de la Historia y Milagros hechos a invocacion de nuestra Señora de Montserrat, sm. 4to. 𝔟𝔩𝔞𝔠𝔨 𝔩𝔢𝔱𝔱𝔢𝔯, *very fine copy, almost uncut*, MOROCCO *extra, gilt edges, from Heber's and Mr. Ford's library*, £5.
Barcelona, Monpezat, 1550
VERY RARE; not mentioned by Brunet nor Nic. Antonio, and not to be found in Salva's catalogues. "A curious monument of Spanish faith, bringing down its succession of 325 miracles to the very year of its publication, during which the last four are recorded to have been performed."— *Ticknor*, 1863, III, p. 251.—This note of Mr. Ticknor refers to an edition of 1556, the only one he knew of; the above edition being six years earlier, and containing 289 miracles, which are carried down to the year 1550, in which six are stated to have occurred.

9714 MORALEJA, el Entretenido, varias flores de diversion, relaciones serias, burlescas, etc. sq. 8vo. *vellum*, 7s 6d *Madrid*, 1741
A strange mixture of odds and ends, written as a continuation part to the *Entretenido* of Sanchez Tortolos.

9715 MORATIN, Obras Dramaticas y Liricas, 6 vols. 12mo. *portrait and plates, calf*, 9s *Barcelona*, 1834

9716 MOSSEH ALMOSNINO, Sepher Henhageth Hakhyis, Regimiento de la Vida, en Español por Sola, Gabay, y Piza, sm. 4to. (?) LARGE PAPER, *fine copy in old red morocco extra, gilt edges*, 18s *Amsterdam*, 5489 (1728)

9717 MOTA (Diego de la) de Confirmatione Ordinis Militiae S. J. de Spata—Principio de la Orden de la Cavalleria de S. Tiago, del Espada, con catalogo de los Cavalleros, 2 vols. in 1, sm. 4to. *vellum*, 9s *Valencia*, 1599

9718 MOYA (Ant. de) Rasgo Heroyco, declaracion de las Empressas, Armas, y Blasones de los Reynos, Ciudades y Villas de España, sq. 8vo. *a very fine copy in Spanish morocco extra*, 18s *Madrid*, 1756

9719 NAIERA (Ant de) Sūma Astrologica, y arte para enseñar hazer prognosticos de los tiempos, sq. 8vo. *vellum*, 10s *Lisboa*, 1632

9720 NARBONA (E.) Doctrina politica civil en Aphorismos : Concejo y Consejeros del Principe por Furió Ceriol, 12mo. THICK PAPER, *fine copy in Spanish red morocco, broad borders of gold, gilt gaufré edges*, 21s *Madrid*, 1779

9721 NAVARRETE, Disertacion sobre la Historia de la Nautica, sq. 8vo. *sd*. 4s *ib*. 1846

9722 NAVARRO (G.) Tribunal de Supersticion Ladina, explorador del poder del Demonio, sq. 8vo. *vellum*, 5s *Huesca*, 1631

9723 Niños (El Maestro de) Carta a Alvarez de Toledo, *Zarag.* 1713—Palacio de Momo, apologia yocoseria por G. Alvarez de Toledo, *Leon de Fran.* 1714—Jornada de los Coches de Madrid a Alcala, ò satisfacion al Pal. de Momo, *Zarag.* 1714—in 1 vol. sm. 4to. *scarce, old calf*, 9s 1713-14

9724 Niños (Maestro de) Jornada de los Coches de Madrid a Alcala, sm. 4to. *vellum*, 6s *Zaragoza*, 1714

This, and the number above it, are singular specimens of burlesque and satirical writing, seasoned with irreverence and profanity.

9725 NODAL (Barth. Garcia, y Gonzalo de) Relacion del Viage al descubrimiento del Estrecho nuevo de S. Vincente, etc., con las Derrotas de America Occidental por Eschavelar, 2 vols. in 1, sq. 8vo. *with the* MAP, *calf, scarce*, 25s *Cadiz* (1766)

9726 NOVELAS ESCOGIDAS, Coleccion de, 8 vols. 12mo. *calf, gilt backs, scarce*, 28s *Madrid*, 1787-91

A collection of 53 Novels, which includes some of the best works of Spanish fiction.

9727 NOVELI, Cartilla de las Reglas para Torear a Cavallo, 12mo. *vellum*, 6s *ib.* 1726

9728 NUÑEZ (Hernan) Refranes o Proverbios en Castellano, revistos por Luis de Leon, 3 vols. 16mo. *calf*, 20s *ib.* 1804

9729 Nuñez DE LEON (Duarte) Genealogia de los Reyes de Portugal, 12mo. *vellum*, 12s *Lisboa*, 1590

9730 NUÑEZ y Quilez (C.) Antiguedades de la Ciudad de Daroca, sq. 8vo. *fine copy, vellum*, 12s *Zaragoça*, 1691

Not in Salva's Catalogues.

9731 OCAMPO. Los quatro Libros primeros de la CRONICA GENERAL de España, que recopila el Maestro Florian do Canpo, folio, BEST EDITION, black letter, *title in red and black with large woodcut, a little stained, otherwise a good copy in vellum*, 36s *Camora, Juan Picardo*, 1543

9732 ——— the same, *a fine clean copy, in vellum*, £2. 10s 1543

Priced, J. Bohn, 1840, £6. 6s ; Heber's copy fetched £3. 17s.

9733 OCAMPO, Los Cinco Libros Primeros de la Coronica General, sm. folio, *bd.* 10s *Alcala*, 1578

9734 OCAMPO Y MORALES. OCAMPO (Florian de) Los Cinco Libros Primeros, *Alcala*, 1578—La Coronica General que continuava MORALES, *ib.* 1574—Los otros dos libros, XIe y XII, *ib.* 1577—Las Antiguedades de las Ciudades de España, *ib.* 1575—Los cinco libros postreros (XIII-XVII. etc.) *Cordova*, 1586 —5 vols. in 4, *a complete set of the Chronicles of Spain by Florian Docampo, with the continuation by Ambrosio de Morales, a few leaves mended*, £3. 3s 1574-86

Priced, 1847, £6. 6s. EXTREMELY RARE to find complete. The Condé copy sold for £11. 0s 6d.

9735 ——— CORONICA DE ESPANA por Florian de Ocampo y A. de Morales, 10 vols. 4to. 1791-93—Historia de los Reyes de Castilla y Leon, 2 vols. 4to. 1792—Opusculos Castellanos de Morales anotadas por Cifuentes, 3 vols. 1793—together 15 vols. 4to. BEST EDITION, *a complete and very neat set in Spanish calf*, £4. *Madrid*, 1791-93

Priced, Salva, 140 fr. Morales continued Ocampo to the union of the crowns of Castile and Leon in 1037—a point from which it was afterwards carried by Sandoval to the death of Alfonso VII. in 1097, where it finally stops. Morales' history, as an historical composition, shows a more enlightened spirit than the work of Ocampo.

"Everywhere it breathes the spirit of its age, and, when taken together is not only the most interesting of the Spanish Chronicles, but the most interesting of all that, in any country, mark the transactions of its practical and romantic traditions to the grave exactness of historic truth."—*Ticknor*, 1849, p. 151.

9736 OCHOA DE LA SALDE, La Carolea, Inchiridion que trata de la Vida y Hechos del Imperado Don Carlos V. hasta 1555, Primera Parte, (*all published*) stout sm. folio, *a little stained and spotted, vellum*, RARE, 18s *Lisboa, Borges*, 1585

9736*OCHOA, Epistolario Español, Cartas de Españoles Ilustres, con notas Vol I. roy. 8vo. 644 pp. *double cols. hf. morocco, joints, gt. edges*, 15s *Madrid*, 1850

9737 OLIVER HURTADO, Munda Pompeiana, memoria premiada por la Academia, roy. 8vo. *sd.* 10s *Madrid*, 1861

9738 Oliveros de Castilla y Artus, por Floresta, 12mo *vellum*, 10s *Barcelona*, 1726

9738*——— the same, 12mo. *vellum*, 5s *Madrid, s. a.*

9739 ONA (Pedro de, *natural de los Infantes de Engol en Chile*) ARAUCO DOMADO, (*poema epico*) stout 12mo. *good copy in limp vellum*, VERY RARE, £3. 3s *Madrid*, 1605

COLLATION: Title, privileges, Sonnets, etc. 16 leaves; folios 1-342; Table, 2 leaves.

9740 ORTIZ Y SANZ, Compendio Chronologico de la Historia de España, 7 vols. 12mo. *Spanish calf*, 25s *ib.* 1795-1803

Priced, 1824, 7 vols. £3. 3s.

9741 ORTIZ (Francisco) EPISTOLAS Familiares, embiadas a algunas personas particulares; con algunas otras obras del mesmo padre, sm. 4to. Black letter, *curious printer's device on the last page*, VERY FINE AND LARGE COPY, *limp vellum*, £3. 3s *Caragoça, Nagera*, 1552
VERY RARE COLLATION. Title in black and red, within woodcut border, prologue, table, etc. 4 leaves; text, folios 1-128; Verses, Oraciones, etc. folios 119 (129) to 136.

9742 ORTIZ DE ZUÑIGA, Annales Eclesiasticos y Seculares de la Ciudad de Sevilla, folio, *Genealogical Table of the " Royal Blood of La Cerda," fine copy, vellum*, 18s *Madrid*, 1677

9743 ORTUNEZ DE CALAHORRA (Diego) ESPEIO de PRINCIPES y CAVALLEROS, en el qual se cuentan los immortales hechos del Cavallero del Febo y de su hermano Rosicler, hijos del Emperador Trebacio, amores de Claridiana y de otros, con la Segunda Parte por Pedro de la Sierra, 1617—TERCERA Y QUARTA parte, por MARCOS MARTINEZ, 1623—together 4 parts in 2 vols. folio, *very fine copy in red morocco extra, gilt edges*, £20. *Caragoça*, 1617;23
A VERY RARE ROMANCE, not in Salva's catalogues. Brunet says of the 4 parts " Ces deux articles, qui ne doivent pas étre séparés, sont rares et fort recherchés 16 liv. Hibbert. Le bel exemple acheté 38 liv. 17 à la vente Stanley, a été revendu £21. 10 sh. chez Heber.

9744 OSSUNA (Fr.) Ley de Amor Sancto, sq. 8vo. Black letter, *vellum, wanting title*, 10s *Sevilla*, 1542

9745 —— NORTE de los ESTADOS; regla de bivir a los Măcebos, a los Casados, a los Biudos, y a todos los Cŏtinentes, sq. 8vo. Black letter, *curious woodcut on title, old binding, very rare*, 36s *Burgos, Junta*, 1550
A scarce and curious work treating on marriage, virgins, widows, etc.; unmentioned by Brunet, Salva, and all bibliographers. Mr. Ticknor mentions the Ley de Amor as "written with great purity of style and sometimes with fervid eloquence."-(1863, II. 13.)

9746 OVIEDO, Historia general y natural de las Indias, Islas y Tierra-firme del Mar Océano, por el Capitan Gonzalo F. De Oviedo y Valdés, Vols. I-IV, sm. folio, *maps and plates, sd.* £3. 15s *Madrid*, 1851-5

9747 [OWEN, (John)] OVEN, Agudexas (Epigrams) traducidas en metro Castellano, por F. de la Torre, sq. 8vo. *calf,* 5s *ib.* 1674

9748 PAPELES CURIOSOS: a collection in 6 vols. sq. 8vo. *containing about 150 pieces on various subjects in* MANUSCRIPT, *with the exception of a few printed tracts, the first vol. bound in old calf, the remainder in vellum,* £5.
Sec. XVII-XVIII.
A most interesting and valuable collection: the greater part being original and unpublished matter, including important documents on obscure points of Spanish History, the secret politics of the time of Philip II. and Philip III. with free strictures on government; Poems, Literary Curiosities, translations and satires upon the great writers of Spain; Criticisms on public events; news from America; and pieces concerning the intrusion of ecclesiastical authority into the political system. There is a series of 15 documents, which begins with a "Papel antique sobre les Particulares que en la orden de S Domingo han escandalizado con su doctrina ó vida," in which a rather curious interpretation is given of the letters *I. H. S.* These tracts handle in a minute and peculiar manner the Immaculate conception and other dogmas of the Church.

9749 PAPELES VARIOS: An extraordinary collection of 25 Official Documents on the COMMERCE of SPAIN and its AMERICAN Dependencies, including some Proclamations, *Printed and MS.* in 1 vol. fol. *limp vellum, from the library of Lord Orford,* £10. 10s
The MS. portion includes the following 3 works: "Informe de la Contradixia general de Indias y Representacion del Comercio de Cadiz; de le " Commercio Libre;" " De la Historia de America de Robertson."

9750 PAPELES VARIOS: Godoy, Discurso serio-iocoso sobre los Pronosticos, 1684 —Escudillas de Pupa, respuestas de Pepa, Tragos de Pipa, Vientos de Popa, y Começones de Pupa, 1683—Arbitrage politico-militar, sentencia de Garena, en el fantastico Congresso, *very curious woodcut*, 1683—Oracion a Inocencio XI de Casimiro Denhoff, Embaxador de POLONIA sobre la Batalla de Viena, 1683; *and other curious Spanish Tracts, together* 17, in 1 vol. sq. 8vo. *bd.* 30s 1683, &c.

9751 PAPELES Varios: Crisol Historico Politico del Arte de Plateros, con las leyes del Oro y de la Plata—Memorial por las dos familias Calzada (having many of its passages obliterated, with the MS. Certificate of the "Inquisidor-General para expungar libros prohibidos," etc. in 1 vol. fol. *vellum*, 7s *Pam.* 1732-44

9752 PARNASO ESPAÑOL. Colleccion de Poesias escogidas de los mas celebres Poetas Castellanos, por D. Juan Lopez de Sedano, 9 vols. 16mo. *sd.* 12s; or, *a fine copy in Spanish calf gilt*, 25s *Madrid*, 1768-78
"A work which, though ill-digested, and not always showing good taste in its selection and criticisms, is still a rich mine of the poetry of the country in its best days, and contains important materials for the history of Spanish literature from the period of Boscan and Garcilasso."-*Ticknor. III.* 184, 251.

9753 PAULO Quadrado, Elogio historico de A. D. de Escaño, imp. 8vo. *sd.* 5s 1852

9754 PEDRAZA (Fran. Bermudez de) Antiguedad y Excelencias de GRANADA, 4to. *vellum*, RARE, 32*s* *Madrid*, 1608
COLLATION: Title, dedication, and preliminary matter, 12 leaves; folios 1-190; Lists of Chapters and Authors, 6 leaves. Chap. 9 and 10, are devoted to a description of the Alhambra.

9755 PEDRAZA, Historia Ecclesiastica, Principios, y Progressos de la Ciudad y Religion Catolica de GRANADA, folio, *engraved title, and first leaf mended, fine copy in calf*, £2. 16*s* *Granada*, 1638
Priced, 1841, H. G. Bohn, £5. 5*s*. This important work is undescribed by bibliographers, and is extremely scarce even in Granada. It contains a complete account of the building and history of the Alhambra. Southey speaks of the book in high terms of praise.

9756 PEREDA, Patrona de Madrid y venidas de nuestra Señora a España, 16mo. *engraved title, calf*, 8*s* *Valladolid*, 1604
A curious work, relating to the performances of a certain miraculous image.

9758 PELLICER Y SAFORCADA (J. A.) Ensayo de una Bibliotheca de Traductores Españoles, con vidas de otros Escritores (Cervantes, Argensola, &c.) sm 4to. LARGE PAPER, *vellum*, 12*s* *Madrid*, 1778
Gives an account of all the Early editions of the Bible in Spanish.

9759 PELLICER, Origen y Progresos de la Comedia en España, 2 vols. in 1, 12mo. *ports. calf*, 5*s* *ib.* 1804

9760 PEREZ (Antonio, Secretario que fue de Phelipe II.) Relaciones (de sus Prisiones y Persecuciones) y Cartas, sq. 8vo. *calf*, 10*s* *Paris*, 1624
Perez' Relaciones revealed so many state secrets, and were so unpleasant to the Spanish Government that they were included in the Index Expurgatorius of the Inquisition even down to 1805.

9761 PEREZ (P. P.) Compendio del Derecho publico y comun de España, o de las leyes de las Siete Partidas, 4 vols. 12mo. *Spanish calf gilt*, 12*s* *Madrid*, 1784

9762 PEREZ DE GUZMAN (Fernan.) Valerio de las Hystorias Scolasticas de la sagrada Scritura y de los hechos D ESPANA cō las Batallas cāpales sm. fol. *title with curious woodcut and border, initial letters*, 𝔅lack 𝔩etter, *a few leaves mended, vellum*, 18*s* *Sevilla, Cromberger*, 1536
Priced, Salva, £2. The real author of this work is the Arcipreste Diego Rodriguez de Murcia. This edition is not mentioned by Antonio.

9763 PEREZ DE HERRERA, Proverbios Morales y Consejos Christianos, Enigmas Philosoficas, etc. sq. 8vo. *woodcuts of emblems, vellum*, 20*s* *Madrid*, 1733

9764 PEREZ DE HITA, Historia de las Guerras Civiles de Granada, thick 12mo. *engraved frontispiece, calf*, 6*s* *Paris*, 1606

9765 ——— Historia de los Vandos y Abencerrages y las Civiles Guerras, con la SEGUNDA PARTE, 2 vols. 12mo. *vellum*, 20*s* *Sevilla*, 1732, *y Madrid*, 1724

9766 ——— the same, 2 vols. 12mo. *vellum*, 18*s* *Barcelona*, 1757, *Madrid*, 1724

9767 PESCARA. VALLES, Historia del Capitan DON HERNANDO DE AUALOS, Marques de Pescara, con los hechos de otros seite Capitanes de Carlos V, con la Conquista de Africa de Fuentes, stout 16mo. *good sound copy, hf. calf*, 25*s*
RARE; not in Salva's catalogues. *Anvers, P. Nutio*, 1570

9768 PETRARCHA (Franc.) de los Remedios contra prospera y adversa Fortuna, sm. folio, *coat of arms on title, large woodcut of the Crucifixion full size of the page, and two pages with woodcut borders*, SUPERB COPY *in vellum*, £4. 15*s* *Valladolid, Diego de Gumiel*, 1510

9769 ——— another copy, sm. folio, *wanting the first eight leaves, vellum*, 15*s* 1510
COLLATION: Woodcut title, 1 leaf; Carta, etc. 2 leaves, obverse of the first is blank, La Vida del Clar. poeta e tabla, 5 leaves, the last of which is occupied with a large woodcut, and sheets b 1 to z 8, and A 1 to F 6.
AN ALMOST UNKNOWN EDITION: not mentioned by Brunet, nor can I find the slightest trace of any copy having occurred for sale.

9770 ——— REMEDIOS contra prospera y adversa fortuna, sm. folio, 𝔅lack 𝔏etter, *woodcut title injured, and last leaf mounted, vellum*, 18*s* *Caragoça, Aleman*, 1523

9771 ——— REMEDIOS contra Prospera y Adversa Fortuna, traducido (por Francisco de Madrid) sm. folio, 𝔅lack 𝔩etter, *woodcut title dated* 1533, *good copy, vellum, rare*, 15*s* *Sevilla, Juan Varela*, 1534

9772 ——— TRASLACION d los seys TRIUMFOS de Frācisco Petrarca de Toscano en Castellão, fecha por Antonio de Obregō Capellā del Rey, sm. folio, 𝔅lack 𝔏etter, *two curious woodcuts, one on the title, the other on reverse of folio iv. margin of the first few leaves stained, otherwise a very fine copy, in the original impressed binding*, £2. 6*s* *Sevilla, Juan Varela de Salamanca*, 1526

9773 PINEDO Y SALAZAR, Historia de la insigne Orden del TOYSON DE ORO, 3 vols. sm. folio, *plate, cloth, bds.* 15*s* *Madrid*, 1787-92
Priced, 1836, Salva's, Paris, 53 fr.

9774 PISA (Francisco de) Descripcion de la imperial Ciudad de Toledo, Historia de sus antiguedades, sus Reis, Arçobispos, etc. 1ra. parte, (*all published*) folio, *old calf, clean copy*, 12*s* *Toledo*, 1617

9775 PLINIO Segundo (Cayo) Historia Natural, traducida por el Lic. Geronimo de Huerta, ampliada por el mismo, con escolios y anotaciones, 2 vols. sm. folio, *with Map of* America, *and cuts, translator's autograph, good copy in Spanish calf gilt,* rare, 25s *Madrid,* 1624-29
Priced, 1843, Salva, 50 fr. Cette traduction est fort estimée, non-seulement à cause des additions faites à l'ouvrage original, mais encore pour la pureté et élégance du style.

9776 PLUTARCO, Morales, traduzidos de lengua Griega en Castellano (por Gracian) sm. folio, black letter, *some of the marginal notes slightly cut into, calf,* rare 35s *Alcala de Henares,* 1548

9777 Poesias : El Cortesano, por Vocangel y Unzueta, 1757—Fabula burlesca de Bulcano y Venus, por Calderon, 1767—Carta de Dido e Eneas, por Zenun, *MS. ; and numerous other pieces of Spanish poetry,* in 1 vol. sq. 8vo. *vellum,* 15s
Madrid, 1740-70

9778 POLO de Medina (S. Jacinto) Obras en prosa y verso, sm. 4to. *vellum, very fine copy,* 20s *ib.* 1726

9779 PONZ, Viage de España, en que se da noticia de las cosas mas apreciables y dignas de saberse que hay en ella, 18 vols.—Viage fuera de España, 2 vols.— together 20 vols. sm. 8vo. *many plates of Church Architecture, Antiquities, Views, etc. bds. uncut,* £3. 3s *Madrid, Ibarra,* 1776-94

9780 —— the same, 20 vols. sm. 8vo. *calf,* £2. 1785-94
Priced, 20 vols. 1825, Salva, £8. hf. bd. £10. 10s: and 1826, £7. 7s, hf. bd. £7. : and 1843, Salva, 144 fr. This curious and interesting work contains a very complete description of Spain; it will be found of great use to geographers and travellers. "Ouvrage curieux dont on trouve difficilement des exemplaires complets."—*Brunet.* "On trouve dans ce voyages des details assez étendus sur les peintres, les sculpteurs et les architectes espagnols."—*Salva.*

9781 Porras, Tratado de la Oraciō, sq. 8vo. Black letter, *last leaf in MS. vel.* 9s 1552
9782 Pujol, Glossa de la carta de Almanzor, y vida de Conrado, sq. 8vo. *vel.* 6s 1677
9783 Pujades, Coronica de Cathaluña, 2 vols. 12mo. *cuts, vellum,* 5s *Barcelona,* 1730
9783*Question de Amor, de dos Enamorados, (dada a luz por Alonso de Ulloa) 12mo. *each page ruled in with red lines, fine copy in red morocco extra, gilt edges, from the MacCarthy collection,* £3. 3s *Venetia, Giolito de Ferrariis,* 1554
9784 Question de Amor y Carcel de Amor, 16mo. *a few leaves at the end slightly wormed, bds.* 5s *Anvers, Nucio,* 1576
9785 QUEVEDO Villegas (D. Francisco) Obras, 6 vols. 8vo. *fine portraits and plates, Spanish calf,* 12s *Madrid, Ibarra,* 1772
9786 —— the same, 11 vols. 8vo. *portrait and plates, hf. vellum, uncut,* 30s 1791-94
9787 —— the same, 11 vols. sm. 8vo. *hf. calf,* 25s 1791-94
9788 —— the same, 11 vols. sm. 8vo. *calf neat,* £2. 2s 1791-94
Priced, 1828, £5. 5s ; 1829, £5. 5s ; 1847, £3. 13s 6d ; 1854, £3. 3s.

9789 Quevedo, Politica de Dios, Govierno de Christo, Tirania de Satanas, Vida del Buscon, Sueños, todos los Diablos, Cuento de Cuentos, etc. 16mo. first edition, *vellum,* 12s *Pamplona,* 1631
9790 Quintana, Santos de la Ciudad de Toledo y su Arçobispado, folio, *title-page engraved with the portraits of* 17 *archbishops, fine copy in calf,* 12s *Madrid,* 1651
9791 Quintana (M. J.) Poesias, 12mo. *red morocco, gilt edges,* 10s ? 1813
9792 Quiros (Franc. Bern de) Obras, sm. 4to. *calf, poor copy,* 16s *Madrid,* 1656
A curious work, containing Poems, Novels and Comedies, unnoticed by Ticknor, and not in Salva's catalogue

9793 RADA (F. L. de) Nobleza de la Espada, cuyo esplendor se espresa en tres libros, segun Ciencia, Arte y Esperiencia, 3 vols. in 2, folio, *engraved title-page, and more than* 60 *plates, fine copy in vellum,* £2. 16s *ib.* 1705
9794 RAMOS, Reynados de Menor Edad, y de grandes reyes, 8vo. *frontispiece and plates, calf or vellum,* 21s *ib.* 1672
9795 Real Sociedad Bascongada. Extractos de las Juntas Generales celebradas por la Real Sociedad Bascongada, en varias ciudades, 1771-76, 6 vols. in 1, stout sm. 8vo. *bds.* 7s 6d *Vitoria, (y Madrid)* 1771-76
9796 Reales Cedulas. Capitulos generales de las Cortes, 1602-40, in 1 vol. folio, *vellum,* 15s *Madrid,* 1610-42
9797 REBOLLEDO (el Conde de) Obras Poeticas, 2 vols. sq. 8vo. *portraits old calf, scarce,* £2. 2s *Amberes,* 1660-61
9798 RECOPILACION, Leyes de, 2 vols.—Autos acordados, 1 vol.—together 3 vols. stout large folio, *vellum,* 20s *Madrid,* 1775
9799 Leyes de Recopilacion, 7 vols. in 9, 12mo. *hf. calf,* 7s *ib.* 1777-76

9800 REJON de Silva, La Pintura, poema, 8vo. *vignettes, calf,* 5s *Segovia,* 1786
9801 REJON de Silva, Diccionario de las Nobles Artes, sq. 8vo. *hf. bd. a useful book,* 10s *Segovia,* 1788
9802 REPRESENTACION contra el pretendido Voto de Santiago, que hace al Rey el Duque de Arcos, con Apendice, folio, *vellum,* 5s *Madrid,* 1771-77
9803 REPROBACION de la ASTROLOGIA judiciaria o divinatoria, sacada de Toscano, 16mo. *title soiled, and slightly stained, calf, rare,* 14s *Salamanca,* 1546
  The translator does not mention either his own or the original writer's name.
9804 RHETORICA en lengua Castellana en la qual se pone muy en breve lo necessario para saber bien hablar y escrevir, sq. 8vo. *the last two leaves in manuscript, vellum,* RARE, 21s *Alcala,* 1541
9805 RIBERO y Larrea, Historia de Don Pelayo Infanzon, Quixote de la Cantabria, 3 vols. 12mo. *calf,* 7s 6d *Madrid,* 1792-1800
9806 RISCO (Manuel) La Castilla, Historia del Cid, 8vo. *sd.* 2s 6d 1792
9807 —— Historia de Leon y de ses Reyes, 2 vols. sq. 8vo. *sd.* 10s 1792
9808 RIVILLA BONET, Desvios de la Naturaleza, Origen de los Monstros, sq. 8vo. *plate, vellum,* 7s *Lima,* 1695
9809 ROBLES (Isidro de) VARIOS EFECTOS de Amor, en onze Novelas Exemplares de diferentes Autores, los mejores Ingenios de España, sq. 8vo. *calf,* 20s *Mad.* 1692
9809*—— Varios PRODIGIOS de Amor, sq. 8vo. *being another edition of the Efectos, calf,* 15s *Madrid,* 1729
  "No work affords more ample proof of the inexhaustible richness of the Castilian language than the present. To write five novels, in prose and verse, under the strict condition of excluding from each of them one of the five vowels of the alphabet, and to accomplish this task in such a manner that the reader does not at first sight perceive the scheme or the fetters with which the author has surrounded his pen, could be only done in a language extraordinarily rich in words and phrases."—*Salva.*
9810 RODRIGUEZ, Guirnalda poetica, 16mo. *vellum,* 6s *Madrid,* 1734
9810*RODRIGUEZ JORDAN Escuela de a Cavallo, sq. 8vo. 23 *plates of Horsemanship, and several cuts, calf neat,* 15s *Madrid,* 1751
9811 ROIG Y IALPI (Juan Gaspar) Resumen Historial de las Grandezas y Antiquedades de la ciudad de GERONA, folio, *fine copy, vellum, rare,* £2. *Barcelona,* 1678
9811*ROIG (Juan G.) Epitome historico de la Ciudad de MANRESA (Catalonia) sq. 8vo. *vellum,* 18s *Barcelona,* 1692
  Unmentioned by Brunet, not in Salva's catalogues.
9812 ROIAS (Pedro de) Historia de la Ciudad de Toledo, Fundacion, Antiguedades, Grandezas, Vidas de sus Arçobispos y Santos, &c. 2 vols. folio, *Spanish morocco extra,* £2. 5s *Madrid,* 1654-63
9813 ROJAS (A. de) Viage Entretenido, stout 12mo. *hf. bd.* 10s *Lerida,* 1615
  This work, written by a famous Comedian, in prose and verse, is very important for the History of the Spanish Stage.
9814 ROMANCERO GENERAL, en que se contienen todos los Romances que andan impresos, aora nuevamente añadido y emendado (por Pedro de Flores), stout sm. 4to. *the title; ' al Lector' 2 leaves; fol.* 1, 33, 482; *and Table,* 2 *leaves,* (*altogether 8 leaves*) *being supplied in manuscript, many leaves stained, old smooth mor.* £7. *Madrid, Juan de la Cuesta,* 1604
9815 —— another copy, sq. 8vo. *consisting of leaves* 91 *to* 425, *calf,* 25s 1604
  Priced, 1837. Payne and Foss, mor. £18. 18s; fetched, Lloyd's, russia, £20. 10s; Gardner's, russia, £14. 14s.
  This volume contains a most curious assemblage of rare old Spanish ballads, and has always been highly esteemed by the literati of Spain. In the collection are included thirty-two ballads relating to the Cid, twelve of which are not to be found even in Escobar. It is more complete than the edition of 1602, which sold in Col. Stanley's sale for £63.
  " L'édition précédente n'a que neuf parties; celleci en renferme seize."—*Brunet.* (*Seize* is here erroneously printed for *treize.*)
9816 DURAN, COLECCION DE ROMANCES CASTELLANOS anteriores al Siglo XVIII: Romancero de Romances Moriscos, todos los del Romancero General, 1828— Romances Doctrinales, Amatorios, Festivos, Jocosos, Satiricos y Burlescos, 1829 —Cancionero y Romancero de Coplas y Canciones, Letrillas, etc. 1829—Romances Caballerescos y historicos, 2 vols. 1832—5 vols. 12mo. *a complete set, hf. calf,* 36s *ib.* 1828-32
9817 —— the same, 5 vols. in 3, 13mo. *with some valuable manuscript notes by Mr. Ford, hf. calf,* 30s 1828-32
9818 —— new edition, the COMPLETE SERIES in 2 vols. roy. 8vo. 1320 pp. *double cols. hf. morocco, joints, gilt edges,* £2. 2s *Madrid,* 1851
9819 —— Romancero de Romances Moriscos—Cancionero y Romancero de Coplas, etc. 2 vols. 12mo. *hf. calf,* 12s *ib.* 1828-29

9820 DEPPING, Coleccion de los mas celebres Romances Antiguos Españoles, Historicos y Caballerescos, ahora enmendada, 2 vols. 12mo. *hf. calf, 7s* 1825
9821 PRIMAVERA y Flor de ROMANCES, ò colleccion de los mas viejos y mas populares Romances Castellanos con introduccion y notas por Wolf y Hoffmann, 2 vols. 8vo. *hf. morocco, uncut*, 18s 6d *Berlin*, 1856
"Selected with great judgment from what is oldest and best, richest and most attractive, in the old collections."—*Ticknor*, 1863, III, 414.
9822 SILVA de Romances Viejos publicada por Jacobo Grimm, 16mo. *hf. morocco, gilt top, uncut*, 10s *Vienna*, 1815
9823 ROMANCES DE GERMANIA de varios autores, con el VOCABULARIO por la orden del a, b, c, para declaracion de sus terminos y lengua, compuesto por Juan Hidalgo, 16mo. *curious woodcuts on title and first leaf, the title slightly injured, calf*, £4. *Caragoça*, 1644
EXTREMELY RARE: not in Salva's catalogues. It is a collection of ballads in the dialect of the Spanish thieves, with a Vocabulary of the phrases.
9824 ROMANCES DE GERMANIA, con Vocabulario, por Hidalgo, discurso de la expulsion de los Gitanos, etc. sm. 8vo. *calf*, 6s 1779
The Germania of Spain is a Spanish Thieves' slang, not Gipsey Proper.
"The Vocabulary of this jargon or dialect is recognised as genuine by Mayans y Siscar."—*Ticknor*, III. p. 29.
9825 ROMANCES VARIOS. A collection of upwards of 100 Romances, Ballads, etc. published separately at various times and places, in 1 vol. sq. 8vo. 100 *curious woodcuts, sd*. £4. 4s 1750-1800
It would be useless to mention the names of a few of the pieces in this interesting collection; all are rare and curious, forming a valuable compilation of the Popular Poetry and Folk Lore of Spain in the last century.
9826 ROMANCES VARIOS. Another modern collection: El Hijo del Verdugo: Cambio de Calzones por Alforjas; Julian de Paredes; La Inocencia perseguida; Doña Josefa Ramirez; La Gitanilla de Madrid: Coplas de la Tabernera y los Borrachos; Los once amores nuevos de una Señora de Andalucia; Doña Ines de Alfaro; Doña Francisca la Cautiva; and others—together 72 curious Romances in 1 vol. sm. 4to. *hf. bd*. 30s *Valencia, Barcelona, Cordoba*, 1822-31, &c.
9827 ROMANCE de los hechos y atrocidades de Estevan de Lucena, *with numerous other curious Romances and Ballads concerning Robbers, etc*. in 1 vol. sq. 8vo. *rude cuts, hf. bd*. 5s *Madrid*, 1750
9828 ROSELL. Historia del Combata de Lepanto, imp. 8vo. *sd*. 4s 1853
9829 RUIZ DE LEON, Hernandia, Triumphos de la Fe y Gloria de las Armas Españoles, poema heroyco, Conquista de Mexico, sq. 8vo. *fine copy in green morocco, gilt edges, by Smith*, £3. 3s *Madrid*, 1755
9830 SAEZ, Demonstracion del valor de las Monedas de España (Enrique IV y Carlos IV) 4to. *sd*. 6s 1805
9831 SALAZAR (Pedro de) Hystoria de la Guerra y Presa de Africa, folio, *original edition, woodcuts, wanting title, and imperfect at the end, vellum*, 7s *Napoles*, 1552
9832 SALAZAR Y CASTRO (Luis de) Historia genealogica de la CASA DE LARA, justificada con instrumentos, y escritores, 3 vols.—PRUEBAS de la CASA DE LARA, 1 vol.—together 4 vols. stout folio, *numerous Pedigrees and Coats of Arms, fine copy, vellum*, £6. *Madrid*, 1694-97
9833 ——— Indice de las glorias de la Casa FARNESE, stout sm. folio, *with Pedigrees, limp vellum, rare*, 36s *ib*. 1716
9834 SALAZAR DE MENDOCA (Pedro de) Chronico de el Cardenal Don Juan Tauera, 4to. *portrait of the Cardinal, fine copy, old calf*, 9s *Toledo*, 1603
Priced, 1824, Thorpe, vell. £2. 2s; 1820, Salva, £1. 1s; 1842, Thorpe, mor. £1. 11s 6d.
9835 SALAZAR DE MENDOZA, Origen de las Dignidades Seglares de Castilla y Leon, relacion de los Reyes, de sus acciones, casamientos, etc. sm. folio, *engraved title, original edition, vellum*, 14s *Toledo*, 1618
9836 ——— Origen de las Dignidades, *second edition, with a list of the creations of Marquises and Counts at the end*—CARILLO, Origen de la Dignidad de Grande de Castilla—2 vols. in 1, folio, *bd*. 10s *Madrid*, 1657
Two important and rare works on Spanish Heraldry; the first was priced, 1826, by Salva, £1. 10s; the second is neither mentioned by Salva, Brunet, nor Ebert, it contains on leaves 9-11 an alphabetical list of 93 Spanish Dukes, Marquises, and Counts, with an account of their estates.
9837 SALAZAR DE MENDOZA, Monarquia de España, desde su origen hasta 1623, con la Historia de Felipe III de Davila publicada por Ulloa, 3 vols. folio, *portrait and genealogical tree of Philip III, and 4 plates of Coins, fine copy in calf gilt, or vellum*, 36s *ib*. 1770-1
The third vol. is often wanting.
Priced, 1806, Salva, £2. 12s 6d; Large Paper, 1822, Thorpe, £5. 5s; 1824, Thorpe, £4. 4s; 1830, Payne and Foss, £4. 4s; 1832, Payne and Foss, £3. 3s. "Ouvrage important pour l'histoire d'Espagne."—*Brunet*.

9838 SALLUST. Cayo Sallustio Crispo en Español: Conjuracion de Catalina, y la Guerra de Jugurta, traducido por el Infante Don Gabriel, Latino y Espanol, con el Suplemento, folio, *Original Edition, fine plates, calf, gilt edges*, £2.
Madrid, Ibarra, 1772
This may fairly be considered as the most beautiful specimen of typography ever issued from the Spanish press. Bayer's Supplement at the end "Del Alfabeto y Lengua de los Fenices y de sus Colonias" is a very valuable work on the Phœnicians, their Language, Antiquities, Coins, etc., illustrated with plates of inscriptions.
"This is rare and dear, as the Prince reserved all the copies for presents."—*Dibdin*

9839 Salzedo (Garcia de) Christales de Helicona, Rimas, sq. 8vo. *stained, vellum,* 6s
Madrid, 1650
Priced, 1826, Salva, 26s. "Ce volume forme la seconde partie des poésies de l'auteur. La premiere a paru a Madrid, en 1624."—*Brunet.*

9840 SAMANIEGO, Fabulas en Verso Castellano, 3 vols. 12mo. *about* 150 *pretty plates after Rodriguez, by Los Vasquez, Marti, Albuerne, etc. calf,* 28s *ib.* 1804

9844 SAMPER, Montesa Ilustrada, Origen, progressos, privilegios, heroes, y Varones ilustres de esta Orden, 3 vols. stout sm. folio, *hf. calf, a little wormed, scarce,* 36s
Valencia, 1669
"Ouvrage peu commun."—*Brunet.*

9845 SANCHEZ (T. A.) Coleccion de Poesias Castellanas anteriores al Siglo XV, con Notas e Indice de Voces antiguadas, 4 vols. 12mo. *calf,* 20s   *Madrid,* 1779-90
"Collection bien faite et d'une belle execution typographique."—*Brunet.*

9846 SANCT PEDRO (Hernando de) Carcel de Amor, con otras obras, 12mo. *woodcut initials, vellum, scarce,* 20s   *Venetia, Giolito de Ferrariis,* 1553

9846*——— the same, 12mo. *Espagnol et Franç. half bound,* 5s   1616

9847 SANDOVAL (P. de) Chronica del inclito Emperador de España Alonso VII, folio, *woodcut Coats of Arms, title soiled and mended, margins of a few leaves stained, vellum,* 36s   *Madrid,* 1600
Priced, 1825, Thorpe, mor. £5. 5s; 1826, mor. £3. 3s; 1826, Salva, £3. 2s. Collation: Title; 'Suma,' Dedication, Prologo and 'Adiciones y Tabla,' 11 leaves; Text, page 1—491. Pages 1—181 contain the Chronicle of Alonso; the remainder, being more than half the book, contains the histories of the noble houses of Sandoval, Osorio, Aculla, Belasco, Castro, Zuniga, Guzman, Haro, Mendoça, Manriques, Padilla, Ponces de Leon, Quinones, Toledo, Touar, with their coats-of-arms.

9848 Sandoval, Historia de los Reyes de Castilla y de Leon, (Fernando el Magno hasta a Alonso VII) sm. folio, *bottom of title cut, Coat of Arms on the back of the title, old calf, arms on sides,* 18s   *Pamplona,* 1615

9849 ——— the same, *new issue, title discoloured and mended,* 1634—Historia de los Obispos Idacio de Badajoz, Sebastiano de Salamanca, Sampiro de Astorga y Pelagio de Oviedo, 1634—2 vols. in 1, folio, *russia extra, gilt edges,* £2. 16s
Pamplona, 1634
Priced, 1824, Thorpe, in vell. the two works, £6. 6s; 1826, Salva, £3. 3s. "Ouvrage estimé."—*Brunet*

9850 ——— Antiguedad de la Ciudad, y Iglesia de Tuy, y de sus Obispos, sq. 12mo. *old calf,* 14s   *Braga,* 1610

9851 SANTOS (Francisco) Obras en Prosa y Verso, 4 vols. sq. 12mo. *calf,* 25s   1723
Priced, 1824, Thorpe, £2. 2s; 1826, Salva, £2.; 1822, Salva, vell. £1. 10s.

9852 Saynetes, Coleccion de, representados en los teatros, 2 vols. sq. 8vo. *bd.* 9s 1791

9852* SEBASTIAN (Pedro Cubero) Peregrinacion de la mayor parte del Mundo, con las cosas singulares que ha vistas, sq. 8vo. *vellum,* £2. 2s   *Zaragoza,* 1688
Colonel Stanley's copy fetched £6. 6s. This rare book contains many curious particulars relative to Russia and Poland.

9853 SEMANARIO ERUDITO, que comprehende varias obras ineditas, criticas, politicas, historicas, satiricas, y jocosas de nuestros mejores autores, dalas a luz Don A. Valladares de Sotomayor, Vols. I-XXXIV, sm 4to. *wanting XXXII, calf, gilt edges,* 30s   *Madrid,* 1788-91

9854 Semanario Pintoresco Español, Enciclopedia Popular, Enero de 1850 hasta Deciembre 1851, 2 vols. sm. folio, *an entertaining weekly Magazine, with several hundred woodcuts of Portraits, Views, etc. cloth,* 12s   1850-51
Containing articles by Fernan Caballero, P. de la Escosura, and other celebrated writers.

9855 SENECA, Epistolas en Romance, con Introductio de Philosophia Moral por Leonardo Aretino, folio, *beautiful woodcut title, calf, very fine copy,* 36s
Alala de Henares, 1529
Priced, 1822, Salva, £2. 2s.

9856 Seyner, Historia del Levantamiento de Portugal, sq. 8vo. *sd.* 5s *Zaragoça,* 1644

Siete Partidas—*see* Alonso.

9857 SOLIS, Historia de la Conquista de Mexico, poblacion y Progresos de la America Septentrional, 2 vols. 4to. best edition, *two maps, superb portraits, that of* Cortes *after Titian, engraved by F. Selma, and a beautiful set of plates, engraved by Moreno Tejada, after designs by Ximeno, calf,* £2. 5s   *Madrid, Sancha,* 1783-84
A masterpiece of Spanish typographical and artistic skill, unsurpassed by any other Spanish work, and scarcely rivalled by the illustrated Don Quixote, 4 vols. 4to. *Ibarra,* 1780. Priced, 1837, Payne and Foss, £6. 6s; 1848, mor. £5. 5s, and calf, £4. 4s; large thick paper, 1848, Payne and Foss, calf, £5. 5s.

9858 SORIA Giron (D.) Fabrica de la Esperiencia, sq. 8vo. *500 curious Epigrams, almost all beginning with the letter N, printed within a woodcut border, engraved title, vellum*, 21s *Naples*, 1649
Rare; unmentioned by Brunet and Salva.
9859 SOTA (Fray Francisco) Chronica de los Principes de Asturias y Cantabria, folio, *bound*, 25s *Madrid*, 1681
Priced, 1829, Salva, £2. 2s; 1855, Lord Stuart de Rothesay's sale, a copy fetched £3. 5s. This chronicle extends from the conquest of Spain by the Moors, to 1200. At the end is an Appendix of ancient documents relating to the kings and nobility of Castille, taken from the Archives of Cathedral Churches, and Monasteries of St. Benedict. "Appendix operi adjecta, quam plurima eaque pervetusta diplomata exhibens, multum lucis tum historiae, tum rei genealogicae hispanicae foeneratur."—*Meusel*.
9860 SUAREZ de Chaues (L.) Dialogos de varias Questiones en Dialogos y metro Castellano sobre diuersas materias, con un Romance, stout 16mo. *title slightly injured, vellum, gilt edges*, 25s *Alcala, Juan Gracian*, 1577
Very rare; priced by Salva, £2. 2s.
9861 Suarez de Figueroa (C.) La Constante Amarilis, *Espanol y Frances*, por Lancelot, stout 12mo. *engraved title, coloured vellum*, 10s *Lyon*, 1614
9862 Sue (Eugenio) Misterios de Paris, traducidos por Cortada, 5 vols. 8vo. *plates, sd.* 7s 6d *Barcelona*, 1844
9863 —— Misterios de Paris, traduccion de Tió y Solá, 5 vols. 12mo. *hf. calf neat*, 10s *Barcel.* 1844
9864 —— Martin el Esposito, traducido por El Doncel, 14 vols. in 7, 16mo. *woodcuts, hf. morocco*, 15s *Madrid*, 1846-47
9865 Tamaio de Vargas, Historia de España de Mariana defendida contra Pedro Mantuano, sq. 8vo. *clean copy, uncut, bd. rare*, 10s *Toledo*, 1616
Rare; priced, 1822, by Salva, £1. 6s.
9866 —— Restauracion de la Ciudad del Salvador i Baia de Todos-Sanctos en Brasil, por las armas de Philippe IV, sq. 8vo. *vellum, rare*, £2. 2s *Madrid*, 1628
9867 Tapia, Historia de la Civilizacion Española, 2 vols. in 1, 12mo. *cloth*, 5s *ib.* 1840
9868 Tapia i Robles, Ilustracion del renombre de Grande, sq. sm. 8vo. *lives and portraits of persons who have been styled "the Great," with fine large portraits of the author and Philip IV, after Velasquez, fine copy, vellum*, 10s *ib.* 1638
Priced, 1826, Salva, £1. 11s 6d.
9869 Tarsis, Conde de Villamediana, Obras (Comedias, etc.) sq. 8vo. *vel.* 5s *ib.* 1634
9870 Teresa (Santa) Vida por F. de Ribera, sq. 8vo. *vellum*, 6s *ib.* 1602
9871 Terreros, Paleografia Española, 8vo. 18 *plates containing numerous facsimiles of ancient Spanish and Moorish writings, vellum*, 10s *ib.* 1758
9872 Tesoro de Escritores Misticos Espanoles, publ. por Ochoa, 3 vols. 8vo. *ports. hf. calf neat*, 14s *Paris*, 1847
Contents: I, Obras escog. de Santa Teresa; II, Alejo Venegas, Joan de Avila, Luis de Granada, Juan de la Cruz; III, Diego de Estella, Luis de Leon, Poesias espirituales, etc.
9873 [TEXEDA] Carrascon, segunda vez impreso con coreccion, con observaciones sobre su vida, etc. sq. 12mo. *with a MS. account of the author and his works, by B. Wiffen, Esq. inserted at beginning, hf. morocco, uncut*, 15s *s. l. et a.* (*ca.* 1843)
This is a reprint of the excessively rare original printed at Norwich in 1633.
9874 Toledo. Ramon Parro, Toledo en la mano, 6 descripcion de su Catedral, y de sus Monumentos y cosas notables, 2 vols. sm. 8vo. *hf. cf. uncut*, 12s *Toledo*, 1857
9875 TORENO (Conde de) Historia del Levantamiento, Guerra y Revolucion de España, 5 vols. stout 8vo. (pub. at 70 *francs*) *Spanish calf*, 36s *Madrid*, 1835-7
9876 Tornamira de Soto, Sumario de la Vida del Rey Jayme I, el Conquistador, 2 vols. in 1, 12mo. *morocco extra, gilt edges*, 14s *Valencia*, 1806-7
9877 TORO (Gabriel) Thesoro de Misericordia diuina y humana sobre el cuydado que tuvieron los antiguos de los necessitados, sq. 8vo. *some old MS. notes on the margins, calf, poor copy, rare*, 30s *Salamanca, Junta*, 1548
Not mentioned by Brunet or Ticknor, and not in Salva's catalogues. Sam's copy fetched, £1. 1s.
9878 TORRE Farfan, Fiestas de la Iglesia Metrop. de Sevilla al nuevo Culto de Fernando III, sm. folio, *portrait and numerous plates, vellum*, 10s *Sevilla*, 1671
This is a minute description of the cathedral of Seville.
9879 TORRES Villaroel (Obras) Libros en que estan reatados Quadernos Physicos, Medicos, Astrologicos, Poeticos, Morales y Mysticos, 14 vols. sq. 8vo. *portrait of Ferdinand VI. hf. calf, almost uncut*, 30s *Salamanca*, 1752
9880 TOSTADO (El, Don Alonso de Madrigal, Obispo de Malaga) Las XIII Questiones, 12mo. *fine copy, old calf*, 20s *Anvers, M. Nucio*, 1551
Priced, 1830, Payne and Foss, £2. 12s 6d. Very curious, the author compares Scripture History with Classical Mythology, rarely done by Spanish authors.
9881 Trolopp (Sir Francis) Misterios de Londres, traducidos por Arrenolas, 3 vols. sm. 8vo. *plates, hf. bd.* 10s *Barcelona*, 1845

9882 TUTOR Y MALO, Compendio Historial de los dos NUMANCIAS, sus grandezas, y Trofeos; y Vida de S. Saturio; 2 vols. in 1, sm. 4to. *sound clean copy*, RARE, 32*s* (? *Soria*), 1690
"This is the first part of a greater work, which the author meditated on the history of Soria; it contains amongst other things, book 1, cap. XIV—XXIII. inclusively, a notice of 12 illustrious families, with their arms, and of the illustrious men of this city. In the second part the author promised to examine these matters more extensively; this part, however as far as we know, has not been published." This work contains genealagies and descriptions of the coats-of-arms of the Salvador, Cancilleres, Morales, De Velo S. Lorente, Santa Cruz, Caltanazor, Santisteban, and Barnuevos families.

9883 UBEDA (Francisco de) Libro de Entretenimiento de la PICARA JUSTINA, 12mo. *calf, rare*, 25*s* *Brucellas*, 1608
Second edition, equally rare with the first which was printed at Medina del Campo in 1605.

9884 UBEDA, la Picara Montañesa llamada Justina, 8vo. *vellum, or calf*, 14*s* *Mad*. 1735
"A work whose tendency is obviously mischievous. The best edition is probably that of 1735 by Mayans y Siscar."—*Ticknor*.
The real author of this licentious romance, written in imitation of Guzman d'Alfarache, was a Dominican monk, Andreas Perez de Leon. It contains a great number of Spanish proverbs, and of those peculiar verses in which the last syllable is cut off, and the precedence in creating which was disputed between Cervantes and Perez.

9885 ULLOA PEREIRA (L.) Obras, prosas y versos, sq. 8vo. *vellum*, 12*s* Madrid 1674
9886 UNANUE, Observaciones sobre el Clima de Lima, sq. 8vo. *calf*, 5*s* *ib*. 1815
9887 UZTARIZ, Theorica y Practica de Comercio y de Marina, sm. folio, *portrait, vellum*, 12*s* *ib*. 1742
9888 VALDIVIELSO, ROMANCERO Espiritual, en gracia de los esclavos del santissimo Sacramento, para cantar, quando se muestra descubierto, 16mo. *hf. bd.* 18*s ib.*1663
9889 [VALERA (Cypriano de)] Dos Tratados, el primero es del PAPA y de su autoridad, el segundo de la MISSA, enxambre de falsos Milagros, stout 16mo. *folding Table of observations on the Eucharist, hf. bd. Southey's autograph*, RARE, £2.
(*Londres*) *Ricardo del Campo* (*R. Field*) 1599
This rare and curious work was anonymously published by one of the early translators of the Spanish Bible. This edition is more complete than that of 1588.

9890 VALERIA, Engaños desengañados, Poesias sacras, misticas, y Funebres, 12mo. *vellum*, 6*s* *Napoles*, 1681
9891 VARGAS (Pero Thome de) Vergel de Plantas Divinas, 16mo. *title supplied in MS. Spanish goatskin, gilt back and sides, rare*, 28*s* *Salamanca, Bonardo*, 1593
One of the early and celebrated Spiritual Cancioneros which form such a feature in Spanish Literature. Collation: Title wanting; 387 leaves numbered: Tabla, leaves 3 and 4 (1 and 2 wanting.)

9892 VELASQUEZ, Ensayo sobre los Alphabetos de las Letras desconocidas en las antiguas Medallas y Monumentos de España, sm. 4to. 20 *plates of Coins, vellum*, 7*s* 6*d* *Madrid*, 1752
9893 —— Origines de la Poesia Castellana, sm. 4to. *a highly esteemed work, bound*, 9*s* *Malaga*, 1754
9894 —— segunda edicion, sq. 8vo. *hf. bd.* 7*s* *ib*. 1797
9895 VERA Y FIGUEROA (Conde de la Roca) el Fernando, ò Sevilla Restaurada, poema heroico, sq. 8vo. *engraved title page and* 20 *plates, calf neat or vellum*, 25*s* *Milan*, 1632
The origin of this poem is rather curious. The author, who was Ambassador at Venice, prepared a translation of Tasso's Jerusalem Delivered, but, just before publication, altered his purpose, and converted his work into "Sevilla Restaurada," by the changes of names, and substitution of episodes, but the metamorphosis was effected by no small material alteration.

9896 VERGARA SALCEDO, Ydeas de Apolo, sq. 8vo. *poems, vellum*, 6*s* Madrid, 1663
9897 VIDAL (Salvador) Respuesta al Historico VICO, sq. 8vo. *vellum*, £2. 4*s* *Venetiis*, 1644
VERY RARE, not mentioned by Brunet and Salva: written in answer to Vico's History of the Kingdom of SARDINIA, printed in 1630-40; Vidal quotes the objectionable parts of Vico, and then gives a lengthy reply to each.

9898 VILLANUEVA (J. L.) Viage Literario a las Iglesias de Espana, con observaciones, 22 vols. 8vo. *plates of inscriptions, monuments, etc. sd.* £2. 15*s* *Madrid, Real Academia*, 1803-52
9899 VILLAVICIOSA, la Mosquea, poetica inventiva, en octava rima, 8vo. *Large Paper, portraits, calf, gilt edges*, 6*s* *ib*. 1777
9900 VILLEGAS (Estevan Manuel de) Las Eroticas y Traduccion de Boecio, 2 vols. sm. 8vo. LARGE and FINE PAPER, *frontispieces and fine portrait, red morocco, gilt edges, from Dr. Hawtrey's library*, 32*s* *ib*. 1774
VERY RARE; very few copies were printed on Large Paper, and those only for presents.

9901 VILLERGAS, Los Misterios de Madrid, 3 vols. 12mo. *portraits and woodcuts, hf. morocco neat*, 10*s* 6*d* *ib*. 1844-45
9902 VIRUES (C. de) el Monserrate, poema, 16mo. *title and preliminary leaves wanting, fine copy, calf*, 18*s* *ib*. 1587

9903 [VIVES (Ludov.)] Instruccion de la Muger christiana, traduzida de Latin por Justiniano, sm. 8vo. *woodcut title,* 𝔟𝔩𝔞𝔠𝔨 𝔩𝔢𝔱𝔱𝔢𝔯, *dedicated to Catherine of Aragon, Spanish morocco*, 10s *Zaragoça*, 1555

9904 WHITE (J. M. BLANCO) EL ESPAÑOL, publicado cada mes, desde su principio en April de 1810 hasta a Noviembre de 1812, Nos. I—XXXI, Vols. I—V, 8vo. *hf. bd. scarce*, 36s 1810-12

    This excellent periodical is the only work which gives full details of the Revolutions of the Spanish Colonies in America.

9905 XIMENA, Catalogo de los Obispos de Jaen, sm. folio, *engraved title, plate and cuts of Arms, vellum*, 20s *Madrid*, 1654

9906 XIMENO (Vicente) ESCRITORES del Reyno de VALENCIA, chronologicamente ordenados, desde 1238 hasta 1747, 2 vols. 8vo. folio, *vel.* 30s *Valencia*, 1747-49

    Priced, 1837 and 1840, by Payne and Foss, mor. £3. 13s 6d ; 1855, Lord Stuart de Rothesay's copy, £2. 15s

9907 YRIARTE (Tomas de) Coleccion de sus Obras en verso y proso, 8 vols. 12mo. *portrait, calf,* 18s *Madrid*, 1805

9908 —— —— la Musica, poema, large 8vo. 6 *beautiful plates, calf,* 4s *Madrid*, 1784

9909 ZAPATA, Dissertacion medico-theologica, 12mo. *beautiful portrait by Palomino of the* PRINCESS OF BRAZIL, *to whom the work is dedicated, bound in velvet, gilt edges,* 16s *Madrid*, 1733

9910 ZARATE (Franc. Lopez de) Obras varias, sq. 8vo. *vel. fine copy,* 18s *Alcala*, 1651

9911 —— —— Obras varias, *Alcala,* 1651—Invencion de la Cruz, poema heroico, *Madrid,* 1648—2 vols. in 1, stout sq. 8vo. *vellum*, 25s 1648-51

    Zarate was one of the excellent poets of the commencement of the 16th Century. His *Obras Varias* comprise a Tragedy, Sonnets, Lyrics, two Silvas, etc. ; but his longest poem is the Epic on the Discovery of the Cross, printed three years previously.

9912 ZAYAS Y SOTOMAYOR, Primera y segunda Parte de las NOVELAS AMOROSAS y exemplares, sq. 8vo. *fine copy in calf extra, gilt and marbled edges, by Niedrée,* 28s *Madrid*, 1659

    Priced, 1840, Payne and Foss, £2. 2s. "One of the stories, although written by a lady of the court, is the grossest I remember to have read."—*Ticknor.*

9913 ZORRILLA (José) Obras, con su Biografia por Ovejas, 2 vols. 8vo. *portrait, hf. morocco gilt,* 13s 6d *Paris*, 1847

9914 ZURITA (Geronymo) ANALES de la CORONA DE ARAGON, 6 vols. folio, *woodcuts on titles,* ORIGINAL *and* BEST EDITION, *vellum,* £4. *Caragoça*, 1585, 1578-79-80

    "Cette edition est la plus belle et la plus rare de toutes."—*Brunet.*

9915 ZURITA, Anales de Aragon, 6 vols. 1610—Indice, 1 vol. 1604—together 7 vols. sm. folio, *woodcuts on titles, bound,* £3. 3s *Caragoça*, 1610-4

9916 —— —— the same, 6 vols. 1610—Indice, 1 vol. 1604—Index Rerum Gestarum ad annum 1510, 1 vol. 1578—together 8 vols. sm. folio, *vellum,* £3. 10s

    "Edition que l'on préfère."—*Brunet.* *Caragoça*, 1578-1610

9917 —— —— Anales de la Corona de Aragon, 6 vols. 1669—Indice, 1671—together 7 vols. sm. folio, *vellum,* £2. 5s *Caragoça*, 1669-71

    "On y a rajeuni l'orthographie des mots et corrigé les fautes d'impression."—*Brunet.*

9918 **CATALAN and Valencian.** BALLOT y Torres, Gramatica Cathalana, 12mo. *vellum,* 6s *Barcelona*, 1814

9919 BOSCH, Summari, Index o Epitome dels admirables y nobilissims Titols de Honor de Cathalunya, Rossello y Cerdanya, gracies, privilegis, llibertats, immunitats, etc. sm. folio, *vellum,* £2. *Perpinya, Amy* 1628

    1858, I sold a copy, cf. gt for £4. 10s. This book contains an interesting account of the difference between the Limosin and Catalan dialects, and of the dialects of Rossillon and Cerdagne.

9920 CAPITOLS dels DRETS y altres Cosas del General de Cathalunya, Rossellò y Cerdanya fets en Corts, 1481-1564, sq. 8vo. *in the Catalan dialect, vellum, rare,* 10s *Barcelona*, 1685

9921 CARBONELL (Miquel) Chroniques de Espáya fins aci no divulgades, que tracta d'ls Reys del Gots, Côtes de Barcelona, Reys de Arago, etc. folio, 𝔟𝔩𝔞𝔠𝔨 𝔩𝔢𝔱𝔱𝔢𝔯, *fine copy in vellum, very scarce,* £11. 10s

Barcelona, per Charles Amoros, 1546

    Written in the Catalan dialect. On the title-page there is the date of 1547, which circumstance has led bibliographers to imagine that there were two distinct editions of 1546 and 1547. The Condé copy fetched £21.

9922 COMA (P. Martyr) Doctrina Christiana utilissima a los faels Christians, augmentada per Salas, 12mo. *in Catalan, vellum,* 7s 6d *Barcelona*, 1609

9923 CONSOLAT DEL MAR. Libre de Cōsolat, tractāt dels Fets Maritims, &c. sm. folio, *large woodcut of a ship on the title, five leaves of the supplementary portion " Capitols del Rey en Pere," wanting and the 8th leaf partly destroyed, old binding, very rare,* £4. 4s *Barcelona, Johan Luschner,* 1502

The only copy I can trace as having occurred for sale in England, is in Salva's Catalogue for 1826, but without a price. " This is the extremely scarce edition, of which Capmany speaks in the ' Suplemento y aviso Singular al Codigo de las Costumbres maritimas;' the same which he himself had before him for the publication of the above mentioned 'Codigo,' and the one which was generally believed to be the first edition, until a copy of another edition of an uncertain date, but unquestionably of the XVth century, was some time ago discovered."—*Salva.*

9924 FUSTER, Vocabulario Valenciano-Castellano, 12mo. 142 *pp. sd.* 5s *Valencia,* 1827
9925 LACAVALLERIA ET DULACH, Gazophylacium Catalano-latinum, dictiones phrasibus illustratas, etc. comprehendens, cum irregularium Verborum elencho, folio, *with autograph of Vinc. Casanova, title and last leaf mended, vellum, rare,* £2. 10s *Barcinone, A. Lacavalleria,* 1696

Collation: title, 3 prel. leaves and pp. 1-1047. Not mentioned in any of Salva's Catalogues. "Annoncé comme un livres très-rare dans la Bibl. Heberiana VI. No. 2179, où il est porté à 3 liv. 11 sh."—*Brunet.* "Ouvrage volumineux rempli de détails *infiniment precieux* pour l'etude de la langue Catalane."—*Jaubert de Pasa, sur la langue Catalane, Paris,* 1831.

9926 LACAVALLERIA, Dictionnaire Español-Français-Catalan, oblong 12mo. *treble columns, vellum, rare,* 32s *Barcelona,* 1647

Containing Dialogues, etc. and at the end a small Grammatical sketch and directions for pronunciation, of the three languages.

9927 MUNTANER (Ramon) Chronica o Descriptio dels Fets e Hazanyes del inclyt Rey Don Jaume primer, Rey Darago e de sos descendents, sm. folio, *in the Limousin or Valentian Dialect, second edition, the margins in many places wormed, recently bound in calf extra, gilt edges, rare,* 32s *Barcelona, Cortey,* 1562

Priced, 1829, Salva, russia gt. £13., another copy, stained and mended in the margins, £4. ; 1857, Quaritch, sound copy in vellum, £6. 6s ; Nicol's copy fetched £7. 2s 6d.

Il serait fort difficile de décider si ce livre precieux intéresse plutôt l'historien que le philologue. Cet ouvrage est le document le plus authentique que doivent consulter ceux qui s'occupent de l'histoire d'Aragon, de Catalogne, de Valence, des Isles Baléares et de la Sicile. Le linguiste aura dans ce volume le monument le plus parfait du dialecte usité dans ces différents pays, et celui qui cultive les belles-lettres aura les compositions poétiques les plus anciennes de ce langage dans les conseils *en vers* que Muntaner donna à l'infant Don Alphonse.

9928 MUNTANER (Ramon) Chronik, Catalanisch, von Lanz, 8vo. *bds.* 9s *Stuttg.* 1844
9929 PARTINOBLES. Historia del esforçat Cavaller Partinobles, traduhida de llengua Castellana, 12mo. *a little wormed, vellum, rare,* 18s *Gerona, n. d. (ca.* 1700)
9930 PUIADES (Hieronym) Coronica Universal del Principat de Cathalunya, folio, FIRST EDITION, *fine copy in old calf gilt, the Cypher N. with a Crown on the back,* £2. 16s *Barcelona, H. Margerit,* 1609

Collation: Title; 11 preliminary leaves, containing Poems in Catalan: Coronica, fol. 1-361; Canc'o and Tavla, 23 leaves. "Cette chronique estimable * * * est très-necessaire pour étudier, non seulement l'histoire de la principauté de Cataluna, mais encore l'histoire générale d'Espagne, particulièrement des Arabes."—*Salva.*

9931 ROIG (Jaume) Lo Libre de les Dones e de Concells donats a son Nebot En Balthasar Bou, Senyor de Callosa, sq. 8vo. *vellum,* 25s *Valencia, J. Garcia,* 1735
9932 —— the same, sq. 8vo. *calf extra, by Kœhler, scarce,* 36s 1735

In the Limousin dialect. Roig was one of the most distinguished of the Valencian poets of the XVth century.

9933 **SPAIN, Books relating to.** ALVA. Histoire de Ferdinand-Alvarez, Duc d'Albe, 2 vols. in 1, stout 12mo. *portrait, calf,* 5s *Paris,* 1699
9934 ARMERIA REAL (La) ou Collection des principales pièces de la Galerie d'Armes Anciennes de Madrid, dessins de Sensi, texte de JUBINAL, 2 vols. roy. folio, 62 *woodcuts and* 82 *large plates of Gothic, Moorish, and Spanish* ARMOUR, *etc. hf. bd.* £5. 5s *Paris* (1840)

A splendid work, being a fit companion to Meyrick and Skelton's Ancient Armour.

9935 ARMERIA REAL, Catalogo de la, con Glosario, 2 vols. in 1, 8vo. 10 *plates containing about* 430 *figures, sd.* 10s *Madrid,* 1849
9936 ASCHBACH, Geschichte Spaniens zur Zeit der Almoraviden, 2 vols. in 1, 8vo. *cloth,* 3s 6d 1833-37
9937 —— Geschichte der Ommaijaden in Spanien, 2 vols. 8vo. *calf gilt,* 5s 1829-30
9938 CONDE, Histoire de la Domination des Arabes en Espagne, traduite par Marlès, 2 vols. 8vo. *hf. calf,* 6s *Paris,* 1825
9939 COOK's Sketches in Spain, 1829-32, 2 vols. 8vo. *bds.* 6s 1834
9940 COOPER (Purton) Catalogue of Books on the Laws of Spain, roy. 8vo. *cloth, only printed for the Lincoln's Inn Society,* 5s 1847
9941 COSTUMES OF SPAIN. Coleccion de los TRAGES en la actualidad usados, 12mo. 112 *coloured plates, calf,* 35s *Madrid,* 1801
9942 DELICES de L'ESPAGNE et du Portugal, per COLMENAR, 6 vols. in 4, 12mo. *map and numerous pretty plates of views, etc. calf,* 15s *Leide,* 1715
9943 DEPPING, Histoire de L'ESPAGNE, 2 vols. 8vo. *map, calf neat,* 4s *Paris,* 1814

9944 DOZY (R.) Recherches sur l'Histoire et la Littérature de l'Espagne pendant le Moyen Age : 2e édition augmentée, 2 vols. sm. 8vo. *sd*. 14*s* *Leyde,* 1860
9945 ———— Histoire des Musulmans d'Espagne jusqu'à la Conquête de l'Andalousie par les Almoravides (711—1110), 4 vols. sm. 8vo. *sd*. 24*s* *Leyde,* 1861
9946 FLÉCHIER, Histoire du Cardinal Ximenes, 2 vols. in 1, 12mo. *calf,* 7*s* 6*d* 1693
9947 FRANCKENAU, Bibliotheca Hispanica Historico-Genealogico-Heraldica, sq. 8vo. *hf. bd.* 15*s* ; *Spanish morocco,* 21*s* *Lips.* 1734
A valuable catalogue raisonné of works on Spanish Heraldry.
9948 FRANCKENAU, Sacra Themidis Hispanæ Arcana, cum Indice Auctorum, sm. 8vo. *bd. gilt top, uncut,* 10*s* *Matriti,* 1780
9949 HUMBOLDT, Prüfung der Untersuchungen über die Urbewohner Hispaniens, vermittelst der Vaskischen Sprache, 4to. *presentation copy from the author,* WITH HIS AUTOGRAPH, *hf. bd. uncut,* 20*s* *Berlin,* 1821
9950 MARIANA, Histoire d'Espagne, en françois, avec des notes, par Charenton, 5 vols. in 6, 4to. *maps, old calf gilt, Lord Walpole's copy,* 18*s* *Paris,* 1725
Bound up with Vol. V. is "Mahudel, Monnoyes antiques d'Espagne, 1725, 16 plates of coins."—Priced, L. P. 1831, Bohn, £3. 13*s* 6*d* ; 1841, Rodwell, £2. 2*s*. Fetched, 1854, morocco. £3. 5*s*.
9951 OIHENART, Notitia utriusque Vasconiæ, tum Ibericæ tum Acquitanicæ, sq large 8vo. *vellum,* 20*s* *Paris,* 1638
COLLATION : 6 prelim. leaves ; pp. 1-558 ; Index, 10 leaves. " Un des meilleurs ouvrages que l'on ait écrits sur cette province."—*Brunet.* It was issued with a new title page again in 1656.
9952 MÜNCH-BELLINGHAUSEN, Über die älteren Sammlungen Spanischer Dramen, impl. 8vo. *presentation copy, hf. calf,* 9*s* *Wien,* 1852
9953 SANCTII (Alfonsi) de Rebus Hispanicis Anacephaleosis Libri VII, sq. 8vo. *frontispiece, fine tall copy, morocco, gilt edges, by C. Lewis,* 36*s* *Compluti,* 1634
A rare work unmentioned by Brunet and not in Salva's catalogues, containing an account of the Discovery of America.
9954 SCHACK's Geschichte der dramatischen Literatur und Kunst in Spanien, 3 vols. 8vo. *cloth, uncut,* 12*s* *Berlin,* 1845-46
SCHOTTI Hispaniæ illustratæ—*see No.* 6218.
9955 SCHOTTI Hispaniæ Bibliotheca ; item Nomenclator Hispaniæ Scriptorum, sm. 4to. *calf, with note by Mr. Ford,* 6*s* *Francof.* 1608
9956 SEMPÉRÉ, Grandeur et Décadence de la Monarchie Espagnole, 2 vols. in 1, 12mo. *hf. calf,* 4*s* 1826
9957 TICKNOR'S (G.) History of SPANISH LITERATURE, 3 vols. 8vo. (pub. at £2. 2*s*) *cloth,* 14*s* 1849
9958 ———— the same, *new, corrected and enlarged edition,* 3 vols. sm. 8vo. *cloth,* 21*s* 1863
An exceedingly valuable work, the best ever published on Spanish bibliography.
The present edition of the History of Spanish Literature differs materially from the preceding editions, it *omits* nearly the whole of the inedited, primitive Castilian poems which have heretofore filled about 70 pages at the end of the last volume ; but in other parts of the work a corresponding amount of NEW MATTER has been introduced.

PORTUGUESE BOOKS.

9959 BARBOZA, Grammatica da Lingua Portugueza, sq. 8vo. *cloth,* 7*s* 6*d* *Lisboa,* 1830
9960 BLUTEAU (R.) VOCABULARIO PORTUGUEZ e Latino, 8 vols. *Coimbra,* 1712-21— Supplemento, 2 vols. *Lisboa,* 1727-28—together 10 vols. sm. folio, *fine copy in old calf, rebacked and gilt,* £5. 1712-28
"Peu commun. Vendu 120 fr. La Serna ; £7. 7*s* Heber ; et plus cher autrefois."—*Brunet.*
9961 BORDO, Diccionario Italiano-Portuguez e Portuguez-Italiano, 2 vols. sm. 8vo. 1000 *pp. double cols. sd.* 20*s* *Rio de Janeiro,* 1853-54
9962 MORAES SILVA, DICCIONARIO da lingua Portugueza, com Grammatica, *quinta ediçao,* 2 vols. roy. 4to. *calf,* £2. 5*s* *Lisboa,* 1844
9963 VIEYRA'S Portugueze-English and Englsh-Portugueze Dictionary, interspersed with Phrases and Proverbs, new edition, enlarged by Aillaud, 2 vols. 8vo. *about* 700 *pp. treble columns, calf neat,* 28*s* 1813
9964 ———— new edition, corrected and improved by Do Canto, 2 vols. 8vo. *calf neat,* £2. 1827
9965 ———— Portuguese Grammar, sixth edition, 8vo. *bd.* 2*s* 6*d* 1808
9966 ———— the same, ninth edition, by Aillaud, 8vo. *calf neat,* 3*s* 6*d* 1813
9967 ———— the same, tenth edition, 8vo. *calf,* 6*s* 1827
9968 NUNEZ DO LIÃO (Duarte) Orthographia de Lingoa Portuguesa, obra util para bem screver a lingoa Hespanhol, a Latina, y outras, sq. 8vo. *first edition, limp vellum,* VERY RARE, 30*s* *Lisboa,* 1576
Priced, 1831, H. G. Bohn, £4. 10*s* ; Sams' copy fetched £5. 2*s* 6*d*.

9969 SANTA ROSA DE VITERBO, Elucidario das Palavras, Termos, e Frases, em Portugal *antiguamente* usados e hoje ignorados, para entender sem erro, os documentos mais raros entre nos conservados, 2 vols. in 1, stout sm. folio, *calf*, £2. 2s *Lisboa*, 1798-99
Heber's copy fetched £3. 3s.

9970 SOUSA (Emmanuel de) Dictionnaire François-Portugais, augmenté par Da Costa, seconde édition par Da Cunha, 2 vols. 4to. 1421 *pp. treble columns, calf*, 18s *Lisbonne*, 1811

9971 **Macaroneana.**—MACARRONEA LATINO-PORTUGUEZA, quer dizer: Apontado de Versos Macarronicos Latino-Portuguezes, *segunda impressam*, 12mo. *green morocco gilt*, 10s 6d *Lisboa*, 1786
A curious collection, containing various pieces by Duarte Ferrao and other writers.

9972 ALBOQUERQUE. Commentarios de Affonso d'Alboquerque, capitaõ geral das Indias Orientaes, 4 vols. 12mo. *portrait and map, calf*, 10s *Lisboa*, 1774

9973 BARBOSA MACHADO (Diogo) BIBLIOTHECA LUSITANA, na qual se comprehende a Noticia dos Authores Portuguezes, et das Obras que compuzeraon, 4 vols. folio, *portrait*, 24 *leaves in Vol. III. supplied in MS. otherwise a good copy in old calf neat*, VERY RARE, £12. *Lisboa*, 1741-59
Conde's copy fetched £12. 12s; Heber's, £11.; fetched at Sotheby's in 1851, £11. 11s.
The extreme rarity of this great work, the highest authority upon Portuguese Bibliography, arises from the circumstance that a large proportion of the first three volumes perished by fire at Lisbon in 1755.

9974 BARBOSA (J.) Catalogo das Rainhas de Portugal, e seus filhos, 4to. LARGE PAPER, *numerous engravings of the Arms of Portuguese Families, old calf gilt*, 18s
Priced, 1860, 25s. *Lisboa*, 1727

9975 CAMOES, Obras (Lusiadas Comedias, etc.) por Coelho, 4 vols. 12mo. *old calf gilt*, 12s *ib.* 1779-80

9976 ——— Obras, con discurso e vida, por Aquino, 4 vols. in 5, 16mo. *portrait, calf*, 7s *ib.* 1782-83

9977 ——— the same, 5 vols. *pretty copy in calf gilt*, 10s 1782-83

9978 ——— Obras completas correctas e emendades por Barreto Feio e Monturo, 3 vols. 8vo. *portrait, hf. calf elegant*, 21s *Lisboa, Baudry*, 1843

9978*——— Os LUSIADAS, commentados pelo Licenciado Manoel Correa, sq. 8vo. *in good condition, old calf*, RARE, £2. 5s *Lisboa*, 1613
Priced, Thorpe, 1834, £3. 3s.

9979 ——— LUSIADAS, commentados por Manuel de Faria i Sousa, 4 vols. in 2, small folio, *portrait and plates, very fine copy in rich old red* MOROCCO, *from the library of the celebrated Colbert*, RARE, £6. *Madrid*, 1639
Priced, 1824, Rivington, £10 10s.
A rare and valuable edition, containing the "Adiciones," Leciones, varias, etc.

9980 CAMOENS (Luis de) Os LUSIADAS, nova ediçao correcta, por Dom J. M. de Souza-Botelho, *head of the poet, after Gerard, Paris*, 1819—The Lusiad, translated from the Portuguese, with notes, by MICKLE, 2 vols. 1798—J. ADAMSON's Memoirs of the Life and Writings of Camoens, 2 vols. *portrait*, LARGE PAPER, 1820—together 5 vols. 8vo. *uniformly bound in brown calf extra*, £2. 4s 1798-1820

9981 FARIA, Lusiadum libri X, authore Thoma de Faria, Episcopo Targensi, 12mo. *vellum*, VERY RARE, 15s *Ulyssipone*, 1622
Fetched at Sotheby's in 1856, £1. 13s. Brunet quotes this translation as "fort rare," but it is evident that he never saw the book, from his adding to the title "in Latinum carmen interpretati." So far from acknowledging that his work was a translation, Bishop Faria does not even mention Camoen's name anywhere in the book.

9982 CANCIONEIRO GERAL, Altportugiesische Liedersammlung des edeln Garcia de RESENDE, neu herausgegeben von Kausler, 3 vols. 8vo. *facsimile and coat of arms, privately printed, French bds.* £2. 2s *Stuttg.* 1846-52
This work forms Vols. 15, 17, and 26 of the "Bibliothek des literarischen Vereins in Stuttgart." It is a collection of the rare pieces of Spanish and Portuguese poetry of the XVth century.

9983 CHRONICAS: Galvaõ (Duarte) Chronica de Affonso Henriques, primeiro Rey de Portugal, publ. por Lopes Ferreyra—Ruy de Pina, Chronica de Sancho I, Affonso II, Sancho II, Affonso III, D. Diniz, 6 vols. in 1, sm. folio, *good copy, calf*, 12s *Lisboa*, 1726-9
A collection of Chronicles of the first six kings of Portugal. The first was written at the beginning of the 16th century; the five others by Ruy de Pina are posthumous, the author died in 1515; they are quoted by the Lisbon Academy as classics.

PORTUGUESE LITERATURE.

9984 CORREA DA SERRA (José) Collecçaõ de Livros Ineditos de Historia Portugueza, dos Reinados de Joaõ I, Duarte, Affonso V, Joaõ II, Dinis, Affonso IV, Pedro I, e Fernando, 4 vols. in 2, (without the additional Vol. V), stout sm. folio, *hf. bound,* LARGE PAPER, *uncut,* £3. *Lisboa,* 1790-1816
"Collection très-importante pour l'histoire de Portugal: elle est bien imprimée, et se trouve difficilement." *Brunet.*

9985 DAMIÃO DE GOES, Chronica de Dom Emanuel, folio, *calf,* 7s *Lisboa,* 1749
9986 ELPINO DURIENSE, Poesias, 3 vols. sq. 8vo. *hf. red morocco, uncut,* 12s 1812-17
9987 ESCOBAR (Gerardo de) Doze Novelas, sq. 8vo. *good copy, calf, gilt back,* £2.
A very rare volume, partly in verse, not mentioned by Salva. *Lisboa,* 1674
9988 FARIA (Manoel Severim de) Noticias de Portugal acrescentadas por J. Barbosa, sm. folio, *cuts of Coins, a few leaves damaged at the end, old calf, gilt back, rare,* 24s *Lisboa,* 1740
"This copy contains the whole of the VIth Discourse relating to the progress of Christianity among the inhabitants of the Portuguese possessions in Africa, which was suppressed July 18, 1740."—*Note in Pencil by Viscount Strangford.*

9989 FIGANIÈRE, Catalogo dos Manuscriptos Portuguezes no Museu Britannico, 8vo. 416 *pp. with Index, sd.* 8s *Lisboa,* 1853
9990 HERCULANO, Origen e Estabelecimento da Inquisição em Portugal, 3 vols. 12mo. *sd. new,* 15s *Lisboa,* 1854-59
9990*LISBON ACADEMY. MEMORIAS, HISTORIA e MEMORIAS, MEMORIAS dos Socios e dos Correspondentes da ACADEMIA REAL das SCIENCIAS de LISBOA, desde 1780 até 1837, Vols. I-XII, sm. folio, *plates and tables, hf. calf, uncut,* £6. 6s *Lisboa,* 1797-1839
Priced, 1845, Bossange, 180 fr.; 1817, 11 vols. sd. £7. 17s 6d.

9991 —— the same, Vols. 10, 11, 2 vols. folio, *bds.* 30s 1827-31
9992 —— MEMORIAS de Litteratura Portugueza, publicadas pela Academia Real das Sciencias, de Lisboa, 8 vols. in 4, stout sq. 8vo. *half calf,* £2. 1792-1812
9993 —— MEMORIAS ECONOMICAS, para o adiantamento da Agricultura, das Artes etc. 3 vols. sq. 8vo. *half calf,* 12s *Lisboa,* 1789-91
9994 LOBO (F. R.) O condestabre de Portugal, D. N. Pereira, 12mo. *calf,* 4s 1785
9995 —— Corte na Aldea e Noites de Inverno, 16mo. *calf,* 6s *Lisboa,* 1649
9996 —— Corte na Aldea, Obras Pastoris (Primavera) e o Pastor Peregrino e Desenganado, 4 parts in 2 vols. sq. 8vo. *calf,* 18s *Lisboa,* 1721-22
"One of the most tuneful swans of the Portuguese Parnassus, who has represented rural life in the most natural manner."—*Barbosa.*

9997 MENEZES, Chronica de D. Sebastiaõ, decimosexto Rey de Portugal, sm. folio, *calf,* 12s *Lisboa,* 1730
The author of this work was J. Pereira Baiao, who wrote under the name of Menezes.

9998 NUNEZ DO LIAÕ, Chronicas dos Reis de Portugal, primeira parte, 2 vols. in 1 —Cronicas dos Reys Joaõ I, Duarte XI, e Affonso V, 2 vols.—together 4 vols. in 3, sq. 8vo. LARGE PAPER, *cloth,* 30s *Lisboa,* 1774-80
This is the complete series of Liao's Chronicles of Portugal.

9999 PALMEIRIM DE INGLATERRA, Cronica de, por Francisco de MORAES, a que se ajuntaõ as mais Obras do mesmo autor, 3 vols. sq. 8vo. BEST EDITION, *fine copy in old Spanish calf,* 30s *Lisboa,* 1786
Priced, Thorpe, £2. 2s; fetched, 1858, £1. 14s.

10000 PARNASO LUSITANO ou Poesias selectas dos Auctores Portuguezes antigos e modernos, illustradas com uma historia da Lengua e Poesia notas, etc. 6 vols. 24mo. *calf gilt, pretty copy,* 25s *Paris,* 1826-34
10001 PEREIRA de Figueiredo, Catalogo de suas Obras impressas e Manuscritas, 8vo. *hf. calf,* 7s 6d *Lisboa,* 1800
10002 RESENDE (Garcia de) Chronica de Joam II, sm. folio, *fine copy, cf.* 7s *ib.* 1752
10003 SA DE MENEZES, Malaca Conquistada, poema com os argumentos de Ferreira, sq. 8vo. *best edition, sd.* 4s; *calf,* 6s *Lisboa,* 1779
10004 SEABRA DA SYLVA, Deducçao chronologica e analytica, 2 parts in 3 vols.— —Provas, 2 vols.—together 5 vols. 12mo. *old calf gilt,* 12s *Lisboa,* 1768
Shewing the miseries caused by the Jesuits in Portugal until their expulsion in 1759.

10005 SILVA (Innocencio Francisco) Diccionario Bibliographico Portuguez, estudos applicaveis a Portugal e ao Brasil, 7 vols. 8vo. *portrait, new hf. calf gilt, uncut,* £6. 6s *Lisboa,* 1850-62
This valuable work completes the last letter of the alphabet in its seventh volume. A supplementary volume will appear soon.

10006 SILVA (Jose de) Principios de Direito Mercantil e Leis de Marinha, 6 vols. in 2, sm. folio, *old calf*, 20s *Lisboa,* 1801-3

10007 SOARES DE SYLVA, Memorias para a Historia de Portugal que comprehendem o governo de Don Joaõ I, 1383-1433, com Collecçam dos Documentos, 4 vols. roy. 4to. LARGE PAPER, *frontispieces, portrait, and vignettes, with Genealogical tables, old calf*, £3. *Lisboa,* 1730-34

10008 SOUSA, Documentos Arabicos para a Historia Portugueza, sq. 8vo. *Arab. e Portuguez, calf,* 7s 6d *Lisboa,* 1790

10009 SYLVA E SOUSA, Instrucçam Politica de Legados a Dom Afonso, stout 16mo. *the first leaf of the dedication wanting, vellum,* 10s *Amburgo,* 1656

10010 TELLEZ, Historia geral de Ethiopia a alta, ou Preste Joam, composta na mesma Ethiopia pelo P. Manoel d'Almeyda; abreviada com nova releyçam pelo P. Balthezar Tellez, sm. folio, *frontispiece which has been coloured, and map of the Nile Sources, but not the large map of Ethiopia, fine copy in limp vellum,* EXTREMELY RARE, £2. 10s *Coimbra,* 1660

"On trouve difficilement cette histoire, qui passe pour fort exacte."—*Brunet.*
Heber's copy fetched £11. 15s; Lord Rothesay's £9.; copies have sold as high as 30 guineas.
This is the work which Bruce the traveller is accused of having pillaged and then destroyed, supposing his own copy unique. The suspicion arose from the circumstance that some of his discoveries are anticipated in this volume.

10011 TRATADO DE TORDESILLAS, 1496—TRATADO de Limites das Conquistas entre Joaõ V. de Portugal e Fernando VI. de Espanha, etc. assignado em Madrid, 1750, sm. 4to. *hf. bound,* 12s *Lisboa,* 1750

This is the treaty which abrogates that of Tordesillas, 1494, and the Agreement of Saragossa, 1529, regulates the rights of the two crowns, and fixes the new boundaries of their possessions in South America, the Philippines, etc.; with copies of the original documents.

10012 VICENTE (Gil.) Obras, nova edição por Barreto e Monteiro, 3 vols. 8vo. *sd.* 15s *Hamburgo,* 1834

Best edition of the works of the greatest modern Poet and Dramatist of Portugal.

10013 XAVIER (Felippe Nery) Viagem de 2000 Legoas pelo Sr. C. Lagrange Monteiro de Barbuda, enriquecida com peças—Instrucção do Vice-Rei Marquez de Alorna ao seu successor o Marquez de Tavora, com notas—Defensa dos Direitos das Gaõ-Carias, Gaõ-Cares e seus privilegios—3 vols. sm. 8vo. *half morocco,* 36s *Nova Goa,* 1848-56

These three words are by a writer intimately acquainted with every thing relating to the Portuguese possessions in India.

10014 **Heraldry.** ORDEM DE SANTIAGO, REGRA y Statutos Estatutos que fez ho mestre dom Jorge filho del rey dom Joam ho Segundo—2 parts in 1 vol. sq. sm. 8vo. *woodcuts, elegantly bound in red morocco, gilt edges,* £3. 10s *Lixboa, Germão Galharde frances,* 1548

This book appears of the greatest rarity, and is supposed to have been the copy belonging to the Order, as no bibliographers mention it. Collation: 4 preliminary leaves, including title and 2 woodcuts the size of the page; fo. i-xxxv; 'Dos dizimos' and 'Tavoada,' 3 leaves; Statutos de Dom Jorge, fo. i-xxxviii; Table and Colophon, 4 leaves.

10015 **Portugal.** ADAMSON'S Memoirs of the Life and Writings of CAMOENS, 2 vols. sm. 8vo. *with the three different portraits of Camoens and the portraits of Inez de Castro and Faria e Sousa, which are often wanting, bds.* 25s 1820

10016 ——— Bibliotheca Lusitana, a Catalogue of Books relating to the History, Literature and Poetry of Portugal, in his Library, sm. 8vo. *bds.* 15s *Privately printed, Newcastle,* 1836

10017 BELLERMANN's Alte Liederbücher der Portugiesen, XIII-XVI. Jahrhund. 4to. *sd.* 5s *Berlin,* 1840

10018 SAINCTHE-MARTHE (Scevole and Louis de) Genealogical History of the Kings of Portugal, and the Houses branched in masculine line from that family, translated and continued to 1662, by Francis SANDFORD, folio, *Genealogical table,* 2 *plates, and numerous coats of Arms, good copy, calf, scarce,* 25s *Lond.* 1662

According to Lowndes, "This work was published in compliment to Catharine of Braganza, Queen of Charles II. It was principally taken from a French work by Louis du May." This latter statement is a mistake for Louis de Saincte Marthe. The Townsend copy fetched £2. 5s; Fonthill, £2. 18s.

10019 SCHÄFER's Geschichte von Portugal, Vols. I-IV. 8vo. (pub at 8 Thalers) *sd.* 15s *Hamburg,* 1836-52

10020 WOLF, Le Brésil Littéraire, Histoire de sa Littérature, avec un choix de morceaux, 2 vols. in 1, 8vo. (pub at 3⅔ Thal.) *sd.* 6s *Berlin,* 1863

GENERAL INDEX

OF THE CHIEF BOOKS, AND ALL THE CLASSES AND SUB-DIVISIONS.

Abbotsford Club Books 14, 447-48
Abd-Allatif, Relation d'Egypte 289
Abrégés Historiques 405
Abulpharagii Chronicon 315
Academies 14-54
Académie Celtique 38
Académie des Sciences 14, 220
Acosta, Historia de las Indias 290
Acta Eruditorum 35
Acta Tomiciana 319
Adamson, Mousôn Eisodia 109
Adelung, Mithridates 138, 193
Aelfric Society 15, 504
Africa 289-90
African Languages 190
Agassiz, Poissons Fossiles 221
— Bibliographia Zoologiae 249
Agincourt, Monumens de l'Art 349
Agricola, Res Metallica 221
Aguado Gallery 360
Albanian 196
Albertolli, Ornamenti 388
Alcala, Arte Arauiga, etc. 307
Alcock's Tycoon 154
Alder and Hancock's Mollusca 44, 249
Aldrovandi Opera 221, 260
Alf Leileh wa Leileh 167
Alf Leileh, MSS. 157
Alford's Greek Testament 82
Alsedo y Herrera, Guayaquil 290
Alvarez, Etiopia 289
America, Works on 290-306
American Ethnological Society 503
American Languages 190-92, 290-306
American Learned Societies 15-16
American Oriental Society 138
Amharic 166, 504
Ammon (Jost) Works 385
Amsterdam Academy Trans. 16-17, 222
Amsterdam Institute 16
Ancien Theatre François 405
Ancient Laws of Engl. & Wales 45, 203
Anderson, Diplomata Scotiae 10, 340
— Royal Genealogies 448
Angelico (Fra) 349
Angling 124
Anglo-Saxon 75, 202-4, 504
Annalen der Physik 17
Annales des Mines 17
Annals of Natural History 17
Anquetil du Perron 57, 60
Antiquaires de France, Mémoires 39
Antiquaires du Nord 40-41, 209
Antiquities 319-380
Antonini Confessionale 429
Antonio, Bibliotheca Hispana 112, 516
Anvári Soheily 183
Apiani Cosmographia 282
Aquinas (Thomas) 62
Arabian Nights, by Lane 138, 448
Arabic Bible 75
— Literature 166-72, 307, 421, 505
— MSS. 155-161, 307
Arago, Oeuvres 223
Archaeologia Cambrensis 17
Archaeologia Cantiana 319, 449
Archaeologische Zeitung 17
Architectural Society 17, 388
Architecture 388-93, 497-99
Arenas, Manual Mexicano 291
Argote de Molina, Monteria 126
— Nobleza 319, 516
Aringhi Roma Subterranea 63, 355
Armenia 139, 307
Armenian 71, 172, 505
Armeria Real de Madrid 546
Armour 350
Arrowsmith's London Atlas 282
Art 349-88, 497-499

Art de Verifier les Dates 17-18, 340
Art Treasures of the United Kingd. 350
Arthur (King) 449
Arts Somptuaires 350
Arundel Society 18-19, 350
Ashmole's Order of the Garter 319
Asia, Works on 138-55, 306-318
Asiatic Researches 19, 139
Asiatic Society of Bengal 19, 139
— of Great Britain 19-20, 139
Assemanni Italiæ Scriptores 319
Assyrian 161, 172
Astle on Writing 10, 449
Astronomical Society 20
Athenæum (The) 20
Atlases 282-84, 449, 499-500
Atlas of Ulster 52, 283
Atti dei Scienziati Italiani 260
Audubon's Works 223, 507
Australasia 360
Australian Languages 192
Autographs 9
Austrian Academy 20
Avila, Arte Mexicano, etc. 291, 294
Ayeen Akbary 150
Aymara Language 190
Aztec 191
Baber's Memoirs 150
Bagster's Polyglott Bible 74
Baines' Lancashire 450
Balbi, Atlas 193
Bankers' Magazine 450
Bankrupt Register 130, 450
Bannatyne Club Books 20, 450
Barante, Histoire de Bourgogne 406
Barbier, Ouvrages Anonymes 112
Barbosa, Bibliotheca Lusitana 119, 548
Barcia, Historiadores de las Indias 291
Barker's Turkish Grammar 189
Baronial Halls 350, 450
Bartoloccii Biblio. Rabbinica 83, 176
Barros e Couto, Asia 265
Barth's Travels 265
Barthema's Travels 265
Bartsch, Peintre Graveur 350
Basque Langu. 22-24, 71, 196-97, 421, 547
Basque Provinces 517
Bataviaasch Genootschap 20, 312
Batthyan, Leges Eccles. Hungariae 62
Bauer et Browne Flora Novae Hol. 223
Bayle, Dictionnaire 113
Beagle Voyage, Zoology 224
Bedae Opera 203
Beechey's Voyage, Zoology 224
Bell's Quadrupeds, Reptiles 224
Belzoni's Egypt and Nubia 147, 289
Bengal Journal 19, 139
Bengali 179, 310
Bengelii Gnomon 82
Bentham (Jeremy) Works 131, 450-51
Beowulf's Poems 203
Berber Language 173
Berbrugger, Algérie 265, 351
Bergamese Dialect 441
Bergano, Bocabulario Pampango 312
Bergeron, Manuel du Tourneur 392
Berghaus, Atlas 173
Berjeau's Dogs 260
Berlin Academy 21
Berlingeri Geographia 266
Bernardo de Nant. Katec. Kariri 71, 191
Berry's County Genealogies 451
Bewick's Works 225, 260, 385, 451
Bhagavat Purana 187, 310
Bible Illustrations 351-52, 508
Bibles 22-24, 25, 74-88, 286, 287, 431, 507-8, 513-14, 518
Bibles (Early Printed) 397-401
Bible, Codices of the 1-9

Bibliography 10-14, 112-24, 420, 499
Bibliotheca Grenvilliana 117
Bibliotheque des Chartes 21
Bibliotheque Elzévirienne 406
Billings' Scotland 378
Biographia Britannica 118
Biographie Universelle 21, 113
Biondelli, Evangeliarium Aztecum 191
Bird's Buddhists 139
Blaeu, Grand Atlas 282
Blake (W. the Painter) Works 352, 497
— Life by Gilchrist 451
Blanchini Evangeliarium 85
Blarrorivo, Liber Nanceidos 385
Bleek's Persian Grammar 183
Bloch, Ichthyologie 225
Block Books, Chinese 173, 308
Block Books, European 384-87
Blome's Gentleman's Recreation 260
Blomefield's Norfolk 451
Blondel, Architecture 388
— Maisons de Plaisance 390
Blume, Flora Javæ 225
— Rumphia 226
Blundell Gallery 360
Blundeville's Horsemanship 487
Bocanegra, Ritual Quechua 291
Bocharti Opera 62
Bodleian Library 21-22, 113
Boece's Chronicles 491
Boeckh, Corpus Inscriptionum 90
Bohemia 285
Bohemian 218
Bolognese Dialect 442
Bombay Branch Asiatic Society 501
Bombay Geographical Soc. 22, 139, 501
Bombay Literary Society 22, 139, 452
Bonaparte (Prince L. L.) Publications 22-24, 193, 197-98, 444
Bonn and Breslau Academy 24
Bonomi, Egyptian Antiquities 147
Books of Prints 349-388
Book of St. Albans 124, 260
Bopp, Comparative Grammar 194
— Glossarium 186
Borlase's Cornwall 457
Bossuet, Oeuvres 62
Bosworth's Anglo-Saxon Dict. 203, 504
Botfield, Prefationes 109
Botta's Nineveh 146, 353
Bouche, Provence 320
Bouchet, Labyrinthe de Fortune 397
Bouquet, Historiens de la France 24
Bourgogne, Histoire de 321
Boutell's Heraldry 320
Bouterwek's Gesch. der Poesie 113
Bradford's Plymouth Plantation 452
Brahminical Worship 57-58
Brandon's Architecture 388
Brasseur de Bourbourg, Mexique 292
Brazilian 191, 294-306
Brescian Dialect 442
Breton Language 198, 421
Breton (Ray.) Dictionnaire Caraibe 191
Brigg's Nizam 150
Brij Bhakha 179
British Archaeological Association 487
British Association Reports 24, 259
British Museum Pubs. 24-26, 114, 507-8
Britton's Antiquities 353
Brockedon's Italy 363-64
Brongniart, Arts Céramiques 343
Browne Fasc. Rerum expetend. 63
Bruce's Travels 266
Bruno (Giordano) 109, 433
Brussels Academy 26
Brydges (Sir E.) Works 114, 453
Buchez, Histoire Parlementaire 417
Buck's Views 353

GENERAL INDEX.

Buddhism	58
Buffon, Histoire Naturelle	227
Bull-fighting	518
Bunda Language	289
Bunsen's Egypt	59, 147
Burckhardt's Arabic Proverbs	168, 402
— Travels	206
Burgmair (Hans) Triumph	386
Burháni Kátyâ	183
Burke's Peerage, etc.	453
Burmese	179, 307
Burmese MS.	161
Burnet's Painting	354
Burney's Hist. of Music	127
Burnouf, Yaçna	139
Burton's Excerpta Hierogl.	59, 147
Butkens, Maison de Lynden	321
Butler (Charles) Works	453
Buxtorfii Opera	83, 176
Byzantine Historians	90
Cabinet Satyrique	407
Cabirism	58
Cailliaud, Méroé	267
Calabrese Dialect	442
Calcutta Journals, etc.	27, 140, 502
Caldwell's Dravidian Grammar	179
Calendar, History of the	340
Calendars	54
Callery, Dictionnaire Chinois	173, 307
Calmet, Dict. de la Bible	63
Cambrian Magazine	27
Cambridge Astronom. Observations	227
Camb. Mathematical Journal	27
Camb. Philosophical Society	27
Camdeni Anglica	27
Camden's Britannia	321
Camden Society's Pubs.	27-28, 487
Campbell's Vitruvius Britannicus	389
Campo Santo	354
Canada, Relation des Jésuites	297
Canaletti's Views	382
Canarese	179, 310
Cancioneros	519, 540
Canova's Works	354
Canti Carnascialeschi	441
Capmany, Obras	519
Caraïbe Language	191
Cardani Opera	261
Cards	124
Carelli Nummi Italiæ	342
Carniolian	285
Carochi, Arte Mexicano	292
Carpentier, Cambray	321
Carte, Rolles Gascons	489
Cartas de Hidalguia	520
Carve, Itinerarium, etc.	490
Casas (B. de las) Tratados	292-93
Casiri Bibliotheca	168, 520
Castanheda Descobrimento da India	267
Castelli Lexicon Heptagl.	140
Catafago's Arabic Dictionary	168
Catalan Dialect	544-45
Catalogues of MSS.	10-14
Catalogues of Pictures, etc.	387
— of Coin Sales	348-49
Catesby's Nat. Hist. of Carolina	227
Causes Celebres	408
Cautley's Ganges Canal	508
Cavendish Society	227
Caxton's Game of Chess	125
Caylus, Antiquités	354
Cean-Bermudez, Bellas Artes	379, 521
Celtic Languages	22-24, 197-202, 505-7
Celtic Society	28
Ceylon	307
Chaldee	176-78, 315-16
Chalmers' Biographical Dict.	28, 114
Chalmers' Caledonia	493
Chap-Books (English)	455
Charles I. Book of Sports, etc.	455
Charlevoix, Œuvres	293
Chenu, Encyclopedie d'Hist. Nat.	228
Cheshire	455
Chess	125
Chetham Society	456, 487-88
Chilian	191

China	146-47, 307-8
Chinese	75, 173, 308, 421, 505
Chinese Drawings	155-56, 228, 354
Chinese Miscellany	307
Chinese Repository	28
Chiromancy	396
Christian Art	63, 355
Chronicles	319-339, 522-24
Chronology	340
Chrysostomi Opera	63
Churchill's Mount Lebanon	59, 140
Ciampini Opera	63
Ciceronis Opera	91
Cicognara, Fabbriche di Venezia	389
Cicognara, Scultura	355
Cieca, Chronica del Peru	293
Circassian	175
Civil Engineer	28, 228
Clarke's Travels	267
Classics, Codices of the	1-9
Classics, Printed	88-112
Claude, Liber Veritalis	355
Clinton's Fasti	91
Clutterbuck's Hertfordshire	465
Cochin-Chinese	175
Codex Alexandrinus	25, 81, 82
Cohen, Médailles Romaines	342
Coin Sale-Catalogues	348-49
Colebrooke's Algebra	228
Colebrooke's Essays	57, 140, 309
Colebrooke's Laws	134, 150
Coleman's Hindu Mythology	57, 140
Collart et Wierx, Icones	355
Collectanea Antiqua	48
Collectanea Topographica	321
Collins' Noble Families	322
Commines, Memoires	408
Common Prayer	71-73
Comparative Philology	193
Concilium zu Constantz	322
Confucian Philosophy	58
Consolat del Mar	546
Contant, Théâtres Modernes	389
Cookery	125
Copenhagen Academy	29
Coptic	175
Cornish	198
Cornwall Geological Society	228
Corpe's Romaic Grammar	217
Cortes, Conquest of Weast India	467
— Nueva Espana	294
Costume	356, 516
Cotton's Fasti Ecclesiæ Hibernicæ	490
Cramer, Stoll, et Voet, Papillons	228
Cresy's Engineering	389
Creuzer, Religions	56, 92
Croatian	71, 218
Cronicas de Espana	522-24
Culdees	58
Cundall's Ornamental Art	352
Curiosa	393-402
Curtis' Botanical Magazine	29, 508
Curtis' Entomology	229, 261
Cuvier's Works	229-30
Cuvilliés, Ornaments	356
Dahlberg, Suecia	356
Dakota Language	191
D'Alembert, Œuvres	230, 409
Dalmatia	285, 329
Dalyell's Powers of the Creator	230
Damiano, Libro di Scachi	125
Dampier's Voyages	268
Dance of Death	356-57, 457
Danish	210-11, 505
Danske Mynter	342
Danske Videnskab. Selskab	29
D'Anville, Œuvres Geographiques	268
Daru, Histoire de Venise	409
Davies' Celtic Researches	58
— British Druids	58
Davila, Tratado Quechua, etc.	291, 294
Dayak	312
De Bry, Voyages	268
De Guignes, Dict. Chinois	173
— Histoire des Huns	141, 306
Delambre, Astronomie	230

Delange, Faïence de Henri II.	359
Delaware Language	191
Delepierre, Macaronéana	109
Delices de divers Pays	357, 516
Denis, Codices Biblioth. Vindob.	115
Denon, Egypte	148
Dennistoun's Urbino	444, 458
De Rossi, Opera	176
Desatir (The)	61
Descartes, Œuvres	56, 409
Description des Arts et Métiers	230
Deutsche Morgenländ. Gesellschaft	53
D'Herbelot, Bibl.	141, 155, 306, 409
Dibdin's Bibliographical Wks.	116, 458
Diccionario de la Academia	514
Dictionnaire de l'Academie	404
Dieffenbach, Lex. Comparativum	194
Dietterlin, Architecture	389
Diez, Romanische Grammatik	214
Diplomacy	130-35
Diplomatics	10-14, 340-41
Directories	54
D'Ohsson, Empire Othoman	154
Domesday Book	45, 51, 458-59
Domingo de los Santos, Lengua Tag.	192
Dominici, Pittori, etc.	373
Donaldson, Architecture Numism.	342
Donovan's Insects	231, 261
D'Orbigny, Dict. d'Hist. Nat.	231
Doré (Gustave) Illustrations	357
Douglas, Nenia Britannica	459
Doutreman, Pedagogo Christiano	192
D'Oyly and Mant's Bible	77
Drake's Voyages	459
Dresden Gallery	361
Druids	58
Druses	59
Dryander, Ca'alogus	231
Duby, Monnaies des Barons	342
Ducange, Glossarium	93
Duchesne, Francorum Script.	30, 323
— Normannorum Scriptores	30, 323
Duff's Mahrattas	459
Dugdale (Sir W.) Works	323, 459, 488
Du Halde, la Chine	146
— China	459
Du Monstier, Neustria Pia	64
Dunlop's Roman Literature	93
Du Paz, Bretagne	323
Du Sommerard, Arts au Moyen Age	357
Dutch	207-9
Dyalogus Creaturarum, 1480	385
Early Prayer Books	394-95
Early Printed Books	397-401
Early Science	396-97
Eastern Europe, Works on	284-88
East India Register	54
Eastwick's Hindustani Grammar	180
Ecclesiastical History	62
Eckhel, Doctrina Numorum	343
Edda Saemundar	211
Edinburgh Royal Society	29, 232
Edmondson's Baronagium	460
— Heraldry	324
Edwards' Uncommon Birds	232
Egypt	147, 149, 289
Egyptians (Ancient)	59
Ehrenberg's Infusoria	232
Eichhoff, Parallèle des Langues	194
Emblems	357-58
Encyclopaedias	14-54
Encyclopaedia Britannica	29, 232
— Metropolitana	232, 460
Engelmann, Bibliothecae	116
Engineering	388-93
England, Books relating to	489
English Bibles	76-78
English Common Prayers, Articles of Religion, Sermons, etc.	71-72
English Dialects	22-24, 444-47
English Language	444-47, 487
English Literature	444-87, 487-88
Englishman's Hebrew Concordance	84
English Historical Society	30
English MSS., Early	1-9
Entomological Society	30, 261

GENERAL INDEX.

:pitaphs	460	
:rasmi Opera	109	
scurial, The	525	
spana Artistica	359	
spana Sagrada	526	
sper's Schmetterlinge	233	
- Pflanzenthiere	233	
squimaux Testament	78	
sthonia	285	
:tching Club	359	
:thiopic	78, 175, 316, 427	
:thnological Society	30	
:truria Pittrice	359	
:ulenspiegel	395	
:uropean MSS.	1-9, 393-4, 477, 520	
:uropean Philol.	138-220, 427-28, 504-7	
:xercises	124-127	
zguerra, Lengua Bisaya	192	
aber's Pagan Idolatry	56, 481	
ablan's Chronicle	461	
.bricii Bibliotheca Graeca	116	
acciolati Lexicon	94	
alconer and Cautley, Fauna Sival.	233	
alconry	126-27	
aris' Arabic Grammar	169	
auriel, Chants de la Grèce	217	
ayence Ware	359	
ebres, Arte Chileno	191	
ellows' Lycia, etc.	270, 461	
enn's Paston Letters	461	
errarese Dialect	442	
erussac, Mollusques	234	
étis, Biographie des Musiciens	128	
ine Arts	349-88, 497-99	
inland	285-86	
innish	220, 265	
irdousi, Shah Nameh	184	
ireworks	136	
isscher's Japaansche Rijk	154	
lacourt, Diction. Malagache, etc.	290	
landin et Coste, Voyage en Perse	270	
lemish	207-9	
leury, Histoire Ecclesiast.	64	
linders' Terra Australis	270	
lora Danica	234	
lorence Gallery	360	
lorio's Fruites	403	
- World of Wordes	428	
oppen's Bibliotheca Belgica	374	
orbes' Bagh o Bahar	180	
orbes' Oriental Memoirs	141, 151, 297	
orbes and Hanley, Mollusca	235	
oreign Quarterly Review	31	
ormosan	312	
orster's Arabia	270	
- Mohammedanism	60	
owler's Mosaic Pavements	360	
ox's Martyrs	64	
rance, Historiens de la	24	
rancisco de S. Joseph, ArteTagala	312	
ranckii Bibliotheca Bunav.	117	
raser, Zoologia Typica	235	
reemasonry	60, 396	
reemasons' Magazine	31	
rench Bibles	79	
rench Language, Works on	404-5	
rench Literature	404-422	
rère, Bibliographe Normand	117	
reytagii Lexicon Arabicum	169	
- Arabum Proverbia	167, 502	
riend of India	31	
risch, Vögel Deutschlandes	235	
risic	207-9	
roissart, Chroniques	410	
– in English	462	
roude's England	507	
ueros	527	
uerst, Concordantiæ	83, 177	
utawa Alemgiri	169	
iale et Fell, Scriptores	79	
Galileo, Opere	235, 261	
Galleries (Art)	360-61	
Gallia Christiana	324	
Gallicarum Rerum Scriptores	24	
Games and Sports	124-127, 260	
Garcilaso de la Vega, Peru	295, 528	
Garibay, Illustraciones Geneal.	325, 528	

Gau, Antiquités de la Nubie	289	
Gazetteer of the World	271	
Geer, Histoire des Insectes	261	
Gell (Sir W.) Works	373, 488, 497-8	
Gems	361-62	
Genealogy	319-39	
Genoese Dialect	442	
Geographiae Scriptores	271	
Geographical Society	31, 271, 500	
Geographical Society of France	49	
Geography	264-318, 421, 499-503	
Geological Society	31, 236	
Georgian	175-176	
Gerbertus de Musica	128	
German Bibles	79-80	
German Dictionaries	422	
German Literature	422-28	
Germanic Languages	202-9	
Geschichte der Künste und Wissens.	31	
Gesenii Thesaurus	177	
Gesneri Res Numaria	343	
Gesta Dei	32	
Ghiberti, Porte del Battistero	360	
Ginguéné, Histoire Littéraire	444	
Gipsey Language	220	
Gladstone's Homer, etc.	463	
Godard et Duponchel, Lepidoptères	236	
Goettingen Academy	32	
Goezen's Bibliographie	117	
Golii Lexicon Arabicum	169	
Gomara, Nuevo Mundo	528	
Gould's Works on Nat. Hist.	237, 261	
Graevii Thesaurus Antiquitatum	32, 94	
Graff's Althochdeuts. Sprach.	205, 427	
Gray's Genera of Birds	237	
— Knowsley Menagerie, etc.	512-13	
— and Hardwicke's Indian Zoology	237	
Greek and Latin Classics	88-114, 505	
Greek MSS.	1-9	
Greenland and Greenlandish	191, 295	
Grenville Library Catalogue	117	
Grenville's Cryptogamic Flora	237, 508	
Griffith's Indian Botanical Works	237	
Grimm's Deutsche Grammatik	205, 422	
Grimm's Deutsche Mythologie	60, 424	
Grimm et Diderot, Corréspond.	411	
Groningen Academy	32	
Grose's Military Antiquities	463	
Grote's Greece	94, 463	
Gruner's Fine Art Works	362	
Guadalupe Ramirez, Com. Othomi	295	
Guarani Language	72, 191	
Guagnini Sarmatia	284	
Guatemala	295	
Guichenon, Savoie	325	
Guillim's Heraldry	325	
Guizot, Oeuvres	411	
Guzjerati	179	
Gwydonis Hystoria Troyana	110	
Gaelic	72, 79, 199, 505	
Hafiz	163, 184	
Haft Kulzum	184	
Hagen's Minnesinger	128, 205	
Hain, Repertorium Bibliograph.	117	
Hajji Khalfeh	169	
Hakluyt's Voyages	271	
Hakluyt Society	32, 272, 464	
Hale's Chronology	340	
Hamilton's Campi Phlegræi	363	
Hammer, Empire Ottoman	154	
Hammer, Literatur der Araber	169	
Handel's Works	128	
Handjeri, Dictionnaire Franç. Arabe, Pers. Turc	189	
Hardiman's Irish Minstrelsy	128	
Harleian Miscellany	33, 464, 488	
Haro (Lopez de) Nobiliario	326, 529	
Harrington's Laws of Bengal	151	
Hartshorne's Salopia	445	
Hart's Beejapore	151	
Hartwell House Publications	41, 480	
Harvey, Phycologia Britannica	239	
Hassall's Fresh Water Algæ	239	
Haug's Parsees	61, 142	
Haughton's Bengali Works	179	
Hawaiian Language	193, 318	
Hawkins' History of Music	128	

Hayes' Osterley Menagerie	239	
Heber's Bibliotheca Heberiana	118	
Hebrew Lang.	82-83, 176-78, 315-16, 505	
Hebrew MSS.	155, 161	
Heeren's Works	94, 465	
Hegel's Werke	56	
Heldenbuch, 1560	424	
Helps' Spanish Conquest	296	
Henninges, Theatrum Genealog.	326	
Heraldry	319-339, 516-50	
Herberstain, Moscovia	287	
Hernandez, Res Med. Nov. Hisp.	239, 529	
Herodotus, by Rawlinson	142	
Herrera, Hechos de los Castellanos	296	
Herrero Grammar	289	
Hertslett's Treaties	465	
Hervas, Catalogo di Lengue	194	
Hewitson's British Oology	239	
Hickesii Thesaurus	203, 504	
Hidayah (The)	142, 502	
Hieratic Papyri, B. M.	148	
Hieronymi Epistolae, Aldus	65	
Higgins (Godfrey) Works	465	
Hindi Language	179-180	
Hindoo Drawings	156	
Hindostani Language	179, 310, 505	
Hindustani MSS.	161	
Histoire Litteraire de la France	33	
Historical Atlas of Ireland	491	
Hitopadesa	186	
Hittorf, Architecture Sicilienne	389	
Hoare's (Sir R. C.) Recoll. Abroad	273	
— Wiltshire	486	
Hoffmann et Kellerhofen, Décorat.	370	
Hofmanni Lexicon	33, 327	
Hogg's Jacobite Relics	129	
Holinshed's Chronicles	465	
Holland, Heróologia	374	
Holme's (Randle) Armory	326	
Homiliae, MS. VIIIth Century	5	
Hooker (J. D.) Works	240	
— (Sir W.) Works	240	
Hope's Costume	363	
Horae, illuminated MSS.	1-9	
Horæ, printed	71-74, 394-95	
Horsfield (Dr. T.) Works	240	
Horsemanship	126, 363, 487	
Hortus Malabaricus	240	
Houard, Coutumes Anglo-Normand.	132	
Household Books	466	
Howell's Letters	374	
Hubbard's New England	296	
Hübner's Schmetterlinge	262	
Humboldt, Asie Centrale	273	
— Cordilleres	297	
— Kawi-Sprache	192	
— Nouvelle Espagne	296	
Humphrey's Illuminated Books	11, 363	
Humphrey and Westwood, Moths	240	
Hungarian	219, 286	
Hungary	286	
Hunter's Doncaster	466	
Hunting	126-27, 260	
Huron Language	191	
Hutchins' Dorset	459	
Hyde, Veteres Persae	61, 142	
Icelandic	211-13	
Ihre, Glossarium Suio-Goth.	209, 288	
Illuminated MSS.	1-9, 155-56, 393	
Illyrian	84, 218, 285	
Inayah	170	
Index Expurgatorius	118, 530	
India, Books upon	150-53, 309-10, 501-3	
Indian Archipelago	312-13	
Indian Botany	511-12	
Indian Languages	179-82, 309-12	
Indian Law	130-35	
Indian Learned Societies	14-54	
Indian MSS.	161	
India Review	33	
InnocentiaVictrix,Chin. Block Book	303	
Inquisition, Works on the	70	
Instituto di Roma	33, 363	
Iolo MSS.	53	
Ireland, Books relating to	489-493	
Ireland, Historical Atlas of	51-52, 283	
Irish	84, 200

2 o

GENERAL INDEX.

Irish Archaeological Society 84
Italian Books 84, 428-44
Italian Dialects 22-24, 441-444
Italian Dictionaries 428-29
Italy 363-64, 444
Jackson and Chatto, Wood Engrav. 386
Jacquemart, Porcelaine 364
Jahrbücher für Philologie 96
Jakout 182
Jameson (Mrs.) Sacred Art, etc. 364
Jamieson's Culdees 58
Jamieson's Etymological Dict. 446
Japan, Works on 154, 313-14
Japanese 182, 314
Javanese 182, 192, 312
Jebb, de Vitâ Mariae Scot. Reg. 110, 494
Jerdon's Indian Ornithology 241
Jesuits, Works on the 70, 297
Jewel (Bishop) Replie 65
Jews, History, etc. 70
John Bull (The) 34
Johnston (Keith) Gazetteer 273
Johnson's Persian Dictionary 184, 506
Jones (Owen) Fine Art Works 364
Jones (Sir W.) Works 142
Jordan, Origines Slavicæ 284
Jost's Israeliten 70
Journal Asiatique 34, 35, 306
Journal des Savants 34, 241
Journal of the Indian Archipelago 35
Juan de la Concepcion, Historia de las Philipinas 313, 530
Juan y Ulloa, America 297, 530
Jubinal, Armeria Real 546
— Tapisseries 364
Junghuhn's Java 274
Jungmann, Slownik Cesky 218
Junii Etymologicum 204
Jurisprudence 130-35
Kabbala Denudata 177
Kaempfer's Japan 142, 314
Kamûs 170
— Terjemeh Turki 189
Kant's Werke 56
Karamsin, Histoire de la Russie 287
— Gosudarstva Rossii 219
Karen Language 310
Kariri Language 71
Keating's History of Ireland 491
Kechua Language 191
Kelham's Norman Dict. etc. 132, 467
Kemble, Codex Anglo-Saxonicus 30
— Horae Ferales 467
Kempis, Imitation de J. C. 365
Kennedy's Origin of Language 142, 195
— Hindu Mythology 142, 195
Kilkenny Archaeological Society 35
King Orfevrerie 365
King's Vale Royall 455
Kingsborough's Antiq. of Mexico 297
Kircheri Oedipus 59, 148
— Musurgia 129
Klaproth, Mém. etc. 142, 274, 306, 308
Knight's Ecclesiastical Architecture 390
Knorr et Walch 242
Knowsley Menagerie 512-13
Koch, Traités 132
Kojalowicz, Historia Lituana 286, 327
Kopp, Palaeographia Critica 11, 97
Koran, translations of 142, 467
Kunst-Blatt 365
Kunstmann's Entdeckung Americas 298
Küssell, Icones Biblicæ 351
Labbei et Cossartii Concilia 328
Laborde, Monumens de la France 365
Laborde, la Musique 129
Lacroix, le Moyen Age 365
Lacroix, Calcul 242, 421
Lacroix du Maine, Bibl. Franç. 118, 420
Lambecii Biblioth. Vindob. 115
Lambranzi, Deliciae Theatrales 129
Lancashire & Cheshire Hist. Soc. 35, 468
Landscape Gardening 390
Landseer's Animals 242
Lanercost Chronicle 328
Langebek, Scriptores Danici 35, 328
Languedoc, Histoire de 328

Lanzi, Lingua Etrusca 97
Laplace, Oeuvres 422
Lapland 285
Lapponic 60, 220, 285-86
Larramendi, Diccionario 197
Lastanosa, Medallas Desconocidas 344
Latham's Falconry 126
Latin Classics 88-112
Latin and Greek Miscellanies 108-112
Lavater, Physiognomy 365
Law 130-35
Lawrence (Sir Th.) Works 366
Layamon's Brut 204
Layard's Nineveh 146
Leake's Works on Greece 98, 274
— Numismata Hellenica 344
Lebrun, Galérie 360-61
Ledebour, Plantae Rossicae 242
Leemius de Lapponibus 60
Legonidec, Dictionnaire Breton 198
Le Grand's Fabliaux, by Way 468
Lelewel, Géographie 274
Lelewel, Numismatique 344
Le Long, Bibl. de la France 11, 118, 328
Le Long, Bibliotheca Sacra 88
Lempriere Family 329
Lenglet du Fresnoy, Géographie 274
Lenoir, Musée des Monumens 366
Leon, Bibliotheca 531
Le Roux, Dictionnaire Comique 404
Le Roy, Castella Brabantiae 367
Lesson, Ouvrages 243
Lettish Bibles 85
Lettres Edifiantes 274
Leycester's Cheshire 455
Lhuyd's Archaeologia 198, 505
Liber Landavensis 53
Libri, Monuments Inédits 118
Lincoln's Inn Library 119
Lindsay's Christian Art 468
Linnaea, Journal 428
Linnaea Entomologica 262
Linnean Society 36, 243, 262, 509
Lionville, Journal Mathématique 243
Lipscombe's Buckingham 453
Lisbon Academy Memoirs 36, 549
Literary History 112-124
Lithuania 286-87
Lithuanian 218
Litta, Famiglie Italiane 366
Liturgical Literature 71-74, 394-95
Livonia 285
Lobineau, Bretagne 329
Londesborough's Ornaments 367
London Gazette 36, 469
London Institution Catalogue 119
Londonio, Works 367
Lord's Persees 469
Loudon's Arboretum, etc. 244
Low German 73-74, 80, 204-08
Lowndes' Romaic Dictionary 217
Lozano, Paraguay, etc. 298
Ludolfi, Lexicon Aethiop. etc. 175, 316
— Historia Ethiopica 142
Lugo, Gramatica Mosca 299
Lusatian 218
Lyndsay (Sir David) Facsimile 494
Lysons' Gloucestershire 367, 469
Lyttelton and Gladstone's Transl. 469
Mabillon, Res Diplomatica 340
Mabinogion (The) 202
Macaroneana 110, 115, 548
Macassar Language 192, 312
MacCulloch's Works 132
Mace's Musick's Monument 129
Machado, Bibl. Lusitana 119, 548
Machiavel's Arte of Warre 470
Machinery 388-393
MacNaughten's Indian Laws 134, 143
Madagascar 290
Madras Journal of Literature 36, 502
Madras Journal of Med. Science 36
Magic 396
Magyar 85, 219
Mahab'harata 186
Mahratti 181
Maillac, Histoire de la Chine 308

Maitland's Early Printed Books 119
Malagasy 290
Malay 182, 312
Malayalim 181
Malcolm (Sir John) Works 143
Malte Brun, Voyages 37, 275
Maltese 182
Mandeville's Travels 275-76
Manipuri Language 181
Mannert, Geograph. d. Griechen 98, 425
Manni, Sigilli Antichi 330
Mantchu 183
Mantuan, Parthenice 397
MSS., European 1-9, 393-4, 477, 520
MSS., Oriental 155-166, 307, 310-11, 316-17, 393
MSS., Catalogues of 10-14
Manx 201
Maori Testament 318
Maps 282-284
Marban, Arte Moxa 192
Marco Polo's Travels 275
Margarita Philosophica, Reisch 245, 250
Marguerite, Heptameron 398, 412
Mariette, Pierres Gravées 361
Marmol Carvajal, Africa 275, 533
Marques, Brasilia Pontificia 299
Marquesan 193
Marryat's Pottery 367
Marsden, Numismata Orient. 143, 344
Martens, Recueil des Traités 132, 413
Martin's Privately Printed Books 119
Martini Storia della Musica 129
Martin's Conchologist and Aranei 245
Mary, Queen of Scots 494
Maseres, Scriptores Logarithmici 245
Massachusetts' Historical Soc. 37, 299
Massachusetts' Language 294
Massillon Oeuvres 66
Massman's Ulfilas 80
Master of the Rolls' Publications 330
Mathematics 220-264
Mather (Cotton) Magnalia 299
Matthaei Paris, Opera 37, 331
Matthaeus Westmonast. 37
Maurice's Hindostan 152
Maximilian (Emp.) Publications 386
Mayerberg, Moscovia 287
Mayhew's London Labour 471
Mechanics' Magazine 37
Medallic History 341-49
Medhurst's Chinese Dict. 174, 309, 505
Mediaeval Glossaries 340-41
Mediaeval History 319-339
Medicae Artis Principes 245
Meibomii Antiq. Musicae Auctores 129
Mémoires de l'Acad. Celtique 331
Mémoires de l'Institut 14
Memoires sur les Chinois 309
Mém. sur l'Hist. de la France 37, 38, 413
Mendez, Typographia Espanola 534
Menestrier, Blason, etc. 331
Meninski, Lexicon 143
— Onomasticum 318
Menou's Laws 186
Mensa Philosophica 398
Mercurio Peruano 39
Merian, Insecta Surinam. 245
Messenii Scondia 289
Meursii Opera 39
Meuselii Bibliotheca 119
Mexico and the Mexican Language 60, 72, 191, 290-306, 555
Meyer's British Birds 246, 262
Meyer's Palaeontographica 246
Meyrick's Armour 367-68
— Heraldic Visitations 53
Micali, Opere 99
Michelangelo 368
Microscopic Journal 39, 246
Miechow, Chronica Polonorum 286
Milanese Dialect 442
Military Sciences and History 135-37
Millin, Antiquities, etc. 368
Milman's Latin Christianity 66
Milne Edwards, Recherches, etc. 246
Mines de l'Orient 143

GENERAL INDEX.

Entry	Page
Mionnet, Médailles Antiques	344
Mirkhond, Rauzat al Sufâ, MS.	316
Mishna Toreh	178
Missals, MSS.	1-9
Missals, Printed	71-74, 299
Modern Greek	217
Mohammedan Religion	60
Mohawk Common Prayer	73
Mohican Language	294
Molina, Vocabulario Mexicano	300
Molinet, Faictz et Dictz	398
Moll et Gayot, Encyc. de l'Agricul.	414
Mommsen's Römische Geschichte	99
Monardes, Historia Medicinal	300
Mongolian	183, 318
Monstrelet, Chroniques	397
Montfaucon's Works	12, 56, 99, 119, 368
Montucla, Hist. des Mathémat.	246, 422
Moor's Hindu Pantheon	56, 143
Moore and Lindley's Ferns	247
Morcelli Opera Epigraphica	99
Morelli Thesaurus	345
Morley's Astrolabe	134, 502
— Digest	134, 502
Morris' Birds	262
Morrison's Chinese Dictionary	174
Moryson's (Fynes) Itinerary	491
Moscou, Société des Naturalistes	39, 247
Mosquito Language	192
Moxa	192
Moyen-Age Monumental	368
Müller (L.) Numis. de l'ancienne Af.	318
Müller's (Max.) Sanscrit Literature	187
— Science of Language	195
Müller's (P.) Saga-Bibliothek	210
Muir's Sanscrit Texts	187
Munich Academy	39
Munich Gallery	361
Muratorii Opera	39-40, 332
Murchison (Sir R.) Works	247, 510
Mure's Literature of Greece	100
Murner, Logica Memorativa	124
Murphy's Arabian Antiquities	369
Murr's Journal f. Kunst-Gesch.	119
Murray's Handbooks	276
Musée Francais, Musée Royal	369
Museo Borbonico	370
Museo Pio Clementino	382
Music	127-30, 444
Nagler's Künstler Lexicon	370
Napier's Peninsular War	137
Nash's Mansions	370, 498
Natali, Evang. Hist. Imagines	351
Natural Hist.	220-64, 421-22, 428, 507-13
Natural History Catalogues	25-26, 507
Naval Affairs	138
Naval Architects' Institution	390
Navarrete, Viages	300
Neale's Views	370, 498
Neander's Kirchen-Geschichte	67
Neapolitan Dialect	442
Nessel, Codd. Biblioth. Vindob.	115
Newcastle's Horsemanship	126, 363
New England Geneal. Register	40, 300
New York State, Hist. etc.	247-8, 300-1
Niceron, Hommes Illustres	40, 120
Nichols' Bibliotheca Topographica	40
— Literary Anecdotes	120
Nicolson and Burn, Westmoreland	473
Niebelungen Lied	206
Niebuhr's Werke	100
Nisard, Livres populaires	415
Nisbet's Heraldry	332
Noceda, Vocabulario Tagala	313
Nodal, Viage	301, 536
Norberg, Codex Nasaraeus	315
Nordiske Oldskrift Selskab	40-41, 209
Norfolk Archaeology	473
Normand, Paris Moderne	391
Norse	211-13
Notes and Queries	41
Noticès et Extraits	12, 307
Nouveau Traité de Diplomatique	12
Numismata	341-49
Numismatic Chronicle	41, 345, 475
O'Brien's Round Towers	56
Old German	204-7, 427
Olivier, Entomologie	248, 262, 422
Olshausen, Bibl. Commentar	67
Oordoo	180
Orbino, Regno degli Slavi	285
Ordem de Santiago	550
Ordnance Survey Maps	284
Ordonez de Zevallos	277
Oriental History	138-155
Oriental Literature	166-190, 427-8, 503-7
Oriental MSS.	155-66, 393
Oriental Societies' Transactions	138-155
Oriental Translation Fund	41-43
Orissa Language	181
Orkney Islands	473
Orme's Hindostan	152
Ormerod's Cheshire	455
Ornaments	370
Ortiz, Arte Tagala	313
Ossian's Poems	200
Ossianic Society	201
Ottley's Engravings, etc.	371
Ovalle, Chili	301
Overstone's Tracts	133
Oviedo, las Indias	301, 527
Ovid, Metamorphoseo	386
Owen (Richard) Works	248
Owen and Blakeway's Shrewsbury	479
Oxford	473
Oxford University Lib. Cats.	113, 120
Oxford and Cambridge Univer.	483
Pageants	371
Painting	349-388
Palaeontographical Society	43
Palaeontographica von Meyer	43
Palaeography	10-14, 340-41
Palestine	154, 315-16
Pali Language	183, 506
Pali MSS.	161-62
Pallas, Vocabulaire Comparatif	288
Pallegoix, Dict. Siamensis	188
Palomino, Museo	380
Panthéon Littéraire	407
Panzer, Annales	120
Paraguay	301
Paredes, Catecismo Mexicano	72, 191
Paris, Armorial de la Ville	333
Parmese Dialect	442
Parry's Voyages	277
Parsees	60-61, 317, 469
Pashley's Crete	474
Passionales	71-74
Pastoret, Hist. de la Législation	133
Patagonian Language	294
Patin (Gui) Lettres	415
Pauly, Klassische Encyclopädie	101
Pearson's Salop	479
Peck's Desiderata Curiosa	333
Pellerin, Médailles	345
Pembroke Coins	346
Pennsylvania Register	43
Penny Cyclopædia	43
Perceval, Hist. des Arabes	144
Percier et Fontaine, Maisons de Plaisance	390
Percy Society	43
Peringskiöld, Monumenta	289
Periodical Publications	14-54, 290, 428, 501-2, 507-11
Persia, Works on	316-17
Persian Lit., Printed	183-85, 316-17, 506
Persian MSS.	156, 162-166, 316-17
Pertz, Monumenta Hist. Germ.	43, 353
Petition for Peace	72
Petitot et Monmerqué, Mém.	37-38, 413
Peutingeri Tabula Itiner.	101
Phenician	185, 317-18, 427
Philippine Isl. & their Lan.	192, 312-13
Philobiblon Society	474
Philological Society	44, 195
Philological Works	138-220, 421, 422, 427-28, 503-507
Philology (Comparative)	138-46, 193-96
Philology, Greek and Latin	88-112
Philosophical Sects	55-62
Philosophical Transactions	46, 511
Piedmontese Dialect	442
Piedrahita, Nueva Granada	302
Pierer's Lexicon	425
Pigault le Brun, Oeuvres	415
Pinto, Peregrinaçao	278
Piranesi, Opere	372
Pistorii Scriptores Polonici	286
Plancher et Merle, Bourgogne	321
Platon par Cousin	415
Plinio en Espanol	539
Pliny's Naturall Historie	474
Ploos von Amstel	373
Plot's Oxfordshire	473
— Staffordshire	474
Poland	286-87
Poliphili Hypnerotomachia	61, 387
Polish	218, 286-87
Political Economy	130-35, 421
Polwhele's Devonshire	458
Polyglott Bibles	74-75, 503-4
Polyglotts	138-55, 193
Polygraphes, Works of	14-54
Polynesian Languages	192, 318
Poniatowski Gems	361
Ponz, Viage de Espana	379
Popol Vuh	191
Portfolio (The)	44
Portraits	373-375
Portugal, Books relating to	550
Portuguese Dictionaries	547-48
Portuguese Literature	547-50
Pothier, Oeuvres	416
Pottery	375
Premare, Notitia	309
Prévost d'Exiles Hist. des Voyages	278
Priapeian Worship	61
Prichard's Works	195
— Celtic Nations	198
Prince's Worthies of Devon	475
Prinsep's Indian Antiquities	152, 346
— Tables	19
Prior's Danish Ballads	210
Private Press Issues	14-54
Proverbs	402-404, 532
Psalters	74-88
Publications of Societies	14-54
Pugin's Works	375-498
Punjabi	181, 310
Punjabi MSS.	166
Purchas' Pilgrims	278
Pushtu	185
Querard, France Littéraire	44, 120
Quichua Language	191, 291-305
Quito Language	302
Rabbinical Bibles	83
Racing Calendar	475
Raczynski, Art Moderne	375
Rada, la Espada	127, 539
Raffaelle, Loggie, etc.	375-76
Raffles' Java	278
Ramon de la Sagra, Cuba	252
Ramusio, Navigationi	279
Raphael Morghen, Ritratti	375
Rasche, Lexicon Rei Numariæ	346
Ratzeburg, Forst Insekten	263
Rawlinson's Great Monarchies	144
— Herodotus	144
Ray Society	44-45, 249
Raynouard, Poesies des Troubad.	215
— Lexique Roman	216
Reale Academia di Torino	52
Réaumur, Histoire des Insectes	250
Record Commission Publications	45
Redhouse's Turkish Dictionary	189
Rees' Cyclopaedia	45, 53, 475
Reeves' Carnatica Dictionary	179
Reeves' Conchologia	45, 250
Reiff's Parallel Dictionaries	219
Relandi Palaestina	154
Relation des Jésuites	297
Religious Worships	55-62
Remesal, Historia de Chiapa	302
Rémusat, Langues Tartares	144
Rennie's Harbours	391
Renouard's Bibliographies	121
Renvalli Lexicon Fennicum	220
Retrospective Review	46
Revolution Française, Tableaux	376
Revue Numismatique	46

GENERAL INDEX.

Reynolds' (Sir Joshua) Works 376
Reysen naar Oost en West Indien 276
Rhind's Papyri, etc. 475
Ribadeneira, Flos Sanctorum 68
Ribas, Triumphos 302
Rich, Bibliotheca Americ. 121, 303, 499
Richardson, Fauna Boreali-Americ. 250
Richardson's Persian Dict. 185, 506
Rietstap, Armorial Général 333
Righetti, il Campidoglio 382
Rig Veda 57, 188
Ritter's Erdkunde 279
Roberts' Holy Land and Egypt 144
Robinson's Ornam. Villas, etc. 390, 499
Roby's Lancashire 476
Roesel, Insecten Belustigung 250, 263
Rodriguez, Polygraphia Espan. 12
Romaic 73, 86, 217, 506
Romance Lan. 214-16, 397-401, 421, 427
Romanceros 540-41
Romanese Dialect 443
Romans 216, 417
Romansch 86, 216, 421
Rommant de la Rose 215, 398
Roquefort, Glossaire Roman 216
Roscoe's Monandrian Plants 251, 263
Rose's Biographical Dictionary 121
Rosenmüller, Scholia 68
Rosellini, Monumenti 149, 377
Rotteck und Welcker, Staats-Lex. 426
Rowland's Armorial of Shropshire 334
Rows' Rol 334
Roxburgh's Flora Indica, etc. 251
— Plants of Coromandel 510
Roxburghe Club 46, 477
Roy's Military Antiquities 476
Royal Academy Catalogues 388
Royal Asiatic Society 19-20
Royal Engineers' Papers 137
Royal Kalendar 55
Royal Society 46-47, 251, 511
Royal Society of Literature 47
Rubens' Works 377
Rudbeckii Atlantica 334
Ruding's Coinage 346
Ruiz, Catecismo Guarani, etc. 72, 191, 303
Rumphii Herb. Amboinense 251, 263
Rundall's Symbolical Illustrations 358
Ruskin's Works 377
Russell's Indian Serpents, etc. 251, 511
Russia 287-88
Russian 218-19, 287-88
Russian Geographical Society 288
Rymer's Foedera 47, 334
Sabda Kalpa Druma 187
Sagard, Dict. Huron 191
Sagus 211-13
Sainct Julien, Bourgongnons 334
St. Petersburgh Academy 47
Saint Simon, Memoires 418
Salazar of Castro, Casa de Lara 334, 541
Sale Catalogues 121
Sandford's Genealogical Hist. 335, 477
Sanscrit 185-88, 310-11, 421, 428, 506
Sanscrit MSS. 166, 310-11
Santarem, Grand Atlas 282
Santarem, Cosmographie 280
Sardinian Dialect 443
Sarmatian Languages 218-19
Savile Scriptores Anglici 48
Saxon Chronicle 204
Saxton's Atlas 283, 449
Scandinavia 288-89
Scandinavian Lan. 209-14, 288-89, 421
Schatzbehalter 387
Scheuchzer, Physique Sacrée 352
Schilteri Thesaurus 206
Schinkel's Architect. Entwürfe 391
Schlagintweit's Buddhism, etc. 477
Schlegel, Fauconnerie 126
Schoenherr, Insecta 252
Schoettgenii Horae Hebraicae 178
Schotti Hispania Illustrata 335
Schroeckh, Kirchen-Geschichte 68
Sciences 220-60, 260-64, 396-97, 421-22, 428, 507-13
Scienziati Italiani, Atti 260

Scloppetaria 478
Scohier, Maison de Croy, etc. 335
Scotland. Books relating to 493-95
Scrope and Grosvenor Roll 336
Sculpture 378, 349-384
Segar's Honor 478
Seir-Mutakherin 153
Selby's Ornithology 253
Sepp's Dutch Insects 263
Sermons and Homilies 71-72
Serpent Worship 61-62
Servian 219
Shakspeare Society 48
Sharpe's Architectural Parallels 392
Shaw's Dresses, Ornaments 378
Shorthand 401-2
Shropshire 479
Siam, Siamese 188, 318
Sicilian Dialect 443
Siebmacher's Wappenbuch 336
Siebold, Fauna Japonica 253
Siennese Dialect 443
Sikh MSS. 166
Silliman's American Journal 16, 507
Silva, Dicc. Bibliog. Portuguez 549
Silvestre, Paléographie 12, 13, 379
Simon's Public Works 392
Sindhi 181, 506
Singalese 86, 181
Singer's Playing Cards 124, 379
Sismondi, Oeuvres 418
Skelton's Armour 367-68
Skinner's Etymologicon 447
Slang, Lingua Furbesca 220
Slavonic Church Lang. 86, 219, 287-88
Sleeman's Thugs 62
Slovak 219
Smith's (Adam) Wealth of Nations 133
Smith's (And.) Zoology of S. Africa 254
Smith (C. Roach) Works 48, 336
Smith's (J.) Catalogue of Painters 379
Smith's (Capt. John) Virginia 304
Smith's (Dr. W.) Dict. 48-49, 105, 479-80
Smithsonian Institution 49, 254, 304
Smyth's Aedes Hartwell. Celest Obj. 489
— Northumberland Coins 347
Snelling's Coins 347
Snorre Sturleson's Heims-Kringla 212
Société de Geographic 49
Society Publications 14-54, 227, 487
Society Atlas 282
Solis, Mexico 304, 542
Somersetshire Archaeological Soc. 49
Somers' Tracts 49
Sommersberg, Scriptores Silesiaci 336
Somneri Dictionarium 204
Songs 127-130, 480
Sotheby's Principia Typograph. 122, 499
Sousa, Casa Real Portugueza 336
Southey's Brazil 480
Sowerbys, Works of the 254, 511
Spain, Books relating to 546-47
Spanish Art 379-80
Spanish Bibles 86
Spanish Dictionaries 514-15
Spanish Literature 514-15
Spano, Bulletino Sardo 337
Specde's England 283
Spence's Polymetis 105, 380
Sports 124-127, 260
Spruner's Historical Atlases 105, 337
Spry and Shuckard, Coleoptera 263
Stade (Hans) 304
Standish, Lepidoptera 255
Statistical Society 481
Steganography 401-2
Stehelin's Rabbinical Literature 70, 178
Stephani Thesaurus 106
Stieler's Hand Atlas 282
Sterling's Artists of Spain 380
— Books of Proverbs 122
Stosch, Pierres Gravées 362
Stothard's Monumental Effigies 380
Stowe's Annales 481
Strabo, Geographia 106, 280
Stradani Venationes 260
Stritteri Populi Septemtrionales 285

Stroobant, Sculpture en Belgique 351
Strutt's Dresses, Sports, etc. 380, 482
Strype's Works 69
Stuart and Revett's Athens 392
Stud Book (General) 481
Stukeley's Stonehenge, etc. 59, 337
Suiceri Thesaurus 69
Suma Johannis 74, 207
Sunda Language 506
Surtees Society 50, 482
Swainson, Zoological Illustrations 255
Swedish 213-14, 506
Swimming 127
Sword Exercise 127
Syriac 87, 176-78, 315-16
Tagala Language 192, 312-13, 515
Tahitian 193
Tamul 181-182, 311
Tanneri Notitia 50
— Bibliotheca 489
Tartary, Tatar 318
Tatar 188
Tauste, Arte Chayma, etc. 304
Taylor (Jeremy) Works 69
Taylor and Cresy's Rome 392
Tchihatcheff, Altai, etc. 280
Tellez, Ethiopia 550
Telugu 182, 312
Temmlnck's Works on Nat. Hist. 256
Tennent's Ceylon 153
Tenore, Flora Napolitana 256
Testaments 74-88, 513-14
Teutonic Languages 204-6
Theatres, Architecture des 389
Theatrical Observer 51
Theologische Studien 51, 69
Theology 62, 513-14
Theurdanck 386
Thevenot, Voyages 281
Thibet, Thibetan 166, 188-89, 318, 421
Thieves' Slang 429
Thomas' Coins 348
Thornton's Gazetteer 153
Thoroton's Nottinghamshire 473
Thorwaldsen's Works 381
Thuani Historia sui temporis 111
Thugs 62, 153
Thurnierbuch 387
Ticknor's Spanish Literature 547
Todd's Cyclopaedia of Anatomy 256
Todd's MSS. at Lambeth 468
Todd's Rajasthan 153
Tooke's History of Prices 133
Topographical Depart. War Office 51
Topography 319-39
Torfæi Res Norvegicæ 210
— Orcades 338
Torquemada, Monarquia Indiana 304
Torres Rubio, Arte Aymara 150
— Arte Quichua 304
Totanes, Lengua Tacala 192
Tradescant Museum 483
Travels 264-318, 499-503
Trésor de Numismatique 52
Trigault, Si Jou Eul Mou Tseu 309
Trikoupê Ellênikê Epanastasis 217
Trithemii Polygraphia 401
Triumph of Maximilian 386
Turberville's Venerie 127, 483
Turin Academy 52, 256
Turin Gallery 361
Turkey 154
Turki-h 189-190
Turkish MSS. 166
Turner's (D.) Fuci 257
Turner's (J. M. W.) Views 381
Turnierbuch (Das) 353
Turning, Works on 392
Twysdeni Scriptores 52, 388, 489
Typography 112-124
Ugrian Languages 219-20
Ulfilas, von Massman 80
Ulster, Atlas of 52
Universal History 52
Upham's Budhism 155, 484
Vaines, Dictionnaire de Diplomat. 13
Vallancey, Collectanea 53

Valencian Dialect	545-46	Wallachian	216	Wilson's (James) Zoology	259
Valentyn, Oost Indien	145, 281	Wallich, Plantae Asiaticae	257	Wilson and Bonaparte, American Ornithology	258
Valerius Maximus, Com. de Burgo	107	Waltheri Lexicon Diplomaticum	13, 341		
Valvasor, Carinthia	338	Walton's Polyglott	74	Wilson (Lea) Editions of Bibles	78
Van Praet, Livres sur Vélin	123	War Office, Publications of the Topographical Department	51, 284	Winckelmann's Werke	384
Vapereau, Dict. des Contemporains	53			Wither's Emblems	358
Vasari, Opere	381, 441	Ward's Hindoos	153	Wood's (Ant.) Athenae Oxonienses	123
Vatican Codex	81	Warner's Hampshire	464	Wood's (W.) Index Entomol. etc.	259, 264, 512
Vaticano (Il)	381-82	Warren's Kala Sankalita	145, 257		
Vecellio, Habiti Antichi	356	Warrington's Stained Glass	383	Wolfii (J. C.) Bibliotheca Heb.	123, 179
Vedas	187-88	Watchmaking	257-8	Wolfii (J.) Lectiones	112
Venetian Dialect	443	Wa'son's Dendrologia	258	Wotton's Misna	70
Venezia e le sue Lagune	264	Watt's Bibliotheca Britannica	123	Wrestling	127
Venice	264, 382, 389, 441	Weale's Early Masters	355	Wright's Court Hand	14
Verdier, Architecture Civile	392	Weber's Northern Antiquities	207	Wright's (Tho.) Vocabularies, etc.	486
Vetancurt, Teatro Mexicano	305	Weever's Funerall Monuments	339, 485	Wyatt's (Digby) Works	384
Vienna Academy	20	Weiss Kunig (Der)	386	Wycliffe's Bible	78
Vienna Gallery	361	Wellesley's Despatches	137	Wyrley's Use of Armorie	339
Viera y Clavijo, Canarias	281	Wellington's Despatches	137	Xeres, Conquista del Peru	306
Villa-Senor y Sanchez	305	Welsh	87, 201-2, 506-7	Xylography	384-387
Vindobonesis Bibliotheca Catal.	115	Welsh MS. Society	53, 202, 507	Yarrell's Birds and Fishes	259
Virgil, by Gawain Douglas	495	Wendish Bibles	87-88	Yorke's Union of Honor	339
Virginian Bible	506	Westphalen, Monumenta	53, 339	Young (Arthur) Works	487
Virtuoso's Companion	484	Westwood's Palaeographia	384	Young's Hieroglyphics	148
Visconti, Opere	382-83	Wharton's Anglia Sacra	70	Yule's Mission to Ava	486
Vishnu Purana	58	Wheaton's International Law	485	Zach, Correspondenz	259
Vitruvius, Architecture	393	Whewell's Sciences	258	Zarlino, Opere Musicali	130
Vocabularius Brevilogus (1490)	108	Whitaker's Leeds	485	Zedler's Universal Lexicon	123
Vocabularius Lat.-Teutonicus, 1479	207	Wierx, Engravings	355, 368	Zeitschr. für Kunde d. Morgenlandes	53
Voet, Coleoptera	257	Wight's Pub. on Indian Bot.	258, 511-12	Zend Language	190, 317
Voyages	264-318	Wilkinson (Sir G.) Works	60, 149, 485	Zend Avesta	60
Vredii (Olivarii) Flandria	338	Willement's Roll, Henry VIII.	339	Zeuss, Grammatica Celtica	198
Wace, Romans de	216, 421	Willems, Belgisch Museum	339	Zoological Journal	264
Wailly, Paléographie	13	Willis's (Browne) Works	70, 485-86	Zoological Society	54, 259
Waldstein, Plantae Hungariæ	257	Wilson's (Dan.) Prehistoric Annals	495	Zulu Grammar	289
Wales, Books relating to	495-97	Wilson (H. H.) Works	57, 145, 348		

THE END.

G. NORMAN, PRINTER, MAIDEN LANE, COVENT GARDEN.

www.ingramcontent.com/pod-product-compliance
Lightning Source LLC
Chambersburg PA
CBHW032012230426
43671CB00005B/54